The edition of *The Complete Works of Frances Ridley Havergal* has five parts :

Volume I *Behold Your King: The Complete Poetical Works of Frances Ridley Havergal*

Volume II *Whose I Am and Whom I Serve: Prose Works of Frances Ridley Havergal*

Volume III *Loving Messages for the Little Ones: Works for Children by Frances Ridley Havergal*

Volume IV *Love for Love: Frances Ridley Havergal: Memorials, Letters and Biographical Works*

Volume V *Songs of Truth and Love: Music by Frances Ridley Havergal and William Henry Havergal*

David L. Chalkley, Editor   Dr. Glen T. Wegge, Music Editor

Frances Ridley Havergal's formal education ended when she was 17, with one term at a young women's school in Düsseldorf, Germany, yet she was a true scholar all her life. Fluent in German and French and nearly so in Italian, she read and loved the Reformers in Latin, German, and French. Knowledge was never an end in itself, only a means to know better her Lord and Saviour and to help to bring others to know Him. The Bible was her only Book, and she studied the Hebrew and Greek texts of Scripture, memorized nearly all the New Testament and large portions of the Old Testament, and loved the Author with all her being.

Frances was brought to a saving knowledge of Christ when she was 14, and the rest of her life was consecrated to her Saviour, the Lord Jesus. Keenly aware of her own sinfulness and inability, her sole desire was to please and glorify Him alone. Very finely gifted, she was truly diligent with her gifts: her poetry is among the finest in the English language, after George Herbert; her prose works are deeply beneficial; a musician to the core, she left behind important compositions. Like her works, her life richly touched the ones near her and countless many who met or heard her. The Lord Jesus Christ was her alone, only beauty, and she glowed Him and His truth. Never wanting attention to herself, Frances' desire of her heart was for herself and for others to know her King, the Lord Jesus Christ. Her works are a gold-mine of help and enrichment. There is life in these pages: her works truly glorify the Lord, truly benefit His people, and powerfully reach those who do not yet know Him.

The Music of Frances Ridley Havergal by Glen T. Wegge, Ph.D.

This Companion Volume to the Havergal edition is a valuable presentation of F.R.H.'s scores, most or nearly all of F.R.H.'s scores very little if any at all seen, or even known of, for nearly a century. What a valuable body of music has been unknown for so long and is now made available to many. Dr. Wegge completed his Ph.D. in Music Theory at Indiana University at Bloomington, and his diligence and thoroughness in this volume are obvious. First an analysis of F.R.H.'s compositions is given, an essay that both addresses the most advanced musicians and also reaches those who are untrained in music; then all the extant scores that have been found are newly typeset, with complete texts for each score and extensive indices at the end of the book. This volume presents F.R.H.'s music in newly typeset scores diligently prepared by Dr. Wegge, and Volume V of the Havergal edition presents the scores in facsimile, the original 19th century scores. (The essay—a dissertation—analysing her scores is given the same both in this Companion Volume and in Volume V of the Havergal edition.)

Dr. Wegge is also preparing all of these scores for publication in performance folio editions.

Frances Ridley Havergal Trust   P.O.Box 649   Kirksville, Missouri 63501

An un-dated photograph of William Henry Havergal (1793–1870).

WORKS

BY

William Henry Havergal.

SIX LECTURES ON THE ARK OF THE COVENANT

SERMONS, CHIEFLY ON HISTORICAL SUBJECTS FROM THE OLD AND NEW TESTAMENTS,

Volume I Old Testament, and
Volume II New Testament

A Third Volume of Sermons by W.H.H. and John East

"A Wise and Holy Child" Poems and Hymns by W.H.H.

A Partial List of Music Scores and Essays on Music by W.H.H., and a Few Examples of His Music

Records of the Life of the Rev. William Henry Havergal, M.A.

by his daughter Jane Miriam Crane

Statements of Appreciation and Articles about W.H.H.

Deep teachings from the Word he held so dear,
  Things new and old in that great treasure found,
A valiant cry, a witness strong and clear,
  A trumpet with no faint, uncertain sound:
These shall not die, but live; his rich bequest
To that beloved Church, whose servant is at rest.

from "Yet Speaketh" by F.R.H. (on page 452)

Taken from the Edition of *The Complete Works of Frances Ridley Havergal.*

David L. Chalkley, Editor Dr. Glen T. Wegge, Associate Editor

ISBN 978-1-937236-27-4 Library of Congress: 2011960055

Copyright © 2011 Frances Ridley Havergal Trust. All rights are reserved.
Frances Ridley Havergal Trust P.O.Box 649 Kirksville, Missouri 63501

Book cover by Sherry Goodwin and David Carter.

CONTENTS.

LIST OF ILLUSTRATIONS.

PREFACE.

William Henry Havergal (1793–1870) was a pastor, musician, scholar, and an example of the believer. His sermons are true gold, so good, fully at the level of rich benefit of sermons by J. C. Ryle, Charles Spurgeon, and D. Martyn Lloyd-Jones. Accounts of his pastoral ministry are true examples, glowing the Lord and His truth.

Born at High Wycombe, Buckinghamshire, on January 18, 1793, he was sent at age eight to a school at Princes Risborough, and later to Merchant Taylors' School in London. He matriculated at St. Edmund's Hall, Oxford, in 1813, receiving his B.A. on February 24, 1816, and an M.A. from Oxford on June 25, 1819.

On May 2, 1816, he married Jane Head. They had six children: Jane Miriam (Havergal) Crane (1817–1898), Henry East Havergal (1819–1875), Maria Vernon Graham Havergal (1821–1887), Ellen Prestage (Havergal) Shaw (1823–1886), Francis Tebbs Havergal (1829–1890), and Frances Ridley Havergal (1836–1879).

Ordained in 1816, he became Curate (assistant pastor) under Rev. Thomas Tregenna Biddulph, Vicar of St. James's Church, Bristol, and Rector of Durtons and Lyng, working in churches in Somersetshire. He was Curate at Coaley, Gloucestershire, 1819–1822. He moved to Astley, Worcestershire, where he served as Curate 1822–1829, and then Rector of Astley 1829–1842. On June 14, 1829, when driving alone, he had a very dangerous accident, throwing him out of the carriage, nearly killing him, causing a brain concussion, a gravely serious injury that caused him very poor health and bad eyesight (at times near blindness) for much or most of the rest of his life. He was Rector of St. Nicholas Church, Worcester, 1845–1860. His wife Jane died on July 5, 1848, aged 54. In July, 1851, he married Caroline Ann Cooke, who survived him, living till 1878. Poor health caused him to resign as Rector of St. Nicholas, and to move to Staffordshire, where he was Vicar of Shareshill Church 1860–1870. His youngest daughter, Frances Ridley Havergal, said that his last conscious day (Saturday before Easter) was "a very climax of peace and brightness in all respects." The next morning apoplexy rendered him unconscious, and he remained unconscious till he died two days later, April 19, 1870.

Like his daughter Frances Ridley Havergal, W.H.H. was a musician to the core, a rarely and finely gifted one. He was a master at the keyboard (his improvisations were profoundly rich), he had a fine, beautiful voice, and he composed valuable scores. Early in his life, he was offered a professorship in music at Oxford University, a very high honor in that day, but he declined that and a career in music to be a pastor. Few could so well compose music, yet he preferred to write a sermon than to compose a score. Though music was so very important to him, and he used music to enrich his ministry and benefit his hearers (he was the music leader in the churches he pastored), yet music was a secondary pursuit to him, and an enjoyment and relaxation, not his priority, unless his physical health precluded pastoral work. Though his priority was pastoral work, he was the foremost church musician in England in his generation (Dr. William Crotch was the generation before W.H.H., and William Sterndale Bennett was not primarily a church musician), and was very highly regarded by knowledgeable people for his compositions and his knowledge of music. The American music leader Lowell Mason wrote concerning his second trip to England, in 1850, that W.H.H.'s church music was the best that he heard, "excellent in all particulars and far in advance of anything that he heard" in England.[1] W.H.H. led the reform of church music, and few today realize the value of his efforts and publications to improve the practice of music in church worship. A generous—though not nearly complete—number of his published scores, his edition of Thomas Ravenscroft's Psalter (London: Novello, 1845), and his musicological treatise *A History of the Old Hundredth Psalm Tune* (New York: Mason Brothers, 1854) are given in Volume V of the Havergal edition (*Songs of Truth and Love: Music by Frances Ridley Havergal and William Henry Havergal*). He was a remarkably gifted organist and pianist, a beautiful singer, a valuable composer, and a true scholar of music.

He was also a finely gifted poet, leaving richly edifying poems and hymns, and a generous—though not complete—number of his poems are given in this volume.

William Henry Havergal preached more than 2,000 sermons over more than five decades (likely approaching or exceeding 3,000 sermons, based on his handwritten record of his sermons from 1816 to 1869), each sermon a true labor of love, a heart work, sermons

[1] *Music* ("A Monthly Magazine Devoted to the Art, Science, Technic and Literature"), Volume IV, May, 1893 to November, 1893, W. S. B. Mathews, Editor and Publisher (Chicago : Published at 240 Wabash Avenue, 1893), page 529. This statement was found in two other places: In *Education* ("A Monthly Magazine, Devoted to the Science, Art, Philosophy, and Literature of Education"), Frank H. Kasson and Frank H. Palmer, Editors, Volume XIV, September, 1893—June, 1894 (Boston: Kasson and Palmer, 50 Bromfield Street, 1894), in an essay on Lowell Mason entitled "Lowell Mason, American Musician" by Rev. James H. Ross, Somerville, Massachusetts (pages 411–416), Ross wrote this same quotation (on page 415) : "He found the musical service, in Rev. W. H. Havergal's church, Worcester, England, 'excellent in all particulars and far in advance of anything that he heard.' " In *The Poets of the Church* A Series of Biographical Sketches of Hymn-Writers with Notes on Their Hymns by Edwin F. Hatfield, D.D. (New York : Anson D. F. Randolph & Company, 1884), page 302, in his entry on William Henry Havergal, Dr. Hatfield wrote this same statement (only without the same quotation marks in Dr. Hatfield's text) : "He [Dr. Lowell Mason] describes the musical service in Mr. Havergal's church as excellent in all particulars, and far in advance of anything that he heard in England." See also page 1492 in Volume V of the Havergal edition.

searched from the Scriptures and taught to him by God, diligently prepared, preached to parish congregations and other audiences. Only four volumes of his sermons were published, all given here; he very likely was ready to publish many more if an opportunity were given, but these that we have are very rich, full of treasure.

Writing about William Henry Havergal's practice of preparation to preach his sermons, his daughter Maria V. G. Havergal wrote these comments at the bottom of an announcement sheet of Two Sermons on behalf of the Church Missionary Society preached on Sunday, October 21, 1860 in the Parish Church of Shareshill:

> One Sermon always written by Wednesday p.m. – the 2nd by Saturday before breakfast. ! (No "hours of darkness" work! N.B. It was my fathers rule to carefully look over all the Scripture, for each Sunday's service, & select his text from these. (Exceptions – also). He generally did so after each Sunday's work over. So getting a clean week to meditate on his texts ! ! [This transcription leaves Maria's precise text as she wrote this, not correcting her mistakes, which are minor.]

Remember that he was a true Anglican, and thus would have been mindful of the Scripture lessons to be read in church each Sunday morning and evening through the calendar year.

His daughter Miriam (the first-born of the six children, and the last one to die, 1817–1898) wrote a richly valuable account, *Records of the Life of the Rev. William Henry Havergal, M.A.* (London: Home Words Publishing Office, 1882). In this biography (original book page 29, page 370 of this volume), Miriam quoted this part from a letter dated October 23, 1821, early in his ministry:

> My parish has called me out a good deal, while my indoor hours have been fully occupied in attending to my pupil and in preparing sermons. In this latter employment my thoughts have little rest. I am an *anxious* sermon writer. Few things are more painful to me than to be obliged to preach a sermon I have used before, and it is so for two reasons: first, every old sermon skeleton rather pains me by its defects; and secondly, I love to preach that which I have felt and desire, and desire to feel that which I preach, and these things are only effected when the heart and the head and the hand have been engaged in the work of preparation.

In the same biography (*Records*, original book page 330, page 439 of this volume), Miriam wrote this of him near the end of his ministry:

> My father was again alarmingly ill early in January, 1869, and expressed himself as distressed at not being able to preach at Christ Church for Dr. Bickmore, as arranged for the very day after his illness began. He frequently preached for his friends in Leamington when at all able to do so, especially at Milverton and Holy Trinity, in which district he resided. He used in his study a folio Bible on a lecturn, and having looked out his text would ruminate on it for a day or two, and then write down the heads of the subject; but in the pulpit delivering the sermon without notes, and enlarging upon it extemporaneously.

One very important part of William Henry Havergal's work was his strong desire and advocacy to promote and advance the work of the Church Missionary Society, to raise awareness and support—money and prayer—for the missionaries bringing the good news of Christ to foreign lands. Over several decades he travelled and preached in many churches, presenting the need and the work of the C.M.S. His daughter Maria, in 1886 before she died in 1887, gave to the Church Missionary Society an invaluable collection of manuscripts and other items by F.R.H. and W.H.H. (now kept in the C.M.S. Archives at the University of Birmingham in England). Among these items was a travelling case with this label handwritten by Maria: "Revd W. H. Havergal's travelling case for C.M.S. in 1824–1828. Many C.M.S. papers & outlines of his speeches were kept in this till his rest from labours. April 19, 1870 Bequeathed to the C.M.S. M.V.G.H. 1886." This case contains handwritten notes, letters, and other manuscripts and items. There was also a bound volume (of pages originally blank, like a bound diary) of W.H.H.'s handwritten notes for sermons, and Maria wrote this on a label on the front cover:

> "One of my beloved father's (Revd W. H. Havergal's) Sermon cases, about 1817. Outlines of his C.M.S. sermons herein, bequeathed to that Society. My father extemporized his carefully prepared thoughts. Bequeathed to the C.M.S. 1886. M.V.G.H."

Maria also bequeathed to the C.M.S. another bound volume with this label handwritten by her on the front cover:

> "Rev. W. H. Havergal's life prints. 'A faithful minister in the Lord.' — The Record of texts & sermons – from March 31.1816. to Janry 3.1869. Sermons from June 5. to Sept 12.1869. not entered'. The last text "The Lord Jesus Christ be with thy spirit." Preached at Pyrmont – Waldeck Sep 1.1869 Bequeathed to the C.M.S. 1886. (M.V.G.H."

This is a golden volume of W.H.H.'s handwritten record of sermons he preached: the first sermon recorded was dated March 31, 1816, preached at Durston on Acts 4:12, and the last sermon recorded was dated January 3, 1869, preached at Milverton in Leamington on Deuteronomy 33:16. This volume is his handwritten record of 160 pages of recorded entries of sermons he preached, recording the place, date, and Scripture text for each sermon. At the end, one of his children wrote this entry:

> My father's last Sermon was preached at Pyrmont Waldeck [in Germany] (C.C.C.S.) Sept 12 1869. text "The Lord Jesus Christ be with thy spirit." 2 Timothy IV.22.

See page 476, and also pages 41, 133, and 467, of this book. All these items were copied in the research on the Havergal edition, but now after years of effort, the lack of time, means, and energy preclude for now the transcription and publication of the true gold in these manuscripts of W.H.H. The bound volume of his handwritten record of his sermons (bequeathed by Maria V. G. Havergal to the Church Missionary Society) had another part: the record of the sermons filled 160 pages, but did not take nearly all of the pages of the volume, and W.H.H. turned over the volume and wrote from the back side forward (inversely from the front, effectively making two books of the single bound volume) 19 pages of handwritten notes on a book entitled *The Art of Logic. on Simple Terms.* This was apparently his notes and reacting comments to John Milton's Latin treatise *Artis Logicae* published in 1672. W.H.H. was a wonderfully brilliant man, and a true scholar with wide interests. This and indeed all of these comments are only a brief, very incomplete description of him, his life, and his work.

Among the Havergal manuscripts and papers was found a copy of *The Work of Jesus Christ, as an Advocate, Clearly Explain'd, and Largely Improv'd, for the Benefit of All Believers. From I John ii.1.* by John Bunyan, this copy printed in London for John Marshall, 1725. In the front of the book this is signed: W. H. Havergal. St Nicholas, Worcester 1847. Below his signature, his widow Caroline Ann Havergal wrote "Last book finished by my blessed husband 1870."

Given next are four quotations from Miriam's biography of William Henry Havergal.

This was written by his second wife, Caroline Ann, on September 23, 1857, concerning a period of W.H.H.'s very severe illness:

> "Wednesday, 23rd.—He was fully dressed for the first time. A kind message from his curate (the Rev. S. B. James) elicited, 'I thank him from the depths of my heart, and pray the Lord to sustain and comfort him.' Poor Fanny had had an alarming attack of erysipelas, brought on by imprudence, but as she was recovering he said, 'God is better than our fears.' I have omitted one little thing: as Fanny one evening bent over him to bid him good-night, saying to him, 'What a gem you are!' he said, 'Hush, hush, my child, your father is unworthy, unworthy—a worm and no man.' " [2]

His wife Caroline also recorded,

> . . . . A lady calling, expressing her thanks to him for his sweet and comforting sermon, he meekly answered, "The Lord make it profitable, and then take all the praise." Another thanking him said it was a precious sermon. "Nothing in itself," he said, "all nothing; but the Lord can make it precious, and may He do so." [3]

His former curate and later successor as Rector of St. Nicholas' Church, Worcester, England, Charles Bullock, wrote,

> Yes, he knew and groaned under the "plague of his own heart." He felt cause enough to lie low before God, whilst he was conscious of his integrity before man; and it was this combination of integrity and humility which

[2] Jane Miriam (Havergal) Crane, *Records of the Life of the Rev. William Henry Havergal, M. A.* (London: Home Words Publishing Office, 1882), original book page 244, page 420 of this book.

[3] Crane, *Records of the Rev. William Henry Havergal, M.A.* (London: Home Words Publishing Office, 1882), original book page 239; page 419 of this book.

gave such power to his testimony to the Gospel of God's grace, and made him not only a preacher in the pulpit, but a preacher in the world—a preacher of what Herbert has beautifully styled 'the visible rhetoric of a holy life.'" [4]

Next is a larger quotation of Charles Bullock's memorial sermon on W.H.H. Note especially the first sentence of the second paragraph, "In all that he did he was emphatically 'real.' "

> Not, indeed, that he was without faults or failings, for "there is not a just man upon earth that doeth good and sinneth not;" but Gospel grace wrought so manifestly in him "the fruits of the Spirit," that, to a remarkable degree, he "adorned the doctrine of God his Saviour:" so that it would be difficult for those who knew him best to specify what those faults and failings were.
>
> In all that he did he was emphatically "real." There was harmony in his character; the counterpart of that harmony of musical genius which gave him a world-wide reputation. [W.H.H. as a church musician was very highly regarded on both sides of the Atlantic.] None could fail to recognize his "godly sincerity." He preached and said what he felt: and from the heart he spoke to the heart, as if he really had a message from God to deliver. He was always the pastor. His was not the ministry of official routine: it was the ministry of the life. His testimony respecting his friend, the Rev. John East, of Bath, when preaching his funeral sermon, applies most truly to himself:—
>
>> The livery of his Divine Master was always and everywhere visibly upon him. Whether in the desk or the pulpit, the committee-room or the platform, the cottage or the mansion, the schoolroom or the sick chamber, the street or the railway, he was always the recognized but unostentatious servant of the Saviour whom he loved. He was not ashamed of his Master, or of His Name, or to speak a word for Him, or to do an act for Him whenever a favourable or fitting opportunity presented itself.
>
> He advised, he admonished, he sympathized; and, to the utmost of his means, he aided those who stood in need of aid. And throughout his ministry he was eminently "faithful." He did not hesitate, though he well knew the cost, to battle manfully with the vices and frivolities of the day. None could hearken to his conversation and think it possible to "serve God and mammon." [5]

Andrew James Symington wrote this in his "Biographical Sketch" of W.H.H.:

> As genial as he was gentlemanly, refined in his tastes, high-souled, and gifted, his own immediate home circle, relatives, and numerous friends, were all perfectly devoted to him; and no one could possibly approach him, even in a casual way, without feeling the radiation of Christian light and warmth from his heart and beaming face; for to the core he was a true man: true to God, and true to his fellow men.[6]

". . . to the core he was a true man: true to God, and true to his fellow men." This is reminiscent of Matthew 22:37–40, the two commandments. Only Jesus Christ alone can do that in a person.

These comments are only brief, very incomplete glimpses of W.H.H. Much more can be said of this genuine disciple of the Lord Jesus Christ. He was a true example, as Paul wrote, "Be ye followers of me even as I also am of Christ." I Corinthians 11:1

He was a true gem, of the Lord's making. Fame or praise of men was utterly of no interest to him, but he greatly desired that others know his Saviour.

William Henry Havergal was a man truly blessed by God and used by Him to bless many others. Similarly to Robert Murray M'Cheyne, John Newton, J. C. Ryle, Horatius Bonar, Alexander Bonar, and other godly ministers of his time more widely known today, W.H.H. is a large, rich gold-mine full of true treasure from the Lord. Thanks be to God. The Lamb is all the glory in Emmanuel's land, the kingdom of God. David Chalkley

4 Crane, *Records*, original book pages 380–381; page 483 of this book.

5 Crane, *Records of W.H.H.*, original book pages 373–375; pages 448–449 of this book.

6 *The Pastor Remembered, and the Brethren Entreated A Memorial of the Rev. W. H. Havergal, M.A.* by Charles Bullock, with the "Biographical Sketch" by Andrew James Symington (London: W. Hunt & Co., S. W. Partridge & Co., and The Christian Book Society, no date, likely 1870), original book pages 52–53, page 492 of this book.

William Henry Havergal, and his first wife, Jane Head Havergal, oil portraits by Solomon Cole in 1845. Married on May 2, 1816, they had six children. She died on July 5, 1848, aged 54.

SIX LECTURES

ON THE

ARK OF THE COVENANT.

By the Rev. William Henry Havergal, M.A.

G. Williams and Co., Printers, Wolverhampton.

PREFATORY NOTE.

THESE Lectures were preached, during the Lent of 1852, in the parish Church of St. Nicholas, Worcester, of which the author was then the Rector.

From that time to the present they have lain untouched, and, consequently, have had a longer sleep than the prescribed literary period.

They have at length been awakened by the kind proposal of a once attentive and grateful hearer, still resident in Worcester. That proposal exempts the author from all risk of loss in their publication.

When the Lectures were preached, many passages were extemporaneously supplemented by practical remarks, which are not now attempted to be supplied. No apology is offered for disregarding the hard and stringent rule of which the late Bishop Marsh was the chief exponent in England, namely, that nothing in the Old Testament is to be considered *typical* unless recognised as such in the New Testament. The opponents of the rule might be mustered into a splendid host, among whom should be reckoned one who seems to have been forgotten, namely, the writer of the homily for Whitsunday.

Should the publication of the present Lectures prove acceptable as a means of spiritual edification, others of a similar character may follow; e.g., on "Job," "Melchisedeck," "The Passover," The "Last Words of David," "The Queen of Sheba," "Gethsemane," etc., etc., etc.

Any profits which may accrue will be devoted towards the erection of a Parsonage House, in the parish of Pipe and Lyde, near Hereford.

Want of sight disables the author from any inspection of either manuscripts or proofs. For this service he is indebted to his kind friend and former helper in the parish of St. Nicholas, the Rev. S. B. James.

PYRMONT, N.W. GERMANY,
August, 1867.

[Note: This volume seems to have been privately printed without an official publisher and without a list of subscribers.]

CONTENTS.

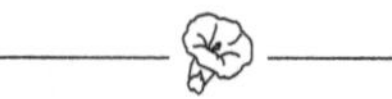

JUST PUBLISHED, PRICE TWO SHILLINGS,

Appendix

TO THE SIXTH EDITION OF THE

REVEREND W. H. HAVERGAL'S

Old Church Psalmody.

THIS small Volume, though nominally connected with one, the most valuable, of our Metrical Tune-Books, is really an "APPENDIX" to every Book of that class in use in English and American Churches and Chapels.

Mr Havergal's "OLD CHURCH PSALMODY," in its latest Edition, contained tunes for 27 different Metres, and few of the Tune-Books in general use contain more than that number: but the present "APPENDIX" contains Tunes for 49 Metres, to suit the translated German and other Hymns now so popular. These Tunes have all been contributed by "living Authors," and many of them have been "specially Composed" by the Rev. Sir F. A. GORE OUSELEY, Bart.; the Rev. W. H. HAVERGAL, and other well-known Church-musical writers: and will be found as worthy the notice of the most refined Choir for their scientific construction, as they are well adapted for Congregational use by their melodic simplicity.

LONDON:

ENOCH AND SONS, 19 HOLLES ST. CAVENDISH SQ. W.

The two separate volumes Old Church Psalmody *(1847) and* A Hundred Psalm and Hymn Tunes *(1859) were published by W.H.H. while he lived. The date of this Appendix is not known. After he died, F.R.H. edited and published the definitive* Havergal's Psalmody and Century of Chants *(1871), adding a number of unpublished manuscript scores by her father and a number of scores composed by F.R.H. See page 292 of this book. These scores, and much other music by W.H.H., are published in Volume V of the Havergal edition.*

THE ARK OF THE COVENANT.

LECTURE I.

"The ark of the covenant overlaid round about with gold, wherein was the golden pot that had manna, and Aaron's rod that budded, and the tables of the covenant; and over it the cherubims of glory shadowing the mercy-seat."—Hebrews 9:4, 5.

THE inspired Apostle, in this part of his epistle, commences a brief description of the ancient Tabernacle and its glorious furniture. Neither the one nor the other were extant in his day; for the tabernacle had been superseded by the temple, and that temple, with the principal articles which adorned it, had been either plundered or destroyed. But, the revelation of what had been was intensely interesting to every Jew. To the Apostle, however, they were more than interesting. They were to his mental eye luminous and invaluable types of either the Saviour or his Gospel. He, therefore, felt a double interest in explaining them to his "kinsmen according to the flesh:" for, it can hardly be doubted that, in some of his many discourses to the Hebrews, he followed out the object of this brief epistle, and largely expounded the evangelical intention of both the furniture and the services of the tabernacle, to which they too commonly attached a carnal meaning.

Fully assured, then, that the record of Jewish rites, and of everything indeed, which pertained to the tabernacle is preserved for Gentile instruction, and that the very soul and spirit of Christianity is contained in them, we cannot do otherwise than well, if, at the present season, we commence a series of lectures respecting that most glorious and most venerable symbol, "The Ark of the Covenant." That symbol was the very heart and core of the Mosaic system. Every service had reference to it. The prosperity of the nation was intimately connected with it: and the history of many ages received its character from it. As a theological subject, therefore, "the ark of the covenant" is beautifully diffuse in itself, and pleasantly inviting to the biblical student. May our contemplation of it be abundantly profitable, and largely sanctified by the Holy Spirit!

I. The Apostle speaks of "the ark of the covenant" as a thing well known to the Hebrews. But it was known to them only as described by report and the written Word of God. For full four hundred years it had been lost to the Jewish nation. Consequently, neither the writer nor any reader of this epistle had ever seen it. Now, as Jewish report was of very uncertain accuracy; but, as the divine record is as full and as authentic to us as it was to them, we are as competent as the Hebrews themselves to form correct ideas of what the ark really was, and for what purposes it was designed.

1. The word ark, though applied, in the English tongue, to the vessel which Noah built, to the bulrush basket or fabric in which the babe Moses was concealed, and the coffer, or chest in which the tables of the law were deposited, is not one and the same word in the Hebrew language. The ark of Noah, and the little ark of the Nile, were each "*Thebat*": whereas the ark of the covenant was "*Arun.*"

2. This ark of the covenant, independently of "the mercy-seat" above it, was simply a chest or coffer, made of cedar wood and gold plates, but wrought with the most exquisite workmanship.

3. The dimensions of it were not at all considerable, nor so large as is popularly supposed, especially as four Levites were appointed to bear it. According to ordinary computation it was only three feet nine inches long, two feet three inches broad, and two feet three inches deep. But, it was fitted for the purpose for which Jehovah designed it: and He, in all His designs, is eminently observable for consulting fitness of operation for the end in view. There is nothing superfluous in any of His works. They are neither too large nor too little; but admirably fitted for their respective ends. Hence, as this ark or chest was intended as a case to contain the tables of the Law, we can well ascertain the size of these tables. Certainly, they were not half so large as some of those tall "Tables of Commandments" which garnish many a chancel of our country churches. They could not have been more than three feet six inches long and two feet wide, being, in fact, like a pair of large folding slates, or thin stone tablets, such as Moses, or any man, might conveniently carry on one arm, when walking up a hill. There were, however, other purposes to be answered by this ark, besides this one of containing the tablets of the testimony. We shall see what they were, when we have seen a little further into the structure of the ark itself.

4. When God gave directions to Moses for building the tabernacle of worship, the first thing which He described, and

the first which He ordered to be made was this ark of the covenant. The details of its formation are set down in Exodus 25:10–16.

> "And they shall make an ark of shittim wood: two cubits and a half shall be the length thereof and a cubit and a half the breadth thereof, and a cubit and a half the height thereof.
>
> "And thou shalt overlay it with pure gold; within and without shalt thou overlay it, and shall make upon it a crown of gold round about.
>
> "And thou shalt make staves of shittim wood, and overlay them with pure gold.
>
> "And thou shalt put the staves into the rings by the sides of the ark, that the ark may be borne by them.
>
> "The staves shall be in the rings of the ark: they shall not be taken from it.
>
> "And thou shalt put into the ark the testimony which I shall give thee."

We here find certain particulars which require attentive observation:

(1.) God Himself is the architect of the ark. Everything respecting it originates with Him. He, also, as a subsequent chapter discloses to us, inspires an artist for the fulfilment of the design: so, as the artist wrought under His inspiration, the workmanship of the ark was truly divine. In Exodus 31:1–7, we read what is recorded on this point.

> "And the Lord spake unto Moses, saying,
>
> "See, I have called by name Bezaleel, the son of Uri, the son of Hur, of the tribe of Judah:
>
> "And I have filled him with the spirit of God, in wisdom, and in understanding, and in knowledge, and in all manner of workmanship,
>
> "To devise cunning works, to work in gold, and in silver, and in brass,
>
> "And in cutting of stones, to set them, and in carving of timber, to work in all manner of workmanship.
>
> "And I, behold, I have given with him Aholiab, the son of Ahisamach, of the tribe of Dan: and in the hearts of all that are wise-hearted I have put wisdom, that they may make all that I have commanded thee;
>
> "The tabernacle of the congregation, and the ark of the testimony, and the mercy-seat that is thereupon, and all the furniture of the tabernacle."

In the thirty-seventh chapter and first verse, we are expressly certified that it was Bezaleel who made the ark.

(2.) The materials of the ark were of the most choice and costly kind, and yet they were, in reality, only two. They were fragrant cedar wood and pure gold. The wood formed the shell of the chest, and the gold overlaid every part of it, both within and without.

(3.) Round the topmost edges of the sacred chest was a projecting rim of gold, called "a crown, or coronet of gold round about." This, though called a crown, was not a lid or cover, (for that was a very different thing, as we have presently to see) but it was a sort of fence or border, parallel with the outside edge, ornamentally formed like a coronet, and intended to fit the mercy-seat, which was put on like a lid or cover upon the topmost edges of the ark.

(4.) On each of the four corners of the ark, Bezaleel was to put a ring of cast gold—to form sockets for the insertion of staves, by which the Levites might bear it on their shoulders. The four rings and the four bearers would necessarily be in four different places; which might be intended for an intimation to the Jews, that the True Ark should eventually be carried to the four quarters of the world.

(5.) The staves, by which the ark was borne, were of precisely the same materials as the ark itself. They were to be of shittim wood or cedar, overlaid with gold. One remarkable injunction was given respecting them, viz.: that, when once put in, they were never to be taken out of the rings, for which they were fitted. They were always to remain in readiness for use: and this might be to testify that the Levites ought always to be in readiness to use them; and that the God, whom the ark represented, was ever ready to rise up on behalf of those who were ready to follow Him.

5. The primary intention of the ark was, as you have heard, and as the Jews were often reminded, for containing the tables of the Law, otherwise called the testimony or the covenant. "Thou shalt put into the ark the testimony which I will give thee."

The ten commandments were a summary of God's mind to man. They described, in brief, all that He required of man. They were the ground of a covenant between Him and the people; and, inasmuch as they were written on two tablets, those tablets were the testimonies of the covenant, because they at once testified God's will to the people and would testify against the people if they failed to keep them. Hence as God's law or testimony was everything to God, we read of "the tables of the testimony" (Exodus 31:18), and "the ark of the testimony" (Exodus 25:22), and "the tabernacle of the testimony" (Exodus 38:21). In after times, the term "testimony" was applied to the whole book of the law, and now it is applied to the gospel also.

But, strange to say, when God directed the ark to be made for holding the tables of the law, those tables were not in existence. Law itself had been given, but the tables, on which it was written, were not yet entrusted to Moses. So provident is the God of providence. He makes due preparation for everything, especially for the preservation of the things which are dearest to Him. He prepared paradise for Adam before he formed Adam himself. He planned Noah's ark long before

Noah was in danger. And now He gives directions for a receptacle for the testimony before that testimony is inscribed on the tables of stone. So, also, (and glory be to His holy name for it!) when He gave the law, which He knew the people would break, He had well provided a mediator and substitute who should perfectly keep it. In the fulness of time, Christ was made under the law, that He might redeem those who were in bondage to the curse of it.

II. In our text, as usually read, it is asserted that, besides "the tables of the covenant," the pot of manna and Aaron's rod that budded were *in* the ark.

> "The ark of the covenant overlaid round about with gold, wherein was the golden pot that had manna, and Aaron's rod that budded, and the tables of the covenant;
>
> "And over it the cherubims of glory shadowing the mercy seat; of which we cannot now speak particularly."

As this apparent assertion is in direct opposition to 1 Kings 8:9, it is proper that the seeming contradiction should be set right. That verse, with emphatic precision, declares that "There was *nothing in the ark save the two tables of stone*, which Moses put there at Horeb."

Added to this declaration is the fact that nowhere in the Old Testament is it said that the pot of manna and Aaron's rod were *in* the ark. On the contrary, it is constantly stated that they were *before* the ark, i.e., by it, near it, in presence of it, within the veil, together with the few other things which were permitted to have a place in the holy of holies. (Exodus 16:33, 34. Numbers 17:10.)

Learned men have spent, perhaps wasted, much time in devising ingenious methods of reconciling the apparent contradiction.[1] Their pains, as Bishop Patrick has observed, might have been spared by a very simple, but very truthful process: for the two Greek terms in our text, translated by one word "wherein," may as properly, and do as commonly mean by which, with which, or near[2] which, as in which or "wherein." A multitude of quotations could be speedily adduced to prove the fact of such meaning of the terms. There is, therefore, no real difficulty in the case—particularly to those who have a due knowledge of the original tongues.

To justify our translation, however, it has been suggested that the word "wherein" refers not to "the ark of the covenant," but to the holy of holies, in which the ark itself was. The passage must then be read in this manner:

> "And after the second veil, the tabernacle, which is called the holiest of all; which had the golden censer and the ark of the covenant, overlaid round about with gold; wherein (i.e., in which tabernacle) was the golden pot that had manna, and Aaron's rod that budded, and the tables of the covenant."

The original Greek may bear this sense, but it is with a strain. The far easier and preferable method is the one already suggested. In corroboration, also, of the pretty plain fact that there was nothing really in the ark but the tables of the law, let it be borne in mind that, if the ark itself was only three feet six inches long, it would be far too short to contain a rod which, in all probability, was nearly double that length.

The supposed discrepancy is just one of those occurrences which should arm humble readers of the Bible against the cavils of infidel objectors; and, at the same time, make them confident in the integrity of Holy Scripture, and thankful for its abundant plainness.

It is proper for it further to be noticed that, in the text, we are told a little additional fact, which is not mentioned in the Old Testament. The pot which contained the manna is described as a "*golden* pot." This is not told us by Moses. But, that a pot or vessel, used for the storing of manna, should be made of gold, is both very likely in itself and quite in keeping with all that surrounded it. Gold was truly fitting for the formation of a vessel which was to hold a miraculous product, and the very preservation of which was itself a standing miracle. The manna, when originally given, would only keep for a single day, or, at the most, for two days, when the second day was the Sabbath. But, when deposited in the golden pot before the ark it was perpetually preserved from putrefaction, and became a type of that "hidden manna" which ever liveth in the true holy of holies for the vital sustenance of the spiritual nation below.

III. Appended to the ark, and, in one sense, part and parcel of it, was the mercy-seat, with the cherubim of glory over it. "And over it the cherubims of glory, shadowing the mercy-seat."

This propitiatory, or mercy-seat, was the grand object of Hebrew awe and solemn veneration. All that was dear to Israel was centred in it, for it was the precise and secret place of the divine presence, as well as being in itself peculiarly significant of great and important truths.

The description of this mercy-seat, and how it was to be made, is recorded in the verses which follow the description of the formation of the ark. (Exodus 25:17–22.)

> "And thou shalt make a mercy-seat of pure gold: two cubits and a half shall be the length thereof, and a cubit and a half the breadth thereof.
>
> "And thou shalt make two cherubims of gold, of beaten work shalt thou make them, in the two ends of the mercy-seat.

[1] "Andrew Sennertus, of Wittemberg, (circ. 1655) compiled a work which contained nearly everything which had been surmised upon the subject."

[2] "*In* the place where He was crucified (meaning, evidently, *near* to the place) was a garden."—John 19:41.

"And make one cherub on the one end, and the other cherub on the other end: even of the mercy-seat shall ye make the cherubims on the two ends thereof.

"And the cherubims shall stretch forth their wings on high, covering the mercy-seat with their wings, and their faces shall look one to another; toward the mercy-seat shall the faces of the cherubims be,

"And thou shalt put the mercy-seat above upon the ark; and in the ark thou shalt put the testimony that I shall give thee.

"And there I will meet with thee; and I will commune with thee from above the mercy-seat, from between the two cherubims which are upon the ark of the testimony, of all things which I will give thee in commandment unto the children of Israel."

1. This so-called "mercy-seat" was the lid or covering for the ark, and was made entirely of gold—pure and solid. It was exactly as long and as broad as the ark itself; and so, fitting it closely on the top, was kept in its place by its own weight, and by the golden rim or coronet-like fringe which went all around the edges of the ark, and so, of course, prevented it, when standing or carried evenly, from slipping off. How thick it was is not stated; but certain circumstances induce the belief that it was firm and strong.

2. At each of the two ends of the mercy-seat was a mystical figure, called a cherub. Each was also made of gold, only not fastened *on* to the mercy-seat, but wrought out of the same metallic mass, and so constituting an inseparable part of the mercy-seat itself. This fact of the cherubim and the mercy-seat being beaten, not molten, out of one and the same mass of gold, was peremptorily commanded of God, and punctually observed by Bezaleel. "He made two cherubims of gold, *beaten out of one piece* made he them on the two ends of the mercy-seat."

The intention of their being thus formed out of one piece is not clear to us. Doubtless, it was mystical and important, as well as worthy of Him, who will, one day, enable us better to understand it. Nevertheless, an opinion or two will presently be stated.

3. What was the exact figure, aspect, and meaning of these golden cherubim has been, and perhaps will, on earth, always be a very hard and disputed point. Various descriptions are given of the cherubim, particularly by Ezekiel 1:4–14, and by St. John in Revelation 4:6, 7, 8, from which it appears that they were "winged beings," with four diverse faces, and one human-like body, terminating in ox or "calf" shaped feet. But, whether this was their peculiar form on the ark is by no means certain. Josephus, (Antiq. 3:6) when speaking of them, says—with no little point—they "were *winged animals, resembling nothing that was ever seen by men.*" That they sometimes resembled an ox is certain from what Ezekiel says in chapter 10:14, compared with 1:10, where the face of an ox and the face of a cherub are reckoned one and the same. And yet *the union* of the man's face with the lion's face is mysteriously significant! Solomon made, for the holy place in the temple, two very large cherubim of olive-tree wood, whose wings shadowed nearly the whole of the area. The cherubim on the ark were of comparatively small dimensions.

As to their mystical meaning, the two principal opinions are these: A small, but goodly number of theologians regard them as symbols of the Trinity in Unity; and support their opinion by, at least, very ingenious and very interesting arguments which, however, are too long and too erudite to be even recapitulated here. Suffice it to add, that the beating out of the cherubim from the same mass of gold as the mercy-seat, is with them a strong fact for the support of their opinion that those cherubim were symbols of deity and not of angelic existences: because, say they, as the mercy-seat was confessedly emblematical of divine graciousness, so must the cherubic figures be emblems of divine powers, inasmuch as they were formed out of the same metallic mass, which is tantamount to being of the same nature.

The generality of divines take a different (I will not say a more satisfactory) view of the case. They consider these figures as intended to represent the persons and services of angels, who derive their being from God, are partakers of His holy nature, and are not only intensely interested in the grant of mercy to fallen man, but are zealously employed in carrying it out.

The turning of their faces downwards and inwards towards each other is taken for a sign of their reverent humility, their deep earnestness respecting God's law and God's mercy to the transgressors of it, and their own perfect agreement with, and inclination towards, one another. The outstretching and overshadowing of their wings are thought to represent their constant readiness to fly anywhere for the execution of God's commands, and their attendance around His seat of glory in heaven.

4. Be these things as they may, we are sure of one thing, which is the great thing of the whole, that the mercy-seat, when placed on the ark, was, to the Jews, the visible throne of the invisible God.—(Exodus 25:22). Here, on the mercy-seat, dwelt the Shechinah, or glorious ray of the divine presence. Before it all Israel trembled. In front stood the high priest once a year, when making a ritual atonement for the sins of the people. And, from it, came forth the voice of Jehovah, when Moses, or any other appointed mediator, consulted the God of the nation.

5. When the tabernacle and all its furniture were completed, a day was fixed for the setting up of the whole in due order. On the first day of the first month of the second year of Israel's entrance in the wilderness, the entire fabric was erected on its dry and burning sands. It must have been a deeply interesting moment in the life of Moses when, with his own hands, he

took the two tables of the law, and devoutly placed them within the ark; for that he so did, and that he also put the mercy-seat upon the ark, we are expressly told in Exodus 11:20.

After this, and during the life-time of Moses, no particular incident seems to have occurred to the ark beyond the ordinary occurrences which were previously arranged respecting it. When the time came for the tribes to leave their encampment at Horeb, the tabernacle was taken down, and the ark was carried forward, in the manner prescribed, to be at once a guide and a defence. An interesting description of what was done and said is given in Numbers 10:33–36. Regarding it then as thoroughly perfect, and placed in its destined position within the veil, let us give a retrospective glance upon it, and what concerns it.

1. View the ark as possessing this remarkable peculiarity. *It was not only the first thing made for the tabernacle, but the chief thing for which the tabernacle itself was made.* It was to the whole Jewish system what the heart is to animal economy. The heart is the first thing formed in man, or beast, or bird; and, to each, it is essential to vitality. Keep the heart in sound and healthy action, and all is well. Take the heart away, and all is gone. So was it with "the ark of the covenant." It was made before the other vessels of the sanctuary, or even the sanctuary itself was made. All was well in Israel when it occupied its proper place as to locality and the affections of the people. But, when it was removed and lost, "the glory departed from Israel," as the dying wife of Phineas too plaintively said. So, afterwards, when the ark was absent from the tabernacle, it was like the absence of Jehovah Himself; for, on that occasion, it is said, (1 Samuel 7:2) "All the house of Israel lamented after the Lord."

2. View the ark as *a beautifully-instructive symbol to the Jewish nation.* It taught them, in substance, what the gospel teaches us. The tables of the law can be approached only by the *mercy*-seat. Unless that mercy covered over human violations of the law, judgment would come forth to destruction.

It taught the Jews, also, that there was no communion with a holy God, but on the ground of His own mercy. These things would induce inquiring to seek further into the truths which respect salvation; and God's good spirit was ever ready to teach them.

3. Seeing, then, that all these circumstances and particulars were divinely prescribed, and have been divinely communicated and preserved, we may be sure of their high importance. For our learning they were written, and God expects us to learn them. We ought, indeed, to read and mark them well, not only on account of their value, but also on account of their extreme interest and profit.

Christians are not universally awake to the benefits of a careful study of Old Testament topics. They are not so interested with them as the Apostles were, for they regarded them as "the lively oracles," and the ancient store-house of saving truth. It will be one object of the present lectures "to stir up pure minds by way of remembrance," and to encourage all to a wider perusal of God's word, and a more pains-taking study of its contents.

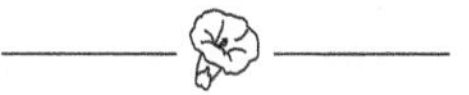

LECTURE II.

"Which are a shadow of things to come, but the body is of Christ."—Colossians 2:17.

THOUGH St. Paul speaks these words with immediate reference to the meats and drinks, times and seasons of the Jewish church, yet he does not, by any means, confine them to those things. He the rather uses them, as elsewhere, with relation to the whole Jewish ritual. Everything in that ritual, as is again and again stated in the epistle to the Hebrews, was intended to foreshadow and prefigure either the person or the truth of Christ. The law, as therein said, had "a shadow of good things to come;" and the tabernacle, with *all* its furniture, "was a figure for the time then present."—(Hebrews 10:1, and 9:9.) Consequently, as the whole includes the parts, and "the law" and "the tabernacle" included "the ark of the covenant," that ark was "a figure" of Christ,—a shadow of the "good things to come" in Him,—a shadow of which the body was Himself. The word "shadow," as used in our text, and in other texts, is variously interpreted. Some divines construe it in the sense of *an outline* such as a portrait painter traces before he begins the filling up. This idea represents everything Mosaic as a mere outline, of which Christ was to be the full portrait. Others, however, regard it as the reflection of an object in a mirror, or by the sun. The shadow only is discerned, but the real object which it reflects is so placed as not yet to be seen. Consequently, the thing discerned is neither real nor satisfactory. It does but represent that which the mind desires. Thus, "the ark of the covenant," though a real object in itself, was not the real object of Jehovah's intention. It was only a shadow of Christ. In the former lecture we considered "the ark of the covenant as to its history under Moses." We are now, according to the plan proposed, to consider "the ark as to its reference to the Lord Jesus Christ." As we have to contemplate the subsequent ages of the ark's historical existence, we shall not anticipate that history, but confine our view of it to the time when it stood, in all its completeness, in "the tent of the testimony," when set up by Moses in the wilderness. It was then a magnificent shadow, of which Christ was the body. But, here, let me meet an objection which less thoughtful persons are wont to raise against the study of such shadows, and which, therefore, applies to a discourse like the present. What need, say these objectors, is there to concern ourselves about the old shadows of the law which have long passed away? Had we not better give our undivided attention to Him, who is the substance of them all, now that He is clearly revealed to us? Why not consider Christ directly and at once—in His manifested person—rather than by looking back to the ark, which has long ago ceased to exist? There is much plausibility in these questions, but there is, also, no little infidelity lurking in them. Our answer to them is this: Though the Mosaic shadows have passed away, the record of them remains. That record is the word of Christ, and is given for our study. If we study it as He explained it, we *must* come to the things of the law; for Himself expounded to the disciples at Emmaus "the things which were written concerning Him *in the law*." When, therefore, we find Christ in the law, that law becomes the gospel to us, and all its incidents and circumstances are only so many interesting delineations of His person and character. In a word, the *figures* of the law are turned into evangelical *memorials*, which are replete with the richest instruction to all who desire to know the fulness of the gospel. There is a remark upon this subject taken by Bishop Home from the writings of the celebrated Pascal, which is so wise, beautiful, and appropriate, that its introduction here is almost unavoidable.

> Under the Jewish economy, truth appeared but in figure: in heaven it is open and without a veil: in the church militant it is so veiled *as yet to be discerned by its correspondence with the figure. As the figure was first built up in the truth, so the truth is now distinguishable by the figure.*—(Bishop Horne on the Psalms. Preface, p. 21.)

In contemplating "the ark of the covenant" in its relation to Christ, the following arrangement will be observed:—First, the ark itself; next, the mercy-seat as placed on the ark; and then, the uses of the ark and the mercy-seat combined. May the God of the ark show us His mercy, and grant us His grace!

I. *The ark itself in its typical relation to Christ.* Without any such typical relation, it would have been a merely splendid and curious fabric, but nothing more. There would have been nothing glorious, nothing instructive, nothing valuable in it. So true is it that every external object is important, only so far as it refers to Christ.

Let us search for the typical relation of the ark to Him in the following particulars:

1. *The ark was composed of only two substances*—cedar wood and pure gold. Nothing else whatever was used in its structure. Now, as cedar wood is a product of the earth, and gold a settled formation, the one is a fit representation of the earthly nature of Christ, and the other of His heavenly origin. In one person He unites two, and only two, natures, the human and the divine, not at all the angelic. Though man, He was God; and in a manner, too, which was shadowed by the union of cedar and gold in the composition of the ark.

The human nature was taken into union with the divine essence. So the gold covered the cedar wood, embraced and embosomed it, as it were, in such wise as to be one with it, and inseparable from it.

The incorruptibility of our Lord's humanity was, also, foreshadowed by the cedar wood; for it is a proverbially durable wood. Pliny, the classical naturalist, called it "the wood of eternity." Fit emblem, therefore, was it of that body which could "see no corruption." United with the gold it became a noble figure of that union of humanity and deity which are never to be separated. The two natures make but one Christ for ever and ever.

2. *The design of the ark was to contain the tables of the law.* It was built for that express purpose, and called after it accordingly. God's law was both a covenant and a testimony—a covenant between Him and the people, and a testimony of His own mind to them for the regulation of their conduct towards Him. The ark was "the ark of the covenant" or of the testimony, because it was the splendid, stately, and solemn receptacle of the tables or records of it.

These tables were, also, a renewed or second set; the first having been broken in anger for the sin of the people. Now, because Adam broke the divine law, when it was first given to him, it was renewed and placed in better hands than his. It was put within an ark which held it safe till all that it demanded had been fully accomplished. Christ was that ark. His incarnation took place in order that He might embody the perfect law of God, and perfectly keep it for the honour of God and the salvation of man. "Thy law (said He prophetically) is within my heart. I delight to do Thy will, O my God." Because of the safety and inviolable integrity of the law, in the person of Christ, all His believing followers fulfil the law in Him, and are justified by the righteousness of Him who fulfilled it.

3. *The ark was the first thing which was formed for the tabernacle, and that very thing for which the tabernacle and all else was constructed.* Nothing else was named before it. It took the precedence of everything, in both the command for its execution and in the execution itself. How vividly does this fact testify the priority of Him who is the true ark of the living God! Is not Jesus "the First" of all beings, and of all things? Is He not the first begotten and the first born? Is He not "*before* all things"? And are not "all things made *for* Him"? Yes, verily, He is First and All. Eternity will unfold His priority and pre-eminence to a degree which our poor understandings cannot now comprehend. But, when we see the true tabernacle, we shall see how it all was built for the glory of the true ark.

4. *The ark had a crown-like border all round its topmost edge.* "Thou shalt make upon it a crown of gold round about." So that, although this crown of gold was for a fence, or enveloping border, to hold fast the mercy-seat, yet did it give to the ark a noble, stately, and regal appearance. What could better represent the regal character of Him whom the ark itself represented? Though despised as a Nazarene, He is the "king of saints." "On His head are many crowns." The Father hath set on Him "a crown of pure gold," and He shall wear it when all other crowns are either cast before Him or crumbled into dust. May we acknowledge His beauty, and bow to His authority!

5. *The ark was a work of inspiration.* The Spirit of God came down upon Bezaleel on purpose for the work. Without that inspiration he would have been unequal to the task; and, as to its mystical intention, he never could have even surmised it. The body of our adorable Saviour was, we must ever reverently recollect, the work of inspiration. The Holy Ghost came down on His virgin mother, and He "was *made* man." We are told the fact, and it is essential to our salvation that we believe it. The whole mystery is super-human. No Bezaleel anticipated it; neither can any unfold it. Curiosity is baffled, but faith is abundantly satisfied. "Great is the mystery of Godliness! God was manifest in the flesh."

6. *The ark, thus constructed, was never to be looked into, nor touched by ordinary persons.* The prying eye and the forward hand were alike prohibited. Death was the penalty for infringing the prohibition. The Hebrews well understood this regulation; and once beheld an affecting proof of its force, when, in after days, Uzzah died, for even his well-intended interference.

This reverence to be observed towards the ark was intended to teach all men that they must honour the Son as they honour the Father. Other types, such as the manna from heaven, and the water from the rock, shewed that Christ was freely to be received, and intimately considered; but this declared that He is, at the same time, to be regarded with the profoundest reverence and the utmost awe. He is the high and lofty one, and His name is holy—so holy that none are to take it in vain, but every knee is to bow down at it.

The type also, in this aspect of it, teaches us to abstain from vain speculation, curious inquiry, and even mere philosophical investigation, respecting those things pertaining to the nature and person of Christ, which are "secret to us."

From this part of our subject let us proceed to contemplate

II. *The mercy-seat as placed on the ark.* The mercy-seat, or throne of propitiation, though considered part and parcel of the ark, was yet, in its structure, perfectly distinct from it. A distinct command was given respecting it. A distinct notice is taken of its formation: and a very precise account is recorded of the act of Moses in placing it on the ark.

Bearing in mind what was said of it in the former lecture, let us search out its typical reference to Jesus the Lord.

1. Being ALL of gold *it represented the Godhead; and being set on the ark it declared the oneness of that Godhead with Christ as the Incarnate Son.* At the baptism of the beloved Son, the Father audibly acknowledged and honoured Him, and the Eternal Spirit came down visibly and bodily upon Him. Indeed, Holy Scripture labours, as it were, to show us that the Father honours the Son, sets His seal upon Him, and rests in His love for Him. The oneness of the Father and the Son was a frequent topic of discourse with our Lord Himself. "I and my Father are one," was that saying which the ark had long whispered to Israel, before Jesus declared it aloud.

2. The mercy-seat was emphatically "*the propitiatory,*" or *the token of the mercy of God to all penitent transgressors of the law.* It was so shaped as to resemble a seat or throne; and Jehovah was pleased to make it His visible throne of grace and mercy. But, being placed over the tables of the law in the ark, it betokened, to every thoughtful Israelite, the grant of mercy to the transgressors of that law, only through a covering or propitiation for their transgressions. Hence it was a clear and intelligible type of Him "whom God hath set forth to be a propitiation for sin, through faith in his blood." He covered the law which was against us—shut up its curses and hushed its thunders—by virtue of that mercy which was like a solid and an impenetrable lid to the ark which contained them. Well might the beloved disciple, when an aged apostle, delight to say (1 John 2:2, and 4:10)

> "And he is the propitiation for our sins: and not for ours only, but also for the sins of the whole world."
>
> "Herein is love, not that we loved God, but that he loved us, and sent his Son to be the propitiation for our sins."

3. From the mercy-seat *God shone forth* in a manner which declared His presence to Israel. So far as we can understand the case, it appears that on the day of the erection of the tabernacle in the wilderness, a luminous cloud descended upon "the tent of the testimony," and that a portion of it took its station between the cherubim on the mercy-seat. The Jews called this bright but softened light the Shekinah; and, in their Rabbinical writings, say much respecting it.

But, this light on the mercy-seat, which marked the certainty of the divine presence, was but a type of "the true light," even of Christ, who declared Himself to be such. He is the manifestation of Deity, "the brightness of the Father's glory," and the only visible image of the God who is light. But, more on this subject, under another division of it.

4. *On the mercy-seat God received supplications, and from it gave answers to questions.* When any went to unburthen their hearts, or seek directions, under the pressure of calamities or perplexities, it was before the ark that they fell down. Suppliants and inquirers were sure to meet with the omnipotent and omniscient Jehovah on His mercy-seat. It was both an oratory and an oracle of the living God for faithful Israelites. What the ark was, in these respects, to them, the Lord Jesus now is to us. He is the only channel of prayer to God, and the only medium of communication from God. Through Him alone God hears us, and speaks to us. "No man cometh unto the Father, but by Him." He, too, is the only "word" of the Father; for the Father's voice sounds to us through Him. Hence all Holy Scripture, though called the word of God, is also called "the word of Christ." In Numbers 7:89, it is said,

> "When Moses was gone into the tabernacle of the congregation to speak with Him, then he heard the voice of one speaking unto him from off the mercy-seat that was upon the ark of testimony, from between the two cherubims."

This "speaking from off the mercy-seat" was the type of God's speaking to His people through Christ: for—Hebrews 1:1, 2,

> "God who at sundry times and in divers manners spake in times past unto the fathers by the prophets
>
> "Hath in these last days spoken unto us by his Son, whom he hath appointed heir of all things, by whom also he made the worlds."

5. If the cherubim, on the ends of the mercy-seat, represented the angelic hosts, then are we to understand that *it is only through the mediation of Christ that angels minister unto us.* Without a propitiation for our sins, there would have been no pathway from heaven to our world. But, because there is a great propitiation for us in Christ, there is angelic access to us at His bidding. Jacob saw it in the vision of the ladder; and the Lord expounded its meaning when he said to Nathaniel—John 1:51—

> "Verily, verily, I say unto you, hereafter ye shall see heaven open, and the angels of God ascending and descending upon the Son of Man."

We pass on to consider

III. *The uses of the ark and the mercy-seat combined.* Not that they were ever, in reality, disjoined; for neither was the ark complete without the mercy-seat, nor the mercy-seat without the ark. They were only spoken of separately for the clearer discernment of their purposes. So God the Father and God the Holy Ghost are never disjoined from God the Son, except in language for the better perception of their respective offices.

Considering, then, the ark and the mercy-seat as one, we may consider its uses, thus:

1. *It was the visible guarantee of Jehovah's dwelling with Israel.* It proved to the nation that God was not a great way off, but nigh unto them, and in the midst of them. And is not this the very purpose for which Christ became man? Was He not expressly called "Emmanuel" that we might be assured of God's *being with us?* He was; and all the true followers of the Lord Jesus rejoice in His explicit promise—"Lo, *I am with you always,* even unto the end of the world." The Jews saw the ark, and, so, virtually saw God. Jesus said—"He that hath seen Me hath seen the Father also." "I am in the Father, and the Father in Me." Christ on earth was God come down from heaven. He was the "tabernacle of God with man."

2. The ark and the mercy-seat were, at once, *the glory, the guide, and the defence of Israel.* A cloud by day, and a lamp of fire by night, hung over the tent which covered it. It was taken up, at God's bidding, to find a place of encampment for the people; and no enemy dared to dispute its march. Invisible death was planted around it.

Such is Christ to His church. He is its glory, its guide, its defence. He is a glory within, and "a wall of fire round about." Only let His people trust themselves in His hands, and they will never take a wrong path, never fall into sin, never run into any kind of danger.

3. The ark and the mercy-seat *concentrated the affection, reverence, and contemplation of the people.* It was their rallying point; their visible "all-in-all." It was to them, in reality, what the idol image of Minerva was to the Trojans in mere vain imagination. So long as that image was in their towering citadel, so long they had something on which to repose their admiration and their confidence. It was their "palladium," and so their boast and their joy.

All this and more than this is Christ to His true Israel. So long as He is in the soul of a believer, that believer is conscious of having a supreme object for his affections, and an adorable presence which commands his awe, and brings him peace. Possessing the ark of Christ's presence, we never want a theme for mediation, or a power to cheer and preserve amidst the hot riot of corruptions within, or the embattled assaults of Satan from without. Israel is safe and prosperous while the ark is with them, and God is in all their hearts.

4. *The ark and the mercy-seat were not commonly seen by the people, but only occasionally.* It was covered by a tent without, and concealed by a veil within. Still, the indications of its presence were always clear and decided. Its staves were, at least, so placed as to be visible, according to some interpreters, to the assembled worshippers. While in the wilderness, as we now are contemplating it, the cloud by day and the fire by night were the incessant index to it. In these circumstances we behold an intimation of the fact that, under the law, Christ was but partially revealed and dimly discerned. As St. Paul says, "The way into the holiest of all was not yet made manifest." The veil was not rent. God was not "manifest in the flesh." Christ was not yet made man. All, therefore, was seen in a sort of faint light—dim and hazy. Occasionally, indeed, the Lord Jesus anticipated His incarnation, and appeared in human form: but that was not the true manifestation of Himself. It was not till angels chanted His birth at Bethlehem that the manhood was revealed to long-expecting eyes. Now that He was come down to us, as bone of our bone and flesh of our flesh, made like unto us in all things, we may see as well as believe.

5. The ark, with the mercy-seat upon it, *had rings and staves for its carriage from place to place.* The whole was, therefore, moveable, and not necessarily restricted to one locality. A glorious truth, and yet a fearful warning, was hereby indicated to the people. The bearing of the ark by four priests, or Levites, seemed to betoken the carrying of the gospel of Christ, recorded by four evangelists, to the four points of the earth. The true ark has long travelled far beyond the coasts of Judea, and is in progress towards every corner of the globe. But, the moveable nature of the ark warns us of the *removable* nature of the gospel. If a people despise it, or make light of it, the God of it will order it to be carried elsewhere. Woe to that nation, city, town, or village, which has enjoyed the bright presence of the gospel ark, but through unbelief and negligence has lost it! No greater scourge can be inflicted on a people, whether many or few, than the withdrawal of the ark of Christ's gospel from among them. May God avert such a calamity from our country, our city, our parish.

And, now, having stated to you wherein "the ark of the covenant" typically represented the Lord Jesus Christ, suffer me to remind you of one or two counterfeit representations. That ark was indeed, a type of Christ, but *it was not a type of His virgin mother.* Roman Catholic books of devotion abound with blasphemous applications of the ark to the virgin Mary. They call *her* "the ark of mercy," and even "the ark of the covenant," as well as the embodiment of other virtues or perfections, of which the ark can be considered the receptacle. We know no such unhallowed touchings of the ark. May God save deluded votaries from the consequences.

Further, in the path of counterfeit, Roman Catholic preachers and orators have a fond practice of insinuating that the ark in the tabernacle was a type of *the pix,* as it is called, on their altar. The pix is the little coffer, chest, or box, in which the consecrated host or wafer is kept, and which is always deposited, as the very body of Christ, on the high altar; and, therefore, to be bowed to, worshipped, and adored by every person who turns towards it. In earlier centuries, as Shakespeare pleasantly testifies, "If a man stole a pix, he was to be hanged outright for the theft." We know no such profanation of scripture types, but account them wicked fables and abominable impostures "to be abhorred of all faithful men."

There are many things connected with the ark which are full of pleasant or profitable meditation:

1. We behold, in the ark of the covenant, *a centre of unity between the old testament church and the new testament church.* The true ark of each is the same; for Christ was theirs as well as ours. Dim as the old dispensation certainly was, there was enough light in it for all general purposes: while particular individuals, as our sagest saints believe, were favoured with clearer powers of perception, and saw much of Him whose types were constantly before them. Thus, then, it is pleasant to reflect on the oneness of the faith, and hope, and love of true christians in all ages. Some divines are of opinion that the two cherubim, on the mercy-seat, were symbols of the two churches—the Jewish and the Gentile—united in one mediator of mercy. Be this as it may, we know that all is one in Christ now; and that true believers of every age and clime find the same mediator on one and the same mercy-seat.

2. We behold, in the main features of the ark, *all our desire, and all our salvation.* We see Jesus displayed as the keeper of the law for us, and as the medium of mercy to us. The law is under His mediatorial throne, kept in its own perfect sanctity, and that sanctity forms a basis for His throne. To this blessed Jesus, as the fulfiller of the law for us, we must come for pardon and righteousness. We have only to approach Him with lively faith, and He will be a lively mediator for us; because, as His seat is all of pure gold, He is the dispenser of golden mercy. The riches of His grace are lavished on us, if we will but gather them up.

3. In the staves of the ark we discern *a joyous token for all lands.* The ark which, after the death of Moses, was borne in triumphant march to a rich but heathen country, symbolized, by its staves, the ultimate intention of its Divine Author respecting the true ark of the new covenant. In due time our ark

shall be carried to every pagan clime. Its staves shall always be in its rings, and the feet of its bearers shall be beautiful on all mountains and high hills. May our hearts be a receptacle for it now.

LECTURE III.

> "And all Israel and their elders and officers and their judges stood on this side the ark, and on that side, before the priests the Levites, which bare the ark of the covenant of the Lord, as well the stranger as he that was born among them."—Joshua 8:33.

"THE ark of the covenant of the Lord" was now in the Land of Canaan. It had been brought thither by Joshua, who, after the death of Moses, succeeded to the lofty duties of the government of Israel.

There were four remarkable events, during the age of Joshua, in connection with which the ark is mentioned. Our text has reference to the last of the four. They were—The passage of the Jordan; the marching round Jericho; the defeat of Israel at Ai; and the division of all the tribes—half on Mount Ebal, and half on Mount Gerizim.

Our former lecture was devoted to the consideration of the typical reference of the ark to the Lord Jesus Christ, when, on its completion under Moses, it beautified the tabernacle in the wilderness. You are now invited to contemplate the ark in its history under Joshua; which portion of its history embraces some of the grandest and most marvellous events, whose bare record ever arrested human ears. We cannot, of course, investigate every particular incident in those events, but only such as immediately depend on the presence of the ark.

I. *The passage of the Jordan* is detailed in the third and fourth chapters of this book. The record of it is of that character which indicates that the inspired writer was peculiarly interested with his subject. He minutely states its facts, recurs to them, and lingers on the ground of them as one whose soul was filled with admiration and delight in the recollection of them.

1. Between the passage of the Red Sea and that of the Jordan a very remarkable difference was ordained. When the Israelites crossed a narrow part of the Red Sea, their passage was effected in haste, in the night, and without any notable preparation. The people were driven to a strait; their hearts were faint, and no particular information was given to them as to the mode of their deliverance. Whereas, when the Israelites were about to cross the Jordan, the most deliberate measures were taken, and the calmest preparation was made. The time selected was in that part of the year when the stream of the river was at its broadest and fullest. Messengers were sent through the host to acquaint every man of what was about to be done; and all was done under the brightest beam of day. Instead, too, of the enemies of Israel being behind them, they were full in front of them, and from their walls and watch-towers discerned every movement of their body. "The people passed over right against Jericho."—(Joshua 3:16.) There probably was a typical intention in these remarkable differences. The crossing of the Red Sea is commonly regarded as analogous to christian Baptism; and the crossing of the Jordan as emblematical of the transit of a believer, by death, into the heavenly Canaan. Now, for baptism, the young Israelite can hardly be said to make preparation. It is prepared for him, rather than he is prepared for it. He is taken through, it may be under a cloud, and with many surrounding pressures. But, when the harnessed and well-travelled believer comes to the end of his journey, he is usually allowed time to prepare for what awaits him. His passage across the full river is often preceded by kindly monitions from his Great Captain; and a bright light and a calm demeanour are vouchsafed to him. May such be our blessed lot when the hour of our departure shall be signified to us!

2. In the passage of the Jordan, the first and last object of universal attention was "the ark of the covenant of the Lord." Every eye was to be directed to it, and every movement regulated by it.

Ordinarily, the Levites were the bearers of it; but, upon this grand and solemn occasion, certain priests were selected for the memorable task. It was an honour to them, and they reverently undertook it.

And, now, their task commences. They bear up the ark as soon as Israel have taken down their tents, and are ready to march. And, as they apply their shoulders to the staves, a hallowed awe fills their breasts; because they know that "the Lord of all the earth," as Himself said to Joshua, was concentrating Himself "on the mercy-seat," between the cherubim, in order to guarantee a clear and safe passage to the youngest and feeblest Israelite.

But, the priestly bearers of the awful and precious symbol must themselves begin the passage by an act of faith. They must not only approach the stream, but actually set their feet in it—(Joshua 3:13). They must believe that, on so doing, the waters would be instantly parted to form a passage for the people. So true and fitting is it that they who bear "the ark of the sanctuary," must be the first to exercise faith in the God of it. The ministers of Christ are to be firm believers in His promises, and their faith is to be visible to all men; otherwise, they are not warranted to expect salvation for themselves, or their people. In all difficult and dangerous times, also, they are to head their people, and lead them on in the path of God's ordaining.

Never did Jehovah fail, and never will He fail, to fulfil His word, when obedience is paid to it. Accordingly, we read—(Joshua 3:14–16)

> "And it came to pass, when the people removed from their tents, to pass over Jordan, and the priests bearing the ark of the covenant before the people;
>
> "And as they that bare the ark were come unto Jordan, and the feet of the priests that bare the ark were dipped in the brim of the water, (for Jordan overfloweth all his banks all the time of harvest,)
>
> "That the waters which came down from above stood and rose up upon a heap very far from the city Adam, that is beside Zaretan, and those that came down towards the sea of the plain, even the Salt Sea, failed, and were cut off: and the people passed over right against Jericho."

Thus the miracle was as instantaneous as it was stupendous. The setting of the feet of the priests in the outer edge of the stream was like the instant gash of a mighty sabre-stroke, or the lightning-like fall of a crystal sluice-gate. Quickly as an eyelid twinkles were the waters from above cut off in a straight, wall-like line, from those which were below. And, what is so wondrously strange, the waters, instead of spreading out at the sides, piled up, as it were, in a heap, increasing every moment, like a glassy wall built up higher and higher by invisible hands. Jehovah could as speedily have congealed the river, and so have formed a path of ice across it for His people: but this would have borne some resemblance to an operation of nature; it would have been like merely bringing down a stream of the north into a channel of the south. This would have been a miracle, but not such a miracle as the one which had no parallel in nature to represent it.

And, now, on the bed of the Jordan becoming dry, the priests advance with the ark into the very midst of it. They take their stand as men who had nothing to fear from the towering flood above them, because the Maker and Master of all was on the ark which rested on their shoulders. They move not till all had passed over—clean, safe, and triumphant.[1] Beautiful pledge this of the presence of Christ in the river of death, when His people are passing through it! And sure token is it that He will not depart, and that not one of them shall fail of reaching the celestial shore!

3. But, though "all the people were passed clean over Jordan," the ark does not yet remove. Something more is yet to be done. God gives command through Joshua for twelve picked men—"out of every tribe a man"—to "pass over before the ark" into the midst of Jordan, and to take from thence as large a stone as each could find, to carry to the spot where the ark should lodge that night, after it was brought out of the bed of the river. Of these stones a pile was to be formed "for a memorial to future generations."—(Joshua 4:6, 7.)

More than this, twelve other stones were gathered, and piled up in the bed of the stream, on the very spot where the priests stood while bearing the ark. And God so modified the force of the returning torrent as not to suffer it to wash them away. Many a boatman, and many a bather, saw them for at least many years after they were there deposited; for it is said, by the writer of this Book, "And they are there unto this day."

4. Thus gloriously and memorably did Jehovah, by His ark, lead His people across the bed of a deep and rapid river. And, doubtless, in the day when his last faithful one shall walk dryshod through a more formidable river, and find, as all his fellows in the faith have found, that the waters have not only not overflown him, but have not even touched him, then will there be such memorials of the event as infinite wisdom will appoint. It cannot but be that every saved believer will vividly recollect the hour of his passage into eternity. He may have appeared to others insensible of what was passing: but the hidden and immortal principle has been awake and watching every incident, especially the presence of the ark as the glory, security, and comfort of the whole.

And now, after due religious celebrations, and further tokens of the Divine Presence among them, the Israelites prepare for the capture of Jericho. But, in this, as in the crossing of the Jordan, every human device is superseded, and wondrously simple and strangely novel methods are prescribed. Amidst them all, however, "the ark of the covenant" is the grand instrument

[1] "And the priests that bare the ark of the covenant of the Lord stood firm on dry ground in the midst of Jordan, and all the Israelites passed over on dry ground, until all the people were passed clean over Jordan."—Joshua 3:17.

for effecting everything. Hence, let us contemplate

II. *The solemn procession of the ark round the walls of Jericho.*

1. For six days, the ark was to be carried, still by priests, around the whole circuit of the city. It was to be preceded by seven other priests, each with a simple ram's-horn trumpet, which they blew as they went. Before them marched a band of veteran warriors, more to clear the way than to guard it: and, then, behind the ark followed the main body of the people. Whether they were to march at the same reverent distance from it, as when they were advancing to the banks of the river, we are not told. While marching thither, they were not to come nearer to the ark than about half a mile, apparently that every individual in a long line of march, might see for himself that which was to be their guide and regulator. (Joshua 3:4.) Be this as it may, one special injunction was laid upon them which had not been laid before. They were to observe the utmost silence. (Joshua 6:10.)

> "And Joshua had commanded the people, saying, Ye shall not shout nor make any noise with your voice, neither shall any word proceed out of your mouth, until the day I bid you shout: then shall ye shout."

2. So singular an arrangement as this must have arrested the attention of the king and warriors of Jericho. They had, as Rahab had previously told the spies, heard of the passage of the Red Sea, and were faint with fear at what they heard. Now, also, the terror of the Lord was upon the city, and though, from what is elsewhere incidentally said, (Joshua 24:11) it is probable that they shot their missiles from their walls, yet none had the daring to sally out and attack the Hebrews.

For a whole army to march, day after day, round the city, with no other sound but a few rustic trumpets, was a military procedure which no General in Canaan had ever heard. But, it is probable that, as those trumpets were blown by the priests of Jehovah, their sound was divinely impulsive, and tremendously thrilling to every ear in Jericho. It is more than probable, too, that the sight of the ark was attended with strange sensations to the men of Jericho, beyond anything of which the men of Israel themselves were sensible. For, as in the passage of the Red Sea, the Lord looked from out of the pillar of cloud and troubled the Egyptians, so may it have been that, from the radiance of the ark, He glanced at the men of Jericho in a manner which conveyed mysterious terror to them. They felt an unspeakable awe, and a dismal foreboding, which, yet, perhaps, no man dared acknowledge to his fellow. The continuance of this silent spectacle might embolden some few monster hearts, and incline them to banter and jest; but it is probable that the majority of them suspected and dreaded something answerable to their own enchantments, or demon-arts of magic. At all events, the six days march must have left them with strange and mingled imaginings, in which their own oracles could give them no aid.

3. But now, on the seventh day, which the Jews generally believe to have been a Sabbath-day, a laborious march is followed by an easy and most triumphant victory. If the day were the Sabbath, we are sure that the Lord of it consecrated it to the special service of the capture of a wicked city, which, though a strange work, was nevertheless the Lord's own work. One at least of the seven days must have been a Sabbath-day. If that day fell on one of the six, then was the march round the city, little more perhaps, than the legitimate "Sabbath-day's journey." Still, in either case, as there was a marshalling of troops, and other secular doings, the pious Hebrew exercised faith in the Lord of the Sabbath, and believed that He had power to vary His own law respecting the sanctity of the Sabbath. The sect of the Pharisees had not yet risen up to trouble honest minds with petty quibbles.

On that day, all the people "rose up early about the dawning of the day," and began a seven-times march round the city. At the end of the seventh circuit, the priests sounded with additional energy, and all the people, at the bidding of Joshua, raised "a very great shout." In that moment, the entire wall of the city, said, by the Jews, to be of seven-fold width, "*fell down flat.*" An unseen hand dashed it all to the ground, instantly, entirely, levelly. Which last circumstance, namely, that it fell down *flat*, or levelly, was not the least remarkable of any, because nothing but a special power of divine exertion could have effected such a phenomenon. Lofty and massy walls, when overthrown by any ordinary means, fall confusedly, and in rugged heaps. But the walls of this God-captured city fall down *flatly*, as though on purpose to facilitate the entrance of the Hebrews into it; for it is significantly added, "So that the people went up into the city, every man *straight before him*, and they took the city." Then followed the work of righteous extermination: righteous, we say, because, sanguinary as it may seem to us, it was executed at the bidding of a holy God.

4. So marvellous a capture, however, was not merely an exertion of divine power, exercised without any reference to human intervention: it was visibly divine, but cooperatively human. Though no skill or strength of man was employed in the overthrow of the walls, yet was the faith of the Lord's people largely expressed. In the army of Israel was a goodly band of spiritual soldiers, who believed and prayed while they gazed or shouted: for St. Paul certifies us that "*By faith* the walls of Jericho fell down, after they were compassed about seven days."

An overthrow so sudden and signal is left on record, also, to furnish us with some idea of those manifestations of Almighty power which will, doubtless, be exhibited in the day of the destruction of Anti-Christ, when it shall be said, "Babylon is fallen, is fallen!" The fall will be as sudden, as awful, as effectual as that of Jericho. Sinners will be as secure in the fastnesses of their superstition, as the men of Jericho were in their apparently impregnable walls. But, their judgment will be as certain, and, probably, as instantaneous.

III. *The defeat of Israel at Ai, and the consequent falling down of Joshua before "the ark of the covenant,"* were consequent upon a forbidden act in the capture of Jericho. The people were commanded, in that capture, to abstain from appropriating a single article of value to themselves. All the gold and silver was to be consecrated to the Lord. Spite, however, of this solemn command, one Achan secreted a wedge of gold. The curse of the theft pervaded the whole camp. It spread as a blight over every effort of the people. The consequence was that, when they went out to attack the next city, they were grievously repulsed. Upon a recurrence of this humiliating disaster, Joshua and all the elders of Israel prostrated themselves before the ark of the Lord[1]—Joshua 7:6. This falling down of Joshua and the elders was for prayerful inquiry of the God of the ark, and not for any superstitious reverence of the ark itself. Jehovah acknowledged the act, and honoured it by an explanatory response. The criminal was detected. The crime was expiated; and Israel was righted. The whole circumstance was calculated to teach all men the evil of covetousness, the omniscience and holiness of Jehovah, and the certainty with which He will detect and punish sin. It, also, very affectingly admonishes us of our liability to suffer the effects of the divine displeasure, through the guilt of intimate connections, on the principle that, if one member becomes gangrenous, the adjoining members are likely to languish.

But, harmless and holy as was the act of Joshua in falling down before the ark, Antichrist steps in and turns it into a plea for superstition and idolatry. Like certain venomous creatures, which first inject poison, and then suck it out, the Papal Antichrist first infuses falsehood into parts of the sacred history, and then parades it for the sanction of blasphemous doctrine.

The case is this: Because there were on the mercy-seat of the ark figures of cherubim, and Joshua in falling down before the ark necessarily fell down before *them*, therefore, say Roman Catholic Doctors, we are justified in doing the like before images of Christ, his mother, and other saints, as well as altars of the host. The plea is formally stated in the note of the Rhemish version of the New Testament, on the word "cherubim," in fifth verse of the ninth chapter of the Epistle to the Hebrews. The plea is as disingenuous as it is wicked; because it keeps out of sight the true facts of the case, as well as foists in ideas which have no manner of relation to it.

Joshua fell down before the ark, not because of the cherubim upon it, but because of the Shekinah which rested between them, as the visible symbol of the invisible God. He, therefore, prostrated himself before the ark not as an *image* of God, but as the seat of God Himself. God was actually there on the ark, and not merely represented by it. But, *is Christ actually in any of the images of Him* which deluded votaries first fabricate and then worship? The question hardly needs an answer. Moreover, when Joshua fell down before the ark, it is more than probable that he neither *saw* the ark nor the cherubim on it. It was covered by a curtain, if not by the tent which was made on purpose to cover it. Here, again, is no resemblance between the act of Joshua and the prostrations of those who gaze intently on the glaring or gaudy figures of Christ and the Virgin Mary.

We must, further, take into our account the immense difference between God's positive command for the building of the ark as one single vessel, for the holding of the law, to be concealed from the people, and the unbidden, or rather the forbidden, formation not of vessels but of images of persons, and those images almost numberless in their amount. Altogether, the perversion of the entire case is as odious, and as sickening, as we fear the crime of it is monstrous and damnable. May God in mercy and pity spare and turn all those who are deceived by the deceiver, lest they be destroyed by the Destroyer.

IV. *The muster of the tribes in two divisions, on Mount Ebal and Mount Gerizim*, when the ark, as our text states, was set between them, was the last of the four instances in which, during the government of Joshua, that ark is mentioned.

As the narrative stands in our Bible, the time of that muster of the tribes was shortly after the conquest of Ai, which had given the people so much trouble. But some commentators are disposed to think that the passage is transposed, and that it ought to be referred to a later period of the history. There is, however, no need for any chronological alteration. At all events, the narrative itself is fraught with solemn and elevating interest. It is briefly of this nature: Moses had strictly enjoined the elders and the people that, upon their establishment in Canaan, they should assemble at a definite spot, which he distinctly described, though he had never seen it. The spot was in Shechem, where two small mountains, or pointed hills, were so near together, that a voice from the intervening valley could be easily heard on either. In this valley the noble and faithful Joshua caused the ark to be brought, and took his station near it. To the people who were posted on the two hills, and in the presence of all the chiefs and worthies of the nation, he audibly recited the curses and the blessings to which Jehovah had bidden the whole multitude to add their solemn

[1] "And Joshua rent his clothes, and fell to the earth upon his face, before the ark of the Lord, until the eventide, he and the elders of Israel, and put dust upon their heads."

and earnest "Amen." It was, in fact, a sort of "Commination Service," as our church uses the phrase; and yet it was accompanied with many circumstances of affecting grandeur. Never did the ark of the covenant cast its golden splendours on a scene more transcendently beautiful. The locality, as travellers report, must have been lovely. Stationed on two such contiguous hills all Israel were seen at once, and saw each other. Veterans and younger warriors, mothers and children, with many a varied individual, were grouped according to their tribes. In the valley gleamed the ark, and stood the princes of the people. Many a heart throbbed with recollections of the wonder-paved way in which God had led them: and many an eye paid its crystal tribute to the gratitude which demanded it. And, then, what more in keeping with the entire scene could there be than the heavenly aspect of the man who was the type of the God-man—Jesus—the true Joshua and Saviour of the Church? There stood he, the Lord's own chosen one, reciting from the standard copy of the Book of the Law, all that Moses had divinely enjoined. But, we must not trace out the solemnly glorious scene any further. May the God of the ark send upon us much of the Spirit which actuated Joshua and all the sound-hearted ones around him.

Suffice it to add that, after this occurrence, no further mention is expressly made of the ark during the life of Joshua. In the eighteenth chapter of this Book, and in the first verse, we are informed that the tabernacle was, at length, set up in Shiloh, and the ark was, of course, deposited in the western end of it—under the tent which was made for it. Shiloh was a central spot, in the lot of the tribe to which Joshua belonged, and which, probably, was the home of his old age. Here the ark continued for nearly three hundred years; during various vicissitudes of Israel's history, to the leading incidents of which, as connected with the ark, your attention will be invited (D.V.) in the next lecture.

In closing the present lecture, it cannot be inapplicable to point out to you

1. *The serial sort of connexion* which seems to exist between these four events which we have been considering. The former two were marked by miracle, the other two by devotion. Of the miraculous incidents, one was miracle rising superior to the regularities of nature, the other was miracle leaping the barriers of human art. Divine power rolled back the stream of Jordan, and the same almighty force threw down in scorn the human-builded walls of Jericho. Of the devotional acts, one was the offering of supplication, and the other the reading of the Word of God. Both these are highly admonitory, and all are particularly instructive. Miracles may dazzle us; but everything devotional should engage and interest us. We should be ready, not only with the Psalmist to look back upon the wondrous scene and exclaim, "What ailed thee—thou Jordan, that thou wast driven back?" (Psalm 114:5.) but we should, also, delight to say, "I will lift up my hands towards thy holy oracle." "Oh how I love thy law, it is my meditation all the day."

2. *The greater wonders which await the eyes of all the followers of the true Joshua.* What the Lord Jesus said to Nathaniel respecting, most likely, the vision of Jacob's ladder, may be fitly applied to us, when rising from the contemplation of what Jehovah wrought in the Jordan and at Jericho, namely, "Thou shalt see greater things than these." God's wonders of old are but pattern shadows of the astonishing realities which His Church is destined to witness. His arm has yet to be made bare in the sight, not of one or two nations only, but of all people. The followers of the Lamb shall walk through a deeper river than the Jordan, and enjoy the protection of a brighter Ark than that which stayed its impetuous flood. They shall, too, behold "the pulling down of strongholds" by an invisible arm, even the fortresses and high towers of Satan's erection, in the Jerichos which for ages he has held and garrisoned. Meanwhile, may miracles of grace be wrought in our hearts, and the True Ark dwell in them!

3. *The necessity of keeping our eye on that True Ark, and the suitableness of a residence brought nearer and still nearer to it, as age advances.* Israel so followed the Ark under the guidance of Joshua, as not only to hear of it, but to see it. The eye of our faith is to be constantly kept upon Christ. And, if we come to be settled in some quiet Shiloh, for a calm old age, let us make it our greatest solace to have that Ark very nigh unto us, so nigh that even when we tread the verge of Jordan, all anxious fears may subside, and our faith rest calmly upon the same sure Ark of our salvation, Jesus Christ the Righteous.

LECTURE IV.

"And when the people were come into the camp, the elders of Israel said, Wherefore hath the Lord smitten us to day before the Philistines? Let us fetch the ark of the covenant of the Lord out of Shiloh unto us, that, when it cometh among us, it may save us out of the hand of our enemies.

"So the people went to Shiloh, that they might bring from thence the ark of the covenant of the Lord of hosts, which dwelleth between the cherubims: and the two sons of Eli, Hophni and Phineas, were there with the ark of the covenant of God."—1 Samuel 4:3, 4.

IT was proposed that the subject of the present lecture should be "The History of the Ark of the Covenant under the Judges." By "the Judges" we are to understand those governors of Israel who followed each other, at broken intervals, from the death of Joshua to the reign of Saul. The times of the Judges stretched over an historic period of more that three centuries. That period was like the gradual approach of an eclipse. The death of Joshua and of the Elders who were his companions, was the signal of its commencement. After them, the sun of Israel soon became dim. Notwithstanding occasional gleams of light, darkness began to prevail. Jehovah was slighted, and the local gods of the land were cherished. Chastisements and deliverances followed each other like alternations of gloom and gleam, from flitting clouds, on the day of an eclipse. At length, during the high priesthood of Eli, when his lewd sons, Hophni and Phineas, hastened on the iniquity of the land, the total obscuration of Israel's sun set in, Philistine darkness swallowed up the light of the ark, and the glory of Israel fell beneath the dank cloud of Dagon.

It is painfully remarkable that, all through the Book of Judges, no mention is made of the ark till the last chapter but one. In that chapter (20:27) it is parenthetically said, that "the ark of the covenant of God was there (i.e. in Shiloh) in those days." Joshua had set up the tabernacle there, and deposited the ark in it. Thither, with more or less punctuality, the people, after his time, continued to go up, according to the law. But, as was predicted of them, they soon began to fall away into foolish and hurtful idolatries. According to prevailing custom, they adopted the gods of the native inhabitants of the land: for, long before and long after their settlement in Canaan, they were infected with the heathen notion that certain deities presided over certain districts. On going, therefore, into a new locality, they were tempted to follow the gods of it. Not that they always or altogether discarded the worship of Jehovah, but added to it the worship of idols. This was the sin of Israel in even the after days of Isaiah and Jeremiah, just as it is the sin of all nominal Christians up to the present hour, who have not the honesty to reject Christ, but aim to unite the profession of His name with the love of the world or some favourite Baal.

Things in Israel proceeded from bad to worse, till Eli became the aged high priest at Shiloh. He was a good man at heart, but sadly irresolute in mind. His sons made themselves detestably vile, but he restrained them not. At length, their conduct, as priests, was so profligate and atrocious, that God issued a sentence of extermination against them and the entire family.

Our text brings us to the period, when, in connexion with the eclipse of the ark, themselves were about to be consigned to utter darkness. But, lo! just as that eclipse and that darkness begin, God raises up a star in the distant horizon, which is to pour its light upon Israel, and to be the harbinger of a brighter day. Samuel is born, in answer to Eli's prediction, and soon he ministers to the Lord, and sleeps near the ark in Shiloh. There the Lord, one eventful night, called him by name, and spoke to him solemn words. It was after midnight, and towards the approach of morning, when the lamps in the tabernacle were burning dimly, and flickering in their last drops of oil. Apt time this to represent the waning state of Eli's priesthood, and Israel's prosperity, as well as the opening dawn of Samuel's prophetic rule.

But, as indicative of that infatuation which precedes destruction, the Israelites, apparently without consulting Samuel, determine to rally a war against the Philistines. They accordingly muster their forces and join in battle. They fight, but conquer not. Four thousand of them are slain, and they fall back to consult with themselves only what to do. They fretfully ask, "Wherefore hath the Lord smitten us to day before the Philistines?" Had they consulted Him at His ark in Shiloh, they would soon have learned why He had smitten them. But, as conscience whispered *why*, they stifled that monitor, and set up their own mad will for their guide. "Let us, (said they) fetch the ark of the covenant of the Lord out of Shiloh unto us, that when it cometh among us, it may save us out of the hand of our enemies."

In the history which follows this insane and wicked proposal, we have to contemplate the desecration and loss of the ark, the vengeance which followed its capture, and the admonitory account of its recovery. May we find abundant profit in reaping the rich instruction with which this history is charged.

I. *The desecration and loss of the ark* formed a melancholy feature in Israel's portraiture.

1. To send for the ark from its quiet resting place, and to force it into the din of a field of battle, was not only an unwarrantable, but a most wicked procedure. The evident intention of those who sent for it was to put themselves under the protection of it as a charm or "*fetish*." That "*it* (said they) may *save* us." Eli, most likely, had no voice allowed him in the matter; and his profligate sons were but too ready to comply with a profane project. They were as willing as the people, whom they had served to corrupt and debase—to venerate the ark merely as a visible symbol: for wicked priests are generally the most zealous in outside formalities. Accordingly, Hophni and Phineas accompany the ark to the field of battle. They went, most likely, not as its bearers, but as its lordly superintendents. When the ark arrived in the camp, "all Israel shouted with a great shout, so that the earth rang again." The shout reached the ears of the Philistines, and gave them a temporary chill; but it did not do with them as when Israel shouted before the walls of Jericho. The God of Joshua was in the shout then, because He was with the ark. But He was now absent from both. The people had sent for the ark, not for Him. They, therefore, had "their heart's desire, but leanness withal."

2. And now the Hebrews renew the battle, and carry the ark into the midst of the fray; just as the ancient heathen used to carry the images of their gods among their fighting men; and as, in some sort, modern Roman Catholics do on the continent, with the canopy of the host, or the images of the Virgin Mary and the Infant Jesus, when a city is besieged, or a neighbourhood is visited with pestilence. The carrying, in fact, of the Bambino, as it is called, from the church to which it belongs to the houses of the sick who can pay for its visit, in the city of Rome itself, is but a wretched mimickry of this carrying of the ark for the securing of victory.

The result, in regard to the people of Israel, was what might easily have been foreseen. Fighting under a false confidence, they sustained a terrible defeat. Their loss, as if to mark their presumption in fetching the ark, was far greater than before. Instead of losing four thousand men, they lost "thirty thousand footmen." Dreadful lesson this to all who depend on a false peace, while, by their continuance in sin, they court a fearful destruction! Besides this loss of men, God suffers His ark to be taken. The Philistines seize it, and bear it off in triumph. Was Jehovah forgetful, or—dare we say it?—unwise, in allowing this? He condescended to show that He was neither. He was preparing a scourge for His enemies, a rebuke for His people, and lessons for them and us. Philistia was to loathe the ark; Israel to long for it; and all Christendom to learn from it. Yes, we are to learn (and the lesson is becoming every day more and more necessary) that God's choicest ordinances are nothing to Him, when His professed worshippers trust in them, and not in Himself. If men trust in sacraments, or any outward symbol, and crave them, send for them, and use them, as Israel, under the countenance of Hophni and Phineas, sent for and used the ark, God will abandon them as He abandoned the ark, and leave His formal and faithless worshippers either to die in their sin, or fall into the hand of their enemy. No greater or surer curse can befal our own beloved church than the prevalence of zeal for the ark without any corresponding zeal for the God of the ark; an increase of reverence for the forms and rituals of Christianity, without a proportionate increase of love for the doctrine and person of Christ. The good Lord save us from such a calamity!

3. Connected with the capture of the ark was the death of kindred, in three very different and yet very painful instances.

(1.) Hophni and Phineas were slain together, apparently close to the ark, and, most likely, in fighting for its defence. They went out with it to the field of fight, like sheep doomed for slaughter. God had said that they should both be slain in one day. They, perhaps, had heard the threat, and despised it. Least of all did they imagine that they *could* die while holding to the ark. But, they did die; and in their death we read this appalling truth, namely, that men may battle unto death for the externals of true religion, and yet be neither believers nor martyrs. Many have stood in the temple, and held to the ark, and cried "Lord, Lord!" without being acknowledged as good and faithful servants. We must judge of faith, confessorship, and martyrdom, by other rules than those of mere external attachments.

(2.) On hearing the news, not of the defeat of Israel, but of the capture of the ark, the aged Eli fell down and brake his neck. He heard of the ark's departure to the camp, and his heart trembled for its safety. A secret boding came upon him. He followed it as far as he was able, to the gate of the city. He there sat down with a boding, an almost breaking heart. The first mention of the taking of the ark increased Eli's anguish beyond endurance; and then followed the heavy backward fall and consequent fracture of the old man's neck. With solemnity, then, and sadness we gaze upon the fact that a really good man may end his days under chastisement and the deepest gloom. A father, too, may die with the love of God in his heart, while his sons perish in their hatred of that God. Awful but salutary lessons for christians, whether children or parents!

(3.) In addition to Hophni, Phineas, and Eli, dies the gentle wife of one of the two wicked sons. Phineas, though a lewd and profligate man, had a chaste and pious wife. She, perhaps, loved him, and doubtless prayed for him. It was her duty to do both. Possibly, she deprecated his going with the ark: and, like her father-in-law, had many a melancholy misgiving respecting it. It was, also, so ordered that the time for the birth of her babe was drawing nigh. The news of the loss of the ark accelerated that time. She became a mother, but heeded not the joy of a man-child being born into the world. The ark of her God was gone, and nothing worth living for remained. She revived and spoke only just so far as to discover her piety and her grief. "She named the child Ichabod," which, in our marginal bibles, is translated "There is no glory;" or "Where is the glory?" In the ensuing verse it is added, "And she said, the glory is departed from Israel, *for the ark of God is taken*."

4. And, now, the Philistines, having seized the ark as their most splendid trophy, convey it to Ashdod, one of their five cities, because the temple of their god Dagon was there. In that temple, and by the hideous image of that no-god, they placed "the ark of the covenant" of the living God. O, piteous spectacle! O, melancholy sight! O, most grievous indignity! How could Moses have endured it? or Joshua, how would he have borne the thought of it? The holy ark set by the side of a filthy idol, and as a trophy, too, in the gorgeous temple of that idol! Did not the hearts of Israel burn to risk their blood in the forcible rescue of it? Did the heavens show no sign of displeasure at such a scene? Was there no falling star, no bursting cloud, no lightning-bolt, to beat down the temple, and set the ark of God free? Alas, for Israel! They had lost their father's piety, and so had lost their father's valour. Jehovah shewed, as yet, no sign. He had other purposes to fulfil.

Let us proceed to contemplate

II. *The vengeance which followed the capture of the ark by the Philistines.*

What they really intended by carrying it to the temple and presence of Dagon is not quite clear. They may have meant to express their belief in Dagon's power as having brought them the prize: or to show honour to their god as alone worthy of such a prize: or to make use of it on some festal day for their sport, as they had done with Samson: or to garnish some triumphal procession when offering sacrifice to Dagon; or, as some conjecture, to worship it in conjunction with Dagon, according to the very common practice of heathen nations. Be these things as they may, the people and priests of Ashdod had only one brief night of quiet, one short dream of triumph, as masters of the ark. They were even eager for that night to be gone, and that dream to brighten into more intense reality; for, it is said, "They of Ashdod arose *early* on the morrow." But now their disasters begin. Like a multitude of dwarfs, making sport around one of their own giants, when slumbering after toil, the Philistines find to their cost that they were sporting with, or glorying in the possession of the ark of God's strength, which, by gradual efforts, soon taught them a strange lesson.

1. On entering their temple early on the first morning, they find their idol prostrate on the ground. In the course of the night, unseen hands had thrown down Dagon flat "upon his face to the earth." The fall was very significant too, for Dagon lay, where themselves ought to have bowed as penitent worshippers, right "before the ark of the Lord." Their annoyance and alarm must have been great. Nevertheless, they do their best to suppress all emotion, and hasten to "set Dagon in his place again." No doubt they make his standing as fast as possible, and frame clever excuses for the catastrophe.

2. But, their work and their wit are fruitless. Another night ensues, and again, in the early morn, they resort to the temple, only, however, to witness a far more surprising and vexatious spectacle. It is thus described (1 Samuel 5:4).

> "And when they arose early on the morrow morning, behold Dagon was fallen upon his face to the ground before the ark of the Lord; and the head of Dagon and both the palms of his hands were cut off upon the threshold; only the stump of Dagon was left to him."

"The stump of Dagon" was the lower or fish-like half of the monster idol; for all historians agree in describing the figure of Dagon as resembling that of the fabled *merman*. The breaking off of the head and the hands was a token to the Philistines that their god had neither wisdom nor might; for the head was the emblem of the one, and the hands of the other.

3. Striking, however, and undeniable as this prodigy was, did it startle the Philistine priests, or turn them from their superstition? By no means; but rather, as is usual in all similar cases, hardened and confirmed them in it. Instead of learning a single lesson from the sharp fact of their idol's head and hands being deliberately placed in the most humiliating part of the temple, on the threshold, where, also, they were compelled to see the severed pieces, they actually convert the incident into a fresh incentive of superstitious reverence. They made it a plea for sanctimoniously stepping over the threshold instead of stepping upon it. This is a striking and an instructive fact for us to ponder in the present day. But, I cannot preferably teach you its general import than by quoting to you a remark of Bishop Hall. "It is just with God that those who want grace shall want wit too. *It is the power of superstition to turn men into those stocks and stones which they worship*. They that make them are like unto them." Never was the genius of superstition more accurately defined than by this masterly exposition of the Psalmist's words. Alas, for its too truthful application to the giant superstition of Christendom! Popery has a mysterious power of turning its votaries into itself. And what is itself? Let Holy Scripture supply the answer. It is a system of ecclesiastical "sorcery," a circle of "seducing spirits," an army of mouths "speaking lies in hypocrisy," an engine which works "with all deceivableness of unrighteousness." In a word, it is an imposture as great as that of Dagon; and it comprises as many absurdities and as much sottishness as that comprised.[1] They who

[1] The flight of the Pope from Rome in 1848, (so ominously anticipated

embrace it gradually become like it: except where the Spirit of God has more influence on the heart than in the head. Upon no other ground can we account for that painfully strange phenomenon which has of late been so frequently forced upon our observation, namely, the fact that, when English clergymen join the Church of Rome, they seem to lose not merely their common sense, but their truthfulness, and that disposition to adhere to fair, open, honourable dealing, which marks and almost makes the character of the English gentleman.

4. After the demolition of Dagon in his own temple, without any sign of change in priests or people, Jehovah began to scourge them strangely and severely.

> "But the hand of the Lord was heavy upon them of Ashdod, and he destroyed them, and smote them with emerods, even Ashdod and the coasts thereof."—1 Samuel 5:6.

This infliction of death and dreadful disease, probably as novel to the Philistines as it was excruciating and annoying, had the effect of urging the men of Ashdod to discern the cause of their visitation, and to take measures for the removal of the ark. The lords of the Philistines determined on its transport to Gath, as though, forsooth, the ark might fancy another city more than Ashdod. To Gath it went, but the same deadly and disastrous consequences followed it. The giants of that city, as well as its dwarfs, fell under the blows of the same mysterious power; for "The Lord smote the men of the city, both small and great." "Therefore, (it is added) they sent the ark of the Lord to Ekron;" where the same terrible inflictions visited them, "for there was a deadly destruction throughout all the city." The consequence was that the Ekronites, as is generally inferred, carried the ark out of their city into the open fields. But, there again, judgment began to work in a new and a startling manner. Enormous multitudes of mice sprang up, spread about, and consumed the produce of the land. Thus, that little elegant creature the field mouse, was employed as God's advocate and executioner. It taught the Philistine farmers WHO was "the Lord of the whole earth," and punished them for not believing in Him.

5. At last, in right earnest, people, priests, and lords, all resolutely set about ridding themselves of so fearful a deity as the ark. Like the Gadarenes of later days, they wish it to depart out of their coasts; and like as with those people, too, the wish was the result of infidel fear, and unrelenting attachment to their own superstitions.

The Philistine project was to send away the ark in a new cart drawn by two suckling kine, accompanied by costly offerings, golden mice, and golden representations of their disease, and to let those kine go whither they pleased; if into the land of Israel all the better, as they would then be sure of the ark being in its proper country. Hence we have now to consider

III. *The admonitory account of the restoration of the ark.*

The Philistine device of untrained kine drawing a new cart at random was a presumption on their part, but an over-ruling providence on the part of Jehovah. He permitted it for the manifestation of His glorious power. The kine, though never yoked before, and while actually lowing after their calves, nevertheless turn away from them, and take the straight road to Bethshemesh, a town of Israel.—1 Samuel 6:12. The entire circumstance was a divine prodigy. It showed not only the Creator's power in restraining the natural instinct of the kine in leaving their calves, but His invisible presence in guiding them along the right road to a town of Israel.

1. And, now, after seven month's absence from that land, the ark returns thereto by the miraculous intervention of that God who had first permitted its capture and removal therefrom.

The kine drew the cart into the field of one Joshua, a Bethshemite. The people in it were reaping, and they "rejoiced," it is said, at seeing the ark. Alas, for their joy, because it had no true-heartedness in it! They had no joy in the God of the ark, and had learned nothing from its absence. In the effervescence of their carnal delight, they slew the kine on the spot, and though a very irregular proceeding, as males only were to be so offered, they burned them in sacrifice with the wood of the cart which they had drawn.[2]

Bethshemesh, it should be remembered, was a city of priests. Levites, therefore, came and first took the ark out of the cart, and set it upon a great stone which was in the field, and which afterwards was called "The great stone of Abel," i.e., of "*weeping*," because of the after weeping of the people of the city.

From either vain curiosity or over officiousness, the men of Bethshemesh looked into the ark, and thus incurred the divine displeasure. They might have pretended that they looked in order to see if the Philistines had molested or marred the tables of the law. But it was not their business or vocation to make such an inquest. We are never warranted to do that which under no circumstances ought to be done. God is the arbiter and responsible dispenser of all such cases. The issue to the Bethshemites was "a great slaughter," either by pestilence or sudden death. It is, too, probable that they were, as a priestly community, an indolent and godless population, for we read not of any pains on their part to lodge the ark, or pay to it such becoming attention as others were eager to render.

by Fleming) instead of being a check to Romanism, was made by its partizans a call for sympathy and greater devotedness. Even the destruction of Rome itself will effect no conversion. See Revelation 18:9.

[2] Possibly they thought that animals which had been miraculously acted upon, and used for so divine a purpose, ought not to return to common uses in a pagan land.

2. The Bethshemites, evidently in an impenitent and querulous temper, sent to the inhabitants of Kirjath-jearim, a town of Judah, to fetch away the ark. They showed their unworthiness of being the guardians of such a treasure, for, instead of humbling themselves, they sought to be rid of a high and hallowed responsibility. The men, however, of Kirjath-jearim were far more noble than they; though it does not appear that they had a single priest among them. They promptly fetched the ark to their town, and lodged it in what we should call the high house of the place; for "they brought it into the house of Abinadab in the hill." This person was probably a Levite, and is said by the Jews to have been a very honourable and very holy man. If so, we may be sure that his honour was increased, and his holiness turned into his greater happiness, by having in his house the ark of the infinitely holy God.

His son—perhaps his only son—was consecrated, or specially set apart, "to keep the ark of the Lord," that is, to keep the apartment in proper order in which it was lodged, and to do everything which reverence and piety dictated to be done. All which bespeaks a high degree of religious propriety on the part of Abinadab, and greatly contrasts with the apathy of the Israelites generally. The consecration of his son was an ecclesiastical irregularity: but the affairs of the nation were so grievously distracted, that little else could be expected. In times of national confusion, the church generally suffers disorder. Sound and faithful men must then do the best they can.

The tarriance of the ark at Kirjath-jearim was long and lamentable. It could not have been for less than forty years; for the twenty years mentioned in 1 Samuel 7:2, referred to the period which elapsed from the removal of the ark to Kirjath-jearim, to the date of the narrative which immediately follows the mention of those years. Towards the end of those years, the people, under the stirring ministry and bright example of Samuel, began to consider their ways, and to exercise godly sorrow for the error of them. It is consequently said, "All the house of Israel lamented after the Lord."

Still, for wise reasons, God did not stir up any one to carry back the ark to Shiloh, or to bring the tabernacle to it. The priests and people of Shiloh had participated too deeply in the sins of Hophni and Phineas, for the Holy God ever again to trust His ark among them. "He forsook the tabernacle at Shiloh." Because He valued true piety more than gaudy formality, He chose to leave the ark in the house of a mere Levite or private individual, rather than to consign it to the charge of even authorized priests; just as He has, many times since, sent His Gospel into a cave or a cabin, when the ministers of a costly edifice have corrupted or cared but little for it.

Suffer me, in concluding this Lecture, to point out to you a few topics for your earnest consideration.

1. *All that we have hitherto been contemplating,* in the history of the ark of the covenant, *is plaintively but most poetically summed up*, by Asaph the psalmist, in Psalm 78:54–68. This is one proof that God wishes the history of His Church to be remembered, and intends His people to cheer and strengthen themselves by the contemplation of His mighty acts and His wonders of old.

2. *It is dangerous as well as foolish to slight or abuse our spiritual privileges.* The presence of the ark was a high distinction and a noble privilege for the large town of Shiloh. Many temporal, as well as many spiritual, interests were involved in its location. But, Shiloh eventually lost them all, because it lost the ark. For a time, indeed, the tabernacle continued to stand there, but its life and glory were gone. The sun had left the firmament, and a dark and deathly night followed. The materials of the tabernacle began, as the Jews say, to decay and rot, after the ark was taken from it, whereas, while the ark was in it, the whole textile fabric, like their apparel in the wilderness, suffered nothing from weather or wear.

Oh that all who hear these things would lay to heart the admonition they convey! If we lose the presence of Christ in our parish, our church, or our home, we lose all that is valuable in life for ourselves and our children. If once we tempt Him to withdraw it from us, He may never allow it to return, just as the ark never came back to Shiloh. "Spare us, Good Lord!"

3. *The vicissitudes of the true Church are not intended to discourage, but to admonish us.* They always carry with them the elements of hope. Out of their darker phases, God has been bringing light, while His people have mourned the while for the want of light. Samuel was in fair training to become a living representation of Jehovah, while Eli was waning, and the ark was trembling on the shoulders of its godless bearers. While the ark, too, was unloved in the land of the Philistines, many a heart was secretly moved to desire it among the thousands of Israel. And while, also, it was lodging in a private dwelling at Kirjath-jearim, that child was born of Jesse, at Bethlehem, who was to prepare a new tabernacle for it in Zion, and to give the plan of a temple for it in Jerusalem. The lodging of the ark in the house of Abinadab, within the precincts of Judah, was, in fact, a quiet step towards its ultimate destination. It was the bringing of it into the lot of that very tribe from which the True Ark was to originate. It was, also, the placing of it in a spot favourable for its transit to Jerusalem. And, yet, at the time, no eye, perhaps, foresaw this; nor did any heart thrill with delight in anticipation of the noble songs which David, by the Spirit, would compose for being sung before it. So true is it that "light is sown for the righteous," during the hours of their darkness: and gladness of heart is being prepared for them, when they are most sorrowful.

LECTURE V.

"Now therefore arise, O Lord God, into thy resting place, Thou, and the ark of thy strength: let thy priests, O Lord God, be clothed with salvation, and let thy saints rejoice in goodness."—2 Chronicles 6:41.

THESE words form the conclusion of Solomon's magnificent address, when he had brought "the ark of the covenant" to its final resting place,—i.e., within the holy of holies of his newly-erected temple. The words, also, occur in Psalm 132:8, where they appear in a curtailed form. Both the longer and the shorter form, however, are said to be Solomon's; for the composition of that Psalm is generally attributed to him. But, as that Psalm contains especial reference to David, as desiring to lodge the ark in a place somewhat worthy of it, we hereby obtain a clue to that series of events which affected the ark, during the reigns of David and Solomon. Those events may be comprised under the following divisions:—first, the commencement of David's preparations for the removal of the ark from its obscurity, and the check which he received in them; second, the renewal of his preparations, and the success which attended them; and, third, the elevation of the ark by Solomon to its grand and final resting place. May our meditation on those topics be sweet and profitable.

It should first be mentioned, by way of reminder, that we have traced the ark from the time of its construction under Moses all through its marvellous progress under Joshua, till he lodged it at Shiloh, and during its tarriance there under the Judges till its capture by the Philistines and its restoration to Israel. In our last lecture we left it at Kirjath-jearim, otherwise called Baale or Baalah, a town of Judah—at no great distance to the west of Jerusalem. Here it was lodged—in the house of Abinadab—who was a Levite, as some think, or only a private but true Israelite, as others say. Here, also, it remained, in comparative obscurity, during the greater part of Samuel's rule, and all through the reign of Saul. That self-willed monarch was too indifferent with regard to divine things to take thought for "the ark of the covenant." It is mentioned only once during the period of his reign—1 Samuel 14:18, in which case it seems that he desired the presence of the ark, now that Samuel had left him, to serve him for divination in difficulties and perplexities. When, however, David succeeded Saul, and found himself well established in the kingdom, he formed the pious design of bringing the ark from its obscurity to his own metropolis. As the man after God's own heart, he dearly loved the things of God, and made the honour and furtherance of them the first business of his life: just as all the genuine people of God delight and glory in the advancement of the cause of God.

I. *The commencement of David's preparations for the removal of the ark, and the painful check which he sustained in them*, are somewhat thus:

1. He consulted with all the leaders of Israel—civil, military, and ecclesiastical—about bringing the ark to Jerusalem. With wondrous unanimity they concurred in his wishes, and most zealously devoted themselves to the carrying of them out. But, as nothing is definitely said of David's *consulting* God in the matter, nor of his taking pains for everything connected with it to be done with due order, we cannot be surprised when we find that the course was not so smooth and favourable as might be expected. We are hereby admonished that, although, in our undertakings, we proceed after extensive deliberation, we are on a very insecure footing, if we have failed in taking counsel with God. Failure in that point may prove a flaw in our writ of success which may subject us to the sharpest disappointment.

2. On a set day, David proceeded with a multitudinous gathering of soldiers and people to the town of Kirjath-jearim. The account is recorded in 2 Samuel 6, and in 1 Chronicles 13, in verses 5 and 6 of which chapter it is more fully stated that

"David gathered all Israel together, from Shihor of Egypt even unto the entering of Hemath, to bring the ark of God from Kirjath-jearim.

"And David went up, and all Israel to Baalah, that is to Kirjath-jearim, which belonged to Judah, to bring up thence the ark of God the Lord, that dwelleth between the cherubims whose name is called on it."

The expression "Whose name is called on it," is worthy of our notice. It is somewhat differently given in 2 Samuel 6:2. Here it sounds as though God bestowed such honour on the ark, that He allowed Himself to be named from it, the God of the ark, the God who sitteth between the cherubim upon the ark. Others read the expression thus: "Whose name is proclaimed;" as though the wonders which had been wrought by the ark, under Joshua, were the means of proclaiming the name of the true God among the surrounding nations. While the expression in the Chronicles—"Whose name is called *on* it"—is thought to allude to the solemn pronunciation of the divine name and titles, by the high priest, on the great day of atonement.

3. Arrived at Kirjath-jearim, which, no doubt, had received due notice of the arrival, David and all his company arrange or witness the removal and procession of the ark. It is reverently placed on a new cart, and drawn—not by kine—but by oxen. This device seems to have been borrowed as a hint from the Philistines, which, as it succeeded well with them, might be expected to succeed equally well with Israel. But, what God may allow among His enemies, in the absence of properly prescribed means, is no rule for what He requires of His fully furnished friends. The Philistines had neither priests of the tabernacle nor Levites among them. To substitute any of the priests of Dagon might be feared as an affront to the dreaded ark. Hence the equipment of a *new cart*, and a couple of untrained kine, was as reasonable a device as any which could be formed. But with David and Israel the case was very different. It had been expressly appointed that none but the Kohathite Levites should carry the ark, and none but the priests should touch it. The Levites, of course, might touch the staves of the ark, but not the ark itself.—(Numbers 4:15.) How it was that David committed so grievous an oversight, or how it was that no one in Israel thought of it in time to correct it, is left to our conjecture only. On David's part, it shows us that the holiest believers never have too much knowledge of the written word. They may always be increasing their acquaintance with it. It is possible that David's discovery of his singular oversight led him to a closer study of the law of his God, and that, as a consequence of that study, he wrote the long and memorable 119th Psalm, in which almost every verse contains some allusion to or some commendation of "the statutes of the Lord." [1]

4. And, now, the procession, being formed, most jubilantly advances. The two surviving sons of Abinadab, or of Eleazar, for the former, at least, seems to have previously died, assumed, or had granted to them, the honour of seeing to the transit of the ark. Ahio drave the oxen, and Uzzah went behind to steady or otherwise help the cart.

> "And David and all Israel played before God with all their might, and with singing, and with harps, and with psalteries, and with timbrels, and with cymbals, and with trumpets." [2] (1 Chronicles 13:8.)

Everything proceeded joyously till they came to a particular spot, when, in a moment, all was stopped. The oxen stumbled, or, in some way, shook the cart and the ark in it, (for there is much criticism on the subject), and Uzzah, to prevent, as he thought, damage or mischief, "put forth his hand to hold the ark." In that instant he fell a ghastly corpse. The Lord smote him, but whether with lightning, or some internal rupture, as many think, we are not informed. The shock was terrible to all Israel, and to none more than to David. The singing and playing soon ceased, and the whole march as speedily stopped. The mirth was turned into mourning. Bright faces gathered blackness, and cheerful hearts heaved with dread; for who could tell what sudden blow might next be inflicted, or on whom it might fall? Even David was not without alarm; for "David was afraid of God that day, saying, How shall I bring the ark of God home to me?" Oh, how well is it, and what a good sign rises out of it, when judgments upon others make men begin to tremble for themselves! It is half the work of sanctification accomplished when we are afraid of bringing home to ourselves what has been chastisement and death to others. To think of our own sins when other sinners are cut down in their sins is a good beginning, and one which carries with it much hope.

5. But, *what* was the sin of Uzzah, that it should be followed by a punishment so sudden and so signal? It was *not* an act of wanton sacrilege or wilful contempt, neither was it an intentional wrong of any kind. In fact, Uzzah meant well. He thought to do God service by saving the ark from a blow or a fall. But, it was not his place to do anything of the kind. It was, therefore, an officious act. It was one which did not pertain to him; for he was, at most, but a Levite, and had no authority to touch the ark on any occasion, or under any pretence whatever. It was, also, a thoughtless act. In fact, the essence of his sin seems to have been irreverence, through a careless and inconsiderate state of mind. He was not, at the time, indulging in high and hallowed reverence for that God over whose ark he was watching. He forgot that, while the cart carried the ark, the ark sustained the presence of Jehovah between the cherubim upon it. The want of due mindfulness of God, especially in those who profess to be patterns of it, is a grievous offence, and an aggravated affront. Besides, as Jewish writers insinuate, Uzzah, by attending on the ark in his father's house, contracted that sort of familiarity with its awful presence which led to an unhallowed demeanour towards it. We are always in danger of the same evil from similar privileges; for the human heart is sadly prone to fall into irreverence, by its habitual association with holy things. Uzzah, too, may have presumed upon his past services to the ark, and so have been tempted of the devil to make a vain display of himself on the occasion. He would appear a great man in the eyes of the multitude to be able to do what none of that multitude dare attempt. Vanity has made victims of many of its votaries.

But, whatever was the real character of Uzzah's crime, the Righteous Lord, against Whom it was committed, saw fit to

[1] Why it was that the priests and Levites participated in the oversight is more easily accounted for. They had, as a body, totally neglected the ark; and long disuse of the forms prescribed for its locomotion, rendered them really ignorant of them.

[2] It is singular that such a diligent student of Holy Scripture as Bishop Hall should say—"I did not *before* hear of *trumpets*," as though there had been no trumpets in the procession round Jericho.

punish it with the instant death of the body. That death is no proof of any perdition of the soul. Uzzah, as a young man, may have been what Eli was as an old man—a true believer—and so have been saved eternally, while he suffered temporally. The punishment was upon one; the fear was upon all. God has perfect right to select His instances of chastisement, as well as His instances of favour.

But, some men will say, "Where is the benevolence and mercy of God in slaying a man for simply touching the ark, and that with a good intention? Can it be wise or expedient to take away life for a single offence, and such an offence as did no injury to any one?" They who question thus know nothing as they ought to know. Their question is next of kin to the infidel question, "Was it fitting to doom Adam and Eve to perdition for eating a single apple?" When we are once correctly informed of the holiness of God, and the lofty majesty of His commands, we shall cease to question thus. We shall see that the divine sanctity cannot endure being infringed upon by the very slightest contact of sin.

6. God's stroke on Uzzah so confounded David, and spread such dismay among the assembled throngs, that the procession was broken up, and every thought of marching further forward that day was laid aside. So unhinged was David by the event, that he fell, for the moment, into infirmity of temper. "David was *displeased*, because the Lord had made a breach upon Uzzah." David had, in consequence, to learn the holy lessons of wisdom and humility; which as the issue proves, he submissively learned. All the Lord's people will have to learn the like, and perhaps at a sharper cost, when they rashly impugn the divine dealings or indulge in fretful and moody feelings respecting them.

Hard by the spot where Uzzah fell was the house of a pious Levite—Obed-edom. There David left the ark, till such time as he could recover himself, and see his way to further proceedings. Obed-edom, too, was willing to receive the ark, though everybody on that day was afraid of it, and even David was unwilling to house it. How are we to account for this conduct on the part of Obed-edom? On the principal of true faith and sterling piety it is easily to be accounted for. "Perfect love casteth out fear:" and the eye of faith sees the terrors of the Lord laid aside, and smiles taking their place. Where there is no mind to transgress, there is no sense of benumbing dread in looking up to God. Obed-edom knew that there was nothing to fear from the ark, if he, as a Levite, did only what Levites might do. Besides, he was not alarmed at the inflictions of God's justice, since he took refuge in His mercy. Indeed, true piety sees, in the justice of God, not reasons for servile fear, but grounds for deeper adoration and more solemn love; as one says, "Even the justice of God is lovely to the true children of God."

II. *The renewal of David's preparations* followed his devout reflections upon the solemn event, and his hearing of the extraordinary prosperity which the presence of the ark brought to the house of Obed-edom. For "The Lord blessed the house of Obed-edom, and all that he had."—1 Chronicles 13:14. The Jews report the most extravagant things of the blessedness which crowned his family and his property.[1] Though their reports may be fabulously exaggerated, yet, without doubt, the personal and domestic prosperity of the good man was very great. So true is it that "Godliness is great gain," and that "the blessing of the Lord it maketh rich, and He addeth no sorrow unto it." Oh, therefore, that men would seek to have God always with them, and that they would believe in the sure prosperity which His presence always brings.

1. And, now, David begins his renewal of pains to bring up the ark to Jerusalem, by an ingenuous acknowledgement of his error about the cart and the oxen on the former occasion. "Then David said, none ought to carry the ark of God but the Levites."—(1 Chronicles 15:2.) We can never set about a renewal of efforts, after some signal failure, more hopefully than by candidly confessing to ourselves and to others the weak or deficient points in our former efforts. With a conviction of his error in his own mind, David openly avowed it to those who were chiefly concerned to repair it.—1 Chronicles 15:11, 12, 13.[2]

After this, David made at once an orderly and very extensive arrangement for the procession of the ark from the house of Obed-edom to the tent, which he had pitched for it, in Jerusalem. The whole staff of priests and Levites, soldiers and elders, singers and instrumental musicians, seem to have been engaged for the occasion. It was thus arranged, because David intended to make the procession as splendid and as joyous as he possibly could. That nothing might be wanting in its hallowed hilarity, himself headed the procession, not in royal state, but habited as sort of lay-priest,[3] wearing a linen ephod, or short white surplice, in order to show that he was more anxious to be

[1] They say that he was blessed with extraordinary health after sickness and a singular influx of wealth. This is not unlikely: but when they say that he had eight married sons, and that the wife of each son bore eight children at a birth, and that within *three* months, (!) they talk as Jewish writers too often talk.

[2] "And David called for Zadok and Abiathar the priests, and for the Levites, for Uriel, Asaiah, and Joel, Shemaiah and Eliel, and Amminadab,

"And said unto them, Ye are the chief of the fathers of the Levites: Sanctify yourselves, both ye and your brethren, that ye may bring up the ark of the Lord God of Israel unto the place that I have prepared for it.

"For because ye did it not at the first, the Lord our God made a breach upon us, for that we sought him not after due order."

[3] Our Henry the Eighth, in the earlier part of his reign, occasionally did the like, in private service. And Sir Thomas Moore often put on a surplice in the chapel at Kensington and took part with the choir.

a believer than a king, and to impress on his subjects the conviction that all he did in bringing up the ark was of a religious rather than of a civil character.

2. Setting out on their homeward course, David was mindful of what he had before omitted. He provided for the offering of sacrifices to Almighty God. (2 Samuel 6:13.) This was the sure way to arrive at a successful issue. May we always prove it so to be! Now that the procession was in full progress, David was to be seen "dancing and playing with all his might." Some kind of harp employed his hands, while his feet were occupied in musical paces, and keeping time to the tune, as well as to the graceful and ecstatic motions of his whole person. The dance of David was wholly of a religious character, and consequently marked with sobriety and devotion as well as with fervour and animation. It accorded with the age of the church and the custom of the times. The Holy Ghost at once sanctified and sanctioned it.[1]

But, it is seldom that an earnest believer escapes censure or contempt for his earnestness. Saul's daughter, who was now David's wife, but who retained too much of the temper of her father, looked out of a window as the ark was passing through Jerusalem, and, seeing her husband dancing and playing, "despised him in her heart." Well, perhaps, would it have been had she kept her feelings within her heart. But, in a fit of ill and contemptuous temper, she told her mind to David. Her quarrel with him was of her own making. God took it up against herself, and pronounced upon her a sentence, than which nothing could be more vexatious to a Hebrew wife, namely, that she should for ever be childless.

3. It has pleased the Holy Ghost to leave on record two, at least, of the divine songs which David composed for the procession of the ark to his city and home. The 24th and 68th are those songs or psalms. The 68th Psalm was probably sung while the ark was on the road to Jerusalem, and the 24th when it reached the tent of its residence. The first verse and the last of the 68th are peculiarly descriptive of the circumstances under which the ark was carried to Jerusalem. "Let God arise and let his enemies be scattered," were words which carried back the hearers to the days of the ark in the wilderness, when, upon its going forward, Moses said, "Rise up Lord, and let thine enemies be scattered!" while the last verse, "O God, thou art terrible out of thy holy places!" seems plainly to allude to the fearful death of Uzzah upon the former attempt to remove the ark. The 24th Psalm is beautifully prophetic of the Ascension of Christ to heaven, from the figure of the ark ascending the holy hill of Zion. When all was ended, as to its safe deposit on that hill, David offered abundant sacrifices, liberally regaled the people, and dismissed them with his fervent blessing. Thus, while he acted as a godly man and a generous prince, he was displayed by God as an eminent type of the Messiah conducting His people to the true Jerusalem, accepting their thanksgivings, and regaling and blessing them in their everlasting home.

It remains for us to contemplate

III. *The elevation of the ark by Solomon to its grand and final resting place in the temple.*

David never intended the tent, which he pitched for it, to be its ultimate abode. A loftier device had entered his mind. He commended that device to his God, who approved it, but directed its accomplishment to be postponed to the days of his son and successor. David's hands had been too much stained with the blood of war to render him a ritually fit person to erect a temple for peaceful worship. Still, he was allowed to communicate the plan of that temple, and to make the most lavish preparation of materials for it. In due time, Solomon applied all the vast resources of both his mind and his wealth to the completion of his father's plan.

1. When the temple was finished, the young king, like his father, made sumptuous and splendid arrangements for conveying "the ark of the covenant" from the tent on Zion to the holy of holies on Moriah. He assembled all the principal men of his empire, and took care that everything should be conducted in due order. He learned what to do from the painful lessons which his royal father had learned before him. Sacrifices innumerable were offered; and priests were the bearers of the ark to the hallowed place appointed for it. The procession must have been eminently gorgeous and grand, and yet intensely solemn and devout. The full account is recorded in 2 Chronicles 5:2–8. In the last two verses it is said—

> "And the priests brought in the ark of the covenant of the Lord unto his holy place, to the oracle of the house, into the most holy place, even under the wings of the cherubims:
>
> "For the cherubims spread forth their wings over the ark, and the cherubims covered the ark and the staves thereof above."

This addition of gigantic cherubim to shadow not only the other cherubim on the ark, but the whole area of the holy of holies, was a magnificent device, full of significance to those who look to the heaven of heavens as filled with all the fulness of divine and angelic beauty.

2. While marching from the tent to the temple, the singers were, no doubt, suitably employed. Whether they repeated the Psalms which David composed for the former occasion, we cannot say; but it is currently believed that Psalms 47 and 132 were used for this last procession, and that each was written by Solomon, or some other inspired person, for that special solemnity.

[1] That religious dances were practised in christian churches during "the dark ages" is notorious. In some of the Spanish Cathedrals even Bishops have headed them.

3. As Solomon made the elevation of the ark to its resting place the first thing in all that he devised for that glorious day, which many believe to have been the chief day of a year of Jubilee, so was it the last thing at which he glanced in the noble and magnificent dedication prayer which he addressed to the God of Israel.

> "Now therefore arise, O Lord God, unto thy resting place, thou and the ark of thy strength: let thy priests, O Lord God, be clothed with thy salvation, and let thy saints rejoice in goodness."

Solomon well knew that, as the temple was nothing without the ark, so was the ark nothing without the presence of the eternal God. With it, therefore, he prayed that Jehovah would condescend to come, and make the holy of holies His "resting place." Jehovah heard the prayer, and allowed the ark to continue as the focus of His presence, for many a generation. The rest which the ark began to have when David lodged it in Jerusalem, was continued in a special manner during the whole of Solomon's reign, "for his God gave him rest round about." No enemy assailed the tent of David, or the temple of Solomon, and no war called forth the ark into a field of battle. Sweet and beautiful emblem this of the repose of Christ after the sufferings of His manhood, and His ascension to the true temple above. When He ascended up on high, it was to enter into His rest; for He had been a man of labours and sorrows on earth. There, as the True Ark, He remains, never again to be personally smitten and afflicted, never again to be taken captive, by wicked men, more cruel than Philistines, and never needing rescue, temporary sojourn, or another ascension. For ever and for ever shall His rest be glorious.

As we have now travelled through the history of the ark, till it has reached its topmost elevation, let us tarry a while to glance at a few prominent points, which the retrospect presents to us.

1. It may be that the main divisions of the history of the ark in Canaan *were intended to foreshadow the main divisions of the gospel dispensation.* If so, we have fresh cause to take comfort in our prospects.

The prosperity of the ark under Joshua, and during the age of those who immediately succeeded him, seems to meet with its counterpart, in the prosperity of genuine truth, from the ministry of our Lord to the death of His apostles and their immediate successors. After Joshua and his companions left the world, an entirely different class of Jews speedily sprung up. "There arose another generation after them which knew not the Lord."—Judges 2:10. So, after the apostolic age men of other minds soon spread over the church, and another gospel crept in. Checks and alternations of light and darkness occurred in Israel, till at length the mass of the priesthood was a mass of corruption, and the ark was separated from the tabernacle. So, with many undulations, the pure truth of Christ sank into obscurity under the darkness of the so-called dark ages; the gospel seemed to be separated from the visible church, and cold indifference generally prevailed. But, there came a great reformation in Israel under David: the ark was restored, and a new era in a new part of the land set in. So our European Reformation restored the gospel, and set forth Christ as the Ark of the new covenant. But, then, that Ark was sent, not to Italy, but chiefly to England. To England all eyes now look as the most favoured spot in the world, and which may prove another Jerusalem, or focus for the outspreading of the light of a millennium, which will answer to the glories of the reign of Solomon.

Be the result as it may, let us watch and wait for the exaltation of that Saviour who is the only glory of His people.

2. The perfect singularity, pre-eminence, and isolation of the ark, should remind us of *the grand peculiarity, which, in every point of view, pertains to Christ.* There was but one ark; everything was formed for it; and, without it, nothing in Israel had life or prosperity. God has studied the like peculiarity with regard to His dear Son. Him, and Him alone, has He set before the eye of His church. All through its ages and its history He is to be the one concentrated object of desire. His presence is everything, and without it we shall in vain look for vitality or blessedness.—Acts 4:12. Oh that all who call themselves christians did but steadfastly hold to the pre-eminence of Christ! Were He, in the estimation of His professed followers, what He is in Himself, "the first and the last," the "all-in-all," there would be neither Popery, feeble Protestantism, sect nor schism, within the pale of the visible church. When Israel held to the ark, and gloried in it alone, there was neither false God among them, nor war to trouble them. Our state will correspond with theirs, when Christ alone is exalted among us.

3. In tracing the ark to its long-intended resting place, we may discern *the joyful certainty of all God's purposes.* Many a time did it seem to go ill with the ark, and the prospect of its ultimate glory appeared most dim and uncertain. But the glorious end was attained. So, when Christ on the Cross, like the ark in Dagon's temple, was given over for lost, who felt confident of the glory which was to follow? Yet the glory did follow. So, many a time does the humble christian seem to himself ready to perish; but, relief comes in due season, and assuredly God will bring him to where his Saviour is. He shall attain the end of his faith, even the salvation of his soul.

LECTURE VI.

"And the temple of God was opened in heaven, and there was seen in his temple the ark of his testament."—Revelation 11:19.

WE hear, in these words, the last mention of the ark in Holy Scripture. But, ere we come to the contemplation of them, we must trace our path through a few other texts, which occur subsequently to those days of Solomon with which our last lecture concluded. For the completion of the plan of these lectures, we have now, finally, to consider "The History of the Ark from the reign of Solomon to the latest mention of it in Holy Scripture." May, then, this last attempt to elucidate an interesting and important topic of divine revelation, be not the least in point of spiritual profit and hallowed pleasure.

I. For full four hundred years we find no mention of the ark in the record of the kings of Judah. True, the ark was to *rest* in the temple; but the exercise of men's affections towards it was to be constant and energetic. It was not to be brought from its place in the holy of holies; neither did any one, except the high priest, and that once a year only, dare to go in to gaze upon it. In this respect it was a notable type of the Invisible One, whom, though not seen, the people were to believe, reverence, and love.

During the days of Solomon all was peaceful and prosperous with Israel. The memorable wonders of the dedication of the temple, and the splendid procession which brought up "the ark of the covenant" into it, lived in the mental eye of many a true worshipper of the God of Israel.

In the reign of his son and successor, Rehoboam, the ark, indeed, continued in its rest, but the first interruptions of that rest were felt, in the dismemberment of the kingdom, and in the establishment of a spurious form of worship for ten out of the twelve tribes. Rehoboam was an unwise ruler, and far more despotically disposed than either justice or prudence required. Taking advantage of this, Jeroboam the son of Nebat was permitted to organize a revolution, which shook the pillars of the empire to their lowest basement. The one nation separated into two kingdoms. Israel mustered ten tribes, and Judah comprised only two. But, then, Judah retained the temple and the ark of the covenant. Jeroboam was too shrewd a man not to perceive the immense advantage which this gave to Judah, and the necessity for devising some substitute for what the people had been accustomed to regard as essential to their security and prosperity. He, accordingly, set up a sort of counterfeit ark, or at least, that sort of imitation of the cherubic figures upon it, which would best engage the thoughts of the people, and satisfy his own idolatrous inclinations. He made "a house of high places," and instituted services and sacrifices after a distorted fashion, so as to beguile the people into the belief that their attendance on them would excuse their going to Jerusalem. But, as the people were familiar with the form of the cherubim, he made and set up "two golden calves," and said, "Behold thy Gods, O Israel!" Now, we are not to suppose that these golden calves were mere likenesses of the animal which we well know by that name, or that the people were, all at once, so befooled and besotted as to worship such creatures. Had they so been, it would have better served their purpose to select a living calf at a far less cost, than to make a golden one. But this was quite foreign to Jeroboam's policy. The cherubim on the ark were made of gold, and as the calves were partial imitations of them, it was expedient for these calves, also, to be formed of gold.

Possibly, however, you are startled at the idea of there being anything cherubic in the calves of Jeroboam. The surprise will cease when you recollect that the first face of the cherubim was that of an ox, and that the feet of the whole were those of a calf. The common figure, too, of a cherub was ox-like, with wings. "He rode on a cherub (a winged ox) and did fly; yea, He did fly upon the wings of the wind." (Psalm 18:10.) Modern discoveries among the buried ruins of Nineveh, have brought to light "the winged bull" of the Assyrian religion, which, like the Apis, or symbolic calf of Egypt, with many another similar device, was, no doubt, a distortion of the patriarchial knowledge of the form of the cherubim, as first displayed at the gate of the Edenic Paradise.

Thus, Jeroboam's counterfeit of the figures on the mercy-seat of the ark, was not so much the substitution of pagan idolatry, as of a spurious form of true Judaism. It was the popery of its day, being a corruption of Jehovah's religion, and in reality antagonistic to it.

But, how came it that such an imposture was so easily palmed upon the people? Jewish historians tell many tales to account for it, but they fail in giving the true reason. It was not the eloquence or cunning of Jeroboam in first winning over the chiefs of the tribes; but it was the hollow-heartedness of the people themselves. Unless they had themselves turned away, in heart, from the God of the ark, they would not so soon and so easily have been turned by Jeroboam to worship his golden calves. All apostacy, like all true religion, begins in the heart. When the inner man is unsound, the outer life will be unfaithful. Israel ceased to love God before they began to love idols. So, to this hour, they who once appeared sound in the faith, but have turned aside to worldly folly, popery, or infidelity, have first turned from the love of truth and holiness in their hearts.

II. In the history of the ark, time leads us on to the beginning of the reign of the young but good Josiah. We read nothing respecting the ark during the many reigns which preceded his. And, yet, there must have been many occurrences which affected it; especially in the reigns of those wicked princes who suffered the temple to fall into decay, and who loved idols more than the ark. How it was preserved during the atrocious usurpation of Athaliah, or what was done with it when Jehoash, under the counsel of the good priest Jehoida, extensively repaired the house of the Lord we are not informed. Neither know we how it fared when the wicked Ahaz,[1] the father of the righteous Hezekiah, perverted every ordinance of God, despoiled the temple, and turned the whole tide of the national religion into heathenism. Neither, again, do we hear anything of it, even when Hezekiah set about a thorough reformation, and restored all the services of the sanctuary. In fact, it is not till the rise of his great grandson, Josiah, (as already stated,) that we find any mention of the ark at all. But, then, that mention of it helps us to understand somewhat of its previous history. The record is found, not in the Book of Kings, but in 2 Chronicles 35:3.

From the wording of this text, we are led to infer that, during the abominable life of Manasseh, and the short but wicked reign of his son Amon, there were some truly pious Levites, holy and devoted men of heart, who had removed and taken care of the ark. It is probable, therefore, that when they saw the horrible impiety of Manasseh, how, amongst other things, "he set a carved image (the idol which he had made) in the house of God," and built idolatrous altars actually within that holy house, that they, most likely at the risk of their lives, secured the ark by carrying it away into the country, and lodging it, as occasion served, in the house of some true-hearted Israelite, who, like Abinadab or Obed-edom, was glad to receive it. It is probable, also, that in order to escape detection, they many times were obliged, reverently to convey the ark from place to place, so that, in the words of Josiah, it seemed to be "a burden upon their shoulders." Most likely, also, they acted under the sanction and direction of the high priest of the day, that good man Hilkiah.

[1] Why Ahaz spared the ark, when he "gathered together the vessels of the house of God, and cut them in pieces," (2 Chronicles 28:24) can only be accounted for by supposing that secret fear of consequences restrained him. He could not be ignorant of the terrible power of the ark in former days, and how Uzzah fell down dead for merely touching it. Some such reason as this, perhaps, prevented invading armies from capturing and carrying it off, till, at length, the visible token of Jehovah's presence (the Shekinah) was withdrawn from it.

How exact a picture, alas, was this of the need of flight and secretion which befel the True Ark, even the Lord Jesus, when to escape the Manasseh of His day—Herod the wickedly great—He was carried into Egypt, and, frequently afterwards, was obliged to hide Himself, or convey Himself away from the grasp of those who sought His life! How painfully, too, has the picture been copied in the lives of the followers of Jesus, "who wandered about in sheep-skins and goat-skins (the ark, when travelling, was covered with badger-skins) being destitute, afflicted, tormented!" May we be spared from witnessing the same sort of wanderings, and enduring the like afflictions!

The ark, once again restored to its rightful place in the holy of holies, had a short rest, during the reign of Josiah. But, that rest was only like the brief lull of a tempest which is about to desolate every spot within its range. The time for the total loss of the ark, or, at least, for its historic annihilation, was rapidly coming on. The measure of the national iniquity was fast filling up, and God was about to give up His vineyard to the wild boar of the wood. But, ere the threatened vengeance is dashed upon the people, their city and their temple, the sweet voice of prophecy is heard, tuning its gentlest strain to a song of future times. To this prophetic song we must now turn our attentive ear.

III. The prophet Jeremiah lived in the reign of Josiah. He saw its beginning and its end. He, consequently, saw the good things which Josiah did; and, among them, the desired restoration of the ark to the renovated temple. This must have been a joy to such a man as Jeremiah. But, much as he may have rejoiced at this time, the Spirit of Prophecy carried him forward to another time, even to the full day of Christ on earth, when neither the temple nor the ark should be objects of desire, because of the knowledge and presence of Him who is greater than both. Thus speaks the prophecy:

> "And it shall come to pass, when ye be multiplied and increased in the land, in those days, saith the Lord, they shall say no more, The ark of the covenant of the Lord: neither shall it come to mind; neither shall they remember it; neither shall they visit it; neither shall that be done any more.
>
> "At that time they shall call Jerusalem the throne of the Lord; and all nations shall be gathered unto it, to the name of the Lord, to Jerusalem: neither shall they walk any more after the imagination of their evil heart."—Jeremiah 3:16, 17.

There are some biblical students, who, viewing distant events with a too considerably shortened telescope, interpret this prophecy as already fulfilled. They imagine that it was fulfilled when, after the captivity in Babylon, the people returned to Judea, re-built the temple, without the ark, and increased and multiplied both in population and prosperity. But, assuredly, in that return to Judea there was nothing like the accomplishment of the many glorious things which Jeremiah foretold, when he spake of the people neither having the ark, nor longing for it. Besides, the broad and palpable fact is, that the Jewish nation did long for the ark, and the other things which, together with it, were missing in the second temple, and for all of which they do long and sigh to the present day. In many of their synagogues they have a holy chest or coffer, in which they keep manuscript copies of the Old Testament, on rolls of vellum or parchment, and which they take out, unfold, and read with great solemnity on special occasions. Without doubt, as the good and the wise, in overwhelming majority, think, the times to which the words of Jeremiah refer are the times of Messiah in His millennial glory. Then the gathered and honoured Jews, having Him for their Saviour and King, and being made altogether a spiritually minded people, shall no longer care for any figure or shadow of Him, such as their ark and other ceremonial forms had presented to their fore-fathers. Oh, happy day, and happy they who see it, when the long-predicted glory of Israel shall fill the earth, and all nations shall flow unto it.

But, we must go back to the dark day of Israel's banishment from the inheritance of Canaan.

IV. After ages of fruitless trial, and unfelt forbearance, Jehovah let His justice take its course. The process, both of the mercy shewn to Israel and of the judgment which terminated it, is thus affectingly described in 2 Chronicles 36:15–19.—

> "And the Lord of their fathers sent to them by his messengers, rising up betimes and sending; because he had compassion on his people, and on his dwelling place.
>
> "But they mocked the messengers of God and despised his words, and misused his prophets, until the wrath of the Lord arose against his people, till there was no remedy.
>
> "Therefore he brought upon them the king of the Chaldeans, who slew their young men with the sword in the house of their sanctuary, and had no compassion upon young man or maiden, old man or him that stooped for age, he gave them all into his hand.
>
> "And all the vessels of the house of God, great and small, and the treasures of the house of the Lord, and the treasures of the king and of his princes, all these he brought to Babylon.
>
> "And they burnt the house of God, and brake down the wall of Jerusalem, and burnt all the palaces thereof with fire, and destroyed all the goodly vessels thereof."

In 2 Kings 25:13–17, a minuter account is given of the spoils of the temple. But in this particular account no mention is made of the ark. All that Nebuchadnezzar took from the temple he carried to Babylon. The meaner spoil of brass he seems to have broken up and used: but all the more valuable articles he deposited in the house of his idol-god. There they continued, apparently catalogued with great exactness, till Cyrus gained possession of them, when he conquered the kingdom. Upon his being divinely moved to let the Hebrews return to their country, he generously gave them back all the gold and silver vessels, amounting to five thousand and four hundred. Still, though many articles are expressly named, no allusion to the ark is made. (See Ezra 1:7–11.) Hence the question very naturally presents itself, What became of the ark, and what was its ultimate lot? This is answered in two or three ways. 1. By some persons it is thought that the ark was not carried to Babylon at all, but that, in like manner as it was secreted by some pious Levites, in the dark reign of Manasseh, so was it secured and privately conveyed away by some equally pious individuals, when the Babylonian storm was seen to be approaching. In this case, it is further supposed, that the ark was concealed in some cave, or covered recess, on lofty hill or in sequestered dale, and that, being of imperishable materials, it remains there to this day, preserved for happy discovery in some bright hour of Israel's joy. 2. Others are of opinion that the ark *was* carried to Babylon, but that, having been in some untold way disposed of, it was not returned to Jerusalem. They even imagine that it may still be extant among the ruins of the temples or treasuries of Babylon, and that, to answer some important object in the day of Israel's controversy, it will be brought to light. 3. Others, again, settle it in their minds that the ark was both carried to Babylon and returned to Jerusalem: for, say they, its not being named among the articles which were taken and then given back, is a thing of no force, because other articles of the larger sort, are, also, not named.

Among our English divines, the principal advocate of this last opinion is Dr. Prideaux, in his well-known work on the Connexion between the Old and the New Testament. In discussing the question whether the second temple had or had not "the ark of the covenant," he takes the affirmative side. His argument is to this effect: that as the holy of holies, and the veil before it, in the first temple, were for containing and concealing the ark, and as the second temple had both a holy of holies and a veil, so, also, it must have had either *the* ark or *one made anew* in resemblance of it. And, further, that as the high priest continued to go, once a year, to sprinkle the blood of atonement in the holy of holies, so there must have been an ark, if not *the* ark before which to sprinkle it.

In reply to this reasoning, it is urged that the Jews universally assert that there was no ark in the second temple, for it was one of the five things which that temple wanted, in comparison with the first temple. They, also, assert that, in lieu of the ark, there was set in the holy of holies of the second temple a large stone, which was dug up from the ruins of the first temple, and supposed to be its foundation, or chief corner-stone.

With this opinion, as to the absence of the ark from the second temple, nearly all the early Christian writers agree. Josephus, also, states that the ark was wanting in it; and that, when Titus, the commander of the Roman forces, captured Jerusalem, and went into the holy of holies, no ark was seen within it.

In corroboration of this opinion, perhaps the following fact, as a new argument, may be admitted: There stands at Rome, to this day, a triumphal arch, "The Arch of Titus," commemorative of the victory of that illustrious general over the Jews and Jerusalem. Within it are sculptured the forms of several of the vessels of the sanctuary, but there is no representation of the ark. Now, it is hardly to be imagined that a Roman artist, in designing such an arch, would have omitted the chief symbol of the Jewish worship, and have selected only secondary objects, if the ark had been known to be among the spoils of the temple.[1]

With the generality therefore, of historians and divines, we may pretty safely conclude that the ark was unknown to the worshippers in the second temple. But, what really became of it after the desolation of the first temple, no man can tell.

We have, however, an authentic revelation respecting Christ as the True Ark, in the vision of St. John, whose words we have now to consider.

V. In our text, the favoured Apostle writes that "the temple of God was opened in heaven, and there was seen in his temple the ark of his testament."

The general meaning of this statement in the Apocalyptic vision, is that at the period referred to, though that period is differently interpreted, there should be an enlarged opening for the spread of true religion, and a clearer discovery of the mystery of Christ. The ark was not seen when it stood in the temple, but was concealed by a veil. As that ark was the symbol of the person and the presence of Christ, so, the throwing of it open, the causing of it to be seen by all eyes, was a mode of stating that the time should come when the mystery of the Gospel of Christ should be more clearly developed, and the distinctive doctrines of Christianity more plainly and forcibly presented to the people. Whether the time intended by the vision referred to the time of the Great Reformation, or, as some think, to the present times, as the continuance of that revival of true evangelical doctrine which has marked the present century, we profess not to determine. Be this as it may, we know, from the text, that "the ark of the covenant" was certainly a type of Christ. And, happy, too, is the knowledge that His doctrine is more fully and more faithfully preached in the pulpits of our land, and more extensively promulgated through the world than in any former age. May it not be that another verse or two in this wonderful revelation, apparently co-significant with our text, has yet to be fulfilled. In Revelation 15:5–8, it is said,

> "And after that I looked, and, behold, the temple of the tabernacle of the testimony in heaven was opened.
>
> "And the seven angels came out of the temple, having the seven plagues, clothed in pure and white linen, and having their breasts girded with golden girdles.
>
> "And one of the four beasts gave unto the seven angels seven golden vials full of the wrath of God, who liveth for ever and ever.
>
> "And the temple was filled with smoke from the glory of God, and from his power: and no man was able to enter into the temple, till the seven plagues of the seven angels were fulfilled."

This filling of the temple with smoke, and the inability of men to enter into it, is thought to mean the mist which will envelope the Church through Anti-christian teaching, and which will prevent souls from entering into the true temple, till after the threatened plagues upon the enemies of Christ shall be accomplished. We know what that mist is doing now. The good Lord deliver us and all ours from its deathly gloom, and keep us in the true light of his dear Son. Sure may we be that, when God manifests the truth to us, it is that we may clearly discern it, and affectionately receive it. To our view "the ark of his testament" has been disclosed. The veil which for ages intercepted our sight of its glories has long been withdrawn. Opportunities for stedfastly gazing upon it and contemplating it in all its wondrous proportions, are amply furnished to us. May our diligence, our earnestness, our gratitude, be commensurate with our privileges! And may the illustrations of the subject which have been presented in these lectures, be one means, at least, of enhancing our estimate of those privileges. Let none forget that, if they regard them only as intellectually pleasant, they dishonour their intention and fail to realize them as spiritually profitable.

Let your renewed attention accompany our winding up of the present lecture, as the last of the series.

1. In the policy of Jeroboam to substitute golden calves for "the ark of the covenant," and thereby to content the people with a counterfeit religion, let us behold *a type of the great apostacy in the Christian Israel, and beware of it.* The one was,

[1] Neither the Coliseum nor the greater part of the monuments now seen from the Capitol, were erected till after St. Paul's death. Of these there is one which, to the Christian or the Jew, must ever be the most interesting at Rome, marking as it does, the final downfall of the Jewish state, and preserving upon its triumphal tablets the only authentic representation in existence of the implements of the temple worship. This is the Arch of Titus, erected, after his death, to commemorate his capture of Jerusalem, and which is, perhaps, the most simple and beautiful at Rome. The ruined frieze bears the triumphal procession of the conqueror, and sculptured on the wall, *within* the archway, is a procession of captive Jews, bearing on their shoulders the spoils of the temple at Jerusalem, the eleven-branched golden candlestick, the jubilee trumpets, the tables of the shew bread, and other details copied, no doubt, from the originals themselves, which, deposited in the temples, are said to have been finally carried away by Genseric into Africa. This sculptured tablet, and the edifice which it adorns, form, perhaps, the most vivid page in monumental history, to be met with in the whole world."—From *Bartlett's Footsteps of our Lord and his Apostles.*

doubtless, intended to foreshadow the other: for, as under the Old Dispensation, there was a great falling away of the majority of the tribes from the worship of the true God, so was there to be a similar defection under the new. For it is written, "that day (the day of the Lord) shall not come except there come a falling away (or a great apostacy) first." That falling away has long been grievously visible in Christendom. The proportion of the spurious to the sound is still as it were, ten to two. Antichrist can boast, like Jeroboam, of numbers. The flock of Christ is still a little flock, but, then, like Judah, they have the True Ark, and as long so they cherish it they shall prosper. In the days of Jeroboam, multitudes of priests, Levites, and people, who loved the ark at Jerusalem, refused to worship the calves, but went and dwelt in Judah. Multitudes, thank God, have left and still are leaving the Church of Rome. To those who stay behind we are with earnest affection to say, "Come out of her, my people, that ye be not partakers of her sins, and that ye receive not of her plagues." (Revelation 18:4.)

Let us hold fast the doctrine of Christ, and never be slack in standing up valiantly for its defence. So long as the ark of God is with us, and we sincerely love it, so long, like Judah, shall we, our Queen and our country, stand and prosper.

2. In the total loss of the ark, and in the entire demolition of the Jewish system, let us discern *the low estimate which God sets upon His own most exalted institutions, in comparison with the living realities, which they were intended to foreshadow.*

The Jewish system of type and ceremony was formed with infinite pains, and at a cost of wisdom and forethought which seemed to draw largely on the divine treasury. It employed the loftiest angels, and the holiest men. It was attended with the most astonishing miracles, and marked the destinies of the world for many ages. All this vast fabric, however, of figurative worship, was accounted nothing in comparison with the simple faith of the simplest believer in the Incarnate Son. When the time for His incarnation was drawing nigh, indications were given of the departure of the types of it. The ark was dislodged from its resting place; and, after a short restoration, was lost to all human observation. Intimation was hereby given that the True Ark was about to appear, that men were to prepare themselves for its appearance, and that all hearts should be ready to welcome it. Yes, nothing is of any value in God's reckoning apart from His beloved Son. Everything gives place to Him. The curious tabernacle was nothing; the gorgeous temple was nothing; and even the wondrous and glorious ark was nothing; for they all were consigned to destruction or oblivion. But the Babe of Bethlehem is everything. He is "all and in all"—unchangeable and eternal. Oh, happy experience, to be a penitent believer in Jesus! He is the Tabernacle which will never decay—the Temple which will never be destroyed—the Ark which will never be lost. All, too, who are found in Him will be what He is. May we be so found!

3. In the visions of St. John, as set forth in our text, *let us see our duty and our joy.* Is the holy of holies thrown open to our view, and the ark of Jehovah's testimony disclosed to us? Let us, then, strive to enter into the one, and never take our eye from the other. The way is laid open by the flesh of Christ; and, by faith, His people walk in it up to the very ark of their salvation. If, in our day, the mists of anti-christianity should thicken around us, and the darkness of the divine judgments appal our hearts, let us take courage in knowing that "the time is short." Terrible as the judgment will be, it will annihilate every foe, and He, whom our souls love, will be alone exalted, according to the force of that covenant which was made before the world began.

Henwick House in 1845. This was W.H.H.'s home after he left Astley Rectory. Henwick is pronounced with the fourth letter w silent (pronounced as if spelled "Henick"). This was drawn by his eldest child, Miriam Crane.

William Henry Havergal (1793–1870), pastor, scholar, musician. A true example, as Paul wrote, "Be ye followers of me even as I also am of Christ." 1 Corinthians 11:1

SERMONS,

CHIEFLY ON

HISTORICAL SUBJECTS

FROM

THE OLD AND NEW TESTAMENTS;

PREACHED IN

THE PARISH CHURCH OF

ST. NICHOLAS, WORCESTER.

BY THE

REV. W. H. HAVERGAL, A.M.

RECTOR OF ST. NICHOLAS'S, AND HONORARY CANON, WORCESTER.

VOL. I.

OLD TESTAMENT.

LONDON:
HAMILTON, ADAMS, AND CO., AND HATCHARD.
WORCESTER: STRATFORD, CHILDE, AND EATON AND SON.
1853.

TO

THE INHABITANTS

OF

THE PARISH OF ST. NICHOLAS,

IN THE

CITY OF WORCESTER

My dear friends and fellow-parishioners,

To you these Sermons are respectfully and most affectionately inscribed. They all were written for you and preached to you.

Individuals among you have read them in manuscript; and they, with many others, have expressed their earnest wish to have them in print. But it is probable that I never should have had resolution to print them, had it not been for the spontaneous and repeated entreaty of a valued friend whose many volumes of Sermons are a "praise in the Church," and especially for the loss of sight with which it has pleased God to visit me. He who by this visitation lays me aside and shows that He can work without me, has a right to do with me as He pleases. To Him I humbly submit myself. But if by the publication of these Sermons your edification or that of others shall be promoted, my loss of sight will be abundantly compensated.

In printing these Sermons I have made no attempt at revision. You have them in all their simplicity, and just as they were written amid the solicitudes and interruptions of a city parish. I prayerfully commend them to Him whose servant I am for your sakes, and

I remain,
Your affectionate Friend and Pastor,
W. H. Havergal.

Gräfrath, Prussia, November, 1852.

SUBSCRIBERS.

The Right Rev. the Lord Bishop of St. Asaph.
Abraham, Miss, Bath. Two copies.
Adams, J., Esq., Bromsgrove.
Aldham, Rev. Harcour, Stoke Prior Vicarage, Worcestershire.
Aldrich, H., Esq., Worcester.
Allbutt, Rev. Thos., M.A., Rural Dean, Vicar of Dewsbury.
Allen, Miss, Glasbury.
Allies, R., Esq., Worcester.
Ames, Mrs., Bath. Two copies.
Anderson, Mr., Worcester.
Astles, Mr. J. W., Worcester.
Bagnall, J. N., Esq., West Bromwich. Six copies.
Bagnall, Thos., Esq., Great Barr, near Birmingham. Three copies.
Barneby, Thos., Esq., Worcester.
Barnes, Miss, Worcester.
Barnett, Mr., R. E., Worcester. Two copies.
Barr, Miss, Hallow-Mount, Worcestershire.
Bayley, Mrs. Thos., Codicote, Herts.
Beasley, Mrs., Brampton, Northamptonshire.
Bethune, Mrs., Leigham Court Road, Streatham.
Bicknell, H. E., Esq., London.

Birbeck, Mr. C. H., Worcester.
Bishopp, Mrs., Thornby Hall, Northamptonshire.
Boissier, Rev. P. E., Malvern Wells, Worcestershire.
Boissier, Rev. P. H., Turville, Bucks.
Bradley, Rev. A., Hale, Farnham.
Bradley, Rev. C., M.A., Clapham. Two copies.
Bradley, Mrs., Clapham.
Bradley, Rev. E., Bath.
Bradley, H., Esq., 2, Harcourt Buildings, Temple.
Bridges, John, Esq., Red Lion Square, London.
Broad, Rev. J. S., M.A., Incumbent of St. George's, Newcastle-under-Lyne.
Brodrick, Hon. and Rev. W. J., Rector of Bath, and Chaplain in Ordinary to Her Majesty.
Burns, G., Esq., Glasgow.
Burrow, Mr. Walter, Great Malvern.
Bury, John, Esq., Bewdley.

Carington, Lord, The Abbey, High Wycombe.
Carden, H. D., Esq., Worcester.
Cary, The Misses, Bewdley.
Cates, Miss, Margate.
Cawood, Rev. J., M.A., Pensax, Worcestershire.
Cawood, Miss.
Chalk, Thos., Esq., Worcester.
Chesshyre, Rev. W. J., M.A., Rural Dean, Rector of St. Martin's, Canterbury.
Child, R., Mr., Worcester. Two copies.
Clarke, Thos., Esq., Northwick Cottage, near Worcester.
Clarke, Miss.
Clutterbuck, Mrs., Worcester.
Cobb, Rev. F. J., Spratton, Northamptonshire.
Cocks, Hon. and Rev. J. Somers, Canon of Worcester.
Colville, Rev. J., M.A., Worcester.
Conyers, Thos. G., Esq., London.
Cook, Mr. Thos., Worcester.
Cooke, John, Esq., Newent, Gloucestershire.
Cooke, Mrs. P. B., Gloucester.
Cooper, Rev. Henry, Flockton Parsonage, Wakefield.
Cooper, Mrs. John, The Oaks, Preston.
Corbett, Mr. George, Worcester.
Corbett, Mr. W. F., Worcester.
Couchman, Rev. J., M.A., Rector of Thornby, Northamptonshire.
Couchman, Mr. W., Cranbrook.
Cowell, W., Esq., Worcester. Two copies.
Cradock, Rev. E. H., M.A., Canon of Worcester.
Crane, Henry, Esq., and Mrs. Crane, Oakhampton, Worcestershire. Ten copies.
Crane, John, Esq., High Habberley, Worcestershire.

Davies, Rev. D., M.A., Vicar of Mamble and Bayton. Worcestershire.
Davies, Mrs., Castle Street, Hereford.
Davis, Mrs., W. H., Worcester.
Davys, Rev. E., Vicar of Peterborough.
Day, H., Esq., Worcester. Two copies.
Day, Rev. S. E., M.A., Vicar of St. Philip and St. Jacob's, Bristol.
Deering, Miss, Powick Court, Worcestershire.
Dent, J., Esq., Sudeley Castle. Two copies.
Dent, W., Sudeley Castle. Two copies.
Dent, W., Esq., Streatham Hill.
Done, Miss, Abergavenny.

East, Rev. John, M.A., Rector of St. Michael's, Bath. Ten copies.
Edgecombe, Mr. W. J., Worcester.
Edwards, Mrs., Worcester. Two copies.
Egan, Miss, Worcester.
Eaton, Mr., Worcester.
Evans, Mrs., Worcester.

Faber, Rev. G. S., B.D., Master of Sherburn House, Durham. Two copies.
Fortescue, Hon. and Rev. J., M.A., Canon of Worcester, etc.
Fanshaw, Rev. C., Vicar of Coaley, Gloucestershire.
Foley, Miss, All Saints' Parsonage, Derby.
Fox, Miss, Worcester.
Fox, Mrs. F., Brislington House, Bath.
Friend, A., by the Rev. C. Bradley. Eight copies.

Gabb, Mrs., Bewdley.
Garrard, Rev. S. E., Park Hall, Evesham.
Gauntlett, Rev. F., Rector of Fladbury, Worcestershire.
Gillbee, Rev. W., Vicar of Gwennap, Cornwall.
Godfrey, Rev. W., M.A., Rector of Martin-Hussingtree, Worcestershire. Two copies.
Grace, H., Esq., Stockwell. Two copies.
Grace, Mrs., Stockwell. Two copies.
Greaves, Rev., Joshua, M.A., Vicar of Great Missenden, Bucks.
Green, Mr. Coker, Worcester.
Green, Mr. Edward, Worcester.
Green, Mrs. S. P., Worcester.
Griffith, Mrs. Davies, Craig-yr-halen, Menai-bridge. Two copies.
Griffiths, Mr. W., Worcester.
Gross, Mrs., Ayr.
Guise, Mrs., Worcester.
Gutch, J. M., Esq., Worcester.

Hall, Rev. John, B.A., Hon. Canon of Bristol and Rector of St. Werburgh's.

Halsted, Mrs. George, Slindon, Arundel, Sussex.
Halsted, Mrs. John, Slindon.
Hammond, Mrs., Shrawley, Worcestershire.
Hanbury, Rev. J., M.A., Rector of St. Nicholas's, Hereford.
Hanbury, Robert, Esq., Ware, Herts.
Hancocks, Mrs., Wolverley Court, Kidderminster.
Hancocks, W., Esq., Blakeshall House, Kidderminster.
Hancocks, Mrs. W.
Hardy, Mrs. J. C., Pinner.
Hart, G., Mr., Tottenham.
Hart, J., Mr., Hatton Garden, London.
Harrison, Mrs., Precincts, Canterbury.
Harrison, Rev. H., Norham; Berwick-on-Tweed.
Harrison, J. E. R., Mr., Worcester.
Harrison, J. N., Esq., London.
Hastings, Sir Charles, M.D., Worcester.
Hastings, Rev. H. J., M.A., Hon. Can., Rural Dean, and Rector of Areley Kings, Worcestershire.
Hastings, Miss, Worcester.
Hatchard, Rev. J., M.A., Vicar of St. Andrew's, Plymonth.
Hawkins, Rev. Charles, Can. Res. of York, and Vicar of Stillingfleet. Two copies.
Hay, Rev. C. R., Herts.
Hayes, Rev. C., Brampton, Rotherham.
Haynes, Miss, Powick Court, Woreestershire.
Head, R. J., Esq., Peterborough.
Head, Miss.
Higgs, Mr. W., Worcester.
Hill, Rev. J., Wyke Regis, Weymouth.
Hill, Mrs., Broad Street, Worcester. Two copies.
Hill, Miss, Worcester.
Hill, Mrs. R., The Foregate, Worcester.
Hobbs, Mrs., Worcester.
Hodges, E., Esq., Mus. Doc., New York.
Holmes, Rev. S., Foot's Cray, Bexley.
Hooper, Alfred C., Esq., Worcester.
Hooper, Francis, Esq., Red Hilt House, Worcester. Two copies.
Howard, Mrs., Greystoke Castle, Cumberland.
Hozier, James, Esq., St. Enoch Hall, Glasgow.
Hozier, W., Esq., Dunoon.
Hudleston, Andrew Fleming, Esq., Hutton St. John, Penrith.
Hudleston, William, Esq., Hanley House, Bath.
Hughes, W. S. P., Esq., Worcester.
Hunt, Rev. W., Weston-super-Mare.
Hutchesson, Rev. Henry, M.A., Canterbury.
Hutton, Mrs., Balham Hill.
Hyde, Miss E., Worcester.
Hyde, Thos., Esq., Worcester.

Jarrat, Rev. J., M.A., Vicar of North Cave, Brough, Yorkshire.
Jaeger, Mrs., Spark Hill, Birmingham.
Jeffery, Rev. F., M.A., Sway Parsonage, Lymington, Hants. Two copies.
Jeffery, Mrs. F.
Jennings, Reginald, Esq., Hereford.
Jones, Rev. James, M.A., Vicar of Naseby, Northamptonshire. Two copies.
Jones, Mrs. (Dr.), Antra Hill, Monmouth.
Jones, Miss, Penlan, Glasbury.
Jordan, Miss, Worcester.

Kershaw, Rev. G. W., M.A., Rector of Thwaite, Suffolk.
Kingscote, Colonel, Kingscote Park, Gloucestershire. Two copies.
Kingscote, R. A. F., Esq., Uley, Gloucestershire. Two copies.
Kirkpatrick, Mrs., Balham Terrace.
Knight, Mr., Droitwich.
Knight, Miss, Bromsgrove.

Latrobe, Rev. J. A., M.A., Kendal.
Landon, Mrs., Bath.
Lea, Rev. F. S., Fellow of Wadham College, Oxford.
Lea, J. W., Esq., Lansdowne Crescent, Worcester. Five copies.
Lea, T. Simcox, Esq., Astley Hall, Stourport.
Lea, Miss, The Lakes, near Kidderminster.
Leach, W., Esq., Blenheim House, London.
Lee, James, Esq., Clapham.
Lemoine, Mrs. Captain, Thornhill Villa, Southampton.
Lewis, W., Esq., The Mount, Worcester. Two copies.
Lewty, Mr. E., Stourport.
Lightfoot, Mrs., Balham Hill.
Linsham, Thomas, Mr., Worcester.
Linton, Miss, Southborough.
Linton, Rev. H., Vicar of Diddington, Huntingdonshire. Two copies.
Little, Mrs., Worcester.
Lockett, Mr. S. A., Worcester.
Lowe, John, Esq., Astley, Stourport. Three copies.
Ludlam, Miss, Pinner.
Ludlam, Rev. J., St. Mary's Rectory, Guilford. Two copies.
Lyttelton, Hon. and Rev. W. H., M.A, Rector of Hagley, and Hon. Can. of Worcester.

Macbride, Dr., Principal of Magdalen Hall, Oxford.
Mackay, Mr. J., Worcester.
Mackay, Miss, Worcester.
Maitland, E. T., Esq., Henley, Oxon. Three copies.
Malpas, Mrs. S., Worcester.
Malpas, Mr. T., Worcester.

Manning, W., Mr., Worcester.
Mason, Lowell, Esq., Boston, U.S. Two copies.
Mence, R., Esq., Worcester.
Metcalfe, Rev. John, M.A., Precincts, Canterbury.
Mills, Miss, London.
Minchall, Mr. T., Worcester.
Moilliet, Mrs., Abberley Hall, Worcestershire. Two copies.
Moore, The Ven. Archdeacon, Isle of Man. Five copies.
Moore, W. F., Esq., Douglas. Two copies.
Morgan, Rev. D., Ham Rectory, Hungerford.
Morris, Mrs. W., Clay Hill, Walthamstow.

Needham, Mr. F. H., Worcester.
Newland, the Misses, Slindon, Sussex. Two copies.
Nicholson, Miss, Warnley Abbey, Farnham.
Nott, the Misses, Lansdowne Villa, Worcester. Ten copies.

Papendick, Mrs., Glasbury House.
Parker, F., Esq., Sydenham, Kent.
Passey, Mrs., Worcester.
Paul, Sir John Dean, Bart., London. Two copies.
Paynter, Rev. S., Stoke Hill, Guildford. Two copies.
Pearson, Rev. Thomas, M.A., Hector of Great Witley, Worcestershire.
Peel, Mrs., The Deanery, Worcester.
Peers, Rev. T. W., Tetsworth.
Pennethorne, the Misses, Albany House, Worcester.
Perran, Rev. G. J., M.A., Clymping, Arundel, Sussex.
Perrins, Mrs. Nicholas, Worcester.
Perrins, W., Esq., Lansdowne Crescent, Worcester. Four copies.
Phillips, Rev. A., D.D., Henwick House, Worcester.
Pidduck, Mr., Stourport.
Powell, Mr., Avenue House, Worcester.
Powell, Mr. A., Avenue House, Worcester.
Prestage, Mrs., High Wycombe, Bucks.
Prestage, J. E., Esq., Russell Square, London.
Prime, R., Esq., M.P., Walberton House, Arundel, Sussex.
Pritchard, H., Esq., Clapham.
Proctor, Rev. G., D.D., Hadley, Middlesex.

The Very Rev. the Dean of Ripon.
Rasch, Esq., Upper Bedford Place, Russell Square, London.
Read, J. B., Esq., Worcester.
Redding, Miss, Worcester.
Richards, Miss, Dursley, Gloucestershire. Six copies.
Riddle, Rev. J. E., Tudor Lodge, Cheltenham.
Ridley, Rev. W. H., M.A., Rector of Hambledon, Bucks.
Ring, Mrs., Shirehampton, Bristol.
Roach, Mrs., Worcester.
Rogers, Arnold, Esq., Hanover Square, London. Two copies.
Rogers, J. C., Esq., Stourport.
Rogers, Joseph, Esq., Arley House, Worcestershire. Two copies.
Rose, W., Esq., High Wycombe, Bucks.

Sadler, Mrs., Britannia Square, Worcester.
Sawer, Thos., Esq., Lansdowne Villa, Clifton.
Scott, Mr. J. W., Victoria House, Worcester.
Severne, Rev. F., LL.B., Rector of Abberley, Worcestershire.
Severne, Rev. W., M.A., Rector of Rock, Worcestershire. Two copies.
Shelton, J. C., Esq., Worcester.
Shrimpton, Mr., Worcester.
Shuck, Miss, Worcester.
Simcox, Rev. T. G., Vicar of North Harborne, Birmingham.
Sims, Rev. W. F., M.A., Lee, Kent.
Skarratt, Mr. J. M., Worcester.
Smallbone, Thos., Esq., Balham Hill, Surrey.
Smelt, Rev, M., M.A., Rector of Binstead and Slindon, Sussex.
Smith, Abel, Esq., London. Two copies.
Smith, Rev. Jeremiah, Long Buckby, Daventry.
Stallard, —, Esq., Blanquetts, Worcester. Two copies.
Stallard, John, Esq., Worcester.
Stallard, Josiah, Esq., Worcester.
Stenning, E., Esq., Straiten House, Godstone.
Stephenson, Mrs., Worcester.
Stephenson, Rev. J. H., Lympsham Rectory, Weston-super-Mare.
Stevenson, Rev. H. J., Vicar of Hallow, and Hon. Can. of Worcester.
Stratford, J., Mr., Worcester.
Stratton, Rev. Joshua, Precincts, Canterbury. Two copies.
Strickland, Rev. John, M.A., Rector of Christ Church, Bristol.
Stuckey, Mrs., Russell Square, London.
Swete, Rev. John, D.D., Rector of Blagdon, Somerset.

Tappenden, F. W., Esq., Rainbow Terrace, Worcester.
Taylor, Mrs., Worcester.
Tebbitt, Mrs., Clapham Common.
Tebbs, H. V., Esq., Doctors' Commons. Six copies.
Teed, Mrs., Bath.
Thomas, W. H., Esq., Worcester.
Thompson, Miss, Bristol.
Thompson, Rev. J. H., Worcester.
Thornton, John, Esq., Clapham.
Townsend, Rev. A., Bath. Four copies.
Tritton, Mrs. Bloomfield, Norwood, Surrey. Two copies.
Tucker, Rev. S., British Chaplain, Düsseldorf.
Tudor, Mrs. Henry, Hyde Park, London.
Turk, Mrs., Worcester.

Turley, Mr., Worcester.
Tymbs, H. B, Esq., Britannia Square, Worcester.
Tyndale, Rev. Thomas, Rector of Holton, Oxfordshire.

Upton, E., Esq., Sydenham, Kent.
Usborne, Mrs. Major, 9, Upper Bedford Place, Russell Square, London. Three copies.

Vernon, H. C., Esq., Weymouth.
Vignier, Mdlle., Norton Villa, near Worcester.
Vowler, John, Esq., Parnacott, Holsworthy.

The Right Rev. the Lord Bishop of Winchester.
The Right Rev. the Lord Bishop of Worcester.
The Very Rev. the Dean of Worcester. Two copies.
The Ven. the Archdeacon of Worcester.
Wakefield, Mr., Worcester.
Wakefield, Mrs., Ludlow.
Walker, G. A., Esq., Norton Villa, near Worcester. Two copies.
Walker, Miss, Clapham.
Waller, Rev. S. R., Stourport.
Webb, Rev. John, M.A., Rural Dean, Rector of Tretire, Herefordshire.
West, Mrs., Pinner.
West, F. G., Esq., Pinner.
Wharton, Rev. C., B.D., Vicar of Sturry, Kent.
Wharton, Rev. J. C., B.A., Dover.
Wheeler, Rev. D., St. Paul's, Worcester.
White, Mrs., Wolverley, near Kidderminster. Two copies.
Wilkinson, Mrs., High Wycombe. Two copies.
Williams, Rev. D., D.C.L. The Warden of New College, Oxford. Two copies.
Williams, Mrs., Pitmaston, Worcestershire.
Wilson, W. W. Carus, Esq., Casterton Hall, Westmoreland.
Wither, Mrs. Bigg, Winchester.
Witherington, Mr. Thos., Worcester.
Wood, Mrs., Swansea.
Wood, Mr. A., Worcester.
Wood, Rev. J. E., M.A., Vicar of St. John's, and Canon of Worcester, etc. etc.
Wright, John, Esq., Dunley, near Stourport.
Wylie, Miss, Broadway, Worcestershire.

Yeadon, Mrs., Regent Street, Leicester.

Zachary, Thos., Esq., Broomy Hill, near Stourport.

Faithfully Y^rs
W: H: Havergal.

In the Sermons that follow, the capitalization of pronouns and the lack of capitalization of pronouns (which are not always consistent) referring to God are left in this newly typeset book (taken from Volume IV of the Havergal edition) just as they were done in the original Volumes of Sermons by W.H.H. He was a truly reverent believer, and though in our day we would capitalize all pronouns referring to the Lord, the editor and typesetter of the Havergal edition concluded that it was better to leave the pronouns as they were originally done.

David Chalkley, Thomas Sadowski.

CONTENTS.

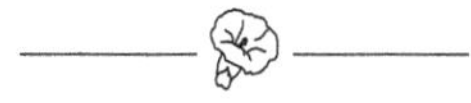

1846

March 29. M. St Mich. — Deut: 33. 16.
— E. Do — Philemon 11.
April 5. M. Do — Matt 27. 19.
— E. Do — Exod X. 27.
Good Frid M. Do — John XIX. 30
— E. Do — 1. Pet: II 24
Easter Day M. Do — 118. Psalm 24
19. M. Do — Acts XVI. 14.
— E. Do — II. Pet: II 16.
26. M. Do — John X. 16.
— E. Do C.M.S. — Do
May 3. M. [illegible] — 1. Pet: II. 17.
— E. Do — Deut: V. 5.
7. Th E. Do — I Kings XIX. 12
10. M. Do — Matt VIII. 20.
17. M. Do — Deut: VIII. 5.
— E. Do — Rom: XVI. 7.
21. M. Ascen: Day — Luke XXIV. 51.
24. M. Do — Deut: XII. 9
— E. Do — II Kings II. 11th.

This is a page from W.H.H.'s Sermon Record Book. The last entry on the page is the Sermon XXV on II Kings 2:11, the evening Sermon preached on May 24, 1846.

CONTENTS.

SERMON I.

THE CREATION OF GRASS AND ITS LESSONS.

GENESIS I. 11.

 Feb 16 1851

SERMON II.

THE TREE OF LIFE.

GENESIS II. 9.

 Jan 29 1850

SERMON III.

EVE AND THE FORBIDDEN FRUIT. Feb 11 1849.

GENESIS III. 6.

CONTENTS.

SERMON I.

THE SALUTATION OF GABRIEL TO THE VIRGIN MARY.

LUKE I. 28. Lady-Day 1849

SERMON II.

THE VISIT OF THE WISE MEN TO THE INFANT JESUS.

MATT. II. 11. Jan 6, 1850

a 3

The first page of the list of Contents for Volume I, the Sermons on Old Testament texts, and the same first page of Contents for Volume II, the Sermons on New Testament texts. The date for each Sermon was written by hand next to each Sermon in the Contents pages.

SERMON I.

THE CREATION OF GRASS AND ITS LESSONS.[1]

GENESIS 1:11.

"And God said, Let the earth bring forth grass."

THE reading of the first chapter of Genesis, on the present Sunday, can hardly fail to arrest the attention of a churchman. It tells him that another year is gone, and that another season of the church is again come round. It reminds him too, that the minister of his Church has turned back the leaves of the great Bible, and has begun it again, with the reading of its very first page. And then the solemn recital of the origin of our world, which no other book can tell us, is itself an interesting circumstance. What is more, it is impossible for a really thoughtful mind to hear that chapter annually read, without finding some new topic start up for contemplation.

But who, on hearing of the wonders of the creation-week, gives a thought about the production of so simple and so common a thing as *grass?* And who thinks of making a sermon upon it? Many a whispering heart is ready to reply, the grass we tread on is so common a thing, that nothing need be said about it; or, if anything is said about it, it can amount to no more than what every child knows, and every rustic well understands.

But how unwise are such whisperings, and how prone are we to forget that the commonest things are often the most important, and the most instructive! Were an angel to come down from heaven, and call around him a class of the cleverest natural philosophers in the world, how would they be astonished at the thousand things which he could tell them about a single blade of grass! And, if he were to summon a conclave of the most learned theologians, and proceed to preach about that blade, what babes in divinity would they all appear!

Dear brethren, the mysteries of grace, and the practical truths which are represented by the grass which God made, are worthy of an angel's teaching, and absolutely necessary for our learning. It is only our ignorance, or our iniquity, which makes us insensible to the instruction which God has attached to the commonest things around us. Our blessed Lord often took the text of his parables, or discourses, from those very things: he consequently preached about sparrows, ravens, lilies, *grass.* Let none then despise what such things, by the aid of the Bible, teach us. May the great Teacher help us, at this present, to understand and receive his own lessons upon *grass. "And God said, Let the earth bring forth grass."*

Hence a series of observations.

I. *Grass, as to its author, its variety, and its growth, is an emblem of divine grace.*

1. Strange as it may sound, it is strictly true, the God of the grass is "the God of all grace." He, who created the one, imparts the other. Both are utterly beyond the power of man to produce. Were all the philosophers and all the agriculturists in the world to meet together, they could not of themselves make one blade of grass. Neither could all the angels in heaven, or all the divines upon earth, bestow one particle of grace to a sinful soul. All is of God. He is jealous of his power, even with respect to the production of grass. Though men, under the name of science, talk arrogantly, or, through forgetfulness, speak flippantly, yet does God constantly assert his sovereignty with respect to the gift of grass. The creation of it is, in the chapter before us, as solemnly announced as the creation of light, or the formation of the sun and the moon, or of any of the grandest objects in our universe. In Deuteronomy 11:15, Jehovah says, "I will send grass in thy fields for thy cattle." In Psalm 104:14, David says, "He causeth the grass to grow for cattle." The like in Psalm 147:8, "Who maketh grass to grow upon the mountains." And our Lord, in his sermon on a mountain, reminded his hearers that it was God who clothed the grass. Equally, too, is God the sole author of all grace. It requires the same power to produce a blade of grass as to create a soul and save it. This is what the Bible everywhere asserts, and what every saint feels. "Thou renewest the face of the earth," says David: and who but the same God can renew the heart of sinful man? "By the grace of God I am what I am," is the grateful and

[1] Preached Sunday Morning, February 18th, 1851.

adoring acknowledgment of every saved sinner. Let thoughtless ones also be reminded that, as grace is covenant grace, so also is grass *covenant grass*. The very verdure of our meadows can come round to us, in coming months, only by virtue of that covenant which God made with Noah. "While the earth remaineth, seed time and harvest, and cold and heat, and summer and winter, and day and night shall not cease." (Genesis 8:22.) With what double, yea, more than double interest then, does the *spiritual* naturalist look upon the pleasant green of the springing grass, beyond anything that the mere *natural* naturalist can possibly feel!

2. As to *the value* of grass, who can estimate that? Were God to destroy it, all the world over, what an upturn and overthrow would it make in all the essential departments of animal life. What then the earth would be without grass, the church must be without grace. Where grass has been withheld, there a desert has been formed; and where grace has been stopped, there a moral wilderness has followed. What is a heathen land but a graceless country? It is a desert in which grows no grass. Ah, and what are graceless hearts but dreary wastes of sin and evil imagination? Grace is everything to us, much as we may slight it, and little as we may seek it. Grass is provender, and grace is our very life. If the cattle perish without grass, so do we die the second death, if destitute of saving grace.

3. Though grass is so common, and we speak of it as one and the same thing, yet are its varieties both numerous and wonderful. Botanists tell us of not merely scores of species, but hundreds of varieties; and yet countless as are the blades of all those varieties, *not two are alike*.

After the same manner, the grace of God is very diversified, both in itself and in its effects upon different persons.

When too all the sons and daughters of God shall be assembled in the last great day, and they shall be spread out like a beauteous field of grass which the Lord hath blessed and scented, not one will be found exactly like another. All indeed will resemble Christ, and be one with him, but each will bear a distinct and separate likeness: so wonderful will the wisdom and the power of our God be in the article of variety alone!

4. *The growth* of grass, like the growth of grace, is not only remarkable but mysterious.[1] We often speak of seeing the grass grow. The process of its growth certainly is at times rapid; still no human sight can perceive its actual gradations.

[1] Grass is remarkable as being a sort of universal vegetable. The earth everywhere produces it. It grows, more or less, in every clime and during every season. In like manner divine grace is subject to no restrictions of time or place. The Holy Spirit dispenses it "to every man severally as he will." Hence the heathen wilderness and the christian city are alike capable of receiving its implantation and witnessing its growth. "There shall be a handful of corn in the earth upon the top of the mountains; the fruit thereof shall shake like Lebanon; and they of the city shall flourish like grass of the earth."—Psalm 72:16.

Far more mysteriously does divine grace advance its growth in the human heart. "It groweth up," as our Lord said of the sower sowing grain, "he knoweth not how." This however we all know, that Christians are to "grow in grace;" that their growth in it will be perceptible, if not always to themselves, yet often to others; and that some things hinder, and other things forward its growth.

Think for a moment of this last named fact! The frost and the chilling wind check the growth of grass, while a rainless and scorching sky soon parch it up. On the other hand copious dews, warm rains, and genial suns promote its growth abundantly.

And does not sin and evil passion of every kind, from rampant lust to sordid covetousness, check, even to annihilation, the growth of grace in the soul? Will not even pride and prejudice do much the same? And, as to pleasure and prosperity, who has not beheld the seemingly fair and verdant professor gradually drained of all spiritual moisture by them, so as to become like scorched grass, useless for all the purposes for which it was destined? If, dear brethren, we would grow as the grass, which rejoiceth the cattle and repayeth the husbandman, we must both pray for the outpouring of the Holy Spirit upon our souls, and cherish it carefully, when it has been vouchsafed to us.

II. *Grass, in the beauty of its freshness, and the luxuriance of its tender springing*, is an emblem of the Lord Jesus, and of the rich and pleasant provision which God makes, in the gospel, for his people. It is remarkable that the margin for our text, as the literal Hebrew, is "*tender* grass."

1. When David was departing this life, he uttered one of the most beautiful of all his prophecies. The inspiring Spirit nerved and brightened him for speaking thus of the Messiah:—"And he shall be as the light of the morning, when the sun riseth, even a morning without clouds; as the tender grass springing out of the earth by clear shining after rain." (2 Samuel 23:4.)

Rarely has the character of the Saviour for loveliness, gentleness, and tenderness, been so happily exhibited, as by this simile of "*tender grass* springing out of the earth, by clear shining after rain." Who has not gazed upon the beauty of such grass, when such shining has freshened it up? What an aspect of health does it put on; and how is that health adorned with dewy gems of inimitable hue; and how inviting to the pearly teeth of the suckling lamb, or promising in the thirsty scythe of the husbandman! Who has not seen all this? But, who has thought of Him, who not only made it all, but has by it intended us to learn living lessons of himself? Who thinks of that "tender grass" as an emblem of his tender frame and gentle nature, springing up from our vile earth, and presently to be trampled under foot of Jews and gentiles, or mown down with their rude and ruthless hands? Who thinks of its sunny freshness, and spangled verdure, as types of his healthful grace and spiritual comeliness, which he sustains for his believing people? Henceforth let us after this manner think of him, when returning spring presents David's picture of him to our eyes.

2. In Psalm 23:2, the Psalmist shepherd-boy, comparing Jehovah to a shepherd, and himself to a sheep, says, "He maketh me to lie down *in green pastures*;" which literally, and as translated in the margin, is "in pastures of *tender grass*."

When therefore you see a field or plot of young, juicy, healthy shooting grass, you see an exhibition of the sweet food, and pleasant blessings which God has provided for the sheep of his pasture, for all true believers, in his holy word, his holy ordinances, and especially in his holy gospel. O how rich are they, how wholesome, how palatable, how nutritious, how joyously pleasant! And never we may truthfully say, does sheep or lamb luxuriate in green pastures of tender grass, half so much as the lively believer delights himself amid the wholesome verdure of a faithfully preached gospel.

Let us now turn to another class of topics, which the Holy Ghost teaches us from God's creation of grass.

III. *Grass, in its over luxuriant and rank state*, is an emblem of wicked men in prosperity. This is revealed to us in Psalm 92:7: "When the ungodly are green as the grass, and when all the workers of wickedness do flourish, then shall they be destroyed for ever."

How fearful are these words, and yet how easy to be understood! Every observer of a field or meadow knows that grass, in certain spots, grows so coarsely, and so rankly, and harbours so many weeds, that it is cut down for the dunghill. Thus sinners, who grow wild in sin, or rank in iniquity, are no better than the offal grass of the swamp, or of the boggy spot of a meadow. They are not only useless, but injurious. Like the grass now described, they occupy the place of better vegetation, and only spread mischief, so long as they remain in it. But then their end, what is that? It is that they shall be cut down, and "be destroyed for ever."

O that all therefore, who hear these things, would take heed respecting them! Let no sinners mistake their character or position, by falsely comparing themselves with other sinners. They may not be so gross, or so daring, or so hardened, as many whom they know: but they are in the way to become such. A patch of rank and worthless grass is not composed of tufts of only one size, nor of only one sort. Many a tuft may be coarser and more towering than another; and many a younger shoot, or milder blade may be found among them. But they all are bad together: they partake of the same root, grow in the same soil, and perpetuate the same mischief.

Let all sinners then remember that the great Husbandman may send his workman, Death, with his inevitable scythe, and cut them off in all the horrid freshness of their guilt. Their only safety is in repentance towards God, and faith in his dear Son.

IV. *Grass, in its withered state,* is an emblem of two things:

1. *Of the sorrow and faintness of an afflicted heart.* This is most pathetically and touchingly set forth in Psalm 102. That psalm is called "A prayer of the afflicted, when he is overwhelmed, and poureth out his complaint before the Lord." After a lengthened description of his sorrowful state, and the use of many similes to illustrate it, among which is that of withered grass, the Psalmist closes the whole by repeating that one similitude, "My soul is withered like grass." (Compare Psalm 102:1–12.) How many a sorrowful spirit realises all that is here described! And how often have individuals, now present, had to say in secret, "My heart is smitten, and *withered like grass*." Their comforts seem dried up; and that, which was once flourishing within them, appears sapless and parched. "Withered grass" is the very thing which represents the state in which they feel themselves to be. And no marvel, for it was the state of him who was *the afflicted One*, and whom Psalm 102 prophetically described. For us and for our consolation, was the tender heart of the Saviour "smitten and withered like grass." The sharp blast of Almighty wrath fell upon him, and he was dried up like a potsherd, and withered like a tuft of tender grass which the lightning has scorched.

His spiritually minded people must expect similar tribulation. He often tries them as himself was tried, to constrain them to see that they have nothing in themselves, and that all grace, comfort, and help, must be sought from him. Other persons cannot understand these things. "They are foolishness unto them." But they are truthful realities, and wise experiences with those who are destined to survive all witherings, and to flourish for ever in the field above.

2. *Grass in its withered state is an emblem also of the frailty of human life, and the suddenness with which it is liable to be cut off.* "The voice said, Cry. And he said, What shall I cry? All flesh is grass, and all the goodliness thereof is as the flower of the field." "The grass withereth, the flower fadeth: but the word of our God shall stand for ever." (Isaiah 40:6, 8.) The picture here drawn is vivid and complete. Look on the pleasant meadow. See the health, strength, and beauty of its crop, as the wind gently waves its surface. But think how the next frost can nip it, or the next blast level it, or how certainly, if it reaches to ripeness, the mower will one day cut it down. And then bring away your eye from that scene, and let it gaze on the great company of mankind, on this city, this parish, this congregation, on yourselves. Like grass we perish, for "surely the people is grass." Yes, let no one take refuge in generalities, but

let each one say to himself or herself, "I am but as a blade of grass, and shall and must as certainly die, as all grass withereth, and every flower fadeth."

They and they alone, who have wisdom and faith to say this, and to act consistently therewith, will be prepared for the comfort of a closing thought or two.

1. Though the grass withereth, "*the word of the Lord endureth for ever.*" This was Isaiah's consolation. St. Peter took it up, and by inspiration added to it, saying, "And this is the word, which by the gospel is preached unto you." Not one syllable of all that God stands pledged to perform shall fail or perish. His gospel is yours for ever.

2. That which *resembles* grass, in the visible church, may be withered and cut down, but the *living* grass of the living church, "*shall never perish.*" "And there came out of the smoke locusts upon the earth: and unto them was given power, as the scorpions of the earth have power. And it was commanded them that they should not hurt the *grass* of the earth, neither any green thing, neither any tree, but only those men which have not the seal of God in their foreheads." (Revelation 9:3, 4.)

In coming times, the Son of man will clear out of his field only that which offends. The false professor, as well as the profligate,—all who bear not the stamp of godliness, will be clean cut down. But, the godly, the green, the living grass of the true field, shall not be hurt: they shall abide for ever.

3. The wonders of the world's first week *will never cease to be admired* by those whom God creates anew in Christ Jesus.

And, if *grass* be a wonder, how wonderful must that parent mind be, which saw, from the beginning, all that it was to teach us until the end! Then let us say, "Thou art worthy, O Lord, to receive glory, and honour, and power; for thou hast created all things, and for thy pleasure they are and were created." (Revelation 4:11.)

SERMON II.

THE TREE OF LIFE.[1]

GENESIS 2:9.

"The tree of life, also, in the midst of the garden."

THE garden here mentioned is, as we knew from our childhood, the garden of the Lord's own planting, in the land of Eden. Our fathers or mothers, or other earliest teachers, told us of that garden when our young imaginations filled it with all the beautiful things with which we were acquainted. But we may be assured, that no imagination, not even that of the sublimest genius, ever came up to the reality of what that garden was. A garden of Jehovah's formation and arrangement, and which he intended for an emblem, in after days, of his own celestial paradise, must have been transcendantly beautiful, and exquisitely perfect. No marvel therefore that, under the gospel, pointed allusion is made to it. The crucified convert was to be with Christ in paradise. St. Paul, whether in the body or out of the body he could not tell, was caught up into it. And St. John in the Revelation beheld it, and spake of it. Ourselves, if saved in Christ, will see it and dwell in it, to all eternity.

Well therefore may we apply our thoughts to the original type of our future bliss, and endeavour to learn from it such things as will further our attainment of the bliss itself.

In the original garden were two principal objects; but one of them far surpassed the other. "The tree of knowledge of good and evil" had an awful though a charming aspect for the time. When that fell time had passed away, we hear no more of it: but "the tree of life" will be heard of, and seen for ever. The purpose of the present discourse will therefore be the advancement of your scriptural knowledge, and your spiritual edifica-

[1] Preached Sunday Evening, January 29th, 1850.

tion. May the Lord aid and bless!

I. "*The tree of life,*" *as to its historical or original character.* Learned men have found a great deal to say respecting this tree. We cannot wonder at the circumstance, seeing that everything relating to the tree is itself so wonderful. It is not my aim to give you merely curious information, there will be little profit in that, but to tell you such things as will, by God's blessing, induce you to attend to other things, and such as, at the same time, will show you what worthy and interesting subjects for thought are set before us in the Bible.

1. *The very name,* "TREE OF LIFE," has given rise not only to many fancies about its kind or sort, but to many suggestions about the word "*life.*" From certain peculiarities in the Hebrew text, scholars say the tree was a species of oak. We may leave that point. We are sure it was as a vegetable production excellence in perfection.

But the word "*life*" is certainly plural; and, therefore, we may say, "the tree of lives," as in verse 7, "the breath of lives." "The tree of lives" may either be a putting of two or more for one, as the Hebrews do to denote eminence or excellence; or an indication of the *length* of life, which the eating of it should secure to man, as though that length would be equal to many after-lives; or, say others, to symbolize or betoken to man the happy continuance of his life on earth, and of his life in heaven, provided he remained obedient.

Others, again, say that it should be translated "the tree of *the living ones,*" and that it was a sort of sacramental image of the Trinity in Unity, as the figures of the cherubim afterwards were in the tabernacle. Of these things you may *think.*

2. *The tree evidently had certain external peculiarities.* As the garden abounded with trees "pleasant to the sight and good for food," this "tree of life" must have been pre-eminently such. It stood "in the midst of the garden," that is, in the most central, most conspicuous and honourable part, and so was likely to be the most beautiful, most noble, most attractive, and most commanding object in the garden. Whether it was a single tree, or a cluster of trees of the same sort, and of one name, as St. John seems to represent, learned men, and good men too, have said a great deal, but have not settled the question. We may leave it, only, let me add, it is well to stand by the simple text of scripture, where there is nothing positive against our so doing.

3. *The intention* of the tree, as it related to Adam, is in some respects an easy, but in other respects, a difficult point. It is easy to see that it had an important relation to himself, and that he fully understood it, and, further, that it had respect in some way to his *life.* But it is difficult to say what was that way. Many of the fathers, and many modern theologians also, are of opinion that the tree possessed certain virtues, which, upon proper application, would renew human life, and preserve it from decay or dissolution. Even the very leaves of that tree of life which St. John saw were "for the *healing* of the nations." Certainly it was as reasonable and as easy for God to create a tree of such virtues, as it will be to re-create our bodies with immortality in themselves, in the morning of the resurrection.

What is said in Genesis 3:22–24, seems, I must confess, to favour the opinion that the tree was not only a sacramental *sign* of immortal life, but also the *actual instrument* of conveying it to all who should eat of it. "And the Lord God said, Behold, the man is become as one of us, to know good and evil: and now, lest he put forth his hand, and take also of the tree of life, and eat, and live for ever, therefore the Lord God sent him forth from the garden of Eden, to till the ground from whence he was taken. So he drove out the man; and he placed at the east of the garden of Eden cherubims, and a flaming sword which turned every way, to keep the way of the tree of life." The excellent Matthew Henry, however, considers the Lord God as speaking *ironically* of Adam's taking and eating of that tree, to which he had forfeited all right: as though God would not allow him "to dare to eat of that tree, and so profane a divine sacrament, and defy a divine sentence, and yet flatter himself with *a conceit* that thereby he should live for ever." But we must recollect that God did actually set a flaming guard to keep Adam from "the tree of life," it is not said for the prevention of profaneness, or the annihilation of conceit, but lest he "eat and live for ever."

From this it would appear that, while Adam was prohibited from eating of "the tree of knowledge of good and evil," it was at his option to eat of "the tree of life;" but that, in the freshness of his creation, he felt no need of it; and, in the confusion of his fall, he either forgot it, or failed to avail himself of it. Thus we were shown, from the very first, that fatal proneness of our fallen nature to flee to any remedy, the fig leaf, or the shade, rather than to go at once to what God has plainly set before us.

4. *What became of the "tree of life"*? may be fitly asked, ere we pass on from this part of our subject. Judging from what is written, we may conclude that, immediately after the fall, he who planted the garden so secured it, and barred all approach to it, by means of terrific cherubim, that no foot ever again entered it. And then at the deluge, after which a new order of things was to follow, the whole was swept away, or otherwise so removed, as the wisdom of God ordained.

Such a termination is a lesson to us, that all God's external arrangement for his church on earth will be treated as but the scaffolding of a building, when the great work is completed, and when the destruction of the world shall arrive.

But "the tree of life" lives for ever. We read of it in the very beginning of the Bible, in the very middle, and at the very end. Moses in Genesis, Solomon in Proverbs 3:18, Ezekiel in his prophecy, 47:12, and John in Revelation, set it before us. We may take this as a passing intimation of a great fact, that what "the tree of life" represents to us is to be the first and last, as well as everything intermediate, with us. Let us, therefore, study

II. *"The tree of life" as now spiritually planted before us.*

1. If the earthly paradise were a type of the heavenly, we may surely say that it also was *a type of God's spiritual church among men*, since the fall of the first man; because the church below and the church above are in essence one.

Yes, God's spiritual church is God's spiritual garden. His garden is not all the world, as Eden was only a district of the earth. Neither was all Eden paradise, for paradise was a garden (a place of pleasure or delight, as the original means) *in* Eden. So, the true spiritual church of the living God is not his whole Eden, not his whole visible or nominal church, but an inclosure, or walled garden (as Solomon calls it), within a larger circuit. All were not Israel who were of Israel, neither now are all Christians who are of the visible Church of Christ.

2. As in the garden of Eden there was *one* superlatively precious and life-conveying tree, so in the church of God is there *one and only one*, source of life to all believers. What "the tree of life" was to Adam, Christ is to all his people. "In him was life." It was his own underived life; for, as he said, he had "life in himself." He, therefore, can *give* life and light to whom he will. He is "the bread of life," "the prince of life," and "the author of life," to all who are quickened from the death of trespasses and sins. "I am come that they may have life, and that they may have it more abundantly." "I gave unto my sheep *eternal* life." Such life he could not give unless he had it "in himself."

All that was noble, useful, and beautiful in the original tree did but faintly picture the excellences of the Lord Jesus. Is he not "pleasant to the sight, and good for food"? Verily he is "fairer than the children of men," and his "flesh is meat indeed." There were other pleasant trees and delightful fruits in the garden, but this one tree combined and surpassed them all. God made ample provision for the reasonable gratification of his creatures; and he still suffers them to enjoy his temporal gifts, in connexion with and in subserviency to his spiritual provisions. Still to the man of living religion his Saviour is the "all and in all." "The tree of life" is his highest joy and his noblest delight. He loves no other shade like its shade, and he desires no fruit like that which grows upon it. "Whom have I in heaven but thee? and there is none upon earth that I desire beside thee." (Psalm 73:25.)

We should not fail to remark the superiority of "the tree of life," as revealed in the gospel, compared with the original tree in paradise. From the description of it in Revelation 22:2, it seems as though, like everything under the gospel, it had expanded and gained additional excellences: for St. John saw the tree *on each side* of a river, bearing twelve sorts of fruit, and that every month, while the very leaves had healing virtue for whole nations. Let this at least teach us the superlative benefits to which the coming of Christ has introduced us, beyond what were enjoyed under any former dispensation. There is great variety of spiritual food, pleasure, and comfort in the one only Saviour, with, at the same time, a freshness and a constancy which leave the penitent sinner nothing to desire. And, if the mere leaves of the tree are for the healing of nations, what estimate ought we to form of what we are too apt to think the unimportant parts of the gospel? "Every word of" that gospel "is precious," as every leaf of the living tree is a healing medium. If the leaves emblemize *ordinances*, how should we value those ordinances.

3. As "the tree of life" would, according to general opinion, have secured immortality to Adam, so will Christ secure eternal life for us, if we "take and eat" of him. That he is able so to do, because of having "life in himself," you have heard. But there is something which he requires of us. Adam, it seems, having "the tree of life" at option, failed to avail himself of it. Christ is set forth not at our option, but at our imperative duty. *We must* take of him, and eat at once, or we are dead while we live, and liable to be sent to the bitter pains of eternal death at any instant. Now, the only way in which we can so take and eat is *by faith*. Himself described believing on him by the acts of eating and drinking. John 6:35.

4. As "the tree of life" was "in the *midst* of the garden," so is Christ the centre of all divine revelation.

When, as the first begotten, he was revealed to the angelic hosts, and set before them as the supreme object of all admiration, it was said, "Let all the angels of God worship him." At the fall in the garden, he was manifested as the only hope of the fallen ones. In the wilderness he was typically *lifted up* or *spread out* in the *midst* of the camp; for the brazen serpent and the manna were representations of him. In the land of Canaan, the cities of refuge were appointed *conspicuously* among the people.

And where, in the gospel, is he not set forth with all the plainness and clearness which the dullest understanding or the darkest eye can require? "Say not in thine heart, Who shall ascend into heaven? (that is, to bring Christ down from above:) or, who shall descend into the deep? (that is, to bring up Christ again from the dead.) But what saith it? The word is nigh thee, even in thy mouth, and in thy heart: that is, the word of faith, which we preach; that if thou shalt confess with thy mouth the Lord Jesus, and shalt believe in thine heart that God hath raised him from the dead, thou shalt be saved." (Romans 10:6–9.)

And O, let us not, as churchmen, forget that "the tree of life" stands in the very midst of our liturgical garden. In what part of our liturgy is not Christ made the one great object of a sinner's hope and a believer's joy? Our prayer book is full of Christ. May our pulpits and our hearts be so too!

5. St. John, in vision, beheld a river of water fast by "the tree of life;" and we read, in the chapter before us, that "a river went out of Eden to water the garden."

Where, in the gospel, do we find the doctrine of Christ without the gift of the Spirit? Nowhere. He who revealed himself as "our life" brought to us a greater manifestation of the Spirit than had ever been previously given. Did he not say of every contrite believer, "Out of his belly shall flow *rivers* of living water"? meaning the gift of the Spirit in copious abundance.

Yes, he who eats of "the tree of life" shall drink of "the river of God." Himself shall be as a tree planted by the river side, and his leaf shall not fail; and all this shall be, because of his secret derivation of vitality from the tree and the river which are from eternity to eternity.

Take a few practical hints with you, in recollecting what you have heard:—

1. Our first care should be to ascertain, *if indeed we are partaking of "the tree of life."*

What availed the presence of the tree, in all its glory in the garden, if Adam ate not of it? And what will Christ avail you, if you take not of him? It will but fill you with bitter remorse some day: too late, perhaps! You cannot be at ease, if you do not ascertain your part in Christ. Then begin the inquiry.

2. *"The tree of life" will not always be accessible to you.* If you continue in sin, God will exclude you from it: the fiery sword of justice will bar you from its virtues. Think of 2 Corinthians 2:15, 16: "We are unto God a sweet savour of Christ, in them that are saved; and in them that perish: to the one we are the savour of death unto death, and to the other the savour of life unto life: and who is sufficient for these things?"

3. *Learn to exalt the Saviour, and to set him "in the midst."* Make him your *all.* Let him hold the centre of the garden of your soul. This is your work.

4. *Rejoice in hope of eating of the tree for ever.* You will see it in paradise. No flaming sword will intervene: the Lamb will for ever be in that paradise. He will be your life and your song. "To him that overcometh will I give to eat of the tree of life, which is in the midst of the paradise of God." (Revelation 2:7.)

SERMON III.

EVE AND THE FORBIDDEN FRUIT.[1]

GENESIS 3:6.

"And when the woman saw that the tree was good for food, and that it was pleasant to the eyes, and a tree to be desired to make one wise, she took of the fruit thereof, and did eat; and gave also to her husband with her; and he did eat."

IT is natural for us to be affected at tidings of a deeply afflictive and strangely calamitous character. Should an earthquake occur, or a shipwreck, or fire, or some other catastrophe befal our connexions, so that valuable lives, and interesting edifices, and immense property are destroyed, who does not shudder, who does not grieve? Were hostile armies to fight their battle in our neighbouring fields, and leave those fields covered with the carnage of the brave and the loved, how sorrowfully should we gaze on the scene! What then ought we now to feel, when invited to contemplate a calamity in which all such scenes had their origin, and compared with which they shrink into the veriest insignificance? The disobedience of our first

[1] Preached Sunday Morning, February 11th, 1849.

parents "brought death into our world, and all our woe." This is that mighty moral catastrophe, in which not merely every human being, but the world and all its creatures, are involved. This is the dark beginning of all our unhappiness as men, and of all our misery as sinners. Upon a right understanding of the doctrine of the fall much depends with regard to the correctness of our views on other important points. The history of the mournful event is affectingly interesting, and not less affectingly instructive. Let us now, comprehensively, study the history, and gain the instruction. And may God the Holy Ghost graciously aid and bless us!

I. *The history* begins with the chapter. We must therefore go through its verses.

At the close of the preceding chapter we behold our first parents innocent and happy, in all the beauties of holiness, and in all the luxuries of Eden. Satan, however, was too jealous of their felicity, and too hostile to their Creator, to suffer them to continue undisturbed. How long they kept their first estate, or whether Satan assailed them in any other way previous to the one recorded, we are not told. From hints, which are subsequently given, there is some reason for supposing that the perfection of our first parents was very short-lived. Even the first verse of this chapter is concurrent with that opinion; for it comes in the narrative, just after the mention of Adam's giving a name to every beast and creature of the field. Hence, on the appearance of all animals before him, and the presentation of Eve to him, it is immediately said, "Now the serpent was more subtil than any beast of the field which the LORD God had made. And he said unto the woman, Yea, hath God said, ye shall not eat of every tree of the garden?" We are not to suppose that the serpent spake of itself; for there is no reason to think that it was created with the faculty of speech. It was Satan in the serpent who was the speaker; somewhat as he was in many a human being in our Lord's day. The devil, we are told, spake in and through those whom he possessed.

One reason is assigned for his possession of the serpent. It was "more *subtil* than any beast." It possessed superior sagacity, and was therefore better suited to serve his ends. Hence the serpent has always been the hieroglyphic for prudence. Our Lord also said, "Be ye wise as serpents." Satan, in after times, was called "the dragon," "the serpent," and "the old serpent," because of this transaction. Revelation 12:9.

But how was it that Eve evinced no surprise at being accosted by a serpent? There are various answers, though the narrative assigns none. The question, however, is legitimate; and we may modestly attempt a reply. Satan might have invested the serpent, naturally beautiful, with some extraordinary fascination. That he has power so to do, seems likely from St. Paul's saying that "Satan himself is transformed into *an angel of light*." It is remarkable too, that in the Hebrew tongue the word *seraph*, or winged *angel*, is the same as that which is translated "a fiery flying serpent." Hence it has been conjectured that Eve mistook the serpent for some one of the celestial seraphim. Or it may be that, as she was not created when the animals were named by Adam, she did not so fully understand their several capacities and endowments as he understood them, and so, for the time, might have supposed that the serpent was favoured with the faculty of speech. This is not improbable, especially on the hypothesis that little time elapsed from her creation to her temptation.

And how did the tempter proceed? He first took care to accost Eve *when by herself*. The occasion of her solitariness is a theme for poets. Sober divines know that, as nothing is said about it, all must be mere fancy respecting it. We are only sure, spite of Miltonic surmise, that there could have been no impropriety in it. But, the fact of her being alone when Satan succeeded against her is proof that, though "solitude is sometimes best society," it is no security against temptation. The cell and the cloister are not a whit more barred from the tempter's intrusions, than the home or the social party.

The tempter, on first breaking speech, insinuated a doubt respecting the divine prohibition, "Yea, *hath* God said, ye shall not eat of every tree of the garden?" as though Satan meant to say, Hath your God really said so? May you not be mistaken as to what he said? or, do you not take the command too literally or too rigidly? Is it likely your great Creator would impose such a trifling restraint? Such is Satan's artifice. He undermines, before he assails. He teaches men to quibble, to question, and to doubt, ere they take a bolder course. He suggests a flaw in God's truth, sets them on renouncing it. Hence, show me a man who begins to question or to twist plain truth, and I will show you a man who begins to be an infidel. Sceptics go by steps, not by bounds.

(Verses 2 and 3.) "And the woman said unto the serpent, We may eat of the fruit of the trees of the garden: but of the fruit of the tree which is in the midst of the garden, God hath said, Ye shall not eat of it, neither shall ye touch it, lest ye die." Here was the commencement of Eve's ruin. *She replied*. She should have withdrawn, in silent abhorrence. To parley with temptation is to invite it. He who hesitates in this warfare is all but subdued. Though Eve, by her reply, showed that she clearly understood the divine prohibition, yet, by the fact of that reply, she betrayed her rising inclination to listen, and to yield. It is observable also, that she passed over the goodness and the positiveness of her divine Creator. She omitted the words "*freely*" and "*surely*," when quoting his beneficent grant, and solemn denunciation, Genesis 2:16, 17. It is no marvel therefore that, when Eve overlooked God's bounty and severity, she forgot to be thankful and watchful.

(Verses 4 and 5.) "And the serpent said unto the woman, Ye shall not surely die: for God doth know that in the day ye eat thereof then your eyes shall be opened, and ye shall be as gods, knowing good and evil." Now Satan plumes his crest, and advances with greater confidence. He disputes the threatening, maligns the motives of the Creator, and lays a snare, baited with pride, to catch the unwary woman. "Ye shall not surely die!" as though he had said, there must be some contingency, and no certainty; or, the Giver of life cannot mean death in reality, especially for so slight an offence: he must mean something else, as it is not reasonable to suppose that he will destroy so fair a being as yourself for the sake of this inanimate fruit. Thus Satan tempted Eve; and thus he tempts us to think lightly of God's threatenings, and then to think lightly of sin itself.

Next, the tempter artfully reflects on the goodness of God, and assures Eve that her eating of the fruit will be followed by the enlarged happiness of her husband and herself, in an amount of knowledge which will equal them to gods. "God," said he, "*doth know*" that such will be the case; implying that God knew the fact, but jealously kept them in ignorance of it, and thus passed a rule for preventing the expansion of their faculties. "Your eyes shall be opened," said the traitor. Vain and proud desires after superior knowledge and power had now risen in the mind of Eve. Satan thus instigated them in her, and he still endeavours to excite them in us. Doubtless Eve would have known more of all things, had she waited patiently, in learning what she had to learn, and in obeying the divine will. Haste and impatience for any supposed good are evils of daily occurrence. Even the haste to be wise has its dangers; and the being "wise above what is written" is sure to lead to disastrous consequences.

Our text, as the succeeding verse, shows us how fatally the devil prevailed, and how easily the woman yielded: "And when the woman saw that the tree was good for food, and that it was pleasant to the eyes, and a tree to be desired to make one wise, she took of the fruit thereof, and did eat, and gave also unto her husband with her; and he did eat." All that is affecting, humiliating, lamentable, and woeful is comprised in these words. They are the history of the ruin of a whole world, in a single verse. They tell us of the origin of sin as to man's own self. That origin is to be looked for in the irregularity of the affections. "The lust of the flesh, and the lust of the eye, and the pride of life," all germinated in the mind of Eve when she gazed with wistful eye on the fatal fruit. She saw it was fair and beautiful as an object of sight; and as it was, at the same time, supposed to be both delicious to the taste and desirable for the mind, she rashly and infatuatedly gratified her heart's desire.

"She took of the fruit and did eat." We might dwell on the melancholy scene, as they are wont to dwell on some harrowing spectacle, whose minds are intensely pained, but whose power of giving relief is altogether nugatory. There is no altering the fact, and no averting the consequences. The sin was committed; and Eve, in one short minute, sealed the doom of myriads for eternity. Satan's dark plot, however, was not complete in the fall of Eve alone. By some additional artifice, which is not detailed to us, he brought about the fall of Adam also.

The woman "gave also unto her husband with her, and he did eat." Upon this, Satan's first work was horribly finished. He had the cruel delight of seeing all the glories of creation spoiled at a stroke. Still the Creator was greater than he; and plans were already ripe in the divine bosom for the development of infinite good out of this mighty evil. But we must not now pursue this branch of the extensive subject. Neither may we stay to indulge a vague curiosity in asking, how it came that Adam joined his wife in her transgression? Or, what would have been the state of things if he had continued in his integrity, and left Eve alone in her fall? All such inquiries are vain. Though they have often agitated particular sections of the church, yet have they rarely profited it. It is enough for us to know that "Adam was not *deceived* as was the woman:" (1 Timothy 2:14) but, whether he joined her in her sin, by the force of sudden desperation, or inordinate affection, we probably shall not learn till we see themselves in the paradise above. Our part is to study what is revealed, and to derive from it the instruction for which it was revealed. Here let us attend with freshened interest.

II. *The instruction of the heart is the grand object of all biblical history.* The history of the fall is remarkably brief; but it is so wonderfully constructed as to furnish us with ample lessons for all the great purposes of life. Among other things we learn

1. *The author of evil and the origin of death.* Satan was that author, and not God. "As saith the proverb of the ancients, Wickedness proceedeth from the wicked" (or the wicked one). 1 Samuel 24:13. "Let no man say when he is tempted, I am tempted of God: for God cannot be tempted with evil, neither tempteth he any man." James 1:13. The devil tempted Eve. This should satisfy us. Speculations about God's permission for the entrance of evil into our world are vain in the extreme. We have no premises, and therefore we can arrive at no conclusion. We can no more tell why God permitted Satan to enter Eden, than we can tell why he permitted sin to enter heaven; for Satan was a sinner there before he became a tempter on earth. "Vain man would be wise (in such mysteries), though he is born as a wild ass's colt." Our truest wisdom, in all questions about sin, is not how it originated, but how it may be eradicated. The fact of its existence in ourselves furnishes a world of practical study and diligent effort, to the contrite child of God.

Besides, the fatal consequence of sin, in the death of both body and soul, is always a solemn topic for such an one. Like Paul he will recur to the cause of that death, and look back into the history of the fall to discern it: "Wherefore by one man sin entered into the world, and death by sin; and so death passed upon all men, for that all have sinned." Romans 5:12.

Hence we learn also

2. *The universality of guilt and woe.* The penalty annexed to Adam's disobedience was death. As remarked to you on Sunday last, it could hardly be that Adam was ignorant of the fact that such penalty would extend to all his posterity. We at least know it. "In Adam *all* die." Like him, we all have, by actual transgression, forfeited our original right to immortality. We have sold our birthright, and flung away our happiness. Not one among all his sons and daughters has escaped the common sentence. Guilt hangs on every soul, and misery is the inheritance of all from whom it is not removed. With Adam we partake of an evil nature. The Holy Spirit forsook our bodily temple, and comes back to it only on the taking place of a new creation.

How awful is the picture of our fallen state which St. Paul sketches in Romans 3:10–12. "As it is written, There is none righteous, no, not one: there is none that understandeth, there is none that seeketh after God. They are all gone out of the way, they are together become unprofitable: there is none that doeth good, no, not one." And, where may we see this picture verified? Alas! in ourselves. The truth of which induced an old divine occasionally to exclaim, "O Adam, Adam, what hast thou done!"

3. *The deceitfulness of sin* is forcibly taught in the fall of Eve. Sin, like its author, is insinuating, and advances unawares. As that author was a deceiver from the beginning, so his progeny, sin, is deceitful in its workings. It first deludes its victim, leading it imperceptibly from bad to worse, and making one false step an incitement to another. It was thus with Eve. She parleyed, she doubted; she next slightly disbelieved, and indulged the risings of pride and discontent. Soon she grew impatient, ceased to reflect, and wickedly fell. Thus from little beginnings fatal endings ensue. David, in his first gazings on the housetop, had, it is probable, no purpose of either adultery or murder: and Judas, in his first pilferings of the bag, little thought that he was paving his path for the mercenary betrayal of his Master. Then take heed and ponder what is said in Hebrews 3:13, "But exhort one another daily, while it is called To-day, lest any of you be hardened through the deceitfulness of sin."

4. *The necessity of habitual watchfulness, of constant dependance on God,* are plain lessons taught us by this narrative. Eve was off her guard, and Satan knew it. It was, perhaps, the chief hope of Satan to catch her by some sudden impulse. Had there been the risk of a second opportunity, he could hardly have hoped for success. Time for reflection must have balanced the slightest wavering in the mind of one constituted as was Eve.

For a moment Eve forgot her position, and the hand which would have supported her. Thus it was with Peter. The temptation caught him unawares. Having said No, once, he said it thrice. He therefore says, 1 Peter 5:8, "Be sober, be vigilant; because your adversary the devil, as a roaring lion, walketh about, seeking whom he may devour."

The second Adam, who had encountered the very tempter of Eve, left this injunction for all his followers, Mark 13:37, "And what I say unto you I say unto all, Watch." With this accords the direction of St. Paul, Colossians 4:2, "Continue in prayer, and watch in the same with thanksgiving." Satan, my brethren, watches you: therefore watch him.

5. *The ultimate end of the fall of Adam and Eve* should never be overlooked. God's lesson respecting it was taught ere the day of the fall had closed. He gave a mortifying intimation to the tempter, that the success of his fraud should only lead to his own destruction; while he announced the outlines of a plan, by which a fairer creation should arise without the possibility of its ever being marred. Like an artist who places his exquisite work in a dubious position, and sees it crushed by a fall, the great Creator restores his beauteous creation; and, as that artist may be supposed to act, fixes it, ever after, on such a footing as to render a similar catastrophe impossible. All this is done for us in Christ, the second Adam. He has more than repaired the fall. John 10:10—"I am come that they might have life, and that they might have it more abundantly." Romans 5:20, 21—"Moreover the law entered, that the offence might abound. But where sin abounded, grace did much more abound: that, as sin hath reigned unto death, even so might grace reign through righteousness unto eternal life by Jesus Christ our Lord." Let all then, who know this life and this grace, praise him to whom they are owing. At his table and in their lives let them say, "Glory be to God on high, and on earth peace, good will towards men. We praise thee, we bless thee, we worship thee, we glorify thee; we give thanks to thee for thy great glory, O Lord God, heavenly King, God the Father Almighty."

SERMON IV.

THE SEED OF THE WOMAN BRUISED, BUT TRIUMPHANT.[1]

GENESIS 3:15.

"And I will put enmity between thee and the woman, and between thy seed and her seed: it shall bruise thy head, and thou shalt bruise his heel."

WE all know the interest which, after the lapse of ages, is taken in the discovery of the original specimen of some important invention. Could the first book which was ever printed be found, or the first watch which was ever made be discovered, how highly would it be valued, and with what interest would it be regarded!

Upon this principle of human feeling, we ought to regard the text before us as one of the most remarkable, and the most deeply interesting, in the whole Bible; because it is the *first* which contains the hope of salvation. The revelation of it was the beaming of the primal ray of light, which shone upon the world after sin had darkened it. It was, in essence, the gospel declared, for the first time, to our guilty and ruined race.

To the early believers it was a sort of sacred riddle. After ages gradually unfolded its meaning. To us, however, the entire mystery is fully explained; for we have "the revelation of the mystery, which was kept secret since the world began, but now is made manifest, and by the scriptures of the prophets, according to the commandment of the everlasting God, made known to all nations for the obedience of faith." (Romans 16:25, 26.)

The affecting narrative, connected with the text, has been read in your hearing. It tells us of God's sentence upon the tempter and the tempted. The serpent, whom God addresses in the text, was, as Satan's agent, to suffer perpetual degradation, while Satan himself, after wounding the manhood of the Messiah, was doomed to destruction.

In unfolding to you the meaning of the figurative language before us, it becomes me to invite your attention to

I. *The two parties who are opposed to each other*, namely, the serpent and his seed, and the woman and her seed.

1. In former sermons from this chapter, and at this season of the year, explanations have been given to you respecting Satan's employment of the serpent, for carrying out his purposes of ruin; respecting, also, the probability of the serpent's being originally a winged, or an erect animal, and one of the most seraph-like and fascinating creatures in Eden.

But now that serpent is exhibited to us, as only another name for Satan himself. Hence we read of "that old serpent which is the devil." And, because subtlety was the prime feature of both the serpent and Satan, in the temptation of Eve, we all are, to this hour, warned to take heed of "the wiles of the devil," or as our Church turns the phrase, "the craft and sublety of the devil or man," when man becomes his slave and agent.

2. Satan then is the grand opponent of whom Jehovah warns us. Powerful by virtue of his original creation and God's permission, he exists for the manifestation and operation of evil. For reasons which at present we only dimly discern, he is allowed to stand up as the daring foe of Christ and his church. God might have put him down for ever, ere he withdrew from the conference in Eden. He not only could, as he did, degrade the serpent; but he could have chained, or even have destroyed Satan, had his wisdom seen fit so to do.

But Satan retains his existence; and he has a posterity too. The seed of the serpent are otherwise called "the children of the devil," and a "generation of vipers." Those expressions designate not so much all mankind by nature (who are indeed "children of wrath"), as that portion of mankind who never attain unto saving grace, but who in heart disbelieve the gospel, and in life practise sin. The number of such is *legion upon legion*, and includes, alas! multitudes who but little suspect it.

3. The woman and her seed are the defined antagonists of the serpent and his seed. By the woman and her seed, we are to understand, in the first instance, Eve and all her lineal posterity, between whom and the serpent race there is, and always has been, a strong and an instinctive antipathy. In the next instance, we must understand by the woman that pure virgin of whom the Saviour was born; still, not in any personal pre-eminency, nor with respect to any especial power on *her* part; but as that daughter of Eve who, in the fulness of time, was selected for the incarnation of him, to whom all pre-eminence and all power belong. The woman also is, in this text, as afterwards in St. Paul's Epistles, and the Revelation of St.

[1] Preached Sunday Morning, February 23rd, 1852.

John, a personification of the true and pure church, and all its true and pure members. That church and those members have always been the special, if not the sole, objects of the old serpent's hate.

But, unquestionably, all these interpretations are only secondary to that one grand object of Satan's animosity, the seed of the woman, the Messiah, who is emphatically *her* seed, and not the offspring of Adam. Christ was the intended person in this mystic text. He was "*made of a woman,*" born of a pure virgin, and became "incarnate by the Holy Ghost of the Virgin Mary."

By this miraculous and altogether singular provision, the Lord Jesus was literally and emphatically "the seed of the woman." As St. Paul said of Jehovah's promise to Abraham, so may we say of his words in our text, "He saith not, And to seeds, as of many; but as of one, And to thy *seed, which is Christ.*"

Thus, as the woman was the first sinner, so was she in a manner the first saviour. Not that she herself, and of herself, was in any respect a saviour of us, but she was the medium of the birth of him, who was the only Saviour of herself and of all who believe in him. It is this astonishing and adorable fact which gives such peculiar emphasis to that saying of St. Paul to Timothy, which, as many eminent divines consider, is imperfectly translated in our English version. Read 1 Timothy 2:14, 15. That passage, instead of being translated, "She shall be saved *in* child bearing," should follow the original Greek, and read thus, "She shall be saved *by* (or *through*) *the* childbearing;" in evident allusion to the promised childbearing,—the predicted "seed of the woman," as revealed in our text. If women, as daughters of Eve, believe in that childbearing, and in all that it includes, they shall be saved, notwithstanding that, through the woman's being deceived, all mankind were lost.

Verily how "great is the mystery of godliness. God manifest in the flesh," Jesus "made of a woman," and all "for us men and for our salvation!"

Let me now lead you to consider,

II. *The conflict in which the two opposite parties were to engage, and the events which should attend it.* "It shall bruise thy head, and thou shalt bruise his heel."

This, indeed, is the grand issue of the conflict: but an animosity is to precede it, which nothing can mitigate, so long as sin is sin, and holiness is holiness.

1. "I *will put enmity* (says Jehovah) between thee and the woman, and between thy seed and her seed." To lay any great stress upon the fact of universal antipathy between mankind and the serpent tribe, as before alluded to, would only weaken the force of that momentous fact which is principally intended to be pressed upon us. God puts irreconcilable enmity between sin and holiness, and between *the natures* of those two grand divisions of the human race, sinners and saints. We say, "*between the natures,*" because sinners and saints, though immeasurably separated in character, are to grow together in all kindly conduct. Sinners, indeed, cannot love *saints as such,* nor can saints love sinners *as sinners,* but they must love them as immortal beings, and, though opposed to their principles and their practices, must labour and pray for the salvation of their souls.

Here, indeed, lies the difference between the enmity of the two parties in its relation to each. On the one side, it is positive and active; on the other, negative and passive. The enmity of the serpent's seed against the woman's seed, that is, the hostility of sinners against saints, is deadly and energetic. When left to its own unbridled fury, it amounts to persecution and death: though, under that restraint which God generally lays upon it, it seldom arrives at more than wrath, hatred, injury, evil report, taunt, ridicule, and slight. On the side of Christ's seed, this "*enmity*" is always removed from the persons, and laid on the practices, of those who, alas! are of another seed. Instead of harming sinners, the saints of God in Christ are bound to do them good. We are to pray for those who despitefully use us, and even to love our enemies.

2. But, in Jehovah's prophetic detail, the severity of the conflict is principally confined to Satan and Christ. "It (the seed of the woman) shall bruise thy head, and thou shalt bruise his heel." On the cross it was that these words received their virtual accomplishment. There it was that Christ conquered Satan, and Satan wounded Christ. But, as a fuller explanation of the terms of the text is requisite, it will be my endeavour to give it.

i. The bruising of the serpent's head is a figurative speech for the destruction of Satan's power and empire.

It is well known to naturalists that the crushing of a serpent's head is the sure destruction of its vitality. The words of Jehovah therefore certify us that Christ, as the seed of the woman, should utterly destroy all that is vital in the power and government of Satan. The celebrated Joseph Mede has well said that, by the bruising of the head of the serpent, we are to understand the annihilation, not of Satan's existence, but of Satan's sovereignty; and, let me add, of Satan's subtlety too. It is remarkable that, in the apocalyptic account of the coercion of Satan, the cessation of his subtlety is expressly mentioned. "And I saw an angel come down from heaven, having the key of the bottomless pit, and a great chain in his hand: and he laid hold on the dragon, that old serpent, which is the devil, and Satan, and bound him a thousand years, and cast him into the bottomless pit, and shut him up, and set a seal upon him, that he should deceive the nations no more." (Revelation 20:1–3.)

As, therefore, the vitality and the subtlety of the serpent are seated in its head, so the bruising of that head, in the old serpent, is the annihilation of Satan's power to reign and to deceive.

ii. But, how did Christ thus bruise the head of Satan? Not, we answer, as he might have done, in some triumphant spectacle, before Adam and Eve, and all the elect angels—not in any way which accorded with human notions of the grandeur of conquest. He effected it by means, not only the least likely in appearance, but by such as seemed altogether nugatory, and even contrary to the end intended. He bruised Satan, by allowing himself to be bruised. He conquered death, and him who had the power of death, that is, the devil, by himself dying on the accursed tree. Here was mystery indeed. The blessed effects of it we may realize every hour. Its glorious results are reserved for the last day; when, before the assembled universe, Satan's overthrow shall be openly exhibited, as one of the closing solemnities of that dread period. We read the prophetic assurance of it: "And the devil that decieved them was cast into the lake of fire and brimstone, where the beast and the false prophet are, and shall be tormented day and night for ever and ever." (Revelation 20:10.)

iii. But, as error always is expert in undermining truth, and Antichrist is ever on the watch to thrust out Christ, so Popery has made, and continues to make, a blasphemous attempt to pervert the text before us. Taking advantage of some errors of copyists, and of the fond translation from the Greek in the Latin Bible, the Douay Bible, as it is called, of the Romanists, renders our text thus:—"I will put enmities between thee and the woman, and thy seed and her seed: *she* shall crush thy head, and thou shalt lie in wait for *her* heel." By this stealthy rendering of the passage, the woman is substituted for "the seed of the woman;" and, as a little more conjuring turns that woman into the virgin Mary, so the virgin Mary is put in the place of Christ, in this very first revelation of his gospel! If such be done with the first text of that gospel, who can marvel at the like being attempted wherever practicable?

3. The temporary triumph of Satan is predicted in the subsequent words of the text, "And thou shalt bruise his heel." The chief meaning of this is, that Satan should have power to wound the lower or inferior part of the Messiah—his manhood or human nature. How cruelly his very feet were lacerated, when spiked to the cross, his evangelists have told us. That was Satan's hour, and the period of his short triumph. But the crushing of his own head followed the bruising of the Saviour's feet; while the head of Christ, not being bruised or crushed, was a token and figure that his vitality, his sovereignty, his infinite wisdom and power, were to remain unimpaired to all eternity.

But Satan's power to bruise the heel or body of Christ might also betoken his power to harm the bodies only of Christ's saints, without any corresponding power to injure their souls.

Hence, though the old serpent has often prevailed in afflicting or killing the bodies of believers by malady or martyrdom, he has never been able to destroy the soul of one of them. The conqueror of Satan knew this when he said, "My friends, be not afraid of them that kill the body, and after that have no more that they can do. But I forewarn you whom ye shall fear: Fear him, which after he hath killed hath power to cast into hell; yea, I say unto you, Fear him." (Luke 12:4, 5.)

But, in telling Satan that, as a serpent, he should bruise Messiah's heel, a severe and cutting rebuke was given to the meanness, cowardice, and contemptibleness, of both Satan and all his seed of "enemies, persecutors, and slanderers." A beast of noble and generous nature attacks full front. The crawlers and the sleeve-creepers, and the backbiters, cannot endure a manly gaze, and so fly at the heel, when the face of the passer-by is looking upward, or turned in some other straight forward direction.

But, let our warmest thoughts be given to him, who, according to the spirit of our text, "was manifested that he might destroy the works of the devil." Standing, as we do, a long way off from the time of that manifestation, let us look back and contemplate the results of it. They are these:

i. *The absolute rule and government of Christ as a conqueror.* His bruising of the serpent's head attests his own undivided sovereignty. He now is the Head of an empire which shall know neither limits nor end. Satan is his vassal,—a maimed and crippled felon, existing only by sufferance, and awaiting his full destruction.

ii. *The redemption of fallen man.* Satan, by his successful subtlety, caught, as it were, our first parents in a horrid net of bondage. Jesus came as one "stronger than he," broke the meshes of that net, and set the captives free. Redemption is now the watch-word of the church on earth, and the song of that in heaven.

iii. *The salvation of all that believe.* By Christ's predicted victory over Satan, Adam and all the Old Testament saints were spared and saved. Through faith in the actual achievement of that victory, all penitent souls may now obtain salvation.

iv. *The certain accomplishment of all those promises which were included in this first promise.* The conquest of Satan, by the Lord Jesus, is the pledge of the evangelization of the whole world. Satan knew this. The sound therefore of our text, when originally uttered by Jehovah, rang not only through Eden, but through the lowest depths of hell and the loftiest heights of heaven. Hell has not dared to repeat the sound; but it came back again from heaven, increased and cleared by its own sweet echoes: "Glory to God in the highest, and on earth peace, good will toward men." (Luke 2:14.) Nor shall those echoes cease, until they swell into this full chorus, "The kingdoms of this world are become the kingdoms of our Lord, and of his Christ; and he shall reign for ever and ever." (Revelation 11:15.)

But present duties are loud in their call for present attention. And what are they?

1. *Humiliation and repentance.* Adam's fall was our own. We would have done as he did. His guilt is therefore ours. His humiliation and repentance must be ours also.

2. *Lively faith in the Conqueror.* The revelation of him was made to Adam for that purpose. It is made to us for the same. Unless it had been made, Adam could have had no hope, and we should be in despair. But it is made; and our faith in it should be as Adam's was.

3. *The surrender of the heart and life to Jesus.* He who conquered for us has every claim upon us. All is due to him. His table is a meet place for the surrender of ourselves.

4. *Courage in meeting the last struggles of Satan.* Those struggles will end in no dubious conquest. A glorious and an everlasting victory will terminate them, because the Lord Jesus has conquered not only death, but that arch-fiend, who for a while has "had the power of death." There is nothing therefore, which the dying believer has really to fear. Death is now his, because of the death of Jesus on the cross. (Hebrews 2:14, 15.)

SERMON V.

THE AGE AND DEATH OF METHUSELAH.[1]

GENESIS 5:27.

"And all the days of Methuselah were nine hundred sixty and nine years: and he died."

WITH such brevity did it please the Holy Spirit to sum up the history of the man who, as far as we know, was the longest liver of all the descendants of Adam. In a manner equally brief, excepting the instance of Enoch and that of Lamech, are the histories of all the patriarchs from Adam to Noah recorded. And why, it may be asked, were their names recorded at all, if nothing be said of their character or conduct? Why the Holy Ghost saw fit not to transmit to succeeding generations any account of their lives, we presume not to inquire; but why he has registered their names in the Bible may be explained on grounds which are full of importance and comfort to the true church. These patriarchs were, according to the flesh, the ancestors of Christ, in a direct line from Adam, to whom the promise of his birth was originally made. Bearing this fact in mind, we shall not regard passages like this in the chapter before us as a string of dull and uninteresting genealogies, but as a portion of the divine word in close connexion with the gospel. Herein we read the names of the holy seed, the names of the good men who kept up the worship of the triune God, who perpetuated the recollection of the grand promise made to man, and successively handed it down from the old world to the new. *Their* names are thus recorded, while the names and achievements of the giants, and other mighty ones of the same days, are buried in the deepest oblivion.

The subject however, to which this discourse will be principally directed, is the great age of Methuselah, as the most venerable of all the antediluvian patriarchs. The fact of our ending, on this evening, another Sunday-year of our lives, and that those lives, according to their average term, are but the length of a childhood compared with his, are circumstances well calculated to awaken our interest, and, by God's sanctifying grace, to further our edification. They will also, I trust, impress us with a holier wonder, and a deeper reverence, in consulting the Scriptures of truth, as comprising the most astonishing fulness of matter within the compass of a few ordinary words.

[1] Preached Sunday Evening, December 30th, 1849.

I. *The years of Methuselah were, we are told, nine hundred and sixty-nine.* The amount startles us by its magnitude; and, because of our present allotted span, we are ready to question the fact of its being the true amount, and to surmise some method of accounting for it, so as to square with our prejudices. Indeed some individuals, who are slow to believe but quick to dispute, have arrogantly attempted to set aside what they call the vulgar notion of reckoning such enormous amounts by popular computation. They consequently presume to assert that a shorter period than our solar year, of three hundred and sixty-five days, is to be taken for these patriarchal years. And yet, on the other hand, when it suits the purpose of a baffled man of science, he contends that by a day, in the six days of creation, a very long age is intended, perhaps a thousand years for each.

Friends, be not deceived; for God's word is not written to deceive us, or so to clash with the settled apprehensions of all mankind, as to teach in plain terms what is not to be plainly understood. Beware of all tamperings with the Bible; and be very careful in watching against the many false, though plausible methods of getting rid of what ill accords with self-willed and unsanctified minds.

To prolong the age of man is perfectly easy with God; for assuredly he who had power to create has power to sustain. Besides, there was a valid reason for his so greatly elongating the days of the antediluvians, compared with his shortening of the term of human life in subsequent times. One reason may have been the more speedy increase of the population of the earth. Another, the more direct and secure transmission of his early revelations to man. It needed but two or three individuals, at the most to be the links of pure tradition from Adam to Noah. Then a third, and by no means the least important reason, may have been the exhibition to the very first generations of sinful man of the riches of his patience and long suffering.

But the great age of the first patriarchs may have been occasioned instrumentally by certain natural agents. The salubrity of the atmosphere, partaking somewhat of its original qualities, the superior fitness of fruits for food, and of herbs for medicinal purposes, all well known to Adam, and their secrets familiar to him, could hardly fail of having great influence over the health and so over the longevity of mankind. The simplicity also and general temperance of their mode of living might have added to that influence, especially as it is a question whether animal food was allowed, or fermented liquors known before the deluge. Still, be these things as they may, the issues of life and death were always in God's hands, and no natural causes could avert the doom which man brought upon himself as a rebel. Hence

II. We read that, aged as Methuselah was, "*he died.*" And, had he lived his years twice over, his existence would have been equally vain, and the end of it quite as certain. The longest period of time cannot shield our lives from the far-deceiving and inevitable dart of death. The judicial sentence of mortality was indeed suspended in its execution before the flood; but the reprieve, however protracted, had its limits. Methuselah, though one of God's elect people, was a partaker of Adam's guilt, and *therefore* "he died." It was *sin* which brought death into the world. The world would fain forget the fact; but God has written it in terrific type on the heart of every man, and his word presents a legible transcript of the inward writing. "Wherefore by one man sin entered into the world, and death by sin; and so death passed upon all men, for that all have sinned." (Romans 5:12.) Let us then beware of subscribing to that fond but false tenet, which is every day meeting our eyes or our ears, that death is *the debt of nature.* No such thing: that tenet is a lie, which "the father of lies" has been palming on the world up to the present hour. So often as he can get a newspaper, or a magazine, to say of some departed worldling, "he has paid the debt of nature," so often does he send forth an illusive and God-defaming scrap of error from the dark pages of his own infernal volume. Death is not the debt of nature, but *the penalty of sin.* Man must be told the unwelcome truth; and if he resists it, all we have to do is to tell it him again. It must be rung in his drowsy ears till either he starts into newness of life, or sinks beyond our reach into the unseen regions of death.

Methuselah, though spared for such a protracted period, did not reach his *thousandth* year. "He died" when wanting thirty-one of it. It is probable, yea, it was a current tradition in earlier days, that no one ever lived to the age of a thousand years. The reason of which, as St. Augustine has stated, is said to be that no man might appear to live to a perfection of time. A thousand years with God are but a *day*: "For a thousand years in thy sight are but as yesterday when it is past, and as a watch in the night." (Psalm 90:4.) And man, say early writers, attained not a thousand years, because God had declared to Adam that "*in*, (or *within*) *the day* thou eatest thereof (that is, of the forbidden tree) thou shalt surely *die.*" It is proper for me to warn you that all this is mere conjecture; and yet it may be turned to a profitable account. Any thing is good for us which humbles us, and leads us to think reverently of the awful and eternal God.

III. *There is much that is calculated to humble the pride of our hearts* in the reflection that so long a life as Methuselah's should be summed up in so few words: "And all the days of Methuselah were nine hundred sixty and nine years, and he died." The Jews have many traditions respecting him. They say he was a very learned man; that he spent a hundred years in the school of his father Enoch; that he was the author of many works, and of three hundred and thirty parables. One learned rabbi asserts that he died only seven days before the flood, just time enough for his grandson Noah to lament him; and that then certain sounds were heard from heaven, as though the angels themselves bewailed his death.

But in all these things there is not only no certainty, but most likely a great deal of fable. They may, however, show us that a few words of inspired certainty are better than volumes of babbling tradition. We shall know about Methuselah when he knows us.

Soon indeed will our history be as brief as Methuselah's. "He lived and he died" will, ere long, be *all* that many will know of us. "*All*" do I say? Little as that "*all*" is, it will dwindle into *nothing*. It will not be known in the spot where we once lived, that we ever lived at all. This is the humiliating lot of man in what, for the time, is often his highest estate. Millions of once illustrious persons are consigned to the darkest obscurity. Their very names have perished, and no trace of their existence is to be found. Occasionally the coffin, or the bones, or the armour, or some other relique of the mighty dead are discovered; but that is all. Therein we behold the dumb proofs of former greatness, but we know nothing more. To whom they pertained, or when they were deposited in their hiding-place, is impossible, by human means, to be ascertained.

It is not long ago that the force of such things as these was keenly brought home to me, even with respect to our own parish. Looking back into our oldest parochial records, in search of information respecting our charities, I was struck with this circumstance. In the accounts of the vestry meetings of our forefathers certain names would be signed. One or two leading names would be traceable for a length of years, and then they cease to appear. At first the name is written towards the bottom of the list. Then, as age and standing advance, it is seen at the very top. For a time the original vigour of the handwriting maintains its aspect; but gradually the pen is observed to become tremulous, and the old and dying man is marked in the feebleness and zigzaggedness of the signature. At length that signature is never again added. The old and respected parishioner is dead. For a little while his last attendance at the vestry is remembered; but soon all is forgotten. And now we, who are filling his place and our own short day, read his name when casually brought to light, and we say, "We know it not; we never heard the name before!" "He lived and he died," that is all that can be told respecting him. Such is the vanity of human life, and such is the contempt which the God of eternity puts upon all things which sin has made perishable. In the case of even his holiest and dearest people, he sums up their temporal life with significant conciseness, in order to admonish them that their best estate on earth is but a shadow, a trifle, a very nothingness, compared with that better life which awaits them in heaven. And yet, short as his record of their earthly life is to our eye, not a single incident of it is forgotten by himself. Every thing respecting them is written down in his "book of remembrance." The lives of his saints are recorded with imperishable ink; and the chronicles of heaven will tell every true saint what he humbly and modestly forgot of his own doings and feelings in this world. O what a profound depth of animating meditation do these things open to us! Let us often employ ourselves in it. Our life will then assume an interest which nothing but God's grace can impart to it.

IV. *To a mind which is unrenewed and unsanctified, a life as long as Methuselah's seems greatly desirable.* But the man whose affections have been chastened and spiritualized accounts it a very valueless thing compared with the life of eternity. He who aspires to that life, says, "I have a desire to depart and to be with Christ, which is far better."

The long and lingering existence of the first patriarchs was possibly a severe trial to many of them. Sin and sorrow would not be diminished by a great increase of years. Jacob, when only one hundred and thirty years old, described all his days as "*evil.*" (Genesis 47:9.) God also has frequently testified his love by taking to himself many of the excellent of the earth before they have arrived at old age. An instance of such love was given in the case of Enoch. "He pleased God," and so God "took him" away from earthly vanities in the very prime of patriarchal life. He was, as an antediluvian might say, *but* three hundred and sixty-five years old when "he was not." God's best children therefore may be thankful that the average term of human life is fixed at three-score years and ten (nine hundred, all but one, less than what Methuselah saw), long time enough to enjoy what little the world can afford, and sufficient to learn the way of salvation.

The extended existence of the antediluvians probably had the effect of hardening sinners among them, and of inclining them to carelessness and procrastination. Centuries spent in iniquity, while other centuries were anticipated, must have made the worldly-minded of those days giants in sin, as many of them were giants in stature. Our shorter time should be an argument for our instant repentance, and for a readier improvement of the scanty space allotted to us. O that it may be such with some, who are present at the last service of this year, but who may not be alive when the last service of the next comes round!

V. It would be well to make another remark respecting *the period when the death of the aged Methuselah took place.*

According to our best chronologists that period was at a time which, while in one respect shows the unsearchable sovereignty of God in afflicting his people, nevertheless marks the kind providence which he exercises in closing their lives.

Methuselah survived his son Lamech, who was the father of Noah, about five years. What a trial, what a bitter affliction was here! For the oldest man in the world to be left, in his five last years, without the son of his heart, who he hoped would care for him to the end, and then lay him in his grave, surely this was a grief indeed! And yet it is one which the same God has often sent on the same sort of persons who are dear to him. May he comfort those abundantly whom he afflicts thus grievously! But Jehovah remembered Methuselah in another way; for he called him to depart hence, either in the year before the deluge, or in the very year in which it occurred. So true was it even then, as Isaiah many years after said, "The righteous is taken away from the evil to come." He still does the like, even under our own eye, and the observant have frequent occasion to remark it. May his grace make and keep us ready for all events, be their character what it may! And now, closing as we do this evening the services of another year, let our concluding remarks be in character with so solemn a season:

1. Another year is ending, and *a long catalogue of mercies and trespasses has to be remembered.* Let the one be remembered with fervent gratitude, and the other with godly sorrow.

2. Many who began the year *have not seen its end.* Thousands among them little thought that it would be said, He or she "*died*" in the year 1849. Then be not thoughtless yourselves! You will die.

3. There are *aged persons among us.* Some are at home, some are at church. Let us pray for the absent, and let me admonish those who are present. Friends, you are our Methuselahs. But what say you of your long life? Is it not a dream? Then tell your younger ones the fact. Would you "live always"? as Job said. No, say you. Then tell your younger ones that. Is your "hoary head a crown of glory"? If not, you have lived long in vain. Tell yourselves that.

4. Before the year actually ends *there is time for it to be said of us,* He or she *died!* Yes, the last day of the year is the last day of many a life. There is time also for eternal life. O seek it!

SERMON VI.

GOD'S VIEW OF THE WICKEDNESS OF MAN.[1]

GENESIS 6:5.

"And God saw that the wickedness of man was great in the earth, and that every imagination of the thoughts of his heart was only evil continually."

WHILE the population of the old world was small, sin was kept in check, men "called upon the name of the Lord." (4:26.) But, as we read in the first verse of this chapter, "when men began to multiply upon the face of the earth," then sin abounded, and universal degeneracy soon followed. So true is it, that in this evil world an increase of population generally brings an increase of moral corruption. That which might be a blessing is turned into a curse.

The chief occasion of the universal degeneracy alluded to was the marriage of the religious with the irreligious. "The sons of God" took to themselves wives of "the daughters of men." But the root and ground of it all was the natural corruption of the heart of man. For, after iniquity had pervaded all classes, and the bad had swallowed up the good, the Almighty God not only saw the great wickedness of man, but resolved it into its true cause. The life was altogether wrong, because the heart was altogether bad. The text certifies us of these facts: "And God saw that the wickedness of man was great in the earth, and that every imagination of the thoughts of his heart was only evil continually." Hence let our meditation be,

I. *The state in which God beheld the human race.* He "saw

[1] Preached Sunday Evening, February 15th, 1846.

that the wickedness of man was great in the earth." Every part of this sentence is fearfully emphatic. Let us notice each.

1. "*God saw.*" He was the judge of all men, because he had been the creator of all men. He therefore saw for himself. "He looked down from heaven," says David, "*to see* if there were any that would understand." As his eye is all-seeing, he could make no mistake. He needed no testimony from witnesses, and could not be deceived by dissemblers. As then, so now, "the eyes of the Lord are in every place, beholding the evil and the good." And what met the eye of the holy Observer?

2. He saw "*wickedness.*" His creatures and their doings were no longer "very good," but "all flesh had corrupted his way upon the earth." Himself was then, as he always was before and ever will be, "of purer eyes than to behold iniquity:" but ungrateful man wearies him with "wickedness." That *wickedness* is the very thing which is most abhorrent to his nature. He is a God of holiness; of such holiness, too, as fills the purest beings around his own pure throne, with the deepest awe. And yet "wickedness" was the principal thing which was to be seen on the earth when he looked down upon it. Now "wickedness" here means *practical* sin, or the commission of things which are contrary to his law, and injurious to both the souls and bodies of his people. "Wickedness" is the doing of "the works of the flesh;" and what they are St. Paul tells us in Galatians 5:19–21: "Now the works of the flesh are manifest, which are these; adultery, fornication, uncleanness, lasciviousness, idolatry, witchcraft, hatred, variance, emulations, wrath, strife, seditions, heresies, envyings, murders, drunkenness, revellings, and such like: of the which I tell you before, as I have also told you in time past, that they which do such things shall not inherit the kingdom of God." Without doubt these evil deeds were horribly rife among men, and, added to the lawlessness and violence of the apostate giants who were then in the earth, rendered society one mass of terrific corruption.

3. This wickedness was "the wickedness *of man.*" It was not the fault and failing of individuals, but of the entire species: for it is not said "the wickedness of *men,*" but "of *man,*" that is, of man both individually, collectively, and generally,—of man in his very nature and constitution. Into this we shall see more fully as we proceed. But this we may say for the present, "wickedness" is man's element; and wherever he is unchecked by civilization or conscience, there he indulges in that element. And verily, what others indulge in, we ourselves would follow, if left to ourselves. The only secret of our individual preservation from enormous wickedness is God's free and upholding grace.

4. This "wickedness of man was *great.*" It was no slight or ordinary degree of moral impropriety. It was moral disorder of the most atrocious and the most extensive kind. It had reached a height which admitted of no partial remedy. It was like a disease for which there is no cure but death, or like the firing of a house, wherein the mischief is so great that nothing can be saved, all must come down, and the whole be built afresh.

And truly "wickedness" is still "*great,*" wherever the power of the gospel has no exercise. See a country where God in Christ is not known, or where the light of revelation is grown faint, or where law and civlization have little influence, and you will see a modified picture of the old world. True it is that external circumstances may vary the wickedness of man, but as its nature changes not, excess may follow upon the removal of any restraint. There is always wickedness enough among the wicked of every place, to throw all things into dreadful disorder, were God at any time to withdraw his check. Our country, and our city too, saw this only a few years ago. A popular outbreak, a rush upon sacred institutions, a shout for infidelity, or a declaration for Popery, are things easy to be done any day, because there is wickedness enough among us for them, if God in judgment cease to restrain that wickedness.

5. It is added in this part of our text, that this wickedness of man was great "*in the earth;*" that is, it was not confined to any particular district, or any singular locality, but was general, extending to the entire population of the globe. What the amount of that population was many have presumed to guess, but none can possibly tell. It is one of the secrets which we may well be content to leave. This however we know, that "the earth was filled with violence;" that the godly were gradually removed from it, till at last one family alone was left to be a witness on God's side, and to serve as seed for the planting of a new world. Such then was the state of the human race when God came to inspect it. He saw the outward condition of man; and he also saw what was the cause of it, the *inward* condition. Let us then next contemplate

II. *The prolific cause of the wickedness of man on the earth.* It was the evil state of his heart: for "God saw that every imagination of the thoughts of his heart was only evil continually." Here again, every word in the fearful declaration is most emphatic. Only see to them:

1. We hear of the "*heart*": and that is spoken of as the fountain to which all wickedness is to be traced: for, being itself altogether evil, no good thing can proceed from it.

But, according to the figurative style of the Hebrew tongue, the heart is here regarded as a weaver's workshop. It is the place in which thoughts and imaginings are fabricated. It is the seat of all desire, and the nursery of all motives. As a workshop it is a dark and loathsome apartment. Something bad is always going on in it. Even the proprietor is never fully aware of the evil things which are hidden in it, and of the hiding places which it contains for those evil things. "The heart is deceitful above all things, and desperately wicked." God alone can thoroughly search this dark and deceitful heart. It is one of his peculiar offices so to do. And, verily, he *does* search it. He saw it before the flood, and has seen everything in it ever since. And what did he see?

2. He saw "*the thoughts*," the *motives* to action, the *purposes* of life, and the *intentions* of man. The heart is the great loom in which these are woven, or the weaver himself who fabricates them: for, properly speaking, the word translated "thoughts" signifies "the textures formed by the art of a weaver." Hence, figuratively, they mean meditations, or a series of thoughts. And, alas! in this series there is no intermixture of holy threads; the warp and the woof are alike entirely bad. The heart weaves wickedness from morning to night, and even in our dreams it fabricates its gossamer of iniquity.

3. But, to add force to no slight intensity of description, the sacred historian is prompted to employ even an extra word; he says the "*imagination* of the thoughts," that is, as the word means, the very *moulding* or *forming* of the thoughts. That too is evil, somewhat like man himself: he is not only sinful as being born in sin, but he was sinful even before his birth! "Behold, I was shapen in iniquity and in sin did my mother conceive me." (Psalm 51:5.)

So this *shaping* of the thoughts, this *imaging* of them, this *moulding* of them, in the heart, is itself an evil process. And, lest any admirer of "the dignity of human nature" (as it is vainly called) should raise an objection, and say that the historian does not mean any thing so sweeping as that all the thoughts of our hearts are evil, but only in general they are too much so—the sacred historian does positively say, "*every* imagination of the thoughts of his heart are only evil continually."

4. Hence there is no limitation; and vain man has no escape from the grasp of that truth which tells him of his real state, and his real self. It is a truth which the godly alone admit, because they are taught to see it in God's word, and to *feel* it in themselves. They see and feel that of their own nature they are inclined only to "*evil*," and that, even after their hearts have been savingly renewed, not one thought of the most eminent saint among them can bear the divine scrutiny. Some mixture of imperfection or evil will always be found in their best thoughts.

5. Nor must we omit to point out to you the *gradation* of which we read in this account of our evil hearts. The imagination of their thoughts is more than evil, it is "*only* evil." It is more, too, than "*only* evil," for it is evil "*continually*." Where then is there room for fond objection? There is none. The self-flatterer may say, "If it be of necessity allowed, that there is *some evil* mixed with the imaginations of the thoughts, there may be *some good* to qualify that evil." No; such a plea is at once silenced. The voice of inspiration declares the imaging or shaping of the thoughts to be "*only* evil." "But, perhaps (as it may be soothingly whispered) this is the case only *occasionally*, when temptation rises into fury, and corruption is lashed into a storm." No; this plea also is quickly silenced. The infallible judge says, "It is only evil *continually*." Brethren, this you will say is a dark picture. Be assured it is none of my painting. The portrait was drawn before the deluge, and has been drawn again and again by inspired hands since that tremendous event. If you are therefore disposed to think that such an awful description of the human heart is to be confined to the world before the flood, I must remind you of what has already been alluded to, that the word "*man*," in the text, stands for *human nature*. There can be no doubt of that. Now human nature is the same in all ages and in all climes. Circumstances may alter or bias its operations, but they cannot change itself. The grace of God imparts a new nature, but the infection of the old man "doth remain even in them which are regenerate." Meditate on Genesis 8:21; Psalm 51; Psalm 53:1, 2, 3; Romans 3:10–12, and you will discern the same descriptive hand at work after the deluge as before it. As to copies from the original, you will find none more true, nor any depicted in stronger colours, than in the Homilies of our own church. Even in our daily formularies there are expressions which little suit the taste of those who know not "the plague of their own heart." "There is *no health* in us," sounds awkwardly from persons who feel not that they are spiritually sick: and, "Have mercy upon us *miserable* sinners," comes strangely from the lips of the wanton or wicked in heart. But, to the truth, whatever men may imagine or say, their character, as seen by God, is described in our text. From our contemplation of that text, let us come to a profitable inference or two.

1. *How great necessity was there for redemption by Christ*! Man's depravity was as great as it could be: and God's justice was righteously inexorable. By sin we became as unwilling to love God, as we were unable to propitiate him. With such a constantly evil heart as ours we could devise nothing, we could do nothing. There was *need*, therefore, for some mighty and generous helper to interpose. Otherwise the evil heart must have remained evil for ever, and all the terrors of the divine justice must then for ever have consumed it.

2. *How inestimably precious ought Christ to be to us!* He hath done for us all that our sin rendered necessary. He allowed his own heart to be pierced, that the evil of ours might be repaired. The blood of that heart was shed for the provision of a laver in which all the defilement of our thoughts, and all the unclean recesses of the hearts which orginate them, may be washed and purified. His atoning death, and his sanctifying Spirit leave us in want of nothing but faith to apply them, and love to be grateful for them. And faith he will give if we ask it;

and love he will shed abroad if we cleave to him, and walk with him, and pray to him.

3. *How self-abased should we be, and how constantly seek for renewing grace!* No man who views himself in the glass of God's word, will entertain a particle of admiration of himself. He will soon say as Job said, "Behold, I am vile: I abhor myself." He will, if honest with himself, always discover enough evil in his breast to make him ashamed, and to keep him humble. Instead of "laying any flattering unction to his soul," he will rather bemoan himself with Ephraim, and be lowly in his own eyes. Nor will he omit to seek the daily renewal of his heart: for he will find that it is not to be trusted, and that, on this side the grave, it is never cleansed so perfectly as he wishes. He still finds that, when he would do good, evil is present with him, and that nothing but the Saviour's grace can keep him pure, or uphold him from falling. He is not therefore one of those who substitute external acts for internal operations,—"the putting away of the filth of the flesh, for the answer of a good conscience towards God." He trusts not in the ceremony, but anxiously looks for the grace which faith finds in it. He knows that the dislodgment of evil from his heart is the work of his life: and as he lives by faith, so does he pray that God will purify his heart by faith. He loves that prayer of our Church, "Cleanse the thoughts of our heart by the inspiration of thy holy Spirit." He prays for that cleansing, because he knows that the absence of it in man is the cause of all crime, disorder, and misery.

Then seek it, dear brethren; and may you carry to your homes this evening those views respecting it which will give energy to your search for it, and to your praise of Him who is the author of it.

SERMON VII.

THE RAINBOW AND THE EVERLASTING COVENANT.[1]

GENESIS 9:16.

"And the bow shall be in the cloud; and I will look upon it, that I may remember the everlasting covenant between God and every living creature of all flesh that is upon the earth."

JEHOVAH has ever shown himself to be "the Father of mercies, and the God of all comfort." He always has seasonably manifested himself to his people, and has never suffered them, when faint or feeble, to be destitute of support or encouragement.

When Noah came forth from the ark, nothing but desolation met his eye. It is therefore probable that much sadness occupied his heart. His position on the wild and lofty peaks of Ararat, in the centre of a lonely world, must have been a trial for the strongest faith and the firmest nerve. At this juncture God revealed himself to him in a manner which must have greatly consoled and strengthened him. By voluntarily making a covenant with him, and exhibiting a beauteous and commanding token of it, Jehovah both healed his sorrows for the past, and banished his fears for the future. The entire narrative has been read to you; and now your attention is called to the closer consideration of it. May the God of Noah teach us rightly to understand his own doings! Let us consider

I. *The covenant which God made with Noah, and the rainbow which he constituted the token of it.*

1. The covenant itself is *a temporal covenant.* It is to last only for a time, and it respects only temporal objects. Those objects are the preservation of the life of man and beast from

[1] Preached Sunday Morning, February 18th, 1849.

at least another general deluge, and the regular succession of seed-time and harvest, summer and winter, night and day, to the end of the world.

2. The covenant is also *general.* It is not special to individuals or localities, but broad and comprehensive to men and things, as a whole. Hence the covenant is not intended to be a security against the death of individuals by flood or famine, but only against that of all mankind at once.

3. The covenant includes *unconscious infants* as well as intelligent adults. It even embraces, and that in a very large proportion, irrational creatures.

"And I, behold, I establish my covenant with you, and with your seed after you; and with every living creature that is with you, of the fowl, of the cattle, and of every beast of the earth with you; from all that go out of the ark, to every beast of the earth. And I will establish my covenant with you; neither shall all flesh be cut off any more by the waters of a flood; neither shall there any more be a flood to destroy the earth." (Genesis 9:9–11.)

Thus then, not only did God extend his covenant to those who could hear and understand and believe it, but also to such of the seed of Noah as were unconscious of it, and so had no power to believe it. Infants were destroyed by the curse of the deluge, and now they are to be preserved by the blessing of the covenant. Their parents represent themselves; and thus they share in all the bounties of the covenant which God makes with those parents. It was thus in after times when God made a covenant with Abraham. His children inherited, as children, all the promises of it; and never has the procedure been annulled or altered up to this day. These remarks are for the strengthening of our satisfaction in bringing our children to holy baptism.

4. This covenant is *not to be considered in itself as "the covenant of grace,"* but as an appendage to it. "The covenant of grace," on which eternal life depends, was spoken of to Noah long before the flood. In the sixth chapter it is said, "Noah found *grace* in the eyes of the Lord." And God said to him, "With thee will I establish my covenant." It was this covenant which secured to Noah all his privileges as a believer in the promised "seed of the woman;" and the manifestation of it to him was like another ray of the spiritual dawn which broke on the world, and which gradually expanded itself into the perfect day of Christ. It was therefore, on this former covenant, renewed with Noah before the flood, that the covenant after it was grafted. This after-covenant, having respect only to temporal mercies, was dependent on the original or eternal covenant, which primarily had regard to spiritual benefits. Never did a temporal mercy reach us but through a spiritual channel. Had not God made a covenant with Christ, to save believers "from curse and damnation," the world would never have been insured from universal famine and watery desolation. But for God's covenant to save them in Christ, not one of the rest would be spared for an hour. "All the blessings of this life" fall into their cup, only because they are mixed up with those for whom God has covenanted eternal life.

5. The covenant with Noah *did not originate with Noah.* It was not his suggestion, neither did he in any way make preparation for it. It was wholly of the Lord: his wisdom devised it, and his love freely gave it. "Behold," said he, "I establish my covenant with you." Christians should always carefully and gratefully mark such facts. To overlook them is a sad sign of spiritual dulness, and brings down upon us the apostolic rebuke, "Some have not the knowledge of God: I speak this to your shame."

6. This covenant with Noah is expressly referred to by Jehovah, *as a token of the stability of that better covenant by which the church of Christ is upheld and saved.*

When God comforted his church in the days of Isaiah, and so prospectively comforted us as faithful members of it, he said thus: "In a little wrath I hid my face from thee for a moment; but with everlasting kindness will I have mercy on thee, saith the Lord thy Redeemer. For this is as the waters of Noah unto me: for, as I have sworn that the waters of Noah should no more go over the earth, so have I sworn that I would not be wroth with thee nor rebuke thee. For the mountains shall depart, and the hills be removed; but my kindness shall not depart from thee, neither shall the covenant of my peace be removed, saith the Lord that hath mercy on thee." (Isaiah 54:8–10.)

Here then we come to see the importance of the covenant to which the text of this discourse leads our thoughts. It is a grand and striking event for the finger of faith to point to, when all things lower and threaten in our spiritual horizon. He who has never yet forgotten the covenant with Noah, will surely never forget that which he made for us with Christ!

7. The *token, sign, or seal of this covenant* is one of the grandest and most beautiful objects on which the eye of man ever rests. It is God's bow, meaning the rainbow, and is called his bow both because he alone can form it, and because he has appointed it for a special intention.

We are apt to talk of there being rain because our almanacs prognosticate it, and our barometers indicate it; but it is God who really gives impulse to all second causes. Hear what he says in verse 14: "And it shall come to pass, when I bring a cloud over the earth, that the bow shall be seen in the cloud."

No cloud comes charged with rain without the hand of God to bring it. Nor does a drop of spiritual dew fall on his church apart from his sending.

In the 13th verse God says, "I do set my bow in the cloud." From this, and from what is previously said just after the creation about the ascending of a mist from the earth to water the whole face of the ground, it has been inferred that, previously to the deluge, there was no rain; and consequently, that no rainbow had ever been seen till the date of this covenant with Noah. Such a conclusion has no certainty in it; for God, in saying, "I do set my bow in the cloud," may intend us to understand, not that he then, for the first time, caused the bow to appear, but that he gave to its appearance a new purpose, constituting, what it had not been before, the visible token of an additional covenant.

The time *when*, and the place *where* God's bow is visible, deserve our notice. It can only be formed when it rains in one quarter and shines in another. When the clouds darken, and the showers thicken, then comes the sun and lightens up the beauteous bow of promise. Thus its appearance is seasonable and opportune; and thus God deals with his people in their afflictions and griefs. When those afflictions are thickest, the light of his comfort is brightest. Without them, half the beauty of the gospel would be undiscovered by us. Then, where is the bow to be seen but in the upward sky? And where should it be seen except where our happiness lies, and whither our hearts ought to ascend?

The notice also, which God himself takes of the bow, should not be unnoticed by us. He says in our text, "I *will look* upon it, that I may *remember* the everlasting covenant." This is God's language brought down to man's capacity. We are sure that the omniscient God stands in no need of anything to remind him of pledge or promise made by him. We must conclude therefore, that this condescending language is entirely for our sakes. While it invites us to commune with Jehovah as a father and a friend, it admonishes us especially of two things: the first is, that when God establishes a sacramental sign, and gives visible pledges, such as the rainbow is, he does not fail to regard them, but graciously binds himself by them. The second thing is that, if God does thus, we ought correspondingly to do likewise. The visible signs and seals of his covenant should quicken us more earnestly to believe the covenant itself, and more carefully to conform our whole conversation to it. These are the true lessons which we should learn, as often as we see water in that font, or bread and wine on this table. If we religiously bore these things in mind, we should oftener think of other things than the magnificent span, and the brilliant colouring, and the generally interesting character of the rainbow, when we happen to be in a position favourable for viewing it. Jews of old say, some of their doctors used never to see a rainbow without lifting up their hands, and blessing the God of Noah and Israel. Certainly a devout Christian cannot look on that bow without thinking that God is looking on it too. The sight therefore is one of solemnity as well as of beauty. This feeling will increase upon us by considering, next,

II. *The rainbow as a symbol of that "better covenant" by which the spiritual salvation of all true believers is secured.*

1. This "better covenant" *was framed before the world began.* It was the covenant of the Godhead with the eternal Son to become man, and to save from destruction a seed which should be given to him. It comprised every other covenant which, in the course of time, was made with individuals or people, and embraced the greatest and the minutest mercy which ever came down to man.

2. That the rainbow is, to this day, a symbol of this better covenant, we gather for certain from the vision of John the Divine. He first saw "a rainbow round about the *throne*" (Revelation 4:3); and afterwards, when he beheld the great Angel of the covenant, he saw that "a rainbow was upon *his head*" (Revelation 10:1). So that the beauteous symbol is traced from the days of Noah all through the times of the law, and the dispensation of the gospel, to the fulness of heaven and the scenes of eternity.

3. Here it is fitting to remark to you that the *bow*, as used among men, is an instrument and a symbol of *war*; but the *rainbow* is eminently a token of *peace*. God's bow, when suspended in the heavens, is a bow without either string or arrow. It, therefore, is not intended for war, but altogether for peace. It is God's picture of the gospel, hung up in the heavens to cheer the heart of his contrite ones on earth. It is in fact a representation to the eye of what the song of the angels at Bethlehem was to the ear. The declaration of both is the same, namely, "Peace on earth, good will towards men." It may not be inopportune to mention that even among barbaric nations a bow well strung, and a bow unstrung, were anciently the heraldic symbols of war and peace. In the Cambrian Antiquities it is stated that such bows were sent round the country, as proclamations of war or peace, according to the circumstances of the case.

The representation of "a rainbow *round about the throne*," as seen by St. John, indicates that he who sits upon that throne is a reconciled God, a God at peace with penitent sinners. And, because "a rainbow was *upon the head*" of Jesus, he is thereby marked out as the divine and glorified reconciler of such, yea, "the Prince of Peace," the Mediator of "the covenant of peace."

4. The rainbow, we familiarly know, is composed of several colours so harmoniously blended as to be at once perfectly distinct, and yet *not divided.* Thus, in the covenant of grace, the divine perfections, which seemed opposed to the salvation of rebel man, are united in wonderful harmony. "Mercy and truth meet together; righteousness and peace kiss each other." Like too the bow in Noah's day, this brighter bow is *all of God.* As Noah did not suggest the one, so did neither man nor angel devise the other.

5. During our sojourn on earth our sight of God's "bow in the cloud" is attended with certain imperfections. For instance, viewed from the earth, the full orb of the bow is never seen. It is beheld only in part. But in heaven the entire bow is seen round about both the throne and the head of Christ. Thus, on earth, we see and know the covenant of our peace only in part. Our highest attainments in the things of God are but the halves of what they will be, when we shall see Jesus as he is, and the throne on which he sits.

We also well know that we do not see a rainbow every day; nor do we always see it so vividly at one time as at another. Such facts may well certify us of the deficiency and imperfection of our present state. We often, as the saints of the Most High, fail to realize eternal things, or to enjoy bright views of the covenant of our redemption. In the land of glory, however, the rainbow will be stationary. It will never remove from the throne, nor vanish from the eye which sees it on the head of Jesus. Moreover, there shall be no *cloud* then. Sorrow and sighing will be gone, and the light of the Lamb will alone remain.

The subject must not end without admonition.

I. Let it be borne in mind that *it is one thing to hear these interesting truths, but quite another to be suitably affected by them.* Ere Noah and his compact family came down from the top of Ararat, there was one wicked person at least who heard all that Jehovah said about the rainbow; and yet that wicked man was not a whit the better for what he heard. Noah's own son, Ham, cherished an unsanctified heart, even when blessed with the protection of the ark. Jehovah's words therefore fell without effect on his ear, and the rainbow gave no hallowed pleasure to his eye. Then take heed lest there be "an evil heart of unbelief" in any of you. If, like Ham, you harden your soul under the gospel, as he did at his father's altar, and under Jehovah's word, judgment will overtake you as it overtook him. God will string his bow, and shoot his arrow at you. Be warned then, and remember that, though the earth will not again be destroyed by water, it will be burnt up with fire, when "all the wicked shall be turned into hell with all the people that forget God."

2. *Let no man say, "Peace, peace, when there is no peace."* The rainbow is so strikingly beautiful that thousands admire it without thinking of him who looks upon it, or that they can be saved only by what it represents. Thus the gospel has its attractions; and many see its beauties, and hear its glorious truths, and even admire and assent to them, without deriving any saving benefit from them. They see the bow, and in a certain way welcome its peace; but they never receive it in a broken and sanctified heart. The consequence is that, after all, they have no true peace. The name contents them, and they delude themselves by it. Then awake; search and try your ways, and know that there is no peace without repentance, and the pardon of the great Peace-maker.

3. *Let the spiritual seed of Noah rejoice in their covenant.* It was made for their joy. It was all David's "salvation and desire," and it should be theirs. They will find in it abundant consolation and good hope through grace.

Yes, ye afflicted ones, the bow of peace is your solace. And your babes, bereaved ones, your unconscious infants are saved by it. Soon you will see it, as John saw it. Amen!

SERMON VIII.

THE CALL OF ABRAM AND HIS OBEDIENT DEPARTURE FOR CANAAN.[1]

GENESIS 12:4, 5.

"So Abram departed, as the Lord had spoken unto him; and Lot went with him: and Abram was seventy and five years old when he departed out of Haran. And Abram took Sarai his wife, and Lot his brother's son, and all their substance that they had gathered, and the souls that they had gotten in Haran; and they went forth to go into the land of Canaan; and into the land of Canaan they came."

[1] Preached Sunday Evening, February 22nd, 1846.

THE origin of great things is generally regarded with great interest.

The call of Abram is a very important circumstance in the history of the church. It was the beginning of a new order of things. It was the setting apart of a family to receive and transmit to succeeding ages the saving truth of God. The circumstances therefore of Abram's separation from the world, and of his call to be the founder of the after church, cannot fail of being interesting to all the true members of that church. May the consideration of them, at this time, be made profitable to us.

Sundry points await our notice: let us consider

I. *The position in which Abram originally was, and the character of God's call to him.* The family of Abram had settled in Ur of Chaldea. All the surrounding population were idolaters; and there were idols even in his father's house. It is probable therefore, that the relatives of Abram followed idols, and lived as the world lived. Himself therefore was likely to be infected with the prevailing spirit.

In this position God communicated his will to him. How that communication was made we are not told. All we know is, that "the Lord had said unto Abram, Get thee out of thy country, and from thy kindred, and from thy father's house, unto a land that I will shew thee." Now the command here given was singularly trying. There were gradations too, or steps, in that trial; each one increasing the intensity of it as they advanced. Notice them. 1. "*Get thee out:*" implying that he was in a place of danger. "And Lot went out, and spake unto his sons in law, which married his daughters, and said, Up, get you out of this place, for the Lord will destroy this city: but he seemed as one that mocked unto his sons in law." (Genesis 19:14.) 2. "From thy *country.*" 3. "From thy *kindred.*" 4. "From thy *father's* house." 5. "Unto a land which I will *shew* thee," that is, a strange land, an unknown land, one too which he should only see and examine, and yet not possess. "By faith Abraham, when he was called to go out into a place which he should after receive for an inheritance, obeyed, and he went out, *not knowing* whither he went." (Hebrews 11:8.)

Thus Abram was commanded to give up everything and forsake all. Surely this was *trying.* And it is so still; for *our* position resembles Abram's; and God's call to *us* is essentially the same. "Wherefore come out from among them, and be ye separate, saith the Lord, and touch not the unclean thing: and I will receive you." (2 Corinthians 6:17.) Let us now observe

II. *The obedience of Abram, and the principle from which it proceeded.* "So Abram departed as the Lord had spoken unto him." It is certain that Abram was willing to leave both his country and his kindred. But, because of this willingness, God graciously mitigated the pain of leaving them: for it is evident that, when Abram had decided on leaving his kindred, God inclined some of the dearest of them to accompany him. His father Terah[1] joined him in his singular emigration, and Lot, his brother's son, went with them. As attendants on them, many a valued servant doubtless followed. Such companionship must have been a great alleviation to Abram as he passed the borders of his native land. Thus we may feel assured that, when we are willing to bear our trials, God will devise means for the mitigation of them. After their departure from Ur, they halted half way between Chaldea and Canaan, and called the place of their halting Haran, or, as St. Stephen properly names it, Charran, in memory of the deceased brother, who had died at their native Ur. At this Haran they stayed, it is probable, a considerable time. There Terah died. At length, as we shall soon see, Abram set out again in right earnest for the land of Canaan.

But let us briefly revert to Ur in Chaldea. Abram *obeyed* the call of the true God. In doing this how likely was he to encounter ridicule and opposition. Those who had no power to thwart his resolves would, in all probability, either openly misrepresent it, or secretly scoff at it. And what is this but a picture of the lot of those, who in the spirit of Abraham renounce the friendship of the world for the service of Christ? If persecution has no license to check them, taunt and sarcasm will use many an expedient to discomfort them. The language in which the call of Abram is described, though simple, is forcible, and in many respects remarkable. "*So* Abram departed, *as* the Lord had spoken unto him." It implies great submission and ready compliance. "*So* Abram departed,"—"*so,*" just like a child, a good and dutiful child,—"*so,*" without *murmuring* or *questioning.* Just too "*as*" God said, so he acted. He obeyed fully, entirely, truly: he made no exceptions to the command, but followed it out manfully.

This was worthy of the grace of God in him who was selected to be "the father of the faithful," and a pattern for all ages. But whence was this? how do we account for it? Great and precious promises, brethren, were made to him. These promises *he believed:* "And I will make of thee a great nation, and I will bless thee and make thy name great; and thou shalt be a blessing: and I will bless them that bless thee, and curse him that curseth thee: and in thee shall all families of the earth be blessed." (Ver. 2, 3.) Let it be well observed, the pith of God's promises to him was *the gospel:* "In *thee* shall all families of the earth be blessed." Here was a revealing of Christ, and of all blessings through him.

[1] In Genesis 11:31, Terah is represented not as the follower, but the leader of Abram. "And Terah *took* Abram his son and went." This, however, must be regarded as the language of reverence for parental age and authority. It is probable that the compliance of Terah was consequent on the conversion of Abram, and that when Terah had determined on accompanying his son, the ostensible leadership was dutifully transferred from the son to the father.

Thus our God deals with us, and thus we should act towards him. He *calls*, and we should *obey*. He *promises*, and we should *believe*. But no obedience, no resignation, is genuine, except that which springs from divine faith in divine promises. And how many and blessed are they! And how wise and good is our God! You see, when he gave Abram a command, he attached a promise to it. This is what he has done for us in every part of his gospel.

But here let it also be observed, as with Abram so with us, our calling and our faith to obey that call are both equally of God. "For by grace are ye saved through faith, and that not of yourselves: it is the gift of God." (Ephesians 2:8.)

And then, why was Abram called, and not his brother Nahor? The reply should be as frank as it must be humiliating: "Even so, Father, for so it seemed good in thy sight." "He doeth according to his will, in the army of heaven, and among the inhabitants of the earth." "He putteth down one, and setteth up another." The great practical end is, for us to acknowledge that "all is of God." (Ephesians 2:9.)—Let us also mark,

III. *The blessings which Abram attained in obeying God.* He and all his "went forth to go into the land of Canaan, and into the land of Canaan they came."

The man of faith realised all that he believed and expected. He was conducted on his journey safely, and arrived at the end of it surely. But wherever he went, he carried his religion with him; for, as the subsequent verses certify us, at every resting place "he built an altar unto the Lord who appeared unto him." Thus he was kept and comforted wherever he was. And though he tarried half way, a little too long at Haran, yet he was not suffered to stay altogether too long. Mercy helped him, and urged him, and never forsook him. "Into the land of Canaan they came." And, when there, Jehovah again visited him, and said, "*Unto thy seed will I give this land.*"

While he lived he enjoyed as much of the land as sufficed for a sojourner; for he became a great and wealthy man. And when he died, his bones were laid in it, as a pledge that his posterity should possess it. As during his life "he looked for a city which hath foundations," so, at the end that life, did he ascend to the true Canaan, and enter the eternal city of the living God.

Thus, dear brethren, it still is, that "godliness is profitable for all things, having the promise of the life which now is and that which is to come." And Jesus has promised: "There is no man that hath left house, or brethren, or sisters, or father, or mother, or wife, or children, or lands, for my sake, and the gospel's, but he shall receive an hundred-fold now in this time, houses, and brethren, and sisters, and mothers, and children, and lands, with persecutions; and in the world to come eternal life." (Mark 10:29, 30.)

During the life that now is, God will sustain his pilgrims, and keep them as the apple of his eye. At the end of it, when to Canaan they come, he will give them "an inheritance incorruptible, undefiled, and that fadeth not away."

But remember you must not halt. Wherever you are, you must not be ashamed to confess your Saviour, and take care not to go where you cannot consistently confess him.—Observe again,

IV. *The privileges which they enjoyed who accompanied Abram.* His household, we perceive, consisted of relatives and servants. Lot, as Abram's nephew, the only one with him, must have been peculiarly favoured. The society of such an uncle, in the prime and vigour of life, must have been no mean privilege. Most likely it was a time of saving health to the nephew, and the means of producing in him that genuine religion which, in after days, preserved him in Sodom. Let then younger relatives set a high value upon older friends who love and fear the Lord. Let them listen to their kindly cautions and admonitions, and not think it grievous to be checked by wise authority amidst evils and dangers.

Abram's servants too were a highly privileged company. There were many of them, not less than three hundred and eighteen, as we learn from Genesis 14:14.

Now these servants must have enjoyed many mercies which their fellows knew not in Chaldea. Themselves too might have been left behind, and so have lived and died in idolatry. But themselves were favoured with bright opportunities: they had the example of Abram, the sacrificial altar, holy teaching, and a well ordered family, in which religion was the rule of all things: "For I know him, that he will command his children and his household after him, and they shall keep the way of the Lord, to do justice and judgment, that the Lord may bring upon Abraham that which he has spoken of him." (Genesis 18:19.)

Then, ye servants, be assured that to live in such a family is your greatest benefit, and your best portion. Let your conduct be in accordance. Be not given to change. Especially avoid evil companions on a Sunday, and those habits by which, when you waste its precious hours, you rob your own souls.

The practical sum of the discourse is,

1. *That God calls you.* He calls you from sin to himself, and *promises* you all blessedness. What if you refuse to obey?

2. *That believers are a blessing to all around them.* Abram was such while he lived, and to this day we are blessed through him. Then value and aid the good.

But *what* of unbelievers? They have no blessedness in themselves, and therefore cannot become blessings to others. They are the brambles of society. True believers alone are its fragrant and nutritious plants.

3. That a land of life awaits the righteous. "To Canaan they came." The promise of Canaan was in a type the promise of heaven. Not more surely did Abram reach the one, than shall all his spiritual seed reach the other. As Abram took possession of the temporal Canaan for his posterity, so has Christ, as our forerunner, entered heaven to prepare a place in it for all his people. Thither, in his own due time, each one of them shall come.

SERMON IX.

JEHOVAH THE PRESENT SHIELD AND EVERLASTING REWARD OF HIS PEOPLE.[1]

Genesis 15:1.

"After these things the word of the Lord came unto Abram in a vision, saying, Fear not, Abram: I am thy shield, and thy exceeding great reward."

THE pen of inspiration has recorded more concerning Abram than concerning any other patriarch. That there should be a greater amplitude of detail in his case, as compared with other cases, is not surprising, seeing that Abraham is one of the larger links of that chain by which the world is kept together. He was "the father of the faithful," and "the friend of God." Take away such men from the earth, and the whole framework of society will soon fall to pieces.

The text introduces him to our notice at an early period of his religious history. He had returned from his sudden and successful expedition against the confederated kings who had captured Lot and all his household. He had been exposed to unusual excitement, and to no common peril; and now that he had laid aside his unwonted use of arms, he was dwelling in his peaceful tent on the plain of Mamre, where he worshipped Jehovah, and waited for the revelation of his will. "After these things the word of the Lord came unto Abram in a vision, saying, Fear not, Abram: I am thy shield, and thy exceeding great reward." The plan of the present discourse will be, first, to offer some remarks upon the time and manner in which God revealed himself to Abram, and then to consider the import of the revelation itself which God made to Abram. I proceed,

I. *To offer some remarks upon the time and manner in which God revealed himself to Abram.*

In meditating upon "the lively oracles," we should be fully persuaded that every word is precious, and that even minute incidents are charged with valuable instruction. By diligent study we may learn much from the brief hints and passing remarks of the sacred historians. Those hints are like the smaller avenues of a mine which, if diligently explored, lead to the choicest ore. The Spirit too who spake by those historians is a Spirit of wisdom; and often has he invited our search by concealing the richest treasure in the most unlikely parts of the mine.

The text opens by saying *"After these things the word of the Lord came to Abram in a vision."—"After these things;"* that is, *after* the event, recorded in the preceding chapter—*after* Abram had subdued the marauder kings—*after* he had received the blessing of Melchizedek—*after* he had refused the offer of goods from the king of Sodom—*after* a season of considerable agitation and interruption, wherein both body and mind had been very severely exercised. At this juncture the Lord visited him with words of encouragement and consolation. The revelation which Jehovah made to him was, as will presently be noticed, most wisely and wonderfully adapted to his circumstances. It was mercy in season, and grace in time of need.

And thus does God, even to this day, frequently deal with his people. When, like Abram, they have endured extraordinary trials, or have exerted themselves for his honour—or, by renouncing some offer of the world, have magnified his grace, then will

[1] Preached Thursday Evening, January 8th, 1846.

he appear for their refreshment, and will manifest himself unto them as he does not unto the world. During the season of effort and trial the God of their hearts sustains and strengthens them; but when the trial is past, and the conflict ended, when in quietness we sit down to ponder and reflect upon all that we have gone through, then is it that our God chiefly imparts his consolations, and sends his encouragements. "Now no chastening for the present seemeth to be joyous, but grievous: nevertheless afterward it yieldeth the peaceable fruit of righteousness unto them which are exercised thereby." (Hebrews 12:11.)

It was precisely thus with our beloved Saviour when, as a man of sorrows, he submitted to trials and temptations. "Then the devil leaveth him, and, behold, angels came and ministered unto him." (Matthew 4:11.) These things teach us to be patient and persevering. In due time either our consolations will abound, or our acquiescence in the divine will will become more entire. The storm may be dark and terrific, but there will come the "clear shining *after* rain."

The *season* too, at which God thus visited Abram, induces the remark, that, in the *dispensations of his love the Lord usually reserves the brighter manifestations of himself till his people have attained some degree of maturity in the Christian life.*

About twelve or fourteen years had, it is thought, elapsed from the call of Abram to this special revelation. During this interval the patriarch had been growing in grace. He had not been without his trials, nor without those changes which are intended to school the heart. He had had opportunities of seeing human nature in its fallen state, as well as of studying the intimations of its recovery by a future Redeemer. He had been into Egypt, and had looked around him amid the risings of a mighty community.

Thus, after a series of hopes and fears, after ten years spent in separation from the spirit of the world and in the exercise of many duties, the Lord visited him in a more remarkable manner than he hitherto had done.

Hence our younger friends in the faith may expect that, as they advance in the divine life, walking holily and consistently, the Lord will enlarge their views of his goodness and truth, and by his Spirit animate and comfort them beyond their present experience. Well may they take courage therefore and press forward, minding present duties, and waiting on God. They must not shrink from difficulties, nor turn aside from irksome obligations, but trust that as their day is so their strength shall be, and that when God deems best their consolations will come.

"*The word of the Lord came to Abram.*" Some excellent divines interpret this expression as implying the personal appearance of Christ to the patriarch, understanding by "the word of the Lord" him who is called "the Word of the Father," "the angel or messenger of the covenant." Without doubt that Word, even Christ as the eternal Son, was the speaker; but there is no positive ground for concluding that, on this occasion, he assumed an incarnate shape. As the Word of the Father, he revealed the will of the Godhead: for "no man hath seen God at any time; the only begotten Son, which is in the bosom of the Father, he hath declared him." (John 1:18.) But revelations were frequently made to the early believers, without the assumption of a visible form by the adorable revealer. There probably was an indication of the divine presence, without the appearance of a personal form. Hence it is said that "the word of the Lord came unto Abram *in a vision*," not in a dream when asleep, but in a sort of ecstacy when fully awake. Either he beheld what the Jews call the Shechinah, a glory or brilliant light, filling an apartment or occupying a particular space, or he saw some other mystic token of the presence of Jehovah.

A short while before this vision the king of Sodom, with gifts in his hand and pomp in his train, had gone out to meet Abram; but now the King of kings, with his invisible retinue, comes to him. Melchizedek too, the priest of the Most High God, had given him his blessing; but now he receives the benediction of the true Melchizedek, even of the Most High himself. So truly may Abram, even at this period of his history, be called "the friend of God;" and so certainly may we conclude that they who honour God will be honoured by him.

It is remarkable that, although the patriarchs possessed, or seem to have possessed so little spiritual light, they nevertheless evinced the most fervent piety, and an enviable degree of religious devotion and heavenly-mindedness. The circumstance may perhaps be accounted for by *the manner* in which they received and retained the knowledge of the true salvation as the source of every privilege and the spring of every duty. They had not, be it recollected, any record of the divine will which they could with ease consult at any time. Memory, not reading, was their practical resource. Hence they were *constrained to be attentive*, and to recur continually to their mental storehouse for information and consolation.

From time to time they received also fresh communications from Jehovah; and those communications were generally made in a manner which was at once awful and imposing, as well as calculated to produce the deepest impression, and to excite the profoundest reverence. Moreover the time of the recurrence of a vision, or a dream, was to themselves wholly uncertain; and, as it was their grand privilege, and an event most likely of constant expectation, they would naturally wait for it with eager desire and serious preparation. For, in truth, the patriarchal believer could never tell when an angel of God, or even God himself, might meet him. He might be journeying alone, or going into the field to meditate at eventide, or retiring to his bed, when he would be likely to say to himself somewhat thus: "Perhaps on this journey, or during this meditation, or in the course of the night, the Lord God may call to me, or appear to me, or send his angel to me!" Surely such an expectation would greatly tend to foster a devout and hallowed frame of mind.

And verily, brethren, what is more conducive to spirituality of affection than earnest recollection of God's holy word, and fervent desire for communion with Christ, and devout preparation for it?

Let every hearer bear in mind that, although visions and revelations have ceased, the plain and infallible word of God is always with us, and may always be enjoyed. "The word is nigh, even in thy mouth and in thy heart, that is, the word of faith which we preach." (Romans 10:8.) And assuredly, if men believe not that word, neither would they believe were they to see visions and receive revelations. The principle of *saving* faith is in both cases the same. Do we then believe the word of him who hath spoken more clearly to us then he ever spake to Abraham? The Lord Jesus hath appeared, and hath spoken those things which Abraham longed to hear. Our peril is great if we reject his word of salvation, or turn a deaf ear to all his offers of mercy.

II. *Let us now consider the import of the revelation itself which God made to Abram:* "Fear not Abram: I am thy shield, and thy exceeding great reward."

These words comprise an encouraging injunction and a most consolatory promise.

1. The injunction is "*Fear not*, Abram." Now to see the fitness of such a command, we must recollect that Abram, by his success in the battle with the kings, had so signalized himself as to become the dread of one party and the envy of another. There was danger lest the vanquished party should rally and take revenge, and lest the king of Sodom should covet the wealth which a mere stranger had accumulated in his own territory. Abram therefore had considerable reason to *fear* an attack, or at least some attempt to plunder his property or injure his person. How *fitting*, then, and *suitable* was the word of Jehovah to him, "*Fear not*, Abram!"

A similar injunction was given to many individuals among the faithful posterity of the patriarch; till, at length, its authority and force have been augmented by those simple but animating words of our Lord, "Fear not, little flock, for it is your Father's good pleasure to give you the kingdom." And truly, how *necessary* is such an admonition at all times, and how *suitable* is it to individuals at special seasons! How necessary, because how many are our spiritual foes, how great their power, how clever their artifices! How suitable too, when the difficulties of the life of faith discourage us, and dangers and dark providences alarm us! Let no one however imagine that the divine bidding, "Fear not," is a ground for presumptuous confidence or careless conduct. In telling us not to fear, God does not tell us to cease to watch. He would have us know our enemies and our dangers, and gird ourselves for coping with them; but, at the same time, he would have us confide in himself, and be courageous because of his word. Obedience to the injunction will prepare us for a realization of the promise, which is

2. "*I am thy shield, and thy exceeding great reward.*"

This magnificent saying is composed so as to suit the present wants and the future expectations of every contrite believer. "I am (or I will be) thy shield." When this protective help was promised, Abram had a large household, and numerous flocks and herds. Around his tent, and within it also, was much valuable property, which an enemy would regard as desirable booty. Now all these things were not collected within a city, nor were they protected by walls or fortresses, nor even by any natural fastnesses; but they lay in a plain, in an open and shelterless country, and covered not by strong-walled houses but by fragile tents. What revelation then could be more *suitable* for Abram than that which Jehovah made, "*I* am thy *shield*"?

My brethren, the more we resemble Abram, as a man of holy faith, the more shall we need the divine protection. The world will hate us if we part hands with it, and the flesh and the devil will find darts enough to assail us at many an unsuspected opening. Besides we are of ourselves feeble and defenceless. Constantly therefore do we need the shield of the Lord of hosts to be held over us. And herein is our comfort,—God has *promised* to be *our* defence; for the promise in the text extends from Abram, the father, to all believers as children. "He shall cover thee with his feathers, and under his wings shalt thou trust: his truth shall be thy shield and buckler. Thou shalt not be afraid for the terror by night; nor for the arrow that flieth by day; nor for the pestilence that walketh in darkness; nor for the destruction that wasteth at noon-day. A thousand shall fall at thy side, and ten thousand at thy right hand; but it shall not come nigh thee." (Psalm 91:4–7.) If then the fiery darts of the wicked one are hurled against you, only cry to the God of Abram, and he will cover you with his favour as with a shield. No weapon which is formed against you can then prosper, because the shield of his love is invulnerable.

3. The other portion of the promise is vast indeed—"And thy exceeding great reward." Abram had nobly refused to receive any recompense from the king of Sodom. "And Abram said to the king of Sodom, I have lift up mine hand unto the Lord, the most high God, the possessor of heaven and earth, that I will not take from a thread even to a shoelatchet, and that I will not take anything that is thine, lest thou shouldest say, I have made Abram rich." (Genesis 14:22, 23.) He looked indeed for a better boon, and was not disappointed, for Jehovah soon after said to him, "*I* am thy shield and thy exceeding great reward."

This same Jehovah is still the portion of his people. In him, as revealed in Christ, is all their satisfaction. Everything else is but as the small dust of the balance. But, alas! long time it too often is, ere we are brought to this mind. We seek our portion in the creature, and find disappointment. We try pleasure, and it ends in sorrow. We ask the world for its reward, and it gives us vanity and vexation of spirit.

We can however appeal to the Christian, as a genuine son of Abram, whether it be not true that there are seasons in which every thing temporal appears in its own proper littleness, and when nothing short of God in Christ can give the soul one particle of satisfaction?

The mention of a reward indirectly reminds the believer of his entire unworthiness; for it is a reward not of merit but of mercy. God imparts himself only to the soul which feels its own demerit. Not the self-sufficient therefore, but the self-abased, receive him as their "reward."

This reward is described as being "*exceeding great.*" Such it must necessarily be; for our God is infinite; and, if he gives us himself, what greater possession can he bestow? But here all language fails, because our reward is so great that the most capacious mind cannot comprehend the half of it, nor will eternity itself diminish or impair it. But the grand point does not consist in defining the extent of the reward, but in ascertaining how it may be possessed, and whether we are likely to possess it. Are you then anxious on this point? Your anxiety will find every relief, if you only mark the character of Abram, and copy it. He believed the word of the Lord, and obeyed his call. He renounced the world, and sought earnestly that better portion, which is now set before *you* in the gospel of Christ. Do likewise, and the "exceeding great reward" will be yours.

In conclusion, suffer me to retouch a topic already set before you. It is,

1. *The gracious wisdom of God in adapting his word to our wants.* It was stated that in what God said to Abram there was a remarkable *suitableness.* And truly in the unseen and untold movements of a Christian mind, how frequently does it occur, that a sentence of the Bible is applied to the heart with all the freshness and fitness of an original revelation? We may have read the passage many times, but we never before saw in it that which now exactly suits our case.

Affliction too often brings to notice words which God has spoken, but which we have passed over. We stumble, as it were, upon them; and a prayerful and believing spirit finds in them a blessed and refreshing suitableness to our respective wants.

It may be that the text before us has come with great force and fitness to some heart in this congregation. Some downcast and troubled soul may be feeling the value of a word in season. Then let your praise abound to the God who sent it.

All of us may very fitly take hold of the text, as one which, at the outstep of a new year, will prove a staff and a lamp as we pass through it. A trackless path is before us. Foes and afflictions are lying in ambush about it.—"After these things the word of the Lord came unto Abram, in a vision, saying, Fear not, Abram: I am thy shield, and thy exceeding great reward."

2. *The pitiableness of their state who have not God for their shield and reward.* And all are in that state who have not the faith of Abram. Being destitute of protection they are the prey of *fear.* Without hope of reward, they are strangers to peace and joy. And then, when their attempted bravery is over, and their fear cometh, how terrible will that God be whom they have despised.

3. *The encouragements to our becoming the friends of God.* How evident and eminent are they! The blessedness of the patriarch is itself an invitation. God in Christ beseeches you to be reconciled. Everything connected with religion is intended to persuade men to love God and seek him for their shield and reward. Age is no obstacle; for Abram was seventy-five when he was called.

4. *The honour and happiness of the true Christian.* How little do all the great men of antiquity appear when contrasted with Abram! His intercourse with God made him the greatest man in the world. The like case is still extant, for "a Christian is the highest style of man."

When Abram had God for his "*shield,*" how contentedly could he emigrate; how peacefully repose at night, and how happily pass his hours at home! So now.

Anticipation too of his reward was always a feast for his thoughts. Then *believe* the promise: continue steadfast, and hope to the end.

SERMON X.

LOT ADMONISHED TO ESCAPE FOR HIS LIFE.[1]

GENESIS 19:17.

"And it came to pass, when they had brought them forth abroad, that he said, Escape for thy life; look not behind thee, neither stay thou in all the plain; escape to the mountain, lest thou be consumed."

IT has frequently been felt almost a wonder, that wicked men so little regard, and so soon forget, the judgments which they have witnessed. The real and the only solution of the wonder is this, sin hardens the heart, as well as destroys the soul.

Thus it was with the ungodly portion of mankind, very soon after the flood. When the posterity of Noah began to increase, they rapidly declined from the true God, and greedily practised those very sins for which the former world had been so terribly destroyed. In little more than four hundred years after that destruction, the inhabitants of Sodom and Gomorrah had become "wicked, and sinners before the Lord exceedingly." God therefore determined to destroy them with fire, as he had destroyed their predecessors in sin with water.

The preparations for this fiery destruction, and the manner of its accomplishment, have been read to us in the lesson from whence our text is taken. In the process both of preparation and accomplishment, one individual in Sodom is selected for signal exemption. Angels were sent to him. God's grace enabled him to follow them, while others of his family stayed behind. On the morning of the fatal day they brought him and part of his family outside the devoted city. The words of our text were then addressed to him, "Escape for thy life; look not behind thee, neither stay thou in all the plain; escape to the mountain, lest thou be consumed." Let us, first, attentively consider these words, and then apply them for our spiritual instruction and profit.

I. *The words of the narrative* invite our attentive consideration.

1. "And it came to pass when *they* had brought *them* forth abroad, that *he* said, Escape for *thy* life." We here instantly recognize a transition from the plural to the singular, both as regards the angels and the refugees. The transition is this, *they* (the angels) brought *them* (Lot and his wife and daughters) forth abroad, and then *he* (one angel only) said to *Lot* himself what he did say.

There is mystery in this; and yet, in our day, it is made plain to us.[2]

Of the three angels who went to Lot, one was far different to the other two. That one proved himself to be "The angel of the covenant." He was the Lord of angels: the other two were only his servants, though he condescended and they were commanded to appear as men. Hence, when all three had brought the family of the four out of the city, the one great speaker began to speak with authority. He addressed himself to Lot, as the head of his house; and through him the wife and the daughters were to hear.

We are but little competent to speculate upon the visible appearance of Christ, prior to his incarnation. But we know the fact: for, again and again, during the patriarchal and the earlier part of the Jewish dispensation, did he anticipate, as it were, his manhood, and appear as man to men. The fact is full of significance and comfort in the wondrous scheme of our redemption. It taught the early believers to look at what was coming; and it comforts us, in the retrospect, to see the constant mindfulness which the Redeemer entertained of the great work which he had engaged to carry out.

2. The words of the divine angel to Lot are stirring and admonitory. Let us take them in their separate parts.

i. "*Escape for thy life.*" Lot was not suffered to take his *goods* with him. His life was all that he was permitted to save. Why was this? It was for admonition and chastisement. It was to remind him that he once had lost his goods, when the four marauding kings, whom Abraham slew, had vanquished the king of Sodom, and taken Lot prisoner with every thing belonging to him. Upon Abraham's victory, Lot had all his goods restored to him. But instead of gladly and gratefully staying with Abraham, he went back again to Sodom. Here was Lot's second great fault; greater, too, than his former fault of separating from Abraham and settling in Sodom, *because it was his second.* Lot did not profit even by punishment. He had felt the smart of God's scourge, but he learnt nothing from it. As soon as the scourge ceased its blows, he returned to his folly. He went

[1] Preached Sunday Morning, March 9th, 1851.

[2] See note at end of Volume I of the Sermons, p. 127 of this book.

back to Sodom. Perhaps he listened to the entreaties of his wife and children, who fascinated with the gayeties of Sodom disliked the pious habits of Abraham, and the hallowed solemnities which they had seen pass between him and Melchizedek.

For this sin and folly, Lot is now to lose all his goods, his wife, and many of his children. Two only are left to him, and they for only further chastisement.

Alas, how little dare the children of God depend upon themselves! Lot was one of his children, but he is held up to us as a specimen of a weak and wayward child. He did not love sin in itself, but he did not resist it in others. He was easy and compliant, though inwardly vexed with the wickedness which was rampant around him.

Now therefore Lot must lose all but his life: and for that he must "*escape*." Judgment was close at his feet. He must hasten in flight to escape it, because, as the command implies, Lot was living where he ought not to have lived. His life was in danger from the locality in which he had chosen to lodge. To how many is this tacit reproof applicable in every community! Men place themselves in businesses, offices, or connexions, which they cannot carry on but at the peril of their souls. Their spiritual life is in danger, and their souls on the border of destruction. Let every professor take warning.

ii. "*Look not behind thee*." Whatever might have been the true reason for this injunction, it was Lot's duty to obey it. We are not to question, but to follow the divine commands. Perhaps, however, the injunction was meant as a moral test and practical trial. It would prove whether Lot really believed the divine threat, and whether his heart retained any hankering after what he had left behind. It might also have been for a check upon vain curiosity. We are to guard our eyes as well as our hearts.

iii. "*Neither stay thou in all the plain*." It would be easy to make an excuse for staying, but no excuse would be allowed. The plain was to become a sea, even "the dead sea," both from the many dead which it should cover, and from the extremely acrid character of its waters, which should be prejudicial to marine life, and to everything around it. If Lot staid at all in this plain, he might stay a minute too long, and so give time for some blast of the fiery tempest to overtake him. Here was mercy therefore mingled with the sternness of the commanded speed.

iv. "*Escape to the mountain lest thou be consumed*." Again Lot is bidden to haste; a spot is pointed out to him, and a motive is urged upon him. Thus have we need to be admonished again and again; for life is to be saved, and yet death is close upon us.

But when we hear the great angel saying, "Lest thou be consumed," we speedily ask, But could Lot, as a righteous man, have been consumed? The answer is as ready as our question: Lot *might and could* have been consumed, as a chastisement on the body, though God would have saved his soul. In times of peril from plague, fire, earthquake, or shipwreck, or in any such cases, the righteous have no patent of exemption. All such things (as Solomon was wont to say) "happen alike to all." But when the people of God place themselves in a forbidden position, and externally mix themselves up with the bands of the wicked, they may with them be consumed by temporal judgment, though themselves shall be saved in the day of judgment.

II. *The application of our text*, thus expounded, will tend to our instruction and profit, in some such manner as the following. Take a series of remarks:

1. That *a destruction, more terrible than that of Sodom and Gomorrah, is reserved for the ungodly*. It is called "the day of wrath;" "the day of perdition," the time of "destruction from the presence of the Lord." David spake of it: "Upon the wicked he shall rain snares, fire and brimstone, and an horrible tempest: this shall be the portion of their cup." (Psalm 11:6.) Malachi also speaks of it in his prophecy: "For, behold, the day cometh that shall burn as an oven; and all the proud, yea, and all that do wickedly, shall be stubble: and the day that cometh shall burn them up, saith the Lord of hosts, that it shall leave them neither root nor branch." (Malachi 4:1.) St. Peter, who had the deluge of Noah and the destruction of Sodom in his mind's eye, very graphically tells us of the character of that day: "The day of the Lord will come as a thief in the night; in the which the heavens shall pass away with a great noise, and the elements shall melt with fervent heat, the earth also and the works that are therein shall be burned up."—(2 Peter 3:10.)

Without question the chapter of Moses, now before us, was written for the warning of the world; and that, not only of God's power to punish any wicked city, at any time, but of his resolve to burn up the whole earth and everything which sin has tainted in it.

It is probable that all in Sodom were not equally wicked; and yet all perished alike. God, in the day of that vengeance, made no distinction between venial sin and mortal sin. It is only Antichrist who falsely contends for such distinction. Now also all sinners are not sinners of the same degree: but all sinners will perish alike, although their after stripes will be regulated by him who will be the judge of their many offences.

But let the whole truth be fearlessly told, though it may not be believed, and though he who tells it may seem as it is said of Lot, "like one that mocked."

There are those among the holiest, discreetest, and wisest of the church in its several ages, who are firmly and calmly of opinion that the fiery destruction of Sodom and Gomorrah was intended for a type of the destruction of that modern city which, in Revelation 11:8, is prophetically called Sodom, as well as Egypt and Babylon. In Isaiah 34:9, 10, we read the beginning of a terrible consuming of a certain locality. Respecting this description of the prophet, one of the best of our commentators sums up the opinions of his fellows, and says thus: "The metaphors are taken from Sodom and Gomorrah, if indeed they be metaphors: but probably they will be literally fulfilled; and Sodom will appear to have been another emblem of that devoted city—anti-christian Rome. Perhaps subterraneous fires will consume the seat of Antichrist, (indeed plentiful provision is evidently made in that part of the world for such an event,) and a continual burning and smoke in several places may perhaps mark out the place on which that city stood."—(Thos. Scott, *in loco.*) We cannot, we dare not, in these days, be ignorant of that burning of Babylon (which name the Pope himself is obliged to confess is a figure of Rome), and which burning, sudden, terrific and signal, is predicted in the 18th chapter of Revelation.

But let me next remark,

2. That, as God mercifully sent to apprize Lot of his danger, and to point out a place of refuge, *so does he warn us to flee from the wrath to come, and set before us the hope of salvation in the gospel.*

God's ministers are as God's angels, sent to different places and parishes, to utter the note of warning. We may not say of any particular spot, (except one in the world,) "Up, for the Lord will destroy *this place:*" but we are bound to say to you, "*Up*" from your sins, your vanities, your heartful lusts, and your foolish pleasures, or "the Lord will destroy" *you!* We are to say, "Escape for thy life!" for the injured and insulted law of God is aroused against you; death is let loose after you; and a day of judgment is fast coming upon you! But we say more: we tell you whither to escape; we preach Christ to you, as both the mountain of refuge for you, and the giver of all grace to enable you to reach it. As a mountain, he can lodge you far above the fiery inundation of the plain. There is a wide and a secure refuge in him not only for the little company who are called out of the world, but for the whole world itself. They alone however who escape to him will be saved.

Now mark the mercy which shines out in both the type and the antitype. Like Lot, we *deserve* destruction: but, lo! we are directed to a place of safe retreat. That place is like a mountain, it is *visible* to all; we cannot mistake it, if in earnest to reach it, for the way to it is well marked out.

How gracious, then, is our holy Saviour! He makes all plain to those who will see.

3. That, if we would save our souls, *we must cast away excuses, and make no delay.* Something, alas! worse than delay is rife among us. It is *unbelief.* There are many, as St. Peter foretold, who by lip or heart are saying, "*Where* is the promise of his coming? for, since the fathers fell asleep, all things continue as they were from the beginning of the creation."

Delay however in those who speak, and profess to think, differently, is a frequent source of ruin. Looking behind and staying in the plain is an every-day folly. It is a sign of that remaining love of the world, and that yet unaccomplished deliverance from the power of all sin, which leads so many to the hushings of conscience, and to those inexpedient compliances with the ways of the world, which have an inevitable tendency to deaden the soul. If we would be saved, we must eschew these things; we must be earnest and instant, or our professions go for nought, and our souls to perdition. Escape then, while you can! To-morrow may be too late.

And now that, on our sacramental Sunday, the table of the Lord is spread for us, let us look on its contents.

1. *As a memorial of him who is the mountain of our refuge.* He saw the impending tempest of wrath and fiery indignation, and interposed himself as a shield from its force, and a refuge from its reach. The Lord Jesus, by his death and passion, made infallible provisions for the salvation of all who come to him. None who escape to the mountain of his atonement fail of eternal life. But let us never forget what it cost him to raise up *that* mountain. Other mountains were formed at a word; but this was prepared by strong crying, and groans and tears, and with out-poured blood from wounds and death. Let the bread and the wine tell us of these things.

2. *As a token of spiritual communion between all those who have secured their escape to the true mountain.* Well is it for us often to look down upon what we have escaped, well too to look on one another as monuments of sparing mercy. Let love abound.

SERMON XI.

JACOB'S VISION OF THE LADDER.[1]

GENESIS 28:12.

"And he dreamed, and behold a ladder set upon the earth, and the top of it reached to heaven: and behold the angels of God ascending and descending on it."

THE varied ways in which Jehovah revealed himself to his earliest people were worthy of his wisdom and of his compassion. Excellently well were they adapted to the infant state of the Church, and very admirably were they calculated to make, on the minds of his worshippers, deep and vivid impressions. Through the medium of the senses it was that God chiefly manifested himself to them. Either they heard his voice, or saw some glorious symbol of his presence, or in vision beheld some emblematical occurrence, when as yet they had no written revelation. In all these ways our God is to be adored as wise and compassionate. He dealt with his people then, as we deal with our children now. We can most readily convey instruction to them by means of pictures, or by any audible or visible representation of things.

After this manner, and in the childhood of his church, he dealt with the patriarchal believers. In the instance of Jacob, as recorded in this chapter, he revealed himself in a singular manner, and in a very unlikely place. Jacob was journeying from his home, to certain relatives in a distant land. Terror and expectation were his companions. He dreaded the muttered threat of his brother Esau, and yet hoped for a tender welcome in the house of Bethuel, his mother's father. Laying him down to sleep in "a certain place," possibly a grove of large-leaved almond trees (as Luz, the original name of the adjacent city, means *an almond*), "he dreamed; and behold a ladder set upon the earth, and the top of it reached to heaven; and behold the angels of God ascending and descending upon it."

This singular and interesting scene of a ladder reaching from earth to heaven, with angels ascending and descending upon it, was not designed merely to excite his wonder, or to be a pictorial embellishment of the vision, a something on which his fancy alone might ruminate; but it had a worthier and more exalted meaning, a meaning which he most likely was taught to understand; while the recollection of the whole afforded him a constant subject for meditation. May *our* meditation upon it, at this present, be made profitable and sweet, by the Spirit of that same God who spake in vision to Jacob, and who now speaks to us by his dear Son. Let our first thought be given to—

I. *The emblematical intention of the various parts of Jacob's dream, especially the ladder and its appendages.* There are not many incidents in the Bible respecting which more fanciful interpretations have been given, than respecting this vision of the ladder and its angels. The very spokes of it, if not counted, have yet been pretendedly accounted for. As steps in the way to and from heaven, all sorts of notions have been affixed to them: while the two uprights, as we say, which held them together, and in which they were grooved, have been converted into types of God's electing love and providential support, with many other couplets, which fancy has culled from God's garden of graces. But there is no need to resort to fancy, when the Spirit of truth condescends to instruct us. The words of our Lord to Nathaniel are luminous enough to lead us to the true interpretation of our text: "Jesus answered and said unto him, Because I said unto thee, I saw thee under the fig tree, believest thou? thou shalt see greater things than these. And he saith unto him, Verily, verily I say unto you, Hereafter ye shall see heaven open, and the angels of God ascending and descending upon the Son of man." (John 1:50, 51.)

These words are generally thought to indicate that Nathaniel, while reposing beneath the cool shade of a fig tree, had been reading or considering the record of Jacob's dream; and that the Lord Jesus, by the power of his Godhead, both saw him and knew the tenor of his meditations. By telling him all that had been passing in his mind, and by explaining the purport of the ladder and its angels, as being a representation of himself and the ministry of angels through him, the Saviour confirmed his new disciple in the fullest faith of his divine mission.

A sound and an ingenious commentator paraphrases our Lord's words thus: "I certainly assure (you Nathaniel, and) all of you ("λεγω ὑμῖν") my disciples, that in a little time ye shall see the accomplishment of Jacob's vision in me. As he beheld the angels of God ascending and descending by a ladder set

[1] Preached Thursday Evening, October 11th, 1849.

upon the earth, the top of which reached to heaven, so while I, the Mediator between God and man, am, in my human nature on earth, my Godhead reaches to heaven (John 3:13): and ye shall see such manifestations of my glory, in the great and wonderful miracles I shall work, in the divine wisdom and knowledge which I shall display, and in the friendly intercourse which I shall set on foot between God and man, that all things in heaven and in earth shall as evidently appear to be under my control, as if ye saw the angels of God perpetually coming and going from heaven to me, and from me to heaven, to carry on a correspondence between my father and myself. And, some time hence, ye shall really see the angels, in a literal sense, attending to pay their honours to me."—(*Guyse.*)

In this view of our Lord's words to Nathaniel, we may consider Jacob's ladder,

1. *As typical of the person and mediation of Christ.* The grand object of all ancient revelations was to set forth the way of salvation through the Messiah.

Now a ladder, reaching from earth to heaven, was a very significant emblem of that way. It taught men to perceive that access to God and heaven could be prepared only by God himself, and that the grand medium of it, the promised Messiah, would be infinitely superior to both the human and the angelic race. It was no inconsiderable intimation also of the union of the human and the divine nature in the person of Christ, that Jacob saw this ladder based on the earth, but mounting to the very heavens. None but God could provide such a ladder, and none but his beloved Son could unite heaven with earth, by being at once divine and human.

That the ladder also prefigured to man his only means of communing with God and of reaching heaven, we ought not to doubt, after hearing our Lord say, "I am the way; no man cometh unto the Father but by me." Through Jesus alone, the Mediator of the new covenant, can the contrite sinner approach the Father's mercy-seat, and the peaceful saint maintain his peace and secure his fellowship. Not a prayer, nor a thanksgiving, ever ascends to the ear of God, but through this channel of communication.

Brethren, the Lord God sets this ladder before us in the gospel, more evidently than he placed it before the mental eye of Jacob in a dream. Have we set our feet on this ladder? Are we walking *in* Christ and *on* Christ? that is, not only living in him, but daily advancing to heaven by him, as though we were stepping higher and higher on the golden treadings of some royal ascent? The Christian life is a perpetual ascent from earthly things to the heavenly estate.

The ascending and descending of the angels upon the mystical ladder, may be construed

2. *As typical of their ministry to Christ, and of their agency in the providential dealings of God with his people.*

i. As an important part of the circumstances which attended the manifestation of Christ in the flesh, St. Paul mentions his being "*seen of angels.*" His conception and birth were announced by them. They ministered to him, during his childhood, after his temptation, and in all his agonies at Gethsemane and Calvary. They were constantly at his beck, when working his miracles, or encountering his enemies. "More than ten legions" of them were always marshalled to obey his instant word. They watched over his sepulchre, and rolled away the stone from it when the minute for his resurrection arrived. At his ascension especially they verified what in the text was prefigured of them, and Nathaniel beheld the partial fulfilment of his Master's words. But even greater things than these will be seen by every eye, in the dawn of the last great day. "In like manner" as the angels ascended with him into heaven, shall they, only in surpassing multitudes, descend with him from heaven, to judge the earth, and all who ever dwelt upon it. And "when the Son of man shall come in his glory, and all the holy angels with him, then shall he sit upon the throne of his glory." (Matthew 25:31.)

ii. That God's angels are extensively employed in fulfilling his providential will, and in forwarding the welfare of his people, we are everywhere taught to believe. Jacob had personally abundant proof of the fact; for when he was at Mahanaim "the angels of God met him;" and when he saw them he said, "This is God's host." Both before and after that event, God constantly engaged them in various services for his elect people, as many scriptures testify. Though, during the present age of the church, and when divine revelation is full and amply sufficient as a witness among men, angels are not permitted to assume a visible form, yet it cannot be doubted that, for judicial or merciful visitations, they are as much employed as ever. The declarative interrogation of the Apostle leaves us no room to hesitate at the fact: "Are they not *all* ministering spirits, sent forth to minister for them who shall be heirs of salvation?"

All their ministrations however are through the mediation of Christ. It was *on* the ladder that Jacob saw them passing and repassing. There was no other way for their transit. So we may be assured that, but for the incarnation and atonement of Christ, not an angel would visit our earth, or ever be sent on an errand of love to the desolate or the contrite. This fact puts to flight all those dreamy notions of a certain class of religionists, about the *roamings* and romantic watchings of angels in churches and hallowed places, and over the favoured living and the pious dead; as though those celestial beings were a sort of independent and non-commissioned host, who go whither they please, and do what they please: whereas, having no access to us but through Christ, they can do us good *only* at his bidding, and his permission. All our adoration therefore is due to him, and not to them.

From the fact also that the ladder, which Jacob saw, was "set on the earth," and not reaching *beneath* it, we may infer that the atonement of Christ pertains only to man, and not to fallen spirits. It is a solemn and an affecting truth, but truth it is, that God passed by beings who were made higher than ourselves, and visited us alone. It should fill us with holy humility and lasting adoration.

Let me now lead you to mark and receive

II. *The blessed truths, as well doctrinal as experimental, which the vision of Jacob conveys to us.* Taking into consideration the peculiar circumstances of Jacob's character and condition at the time of the vision, we may gratefully and admiringly infer,

1. That *very great indeed is the Lord's mercy to even his dearest people.* Jacob, a short while before he set out on this journey, had acted an ungenerous and very censurable part towards his brother Esau. By an act of subtlety and deep-stained prevarication, he had supplanted him in the gaining of the birthright blessing. And now he was fleeing, while opportunity served, from the revenge which he dreaded. In this pitiful, unwelcome, and somewhat disreputable position, did Jehovah appear to him. And, truly, with what justice might he have appeared with tokens of displeasure and words of reproof! How fitly might he have sent him back, to reconcile himself with his brother, and to make such compensation as he could! But the Lord's thoughts are not as our thoughts, neither are his ways as our ways. We are left to see and admire the goodness and gentleness of our God. The revelation of himself to Jacob was all loving-kindness and tender mercy. His words were peace and consolation: "And, behold, the Lord stood above it and said, I am the Lord God of Abraham thy father, and the God of Isaac: the land whereon thou liest to thee will I give it, and to thy seed: and thy seed shall be as the dust of the earth, and thou shalt spread abroad to the west, and to the east, and to the north, and to the south: and in thee and in thy seed shall all the families of the earth be blessed. And, behold, I am with thee, and will keep thee in all places whither thou goest and will bring thee again into this land; for I will not leave thee, until I have done that which I have spoken to thee of." (Ver. 13, 14, 15.)

Now this discovers to us much of God's peculiar method of dealing with his peculiar people. With others he often deals very differently. When the angel of the Lord appeared to Hagar in her flight, he ordered her to return and *submit herself* to her mistress. But, when God appeared to Jacob, he encouraged him to go forward, and said nothing about returning to his brother. He, as it were, settled the difference with his brother for him, by giving to Esau a milder temper and an altered purpose. Most likely the Lord saw in Jacob great relentings of heart, and a secret shame for his conduct. Mercy therefore passed by his transgression, and rejoiced against judgment to do him good.

To this hour our God is waiting to shew the like grace to every penitent spirit. He will pass by innumerable infirmities and errors, where he beholds "truth in the inward parts." It is the sincerity of his people which attracts his mercy. Still let them not presume on their sincerity: for few sins will be accounted more presumptuous than that. Neither let them forget that mercy shown to their infirmities is mercy granted to their endeavourings, and that for them they are to be as humble as the veriest sinner whose soul is spared.

2. *That God frequently sends his consolations to us at a time or place in which we least expect them*: "And Jacob awaked out of his sleep, and he said, Surely the Lord is in this place; and I knew it not." (Ver. 16.) It cannot be supposed, from this speech, that Jacob had such mean and imperfect ideas of Jehovah, as not to believe that his presence filled every place and at all times. What we must conclude from it, is this,—that Jacob, when he lay down to sleep, little thought that the Lord would there and then, in such a spot and at such a season, manifest himself so gloriously to him. He evidently had gone to sleep without anticipating, and so without preparing himself for such a scene and such a visitation. His expression therefore may be taken as indicative not only of admiration, but of self-chiding. He was filled with astonishment at the goodness, glory, and condescension of Jehovah, and with earnest humiliation at his own want of preparation for their exhibition.

Are these things uncommon in the present age? Visions and angel-visits may be, but the manifestations of God's grace are not. Oftentimes, when sorrows have encompassed us, and loneliness has been our portion, the presence of "the Father of mercies and the God of all consolation" has been largely vouchsafed to us. What Christian has not had to bear witness that mercy, or comfort, or help of some kind, has come to him very unexpectedly, at a time or from a quarter which had previously been very little in his thoughts? Many a believer, like Moses in Midian, or the widow at Zarephath, has gone out oppressed or saddened, and met with the presence or help of God in a manner which has made them ashamed of their fears, or astonished at his goodness. At this we cannot marvel, when we think of our forgetfulness in trusting him, and of his continuance in watching over us. The words of Hanani, the seer, to Asa, king of Judah, should never be forgotten by us: "The eyes of the Lord run to and fro *throughout the whole earth*, to show himself strong in behalf of them whose heart is perfect towards him." (2 Chronicles 16:9.)

3. *That the enjoyment of God's presence is the great solace and strength of the Christian pilgrim.* How animating and invigorating was the vision of God to Jacob! His spirit rose, and his heart rejoiced, and his whole soul was made strong, in the

waking retrospect of what had passed. True, he was filled with dread, but it was a holy dread, a delightful dread, such a dread as an angel feels, when the smile of his Maker falls upon him. Therefore Jacob "was afraid, and said, How dreadful is this place! this is none other but the house of God, and this is the gate of heaven." (Genesis 28:17.) After this, how nimbly and cheerfully did he resume his journey! Though every step of the way was new to him, and he was treading where, in those times, human feet seldom or never trod, yet was he vigorous and joyous, and, what is more, confident in the unseen hand which was guiding him. Therefore it was said, in the first verse of the next chapter, "Then Jacob went on his journey, and came into the land of the people of the east."

And do not *we* meet with seasons of refreshment from the presence of the Lord? Do *we* not know what it is to rise from our knees, or to leave our chamber, or to retire from the house of our God, with hearts warmed by that glow which gave to Jacob's lip the fervour almost of heaven itself? Some at least of us do, I trust, know the power and solace of such seasons. Some, I fain would hope, have heretofore said as David said, in Psalm 40:1, 2, 3: "I waited patiently for the Lord; and he inclined unto me, and heard my cry. He brought me up also out of an horrible pit, and out of the miry clay, and set my feet upon a rock, and established my goings. And he hath put a new song in my mouth, even praise unto our God: many shall see it, and fear, and shall trust in the Lord." Assuredly we may oftener so say, and oftener set to our seal, that God is mindful of us, and doth bless us, if we only love and trust him more, and follow and serve him better. In all your sorrows then, in all your difficulties and perplexities, think of the vision of Jacob, and be comforted and strengthened. The same Lord God who "stood above" the ladder is ever standing above you. In the person of his dear Son, he speaks to us all that he spoke to Jacob: for the sum of what he said to Jacob constitutes the standing promise of his love to all his people. He will be with them, and keep them, in all places whither they go: for did not his beloved Son and our only Saviour say, "Lo, I am with you alway, even unto the end of the world"? He did; and never will a true disciple of his have to say, "I am forsaken: the Lord hath forgotten to be gracious."

4. That *we should cultivate a grateful recollection of the kindness which the Lord shews us in the day of our distress.* Jacob's condition, at the time of the vision, was, as we have seen, very disconsolate. His leaving home, his rending himself from the society of a fond mother and a saintly father, and his being now a solitary traveller to an unknown land, constituted, most likely, the first severe trial of his life. Such trials, when they occur to ourselves, generally leave a deep and tender impression on our minds. It is therefore no uncommon thing to hear a person say, "Ah, I shall never forget the hour when that trial came upon me, how it affected me, how I was ready to sink under it!" The recollection of it does not depart; and the mind soon catches up the returning sensations respecting it. It is very likely also, that the vision of the ladder was the first special revelation with which God had favoured the young patriarch. It evidently excited his warmest affections, his devoutest desires, and his most vigorous resolutions; for, in the fulness of his heart, he vowed a vow of gratitude, and bound himself with great solemnity to cleave to the Lord as his God. How he bore the circumstance in mind is shewn us, in his memorable conversation with Leah and Rachel, respecting the unkindness of their father to him: "I am the God of Bethel, where thou anointedst the pillar, and where thou vowedst a vow unto me: now arise, get thee out from this land, and return unto the land of thy kindred." (Genesis 31:13.) And how he fulfilled his vow is recorded for our learning in Genesis 35:6, 7, "So Jacob came to Luz, which is in the land of Canaan, that is, Bethel, he and all the people that were with him. And he built there an altar, and called the place El-bethel, because there God appeared unto him, when he fled from the face of his brother."

Again we may remark, that our first experiences of the Lord's favour, and the first manifestations of himself to our hearts, are generally those which leave the deepest and most abiding traces on our minds. Where such dealings of God with us, in any marked manner or singular degree, have occurred, they cannot be forgotten. If we slight them, we are sooner or later constrained to say, "O that I were as in months past, as in the days when God preserved me; when his candle shined upon my head, and when by his light I walked through darkness!" To call to mind such months and such manifestations as Jacob called them to mind, is a great means of deriving support under any present difficulties or discouragements. "I will call to mind thy wonders of old, I will meditate on all thy doings," is the resolve of one who knew what it was to look back along the path of his pilgrimage, and to take courage from the sunshine which gilded its first or earliest stages.

5. *That every promise and every help from heaven is given to believers alone, and to them in Christ Jesus the mediator between God and man.* Profane Esau dwelt at home and enjoyed his ease, but God made him no spiritual promise. Pious Jacob had to labour for his bread, but the God of heaven crowned him with loving kindness and tender mercy. But then the pledge thereof was given to him from the top and down the incline of the mystic ladder. Christ was that ladder; and through his mediation alone is it that God speaks to man, and sends him grace to help in time of need.

Then let the worldling see and feel his real destitution, amid the pleasures of sin and the prosperities of life. And let every believer testify to all around him, and say, "Blessed is the man that hath the God of Jacob for his help!"

SERMON XII.

THE CERTAINTY OF GOD'S PRESENCE WITH HIS PEOPLE.[1]

Exodus 3:12.

"And he said, Certainly I will be with thee."

THIS chapter is not more remarkable for the miracle of the burning bush, than for the renewal of God's open intercourse with his church, in the person of Moses. From the time that Jacob went down into Egypt, to this period of forty years after Moses had fled from it, there was not, so far as we know, "any open vision," any visible apperance of Deity, or any appointment of a standing prophet. The long sojourn of Israel in the land of their bondage was a dark and disastrous season for the church of the living God. Without doubt that church was continued, and faithful members were not wanting to perpetuate its vitality: but those members were few, and that vitality was feeble. Now however, that the destined period had arrived for a new impulse to be given to the cause of the chosen people, Jehovah, on a sudden and with great singularity, revealed himself to Moses. After the first suprise of Moses had subsided, the Lord God proceeded to converse with him. He especially detailed to him the plan for the deliverance of the people from the tyranny of Pharaoh, and revealed the process of its accomplishment, by Moses himself being commissioned to carry it out.

Startled and awed at the magnitude and difficulty of the commission, "Moses said unto God, Who am I, that I should go unto Pharaoh, and that I should bring forth the children of Israel out of Egypt?" (Exodus 3:11.) Upon this, Jehovah majestically replies, "*Certainly I will be with thee,*" meaning to say: My presence shall acompany you, and that will obviate every objection and insure success. Hence let our hearts ponder

I. *The position of Moses, and the workings of his mind, when the text was addressed to him.* There was great peculiarity in that position which makes it worthy of our careful consideration. The workings of his mind would, of course, derive their character from it; for our thoughts and feelings generally correspond with the circumstances in which we are placed. At the time then when the text was addressed to him, we may discern his position to have been somewhat of this kind:

1. *He was no stranger to the true God.* He was not a novice in "the faith which bringeth salvation." Consequently, though he was struck with the strange or "*great* sight" of a bush burning and yet not burnt, he was not perplexed when the Lord spake to him out of it. Instead of saying, with Saul of Tarsus, "Who art thou, Lord?" he readily replied, "Here am I."

While in Egypt, and when but a young man, he had nobly decided for God and true religion. He seems to have had, as traditionally reported, the crown of Egypt at his command. Certainly he might have enjoyed the highest honours and the choicest pleasures, had he allowed himself to be legally regarded as "the son of Pharaoh's daughter." But he renounced them all, and "chose rather to suffer affliction with the people of Christ, than to enjoy the pleasures of sin for a season." "The treasures of Egypt" were worthless to him, in comparison with a pure conscience, and the hope of heaven. In all this a holy and a saving faith was with him the spring of action. We are expressly told it was, by that Spirit who inspired the writer of the Epistle to the Hebrews. Hence Moses had not now to learn who Jehovah was, and what religion ought to be.

2. *He had been subjected to long and trying discipline.* He had left the court of Egypt for the wilds of Midian, the palace of a sovereign for the hut of a shepherd, the luxury of faring sumptuously and of being waited upon by a staff of servants for the hardness of the most homely food, and of himself being the servant of another man. Instead too of mingling in public life, he was inured to privacy, obscurity, and even loneliness: for, when the Lord met him, he was keeping sheep on the slopes of the wildest of mountains, in the very back part of a desert. This had been his lot for the last forty years: for, as Stephen tells us, he was forty years old when he fled from Egypt, and it was not till another "forty years had expired," that the Lord appeared unto him. Thus had he spent the riper half of his life in suffering affliction with the people of Christ. Surely this was discipline indeed, and such as could hardly do otherwise than bend him to the divine will, and, in conjunction with his splendid acquirements, prepare him for any service.

3. *He had, when a younger man, been a bold, zealous, and, perhaps, a self-confident champion of the cause of God and his brethren: but, now, he evidently had become an humble, wise,*

[1] Preached Sunday Morning, April 6th, 1851.

and self-diffident professor. He had, as he no doubt thought, justifiably killed and hidden in the sand an insolent and murderous Egyptian. But now he is even backward in facing strangers, and in speaking to a king. Formerly he thought the Lord had commissioned him to act, when really the Lord had not. But now that, after a long check, he finds the commission actually laid upon him, he hesitates, trembles, questions, and virtually declines! The grace of God, when operating in conjunction with protracted discipline, has a wondrous effect in changing our dispositions, and in making us very different beings to what we were years ago.

4. *Moses however was, after all, the fittest man in the world for the great undertaking which Jehovah had planned, though himself was the last to believe such of himself.* Who so fitting to visit a court, as one who had been brought up in it? or so competent to treat with the philosophers of it, as he who was early "learned in all the wisdom of the Egyptians, and mighty in words and deeds"? or who so adapted to converse with a king, as the man who had been trained by the daughter of a king, and who possessed a most kingly aspect and royal bearing? And yet this very man, on God's proposing to send him to Pharaoh, said "Who am I, that I should go unto Pharaoh?"

From all this we may derive rich and beneficial instruction.

i. *We see the value and importance of true religion in early life.* By the power of it Moses was kept from falling amidst the dangers of an Egyptian court. When betrayed into an error of judgment, and thereby driven into very adverse circumstances, he speedily contents himself with them, bears up under them, and begins to be benefited by them. How blessed a thing is it for us, when forced into a new and trying position, not to be at a loss in finding God, not to have to learn the first principles and the first duties of true religion! "'Twill save us from a thousand snares" (and from a thousand sufferings too!) "to mind religion young."

ii. *We discern the intention of God in visiting us with trials, and in subjecting us to discipline.* True, thousands journey onward without meeting with any particular check, or sustaining any very noticeable affliction. But the contrary is the usual lot of life: only it is not the usual wisdom for it to be observed and improved. Still the divine intention of all trials, checks, and afflictions, remains the same. It is the discipline of the heart, the sanctified bending of the soul to God and his service. How many an individual has had to say, "But for that illness, but for that loss, but for that bereavement, what might I have been? Any thing perhaps, but what I hope I am!" And how often too have persons, who have long been under reverses, or trying dispensations and positions in life, had to see, in the occurrence of some bright issue, the intention of God in having so placed them! It was to chasten them, test them, school them, and fit them for something better and greater than they had ever anticipated. Wise and gracious indeed is our God in all the varied methods which he takes to make us other than we were, happier than we thought to be, and fitter for some post or some duties in life, than really we before were.

iii. We perceive, in the hesitation of Moses, the infirmity of even a sound and steadfast believer. He could not deem himself qualified for an undertaking to which God had called him. This was a virtual, though perhaps an unwitting reflection upon the wisdom of God; for surely God would not manifestly call an individual to fill a post, which that individual was incompetent to fill, or which he would not enable him to fulfil. There is great reason, dear brethren, for us carefully to distinguish between a sense of our unworthiness and of our own unfitness, and that timidity and despondency which border on forgetfulness of God's enabling grace. While we are never to let go humility, modesty, and discretion, we must lay fast hold upon divine promise, cheerful hope, and believing confidence. We always increase our difficulties, and diminish our comforts, by looking too much upon our own drawbacks, and too little upon God's gracious help. Humbleness of mind, and a constant reliance on that in which we know we may confide, are as desirable for us, as they are compatible in themselves. Happy and blessed for us is it, that we have a God who knoweth our infirmities, and who will not only pity and pardon them, but sustain us under them. Hence ponder

II. *The reply which God promptly and graciously made to Moses*, when, through remaining infirmity, he forgot his true position. "*Certainly I will be with thee.*" There is much in this which invites our meditation.

1. *It was condescending and tender on the part of God to give any reply at all.* When we call our servants, and becomingly bid them perform some honourable service for us, we are not usually pleased if they excuse themselves, and show reluctance. "Not answering again," we consider the wide rule of their duty. Nor would it be thought a very unreasonable thing for us to say no more to them, but to employ some other persons. Thus did not the great Master with his servant Moses. He had patience with him, bore with his infirmity, and generously replied to all he said. Our hearts can perhaps affectingly tell us, how often he has dealt in like manner with us.

2. *It was a reply which met every difficulty which had started in Moses' mind.* The servant said, "Who am I?" The Master with dignity and significance named himself, as though in reply he too said, "And WHO am I? You look at yourself: look rather on ME. *You* feel yourself nothing: believe that *I* am everything." This was enough: for the presence of our God, God in Christ, is the only thing that we really need, because it brings with it all else that we can possibly require or desire. Moses, in

returning to Egypt, would want neither guard for his person, nor wisdom in his interview with Pharaoh, nor energy for surmounting obstacles, if only Jehovah were with him. Hence the brief sentence, "I will be with thee," was full enough for every purpose which the case required.

3. *It was a reply which brought with it an infinite weight of assurance.* It began with a word which swept away all doubt at a breath. "*Certainly* I will be with thee!" Unbelief is never moved by any word of God, however strong: but faith is always roused by it; and, when it falls on the heart with its strongest tones, that heart is startled out of its hesitation, and elevated beyond itself. "*Certainly!*" How excellently kind of our God to back even his own promise with a protestation of infallibility! There was no need on his part so to do; for his gentlest word is firm as eternity. But he did it in consideration of human weakness. It was like giving to a fainting traveller, not only a staff to support his faltering steps, but wings to bear him aloft, and speed him on his way. It was the clenching of that nail, which already had been driven in a sure place. Such however is our God's good pleasure.

4. *It was a reply which was grounded on a standing promise, and which was to be a lasting encouragement.* "I am, or will be with thee," was the early word of God to his saints, long before Moses was added to their number. While it stands, all who are of that number have nothing to fear, and will have nothing to want. Moses learned its strength and its sweetness, by often recurring to it. He seems never to have forgotten it; especially as the event, recorded in this chapter, was his first special reception of it. In the after course of his mission, he pledged Jehovah to the fulfilment of it: "If thy presence go not with me, carry us not up hence." He knew the value of that presence by the proof which he had had of it in Egypt: and therefore he craved it as essential to his comfort and well-being, in every future step of his way. When a veteran in the wars of the Lord, and when about to retire from all earthly service, he encourged Joshua, as his successor, by repeating the very same promise: "And Moses called unto Joshua, and said unto him in the sight of all Israel, Be strong and of a good courage: for thou must go with this people unto the land which the Lord hath sworn unto their fathers to give them; and thou shalt cause them to inherit it. And the Lord he it is that doth go before thee; he will be with thee, he will not fail thee, neither forsake thee: fear not, neither be dismayed." (Deuteronomy 31:7, 8.)

A review of the entire subject, with the brief remarks which have been made upon it, will enable us, by God's blessing, to arrive at further truth, and I trust further profit.

i. *We are not to be surprised at hesitations rising in our own minds, or at witnessing infirmities in others, on the first presentation of arduous and important duties.* Though Moses hesitated, he had some reasonable ground for such feeling. The work to which he was called demanded energies and talents which he had not been exercising for forty years. It required great address and would expose him to much publicity: whereas he had been in the deepest retirement, and amongst a class of persons whose humble and quiet pursuits were totally opposed to what was now before him. The indiscretion of his younger years, in slaying an oppressor, might rouse his fears of retaliation from some yet surviving relatives. The notorious haughtiness and despotic cruelty of Pharaoh was an appalling thing of itself; and the recollection of his having formerly been rejected by his nation, as a deliverer, might, fairly enough, contribute to his diffidence in undertaking the proposed duty.

The God of love will pardon the diffidence of his people, when it does not proceed from deficiency of love to himself; and especially when it is not indulged, but rather deprecated. In what a variety of cases such diffidence may befal us, it would be tedious, and perhaps impracticable to enumerate. In every department of Christian society there are temptations to it; and individual history is rife with it. Some minds are more liable to it than others; and the same persons are more under its influence at one time, and in one case, than at another. They say, "Why is it thus with me? I never recollect being so timid or so disheartened on any former occasion." It was thus with Moses. In early life, as you have heard, he was forward and zealous: in riper years, he was retiring and cautious. Trial had shown him more of himself, and discipline had lowered that high-mindedness and fond conceit which his Egyptian rank would naturally engender. Thus anything is good which brings us to a lowly level in the presence of God, or in the contemplation of any thing which befals us from him. Still we never are to let our humiliation sink into over-timidity, or urge us to irresolution. There is evil enough in the world to be resisted, and good enough to be disseminated in it, to call for decision, promptness, and energy, on the part of all who, like Moses, desire to serve the Lord.

ii. *We should learn habitually to covet the presence of our God, and to set the highest value on it.* It is, in itself, the choicest and most comprehensive privilege, which tongue can name or heart desire. "The Lord be with you!" is, as a prayerful salutation, equal to anything which cherubim or seraphim could devise for us, or angels or archangels pronounce over us. It is one of the most lovely sentences which the church puts into the lips of her ministers, when they, with their people, are about to kneel in renewed prayer to the triune God. And highly becoming would it be, if all congregations, and our own among them, were not to adjust themselves for kneeling, till they have calmly and affectionately responded to the minister's expression of his wish, by saying, "And *with* thy spirit!" If the Lord be with us, we shall want neither energy in prayer, nor company in solitude, nor safety in publicity, nor prosperity in business, nor success in any undertaking. All will be well, when he is with us for that upholding, guiding, and strengthening, which we so continually are needing. None but the true servants of God know the blessedness which a sense of that presence imparts to them, when, like Moses, they are about to engage in some high and important service, or perform some arduous and responsible duty. Who, when called upon to advise in some perplexing case, or to discharge some delicate and painful task, or to negotiate some considerable business, is not likely to do it all the better, if conscious of, at least asking for, the aid of the divine presence? How many a professional man has found the inestimable value of so doing! How many a student or candidate has proved it in the trying stages of an examination! How many a traveller "by land or by water," on leaving home for an eventful journey! And how continually should we all prove it in our respective stations in life! In *viewing our difficulties*, entering on our engagements, and in even making our calls, can we realize anything better than Jehovah's word to Moses, "Certainly I will be with thee"?

iii. *We must carefully bear in mind who, and who alone, they are, who may expect the Lord to be with them.* It is said of the worldly and the wicked, "God is not in all his thoughts." Can he then expect that God will be with *him* in any of his ways? He may imagine it; but he cannot realize it. God will not be with us unless, in heart and mind and life, we are habitually with him, and that with an abiding recognition of the mediation of his beloved Son. Clear and striking testimony to this fact is found in 2 Chronicles 15:1, 2: "And the Spirit of God came upon Azariah the son of Obed. And he went out to meet Asa, and said unto him, Hear ye me, Asa, and all Judah and Benjamin: The Lord is with you, while ye be with him; and, if ye seek him, he will be found of you; but, if ye forsake him, he will forsake you."

Sure then are we that worldly minds cannot feel what Moses felt when Jehovah addressed to him our text. They go to their businesses or their duties without God. They are left to themselves. And if they die as they have lived, without the Lord being with them, *what then?*

SERMON XIII.

LIGHT IN THE CHURCH, AMID DARKNESS IN THE WORLD.[1]

EXODUS 10:23.

"But all the children of Israel had light in their dwellings."

WE well know that the present day is the shortest day of our year. We may therefore say as Job said, "They change the night into day: the light is short because of darkness." (Job 17:12.) But we should not be content with knowing this fact, and saying these words, we should endeavour to obtain from them holy and practical instruction. God has wonderfully ordered everything to be capable of affording spiritual improvement; consequently the shortest and darkest day of our year will, if duly contemplated, lead us to that light which can purify and rejoice the heart.

Darkness is God's emblem for sin, and light is his emblem for holiness. Never were these emblems so wonderfully exhibited as in that history which is connected with our text. The terrific plague of darkness is as remarkable as any of the plagues which were inflicted upon the land of Egypt. What adds to its remarkableness is the contrast which existed between the houses of the Israelites and the homes of the Egyptians. The inspired account of the whole is as forcible as it is brief. "And the Lord said unto Moses, Stretch out thine hand toward heaven, that there may be darkness over the land of Egypt, even dark-

[1] Preached Sunday Evening, December 21st, 1845.

ness which may be felt. And Moses stretched forth his hand toward heaven; and there was a thick darkness in all the land of Egypt three days: they saw not one another, neither rose any from his place for three days: but all the children of Israel had light in their dwellings." (Ver. 21, 22, 23.)

This singular exemption of a singular people, from a surrounding visitation, was recorded for our learning. May our present meditation upon it lead us, by God's blessing, to many lessons of saving truth.

Let us first think of

I. *The surrounding visitation.* It was a plague of darkness; that is, the enshrouding of the whole land of Egypt with dense impenetrable gloom. The like had never been known. It was as strange as it was terrible; for, being a divine visitation, it was no doubt as intense and dreadful as divine vengeance saw fit to make it.

1. How the darkness was instrumentally produced there have been many conjectures. Some writers tell of a supernatural eclipse, extended for three days, and accompanied with dense clouds. Others say the darkness was occasioned by a mustering of all the clouds from above, and a rising of all the vapours from beneath; the one covering the face of the sky with stratum upon stratum, and the other ascending to meet them from every pore of the earth. Philo, a Jewish author, relates that the preceding part of the day had been beautifully serene and clear; and that, suddenly, a horrible gloom fell upon every spot: so that wherever the Egyptians were, when they were overtaken by that gloom, there they were obliged to remain, as well through inability to grope a step, as through fright at horrid visions which served to make the darkness visible.

2. In all this there is nothing at variance with God's own word. The means were of course all his own, but the effect he has himself described. The darkness was "*thick darkness,*" such as might "be *felt;*" that is, it was clammy and densely damp, so as not only to hide all objects from eyes which could have seen, but which so clogged and clammed the eyes themselves as to prevent all exercise of vision. And then, as all natural light was banished, so also no artificial light would burn. Either the thick damp of the darkness put it out, or the presence of certain gases prevented its flaming. Hence the Egyptians "saw not one another, neither rose any from his place." They were doubly bedarkened, while a horrible dread overwhelmed them; for God, as the Psalmist certifies us, "sent evil angels among them," and scared them with spectral sights and sounds. The consequence was that under this plague the Egyptians suffered without help or sympathy. Under their other visitations they had power to condole with or aid one another; but under this they were bound in an adamantine chain of darkness. They were as prisoners in *solitary* confinement, and that amidst starvation, filth, and terror.

The apocryphal author of the Book of Wisdom gives at least a very graphic description of their horridly doleful condition. (Chap. 17.)

3. And what, brethren, is all this but a picture of the world lying in the darkness of sin? For the time it was a type of Egypt itself; for, although that land was "the mother of science," yet was it also "the house of gods." The light of her science was but a glow-worm light, and the darkness of her idolatry extinguished it. Pharaoh had done his utmost to obscure the glory of Jehovah; but now Jehovah humbled him in deathly gloom. And, if we turn to heathen lands, what do we see save gross darkness covering the people? They too are in terror from their idols, and yet they "move not from their place" to help one another; for they are fast bound in deepest gloom, and there is no sympathy among idolaters. Their habitations are cruel as well as dark. And further, is not the darkness of Egypt a representation of that spiritual gloom which spreads itself over the mind of every unrenewed person? Is not the "foolish heart" of every such person "darkened"? Does not the god of this world blind his eyes? And is he not unable to discern spiritual things? These questions can be answered only in the affirmative; for, proud as the sinner may be of his taper of intellectual light, he is pronounced to be "poor and *blind* and miserable and naked." But the type of greatest terror remains to be told. The darkness of Egypt is the shadow of that "blackness of darkness" which fills the bottomless pit. It always has been regarded as such by the good and the wise in all ages of the church. But all comparison fails of approaching reality. What is the darkness of our darkest December compared with that of Egypt? And what is that of Egypt compared with the tormenting and enchaining gloom of hell, where evil angels will afflict those who are cursed with impenitence and unrelenting hardness of heart? O think of this, ye thoughtless ones, who come hither irreverently and wantonly; *ye*, I mean, who come with eyes full of adultery, and which cannot, because they will not, cease from sin. Think of it, yea, ponder it well, ye who enter this holy house only to sport yourselves in your own deceiving, to beguile unstable souls, though all the while you are weaving a shroud of prickles for your death-bed, and twisting a lash of scorpions for your never-dying souls. If ye repent not, ye will find the "blackness of darkness" reserved for you for ever! God grant you "repentance unto life!" Next think of

II. *The peculiar people who were exempted from this surrounding visitation.* In the text they are called "the children of Israel."

1. These people are constantly described as having been chosen of God to be a holy and a peculiar people unto himself. Not that they were individually holy in the saving sense of that

term, but were as a nation accounted such, because they possessed a holy creed and a holy worship, and in their collective capacity believed the one and followed the other. They were also a peculiar people, peculiar as to their features, their habits, and their entire separation from the rest of mankind. They were not to intermarry with other nations, nor were they allowed to follow their customs, but were, with great strictness, to avoid all intimate society. Other people might join them, but they might not join other people. All these marks and singularities were not inherent. They did not originate with themselves. All was the result of God's choice and appointment. Their father Abraham was like other men; but when God selected him as the founder of a peculiar family, that God took care to set his own mark upon that family.

2. In these respects, as well as in others kindred to them, the children of Israel were a type or representation of the Christian church. That church, as the original word means, is a company of persons selected or called out from the godless world. Those persons are constituted "a holy nation and a peculiar people," as well as being "a chosen generation" and "a royal priesthood," in comparison with the great mass of mankind. For, as the children of Israel were but a small population compared with the Egyptians, so are Christians but an inconsiderable body when matched with the heathen and Mahommedan world.

3. But the comparison must not rest here. A greater mistake can hardly be made than the confounding of the true Israel with the nominal Israel, the spiritual church with the visible church. Holy Scripture labours to keep men mindful of the distinction between the two: but unrenewed minds are unwilling to see the distinction, and teachers who borrow their light from earthly sources are perpetually mistaking and mis-stating the simple truth.

The fact is, as St. Paul avows, "*all* who are of Israel are not Israel;" and "he is not a Jew who is one outwardly, but he is a Jew who is one inwardly." (Romans 2:28, 29.) Hence among the very children of Israel there was an election from an election, a choosing from out of the chosen, a circle within a circle. In like manner there is a church within a church, the true within the nominal, the real within the visible. Men therefore may belong to the one but not to the other; they may call themselves Christians without having the Spirit of Christ; or, as St. Paul expressly says, they may "have the form of godliness while they deny the power thereof."

Careful therefore must we be to take Holy Scripture as we find it; and, without regard to what is called Calvinism, Arminianism, or any other theological distinction, to receive simple truth in all the clearness and positiveness of its divine revelation. God chose himself a people, the children of Israel. His choice of them to external privileges was like his choice of us as a Christian people to Christian privileges. But as with Israel so with us; "there is a remnant according to the election of grace," a "little flock" within the great sheepfold, a company of honest hearted people who are in right earnest about Christ and his salvation.

Next let us contemplate

III. *The privilege of God's peculiar people.* In Egypt it was an exemption from the surrounding visitation. "All the children of Israel had light in their dwellings." The same power which spread impenetrable darkness around their dwellings prevented its entrance within them. Thus, while the Egyptians were fast bound in gloom and horror, the children of Israel, though their captives, were enjoying light and freedom. It might indeed be said of them then, as was said of them afterwards, in the days of Esther, "the Jews had light, and gladness, and joy and honour." (Esther 8:16.)

1. And what, we may as before ask, what is this singular privilege of light in the Hebrew dwelling-house but a representation of the existence of divine truth in the church of the living God? The only real light in the world is that which is found in the Christian Israel. Without that light (and it "cometh down from above") men grope in darkness, they "stumble on the dark mountains," and know nothing as they ought to know. "The lively oracles" were committed unto the Jews, and are now, with the additional light of the New Testament, intrusted to the Christian church. That church therefore is the great candlestick of the world. It holds the lamp of life, and presents the spectacle of a house full of light, in the midst of a "darkness which may be felt."

2. But as again in the former instance, so in this, we must not confound things which are essentially distinct. The light of the church of Christ is not always found in the souls of the members of that church. In our Lord's day on earth the Jews boasted of their light: but he said to them, "If the light which is in you be darkness, how great is that darkness!" So in Egypt a large proportion of the children of Israel who had light in their dwellings had darkness in their hearts; for afterwards they perished, through unbelief, in the wilderness. And thus, alas! it still is many who are baptized, and enlightened in the church, fail of seeing Christ with the eye of the soul, and of thereby having "the light of life." St. John tells us of many a one who is called a Christian brother, "walking in darkness, and knowing not whither he goeth, because that darkness, (like the damp gloom of Egypt,) hath blinded his eyes." (1 John 2:11.)

3. It therefore is only the true Israelite, the Christian in deed as well as in profession, who has "light in his dwelling," such light, at least, as will suffice him in "the valley of the shadow of death." Such an one has those graces of the Spirit of which light is the constant emblem. He has knowledge and

freedom, and purity and comfort. In a word, he is the child of light, for he has God for his Father, who is "the Father of lights;" and he has Christ for his portion, who is "the Light of the world," and the "very Light of life."

How true is it also, that the Israel of God, as opposed to the families of the world, have light in their dwellings. Truly Christian families are conducted upon principles of light. They set up the Bible as the lamp of their household, and study to work and walk in its light: whereas, in a worldly family, where is only nominal Christianity but no religion, the light of the Scriptures sheds no sanctifying and calming ray. The Bible may indeed be in the house, but it is there to no purpose. It is a light put under a bushel. It is put away on the shelf, in the drawer, or the closet, and if wanted is hard to be found. And, as for reading of it daily before the entire family of children and servants, that each may, as it were, kindle their lamp afresh in the midst of a dark world, how few, alas, practise this!

Then, dear brethren, suffer the word of exhortation, and receive it candidly and feelingly.

1. *Take heed of being, like disobedient Israel, none the better for your light.* Your external relation to our Israel is a great privilege; but that external relation is only temporal. The light which shines around you lasts at the longest no longer than death; and then if death comes and finds no light *in you*, how terrible will be your darkness! The right improvement of your privilege is the great business to which you have to attend. Be content with nothing short of that illumination of the inner man which will keep the dwelling clean and pure, and ready for the Master's entrance.

2. *Let the children of light rejoice in the light, and walk in it too.* There must have been great gladness in Goshen while God was permitting light to shine and fire to burn only in the dwellings of Israel. It was common light with very uncommon interest; for it then became a miraculous light, and a special token of the divine presence. Just so is it with true spiritual light. It is a daily miracle. It is a token from the Saviour. We may be glad and rejoice in his tokens; for the light he gives now is only a ray of that splendour which shall light his own temple.

And now, to give an allowable turn to the words of the text, and from them to admonish our poorer parishioners, let me say,

3. *Be thankful, my friends, for the bountiful light which St. Thomas's dark day always brings to your dwellings.* It is a season of light and gladness to our poor, because of those charitable "gifts" which then abound to them.

Few parishes have such light. While many poor are pining in want, on these dark days, most of you have something to cheer you. Then be thankful; and let your thankfulness be shown in doing the works of light. Recollect also, it was God who *provided* these gifts, and who has *preserved* them too. Do not abuse them by pride, quarrelling, or excess. "Labour not for the meat that perisheth, but for that which endureth to everlasting life."

SERMON XIV.

UNHOLY HEARTS RIGHTEOUSLY HARDENED BY A HOLY GOD.[1]

Exodus 10:27.

"But the Lord hardened Pharaoh's heart, that he would not let them go."

THE scriptures of truth record the lives not only of the eminently good, but of the notoriously bad. They tell us of monsters of iniquity, as well as of exemplars in piety. And this they do, in order that we may tremblingly adore the severity of

[1] Preached Sunday Evening, April 5th, 1846.

God in the destruction of the one, and joyfully admire his goodness in the salvation of the other. Hence the biographies of the Bible are not to be read as we read tales and narratives in other books: but they are to be pondered and studied, and that with all seriousness and personal application. Now of all the histories of human enormity, which the pen of inspiration has recorded for our learning, none are more awful, and few are more solemnly instructive, than that of the Pharaoh mentioned in our text. As the hardening of his heart is repeatedly attributed to God, explanation becomes necessary; and the more so, as the fact is sometimes misunderstood by the godly, and generally misrepresented by the godless. Since then it is said, "The Lord hardened Pharaoh's heart, that he would not let them go," let us first inquire, what are we to understand by this statement? and then, what may we learn from it?

I. *What are we to understand by the divine hardening of Pharaoh's heart?*

Whatever the statement in the text *may* mean, every devout mind feels at once that it *cannot* mean any thing which can cast imputation upon the goodness or holiness of God. Those perfections must remain unsullied, however unable we may be to understand what seems to be opposed to them. But, before coming directly to the question, let me remind you that, in other parts of the Bible, things are said of a nature similar to what is said in our text. Thus, in the vision which Isaiah saw, and which is recorded in the 6th chapter of his prophecies, it is thus said, in verses 9 and 10, "Go and tell this people, Hear ye indeed, but understand not; and see ye indeed, but perceive not. Make the heart of this people fat, and make their ears heavy, and shut their eyes; lest they should see with their eyes, and hear with their ears, and understand with their heart, and convert and be healed."

These fearful words are quoted or referred to, no less than six times in the New Testament, principally however by John the evangelist (12:40), and Paul the apostle (Acts 28:26). This same apostle also, in his epistle to the Romans (9:18), said of God, "Therefore hath he mercy on whom he will have mercy, and whom he will he *hardeneth*." Now, in these, and in whatsoever corresponding passages may be adduced, we may be instantly sure that God cannot be the author of evil, and therefore that he cannot capriciously, wantonly, or wilfully, harden the heart of any man. We may be sure too that every part of his revealed word is really and truly accordant with itself, and that whatever difficult or discrepant things we discern, or fancy we discern, in it, all is easy and harmonious to him.

To harden a man's heart therefore, is no *positive* act of God. He has no moral power, so to speak, to infuse evil into any creature, because there is no evil in him. It is foreign to his nature, and altogether opposed to his perfections. "He is the Rock, his work is perfect; for all his ways are judgment: a God of truth and without iniquity, just and right is he." (Deuteronomy 32:4.) Wherefore, as though it were intended to meet every objection, it is said, "Let no man say when he is tempted, I am tempted of God: for God cannot be tempted with evil, neither tempteth he any man." (James 1:13.) Hence we come to a direct answer to the question, *How did God harden Pharaoh's heart?* We reply,—simply by leaving that heart to its own wickedness. It requires no *positive* act on the part of God to harden the human heart. Its own innate tendencies will accomplish that dreadful work, if they only are allowed to have their own course. The human heart will always harden itself, if God at any time simply leaves it to itself; just as in nature the whole surface of our globe would be hardened into ice, if God were to withdraw his sun. Leave the earth to itself, and darkness, deadness, and desolation, would soon ensue. When therefore it is said, "The Lord hardened Pharaoh's heart," we are to regard the expression as another mode of saying that God, in judgment to Pharaoh for his crimes, left him to fall into that hardness of heart, which he really loved and actually produced: for the earnest inquirer, as well as the perverse caviller, must be reminded that, ere God said, "I will harden his heart" (Exodus 4:21), he had declared (Exodus 3:19) "I am sure that the king of Egypt will not let you go." Here God's foreknowledge and prediction were not the cause of Pharaoh's sin, but the divine foresight of it was the ground of his foretelling it. Besides it is expressly said, again and again, that *Pharaoh hardened his own heart.* (See Exodus 8:15–32.) In truth Pharaoh, who seems often to have heard of the God of Israel, from the very first despised and spurned him. When Moses and Aaron were introduced to him, and mentioned God's demand, the wicked monarch said, "Who is the Lord, that I should obey his voice to let Israel go? I know not the Lord, neither will I let Israel go." (Exodus 5:2.) Thus by his pride, obstinacy, and horrible blasphemies, he provoked the Most High. He tempted the thunder of his judgments by resisting the appeals of his mercy: for, as soon as any plague was withdrawn, the chastised criminal only hardened his heart the more. This is repeatedly declared, but in no part of the narrative more forcibly than in Exodus 9:34: "And, when Pharaoh saw that the rain and the hail and the thunders were ceased, he sinned yet more, and hardened his heart, he and his servants."

Thus God's hardening the heart of Pharaoh was a judicial act, a punishment for having, of his own free will, hardened himself. This is implied in even the latter half of the text, that Pharaoh "would not let them go." In all this Pharaoh felt no constraint laid upon him, no force of any necessity, no power of any decree. He acted agreeably to his inclination, and God in righteous judgment allowed him so to do.

After the same manner the unbelieving Jews, both in Isaiah's time, and in the time of the apostles, were chastised and rejected. They had made their own hearts fat, and shut their own eyes, and closed their own ears, before God in judgment issued his mandate to the same effect against them. Only refer to the chapter of Isaiah's prophecies (the 5th), which *precedes* the one containing the vision and the denunciation, and you will see how grossly the people had sinned, and how wilfully they had aforetime hardened their souls.

This then is the mode of God's judicial operations with sinners, such as Pharaoh. He hardened his heart, not by making him a bad man, but by judicially allowing him to make himself worse, and to sink into a callous and reprobate state of mind.

II. *What then may we learn from these facts?*

Everything in the Bible carries its lesson; and every man is under obligation to learn it. From the hardening of Pharaoh's heart we have many things to learn. See

1. *The thorough depravity of the human heart.* The root of all the impiety in Pharaoh's history was that spiritual corruption which came down to him from Adam. That corruption comes down to each of us. Every man is a Pharaoh by nature. Our hearts contain the seeds of those diabolical acts which were matured in his life; for, left to ourselves, the iniquity, which lies hidden within us, would soon be brought out in the visible conduct. Temptation and opportunity are sure to elicit our native character, unless the grace of God intervene, and keep it under check. Hence no man is safe who does not know this fault of his nature. Ignorance of our true state will be sure to lead us to a false confidence. We shall trust in ourselves and fall. Come then to the looking-glass of God's word. Our portrait is correctly drawn in it; and we may see it at length, if we do but take from our eyes that veil of self-love and fond esteem which Satan strives to cast over them. In that faithful mirror we shall see that our interior person is as deformed as was the outward life of Pharaoh. We shall see that our heart is stone, our thoughts evil, and only evil continually, and every preparation of them as ready as possible for saying and doing as Pharaoh said and did. Learn also

2. *The danger of indulging an evil heart, and of resisting better convictions.* Evil weeds grow fast enough of themselves; but if watered and encouraged they soon choke up all useful vegetation. Thus, if the wickedness of the heart be indulged and cherished, it will speedily become enormous, and overpower every better feeling. The individual who begins with what are called *little things* advances to greater: and crimes, at which that individual would once have shuddered, become shockingly familiar. "Is thy servant a dog that he should do this thing?" said one, who did not *then* believe himself capable of doing what was described to him; but who, nevertheless, in process of time, *did it.*

Then take heed of Pharaoh's sin. Take heed of stifling convictions of right and wrong, and thereby hardening your heart. Every instance of resisting such convictions is an aggression upon the soul, by that fierce enemy who is ever seeking its destruction. It leaves the heart more insensible than it was. It takes away a portion of power, and blunts every energy for using what remains. Beware then of provoking God by your inattention to his warnings, by your neglect of his means of grace, by your deafness to the reproofs of conscience and the lessons of providence. Beware too of infidel cavillings. Especially take heed of that most fearful part of Pharaoh's conduct, the despising of mercy and respite in succession, and the becoming worse and worse, after protestations of repentance and professions of amendment. Alas, how often is the minister of Christ called to lament over this wickedness of the human heart, and to see the most profligate conduct follow fast upon the kindest deliverances or the most solemn warnings! Take special heed of this grievous sin; for it is the very sin which will sink you into that reprobate state which engulphed Pharaoh, and which still engulphs its tens of thousands. Hence forget not to observe

3. *The certain destruction which awaits all who harden their hearts against God.* Plague after plague was sent upon Egypt; under any one of which Pharaoh might have lost his life. Every hour was an hour of danger to him. Judgment might have dashed upon him in a moment: and even the mercy which spared him only paved the way for his more signal destruction. At length that destruction came; and when it came it was in a form as novel as it was terrible, as overwhelming as it was unexpected. Thus it still daily is. Impenitent sinners are cut down silently, or cut off openly, and sent to the perdition which they would not avoid. For verily who ever hardened himself against God, and as to his soul prospered? Who ever strove with his Maker and came off unscathed? Who ever said, in his heart and life, "I know not the Lord," and then died with the salvation of the Lord in his hand? None! none!! none!!! Then take this warning word into your best recollection, ponder it, and pray over it. And may the God of mercy save you!

Another lesson which we must most carefully learn is

4. *The need in which we stand of renewing grace.* With hearts naturally depraved, and with inclinations ready to welcome temptations, how can we, of ourselves, escape that hardness which merits divine wrath? There is nothing which we can command, whereby we may be saved from it. Neither have external things any such force, however exciting or remarkable they may be. All the miracles which Moses wrought were unavailing for the conversion of Pharaoh and his servants. Even the severest sufferings and losses, and the most appalling sights and sounds, were incapable of softening a single soul.

Thus it ever has been; and thus it still is. Nothing but the grace of the Spirit of God can affect the heart of man in that way which will make him a new creature. Without that Spirit we shall continue dead while we live, and fall into a living death when we die. The Jews witnessed our Lord's miracles, and heard his beautiful words: but, excepting where his Spirit entered the heart, no saving efficacy followed.

Then let me warn you of your need of that Spirit, and show you how you may obtain it. It is not your coming to church, and listening to singing, or hearing a sermon,—neither is it your reading in private, nor observing any devout custom, which will change your heart and cleanse it. Those things are blessed means indeed, but they are not the efficient blessing itself. You must look through them all, for the Holy Spirit of Jesus to soften and sanctify you. And that Spirit will be sent into your heart, if you do but earnestly, honestly, and perseveringly, seek for it: for, "the Father will give his holy Spirit to them that ask him." (Luke 11:13.)

But let us not leave off till we have learned

5. *The fact that in all these things there is glory for God, and encouragement for the true Christian.* Amid all the impieties of the king of Egypt, God was consulting his own spotless honour. The Egyptian strove, and rebelled, and blasphemed; but God had him in his omnipotent grasp, and turned him and all his impiety into that course which ended in the greater glory of the King of kings. Yea, in the very midst of all the wicked hardness of Pharaoh, God sent a message to him by Moses, to admonish him that all his opposition to the divine will would tend only to the manifestation of the divine honour: "And in very deed for this cause have I raised thee up, for to shew in thee my power, and that my name may be declared throughout all the earth." (Exodus 9:16.) Thus it still is: "the wrath of man will be turned to the praise of God;" and all the opposition of ungodly men will end in the greater deliverance of the godly, and the brighter glory of God. In a wonderful manner, God will bring round all the spite and persecution and hindrance of his enemies to tell for his own honour. In some way or other it will be made to contribute to his praise.

Then, Christian brethren, take courage under your own griefs, and under the sorrows of the church. God will not fail you: but, if he has begun a good work in your heart, he will not leave it unfinished, but perform it unto the day of Christ. Only be not discouraged. Say not bitter things of yourselves, beyond what is fitting for a contrite spirit to say. Say not that you are hardening your heart, when perhaps you really are grieving at its remaining hardness. Say not you are going to destruction, when you are longing to be delivered from it. Such fears and such feelings are not the usual marks of a reprobate mind. If you are not cleaving to old ways, not taking pleasure in sin, not hating reproof, not despising the calls of God and the exhortations of his ministers, you ought rather to look up with faith, than bend down with despondency. Let your greater concern be the more thorough softening of your heart, the more devoted obedience of your life. In spite of doubts and drawbacks, repose with babe-like confidence on the arm of the God of Israel. He will bring you out of Egypt, and will conduct you far away from Pharaoh to the celestial land.

SERMON XV.

THE ANGEL JEHOVAH OUR GUIDE TO BE FOLLOWED, AND OUR GOVERNOR TO BE FEARED.[1]

Exodus 23:20–22.

"Behold, I send an Angel before thee, to keep thee in the way, and to bring thee into the place which I have prepared. Beware of him and obey his voice, provoke him not; for he will not pardon your transgressions: for my name is in him. But if thou shalt indeed obey his voice, and do all that I speak, then I will be an enemy unto thine enemies, and an adversary unto thine adversaries."

[1] Preached Thursday Evening, February 8th, 1849.

THESE words were spoken by Jehovah to Moses, amid "the thick darkness" which shrouded mount Sinai. They were words of light and life, compared with the gloom of the scene, and the deathly tremor which had seized the people. They comprised a comfortable assurance to those people as wanderers, and a needful caution to them as frail and fallible beings.

Now what they were to Israel they are to us; for they were written for our learning, and are in substance repeated in the gospel revelation. That revelation has indeed both freshened and increased their meaning, as well as set it forth to us with wondrous and touching energy. Let us then give our devoutest attention to the words themselves, as presenting to us a gracious announcement, a solemn caution, and an encouraging promise.

I. *The gracious announcement* is contained in the twentieth verse. Herein we are addressed as travellers to a destined abode. An angel, we are certified, is sent before us, at once to pioneer our way, to keep us in it, and to secure our arrival at the end of it.

1. *We are travellers.* Israel, while in Egypt, were comparatively settlers. They abode, for many generations, in the home of idols, the house of bondage, the land of death. As soon as they were ransomed from this evil plight, and brought out of it, they entered on an entirely new mode of life. They became travellers instead of settlers, and pilgrims instead of hereditary bondsmem. True, they were led into "a waste howling wilderness;" but they breathed its air freely, and walked through its wastes in the sandals of liberty. Thus it is with ouvselves. In our natural estate, which is one of cruel sin and deathly bondage, we are settlers, sleepers, idlers. We may be described as sour wine settled on its lees, and are inactive and unstirring as to anything good. When our Redeemer's grace awakens and rescues us, then we rise, go forth in the full liberty of the gospel, and, shod with the preparation of its peace, commence a journey, of which the journey of the Israelites was a type and figure.

2. *Our destined abode is a place which God has prepared for us.* Canaan was selected as the homeland of Israel. Heaven is the rest and inheritance of all true believers. He who prepared the nether home prepared the upper. Canaan was marked out for Israel, long before they or even their great ancestor set foot in it. "When the Most High divided to the nations their inheritance, when he separated the sons of Adam, he set the bounds of the people according to the number of the children of Israel." (Deuteronomy 32:8.) So heaven, the true Canaan, was prepared for "the followers of the Lamb," from even "before the foundation of the world." When Israel departed from Egypt, it was no new or sudden project to lead them to Canaan. The entire plan had long before, even antecedent to their bondage, been well ordered and made sure. In like manner the method and end of our redemption had been arranged and secured, even prior to our fall in Adam. All the antediluvian patriachs had looked for a new paradise; and Noah and Abraham, and all their fellows in the faith, had waited for a world and city which hath immovable foundations. Their God had prepared for them all that they desired to find; and now the realities of that preparation are set forth to us in the gospel.

3. *An angel is sent before us,* and that for the threefold purpose (as already intimated) of arranging our path, keeping us in it, and securing our perseverance to the end of it. And *who* is that angel? He is Michael, or some other pre-eminent but created angel, say a certain class of divines, who *seem* to take pleasure in putting Christ under a bushel whenever they can. But even Jewish Rabbins put them to shame; for they freely confess that the angel, here and similarly elsewhere revealed, can be none other than "the Angel of the covenant," "the Redeemer of Israel." Simple minded Christians can be at no loss to determine what angel is meant in the passage before us, because Jehovah calls him "mine angel," and says, "My name is in him." He also attributes to him the power of forgiving or not forgiving transgressions. And "who,"as the Jews in after days aptly concluded, "who can forgive sins but God?" Confidently therefore do we believe that the angel announced was that very "Angel who redeemed Jacob from all evil," who "appeared to Moses in a flame of fire in a bush," and who also discovered himself to Joshua, for the purpose of completing, as the divine Captain of the host, what Moses had begun. This Angel, it cannot be denied, claimed to himself the titles and perfections of the Godhead. He could therefore be no other than the Angel Jehovah, the second person in the united Three, the very Messiah himself. Besides the offices here assigned to the promised angel exactly coincide with those which are attributed to our Saviour Christ. In the journey of the church to the true Canaan, Christ is our forerunner. He makes all arrangements for our travel and progress. He heads the line of march, and always walks onwards in the far van, to remove difficulties, deter or disable enemies, and to provide all that our necessities require. Blessed be our divine and sovereign Angel! He orders the course of this world, ordains its events, and by his "never-failing providence" so tempers every storm which falls on his true church, and so wonderfully sustains and helps it that, while all things work together for its good, nothing prevails against it. And what is true of our Israel collectively is true of ourselves individually. The Lord Jesus goes before each one of us, if we are his faithful people, to mark out our path, and to order our footsteps in it. Nothing befals us but what has his previous cognisance and approval.

What is more, he *keeps us* in the way. But for this keeping, what would have become of Israel, and what would become of us? Ten thousand things would seduce us from it, or our own wilfulness would turn us out of it. There was no path in the wilderness through which Israel journeyed: and all our steps in the way of life are new and untried, till the moment we enter upon them. Greatly therefore do we need to be kept and upheld from hour to hour, and from step to step, as we cannot tell what the one may bring forth, or to what the other may lead.

And then, what is still more cheering and glorious, our Angel "ever liveth to make intercession for us," and to *bring us* safely to the promised rest. Left to themselves Israel would never have reached Canaan, nor have conquered it. Because the Angel was with them they did both. Thus is it, and thus will it be with us. Left to ourselves our carcases would soon fall in the wilderness. Amalek would soon smite and overcome us, and the goodly land would never greet our eyes. But the Lord Jesus is in the midst of his little band; and because he is with them they enter the promised inheritance, and take possession of it with a song and a shout. And when we reach it what will it be? Canaan was prepared for Israel. God, in his providence, so ordered the course of events, as to allow the Canaanites, amid all their enormous wickedness, to revel in astonishing prosperity. They had splendid cities, goodly towns, and a land flowing with milk and honey. All these things were prepared for Israel, without any forethought on their part. "The wealth of the wicked was laid up for the just;" and Israel inherited that wealth at the bidding of the Lord of the whole earth. All this marvellous preparation was but a faint picture of what the gospel tells us, concerning the ready state of heaven for all who are destined to enter it. Its mansions are ready, its banquet is spread, and all the glories of eternity beam upon it. But who has done all this for us? None other than he who speaks in our text, only it was by a very different process. The Angel of the covenant became incarnate. In our own nature he effected our redemption, and now is gone first into the land of glory, "to prepare a place for us" individually, where all is prepared for Israel collectively.

II. *The words of caution* which follow the gracious announcement are these:—"Beware of him and obey his voice, provoke him not; for he will not pardon your transgressions: for my name is in him." (Exodus 23:21.)

Though God does everything for us, yet are we required to do what he bids us. All his commands are grounded in truth and wisdom and have respect at once to his honour and our welfare. There is too a certain *fitness* in them, which commends itself to the judgment of every enlightened believer. Thus his angel is holy, and the people of his charge must be holy also. He does not gather his Israel that they may live as they list, but that they may live to his praise. He has bought them with a price: they therefore are to serve him in love. Without obedience to his will they can neither prove their love, nor show forth his praise. Hence Jehovah will have them reverence his beloved Angel. He will have us, like Israel, "beware of him, and obey his voice."

The will and the voice of the Angel of Israel were recognised in divers manners in the wilderness. Himself dwelt among the people, locally, and visibly, by means of a mysterious and marvellous cloud, which pillared up itself into a lamp-like flame by night, and, as a grateful canopy, expanded itself for shade by day. From this cloud a voice, it seems, was often heard. The Angel "spake" to Israel, we are told, from out of "the cloudy pillar;" and Israel either to their benefit obeyed, or at their peril disobeyed what was spoken. This pillar of cloud, as the symbol of the divine presence among them, also intimated the will of their Angel-guide by moving or resting, according as the people were to march or halt. All which things they were carefully to observe, and obediently to follow.

God's command for us to observe and obey this same Angel, as his only begotten and well beloved Son, was repeated at his baptism in Jordan, and at his transfiguration on mount Tabor: "This is my beloved Son, in whom I am well pleased: hear him." Every page of the gospel is charged with commands to believe in and obey this beloved One. The utmost stress is laid upon the article of our obedience to him in all things. Himself made such obedience the test and proof of our adhesion to him. "If ye love me keep my commandments." Should we, with some professors, fancy that we can pursue our spiritual course, without the mention of law, or caution, or admonition, we are in danger of being taught a sharp and bitter lesson, by being left to ourselves. Some unwary slip, or humiliating fall, may be commissioned to teach us that we are not so angelic as to be above the need of constant remindings and arousings to duty. Were such things unnecessary for even the best of saints in this evil world, the apostolic epistles might be reduced to nearly half their length. But he who knows us better than we know ourselves has seen fit to record many a memento in them, respecting even the commonest duties and the worst sins. It is no marvel then that in the text it is said to Israel of the Angel whom they were to obey, "*Provoke him not*; for he will not pardon your transgressions." Alas, how often did Israel do this very thing, "by their hill-altars," and their other idolatries, by their murmurings, lustings, and rebellions! And how great is our danger of doing the like! Others may boast as they please: but the man who knows the plague and treachery of his own heart, and entertains exalted views of the holiness of his Saviour, knows full well the innate proneness of his nature to rebel against that Saviour, in either the purity of his precepts, the spirituality of his laws, or the wisdom of his corrections. But, while it becomes us to be well aware of this proneness, there is ground for comfort in the assurance that no vigilant, earnest, affectionate, spiritually-minded Christian is likely to *provoke* him whom his soul loveth. Should such an one fall, it will be through infirmity, and not from deliberate intention. The infinite charity therefore of the great Redeemer will not, in *such* case, be so provoked, as to call for any correction in *anger*.

There are however multitudes in the camp of our Israel to whom we, as the echoes of God's voice, are bound to say solemnly and loudly, "*Provoke him not;* for he will not pardon your transgressions." A profession of something like pure and spiritual religion, when tarnished by inconsistencies, must be very displeasing to the holy Saviour. When those who profess to love him, his house, and his people, join hands with the world, because they have not resolution to withstand the force of its allurements, its maxims, and its invitations, this is very likely to provoke his displeasure, and call for his denial of pardon. In like manner a careless spirit beneath a decent exterior, and a lax and self-indulgent conduct in private, cannot be otherwise than offensive to him who "is of purer eyes than to behold iniquity." The sins of benighted heathen cannot carry with them half the provocation that the inconsistencies of professedly enlightened Christians must carry. It was because the favoured Israelites, who had many times acknowledged the Lord to be their God, disbelieved his word, and contravened his will, that he forgave not their transgressions, "but sware in his wrath that they should not enter into his rest."

Then let these words ring in your hearts, and help to regulate your homes, "*Provoke him not,* for he will not pardon your transgressions." On the other hand, let every humble and faithful Israelite, who follows the Angel of our redemption, take good cheer from what remains for our consideration, namely

III. *The encouraging promise,* which is appended to the caution, in the 22nd verse: "But if thou shalt indeed obey his voice, and do all that I speak, then I will be an enemy unto thine enemies, and an adversary unto thine adversaries." Then follows an enumeration of the manifold blessings which should constantly accrue to the people, as the willing and obedient servants of the Angel, the Holy One of Israel. The blessings are so varied and comprehensive, that a nation in the enjoyment of them could not fail of rising to the highest level of happiness and prosperity. The record of them is an important and an inviting memento to our own nation, and to every nation under heaven, that the truest hope of national prosperity is national godliness. Text on text might easily be adduced in proof of this position. Suffice it to remind you that St. Paul, with the Old Testament in mind, deliberately declared that "godliness is profitable for all things, having the promise of the life that now is, and of that which is to come." Godly nations shall possess the one, and godly individuals both the one and the other. Everything however depends on obedience: "If thou shalt *indeed* obey his voice, and do all that I speak." This is the hinge on which the promise turns, and we must ourselves take care to turn it aright. Though all Scripture makes it clear that the benefits of the gospel are in some sense conditional, yet certainly not in that sense which, traced to its legitimate issues, would make man his own saviour. "Believe on the Lord Jesus Christ, *and* thou shalt be saved," is only the evangelical version of our text. It makes salvation depend on believing, which is one sort of obeying; and assuredly there is no salvation for us without it. But then the self-same Spirit who said, "Believe and be saved," has admonished us that, while faith is our *duty*, it is God's *gift*. We stand not on quibbles and profitless questionings, as to the reconciliation of these things; but we solve them all, with thankful satisfaction, by one text: "For by grace are ye saved through faith; and that not of yourselves: it is the gift of God." (Ephesians 2:8.)

With the faithful and obedient Israelite God will, as it were, form an alliance offensive and defensive. "I will be an enemy unto thine enemies, and an adversary unto thine adversaries."

The promise was every thing to the literal Israel; for they were surrounded with wonderfully powerful enemies, and were themselves totally inexperienced in the arts of war. To us that promise, in its spiritual bearings, is still more important and cheering. Our enemies are those real foes, of whom the foes of Israel were but shadows. Our Amalek is a mighty spirit, whose legions are untold: and we have more adversaries within us than Israel ever had in all their tribes. And what is our strength for wrestling with them? It is pitiable weakness. Unaided and unsupported by our Angel captain we should perish in an hour: but in his strength our weakness is made strong, and through his grace we can "wax valiant in fight." Satan is our enemy, but our Angel will bruise him shortly under his feet. The world is our adversary: but that same Angel said, "Be of good cheer, I have overcome the world." Sin is our besetting foe, but the same Saviour vanquished it on the cross. Even death himself is foiled of his prey, for the Angel of life has crushed his head, and drawn his sting. And as to all inferior ills, who or what shall harm us, if we are followers of that which is good? Afflictions may cast us down, but they shall not destroy us. Bereavements may pierce our souls; but the smart shall turn to our joy, by the lightening of those souls in their upward flight to the things which are not seen. In a word, "All things work together for good." "All things are yours, whether Paul, or Apollos, or Cephas, or the world, or life, or death, or things present, or things to come,—all are yours; and ye are Christ's; and Christ is God's." (1 Corinthians 3:21–23.)

Let a few reflections form the conclusion of this discourse:

1. *How adoringly ought every eye and every ear to be fixed on Christ, the Angel of our salvation!* What the Israelites knew of him indistinctly and imperfectly we know clearly and fully. They chiefly knew his power and terribleness. We know his love and tenderness. They beheld him mystically in a pillar of cloud. We see him on the cross, and on the throne of the majesty on high. Ten thousand affecting considerations unknown to them meet us at every point, and call us to love him with all our love, and to obey him in thought, and word, and deed. He comes so nigh unto us as to stand at our heart's door and knock for admittance within us. He spreads a table for us in his sanctuary, and invites us to the feast. He provides the viands, even his own body and his own blood, sacramentally presented for the eating and drinking of the children of faith. From that table he leads us, as it were, afresh along the journey of life, and strengthens us for its roughnesses, and refreshes us under its burthens. Then meet him where he presides, and whither he bids you come.

2. *How perilous is unbelief in even its milder forms!* Among the myriads who fell in the wilderness there doubtless were not a few who did not, in their murmurings and hard speeches, go the length that others went. Yet these also were excluded from Canaan: "they could not enter in," because they were not altogether obedient to the Angel of the covenant. Thus, to this day, the unsteady and irresolute professor is in as great danger of perishing as the most daring profligate. Their positions differ only in their own eyes, not in the eyes of God.

Let then no man think to be saved by virtue of what may be called *generalization.* It is not enough to be *of* Israel: we must *be Israel.* It will not suffice to be *among* Christians: we must *be* Christians. Each one must believe for himself, and obey for himself: otherwise he will find no salvation for himself.

3. *How cheerfully should every believer follow the Saviour as his guide and protector!* That Saviour goes before him. Hence all providences are arranged for him. HE is with him to keep him in the way. Then let the believer walk with him and pray to him. HE is with him too, to bring him securely to Canaan. Then let him mount his Pisgah and forecast that Caanan.

God has provided more for him than he promised to Israel. "For since the beginning of the world men have not heard, nor perceived by the ear, neither hath the eye seen, O God, beside thee, what he hath prepared for him that waiteth for him." (Isaiah 64:4.)

SERMON XVI.

THE SAFETY OF ISRAEL IN JOURNEYING TO JERUSALEM.[1]

EXODUS 34:24.

"Neither shall any man desire thy land, when thou shalt go up to appear before the Lord thy God thrice in the year."

THE facts to which this Scripture refers were these. Three times in each year all the Hebrew males of sufficient age were to leave their homes, and to go, for solemn worship, to the spot which God might select for his tabernacle or temple. Those three times were the Passover, the Pentecost, and the Feast of Tabernacles; answering, in general description, to our Easter, Whitsuntide, and Michaelmas. To obviate all objections and allay all fears, Jehovah solemnly promised especial protection during the time of absence from home. Such a promise could never have been made except by the true God; for, had any false prophet ventured on such a test, the chances, so to speak, would have been so greatly against him, that none but madmen would have believed him. The promise therefore was a bold appeal to the knowledge and faith of Israel, and was intended to put that knowledge and that faith to a constantly recurring proof. The whole arrangement was wonderful in it-

[1] Preached Thursday Evening, February 10th, 1848.

self, and worthy of the God who devised it. It is full of wise and holy and profitable instruction. May we reap its richest product. The things which this arrangement for Israel was calculated to effect were important in themselves, and gracious in their tendencies. It was well adapted

I. *To keep all parties in vivid mindfulness of the unseen God.*

The great object of each journey was "to appear before the Lord their God." It was to bring them to the place where he had recorded his name, and where he especially manifested his presence. This spot was, in the progress of time, settled at Jerusalem, where alone all the high solemnities of their holy religion were allowed to be performed. The Lord God then was to be the great theme of their thoughts. The God of their fathers, the Holy One of Israel, the author of their wonders, and the giver of their mercies, was to be present in their hearts: for him they were to leave their homes, and for inspection, as it were, before his eye, they were to travel to Zion.

Thus Israel had always something to remember, and something for which to prepare, as each returning season approached. And yet the Lord God was the grand object to be kept in view. When any one of the three seasons approached, there was need of many little arrangements which would necessarily interest and affect all the members of a family. The husband would have to prepare for his journey; and the wife would have to forward that preparation, and to see to the going of her elder sons. And, as some were setting out "to see God in the sanctuary," and others were staying at home to be under his immediate protection, all these things were of a nature to affect the heart, and lead it to God.

And verily, brethren, in this thoughtless world is not any thing good which will lead sinners to think of God? To make the careless heart pause and ponder amid its whirl of business or round of pleasure, is of all things most desirable. Only let men "set God always before them," and there will not be much amiss. For this purpose, what we now call our great festivals are really designed. Our Christmas, Epiphany, and Good Friday, our Easter, Ascension Day and Whitsuntide, are only so many prominent periods for our especial appearing before the Lord our God. They are times for our more solemn travel up to the spiritual Zion, up to that spot in the gospel Palestine where our salvation was wrought out by the beloved Son of God. Unlike the Hebrews, we go in heart and mind to see realities, and not merely to contemplate shadows and perform figurative ceremonies. Every thing in the Christian church is designed to conduct us to Christ, and to centre all interests and all affections in him. This prescription was also adapted

II. *To remind every individual of the constant and universal rule of God.*

The Hebrew father left his wife and babes, for an interval of some weeks, and felt confident of their safety. The Hebrew mother saw her husband depart, and had no fears about herself or her little ones. The promise of their God was clear and sure; for he had said, "Neither shall any man desire thy land." What a beautiful and living lesson was this to every heart to confide in the fidelity of God as the sole Preserver of men! The nearer too any families were lodged on the borders of the land, the closer would this lesson come home. Some would be located in sight and sound of enemies, and yet all alarm would cease. The God of the family was a wall of fire round about the homestead; and the mother and her daughters, the housewife and her maidens, might go in and out, and lie down to rest, in security and peace. No man among the haters of Israel should think of doing them harm, for God would put it out of their thoughts. He was the Ruler of their jealous enemies, and without his sufferance they could do nothing.

Now to ourselves, dear brethren, the same deep and earnest convictions of the divine rule and governance are absolutely necessary. We can never look abroad without entire dismay, unless we carry with us a vivid assurance that "the Lord God omnipotent reigneth." If we turn our eye from him and his promises, we shall see nothing but confusion and terror, enemies ready to swallow us up, and circumstances dark and full of overwhelming difficulty. But the belief of Christ's power over all things will keep us steadfast, and peaceful, though we dwell as it were on a border land, and nothing but a brook or a hillock separates the Philistine, the Ammonite, or the Perizzite, from us. This rule of the God of Israel over all lands had respect to the very hearts of the enemies of Israel. No man was to *desire* their possessions. And yet the land of Israel was always desirable. So true is it that God has all hearts in his hand, that he can curb unruly desires, and check and chain the most wicked purposes of the most wicked men. Then what can he not do for our hearts, and for the multitude of their thoughts? If he can restrain a sinner, surely he can urge a saint! If he can prevent covetous desires when wicked men would harm us, he assuredly can impart and foster holy desires when we seek to do them good. In these considerations let us find comfort, and take courage. The arrangement was further adapted

III. *To enliven the dulness and monotony of Hebrew life in remoter districts.*

We must recollect that, although the cities, towns, and larger villages of Judea had their synagogues, there yet was only one tabernacle or temple at which sacrifices were offered and fuller services performed. The consequence was that numerous families of females, and sickly and infirm persons, were debarred from those privileges which males of good age and good health alone enjoyed. Books too were rarities, and intercourse between one place and another was comparatively scanty. It therefore is easy to imagine that husbands and elder sons, who went up to the festival, would, on their return, have much that was refreshing to tell to pious wives and others among the sick, the aged, and the bereaved. Accounts of the various sacrifices would be like descriptions of sermons; and the repetition or report of some new psalm which was sung, or some fresh prophecy which was uttered would be intensely interesting, and religiously reviving to many a gracious heart. Thus kind and considerate was the God of heaven towards the thousands of his Israel. By such means he seems to have kept up the knowledge and reverence of himself, in the more distant parts of the land, and to have provided for the spiritual refreshment and sustentation of souls which had tasted the grace of his covenant.

And who will say that our God is not equally good to his people, when secluded from society or deprived of facilities in the present day? Is he not as thoughtful for the followers of his dear Son as he was when his people looked to Moses his servant? Verily he is. It requires not an unusual extent of information to discern how the Lord, by his Spirit, comforts those who love him, even when they are cut off from the ordinary privileges of his church. If they cannot go up to appear before him, he will condescend to come and manifest himself to them. The sick chamber, or the distant cottage, at the far extremity of a spacious parish has a thousand times borne witness of the freedom and abundance of his grace. Often too has it been found that individuals, in the least favoured parts of our Israel, have grown in grace and thriven in holiness, with also an enviable fervency and simplicity of spirit beyond what is commonly discerned in localities where every privilege abounds. The custom of Israel, alluded to in the text, was also intended

IV. *To teach the people certain moral lessons of great moment.*

1. It taught them *social duties and brotherly kindness.* Many of them living in different quarters, and yet at the distance of a tedious journey, found it a matter of convenience and comfort to travel together in companies. The early history of our blessed Lord tells us this fact; for while he, as a youth, stayed behind in Jerusalem, Joeseph and Mary, "supposing him to have been in the company (that is, the little band of fellow travellers homewards), went a day's journey, and sought him among their kinsfolk and acquaintance." Thus the festival journeys of Israel were made companionable, and one neighbour and acquaintance helped another in them. So also we learn from Isaiah that as these companies, in the hotter months, travelled by night, they cheered and enlivened one another with holy song, as well as with instrumental music. "Ye shall have a song, as in the night when a holy solemnity is kept; and gladness of heart, as when one goeth with a pipe to come into the mountain of the Lord, to the mighty One of Israel." (Isaiah 30:29.)

2. It taught them also, when assembled at the place of meeting, *the importance of national unity.* The different tribes all meeting together in one spot gave an opportunity of kindly recognition and good understanding. It furnished a fine season for settling little differences, and soothing partial animosities, and allaying embryo jealousies among border tribes. Especially would it present to them the beauty of union, as a favoured people separated from the rest of the world. The writer of the hundred and twenty-second Psalm seems to have glowed with this very thought as he penned his beautiful lines. Read that entire psalm.

3. It above all taught the Hebrews *to look for better things.* Their constant journeying to Zion reminded them of their pilgrim state, and stirred them up to long for rest, and a settled residence with their God. It inclined them to say, "Blessed are they that *dwell* in thy house; they will be *still* praising thee." And then their assembling in one religious band in Zion was calculated to lead their thoughts to that "city, whose builder and maker is God." They might sing or say, in an exalted sense, "They go from strength to strength, every one of them in Zion appeareth before God." (Psalm 84:7.) High and rapturous themes are here presented to our hallowed meditation. The church of our Saviour, though composed of many tribes, is but one; and all its tribes *ought to feel* as one in him. Love is to be their hearts' delight, and their daily study. They are to cultivate "brotherly kindness," and not to sacrifice unity of spirit for things of trifling consideration. All the imperfections of their worship now are to remind them that "as strangers and pilgrims," they are to look for a better service in a better temple. Thither we hope one day to go up, and join in an assembly which shall never separate. But we have somewhat yet to learn, and we can never set it in too strong a light before our mental eye. It is a great practical truth, which the regulation named in our text was eminently fitted to force on the attention of the Jews: for, lastly, that regulation was adapted

V. To *exhibit the intimate connexion of faithful obedience and individual prosperity.*

God gave a command to the Israelites, and attached a promise to the observance of it. They were to leave their homes, *on his service,* thrice every year. But, though obedience to that requisition might seem to involve great risk and much loss of time, God pledged himself that no ill should ensue. "No man should desire their land;" as much as to say, "Go ye as I command, and I will prosper you as ye desire: appear at my temple, and I will take care of your home."

And, what is worthy of our close attention, there is not, throughout the whole history of the Jews, any record, nor even any intimation of an infraction of the divine promise. On no one occasion does it appear that the enemies of Israel ever made an incursion into their land during the absence of the male population in appearing before the Lord their God. Glad would infidels and gainsayers, both ancient and modern, have been, had they been able to discover any instance in which Israel obeyed, and Jehovah failed. Here then let us rejoice: "Our God is a rock." None ever trusted in him and were made ashamed.

His rule of moral dealing is the same with his Christian children as with his Jewish family. He says to us, in Christ Jesus, "Who shall harm you if ye be followers of that which is good?" "If God be for us, who shall be against us?" "Fear not them which kill the body, but are not able to kill the soul." (Matthew 10:28.) In a word, as David said in his day, so is it still to be said in our day, according to our new version translation,

> "Fear him, ye saints, and ye will then
> Have nothing else to fear;
> Make ye his service your delight,
> He'll make your wants his care."

Let us not depart without bearing in mind,

1. *That our privileges and securities are far greater than any which were known in Palestine.* He, whom the children of the law but dimly discerned, is now made conspicuous to us under the gospel. Christ Jesus is plainly set forth to our eyes. All that ancient believers desired to see and know, we see and understand. We have not to go up, thrice a year, to some central spot even to hear the full gospel; but it is preached, near to our homes, at least "every Sabbath-day." Our wives and our little ones are not debarred from attending, because of a long and toilsome journey; but all may join in the services of the Christian sanctuary. These things should be more highly esteemed than, alas! they too generally are. Many a Hebrew mother will rise up in judgment against the careless daughters of Christendom: for the Hebrew women occasionally took the long journey to the temple, but many a Christian female will not take a few steps to worship and hear in the house of the Lord. And remember,

2. *That we still need a protector for our homes.* We can have no security for them unless we have the Lord for our guardian. Nothing is safe without his keeping. But what a comfort to a Christian parent, when he or she is called to leave home for a season, to be able to commend all who are left to the Keeper of Israel, who never slumbers! In vain will any one desire our goods if he be the watcher over them. So, as to what is now called "our national defences," though every prudent patriot will do what is prudent, yet our highest wisdom will be to make the Lord our defence. Let England *trust* in him, and our shores are safe.

3. *That we all must appear before the Lord our God.* We must come up from the grave, and stand before him. The homes of the dead must be left once for all. None can remain in them. Every tenant of them must go forth at the voice of the "Archangel and the trump of God." There will be neither power nor practicability to disobey *that* call. But all the tribes of Adam, from his first to his last born son, will be compelled to meet their God. Multitudes however will be denied admittance to the heavenly Jerusalem. Because they refused to meet him in the day of the gospel, they will be driven from him in the day of judgment. They believed not his promises. They trusted not their all with him. They went not up to his throne of grace to meet him. They will therefore be bidden to depart from him. Still a countless throng *will* enter the everlasting city, never again to return from it, or to leave its unutterable pleasures.

With whom then are you, as individuals, likely to be joined when the great gathering of souls shall come, and their unending destiny be determined?

SERMON XVII.

THE BITTEN ISRAELITES AND THE BRAZEN SERPENT.[1]

Numbers 21:8.

"And the Lord said unto Moses, Make thee a fiery serpent, and set it upon a pole: and it shall come to pass, that every one that is bitten, when he looketh upon it, shall live."

[1] Preached Sunday Morning, January 19th, 1851.

THE Israelites, when on their march from Egypt to Canaan, were not more remarkable for God's mercies shown to them, than for their murmurings expressed against him. Like their posterity in the days of the Lord Jesus and John the Baptist, they could never be pleased or made content, no, not with even the possession of all that they craved. No sooner was one want supplied, but they complained of another.

Thus, after years of miraculous protection and sustentation, they fell into fresh complainings. Loathing the very bread and the water for which they had dyingly cried, they "again spake against God and against Moses." To correct and humble them, "the Lord sent fiery flying serpents among the people; and much people of Israel died." As he had fed them miraculously, so he punished them miraculously. They had seen fiery serpents, and scorpions also, before; for, as Moses says in Deuteronomy 8:15, the desert through which they travelled abounded with them. But it does not appear that they suffered the slightest ill from them. Now however, that their fresh sin required a fresh chastisement, God takes off his restraint from these venomous creatures, and sends them as his new army against his old rebels. He sends too (as there is reason to believe) the winged sort, that their aspect might be as terrific as their bite was mortal. The whole circumstances were written for our learning. They were written to admonish us of the wickedness of murmuring against God, and of the danger of tempting him by ingratitude and unbelief. "Neither let us tempt Christ, as some of them also tempted, and were destroyed of serpents. Neither murmur ye, as some of them also murmured, and were destroyed of the destroyer." (1 Corinthians 10:9, 10.) But not only this. In the lifting up of the brazen serpent upon a pole, we look back upon one of the fine old glorious types of the gospel; while we recollect that the great Antitype himself has taught us how to understand it: "And, as Moses lifted up the serpent in the wilderness, even so must the Son of man be lifted up." (John 3:14.)

Hence, let me invite you to consider

I. *The position of the Israelites as representing the moral condition of mankind.* Their position may be characterized thus:—

1. It was *fearful and tormenting.* To see the air filled with hideous and furious serpents,—to hear them whirring and hissing all around, and to see multitudes of themselves writhing and dying under the agony of their bite, must have formed a scene as terrible, and even as horrifying, as the most spectral painting mind can picture.

The serpents are called "*fiery*," either from their colour, or from the burning sensation occasioned by their poison. There is reason also to think that their fieriness, whether it meant their colour, their flame-like breath, the fury of their attack, or the power of their bite, was intended to contrast with that refreshing water which the Israelites had despised. No uncommon thing is it for God to punish sinners by that sort of torment which is antipodal to those mercies which they have abused or trodden under foot. Dives, whose palate indulged in sumptuous fare, was reduced to the torment of wanting even one drop of water to cool his burning tongue.

But it is worth our notice that, in the Hebrew, these "*fiery* serpents" are called *Seraphim*; who are so named because, though we know not exactly what it means, they are *the burning ones.* Hence these specially sent serpents are supposed to have been not small but large creatures, and therefore both the more terrific and the more destructive.

They are described as "*flying*" serpents (see Isaiah 14:29, and Isaiah 30:6); and we dare not doubt that they were literally such. The analogies of nature accord with the fact; for, if the sea has its flying fish, the earth may have its flying snakes. Besides ancient history, not to adduce modern testimonies, is so distinct upon the question, that it cannot be evaded by German neologists or French infidels. Herodotus, who lived nearer to the times of Moses than any other historian on whom, for such things, we can depend, tells us (book 2, chap. 75, 76) that in the course of his Egyptian travels he went near to the city Buto, on purpose to see the *winged serpents* of which he had heard. He describes them as resembling those which the Greeks called *hydræ*, water-snakes. He also states that near to Buto were large heaps of the spinal bones of those serpents, which had been killed and devoured by the bird called ibis. He mentions too, that the wings of these flying monsters were not feathery but membraneous, like those of a bat and not of a bird. Further than this, the theologian need not proceed.

It is our part, at this present, to think of the terror and torment of the Israelites, as furnishing a picture of our own morally miserable plight. We are bitten of "that old serpent, the devil." He flies about (often indeed as a seraph or angel of light) seeking whom he may devour. Not one, alas! has escaped the poison of his original bite. We all are infected by it. Through every vein and over the whole inner man has it spread, and will continue to spread till the one sovereign remedy is applied. Men may not always be sensible of the deadly infection, but that is one proof of its deadliness. It stupifies ere it kills.

2. *It was altogether hopeless.* The bite of the serpents, if unchecked by the one only process, was inevitably fatal. A bitten Israelite was a man of doom. As the poison entered his body, hope fled from his soul. He had nothing to do but to lie on the sand, agonize and die. Precisely thus is it with us as sinners. The poison of sin is mortal. For a time God's permission may spare the body, and art may strengthen or revive it: but the issue is not to be averted. Death is the penalty, of which sin is the poison; for "the sting of death is sin, and the strength of sin is the law."

3. *It was also entirely helpless.* The bite of the flying scourges admitted no human remedy. There was no practised leech in Israel for the cure of such a novel infliction. Gilead had not yet been heard of, and neither balm nor physician were to be found in the desert: so true also is it, that no human device can heal the hurt which sin has made in the soul. The wounds of that soul defy all the magic and all the medicine of the pretenders to spiritual pharmacy, whom the world has ever produced. Proud man has frequently attempted to be his own physician, but in vain. Popery is but a college of spiritual quackery; and Socinianism is only a less imposing pretence for effecting what neither can achieve. "*Physicians of no value*" must, as Job felt, be the appellation of all the motley throng of Antichristian healers of the bite of the old serpent. Their arts are mere artifices, and their curious books, so full of dangerous and even deadly prescriptions, are fit only for the fire: because all attempts at rectifying the empoisoned souls, by the merit of any sort of human doing, will only give the malady tenfold virulence. Thus helpless as well as hopeless are all of us by nature.

4. *It was full of mental torture,* because they knew that their evil plight was occasioned solely by their crimes. It was one thing for their sufferings to be the effect of their sin, but it was another for them to *know* and *feel* that it was such. Their discontent and their murmuring brought bite, torture, and death to them: but they would have braved these consequences, had not their spirits been more deeply wounded than their bodies. "A wounded spirit who can bear?" Ah! brethren, while all the misery of man is occasioned by his guilt, it is the bitten conscience which brings that misery home to him. And, sooner or later, every one of us will know the smart of *that* bite, to be followed with either everlasting cure or everlasting death.

Such, generally speaking, are the points of resemblance between the condition of the Israelites and of ourselves. But there is one circumstance in which only few among us can be said to act as they acted. When the people felt their torment, they came to Moses, and said, "We have spoken against the Lord and against thee: pray the Lord that he take away the serpents from us." (Ver. 7.)

To feel our spiritual misery, and to go to our great Intercessor for its removal, are the first steps in the path of restoration to that health which is destined to end in a glorious immortality. The good Lord open many a prayerful heart in this congregation! Then will no prayer fail of its earnest desire. But, till we feel the smart of our sin, and cry to the one only Healer to have mercy on us, we shall be but as the dying Israelites, who perished before help came to them, or who refused it after it had come.—Now consider

II. *The relief which was provided for the Israelites as emblematical of the salvation which is provided for us.* Our blessed Lord's manifestation of the truth of this Old Testament shadow happily spares us from difficulty in tracing the mind of the Holy Ghost, with respect to its specific intentions. We have only to mark the incidents which our text comprises, and, if our eye be spiritual, we shall presently discern their evangelical bearing. Let it then be observed, that

1. The Lord directed Moses to make *a serpent of brass,* that is, a representation of the shape and colour of the very animal which inflicted the mortal bite. This, at the first glance, may seem an anomaly—an apparent confusion of purposes: for, as the serpents which bit the Israelites were evidently types of Satan and the fallen angels, so it might be supposed that an image of those serpents would be a representation of those evil ones. But that such is not the case we must certainly believe; for our Lord's exposition of the narrative obliges us to regard the brazen serpent as a lucid emblem of himself. He who giveth no account of his ways is often pleased to adopt methods at which human reason starts back with surprise. Nevertheless for this apparent inversion of things a reasonable account may be given. In the first place the eternal Son, though perfectly holy and innocent, took upon him "the likeness of sinful flesh," and so became a sinner by imputation and in appearance. In the next place he undertook to become "*a curse for us.*" The serpent was the first thing *cursed.* The figure of a serpent therefore was a fitting emblem of him who bore our curse. Moreover, by assuming our nature he bore the resemblance of those who are by birth "a generation of vipers," "a seed of evil doers."

The serpent, be it observed, was made of an inferior metal. It was constructed of *brass,* not of *gold.* So our Lord took upon him not the nature of angels but that of men, not the superior but the inferior rank of created beings. The process of the manufacture we are not told. Its fabrication must have occupied some time. During that interval the serpents were unchecked, and the work of death was going on. In like manner there is great mystery attending the incarnation of our Lord. We are told the fact but not its mystic incidents. Time had to reach a certain fulness, ere he was manifested to "destroy him that had the power of death, that is, the devil." But though the Israelites continued to die, yet doubtless the divine mercy spared its objects, while divine justice selected its deserved victims. It might have been that they alone died, who were and who *would* continue to be unbelievers and hard hearted. So before the coming of Christ none we may believe perished, but those who would have despised him, had they lived till his coming.

2. *The brazen serpent was elevated on a pole.* This was an important and even an essential part of the procedure. It was such both as a circumstance and as an emblem. It was necessary for it to be raised to a certain height, that the distant parts of the encampment might easily see it. That necessity was an emblem, not only of our Lord's crucifixion, but of the duty

of his ministers to lift up, as it were, the doctrine of his cross: "And I, if I be lifted up from the earth, will draw all men unto me. This he said, signifying what death he should die." (John 12:32, 33.) But here is no warrant for that blasphemous elevation of a wafer which the Church of Rome practises. As our more primitively constituted church says, "the sacrament of the Lord's Supper was not, by Christ's ordinance, reserved, carried about, *lifted up*, or worshipped." The lifting up of Christ, which his ministers are now to perform, is the preaching of his crucifixion, the exhibition of his gospel, and the unfaltering exaltation of his finished work. It is this that is the lifting up by which he draws to him those who are afar off, whether in sin at home or in heathenism abroad.

3. *To the serpent thus elevated all bitten sufferers were directed to look.* We are not indeed told how Moses made known the will of the Lord, whether by open proclamation or quiet message. Possibly he adopted more methods than one, though a public proclamation seems the more probable means. Something of that sort of communication must have been adopted; for how else would the people know what they were required to do? The brazen gleam of the suspended serpent might have flashed in the rays of the sun upon many an eye; but no such gleam would of itself have sufficed to heal a single individual. It was necessary, according to the divine stipulation, for each sufferer to raise a conscious and a willing eye to the elevated type. But how could the duty be known unless it were told and explained? In the gospel all is made plain to the meanest understanding. The command to preach that gospel stands out in fullest brightness: and the grand requirement of it is equally clear, "Believe in the Lord Jesus Christ, and thou shalt be saved;" "look unto me, and be ye saved, all the ends of the earth; for I am God, and there is none else." (Isaiah 45:22.) Yes, "all the ends of the earth," and the guiltiest sinners in the remotest of those ends, are at once directed and encouraged to look unto Christ. Ah! and they *must* look, spite of weakness, spite too of prejudice against the simplicity of the means, or they will die the second death: they must look too each one for himself. There was no looking by substitute or proxy on the brazen serpent; and verily there is no such thing as believing for salvation in another's stead. It is all a cruel fable to substitute priestly faith for personal belief. Faith in Christ for eternal safety must be our individual act and deed. The stipulation in the wilderness was that the anxious sufferer should look not on the pole, but on the typical serpent. So in the gospel it is Christ, and not the church, on whom the eye of faith is to dwell. The church is but as the pole to the brazen serpent—it is but a means to an end,—a means for the fitting elevation of him who alone can save. Mark well the mighty difference.

4. *They, among the bitten Israelites, who looked were healed and lived:* "And Moses made a serpent of brass, and put it upon a pole, and it came to pass that, if a serpent had bitten any man, when he beheld the serpent of brass he lived." It must have been a thrilling sight to behold here a group, and there an individual, starting up into "health and cure," at the cost of only a single glance. The restoration of one perhaps encouraged another; while we hear of no exceptions, in consequence of distance of situation or dimness of sight. All who looked lived. That was the masculine fact. Such certainty is still extant in the gospel. One true glance from the eye of faith saves the whole soul, or at least secures to it that pledge which is tantamount to its salvation. Weak faith too will bring the same security, though it may not yield the same comfort. The measure of faith is no where defined to us, but only its quality. If it be but holy it will save.

5. *The entire arrangement originated not with Moses, but with God,* whose appointment alone gave efficacy to every look. In like manner the salvation of sinners is not of man, nor of the will of man, but wholly of God. The crucifixion of Christ was the scheme of eternity; and all its virtue comes to us from the sovereign appointment of the eternal God. It was he who, instantly and mysteriously, in every case of recovery from the poisonous prostration conveyed the marvellous gift. And he it still is, who secretly imparts life and health to believing souls, in a manner which they know not. The brazen serpent was not set up as a charm, but as God's appointed means. Why he selected it is no part of ours to inquire. In like manner his sacraments have no inherent power, but require his special intervention to make them efficacious to the soul. But, like the brazen serpent, they are efficacious to every true believer.

In conclusion, suffer me to say that

1. *Historically* this subject may teach us what heathen mythology cannot, and what the church of Rome will not. Christ is the true Æsculapius;[1] though Moses, there is good reason to suppose, was made the real foundation of the Greek fable, concerning the God of the healing art. Æsculapius, with his staff entwined by a serpent, is only a mythological perversion of Moses dispensing health, as it were, through a serpent on a pole. The notions attached to the serpent of Æsculapius, as indicating the skill and sagacity by which he and his fraternity restore health, and procure longevity, are only poetical embellishments. The true reference is corroborated by the fact, that the medical Æsculapius is said to have been own brother to Mercury, the messenger of the gods. Now what was this but another perversion of another part of the office which Moses sustained? for was he not the messenger of the true God to the

[1] This mention of Æsculapius, as the congregation generally understood, was supplementary to some remarks which had been made in an interesting lecture, on the "Natural history of serpents," delivered in the room of the Worcester Natural History Society, on the preceding Friday evening.

Israelites? Be thankful, brethren, that we follow truth, and not any "cunningly devised fable." The true brazen serpent is the true source of our truest health.

But what became of the brazen serpent? It was preserved, no doubt, by divine permission. For a long time no harm ensued; but at length it became a snare to Israel. The people reverenced it, bowed down to it, and offered incense before it. At this crisis, the Spirit of God moved king Hezekiah with every mark of contempt to destroy it. (2 Kings 18:4.) In like manner and as an irrefragable verity, we ought to destroy the very cross of Calvary, if we had it, in case the people were similarly ensnared by it. This the Papal Church would not tell us.[1] Your own common sense will proceed to other and similar applications.

2. *Doctrinally* the subject is replete with richest truth. The glorious type flashes not a brazen, but a more than golden splendour, across the deathly wilderness of this world's march. It has taught salvation and imparted comfort to many a bitten but penitent pilgrim. And so long as "Christ crucified" is the watchword of the militant and travelling church, it will be a fruitful and a cheering theme for meditative hearts. Be it so for ours!

3. *Practically* it suggests a thousand duties. Sinners are dying from the great snake-bite. They must *look* ere their eye fails. Christians should *bless* God for the substance of which Israel saw the shadow. They should also *labour to improve* their clearer view of gospel truth. Never must they cease "looking unto Jesus!"

[1] In the Rev. M. Hobart Seymour's "Pilgrimage to Rome," chap. 1, the following facts are related:—"It is said that in the church of St. Ambrose, at Milan, the original serpent of brass which Moses lifted up is deposited. It is placed on a lofty column in the body of the church, and is regarded with superstitious veneration. It is a perplexing inquiry to ascertain how, unbroken and entire, it was presented to this church, seventeen centuries after it had been broken to pieces by Hezekiah, to prevent such idolatrous tendencies! But difficulties and perplexities of this kind are easily resolved under an Italian sky. When the reverend sacristan called our attention to this relic, and would persuade us it was the original serpent, my wife reminded him that had been broken in pieces by king Hezekiah, when he smartly replied, "Non e certo." [not and it is certain (or "No, certainly" or "No, and that's for sure.")]

SERMON XVIII.

THE CITIES OF REFUGE EMBLEMS OF A BETTER SAFETY.[1]

DEUTERONOMY 4:41, 42.

"Then Moses severed three cities on this side Jordan toward the sunrising; that the slayer might flee thither, which should kill his neighbour unawares, and hated him not in time past; and that fleeing unto one of those cities he might live."

IT was as likely as it was fitting, that he who made man should evince a high regard for the life of man. The Triune God held council respecting the formation of man, and accompanied his creation with every circumstance of dignity and honour. That God formed him in his own image, and breathed into him his own breath. Consequently man, being God's property, can lawfully be put to death only by God's permission. He alone who gave the life of man can rightly take it away from man. But then he can exercise that right in just such way as he will. He is at liberty to withdraw man's life by natural or supernatural means: and, if one man wilfully and wickedly presumes to deprive his neighbour of it, he may punish that man either by his own almighty but invisible hand, or by employing some other man as his visible agent and representative. In every case and form of murder, he has always manifested his holy and utter abhorrence of the crime itself. For ages after the first declaration of his will respecting blood being judicially shed for blood, historical record is so scanty that we know but

[1] Preached Sunday Morning, April 25th, 1849.

little respecting either occasions for its observance or the manner in which that observance was carried out. But, when his church began to assume a settled form, he propounded a settled method for more effectually screening the innocent manslayer, and the more vigorously punishing the wilful murderer. He directed Moses to set apart certain sanctuary cities in different districts of the promised land, in order that the man who by pure accident killed his neighbour might, by fleeing to one of them, be protected from all private vengeance at the hand of some surviving relative. But these sanctuary cities afforded no protection to the wilful murderer, not even if he held fast to the horns of that most preservative of all localities, a sacrificial altar. Nothing could screen *him*. Vengeance, not human but *divine*, was reserved for him. On the other hand all protection, pity, and provision, were furnished for the innocent homicide. Nevertheless, to keep up the national abhorrence of even the semblance of murder, God interposed certain painful duties and severe restrictions upon those whose lives were spared by flight to a city of refuge.

Connected however with the temporal intentions of these cities were certain great spiritual truths, which are as clear and important as ever. It is our duty always to learn those truths; and it will be my object at this present both to state them to you and to urge them upon you.

Our text is the record of what Moses did, in accordance with the divine command, as stated in Numbers 35:9–15.

Hence let our first consideration be

I. "*The cities of refuge," as typical of the great gospel refuge in themselves, and in the design and authority of their appointment.* That these cities had a typical reference to better and greater things than those for which they were temporally appointed we cannot doubt, after the reference which is made to them in the epistle to the Hebrews: "That by two immutable things, in which it was impossible for God to lie, we might have a strong consolation, who have fled for refuge to lay hold upon the hope set before us." (Hebrews 6:18.)

1. *The cities were six in number, and their position being in different parts of the land was favourable for the flight of the hapless manslayer.* Thus there is ample provision in the gospel for the salvation of the sinner who is the spiritual manslayer. There is no lack of refuge for him whose life is forfeited to the divine justice. Mercy has devised an abundant facility for his complete security and comfort. Nothing but faith and earnestness are wanting to render his preservation as blessed as it be everlasting. In a land like Britain the refuge of the gospel is everywhere to be found. It is not with us, as in a heathen country, that a soul may cry out, "What shall I do to be saved?" and no response can be heard. The true answer *can* be obtained by all who are in right earnest to obtain it. It is this fact which makes the mighty difference between heathens abroad and heathens at home.

2. *The names by which the six cities were called are remarkably significative of the excellencies of him who is our true Refuge.* Those names in their literal meanings are, to say the least, very applicable to the person or offices of Christ. They mystically described to the Israelite certain qualities or excellencies which were to be looked for in the character of the Messiah. They now help us to know him more distinctly by the aid of that added light which the gospel supplies. Thus the cities which Moses set apart were called Bezer, and Ramoth, and Golan. Now *Bezer* signifies "a strong-hold." And is not Christ "a strong-hold" to his people? Is not his name "a tower of strength" to all who believe in him? Is it not truly that very refuge into which "the righteous runneth and is safe"? It is: and therefore we say to all sinners, what was said to all the Hebrew captives, "Turn you to the stronghold, ye prisoners of hope." (Zechariah 9:12.) *Ramoth*, the next name, signifies "exaltations;" and Christ Jesus the Lord is not only the exalted of God, the throne-seated Prince and Saviour of Israel, but he is worthy of *every* exaltation to which heaven or earth can call him. Yea, saith the apostle, he is "made higher than the heavens." His exaltation "to the right hand of the Majesty on high" is the assurance of all our hopes, as to the fulfilment of what is promised to those who flee to him for refuge.

The other name, *Golan*, means "exultation, gladness, joy, delight." And whither shall a disconsolate and terror-smitten sinner flee for such reliefs, but to him who is the joy and "strong consolation" of all true believers? It is only when found in him, that the once condemned sinner can exult and be glad. He is the *Golan*, the source of triumphant delight to all who despair of safety but in himself.

A similar application may be made of the names of the other three cities which Joshua afterward set apart, when Canaan was brought into subjection to Israel. Those cities were called Kedesh, and Shechem, and Hebron. The first, named *Kedesh*, signifies "holy:" and what name can be more appropriate for the refuge of the guilty than "the Holy One?" But Jesus is "the Holy One of God," who is "made unto us *sanctification*," as well as righteousness and redemption. The word *Shechem* means "a shoulder," as the emblem of strength and government. Christ is the strong One, on whom God has laid help for his Church. "The government," says Isaiah, "shall be *upon his shoulder*:" and himself said, "All *power* is given unto me in heaven and in earth." Hence every spiritual refugee is made "strong in the Lord and in the power of his might:" and the rule and governance of the whole community of saints will never be triumphantly violated by any power of earth or hell. The remaining name, *Hebron*, implies "fellowship;" which is exactly what the gospel reveals to those who, being alienated from

God by sin, are brought into fellowship with him by Christ: "That which we have seen and heard declare we unto you, that ye also may have fellowship with us; and truly our fellowship is with the Father, and with his Son Jesus Christ." (1 John 1:3.)

Thus the Hebrew refugee was, as it were, under shelter of some pleasant name, according to the city to which he had fled. That name, whatever it might be, was calculated to furnish him with pleasant associations and profitable meditations, in the right exercise of which he might gain many a refreshing glance of better things to come. But here is the important difference between the privilege of the literal and the spiritual manslayer: The Jew could be in only one city at once, and so have the cheer of only one name: but the Christian has, in Christ, all the associate names together, and all their combined blessedness. Thus pre-eminently does the gospel set forth to us all things *at once* in the refuge which is now provided for us.

3. *The design of refuge cities was simple and definite*: it was the preservation of the manslayer's *life*, "that fleeing," says the text, "unto one of these cities, *he might live*." The like design is presented in the gospel plan of salvation. Every thing in it is for one ultimate object, the preservation of the life of the soul from eternal death. As an offender of the most capital class, the sinner is exposed to divine vengeance. The wrath of God abideth on him, and justice is in pursuit of him. One method of escape is set before him; and one way of securing life is opened to him. Flight by faith to Christ, the City of our salvation, will secure the soul from every penalty, and win for it eternal life.

No doubt the Hebrew refugee was urged by many considerations to make good speed: but the preservation of his life was the all-absorbing motive. So, in embracing the gospel, there are many blessings to be reckoned upon, but the life of the soul is the grand and comprehensive object: "that fleeing he might *live*."

4. *The authority on which the appointment of these cities rested* was no ambiguous topic, but one as clear as the sun in the firmament. It was not to Moses that so benevolent a provision was owing, but solely to the God of Moses. It was a project worthy of the wisdom and the love of him who, though always righteous, is always merciful. So the plan of our redemption in Christ Jesus, equally with the system of refuge for the Jew, is wholly to be attributed to the triune God. It was no device of angel or man, but that of God alone, who "so loved the world that he gave his only begotten Son, that whosoever believeth in him should not perish, but have everlasting life." (John 3:16.) In vain would the manslayer have fled to any city in Israel, which *God* had not appointed: and equally in vain will the sinner seek for succour in any one or in any thing, but that only Saviour whom he hath sent to us and set before us; "neither is there salvation in any other, for there is none other name given among men whereby we must be saved." (Acts 4:12.) How pitiable must have been the plight of the manslayer who had mistaken some other city for a city of refuge! But incomparably more pitiful will be the condition of multitudes who make saviours for themselves, to the neglect of that one "great salvation" which God has made for them. May we both be sure of our city, and make sure in fleeing to it! Our next consideration is

II. *The flight of the manslayer to a city of refuge, at least in its principal circumstances, as emblematical of many things connected with the way of our salvation.*

You heard it said that, from the first, God manifested his abhorrence of every sort of murder. We may add that he still manifested that abhorrence, even when he provided a method of exemption from penalty in the case of manslaughter. In like manner the same God has always manifested his abhorrence of sin, which is virtually the murder of the soul. That abhorrence is not diminished, though he has mercifully set forth a propitiation for it. Sin is as much his detestation as ever. The sufferings of his dear Son have not reconciled him to sin, but only to the person of the penitent sinner. Sin is still spiritual murder. The impenitent sinner is as an unpardoned murderer. The *penitent* sinner alone is like the refuge-seeking manslayer. There is salvation for him; and he has only to flee to it.

But here the parallel begins; and first let me remark

1. *That, until the manslayer reached a city of refuge, he was liable to be put to death.* The avenger of blood had absolute power over his life, if he overtook him outside the walls of the sanctuary city. Thus it is with sinners. It is not enough that they know the city of refuge as revealed in the gospel, or that they are willing to enter it, and intend to set out for it. Till they have actually entered it, till by a lively faith they have fled to Jesus as their only Saviour, and are really and truly "found in him," avenging justice may seize them and cut them off for ever. Then lay this fact to heart, ye who linger between Christ and Belial, ye who come near enough to the gospel city to mark its walls and count its bulwarks, but have not yet entered the city itself! Be assured that, if you are only "almost Christians," ye are yet in your sins, and are in peril of your souls. "He that believeth on the Son hath everlasting life: and he that believeth not the Son shall not see life, but the wrath of God abideth on him." (John 3:36.) Observe again

2. *That roads were well prepared and directing posts set up, in order to facilitate the flight of the manslayer to the city of refuge.* Jewish historians report that these roads were of extra width, and kept in the best repair, and that at convenient intervals an index-board was set up pointing to the city, and bearing a suitable inscription. After this manner is facility furnished for the flight of sinners to the refuge for their souls. Repentance and faith constitute the high road which leads to the Saviour; and

the Bible and the ministers of the gospel are appointed by God to direct inquirers in the right way. The refuge cities belonged to the Levites, who had the charge of the refugees. The church is now chargeable with the duty of keeping the prescribed facilities in a proper state, of opening her sacraments, her scriptures, and her evangelical deposit, in such wise as shall urge and aid sinners to flee from the wrath to come. What St. Paul said of himself is applicable to every minister of the church: "Woe is me, if I preach not the gospel!" If we preach any other refuge but Christ, or direct men wrongly to it, their blood will be required of us.

3. *The cities of refuge always stood open, and admittance to them could not be refused.* This is but a figure of that noble reality of the gospel, the freedom of divine grace in admitting sinners to salvation. There is no impediment but their own unwillingness. The great Saviour himself keeps the gates of the gospel city: "he openeth and no man shutteth." He even "waits to be gracious," and condescendingly and cheeringly says, "Him that cometh unto me I will in no wise cast out."

4. *As soon as the manslayer entered the city he was safe, and the judges, upon examination, acquitted him of all guilt.* The power of the avenger of blood extended only to the threshold of the gate. No weapon of his dared to wound or slay beyond it. One step across it rendered the breathless fugitive a happy man. His fears were gone, his danger was over, his anxieties were ended. He could now face even the dreaded avenger, and receive the visits of his friends: for, after examination of the case was held, and his innocence declared, he was not only at full liberty to go whither he pleased within the city, but accommodation and provision were made for him, as a refugee who was entitled to all commiseration and sympathy. The time, dear brethren, would fail us to unfold all that these beautiful incidents emblematically describe to us of the security, freedom, happiness, and sustenance, which the believing penitent finds in Christ Jesus his Saviour. Once in him, by a living faith, he saves his soul alive; for his guilt is cancelled, and unnumbered bounties await his enjoyment. The wrath which rested upon him is withdrawn, and he is declared to be a righteous man. The accuser can bring no further charge, and the avenger has no longer any power against him. The words of St. Paul seem almost framed to describe the case of the spiritual refugee: "There is therefore no condemnation to them which are in Christ Jesus, who walk not after the flesh, but after the Spirit." (Romans 8:1.) But remember

5. *That the manslayer, though acquitted and protected, was safe only while he abode in the city.* If he went through the gate, or was found anywhere outside the walls, his life was in peril, for the avenger of blood might then slay him with impunity. Now it ought never to be forgotten that the Saviour has said, "Abide in me, and I in you. As the branch cannot bear fruit of itself except it abide in the vine, no more can ye except ye abide in me. I am the vine, ye are the branches: he that abideth in me and I in him the same bringeth forth much fruit: for without me ye can do nothing. If a man abide not in me he is cast forth as a branch, and is withered: and men gather them, and cast them into the fire, and they are burned. If ye abide in me, and my words abide in you, ye shall ask what ye will, and it shall be done unto you." (John 15:4–7.) This is for the warning of all nominal Christians who *seem to* be in Christ, but who really are disjoined from him. It is also for the admonition of even true Christians, who are safe only while they abide in him. It is well calculated to teach them circumspection, not to place themselves in dangerous positions, not to poise themselves on the lofty walls of their city, not to loiter about the opening of the gates, nor to hold parley with those who are on the wrong side of them. We may lose our balance and fall, or take one false or forward step, and receive lasting damage or irreparable harm. Careful therefore must we be to *abide* in Christ, never listening to dulcet sounds which would withdraw us from him, nor to promises of greater liberty outside the walls of his spiritual presence: "Little children, *abide* in him." Observe too

6. *That the manslayer could obtain full release only by the death of the high priest.* While a refugee he was, though an acquitted person, under certain restrictions. He could not go to his friends or his possessions. But, while he might be kept from them for many years, he might by the uncertainties of life be soon restored to them. Thus he lived in hope and expectation. The death of the high priest was the event on which he meekly and submissively kept his eye. This part of the type was peculiarly significant to the ancient Jews. It taught them to look for spiritual liberty, for the remission of sin, and the enjoyment of their heavenly home, only through the death of their promised Messiah, the true High Priest of the one true church. And truly it teaches us precisely the same things; for the *atoning death* of Christ is the only ground of our restoration to the full glory and the full liberty of the sons of God. It is only by it that we can be released from present hindrances and infirmities, and have a free passage given to us, for an abundant entrance on that inheritance and home which as manslayers we had forfeited. For "Christ was once offered to bear the sins of many; and unto them that look for him shall he appear the second time without sin unto salvation." (Hebrews 9:28.)

Our conclusion will have reference to the only two classes into which all men are divided, namely those who have *not* fled and those who *have* fled to the refuge set forth to us in the gospel.

i. They who have *not* fled to Christ, as our only sanctuary, are in a position which is beyond description perilous. There is not an hour's certainty in their present standing. The avenger of blood is in pursuit of their souls. If mercy withdraws the shield, they have no power to ward off a blow. Hence at their next step they may be overtaken and cut down. O that men would consider their guilt, their danger, and the only way of escape! You come hither to be told of these things, and to be set right respecting them. As God's ministers, it is our part to point out to you the peril which surrounds you, and the refuge which is provided for you. It is natural to suppose that the Hebrew manslayer, on discovering his peril, would be in haste to avert it, by fleeing at once to the appointed city. Thus ought it to be with us. Anxiety and effort should be in our right hand and in our left. We should not linger, lest we die. St. Paul uses a strong word, in describing the haste of the spiritual refugees under the gospel. He speaks of them as they "who have *fled* for refuge." They speed with all the rapidity of a timid bird pursued by a hawk, or a fugitive running for his life. Such should be our haste. God grant it may.

ii. They who *have* fled and found refuge are especially bound to be *thankful*. But for grace to help they might still be in their sins and their perils.

Esteem your admittance to the common refuge as a blessing which *counterbalances* every trial and privation.

Remember you are entitled to "strong consolation." (Hebrews 6:18.) *Abide* in Christ, and wait patiently till your change cometh.

SERMON XIX.

GOD'S COMMINATION TO BE APPROVED BY OUR AMEN.[1]

Deuteronomy 27:26.

"Cursed be he that confirmeth not all the words of this law to do them. And all the people shall say, Amen."

THESE words are recorded in connexion with an interesting and instructive ceremony. That ceremony, as instituted by God, may at *all* times be profitably contemplated by all Christians. But, as the church follows the spirit of it in her service for Ash Wednesday, we may with great propriety make it the subject of our contemplation on the evening of that day.

May the Spirit of him who bore every curse, and purchased every blessing for us, cause your meditation to be sweet, and our instruction effective! In explaining the ceremony alluded to, let us consider the text, first, as to the curse which it pronounces, and, secondly, as to the duty which it enjoins: "Cursed be he that confirmeth not all the words of this law to do them: and all the people shall say, Amen." Consider then

I. *The curse which the text pronounces.* In the preceding verses, Moses directed the Israelites in their settlement in Canaan to proceed to mount Ebal and mount Gerizim, and there in solemn concourse to recite and ratify certain curses and certain blessings. These two mountains were in that district of the Holy Land which was called Samaria. They are described as rising opposite to, and within a very short distance of, each other. A narrow valley lay between them, so narrow that the human voice could be distinctly heard from the one to the other. This spot God selected for the scene of a very solemn occasion. The twelve tribes of Israel when assembled there were to divide themselves into two companies. Six tribes were to stand on Mount Gerizim to bless the people, and six on Mount Ebal to curse. As each blessing and as each curse was pronounced, all the people were to answer and say, "Amen."

The object of this ceremony was evidently to impress the memory and affect the heart. And this, dear brethren, is the object of all the simple ceremonies of our apostolical church. It should too be the one grand object of every Christian in at-

[1] Preached Ash Wednesday Evening, 1847. commination: threat, threatening denunciation

tending ordinances, joining in worship, or hearing sermons. In vain shall we call ourselves either Christians or churchmen, unless we earnestly seek for holy improvement in all we do. To profess an observance of Lent, or of any other ecclesiastical season, will be profitless to our souls, without a vigorous effort to enter into their spirit, and to obtain the true grace of God. Ecclesiastical observances without the sanctified affections of the heart resemble clear weather without warmth, or statues without life.

The directions which Moses gave respecting the ceremonies in question were fulfilled by Joshua and all Israel, after their conquest and allotment of Canaan. The event is recorded in Joshua 8:30, where we find that the tribes of Israel, with even their wives and little ones, assembled at the appointed spot, and solemnly obeyed all that they had been enjoined. The scene must have been both imposing and impressive. Picture to yourselves a vast assemblage of warrior Israelites, covering the sides and crowning the summits of two closely opposite mountains. Behold them in the prime of manhood, or in the buoyancy of youth, (for all the old men had died in the wilderness,)—behold them grouped into tribes, fresh in their recollection of the wonders of past days, and devoutly joyous in the possession of magnificent benefits. See them viewing each other's array, and gazing on the thrilling sight in the little valley below. There were the priests of the Most High God, clad in their splendid vestments of office,—perhaps the very vestments which had been wrought under the eye of Moses the man of God. There were also the Levites and officers and judges, in simpler but not less hallowed garb. And there, in the midst of them, was that awful but beloved symbol of Jehovah's presence, the ark of the covenant; and there too conspicuous above all was one old man, eminent for valour, faith and sanctity. It was Joshua, the successor of Moses, the captain of Israel, the type of Christ. There stood he, aged but not feeble, triumphant but not haughty. And then, perhaps as he waved his staff or his spear, every spectator was motionless, and every tongue silent. The original roll of the Pentateuch—Moses' own copy of God's law—was then held forth, and from it either Joshua himself, or the Levites for him, read the blessings and the curses—the former from the side of Mount Gerizim, the latter from the direction of Mount Ebal. And then, as each curse or each blessing was pronounced, the air resounded, or the earth rang, with a solemn or joyful Amen!

The scene, we said, must have been impressive as well as imposing. To many a heart it was doubtless extremely affecting. It seems indeed to have been followed by good and lasting effects; for "Israel served the Lord all the days of Joshua, and all the days of the elders that overlived Joshua, and which had known all the works of the Lord, that he had done for Israel." (Joshua 24:31.)

To this account of the ceremony under consideration a remark or two may be fitly appended. It is observable

1. *That the division of the tribes on the two mountains was very precise and significant.* The tribes stationed on Mount Gerizim, from which the blessings were to be pronounced, were the descendants of the wives of Jacob, and not of his concubines: whereas the six tribes on mount Ebal, the mount of cursing, were mainly the descendants, not of Leah and Rachel, but of Zilpah and Bilhah, their maid servants. At least four tribes were such, and the six were made up by the addition of the descendants of the guilty Reuben, and of Zebulon the youngest of Leah's children. (Ver. 11–13.) Now, may it not be that there was a mystical intention in this very precise arrangement? We know that the history of Sarah and Hagar, and their respective children, was an allegory. And surely there could be nothing forced or foreign in regarding this as one also. The cases are certainly of the same class. Their import therefore may illustrate the same truths. Hagar and her son Ishmael allegorically represented the spirit of bondage under the law; while Sarah and her beloved son Isaac shadowed forth the spirit of liberty under the gospel. In like manner the descendants of Bilhah and Zilpah, standing on Mount Ebal, might be designed for a figure of the legal dispensation which abounded with prohibitions and curses: and the descendants of Leah and Rachel, stationed on Mount Gerizim, might contrariwise be for an emblem of the privileges and blessings of the gospel dispensation. At all events it is more than probable that the tribes themselves would notice the peculiarity of their division. Their apprehensions of its spiritual meaning might be faint and dim, for they lived in an age of shadows: some might suspect in it a lesson on the sanctity of marriage; but many a devout and thoughtful Hebrew might ponder it in his heart, and gain a comfortable glimpse of evangelical times. God grant that our own souls may gather comfort at the very mention of these topics! Hence observe

2. *That a marked difference exists between the Jewish and the Christian dispensation, as to the clearness and blessedness of the way of salvation.* Under both dispensations there is but one and the same salvation: only before the day of Christ that salvation was differently set forth, and its consolations far less prominently disclosed. In the solemnities of Gerizim and Ebal we have a latent but remarkable proof of this fact. In the record of injunctions of Moses the curses alone are enumerated, and not the blessings. True it is that we read of Mount Gerizim as the mount of blessing; but then the blessings themselves are not written down,—the curses alone are registered. The one indeed implies the other, and hence it is supposed that the mere substitution of "BLESSED is he" for "CURSED is he," omitting or inserting a negative, as the sense required, was all that Israel heard from Gerizim. Still here is the fact, that Moses passed

over the blessings in silence. Now we know that the silence of Scripture is often mystical and significative. It is so in the case of Melchisedec. In the ceremonies of Ebal and Gerizim, that silence was well calculated to attract the notice of the people, and to draw the eye of their faith toward another Joshua and another mountain,—even to Jesus the Messiah, and to that mount on which his sermon of blessings without curses was delivered. May the Spirit of Jesus inspire us with gratitude for the abundant light which beams on us, and for the ten thousand blessings which mark our evangelical day!

Let us not proceed without further noticing

3. *That the ministers of Christ are charged with a two-fold duty.* They must tell men of judgment as well as mercy. The Levites were to pronounce curses as well as blessings; and we, dear brethren, are to proclaim the terrors of the Lord in conjuction with the riches of his grace. To be partial in our preaching is to be somewhat selfish or forgetful. To withhold one duty, and to cleave to the other, is an act of unfaithfulness to souls and to their Saviour. It may be more pleasant to our feelings to dwell on the cheering truths of Christianity and the happiness of Christians: but it is essential to our fidelity to tell sinners of their danger, to warn them of threatened judgments, and to call them to repentance. O that some heart may be smitten *now* under a sense of God's curse, and so find its way to the fulness of the blessing of the gospel of Christ!

In the catalogue of curses pronounced from Mount Ebal our text is the last; and yet it includes all which precede it, for it denounces a curse on those persons who neglect or refuse to confirm all that had been spoken: "Cursed be he that confirmeth not all the words of this law to do them: and all the people shall say, Amen." St. Paul, in his epistle to the Galatians, translates this text from Hebrew into Greek, which Greek version, according to our own rendering, runs thus: "Cursed is every one that continueth not in all things which are written in the book of the law to do them." (Galatians 3:10.) Hence we learn the mind of the Spirit, and clearly understand that by *confirming* all the words of the law is meant *continual obedience* to it. A devout Israelite would soon perceive his inability to render such obedience as must be both perfect and constant; and therefore, like his father Abram, he would seek "*the righteousness of faith.*" In vain will any sinner, whether Jew or Gentile, hope for salvation by any other process. "The righteousness of the law" may be sought after by those who trust in themselves, while they of necessity fall infinitely short of it: but if a man would be saved he will seek for righteousness in his great Mediator, and study for love's sake to obey his will with heart and mind, and soul and strength. In this way alone will all the curses of the law be escaped, and all the blessings of the gospel be secured. May the finger of God write the law upon our hearts, and may our lives exhibit its holiness; that denying ungodliness and worldly lusts, and continuing in cheerful and conscientious obedience, we may find peace now, and a reward hereafter.

Let us next consider

II. *The duty which the text enjoins.* "All the people shall say, Amen." The injunction is God's, and therefore we may be sure that it is consistent with infinite holiness, perfect love, and eternal truth. Ignorance indeed has sometimes misunderstood the meaning of this "Amen;" and prejudice has not unfrequently perverted it. Thus in its use, during the commination service of our church, thoughtless or frivolous persons profess to see sundry objections. "We do not wish" say they, "to go to church on Ash Wednesday, in order to curse our neighbour; nor is it likely that we should wish to curse ourselves; and moreover there is no need for this pronouncing of curses, and saying, Amen, because we read that Christ was made a curse for us, and bore the curse in our stead." Such are the objections of either inconsiderate or unholy persons. One answer might suffice for all; but, in addition to that answer, we will give an explanation. It might suffice then to say that it is impossible to object against the commination service of the church, without objecting to the institution of God himself, as recorded in the chapter before us: the service of the church is but the clear echo of the institution of God. "And who art thou, O man, who repliest against God?" Can there be the shadow of error in using the words of God, in precisely that sense in which Joshua and the priests and people of God used them? Every honest man must say, "*I trow*[1] *not.*"

Hear now the explanation. The word, "Amen," does not, in its use here, imply a wish or an imprecation. It does not mean, "May God curse me, or may he curse my neighbour!" On the contrary it implies only an assent or affirmation. "Amen," as a response to the curse, is an acknowledgment of its truth and its justice. The pronouncing of the curse is the pronouncing of a sentence in the presence of a righteous jury against penitent criminals. The jury will say, "Amen," as a token of their assent to the justice of the sentence: and the penitent criminals will say the same as an acknowledgment of their desert of condemnation. Hence, as churchmen, we justify two things in our Book of Common Prayer: the first is the commination service, of which we have been speaking; and the second is the opening of the service for the holy communion, where, after the recitation of each commandment, we say, "Lord, have mercy upon us." Both these solemnities are very impressive. Both are designed and adapted to awaken the careless, and to quicken the formal, to deepen repentance and enliven faith, to inflame our love and confirm our holy obedience: all which strictly accords with the duty enjoined in our text. That duty comprises

[1] trow: trust or believe

1. *A profession of faith in the certainty of God's threatenings.* The Author of the promises of the gospel is the Author of the curses of the law. One God hath spoken both, and one Mediator hath ratified both. Jesus, the friend of publicans and sinners, denounced Pharisees and lawyers. He who said "*Blessed* are ye that mourn," also said, "*Woe* unto you, hypocrites! how can ye escape the damnation of hell?" Now in saying, "Amen," to the divine denunciations, we attest our faith in their reality and certainty. And to do this how great faith is necessary,—what a mighty effort of the heart is requisite! To assent to God's promises as true is a comparatively easy thing in the Christian life, because our personal comfort is at stake: but humbly and steadfastly to believe that all his threatenings are every whit as certain as his promises is a more trying effort of the sanctified heart; because such belief puts the knife to the throat of all our lusts, passions, prejudices, and sins of every sort. Many a man is content to say, "Thou art the King of glory, O Christ," who still falters or quakes as he adds, "We believe that thou shalt come to be OUR JUDGE."

2. *An assent to the equity of God's curse.* It is not enough to believe the certainty of that curse: we must perceive its justice, and cheerfully though meekly assent to the equity of God in inflicting it. This is required of every believer now; and in the last great day their assent will be openly and unanimously declared. God in all his judgments is to be justified and glorified. Hence, if a believer falls into sin, he is to look up and say, "Against thee, thee only have I sinned, and done this evil in thy sight, that thou mightest be justified when thou speakest, and be clear when thou judgest." (Psalm 51:4.) But in the great assize, when the right hand and the left of the Judge shall constitute the Gerizim and Ebal of the whole world, and when it shall be said to the one, "Come ye *blessed* of my Father," and to the other, "Depart ye *cursed* into everlasting fire," then shall the glorious company of the redeemed lift up their crystal voices in a loud Amen, and say, "Great and marvellous are thy works, Lord God Almighty; just and true are thy ways, thou King of saints. Who shall not fear thee, O Lord, and glorify thy name? for thou only art holy: for all nations shall come and worship before thee; for thy judgments are made manifest." (Revelation 15:3, 4.)

3. *A penitent confession of sin.* To hear the curse of God pronounced against various transgressors will be sure to excite in the breast of a penitent a consciousness of his own individual guilt as a sinner in heart if not actually in life, as an offender in thought if not positively in deed. "Amen" therefore appended to a curse implies much the same as "Lord have mercy upon us" after a command. Both amount to an acknowledgment of our need of mercy, because of our desert of chastisement. Then let us probe our own hearts with a determined hand. Let us view our sins without partiality, and repent of them without hypocrisy. The duty further implies

4. *A solemn resolution of future obedience.* Repentance is not merely a sorrowful confession of sin, but a hearty forsaking of it. It has therefore been well said that "repentance is a breaking of the heart *for* sin and *from* it." Vain and fallacious indeed is the hope of forgiveness without a corresponding desire after holiness. Consequently he who would say, "Lord, *have mercy* upon us," must earnestly and sincerely add, "And incline our hearts to keep this law." He who lifts up his voice, and says, "Amen," to a divine curse, must resolve with his heart to shun that sin which brings down the curse. Let these truths be lastingly impressed on our minds, and then neither sin nor Satan will have dominion over us; but through the grace of the Spirit our path through life will be strewed with religious pleasantness, and our end will be marked with heavenly peace.

Bearing in mind what has been adduced, let us take a comprehensive view of the subject as presenting to us

1. *A test of spiritual regeneration.* "He that is born of God sinneth not;" that is, he does not live in sin; it is neither his habit nor his choice to follow sin. Consequently the child of God consents to the law that it is good. He studies it, loves it, delights in it. He consents to it *entirely*, regarding what it prohibits as well as what it enjoins. He consents to it in all its *spirituality*, marking its reference to the heart as well as to the life. He consents to it too with all its evangelical sanctions; for with the eye of faith he sees the Lawgiver in the mercy-seat, the Judge on the cross; and when he sees that wondrous sight his soul is melted within him, and the God of the awful curse appears infinitely adorable and lovely.

What then is our state when brought to this test? Do we consent to the law after this manner? Are we ready to confirm the curse though its thunders should be levelled at ourselves? Are we ready to fall down as guilty before God, and yet to look up and say, "Though he slay me, yet will I trust in him"? Brethren, these are questions of life and death!

2. *A memento for impenitent sinners.* They hear of a curse: that curse is the curse of God, and therefore it is infinite and everlasting. And what is an infinite curse? It must be one so amazingly terrible, so fiercely consuming, and so overwhelmingly destructive as to leave all human imagination baffled in the attempt to span its horrors. But we are told enough, if man will but listen. We are told that, if a man will not turn when mercy calls, the curse of God, like a whetted sword will cut him off. "God" says St. Augustine, "has woollen feet, but iron hands;" that is, in inflicting his curse on sinners he advances softly, but strikes irresistibly. Are *we* sinners, secret, unthinking and unsuspecting sinners? O let each one hasten to escape

the curse: for how shall we dwell with the everlasting burnings, how bear the gnawing of the worm which dieth not, how endure the tormentings of the devil and his angels? Ah! dear friends, better is it to sigh and sorrow now than to mourn at the last and for ever. Lord, smite us, but heal us; alarm us, but comfort us; shake thy curse over us, but "show us thy mercy, and grant us thy salvation!"

Finally let us derive from the text

3. *An appeal to him who bore for us every curse, and purchased for us every blessing.* To make this appeal would be the natural effort of every cross-signed soul. On hearing the curse such an one will say, "Lord, I am vile, and I know that thy holy law justly condemns me; but I believe: O help my unbelief in looking to Jesus as *made a curse* for me!" Such language comes, I trust, within the experience of some of us. Assuredly it accords with the spiritual and evangelical teaching of our church. Hence the reason why she ordains both tables of the law to be recited at the commencement of her communion service. It is to lead us from Ebal to Gerizim, from the consideration of that law which we have violated to the Saviour who has fulfilled it for us, that by faith in his broken flesh and outpoured blood we may find the curse turned into a blessing.

Happy are they who are familiar with this appeal from the curse of the law to the atonement of Christ.

Happy too are they who see in the simple ceremonies of the Lord's table a more imposing, a more impressive, a more affecting sight than any which Israel saw on Ebal or Gerizim. O look unto Jesus! love him, live to him, praise him!

SERMON XX.

THE DEGRADATION OF ISRAEL MARKED BY THE ABSENCE OF A TRADE.[1]

1 Samuel 13:19.

"Now there was no smith found throughout all the land of Israel."

AND *why* was there not? Because there was, generally speaking, no *godliness* to be found in the land. This simple question and this plain answer furnish a clue to the sum of the present discourse. They who forsake God forsake their own mercies. Prosperity, whether national or individual, temporal or spiritual, depends on our adhesion to God and to the things of God. To teach us this truth the passage before us was written: and, that all the members of our church may periodically hear it, the entire chapter was doubtless appointed to be read. Let us

I. *Take a view of the position of the nation of Israel, when no smith was to be found in their land.*

From the first the people of Israel were a peculiar people. Their entire history presents as much variety as any history in the world. It exhibits a succession of provocations and mercies, judgments and respites. In Egypt that people were reduced to the most abject condition: and under Solomon they attained the highest elevation. But they attained this height only after considerable undulations and depressions. Their national exaltation, like a thermometer, was regulated by the fervency of their national attachment to the worship and service of God. How fickle and how heartless that attachment too frequently was, we may easily read. But "all these things happened unto them for ensamples, and were written for our learning." After the death of Joshua and his fellows in the faith, the condition of the people gradually became worse and worse, till the rebellion of Saul, whom they foolishly admired as their king, brought them into the most pitiable plight. Their old enemies, the Philistines, whom they indolently suffered to remain in the land, were permitted to bring them into subjection. So abject were the oppressed, and so politic were the oppressors,

[1] Preached Sunday Evening, July 5th, 1846.

that every man who followed the occupation of a smith was either put to death, disabled, or removed to a distance. The policy of the Philistines, in inflicting this privation, was to prevent the people forging weapons, or flourishing in agriculture: "for the Philistines said, Lest the Hebrews make them swords or spears." It also gave the Philistines a power of closer inspection and greater gain, because it compelled the Israelites to go down to them, whenever their larger and heavier implements of labour required repair. This compulsion to go to the towns or garrisons of the Philistines for any sort of iron work must have been peculiarly galling to the proud hearts in Israel. But, when persons through sin and folly bring themselves into trouble, God will be sure to humble their hearts if he secretly has a favour for them. But amid the privations to which the Hebrews, through contempt of God and love of idols, had brought themselves, *some* relief was allowed. Though they had neither forges nor anvils for new formations or larger repairs, "*yet* they had a file for the mattocks, and for the coulters, and for the forks, and for the axes, and to sharpen the goads." (Verse 21.) This indeed was but slight mitigation of their grievous degradation. Still it was a mitigation. It did afford some facility to the industrious husbandman: and perhaps some of that class among the Hebrews were still piously disposed towards the God of their fathers. If so, they would thankfully receive the mitigation as a mercy amid their judgments.

To such an extent had the Philistines carried their endeavours to humble and depress the Israelites, that "it came to pass in the day of battle that there was neither sword nor spear found in the hand of any of the people that were with Saul and Jonathan: but with Saul and with Jonathan his son was there found." (Verse 22.)

Truly how humiliating was this state of things! How different from their position at the Red Sea, when they walked as lords through its proud waves, and saw their enemies prostrate on its beach, and heard its shores resound with their chant of triumph, and their song of victory! How different too from the day when Deborah and Barak led their hosts to splendid conquest, and left them masters over their oppressors. Once so exalted, now so low! Once so well armed, now destitute of a single sword or spear! They probably used only slings or simple bows and arrows, such weapons as they could fabricate in secret, and without the aid of an artificer. Hence we may account for David's skill as a slinger: for he was at this time a shepherd-boy in the pastures of Bethlehem, and, with no suspicion on his part, was retiredly training for that great feat which was to distinguish him for ever. Thus God has wheel within wheel, and is often preparing great things by the smallest wheels of his mysterious machinery.

We say, how different the position of Israel to that of former times! And have not some of you, dear brethren, lived to see differences, comparatively as great, befalling individuals, who once were neighbours or associates? Profligacy or folly, or irreligion in some shape, has often sunk a man to a depth of poverty or shame, which it once seemed incredible to anticipate. All such cases should bring our hearts to say, "Verily there is a God that judgeth in the earth!" they should also fasten our hold on Christ, the only friend of sinners, and the great preserver of man.

But to complete the infatuation and misery of the Hebrews, they had declared a revolt from their masters, while their king had himself revolted from God. The spoilers were consequently sent out upon them, and a destructive attack was every day feared. And now the fact of there being, throughout all the land, no such humble artizan as a blacksmith, began to be felt as a terrible privation. It cut them off from all hope of preparing a single weapon of iron for the coming war, and left them to anxious dread and bitter dismay. So true is it, that when God is chastising us trifles become momentous matters, and little things are made to shew us our gigantic sins.

Let us proceed to

II. *Educe some useful instruction from this view of the position of the Hebrews.* And this is exactly what the ministers of Christ are appointed to do, among their respective people. We are to the best of our ability to expound Holy Scripture for their learning, and to induce them to think of it, and to search out instruction for themselves. And if, by calling their attention to some simpler passage of the Bible, which they have passed over as of little account, we succeed in showing them how great things are wrapt up in it, then we haply, by God's grace, may lead them to that nobility and profit which the Bereans attained, who "were more noble than those in Thessalonica, in that they received the word with all readiness of mind, and searched the scriptures daily, whether those things were so." (Acts 17:11.)

Now from what we have heard we may learn

1. *That sin is the fruitful source of all the evils which we suffer.* When we forsake God and follow our own sinful inclinations, we provoke him to withdraw his mercies from us, and thereby expose ourselves to certain but unknown distresses. Sin ruins individuals as well as kingdoms: and the very sins which brought Israel into misery and dismay are the same which, under different disguises, work in us to our injury and discomfort. Israel was self-willed, eager for idolatry, and bent on earthly things. It was these evils which brought them under the iron yoke of Philistian bondage. They *would* have a king, like Gentile nations, instead of being under the rule of God's priests and prophets. They madly worshipped the very gods of their enemies, and sought their happiness in luxury, wantonness, and pride. Thus "they were minished and brought low." And ver-

ily how like Israel are mankind in the present day! Are not we fond of self in all its shapes? Do not our evil hearts cast off allegiance to God, and prefer any rule to his laws? "We have followed too much the devices and desires of our own hearts," say we in confession: and yet, in the teeth of that confession, how do we continue to indulge our rebellious inclinations! How many an individual in this city (alas, in this congregation perhaps!) who has uttered these words of confession to day deliberately means to follow idols and lying vanities to-morrow and the rest of the week! That individual seriously intends to frequent places and scenes which answer to the captivating festivities and idolatrous revels by which the Philistines entrapped the Hebrews. Unquestionably the idols of the heathen had many attractions for the lovers of pleasure. But the idols of the heart are more tyrannical than any other idols; and we are more infatuated than the Hebrews in following them. These idols call, and tempt, and demand: and we with open eyes run into the meshes of their net, and court our destruction. This is our infatuation: for where sin is loved, and hearts are set on following it, there God says, "Let him alone!" The sinner indeed has his way, but "hell and destruction" are at the end of it. As then with Israel so will it be with us: iniquity will pave the way for our ruin, if we walk in it; and departure from God will be the leaving of the only arm which can protect and save us. Even in the commonest walks of life we daily see the case of the Hebrews exemplified. We have only to go into families around us to see what misery sin occasions, and how many sufferings and distresses it brings on parents and children. Go into the lanes and alleys of our city, and you will see a picture of Israel when there was no smith in all the land. You will hear strife and discontent, and see dirt and destitution. Misery will start up in many forms, and wretchedness will look out of dark corners and broken windows. And why is all this? Because the people have brought themselves into the bondage of sin. They are living in sin and love it. They either practise wickedness, or wink at it, in their children and neighbours. Who then can wonder at their wants or woes? There is no marvel in it except the hardness of their own hearts under the stings which pierce them.

But, turning to another view of the case of Israel, we may learn

2. *That a time of humiliation is a school time for the soul.* The Hebrews would never learn in prosperity. They "waxed fat and kicked." When things went well with them, themselves went ill with God. They forgot his works, and turned his mercies into occasions for licentiousness. It was only when they were sickened of their sin, by smarting under its consequences, that they at all bethought themselves and sought after God. It is ever much the same with us. Prosperity is rarely good for us. We thrive better in adversity, when the thoughts are called away from vanities, when the heart sinks within itself, and the spirit feels how poor and pitiful every thing is without God. For this beneficial cause it is that God sends afflictions to his people. It is that by them they may learn what they perhaps would never learn without them. Our unwillingness to abase ourselves constrains him who loves us to bring us into trouble. Then it is that we see and acknowledge how all things are dependent on him, how desirable it is to hold fast by him, and how utterly worthless every thing is for our real happiness which does not proceed from him and lead to him. Besides, as the Hebrews in their humiliation were made to see the cause of it, so is it well for us to ask why our afflictions come, and to probe those recesses of the heart in which the evils lie which mostly cause them to come. Rely on it, we learn but little in a time of humiliation unless we learn how little trustworthy our own hearts are, and what need there is for their being cleansed by the Spirit of Christ, and kept by the power of Christ. Study then under every tribulation to make that advance in wisdom, stability, and holiness, which will insure you a happy issue out of it.

You will further see that we may learn

3. *That in trying circumstances there generally is something which alleviates or mitigates the trial.* It cannot be that the little incident about *a file* is recorded in the 21st verse without a gracious intention: "Yet they had a file for the mattocks." That file chiefly benefited the pious and the industrious: and God will always bless piety and industry. The permission to possess a file was an alleviation to the husbandman: it spared him many an annoying journey to the forges of the Philistines, and enabled him to renovate the edge of certain implements at his pleasure.

Hence the little word "*yet*" is full of meaning. It is charged with instruction for ourselves. It tells us a high tale of sparing mercy and mitigating grace. By its single syllable it preaches a sermon of many truths,—truths so precious that the Christian in affliction would be poor and wretched indeed without them. "Yet:"—and is there not in every sentence of fatherly or judicial chastisement a "yet" inserted? Does God ever send trial *too* heavy to bear, or vexing temptation from which there is *no* way of escape? No. There is always a *yet*, a something to mitigate or lighten in every distress. Does the Lord lay you low? *Yet* there is hope of rising, or many comforts left which might have been denied. Does he take from you health? *Yet*, perhaps, he gives you peace. Does he make inroad on your property? *Yet* he leaves you *something*. Does he bereave you of a relative or friend? "*Yet*" he grants you a joyful hope of the departed, or gives you grace to seek life eternal yourself.

Thus we might travel through the whole region of human distress, and everywhere find this little word "yet" marking some exception or pointing to some blessedness. Then, dear brethren, be thankful for your alleviating mercies, and make good use of them. Never is God more ready to give us greater mercies than when we thankfully use the smaller.

4. *God frequently overrules our folly for the display of his wisdom, and our sin for the setting forth of his grace.* The Hebrews foolishly desired a king: but how pitiful was their muster under him! Their destitute and defenceless condition however made God's intervention more desirable and more signal. When their folly in choosing a king had been exposed, he presented to the kingdom "a man after his own heart." This king, who was also their deliverer, was being prepared for both their deliverance and their government while their distress was going on. How true a picture is this of the infinite wisdom and grace which provided for mankind "a Saviour and a great One," while they were perishing in their sin, and were unconscious of the approach of salvation! How little did the Jews suspect, in the midst of their galling subjection to the Romans, that One who appeared as a carpenter boy of Nazareth was "he who should redeem Israel," and spiritually "restore the kingdom!" But thus it was; and thus often in our own cases are God's deliverances wise and wonderful. Our folly makes way for his wisdom: and where our sin hath abounded his grace has much more abounded. Then

i. If we are in any present *distress*, let our first concern be *humility* and *repentance*.

ii. If like Israel we *suffer for past sins*, let us not be only humble and penitent, but *earnest also in looking to Jesus* for pardon and restoration.

iii. If we would *escape the smarting pangs of God's displeasure*, let us carefully avoid *those things which bring it down*. The words of Samuel at the close of the former chapter point out our strength and security: "Only fear the Lord, and serve him in truth with all your heart: for consider how great things he hath done for you." (1 Samuel 12:24.)

SERMON XXI.

YOUTH NO BARRIER TO REAL GREATNESS.[1]

1 Samuel 17:42.

"He was but a youth."

IT is extremely common for the follies of youth to be fondly excused upon the score of youth. "He or she is but young, so you must make some allowance," is the familiar apology for youthful giddiness or early delinquency. Such excuses and such apologies however derive no countenance from the word of God. Youth is no excuse for sin, but rather an urgent reason for holiness. God is as much the God of the young as he is the God of the aged. His grace is equally ready for both, and equally availing too. We consequently find in the word of God instances of illustrious piety among the young as well as among the old. There is one such instance in the chapter before us. Its beautiful narrative tells us of a youth, whose doings would have astonished the world, if the piety of that world had only been equal to his own. Standing forth, on a sudden, as the champion of his country, David was an unparalleled instance, not only of true magnanimity, but of all the virtues which adorn a good man. It is said of him in the text, that "he was but a youth:" but then what sort of youth was he! how much more than even a very noble youth! True, he was going forth in all the simplicity of a stripling champion to face a powerful and haughty giant. All his artillery was a rustic sling and a few pebbles, which had been polished by the running brook. His opponent was clad in all the pride of armour, and was brandishing a huge and glittering spear. And yet this youth, this mere shepherd boy, was more than a match for him who had been "a man of war from his youth." But it is not as a youthful warrior that Da-

[1] Preached Sunday Evening, June 22nd, 1845.

vid is chiefly pre-eminent. He is resplendent in far higher honours; for though "but a youth," and the generous champion of his people, he was at that very time, although perhaps little suspected by those who saw him, the most highly favoured and the most important personage in the whole world. "He was but a youth;" but then he was "the man after God's own heart," "the sweet psalmist of Israel," the living type of that Messiah who was to come. More than this, he was a conspicuous pattern for the youth of all generations in after times. Let us at this present contemplate him in these capacities; and may the God of David bless the contemplation to both old and young.

I. *David was, at this early period of his life, "a man after God's own heart."*

King Saul, in consequence of his disobedience, had been rejected of God. The prophet Samuel was therefore commissioned to say to him thus: "Now thy kingdom shall not continue: the Lord hath sought him *a man after his own heart.*" In a political point of view this might be construed as meaning that David, as an earthly ruler, should fulfil God's heavenly will by living religiously, reigning righteously, and forwarding the development of Messiah's kingdom. But in its moral sense it means something of still higher importance. It implies that David was an eminently holy youth, and an especial object of the divine approbation. For surely he who is a man after God's own heart must be a man after God's own image. That image, we are told by an apostle, consists in "knowledge, righteousness, and true holiness."

That David was what he was, could be attributed only to the grace of that God who chose him for his servant. He well knew that by nature he neither possessed God's image, nor accorded with his heart. "Behold," says he, "I was shapen in iniquity, and in sin did my mother conceive me."

The great change was wrought in him just as it is wrought in us. The Holy Spirit made him a new creature, and transformed him into a spiritual child of God. Of that mighty change circumcision was to him the "sign and seal." To us holy baptism is a similar witness, only with all the brighter and more blessed privileges of the new dispensation.

In consequence of this spiritual change, and not from any naturally amiable disposition, he loved and reverenced the God of Israel. It may indeed have been that he was a youth of a lovely disposition: but it must ever be borne in mind not only that such disposition is not religion itself, but that it frequently exists without any religion at all. There are amiable heathens abroad as well as amiable worldlings at home. The young ruler was in disposition so lovely that even the Lord Jesus loved him; but he had not the loveliness of a renewed mind. No naturally pleasing qualities can compensate for the absence of the image of God in the soul, nor can anything short of the grace of God accomplish that image. The renewing of the Holy Ghost is the grand agency in that momentous work.

Pray then my hearers, and my younger hearers especially, for the gift of that Spirit who alone can make you what David was. To be a man after God's own heart is what an angel may prize; for there is no higher honour in heaven, and no greater blessedness on earth. But you never can attain either the one or the other without giving up your sins, and seeking for the Holy Ghost. Should it seem to you to be a hard thing to give up "the pleasures of sin," and "the pomps and vanities of this wicked world," remember that David made this sacrifice, and yet "he was but a youth." What therefore one youth did another may do. Then "seek and you shall find." Pray for David's grace, and David's blessedness shall be given you.

II. *David, when our text speaks of him, was "the sweet psalmist of Israel."*

"He was but a youth;" but already he was a poet and a musician. He was more—he was a *divine* poet and a *sacred* musician. "He appears (as a writer of our own Church remarks) to have had almost from his very childhood the sublimest talents for poetry, and an exquisite taste in music. His harp therefore was probably his frequent companion in the fields when he exercised the occupation of a shepherd. And, having experienced the inestimable blessing of early conversion, he did not debase his poetic genius nor prostitute his musical skill, by devoting either of them to the contemptible purposes of versified nonsense and unmanly dissipation; but, his heart being as rightly tuned as his harp, his happiness and his highest recreation were to sing the praises of the God he loved."

In regarding David, while yet so young, as "the sweet psalmist of Israel," we must bear in mind that, having been anointed by Samuel, he was under the inspiration of the Spirit. There is much reason for concluding that many of the psalms now extant were composed by him while tending his peaceful flocks on the pastures of Bethlehem. The twenty-third Psalm, for instance, is evidently the composition of a pastoral poet. But, while it is the composition of one who borrows his images from the moonlight scenes of a shepherd's life, it is also a most sublimely prophetical hymn addressed to the Son of God, as the great and good Shepherd of the flock of God.

As a musician too David excelled, because the "Spirit of the Lord was upon him." His master-powers rivetted the astonishment of all who heard him. This circumstance was the occasion of his introduction to Saul; for, when evil melancholy and infuriate passion came upon the unhappy monarch, David was sent for as a minstrel of surpassing skill. The tones of the stripling's harp "expelled the raging fiend."

Thus David, though "but a youth," was the honoured instrument of teaching, by his psalms, the church of the living

God, and of asserting the power of the Holy Spirit over the spirits of the wicked one. And thus, in at least some humble degree, may our own sons and daughters honour the God of their salvation. Without being either such poets or such musicians as the youthful David was, they may be such as the true David, the Lord Jesus, proved himself to be. They may love the poetry of the Scriptures, and sing its hymns as he did, when a man of sorrows in our evil world.

It is a fearful disgrace to us, as a Christian nation, that poetry and music of the most earthly character are far more common among us than either "the songs of the temple," or "the music of the church." While time and money are lavished on the former, they are doled out with scantiest moiety on the latter. It is too an unwelcome reflection on us as churchmen that, generally speaking, so little attention is paid in our congregations to the worship of God by singing. Hundreds who can sing and do sing elsewhere make no effort to sing in the house of God. They must answer for the neglect to him who claims our praises, and who has commanded us to sing them with understanding. God grant that in our own congregation both "young men and maidens, old men and children," may take pleasure in praising the name of the Lord!

III. *David, when "but a youth," in the camp of Israel, was an illustrious type of the Messiah.*

To trace that type in all its relations is far too copious a subject for the present sermon. A brief notice of its principal bearings, as exhibited in this very chapter, is all that can be attempted.

David in his very *name* foreshadowed the Messiah; for the word David signifies "*dear* or *beloved*." He was the youngest son of his father, and most likely the one in whom he especially delighted. Now we know what Father it was who said, "This is my *beloved* Son." David had been sent by his father to visit his brethren in the field of expected battle. And we know too what Father sent his Son into our world of strife to visit us as his brethren according to the flesh. That beloved Son was born at Bethlehem; and David had been born there before him, for David was the son of Jesse the Bethlehemite. That good man did not send his stripling son empty handed to his other sons. He sent him with "parched corn, and loaves, and cheeses." God the Father sent his beloved Son to us with the bread of life. Yea, himself was that bread, and he brought it down from heaven for the refreshment of a famishing world.

When David entered the camp of Israel he wore a common garb, but he was no common individual. He was a king in disguise. He had been anointed by Samuel to fill the throne of Israel, though that circumstance was either forgotten or not understood. And who was he who walked through the cities and villages of Judea in "the form of a servant," and yet all the while was the King of the people, yea the very King of kings, and Lord of lords? It was Jesus of Bethlehem and of Nazareth, "David's Son" and "David's Lord!"

As soon as David, on entering the camp, began to ask questions and excite surprise, the anger and the envy of his brethren were keenly aroused against him. "I know thy pride," said one of them, "and the naughtiness of thine heart." And what did not the angry brethren of Jesus say to him when the Spirit which was given to him without measure began to exert itself in teachings and miracles? One said, "he had a devil." Another, that "he cast out devils by Beelzebub the prince of the devils." A third said or thought, he was "beside himself;" and a multitude cried out "Crucify him, crucify him!"

In the estimation of the spectators David appeared a very unequal match for the Philistine of Gath, while his weapons and his plan of attack were objects of ridicule. So to the carnal Jew, and the philosophic Greek, Christ was derision and his cross foolishness. And further, as David fought all alone for Israel, and won deliverance for them, so the arm of the Lord Jesus, without any assistance, fought our battle and secured our redemption.

But mark some points of contrast. David, in going to the combat, went in all the health and vigour of youth. "He was ruddy and of a fair countenance." How different was it with the Saviour! "Many were astonished at him, his visage was so marred more than any man, and his form more than the sons of men." Agony and sleeplessness and scourging and cruel insults had so debilitated his sinless frame, that it sank beneath the weight of the cross which he essayed to carry.

Admiration and plaudits followed the discharge of David's sling; but mockery and scorn surrounded the cross of the suffering Jesus. In a word, while David only risked his life, our champion laid *his* down! O that, for this consideration, the hearts of old and young would cleave to him in love, and follow him in faithful obedience!

IV. *David, as a youth, is an illustrious pattern for the youth of all generations.*

It may too be remarked that his piety never shone more brightly than at this period of his history. After he entered on public life, and became the king of Israel, cares and temptations darkened his path: so little conducive, generally speaking, is publicity and greatness to purity of heart and heavenly mindedness. Let youth then well improve its rapidly passing hours, and use them in securing what will balance riper years, and be a blessing to old age.

As a son, David was evidently worthy of his name, the *beloved* one; for he seems to have taken delight in obeying his father's wishes. When Jesse told him to go and take certain articles of provision to his brethren in the camp, David acted with great readiness and alacrity. "He rose up *early* in the morning, and," like a *thoughtful* youth, "left the sheep with a keeper, and went as Jesse had commanded him."

And truly how lovely and commendable a thing is it for older as well as younger children so to love and reverence their parents as to render a cheerful and instant compliance with all their wishes or directions. "Honour thy father and thy mother" is "the first commandment *with promise*."

As soon as David entered the camp the prevailing temper of his mind began to evince itself. When he saw and heard the boasting giant, he said, "Who is this uncircumcised Philistine that he should defy the armies of the living God?"

Observe, he does not call them the armies of his king or of his country, but of his "*God*," yea of even the "*living* God," as opposed to Dagon and other dumb idols. How enviable a thing is it for our youth so to know God as to love him, to be zealous in his service, and ever ready to vindicate his honour!

The peculiar gentleness of David's spirit, under very unjust and very unkind aspersions, affords a fine pattern to the young Christian. When his eldest brother, Eliab, angrily and sarcastically addressed him, his calm and meek reply was, "What have I now done? Is there not a cause?" How happy would it be if this "ornament of a meek and quiet spirit" were more carefully cultivated in the families of our Israel! How greatly would it conduce to the well-being of brothers and sisters, and what a fragrance would it shed in many a home!

But we must not overlook the modesty, the courage, the patriotism of David. When Saul objected to his youth and inexperience, he modestly related his successful encounter with a lion and a bear, adding, with the dignity of true courage, "This uncircumcised Philistine shall be as one of them, seeing he hath defied the armies of the living God." Thus he avowed his humble confidence in God on the ground of past deliverances and former helps. Nothing can surpass the Christian beauty of this meek and modest profession, especially when coupled with his declining the military habiliments of the king, and preferring his own plain attire.

When the Philistine drew nigh, and the dread encounter was at hand, then every excellency in David's character appeared, like stars in a gathering storm, even greater and more resplendent. His confidence was reposed in the Lord of the battle: and therefore with uncommon magnanimity he said to the haughty foe, "Thou comest to me with a sword, and with a spear, and with a shield: but I come to thee in the name of the Lord of hosts, the God of the armies of Israel, whom thou hast defied." So true is it that godliness is the best foundation for moral courage; "the righteous is as bold as a lion." Nor was David deceived in his religious confidence. He selects one of his pebbles, takes a good aim, and thinks all the while of his God. The hand of that God guides the stone, and the giant falls! Thus he, who "was but a youth," overcame him who was "a man of war from his youth." Thus too the Lord honoured the young servant who had honoured him, and thus will he honour all who act like him.

How fitly then may I say to all young persons now present, and especially to *the candidates for confirmation*, Take this godly youth as your pattern, and believe that in imitating him you will reap a rich reward. Whatever your position in life may be, you can hardly be so circumstanced as not to find, in what you have been hearing of David, somewhat that is applicable to yourselves. Like him you may seek to be renewed more and more in the spirit of your minds; that, being transformed into the divine image, you may become the sons and daughters of the Lord Almighty, and thus be children after his own heart. Like David, you may do much to promote and adorn the worship of God, whether by unreservedly singing his praises in the great congregation, or zealously and devoutly repeating such parts of our beautiful service as claim the humble and lowly voice. A hundred such voices from among only the David-like young of this congregation, would be very grateful to my ear, and very animating, I trust, to all true hearts. Especially may you, my young friends, do much for God by standing forth, like David, as witnesses of his truth and supporters of his honour. Ever nobly protest against Philistine impiety, whether in the shape of false religion or worldly vanities. We need such protestations among our youth; for the more I see of Worcester the more need do I discern of calling upon our rising population to "flee youthful lusts," to avoid the haunts of sin, and to turn away from the stranger "whose feet go down to death, and her steps take hold on hell."

Further let every candidate for confirmation remember that what David did is precisely that which our blessed Church desires them to do, namely to make an open and earnest profession of the one true faith. David, before Saul and Abner and the great men of the army, declared his trust in the God of Israel. Your part and duty is to take upon yourselves all the pledges of a Christian, and to say before the bishop and the assembled clergy, that you "renounce the devil and all his works, the pomp and vanities of this wicked world, and all the sinful lusts of the flesh." Then think of these things, and let *me* say, as Saul said to David, "Go, and the Lord be with thee!"

Finally let older friends remember that the text could *once* be truly said of each one of them. But how has our youth fled like a dream! And yet, by God's arrangement, *no man forgets his youth*. Pray against judgment for its sins, and improve remaining years.

SERMON XXII.

THE MAN OF GOD SLAIN BY A LION.[1]

1 Kings 13:24.

"And when he was gone, a lion met him by the way, and slew him: and his carcase was cast in the way, and the ass stood by it, the lion also stood by the carcase."

THIS text is an affecting part of a singularly awful narrative. The whole chapter indeed is of a solemn and searching cast, inasmuch as it reveals not only the anger of God against wicked men, but his displeasure also at sin in even his own people.

The entire history has been read in your hearing. May you have so marked it as to be ready inwardly to digest it, for such readiness is what the Church desires in all her members when her scripture lessons are recited to them.

Your devout attention will be directed, first, to *the character* of the prophet who was slain; then to *the reason* why he was slain; and, thirdly, to the *remarkale manner* of the lion which slew him.

I. *The character* of the prophet who was slain is an object of great importance. It is in fact the pivot on which the entire narrative turns, and forms the pith of our practical application of it. For, if the prophet be found to be a bad man at heart, our conclusions must be of one sort; but if we decide on his being unquestionably a good man, our conclusions must be widely different. Without fear then of mistake, we may assert that he was, in the highest sense of the expression, "*a good man*."

1. In the first verse of this chapter he is emphatically called "a man of God:" and he seems to be so called, on purpose to distinguish him from another prophet, who is brought on the stage of this narrative as a man of the world.

2. To be denominated "a man of God" is to be called by the highest title which can be given to one of our race. It is a title which describes the interior character of a man more than his external office. It implies the influence of divine grace over the soul, and the devotion of all its powers to the cause of God. Names which are descriptive of office, such as prophet, priest, and apostle, do not necessarily imply the existence of a holy principle. But the expression, "a man of God," is never in holy Scripture applied to an individual who is not a partaker of the saving grace of God. Balaam was a prophet, Hophni and Phineas were priests, and Judas was an apostle, but not one of them was "a man of God." The highest official appointment in God's church neither secures the presence, nor supplies the absence of God's grace. The former may answer certain purposes of God, but the latter alone adorns his doctrine and saves the soul. This momentous distinction is observable in the narrative before us: for, while he whom the lion slew is called "the man of God," the party who deceived him is simply described as "the old prophet."

3. As to this "old prophet who dwelt at Bethel," there is no reason for concluding that he was a genuinely religious man. His living contentedly in the neighbourhood of Jeroboam's wickedness, and his suffering that wickedness to proceed without protest or reproof, and at the same time his not even restraining his sons from joining it, together with the deliberate falsehood by which he deceived "the man of God," forbid us to believe that he was personally a holy man. His motive for wishing to bring the good prophet to his house, at the expense of a lie, is not specifically told us. Possibly it was the gratification of a vain and ostentatious feeling in having for his guest a man who had wrought a miracle of both judgment and restoration upon the person of the king. Or he might be anxious to screen his own character, by having for his associate a better man than himself, or to purchase a little self-complacency by a cheap token of respect for a really good man: because it is certain that corrupt human nature will both tolerate piety, when self-interest is at stake, as well as allay the irritations of an uneasy mind by the semblance of respect for what is holy.

4. Hence, dear brethren, we may fitly infer, and that with more explicitness than by a former remark, that neither sacramental dedication, nor education, nor official institution, nor even the profession of a correct creed, is any proof of, or any substitute for, a participation of saving grace. No outward station, compliance, or calling, can impart that grace. It must come from another quarter. The Spirit of Christ is the only agent of the grace of Christ in the heart of a sinner: and that Spirit, we are told, "divideth to every man severally as he will." That "the man of God" before us was a partaker of that Spir-

[1] Preached Sunday Morning, July 25th, 1847.

it, we have no reason to doubt. His conduct in the presence of Jeroboam, boldly facing the king and denouncing his false religion, as well as nobly refusing his invitation, betokened a man of principle. His conscientious adherence also to the injunctions of his mission, till he was deceived by a solemn lie, also tends to establish what is important for us to ascertain, namely the genuineness of his religious profession. He was an honest and holy man of God.

Why then, we ask, was such a man visited with such a death? This leads us to consider

II. The *reason why the good prophet was slain by an evil beast.*

It is no mean part of our office "to justify the ways of God to man," and to show that, amid the mystery of his doings, there is a holy and rightful wisdom which we are bound to adore.

1. The truth of God required proper vindication in the case of this good but disobedient prophet. A positive injunction had been given to him by God: "Thou shalt eat no bread, nor drink water there, nor turn again to go by the way that thou camest." This injunction the good prophet had confessed both before the king and other witnesses. Besides he sustained a high character, and had been employed in a high commission. Many of the enemies of God had their eye upon him, and he had been divinely honoured before them. Hence any swerving from duty would be a delight to them, and a scandal to his profession. It consequently was a reasonable expectation that disobedience in him would be followed by proportionate chastisement.

2. Now the good prophet, though for a long time earnest and staunch, at last, through want of due caution, fell into a snare and violated the divine command. He suffered himself to be deceived by the fair speeches and mere appearances of the old prophet. While the good prophet was sitting at table with that deceiver, the Spirit of inspiration, as if to add shame to the sentence, by putting it in the lips of a bad man, caused that very deceiver to denounce the conduct of his victim, and to declare a terrible award: "Thy carcase shall not come to the sepulchre of thy fathers;" meaning that, because of his disobedience he should die elsewhere than at home, that violence should attend his death, and that strangers should bury his corpse.

3. Clear however as the sin of the good prophet certainly is, there is much in his position which human reason could plead as an excuse. It might urge the severity of the prohibition, and its unreasonableness also; for it would seem hard that he who had travelled so far, and laboured so excitingly, should take no refreshment afterwards. It might argue the apparent unimportance of simply taking the simplest food in that place, and of not returning by exactly the same way. It might further lay great stress on the counter-command of the old prophet, who positively professed himself commissioned by God. But, dear friends, when human reason questions divine wisdom it only discovers its own folly: "Our God is the Rock, his work is perfect, for all his ways are judgment: a God of truth and without iniquity, just and right is he." (Deuteronomy 32:4.) The man of God had received a positive order from God, and nothing merely second hand or traditional, nothing coming without palpable evidence of authenticity, should have induced him to depart from that which had been plainly revealed to him. He should have demanded proof, and not hastily have relied on assertion, especially when that assertion came from a questionable party; for the life and conduct of the old prophet were not such as to warrant implicit credit. Probably also in yielding to the old prophet's invitation, he was yielding to the importunities of hunger and thirst. His self-denial, therefore, was not proof against temptation.

4. But, alas! who among ourselves will venture to cast a stone at the good prophet? Rather let us ponder our own dangers and infirmities. Better and safer also will it always be for us to obey what we know to be the divine commands, than to listen to uncertain declarations, or to question the force of any divine rule which it is difficult to mistake, but easy to dislike.

Great purposes are often concealed by God under apparently trivial commands. "Eat no bread, drink no water," was as though God had said, 'Hold no intercourse, acknowledge no communion with people who set at nought my religion, and set up one of their own!' So also, "Turn not again by the way that thou camest," was virtually saying 'Court not ostentation, by returning along a road in which people will recognise you and point at you, as the prophet who had faced and frightened the king, and wrought a double miracle upon him.'

Our God is jealous of his word, and will not allow his people to disobey it with impunity. This is why every erring child of God is made to smart "in mind, body, or estate," for wilful errors. Disobedience is the very essence of sin. When such sin is committed by a believer in an elevated position, his chastisement may reasonably be signal. It was thus with the good prophet. He stood, while in office, on a pinnacle. He must therefore in suffering be made a spectacle. Hence he was slain by a lion, under circumstances so singular that all Israel heard of it.

Such an act of penal chastisement on the person of the good prophet was especially fitting in order to vindicate the authority of God as being the Lord of his prophets, and also to give force to the prophecy which, just before, had been delivered against the altar of Jeroboam. For, had the failure of the prophet himself been unreproved, the effect of his inspired words might have been weakened amongst those who heard them. It might moreover be intended as a strong warning to the old prophet and his idolatrous sons.

Such then were the reasons for the chastisement. Let us next contemplate the peculiarity of the chastisement itself.

III. *The manner of the lion who slew the good prophet is, in every respect, most singular,* though the singularity is not noticed by every reader of the affecting narrative.

1. From what is told us it appears that the good prophet, after his repast at the home of the old prophet, rose up to go on his way. He must have set out on that way with feelings of the deepest sadness. As a good man, his heart must have pained him, because of his failure toward God, while the thought of the sentence which had been uttered against him must have weighed heavily on his mind. He knew that he was doomed to meet with a strange death in some strange place. The time also he knew not. This would keep him in constant suspense. Thus, in the multitude of his thoughts, he proceeded on his homeward course, little suspecting, it would seem, that he was never to see his home again. In an instant God's executioner met him. The appointed lion, guided by supernatural instinct, sprung upon him, and at a blow took away that life which disobedience had forfeited: "And when he was gone a lion met him by the way, and slew him: and his carcase was cast in the way, and the ass stood by it; the lion also stood by the carcase."

2. From the circumstances mentioned in the text, and cleared up by further mention in verse 28, it is evident that every natural instinct of the lion was powerfully suspended, in order to mark the especial service in which God employed him: "And he went and found his carcase cast in the way, and the ass and lion standing by the carcase: the lion had not eaten the carcase, nor torn the ass." (28th verse.) In ordinary cases that lion would have killed both man and ass, and have eaten one or mangled both. But in this case he killed only the prophet, though the ass continued to stand close by. What is more, he did not eat the body, but merely killed it. It is further observable that, after the work of death, the lion did not hurry away, but calmly stood by the corpse on one side, while the ass, without any of its usual alarm, stood quietly on the other. So also, when travellers passing by beheld the spectacle, the lion did not molest them; neither did he alarm the old prophet when, after a long interval, he came to take up the body for its burial. All these are extraordinary events, and quite beyond the customary habits of the king of beasts. And why did things so strange come to pass? One answer alone can be given: they were all ordained to show the real hand which had been at work. They formed a miraculous evidence to hard souled apostates that the lion was God's agent, and that he who had created the noble animal had employed him for one simple purpose,—the slaying of a good man because of his sin.

Here is abundance for us to learn. O Lord God, give us grace to learn it! Then let us learn what we cannot fail of seeing,

i. *That, God notices sin in his people, and will scourge them for it.* Because it is said, "He hath not beheld iniquity in Jacob," some unwise professors have dared to assert that God sees no sin in his people, and that, when once it is pardoned, they have no need to be further concerned about it. But all such expressions as the one just quoted are applicable to the Lord's people only in their final state, or as standing in the eye of God at that point at which they shall stand when all is ended. The whole Bible is a testimony against sin in the heirs of salvation; and such narratives as the one before us are exemplifications of that testimony. In fact the glory of the divine character, the honour of redemption, the good of offenders, the discipline of the catholic family, all require chastisement for sin. God may inflict it even unto death, and that without the slightest imputation on his mercy. For, though the covenant of grace insures the salvation of the soul of every believer, yet is it consistent with that covenant for the body to suffer death under the correcting rod. But let it ever be borne in mind that the rod smites not for atonement, but simply for sanctifying correction. The blood of Christ alone atones for sin. Chastisement makes us hate and abjure it.

ii. *The strictest obedience in some things will not excuse disobedience in others.* How noble and exemplary was the conduct of the good prophet before the sin-causing Jeroboam! How boldly did he protest against his defection from the God of Israel! and how beautifully did he act as a true servant of his, amid dangers and provocations! But all this did not exempt him from obligation to obedience in remaining particulars. We must, dear brethren, fulfil all righteousness, and study to obey our Saviour in every tittle of his perfect law.

iii. *A really good man may, as the phrase is, "die under a cloud."* We are too apt to think this impossible. It may not be very common: but many a fact, in both the Bible and the history of the church, proves it be very possible. Jehoshaphat was a case in point: and the one before us is proof positive. Then let us not by harsh judgment add darkness to a neighbour's dark end; but let us seek to have our own end clear and satisfactory. Many a sun which has set with us in deepest shade has risen in another hemisphere in glorious light. Let us however pray that we may obtain, not only "an abundant entrance" into heaven, but a happy departure from earth.

iv. *No external circumstances determine inward character.* The wicked old prophet lives at his ease in Bethel, long after the man of God dies by the paw of a lion. So Lazarus lingers and expires on a dunghill, while Dives is nursed and departs on a bed of down. We must not be deceived by any thing of this sort which befals either good or bad men. (Ecclesiastes 9:1, 2.) Then judge nothing before the time, but rather judge yourselves, that ye be not judged of the Lord.

v. *Vigilance and prayerfulness should be our constant effort.* And these should be our effort especially after seasons of honour, success, or enjoyment. It was at the close of the prophet's noble demeanour that the enemy prevailed against him. He had performed his commission, and was departing with honour, when temptation overtook him and he fell. Then "watch and pray" and that without ceasing. Study your dangers and that will quicken your prayers.

SERMON XXIII.

ELIJAH'S REMONSTRANCE AGAINST HALTING BETWEEN TWO OPINIONS.[1]

1 Kings 18:21.

"And Elijah came unto all the people and said, How long halt ye between two opinions? if the Lord be God, follow him: but if Baal, then follow him. And the people answered him not a word."

FOR three years and six months there had been no rain in all the land of Israel. The privation was a judgment on the people because of their idolatrous practices or propensities. But the judgment had not turned their hearts. There was no dew of the spirit on *them*. They therefore remained as insensible as the rainless ground was hard. At length, when all was hopeless on the part of the king and the people, Jehovah tries another experiment, and makes bare his arm for success in it. He sends Elijah from his retirement at Zarephath, brings him into contact with Ahab, and inspires him with the loftiest wisdom and the noblest zeal, for one of the most singular and interesting controversies which the world ever witnessed.

The good prophet proposed to the wicked king a congress of all the people, but especially of all the Baalite priests, on the splendid heights of mount Carmel. The proposal was accepted, and the congress met. The fainting multitudes no doubt expected that the prophet was about to do some great thing *for* them. And so he was: but he was first going to do a great thing *with* them. He must school their souls and, by God's grace, turn their hearts, before he relieves their bodily wants. He went to the root of their evil plight ere he adjusted its branches. He startled them by the force of a great practical question. Their smitten conscience stopped their mouth, and no answer could be given. From our text three remarks will, as propositions, be deduced for our devout consideration. May we be "swift to hear," and, if smitten in heart, "slow to speak," as the people were; but like them, when the truth is set before us, may we be prompt and firm to act! Let us observe first

I. That, as *it respects the things of God and religion, there are really but "two opinions."*

The wickedness of the human heart prompts it to imagine that there are more than two, and that the line of distinction between the true and the false is not so finely drawn as it is represented to be. But since the entrance of sin into the world there have been two, and only two opinions in it, as to the grand interests of the soul and the honour of God. The fact was established as soon as there was room and opportunity to establish it. The history of Cain and Abel proved it: and every subsequent age has added to the proof.

1. In the time of Elijah the worship of Baal, a personification of the sun and of the solar powers, was generally adopted, in opposition to the worship of Jehovah. The one system was of Satan, the other of God. The one suited the natural heart, the other opposed it. The one winked at sin, the other commanded holiness. This melancholy change in the religious

[1] Preached Sunday Morning, July 28th, 1850.

aspect of Israel was effected chiefly by the arts of an elegant and fascinating queen. Jezebel was a devotee to the gods of her native Zidonia. She perverted her husband, crowded his court with priests, and fostered their influence over the people. So great a zealot was she that, even while judgment was consuming the country for her sin, she persecuted the servants of Jehovah. So true, therefore, is it, that even under the fairest form the natural heart is "desperately wicked."

2. In the present day, as in every other day since Christianity became the law of the earth, there are but "two opinions," two states, two sides, opposed to each other. Light and darkness, holiness and sin, Christ and Belial, still divide the world: and every man is in reality ranged on the one side or the other.

The difference between the "two opinions" is broad and very definite. It stands not in any niceties of ecclesiastical or theological sentiment. It does not consist in holding this view or that view,—in joining this party or that party. It is altogether of *another sort* of difference. It is a *spiritual* difference, discernible indeed by its effects, but not always so clearly as to be determined by the human eye. The heart is its seat: and he alone who searches the heart can accurately discern the opinion or thought, as the word also means, which most sways the heart. But he *does* discern it. He knows if it inclines to himself or to another master,—if it sides with holiness or with sin,—with the love of heavenly or of earthly things. He knows too, what we are so unwilling to admit, that all the shades and varieties of moral thought and opinion, when resolved into their proper character, range themselves into one or other of these two and only two classes. We are of opinon that "the Lord he is God," or that some Baal of our own making is worthy of being our God. We are either serving the creature, in some shape or other, or giving up ourselves to the one only Creator. Quibble too, and plead, and refine, as we may, we cannot make more "opinions" than divine infallibility has made. There are but "two."

Notwithstanding however this simple and certain division of things, mankind are not always so simple or so certain in their choice between them. Hence our second remark or proposition,

II. *That we are prone to be wavering and undecided as to the part which we mean ultimately to take.* "How long halt ye between two opinions?" Though it is certain that, in the sight of God, we *are* of one opinion only, yet is it equally certain that many who are not of the right opinion are, in themselves, wavering about it. They have not deliberately made up their minds openly to avow themselves religious or irreligious, but halt between the two states, inclining to the one or the other as times, opportunities, or associates influence them.

1. Society assumed much of this aspect in Israel, when Jezebel perverted the nation. The mass of the people either wavered or apostatized. A few thousands, not more than seven, were firm in heart, but fearful in life. They did not really bow the knee to Baal; but they had not resolution to protest against his worship. Others went with the stream, either justifying or excusing their defection, sometimes worshipping God and at other times favouring Baal, as though conscience and interest kept them in a struggle. Thus they halted between two ways, and so neither honoured God nor satisfied themselves.

One transition of the Hebrew text is peculiarly expressive of the indecision of the people. Instead of "How long halt ye between two opinions?" the supposed more literal rendering is, "How long *hop* ye from spray to spray?" as though Israel were like a fickle, restless, "light-minded" bird, springing from one twig to another, and settling on neither.

2. And truly how exact a picture is this of many individuals in our Israel! Even ecclesiastically there are always some to be found who are hopping from spray to spray, fluttering to and fro between the church and the chapel, the established religion and dissent, protestantism and popery; while, alas! far greater numbers are acting the part of inconstant birds as to the great realities of life and death, time and eternity. Multitudes have neither the heart to serve God, nor the honesty to deny him. They do not love his service, and yet they would not be thought to hate it. They care not for Christ but they dare not declare for Belial. At the same time, while they thoroughly love the world, more thoroughly than they quite like to acknowledge, they still see that they must pay some little deference to at least the Sunday forms of religion. The man of all absorbing business, and the lover of pleasure, must be seen at church, or their principles may be suspected. The devotee of the convivial or gambling party must be a little decent, and must come to church now and then, else conscience will goad a little more than it does, and character may be too much damaged. Such compromises are effected, even when the guilty ones have not reached their homes till the clock has told that the Sabbath morning is come.

3. Looking at another range of the halting and undecided, do we not see individuals at one time thinking solemnly, and then turning to thoughtlessness? Sickness perhaps has seized them; and more than that it has alarmed them. O how near to decision for God do they seem to come *then!* Resolutions and promises are speedily and abundantly sown: but they have only a mushroom growth. The sickness subsides, and the new prayer and the recent promise make way for old thoughts and former devices. The convalescent begins again to "hop from spray to spray;" he halts between what he dreads and what he loves.

And is it not also a frequent sight, for some sharp or affecting affliction to befal one who is in as full love of the world as he is of health? Do we not see such an one appalled, amazed, aroused? Property perhaps has, beetle like, suddenly unfolded a hidden wing, and, before we suspected that it had one, has taken flight and left us. Or, what is as common and far more piercing, because there is no hope of return, some beloved relative or friend has been snatched from us, the most loved of all perhaps, and the very one whom of all others we were least prepared to part with. And what do we then see? The man who halted turns round in the right direction. He is in an agony. He flings himself on his knees. He is wrong. He *knows* he is wrong. He has been a foolish, erring, inexcusable sinner. He has seen and acknowledged the good, but has chosen the evil, and followed it, alas! Now he *feels* it. Now he cries for mercy, pardon, and help. He *will* be altogether different. He longs to be as the beloved dead was, and will so be, if the Lord only spares and helps. He half commits himself to this course, in the hearing of some Christian acquaintance. But what does it all amount to? The heavy finger of God's chastisement has been upon him, and has pressed down the elastic worldliness of his heart. Under the pressure he has relented, and talked like an altered man. But time steps in, and circumstances follow at intervals, and they both with easy and unobserved effort take off the weight that lay on the man's heart. The *steel* spring within it rises and rises, till some day it darts up to its original height, and the man smiles to find himself *recovered* as he calls it! He begins to halt afresh; and perhaps, after a little, he is found further from the one true opinion than he ever was.

All this is nature,—original, corrupt, unrenewed nature. It is *that* which prompts us to halt and waver when we ought to be progressing and decided.

4. Elijah probably gave a peculiar force to the words "*How long*." It was as though he said, "The judgments of God have been upon the land for three years and six months: 'how long' would you have them to continue? God has borne with your indecision all this time: 'how long' will you tempt him to punish you for it?"

Alas, how many halt and waver even under the chastisements of God! Those chastisements are sent on purpose to end our halting, and to urge us to the right side. But earthly hearts see not the meaning and intent of God's "*tokens*," whether of a personal, family, or national character. A little moralizing, or a brief emotional stirring, is all that *usually* follows such "tokens," as England and America have just been simultaneously witnessing.[1] Jehovah, as said by Isaiah (3:2, 3), takes away "the prudent and *the ancient*, the *honourable man, and the counsellor, and the eloquent orator*" (or, as in the margin, the "*skilful of speech*"). But who thinks that himself may be taken next, and so ceases to halt between two opinions, lest he should be found siding with the wrong, and death give him no time to change to the right? Whoever among the thousands of our Israel may not do thus, let *us* do it *ourselves!*

Our third remark or proposition now finds its proper place:

III. *That a firm and an instant decision is expected of us.* Elijah spake for this fruit, on the part of Israel, when he boldly said, "*If* the Lord be God, follow him: but if Baal, then follow him!"

1. The good prophet said not thus because he had the glance of a doubt as to who was the true God. He risked not an hypothesis in so solemn a business. There was no "if" in his own mind. He knew that the God alone of his fathers was the one true God, and that Baal was a lie and an abomination. But he was willing to put the people on some test, and to have an opportunity to demonstrate to them where the truth infallibly lay.

2. In like manner the ministers of Christ are, or ought to be, prepared to assert, illustrate, and defend the truth of Christ. They are not needlessly to invite controversy but they are manfully to meet it. They are to declare the truth, and to contend for it. But, as it respects the one comprehensive and constant question, the decision of the soul for God, in opposition to the love of sin and the world, we are always to be urgent, confident, and peremptory. We are to say, "Behold we 'set before you' good and evil, life and death, heaven and hell! 'Choose ye, this day,' between them. 'Choose ye whom ye will serve.' Be not wavering, but honestly take your side, and let us see who and what you are!" Now who will doubt to whom our hearts should be given, and on whom and on what our affections ought to be set? There is but one conclusion, and we hear it in verse 39: "And all the people said, The Lord he is the God; the Lord he is the God." Hence, as ministers of Christ, we ask you to decide for Christ. Decide for him and he will decide for you!

We may urge our call also on further grounds:

i. *Indecision is unwise in itself.* There is no peace in it; there is no profit from it; there can be no desirable end of it. "He that wavereth is like a wave of the sea driven with the wind and tossed: for let not that man think that he shall receive anything from the Lord." (James 1:6, 7.)

What a really terrific picture is this of the folly of indecision! To be all through life tossing about, ebbing and flowing, heaving and sinking, and then to receive nothing of the Lord! The life disquiet, the end loss!

ii. *Indecision is hateful to God.* He regards it as practical indifference, and a proof of worthlessness: "I know thy works, that thou art neither cold nor hot: I would thou wert cold or

[1] In allusion to the deaths of Sir R. Peel and the President of the United States.

hot. So then because thou art lukewarm, and neither cold nor hot, I will spue thee out of my mouth." (Revelation 3:15, 16.) This shows us that God accounts indecision as insincerity, and that he will treat it accordingly.

iii. *Indecision is criminal and therefore destructive.* What has just been said might suffice to prove it to be such; but there is more to be added: "He that is not with me is *against me*," said the Lord Jesus. Consequently indecision is, in fact, hostility and positive rebellion. It is being *against* Christ! And what does he say of such? "Those mine enemies which would not that I should reign over them bring hither, and slay them before me." (Luke 19:27.) Let me add, the danger of this destruction is increased by delay, because indecision easily becomes a habit—a chain of adamant.

And now, from the question contained in our text, let us conclude the present discourse by looking at the prophet who put that question. We find reason to say

1. *The man who asks for decision in others must himself be decided.* Without sincerity and firmness on our own part, we injure Christ's cause by demanding them from others. We are to be and to do what we ask them to be and to do. The work of the ministry, if it be not coupled with sincerity and firmness, is a work of inward misery. It was no such thing with Elijah. Everything proved that he was not "halting between two opinions." His very position proved his staunch and intrepid adherence to the one true opinion. There stood he, single handed, before crowds of opponents, and nobly declared for God. His sincerity commanded attention. He had a right to put the question which he did put, and consciences felt that he had that right. The Lord make our Church a mount Carmel!

2. *The servants of God may glorify him in very varied acts of service.* Elijah was just as much his servant while doing *nothing* at Cherith, as he was when doing *something* at Zarephath, and *working wonders* on Carmel. The silence and seclusion of a minister of Christ may be as valuable in his omniscient estimate, as the most devoted efforts in pulpit, press, or platform. The Master best knows how to employ the servant. He lays him aside or brings him forward just as is best for his church. But all of *us* can always serve the Lord by being on his side, manfully yet modestly, wherever we are.

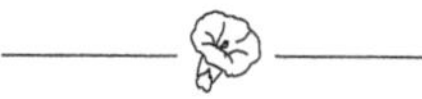

SERMON XXIV.

THE BOW DRAWN AT A VENTURE.[1]

1 Kings 22:34.

"And a certain man drew a bow at a venture, and smote the king of Israel between the joints of the harness."

THE arrow, which was thus carelessly shot, proved the death-pang of a king who was remarkable for the mercies he had received, the sins he had committed, and the warnings he had despised. Ahab knew what was right, but followed what was wrong. Occasionally he seems to have acknowledged the truth of God, and the folly of his own ways. But, though conscience often smote him, his heart was never subdued. Consequently all his temporary convictions and resolutions were but as blossoms nipped by a northern wind. At one time, when he heard the threats of divine vengeance like thunder over his head, his spirit sank within him, and he *seemed* like a penitent man. He went so far as to put on sackcloth; and God said to his own prophet, "Seest thou how Ahab humbleth himself?" But as soon as the thunder of the divine threatening had ceased, and the sentence against him was suspended, he fell back to his former self, and recurred to his former ways: so hard is it to break off from besetting sins, and so little trustworthy are the resolves of a man who does not thoroughly love the

[1] Preached Sunday Evening, August 16th, 1846.

things of God. Shortly after, when unwelcome truth was told him by the honest Micaiah, he insulted that faithful prophet. "And the king of Israel said, Take Micaiah, and carry him back unto Amon the governor of the city, and to Joash the king's son; and say, Thus saith the king, Put this fellow in the prison, and feed him with bread of affliction and with water of affliction, until I come in peace." (1 Kings 22:26, 27.)

From the date of this wickedness the measure of Ahab's iniquity began fast to fill up. He went into the battle-field both armed and disguised; but vengeance singled him out, shot an arrow at him, and dashed away his life. A Syrian warrior drew his bow "at a venture" (in the margin it is said, "in his simplicity"), shooting at random and aiming at no one in particular. But by that very random-shot arrow did the hand of God accomplish the prediction of his own prophet: "And thou shalt speak unto him, saying, Thus saith the Lord, Hast thou killed, and also taken possession? And thou shalt speak unto him, saying, Thus saith the Lord, In the place where dogs licked the blood of Naboth shall dogs lick thy blood, even thine." (1 Kings 21:19.) Then let us take this fact as the concentration of a great lesson, and learn from it sundry truths which bear at once on Christian doctrine and Christian practice. Learn this,

I. *That what appears accidental to man is providential with God.*

Though the Syrian archer shot at a venture, yet the finger of God was upon the string of his bow. The arrow flew through the viewless air; but its course was guided by a divine hand more surely than if the most dexterous aim had been deliberately taken. None around were conscious of this invisible guidance; and all would naturally attribute the infliction of the wound *to chance*. But God's providence was as certainly at work as in any of those more ostensible events which none presume to deny.

1. Now the doctrine of a particular and especial providence is as *consolatory* as it is *important*. It stands out with more than gilded prominence in the great structure of evangelical truth. "Known unto God are all his works from the beginning of the world," is a declaration which, however puzzling to our puny understandings, is full of unsearchable fact and comfortable truth. We are ready enough to admit both the fact and the truth as applicable to what we call *great* events; but we hesitate and halt at admitting their application to the minuter circumstances of individual history. But our blessed Lord schooled his disciples in the entire doctrine. The very hairs of their head, as worthless as humanly they were countless, were all numbered. And the very sparrows, those commonest and cheapest of birds, were so known and protected that not one of them fell to the ground without the will of the great Father of heaven. The habit of tracing the hand of God in *all* that befals us is a very gracious habit. Its cultivation is precious.

2. The child of God should *well study* this doctrine, and ever bear it in mind. It will be to him an anchor and a compass; an anchor to hold him fast amid the tempest turmoils of life, and a compass by which he may safely pass the rocks and quicksands on which others make shipwreck. He can never be at a loss for either calmness or contentment when he feels assured that his God is guiding all things. To be able to say "*It is the Lord!*" will turn the edge of any calamity.

3. The Christian too should advocate the doctrine of his Saviour's providence, for the honour of God, in opposition to the infidel notion of chance. We may talk of "time and chance happening to all men;" but then it should be in the sense in which Holy Scripture speaks of such sort of accident. Nothing is accidental or fortuitous on God's part; things are apparently so only with reference to our inability to tell what a day may bring forth. Hence what is accident with man is providence with God. Many illustrations of this truth are recorded for our contemplation in the oracles of God. Saul went in search of his father's asses; but God meant him to find the kingdom of Israel. David went as his father's errand-lad into the camp of the Hebrews, but found himself the conqueror of the Philistines. The widow of Zarephath walked out to gather a few sticks to dress her last meal, when she met the prophet of God, who secured for her an ample store. And the widow of Nain carried forth the corpse of her only son, and fell in with him who proved to be "the Resurrection and the Life." These all, as it were, drew their bow at a venture, but God directed the arrow to his own mark.

4. *The histories of private individuals* furnish convincing proofs of that which is accident with man being purpose with God. Many of the most important or most interesting events of our lives have often originated in what we call accidental circumstances. The accidentally calling here or there, going in this direction or in that direction, or not going at all, the casually seeing this person or that person, or hearing this or that intelligence,—have proved so many bows drawn at a venture, but carried to a mark which God had destined for us.

My brethren, this truth, which lies covert in the text, demands, when elicited, great thought of heart and much seriousness of soul. It discovers to us a very solemn reality, namely, that God is in every thing, and that his hand is at work either where men think it is not, or where they consider that chance operates.

5. In our text, as suggestive of these thoughts, there are two things, or rather the presence of one thing and the absence of another, which a careful eye will not overlook.

i. It is said that "*a certain man* drew a bow at a venture," but the name of this certain man is not told us. In all probability it was never told; because most likely the man himself did not know what he had done, and in the confusion of the battle and the dispersion of its hosts there was no practicability for making inquiry. But God knew the man, and his recording angel marked his name. That "certain man" is as well known amid the numberless ones of the world of spirits as any name that is known to us. Like him perhaps we shall eventually find that during some period of our brief generation on earth we have been the unconscious instruments of a mighty providence.

ii. The fact of the death-charged arrow being shot at a venture is told us *without the expression of any moral or admonitory sentiment.* It is a simple record, unaccompanied by even a syllable of teaching or instruction. There is no effort to give it force, nor any attempt to parade it on our notice. And *why* is this? Because it is all of God; it is thoroughly divine. It is just the method which a holy God takes with a thoughtless world. He will not always explain where men *ought* to understand; neither will he teach openly where his people, by prayer and thought, can learn secretly. He gives the fact as we may give a text, and says, "Consider it:" "whoso is wise will *ponder* these things."—Let us next learn

II. *That no human devices can thwart the purposes of God.*

King Ahab knew what God had threatened against him: but either he thought that the threat would glance off into nothing, or that he, by prudent precaution, could avoid a violent death, and avert so strange an occurrence as for dogs to lick up his blood from the spot where Naboth was murdered. He therefore, in going down to battle, very wisely, as he thought, adopted two precautionary measures. He put on armour, and at the same time disguised himself. All probabilities were in his favour, and his usual good fortune he perhaps imagined would certainly attend him. But the wisdom of man is folly when arrayed against God; and all our schemes to avoid or avert deserved vengeance are but as a barricade of cobwebs against a battery of cannon. Ahab was *disguised*; but the eye of judgment discerned him as clearly as if he had been clothed with sunbeams. He was clad with well fitting armour, but God's arrow smote him in an unsuspected opening. The joints of his harness, the small bendings of his breast-plate, furnished opening enough for death to enter.

"How singular!" we are apt to say. But how easy is it to be understood when we bear in mind that God, as omniscient and almighty, knows the vulnerable part of every wicked man, and can wound his enemies where they think themselves most secure. Besides how truly it is said, "Thine hand shall *find out* all thine enemies!" No disguise can mislead his eye, no encasement of steel or adamant can thwart his arm. He knew Achan in the spacious camp of Joshua, and Judas in the little company of Jesus. And at the final mustering of all mankind he will see and separate them as easily as a shepherd divideth the sheep from the goats. On the other hand how blessed is the fact of the divine omniscience to the true people of God! The poor woman who touched Jesus' garment, and modestly thought herself hid by the press, was as well known and as accurately observed as they who let down the paralytic man through the roof of the house.

It is also a blessedness to know that spite of all impediments the purposes of God will be accomplished. Jehovah says, "I will work, and who shall *let* it?" The saying holds good not only in cases where judgment calls for the death of the offender, but in all other cases in which mercy is pledged to fulfil a great work both in the world and in the Christian's own soul. As no device of Ahab could prevent the accomplishment of God's purpose, so will no stratagem, "which the craft or subtilty of man" can devise, ever be able to retard God's purposes in his church one moment longer than he sees fit to allow.

What secret misgivings Ahab may have had we cannot tell, but the fact of his disguising himself is a half whisper of his inward fear. The bodings of wicked men are often, no doubt, as torments to them before their time. Their cunning carries with it an uneasiness which they dare not disclose to even their nearest associates. They are obliged *to appear* confident, while they are within themselves "horribly afraid." Hence such opponents of God are not unfrequently most bold and vociferous when they have the least ground for courage. Their disguise and their cunning are wont to promise them most when their exposure and confusion are nearest.

It wants no prophet-eye to discern the end of many of the disguises and of much of the cunning of the controversies of passing days. Truth perhaps is seldom in less danger than when its opponents are most confident of crushing it. Ahab is smitten when most secure. This leads us to remark

III. *That our God will never suffer the word of his servants to fail.*

All that befel Ahab befel him according to the word of Elijah and Micaiah. (Ver. 37, 38.) God had spoken by his persecuted prophets; and for their sakes, as well as for his own truth's sake, he would not suffer his word by them to fall to the ground. All therefore which they had predicted came to pass. And thus everything will come to pass which either judgment or mercy has spoken by the lips of God's authorized servants. In the process however of such accomplishment there are sundry things which generally happen.

1. *There may be a long interval between the word and the blow*—between the prediction and the fulfilment. Ahab had a considerable respite, long enough to induce a forgetfulness of impending destruction. The same thing occurred in both the destruction of the old world and the overthrow of Jerusa-

lem. For one hundred and twenty years the *one* was in abeyance, and for forty years the other was suspended. Thus we still not unfrequently see a wicked man going on for a long time in his wickedness.

2. *There may be many things to make the predicted accomplishment seem unlikely.* Ahab continued to reign as king. His health and luxury and splendour suffered no diminution. He seemed indeed to prosper, for he secured the good Jehoshaphat as his ally, and sat in state with him before all the people. A multitude also of priests and prophets favoured his projects, and boldly, as if by genuine inspiration, said, "Go up and prosper!" Thus it has been on many memorable occasions. Everything for instance, which prophecy had declared respecting Jesus of Nazareth, once seemed unlikely of any favourable issue. The seal upon his sepulchre seemed to his disciples a strange but sure token of insuperable failure. So, in the present day, it would be easy to call up seeming tokens of difficulty, hazard, and defeat, as to the great strife between Christ and Belial. But all is safe. Hence

3. *There may be, and generally there is, many a trying hour of suspense and apprehension to the servants of God.* Doubt they cannot as to the ultimate issue of things: but, somehow, Satan contrives to harass them with fears, while things are apparently at a stand-still, or when the struggle is most intense. Elijah and Micaiah had trials of their faith with regard to Ahab: and the ministers of Christ have trial of theirs also with respect to God's dealings among his people in the present day. But, amid all our waverings and tremblings, the word of the Lord for good or for evil, for judgment or for mercy, stands as a rock of certainty, which nothing can shake or turn aside. So far as we preach in accordance with that word, will God fulfil all that we declare. Every threatening as well as every promise which you hear will inevitably be accomplished. Not one jot or tittle of either will pass away without receiving such accomplishment as will honour God. Then, inasmuch as God's promises are like those fruits which are altogether delicious and good for food, and his threatenings like those plants which though deadly in themselves can, by chemical art, be converted into useful medicines, see that you have grace to enjoy the one, and holy skill to improve the other.

Let me now entreat you

i. *To think of what God says to you by the prophets of his gospel, and how he frequently employs them as men who draw a bow at a venture.* God commissions us to tell sinners of the error of their ways. Every man is an Ahab by nature; and we, like Elijah and Micaiah, are to speak to each with all plainness, fidelity, and decision. We are to warn sinners to flee from the wrath to come: and, "whether they will hear, or whether they will forbear," we are to say to the wicked, "Thou shalt surely die;" vengeance *will* overtake you, if you repent not. True, we have not an individual message for every sinner whom we meet; but we have one common message which we are individually to apply, and God warrants our applying it with all the force of an especial errand. At the same time our commission includes a message of peace. We come to you with words of tenderness and love. We tell you of God's love and pity in Christ Jesus, to every contrite and prayerful sinner. We appeal to you beyond what Elijah and Micaiah appealed to Ahab. Then welcome the appeal: and when Christ offers you pardon, accept it with all thankfulness. But recollect how entirely we depend on God for all we preach to you, or say among you. Our preaching is very much like drawing a bow at a venture, the arrow of which God alone must direct. Often, like the Syrian bowman, we shoot our words "in our simplicity," without aim at any individual, and in utter unconsciousness of the mark which they may hit. But, we know that, by such means, many a heart has been infixed by an arrow which God has made the death of sin. Often has the utterance of some Scripture text or simple speech been carried home to the inmost bosom, and made a blessing beyond what worlds can give. O that many such arrows may be shot from this pulpit! Pray that many may.

ii. *Take heed of doing like Ahab, reverencing God in profession, but despising him in heart.* Ahab when alarmed bent his head, and apparently repented. But the man was not changed; for, when prosperity returned, every evil disposition returned with it. Such cases are fearfully common: but they are also fearfully dangerous, so dangerous that escape from them is a rare circumstance. Then look a little into your real state before God. There is every need for this, because Ahab deceived himself; and self-deception is as easy to us as it was to him.

iii. *Make the God of salvation, with all certainty, your friend*: then will no uncertainties, no accidents, alarm you. "The arrow that flieth by day, and the terror which walketh by night," will have no power over you. All will be ordained for you in that manner which, however unexpected its coming may be, will end in peace and good. God will guide every contingency, and give every blessing. Malady, such as is now prevalent, even should it be turned into pestilence, will never shoot its arrows *at a venture* upon you. Your God will be at hand to turn every shaft, or to make the harm of the body the gain of the soul.

SERMON XXV.

ELIJAH'S TRIUMPHANT ASCENSION INTO HEAVEN.[1]

2 Kings 2:11.

"And it came to pass, as they still went on and talked, that, behold, there appeared a chariot of fire, and horses of fire, and parted them both asunder; and Elijah went up by a whirlwind into heaven."

THE prophet Elijah was an extraordinary man, raised up for extraordinary times. In disposition he was somewhat severe, but in principle he was nobly determined for God, and most uncompromising toward wicked men. Toils, perils, and privations were alike familiar to him. That he was uniformly perfect cannot be affirmed; but he was uniformly faithful, and God made him eminently successful. As therefore his life was marked by much that was marvellous, it was not unlikely that his departure from the world would be proportionably uncommon. Apprized by the Spirit of God that the time of his removal was at hand, he wished to spend his last hours alone: he at least expressed a wish to that effect, though he probably expressed it more as a trial of Elisha's attachment than as the really strong desire of his own heart. Elisha however could not be induced to leave him. In company therefore together they visited Bethel and Jericho, for the sake of the sons of the prophets, or, as we say, for inspecting the divinity students of the colleges established in those towns. A good man, in older life, may well address words of admonition to younger men who are staying in that world which he is about to leave.

After miraculously crossing the Jordan, "it came to pass, as they still went on and talked, that, behold, there appeared a chariot of fire, and horses of fire, and parted them both asunder; and Elijah went up by a whirlwind into heaven."

May we find much profit in contemplating two things:

I. *The conduct of the prophet in his last hours on earth.*

He "went on and talked" with Elisha. This fact certifies us that preparation for heaven does not consist merely in quiet contemplation and in solitary seclusion, but that it is fully compatible with open duties and active energies, even to the very last. Men and women gain nothing by shutting themselves up in monasteries and convents. They may perhaps, but only perhaps, escape a little turmoil and annoyance, but they lose "the luxury of doing good," and the opportunity of honouring the Saviour in an evil world.

True religion, while it indeed comprises holy meditation, secret prayer, and self-examination, is nevertheless a life of practical exertion and vigorous duty up to its very end. The Christian, like Elijah, should be going on his way, and talking of the things of God, so long as he is continued in the land of the living. And, when his departure is at hand, his lips, if he has strength to exercise them, will find abundance to utter, either in testimony of the gracious dealings of God, or for the benefit of relatives and friends. This is in accordance with the mind of our Saviour Christ, who said, "Blessed is that servant whom, when his Lord cometh, he shall find *so doing*." Indeed the whole tenor of his admonitions respecting the day of death or of judgment shows that it is well for his people to be adorning his doctrine when the hour of their summons shall come. Consequently death at short notice, or even sudden death itself, is not to be regarded as an evil, provided the heart be in a prepared state, and the life be occupied in proper duties. Dorcas, as a good woman, was "*full* of good works and alms-deeds" up to the very last: for some translators are of opinion that, even on her death-bed, she *was making* "coats and garments" for the poor ("vestes, quas faciebat").

Many holy men, in sundry ages of the Church, have wished to die under some such circumstances as would best accord with the prevailing bias of their minds towards God. That holy man, Archbishop Leighton, long entertained a wish that he might die on a journey, or at an inn, in order that he might leave the world as a pilgrim. His wish was granted, for he was taken ill and died at a travellers' inn in London. Many a clergyman has desired, as the phrase is, "to die in harness," when preaching the gospel, or otherwise ministering, in accordance with it, to his people. Their desire has not unfrequently been accomplished. Others, in the privacy of Christian life, have coveted death, like as it was with many of the patriarchs, "in the presence of all their brethren," pronouncing blessings on them, and magnifying the mercy of God. In fact every real Christian desires to glorify God in the day of his death, be the mode of that death what it may: nor will such a Christian be very concerned respecting that mode, so that it comes upon

[1] Preached Sunday Evening, May 24th, 1846.

him when engaged in honest duties, or found in honest company. For a lively Christian to sink into the arms of death in the shop, the field, the mart, or the friendly circle, is nothing which will alarm him in the last gleams of departing consciousness, or cause a secret shudder to his friends who attend him to his grave. Even worldly men think it nothing very dreadful or unwelcome for themselves or their friends to die under similar circumstances: but there are other scenes and places in which *they would not exactly like to die.* It is not a *very* agreeable thing to die in a ball-room, a theatre, a revelling tavern, or a gambling-house! Nor is it *very* desirable to pass into eternity from a grand-stand, or in the midst of some "vanity fair." And *why* not? You *know* why not. Conscience tells you why not, louder than I could declare. Then let conscience be heard, and may the Spirit of Jesus sanctify the hearing.

What it was about which Elijah "talked," as they "went on," we are not told. Such a man as Elijah, at such a time and under such expectations as then were present with him, could be at no loss for topics of conversation. On the threshold of heaven every thought and every word must have been heavenly. Or, if not permitted to talk of its glories and realities, there was the blessedness of a life of faith, which now was at its close with him; there was the state of the church of God in Israel, which required all the zeal and holy skill of a prophet to regulate; and, above all, and connected with all, was the promised coming of the Messiah. That was a topic which we are sure occupied the best affections, and therefore employed the earnest lips of Elijah; inasmuch as he alone of all the prophets was elected to be the companion of Moses on the mount of transfiguration, when they talked with the very Messiah himself "respecting his decease, which he should accomplish at Jerusalem."

Whatever the topic was, we can hardly doubt that it was such as *became* the position of a man of God, who was going to God. A dying Christian, with the full assurance of hope in his heart, and with all heaven opened to his mental eye, will hardly fail to speak, if he can speak at all, of the Saviour whom he loves, and with whom he knows that he soon shall be. If we, dear brethren, more habitually than we are wont, set Christ before us, and the day of our departure to him, or the day of his coming to us, our tongues would never want a topic, nor our spirits refreshment. But, in alluding to the last earthly hours of Elijah, let it not be thought that a deathbed seriousness, or a sort of an eleventh-hour religion, is all that is intended for your imitation. Elijah had not then first taken up with a devout and hallowed turn of mind. He had long been conversant with godliness, and had exemplified its power through many a year. Ah! brethren, it is not the transient flush of hasty profession, but it is this uniform and habitual cultivation of holiness, which makes last hours best hours, and which, amid the darkness of dissolution, gilds the surrounding scene with the calm brightness of a "good hope through grace." May you prove the truth of this remark by a blessed experience, and may I prove it with you!

Let us next consider

II. *The translation of Elijah to heaven.* "There appeared a chariot of fire, and horses of fire, and parted them both asunder; and Elijah went up by a whirlwind into heaven." The scene is beyond the powers of the most vigorous and chastened imagination adequately to conceive. Painters have attempted to delineate the chariot and horses on canvass, and admirers have been found for their skill in depicting the elegance of the one and the symmetry of the other. But how utterly childish are all such efforts of even the most gigantic genius! An artist may indeed describe what he can discern. Earthly himself he may picture earthly things, and picture them too with admirable truth and precision. But, because a man can paint an earthly car and earthly steeds, such as draw kings and conquerors along terrestrial streets, is he able to paint such a chariot and such horses as can mount the skies, and roll and prance among the stars?

Let us be content with what is written, and wait for the full understanding of it till we can talk with Elijah himself.

The scene however is so described as to give us some faint idea of the majesty and power of God, as well as of the honour which he puts upon his saints. A chariot of fire and horses of fire, things surpassingly bright and ethereally beautiful—made too as transcendantly noble as human eyes could, for a few short glances, sustain—were worthy of the majesty and kindness of that God who intended to honour the man who had honoured him. The whole was, no doubt, effected by the instrumentality of angels, who are God's "ministering spirits," and whose appearance, when revealed to mortal eye, is like "a flame of fire." The countenance of one of them, when seen at our Lord's sepulchre, "was like lightning." The very look of such bright and holy beings will no doubt add to the terror of the impenitent, when they are gathered by them, as bundles of tares, in the morning of the resurrection. And, as angels will gather the wicked, so will they gather the righteous; and, because they will gather the righteous then, we conclude that they, in the form of chariot and horses, conveyed Elijah to heaven. The accomplishment of their errand was, it is probable, marvellously quick. "In a moment" perhaps, or little longer than "the twinkling of an eye," Elijah was caught up in the chariot and wafted, with the speed of a whirlwind, into heaven. This rapid translation most likely had respect to the earthly infirmities of Elisha: for, had the angelic effulgence lingered before his eyes, he must have been overwhelmed with its insufferable splendour. Thus while Jehovah honoured one servant he had compassion on another: and thus he deals with us, making a difference according to what we are able to bear. But why, it may be asked, in translating Elijah to heaven, was it so ordained that the vehicle should be *a chariot?* Why not a ladder, as in Jacob's vision, or a couch upon a cloud, or a cherub with wings? Jehovah is as independent as he is wise in choosing his own means. But we are at liberty to trace that wisdom, while we bow to his sovereign independence. Now a chariot was anciently, even long before Elijah's day, the characteristic equipage of princes and conquerors. As Elijah had fought the battles of the Lord against Baal and his priests, and had come off an abundant conqueror; and as he had, as a prophet-servant, honoured his master, the "King of kings," that gracious Master and all benevolent Sovereign gave him a princely and triumphal entrance to his heavenly palace. He raised his faithful servant's head, and "set him among princes." In the eye of the world he honoured him as a victor over that corrupt religion which he was leaving, and as a prince in that region to which he was going. A chariot and horses, such as neither potentate nor conqueror ever mounted, triumphantly wafted him to heaven. That he went direct to heaven is plainly declared. "Elijah went up by a whirlwind *into heaven.*" Hence we are certified that heaven, as we understand the word, is not only a state, but *a place*—a place too capable of lodging a human body when spiritualized. It is also a place above the sky. Elijah went up to it, as did our Lord, and sundry angelic messengers in the old time before them. But when *we* talk of heaven, how must angels pity the meanness of our conceptions, if they are cognizant of them! In all probability the loftiest and most sanctified intellect among us is no more capable of forming an idea of the real glories of heaven, than a spider in a cellar beneath a royal saloon, or a worm in a crypt under a gorgeous cathedral, can conjecture what is above them. But if we cannot tell what heaven is we can feel what it is not. It is not what our earth is, a place of sin and sorrow, defilement and wretchedness. In entering heaven Elijah left behind him his naturally *vile* body, his *evil* heart, his carnal mind, and all the ills to which flesh and spirit are heirs. And surely, as the considerate Christian often feels, it must be a heaven of itself almost, to be delivered from these! But the positive happiness of heaven is even greater than such deliverance. It will be all that the God of love can make it for those whom he loves.

And now, in conclusion, let us glance at the singular event before us under sundry points of view. View it then

1. *As a typical representation of the ascension of our Lord.* In this respect it is very remarkable. Elijah, let it be noticed, was admonished of his ascension; he walked away from the city; he was attended by his successor; he conversed with him, and implored a blessing for him; and, while in the act of these things, was parted from him and carried up into heaven. How wonderfully all these doings were done again in greater efficiency, we learn from the evangelists, who wrote the brief history of our Lord's ascension. "And Jesus led them out as far as to Bethany, and he lifted up his hands and blessed them: and it came to pass, while he blessed them, he was parted from them, and carried up into heaven." (Luke 24:50, 51.) Moreover, as fifty of the sons of the prophets were on the look out for Elijah's ascent, so did five hundred brethren at once "see the Lord Jesus after his resurrection," while one hundred and twenty disciples testified his ascension. And as Elijah let fall his mantle, for a token of a double portion of his spirit descending on Elisha, so did Jesus shed forth upon his apostles a flood of gifts beyond what himself saw fit to exercise. But mark the contrast. Elijah ascended without pain or death. He ascended too for rest from his labours, and for his own individual happiness. The Lord Jesus tasted death in its bitterest form. He descended to the cold grave, and now ever liveth to complete the work which he advanced on earth. This is the glory of his ascension: He liveth to make intercession, and to elevate us!

Consider further the translation of Elijah

2. *As an intimation of the certainty of an immortal existence.* Immortality and future life were but dimly discerned under the Old Testament. But what other inference could the sons of the prophets draw from the ascension of Elijah but the fact of immortality in heaven? As to what change the body of Elijah underwent all is conjecture. But we know what light the inspired apostle Paul, in after times, has thrown upon the entire subject. For hereafter "we which are alive and remain shall be caught up together with them (which had slept in Jesus) in the clouds, to meet the Lord in the air: and so shall we ever be with the Lord." (1 Thessalonians 4:17.) Then be thankful for this light. It all came by Jesus Christ. Besides it is better than all speculations to rest in the fact that, where Elijah *is*, all Christ's servants *shall* be.

Regard the translation of Elijah also

3. *As an exhibition of the regard which God takes of his faithful servants.* Elijah was a holy man and a great prophet. As such God honoured and rewarded him. But he was also *a suffering* believer. God therefore made his end blessed indeed. God still regards his servants, though not in the same way. He will however send his angels to their death bed, and thus convey them to where himself is.

Sinners, "it is appointed for you to die:" but, if you die in your sins, where Elijah is you never will be: no angel wing would waft you to the Saviour's bosom, but fiendish arms would drag you to the bottomless abyss. You are still however where Elijah once was—in a world of mercy, where voices as authoritative as his call you to repentance, and proclaim to you pardon. Use then the present hour as it ought to be used, and you will escape an endless despair. If angels rejoice over you as penitent suppliants, you shall rejoice with them as glorified spirits.

[This Note with text and footnote was printed at the end of Volume I of the Sermons. This refers to the sixth paragraph of Sermon X, on page 72 of this book, page 120 of the original Volume I.]

NOTE.—The MS. of these Sermons was sent from Prussia. In the transit, a slip was overlooked or lost, containing some such remarks as the following, and which should have been printed immediately after the paragraph in page 120, commencing thus—"There is mystery in this":—

Some divines are of opinion[1] that, although only two angels passed the night, as Lot's guests, in Sodom, the third angel, who is expressly called "The LORD," or JEHOVAH, and who staid behind to converse with Abraham, overtook them in the early morning, either within the city, or at its suburbs. Of the three angels, then, who went to Lot, etc., etc.

[1]The grounds for this opinion are of this sort:—The ANGEL JEHOVAH had said "*I will go down now* (i.e., to Sodom,) *and see whether they have done altogether according to the cry of it.*" Surely, then, He kept His word, and went to Sodom. In the morning Lot lingered, but was urged onwards, "*The LORD* (as is said) *being merciful unto him.*" Speedily after, Lot addressed to the principal ANGEL these words, "*Thou hast magnified thy mercy which thou hast showed unto me, in saving my life.*" To admit that language so lofty as this was listened to and answered by a created angel, would be to yield all that the worshippers of angels can desire. It is subsequently said, "*Then the LORD* (the same LORD as spake to Lot) *rained brimstone and fire from the LORD out of heaven,*" i.e., the Eternal Son in earth, from the Eternal Father in heaven.—*See Poole, Ainsworth, Hughes, etc., in loco.*

W. H. H.

END OF VOL. I.

This four-page letter was written by Rev. R. Jarratt to W.H.H. (and was placed by Maria V. G. Havergal in her Photograph Album given to the Church Missionary Society in 1886). See also pages 130 and 134.

Wellington Somerset

June 19th 1826.

My dear Sir,

As you have requested by my son Samuel that I would write to you to say about some benefaction to our Church Missionary Society, I send you the following account. But first, I must inform you that my son Samuel reached Wellington to our surprise on Friday afternoon in safety & William on the following day. William appears to me as well as I expected, & I would pray to God, in submission to his will, that his strength may be restored & his life prolonged. [This was only the first page of the letter. See page 1430 for the next two pages. Below the original letter, Maria V. G. Havergal wrote this next note:]

A most striking fact in 1826 given in the above from the Rev R. Jarratt to my father W.H.H. A poor woman bringing first £ 14..0..0 – her own day labour being 7 s per day! In the parcel of money was a ragged slip of paper "This money is for the mishnery (sic) "look unto Me and be ye saved all ye eands of the earth." In six months she again brought £ 20 and again £ 6—from a small annuity left her. Shall not this be told "for a memorial of her?"

SERMONS,

CHIEFLY ON

HISTORICAL SUBJECTS

FROM

THE OLD AND NEW TESTAMENTS;

PREACHED IN

THE PARISH CHURCH OF

ST. NICHOLAS, WORCESTER.

BY THE

REV. W. H. HAVERGAL, A.M.

RECTOR OF ST. NICHOLAS'S, AND HONORARY CANON, WORCESTER.

VOL. II.

NEW TESTAMENT.

LONDON:
HAMILTON, ADAMS, AND CO., AND HATCHARD.
WORCESTER: STRATFORD, CHILDE, AND EATON AND SON.
1853.

[Page 2:] I think it is about 3 years ago, when a Woman called upon me. I went to her to the door. She said that she wanted to give something to the Missionary. Thinking that she was going to give me a 1/- or 2/6 I professed my willingness to accept it. But this did not seem to satisfy her. I had not asked her into the house. I was then engaged. She said, if I was busy, she would call again. In the course of an hour or two she called again. I took her into my room. Then she said that she had brought something for the Missionary. She gave me a brown paper parcel. & when I opened it, to my utter astonishment I found it contained fourteen Pounds in Bills and Silver. I expressed my unwillingness to receive such a sum from her, thinking that it would be necessary for her maintenance, as she goes out to work for [Page 3:] 7 s [unclear here, but indicated in Maria's note, on page 1428] 7 s per day & her victuals. She replied, never mind you that. I talked to her a good deal on this subject, remarking that the Society did not wish for people thus to give out of their poverty. However, she was urgent with me to take the money. I mentioned to have the money entered as from a "Friend." She replied with great humility, if I am worthy to be called such. She told me that her Father on his death bed, mentioned that passage of Scripture, preach the Gospel to every creature. If you had seen her manner, her eyes, her thread bare Cloak, you would have been astonished. I never met with such a case, as so filled me with amazement. After she was gone, I knelt down & thanked God. In the parcel was a ragged slip of paper with these words written. "this money is for the mishnery look unto me & be ye saved all ye eandes of the of the earth". This woman has a small annuity left her. About ½ year afterwards she brought me £ 20 & this last Spring £ 6. I again talked to her about the Society's wish, that she should not impoverish herself.

See pages 128 and 134 of this book. These are the second and third pages of the letter from Rev. R. Jarratt to W.H.H. This is reminiscent of Luke 7:36–50 , Matthew 26:6–13, and Mark 12:41–44.

CONTENTS.

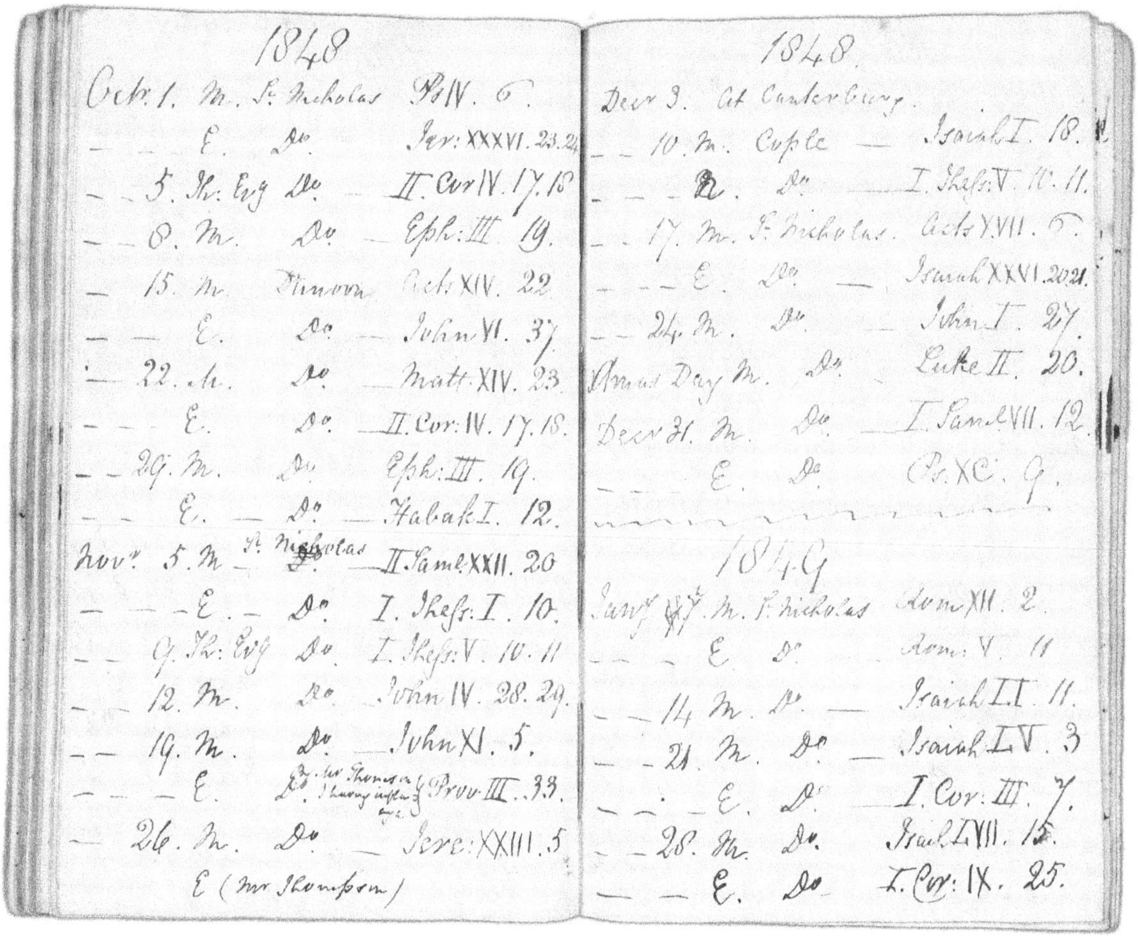
1848
Octr. 1. M. St. Nicholas Ps. IV. 6.
— — E. Do. Jer: XXXVI. 23.24
— — 5. Th: Evg Do. II. Cor IV. 17.18
— — 8. M. Do. Eph: III. 19.
— 15. M. Acts XIV. 22
— — E. Do. John VI. 37
— 22. M. Do. Matt XIV. 23
— — E. Do. II. Cor: IV. 17.18.
— — 29. M. Do. Eph: III. 19.
— — E. Do. Habak I. 12.
Novr. 5. M. St. Nicholas II Saml XXII. 20
— — E. Do. I. Thess: I. 10.
— — 9. Th: Evg Do. I. Thess: V. 10. 11
— 12. M. Do. John IV. 28. 29.
— 19. M. Do. John XI. 5.
— — E. Do. Prov. III. 33.
— 26. M. Do. Jere: XXIII. 5
E (Mr Thompson)

1848.
Decr 3. At Canterbury.
— — 10. M. Cople — Isaiah I. 18.
— — E. Do. I. Thess: V. 10. 11.
— — 17. M. St. Nicholas. Acts XVII. 6.
— — E. Do. Isaiah XXVI. 20.21.
— — 24. M. Do. John I. 27.
Xmas Day M. Do. Luke II. 20.
Decr 31. M. Do. I. Saml VII. 12
— E. Do. Ps. XC. 9.
1849
Jany 7. M. St. Nicholas Rom XII. 2.
— — E. Do. Rom. V. 11
— — 14 M. Do. Isaiah II. 11.
— — 21. M. Do. Isaiah LV. 3
— — E. Do. I. Cor: III. 7.
— — 28. M. Do. Isaiah LVII. 15.
— — E. Do. I. Cor: IX. 25.

These are two pages from W.H.H.'s Sermon Record Book. The third entry on the right page is the Sermon XXIV on Acts 17:6, the morning Sermon preached at St. Nicholas Church in Worcester on December 17, 1848.

~~But~~ If I had not taken the money, she would have given it, I have no doubt, to some other [S.M. ? illegible]. With the last money I had a scrap of paper with the following words written.

"I gave you many thanks the first-was 14
"the next was 20 this es [is ?] 6 all together 40 pounds
"pleas to send it safe I gave you many thinks [thanks ?]
"for your trouble pleas to lit [let] me know where i come
"the right time for you to sen it away."

Rev. W. H. Havergal Astley Stourport Worcester

I have not mentioned these donations at the meetings in this place, ~~not wishing~~ out of regard to the feelings of my Friend, who wishes to remain secret. I write in haste to save this post.

With kind regards to Mrs. Havergal, in w^h [which ?] my C^hn [Children ?] join

I remain dear Sir, your's sc [sincerely ?] R Jarratt

This is the final page of the letter from Rev. R. Jarratt to W.H.H. See pages 128 and 130.

SERMON I.

THE SALUTATION OF GABRIEL TO THE VIRGIN MARY.[1]

Luke 1:28.

"And the angel came in unto her, and said, Hail, thou that art highly favoured, the Lord is with thee: blessed art thou among women."

THE Reformers of our Church were themselves originally unreformed. They were born and bred, trained and taught, amid the dark doctrines and unscriptural practices of the Italian Church. When therefore they were brought out of darkness into marvellous light they followed the light, though they well remembered the darkness. In few things more than in the idolatrous abuse of the present day, popularly called "Lady Day," did they evince their right-mindedness, their knowledge of ecclesiastical antiquity, and above all their correct understanding of the word of God. They knew that what is called "the worship of the Virgin," however softened down before opponents and controvertists, was actually, and in all popular practice, as much a real worship of the creature as any which was offered to the Creator. When therefore they brought back the British Church to something like what it was ere a Roman missionary set foot on the land, they carefully removed all superstitious references to the blessed mother of our Saviour Christ, and placed every memorial of her in the modest and instructive position in which she had placed herself, as the holy, grateful, and humble "hand-maid of the Lord." Accordingly the two festivals, instead of four which some Churches keep in memory of the virgin-mother, though they carry with them some remembrance of herself, yet do they more peculiarly refer to her Son and Saviour. The titles of the two festivals, the Annunciation and the Purification, bear indeed her name (because those titles, as associated with her name, were familiar to the common people); but all the substance and all the honour of them are transferred to Him to whom she herself would and did transfer all adoration and praise. In no prayer is her name so much as mentioned. This significant procedure on the part of our Reformers should be attentively studied by all the members of our Church. Let it guide us in our present contemplation of the words of the angel, which meet us in our text from the gospel for the day. It will be my purpose, first, to expound those words, and then to deduce from them some remarks for our edification.

I. *The exposition of our text* must commence with reminding you that the great subject connected with it is the blending of the loftiest majesty with the lowliest humility, the uniting of the mysterious Godhead with our most mean manhood. This was to be effected by the second Person in that Godhead becoming a partaker of manhood, through the medium of an earthly mother, without the intervention of an earthly father. The individual selected as that medium was a virgin daughter of the family of David, sunk from former royalty into obscurity and poverty. Her name, we are told, was Mary, an ancient name in Israel, though not apparent as such to an English, or even a Latin reader. Miriam, in the Hebrew tongue, is the Mariam of the Greek, the Maria of the Latin, and the Mary of the English. She was living far away from the abode of her ancestors, not in Bethlehem or Jerusalem, but in Nazareth, an ill-reputed locality in Galilee. All these circumstances, coupled with the sterling excellences of her character,—her modesty, her purity, her piety, and especially the deep humility of her soul,—all conspired to show God's low estimate of mere earthly distinctions, and his preference for heavenly virtues. To this Mary an angel was sent, to announce Jehovah's intentions towards her. It was the same angel, even Gabriel, "the strength, or strong one, of God," who had been sent to instruct Daniel, and also more recently to apprise Zacharias of the birth of John the Baptist. Angels had before announced miraculous births, as in the case of Isaac and Samson. It was fitting that no less an honour should be exhibited in the case of Him who is above all honour. Still he was content that his virgin-mother should receive no higher honour, in this instance, than others had received, lest human indiscretion should exalt her above measure, and so turn the honour into sin. It was fitting also

[1] Preached Sunday Morning, March 25th (Lady Day), 1849.

that, as an evil angel had assailed Eve for our destruction, so a good angel should visit Mary for our salvation. The mission of Gabriel to her was simple, unostentatious, and edifying. Respecting it, the learned editor of Calmet, a Benedictine abbot, thus speaks:—"This subject has been so often set before our eyes by the representations, or rather *mis*representations, of the pencil, that it seems necessary to guard ourselves against false ideas received from prints and pictures; to dismiss the cloud attending the angel, the wings, the flowers, the brilliancy, and all such artificial and artful accessories, and to reduce the story to the simple narrative of Luke: by which it appears that Mary was in a house, and probably in private (but this is not said, nor in what part of the house, neither how she was occupied), for the angel *entered* and advanced towards her; that he did not appear in splendour, nor in any *extremely* disturbing manner, so as to *astonish* Mary, but gave her time to consider, that is, to reason with herself respecting his saying (for it was *that* which 'troubled' her, not his appearance). It does not appear that she knew him to be an angel" (any more than Sarah and the wife of Manoah knew a similar fact at the time) "else she would have acquiesced in his words without hesitation; but after he had, as a sign, given her information respecting her cousin Elizabeth, be departed; he did not *vanish*,but (ἀπηλθεν) went away."

And what said Gabriel to her? "*Hail*, thou that art highly favoured, the LORD is with thee: blessed *art* thou among women." He said "*Hail!*" This was the ordinary, and nothing more than the ordinary and respectful salutation of the clime and the country, and yet the church of Rome has most absurdly turned it into *a prayer*, and taught her millions to use it as such. The words "Ave Maria," (simply Hail Mary) have, as Luther was ingeniously wont to say, been made "very great martyrs;" for not only have they been tortured into a prayer (*ten* Ave Marias being said for *one* Pater Noster), but they have been twisted and turned into all sorts of fanciful and ridiculous puns, anagrams, and riddles, for the amusing of poor souls, and the drawing them away from saving truth.

"Hail, thou that art *highly favored!*"To answer an idolatrous and impious purpose, the church of Rome persists, in spite of all lingual propriety and common orthodoxy (following the erroneous rendering of the Vulgate), to translate the words, highly or freely favoured, "*full of grace*."The object of this translation is, not to show that the blessed virgin was a most gracious person, and as full of divine grace as poor human nature could be, but that she was as *full of grace as a fountain*, for the supply of other souls. Such notion and such intention are utterly opposed to the whole tenor of the gospel, and most palpably at variance with the virgin's own *Magnificat*,in which she rejoices in nothing but in God her Saviour, and his unmerited grace. The expression in fact is, as Dr. Burton well observes, clearly explained by Gabriel's own subsequent remark in the thirtieth verse, "Thou hast found favour with God." In truth the like thing had actually been said, by the very same angel, to the prophet Daniel, "ODaniel, a man *greatly beloved!*"

"*The Lord is with thee*."He had, by his holy Spirit, been with her, to prepare her, as the predicted virgin, for that sacredness and purity of character which befitted her high calling; and now he was with her, at the instant, to enable her rightly to receive the message which was awaiting her: and, as he was with her in mind, so would he be with her in body, for all the exalted and mysterious purposes of Messiah's incarnation. As though Gabriel had said, "I am sent from God, and so the Lord is with thee, but much more by some more eminent operation. God the Father is with thee, *highly favouring* thee, making his Son thy Son: God the Son is with thee, for thou shalt bear and bring Him forth as man: and God the Holy Ghost is with thee, for He shall come upon thee, and the power of the Most High shall overshadow thee." (Dr. Sparkes.)

It was added, "*Blessed art thou among women*."Mary had been "highly favoured" by being selected, above all the matrons of past days, and the virgins of her own day, for the exalted and long-envied honour of becoming the mother of the Messiah. She had been "highly favoured" too in the abundance of spiritual grace bestowed upon her; but now she is declared to be "blessed among women," that is, the greatest, most distinguished, most happy of her sex—a being whom angels might envy, and a fellow-creature whom all mankind may reckon preeminently privileged, and incomparably blessed. Blessed was she as being a mother and yet a virgin; blessed as a wife among wives, and yet honouring the maiden state; blessed in being protected from all scandal by a wonderfully superintending Providence; blessed in surpassing all the wedded and the unwedded, in past, and present, and future times; blessed in being allowed to be *called blessed* throughout all generations.

II. *The remarks*, which a desire for your edification in sound doctrine and holy practice will dictate, are summarily three.

1. *That we should take the blessed virgin for a bright example in the ways of faith and godliness*.What is recorded concerning her is, like all Scripture narratives, recorded for our learning. We hear nothing of her till we hear the angel's annunciation to her of the high honour which Jehovah had destined for her. But the instant she is brought to our view she stands forth in all the beauty of true religion. The mission of Gabriel did not *make* her religious. She was such before. He did not come to bring her grace, but to prove and honour that which had already been imparted to her. She was a blessed believer ere she became a "blessed"and distinguished personage. All then that we discern in her spirit, mind, and conduct, is what should be discerned in ourselves, and what may exist if we seek the

same grace as she sought and found. The grace which shone so conspicuously in her was the grace *of humility.* When the high honour from heaven was announced to her, her first thought seems to have been her unworthiness of it. "Behold," said she, "*the handmaid* of the Lord!" Though told that she should be the mother of "the Son of God," she caught at no lofty title, but meekly called herself "the *handmaid* of the Lord." When pouring out her grateful spirit in a strain of direct inspiration, she was taught to teach us that Jehovah had regarded, not merely the lowness of her temporal condition, but the humbleness and meekness of her soul. What a pattern is this for all hearts, but especially for the daughters of our land, in this day of pride, vanity, and petty self-esteem! Mary, in her original retirement, was well acquainted with the Scriptures of truth. She had marked, learned, and inwardly digested them. This we ascertain from the fact of her declaring that God, in his dealings with her, had remembered his mercy, according to what he had spoken to the fathers. How profitable, brethren, is Holy Scripture, even that very older portion of it which Mary had pondered for her soul's health and strength! And how well may all her sisters in the Christian Israel do likewise, to the banishment of frivolous reading, and the attainment of sound wisdom and true profit!

We cannot wonder that the favoured Mary had learned to entertain right views of the God of Israel. She knew him to be the *Holy* God, as well as the God who keepeth covenant and mercy. "And *holy* is his name," said his holy and highly-favoured daughter. Her holiness was derived from him, just as ours must be derived. Without just such holiness as hers we shall not see him, nor shall we see her: neither can we rejoice in him, as she rejoiced from knowing him to be her Saviour. No doubt she had rejoiced before; but now that the mystery of the gospel, "which had been hidden for ages," was revealed to her by an angel, and herself shown to be instrumentally connected with its furtherance in a most singular and wonderful manner, then was her joy both intense and ecstatic, and her whole soul magnified her adored and beloved Lord. We, in at least some humble measure, must do likewise. Let us next remark,

2. *That, in imitating the blessed virgin, we must not invocate or idolize her, but carefully abstain from what she would repudiate, and even abominate.* As though God foresaw the insult to himself which was likely to occur in the inordinate exaltation of the mother of our Lord, he seems to have taken every precaution, consistent with circumstances, to prevent all countenance to it. Gabriel neither said nor did anything in favour of it. The magi, when visiting the manger at Bethlehem, bowed down and offered gifts to the holy babe, but did neither to the virgin-mother. Herself was suffered to betray remaining infirmities toward him in riper years. When one also said to him, "Blessed is the womb that bore thee!" he replied, "Yea, *rather* blessed are they that hear the word of God and keep it!" "Behold" (said he, pointing to them that *believed* in him) "my *mother* and my brethren!" At his death he committed her to the care of a disciple, and not his disciples to her care. After his ascension, she is cursorily mentioned as among his believing followers, but not a single apostle has written her name or made the slightest allusion to her. John the Divine, who had the charge of her and wrote the Revelation after her decease, makes no mention of having seen her, though all heaven was opened to his gaze. And then, for the first three ages of Christianity, no one thought of making her a goddess. But, as soon as the mystery of iniquity came into fuller operation, then began the cunning artifice of Antichrist for annulling the mediation of the Son, by substituting the pretended advocacy of the mother. The device has filled Christendom with infidelity, and, in conjunction with kindred errors, is saturating it with the blood of souls. The falsehoods, the forgeries, and the abominable perversions of all sanctity and common sense, to which the invocation of the virgin-mother has led, would be enough to make her feel that the honour at least of her blessedness has been turned into a curse, if her saintly mind could converse with believers on earth as to the sad turn which has been given to it. We who breathe in a Reformed community, may be grateful for deliverance from the spiritual snare, but we should not be insensible to the snare itself. If we think that as a body we stand in no need to be warned of it, we are ignorant both of Satan, ourselves, and half our duty. One part of that duty is to keep up a holy and lively abhorrence of the sin of idolatry, be it smoothed over or softened down as it may. O how great would that abhorrence be if the invocation of the Virgin, and all its monstrous applications, had never been heard of till yesterday! We should have been startled into utter detestation of a practice so abhorrent to all that stands on the page of inspiration. It is by our familiarity with the error and the evil that Satan keeps off the burst of indignation from the Church upon them. God grant us safety from the spirit of "strong delusion" and give grace, for escaping it, to those who are under it! Our last remark is

3. *That all our adoration and our prayers should,* as our collect teaches, *be addressed to the Godhead alone.* Well may that adoration be fervent on a day when we commemorate the annunciation of the incarnation of Christ to her who was to become his mother. It is a beautiful saying of St. Chrysostom to this effect: "That Christ should die when he *had* become man was a thing of almost natural course; but that, when he was God, he should be *willing to* become man, this is indeed wonderful and astonishing in the highest degree. In admiration of it St. Paul, as it were in rapture, says, 'Without controversy great is the mystery of godliness, God was manifest in the flesh.'"

With apostles then and all other saints who have rejoiced in the message brought by Gabriel to Mary, and who were saved by its blessed results, let us, from our inmost souls, adore the Lord Jesus as the *only* Redeemer, Mediator, and Saviour of his Church. We shall desire no other Intercessor or Advocate when we spiritually know him as he is to be known, and must be known. In the quaint lines of a chaplain to Charles II we shall say—

> "It derogates from Christ, religion taints,
> To worship or invoke the blessed saints:
> But, when their pious steps our souls do raise,
> We honour them in giving God the praise."[1]

Our collect teaches us to pray for the infusion of divine "grace into our hearts." Hence the clearest understanding of Gabriel's message and Mary's blessedness, and all to which they pertain, will profit nothing unless God "pour his grace into our hearts." This alone will prepare us, through Messiah's cross and passion, for the glory of his resurrection. God grant us faith now, and that will ensure us joy then.

[1] Dr. Sparkes.

SERMON II.

THE VISIT OF THE WISE MEN TO THE INFANT JESUS.[1]

MATTHEW 2:11.

"And when they were come into the house, they saw the young child with Mary his mother, and fell down, and worshipped him: and when they had opened their treasures they presented unto him gifts; gold, and frankincense, and myrrh."

THE *abruptness* of Holy Scripture is often very instructive. An instance is presented in the opening of this chapter. In verses 1 and 2 it is said, "Now when Jesus was born in Bethlehem of Judea, in the days of Herod the king, behold, there came wise men from the east to Jerusalem, saying, Where is he that is born King of the Jews? for we have seen his star in the east, and are come to worship him." We here read of certain "wise men;" but we are not told either their names or their number, nor is their country described, but only the quarter in which it lay. A star too is spoken of; but of what sort it was, or when the wise men first saw it, or how they knew that it had reference to the Messiah, no intimation is given. For such a passing over circumstances, which human curiosity would be likely to pry into, there must have been a wise intention. That intention will, in some degree, be answered, if we learn to withdraw our curiosity from unimportant topics, and devote our earnest attention to such as are clearly revealed. Reminding you then that these magi, or wise men, are generally believed to have been devout and reputable persons, of some sect of oriental philosophers, and that they were acted upon by the Holy Spirit, either in dreams or by some other mode of communication, it will be my endeavour to guide your thoughts to a profitable meditation of what the text presents to us as the main points of the entire narrative.

I. The first incident of which we read is the coming of the wise men "*into the house*." "And when they were come into the house."

When the shepherds hastened to Bethlehem, they found the holy child not *in the house*, but in some hovel or stable belonging to it. As some little time must have elapsed between the date of their visit and that of the magi, it is not unlikely either that room was at length made in the inn, or, if at a later period, in some other dwelling, for the holy family; especially

[1] Preached Sunday Morning, January 6th, 1850.

as the testimony of the shepherds aroused great attention, and produced much wonder. The fact however has not been regarded by some of the great painters of Christendom, in their delineations of the scene. But human art and divine truth are not always faithfully allied.

Still what must the oriental visitors have felt at finding themselves guided by the star, not to a palace, but to an inn or a mean abode in one of the decayed towns of Judea? Had they been left to the natural pride of their hearts, they would have felt just as we are apt to feel when we are compelled to bring down some high notion which we have been too fondly cherishing. It is however God's usual method to make humility the first lesson in the school of the soul. The wise men of the east therefore were made wiser by learning that the God of heaven sets little account upon the great things of earthly minds. Never indeed is true wisdom found where the heart is set on the vain elevations of a perishing world. "With the lowly," said Solomon, "is wisdom." (Proverbs 11:2.)

II. In the house the wise men "*saw the young child, with Mary his mother.*" And never did earthly house contain such a young child before! It was the bringing down of all heaven into the common chamber of a common house; the compressing of the Ancient of days into an Infant of hours; and then, as it were, circumscribing the God of the universe within the sorry walls of a homely dwelling or a country tavern. But the wise men were made wise to understand, or at least to adore, this mystery. Hence, as they were content with the house, they were not offended at seeing the everlasting King of the Jews an humble babe in the arms of an humble mother.

"*They saw the young child,*" and in so seeing him became notable witnesses of his incarnation, in that stage of it which few persons of eminence had either the opportunity or the inclination to remember. It is not at all probable that they ever again, with bodily eyes, beheld the Saviour of the world; but when, in the day of his appearing, they shall see him as he is, they will recognise him as that very "young child" whom they saw in the house at Bethlehem. The wisdom of God has thus taken care that there shall be wise witnesses of the identity of his beloved Son. When we come to where those witnesses are, they will answer all the questions which our warmest and most hallowed curiosity can address to them respecting the appearance of "the young child," and their own emotions at first seeing him.

They saw also "*his mother.*" It is not said that they saw his reputed father, although, when the shepherds visited the manger, it is expressly said that "they found Mary *and Joseph.*" It has been reverently conjectured that, when the wise men arrived, Joseph was providentially absent, in order that these gentile strangers, who were not conversant with the customs of the Jews, and had heard nothing of the previous history of Mary and Joseph, might not mistake Joseph for the real father of the babe, but give the readier credence to the fact of his being the virgin-born, the promised "seed of the woman." This exalted peculiarity, this incomparable singularity, as to the birth of "the young child," was of old God's sign to his Church of the certainty of his word of promise, and his fulfilment of all that stands connected with it. There is nothing therefore to excite our surprise in the fact that his mother alone is mentioned in this narrative.

III. When the wise men "saw him, they *fell down and worshipped him*;" and this, as the structure of the original phraseology implies, they did *instantly.* Being filled with heavenly wisdom, their faith quickly discerned in "the young child" somewhat of that majesty and glory at which all heaven bows with awe and adoration. They therefore, without any formal pause or cold deliberation, prostrated themselves before the infant King, and paid him that homage which the Holy Spirit impelled them to pay.

If then "the young child" had been nothing more than a young child, although the heir of a temporal universe, this act of the wise men would have been an act of folly, and of gross, deliberate idolatry. But, as the act was approved, it must have been an act of wisdom and exalted propriety—only however on the ground of "the young child" being "the mighty God, the everlasting Father, the Prince of peace."

Such was the truth, and thus early did the true God take care to have it recognised and acknowledged. He who had said "Let all the angels of God worship him," now brought these eastern sages on their knees and faces before him, that all Judea, and afterward all the world, might know whom to worship and obey.

And O what a time will that be, what a scene will that present, when not only the sages of the east, but every knee from the north, and west, and south also, shall bow to him, and the tongues of an assembled universe shall confess that he alone is God, to the glory of the eternal Father! May we be prepared for it now, by the right reception of himself into our hearts through faith, and by that love of and obedience to him which are the proper fruits of a true acknowledgment of his true and essential Deity. Only indeed let such faith and such love find entrance into our bosoms, and, like the wise men, we shall be *instant* in our submission and adoration. There will be no parleying with self, no balancing of interests with the world, no computing as to how long there may be "time enough yet;" but there will rather follow a quick and cheerful surrender of the "whole body, soul, and spirit" to the never-ending service of the one only Redeemer. One real discovery of Christ to the soul, one genuine sight of him as "made man" for us, will promptly bring us into that lowly attitude before him in which we should willingly remain to all eternity.

Let it be well observed, and the observation is growingly necessary, that a very pointed, and apparently a very intended distinction, is made between "the young child and his mother." She is *merely* mentioned. Not a syllable of additional reference is made to her. Without doubt she was regarded by the wise men with becoming interest and esteem; and, in all probability, she heard and received from them the first fulfilment of her own prophecy, that all nations should call her "*blessed.*" But there her case ended. Not a breath of adoration is heard, not the veriest symptom of worship is seen, at the mention of herself. To her Son, and to her Son *alone*, was the falling down made, the worship offered, and the gifts presented.

We know how these facts are pitifully evaded when Romanists and others are reminded of them. It is like thrusting a sword into a sensitive part, and yet meeting with such tact and self-possession as conceal the real pain! But every careful observer of what is passing in Christendom cannot fail to discern that "The worship of the Virgin," as it is called, is becoming more and more the mill-stone about the neck of the church of Rome, and which will one day help to sink her in that unfathomable depth to which, as our own Church believes, St. John the Divine has prophetically assigned her.

IV. After their prostration and worship, the wise men proceeded to open "*their treasures*," or such little store of valuables as they had brought with them for defraying the costs or facilitating the progress of their long and toilsome journey. Having done this, "they presented unto *him*" (that is, the young child, *not* his mother) "gifts, gold, and frankincense, and myrrh." Some of the early fathers, as has often been remarked, were fond of representing these gifts as bestowed with a typical intention. "Gold," say they, was presented to him as a king, "frankincense" as to a God, and "myrrh" as to a man: because, "gold" (as writers say) "is the symbol of royalty, frankincense of Deity, being offered in sacrifice to God, and myrrh of dying humanity, inasmuch as it is the principal ingredient with embalmers." To this we can give no positive credence. It may be received or not, as men's minds dispose them. But no sort of credit is to be attached to the popular Romanist tradition, that these three sorts of gifts were presented in succession by the three, and *only* three, wise men, who by that tradition are called *kings*, and named "Melchior, Gaspar, and Balthasar." There is no more truth in this tradition than in that which prevails in the far-famed city of Cologne, where the images of the three native kings who went to Bethlehem are shown to all inquisitive visitors. Here the abruptness of Holy Scripture, as noticed at the outset of this discourse, shines forth in frowning grandeur upon all such fanciful fillings up of the written word. Enough is told us for our edification in reading that word, though multitudes, alas! prefer the silly garniture of a groundless tradition to the solid and satisfying simplicity of the truth of God.

The gifts were, in all probability, either the produce of the country from which the wise men came, or the principal articles of its commerce. Thus the presentation of them to the young child was an acknowledgment of his being the Lord of the earth from which they grow or were derived, as the prostration of their persons was a token of their entire surrender and devotion to him as the Saviour of their souls. There is reason also for thinking that the gift of costly articles was ordained of God to be a timely provision for the expenses of the flight of the holy family into Egypt, which seems to have ensued immediately after the departure of the wise men: so adorable is our God in ordering all things for the welfare of his people when his own purposes are at stake. Such timely provision gives comfortable assurance to all the true followers of Christ that their God will take thought for them in times of privation or pressure. Besides he will never call us to fulfil a difficult duty, such as was the flight into a foreign land, without pointing out and providing some means for the accomplishment of it. Thus again, while God made ample provision for Joseph and Mary, he taught them two great truths, which they were afterward more fully to understand. The first was, that Messiah, "though he was rich," yet, for their sakes and our sakes, "became poor," so poor as to need the charity of eastern strangers: the other was, that themselves, and we also, receive nothing *but through him*. The gifts were given to him, and not to them, though, from the nature of things, they had the disposal of them. O that we always bore in mind that the only channel of mercy to our sinful selves is the Lord Jesus Christ!

From our text, thus expounded to you, three principal topics are deducible. To them I crave your attention in conclusion.

1. *The paramount duty of all men* is indicated to us in the going of the wise men to Bethlehem. These excellent persons obeyed a divine summons. They took pains and incurred cost to obey it. They were happy and blessed in so doing. Now to us is a summons given, in the gospel, to go unto Christ. He is set forth to us, not as a young child in a remote and an obscure dwelling, but as the God-man Christ Jesus, who, having made atonement for us, is set down at the right hand of the Majesty on high, to plead for help, and save all who come unto God by him. A brighter star than the sages saw points him out to us. Every assurance is given that we shall not approach him in vain. Not one individual shall be cast out who in true faith goes to him. There may be difficulties and hindrances in search for him, just as the wise men failed in going to Jerusalem: but let the honest and humble seeker persevere, and light shall arise to

him in darkness, and never leave him till he reaches the object of his supreme desire. Only let him beware of the entanglements of the world, and of the delusions which are sure to beset him, if he once withdraws his eye from the true star, and turns to those parties who have no sympathy with his search.

And, as the wise men were filled with joy, and saw what they desired to see, and were instructed of God, so shall all who have the holy daring to be singular in searching for and inquiring after Christ, find abundant joy and peace in believing. But despisers shall perish, and none who "neglect so great salvation" will be able to escape. Let all then, on whom the Star of Bethlehem again, as on this day, dawns, haste to leave their sins and sinful companions, and come with true repentance and lively faith to him who can save their souls.

2. *The nature of true charity, in a generous bestowal of our property, and the manner in which it should be exercised,* may be learned from what the wise men did. In coming to Bethlehem and visiting the holy child, they adopted no indirect, no semi-selfish, no questionable method of testifying their good-will to him, neither did they keep back that best of all testimonies of affection and allegiance to the infant King, the surrender of themselves. In the language of an apostle in after times, "they first gave themselves to the Lord," by an act of prostration before him, and then frankly, freely, and with noble *directness,* presented their gifts *to himself.* They did not, be it well observed, even give them to his mother to give to him, or to use for him. They gave them to himself *at once,* without any second-hand intervention. Least of all did they dream of inducing the Bethlehemites, by any pleasurable scheme, to join them in contributing to the same purpose as that to which their own gifts were devoted. These good men knew of no such false principles of charity, nor any such evil modes of doing a good thing. They had learned wisdom in a wiser school. They knew, as the people of Christ in all ages have known, that just in proportion as our charities are mixed up with carnal pleasures or selfish gratifications they become contemptible in the eye of God; that "God loveth *a cheerful* giver," not one who gives "grudgingly or of necessity," or even under the enticements of pleasure. He will have his people "*ready* to give, and *glad to distribute,*" "for with *such* sacrifices he is well pleased." In a word, as his apostle saith, "He that giveth, let him do it *with simplicity,*" that is, in the same simple, hearty, and direct manner as the wise men adopted, and which God has set forth as an example for all men to follow.

3. *The conversion of the Gentile world to Christ* is brightly shadowed forth in the contents of our text. The wise men were led from the east to Judea, as a sort of first-fruits of the immense harvest which is to be gathered from among all nations. Very properly does our Prayer-book therefore interpret the word "epiphany" as "the manifestation of Christ to the Gentiles." In due time that manifestation will be extended and completed. "All shall know him from the least to the greatest:" and "all the families of the earth shall be blessed in him." But who can tell what shakings and siftings will occur before the glory of that day shall beam upon the earth? May we be prepared for them! Above all let us be sure that Christ is manifested to our own souls in the only way which will save them.

SERMON III.

THE PRESENTATION OF CHRIST IN THE TEMPLE.[1]

LUKE 2:22–24.

"And when the days of her purification according to the law of Moses were accomplished, they brought him to Jerusalem, to present him to the Lord; (as it is written in the law of the Lord, Every male that openeth the womb shall be called holy to the Lord;) and to offer a sacrifice according to that which is said in the law of the Lord, A pair of turtle-doves or two young pigeons."

[1] Preached Sunday Morning, February 2nd, 1851.

THE incidents which this text comprises are historically most interesting, and doctrinally most important. As our Church selects them for our special meditation on the present day, let them be met with our devoutest attention. May that Almighty Spirit, who caused them to be recorded for our learning, graciously help us to derive from them all that their history and their doctrine are intended to impart.

I. *Historically the incidents are most interesting.* And yet, alas, earthly minds see no interest in them! They pass them over as things of very little moment, and not at all to be compared with the histories of human affairs, or with even the novels of human invention. But to spiritual minds there is a glowing attraction in every incident connected with the childhood, youth, and manhood of Christ, which surpasses all that elsewhere exists. To hearts which thrill with the love of Christ, even the minutest incidents of his life on earth are capable of yielding meditations of incomparable sweetness and satisfaction.

The text opens thus:

1. "*When the days of her purification, according to the law of Moses, were accomplished.*" She of whom this is said was, as you readily understand, the virgin mother of our Lord. "The days of her purification" mean the forty days from the birth of her Son, which every Jewish mother was obliged to pass before she could be regarded as ceremonially pure, and admissible to public worship. The law of Moses laid down the restriction, and doubled the forty days' separation when the offspring was a daughter instead of a son. This was a part of that yoke which pressed heavily on the mothers of Israel, but which is altogether removed by the gospel of the New Testament.

2. When these days were "accomplished," "they (his parents) *brought him to Jerusalem.*" A question of some moment, and of no small difficulty, here starts up. The question is this: How does this statement harmonize with what we are told of the wise men and Herod, and of the flight of the parents and the child into Egypt? On reading St. Matthew's narrative, we speedily infer that, soon after the birth of Jesus at Bethlehem, the wise men arrived there; and that, on their departure, Joseph and Mary, according to the warning dream, fled with the holy babe into Egypt. But this relation of incidents by St. Luke interposes a difficulty as to the time when those incidents occurred; for, if the holy family went from Bethlehem into Egypt, how could they, at the end of forty days only, have been present at Jerusalem? The thing appears an impossibility: and so "vain man, who would be wise," presumes to scoff with infidel derision. But here, as elsewhere, "the wisdom of man is foolishness with God."

Among many attempts at solving the difficulty, the following, because it is the simplest, appears to be the best. St. Matthew does *not* say (what has been taken as said) that the holy family went direct from Bethlehem to Egypt. Not a word is written to show that the wise men, in being admonished not to return to Herod, knew his murderous intention, and gave any intimation of it to Joseph and Mary. Consequently there is ample room for concluding that, at the end of the forty days, Joseph and Mary, without either fear or suspicion, went up to Jerusalem, and that they went during the time that Herod was waiting for the return of the wise men. Then, on the night after their visit to the temple, Joseph was warned, in a dream, what to do and whither to go, and he instantly obeyed. Thus the incidents mentioned by St. Luke merely complete, not oppose, the facts recorded by St. Matthew.

But what a flood of thought follows the fact, that his virgin mother and his reputed father "*brought him to Jerusalem!*" Instead of going first to their own city, they travel fast to the city of their God. Jerusalem, not Nazareth, is their hearts' desire, because they loved the God whose law directed them thither.

But whom take they with them? An infant of only forty days' old, the son of a poor mother, (who was hardly recovered from his birth,) while he was altogether such a babe as no one stopped at the gates to ask about, or in the streets to gaze upon. Unlike Moses, he possessed "no beauty," that any of the matrons of the city "should desire him."

But who in reality was he? He was "the Ancient of days" in the form of an infant of forty[1], the rightful and lineal King of the city though entering it as its meanest subject, yea, the child of whom prophets preached and angels sang and wise men heard afar off in the east. And yet no one knew him in Jerusalem! Herod had sent to inquire after him, little suspecting he was near his palace gates: so effectually did God conceal his beloved Son, when the policy of his holy purposes required the concealment. And then, secret as was his first visit to Jerusalem, the Holy Ghost had prepared witnesses of it, and was inspiring a song for the celebration not only of it but of all that glorious sequel to it which followed in due time.

3. But *for what* did they themselves come, and also bring him, to Jerusalem? It was "to present him to the Lord, and to offer a sacrifice according to that which is said in the law of the Lord, A pair of turtle-doves or two young pigeons."

i. Since the slaughter of the first-born in Egypt, God had claimed to himself the first-born of every Jewish mother. Such child was to be solemnly brought to his holy house, and submissively presented to him. A sort of fine, paid by all alike, whether rich or poor, mounting to five shekels, or eleven and sixpence of our money, was the ransom price of the presented babe, on being returned to the purified mother. As the beloved Son "was made (man) under the law," the eternal Father would have all things fulfilled for him, as well as by him. Thus the infant Jesus, though the Lord of all worlds, and he to whom all

[1] W. H. H. meant here forty days.

souls were presented for redemption, was himself presented in the temple as one who needed to be redeemed. O the depth of that condescension which was required as an atoning contrast to the pride of sinful man! The true Melchizedek allowed himself to be brought before the successor of Aaron! The Lord of the temple suffered the mere priest of it to receive a fee for his own priceless presentation. He, for whom the temple was built, and of whom it was a figure and a type, comes into it as one of the meanest suppliants who ever entered it. Would that our proud hearts were startled into humility by the mention of such facts as these!

ii. But the virgin-mother came to the temple, not only to present her first-born, but to offer for herself[1] the requisite offerings according to the Jewish law. (v. 24.) Had she been a rich person, she *must* have offered a lamb; and that vile thing—as at least it too generally is—which we call *respectability* would have prompted the more costly offering. But the mother of the King of kings was *a pauper*; and the evangelist well knew it; for, with significant simplicity, as though in her case it was a matter of course, he says nothing of what the law says about a lamb, but mentions only the doves or the pigeons. Hence there is no *disgrace* in being poor. The happiest mother and the holiest Son were among the poorest of our race.

iii. In point of equity the mother of our Lord might have claimed exemption from the claims of the law. The offering required from Jewish mothers was for *purification*; but she needed no maternal purification, because her offspring was neither conceived in sin nor shapen in iniquity. The Holy Ghost had sanctified her for the spotless incarnation of the infinitely holy Jesus. But, though she might have claimed the exemption, yet not only did she *not* claim it, but the thought of it does not seem to have crossed her mind. Indeed there is ample reason for believing that, as in other cases, after her one song of inspiration, the Holy Ghost never again actuated her beyond his ordinary inspiration of ordinary believers. In no other way can we account for her apparent ignorance of both her own position and of the real character of her son Jesus.

This however is now said not so much as a thing which is often considered (if indeed it has been considered at all), but as one thrown out for consideration. Eventually perhaps it will be found to be one of those measures of divine forethought which were taken for the prevention of that idolizing reverence which has since been paid to her, and which, in these days, is one of the distinguishing marks of the great apostasy.

iv. How admirably our own Reformed Church follows the rule of this divine forethought we ought in the present day especially to mark. In calling this day "The purification," it is plain that our Reformers used the title more as one of popular custom than anything else. It was the almanack appellation and the ecclesiastical heading; for, beyond the mere use of the term for those purposes, no further attention is paid to it. The case is so remarkable that our Protestant vigilance should be directed to it. On referring to the Prayer-book, you will see that, although "The purification of the virgin Mary" is the popular title of the day, "The presentation of *Christ* in the temple" is the truthful reality. The heading of the collect and what follows is this, "The presentation of Christ in the temple, *commonly called* The purification of St. Mary the virgin." And then, following out this significant hint in the heading, our Church drops all allusion to the purification, except the one Scripture text before us, and turns the whole tide of attention to Christ as the great Purifier and the grand object of all adoration.

May every heart be given to him, and every prayer be offered alone through him, and that very earnestly and very particularly at this time, seeing that the great senate of the nation will in the ensuing week be summoned[2] to resist the progress of that specious but wicked system which insults God and ruins man.

II. *Doctrinally our text is full of important matter.*

Even what it does *not* teach us is important for us to consider. It does *not* teach *anything* for the countenance of that fable which the church of Rome, after long winking at, now openly supports. The pope, his cardinals, and the whole Romish episcopate, are bent on making what they call the immaculate conception of the virgin Mary—that is, that she herself *was born* spotless of all sin—as much an article of faith as any in the Apostles' Creed. The text is abhorrent to everything of the kind; as are those passages also which describe to us the annunciation of her becoming the mother of the Messiah. The very fact of her ritual purification, and of Joseph's having been previously minded "to put her away privily," are proofs of unconsciousness, on *their part*, of any *such* sanctification.

But to the doctrines taught us:

1. *The reality of our birth-sin* is taught us by that purification to which the virgin-mother submitted.

Though "matrimony" is justly called "*holy*," yet is the birth of offspring a memento of our *sinful* state. The ritual purification of the purest mother was designed to teach the Jews the fundamental doctrine of original or birth-sin. This is that doctrine which our hearts deny, spite of their constant witness to it. Our original sin is our lasting taint. It is that "infection of nature which doth remain in even them that are regenerate."[3]

[1] Our translators do not regard Origen and Jerome's reading.

[2] An allusion to the "Ecclesiastical Titles' Bill," consequent on the Papal Aggression of the preceding year.

[3] Ninth Article of the Church of England.

Unless it be felt, and lamented, and confessed, the gospel will be no gospel to us.

2. *The necessity of more than ceremonial purfication is, in the text, intimated to us.*

St. Paul has clearly demonstrated that no legal purification could affect the conscience of any one. It could benefit only the outward state. Now when the virgin Mary went to the temple, for the rites of purification, *who went with her?* HE, we answer, who alone could really purify her or any other descendant of Adam. Her own Son, he whom she presented in the temple, was the sole Purifier both of that temple, of the very temple above, and of all true worshippers in them. Hence the primitive Church, and our own Church as succeeding it, most appropriately joins the reading of the prophecy of Malachi with the narrative of Luke. The predicted Purifier and the evangelic purification are brought together for our reading, as truly as they were actually brought together into the temple for Simeon and Anna's observation:—"Behold, I will send my messenger, and he shall prepare the way before me: and the Lord, whom ye seek, shall suddenly come to his temple, even the Messenger of the covenant, whom ye delight in: behold, he shall come, saith the Lord of hosts. But who may abide the day of his coming, and who shall stand when he appeareth? for he is like a refiner's fire and like fuller's soap. And he shall sit as a Refiner and Purifier of silver: and he shall purify the sons of Levi, and purge them as gold and silver, that they may offer unto the Lord an offering in righteousness." (Malachi 3:1–3.)

Whence then will you seek for holiness but from Christ? The virgin Mary has none to bestow, because she had none but what she received. Christ alone is its fountain and source. He, as the infinite Purifier, sends his holy Spirit to cleanse and perfect all his penitent ones. The process will always be searching. It is compared to a refiner's fire. But, happily for tender believers, that fire is watched and regulated by the tenderest of purifiers. "The Lord himself" (says Malachi) "whom ye seek," "whom ye delight in," "he shall sit," in loving watchfulness, "as a refiner and purifier of silver."

3. The presentation of Christ in the temple *admonishes all Christian parents to present, formally as well as spiritually, their infant children to the Lord.* It is a *great* mistake on the part of those who call themselves Baptists, to decide that any one essential principle of the Church of Christ from the beginning may be repudiated because it was not afterwards distinctly recommended. Jehovah established the right of infants to a share in his covenant. That right has never been withdrawn. Christ himself, as our pattern, sanctioned it by coming under it. His circumcision and presentation are clear warrants for corresponding rites to our children. Let parents then devoutly see to the baptism and confirmation of their sons and daughters, and ever after show a becoming anxiety that both they and themselves may frequent the temple of the Lord, and, especially at his table, say with true fidelity, "And *here* we offer and *present* unto thee, O Lord, ourselves, our souls and bodies, to be a reasonable, holy, and lively sacrifice unto thee."

Let it not be overlooked, that the attendance of Mary and Joseph in the temple was met with a signal blessing from the God of that temple. The Spirit of inspiration fell on Simeon, and probably on Anna, to the great encouragement and comfort of the real mother and the reputed father. Moreover let it be noticed (novel as the remark may be) that Simeon blessed the virgin Mary, *not* that the virgin Mary blessed *him*. (See verse 34.) Unwelcome perhaps is the notice to those who vainly repeat more Hail-Mary invocations than any other prayer! But Bible truth should always be told to the shame of deceivers and the deceived.

Possibly the minds of some among us have been pained at what took place on Monday last, when, in our diocesan temple, a heathen child was presented to our bishop for holy baptism. That much occurred which is greatly to be deplored we all feel, but that the blame of it has been laid on the wrong quarter every considerate and candid person must admit. According to ecclesiastical rule, the baptism was right in itself; because, if even the parents themselves were unbaptized, the babe was born in a Christian land, and was represented by at least nominally Christian sponsors. Eager partisans make no allowance for the rush of sudden occurrences, and the consequent confusion and excitement. The real blame, my brethren, rests on all who are chargeable with the spiritual and moral condition of the lower orders (as they are called) among us. The rich are, to a certain extent, responsible for the poor, the educated for the uneducated, the churchgoing for the non-church-going. Let *us* take our share of the shame: for what hitherto has the parish of St. Nicholas done toward teaching the poor in schools, or "how to behave" themselves in the house of God? I cannot answer the question as I would desire. Well may such a baptism remind us of our duty toward *the heathen!*

4. The text further teaches us this very important truth, namely, *Divine prophecy may, as to time and manner, be very unexpectedly fulfilled.* Not one of all the princes or priests in Jerusalem were conscious that, when Joseph and Mary brought their babe to the temple, the prophecy of Malachi was fulfilled. The fact was not known to either Mary or Joseph. It was revealed to only two aged persons, who might by scoffers be thought in their dotage. But fact it was, that the Lord came suddenly and unsuspectedly to his temple. And fact it is, that he will soon come suddenly and unexpectedly upon us. His coming will be "unawares" and "as a snare." Are we ready for it? Let Simeon and Anna be patterns to us.

"Now unto him that is able to keep you from falling, and to *present you faultless* before the presence of his glory with exceeding joy, to the only wise God our Saviour, be glory and majesty, dominion and power, both now and for ever." (Jude 24, 25.)

SERMON IV.

HEROD'S SLAUGHTER OF THE BABES OF BETHLEHEM.[1]

MATTHEW 2:17, 18.

"Then was fulfilled that which was spoken by Jeremy the prophet, saying. In Rama was there a voice heard, lamentation, and weeping, and great mourning, Rachel weeping for her children, and would not be comforted, because they are not."

THAT which is here said to be the fulfilment of a prophecy was the cruel slaughter of a multitude of infants in Bethlehem and its neighbourhood. The circumstance itself is painfully remarkable, and the instruction which it furnishes is as varied as it is important.

Our consideration of the history, and of the prophecy which that history accomplished, will be guided by tracing, first, the fulfilment of which the text speaks; next, the observance which our Church makes of it; and then the prophecy itself, with such reflections as are suggested by it.

May he who told Jeremiah to prophesy help him who preaches and all who hear!

I. *The fulfilment* of Jeremiah's prophecy was that atrocious massacre which is briefly detailed in the 16th verse: "Then Herod, when he saw that he was mocked of the wise men, was exceeding wroth, and sent forth and slew all the children that were in Bethlehem, and in all the coasts thereof, from two years old and under, according to the time which he had diligently inquired of the wise men."

1. The Herod here mentioned was the first of three who bore that odious name. He was flatteringly, but falsely called "The great." As though the God of Providence intended him for a contrast to the beloved Son, he was a monster of vice, cruelty, selfishness, and impiety; and yet, withal, he made some pretensions to religion.

When the magi, or wise men, came from the east to Jerusalem, and inquired for the newly born King of the Jews, the craft of the odious monarch was as prompt as his fears. "Go and find him," said he; "then come back and tell me, that I also may worship him." Yes, he would have worshipped him as the murderer worships the victim for whom he has long laid in wait, or as the hyæna worships the gentle gazelle, when he steals on its unwary slumbers!

By profligate Pharisees and others of their serpent sort Herod had been flattered into the notion that himself would prove their Messiah. He at least connived at the blasphemous imposture, for his own belief of it was an impossibility. But, as it answered his purposes to be considered a sort of demi-god, he allowed the wicked conceit to spread, and to become the doctrine of a set of hypocritical followers who were called "the sect of the Herodians." Regarding himself then as virtually the king of the Jews, and yet wishing to be on good terms with the Roman emperor, he instantly meditated the destruction of the babe whose birth had been so startlingly announced to him. But the eternal Father of that babe frustrated the design by sending him, under charge of Joseph and Mary, into Egypt. Baffled by the return of the wise men to their own country, without coming to his court, and imagining that as the babe was born in Bethlehem he would continue in that city or its vicinity, Herod sent out a band of assassins, with orders to kill every infant (that is, according to the original word, every *male*

[1] Preached Sunday Morning, December 28th, 1851.

infant) of the age of two years and under. He thought that by taking this age (for Jesus could not be much more than a year old), and murdering all who came within it, he should make sure of destroying the dreaded intruder, and at the same time testify his zeal for the interests of that party whose watchword was, "We have no king but Cæsar."

Speedily, alas! the blood of babes, in all their innocency and loveliness, stained the quiet homes of the Bethlehemites. The horrid massacre must have been attended with scenes as heart-rending as they were diabolical. But the spirit which actuated Herod is only the spirit of every antichrist; for, whenever antichristian persecutors fail to accomplish their ends by policy, they fly to the exercise of such power as they possess. What that spirit of persecution has done, since the days of Herod, let the foul tragedy of the Sicilian vespers, and the Parisian vespers, the atrocities of St. Bartholomew's Day, and many another dark hour, tell our too drowsy ears. That the same spirit is as rife as ever wants no proof. If evidence should be needed, the periodical organ of the French Jesuits will presently furnish it.

Respecting the number of the slaughtered infants we have nothing but conjecture to guide us. To venture on such guidance however would be as vain as it is unnecessary.

The Greek tradition and the Ethiopic missal fondly assert that the number amounted to fourteen thousand. This is so extravagant a computation, that common sense at once rejects it. There could hardly have been that number of male infants under two years of age in all the south of Israel, as our best writers on population will allow. It shows however the uncertainty of mere tradition, and how little it is to be regarded apart from other evidence. A far more authentic report is this: that Herod, in either the madness of his wrath, or the recklessness of his barbarity, forgot that a son of his own, by a Jewish wife, was being nursed in the neighbourhood of Bethlehem at the very time that he sent out his armed fiends. The consequence was that his own assassins slew his own son. This gave rise to the Roman jest, that "*It was better to be Herod's swine than Herod's son.*" The one he did not kill (out of compliment to the Jews), but the other he inhumanly murdered.

Such cruel atrocities were the fulfilment of a divine prophecy. The God who directed the utterance of it kept his eye on the monster who fulfilled it, and soon brought him, for it, into the pangs of a most obscene and horrid death. Herod died, a spectacle of the most loathsome degradation of which the human frame is capable.

II. *The observance which our Church makes of this slaughter of the infants* is worthy of a churchman's best attention.

1. In the first place she regards their cruel death as a species of holy martyrdom, and appoints a service for the commemoration of it. The third day after Christmas she calls "The Innocent's Day."

Each, however, of those three days is devoted to the contemplation of the same sort of subject. Martyrdom is the theme of each, according to its tripartite ratio. He is a martyr of the first class who suffers in both will and deed; he of the second who suffers it in will, but not in deed; and he of the third who undergoes it in deed but not in will. St. Stephen is accordingly ranked, as to the commemoration day, immediately after Christmas, because he suffered in both will and deed. St. John is placed next, inasmuch as he suffered in will though not in deed, being cast into a cauldron of boiling oil, but preserved from it. On this the third day, come the innocent babes of Bethlehem, who were too young to yield any conscious assent to the martyr's lot, but who nevertheless suffered it.

Now this is a truly remarkable arrangement, and is fraught with the most salutary lessons. Many an aspirant for ecclesiastical exactness may observe the outside arrangement, but will perhaps overlook the inward and spiritual intention. The one and the other are these: immediately after the most joyous festival of the church is ended, yea, as soon as the morning of the following day is on the dawn, another kind of sound is heard, a solemn though not a mournful note is struck. Martyrdom mingles its grave and affecting tones with the expiring echoes of the angelic song. The touching cases of St. Stephen, St. John, and the Bethlehemite babes, are successively set before us. And for what purpose can this be, save the great and necessary purpose of reminding us that he who rejoices at the birth of the Saviour must be prepared to weep with him in his sufferings, and to be himself baptized with the baptism of blood? Yes, verily, it teaches us to "rejoice with trembling," and to be very careful how we let into our hearts the notion that Christmas really *is* a time for *carnal* mirth. Time for cheerfulness, hospitality, mercifulness, bountifulness, and all the amenities of life it certainly is; but it is not a time for "chambering and wantonness, rioting and drunkenness," "revellings and *such like*" procedures. Not, least of all, is it a time for that most inconsistent and most pitiful prostitution of the fair and hallowed name of charity—a charity ball.

Let it then be a question for our hearts to answer, Are we Christians according to the true spirit of Christmas, and are we churchmen according to the *spiritual* and *godly* mind of our Church? Hot and empty churchmanship is but as a crackling flame. True, solid, consistent piety, always glowing and always generous, is the only churchmanship which will either honour and increase the Church, or warm the hearts of her members in a wintry time of peril, perplexity, or persecution.

2. For the furtherance of her hallowed purpose our own Church has framed a collect, upon the model of her other collects, by which, in a few brief sentences, we are taught to pray

for those things which most concern us to learn and attain, in the consideration of the case of the martyred infants. This collect was cast in its present mould at the era of the Reformation. The celebration however of the day itself is of immemorial prescription; for Origen, before the end of the second century, mentions it as one of the settled observances of the Church.

God grant that "all vices" may be slain in us, and that every churchman may be an "innocent" churchman, that is, holy, harmless, and an undefiled Christian in the midst of a wicked world, "innocent," as David says, "of the great offence," and "blameless" before our Lord Jesus Christ!

III. *The prophecy itself,* which Herod unconsciously fulfilled, occurs in Jeremiah 31:15. "Thus saith the Lord: A voice was heard in Ramah, lamentation and bitter weeping; Rahel weeping for her children refused to be comforted for her children, because they were not." It primarily referred to quite another event, namely the slaughter of some and the dispersion of others of the captive Jews whom Nebuzaradan brought to Ramah after the spoiling of Jerusalem. (Jeremiah 41.) Ramah was a city of Benjamin, as Rahel or Rachel, the figurative name for Bethlehem, was in Judah. They were adjacent places. Bethlehem was also the site of Rachel's sepulchre. Her descendants were living around it; and as she was an anxious mother, often weeping for the want of children, and as she died at the birth of her second child, those mothers who had seen their infants slain by Herod's command are touchingly represented as Rachel herself. Their bitter sorrow and inconsolable weeping could not be more affectingly described than by the prophet's elegant allusion to the grief of the beloved wife of Jacob. Her story was the most tenderly interesting of all their national stories; and the very name of Rachel, as the model of Jewish beauty, was sure to awaken all the sympathies of the Jewish heart.

1. *Such a fulfilment then of the prophecy,* a second fulfilment after the first, and such an one as no individual had perhaps anticipated, *should awaken our attention to the wondrous texture of Holy Scripture.* None but an omniscient Spirit could have framed passages of such singular adaptation to such different events, and yet both occurring in the same locality. The God of the Bible is he who sees all things from the beginning to the end. In perfect fitness therefore he adapted the word of prophecy to hold good to a series of similar events in very different ages of the world. The recognition of this principle is of great importance, because so many prophecies relating to Jew and Gentile, Rome and Jerusalem, Christ and Satan, have yet to receive a fuller accomplishment than hitherto witnessed.

2. *Prophecy,* be it well observed, *does not justify the wickedness of those who fulfil it.* Because it was said that Rachel should weep for her children, Herod was not held in excuse for killing them. The eye of prophecy only foresaw what would come to pass; the prophet wrote it down, and Herod was a wilful agent in accomplishing it. That there is a profound mystery as to the union of God's ordaining all things, and wicked men working out his decrees while they indulge their own iniquitous desires, must ever be acknowledged. It must stand fast with us too that the fulfilment of prophecy by the wickedness of men is no impeachment of the righteousness of God. (Deuteronomy 32:4.) A few practical reflections await our attention:

i. *How true is it that children suffer from the taint of Adam's sin, and are saved by the atonement of Christ!* Had not these children of Rachel been born in sin they would not have been vulnerable by the weapons of Herod's troop of assassins. But our children die because we have, alas! transmitted to them a sinful nature. "Wherefore by one man sin entered into the world, and death by sin; and so death passed upon all men, for that all have sinned: for until the law sin was in the world; but sin is not imputed where there is no law. Nevertheless death reigned from Adam to Moses, even over them that had not sinned after the similitude of Adam's transgression, who is the figure of him that was to come." (Romans 5:12–14.) Our children "have not sinned after the similitude of Adam's transgression," because, being unconscious of good or evil, they cannot be guilty of disobedience. Yet are they the subjects of suffering and death. This fact often so affecting to witness, is a call to us for the exercise of two things—deep humiliation and repentance whenever we see our little ones suffer or die, and reverential awe of the divine holiness, justice, and truth, in causing them to feel the penal consequences of the original transgression.

But then let Rachel—like mothers, resist the temptation not to be comforted. The second Adam embraces little children in the arms of his love. If he smites them with death, it is the sooner to bring them to eternal life. When their gentle spirits depart hence he receives them to himself. This we are warranted to say with great earnestness in all cases where infants have, by the appointed ordinance, been brought within the covenant. The innocents of Bethlehem were, in all probability, under the seal of circumcision; and our church which celebrates them says: "It is certain, by God's word, that children which are baptized, dying before they commit actual sin, are undoubtedly saved."

A very wise and a very sober decision is this; alike opposed by its scriptural silence, as to unbaptized infants, to the dogmas of Rome and the leanings of some among ourselves.

ii. *How true also is the paradox that the Prince of Peace "came not to send peace on earth, but a sword!"* These words of his do not mean that it was not his mind and desire to spread peace among men. Far otherwise: only he knew that the peace, of which he is the Prince, is a *holy* peace. Now men by nature hate holiness; and therefore they quarrel with its peace, and as far as they can persecute those who promote it. This is the true solution of the paradox. The sword which Messiah came unwillingly to send through the earth was very early unsheathed. The little ones of Bethlehem were the first to taste its smart. They were, as St. Augustine pleasantly called them, "*The primroses of martyrdom*," early flowers, betokening the character of those which are to follow.

Christ's sufferance of the indignities inflicted on his people is a profound subject. But it will be made clear in the day of their reward. Meanwhile let them prepare for the jest, the taunt, the misrepresentation, the lie, and perhaps the prison, and the last struggle. But let them also *pray* for those who inflict them, assured of the crown that awaits themselves.

iii. *How great the contrast between the earthly and the heavenly estate!* While babes were dying, and mothers crying, the holy child Jesus was fleeing into Egypt. All *seemed* marked by confusion and sadness, and yet all was working aright for order and joy. The eternal Son was still in heaven, and fast as the infants expired he received them. "These were redeemed from among men, being the first-fruits unto God and to the Lamb." (Revelation 14:4.)

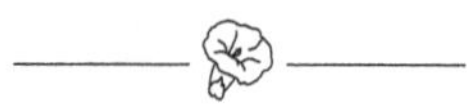

SERMON V.

THE THOUGHTFULNESS OF THE VIRGIN MOTHER.[1]

LUKE 2:51.

"But his mother kept all these sayings in her heart."

THIS gospel was, no doubt, selected for the first Sunday after *the* Epiphany because it contains *an* epiphany, or one of those occurrences in which Jesus manifested his divinity. He had accompanied his reputed father and his real mother to the feast of the Passover at Jerusalem. On their return he lingered in the temple. His parents went on their homeward way, a little too easy, as is generally thought, respecting their remarkable child. Supposing him to be in the company of some of their relatives or neighbours, who loved the society of so sweet a youth, Joseph and Mary were content. But his lengthened absence alarmed them, and sorrowful anxiety urged them to go back to Jerusalem. After searching for two full days, "they found him in the temple, sitting in the midst of the doctors, both hearing them and asking them questions."

Though all were struck with astonishment and admiration at the wonderful child, yet his mother, in the agitation of the moment, chided him. His reply was prompt and gentle, but more wondrous than all which hitherto she had seen or heard:—"And he said unto them, How is it that ye sought me? Wist ye not that I must be about my Father's business?" But, it is added, "they understood not the saying which he spake unto them."

His mother however kept it and all that passed in her heart. As this is exactly what we should do, let us devoutly consider the subject: and may the holy child Jesus give us grace and wisdom rightly to understand it!

I. *Every thing which the holy Jesus said or did is in itself, and ought to be to us, supremely interesting and important.* Nothing is *really* interesting and important but what concerns him. All else is passing and perishing. If we see not this truth during the present life, eternity will force it upon us, either with terror or sorrow, or both. Of the childhood of Jesus very little is told us. Holy and sweet and beautiful that childhood no doubt was; and, though there were some witnesses of it, yet it seems that they were not permitted to make much of it, lest the purposes of God should be hindered by human interference. There are many apocryphal stories told about his childhood, which

[1] Preached Sunday Morning, January 11th, 1840.

corrupt or apostate churches cherish more than authenticated facts. But we may be sure that, if God had seen fit to perpetuate a fuller account of his childhood, that account would have been written by his own evangelists. Besides, if we do not earnestly believe what is told us, neither should we believe if more were told us. Let us then be content with what is written, following the good old rule: "Where the Scriptures have no tongue, let us have no ear: when they speak, let us mark and learn." The sayings which Mary could not understand, but which she nevertheless stored in her thoughts, were these: "How is it that ye sought me? Wist ye not that I must be about my Father's business?" "*How* is it that ye *sought me?*" As though he had said, "Have you not long ago seen and known enough of me to be persuaded that I am safe everywhere? that angels have charge over me, to keep me in all my ways? Did not the shepherds tell you, when I lay in the manger, that I was born to be the Saviour of men? And did not Simeon afterwards confirm all which they said? How could you be so forgetful, and then so anxious? I would certainly have returned to you." And so without doubt he would have returned, even had they not come for him. Omnipotence would have made easy work of his conveyance to Nazareth.

And then he added, "Wist ye not that I must be about my Father's business?" As much as to say, "Know ye not that Joseph is not my real father, but, as the angel told you, that God is my Father, and that I am his only begotten Son? Have you forgotten this also? and do ye not understand that the service of my true Father is my true and proper business?"

Alas, dear brethren, how often is it that we very imperfectly understand that which a little consideration would make clear to us! How many among those who profess and call themselves Christians, mistake and confound things which, to a certain extent, they really know! Take the case in point, the very "business" of which Jesus spake. By that "*business*" he meant, as the original means, the things or affairs of God, his worship, his service, his cause in the world.

Now how many know that God has such a cause, such a kingdom, such a great business in the world, and yet, like Joseph and Mary, have no clear perception of its nature, or of its dependence on Christ! And what with others is far worse, though, like Mary and Joseph, they understand not what they might be supposed to understand, yet they have not the gracious disposition or the holy desire which Mary and Joseph had. That blessed couple indeed, though not very enlightened, were truly sanctified: but men are now content with little knowledge and no sanctification.

My brethren, the "business" of our heavenly Father is a great business, and one which concerns ourselves. Yea, for our sakes it is that Jesus undertook it, and was engaged in it, and is still forwarding it. Greatly therefore does it become us to know it well, and ourselves also; for, unless we understand our position as sinners, we shall never clearly perceive the nature of that business which, as a Saviour, he undertook for us.

II. *Our duty then is, like the virgin-mother, to keep all these things in our hearts.* Though she did not at the time understand what her adorable Son said, yet she did not discard it. She kept it in her heart, that is, she carefully stored it in her mind, and diligently pondered it. It was not banished from her thoughts, but cherished in them. Nor was it with her a new thing so to do. From the first she was a *thoughtful* mother; for, when the shepherds came from the field, and told in Bethlehem the marvellous things which they had seen and heard, Mary "kept all these things and pondered them in her heart," while other persons only "wondered." (Luke 2:18, 19.)

It is, alas! as common as it is dangerous, for persons to act a totally opposite part to that of the virgin-mother. The doctrines of Christianity for instance, or the unpalatable truths of the gospel, after being faithfully expounded, are urged on their attention: and what do they think or say in reply? Is it not, using familiar terms, somewhat thus?—"These things may be so, but I do not understand them. They are all very well for clergymen to discuss, but we laymen have something else to think about. Business must be attended to. Perhaps I shall be able better to consider them another day." And then the earthly soul whispers to itself in this strain: "What a stir is made about these things! They are a little beyond my comprehension, and not at all to my liking. I see no need to be troubled about them—at least I do not mean to trouble myself with them. I have always been accustomed to go on as I am going, and so I shall continue to the end of the chapter. I shall take my chance, and make the best of it."

In all this there is an utter want of spiritual taste for the things of the Lord Jesus. There is not only no keeping them in the heart, but no interest in them—no concern about them. What the consequences of such indifference will surely be we shall presently discern.

Few things, dear brethren, more plainly mark the genuine Christian than the temper and conduct of the mother of our Lord. What she did not understand at the time she hoped to understand at a future season. She therefore made her heart the ark of her soul, and deposited in it things which were likely to be of consequence hereafter. Thus many an humble Christian hears a saying from the pulpit (from whence we speak by Christ's commission and in Christ's name), but the saying is not understood; still it is kept in mind, because there is a gracious principle in that mind. The saying becomes the subject of thought, and perhaps of inquiry. In due time it is cleared up, and the saying loses none of its interest by being kept long in the heart.

Few things give greater pleasure to an earnest preacher than to explain his meaning more fully in private, when, from some cause or other, that meaning has not been understood in public. It is always gratifying to find attention, even where there is not full understanding. It is the very thing which "the Father of spirits" delights to see in his people. "If any man lack wisdom, let him ask of God, who giveth liberally and upbraideth not." "The Father *will give* his holy Spirit to them that ask him." It is the desire for wisdom and grace which he approves and loves. Hence the Saviour himself said, "If any man will do his will, he shall know of the doctrine, whether it be of God, or whether I speak of myself." (John 7:17.)

III. *They who close their hearts to the sayings of Jesus are likely to lose the salvation which those sayings contain.* All his words are life. In even what he said to his beloved mother there was salvation to be found: for, only let a man think of what Jesus called his "Father's business," and he will perceive that it is the business of the soul for eternity; because the faithful service of God now will lead a man, through Christ, to the saving health of heaven hereafter. But, if men think scorn of sayings which they will not understand, what can they expect but the wrath of him who has spoken them? To find no room in the heart for the sayings of Jesus, is to shut out all room from that heart for the grace of Jesus. If therefore Mary did well in keeping in her heart the sayings of her holy Son, what must we say of those who cast his words behind their back, who will have none of his counsel, and neglect his great salvation? There can be but one conclusion. What that conclusion is let every man's conscience tell.

But think of the text in another respect. "His *mother* kept all these sayings in her heart." Now a mother's heart is always a little chamber of tender solicitudes. She keeps in it many anxious thoughts, and stores up many an interesting recollection of the childhood of her beloved ones. She can remember the sayings and doings of her children long after they have ceased to be children. But no mother ever had such sayings to keep in her heart as the mother of Jesus had. And Jesus himself knew this; for, though his mother did not understand him, he understood his mother. And, dear Christian mothers, this same Jesus understands all that you keep in your hearts. He knows your solicitude for your children, and sympathises with it too. He understands your thoughts about them, even though he be afar off. Then cast all your care on him. Keep his sayings in your heart, and he will be the more likely to keep yourselves and your children in his hand and from all evil. At this present especially may we all bring forth from our hearts that one saying of the Saviour, which ought always to be kept in them: "This do in remembrance of me." His disciples did not fully understand the saying at the time, but they kept it in their hearts, and well understood it afterwards. Now, if we discard this saying and put it from us,—if practically we make it of no account, how can we reasonably expect that he will regard us? If we keep not his saying, will he keep our souls? If we neglect his request, will he hear our prayers? O for the time when all hearts will be his, and when men will come to his table "as doves fly to their windows!" (Isaiah 60:8.)

SERMON VI.

THE HUMILITY OF JOHN THE BAPTIST.[1]

JOHN 1:27.

"Whose shoe's latchet I am not worthy to unloose."

IT was to be expected that the ministry of John, so startling, so uncompromising, and so mysteriously commanding, would arouse the attention of the authorities in Jerusalem. Individuals among them were likely to be still living, who in

[1] Preached Sunday Morning, December 24th, 1848.

younger life had heard the prodigies which attended his birth. "All they that heard them laid them up in their hearts saying, What manner of child shall this be!" (Luke 1:66.) Accordingly, when the doings of John at the Jordan reached the ear of the Jewish Sanhedrin, they sent a deputation to him, to make inquiries as to who he was and what he meant. He replied with great frankness to all their interrogations, and at length gave them such an answer as must have left them in greater astonishment than ever. He declared that he was but the vocal herald of One who infinitely surpassed himself, and who, without their observation, was actually living among them. He testified his own sense of the amazing dignity of this unrecognised personage, by adding that himself was not worthy to do for him even the most menial office, the unloosing of the latchet of his shoe. This instance of pure humility is not more remarkable in itself than it is instructive to us. Let us view it in its nature, its origin, and the time of its manifestation.

I. *The humility of John was singularly beautiful and severely tested.* John himself was called "a burning and a shining light." The words of our text, as they beamed from his lips, are not the least brilliant part of that light. His austerity, his boldness, his fidelity, are each strong rays of his light; but his humility gives it that chastened and winning lustre which nothing else can supply.

No man ever had more plausible grounds for self-elevation than John the Baptist. For a solitary individual of only thirty years of age to see a whole territory paying him breathless attention, submitting to his sharpest rebukes, and obeying his sternest biddings, and that on the part of all sorts and all classes of persons, was a temptation to such self-elevation, and an excuse of no ordinary degree. When however a deputation from the haughtiest assembly in the world came all the long way from Jerusalem to him, his humility must have been enviably great, for him to have remained unmoved in it. But when from their queries he gathered that he might have passed for even the Messiah, nothing but "grace for grace" could have kept him in his integrity.

More than this: when all their suppositions as to who he was were shown to be erroneous, and it remained for him to announce his real character, instead of describing himself in the lofty terms which, from prophetic Scripture, he might have done, he used only the simplest and meekest terms. Had he acted in the spirit of many an after ecclesiastic he might, as to his real standing, have said to the deputation: "Instead of yourselves let your high priest come hither and place his neck under my foot. I am greater than he. I am the very vicar of the Christ. I am sent to hold his sceptre till himself appears to take it. I was foretold by prophets. An angel predicted my birth, and nature forsook her course to forward it. Let your high priest and your whole Sanhedrin come to me!" But did John speak thus? Far otherwise. Not one word which tended to exalt himself fell from his lips. He even shrunk from mentioning the august prophecy of Malachi, in which he was expressly called Elijah, and chose the humbler words of Isaiah: "I am," said he, "the voice (the mere airy, flitting, passing) voice of one crying in the wilderness." And then proclaiming the greatness of his Lord, who was dwelling as a stranger among them, he added, "Whose shoe's latchet I am not worthy to unloose."

How far beyond us, dear brethren, is all this! When do we find in ourselves humility *like* this? Who among us is always wise enough to be *humble?* Who, when vanity throws her bait before us, is too lowly ever to be caught by it? How hard is it to be called of God to fulfil for him some high duty, or to hold for him some enviable talent, and yet not to be elated by our commission or our ability! John however did all this, in a degree too which we are scarce competent to measure. Probable is it that those humblest of beings, God's holy angels, never saw a nearer approach to their own perfect humility than when the Baptist uttered the words of our text.

II. *The origin of this precious and beautiful grace in John was twofold.* It was the product of the Holy Ghost in his heart, and was matured by a clear and an impressive knowledge of the character of Christ.

1. John, from his very birth, was the subject of especial sanctification. "He shall be filled (said the predicting angel to his father), with the Holy Ghost, even from his mother's womb." One of the sure works of that Holy Ghost in the elect people of God is meekness, lowliness, humbleness of mind. The pride of our fallen nature is a part of our original sin. Humility, as opposed to it, is a branch of that holiness which the eternal Spirit alone can produce. The hand of an Almighty agent is requisite for the production of a principle which is most antagonistic to our natural bias. Who but such an agent can take the pollard oak and bend it to the pliancy of the weeping willow? Equally necessary is it for Almighty grace to deal with us, when our stout hearts are to be made tender and lowly. Generally it is the work of years to bring us down to that habitually humble point which best accords with the present perfection of the Christian character. The older Christians grow, and the nearer they attain the maturity of spiritual life, the more discernible will their humility become, if not always to themselves, yet generally to others. But, in the case of John, the work of humility began with his childhood. It was highly becoming that he who was to be the harbinger and herald of the meek and lowly King of Saints should himself be a pattern of humility. No marvel then that the herald spake not of carrying the *crown* of that King, but rather of *not being worthy* even to unloose the latchet of his shoe.

2. John however, in learning humility, kept his eye on One who awes as well as teaches. It is evident that although, as it is thought, he had not yet seen Christ he had reverently studied his character. He had read the book of the prophet Isaiah, which was a history, by anticipation, of that very Christ. He read it too in long and deep retirement, and under an interpreter who could not mistake. The wilderness was his study for the prime of his younger manhood, and the inspirer of all he read was his infallible guide. From the Book of Isaiah he could learn both the divine and human character of his Lord; and by the help of that Spirit which filled him, he would foresee all that pertained to the union of the human and the divine in that Lord. This accounts to us for his accurate perception of the combination of greatness and humiliation in the character of Christ. He spake of him therefore, to the deputation from the Sanhedrin, as "the Lord," that is, the Jehovah, and yet recognised his lowly incarnation by alluding to the latchet of his shoe. O strange and wonderful fact! He who walks upon the wings of the wind, and treads that path which the vulture's eye hath not seen, condescends to wear an earthly shoe! Ah, dear brethren, for whom did he this? He walked on earth while under a curse that he might bless it and those who dwell upon it. He fastened the latchet of his shoe that he might "go about doing good," and after he had done it might ascend to where he had walked before, for the perpetual increase of it.

With these views of Christ in his mind, how could John be otherwise than humble? The right perception of his Saviour's greatness would speedily show him his own littleness: and the thought of that Redeemer's humiliation as a sandalled sojourner among men would as speedily tend to abase him in his own heart. The period of John's ministry at the Jordan must have been one of deep and intense interest to his soul. He could not but feel that he was standing at the junction of two mighty causeways in the high path of the Church, and that he was the bridge which joined them together. The old dispensation and the new met in his person. With one hand he bade farewell to Moses, and with the other he saluted Christ. And, as he stood preaching and baptizing on the running stream, he felt that a crisis was every moment to be expected, which dated all its consequences from eternity to eternity. Conscious of his descent from apostate Adam, and that he now was what he was only by the grace of Messiah, how could he feel otherwise than "*unworthy*" at his singularly honourable position?

My brethren, we never can know what true humility is, till we know the Lord Jesus Christ as the mighty God and the sorrowful man. John might have lodged in the desert, and have worn his raiment of camel's hair, till his age was gone and his haircloth worn out: but, unless the eternal Spirit had taught him to know the eternal Son, he would have looked for true humility in vain. "Voluntary humility," both in heathendom and christendom, has done its feats and gained its honours: but true humility has only been obtained when the soul has been filled with that love for Christ and admiration of him which are followed by the laying down of every honour at his feet. We accordingly find that in the New Testament the study of Christ is enjoined as the sole method of learning humility. Hear St. Paul's testimony: "Let this mind be in you, which was also in Christ Jesus: who being in the form of God thought it not robbery to be equal with God, but made himself of no reputation, and took upon him the form of a servant, and was made in the likeness of men: and being found in fashion as a man he humbled himself, and became obedient unto death, even the death of the cross. Wherefore God also hath highly exalted him, and given him a name which is above every name, that at the name of Jesus every knee should bow, of things in heaven and things in earth and things under the earth, and that every tongue should confess that Jesus Christ is Lord, to the glory of God the Father. Wherefore, my beloved, as ye have always obeyed, not as in my presence only, but now much more in my absence, work out your own salvation with fear and trembling." (Philippians 2:5–12.)

Our thought then of the Saviour's "great humility," and our study of his deep humiliation, are the instrumental means of our becoming, like John, sensible of our utter unworthiness to do any thing, even the least thing, for his honour and glory. Possessed of this spirit of the Baptist we shall like him "walk softly," and yet labour earnestly, blending also, in the process of our salvation, "fear and trembling" with joy and hope.

III. *The season at which the humility of John was especially exercised is replete with solemn admonition.* It was just at that point when the Lord Jesus was about to step from obscurity into publicity. He was among the people; but as the Messiah he was not known by the people. The very next day after John declared him to the people. Then did a new era begin. The seal of Jehovah was set upon the man Christ Jesus; and from that day the world was left without excuse as to the knowledge of the one only sacrifice for its sin. "Behold the Lamb of God which taketh away the sin of the world!" Then did the proper work of his first advent commence. The gospel of the kingdom was heard from the lips of him who "brought life and immortality to light."

1. If then, at such a juncture, John was conscious of the propriety of self-abasement, may we not dutifully acknowledge the wisdom of our Church in calling our attention to his case at the season of Advent? There is great wisdom in the call. May we be equally wise in obeying it! It is a vain thing to expect any profit from the contemplation of any advent of our Lord, unless we come to it with humility of heart: and, to invert the sentence, it is little likely that we shall feel at all as John felt,

that is, that we shall possess humility of heart, unless we ponder the advent of him who, though the Highest of all, became the lowliest of all.

2. As, like John, we are standing in an expectant position, and men's minds are musing on the things which are coming to pass, there seems a peculiar fitness in so chastening our own spirits as not to think more highly of ourselves than we ought to think. Whatever development of the kingdom of Christ is in progress or at hand, we are sure that "humbleness of mind" is one of the best preparations for it. Be the development as it may, it is quite certain that the kingdom itself is not changed. It is still, as in the days of John, a holy and spiritual kingdom, and can be met in its joy only by holy and spiritual subjects.

3. As further the final advent of the Saviour will come upon the world, and we *must* take our part in it, we should be admonished that every thing lofty will be brought low, and nothing but humility will serve us then. This was foretold, with great grandeur of imagery, by the prophet Isaiah: for, while his words are applicable to any advent by which God humbles the proud, they will rest, for their full accomplishment, on the advent of Christ in the last day. "Enter into the rock and hide thee in the dust, for fear of the Lord, and for the glory of his majesty. The lofty looks of man shall be humbled, and the haughtiness of man shall be bowed down, and the Lord alone shall be exalted in that day. For the day of the Lord of hosts shall be upon every one that is proud and lofty, and upon every one that is lifted up; and he shall be brought low: and upon all the cedars of Lebanon that are high and lifted up, and upon all the oaks of Bashan, and upon all the high mountains, and upon all the hills that are lifted up, and upon every high tower and upon every fenced wall, and upon all the ships of Tarshish, and upon all pleasant pictures. And the loftiness of man shall be bowed down, and the haughtiness of men shall be made low: and the Lord alone shall be exalted in that day." (Isaiah 2:10–17.)

Where shall pride, vanity, self-conceit, or high-mindedness of any description, find space to stand on, when the Judge who appeareth shall be the Searcher of hearts? How abject will the haughtiest sinner be, when the terrible array of the last scene shall startle his eyes! And who will be so appalled as they who, having been stout in the pride of their own righteousness, have refused to submit themselves to the righteousness of God? And how will they be scared who were foolish enough to make a mock of sin, instead of humbling themselves for it! The Baptist had both these classes in his eye when heralding the arrival of Christ: "And think not to say within yourselves, We have Abraham to our father: for I say unto you, that God is able of these stones to raise up children unto Abraham. And now also the axe is laid unto the root of the trees: therefore every tree which bringeth not forth good fruit is hewn down and cast into the fire." (Matthew 3:9, 10.) To the others he alluded when, speaking of the baptizer with fire, he said, "Whose fan is in his hand, and he will throughly purge his floor, and gather his wheat into the garner; but he will burn up the chaff with unquenchable fire." (Matthew 3:12.)

In conclusion,

i. *Let these things arouse us to think of sins which oppose humility.* What an amount of pride is there in our wicked world! How full of it are our hearts, our streets, our drawing-rooms, and even our halls, and the many far inferior dwellings of our land! How little sense of unworthiness marks the demeanour of many persons as they enter a church, or take their seat in a pew! How little do they *seem* to think themselves *unworthy* to loose the latchet of Messiah's shoe! Let us apply these brief words to *ourselves*, and not add sin to sin by fancying how applicable they are for other persons.

ii. *Let the things of our text encourage us in the cultivation of humility.* John thought meanly of himself: but his Master said that among all who had been born of woman there had not been a greater than he. Yes, the Lord hath respect to the lowly: he will deal with them as he deals with vallies, that is, let the flowing rains fertilize them, while the towering hills lift their heads with only *barren* grandeur. And as life advances, and sanctification increases, they shall find good evidence of their acceptance with God in the ease with which their souls bend and bow to his will. A fruitless branch will shoot aloft; but that which is laden with fruit bends downwards. The increase of humility is a sign of a nearer approach to heaven. At an early period in his ministry St. Paul said, "I am unworthy to be called an apostle:"—just before his martyrdom, "I am the chief of sinners."

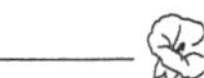

SERMON VII.

THE WOMAN OF SAMARIA.[1]

JOHN 4:28, 29.

"The woman then left her waterpot, and went her way into the city, and saith to the men, Come, see a man which told me all things that ever I did: is not this the Christ?"

OUR Lord as the Sovereign of his Church laid down rules for his own mission into our world. "I am not sent (said he) but to the lost sheep of the house of Israel." But, as the rule was one of choice, and not of moral obligation, he who made it had power to go beyond it. Accordingly we find him extending salvation in one instance to a Syro-Phœnician woman, and in the chapter before us to a Samaritan. His grace is not limited to sections and parties, but is bestowed as he will, and often where we imagine that it cannot be bestowed. "The Jews had no dealings with the Samaritans," but treated them as an heretical faction. The Lord Jesus gave no encouragement to the spirit of exclusiveness; but, when a woman of Samaria found him sitting at Jacob's well, he instantly began the work of her conversion. Though she was but an individual, he spoke divine truth to her as eloquently and as earnestly as if a multitude had stood before him.

From the simple circumstance of drinking the water of a public well, Jesus taught the poor woman all that concerned her to know of the mysteries of the Spirit, and of the way of salvation by himself. He also told her more than he saw fit to tell the great and the mighty in Israel. He told her plainly what he would not plainly tell the haughty Jews, that he was the Messiah. "*I* (said he) that speak unto thee, am he!" And often to this day does he reveal deep and precious truths to the lowly and inconsiderable, while the lofty and the noble are sent empty away. This is *his* way, and he will justify it, though a proud world may despise it.

We shall find ample store of thought for the present discourse in reviewing the conduct of this woman of Samaria, when she left her waterpot and went her way to tell others of the Christ whom she had found.

I. "*The woman then left her waterpot.*" She had come in an ordinary manner for an ordinary purpose, but she met with most extraordinary incidents. Instead of a talkative throng, as was usual in "the places of drawing of water," she found a mysterious individual, who discoursed to her upon subjects to which she had given but little attention. Often now is it that the high and momentous truths of salvation are presented to our notice unexpectedly, at a strange time, or in an unlikely place. And yet never is time or place inopportune, when the Spirit of Christ is waiting to bring those truths home to our hearts. The poor woman came for only the water of the well of Jacob: but she returned with the water of life from the well of the God of Jacob. Jesus taught her that the water which quenches our natural thirst is a type and an emblem of that grace which, flowing from himself, is as water to the soul. (Verses 13, 14.) These words, accompanied by the secret power of him who spoke them, went to the heart of the hearer. She prayed for the gift which Jesus revealed to her: "Sir, give me this water!" And thus, by attentively hearing the gospel, and then earnestly praying for its grace, faith in all its power is imparted to us. "Faith cometh by hearing, and hearing by the word of God."

The Lord Jesus next probed the hidden thoughts of that heart into which he had poured the water of his grace. "Jesus saith unto her, Go, call thy husband, and come hither." The mention of a husband touched the woman's feelings. She was a widow, of repeated widowhood, but she was then living in sin, and cherishing an iniquitous connexion. But, as one in whom a new principle was beginning to work, she attempted no denial of the fact. She frankly replied, "I have no *husband*." It is always encouraging to meet with ingenuousness; and, when we find it in sinners with whom we plead, it kindles a hope of ultimate benefit. "I said, I will *confess* my sin unto thee, and mine iniquities have I not hid," were the sayings of one who found forgiveness and peace.

Upon the woman's frank admission of wrong, the Saviour passed a word of commendation, and told her enough of her past and secret history to startle her with the full belief that he knew the whole. "Sir (said she, with no doubt a solemnly tender accent), I perceive that thou art a prophet." She then proceeded to touch the vexed and vexing question which was daily rife between the Jews and the Samaritans. *Where* ought men to

[1] Preached Sunday Morning, November 12th, 1848.

worship, in Samaria or at Jerusalem? This was the great controversy of the day. The Messiah settled it by showing that things of far greater importance to both parties were at hand. Jews and Samaritans must "worship God in spirit and in truth," since no locality could confer his grace. It is not, as to country or city, *where* we worship, but *what* and *how* we worship, which constitutes the grand point in our acceptable approaches to the eternal God. Still our Lord gave righteous judgment, and tried the grace of the woman by deciding against her prejudices. He plainly said to her, "*Salvation is of the Jews;*" meaning that historically, evangelically, and perhaps prophetically toward the end of this dispensation, the Jewish nation, and not the Samaritan stock, would prove to be God's selected instrument for the salvation of other kindreds, tongues, and people. The prophets were Jews, and all the writers of the Old and New Testament were Jews; for there is greater probability that St. Luke was a Jew than that he was a Gentile, and what is the most affecting of all considerations the Saviour himself was a Jew, and all his apostles likewise. The gospel therefore is of the Jews, and in the same sense salvation also. Through them it has been given to us. Hereafter too it will doubtless be seen that the salvation of future myriads will yet be of the Jews. There is a mystery in the singular preservation of that people, which it is folly to overlook, and infatuation to deny. Our duty and our interest as Christians, and eminently as Christians of our national church, plainly require us to watch, and to further the development of that mystery, by all those legitimate means which divine revelation sets before us. The discourse of St. Paul on this subject, in the eleventh chapter of the Epistle to the Romans, explains our Lord's words to the woman of Samaria in their prophetical and most lofty sense. Let one sentence suffice: "For, if the casting away of them be the reconciling of the world, what shall the receiving of them be but life from dead?" (Romans 11:15.)

To this subversion of her prejudices the awakened woman seems readily and meekly to have submitted. And truly, though the prejudiced mind is like a coat of the thickest mail, the flexile arrow of divine grace can easily penetrate it. No prejudice can withstand the force of scriptural truth, when God accompanies it with his softening, enlightening, and purifying grace.

Upon the woman's acquiescence in our Lord's doctrine, and on the profession of her right faith as to the character of the Messiah, he graciously told her who he was. Just at this point, which was of brightest and fullest interest, the conversation was stopped by the arrival of the disciples. It mercifully was not ended till the sum of all that needed to be said was said: so careful is the Saviour of our souls not to leave them in the first hours of their conversion, till he hath communicated enough to them for their stability and comfort.

"*Then* the woman *left* her waterpot,"—that is, when her heart was full, and when she saw that the disciples had brought refreshment for their Lord and Master. She had received a new treasure, a new principle, a new impulse: and under her strong and ardent feelings at all that had transpired, she very excusably delayed her errand, left her waterjar, and gave up her whole self to higher and better objects. The Messiah saw her leave her waterpot, and knew for what purpose she was hastening to the city; but he said not one word of disapproval or counter-direction. It is possible that the woman left the waterpot in humble courtesy to Christ, that access to the well, for the allaying of his weary thirst, might be easy for him and his disciples. Be this as it may, he clearly suffered the woman to leave it. Thus, dear brethren, we are not to wonder at warm feelings and earnest actions at the first coming of *true* religion into the soul. Neither are we coldly to censure those who indulge them, lest we thwart that in them which Christ delights to encourage. Nothing *great* is done in the world without enthusiasm. Can we expect that without earnestness any *good* will be done by any one? "I trow not." "The woman *left* her waterpot." Disciples had already left all to follow Christ; and we, in will and inclination, must be ready to do the like, if we would be crowned by him. Nor indeed is there a doubt that like this poor woman, we shall be right glad to leave in the hands and under the care of Christ that which is as a waterpot to us. We shall for the love of him be willing, at fitting seasons, to close our shops, to postpone our little businesses, and forego our greater pleasures, so that we may carry out the grace which he has given to us, either by coming to his holy house, retiring to our own closets, or joining in the furtherance of some undertaking which angels would rejoice to promote. We must make sacrifices for Christ, if we would prove ourselves worthy of Christ. We are next introduced to another portion of the woman's conduct; and most beautiful and instructive is it:

II. The woman forthwith "*went her way into the city, and saith to the men,* Come, see a man which told me all things that ever I did: is not this the Christ?" The city was a memorable and finely situated spot. Some of us heard the interesting description which a year ago a traveller in Palestine gave us vividly of it, under the corrupted name of Nablous, for Neapolis, being the ancient Sychem or Sychar. Into this city, the place of her home, the woman speedily went, and told "the men" of it the simple but astonishing facts of her interview with the Christ.

By "the men" of the city we are, according to the sense of the Greek term, to understand not the male population solely, but the inhabitants generally. Some indeed suppose that by "the men" are meant "the magistrates, the aldermen, the authorities of the city." But the ordinary use of the Greek word does not fully warrant that application of it. Rather we conclude that the woman addressed herself to all sorts of persons with whom she met. This shows great firmness for one in her station. It required no little nerve for a questionable individual like herself, unsupported by a single witness, to call up a whole town to go out and see a stranger of whom she told such strange things. But that stranger had given her heart full strength for the new and singular task. She therefore set about it not only resolutely but discreetly. She did not pledge the citizens on her own assertion, but challenged them to see, and examine, and judge for themselves. (Ver. 29.)

In all probability our Lord said *much* to the woman which is not recorded, he may have rapidly and graphically pictured to her her whole life, its general tenor, and its most secret incidents. Thus she felt that he knew every thing, and had virtually and comprehensively told her every thing. And who but a divine being can do this of himself? But Christ did it of himself; for " he knew what was in man, and needed not that any should testify to him of man." The woman therefore did admirably well in seizing on one of the most striking perfections of Deity, the perfection of omniscience, and holding it up as a proof that he who then was sitting at Jacob's well was the Shiloh of whom Jacob prophesied, the very Messiah of God himself. How solemn then is the fact that the Saviour of our souls knows all that ever we did! We forget many things which we have done: but he forgets nothing. All is naked and open to the eye and the remembrance of him with whom we have to do.

The woman's earnest appeal, " Is not this the Christ? " aroused the attention of those who heard her. God's Spirit made her single voice effectual in doing that which, in some instances, even the voice of Christ failed to do. When he called to Chorazin, Bethsaida and Capernaum, the people refused to hear: but, when this poor woman went to the men of her city, she was made the instrument of bringing them speedily and savingly to Christ. They went out to him, brought him in, and for two days entertained him; while many believed on him, first from the woman's testimony, and then from his own words.

This, dear brethren, is precisely as it should be with us. If the Saviour by the power of his gospel manifests himself to us, we are not to be indolent recipients of the benefit. Our duty is to spread the savour of his truth and the knowledge of his grace wherever we can. The Samaritan woman by her simple but forcible invitation and statement did more for the people of her town, than even the disciples of our Lord who went into it to buy food for their Master. The Spirit of God can work mightily by the feeblest means, and can make the most unlikely agents wonderfully efficient for his glory. Such a case in our Lord's day would tend to show to the disciples their Master's power, apart from their ministry, and so teach them to depend on his power more implicitly, and to pursue their ministry more industriously. If we deny the truth which is involved in these things, we may assert our official authority, but the *blessing* of him who authorizes the office will descend elsewhere. While the ministers of Christ pursue their high calling, they must promote among their people a spirit of *active* piety, and above all must pray for the Spirit of Christ to actuate both themselves and their people. In no other way has success ever followed either those that teach or those that learn.

How far then are we acting like the woman of Samaria? Are we, like her, willing to listen to Christ, and to be taught by him, though it be at the cost of probing our consciences, and subverting our prejudices? And, if professing to know him as the Chirst, are we willing to leave our waterpot, or any thing which is answerable to it, so that we may labour for him and tell others of him? What have we of the missionary spirit of this poor woman? Missionary spirit hers indeed was, exactly of that kind which must actuate and does and will actuate every real Christian. She received the gift of God, the saving knowledge of his dear Son; and instantly she was willing to let go and forego all other things, so that she might communicate that gift to others. Let us, if it be in only some humble measure, still do likewise; and present comfort and future reward will follow.

And now, dear brethren, come and see that which, by God's grace, will effectually remind you of him whom the Samaritans saw and welcomed. Here is his mystical body and blood. Here is one of " the wells of salvation " opened to us to-day: and Jesus sits at it to give us the water of life. Draw near with faith, and drink with joy.

SERMON VIII.

THE SHEW-BREAD.[1]

MATTHEW 12:4.

"And did eat the shew-bread."

BY the argument with which these words are connected our Lord taught the Jews and ourselves that "necessity knows no law." He showed that the law of God is administered according to common sense, and that consequently all ceremonial and ecclesiastical rules are to give place to natural, moral, or religious claims. The shew-bread in the tabernacle was, under ordinary circumstances, to be eaten only by the priests: but, when a band of men were famishing, the rule might be broken rather than any life should sink.

David "did eat the shew-bread." We read the fact, but do we understand it? We hear of this peculiar bread: but have we searched the Scriptures to know what it was and what it really meant? The object of the present discourse will be to remind you of the one and to inform you of the other. May he who is the "Bread of life" teach the teacher and sanctify the taught, that the souls of all may be satisfied with his own fulness!

I. *The history of the shew-bread, and the reference which it bore to the Jewish nation,* was summarily this:

Every sabbath day twelve cakes or loaves, made without leaven but of the very finest flour, were to be reverently placed by the priests on a certain table, which was called "the golden table," and which stood in the holy place of the sanctuary. The table itself was made of choice wood, and overlaid with pure gold. The loaves were prepared, with great care and nicety, in square golden frames or moulds, and were baked in the outer court, under the inspection of the priests, assisted by the Levites. Each loaf was perfectly square, having its four sides or faces all alike. Each was of goodly size, consisting of two homers, or about two half-pecks, which were double the allowance of manna for each man a day.

When placed on the golden table, they were set six and six beside each other, plates, or as some say pipes, of gold being laid between them, in order to let air so circulate among them as to preserve them fresh and sweet to the week's end. When changed for a new supply, the officiating priests divided them for their own eating, the high priest taking half for himself, and the other priests appropriating the remainder. Upon the two rows of the bread were set cups of the purest frankincense, which frankincense, upon the removal of the bread itself, was burnt on the incense altar as a memorial to the Lord.

The Jewish doctors describe many additional incidents, either explanatory or supplementary: but the present statement comprises all the chief outlines of the institution. See Leviticus 24:5–9.

The intention of the institution, so far as the Jewish people were concerned, appears to have been this:

The loaves, being twelve in number, represented the twelve tribes of Israel, as did the twelve stones on the oracular breastplate of the high priest. The placing of the loaves on a special table before the Lord, and the quality and shape of those loaves, had an interesting and important signification. The Hebrews learned from those facts that their tribes were dear unto God, that they were always in his sight, and always reckoned as choice and precious before him, as the finest of the wheat was reckoned to themselves. As the loaves were made without leaven, so were God's people to be without anything ill which leaven usually represents: "Not with the old leaven, nor with the leaven of malice and wickedness, but with the unleavened bread of sincerity and truth."

And because these loaves were square, and consequently faced the four corners of the earth, the people were thereby reminded that, as their God was everywhere present, so ought they to be everywhere the same. They were to carry the same face, to sustain the same character, wherever they might turn or sojourn. But the main circumstance of all was that which has been only just glanced at; it was that for which the loaves were expressly called "the *shew*-bread." Literally that expression means "the bread of *faces*," or, as some render it, "the bread of *proposition*," or "*exhibition*," meaning that, as the faces of the bread were set in the holy place before the Lord, so were the faces of his people always familiar to his eye. It meant that they were set before him, proposed to him, exhibited or *shewn* forth to him. Hence "the *shew*-bread." But as this bread stood on a costly table, and not on the floor, so were the Jews reminded that they could not stand on their own footing before the Lord,

[1] Preached Sunday Morning, May 14th, 1848.

but that they needed a mediator to be the ground of their support and the medium of their presentation. Constantly were they told that the Lord did not choose them *because* they *were* a holy people, but because the Lord, having loved them, *made* them a holy people, and set them as such before himself. The burning of the frankincense which crowned the loaves was a sign that the tribes of Israel were to be an offering of a sweet-smelling savour unto God, and that all their services were to be accompanied with the incense of prayer and praise.

The removal of the loaves for fresh ones was to teach the people, either that God would maintain a continual succession of his true Israel in all ages, or that their spiritual state and condition before him is always to be that of purity and freshness. And, because the priests alone were to eat the loaves at their week's end, the people should be willing of their substance to furnish ample provision for God's ministers. But then, as the priests were to eat this pleasant bread only within the precincts of the sanctuary, so were God's ministers taught that they are never to squander their stipends on the pomps and vanities of the world, but to expend them in such way as accords with the sanctity of their calling.

Such briefly was "the shew-bread," and its varied intention as regards the Jews. But, as it was among those things which were figures of greater and better objects to come, it is our duty to search out the blessed truths which the memory of it still brings before ourselves. All the furniture of the tabernacle was devised by God himself, with an admonitory purpose. Instruction was connected with everything. We may not always be accurate in eliciting it, but we can never be wrong in *endeavouring* to find it out.

II. The *typical intention of the shew-bread, as standing on the golden table*, may be regarded in a twofold point of view. The whole may be considered as a figure of Christ in himself and toward his people, and also as a representation of both him and his people. Either view will be found beautiful and pleasant to the spiritual eye.

1. As a type of Christ himself, in his relation to the true Israel, we see in the golden table and the bread upon it a figure of his personal excellencies, and of the rich benefits which he possesses for all true believers.

Gold is the constant emblem of Divinity. The table of gold, therefore, shadowed forth the divine nature of the Messiah. It represented his infinite worth as a Mediator of every perfection. Crowned with frankincense, it denoted his priestly dignity as our royal incense Offerer, who, in the rich perfume of his boundless merit, is well pleasing to Almighty God. The excellency and abundance of the bread displayed the goodness and sufficiency of his gospel for all his people. Every truth in that gospel is as fine flour, compared with other flour, which is as other truth. All truth is like valuable meal, but gospel truth is as "the finest of the wheat." Its quality is of the best and first sort. And then the large loaves aptly exhibit the large supply of that living bread which Jesus prepares for his people. A loaf too for a tribe is one mode of telling us that provision is made for believers, both severally as well as collectively. "Of his *fulness* have we *all* received, even grace for grace." Still, differ as they may in their tribes, the *same* spiritual bread is prepared for them all. The shew-bread, though divided into many parts, was all one in quality; for Christ, who is himself that bread, was the very unity of perfection. Christ is one, always "yea," and never "yea and nay." As the fine flour was in every part of every loaf, so is the Saviour's perfect excellence to be found in every act of his life, and in every gift of his hand. There is no coarse admixture in anything pertaining to him. His enemies could find no bran, no sin or fault, in him at all. Neither can his friends complain that the bread with which he feeds their souls is other than sweetness itself. As the table and the bread upon it were continually before the ark of the divine presence, so is Christ continually in his Father's sight; for he is gone, as St. Paul writes, "to appear in the presence of God for us." As the true Shew-bread, he stands in all the worthiness of his person, and in all the excellency of his benefits, before that ark of the Godhead of which he is the sole Mediator.

Nor must we overlook the weekly renovation of this bread, and its consumption by the priesthood. Though Christ and his gospel are always to be set forth among his people, yet on the sabbath of the Saviour are his ministers to bring him forward with that freshness which stewards are bound to seek for when the treasure of the gospel is entrusted to them. And, while they preach and present Christ as the bread of his people, they are themselves to feed on him whom they so preach and so present. For Christ is the common food of *all* his people, who under the new dispensation are made kings and priests unto God.

2. As a type of Christ and his people, we see in the shew-bread, as placed on the golden table, a representation of believers forming one bread in him, who is the support and Mediator of them all. The twelve loaves were, under the law, the twelve tribes inclusive of all the families of each; but, viewed from the gospel, those tribes become the twelve heads of the Christian church, including all who believe in Christ through their word. St. Paul seems to have had the shew-bread as well as the manna in his mind's eye when he said to the Corinthians (1 Epis. 10:17), "We being many are one bread." The loaves on the table were twelve, and yet they formed but *one* shew-bread. True Christians are one body in Christ. Though separated by many accidents and circumstances, they are united in him on whom they rest for presentation to God, as the loaves were set on the table before the Lord. Their appearance before him, and

acceptance with him, entirely depend on the Mediator of his appointment. The frankincense upon the loaves becomes mystically the perfume of holy praise and prayer, coupled with that divine incense which the great High Priest offers for his people. The arrangement of the loaves in two rows may well admonish us of that orderly conduct and well-regulated position which the members of the church should study to maintain. The weekly removal of one relay of loaves for another should remind us of the rapid succession of generation after generation. But it may teach us the comfortable truth of the sure perpetuation of God's saints to the end of time. Their number may at intervals be diminished, but their germ remains. Even after the separation of the ten tribes from the temple at Jerusalem, the twelve loaves still continued to be placed on the golden table. It was a beautiful and an affecting incident. It was as though the true worshippers of God would not despairingly give up those who had separated themselves from them, but still hoped there were some whose hearts were with them, and who some day might come back to them. And if, dear brethren, when the short week of our lives is ended, we do but become the portion of the true Aaron, and instead of being cast away be taken into his hands as the bread of his delight, we may well be content to be succeeded by others in that part of his Church in which he placed us.

The sum of what has been advanced is this: "The shew-bread," in its mystical intention, was both an exhibition *for* us and an exhibition *of* us. It was a shewing forth of Christ as the fine and true bread provided *for* all the tribes of his Church, and it also was a shewing forth *of* Christians as forming one bread in him. Then let us come to the great practical purposes of these holy mysteries. The table of the Lord, more excellent than the gold and cedar table made by Moses, is from time to time spread before us. As oft as it is so spread, yea, as oft as the gospel of it is preached to us, the Lord Jesus is presented as the bread of life for our souls. But he is not so presented for our indiscriminate and profane eating. We must become his kings and priests ere we dare to touch his shew-bread or attempt to eat it. Holiness becometh his house and his table for ever. So also, when we eat the bread of his table, we hold communion with him and with one another. In heart and mind we are to be "one bread." May all these high purposes be fulfilled in and by us at this very present!

SERMON IX.

THE RAISING OF THE SON OF THE WIDOW OF NAIN.[1]

LUKE 7:14, 15.

"And he came and touched the bier: and they that bare him stood still. And he said, Young man, I say unto thee, arise. And he that was dead sat up, and began to speak. And he delivered him to his mother."

IT was justly said of the despised Jesus that he "went about doing good." During the short period of his public ministry he seems to have spent no day without imparting special good to either the bodies or the souls of men. And, though the half of what he did is not told us, yet is sufficient recorded to induce our faith, our love, and our adoring admiration. The day before that on which he raised from the dead the young man of whom we hear in the text, he had wrought an act of compassion, gracious and wonderful in no ordinary degree, by restoring to perfect health, without even seeing him, the dangerously sick servant of a Gentile centurion: and now, on the following day, he banishes not only sickness but death himself. The case of the widow of Nain and her only son is as replete with touching interest and deep pathos as any narrative of the sort on record. May we find it full of searching and profitable instruction!

[1] Preached Sunday Morning, September 23rd, 1849.

For this purpose let us review

I. *The principal incidents of the beautiful and affecting tale.*

Attended by many disciples and much people, the Saviour drew nigh to the gate of the city of Nain, situate in the northern part of the Holy Land, at the foot of mount Hermon. For what purpose he was going thither we are not told; but we see that in his providence he had arranged the time of his approaching the city, exactly to suit that of the funeral procession on leaving it. This coincidence might seem the effect of chance to the spectators, as similar coincidences often so appear to us; but the God of eternity arranges all the incidents of time, while it is only our ignorance which attributes them to chance. Many of us have unexpectedly lighted upon a funeral in a road, passing to a neighbouring grave-yard. The incident had its intention, whether we discerned and felt it or not.

In the case before us the season, the circumstances, and the spot, all were favourable to the exercise of the Saviour's goodness, and to the advancement of his glory. "Now when he came nigh to the gate of the city, behold, there was a dead man carried out, the only son of his mother, and she was a widow: and much people of the city was with her." (Verse 12.) Thus *the season* was to the widowed mother an affecting crisis to her feelings. She had left her home, and had crossed the threshold where her son, when a child, had often played. Then however she was still in the city; but now the corpse of her beloved one was just carried *out* of it, and the last links of home associations were breaking.

The *circumstances* too were such as tended to spread solemnity and seriousness over every mind. A widowed mother following the corpse of her only son, and that son a *young* man, was itself sufficient to awaken the tenderest sympathies of all who knew the case. The fact of "*much* people of the city" accompanying her, proved that she was herself respected, and that a feeling of deep pity was prevalent for her: while the spot too where our Lord met the mournful company was well adapted to give proper effect to what he was about to do. It was *without* the city, away from noise, interruption and worldly occupation, where less of man's works and more of God's were to be seen. And let us pause, for a little moment, to contemplate this scene. It was painted, so to speak, for our learning; and our Church brings forward the picture, not on perishing canvass, but in the sure gospel for the day. And what see we in this picture? There is conspicuously "*a widow*," who, if she were "a widow *indeed*," had tasted a bitter cup before she wept for the loss of her son. She must have wept, with agony of heart, over another corpse ere she wept over his. She had lost one who was even nearer to her than was this one. Thus her grief was at its double. But "*a widow*,"—if anywhere she be such "*indeed*,"—then do we see in her person God's type of our deepest affliction, and an object of his most tender regard. We cannot see a widow, without being reminded of the afflictions of this life, any more than we can see a soldier without being tacitly told that there is sin and insubordination in the world. God is emphatically called "the God of *the widow*;" a title, the like to which is not once given to any mourner of the other sex.

And then what else in this picture do we see? "A *young* man" a *corpse!* When an old man dies we count it a thing of course, and think of death as a sort of *natural* issue to a long life. We cheat ourselves into the belief that there is nothing remarkable in it, because it is nature and common lot, and even perhaps a thing to be desired. But when opening manhood is cut down, and the young and the strong die, we are obliged to think of some other cause than nature or common lot. Whether we think or not, God shows us that death has something to do with sin and a certain curse; and that his *will* also is concerned, and not mere necessity.

But what else see we? A crowd meeting a crowd; "much people" coming out of the city, and much going toward it; some weeping with the desolate widow, and others watching the wonder of Israel. What a mingled world is ours; and how near to each other may persons be who are yet far apart in disposition, purpose, and feeling! We all, brethren, help to make up the crowd of souls which is passing on to eternity; but he who made us sees us and knows us as distinctly as though we were standing in a desert alone, or on the point of a mountain by ourselves.

But who in the picture is he beside whom all other objects wear only a secondary interest? It is he who hid his glories that he might display his bounties; he without whom the world itself, like this picture, would fall to pieces, and become nothing. On him we must gaze in silent adoration, while we proceed to notice what he did. And when "the Lord saw her, he had compassion on her, and said unto her, *Weep not*."

Amid the mournful throng the bereaved one seems at once to have caught and fixed the eye of him who alone could help her. It may be that her grief, and her mourning veil, prevented her seeing him till she heard his voice. But he saw her. He knew too all the bitterness of her soul, and that keen smart which she smothered to enable her to follow the last journey of her son. And then he showed that he *felt for her* too. He proved himself to be one of us, having as man all our kindliest and tenderest feelings, without one of our imperfections or infirmities. It does not appear that he began any conversation, or uttered any preliminary remark, but that he at once said to her, "*Weep not!*" The early Christians cherished a tradition that our Lord was remarkable for a most sweet and tenderly thrilling voice. Can we imagine it ever to have been more so than when he uttered these two simple but soul-soothing words, "*Weep not*"? There must have been a power of sweetness in their utterance which no tongue can define. Ah! dear brethren, anything from Christ, be it but a look, a touch, or a word, carries with it a world of might, and penetrates where nothing human can.

What emotions these wondrous words instantly aroused in the poor mother's heart we are not told, but we *may* imagine, because her heart was moulded like many another heart. It is not unlikely that she had heard of Jesus of Nazareth; because when he was living at Capernaum she was at no great distance from him: and therefore it may have been that, when her son lay a dying, she many times longed for the Son of David to come to her city. Thus there would be a rising faith in her soul, and a readiness to welcome him, if only she could meet him. And now she, on a sudden, heard a strangely tender voice, which with her first glance sent flashing across her mind this thought, O is it HE? The mysterious glow which came over her assured her that it *was* he: for how else could she feel such sudden joy, and find the fountain of her tears so marvellously sealed? For the present nothing more was said. Her sweet surprise, and his kind intentions not long to be deferred, were enough. By staying her tears before he revived her son he showed, not only the warmth of his compassion, but his quickness in manifesting it to his people. He will not suffer them to weep longer than he can wisely help.

And now "he came and *touched* the bier," or the litter on which the young man lay. He did so as a token of his right to do as he pleased, and as a gentle method of conveying his command to stop. The Divinity of his very manner no doubt produced a wondering awe among the bearers, so that they immediately "*stood still.*" No marvel is there in their pause, seeing that he, at whose touch they stood motionless, will one day stop the sun and the moon, and our earth and all our stars. At his invisible touch they all shall stand still in their courses, and then melt with fervent heat, or pass away with a great noise.

At length, though apparently with little delay, a ray of his Almighty power beamed forth, and he was beheld as the God-Man whom all things are to obey. "And he said, Young man, I say unto thee, arise!" Ah, how might the Pharisees, and Sadducees, and the unbelieving populace have laughed him to scorn had he been a mere man, or as they blasphemously said, "a sinner!" But conscience testified who he was; his very manner declared him to be divine, and death acknowledged his Godhead. His word was *life*; for the departed spirit returned (we know not how, it is all mysterious to us), and at his bidding the dead corpse revived, for the young man "sat up." Prophets before, and apostles afterward, raised the dead, but not as Jesus raised this young man. They all had to pray, and to ask for power to affect the dead; but the Lord Jesus acted in his own might, and had no need to pray. "Young man *I* say unto thee, arise!" This was his lofty bidding, this the easy expression of his supremacy! The highest archangel in the highest heaven would tremble to take upon himself such authority, or to use such language. But it was natural and rightful to him who "thought it not robbery to be equal with God," and who will in due time bid all the dead arise from their deepest or most ancient graves.

"And he that was dead *sat up*, and began to speak." From our mode of burial inaccurate notions commonly exist about the feasibility of a corpse instantly sitting up and speaking. We think of the obstructions of a coffin-lid, and fancy other relative difficulties. But there was no coffin in the bier. The custom in those parts was, as it still is, for the dead person to be laid in appropriate clothing on a palanquin or bier, and carried in that simple fashion to the grave. Modern readers will find details respecting this mode of burial in the well known "Diary of an Invalid," by a deceased clergyman named Matthews.

When the young man proved to all that he was indeed alive, the Saviour "delivered him to his mother." It was doubtless an affecting and joyfully solemn act; but it was also full of significance and meaning. It admonished both mother and son to recollect whose they were and whom they ought to serve. It told the son to obey and cherish his mother, and the mother to devote the gift to the Giver.

The issue is briefly described to us in the 16th verse. Well might they so feel and speak, and well it will become us to do likewise. Unless we rise from the contemplation of such facts with a holier love, a devouter awe, and a warmer adoration of Christ Jesus the Lord, those facts are recorded in vain for us. But may no such fatal consequence be true of us! Rather may it be that we are prepared to welcome a practical application of what we have been hearing. Hear then

II. *The principal points of spiritual instruction which this narrative contains.*

Prominently and forcibly are we taught

1. *Our own mortality and our constant liability to the sharpest trials.* To the young especially the case speaks with an earnest voice. Their youth is no preservative against death. God teaches us this truth in a variety of ways. The field and the flower garden are his mildest monitors of it. The graveyard, with its narrow cells of unequal length, is a sterner instructor. But the actual death of the young among us, especially when feminine beauty or masculine vigour are made the prey, compels the living to sigh, however reluctant they may be to learn.

Young friends, you are mortal! You may never see maturity. Death may at this instant be secretly lodged within you, while he puts a little colour on your cheek or a little sprightliness in your frame, *just to deceive you.* Then be wise, by considering Christ and your latter end!

And ourselves, dear friends, the older among us, not one is there but what might have died while we were young! Have we devoted the sparing of our lives to him who has showed us mercy? And are we mindful that death may come to us as ruthfully[1] as he came to the widow of Nain, and snatch away our dearest, or even our *only* ones, and leave us as desolate as she was? He may so do; or varied affliction, as sharp as any arrow of his, may pierce us without warning. Such is the fact, whether we believe it or not. Our only security is "the Rock of ages," "the Lord of life," the Saviour of the soul.

Very prominently and forcibly also are we taught

2. *The wondrous grace and compassion of our blessed and beloved Jesus.* We have spoken somewhat of this already: but can we ever speak enough? Who shall exhaust that which is exhaustless? Or how can we dwell too much on that which dwells with us at every breath we breathe? The tender pity which the Saviour showed toward the bereaved widow was but a drop from that fountain of compassion which he unsealed in his heart when he came to redeem us. What is said so beautifully of his compassionate dealings with Israel may be said of his dealings with us: "In all their affliction he was afflicted, and the Angel of his presence saved them; in his love and in his pity he redeemed them: and he bare them, and carried them all the days of old." (Isaiah 63:9.) It should not be overlooked that his compassion to the bereaved widow was singularly spontaneous. No one sought it, no one asked it; but, before even the widow herself had time to think of it, its fullest tide flowed upon her. How wondrously did this verify the words of his prophet concerning him, "I am sought of them that asked not for me, I am found of them that sought me not:" "before they call I will answer, and while they are yet speaking I will hear." (Isaiah 65:1, 24.)

It is perhaps worthy of our considerate attention that the compassion which our Lord showed in the three and only three instances in which he raised the dead was a compassion which befriended strong human affection, when centred in one beloved object. The daughter of Jairus was his "one only daughter:" and how must he have loved her! Lazarus was the only brother of Martha and Mary: we are told by their own tears how they loved him. And here the young man of Nain was "the only son of his mother:" who can question her love for him? The God of love befriends such love in his children. It is pleasant in his eyes. But then if he sees it becoming inordinate, and therefore dangerous, he will either severely try it or remove the object which engrosses it. Still, let him do what he will, "his compassion fails not."

Not less strikingly are we required to notice

3. *The sovereign power of the Lord Jesus.* When we read of God's saying, "Let there be light, and there was light," we seem instantly to say, "This is wonderful; this is past understanding; this is Omnipotence!" Just so should we say on hearing the words of the lowly Jesus, "Young man, I say unto thee, arise!" For the young man did arise, and became a monument of that very same Omnipotence which the days of creation witnessed. There was as much wonder, as much incomprehensible miracle in the return of light to the eyes of him who was dead, as there was in the bursting of the first created beam upon the world when "without form and void." The power was the same, and that same power is still in the same hands. It is hourly exercised in upholding all things, and is always on the watch to rescue sinners from the death of trespasses and sins. In dependence on that power we preach the gospel and say, "Awake thou that sleepest, and arise from the dead, and Christ shall give thee light!" Every spiritual conversion is a spiritual resurrection, and in Jesus alone does the power of it dwell. May it be exerted among us! Very especially should we give attention to

4. *The practical reverence which, if we would be saved, we must exercise towards the Lord Jesus.* The contents of the verse following our text are very admonitory, and therefore we repeat them: "There came a fear on all: and they glorified God, saying, That a great prophet is risen up among us; and, That God hath visited his people." It is this "fear," this holy and reverential awe which we desire to witness in all who hear from our lips the gospel of Christ. Levity or indifference under the sound of that gospel, will call up heathens and barbarians in judgment against us. Greater works than the resurrection at Nain are done before us in our own localities. As a prophet Christ is still spiritually among us to heal the broken in heart, and raise the dead in sin. To him we are to hearken. All the precepts of his Father's word direct us to obey him. The soul which refuses that obedience is in danger of being cut off. Then hear, obey, and follow!

And what if he has been gracious and compassionate to ourselves? Shall we not give our whole hearts to him, and desire to know more of him? No doubt the widow in her joy did this, and we in gratitude should do the same.

[1] ruthfully: full of sorrow, woefully; alternatively, full of ruth, pitifully

SERMON X.

THE DEATH OF JOHN TOLD BY HIS DISCIPLES TO JESUS.[1]

MATTHEW 14:12.

"And his disciples came, and took up the body, and buried it, and went and told Jesus."

THERE is much in the character of John the Baptist which merits universal admiration and imitation. His separation from the world and devotedness to God; his simplicity, humility, and fervency of spirit; his boldness in reproving sinners, and his earnestness in advancing the glory of his Lord and Saviour, are worthy of all men to be marked and followed. With good reason therefore has the Church appointed a day for the commemoration of the life and death of so eminent a saint.

Our text is, as it were, the last line of his short but memorable history. It tells us how after his cruel death his disciples testified their love for his person, and acted in accordance with his ministry. They first went to the prison where he had been wickedly beheaded, boldly took up his body, and affectionately buried it. Afterward they did the best and wisest thing which they possibly could do; they "went and told Jesus." Not that he needed telling; but it was a becoming act on their part to lose no time in communicating their griefs to him who alone was able to soothe and sanctify them.

And would that we in all our troubles and perplexities were fully persuaded to "go and do likewise!" Our sorrows would then lose half their bitterness, and our comforts would be doubly sweet. "And his disciples came, and took up the body, and buried it, and went and told Jesus." From these words a series of remarks will be deduced, with the view to your instruction in the ways of God, and your preparation for those dealings with which he may meet you.

Depending on his grace let me first remark

I. *That very startling and mysterious events may befal the most eminent and the most devoted saints.* This remark is grounded not on speculation, but on fact. God has in all ages shown that it is one of his unsearchable ways to chastise those the most whom he loves the best. Abel, the fairest hope of fallen but penitent parents, was suddenly cut down by the murderous hand of his brother. Joseph, the heart's joy of the godly Jacob, was sold away as a slave, and thrown into a prison. Holy and upright Job was stripped of his wealth, and bereaved of his children, and plunged into loathsome maladies. And here we behold the relative and herald of Messiah cut off, without warning, at the instigation of a revengeful adulteress. Now give your best attention to this event, for it is perhaps the most mysterious and affecting event which the world ever witnessed.

John the Baptist was a man of the most marked notoriety. As a prophet he was himself the subject of prophecy. Isaiah, the first in eloquence, and Malachi, the last in time, had foretold his appearing. An angel announced his birth under circumstances of mystery and miracle. From his infancy he was a Nazarite. His growth and early manhood were spent in retirement and self-denial. He entered on his public ministrations by a direct impulse from God. He wrought no miracle, but awed a whole nation by his solemnity and earnestness. His Master bore witness to his superlative devotedness and fidelity. He called him "a burning and a shining light," that is, a light which while it lightens others consumes itself. And yet this brilliant light, this morning-star of the gospel-day, is suddenly extinguished in a dungeon! This greatest of men is sacrificed to the malice of the basest of women! Surely this is awfully mysterious. It may seem to furnish arrows for the quiver of the infidel to shoot against the doctrine of a superintending and equitable providence. But know, O vainest of men! that our faithful God will laugh to scorn all your impugnings of his moral government. Even now his obedient people can discern enough in the mystery of John's death, to believe that eventually the divine wisdom will be fully and beautifully justified. As in the case of John's birth, so in his death, it seems that a bold and vivid contrast was intended between him and the Lord Jesus. John, as the servant, was born of an aged and a barren mother, and was put to death silently and privately in a prison cell. Jesus, as the Lord, was born of a youthful virgin, and was crucified amid much commotion, at the instigation of the highest authorities, and in sight of all the people. The death of the one is not again alluded to, that of the other *always*. John too, as himself said, was to "decrease," while Jesus was to "increase." Hence, as John had been mistaken for the Messiah, the mistake must be annihilated. The servant must

[1] Preached Sunday Evening, June 24th, 1849.

be removed, that there may be no doubt who is the Lord. The herald had performed his part; and he who sent him withdrew him, not like another Elijah, as we should have surmised, but in a way peculiarly his own. We call this mystery: but mystery in such case is only another word for our ignorance. We express no wonder at seeing the bright and morning star suddenly become dim, when the first rays of the sun dart across the heavens. Neither do we think it strange at beholding a brilliant insect, which has laboured through several inferior forms, caught up by an ignoble sparrow, ere its first day of winged life and beauty has reached its centre. And yet all such things are mysteries in their degree, and are a part of the ways of the same God who allowed his servant John to die as a felon dies.

Hence, when dark and fearful providences befal the people of God, let us neither charge him with injustice, nor them with sin. The most holy and the most useful men may be as strangely and as suddenly cut off as was John the Baptist, and yet without guilt on their part or displeasure on God's. Such events have a present purpose, and they will have a future clearing up. The great day will manifest the wisdom and the love of God in them. The veil which covered the mystery will then be removed, and the supposed darkness of it will shine out in adorable lustre. The song of Moses was, "His work is perfect; for all his ways are judgment: a God of truth and without iniquity, just and right is he." (Deuteronomy 32:4.) The song of the redeemed is, "Great and marvellous are thy works, Lord God Almighty; just and true are thy ways, thou King of saints." (Revelation 15:3.) Observe next

II. *That the saints of God must be prepared for the afflictive providences of God, and expect trials and bereavements.* It has ever been the lot of the righteous to suffer, because, as previously intimated, it has always been God's method to chasten those whom he loveth, and to scourge every son whom he receiveth. This is fully accordant with the nature of things pertaining to us; for our present state is a sort of school-time, a season of training and discipline. Even our beloved Lord himself, when a servant on earth, "learned obedience by the things which he suffered." Before he left the scene of his trials, he admonished his disciples to expect tribulation. "In the world ye *shall* have tribulation." We are not to dream of dwelling at ease, or of marking a circle around us as a charmed bulwark against the inroads of affliction. We are not to say with Babylon, "I shall be a lady for ever; I shall not sit as a widow, neither shall I know the loss of children." All such security is vain; for it generally happens that, when we begin to think our mountain so strong that it can never be moved, the God of our salvation is about to hide his face from us, and to cast us into trouble. All things admonish us of change, and of our liability to experience even strange vicissitudes and bitter reverses. The fairest mornings, as at this season of the year we often see, are sometimes followed by a cloudy noon, and a tempestuous evening. Thus it may be that some dire disaster, some fearful visitation, is lying in ambush to catch unwary souls among us, before the present week has seen its close. Let the careless and those who live at ease be aroused to a sense of their peril.

The disciples of John, most likely, thought it very improbable that such a man as he would be vilely put to death. They would naturally think that one so holy, so eminent, so beloved and so feared, would never be murdered in a jail. But their thoughts were not God's thoughts. Affliction, sudden and grievous, came upon them. Neither the sanctity of John, nor their attachment to his person, could exempt them from bereavement and sorrow. He had fulfilled his ministry, and they had advanced by it as far as he could lead them. His Master took him, by a speedy martyrdom, to rest and glory, but left them to follow by a slower sanctification.

After this manner, dear friends, the Lord may deal with us. He may see fit to take from us those whom we most love, or those on whom we most depend. The pillars on which we have most confidently leaned may soonest be removed from their position; and we may unawares be left to contemplate the ruins which lie spread around us. But, if this be our lot, it will be God's intention in it to show us the greater happiness of those who supremely love himself, and the superior stability of such as depend only on his support. It is no easy task to relinquish our hold on visible helps, and cautiously to enjoy allowable delights. We therefore often stand in need of loud warnings or sharp rebukes, to make us wise and obedient. It sometimes is not a little which will accomplish this: and consequently our heavenly overseer deems it necessary to send us some heavy or stunning blow, that we may the more effectually realize the truths which we were too unwilling to learn. Happy however is it, if at any cost we break away from the creature, and lay fast hold on the Creator. All God's afflictive visitations have an eye to this end. They are sent for that best and greatest of all profitable things, the bringing us closer to himself. This was the result, and therefore we may consider it the design of John's unlooked-for death, so far as it affected his disciples. It was the motive for their going at once to Jesus, and seeking his counsel and blessing.

Hence it becomes us next to remark

III. *That the Lord Jesus is the only refuge of the afflicted, and the sure succour of all who appeal to him.* We read that John's "disciples came and took up the body, and buried it, and went and told Jesus." And what better could they have done? To whom else, as Peter once said, should they go? He had "the words of eternal life," and was able to do for them abundantly more than John ever did or possibly could do. They went to him who was the Master of their master. They told their sorrows to him who had grace to soothe them. They did exactly what most became the ministry of John, and what was most beneficial for themselves: because, by going to Jesus, they went to him whom John preached as the Lamb of God, and the Light of the world. They in all probability remained with Jesus, and thus shared his sympathy, and all the benefits of his earthly presence. There are indeed traditions respecting some of them, at least as to their adhesion as disciples to Jesus, and their appointment by him to some corresponding labour. But it is enough for us to rest on our text, and to know that they went and told Jesus all that had befallen John and concerned themselves.

After this manner God would have us act, when afflictions or trials befal us. He would have us *go and tell Jesus*. And why Jesus in particular? Why not the Holy Ghost? Because the Lord Jesus is *a* MAN like ourselves, a brother born for our adversities, the very Friend of sinners, and, as such, exalted to be our Mediator and Intercessor with the Father, on purpose that he might send to us " the Holy Ghost the Comforter." Never are believers to slacken their apprehension of him as especially provided to be unto them " a hiding place from the wind, a covert from the tempest," " their arm every morning, and their salvation also in the time of trouble." Strange however is it, and yet not more strange than true, that, although Christ is set forth as the refuge and help of every afflicted spirit, yet comparatively few go to him for the alleviation of their sorrows. Men try every expedient rather than instantly give up themselves to Jesus for the relief of their troubles. They try pleasure, business, change, excitement of any sort, in preference to that one resource which God would have them try. And why is this? The reason is to be found in the state of the heart, at the time that sorrow first comes heavily upon it. The heart has not *sorrowed for sin*, though it may have been sorely distressed under some present suffering. This reason is corroborated by the fact, that John's disciples went at once to Jesus, because they had previously gone to John as the baptizer of *penitent sinners*. They had heard much from him of " the exceeding sinfulness of sin." They had confessed their share in such sin, because they had been baptized of him, and his baptism was a baptism for the remission of sins. This explains why they so readily, and as it were instinctively, went and told Jesus all the sorrow of their hearts. John had told them that he alone was God's sacrifice for sin. This also accounts for the naturalness, so to speak, with which all true Christians turn to the Lord Jesus, when they are brought into " sorrow, sickness, or any other adversity." They have felt that his blood has cleansed them from sin, and therefore they know that his Spirit can alleviate their sadness.

But doubtless, though John's disciples went to Jesus, seemingly at their own impulse and of their own accord, there was a secret grace which inclined and quickened them so to do. He to whom they went had *prevented* them in their coming, that is, he had gone before to their hearts, and, by the sweetly constraining grace of his Spirit, had suggested the good thought to them, and sanctified its entire fulfilment. This is the process with ourselves. None ever go to him without being drawn by him. There is a strong under-current of grace which bears along, on the upper and visible tide, the ark of our affections toward himself. " We love him, because he first loved us." " Draw me, and I will run after thee," is the gracious cry of every soul, which knows the truth, and its own inability to follow it as it ought.

Let sinners and saints mark the lessons of these facts.

1. *There is neither peace nor safety for any sinner but in going to the Lord Jesus*. He alone is still presented to us as John preached him to the Jews. He is " the Lamb of God which taketh away the sin of the world." Apart from him the burthen of sin which he bore will crush our souls: and, till that burthen is taken from us, there can be neither peace nor consolation for us. All who are strangers to him are strangers to every thing which a man most requires: they cannot have inward rest or genuine hope. This we learn from Isaiah 57:20, 21: " But the wicked are like the troubled sea when it cannot rest, whose waters cast up mire and dirt. There is no peace, saith my God, to the wicked." When therefore we see afflicted but worldly persons wretched and miserable, we may be sure that remaining sin is the cause. O that all who hear would ponder and seek! Christ is as accessible now as when John's disciples spoke their first word to him.

2. *There is nothing but a fearful looking for of judgment for all who resemble the enemies of John*. Herod and Herodias, and all who countenanced his imprisonment and death, are still represented by those who hate what John preached. It was lust and the love of worldly things which took off the head of the Baptist. And it is just those very sins which set men in array against the holiness of God and those who preach and practise it. The world is full of such men and women as compassed the death of John. But judgment is on the watch for them, as surely as history says that it overtook the guilty three in the case of John's beheading. And let it not be overlooked that, if God so deals with his holy servants in this life as he dealt with John, he surely will deal most terribly with his opponents in the world to come! If he allowed the preacher of repentance to suffer a vile death, what will he not do to the impenitent?

3. *There is abundant encouragement for every afflicted saint*. Jesus is *waiting* their coming to him. Whatever their grief may be, only let them go and tell it to him. Let them do this *habitually*. Let them go with their tale of sorrow as readily as the little weeping child runs to its mother.

Remember too, not only that he *waits* for your coming, but that trials are his messengers to urge you to come. John's death led his disciples to the Lord of life. He tenderly received them and they confidently rested in him. Go ye likewise to him, and he will likewise receive you. He will one day come to take you to himself and to keep you for ever in his presence!

SERMON XI.

THE REWARD OF RIGHTLY RECEIVING THE MINISTERS OF CHRIST.[1]

MATTHEW 10:41.

"He that receiveth a prophet in the name of a prophet shall receive a prophet's reward."

THIS chapter has been fitly called Christ's Ordination Sermon to his apostles. It commences with a general statement of their commission and the roll of their names. It then enumerates their duties and their trials, graphically describing what they were pledged to perform and what they must expect to suffer. In the prospect of their sufferings many encouraging counsels are given. They were also cheered by the assurance that their labours should not be in vain. Though many would reject them, some should receive them. Whereupon the Lord Jesus glanced at the grace which should follow such recipients. They shall receive a reward. Thus the ministers and people of Christ in all climes and ages are encouraged to persevere, the one to labour and the other to cheer the labourers. Our text embodies the whole, and expresses a general truth of that sort which will never lose the blessed force with which it is charged. That we may at this present profitably contemplate it, let us direct our attention to two inquiries.

I. *What is it to receive a prophet in the name of a prophet?*

1. By "*a prophet*" we are to understand not a seer or predictor of future events, as the name meant of old, but a minister of Christ, especially a preacher or expounder of his gospel. To prophesy, as spoken of by St. Paul, especially in writing to the Corinthians, is not to foretell but to explain. The original word has that double meaning. Even "the prophet of a heathen oracle" was not the originator of the prophecy, but the interpreter, arranger, or expounder of it. Such are we. Our part and duty is to declare to you the will of God as we gather it by prayer and study from his revealed word.

2. Now to receive a prophet is one thing, but to receive a prophet "*in the name* of a prophet" is another. The commissioned prophet may be received with all kindness and hospitality; but, if he be regarded merely as a man, or as a *gentleman*, the reception falls vastly short of our Lord's meaning. Many kind hearts mistake on this point. They think it right to pay all respect to the clergyman of their parish, and they show it by the observance of those attentions which accord with the common notions of his position. They honour his profession; but then their honour does not rise above himself, or at least above the notion that his profession is merely one or possibly the highest of several professions. Thus, while they receive their prophet kindly and respectfully, they fail to receive him as his Master will have him received.

3. To receive a prophet rightly involves not only kindly affections but *spiritual perceptions*. He must be received "*in the name* of a prophet," that is, apart from all considerations of the man, the scholar, or the mere official, and simply and reverently *as the servant of Christ*. There must be a spiritual perception of the truth of Christ, an appreciation of its power and importance, and consequently a becoming esteem for the value of its dissemination through the appointed ministrations of its teachers. Such a reception therefore supposes the prior or coexistent exercise of all those exalted views and holy dispositions which constitute a genuine believer in Christ; for he who re-

[1] Preached Sunday Morning, September 9th, 1849.

ceives a minister of Christ as Christ's minister must necessarily believe in Christ as his Saviour and Judge. Consequently such a recipient will have received Christ in his heart before he receives his minister with either heart, or eye, or hand. He will have loved Christ before he loved his minister, and will love him and receive him for Christ's sake. Hence such a recipient will always have a high, a warm, and an engrossing affection for that which is the great object of the Christian prophet to handle—the *gospel* of Christ. Seeing that all his salvation is comprised in it, he will give it all his desire. And, what is more, he will be anxious not only to secure its blessedness for himself, but that, for the sake of others, he who brings it in the name of Christ may bring it honestly, purely, fully. Such anxiety as this will induce the right recipient of a prophet to accompany his reception of him with earnest prayer for the prosperity of the prophet's work. Indeed, without prayer for that purpose, the reception of a prophet will want half its entireness. It will not be enough for the recipient to say, "Come in thou blessed of the Lord!" he must from his heart add, "The Lord be with thee; the Lord prosper thee! The Lord give thee souls for thine hire, and set his beauty upon thee!"

4. With all this however it must be understood, that the prophet who presents himself for reception should bring with him the reflex image of his Master's person. He must be a man of holiness and not merely a man of office. The minister of Christ must in personal character resemble Christ. No elevation of ecclesiastical rank, no amount of talent or official authority, can compensate for the want of such resemblance. The official acts of an unholy prophet may carry with them validity, but they bring but little comfort; for though in such acts, especially in the administration of the sacraments, Christ's blessing is not tied to character, yet is the pleasantness and comfort of the recipients greatly affected by it. It is very natural that it should be thus, because we are all so constituted as to be ready judges of consistency. Thousands can understand *conduct* who have but little capacity or less inclination to understand *principles*. Besides the most ordinary Christian who hears what Christ said to his apostles, "He that receiveth you receiveth ME," will naturally look for some resemblance between the one and the other. So indeed all his apostles understood him to mean, for in all their after epistles they set up a standard of sanctity for the ministers of the gospel, which they followed themselves and required all others to follow.

To receive a prophet then in the name of a prophet, is to give to the minister of Christ a cordial and prayerful reception, because of his relation to Christ, and from a fervent love of that gospel which he proclaims. Our next inquiry is

II. *What is it to receive a prophet's reward?*

1. By "a prophet's reward" we may understand a two-fold blessing, or a blessing in two different ways. It may mean such a reward as God ordinarily gives through the instrumentality of his ministers, or a share of that reward which he will confer on his ministers themselves: or it may comprise both the one and the other. In all probability it will comprise *both*, for our God is a generous Master, who is wont to give often more than we desire, and always more than we deserve.

2. The reward which may be expected through a prophet is altogether a *spiritual* reward: but it is intrinsically more valuable than any amount of temporal benefit. It is the finding of a treasure in the ministry of the prophet, which suffices for the wants of the soul during the days of its pilgrimage in the body. It is in fact the happy realization of those promises of strength and comfort which God makes to all who hear and love his word. It is the feeling and knowing that the ministry of the prophet is indeed made a blessing to the inner man, and that our spiritual well-being is prospered by it. Christ too can make his prophets instruments of great service to such as are cast down, and are suffering from any of those sorrows of heart which meet us amid the changes and chances of this mortal life. There is moreover the solace of a prophet's supplication before his Master's throne. His "effectual fervent prayer," unworthy as it may be in itself, will not be without avail to those who set a becoming value on it. It was said to one of old, "He is a prophet and shall *pray* for thee."

Besides, if the prophet be what he ought to be, a man of godly conversation, there will be the value of his example to the family or community in which he is received. And what more valuable reward will any family or community desire than such an example as God in some way or other usually blesses to all who come within its observation? When St. Paul sent forth Timothy as an evangelist to the churches, he said to him, "Be thou an example of the believers." The apostle knew the value of such example, and the beneficial influence which by God's grace it carries with it. So that even in this respect the kindly reception of a godly minister insures no mean reward.

3. But, rich and desirable as is a participation of the prophet's reward in all these respects, there is yet another manner and another season for its bestowal. The great reward of every faithful minister is a future reward, one that is laid up for him till that day when it shall be given to him openly and gloriously. What it will be, in all the fulness of its reality, doth not yet appear, but faith is animated to contemplate, in a degree which may suffice for the present, from the rapturous exclamation of St. Paul respecting it: "I have fought a good fight, I have finished my course, I have kept the faith: henceforth there is laid up for me a crown of righteousness, which the Lord the righteous Judge shall give me at that day, and not to me only but unto all them also that love his appearing." (2 Timothy 4:7, 8.)

In these words you hear an echo of our Lord's saying in the text: "And not to me only, but unto *all them also* that love his appearing." Not only shall the preacher of the gospel be crowned, but all who have received himself and his preaching. They who receive the prophet for his Master's sake shall share the prophet's reward: a portion of the honour which will be put on him shall be put on them. If he be given to shine as a sun in the firmament, they shall be graced with the same splendour. If it be said to him, "Well done, good and faithful servant, enter thou into the joy of thy Lord!" they shall hear a similar voice and partake of the same joy.

The reason for such procedure seems to be this: "they who receive a prophet in the name of a prophet" of necessity entertain not only a regard for his person but a sympathy with his work. This sympathy with his work induces them to help him, just as the apostle Paul made honourable mention of many a saint who in true yoke-fellowship aided him. If then it is counted an equitable thing to remunerate those who help our servants and so help us, shall God be less equitable than man? Will he not reward those who have aided his ministers in the work of winning souls and turning sinners to righteousness? Doubtless he will. Our text assures us of the fact, and that on the authority of him who is appointed to be the Judge of quick and dead.

4. Meanwhile, and till the great day arrives, there is a present reward to be shared by the prophet and those who receive him. God does not suffer either his ministers or his people to labour without some passing remuneration. He gives it generally in this manner: he lifts up the light of his countenance on his pains-taking ministers, and strengthens them with a cheering expectation of success in their humble but hearty endeavours. They who receive and aid them in those endeavours share the animating expectation, while they always possess a joyous assurance that, whatever checks or failures may occur in their particular departments, the entire cause shall ultimately prevail. Christ *shall* be received. All the families of the earth shall one day be blessed in him, and his reward shall be abundantly bestowed.

But, in bringing our train of thought to a proper close, we must not too speedily pass over ground which remains to be trodden.

i. We should remember *that the reception of a prophet, and the bestowal of the corresponding reward, have no dependence on human power.* The most heavenly prophet that ever graced the earth would seek in vain for reception unless his way be prepared for him. Not a heart or a door would be opened to him unless his Master's grace went before to open it for him. There would be a constant shaking off of dust from peace-shod feet, were it not that the Spirit of Christ inclines here some and there others to welcome the heralds of truth. All is of God: and the more we all are practically sensible of the fact the better and the sooner will his work prosper with us.

So in the bestowal of the promised reward, though it is often given to individuals in answer to a prophet's prayer, yet is the gift of it dependent not on the will of the prophet but on the will of his God. We can no more command a blessing on our ministry to particular persons, than we can bid the clouds rain, or the sun shine, on particular spots. He who prepares the reward holds it in his own hand, and bestows it in his own time. This should teach us more of that humility of which one word in the text is especially adapted to admonish us: it is said of the reward, not that any favourer of a prophet shall *merit* it, but that he "shall *receive*" it. No man can *deserve* it, nor will any man ever receive it without acknowledging from his heart that he is utterly unworthy of it. The best friends of the ministers of Christ are practical judges of this truth; for it is habitual with them to think that they give but a poor reception to them in comparison with what they ought to give; and thus they discard all imagination of merit in that which they do give.

ii. We should fail in a momentous duty were we to omit apprising you of *the peril of not receiving* "a prophet in the name of a prophet." Christ the Lord does not send his ministers subject to the option of men, but as his representatives whom they are bound to receive. A rejection of them is a rejection of him, and will be visited accordingly. Proofs of this connexion between a rejection of the one and of the other every day meet our observation; for just in proportion as people love Christ or slight him do they love his ministers or slight them. The lovers of the world and its wicked ways and sinful pleasures, secretly if not always openly, dislike those ministers of a holy Saviour who denounce their doings and warn them of the wrath which is coming upon them. But, grieved as those ministers may be at the indifference or contempt of men, their grief would be comparatively unimportant, were it not that the indignation of an almighty Judge will follow it. The voice of that Judge will pronounce a doom which no power can resist, and which every heart should even now hear with trembling, "Inasmuch as ye" received not them, ye received not "ME:" "depart ye cursed!" Friends, be earnest. Receive Christ and his *now*. Another Sunday may be too late! Cholera may sweep prophets and people to the grave.

iii. We should gratefully admire *the tender solicitude of Christ for the welfare of all his faithful ones*, whether ministers or people. He was anxious that the one should be received, and that both should be blessed. He sent his disciples abroad for the benefit of souls. That was all his desire; for he loved souls and died for them. But, in sending his disciples to minister to them, he willed that *they* should be well received, and therefore he put this honour and blessedness on their reception: "He that receiveth you receiveth *me*." O what adorable love and condescension! He is willing to be represented by mere men, and, what is more, to be received by beings who have sinned against him!

Have *we* then "received Christ"? Does he dwell with us, and are we welcoming any thing which reminds us of his readiness to come to us? Truly, dear brethen, we may, with all simplicity and affection say, "Receive *us*; we have wronged no man." We come again to you, after a little absence: "Receive us!" But more earnestly would we say, Let us all receive him, as well at all seasons as at the present opportunity, when at his own table he is waiting to receive ourselves! He is the great prophet of his Church. If sinners receive him they shall receive the Father also.

SERMON XII.

JESUS COMMANDING THE MULTITUDE TO SIT DOWN.[1]

John 6:10.

"And Jesus said, Make the men sit down."

THESE words are part of a narrative which describes a stupendous miracle, and an important conclusion from it. The miracle was the feeding of five thousand persons, to their full satisfaction, from only five loaves and a few fishes, while the very fragments, when collected, made up an amount of food which exceeded the original supply. The conclusion or inference which the people drew from it was, that he who wrought the miracle was that very Prophet whom, from the writings of Moses, they expected to come into the world. The mention of the coming of that Prophet is taken up by the Church as her note of preparation for the contemplation, on Sunday next, of the advent or coming of Christ to judge the world. We are thus taught to close and commence our ecclesiastical year with the first and last subject of all divine revelation and all Christian expectation.

At this present however, and for a somewhat incidental purpose, as will be shown, let us fix our attention on the very simple words, as they perhaps seem to us, which have been announced as our text.—"And Jesus said, Make the men sit down."

Let us contemplate these words first in their reference to the people, and then in their relation to Christ.

I. The words, *in their reference to the people*, were calculated to develop some of the most essential points of the Christian character.

1. They were *a strong appeal to implicit faith*. We must, in order to perceive this fact, call to mind the situation of the persons to whom they were addressed. The people had come on foot, in considerable numbers, from various places, and from a considerable distance. They had been in attendance as earnest hearers or interested spectators for the greater part of the day. It was now "evening," the sun was withdrawing his beams, and consequently "the time was past" for their convenient return. Added to this, they were in a "desert place," that is, in an uninhabited district, remote at least from places where provision could be purchased.

To be told then at such a time and in such a place *to sit down*, might appear to some very unreasonable or very doubtful.

It would be natural for the people to expect to be told anything rather than to sit down. It was time for rising up and going away rather than for sitting down and tarrying longer. Their anxieties therefore might well question the reasonableness of the command. Others might be perplexed and doubt-

[1] Preached Sunday Morning, November 23rd, 1851.

ful as to what was to follow. Whether they were going to be fed or further instructed, or whether they would be required to stay all night, or what among many imaginings might be the true result, no one could tell.

Under these circumstances there was room for practical faith. They had learned to believe that Jesus could do wonders for the sick, but they had yet to learn that he could do equal wonders for themselves. The command therefore to sit down was an appeal to their faith, to even their most implicit faith, for they were required to do what they could see no good reason for doing.

And has not God often required the like of others, and perhaps of ourselves? Did he not require it of "the father of the faith," when he commanded him, first, to quit his native land for an unknown locality, and then to sacrifice his only son? And has he not, in his providence, sometimes compelled some of us "to sit down," as it were, when we should deem it fitting to rise up? Has he not seemed to say, "Be *still!*" when our hearts have been saying, "Up and be doing"? Unquestionably many of us have been so circumstanced, as to feel that we can do nothing, when most we have wished to accomplish something. We have felt ourselves hedged in and helpless. We could only sit down, and believe that our quietness in so doing is the will of our Father concerning us. It has required implicit faith to observe that quiescence, but the result has proved its wisdom. Never can it be that we lose anything, in either time or value, by being content to obey a plain monition from our Father's hand. If that hand beckons us to stand still and see his intervention, we shall be gainers by obeying it. He will reward all faith; but quiet, self-denying, implicit faith generally insures his richest reward.

Of the words of our text we may further say,

2. *They were calculated to raise in all thoughtful minds satisfactory expectations.* Individuals who had strong belief in the despised One would almost intuitively conclude that such a seemingly unreasonable command was only the more really reasonable, because of some latent design which would soon develop itself. They would feel assured that he would not be likely to tell them to "sit down" without having some purpose of mercy to answer by it.

After this model God still deals with his people. If he so places them that they feel their inability to help themselves, and that he plainly bids them to "sit down," as it were, and be content to wait his will, without any factious stirrings to accomplish their own wishes, they may rest satisfied that he is about to do for them something better than they can do for themselves. When God thus prevents our own active endeavours, he does but bid us indulge favourable expectations of his mercy.

Possibly however, when the men began to sit down, they also began to imagine that Jesus did mean to provide refreshment for them. Upon this some would picture one mode of its provision, and some another. And yet, when the provision itself came, the mode of it was beyond all human picturing. Five barley loaves were invisibly and continuously multiplied, in such manner that no eye could trace the operation, or discern how the multiplication was performed.

Thus, in a season of quiet expectation, human imagination is generally very busy. We fancy that our help will certainly come at this time, or from that quarter. We mark out the mode to ourselves, or draw out a variety of plans respecting it. But in the issue we find that God's ways are not as our ways, neither are his thoughts as our thoughts. Our prayers are heard, and our desires or expectations accomplished; but there has been an unthought of procedure, and God has done his work in his own way. This then should teach us, on the one hand, to repress our imaginings, and on the other to increase our prayers. If we expect, we must still supplicate. If we wait, we must do it as they who keep their hearts quiet, and their souls in a heavenward position.

Of Christ's words, with respect to the people, we may also remark that

3. *They were fitted for trying the disposition of the people to obey him.* If they yielded to an injunction which some might deem unreasonable, and all might think questionable, they would at least show their willingness to be led. Their sitting down, at that late hour of the day, would be a proof that they had confidence in his measures, and were not tired of either his presence or his instructions.

Now what does our God delight in more than to see us ready to do his utmost will, and to submit to anything which he may lay upon us? Does he not watch and wait for the tokens of obedient disposition in all his people? He does: and when he sees us ready to obey his unexplained commands, ready to receive his word without questionings, and ready to give our full faith to all his requirements, he will not long leave us without the fulfilment of our wishes, or some satisfying manifestation of his gracious favour.

II. *The words of our text, in their relation to the Lord Jesus,* discover to us several interesting points of his own adorable character.

1. They show us *his own perfect consciousness of power over human hearts.* It is not to be supposed that he who was given to be "a Leader for the people" would issue a command to them which he could not enforce if they were disposed to disobey. Hence, in saying "Make the men sit down," he knew his own divine power over even a large multitude, so as secretly to constrain them to sit down. Far mightier was he than any who then saw him supposed him to be. Occasionally indeed he let it be seen that he possessed power to turn men's hearts

according to his good pleasure—as when the owner of the colt on which he rode, and the proprietor of the guest-chamber in which he celebrated the Passover, readily complied with his wishes, though they were expressed only by his disciples.

In the present instance therefore the command was no sooner given than it was obeyed. "The men sat down;" and, in beautiful keeping with the benevolence and thoughtfulness of the Saviour, it is added, "There was much grass in that place." He who at the beginning formed the grass of the field now appropriated it as a carpet for the convenience of his guests.

But, recurring to his power over the hearts of the multitude, we must never forget that he took that power with him into heaven, and can exercise it as effectually now as then. When he is pleased to bend a nation, a city, or an individual to his will, he can do it without noise or observation. Let him say "Arise!" or "Sit down!" as to anything connected with his gospel, and his Spirit can insure the speediest obedience to the command. Thus we read in David, "Thy people shall be willing in the day of thy power." That time of his power is solely in his own hands. We are to pray that it may always be the time for us, for without his power constantly with us what good thing shall we be able to do?

With reference to the words of Christ, as spoken by himself, we also see that

2. *They disclose to us somewhat of his method in dealing with his servants.* When he said, "Make the men sit down," he had ulterior intentions, but did not intimate them. His disciples were ready to suggest a plan for feeding the people; but it is significantly said, "Jesus himself knew what he would do." He knew, but he saw fit not to foreshow what he was about to do. He had rather, for wise reasons, let his method develop itself than suffer it to be pre-disclosed. Very like to this is his frequent dealing with ourselves. He brings us, as it were, into a desert place. He lets the day pass with us, and the shadows of a coming night surround us. Want of some sort presses on us, and we begin to feel perplexed. Presently expectation comes to us, and we look forward, but still nothing is clear or definite. God has not admonished us of the exact method which he means to adopt in our case. We must wait; and if we do but wait aright all will soon be done for us. But again, as to Christ's words,

3. *They are a part of a memorable illustration of his love of order and method.* The entire transaction, from beginning to end, was conducted with a precision which, as to its spirit at least, all the friends of Christ will do well to follow. First he bids all be seated, and that, as another evangelist tells us, *in rows* of fifty each. He then takes the loaves, pronounces a blessing on them, distributes portions of them to his disciples as his ministering agents, and they hand them to the people. Every thing is done with regularity, method, calmness. At length, when all have eaten to the full, he gives another command, "Gather up the fragments, that nothing be lost." Herein he taught the world a valuable lesson of becoming economy. Though he had miraculously multiplied the bread, and had furnished abundance of it, yet would he have no part of it wasted. The moral of this incident applies itself to a thousand cases in ordinary life. This however is not the time for dwelling further on this part of the subject. The Saviour's observance of order and precision is the topic which, as applicable to even the celebration of divine worship, I now beg to press upon your attention.

It was in the spirit of Christ, and in perfect accordance with this transaction, that St. Paul said, "Let all things be done decently and in order." There are some things which I have long wished to see done in better order and with more decency than they are done among ourselves. I am not about to allude to our parish church, or to any of its unseemly arrangements. On that topic *I hope* never to say another word, at least from this pulpit, except that my mind and my resolution are just as they were, only that I have no power to act. I am like one who is bidden to "sit down" and wait.

For now nearly seven years I have been weary of making alterations, or of even strongly noticing imperfections. I have had my reasons for it. But now, as we this day end, as to Sundays at least, one year, and shall begin another when we next meet, let me kindly and briefly point out to you the principal of those few things in which our order and decency may greatly be improved.

i. In coming to church *in good time* there is much need of more decency. It is an ill thing to be a minute too late, because the beginning of our service is one of its most important parts. It is too the service of the God of heaven; and therefore to be behind in it, except in cases of necessity, is an insult to him.

ii. *In following out the spirit of our beautiful service* there is much lack of order and edifying decency. We are improved certainly, but still we are deficient in fervour, regularity, and *continuance* of our respondings. Few seem to recollect that our prayer is "*common* prayer." They either never join in it at all with their voices, or they do it so feebly and so irregularly that it amounts to little or nothing. If they respond at first, they cease after a while, and then, as the service advances, they seem to make the voice of the clerk their proxy or substitute. "These things ought not so to be."

iii. *In attendance at the Lord's table*, for the celebration of his dying command, too many among us are still sadly in fault. If churchmanship were to be tested by such attendance on that holy ordinance as the church requires, how many among us would be reckoned dissenters! Let a word suffice. More will be added at another time if circumstances require it.

iv. *In the arrangement of our singing* some improvement may be made. As our congregational singing is much increased, I say no more than that it will always be pleasant to observe its progress. But, with the view to facilitate the labour of our children in some part of it, and to quicken our own interest in it, it has been suggested that in our chanting it will be pleasing and improving if we observe a modification of the very custom which we follow when *reading* what we chant; that is, instead of the minister alone and the people in common reciting a verse alternately, that this responsive mode of repeating the words should be maintained in the following manner, namely, for the minister (provided he can chant) and the people on the ground floor to take one verse, and for the choir and the people in the galleries to take another, both uniting in chorus in the doxologies and whenever the organ, by its fulness, gives the signal for so doing. As the children of the choir above and of the Sunday school below will be taught their respective parts, so the people in the galleries will be guided by the little choir, and the people on the ground floor by the Sunday scholars.

Something of this method was adopted during my recent absence. As it seems to be well received, I am willing to give it a fair and fuller trial. The only object in it for which I care is the greater interest and so the greater profit of the congregation in one of the pleasantest parts of divine worship. Our noble hymn the "Te Deum" is fatiguing to young voices when sung *continuously*. They generally get out of tune toward the end. The method now proposed, being *in fact* the original method, will obviate this difficulty, and make the repetition of that hymn easy and animating to all.

As Sunday next will be Advent Sunday, and the first of another ecclesiastical year, it is hoped that these brief remarks will then begin to be reduced to hearty and unanimous practice. May he who said, "Make the men sit down," give us a fresh impulse of soul in every part of his service, and feed our souls with the bread of life!

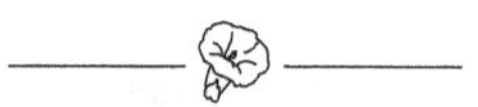

SERMON XIII.

THE THREE WHOM JESUS LOVED.[1]

John 11:5.

"Now Jesus loved Martha, and her sister, and Lazarus."

VARIETY of character is one mark of God's marvellous hand in moulding mankind. Similarity is often found, but identity never, so boundless is that variety to which allusion is made. To know it as a fact is necessarily common enough, but to exercise such discrimination of it as will subserve the high purposes of man's salvation, is a talent of exceeding value. Our blessed Lord, as the great Master in Israel, both knew the fact in its utmost extent, and treated it with inimitable wisdom. He met with great diversities of character; but none ever baffled his penetration or lost his most judicious management. Over all which presented even the semblance of his grace he cast the mantle of his love, while particular cases shared his tenderest and warmest affection.

The pleasant village of Bethany, at an easy distance from Jerusalem, furnished a memorable instance of this variety and of that affection. There was in it a family of three, two sisters and a brother. Each of the three differed as much from the other as well could occur; but the same love from the heart of Jesus encompassed them all: "Now Jesus loved Martha, and her sister, and Lazarus." Taking these three individuals as generic specimens of character, we shall find ourselves introduced to a very large circle of that spiritual family which Jesus always loves.

I. "*Martha, her sister, and Lazarus,*" are types of the three grand varieties which make up the every day character of the

[1] Preached Sunday Morning, November 19th, 1848.

Christian church. Martha was a Christian of many infirmities, Mary a Christian of superlative excellencies, and Lazarus a subject of great affliction. All three were real believers, and Jesus loved each of them; but neither resembled the other. We not unfrequently meet with individuals whom it is not easy to liken exclusively to any one of the three, so mixed are the features of each in those individuals. Still it will be found that infirmity, excellency, and affliction are commonly the component parts of the lot and character of most Christians. The degree of each may vary, but the existence of each is always traceable.

1. Martha was a Christian of many infirmities. Not the shade of a doubt is ever cast upon her as a truly good woman. And yet the pen of inspiration, which is always the pen of impartiality, has described her weak points and personal failings. Martha loved the Lord Jesus as her Saviour, and Mary as her sister; but her love for each did not always rise superior to her indulgence of besetting infirmities in her demeanour towards them. She was prone to that temper which borders on the peevish and the irritable, and which too commonly marks those who are wont to be over anxious about most things, and over nice and over particular in little things. We are too apt to be impatient and fretful and perhaps tart and hasty if we are molested in our supposed good management, or not so promptly assisted or obeyed as we fancy we ought to be, or possibly if we do not meet with quite so much deference and respect as we think should be justly shown us. Thus, on the memorable occasion of Christ's first recorded visit to Martha's house, we hear her intemperate words betraying her ruffled temper and her inconsiderate spirit. "Cumbered about much serving," that is, over intent and over bustling in arranging a mere table entertainment, Martha forgot the rules of spiritual decorum, and, in raising a complaint against her more devout and devoted sister, thoughtlessly impugned the Lord her Saviour: "Lord, dost thou not care that my sister hath left me to serve alone?" And, as though that inuendo were not enough, she must needs venture to dictate to her divinely royal guest: "Bid her therefore, that she help me!" Thus prominent were the infirmities of one who, at heart, was a kind and really good woman. Such anomalies are painful, but not surprising; because God's new principle does not absorb our old nature, but is grafted upon it. The natural disposition of the renewed sinner, is not, by his renewal, annihilated, and therefore, while still dwelling within us, it will strive if not for the mastery, yet for such indulgence as will insidiously betray and injure us. It is remarkable too, that of all infirmities which mar the Christian character those which Martha exhibited, namely, infirmities of temper, are the hardest to be remedied. Indeed, as our great English authoress many years ago sagaciously observed, "it is too frequently *the last* to be corrected." This pertinacity of the infirmity is no excuse for it, but should rather be looked upon as a reason for greater vigilance and deeper humiliation.

2. Mary seems to have been the younger of the two sisters; but she was the maturer Christian of the two. There is no intimation of a want of due consideration on her part for the hospitalities which were due to such a guest as then honoured the home of the three. She was fairly exempt from taking the lead in preparing them, as in all probability Martha prided herself in the cleverness of domestic management.

Mary's heart was set where ours should be. It was set on the things of Christ, and intently devoted to the riches of his doctrine, the interest of the soul, and the realities of eternity. It is probable too that she was a convert of no long standing. Very pardonable therefore was it in the younger sister to remain a listener at the feet of Jesus so long as he thought fit to speak in his usual ravishing strain of the most gracious and the most instructive wisdom. An angel might have coveted that seat of Mary from which the busy tongue of Martha would have dislodged her. The Lord Jesus himself not only discerned the superiority of Mary's task and choice, but openly commended it. He even contrasted it with Martha's ill-timed, though well intended, domestic solicitude: "Martha, Martha, thou art careful and troubled about many things: but one thing is needful: and Mary hath chosen that good part which shall not be taken away from her." (Luke 10:41, 42.) This gentle rebuke contains a standing lesson for the world and the church. It shows the mind of Christ as to our commonest things, and reveals his decided preference for that character and conduct of which Mary furnishes the pattern, beyond the utmost amount of all such solicitudes and attentions as Martha too evidently exhibited. Lively, hearty, and affectionate concern for the truth and cause of Christ, and for all that his gospel comprises as the treasure of our souls, is far dearer and more estimable in the sight of Christ himself than all the busiest efforts of the busiest hands, if the "good part" be not chosen as the first thing, and held to the last.

3. Lazarus, most likely, was the youngest of the family. We know less of him than of them. Of two things however we may be sure—that he was a very estimable person, and a great sufferer. He is marked out to us as the friend of Jesus, whom he especially loved. But we are left to sober conjecture for the peculiarities of his character. That conjecture leads us to conclude that, as Jesus very much loved him, he was a truly godly man of very lovely dispositions and kindly habits. In all probability he was assimilated to that style of character which marked our Lord himself as man among men. Devout and holy he must have been; and if great meekness, kindness, and docility filled up the remainder of his character, it is what we can readily suppose. Our curiosity is not told anything as to his illness. Doubtless he bore it in a becoming manner. Such cases are still extant.

Let us now look to what is said of the bearing of the Lord Jesus towards him and his.

II. "Jesus *loved* Martha, her sister, and Lazarus."

1. As a friend he visited them, and as a friend he loved them; for, as man, he had all the sympathies of man in his holy and immaculate nature.

It is the friendship of Jesus for such persons as comprised this little family which sanctifies all similar friendships among his people on earth. Without such sanctification there can be nothing really profitable in any friendship, nor anything which can look beyond the grave with a feeling of hope or a prospect of happiness.

The love however which Jesus bore to the three in family, though necessarily partaking of earthly sympathies, was eminently and essentially a holy and spiritual love. He loved their souls, and they loved his salvation. His conversations with the sisters exhibited the deepest interest in them as seekers of salvation, and as believers in his word and person for the attainment of it. All the love of Christ to us, and all our love to him, proceeds *now* solely on this foundation. Human sympathies, in their mutual exercise, ceased with his personal presence on earth; though, blessed be his name, his sympathy for us changes not in any of its spiritual realizations.

2. The sisters and the brother at Bethany seem to have duly appreciated the honour of their Saviour's love. They evidently esteemed it very highly, and with all earnestness and meekness testified their sense of its infinite value. Neighbours and acquaintances seem to have been well aware of the mutual esteem. In the case of Lazarus it was particularly well known: "Then said the Jews, Behold *how* he loved him!" This was honour indeed to be recognised, the one as the friend, and the whole as the family, whom the beloved Son of God greatly delighted in and personally favoured. No greater honour can be realized than for Christ in his providence to let it appear that he loves us, and that we love him.

3. But the *manner* in which Jesus testified his love to the three is as singular in itself as it is worthy of our consideration. He did not, be it observed, show that he loved them by everywhere talking of them, and lauding their excellencies, and professing his friendship for them. This would have tended to make them vain and others jealous. Our Lord was a wise Friend, and therefore abstained from what might prove injurious to those who enjoyed his friendship. For this same reason, while he did not extend the fame of the little family, he also did not cause to them an increase of temporal benefits. He who turned water into wine, and multiplied a few loaves and a few fishes into a banquet for thousands, had power by a word or a touch to have filled their house with abundant treasure. It would have been easy for him to let Martha find an entertainment ready to her hands, or her household stores increased profusely, or even her whole culinary apparatus turned into vessels of gold and utensils of silver. But the Friend who loved her and her sister and brother did no such marvels as these. His love met them in quite a different style. Martha he rebuked, Mary he kept in suspense, and Lazarus he permitted to sicken and to die. This indeed accords with the general rule of God's dealing with his people: "As many as I love I rebuke and chasten." He did thus indeed with all the three; only Martha and Lazarus seem to have borne, one the rebuke and the other the chastening, more than Mary. Martha, though loved, was chided in words which must have keenly touched her: "Thou art careful and *troubled* about many things." In common with Mary she was deeply affected at her brother's illness and death. They waited for the arrival of Jesus to whom they had sent when they saw their only brother sickening unto death. Doubtless their suspense was as tender as it was anxious. While one sister would turn to wait on the sufferer, the other would step to a portal or a lattice to look for the expected Physician. All would be increasingly painful as the illness of the sufferer progressed. Many doubts would secretly arise; many a fear would hover where love would not let it lodge, and many little sayings of mingled regret and wonder would be sure to escape those lips which the feelings of the heart would readily open. At length the sufferer draws his last breath and closes his eyes. Jesus is still absent, and the sisters have no alternative but to forward the burial of their beloved one. Thus did the Lord try those whom he loved; and so unlike are his ways to our ways. Eventually his love to the whole three shone forth, like the gradually increasing blaze of the glorious sun from behind a darksome cloud. Martha he instructed and soothed before he went to the grave. Mary he honoured and cheered by going *instantly* to the sepulchre, upon her making precisely the same remark as Martha had made. (Ver. 21, 32.) And Lazarus he called back to life, under circumstances the most remarkable that the world ever saw.

These, dear brethren, are instructive incidents. It behoves us to ponder them ere we let them pass. Let us call up a few reflections from them.

1. *The ministers of Christ should be prepared for the proper treatment of diversities of character.* Their study of Scripture truth is indeed their first labour; but the skill of rightly applying it to persons is their second. To think to treat all shades of character with the same spiritually artistic touch, is as unwise as it would be unprofitable. We must discriminate, and strive to catch the spirit and copy the manner of him whom no variety of human nature ever baffled.

2. *All Christians should love one another, spite of those little diversities which mark their character.* The Lord Jesus has in this

respect, as in all others, set us a noble example. His love was as elastic as human character is varied. He overlooked the little infirmity in the lustre of the greater excellence, and blessed and bound together one family, though comprised of very different persons. Our own families and our own friends generally present the like diversities, or even diversities of a far more serious nature; but parental love and Christian love are to spread, the one its wing, and the other its banner, over all who form our little circle.

3. *The Lord Jesus is himself "altogether lovely," and demands our supreme affection.* Not only did he love the three at Bethany, but the three loved him. Thousands saw the Saviour in Judea without the kindling of a spark of affection in their bosoms for him. This was their cruel sin: they despised and rejected him. If you do *the like* you will be "Anathema Maranatha." If the love of the world, or the love of any iniquity, shuts out the love of Christ from your souls, better will it be that you had not been born. But "love the Lord, all ye his saints!" even this same Lord who "loved Martha, and her sister, and Lazarus." He did not greater things for them than he has done for you.

4. *All families, but especially Christian families, should aim to be like the one at Bethany.* Family love is indeed a comely thing. "Behold how good and how pleasant it is for brethren to dwell together in unity! It is like the precious ointment on the head, that ran down upon the beard, even Aaron's beard, that went down to the skirts of his garments; as the dew of Hermon, and as the dew that descended upon the mountains of Zion: for there the Lord commanded the blessing, even life for evermore." (Psalm 133.) But how distressing and unsightly is it when a family is divided against itself! Such unsightliness is very painful when the love of Christ is "the bone of contention;" but it is sad and shocking when it is occasioned by the want of due regulation of temper in those who profess godliness.

5. *We should expect rebuke and trial, but wait on Christ for the issue.* He will try us. But in the day of the resurrection he will show his love gloriously!

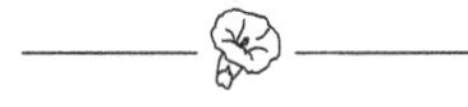

SERMON XIV.

BLIND BARTIMÆUS.[1]

Luke 18:38.

"And he cried, saying, Jesus, thou son of David, have mercy on me."

THIS was the prayer of a man who, though poor and blind, had once, as his very name indicates, been in affluent or honourable circumstances. Blind Bartimæus "sat by the wayside begging." There is not one of us but what may become blind, and even reduced to beggary. Such changes are every day the lot of many. We may experience the like.

Though he went, or perhaps was led, on the morning of a certain day, to his usual waiting-seat, and took it with his usual feelings, yet, without consciousness on his part, very unusual blessings were close to him. When he began the day, he little thought how happily it would end. God's deliverances or blessings are sometimes nearest to us, when we are least expecting them.

Through God's mercy Bartimæus, though blind, was not deaf. He *heard* "the multitude pass by." What is more, he retained his *speech*. "He *asked* what it meant."

How good is our God, even when he afflicts us with ill! It is a rare thing to find the total loss of the three senses at once. Generally a defect in one sharpens the power of another. Let sufferers then be thankful when, under any privation, they find many valuable things still left for their enjoyment.

In reply to his question, Bartimæus was told that "Jesus

[1] Preached Sunday Morning, March 3rd, 1851.

of Nazareth passeth by." The fame of this mysterious person had reached the ear of the blind mendicant. Immediately "his heart was hot within him." Longing desire, coupled with fervent hope, seized his whole soul. He stayed for no further inquiries. The moment was passing, and it might never return. With all his might therefore he cried out; but what did he cry? Not what he had just heard, not "Jesus of *Nazareth*," not Jesus the despised One of a despised town. No: faith raised his affections above the scorn of the world, and carried him to the true dignity of the beloved of God. Therefore he cried out, "Jesus, thou *son of David*, have mercy on me." Seeing then that all which the Lord Jesus did on earth, when the needy applied to him, was designed to show us what he will spiritually do for all spiritual applicants, now that he is in heaven, let us ponder the prayer of Bartimæus, and learn what we may from it.

I. *It was a prayer which proceeded from a deep sense of need, and was accompanied with intense desire for the relief of it.* The poor blind man *felt* that he was blind. It was the burden of his heart. The privation of sight was his great affliction. He no doubt regarded it as far more grievous than his poverty: for it would be natural for him to think that, if he had his sight, he could gain his subsistence. Hence his desire to be relieved of his blindness was intense, and paramount to every other object.

Exactly thus will it be with the awakened sinner. Such an one will be sure to *feel* his spiritual wants. The sense of them will press heavily on his soul. All other things will be light in comparison with them. Remove them, and he thinks he can be happy. His feelings, like the Scriptures, tell him that spiritually he is but a poor blind beggar, that he has lost his original wealth, and that he has been sitting in darkness, under the power of a foolish heart and a wicked world. Can we wonder then that such an one is earnest, anxious, importunate? Is it a marvel that he prays with all his heart, and desires with all his soul? Be assured that, unless you *feel* your spiritual wants as God's word describes them, you will never really pray; and conversely, unless you really pray, you have not yet felt your spiritual necessities. People may talk religion, and even interest themselves about things that relate to it; but, unless they *feel* that they are unhappy and undone without it, and earnestly seek to possess it, they are not religious.

II. It was a prayer *which indicated becoming views of himself, and a due appreciation of Christ.* Bartimæus was conscious that he had no claim on the attention or favour of Jesus. It may have been that his poverty, or his blindness, or even both, had been the consequence of some sin. He may have sunk from his former station through improvidence, or have incurred his blindness by some act of folly. At all events he knew that he had nothing to plead. He therefore appealed to Messiah's "*mercy*." "Jesus, thou son of David, have *mercy* on me."

He further *believed* in Jesus, not as being of Nazareth but of Bethlehem, and by recognising him as the son of David testified to all who heard him, that his faith was in Jesus as the promised Messiah. With Bartimæus then "faith came by hearing."

Now all these things must find a place in us. Our hearts must be humbled. We must disclaim every thought of merit. While our sins should humble us to the dust, our best services, if ever we have done any, should humble us within ourselves. "After ye have done *all*, say, We are *unprofitable* servants." Hence, the plea of Bartimæus must be ours. We must cast ourselves on the mercy of Christ. Whatever we desire must be for his mercy's sake. We must honour him as the free Giver of all that we desire to receive. This is solid truth.

Then, in crying to Christ, we must believe that he is all that we have been told he is. Our hearing must be turned into believing; or the hearing will no more profit us, than the hearing of Bartimæus would have profited him, had he continued to sit where he was, in cold and careless unbelief. It is our want of earnest, soul-felt, heart-stirring faith that keeps Christ from noticing us as often as he passes by us, or we present ourselves before him. "Without faith" in his exalted excellences, it is "impossible to please" him, or to receive any benefit from him. How should this thought startle multitudes of hearers into shame and fear! shame for past neglects, fear of future judgments.

III. It was a prayer *which no impediments could check.* The spirit of an earnest determination breathed in it. It was uttered as a drowning man utters his cry for help, with a resolution to utter it again, as oft and as loud as he can. Bartimæus was told to keep silence: but his prayerful tongue was not to be chained by any earthly restraint: "And they which went before rebuked him, that he should hold his peace: but he cried so much the more, Thou son of David, have mercy on me." (Verse 39.)

Alas, how many checks are attempted to be put on souls which, in the days of their awakening, are absorbingly intent on finding favour with Christ! In their distaste for former vanities, and their anxiety to be right and safe and peaceful, how many a rebuke do they hear, how often are they told to hold their words, and stop their doings, and banish their singularities! But no such impediments avail, where the heart is touched, and the soul enlightened, and the spirit taught to make prayer and supplication. "So much the more" will the impeded suppliant cry, "Thou son of David, have mercy on me!"

There are few things more certain than this: listless prayer will gain nothing; but "effectual fervent prayer" will gain every thing that is really good for us. "Ye ask, but have not, because ye ask amiss:" and nothing is so amiss in asking as coldness, and a mind that is easily diverted from at least its desire of asking. The throne of grace may well be said to be "taken by violence; and the violent taketh it by force."

IV. It was a prayer *which stayed the steps of Christ to listen to it.* "And Jesus *stood!*" says the evangelist.

The sun once stood still, when Joshua by a divine impulse commanded it so to stand: but now the Creator of that sun, the very Sun of Righteousness himself, stayed his course, at the prayer of a poor blind man. This was astonishing condescension; and angels might well have gazed with admiration on it. It should assuredly win our attention, and engage us to adore the compassion and readiness of our Friend in heaven. It should also fix in us a firm persuasion of the willingness of Christ to listen to every suppliant, and to sympathize with us in all our wants and solicitudes. It proves to us too the power of prayer, and the certainty of its arresting the notice of him who is ever "more ready to hear than we are to pray."

One circumstance in the narrative must not escape us in this part of our contemplation of it. When Bartimæus cried to Jesus, a multitude was thronging him; and many voices, most likely, were busily sounding around him. But, spite of the throng, the busy hum, and the many things to occupy attention, Jesus *heard* the man. So now, though surrounded by the hosts of heaven, and intent on the rapturous worship of the countless multitude, the feeblest cry of the feeblest saint reaches his ear. The very sighing of a contrite heart ascends in all its truthful simplicity to him; and he *stands*, as it were, at its lowly summons.

When "Jesus stood," he spoke, "and commanded him to be brought unto him." This shows that the suppliant was at some little distance, and that his blindness was no pretence. He would have sprung forward to him, or have flung himself before him, could he have seen to do it. The miracles of our Lord will always bear the most searching investigation. They were never done in a corner, as those pretended miracles are, with which Antichrist deludes his devotees. In the case of Bartimæus due preparation, we see, was made for the open performance of a great deed. Every body knew and saw that he was blind.

Jesus asked the man, "What wilt thou that I shall do unto thee?" There was no *need* on the part of Christ to be informed; for he knew before hand all the desire of Bartimæus. Still he would have him *express* it. This is ever the Lord's way. He knows the wish of our hearts, better than we know it ourselves, but he will have us tell it to him in prayer, as much as though his knowledge depended on our prayerful telling. The expression of our mind and meaning, whether to God or man, gives emphasis, and betokens sincerity.

Thus interrogated the poor man replied, "Lord, that I may receive my sight." Thus he gave utterance to adoration and faith. By calling him "Lord," who was so poor that he "had not where to lay his head," he acknowledged his *divine* nature: and by the word "*receive*" he showed his firm faith in Christ's power to bestow. He called him "Lord" also, while the Pharisees were calling him "a *sinner*." This, in the face of a multitude (and how many great perons, or how many spies, were in it, the blind man could not see even to guess), this was boldness added to faith. Thus must we also approach the same Lord and Saviour, if we would be accepted of him. We must adore him, believe him, and boldly confess him.

V. It was a prayer *which triumphantly prevailed.* (Verse 42.) Here we behold the son of David acting as "David's Lord." Who but he could in his own strength speak such words? Who but he, who at the beginning said, "Let there be light!" could have dared to say, "Receive thy sight!" But he did say it: and, as in the one instance "there was light," so in the other "sight" followed close on the word: "*immediately* he received his sight." It is not said, immediately he received sight: but it is expressly said, "*his* sight." The difference is great. He instantly recovered not merely the faculty of seeing, or a mere portion of sight, as sufferers with us after an operation on the eyes; but he "immediately received *his* sight;" his former sight, the degree which he had once enjoyed. He did not require to be kept in the shade, or to *learn* to see, to *learn* to judge of distances and other things, and to come to the gradual exercise of his recovered faculty; but he was made whole in his vision at once. And this was testified by his instantly joining the multitude and following his Lord.

What a picture is this of the grace of Christ under the gospel! Sinners cry to him. He hears them. He does for them "exceeding abundantly." They rejoice in recovering their spiritual sight, and quickly exercise it in following him along the path by which he leads them. His work for them is perfect. All who observe it know it, and, best of all, they who experience it. Their concern and effort will be to glorify him who has done such great things for them. They will join his throng of adoring ones, and study to praise him in heart and lip and life. This they will do as a sort of natural result from the spiritual change wrought in them. Jesus said to Bartimæus, "Thy faith hath saved thee." And Bartimeaus proved his faith by his works. This is exactly what every enlightened and saved sinner will habitually aim to do.

In a word, the prayer of the blind suppliant issued in the gladsome light of praise. It testified what myriads of cases before and since have testified, that the prayer of faith always prevails. Let this be our encouragement in fervency and perseverance.

It behoves you to lay to heart,

1. *That the prayer of Bartimæus must be your prayer, or you will never be saved.* "Jesus, thou son of David, have mercy on me," may be said to be the universal prayer of the universal company of Christ's saved ones. None, among adults at least, are saved but what feel their need of him; and all who feel their need of him will say to him, "Have mercy on us!" Monarchs and mighty ones, as well as the meanest and feeblest, must bend their hearts, and lift their cries to him, or perish for ever.

The time will inevitably come to each one of you, dear friends, when you will wish to be as earnest and as successful as was blind Bartimæus. The flush of health will soon fade away. The sands of life will ere long run out, and perhaps unawares. The feebleness of decay and the pallor of death will speedily settle upon us, and they may so settle any day. And what if, when such things come to pass, and you cry for mercy, the Lord should refuse to hear? He says he *will* refuse to hear then, if you refuse to hear now: "Then shall they call upon me, but I will not answer: they shall seek me early, but they shall not find me." (Proverbs 1:28.) How dreadful will it be thus to "mourn at the last!" No beloved relative can help you in that case, nor any steadfast friend make atonement for you under it. They must let that alone for ever. You will be left to yourself, and there will be none to help. Then be persuaded to set about the work of salvation by Jesus in right earnest. Cry to him, "Jesus, son of David, have mercy on me." And believe too

2. That "*now* is the accepted time, *now* is the day of salvation." Bartimæus seized the favourable moment. Jesus was passing by. He never, most likely, passed by that way again. Had Bartimæus indolently sat still, or plied his importunities for begging alms alone, he might have died in his blindness. So, if you are spiritually idle, if you are intent upon your businesses, or any other avocations only, you may let slip your last unsuspected opportunity, and lose your own souls. Now is the Lord's time. O let it be yours! He is present now, and, as it were, passing by. He may never return again to you. Then hear, as though you were never to hear again. Cry to him as though this were your only opportunity. It may in reality be such, for aught you know. Remember also

3. *That all true suppliants should persevere and rejoice in hope.* Let none be daunted by petty rebukes. Meet them forbearingly, and turn them into incentives for greater earnestness. And, now that the symbols of the presence of the son of David are before us, let us seek for his mercy with greater fervour. And let us look forward to the day when a great multitude, which no man can number, shall follow him to the inmost heaven. Can we see ourselves among them?

SERMON XV.

JESUS WEEPING OVER JERUSALEM.[1]

LUKE 19:41, 42.

"And when he was come near he beheld the city, and wept over it saying, If thou hadst known, even thou, at least in this thy day, the things which belong unto thy peace! but now they are hid from thine eyes."

THE position of our Lord, when he spake these words, was wondrously majestic and deeply affecting. He was on his way to Jerusalem. He was going thither for the last time, and that on purpose to meet the atoning crucifixion which he knew awaited him. But he was fulfilling an ancient and an important prophecy. He was riding on an ass, and yet, amid the acclamations of the multitude, was advancing as a king. His meekness was abundantly manifested, his rightful claim to sovereignty was openly acknowledged, but his real dignity was purposely concealed. Arriving however at a point of the hilly

[1] Preached Sunday Morning, November 3rd, 1850.

road, from whence Jerusalem was nearly[1] and clearly seen, he paused, not so much to gaze on its beauty and magnificence, as to weep over its enormous iniquity and inevitable misery, as though his human mind grasped its grandeur and its sin, its unparalleled privilege, and its almost unequalled profligacy: and then, forecasting the horrid sufferings and the thorough desolations which were preparing for it, he threw a last sad look upon it and wept, as no human eyes had ever wept before. Let the text, with its own touching simplicity, place the whole scene before us: "And when he was come near he beheld the city and wept over it, saying, If thou hadst known, even thou, at least in this thy day, the things which belong unto thy peace! but now they are hid from thine eyes." This was written, not merely for our historical information, but for our spiritual learning. May we be willing and prayerful learners of what, by God's enlightening and enabling grace, we hope to teach you.

There are four things to which, as contained in the text, your attention will be principally directed. The first is

I. *The compassion of the Lord Jesus toward the sinful and the perishing.* "He *wept* over it!" Tears are the relief of a burthened spirit when not actually fast bound in iron misery. The very sympathies of our nature are so many sisters to even manly tears. For never is it a weakness to weep, when a man's best feelings are strongly stirred. A man without a tear is a man almost without a soul. Stern and strong he may be, but angelic or amiable he cannot be.

It may be worth the expenditure of a little minute to remind you that the noblest and highest of our race have *wept.* Patriarchs and prophets were men of tears. Monarchs and warriors have been the like. History tells us of Xerxes weeping at the sight of his immense armament, because he thought that not a man of it would be living when a hundred years were gone. The Roman Claudius Marcellus wept as he looked down upon Syracuse, and revolved in his mind the horrors of sword and flame, which his soldiers were about to bring on that splendid city. And king David wept, yea, wept very bitterly, when going as an exile up the very hill, the ancient Olivet, down which the Lord Jesus was going as a royal but guiltless malefactor, when he wept as recorded in our text.

But why are these things named? It is the more forcibly to impress upon you the momentous doctrine of our Lord's humanity. It is as much a fundamental article of our creed that he "was made man," as that he is "God of God, very God." Without his perfect humanity there could be no sympathy toward us; and without his Godhead there could be no salvation for us. The two natures united in one person constitute the Christ, the only Mediator between God and man.

Now the fact of our Lord's weeping over Jerusalem abundantly attests his perfect humanity, and shews how thoroughly he partook of our nature. He wept as Hebrews and heathens weep, though they could not possibly weep as he wept. There was a depth, an intensity, and a meritorious value in his tears, which by no possibility could be found in the tears of any mere man.

And then *why* and at *what* did he weep? It is a mighty question. He wept, not as a selfish man, but as a true patriot, and as one whose soul was grieved for sin. He "wept over" Jerusalem. He did not weep at the prospect of the indignities and death which he was to suffer at Jerusalem, but at what Jerusalem itself would suffer because of its iniquities. Here was his amazing compassion for the guilty, the doomed, and the perishing! He wept over the so-called "holy city" because it had become "the cage of every unclean bird," and was about to be "swept with the besom of destruction." And where is that compassion now? It is exactly where it was, in the infinite capacities of his own immaculate bosom. On the throne of his mediatorial intercession he exercises all the sympathies of manhood, with all the wisdom, truth, and holiness of his Godhead. He is grieved for sinners. He willeth not the death of one of them, but rather that they should repent and live. But, when they *will not* repent and turn to him, his compassion, though not changed, is superseded by his justice. He will by no means, because he cannot consistently by any means, clear the impenitently guilty. Let this thought sting the heart of many an one who "goeth on still in his wickedness," if haply the smart may lead him to seek the only balm which can assuage it. Next in course of consideration is

II. *The equity and mercy of God in granting sinners opportunity for salvation.* Jerusalem had long been the sink of iniquity, the slaughter-house of the prophets, and the grave of true religion. Still the offended Jehovah would not destroy without warning, nor bring a last day without giving a previous day for thought and repentance. Jerusalem therefore had had her day. It had been a long and latterly a very bright day. The Light of life and the Prince of peace had come down to her. But, instead of being loved and received, "he was despised and rejected." The day consequently was all but gone, and the doom was virtually sealed: "If thou hadst known, even thou, *in this thy day!*" How characteristic, but how affecting, is the emphatic repetition of the word "thou, *even thou!*" It is as though the weeping Saviour had said, "Wicked as thou art, '*even thou,*' the most wicked of all wicked cities, because the most highly favoured, 'even thou' hast had a long day of respite and a winning call to reconciliation!" Yes, it was indeed a day for Jerusalem, when her streets, her suburbs, and her daughter-towns and villages were visited by him who was the Beloved of Jehovah, the Friend of sinners, who spake as never man spake, who went about doing marvellous good to souls and bodies, and by

[1] W. H. H. here meant not "almost" but nearness. This may have been a typesetting error for "nearby" in the original book.

whose quiet presence "the whole city was moved, saying, Who is this?" Yes, it was a day, the brightest parts of which were when Herod the king was visited by the wise men who told of his birth; when, as a child, he astonished the sages of the Temple; and when, at his passover visits and at other seasons, he preached, conversed, argued and wrought miracles. These were the cardinal hours of a day, which, as it had a beginning, had also an end. It was a day which magnified the mercy of God who gave it, and proved the night of those who closed the eyes of their heart against it.

To sinners of every locality does the same God grant a similar day. To how many of you is he granting it now! With how many is he still bearing, amid their habitual frivolity and constant earthliness! What multitudes are there, in even our own city, who by open vice or secret profligacy are daring the God of mercy to cut them down in judgment! And who shall count the number of those who, though they hear Christ, do not believe Christ? who, though they come within sound of his gospel, do not obey it? And how many an individual has been favoured with a day of greater grace than others, and yet knows it not to any profit for the soul! Such an individual has been met with alarming sickness, with afflictive warnings, with checks of fortune (as it is called), and above all with deep convictions. Some circumstance, some providence, or it may be even some sermon, has aroused the slumbering conscience and made it, for the moment, think of repentance toward God, and faith in our Lord Jesus Christ. But Satan, the world, or the flesh, has interposed, quenched the mounting spark, and darkened the rising dawn. The special day has thus been lost, and God may never send another.

But O the equity and the mercy of our God, in granting any day at all! He might righteously cut off the sinner in his first sin, or give him but an hour's warning. On the contrary, what is the whole life of some men but a stretch of God's mercy in sparing them? They sin; he forbears, and they sin the more. Thus their day only ripens them for the "sudden destruction" which is coming upon them. Their self-invited doom is everlastingly dark; but the equity and mercy of our God will, to all eternity, shine forth. Never will a sinner perish who can truthfully say that he received judgment without mercy. In some way or other mercy, it will be found, has met him, spared him, and pleaded with him. So that our God will be clear when unbelieving hearts judge him.

Let us further weigh and practically regard

III. *The unspeakable importance of knowing the things which belong to our peace.* "If," said our Lord of Jerusalem, "thou hadst *known*, even thou, *the things that belong to thy peace!*" Immediately afterward he also speaks of the time of Jerusalem's visitation: "Thine enemies shall lay thee even with the ground, and thy children within thee; and they shall not leave in thee one stone upon another; because thou knewest not the time of thy visitation." (Verse 44.[1]) The two things are virtually the same. The day granted for knowing peace is the time of visitation. Only in the former expression our Lord referred more pointedly to certain things which marked the time of visitation. The things which belonged to the peace of Jerusalem are, in essence, the same as what belong to our own individual peace.

1. It belonged to the peace of Jerusalem *to know its own dreadful hostility toward God.* Instead of knowing this Jerusalem disbelieved it, and not only disbelieved it, but avowed the very opposite. It had a zeal for God, and professed allegiance to him, boasting of his being its king, and itself his most loyal subject. But the foolish heart of the people was darkened. They were "enemies to God by wicked works." They loved not him, but their own carnal notions of him. Consequently, while they gloried in being his children through Abraham, they were, as our Lord peremptorily told them, "of their father the devil." Precisely thus is it with all who know not the truth respecting themselves. They say, "Peace, peace, when there is" not only "no peace," but positive enmity. "For the carnal mind is enmity against God." Men fancy their acquiescence in certain things is a proof of their being agreed in all things. But their mistake is fearful. There is no peace between God and the soul, so long as that soul is set on earthly things, without being humbled, renewed, and sanctified, by the Holy Spirit's application of the blood of Christ.

2. It belonged to the peace of Jerusalem *to acquaint itself with God.* It was a patriarchal maxim, as true as it was ancient, "Acquaint thyself with him and be at peace: thereby good shall come unto thee." It was the duty of Jerusalem, on hearing the voice of John the Baptist, to inquire, not affectedly and hypocritically as, alas! the priests and Levites did, but earnestly, sincerely, and, with hearty affection, as to who the Lamb of God really was. John indeed pointed him out, and all his own demeanour proved the truth of his divine pretensions. But Jerusalem took no pains to search into the case. It rather slurred it over, applied a thicker veil to its own heart, and hated every thing which corroborated the claims of Jesus of Nazareth. It delighted in the vain traditions of men, and spurned the word of God. No peace therefore dwelt in the city, nor was any thing known about it as it ought to have been known.

To this hour earthly hearts professing to know God in works deny him. They contain no honest and unprejudiced desire to be acquainted with him, through the humbling and purifying gospel of his dear Son. One consequence is that they know not, to any practical and salutary effect, the things which continually fall on their ears. They are not willing to acquaint themselves with what runs counter to their will, and so fail of peace with an offended God.

[1] See verses 43–44.

3. It belonged to the peace of Jerusalem *to welcome him who came down from heaven to her.* Her grandees, as well as her other inhabitants, should have done as Simeon and Anna and a few others did. They should have said, "Blessed is he that cometh in the name of the Lord!" He was the great peace-maker between God and man. But Jerusalem had no heart for the welcome of such a visitant. Hence she fell under the wrath of him who did not spare.

Always has it been that the reception of Christ has proved the peace of the soul. There is no fleeing from the wrath to come, but through himself as the way to a reconciled Father. "Christ is our peace," but he is made such to us only when welcomed by faith in the soul. If we fail of knowing him, we fail of knowing either peace now or salvation in eternity.

But happily the soul which welcomes the Son of God shall be saved. Our Lord's words over Jerusalem imply this. Scholars recognise in those words a form of speech called *aposiopesis*, that is, a sudden silence, or abrupt breaking off, when something either very bad or very good is intended: "*If* thou hadst known!" The thing implied is, that the greatest benefit would have followed a right knowledge of duty and a right improvement of privilege. Hence the unspeakable importance of seizing the gracious opportunity, and not letting slip the day of visitation. But this is enhanced by

IV. *The certainty that mercies despised will seal our condemnation.* "But now are they" (the things which belong unto thy peace), "*hid from thine eyes!*" To pronounce such a sentence, and to know that it is inevitable, is fully enough to open the fountain of any eyes. Well might the channel of all compassion be itself choked with grief, at uttering words so awful! Divine truth however is infinitely energetic; so that the lips which said, "Him that cometh unto me I will in no wise cast out," will not falter when compelled to say, "Depart from me, ye cursed!"

Still it is always a searching task to any preacher, who feels that himself is unworthy of any mercy, to tell others that, if they despise their mercies and disregard their privileges, their eyes will be judicially blinded, and their souls irretrievably lost. How fearfully the bandage of reprobation was bound over the eyes of the great men of Jerusalem, we can plainly discern in their horrid hard-heartedness, at mocking and taunting the meek and holy Jesus, when he hung upon the agonizing cross. The things which belonged to their peace through him were so hidden by judgment from their eyes, that they *could not* relent. Their determined impenitence became a part of their settled punishment. And so will it be with even yourselves, if you trifle with your spiritual opportunities, and either despise or let pass unimproved your day of grace and your time of visitation. When parishioners and hearers come within the range of a prayerful and painstaking ministry, and hear the truths of eternity (for our gospel is the everlasting gospel) faithfully (no matter how humbly if but faithfully) expounded, they will certainly be in danger of judicial indifference and penal unconcern, if they take no pains to *know* the things that are done for them and spoken to them. As they grow older they will grow harder. The inner eye will become duller and duller, and God will either close it up, or remove the things which it once saw. O that the trifling, the scornful, the negligent, the prejudiced, would think of these solemn truths!

Recurring to our text as a portion of a remarkable and memorable narrative, we shall be at no loss to find other topics for the gravest thought.

1. *The text is a link of a tremendous prophecy.* That prophecy was fulfilled to the utmost of the very letter. The text therefore is one of the pillars of the New Testament, as to its perfect authenticity and divine inspiration. All that befel Jerusalem in the day of its destruction was clearly foreseen, and graphically foretold, by him who wept over it. Hence the infidel is challenged to stand to his infidelity if he can, while the page of profane history confronts him with the seige of Jerusalem under the Roman Titus.

2. *The text is also a manifestation of the wonderful love of Christ for the Jewish nation.* Why went he not to any of the greater cities of the world to weep over them? The answer is to be found in the fact that Jerusalem was his metropolis, that himself was a Jew, and that the very humanity which he carried with him into heaven, and which he still sustains, was and is after the Jewish form. He also was and is the King of the Jews. Many a strong verity is pledged for the restoration of his Israel. St. Paul, though the apostle to the Gentiles, has said that the restoration of the Jews shall be to the world at large "as life from the dead." When the day of that life shall come, then shall the reign of our Saviour Christ be what as yet it is not. It will be acknowledged and felt and loved in every corner of the earth. "Rejoice ye with Jerusalem and be glad with her, all ye that love her; rejoice for joy with her, all ye that mourn for her: that ye may suck, and be satisfied with the breasts of her consolations; that ye might milk out, and be delighted with the abundance of her glory. For thus saith the Lord, behold, I will extend peace to her like a river, and the glory of the Gentiles like a flowing stream: then shall ye suck, ye shall be borne upon her sides, and be dandled upon her knees. As one whom his mother comforteth so will I comfort you; and ye shall be comforted in Jerusalem. And when ye see this your heart shall rejoice, and your bones shall flourish like an herb: and the hand of the Lord shall be known toward his servants, and his indignation toward his enemies." (Isaiah 66:10–14.)

This prophecy opens to us a wide and brilliant field of hallowed expectation. Let us rejoice to sow our seed in it. It may be despised by those who look only upon its present fallow: but when it begins to spring forth and bud they will be ashamed of their neglecting to help its progress. In the course of a few Sundays opportunity, if it please God, will be afforded in this Church for the prayers and alms of those who desire "the peace of Jerusalem."

3. The text, by the force of contrast, reminds us *that the Lord Jesus will never again weep over Jerusalem.* His tears are dried for ever. He is reaping and will reap the joy which his precious sorrows once sowed for him. When he comes again (not on an ass, but in the clouds of heaven), it will be to bow all things to himself. There will be joy indeed in that morning. And you, Christian brethren, shall rejoice with him!

SERMON XVI.

THE DREAM OF PILATE'S WIFE.[1]

MATTHEW 27:19.

"When he was set down on the judgment-seat, his wife sent unto him, saying, Have thou nothing to do with that just man: for I have suffered many things this day in a dream because of him."

THIS text is remarkably comprehensive. It tells us of three individuals, singularly opposite in character, but somewhat relative in their position, Pilate, his wife, and Jesus. It tells us therefore of a husband and a wife, a prisoner and a judge, a governor of a province and "a man of sorrows" who had not "where to lay his head." But then, as to the husband and the wife, the one is a hopeful and the other a hopeless character. The prisoner too is innocent, and the judge is guilty. The governor of the province also had no power but what was given him by the very "man of sorrows," who was in disguise the Governor of the universe.

The text however, besides telling us of these persons, tells us of something mysterious, something connected with the world of spirits—*a dream*—a communication, there is reason to believe, from God himself. The occasion of the dream was this. During the unrighteous trial of the Lord Jesus, divine care was taken to make his innocency plain to even his bitterest enemies. After the Jewish authorities had condemned him in their own corrupt court they led him away to Pontius Pilate, for the purpose of obtaining his sanction and death-warrant. Amid their clamour and Pilate's guilty hesitation a strange and solemn warning was given to all parties, but especially to Pilate himself. "When he was set down on the judgment seat, his wife sent unto him, saying, Have thou nothing to do with that just man; for I have suffered many things this day in a dream because of him."

Let us contemplate from these words

I. *An attestation of the innocency of the Lord Jesus.* Pilate's wife calls him "that *just* man." The Jews indeed *knew* that he had done no wrong. Pilate also "knew that for envy they had delivered him," and was evidently conscious that he was a mysteriously upright person, for he openly said "I find no fault in him." But, that nothing might be wanting to convince the judge of the innocency of his prisoner, his wife is made the instrument of a thrilling appeal to his heart and conscience. By a supernatural dream or vision she is convinced that Jesus of Nazareth, about whom all the city was in an uproar, deserved protection and not punishment. She was certified that he was a fearfully just and holy person.

This strange truth was announced to Pilate at the very time he most needed the assurance of it. Apparently too it was announced by a messenger in the hearing of all.

Thus careful was the Almighty Father of the character of his beloved Son, when standing, for our sakes, as a malefactor before a heartless judge. He was careful to have the innocen-

[1] Preached Sunday Morning, April 5th, 1845.

cy of his Son made as clear as the light of his own heaven, although it was not consistent with his purpose that wicked men should at the time be affected by it. The innocency of Jesus *as man* was essential for the redemption of the world. Prophecy had of old pointed him out as "the Holy One" who should be the grand concentration of all purity and truth. Types too and ceremonies had joined in representing him as the fount of sanctity for the whole family of God. In fact, all Scripture proclaimed him as "the Lord our righteousness," as a sacrifice for sin so unblemished as to insure acceptance, and a surety for sinners so holy in himself as to impart holiness to others. It was necessary therefore that the innocency of the despised Jesus should be attested at the very time of his condemnation for our sakes. His innocency is that blessed fact upon which all our happiness depends, because we have no innocency of our own, and yet "without holiness no man shall see the Lord." As he was "holy, harmless, undefiled, and separate from sinners," he could accomplish for man an innocency and a righteousness which guilty man could not accomplish for himself. Being "made sin for us," while himself knew no sin, we by faith can be made righteous in him. Suffering and dying, "the just for the unjust," he rescues every contrite sinner from the curse of the law, and restores him to the favour of God. Well therefore may we admit the importance of the attestation of the wife of Pilate.

The text also presents to our contemplation

II. A *proof of God's sovereign power over spirits*. The text informs us of a Roman lady—a lady, be it remembered, who was not a Christian, but a pagan—whose mind was powerfully impressed with correct views and deep sympathies respecting One whom she perhaps had never seen, and of whom till recently she had never heard. Amid the occupations and gaieties of a foreign court in a foreign land, she probably had not found many individuals who interested themselves with the tales of a certain singular enthusiast who was going about "doing good" indeed, but teaching doctrines which created confusion and alarm. But by a strange and exciting dream her mind is so wrought upon, that she openly declares her conviction of the sacredness of his character and the truth of his cause. With all firmness, but with all decorum, she befriends the persecuted Galilean, and in opposition to the Jewish rulers attests him to be a "just man."

What was the real extent of the impression made on the mind of Pilate's wife we are not told. Whether she had been one of the honourable women who devoutly favoured Jesus, or whether she afterward became a faithful follower of his doctrine, we have no means of knowing. It is however plain that, for at least the time, the finger of God had powerfully touched her heart.

The means which he used for this purpose was "*a dream*:" "I have suffered many things this day in a dream because of him;" meaning that early in the morning ("this day") she had been much agitated by a dream or waking vision respecting the prisoner then before her husband, and that the dream was of such a nature as to convince her of the innocency of Jesus, and of the danger of having any thing to do with his condemnation. What the dream, as to its particularity of incident, really was, it is useless to conjecture. It is sufficient for us to know that, from its general character, and the manner in which the evangelist notices it, it was, as Theophylact concludes, *not* a suggestion of the devil to hinder the work of redemption by avoiding the death of Christ, but a communication from God for the testimony of his Son's innocence, and for the salvation of the woman's soul.

In the earlier ages of the Church such communications were common. Elihu, at a very early period, describes such a communication: "For God speaketh once, yea twice, yet man perceiveth it not; in a dream, in a vision of the night, when deep sleep falleth upon man, in slumberings upon the bed, then he openeth the ears of men, and sealeth their instruction, that he may withdraw man from his purpose, and hide pride from man. He keepeth back his soul from the pit, and his life from perishing by the sword." (Job 33:14–18.) Joseph, the husband of the mother of our Lord, was twice "warned of God in a dream." In like manner were the magi or wise men who came from the east to Bethlehem.

Not that we are to credit dreams generally; for in most instances they are either capable of easy solution, or from their very nature are shown to be senseless or incoherent. But it would be impious to deny God's power of influencing our own spirits by dreams, or any other means which he chooses to employ. There are some dreams in even the present day which are so remarkable that it is vain to deny the spiritual agency which has caused them. All such dreams however carry with them their own witness, and are not left to the interpretation of our own fancies. Doubtless also there are times and occasions when God, who is the ruler of our hearts and director of our thoughts, so orders our dreams as to make them lessons, warnings, checks, or admonitions, as circumstances may require. There are holy dreams, as well as wicked and licentious dreams. There are also dreams which leave a calm and devout impression on the mind of a Christian as he wakes up into conscious existence; and verily there are dreams which sadly annoy wicked men in their career of worldliness and vice. Those wicked men go to sleep with the thoughts of some licentious project or of some sinful device: their hearts are full of the evil, and their imaginations are polluted with its anticipated enjoyment. "By this time to-morrow," think they, "all will be sure;" but, lo! they fall asleep, and some annoying dream scares them in the night. They fancy they see Satan, or Death, or the day of judgment, or some other scene of terror or alarm.

Now let men always regard *such* dreams as *true*, because they are either the arousings of conscience or the warnings of God.

God's power over our spirits is a wonderful fact. It is beyond our understanding, but not beyond our perception. He can make, not only a dream, but a mere thought, a single word, the glance of an eye, the toll of a bell, the crowing of a cock—yea, the veriest trifles—he can turn them all into mighty instruments of speech to our souls.

But this power of God is the power of a sovereign. He exerts it where he will and as he will. Hence Pilate's wife, and not Pilate himself, is the chosen subject of it: "There shall two be in the field, the one shall be taken, and the other left; two women shall be grinding at the mill, the one shall be taken, and the other left." (Matthew 24:40, 41.)

The text further invites us to contemplate

III. *An instance of good advice faithfully and kindly given*: "Have thou nothing to do with that just man." As a lady Pilate's wife might have readily devised excuses for not sending to her husband about her dream. She might have pleaded his manly wisdom and her feminine character, as well as the impropriety of interfering with him as a judge, or the unseemliness of sending a cautionary message to him when actually administering judgment. But God had touched her heart, and all excuses vanished. He had shown her the truth, and therefore she was in right earnest. Speedily did she obey her honest convictions, and intrepidly and faithfully advised her husband to take no part in the condemnation of Jesus the just.

Now her conduct, dear, brethren, furnishes a bright example for ours. We are to be faithful in admonishing one another. It is an express command and a positive duty: "Not forsaking the assembling of ourselves together, as the manner of some is; but *exhorting* one another, and so much the more as ye see the day approaching."

It is an easy thing to find excuses for the avoidance of this duty: but it will not be an easy thing to cancel their guilt when the day of judgment shall reveal the full extent of our mutual obligation.

If we *know* that a relative, friend, or neighbour is doing wrong, or is likely to do wrong, it is our bounden duty kindly but faithfully to admonish him of that wrong or of his danger in doing it. A thousand cases may occur in which a wife may thus advise a husband, or a husband advise a wife. And if we consider that most common of all wrong-doings, the neglect of the soul and of him who died for it, opportunity will rarely be wanting to follow the example of Pilate's wife. But, as the best advice avails not without God's grace, all our admonitions should be accompanied with consistency on our part, and with earnest prayer for the person admonished.

Pilate, alas! heeded not the admonition of his faithful wife, and so stained his soul with guilt and his name with infamy. But Pilate was left without excuse; and so are all sinners who heed not the call of the gospel or the cry of conscience. As the admonition of Pilate's wife is precisely that which the ministers of Christ may address to their people, suffer me in conclusion to say:

1. "*Have nothing to do with* the condemnation of *that just man.*" See that ye have no part in crucifying him afresh. Sin not against Jesus by rejecting his redemption or perverting his gospel. Put him not to secret shame by an unholy heart, or to open shame by a wicked life.

Alas, how many do in principle what Pilate did in practice! and yet if they allow not the principle they virtually follow the practice. Thousands in every large population are indifferent to the name of Christian. Others, who call themselves by that name, and observe some of the forms of Christianity, are inconsistent in their calling and unsteady in their observances. They do not follow out their calling. "They mind earthly things" beyond their due proportion, and practise vanities which they profess to renounce. They come to church, but not earnestly, not steadily, not under a sense of that duty to which all inferior duties on the Lord's-day are to give place. They also sometimes come, it may be, to the Lord's table; but how many times do they turn away from it, instead of joyfully seizing every reasonable opportunity of partaking of it! All which irregularities are varied modes of not standing up for Christ in the face of a mocking and condemning world. He is the Lord of the sabbath, and the life of the sacrament. Our observance of the one attests his right to the day; and our attendance on the other declares that we "have nothing to do with" his condemnation, because we show that we trust in his innocency for righteousness, and in his death for atonement. Take heed, brethren, for judgment came on Pilate, and it *will* come on you if guiltily ye have any thing to do with "that just man."

2. *Follow the example of this Roman lady, by believing in Jesus, and not being ashamed to confess him.* The very season of our ecclesiastical year invites you to serious meditation upon his sufferings and death.

If you cannot quite stop the engine-wheel of this busy life, you may, without loss, stay it a little. The time thus gained *may* be "profitable for all things."

But take up religion with *sincerity*, as did Pilate's wife. If Christ be the Just One, then *show* your faith in him. Give up everything for him, since he gave up everything for you. O deny him not, but have resolution to confess him before men, and then in the day of his glory he will confess you!

SERMON XVII.

THE REAL NATURE OF CRUCIFIXION.[1]

JOHN 19:17, 18.

"And he bearing his cross went forth into a place called the place of a skull, which is called in the Hebrew Golgotha: where they crucified him, and two other with him, on either side one, and Jesus in the midst."

"THE assembling of ourselves together" this day is a solemn memorial of that momentous and affecting event of the narrative of which our text is the sum. Lightly as some classes of Christians may esteem our observance of Good Friday, we may boldly believe that the annual recurrence of its hallowed services has been a sort of beacon-day to a busy world. Once in the year Christendom reminds itself, and spectators around it, that the Creator of the universe and the Saviour of souls died on a cross. On a set day, generally in a spring week, business in most parts of Christendom is ordered to cease, and pleasure is told that she must pause. The mandate may be unheeded by individuals; but the very giving of it is a most valuable testimony to a fact before masses of people who are always prone to forget it. Yes, the fact of the crucifixion of the beloved Son of God is the great event of our world's history. Himself instituted a memorial of it, to be repeated at convenient seasons; and his Church, soon after his ascension into heaven (apparently without effort, very naturally and very unanimously) adopted the practice of devoting one whole day every year to the especial contemplation of it. But, while ourselves believe the fact, and familiarly speak of it, do we clearly understand it? To say nothing, for the moment, of merely nominal Christians, are there not multitudes of real Christians who rightly glory in the cross of Christ, and yet very imperfectly know what crucifixion was? They believe it to have been *something* very dreadful and shocking, but as to what it was, in all the precision of its horrors, they have but little idea.

Now, as our knowledge of what a friend really and fully suffers for us in rendering us some great benefit, is essential to our entertaining a becoming sense of his great kindness, and will also serve to quicken and deepen that sense in us, so will a greater knowledge of the sufferings of Christ on our behalf tend at least to give us more enlarged views of his love to us and by his grace to kindle anew our love to him. May these desirable effects be produced in us while giving a somewhat minute attention to the several incidents which the text presents respecting the crucifixion of our Lord!

Your meditations will accordingly be directed to the intensity of our Redeemer's sufferings and the ignominy of them on the cross. And verily, if it can this day be said of you, as of the Galatians, "Before whose eyes Jesus Christ hath been evidently set forth crucified among you," may his own holy Spirit abundantly sanctify the setting forth, and cause us at once to crucify sin in ourselves, and to centre all our hopes of salvation in his cross!

Consider therefore

I. *The sufferings of our only Redeemer in being put to death by crucifixion.*

1. Previously to the act of crucifixion there had been everything which could increase its terrors. Great as were the agonies of that act, they were but little in comparison with what had already been endured. The Saviour's bitterest pangs were the pangs of his soul. He had undertaken to bear, not only our sin, but the wrath of God for it. It was the keen and perfect sense of that wrath which agonized him in the garden. The anguish of it was so intense as to force the very blood of his immaculate body through the pores of his skin, and thus to occasion that shocking phenomenon "a bloody sweat"—a sweat of "great drops of blood." Hence we must recollect that the very frame of the crucified victim was exhausted to the utmost; so much so, that it was prophetically said by him, "I am poured out like water," as though his vital powers had flowed out of him in that sanguineous perspiration to which he had been reduced. Added to this, as soon as he rose from his agony in the garden, he had to face all the bitter grief of his betrayal, all the excitement of his apprehension, and all the sad sight of his pledged disciples forsaking him. Then followed the mockery of his trial, with the rough and rude treatment which accompanied it. Supplementary to this were the cruelties inflicted on him as soon as the sentence for his crucifixion was pronounced. There was buffeting, reviling, smiting with sharp reeds and brawny hands, scourging with lashes, and crowning with prickly thorns! All this too was during the night and the early morning, so that the innocent

[1] Preached Good Friday Morning, 1850.

sufferer was thrust to an extremity of endurance for want of rest, sleep, and food. In this grievous plight he was led away to the place of execution. But, that nothing might be wanting to increase his degradation and suffering, the very cross to which he was to be nailed was forced on his mangled shoulders, that, felon-like, he might carry that in life which was to carry him in death. How *meekly* he submitted to the cruel burthen, and how *willing* he was to bear it, is told us in the first words of our text: "And he bearing his cross went forth." What a touching enforcement was this of his own admonitory words, "He that taketh not his cross and followeth after me is not worthy of me!" But outraged nature at length asserted her claims to pity. The weakened frame of the immaculate One sunk under the weight imposed upon him, and the ponderous cross was transferred to a man of whom the world would otherwise have never heard. "They *compel* one Simon a Cyrenian, who passed by, coming out of the country, the father of Alexander and Rufus, to bear his cross." (Mark 15:21.) Happy compulsion, and transcendant the honour which followed it!

Though faint, the beloved One pursued, as he went on his way to death, his work of warning love: "And there followed him a great company of people, and of women, which also bewailed and lamented him: but Jesus, turning unto them, said, Daughters of Jerusalem, weep not for me, but weep for yourselves and your children. For, behold, the days are coming, in the which they shall say, Blessed are the barren, and the wombs that never bare, and the paps which never gave suck." (Luke 23:27–29.) Yes, mighty Saviour, we will weep for thee and with thee! But O teach us to weep for ourselves, lest our sins, which caused thy sorrows, should pierce us with "the bitter pains of eternal death!"

2. Arriving at length where Roman justice had been accustomed to sacrifice its victims, the soldiers, under the eye of the harder-hearted priests, "crucified him."

And now we come to the exposition of what crucifixion means. In offering that exposition, such as St. Paul was evidently accustomed to offer, everything approaching sentimentality, florid declamation, or mere excitation of harrowed feelings, is thoroughly deprecated. We want not the production of those emotions which many a continental church is accustomed on this day to witness. We want not *such* sobbings and moanings and frensied gesticulations as too readily subside in the "pomps and vanities" of the next Sunday opera and the Easter ball. We want you to stand awhile with masculine tenderness, yea, with feminine firmness, like the very mother of our Lord and the two other Maries on the place where the last sufferings for our salvation were sustained.

"*Where they crucified him.*" Crucifixion was not a Jewish but a Roman mode of execution. It was considered the most lingering and yet the most agonizing death which could be inflicted. It was therefore perpetrated only on felons of the foulest cast, or on offenders of unwonted magnitude. The manner of it was this. The cross itself was laid flat on the ground. The culprit was stripped and sretched on it. A large rough spike was driven though each hand and both feet into the wood of it. The frantic struggles and piercing screams of the victim generally required many lusty arms and well-steeled hearts to restrain and endure them. But he who became a victim for us was "led as a lamb to the slaughter, and opened not his mouth." He, we know, "resisted not." When these shocking perforations were completed, the cross, with the criminal on it, was raised slantingly, as we raise a heavy ladder, and, the lower end of it being brought to the edge of a hole dug to receive it, was violently jerked into it, so as to tighten its hold in the ground. When cruelty was added to justice, the jerk was so managed as to put the unhappy creature to the most horrid agonies at once. For such a jerk, when the body was hanging by spikes through the hands and feet, must have thrown the whole weight of the frame upon the muscles of those very sensitive parts, as well as have caused the most excruciating dislocations and distortions. This will interpret to us those words of the prophetic psalm, "All my bones are *out of joint!*" Doubtless it was literally fulfilled in the case of him who, for our sakes, courted no mitigation of the criminal's lot.

Suspended in this unnatural position, the sufferer must have writhed on the slightest motion. The hands and feet, abounding with nerves and tendons, and being with all their lacerations exposed to the sun, wind, and weather, usually became much swollen and inflamed. The whole system was fevered and the whole frame convulsed. But amid every pang there was no relief, not even for a moment, by any possible change of position. The head sank down by its own weight, and that and the heavy trunk kept the arms on the most torturing stretch. From these sufferings the most burning thirst always ensued. This was or was not allayed as the pity or the caprice of the executioners dictated. Surely we shall remember him who mournfully said, "I thirst!" and of whose terrible sense of parchedness the Spirit of prophecy made mention a thousand years before it was realised: "My strength is *dried up* like a potsherd, and my tongue *cleaveth* to my jaws." (Psalm 22:15.) "When I was *thirsty* they gave me vinegar to drink."

Yes, he endured the thirst of the cross that all who believe in him might be delivered from that endless thirst which will torment in the blazing abyss, where there will not be one drop of water to cool a burning tongue. For days sometimes the wretched sufferer on the cross continued thus lingeringly to die, as no vital part was lacerated or touched. An occasional shriek or a hollow moan was all that the throbbing lungs could, towards the end, emit. Death was the only relief, and that was often preceded by delirium or even madness.

Such was crucifixion, and such was that "sharpness of death" which Jesus tasted for the ransom of our souls. He tasted it too willingly and to the full; for when he was offered a bitter infusion—sour wine or vinegar mingled with myrrh, which was usually given to dull the first sensations of pain—he refused to receive it. As though he were meekly resolved to admit of no alleviations, he gave himself up to the fiercest pangs of expiring nature. But even on the cross he died as no one else ever died. He died only at that moment when he was pleased to die. At the destined minute he left his two fellows in crucifixion to die as others died, but by his own power and in his own will "he *gave up* the ghost." Death had no dominion over him beyond what he was pleased to allow. Well might Pilate marvel that he was so soon dead.

We might fitly pause in mental anguish and hallowed sympathy at what we now hear; but we have to remind you, not only of the sufferings, but also of

II. *The ignominy which in all cases, but particularly in our Lord's case, attended crucifixion.* Not only was crucifixion a most barbarous mode of execution, but, as you have heard, the most ignominious and shameful which could be inflicted. All the decencies of nature were insulted. Though painters and sculptors soften to our eyes this violence of shame, yet is there no reason to believe that our blessed Master was treated otherwise than the vilest slave. We know that the soldiers parted his garments among them even while he was alive on the cross. Here then was a grievous part of "the shame" which he endured that he might provide us with the garments of salvation.

But, apart from that, the mere suspension on a cross or gibbet was a black disgrace among the Romans, and to the Jews a curse and an abomination beyond anything that could be named: "Christ hath redeemed us from the curse of the law, being made a curse for us: for it is written, Cursed is every one that hangeth on a tree." (Galatians 3:13.)

The very place too where our Lord was crucified added to the scandal of his death. It was in Golgotha, which is the same in Hebrew as Calvary in Latin. Our devotional use of the word Calvary has softened to us the harsh and shocking meaning of the term itself; but it means, as we hear in the gospels, "the place of a skull," or that place, says an historian, where the bones, but especially *the skulls*, of malefactors were left on the ground, as so many footballs for idle sport.

But notice further the prominent degradation of our Lord. He was not executed alone, and in all the solemnity and pomp of some illustrious state criminal, but was numbered with low and contemptible transgressors. And, as though he were the worst of the three, and deserved the most conspicuous post of degradation, he was placed in the middle: "And he bearing his cross went forth into a place called the place of a skull, which is called in the Hebrew Golgotha: where they crucified him; and two other with him, on either side one, and Jesus in the midst." (John 19:17, 18.) O what unutterable shame was there in the whole transaction! Well might the sun hide his face from it, and darkness come with his pall to cover it! And O that our faces were ashamed when we think of it, and that our hearts would be as sensitive as the very rocks which rent asunder! God grant us grace to make a right and profitable "conclusion of the whole matter!"—We shall be likely to do so if we regard it

1. *As the sum of all doctrine and the motive for all holiness.* The crucifixion of the Messiah was the substance of the gospel in Eden. It was the standard topic of type and prophecy, and is, as it ever has been, the one grand and engrossing theme of Christianity: "For Christ sent me not to baptize, but to preach the gospel; not with wisdom of words, lest the cross of Christ should be made of none effect:" (1 Corinthians 1:17, 18.)—"For I determined not to know any thing among you, save Jesus Christ, and him crucified:" (1 Corinthians 2:2.)—"But God forbid that I should glory, save in the cross of our Lord Jesus Christ, by whom the world is crucified unto me, and I unto the world." (Galatians 6:14.) Where this doctrine of the cross is paramount in the mind and heart, there will be little room, and less inclination, for mere tenets which are either ambiguously revealed, or are "of doubtful disputation." Let a man hold fast to this sheet anchor, and he can afford to let straws and stubble float by him.

When too the soul is intent on "Christ crucified," there will be a constraining power over the best love of the heart, and the fullest obedience of the life. "The love of Christ constraineth us," will be the reason and the plea of every holy effort, endeavour, and undertaking. Hence regard this matter

2. *As a theme for constant meditation.* Our Lord's sufferings are not a mere Good Friday subject; they will be the theme of eternity, and therefore cannot be otherwise than the settled topic of all time. Our Lord's own selected emblems of them are the every-day viands of life. Those viands are not more necessary for the body than the benefits of those sufferings are for the soul. As we cannot live without thinking of and participating in the one, so should we always be intent on the other. Indeed a genuine Christian will find that his thoughts habitually flow in this course. His daily troubles will point him to the troubles of the cross; and his several wants, especially if he be in poverty or strait, will incline him to think of the privations of Calvary. Who can repine with that in view?

View the crucifixion of Jesus also

3. *As the grand truth for the knowledge and salvation of the world.* Two-thirds or more of the human race are ignorant of it. Without the knowledge of it there is no hope for sinners; yea, without the realization of it, there will be no salvation for any one of *us*. Give men what you like, or teach them what you

will, yet if you unfold not to them the gospel of the crucifixion you leave them to perish. God will own no ministry but that which proclaims it to the hearts and consciences of men.

Look on the death of Jesus lastly

4. *As a check to all sin and a call to all duty.* We denounce Pilate, and Caiaphas, and Herod. Let us denounce our sins. They were *the* crucifiers. Remember Christ's sufferings, and sin not. Shun the crime of crucifying him afresh. Live as it were under the cross. Repentance, faith, every grace and every duty will flourish beneath its shade.

SERMON XVIII.

THE BURIAL OF JESUS IN A NEW SEPULCHRE.[1]

John 19:40–42.

"Then took they the body of Jesus, and wound it in linen clothes with the spices, as the manner of the Jews is to bury. Now in the place where he was crucified there was a garden, and in the garden a new sepulchre, wherein was never man yet laid. There laid they Jesus therefore because of the Jews' preparation-day; for the sepulchre was nigh at hand."

IT was a strange singularity for the Sun of righteousness to sink into all the darkness of ignominy; for the Prince of life to suffer death; for him who held the keys of the grave to be bound as the prisoner of the tomb! But the burial no less than the crucifixion of our Lord was an occurrence which divine wisdom had foreordained as accessory to the accomplishment of our redemption. The registry of that burial is contained in our text, and a copy of it ought to be written on the tablet of every heart. For the burial of the Lord Jesus, apart from his death on the cross, and his descent into hades, is at once affecting, admonitory, and consoling, to the highest degree.

In accordance then with the intention of our Church, on this *good* day, let us approach the sepulchre in which his precious body was deposited, and view the scene of his last and lowest degradation. The circumstances of the burial itself; the intention and importance of it as a matter of fact; and the admonitory and consoling truths with which, as an article of faith, it is charged, will constitute the framework of the present discourse.

I. *The circumstances of the burial of our Lord* are simple, yet very striking and affecting. When it was ascertained that Jesus really was dead, Joseph of Arimathea went, with no little courage, and begged of Pilate the grant and disposal of his crucified body. Contrary to the custom of the Romans, who never interred, but ignominiously cast out, the corpses of notorious criminals, Pilate permitted him to take the body, and to do with it as he pleased. No doubt there was in the mind of Pilate, not only a conviction of the innocency of Jesus, but a secret awe of his character. These combined feelings seem to have operated with Pilate in acquiescing with the request of Joseph.

Hence we are led to conclude that, when there is a scripture to be fulfilled, God so prepares his agents, and so overrules the wills of his enemies, that no part of his word is broken. This fact is sufficient to account to us for the singular conduct of many who are not Christians at heart, though they make many concessions to Christianity. But, to the narrative:

"*Then took they* the body of Jesus, and wound it in linen clothes with the spices, as the manner of the Jews is to bury."— In doing this, Joseph and Nicodemus evinced much affection for the person of Christ, but much ignorance of his doctrine. They forgot the prophecies of their own scriptures, and the expositions which he gave of them, when frequently alluding to his death and resurrection. But, when we heartily love the beloved Son, the eternal Father will pardon our ignorances and

[1] Preached Good Friday Morning, April 6th, 1849.

bear with our infirmities. Love for Christ is the grand criterion of character, and the sure plea for acceptance, notwithstanding many imperfections and weaknesses, in the walk and conversation of a believer. Only let him give all his heart to his Redeemer, and he will be neither spurned in displeasure nor corrected in anger.

"*Now in the place* where he was crucified there was a garden, and in the garden a new sepulchre, wherein was never man yet laid." The garden and the sepulchre, as we learn from St. Matthew, were the property of Joseph. The sepulchre was "his own new tomb, which he had hewn out in the rock." (Matthew 27:60.) He had either hewn it with his own hands, or caused it to be hewn, for the reception of his own body, when death should call away his spirit. As the sepulchre was in a garden, it is very probable that Joseph was accustomed to resort thither for devout meditation, as well as for solemn anticipation of his own decease. Such withdrawal from present scenes, and such reflections on future realities are becoming in themselves, and profitable for our souls.

The sepulchre, we are told, was "hewn out of *a rock*;" and with much care we are also told, that it was "a *new* sepulchre, wherein was never man yet laid." These are apparently little things to be described, but they are in reality very momentous facts.

If we bear in mind that the resurrection of Christ was to be the test of all the claims which he had advanced, we shall see that it was requisite for every precaution to be taken against plausible objections. To this the divine wisdom paid every attention. Every thing, even the minutest, was so arranged as to prevent the gainsayer having the slightest advantage in disputing the fact of Christ's resurrection. The sepulchre was in *a rock*: the body therefore could not be easily taken away by the secret removal of a little earth. Nothing but a toilsome excavation through solid rock could effect a passage to the interior of the tomb. Such a procedure was next to impossible, considering the close and constant watch of the Roman guard. Then it was "a *new* sepulchre," wherein no corpse had ever been laid. Consequently it could neither be said that it was the body of some one else, who had revived; nor that it was through contact with the bones of some illustrious saint, that the body of Christ was revived. Cunning and malicious objectors might have pointed to 2 Kings 13:21, and have pretended that something of the sort had occurred a second time, as once occurred by contact with the bones of Elisha. But he who is "a jealous God," and will not leave men with excuse, so far as his veracity and honour are concerned, took care to wrest beforehand all such vain pleas from those who would have been too glad to urge them. May we never, by any prejudices or partialities, weaken the force of any portion of that truth of God which he has guarded with all jealousy and care!

"*There laid they Jesus.*" God, we are told, buried Moses: but now the disciples of Moses bury the beloved Son of God. How interestingly solemn was the deed of these good men! They seem to have been alone and unattended in their hallowed and thrilling labour. They little understood what they were doing, what prophecies they were fulfilling, and for what a glorious triumph they were preparing. They were like two brotherly husbandmen engaged in depositing one single grain of wheat in the ground, but little suspecting that, in a day or two, it would suddenly spring up, and bear the living grains of a countless product for eternity.

"*There* laid they Jesus:" "*there,*" "in the place where he was crucified," that, on the very spot where he ended his sufferings, he might begin his triumphs: "*there,*" in Joseph's tomb; for, as he had no house or home of his own, how should he have a sepulchre? "*there,*" in the grave of a *rich* man, though himself was a poor man, but that the scripture might be fulfilled: "He made his grave with the *wicked*, and with the *rich* in his death," says Isaiah; and, saying thus, the prophet has been construed as speaking *ironically*; as though dying with the wicked, and yet being buried with the rich, were a glaring inconsistency on the part of those who compassed his death. Truly it was; but the irony, if intended for the Jews, was wonderfully instructive for ourselves. It teaches us that, although God allowed his Son, in becoming *sin* for us, to be degraded as a dying offender in company with malefactors; yet, because he was in himself infinitely holy, God so ordered events that he should not be cast out with malefactors, but be buried in the tomb of a rich, an honourable, and an upright man. How lofty, how beautiful, how adorable, is the wisdom of him who planned our redemption in Christ Jesus!

II. *The intention and importance of the burial of our Lord*, regarded simply as a fact, well deserve our consideration.

Usually, and with all propriety, we ascribe our blessedness as believers to the *death* of Christ. His burial however was a most indispensable event, and a large and strong link in that chain of occurrences by which our salvation is held fast.

1. It was the greatest external evidence which could be given to the world of *the certainty of his death*. The enemies of Jesus would not have suffered him to be taken away for burial, had they at all suspected that animation was not thoroughly extinct. Neither would his friends have attempted such burial, if they had not been fully satisfied that life was utterly gone. Thus his burial was the joint certificate of both enemies and friends as to the certainty of his death. On that certainty depended the reality of our atonement with God. We are therefore *sure* of its having been accomplished for us.

2. Jesus was buried *that his humiliation might be complete.* The penalty of sin was not only the death of the body, but the

return of that body to its native earth. The Lord Jesus therefore, as man's substitute in the propitiatory suffering of our penalty, went to the lowest depths of human humiliation, as consistently as circumstances would allow. He indeed was "brought to the dust of death," and laid within the pale of corruption. He was placed as a corpse in the grave, and consigned to the chamber of bodily dissolution. Thus all that was required to complete his humiliation was accomplished. But it was enough for him to be visibly humbled. It was "impossible" for the process to proceed further, because eternal verity had promised security from actual corruption: "For thou wilt not leave my soul in hell; neither wilt thou suffer thine holy One to see corruption." (Psalm 16:10.)

3. Jesus was buried *that his own words might be fulfilled*, and the *scriptures not be broken*. The burial of Messiah was both prophetically and typically declared. David and Isaiah had plainly announced it; and Jonah's entombment in the belly of a whale was a grand and striking type of the fact. Not once only, but "at sundry times and in divers manners," did Christ himself prospectively refer to his coming burial: "Verily, verily, I say unto you, Except a corn of wheat fall into the ground and die, it abideth alone; but if it die, it bringeth forth much fruit." (John 12:24.) And again: "For in that she hath poured this ointment on my body, she did it for my burial." (Matthew 26:12.)

As a fact therefore, the burial of Christ was of high importance; inasmuch as the truth of the Father and of the Son, made known to us by the inspiration of the Holy Ghost, was at stake upon it.

4. The burial of Christ was *a remarkable attestation of his personal innocence*. Had he really been a malefactor, he would have "perished as dung" like other malefactors. Divine Providence would not then have interfered to save him from being cast out for his flesh to waste, and his bones to bleach, on "the place of a skull." But, because he was what Pilate pronounced him to be, an honourable sepulchre was provided for him by a confessedly honourable man.

5. Jesus entered the grave *that he might dispel its terrors, and be its destruction*. Had Joseph and Nicodemus placed an inscription on his tomb, they might with great suitableness have selected it from the writings of Hosea: "O death, I will be thy plagues! O grave, I will be thy destruction!" Death indeed might have exulted over such a prisoner. But death had little cause for exultation. His prisoner was unlike all who had ever before submitted to him. He was omnipotent; and no one had power over him beyond his own permission. In the guise of a captive, he went down to the gates of death, only to demolish them and conquer him. On the cross it was that he broke the sceptre of "the king of terrors;" but it was in the grave that he finished his triumph over him. Like "a mighty hunter," he not only wounded the tyrant of the forest in the open field, but followed him to his den, and therein virtually annihilated him. It is said "*virtually*," because, like the maimed kings whom Adonibezek kept about him, death is a disabled foe, and turned into an unwilling servant. But the hour is fast approaching when his annihilation will be complete, and when all who once were his captives will rise up against him, and chant this pæan over him: "O death, where is thy sting? O grave, where is thy victory? The sting of death is sin; and the strength of sin is the law. But thanks be to God, which giveth us the victory through our Lord Jesus Christ." (1 Corinthians 15:55–57.)

III. The *truths, admonitory and consolatory which the burial of our Lord, as an article of faith, presents to us, are mainly these*:

1. *The malignity of sin and its destructive tendency are fearfully manifested at the grave of our Lord.* Were our sin and apostasy lighter evils than they are, Jesus had never been buried. Had not we, by wilful sin, become the prey of the grave, he had never stooped to enter it for our deliverance from it. Then think of this, you who never think of sin but when you smart under some suffering from it! Think of this, you who love "the pleasures of sin," and are even meditating the enjoyment of them at the coming Easter! Think of this, you who profess and call yourselves Christians, but have no real repentance, no godly sorrow, no aching heart at the ten thousand spears which you have thrust into the side of the crucified and buried One! God grant you repentance unto life!

2. *Our daily duty is to seek a conformity to the death and burial of our Saviour Christ.* The great practical business of life is to prepare for death. But there will be no preparation unless we take our stand at the sepulchre of the holy Jesus. It is there alone that we shall learn what constitutes the beginning, the progress, and the end, of the Christian life. We are to be "*buried* with him by baptism into death." And, being thus "*planted* together in the likeness of his death," we are to be "dead indeed unto sin," like a corpse in a tomb, insensible to all the vanities around it. And then we are so to be conformed to the buried Jesus as to lie passive under the will of our Father, and to rest in hope of all that he has promised. This conformity to Christ in the grave is to be attained only by union of spirit with him. We must be made like to him, and one with him, ere we can enjoy the hope of security from sin, and of safety in the sepulchre. "He that believeth in me shall *never die!*"

3. *All is accomplished for us.* The dying Saviour said, on the cross, "It is finished." But his subsequent humiliation in the sepulchre gave intensity to that declaration, because it gave intensity to his death, which was the ground of the declaration. If the sinner can be certified that all which his soul needs is fully and freely provided for him, because of his Saviour's last pangs on the cross, how much more is he certified of that full and free

provision by the humiliation of the tomb! Sure may we be that the merit of that humiliation will be like a stamp on the pure gold, by which he purchases our salvation.

4. *The grave is now a sanctified repository for the bodies of the saints.* Christ, by entering the grave as our head and representative, consecrated it for our safe reception. Instead of a prison, it is become a passage to a blessed home. "Fear not" then, ye who walk softly, "to go down into this Egypt." Jesus has gone thither before you. He will be with you, and bring you up again from it.

The Christian sepulchre is but a quiet chamber, in which our bodies rest awhile till their redemption cometh. It may be likened to the workshop of a superior mechanist, in which our bodies, so fearfully and wonderfully made, are taken to pieces preparatory to their being fashioned, by the great Artificer, "like unto his own glorious body."

Are you then "in bondage to the fear of death"? Take a near view of Jesus in the sepulchre of the garden; and believe that, if you "only believe," your rest in the grave will be as safe and as peaceful as his. "Death is yours!" saith the apostle, for Christ has made him your servant; and therefore the grave also is yours.

5. *The brightest proof of our Saviour's love beams forth to us from the darkness of his tomb.* The greater his humiliation, the greater the token of his love. The high and lofty One, who inhabiteth eternity, stooping to the recesses of the grave! What more wonderful love can be imagined? How truly overwhelming!

Come then to the commemoration of his burial. He had few attendants on the evening of his interment, and few to weep for him. But now let throngs of penitents draw nigh with faith, and testify that they love him!

SERMON XIX.

THE WALK OF THE DISCIPLES TO EMMAUS.[1]

LUKE 24:32.

"And they said one to another, Did not our heart burn within us while he talked with us by the way, and while he opened to us the scriptures?"

THE walk of the two disciples from Jerusalem to Emmaus was the most interesting and the most memorable of any which human feet ever trod. Disconsolate and perplexed the two friends set out on their village visit. In the way the Lord Jesus, in the guise of a stranger, joined them. He inquired the cause of their visible sadness, and the topic of their earnest conversation. They frankly told him, though not without an expression of surpise at his seeming ignorance of the all-absorbing topic of the day. Presently they were held with amazement at the flow of luminous instruction which proceeded from his lips. Unconscious who he was, they listened with even burning delight, and would have detained him to an indefinite time: but in the act of breaking bread with them he discovered himself, and then vanished from their sight.

They presently, as was natural, fell to talking of all that had passed, and compared their inmost feelings, which fully corresponded the one with the other: "and they said one to another, Did not our heart burn within us while he talked with us by the way, and while he opened to us the scriptures?"

Here notice

I. *Their statement of what Jesus had done.* "He talked with us," say they, "and opened unto us the scriptures."

1. "*He talked*" then with the two disciples. We naturally

[1] Preached Sunday Morning, November 8th, 1846.

ask; Of *what* did he talk, and in *what manner?* We are told the one, and can infer the other.

i. He talked with them *of himself.* In doing this there was no stain of that egotism which too surely stains us, when we talk much respecting ourselves. He spoke of himself because it was of himself that they wished to hear. All their concern was to know the real and entire truth respecting him. They had believed in him, and they loved him: but such strange things had befallen him that, although their love was not diminished, their faith was sorely tried and their hearts deeply troubled. Thus it is with both the newly awakened sinner and the beclouded believer. They both require to know more of Christ. The soul that is aroused into solicitude about its sin is eager to know if Christ can save such a soul as itself: and the believer whose faith is staggered and whose heart is downcast is not likely to be either strengthened or comforted, except he know more of that fulness of grace which dwells in the Lord Jesus. As he then talked of himself alone to these sorrowing travellers, so are his ministers to preach him alone to anxious believers and inquiring sinners.

ii. But in *what manner* did he talk with the disciples? From what is told us the manner may at first sight seem a little harsh. "O *fools*, and slow of heart to believe!" but the word "*fools*," as *now* used, does not mean what it used to mean in even the English tongue. The old English sense of the word corresponded with that of the original Greek, and conveyed the idea of "thoughtless or rather *inconsiderate* persons." Spoken with a kind voice and tender demeanour, the first words of our Lord to the disciples would convey a gentle reproof, rather than a cutting reproach. And how often does our inconsideration deserve reproof! Is not much of our sadness and perplexity owing to our want of due attention to what has long been written for our learning? "Ye do err" (and it may be added, ye do grope and sorrow too), "from not knowing the scriptures."

More than this, as to our Lord's manner, we may be sure that "he neither broke the bruised reed, nor quenched the smoking flax." From what followed also, it is clear that the disciples were charmed with his kind and earnest bearing. And verily who will find fault with the perfection of gentleness? Who can say that, in spiritual fellowship with the beloved Son of God, he ever discouraged a feeble heart or chilled a glowing mind?

The disciples further stated that

2. "*He opened to them the scriptures*," that is, he unlocked their meaning by his exposition of such types and prophecies as foreshowed his sufferings, death, and resurrection. Hence we make sure of two things:

i. *The scriptures are the treasury of all knowledge respecting Christ.* He is the one great object of all knowledge, and they are the only storehouse of that knowledge. Himself had certified both his disciples and the Jews of this fact: "Search the scriptures, for they are they which testify of me." There is no other testimony but theirs: for it is very remarkable that, spite of all the pretensions of tradition (so called), not one single prophecy, nor one extra word or deed, said or done by Christ, has ever been authenticated, beyond what is contained in holy scripture.

The other thing of which we make sure is this:

ii. *Faithful exposition of the scriptures, such exposition especially as sets forth the Saviour, is the only accredited means of winning sinners, and strengthening saints.* We must doubt every thing if we doubt this. Testimony to it is written with sunbeams in all that the apostles themselves said and did. They too only followed their divine Master's example, when they preached him and his gospel wherever they went; for, though Jesus "*pleased* not himself," yet he did *preach* himself. In preaching Christ, with holy affections and honest lips, myriads have been won to him; and countless hearts have been strengthened and rejoiced by (oftentimes) very humble but truly faithful sermons. Of this we shall see somewhat more in considering, with respect to the disciples,

II. *Their description of the effect produced on them by the words of Christ*: "Did not our hearts *burn* within us?" In this simple but frank-souled appeal to one another, they expressed in few words what might have been expanded into a volume. They did not stay to recount what Jesus had said, but bounded at once to the effect which every word, as it fell on their ears, wrought in them. Curiosity would be sure to ask, what texts Jesus expounded and what was his exposition of them. But divine wisdom knew very well that, if we do not believe the texts themselves, we certainly should not believe any account of his exposition of them.

Now notice attentively, in the two disciples, the genuine effects of a gracious faith. They did not begin with any boast of their knowledge. They did not say, "Were not our eyes opened, and did we not see things as clear as light, when he talked with us, and opened to us the scriptures?" No! They came to the right point at once: "Did not our *hearts* burn within us?" This was their first exclamation, because it was their strongest feeling. While their understandings were opened, their hearts were warmed, intensely warmed. They not merely saw the truth of all that Jesus explained to them, but found their interest in it. His atoning death and triumphant resurrection were felt to be springs of joy, because they were wells of salvation to them. Thus, brethren, will it always be, when the words of Christ really enter the heart; for true religion is no chilly languid feeling; at least, it never is where the grace of Christ performs its perfect work. In fact half the quarrel with the world would be at an end if the professors of religion would agree to that temperature which suits an unrenewed heart. But such a compromise will never be made by such disciples as walked with Jesus to Emmaus. Their "hearts" *burned* within them; and they were not ashamed to acknowledge it, by letting the warmth be felt around them. Indeed how can it be otherwise, when the baptism of the spirit is a baptism of *fire*, and "the spirit of burning" is the temper of all who are born from above? (Isaiah 4:4.) They who have "much forgiven" will "love much," and will ever covet that "*fire* of love," for which our Church teaches us to supplicate in her Ordination Hymn.

Some professors are marvellously afraid of what is called enthusiasm. And pray what, properly speaking, is enthusiasm? In plain English it is *doing a thing with all one's heart and soul.* It is just what Jesus approved, when he authoritatively said of God, "Thou shalt love him with all thy heart; and with all thy soul, and with all thy mind." It is just what the two disciples did when their *hearts burned within them.* My dear brethren, there is incomparably more danger of religious indifference, than of religious enthusiasm, as it is called. Where one man is over excited by religious exercises, thousands die under the freezing power of worldliness and unbelief. Because here and there deluded souls run into fanaticism, the enemies of the cross take pleasure in decrying that very enthusiasm, in the article of *true* religion, without which no man ever was saved, or ever will be saved.

If then these things be so,

1. *What a difference is there between the reality of religion and the notions of multitudes respecting it!* The religion of Jesus demands the whole heart, and demands it even to burning within itself. There men of the world stop. "We have no objection," say they, "to a little decent sober profession, but do not talk to us about *hearts burning* within us."

Then, my friends, without putting the Bible under a bushel, the ministers of Christ can preach nothing at all to you. Their commission is to ask for your hearts, to preach to your hearts, and to kindle them into a flame of holy love for himself. If you refuse this work of the heart you die. May you think of this and find life!

2. *But what comfort is there for true Christians in the word of Christ, and in communion with Christ!* The two disciples went from Jerusalem downcast and doubtful: they heard the words of Jesus, and returned with hearts burning within them.

Thus many a true believer goes with a heavy spirit to the sanctuary, but, being met in faith by Jesus, comes away with gladness of heart. In prayer, or in sermon, or in sacrament, the word of Christ has met his case, and he burns with joy and thankfulness. At this present let us recollect the 35th verse. May the Lord Jesus manifest himself to us in our breaking of bread! Then will no heart be without warmth, nor any soul without profit. Amen!

SERMON XX.

THE FAITH OF THOMAS AFTER HIS INCREDULITY.[1]

John 20:28.

"And Thomas answered and said unto him, My Lord and my God."

RESPECTING some of the apostles of our Lord the Holy Ghost has recorded little else than their names. This fact should teach us to be content to live usefully without a trumpet to blazon our fame. Those apostles of whom we know the least may in certain instances have laboured or endured the most: yet, dear as they must have been to their divine Master, posterity cannot praise their doings. Their record is above.

Of those of the twelve, concerning whom most is written,

[1] Preached Sunday Morning, December 21st, 1851.

Thomas is not the last: and yet of him, as of Peter, a main part of the historic record is occupied with a detail of failure and fault. Nothing can surpass the moral beauty of this noble feature in the evangelical narratives. If the evangelists had conspired to write for posterity a cunningly devised fable, they would have kept out of view the fall of Peter and the faith-lacking conduct of Thomas. Their candid description of those dark circumstances is to every ingenuous mind a proof of their genuine simplicity and unflinching veracity.

But, while each of the four evangelists details the fall of Peter, St. John alone describes the failure of Thomas. Why the inspiring Spirit directed this procedure no man can certainly say. Suffice it to remark that, as the fault of Thomas was far less than the fall of Peter, it was not told till after the decease of Thomas. None but apostles were privy to it, and possibly it was not divulged till all but St. John had died.

Our Church appoints the account of it to be read for our learning on the present day. The verse selected from it as our text is the pith of the whole. It is the memorable answer of the forgetful apostle when recovering his faith at the sight of his beloved Master, and at the sound of his gentle reproof. Our spiritual profit will perhaps best be promoted by our considering

I. *The circumstances which led to the emphatic answer of Thomas*: "*And Thomas answered and said unto him, My Lord and my God.*"

St. John commences the account of those circumstances by saying, "But Thomas, one of the twelve, called Didymus, was not with them when Jesus came." St. John gives the two names of the apostle, not as being two in reality but only in tongue. The apostle had but one name, that was *Twin*, according to its meaning in our language; but our "twin" is in Hebrew Thomas, and in Greek Didymus.

The Lord Jesus, in the after part of the day on which he rose from the dead, suddenly presented himself to his disciples when assembled secretly for fear of the Jews. On this occasion he said and did such things as left no doubt of his identity. But "*Thomas was not with them when Jesus came.*" Whether his absence was wilful or accidental we are not told. Be that as it may, the lesson to us is plain—our absence from the assembly of God's saints and Christ's disciples *may* be a serious loss to us. We may, for instance, be absent from church on that very occasion when, if we had been present, the greatest blessedness might have followed.

When the disciples next met Thomas, they said to him, "*We have seen the Lord.*" No doubt they accompanied their statement with a detail of circumstances. Thomas however was incredulous; not that he disbelieved them by any suspicion of their veracity, but supposed them to be mistaken or deceived by some fallacious appearances. Nothing that he said betrays any want of confidence in their truthfulness, but rather shows his own incredulity as to the *possibility*, or at least the probability of the resurrection of Christ; for he said, "Except I shall see in his hands the print of the nails, and put my finger into the print of the nails, and thrust my hand into his side, I will not believe." (Ver. 25.)

It is clear then that Thomas expressed no sort of doubt as to the divine character of his Master, nor as to the authenticity of his mission. There was no denial of these things, nor any approach to the sort of denial of which Peter was guilty. His fault lay in too much self-will, and in too little readiness to accept reasonable and credible testimony. His self-will was in fact opposed to that very principle by which God intended to enlarge his Church among the Gentiles. That enlargement was to be effected by the spread of faithful witness, such witness as Thomas himself was destined to bear to far distant lands.

But, as Thomas was sound at heart, his passing fault was soon to be corrected. Accordingly, at the expiration of a week, the Lord Jesus again suddenly presented himself to his assembled disciples, Thomas being now with them. It was now also the return of the first day of the week, the day of the resurrection; and Jesus, by manifesting himself on it, intended most likely to declare his consecration of the day as the future Sabbath of his Church.

No sort of communication had, it seems, passed between Jesus and the eleven since the preceding interview: and yet as soon as he enters their company he addresses himself to Thomas, and quotes his very words, as though he had been present when they were rashly uttered. (Ver. 27.) This appeal to Thomas, conveying reproof so tenderly, and granting evidence so fully, wrought effectually with him. His heart was feelingly alive to the truth of what he had doubted; and consequently with intense emotion he devoutly and adoringly said, "My Lord, and my God!" Let us then proceed to consider

II. *The meaning of the importance of this remarkable confession.*

Thomas's exclamation was the unburthening of a full heart. It was as though he had suddenly recovered himself after a week's spiritual slumber. All that he had previously heard his Saviour say about being put to death, and rising again on the third day, flashed upon his recollection, not only as so many sayings, but as so many accomplished facts. The crucified One stood before him as his risen Lord. Awe, love, gratitude, with all that the loftiest admiration and the most fervent adoration could produce, rushed over his soul, and forced his lips to breathe a sentence which contains a world of meaning and importance.

1. The plain broad *meaning* of the words, "*My Lord and my God*," one would think so evident that a child need hardly be

told it. But, if children hardly require to be told it, sceptical philosophers and Socinian freethinkers need to be reminded of it with an emphasis which admits of no resistance.

Had Moses, or any other of the favoured ones of old, stood before some manifestation of Deity, and heard the voice of the eternal Majesty addressing them, could they in reply have used words more expressive of deliberate adoration than the words of Thomas to Jesus of Nazareth, "My Lord and my God"? And, had they used those words, who could have doubted that they meant to express by them an unequivocal acknowledgement of the Godhead of the person so addressed? What else can we, in common honesty and common sense, believe that Thomas meant when, without any retraction or qualification, he called Jesus his Lord and his God? Besides what else could Thomas mean when he recollected all that he heard Jesus say, and all that he had seen him do? Did he not hear him utter many a sentence which amounted to his saying, "I am the Lord thy God"? Did he not say, "I and my Father are One:"—"I am in the Father and the Father in me:"—"He that hath seen me hath seen the Father"? And did not Thomas hear him apply to himself the very title by which Jehovah had described himself to Moses, "Before Abraham was, *I am*"? And did he not hear him allow himself to be addressed as Divine, and suffer it to be inferred that he was "very God of very God"? "Who," said the Jews, "can forgive sins but God?" and yet he persisted in saying, "Thy sins be forgiven thee." We make no question then that Thomas, under a gracious impulse, meant by what he said to recognise in the risen Jesus the Lord of his life and the God of his salvation. He meant all that too, not only as a part of a general confession of faith, but as an expression of personal and experimental interest in his beloved Master. For he did not look around on his fellow disciples and pointing to Jesus say, "*Our* Lord and *our* God!" but he addressed himself alone to him and said, "*My* Lord and *my* God!" It was the language of a man who realized his own everlasting interest in the Saviour of sinners. And, oh! let it be borne in mind that this personal realization is the essence of religion.[1]

More than this, the Lord Jesus assented to the address of Thomas. He not only did not reprove or check him for it, but in presence of all his disciples admitted it. The very method also which the advocates of Socinianism adopt for evading the force of Thomas's words is a strong testimony to the truth of the ancient and simple view of them. Those advocates pretend (for it is but a wicked pretence), that Thomas, by saying what he did, merely let fall an expression of surprise, tantamount to a popular exclamation of, "O Lord!" or, "Good God!"

The wickedness of this surmise is only equalled by its blasphemy; for it not only imputes to Thomas a flagrant violation of the third commandment, but makes the holy Jesus an accomplice in the crime, seeing that he never rebuked Thomas for it. May Jesus, the Lord our God, ever keep us steadfast in the faith which his apostle Thomas at length so nobly witnessed!

2. *The importance* of Thomas's confession lies in the grandeur of the truths which it contains, in the caution with which it was made, and in the sincerity with which it was followed out.

i. That a sentence so short as that which Thomas uttered should comprise the grandest truths of revelation is nothing marvellous or uncommon in the estimation of the biblical student. The Bible abounds with pregnant brevities. Some of its briefest sentences contain unsearchable fulness. It is so, because they are of the inspiration of an infinite Spirit.

To acknowledge Jesus to be Lord and God is the great end of angelic and human existence. (Philippians 2:9–11.) It is the eternal Father's delight to honour the beloved Son. It is as though he gloried in the plan of winning all hearts to the admiration and love of him who stooped to the lowest point of human degradation. It is also as though he would have his wisdom adored in that very thing which seemed most to disparage it. That a man whom a nation scorned and crucified should be the Lord of angels, the Saviour of sinners, and the God of both, was a grand and wondrous design. When that design shall be completed in days to come, eternity will be spent in adoring it. The confession of the apostle Thomas was therefore the epitome of the worship of heaven. It was the grandeur of eternal truth compressed in a few simple words.

ii. *The caution* with which the apostle made his hearty confession is a highly important consideration. He had asserted, almost with an oath, that he would not believe in the resurrection of Jesus, not only upon mere hearsay, but upon even the testimony of ten friends whom he knew and loved. He would see for himself, and make too the most minute examination of the risen One. How unspeakably valuable is this fact, as a proof of the exquisite care of the first witnesses of Christianity! Thomas's incredulity was patent to the other ten apostles, and they were present when it was totally removed. It was not in a corner that Thomas, without any one to see or hear him, recanted all he had said; but it was before the whole of that company which had heard his rash declaration. In presence of them all Jesus challenged him to the test upon which he had insisted. (Ver. 27.) It does not appear that Thomas for one moment, after Jesus addressed him, thought of doing what he had proposed to do. Conviction was too powerful to require any petty aids. Independently of seeing Jesus in the attitude in which he presented himself, Thomas must have felt himself carried away as with a flood when he witnessed the omniscience of

[1] "The devil," says an old divine, "can recite the whole creed, but he cannot put '*my*' to any article of it."

his Master in knowing and repeating the very words which he had improvidently uttered. After such evidence flashing upon him, what else could he say but, "My Lord and my God"?

iii. *The sincerity* with which the cautious apostle followed out his confession adds greatly to its interest and its importance. The Holy Ghost has not seen fit to suffer any record of his acts to come down to us. History however, though of course not inspired, is sufficiently authentic to certify us that, of all the apostles, none travelled further or laboured unto death more nobly than the once incredulous disciple.

After travelling through Media, Persia, and the neighbouring countries, he reached as far as the great southern peninsula of India, which is now known to us as the coast of Malabar. He there made converts and established a church, which of all the apostolical churches is the least corrupt and superstitious. It has outlived many a once more imposing and more widely flourishing establishment. "The Christians of St. Thomas," as they still are called, have maintained the faith more purely than they who claim St. Peter for their founder. They were always independent of the Church of Rome; and, though from their isolated position they suffered in learning and fervour, yet have they retained their simplicity and truthfulness. The late Dr. Buchanan visited and almost re-discovered them in the early part of the present century. The tale of their sufferings from the agents of the Pope, and the progress which they have made under the banner of the English Church, is too long for present recital. Suffice it to know that the church which St. Thomas planted is still extant, like a little oasis in the desert of Braminical idolatry, under the enmity of which he suffered martyrdom by darts and spears.

Let the collect for the day direct the conclusion of this discourse.

1. *The doubtfulness of Thomas was suffered "for the more confirmation" of his faith.* This was an instance of God's gracious power for bringing good out of evil. It was an illustration of Samson's riddle (Judges 14:14). If then we ourselves have been suffered to doubt, let us be earnest for the passing doubt to be turned into deeper conviction. Happy will it be if of the many who have been drawn aside and entangled in the Popish snare which has been set within our Church some at least should, like the doubting apostle, escape with even benefit to their souls.

2. *May our own faith be so strong and steadfast as "never to be reproved."* For this blessed end let us avoid all hindrances to faith. Thomas should not have been absent. Let us be always present in the assembly of the saints. Above all let us pray, "Lord, increase our faith!" Jesus increased Thomas's.

Thomas doubted the fact of his Master's resurrection. Let us never doubt his future advent. The one is the assurance of the other; "because he hath appointed a day, in the which he will judge the world in righteousness by that man whom he hath ordained; whereof he hath given assurance unto all men, in that he hath raised him from the dead." (Acts 17:31.) We must look especially to his second coming, as "knowing that there shall come in the last days scoffers, walking after their own lusts, and saying, Where is the promise of his coming? for, since the fathers fell asleep, all things continue as they were from the beginning." (2 Peter 3:3, 4.) Never let our faith be reproved on this ground; but let us "wait for his Son from heaven, whom he raised from the dead, even Jesus, which delivered us from the wrath to come." (1 Thessalonians 1:10.)

SERMON XXI.

THE DAY OF OUR LORD'S ASCENSION.[1]

Acts 1:2.

"The day in which he was taken up."

[1] Preached Ascension Day, June 1st, 1848.

AND this is more than the eighteen hundredth anniversary of that day. Oft as it comes round to us, we *should* meet it with all elasticity and freshness of heart. We should do thus, because the day of our Lord's ascension is a day "much to be remembered" by those whose everlasting interests are involved in it. Think of those interests as often as we may, or even of the circumstances which marked the ascension itself, we shall always find something to think of which we had not thought of before. Every thing relating to our divine Mediator is infinite in its ramifications and bearings. A finite creature therefore need never feel at loss for fresh meditations upon even the oldest themes.

How our text is introduced to our notice by the pen which wrote it, you have already heard in the portion of Scripture "for the epistle." St. Luke began his narrative of the Acts of the Apostles by recurring to the last fact in his Gospel concerning Christ. He described his ascension as taking place while he was in the act of blessing his disciples. He now refers to that fact, and gives a further description of it.

Let us then devoutly think of "the day in which our Lord was taken up." And may he send down upon us grace to think aright!

I. "The day" was *the termination of his mission to us and of his sojourn among us.*

1. His eternal Father had sent him into the world for the accomplishment of an infinitely great work. That work was no less than the redemption of sinners by the sacrifice of himself. This work was his meat and drink, from the first days of intelligent youth, to the last hour of his natural life. But then the work included an unspeakable amount of mental and bodily suffering. He had to expiate sin by enduring all the sorrow and all the torture which it deserved. This he endured to the full: and now that, in his last pang of body and soul, he had judicially and infallibly said, "*It is finished!*" he was about to return to that bosom from which he had come. "He was taken up" from the miry pit in which for three and thirty years he had sorrowfully lain. "He was taken up" from morning wants and midnight dews, from sighings of heart and groanings in spirit, from bitter agonies and bloody death.

2. And now too his sojourn among us had reached its end. The tabernacle in which he dwelt with man was to be taken up and pitched with God. He had "gone about doing good," "eating and drinking" with kindly but hallowed familiarity, all the while teaching heavenly doctrine, and exhibiting spotless and winning example. At length the day for his triumphal departure from his poor but chosen companions dawned on the world. "He was taken up," and bodily eyes, after tracing his ascent as far as they could, saw him no more!

II. "The day" was *the commencement of mediatorial glory to himself, and of mediatorial advocacy for us.*

1. "He was taken up," not only to the glory which he had with the Father before the world was, but to that additional glory which as a faithful servant he had earned, and as a champion-conqueror he had won.

No proof is wanted to assure us that Jesus was "taken up" to all the glories of his home and of his office. Himself declared that he was going to them; and apostle after apostle was inspired to avouch the fact. That "he sitteth at the right hand of God," was the testimony of Stephen, when standing as a confessor for his sake before the Jewish Sanhedrin. No marvel that Stephen had the eyes of an angel to gaze upon the very throne of God, when he had "the face of an angel," as his unrighteous judges acknowledged. "Exalted high at God's right hand," and enthroned in eternal glory, our ascended Lord rules the universe,—heaven, earth, hell, and worlds perhaps unrevealed to us, all being subject to his sovereign behest. But his choicest rule, the empire in which his soul delights, is the church for which he died. In the government of that church he is pleased to concentrate all his glory. He so loved it that he gave himself for it: and now that he has resumed the life which he laid down to purchase it, and has ascended the throne of his glory, he watches over it night and day, that he may deliver it from all the dangers which encompass it, and eventually bring it to the mountain of his rest.

2. But while he reigns amid the plaudits and adorations of celestial beings, and while he wields a boundless supremacy, to even the skirts of which our thoughts cannot reach, he still condescends to be our ministering High Priest. Yes, "he was taken up" "to appear in the presence of God for us." He went up as our representative in the court of heaven. He went up to plead our cause before the God of our rebellious souls; to whisper our sighs in his ear; to send down good and perfect gifts from him; to prepare a place for us with him; and finally to take us up also, that we may for ever stand before him. Still the great leading practical thought which we are to connect with his being "taken up" is the fact of his perpetual advocacy on our behalf. That "he ever liveth to make intercession for us," is to be the ever lively thought of our hearts. Without this thought energetically stirring within us, we shall neither pray nor praise aright, nor shall we do any really good thing, or find any safe prosperity, throughout the daily walk of life. Where will be the contrite sinner's comfort unless, as our Church bids, we can stand up and say, "Hear what comfortable words St. John saith: If any man sin, we have *an Advocate with the Father*, Jesus Christ the righteous, and he is the propitiation for our sins"? Or where shall we find solace for the weeper, and for him whose spirit is wounded by some keen anguish, unless

we could adduce St. Paul as saying, "We have not a High Priest which *cannot* be touched with the feeling of our infirmities, but was in all points tempted like as we are."

III. "The day" *was anticipated under the old dispensation, and may well therefore be remembered under the new.* As it was the last day of Christ's dwelling in sorrow on the earth, and the first of his mediatorial glory in heaven, it was likely that a day of such solemn importance, and of such triumphant magnificence, would be preceded by some intimations of its destined character.

1. Accordingly we find that in the Jewish ritual God provided an annual representation of Christ's being "taken up" to the throne of his priestly glory. On the great day of atonement the high priest, with much solemnity, and before the gaze of the congregation, entered into "the holy of holies." He went in thither to sprinkle the blood of a chief sacrifice before the ark of the mercy-seat. This ceremonial entrance into the most holy place was, as the epistle to the Hebrews informs us, a type of the day of Christ's going into heaven as the High Priest of his people. This then was the stated intimation of "the day," of which the present day is the last anniversary which the church has yet seen.

There were also occasional intimations of a more august description. These riveted the attention of the people, and were as the larger nails of a fabric, "fastened in a sure place." What the taking up of Enoch was is not narrated to us: but the translation of Elijah to the heavenly mansions is minutely described. The entire occurrence was a splendid and memorable picture of the taking up of Christ from amid his disciples to the right hand of God. Prior however to the age of Elijah, there was one other remarkable occasion by which the great event of this day was foreshadowed to the church. That occasion was David's carrying up the ark from an inferior dwelling to a nobler and more exalted position in Zion. This removal and elevation of the ark was marked with both regal pomp and with priestly as well as with popular celebrations. All Israel was aroused to the ceremony, and the pen of inspiration was busy in framing sweet and glorious songs to accompany it. Those songs are our appointed psalms for the day. Some of them you have this morning heard; and all of them you may study at your personal or domestic leisure.

2. If Jehovah then made such arrangements for Israel's *anticipation* of "the day," we assuredly cannot be too careful in our *remembrance* of it. Some Christians affect to despise all such memorials of the leading events in our Redeemer's history. They however who know human nature, how easily it lets slip divine truths, and how greatly it needs to be reminded of every thing which concerns salvation, will not and do not despise any regulation which, with perfect simplicity and freedom from all superstition, reminds men of those few past days in which the destiny of all mankind was involved.

With ourselves the practical point is this: if we "regard the day," let us "regard it unto the Lord." How then shall we best regard it, so as to be honourable to that Lord and beneficial to ourselves?

i. Let it remind us that, though Christ the Lord is "taken up" from us, *he still lives and rules among us.* It was only his *bodily* presence which the church lost by his ascension into heaven. His spiritual presence is as really with us as it is with the saints in heaven. We are not therefore to be like children who, because they do not see the parent whom a curtain alone conceals, think that that parent does not see them. Draw back the curtain of the sky, and we shall see him who always sees us. Yes, Christ is an ever present Saviour and Governor. He is *nigh* to the contrite heart, and to all that call upon him. "He upholdeth all things by the word of his power," and "ruleth among the children of men." One act of his rule and governance we too commonly forget: it is he which "fixeth the bounds of our habitation." It is our ascended Lord who, to speak technically, makes us parishioners of this or that parish. It is his providence which orders all the circumstances of our birth and residence. Then let my fellow parishioners this day go forth in his name to beat or perambulate the bounds of our parish. It is his right and rule over us which, as one section of an ancient city, we are to remember and acknowledge. Without his blessing our respected parish would soon fall into disesteem. A queen, the noblest whom our country had ever seen, once halted before the old church of our parish, and graciously said to the surrounding throng, "Good people, God bless ye all!" That good wish has long been realized. May he who followed it with his blessing renew his good will to us this day, and send also his freshest blessing into every habitation which our circuit is about to embrace!

ii. Let "the day" remind us that *our residence in any parish is short, transient and uncertain.* Our Lord tarried not on earth for half the allotted term of human life. He was "taken up" in the midst of his days. He knew his term and time. We do not. At a moment's notice we may quit our earthly life and be "taken up" to a brighter realm, or sent down to a darker abode. They who traverse our boundaries this day may never traverse them again. Some *must* expect to be in eternity when another season comes round: and many a one perhaps *will* be there, who now little expects any such change.

iii. Let "the day" *admonish us more intently to set our affections on things above.* Whither Christ "was taken up," thither are we in heart and mind to follow him. He is to be our treasure, on which our hearts are to be set. The things which are in the home of his presence are to be our first aim and all our desire. All that our eyes will see in our approaching perambulation are fading and perishing possessions. Not one stone will ultimately be left upon another; but every thing shall be burnt up, and clean dissolved. How wise then will it be to secure an everlasting habitation,—one of those mansions which Christ hath gone up to prepare for them that love him!

iv. Let "the day" certify us that, *like as Christ was "taken up" into heaven, so will he return from heaven.* That time will indeed be "*the* day," the *great* day, the day of universal doom. If we live in Christ and die in Christ, it will be *our* ascension-day. And O what a procession will that be which shall enter and perambulate the eternal city. Christ will head it, and all the company of the redeemed will compose it. May we join it and rejoice in it!

SERMON XXII.

THE JEWS CHARGED WITH KILLING THE PRINCE OF LIFE.[1]

ACTS 3:15.

"And killed the Prince of Life."

STRANGER words than these the world had never heard till St. Peter uttered them. They form a paradox at once so deeply awful, so amazingly sublime, and so affectingly grand, that the wonder is, we are not all subdued and brought to repentance by them. That the Prince (or, as in the margin, the Author) of "*life*" should *die*, and that by violent hands laid upon him, is a mystery as marvellous as any which an angel can study. That he who made all things, and imparted life to all beings, yea, from the meanest reptile to the loftiest archangel, that he should have expired on a cross, is surely an event of such winning strangeness that every heart must be arrested by it. Such indeed *ought* to be the case; but human hearts resemble stones; and so they hear the most stupendous facts, if connected with a holy Saviour, without feeling, without emotion, without one anxious thought as to their own everlasting interest in those facts.

But let *us* not at this present be so insensible. It is our privilege to be members of a community, in which a whole day is annually set apart for the more careful contemplation of the greatest event which earth ever saw, and which heaven will ever celebrate. May our meditation upon that event be accordant with the penitential feeling of our Church, and by the grace of the Holy Spirit be made so profitable to us, that the day may indeed be "a *good* day" for our souls!

Our text is part of St. Peter's address to those Jews who were astonished at the miracle, which he and St. John wrought upon a well-known cripple, who was laid at the gate of the temple for such alms as might be given to him: "And when Peter saw it he answered unto the people, Ye men of Israel, why marvel ye at this? or why look ye so earnestly on us, as though by our own power or holiness we had made this man to walk? The God of Abraham, and of Isaac, and of Jacob, the God of our fathers, hath glorified his Son Jesus; whom ye delivered up, and denied him in the presence of Pilate, when he was determined to let him go. But ye denied the Holy One and the Just, and desired a murderer to be granted unto you; and killed the Prince of life, whom God hath raised from the dead; whereof we are witnesses. And his name, through faith in his name hath made this man strong, whom ye see and know; yea, the faith which is by him hath given him this perfect soundness in the presence of you all." (Verses 12–16.) The circumstances of the crucifixion of Jesus were at this time fresh in the eyes, and ears, and lips of the people. And, as those circumstances were never to be forgotten, so did the apostles never cease to declare

[1] Preached Good Friday Morning, April 21st, 1848.

them to the Gentiles, and to repeat them to the Jews. The reason was, because the life of the world depends on the death of "the Prince of life." We are therefore sure that our text recounts a fact, not only of the deepest interest, but also of the highest practical importance. Hence let me secure your attention to a series of remarks, namely,

I. *That for an event so surpassingly singular, as the killing of "the Prince of life," there must have been both a* CAUSE, *and an* OBJECT. Had all things continued as they were, when God pronounced every thing very good, it could not have been that a nation would have demanded the death of One, "who did no sin," but "went about doing good." There must therefore have arisen some terrible disruption of the concord between God and man, some frightful change (since God changes not) on the part of man himself. Looking at man's original condition, we should say that it was a most unnatural thing for him to hate and persecute a being who was all lovelineess, purity and peace, who never spoke but with tenderness and eloquence, whose presence brought prosperity, and whose touch was life! One would have thought that such a being, wherever he trod, or wherever he breathed, would have been greeted and honoured by all rational creatures. But such was not the case. The reason of the sad contrariety was man's apostasy from his Maker, and the evil which took full possession of all his faculties and affections. This apostasy and this evil placed man under the dominion of death and the devil. From such position there was no release but by an atonement to the insulted majesty of God. A finite being had no power to make that atonement, or to drive death from the dominion which he had obtained. Of necessity a divine person alone could do either. In the forlorn hope of the case, "the Prince of life" interposed, and by willingly engaging to taste death for sinners became able to save to the uttermost every contrite believer. Here was the cause of his death, and the object to be gained by it. The cause was man's apostasy—the object was man's recovery. "Not for himself" did "the Prince of life" submit to death, (for he had done no sin,) but for those who through sin had forfeited present blessedness and eternal bliss. Satan had usurped the rule of this once beautiful and holy world: he ruled it with iron, and rewarded his subjects with death. No hand but one could depose him: nor could that hand effect that object, except by resigning its strength for three days and three nights. This it did; and the result was conquest for us, and everlasting glory both for himself and us. His death has brought us life. His being killed secures our being raised from the dead, if only we believe that he died, and fully act up to that belief.—We next remark,

II. *That the death of "the Prince of life" could not have occurred without his own will and consent.* For the Author of life to be of necessity or casually subject to death, is an impossibility. It is a contradiction of such a nature as involves what never can be reconciled with facts. The self-existing, ever-living God could not be what he is, if destruction could possibly befal him. We are sure therefore, that the Lord Jesus, though incarnate, and made like unto ourselves in every thing but sin, could not be invaded by death, without himself giving permission for such invasion. The reason is to be found in the fact of his Godhead, his own self-existence: for from that Godhead spring his title, "the Prince (or Author) of life," and his power to impart life to others. As man he was *capable* of dying; but as God he must necessarily live. As God-man "he had life in himself," "even as the Father hath life in himself." He had "power also to lay it down" and "power to take it up again."

The Jews indeed "killed him:" but what was the real extent of their power? It was that of the grasshopper; it was less than what the worm possesses over the foot which is raised to crush it in an instant. They had no power over Jesus beyond what he himself was pleased to allow. This truth he very plainly declared to the man who thought he could do as he pleased with him: "Then saith Pilate unto him, Speakest thou not unto me? knowest thou not that I have power to crucify thee, and have power to release thee? Jesus answered, Thou couldest have no power at all against me, except it were given thee from above: therefore he that delivered me unto thee hath the greater sin." (John 19:10, 11.)

The resignation of life by the Lord Jesus, though it was apparently forced by murderous hands, was nevertheless entirely free. His own words, as previously alluded to, declare the fact: "Therefore doth my Father love me, because I lay down my life, that I might take it again. No man taketh it from me, but I lay it down of myself. I have power to lay it down, and I have power to take it again." (John 10:17, 18.) The circumstances of the crucifixion bore remarkable evidence of the fact. When the executioners offered him the usual preparation for benumbing the sense of feeling, their "wine and myrrh," or "vinegar and gall," as it was called, he refused to take it. He had no need of such reliefs, when he had power over death itself, and was resolved to give up himself to all its pangs. Hence, when all the usual inflictions were inflicted on him and death was naturally inevitable, he waited not for the insensibilites of the last lingering hours, but, while possessing full consciousness and sufficient strength to cry with even a loud voice, he "*gave up* the ghost." *He* voluntarily surrendered that life which the Jews thought *they* had taken from him. Here was the anomalous but actual truth, the Jews "*killed* the Prince of life;" and yet "the Prince of life" *consented* to taste death. It was their murder, but his surrender. This surrender, dear brethren, constitutes the wonder of his death. It was "his love and his pity" for perishing man, which induced him to offer his life as a sacrifice to the justice of God. In that free consent to the laying of murderous hands upon him, was comprised a love as vast as it is adorable. We think it a great thing for the prince of a realm to humble himself to the guise of a pilgrim or stranger, that he may carry some needed relief to a cottage or a prison. But when did we hear of the generosity of a prince, who willingly forfeited his very life to save the head of the bitterest enemy of his empire? "The Prince of life" did both. He came in disguise to the dungeon of our world, and laid down his life for the prisoners who were in it. He stood and saw the enemies of his throne fierce in their hostility, but ready to sink into a yawning gulf. To save them from destruction, he cast himself into the gulf, and by his death preserved their life. This was the love of that Prince whom the Jews, with wicked hands, crucified and slew. St. Paul conveys to us his own impressions of that love, when, in his epistle to the Romans, he thus eloquently says: "For, when we were yet without strength, in due time Christ died for the ungodly. For scarcely for a righteous man will one die: yet peradventure for a good man some would even dare to die. But God commendeth his love toward us, in that, while we were yet sinners, Christ died for us." (Romans 5:6–8.) "*While we were yet sinners!*" O that these words were always before us! O that we felt our sin, and loathed it! O that the thought of Christ's being killed because of it would humble us to the dust for it! O that our hearts would melt under the softening power of that unspeakable love, which led him to resign his life for our salvation! Then, and not till then, shall we rise superior to the love of earthly things, and say to the willing Sufferer, "O thou, whom my soul loveth!"

It follows as a very natural remark,

III. *That, upon an event so unparalleled and so strange as the killing of "the Prince of life," it was likely that corresponding results would occur.* And such results did occur. The human mass was insensible, but inanimate creatures felt the shock and the blow of the atrocious deed. The hearts of priests and people were callous and unmoved; but the ground trembled, and the rocks burst asunder. The eyes of evil men mockingly gazed upon him, when expiring in agonies; but the orb of day retired, and withdrew his beams at so fearful and monstrous a sight. The murderers stripped his immaculate body, and cast lots for his clothing; but darkness came, and threw his pall-like mantle over the beloved corpse. Besides, while living men were dead to shame and feeling, the dead and the buried arose from their tombs, and walked, as warning witnesses, into the so-called "holy city." The veil too of the temple was mysteriously rent asunder; Pilate was dismayed and dreadfully uneasy; and philosophers, as history reports, surmised that either nature was at a stand still, or the God of nature was expiring. But what availed these prodigies? They availed but little; for Jerusalem had filled up the measure of her iniquity, and wanted only the rejection of the last offer of pardon, to make it run over the brim. Then, in due but rapid time, judgment came and made inquisition for blood. She found it where the people themselves had placed it,—on their own brazen heads and stony hearts. Then followed desolation and dispersion, universal "hissing and scorn," "the proverb and the by-word." To this hour that judgment frowns on the descendants of those who "killed the Prince of life;" nor will it cease until "they shall look upon him whom they have pierced, and shall mourn" with penitent bitterness and sanctified sorrow.

But other results followed the death of "the Prince of life." A faithful few were raised up to confess his glory even when it was most intensely obscured. A crucified thief expired with joy in his heart and the boldest truth upon his tongue. A Roman centurion became a noble confessor. A rich councillor begged the crucified body; and honourable women brought spices for its embalmment. From that period to this hour, myriads of souls, under every variety of human circumstance, have rejoiced in the death of him who, though killed, willingly laid down his life for their salvation. May the number of those who, amid godly grief, thus spiritually rejoice, receive large accessions all over the world! And, not least, may that number be increased from among ourselves; for, unless we personally and individually swell the number, Good Friday will yield no goodness to us, and our profession of faith in the dying Redeemer will be but a profitless lip-service. Then "do ye now believe?" Let the question meet your earnest thought and your honest answer.

Lastly, let us say, and do you mark,

IV. *That the event, though worthy of a day of special commemoration, is to be the theme of habitual meditation.* The death of "the Prince of life" may well as a fact have its anniversary; but, if that anniversary be set up in the place of daily recollection, man's appointment will only do sad dishonour to God's intention. Never can it be said that we fulfil the divine intention, unless the crucifixion of the Saviour is the grand thought and leading principle of our hearts. To think of him as killed in our stead is to be the perpetual theme of our minds. All our meditations are to branch off from it. Our principles and motives are to be invigorated by it; and, in ten thousand varied ways, are we to be familiar with it. We must rest all our hopes upon it, as well as trace all our mercies to it. It is to be our stay in life, and our song in death. Well indeed may we make it such, because it will be the germ of that life, and the burthen of that song, which await us after death. "Thou wast slain!" will be an eternally repeated declaration, amid the throngs who will be assembled around the throne of the risen Redeemer. But for the present we have solemn facts to weigh, and hallowed duties to perform. It is a fact that every impenitent person stands charged with the murder of the Prince of life. The Jews were only the agents of that deed of blood to which all sinners consent. If they repent not, good for them would it be, had they never been born. Then see to that work of the soul, repentance for the sins which crucify the Prince of life afresh, and put him to an open shame. And let the true believer mind that Prince's command to show forth his death. Let him love to obey it, "in season, and out of season," and expect to find "grace for grace" in so doing.

SERMON XXIII.

CONVERSE WITH CHRIST OBSERVED BY THE WORLD.[1]

ACTS 4:13.

"And they took knowledge of them, that they had been with Jesus."

THE book of the Acts of the Apostles is the missionary register of those days which witnessed, and of those men who experienced, the miraculous effusion of the Holy Ghost. It is the only authentic history of the labours and successes of the immediate followers of our Lord. Without it there would be a blank space in the foreground of the Church, and an absence of many most interesting events and most important truths, which no other part of the New Testament can supply.

It may seem a wonderful circumstance for Gideon's handful of men to have routed the almost countless hosts of Midian: but that a few poor fishermen, obscure and illiterate persons, should have braved the haughty scorn of Jerusalem, and have morally "turned the world upside down," is a fact unexampled in the history of revolutions, and one which will not cease to be felt until the Church militant shall have become the Church triumphant.

Among the bold and faithful deeds of the apostles, the one which is recorded in connexion with our text holds a prominent rank. Peter and John had wrought a miracle in the name of their crucified Master. This, with their energetic preaching of his gospel, aroused the good-will of the people and the animosity of the priests. They were personally seized and formally examined in the ecclesiastical court. The two apostles were enabled to speak with an intrepidity and a power which the authorities could not possibly resist. In their surprise, those authorities recollected that they had seen them in company with Jesus, and so, it seems, attributed their boldness and freedom of speech to their intercourse with him: "And they took knowledge of them, that they had been with Jesus." When we have contemplated these words in their historical bearing, a few instructive and admonitory remarks will very naturally follow. In this work may the Spirit of Jesus be with us!

I. *The historical bearing of the text* has its root in a fact. That fact is, that Peter and John had associated with Jesus, and that the Jewish rulers knew it.

1. Peter and John, together with their ten companions, had not only been in constant attendance on Jesus, but had been chosen of him for that very purpose. Himself said of them and to them, "Ye also shall bear witness, because *ye have been with me* from the beginning." Themselves also solemnly recognised the fact, when after the death of the traitor Judas they in council said, "Wherefore of these men which have companied with us all the time that the Lord Jesus went in and out *among us*, beginning from the baptism of John, unto that same day that he was taken up from among us, must one be ordained to be a witness with us of his resurrection." (Acts 1:21, 22.)

It is remarkable too that, though they were illiterate and civilly unrecognised persons, and though all the time their

[1] Preached Sunday Morning, April 7th, 1850.

Master was with them they were filled with many carnal notions and selfish prejudices, yet was provision made for the counteracting of these evils, and for bringing to their recollection important things which, while under the influence of those notions and prejudices, they were likely not to notice as they might, or not to remember as they ought. Their beloved Lord knew their infirmities, and so made an omnipotent arrangement for the remedying of them. That arrangement was the wondrous gift of his holy Spirit, the Comforter. Of him he said to them, "He shall *bring all things to your remembrance.*" This accounts for our Lord's saying and doing many things which he knew his disciples did not at the time understand. He said and did them fully intending that, in due time, they should understand them. No doubt therefore after his ascension to heaven his sayings and doings came back, as it were, flashingly and vividly to their minds, helping them in many a doubt and comforting them in many a difficulty. So that, although they had been much with Jesus in body, they were now more with him in spirit. Take only a single illustration in the case of each of his two disciples. Peter, in his second epistle, feelingly alludes to the mount of transfiguration, and the rapturous presence of the Saviour, "when there came such a voice to Jesus from the excellent glory, 'This is my beloved Son, in whom I am well pleased:' and this voice, which came from heaven, we heard *when we were with him* in the holy mount." (2 Peter 1:17, 18.) St. John opens his first general epistle with a similar reference to his having been with Jesus: "That which was from the beginning, which we have heard, which we have seen with our eyes, which we have looked upon, and our hands have handled of the Word of life; (for the life was manifested, and we have seen it, and bear witness, and show unto you that eternal life, which was with the Father, and was manifested unto us;) that which we have seen and heard declare we unto you, that ye also may have fellowship with us: and truly our fellowship is with the Father and with his Son Jesus Christ." (1 John 1:1–3.)

Now all such clear and intense remembrance of what they witnessed when they were with Jesus must have greatly aided and animated them in the arduous and trying position to which they were called when the Jewish rulers summoned them to their tribunal. Under the reminding influence of the Holy Spirit they would be sure to recollect the energy of wisdom with which their Lord replied to all the cavils of his opponents, and how, on one occasion especially, his meekness seemed to lose itself in holy indignation against the hypocrisy and selfishness of the scribes, Pharisees, and lawyers around him. They could not also fail to remember that he had admonished them of the coming of just such a time as that which they were then seeing: "They shall lay their hands on you, and persecute you, delivering you up to the synagogues, and into prisons, being brought before kings and rulers for my name's sake. And it shall turn to you for a testimony. Settle it therefore in your hearts, not to meditate before what ye shall answer: for I will give you a mouth and wisdom, which all your adversaries shall not be able to gainsay or resist." (Luke 21:12–15.) This promise was now being fulfilled to them, for they were enabled to speak with a "boldness" which astonished their adversaries, and which, added to the miracle, positively silenced their cavils. (Ver. 13.)

2. The Jewish rulers, struck with the demeanour of the two apostles, "took knowledge of them that they had been with Jesus," that is, they recollected that when they had themselves disputed with Jesus, or seen him in the temple or elsewhere, they had also seen these two disciples with him: and, as they had felt the withering force of his words against them, they naturally imputed the confidence and boldness of these two men to their intimacy with him as their teacher and master. It was as though they familiarly said among themselves: "All this impertinent boldness comes from their intercourse with '*that fellow*' who called us 'vipers,' 'hypocrites,' 'children of hell,' and what not! As with the master and tutor so with the servants and pupils!" Now this was a natural conclusion, but on their part it was an aggravation of their wickedness. It was but likely, and in reality it was true enough, that their having been with Jesus was the secret of their courage and their manly eloquence. The seeds of every requisite qualification had been sown, by his own hand, in their hearts, during his presence with them: and now, on his ascension from them, the dew of his Spirit had quickened those seeds into fruitful maturity. They were a marvel to their persecutors, and probably not less such to themselves. In the case of Peter, we may very properly pause to admire the display of divine grace in him. At the wicked trial of his Lord he was ashamed to avow him. When a simple maidservant took knowledge of him that he had been with Jesus, he timidly but fully denied the fact. But now when put on his own trial for his Lord's sake, and when recognised, not by a mere maid-servant but by the chief authorities of the nation, he fearlessly preached Christ to them, and openly charged them with being his betrayers and murderers. How thoroughly does this prove the sincerity of his repentance, and how beautifully does it manifest the grace of that loving, melting, omnipotent *look*, which broke his heart more effectually than his own bitterest tears, and yet healed it with a sweetness and a perfection which nothing but itself can produce!

But it was said that the conclusion which the Jewish rulers formed was an aggravation of their wickedness. It was such because, in recognising the character of Jesus in the conduct of his disciples, they loved it none the more and hated it none the less. They took knowledge of what they detested; and so, by setting at nought the affecting testimony of his disciples, they rejected the opportunity of that repentance, and the offer of that remission of sins, which he had mercifully and pitifully commanded to be preached "*first* at Jerusalem." (Luke 24:47.)

II. The remarks, to which this review of the historical bearing of our text seems appropriately to lead us, may be commenced thus:

1. That, notwithstanding the resurrection and ascension of our Lord, we *may still be with Jesus*. Though, as St. Paul says, "we know him no more in the flesh," yet may we know him more than ever in the spirit. Himself, on leaving his true followers, said, "I will not leave you comfortless (Gr. orphans); I will come unto you." And all his invitations for poor sinners to come unto him are just as fresh and forceful as in the hour that his gracious lips uttered them. His standing invitation, both to the church and to the world, is to come to him and be with him. "Behold, I stand at the door and knock: if any man hear my voice and open the door, I will come in to him, and will sup with him, and he with me." What is his call to prayer but an invitation to commune with him on the throne of his heavenly grace? What is the preaching of his gospel but a message to sinners and saints to come into his presence, the one for pardon and the other for comfort? And what is the spreading of his sacramental table but a setting forth of his readiness, not only to admit us to his presence, but to bring us into the very interior of his banqueting house, where his banner over us shall be love? And what is the calm and closeted reading of his holy word but a time of converse with him, a being with him in the past but deathless sayings of his lips, and the standard doings of his grace? When "the word of Christ dwells in us richly," we may be sure that himself is not far off. But there is also the steady walk of the Christian life, by which we may always be with Jesus. "Enoch walked with God," that is, held habitual converse with him, was in spirit so familiar with his presence, and had such a realization of it, that his whole life was a companionship with God. Now that the same God is revealed to us in the person of Christ we may say with St. John, "Truly our fellowship (our walk, companionship) is with the Father, and with his Son Jesus Christ."

Let it however be remembered that there is a sort of *negative* mode of being with Jesus, that is, the ceasing to be where he is not wont to be, and the not being with those who never desire to be with him, *plainly*, by our withdrawal from the haunts, the friends, the fashions, the triflings of a vain and wicked world. With equal plainness let it be said, there is very little difficulty in understanding what the word of God means by such expressions as "the world," "the fashion of this world," and "the friends of the world." Apply our text *as a rule*, and all will soon be clear, when dubious cases occur to us. "Can I be with Jesus, in that company, or in that place?" is a question which, if honestly addressed to our hearts, wilt not long leave us in doubt. It is historically said that Alexander the Great, when a manly youth, was one day asked to run in a race with some of the common people. His reply was, "Were I not a king's son I should not regard my company; but being a prince I must keep such company, and do such things, as become the rank which the gods have given me." Christian friends, if you would be one with Christ you must walk with Christ; you must consider your high relationship and act in accordance with it. If you run with the multitude, in the vain race of pleasure, pomp, and frivolity, you may profess to be with Jesus, but he will not be with you.

2. *Being with Jesus will, through the grace of the Spirit, produce in us corresponding results*. Peter and John had insensibly almost at the time caught much of the character of Jesus. Impressions were made on them, and feelings and sentiments were imbibed by them, which, though not influential at the instant, were destined to be permanent, and eventually operative, and all pervading. Character, we well know, receives much of its light and shade by the intercourse under which it is formed. Close intimacy between persons generally produces a similarity of disposition and habit. The like effect must reasonably follow from spiritual association with Jesus. To be in heart and mind with him, and to live, if not always in the light of his countenance, yet habitually under the power of his presence, can hardly fail of producing such effects as will give a character to us beyond what we naturally possess. It will effect in us no inconsiderable change of sentiment, temper, and conduct.

i. We cannot be with Jesus without *un*-learning many *erroneous sentiments*. In the faith and love of one so meek and lowly as he we shall find no room for high notions of ourselves. In the perfection of his righteousness all ours will appear but as cobwebs and filthy rags. In the beauty of his holiness our own will vanish into absolute impurity. Unlearning such fondnesses as these imply, we must of course come to the reception of all saving truth from himself. We shall take him just as he offers himself to us, "The Lord our righteousness," our "All and in all." Not least shall we take him as "The Lord of the Sabbath," and delight to conform our views of the Christian Sabbath to the full sanctity of his. There will be no petty quibblings on that important subject, if we do but heartily keep it with him. Let us be with Jesus on the day of days, and we shall never think that we can give too much of it to him.

ii. *The temper* too of the man who is with Jesus cannot (at least ought not to be) otherwise than improved. "The Lamb of God" is all gentleness, quietness, innocence, and love. To be with him, in the exercise of such qualities, will be a check and a chain to our opposite tendencies. Temper is one of the last things which divine grace conquers: but the religion of Jesus is sure to modify it in *some* degree. It will make a good temper better, and either correct a bad one or keep it from being worse. Peter, before the council, was no longer headstrong and hasty; nor was John inclined to call down fire from heaven upon the Jewish adversaries, as he once was upon the Samaritans. (Luke 9:54.)

iii. In *conduct* too how marvellous will be the change! Who can go about with Jesus doing good, and yet stand spiritually idle all the day long? Who can hear his wisdom, and see his sanctity, and witness his earnestness to save souls alive, and yet feel pleasure in "jesting which is not convenient," and in "foolish talking;" or not feel pain in every instance of sin and neglect of salvation? Assuredly if we are with Jesus we shall do as Jesus does. His conduct will be the model for ours, for verily "he hath left us an example that we should follow his steps."

3. *If our being with Jesus makes us at all like him, we shall be taken knowledge of by those around us.* Peter and John were not more observed by their rulers than we shall be by our neighbours, if like the apostles we are bold for our holy Christ, and opposed to an unholy world. It always has been that sterling and consistent Christians have many eyes upon them. They are in fact as public "epistles, known and read of all men." Their Master compared them to "cities set on a hill." We may be sure therefore that many will walk round about them, not to admire the beauty of their structure as a whole, but to spy out the cracks and crevices of their otherwise stable walls. What St. Paul said of himself and his followers may be said of all true followers of Jesus: "We are made a spectacle to the world, to angels, and to men." There is too a peculiar sagacity in the eye of those who watch that spectacle. Men of the world are quick in discerning the flaws and faults of the associates of Jesus. It is a matter of dark interest with them so to do, because the more faults they espy in the professors of religion the more excuses they think they gain for not being themselves religious. All this is so much argument and admonition for our walking circumspectly, and taking heed that we never bring discredit on that blessed Saviour whom we profess to follow.

4. *Being with Jesus leads to present and future blessedness too inestimable to be told.* Even the disciples, during the comparative darkness of their minds, felt the preciousness of their Master's presence. When he provingly asked them if they also would leave him, their ready reply was, "To whom else should we go? Thou hast the words of eternal life!" Those words he will impart to all who abide with him. His presence renders all things bright and bearable in this homeless world, while companionship with him is the sure pledge of protection for the soul amid all its perils and dangers. Indeed bright evidences, rich consolations, and warm experiences are generally the results of being habitually with Jesus. Many saints who have gone before us to where he now is have left testimony to this fact. One especially, who had long laboured in the church, said as he was dying to friends around him, "You have heard or read the words of many dying men: now these are mine. I have found a life of communion with Christ the happiest life in the world. *Strait* indeed is the gate and *narrow* is the way; but if the way be narrow it is not long, and if the gate be strait it opens into eternal life!" Who then would not be with Jesus? When you hear of dying, you would fain have him with you at your death. But *he* will not come to you then unless you come to him now. You must be with him in life if you would realise his presence in death, and his smile in the day of judgment. Amen!

SERMON XXIV.

THEY WHO TURN THE WORLD UPSIDE DOWN.[1]

ACTS 17:6.

"These that have turned the world upside down are come hither also."

[1] Preached Sunday Morning, December 17th, 1848.

HE who brought his own blessed gospel from heaven told us how it was likely to be received among men. He told those, whom he sent to preach it, that they should be hated of all men for his name's sake. He prepared them to expect, not the plaudits of an admiring world, but the bitter scoffs of a hostile population. When therefore the apostles went forth, "preaching every where that men should repent," it did not surprise them to find their Master's words come true. They were ready for the misunderstanding of their motives, and for the misrepresentation of their conduct, which they too frequently had to bear.

The instance before us was only one of many in which rough treatment accompanied the most absurd calumny. Paul and his companion Silas had simply preached the gospel of a crucified Saviour, in a synagogue of the Jews at Thessalonica. Instantly an opponent party, who hated the holiness of their doctrine, raised a violent clamour against them, and reported them to the magistrates of the place as movers of sedition, and traitors to the government of the land. "These," said they, "that have turned the world upside down, have come hither also:" "these all do contrary to the decrees of Cæsar, saying that there is another king, one Jesus."

As is very commonly the case, those who clamoured these charges were in reality the greatest offenders: for it was notorious that "the unbelieving Jews" hated the decrees of Cæsar, and in heart repudiated his sway over themselves. But, when men reject the truth of Christ, they gladly take up any falsehood that will serve their turn against his ministers or his people.

As the spirit of the charge in question is as fresh in the world as it ever was, let us see, first, wherein it was false, and then wherein, unknown to those who brought it, it was actually true.

I. *Wherein was the charge of turning the world upside down notoriously false?*

1. It was false as to *apostolical principle.* There was no conspiracy among the apostles against the rights of rulers or the liberties of the people. There was no subtle plot for the subversion of order and institution as regards the temporal government of nations. No dark policy, no artful fraternity, existed among them, for discovering state secrets or baffling state plans. They indulged no ambitious projects for grasping power and lording it over regal heads. In a word, it was not their *principle* to concern themselves with secularities. The kingdom which they were commissioned to establish was not of this world, neither did its establishment require the subversion of existing governments as to any thing worldly. There was no need for them to upturn any government in order to reduce it to Christian obedience. They on the contrary aimed at simply instilling Christian truth into men's hearts, well knowing that the reception of that truth would work its own wonders whether with kings or people. They accordingly were friends of order, peace, and equity, and had no thought of dethroning Cæsar or any other ruler.

As to the charge in question,

2. It was false as to *apostolic practice.* Nowhen and nowhere did the apostles either jointly or severally interfere with the kingdoms of the world. As they had no principle to incite them to such interference, so did they follow no practice which accorded with it. They were "not busy-bodies in other men's matters," especially in the greater matters of national rule and government. Consequently they meddled not with *mere* politics. And yet, as was to be expected, St. Paul was accused of doing this. The accusation however was futile; for what his enemies misrepresented as pestilent intervention with the forms of government was simply truthful earnestness in his Master's cause. Both he and all his fellows, as far as their acts are recorded, were worthy of the best thanks of all governments, inasmuch as they strenuously enjoined obedience to civil rulers, and paid that obedience themselves. Whatever the lawful government was, whether imperial or popular, so that it required nothing contrary to godliness, they steadfastly upheld it and honestly submitted to it. Thus they nowhere "turned the world upside down" in the sense which was imputed to them.

II. *Wherein was the charge just and true?* As it was false according to the sense in which the accusers brought it, so was it true in a manner which they little suspected.

The success of Satan in the apostasy of Adam produced such a revulsive change in the world as might well be called a turning of it "upside down." Everything was morally inverted from its original position. Man was no longer what he had been. His heart was out of place, and all things in it were perverted and corrupted. To meet this shocking upturn of the whole moral creation, the God of love devised the plan of our redemption. His gospel was the chosen instrument for turning the world back again to its original position. But because the defection of the world from God has been of such long standing, and sinful hearts "love to have it so," we all by nature regard the present posture of things as its original and rightful condition. Hence, when the gospel produces its proper effects among men, the bystanders call it by ill names, and describe it as a senseless and tumultuous overturning of the due order of things. "Art thou he that *troubleth* Israel?" cries one. "He hath a devil!" says another. "Paul, thou art beside thyself!" exclaims a third. And no lack is there of defamatory imputation when the ministers of Christ are made strong to turn upside down some portion of the world which lieth in wickedness.

Regarding therefore the world in its moral existence, it was most true that the apostles tried to turn it upside down. They aspired to undo what Satan had done; they aimed to turn men back again from darkness to light, to invert the existing order of things as they stand toward God, and to bring about a mighty and glorious change all the world over. That such was the aim of all the apostles we may surely conclude from the commission which was given to the last but not the least of them: "Delivering thee from the people, and from the Gentiles, unto whom now I send thee, to open their eyes and to turn them from darkness to light, and from the power of Satan unto God, that they may receive forgiveness of sins, and inheritance among them which are sanctified by faith that is in me." (Acts 26:17, 18.)

No doubt then the apostle Paul everywhere laboured to fulfil his high commission, and to effect that moral upturning in the world which that commission implied. Taking the charge against him in this sense, he not only would not deny it but would openly glory in it. Thus we perceive how the opponents of the gospel, in their utterance of calumny or falsehood, sometimes unwittingly declare God's truth. Caiaphas little thought that he was speaking the high verities of prophecy when he said, "It is expedient that one man should die for the people." And little did the Thessalonian rabble imagine that, in accusing Paul and Silas of what they had not done, they correctly specified the very thing which, though in a very different sense, they were doing and desired to do.

III. *What are the practical uses which we should make of the text before us?*

To search out those uses and to apply them is our main business in the contemplation of a text so remarkable as the one which we are hearing. The best intellectual perception of scripture verities will avail us nought unless it is followed up by a practical application of them to the heart and life. Let us then regard the present text

1. *As indicating the nature of true religion.* It is something analogous to the turning of a world upside down. It is a thorough subversion of some things and a marvellous introduction of others. It is in fact that mighty change of principles and habits in a man which the Scriptures denominate a new birth, a resurrection, and a new creation. Such terms are most comprehensive, and describe to us such a change as admits of no half or incomplete degrees, but those only which are total and entire.

Here however thousands begin their mistake in opining what true religion is. They settle its standard as a sort of partial alteration or half-measured change. They mistake mere morality for vital piety, decency for devotion, external propriety for internal holiness, things merely ecclesiastical for things savingly spiritual. They are averse to the plain meaning of the plain terms of Scripture, when setting forth the nature and power of true religion in the soul of a sinner. They cannot bear to think that it really is tantamount to a turning of all things upside down in heart and life. But if we would be right in our estimate of true religion we must derive our notions of it from the unerring word of God. In that word we are taught to believe that the effect of the religion of the gospel is an entire change of the whole inner man. We must be made *new* creatures in Christ Jesus, old things must *pass away* with us, and *all* things become new. The inner world of our pride and passion, lust and ambition, with all their satellites and appendages, must be turned thoroughly upside down. In their room and stead must be set up those things which had been kept down. Christ must be placed on the throne of our hearts, and godliness must do homage to him in every part of our lives. This, dear brethren, is the religion which we desire to see paramount among you—a religion which will make you a wonder to yourselves, a joy to angels, and an honour to your God—a religion which alone will bring you satisfaction or salvation.

Then see and examine if you are partakers of this religion, if you really have experienced in yourselves that upturning of things evil and that implanting of things good which our Saviour intended when he said, "Except ye be *converted* and become as little children ye shall in no wise enter the kingdom of heaven."

Regard the text further

2. *As proving the power of the gospel in the ministration of the Spirit.* What was it which produced the strange sensation and the singular effects which the unbelieving Jews compared to a turning of the world upside down? *What* was it? It was simply the gospel of Christ when preached by earnest and faithful men. All that Paul had done was to *reason* with the Jews, and to *prove* to them, from their own scriptures, that Jesus of Nazareth was the very Christ. There was nothing violent, nothing exciting or extravagant on the part of the apostle in his addresses at Thessalonica. On the contrary there was calm reasoning and logical deduction, whatever else there might be as to eloquence of language and earnestness of manner. Still it was the weight and force of the gospel which produced the astonishing changes, and thus excited so much distaste and reprobation. St. Paul well knew this power of the gospel of his Saviour, and had already tested it elsewhere. Writing to the Roman saints, he said, "For I am not ashamed of the gospel of Christ: for it is the power of God unto salvation, to every one that believeth; to the Jew first, and also to the Greek." (Romans 1:16.) It was too a familiar thought with him that God accomplishes great things by simple instruments, and exhibits his infinite wisdom by means which earthly minds count folly. He knew that the ritual-loving Jew and the philosophic Greek looked upon preaching as sheer foolishness. But God by that despised foolishness chose to save them that believe. Such is his choice still: for *never* has he turned any part of the world upside down

but "by the foolishness of preaching." Look where you will, and you will see the first grand move in the up-turn of human hearts brought about by the ministration of the gospel proceeding from the lips of feeble but faithful servants. To this truth our Church directs more than a glance in her collect and epistle and gospel for the day. She calls our attention to the ministry of the gospel mystery, and to John the Baptist as one of the most stirring of all stirring preachers, and in view of those instances prays that the present ministers and stewards of the divine word may, like John, "*turn* the hearts of the disobedient to the wisdom of the just," which is merely a contemplation of that very turning of the moral world upside down which St. Paul effected at Thessalonica. Nothing short of the like to this is, my dear people, what I desire to see accomplished among you. Our ministry will have done but little for you, unless by it God turns you as it were upside down, converting you from sin to holiness, from the love of the world to the love of himself, and so changing you as to impart to you a consciousness that you are what you were not. This will in meekness be evident to you, by your finding that you dislike what you once loved, and love what you once disliked.

Further regard the text

3. *As a noble testimony to the fidelity and zeal of St. Paul and his companion Silas.* For opponents to acknowledge that they had turned the world upside down, though intended as a bitter taunt, was in fact an enviable commendation. It proved that St. Paul, far from being negligent or listless in his work, had earnestly pursued his high calling, and had left no effort untried for the spread of truth and the conversion of souls. When the wicked or the worldly find fault with the successful labours of the servants of Christ, it is a credible token that they have been doing their duty. "The god of this world" cannot look with a favourable eye upon the doings of those who invade his kingdom. But here is a part of his torment: if *he* lifts up his voice against them, it will be turned to their credit and accounted their praise. The wrath of Satan is one honour of the saints.

Well therefore may any minister of the church pause and question his position, when all men speak well of him. The world will let him alone, if he never strives to turn it upside down. But will the great Judge let him alone, in the day when those who have been set to watch for souls must give account? We are sure he will not. The labourers, not the loiterers, will be commended "in that day."

Again consider the text

4. *As teaching all who stand up for God what sort of lot they must expect in an evil generation.* They must make up their minds to be called disturbers of parochial or domestic peace, meddlers or busy-bodies, or to meet with taunt or defamation of some sort or other. This has always been the lot of those who dare to protest against folly, frivolity and sin, and to assert that "without holiness no man shall see the Lord." But none of these things will move the man who lives in awe of his responsibility to God. He will know that the scoff of opponents is a part of his test. Should he shrink from it, and trim his conduct so as to avoid its blast, he will only be likely to make shipwreck by "the blasting of the breath" of the divine displeasure. From that there will be no recovery.

It cannot but be that unrenewed hearts will either openly or secretly revile those who follow Christ in the regeneration. They will wag the head, or shoot out the tongue against them. But they who are thus reviled have nothing to fear. He who sits above the noise of the people will shield them in the world, and remember them when it is clean passed away.

Lastly view the text

5. *As revealing a state of things confidently to be expected and devoutly to be wished.* The turning of the world, in a moral and spiritual sense, upside down is what the word of prophecy bids us look for and forward. Half the Bible may be said to be occupied in pointing to this subject. Holy men of old leaped for joy in the prospect of it. Christ lived and died for the future realization of their hopes. All the apostles and saints of the early Christian church laboured for, and delighted in, the furtherance of the mighty change. We who are come to the days, which form the edge or brink of that change, "ought to give the more earnest heed" to that "sure word of prophecy" which declares that our "God will arise to shake terribly the earth," to confound the sinners, and gather the saints, which are upon it. The aspect of the world in its present position may, at first sight, appear unfavourable to the predicted change; inasmuch as the commotions and heavings of the nations around us present no indications of the increase of truth and holiness. Crime and selfishness, or folly and heartlessness, mark the unsettlings of both princes and people. But these very things, which arise from darkness and diabolical device, are just the sort of things which holy scripture teaches us to expect. The last days are to be dark times. Trouble on the one hand, and scoffing and hate on the other, will, we are taught to believe, make up the sum of the world's short interval before the rightful Lord of it shall turn it upside down. Consonant with the same teaching, we gather that the faithful people of Christ are to arm themselves for a struggle, and yet to look up with great joy because their redemption draweth nigh. The upturning of all things will bring no peril to them: they shall be safe in the hollow of a Father's hand, if only they study to keep their spiritual garments clean, and meekly watch for their Lord.

SERMON XXV.

THANKING GOD AND TAKING COURAGE.

Acts 28:15.

"Whom when Paul saw, he thanked God, and took courage."

AT the date of this text, the great apostle was entering upon the last and most eventful period of his life. He had landed in Italy, and was within a day's journey of Rome. He was going thither as an appellant from the authorities in Judea, to the emperor himself. With what reception he might meet from Christian brethren, or with what sentence he might have to depart from the presence of a cruel and capricious despot, he could not exactly tell. He would therefore naturally feel solicitude. But when the brethren, hearing of his arrival at Puteoli, about eight miles from Naples, came from Rome to meet him on his way, some as far as Appii Forum, about fifty miles from the city, and others to the Three Taverns, about thirty, he was so cheered and refreshed by intercourse with them, that he thanked God for past and present mercies, and took courage for the future. In these circumstances there is much that is deeply interesting and eminently instructive. May a large blessing accompany our endeavours to set before you the true spirit of the text. And, first, let me observe,

I. *That the very business, which interested St. Paul and his friends, is precisely that which should mainly interest us.* They, one and all, were intent on the religion of the Lord Jesus. It was that which occupied their thoughts, their conversation, and their counsel. Paul was going to Rome as "the prisoner of the Lord:" and the brethren regarded him as the champion of their despised and persecuted cause. They therefore gladly left their homes to meet him on his way, and to escort him as an honourable prisoner to the imperial city. His entrance into that city they regarded as far more remarkable and joyful than the triumphal procession of any of the heroes of their land, when returning with the tokens of conquest and of the acquisition of other countries to their empire.

Hence his arrival was a joy to them, as his sight of them was a joy to him. And why was it such? Plainly for this reason: they had one common centre of desire, pleasure, and union. The Saviour of the world was their Saviour. The truths of his revelation were their philosophy. The shame of his cross was their glory. Consequently Christ was all their desire, the progress of his cause was their pleasure, and both together united them in one spirit of holiness and love. Besides these brethren were the persons to whom the apostle had written the most elaborate of all his epistles. How naturally would they rejoice at the sight of the man who wrote it, and at having opportunities to converse with him upon the high and stirring topics which it comprises! And how naturally too would the warm heart and strong mind of the apostle recur to all that he had written, with a readiness to go over with word of mouth the ground which he had marked out with his pen!

Religion then, or the realization of the gospel of Christ, was the great topic of interest with the Roman Christians. And such it should be with us; for we have souls at stake precisely as they had; and God sends us his gospel for all the purposes and with all the responsibilities exactly as he sent it to them. If it was their duty to be so intensely interested with the ministration of evangelical truth, as they plainly were, then is the same duty incumbent on us. If they could leave their homes and their businesses to travel some thirty or fifty miles to meet a minister of Christ, and to testify their respect for his person and his work, preparatory to his actual residence among them, what may be justly expected of us, who have privileges and facilities greatly beyond what they enjoyed? Remember too, these Roman brethren were not bishops, priests and deacons (for we read not of such church-officers at Rome), but were simply "saints," converts to the faith from different classes of society, in modern language, "*laymen*" like yourselves. Would then it were that our zeal and devotedness equalled theirs; and that like them we reckoned all imperial splendours, and civic concerns, and local amusements, (whether in their Campus Martius or their river Tiber) as things of very passing and secondary consideration, compared with the one great business of life, the glory of Christ in the conversion of the world and the salvation of our own souls.

Further observation of the text and its bearings induces the remark,

II. *That our wishes are often, by God's providence, accomplished in a way which we little expected.*

St. Paul had long been desirous of visiting Rome. A considerable body of Christians was resident there, although by what means Christianity was introduced among the inhabitants of that city we do not from scripture know, though Clement says it was through "Barnabas." On the day of Pentecost there were at Jerusalem "strangers of Rome," who *might* have carried back the tidings of salvation which they heard on that occasion: or devout soldiers and converted centurions, who like Cornelius loved the truth of Christ, *might* have spread the knowledge of it among their connexions in the regal city. Certain it is that St. Peter could not have planted the gospel in Rome, otherwise St. Paul would never have used the strong and definite language which he does use in his epistle to the Romans (chap. 15. ver. 20.) Now had St. Peter, as modern Romanists assert, been Bishop of Rome for five-and-twenty years already, it is impossible, upon any principle of common honesty, for St. Paul to have said what he broadly does say. He would not "*build upon another man's foundation.*" In these days of bold assertion and arrogant demand it is well for us to be reminded of such facts, on these topics, as holy scripture infallibly contains. But, to recur to our more immediate thesis, St. Paul had long wished to visit Rome. Two or three years before the date of our text he had said to the Roman Christians: "But now having no more place in these parts, and having a great desire these many years to come unto you, whensoever I take my journey into Spain, I will come to you: for I trust to see you in my journey, and to be brought on my way thitherward by you, if first I be somewhat filled with your company." (Chap. 15. ver. 23, 24.) Hence we discern how, after the manner of men, St. Paul had drawn his plan, and arranged his expectations according to it. He thought to travel into Spain, and call at Rome in his way, anticipating that friends there would forward him to his ultimate destination. But how strangely did the providence of God alter these arrangements, and turn the current of all these expectations! Circumstances arise which place the apostle in a new position. He becomes a prisoner, and in that capacity is conveyed, through perils and trials, to the city which he had long desired to visit: so different was God's method of accomplishing his desire to that which he had marked out for himself. He longed to see the brethren of Rome, and had pictured to himself somewhat of the time and the manner in which he should see them: but how little did he think that they would first meet him at Appii Forum and the Three Taverns! And what is this, dearly beloved, but a foreshadowing of our own little way of doing things, and of God's wiser method of bending us to his will? How often have we drawn our plans, and in imagination traced their progress and witnessed their results; when, lo, God has interposed, and by the lifting of his hand has dispersed all our airy expectations, and brought us to realities of his own wonderful ordering! Who among us has not had to say, "I often wished to see this place or that person, I often thought of doing this or attaining that, but I little thought it would be at this time or in this manner"?

My brethren, all these things are intended to school us in a truth which we are very unwilling to learn. That truth is this: *we are not our own masters*; we are dependent on One "in whose hand is our breath, and whose are all our ways." (Daniel 5:23.) Then let us enter deeply into the spirit of St. James's admonition, and habitually act upon it: "Go to now, ye that say, To-day or tomorrow we will go into such a city, and continue there a year, and buy and sell, and get gain: whereas ye know not what shall be on the morrow. For what is your life? It is even a vapour, that appeareth for a little time, and then vanisheth away. For that ye ought to say, If the Lord *will*, we shall live, and do this, or that." (James 4:13–15.)

The conduct of St. Paul further warrants our remarking,

III. *That a thankful disposition always and peculiarly becomes the people of God.*

Intercourse with the parties to whom St. Paul had written gave him great reason to be thankful to that God who had given them grace, and who had blessed his epistle to them. His gratitude therefore rose above fears and anxieties, yea, even above sufferings and disappointments. Strange as was his position compared with his expectations, he found room to be thankful. And such room shall we always find if we consider two things: first, that events are always better than we deserve to experience them; and, secondly, that they might be very much worse. The great apostle passed a low estimate upon himself. No man was ever more sensible than he of his own personal unworthiness. He thought himself "less than the least of all saints," and "not worthy to be called an apostle." Hence he well knew that the prosperous state of the Roman brethren was in no degree attributable to his own merits or deserts. He too who had suffered from false brethren, and had mourned over apostates from the faith, was equally well aware that the state of things among the Roman converts might have called for lamentation rather than for gratitude. Now if we, amid the events of life, more uniformly acted upon these considerations, we should oftener be content where we are dissatisfied, and thankful where we are ready to repine.

But mark the character of St. Paul's gratitude: it was altogether *a godly* gratitude. He "thanked *God*." As a man of God St. Paul was accustomed to refer everything to God, and to attribute all prosperity to his power and grace. And this is what, in every expression of thankfulness for spiritual or providential mercies, we should be careful to do. A disposition to be thankful, and an actual expression of thankfulness, are excellencies of only a certain extent. When the disposition and the expression have direct reference to God, that is the perfection of gratitude. When the heart feels that it owes everything to the free mercy of God, and when the tongue is joyfully free to give utterance to that feeling, then is the thankfulness of the Christian most like what it ought to be.

How becoming such thankfulness is we cannot fail to see when we glance at our position as sinners, and at our expectation as believers. We have nothing but what is given to us, and we never deserved anything. All the glories of heaven are stored up for the man of a penitent and grateful spirit: but those glories would lose half their enjoyableness were it not that eternity will be spent in giving thanks for them. Thus it also is with us in our present state: we lose much of the sweetness of daily mercies for want of a more thankful temper to him who gives them. Were we more habitually grateful for what is given, we should be far less incommoded by what is withheld. Well therefore did the apostle at Appii Forum "*thank God*," since in his epistle to the Thessalonians he had said, "In *everything* give thanks;" and in that to the Ephesians, "Giving thanks *always for all things unto God, and the Father* in the name of our Lord Jesus Christ."

Passing on to a remaining point in the text, let me remark

IV. *That the strongest Christians may faint in their minds, and need encouragement.*

The apostle not only "thanked God," but "took courage." If then he "took courage," he was exposed to discouragement. And no marvel that he was a little cast down and depressed in spirits. To say nothing of the debilitating toils and perils through which he had passed, his prospects on landing in Italy were dark and boding. He was a prisoner bound for the highest court under heaven. He had to stand before Nero, or the Roman senate: the one was, as he himself afterwards called him, "a lion" for fierceness and inhumanity, and the other was a den of opponents to the cross and cause of Christ. Moreover, as his voyage from Judæa had been circuitous and tedious, he could not tell what malice had been doing at Rome by taking some shorter route to that city. He might have been misrepresented to both friends and foes, and an evil impression might have been made respecting him by calumnies secretly uttered. All these uncertainties would naturally tend to depress the strongest mind, especially on landing, after a sea voyage, on the shores of a foreign country. And truly, brethren, how often and how variedly do events occur to awaken our anxieties and arouse our solicitudes! Like the apostle at Appii Forum, we find ourselves harassed with past trials and present difficulties. We are concerned too about impending events, domestic health, turns in our business or profession, the settlement of some personal question, or the issue of some important point which the next period of time is to determine. All such things cause us to feel faint and weary in our minds. Happy is it if they do but lead us to see the vanity of all earthly concerns, and the desirableness of having a refuge to which we can flee under any pressure of heart or soul. Such a refuge had St. Paul; for, as he "thanked God," so without doubt he "took courage *in God*." The intercourse of Christian brethren and the tidings which they brought him were, it seems, a great relief to him: but doubtless his hope was in Christ, the Captain of his salvation and the preserver of his way. And full right was he in relying upon that unfailing source of support; for "vain is the help of man," and unstable is every staff except that which is put into our hand by the great Eternal himself. These very friends who so solaced the apostle, at their place of meeting, as to raise his courage on entering Rome, proved weak and uncertain, to say the least, when his hour of peril before Nero arrived. They had not the courage to stand up for him, or to stand by his side, when he stood before that stern-souled and fickle-minded tyrant. They all "forsook" him, as himself plaintively says in his second epistle to Timothy, chap. 4. ver. 17, "notwithstanding," as the apostle cheeringly adds, "*the Lord* stood with me, and strengthened me." Then learn, my Christian brethren, to make the Lord your stay. All else is frail and uncertain. He is the strength of his people and their portion for ever. Lean on him, and you will never faint or fall; courage will be given to you, and a grateful heart will always bring its own solace from him who gives it and loves it.

And now let none depart without recurring to the former part of this discourse. The *great* business of us all is true religion, religion in our own souls and in the souls of our fellow men. Many another business may be commendable or expedient, and for temporal purposes even necessary: but this is above every temporal consideration. It is the business for which we were born, and eternity itself depends on the attention we pay to it. Then take a pattern of earnestness and devotedness from the brethren who went to meet St. Paul. Their faith was "spoken of throughout the whole world;" and, though mixed with many infirmities, it was honest and availing. But awake to the assurance that, if you love not and practise not what those brethren made their first concern, you are living without one single security, yea, without a shadow of genuine hope, that when you die you will see God in heaven.

And let Christian brethren bear in mind how greatly they may *encourage* Christian ministers. Our people do not sometimes adequately consider how many things we have to bear and feel, and how weighty our burthens often are *in secret*. A kind word from our people has often cheered us, as St. Paul was cheered. May we then, through you and among you, ever "thank God and take courage."

END OF VOL. II.

To my dear Daughter / Fanny, / with the earnest love / of her Father / W.H.H. / July 1. 1859. [After F.R.H.'s death:] John Henry Crane, / in holy memory / of his Grandfather W.H.H. / & his loving Aunt / Frances Ridley Havergal. / By her wish that some / in memoriam book from / her study sh^{d} [should] be sent. / M. V. G. H.

These two facing pages, William Henry Havergal's inscription to Frances Ridley Havergal (on July 1, 1859, when she was 22), and Maria Vernon Graham Havergal's inscription and note to her (and Frances') nephew John Henry Crane, were found in the front of a copy of this third volume of Sermons by W.H.H.

This third volume of Sermons by William Henry Havergal (and one by John East) was a bound volume. There was no title page for the volume, and the various sermons were printed by different printers. This appears to have been a privately published volume, made of various Sermons printed at different times that were gathered together and bound in one book. The Sermons are listed below.

This was beautifully engraved on the spine outside cover of this book: HAVERGAL'S OCCASIONAL SERMONS.

Astley Wake.*

ON SUNDAY MORNING, THE 22ND SEPTEMBER, 1839.

A SERMON

ON BEHALF OF

THE CHURCH MISSIONARY SOCIETY,

WILL BE PREACHED IN THE

PARISH CHURCH AT ASTLEY,

BY

THE REV. W. H. RIDLEY, A. B.

Student of Christ Church, Oxford.

DIVINE SERVICE WILL COMMENCE AT ELEVEN O'CLOCK.

* Many persons require to be informed and others to be reminded, that a parish WAKE is properly a *religious* festival. It originally was the Feast of the Dedication of the Parish Church; and was kept by watching or *waking*, unto prayer and praise, during the whole of the preceding night, till sun rise.

HYMN I.

"*Blow up the trumpet in the new moon, in the time appointed, on our solemn feast-day.*"‖Psalm. LXXXI. 3.

Our festal morn is come!
And, Lord, we come to Thee:
Thy house shall be our joyful home,
Thy name our melody.

"These temples of thy grace,
How beautiful they stand!
The honors of our native place,
And bulwarks of our land."

Our fathers built this fane,
And watched the live-long night:
They sleep in death; but we remain
To hail a purer light.

Then, blow the trumpet, blow;
The psalm, the psaltery take:
Let ev'ry heart with praise o'erflow,
And ev'ry lip awake.

Sound, sound that sweetest strain,
The gospel-jubilee!
Till bursting from their idol-chain,
The heathen shall be free.

Thus let us keep the feast,
Thus *wake* to righteousness;
And teach the world from sin released,
The Lord our God to bless.*

‖"In the Jewish Church, notice was given of feasts, jubilees, "&c. by sound of trumpet.--We have now our religious feast. "days.---On these and all other solemn occasions, let the "evangelical trumpet give a sound of victory over death, of "liberty from sin, of joy and rejoicing in Christ Jesus our "Saviour,"---BP. HORNE.

HYMN II.

"*The people that walked in darkness have seen a great light: they that dwell in the land of the shadow of death, upon them hath the light shined.*" ISAIAH. IX. 2.

Our Isle in darkness lay,
Remote from Judah's light;
No beam of truth, no holy ray,
Dispelled the Druid-night:

Till o'er the barrier-sea,
Came messengers of good:
They brought the lamp of life, that we
Might hope through Jesu's blood

But, still the heathen lie
In deep and loathsome gloom;
Fast bound in deadliest misery,
And sightless of their doom.

Then up, ye favoured race,
Lift high the beacon-flame,—
The cross of Christ, His boundless grace,
His healing cheering name!

Send, send to lands of death,
That torch of living light;
And fan its blaze with prayerful breath,
The Spirit's inward might.

Rejoice we in that light,
The glory of our land;
And be our works and armour bright,
Till Christ on earth shall stand.

HYMN III.

"*Neither is there salvation in any other; for there is none other name under heaven given among men, whereby we must be saved.*" ACTS. IV. 12.

In vain the heathen bows,
To gods of wood and stone;
No cruel rites or vows
Can e'er for sin atone.
No name but one,
Jehovah gave,
With power to save,
Beneath the sun.

That name! our hope below;
That name! the theme above:
Nor men nor angels know
Aught greater, than its love.
Thy power to save,
Blest Nazarene!
Is sung and seen
Beyond the grave.

All hail Immanuel!
O'er earth uplift thy face;
Let Satan's captives tell
The triumphs of thy grace.
Where idols reign,
Let prayer abound,
And faith be found,
Through thy great name!

No name but Thine shall be
Earth's solace and her song;
When heavenly minstrelsy
Shall dwell her tribes among:
When saved by Thee,
No more to weep,
Thy church shall keep
Her Jubilee.

G. WILLIAMS, PRINTER, STOURPORT.

William Henry Havergal traveled very extensively, preaching in many churches to raise awareness and support for the foreign missions work of the Church Missionary Society. Here is an example when he had another come to the church he pastored to preach on the same need. William H. Ridley was a former student and dear friend of W.H.H., and was the godfather of Frances Ridley Havergal. The three hymns sung in this service were written by W.H.H. (and likely sung to music composed by W.H.H.). *See also page 394 of this book for comments on C.M.S. meetings on the Sundays of Astley Wake.*

APOSTOLIC EXAMPLE IN FINALLY COMMENDING A PEOPLE TO GOD:

A SERMON,

WRITTEN BY

THE REV. W. H. HAVERGAL, M.A.

UPON HIS RESIGNATION OF THE LIVING OF ASTLEY,

In the county of Worcester:

AND PREACHED IN THE CHURCH OF THAT PARISH,

On SUNDAY MORNING, the 13*th MARCH*, 1842,

BY

The REV. J. EAST, M.A.,

OF ST. MICHAEL'S, BATH.

BRISTOL:
PRINTED BY J. CHILCOTT, WINE STREET.
1842.

TO

THE PARISHIONERS OF

ASTLEY,

THIS SERMON

(WRITTEN WITHOUT THOUGHT OF PUBLICATION AND PRINTED PRECISELY AS IT WAS PREACHED)

IS

MOST AFFECTIONATELY

DEDICATED

BY THEIR LATE PASTOR, BUT CONSTANT FRIEND,

W. H. HAVERGAL.

Henwick House, near Worcester,
5*th April*, 1842.

INTRODUCTORY ADDRESS.

THE office with which I am entrusted this morning is as peculiar and painful, as it is honourable and responsible. I might have shrunk from the undertaking had I consulted only my personal feelings. But the voice of duty and friendship demands it at my hands, and therefore I come, reposing on "the Strength of Israel," at the earnest request, I may say the affectionate *bidding*, of my dear friend, the Rector of Astley, to deliver his farewell address to the flock, over which for many years the Holy Ghost has made him overseer. In the afternoon I shall myself address you on the separation that is about to take place between him and you: but this morning I come, like Baruch of old, when Jeremiah commanded him, saying, "I am shut up: I cannot go into the house of the Lord: therefore go thou and read the words of the Lord in the ears of the people in the Lord's house." Your pastor is forbidden, by imperative considerations of health, personally to make this last painful effort for your souls' good. He devolves it upon me as his representative. And may the Divine, Almighty Spirit sow the word in your hearts, with a living power, which shall for ever secure it alike from the dark foe that would take it away, from the worldly cares and pleasures that would choke it, and from the opposing enmity that would destroy it; and so may the precious seed yield a rich harvest of glory to our God, of comfort to my beloved brother, and of grace, peace, and salvation to your souls.

Endeavour, then, to forget that it is my *voice*, and to realize the fact, that your pastor speaks unto you, in the language of St. Paul to the Ephesian elders, in Acts 20:32, "Now, brethren, I commend you to God, and to the word of his grace, which is able to build you up, and to give you an inheritance among all them which are sanctified."

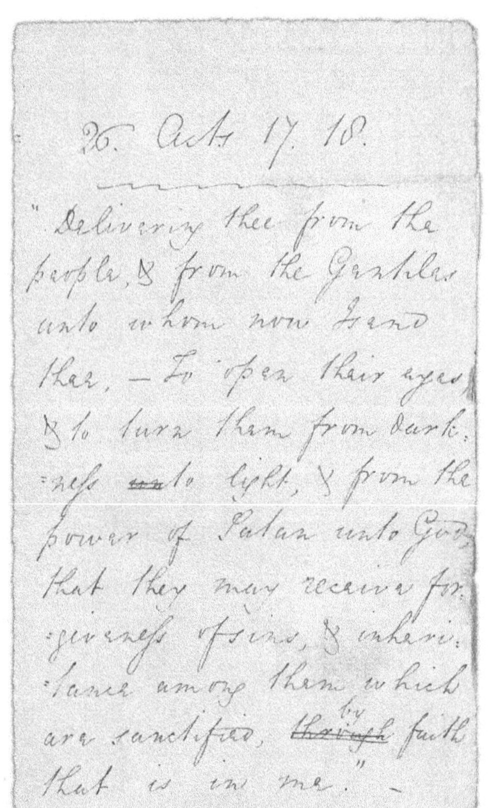

26. Acts 17. 18.

"Delivering thee from the people, & from the Gentiles unto whom now I send thee, — To open their eyes & to turn them from dark:ness ~~unto~~ to light, & from the power of Satan unto God, that they may receive for:giveness of sins, & inheri:tance among them which are sanctified, ~~through~~ by faith that is in me." —

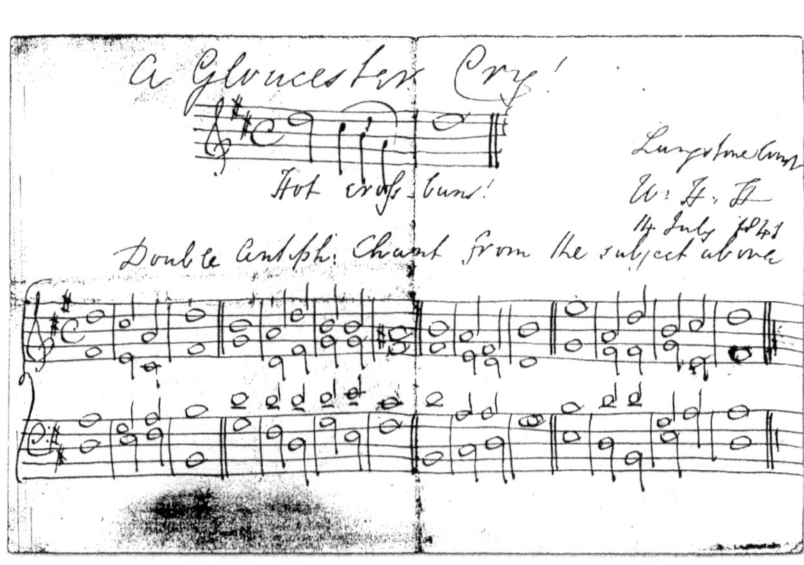
A Gloucester Cry!
Hot cross buns!
W: H. H.
14 July 1841
Double Antiph: Chant from the subject above

W: H: Havergal.

When his physical health prevented him from doing pastoral work, W.H.H. spent more time and attention on music. He was a very fine composer, and money received from his published scores were often or usually given to the Church Missionary Society or other ministries. These are three examples of his handwriting. The first title line means Acts chapter 26, verses 17–18.

APOSTOLIC EXAMPLE IN FINALLY COMMENDING A PEOPLE TO GOD.

Acts 20:32.

"And now, brethren, I commend you to God, and to the word of his grace, which is able to build you up, and to give you an inheritance among all them which are sanctified."

WITH these words St. Paul took his final leave of the elders of the church of Ephesus. He had for the space of three years ministered among them. On his departure from them, he not only admonished them respecting their future conduct, but particularly reminded them of what his own preaching and living had been, during his sojourn at Ephesus. "Ye know (said he) from the first day that I came into Asia, after what manner I have been with you at all seasons." (ver. 18.)

Now we, dear brethren, as far as circumstances admit, desire to imitate St. Paul. For what better example can be taken than that which he has set? And, truly, it is a *merciful* thing that the ministers and people of God are furnished with such an example, when called to take leave of each other.

In accordance, then, with this apostolic example, suffer me, first, to remind you of both my "preaching and living;" and secondly, to "commend you to God, and to the word of his grace." And may the God of all grace give us "grace in addition to grace;" and, by his "good Spirit," so bless the present occasion, that, while it shall tend to your edification, it may add to the joy of angels in the presence of Jesus our Saviour.

After the manner of St. Paul, let me

I. *Remind you of both my preaching and my living.*

The great apostle, in the course of his address, testified that, while at Ephesus, he had "served the Lord with all humility of mind;" that he had "kept back nothing that was profitable;" that he had preached "repentance toward God, and faith toward our Lord Jesus Christ;" that he was "pure from the blood of all men," because he had "not shunned to declare all the counsel of God."

Cautiously and diffidently, dear brethren, as I would apply the apostle's words to myself, I do not hesitate to say, that I have *aimed* at "serving the Lord with all humility of mind." I have not, I trust, either preached to you, or behaved before you, in a vain, self-confident, high-minded manner. It certainly has been my effort always to remember that, before God, "I am a worm, and no man;" and in presence of yourselves, "a dying man amongst dying men." Though I have suffered nothing, as St. Paul suffered, from the lying in wait of any to do me bodily harm, yet have I often grieved over the apparent indifference of many an individual to the good-will which I have studied to shew in the gospel. And yet I heartily thank my heavenly Father that in many instances, I have been spared to see that indifference either greatly modified, or totally removed, when the sands of life began to sink fast, and the footsteps of death to be heard near.

That I have "*kept back* nothing that was *profitable* unto you," my conscience is quite clear. Reserve or concealment has never been in my thoughts. If I deemed it "*profitable*" for my flock, to set before them my own views of passing events, either national or local, I have never shrunk from exhibiting those views. While, as to any truth of God's holy word, I am not conscious of having met with even any temptation to keep it back. "Itching ears" or "worldly minds" may sometimes have been disappointed or offended, but the God of our hearts knoweth that my aim has been your *profit.*

By "*repentance* toward God, and *faith* toward our Lord Jesus Christ," St. Paul intended to express that broad range of gospel duty and gospel privilege, which a faithful messenger of the church will always be anxious to present to his hearers. "*Repentance* towards God" implies a right view of our sinful state, with all its odiousness and peril. It implies, too, that our hearts are "broken for sin and broken from it," and that we loathe that for which we are sorry, and will never again wilfully commit it. "*Faith* toward our Lord Jesus Christ" is the grand exercise of the heart, by which a sinner receives the testimony of God respecting the only method of salvation; and through which he derives from Christ "wisdom, righteousness, sanctification, and (complete) redemption,"—all that can comfort him now, and all that will glorify him hereafter.

How constantly and, as to manner, how variedly, I have testified these things unto you, all will, I trust, readily acknowledge. Ye, too, are my witnesses that I have not knowingly led you into any error. That no soul has perished in this parish through *wrong* teaching, I do most humbly, but most confidently believe. Amidst all the doctrinal fantasies of the age, and the clashing of opinions in the church, I am not conscious of the slightest change of sentiment upon any topic of importance, since the day I first came among you. I have warned you, and advised and intreated you. I have habitually set before you what I believed to be "the truth, the whole truth, and nothing but the truth." I have not confined my preaching to this or that favourite doctrine. On the contrary, I have studied to unfold the different parts of the word of God, so as "to declare unto you all the counsel of God." And this "I have not *shunned*" at any time to do. It cannot be said that fear or favour has influenced me. Smiles and frowns have been alike unheeded. To personalities, I can honestly say that I have *never* descended: while, assuredly, on the other hand, I have never, through a contemptible fear of *being thought* personal, shunned to declare an unpalatable but wholesome truth, which my text, generally from some lesson for the day, has fairly placed before me.

But, dear brethren, in reminding you of these things, with all truth and honesty, my own heart trembles while I think of them. Could I but lift up the vail which has shaded my own feelings, you would see that I have very often been ashamed of the imperfections and infirmities which have attended my ministrations among you. I am deeply conscious that, "after all," I am a most unworthy and most "unprofitable servant." I know that my Master and Saviour will not enter into judgment with me for what I *could not* do, through illness and sundry afflictions; but I am painfully aware that, although I have sometimes exceeded my strength, I have done nothing as it *ought* to be done, and have omitted to do much that *should* have been done. Often have I taken my freshly-written sermon, and locked it up as soon as I have left this pulpit, because I have been ashamed of its poverty and weakness, in comparison with the richness and strength of the gospel of our salvation. I can only intreat you to pray, that the great Head of the church will pardon all my imperfections, and abundantly sanctify my humble endeavours.

Suffer me now to remind you of my manner of life as your pastor and teacher; for, as our church intimates, it is not only by our preaching, but by our *living* that we are to set forth and shew unto you God's holy word. We are to practise what we preach, otherwise a *double* condemnation awaits us.

Upon this subject, the great apostle seems to have been anxious to a degree which amounts almost to sensitiveness. He habitually alluded to the purity, uprightness, and disinterestedness of his conduct. Writing to the Thessalonians he said, "Neither at any time used we flattering words, as ye know, nor a cloak of *covetousness*; God is witness." "We were *gentle* among you, even as a nurse *cherisheth* her children." "Ye are witnesses, and God also, how holily, and justly, and unblameably we behaved ourselves among you." (1 Thessalonians 2:5, 7, 10.) So to the Corinthians he said, "Did I make a *gain* of you?" or "did Titus make a *gain* of you?" (2 Corinthians 12:17, 18.) "I seek not *yours* but *you*." (ver. 14.) Quotation upon quotation might be adduced, as expressing the intense feelings of St. Paul, and of every faithful minister, upon the question of personal character. That he always aimed to shew great disinterestedness of conduct, and was uncommonly solicitous to prove it, is evident from all, or most of, his epistles. He well knew that the credit of his gospel, and the glory of his Master were at stake, and that the keen eye of a malicious world was upon him. Hence, in this very chapter, and in the verse following our text, when taking leave of the Ephesian elders, he would not part with them till he had cleared himself from all imputation of having served them for "filthy lucre's sake." "I have coveted (said he) no man's silver, or gold, or apparel." Nor were St. Paul and his fellow apostles singular in their solicitudes on this point. Long before their time, Samuel, the prophet, had made, towards the close of his life, a stirring appeal to the people of Israel, respecting the uprightness and integrity of his living among them. "Behold, (said he) here I am: witness against me before the Lord, and before his anointed: whose ox have I taken? or whose ass have I taken? or whom have I defrauded? whom have I oppressed? or of whose hand have I received any bribe, to blind mine eyes therewith? and *I will restore it you*." (1 Samuel 12:3.) Confident as I am, that could your answer be openly given to me, it would resemble the answer of the Israelites to Samuel. I nevertheless disclaim, with the deepest humiliation, all self-complacency before you, and all idea of merit before God. I have been but an unworthy steward; I have, indeed, *aimed* to advance your comfort and God's glory in that comfort, but this it was my *duty* to do. I see ten thousand imperfections in my few little doings, and feel that I have urgent need to look up and say, "O Lord, cleanse thine unworthy servant: accept what is thine own, and pardon all that is mine!"

"And *now*, brethren," *i.e.* "now" that, after St. Paul's example, I have reminded you of the past, let me

II. "*Commend you to God, and to the word of his grace*, which is able to build you up, and to give you an inheritance among all them which are sanctified." St. Paul, when taking leave of any of his christian brethren, appears always to have given them his blessing in very affectionate terms. So true is it, that the christian temper is a temper of cordial love and genuine tenderness. Mindful of this fact, "*I commend you to God*." As the long-standing pastor of the parish, I resign you to his care and kind providence. I commit you to him as your Benefactor, Preserver, and Guide, who alone can bless you "in the midst of life, at the hour of death, and in the day of judgment."

And, in thus commending you to Almighty God, I offer many an earnest prayer for your future prosperity in the gospel. I pray that he will remember you in this his holy house, and cause you to see many good days within it. I pray that his most bountiful blessing may rest upon those who shall hereafter minister among you; and that their ministrations may prove a greater benefit to you than any poor and past services of mine.

Nor in this solemn commendation would I pass over any one of any class. Whether you are old or young, rich or poor, I commend you *all* to God. May he "bless, preserve, and keep you," through all "the changes and chances of this mortal life!"

Further, "*I commend you to the word of his grace.*" This comprises two things:

1. I recommend you seriously and habitually to read and study God's holy word, as well for your comfort as your instruction and guidance.

2. I commend you, in faith and prayer, to the faithfulness of God, as to the many precious promises which are recorded in his word.

And let me remind you, that it is a noble feature in the character of the church, that *so much of the pure word* of God is always read in her services. This alone is an urgent reason why you should attend those services. Resolve, then, never to neglect hearing the word of God in this holy temple; whether it be read from the table or the desk, or preached from the pulpit. Rejoiced shall I be to learn that you come to church with even more constancy than ever; for this will be your surest duty, and your truest interest.

But fail not to bear in mind that no merely external means can avail for your salvation. It is God alone "*who is able to build you up, and to give you an inheritance among all them which are sanctified.*" To him "I commend you," for he is the great Builder up of souls for eternity. He alone, by his Spirit, can make his lively word available for your growth in holiness, and your stability and increase on that foundation which is laid in Christ Jesus. He alone, too, has power and authority to "*give* you an inheritance" in heaven. But this inheritance he *will* give to all who are sanctified through his word of truth. In due time they shall join all those who are saints in light; for eternal life is at once his gift and his promise. He gives it to whom he will, and yet promises it to all who seek it through his beloved Son. Then suffer me, for the last time, to warn and exhort you. Much of an admonitory nature, that I might otherwise say, was said to you on Sunday last.[1] O seek this inheritance of the sanctified! You will lose it for ever if you repent not and believe the gospel. Without such holiness as implies a renunciation of the world, and a vital union of heart and soul to Christ, you cannot see the Lord. Then be not deceived by any thing that the world, the flesh, or the devil, may set before you. *Begin* to seek on this very day, or arise to fresh energies in seeking, the kingdom of God and his righteousness. Then shall I not have laboured in vain among you; and then will this my last sermon to you be, like Samson's last effort, the most effectual of any.

And here, dear brethren, I would not fail to offer one other remark, suggested by the text. *How cheering is it when christian friends part, to hear of a place in which they shall meet again!* Perhaps St. Paul so felt, when he spake of "the inheritance of all them that are sanctified." Certainly he was not exempted from the trials of the christian ministry, and therefore he needed the consolations of the christian covenant. To him the act of parting with those whom he loved was evidently most trying. His solace seems to have been the hope of meeting them again in "an inheritance that is incorruptible, and undefiled, and that fadeth not away." Hence, let *us all* learn more and more to "set our affections on things above." The dearest connexions on earth are but transient, imperfect, and frail. Our happiness, therefore, consists in making sure of that heavenly home, where connexions are never broken, and where separations never occur. There the faithful minister and the holy people will meet before the throne of the Saviour's glory: and there shall they dwell together in one fold which shall never be disturbed, and behold and love one Shepherd who shall never be removed. Then let us "thank God and take courage!"

And now, in brief conclusion, it is a genuine pleasure to acknowledge, that I *owe* you much love, so much that I can hardly trust myself to speak of it. It has fallen to my lot, thank God, hitherto to pass through life in the enjoyment of almost uninterrupted kindness. But nowhere have I met with more than in this parish. Astley has been a land of brotherly love and kind heartedness to me and *mine*. Never shall I forget the friendliness of past days, and the willingness to oblige which all classes have shewn me. It may be a rare thing for a clergyman to say, what I am thankful and greatly glad to say, *that I have spent nearly twenty years in a parish, without the recollection of an unkind act, or even an unkind word from any of its inhabitants!* Of late, also, when trials of no common bitterness have come upon me, I have intensely felt the tender and hearty sympathy of every one who has seen me, or any of my household. The simple sayings, too, of many an humble parishioner have gone to my very heart. Brethren and friends, for myself and my family, I *thank* you, I THANK you! My office will soon cease, but my

[1] The sermon in the morning was from Philippians 1:27, "Only *let your conversation be as it becometh the gospel of Christ.*" In the afternoon, from the second lesson, Colossians 1:28, "*Whom we preach, warning every man and teaching every man in all wisdom; that we may present every man perfect in Christ Jesus.*" These were virtually my farewell sermons, though known as such only to myself. The latter of the two was the first sermon I preached at Astley. (30th June 1822.) My object in preaching it once again, and that for the last time, was to *end*, as I had begun and continued, with setting forth and setting forward the salvation of sinners, and the perfecting of believers, only through Christ Jesus the Lord. W. H. H.

affection cannot cease. Many of you I have baptized; many of you I have led to confirmation; and to many, also, have I administered the most comfortable sacrament of the body and blood of our Saviour Jesus Christ. Not a few of your nearest kindred or dearest friends have I tended on a sick-bed, and consigned to the silent tomb. All which things are ties, so fastened by years of kindly intercourse, as not to be dissolved by any earthly severance.

Brethren, *farewell!* Pray for me and for mine. Live for Christ, and you shall die in Christ. Live, also, in peace and love among yourselves, and the God of love and peace shall be with you! Amen and Amen!

SOME GROUNDS OF A MINISTER'S REJOICING ON BIDDING HIS PEOPLE FAREWELL:

A SERMON,

PREACHED IN THE

PARISH CHURCH OF ASTLEY, WORCESTERSHIRE,

ON

SUNDAY AFTERNOON, MARCH 13, 1842,

By the REV. JOHN EAST, M.A.,

OF ST. MICHAEL'S, BATH.

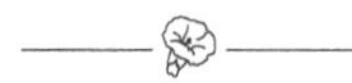

TO

THE REV. W. H. HAVERGAL, M.A.,

THE FOLLOWING DISCOURSE,

DELIVERED IN HIS ABSENCE, AND NOW

PRINTED AT THE REQUEST OF HIS LATE PARISHIONERS,

IS WITH MUCH AFFECTION DEDICATED,

BY HIS LONG ATTACHED AND FAITHFUL

FRIEND AND BROTHER,

JOHN EAST.

Bath, *April* 6, 1842.

SOME GROUNDS OF A MINISTER'S REJOICING ON BIDDING HIS PEOPLE FAREWELL.

2 Corinthians 1:12–14.

"Our rejoicing is this, the testimony of our conscience, that in simplicity and godly sincerity, not with fleshly wisdom, we have had our conversation in the world, and more abundantly to you-ward. For we write none other things unto you, than what ye read and acknowledge; and I trust ye shall acknowledge even unto the end; as also ye have acknowledged us in part, that we are your rejoicing, even as ye also are ours in the day of the Lord Jesus."

ST. PAUL, like his divine Master, the Man of sorrows, was intimately acquainted with grief, and especially with those forms of affliction, which in all ages have attended the faithful discharge of the christian ministry. Indeed from the time of his conversion and his consecration to the apostolic office, he had been shewn how great things he must suffer for the Lord's name's sake. Experience echoed back the prophetic warning. His sufferings for Christ abounded. He was often "pressed out of measure, above strength, insomuch that he despaired even of life." When he was not assailed by the hand of violence, he was by the tongue of malice. His motives and his principles were not understood, or even when known were misrepresented. So that St. Paul and those who acted with him were esteemed and treated as "the filth of the earth and the offscouring of all things," and they had the sentence of death in themselves. But both he and they had comfort in all their tribulation, for they were comforted of "God the Father of mercies," and "the God of all comfort." Their consolation abounded by Christ. They had more than comfort—they had "rejoicing"—springs of joy, to which men in general were utter strangers: as sorrowful yet alway rejoicing, they had joy in God, through our Lord Jesus Christ. *Their* privileges are the privileges too of every faithful servant of God, especially in the ministry of the gospel, and when called to the endurance of severe trials in connection with that ministry.

It would be affectation in me were I to occupy this sacred spot to-day, and to fill up this solemn hour, without a direct reference to the separation about to take place between the flock of Astley and their beloved pastor. Sympathy with him brings me here, to discharge an office of peculiar delicacy and no small pain. But, much as I love him, in a friendship which has sustained no change for nearly thirty years, and tenderly as I feel for him and his family, I would not—I dare not as a minister of Christ, address you from this place today, in *his* name?—nay, in the name of our common Master, unless I could unhesitatingly take up a subject like that I have selected. May the unction of the Holy One, teaching to profit, rest on your souls and on my lips, while I now place before you some grounds of a faithful minister's rejoicing on a review of his labours:—

I. The testimony of his conscience to the motives and principles of his conduct.

II. An assurance of his fidelity in the ministry, and its acceptableness. And,

III. His anticipation of mutual joy with his people in the day of the Lord.

I. The testimony of his conscience to the motives and principles of his conduct, was one ground of the apostle's joyful satisfaction, when he reviewed his labours amongst the Corinthians. "Our rejoicing is this, the testimony of our conscience, that in simplicity and godly sincerity, not with fleshly wisdom, but by the grace of God, we have had our conversation in the world, and more abundantly to you-ward." Before God, indeed, and in the matter of his own soul's acceptance, justification, and hope, Paul had only one, but that a grand and sufficient ground of rejoicing, and that was Christ—His righteousness—His cross. "*We joy in God through our Lord Jesus Christ*, by whom we have now received the atonement." As a sinner he felt and admitted that he was the chief: as a saint, less than the least of all: as an apostle, one born out of due time, not worthy to be called an apostle; in himself a mere "nothing." But his conscience had been purged from dead works to serve the living God, and it now bore a humble but firm testimony to the simplicity of his object as a minister—the glory of God in Jesus and his gospel.—"To me to live is Christ." His conscience bore him witness, that in the tenor of his life, his conversation, and intercourse with the Corinthians, he had not sought "his own profit, but the profit of many, that they might be saved:" that he had served them not "for filthy lucre's sake, but of a ready mind." Nay, he was a man prepared, and his actions proved it, even to serve them without worldly compensation—to preach to them the gospel of God freely. He would gladly have carried on his honest craft as a tent-maker, and have provided for his own temporal wants, could he have proceeded with his favourite work—preaching the unsearchable riches of Christ. *There* was the simplicity of his object, and its grandeur too—*Christ and precious souls.*

Ah! my brethren, had the dear friend whose place I now occupy, lived amongst you only for his own ease, or pleasure, or emolument, leaving behind him no traces of charity in the cottage, and no memorials of large-hearted liberality in the sanctuary of his God: were his name to be hereafter connected in your remembrance only with the dark portrait of a man all selfish in his covetousness, or all selfish in his personal indulgence, how different now must have been the testimony of conscience, and how utterly silent must have been the tongue of faithful friendship. But herein I am bold in my God to say, that the testimony of his conscience is supported by the testimony of your consciences. You know how unselfish has been his conduct "in the world, and more abundantly to you-ward."

Paul, as a deceiver and yet true—a deceiver, a mere hypocrite in the estimation of some—was yet true in "godly sincerity." He made not professions with his lips which his heart and life belied. The smile with which he was wont to meet his people, was that of sincere affection for their souls, no mask of self-seeking hypocrisy. The apostolic robe he wore was not the garb of one well paid to act a part in which he felt no spiritual interest. No: he could say to the men of Corinth, as afterwards he said to the men of Philippi, "God is my record, how greatly I long after you all in the bowels of Jesus Christ." I know, my dear hearers, how "abundantly to you-ward" have flowed the godly sincerities of my beloved friend's earnest desires for your souls' conversion, sanctification, and salvation. He has preached to you what he felt, and felt what he preached. His has not been a ministry of official routine—the compulsory and scanty duties of an hireling, but the willing and more abundant service of a pastor, watching for your souls, and ready to spend and be spent in your spiritual service. I say not this to his praise. *He* feels cause enough to lie low before God. But I say it to the Lord's honour, "whose he is, and whom he serves." He would tell you, that if he has taught your little ones to lisp Emmanuel's praise: if he has turned any of you from darkness to light, and from the power of Satan unto God: if he has recovered any wanderers, and raised up any fallen soul: if he has been the kind, sympathizing comforter of them who mourned: if he has successfully pointed out the atoning Lamb to the trembling sinner, and exalted Him as the alone but sufficient hope of the departing soul: in a word, if your pastor has been a spiritual blessing to this parish, and not a professional curse, as a blind leader of the blind, it has been effected, "not by fleshly wisdom, but by the grace of God:" and you may and must glorify God in him. And *is* it no ground of rejoicing, when that loud and mighty witness, CONSCIENCE, unbribed by passion, testifies that "simplicity and godly sincerity" have furnished the motives and principles of a minister's conduct? It *is high* ground, and the very word of God invites your beloved pastor to take his stand upon it, rejoicing even on the very day of what must be his sorrowful separation from you.

II. But connected therewith is AN ASSURANCE OF FIDELITY IN HIS MINISTRY, AND ITS ACCEPTABLENESS. St. Paul had preached and taught what he now wrote, and what other inspired men had in substance before written, and no other things. "For we write none other things unto you than what ye read and acknowledge; and I trust ye shall acknowledge even unto the end; as also ye have acknowledged us in part." Whether they read his writings, or whether they remembered his preaching and teaching publicly and from house to house, he well knew that "by the grace of God" he had been found faithful. He and his fellow-labourers preached, "not themselves, but Christ Jesus the Lord," and themselves their "servants, for Jesus' sake." His ministry had fully accorded with his determination to know nothing among them but Jesus Christ and him crucified. They "in part," *i.e.* some of them, had acknowledged Paul's fidelity, both in their reception of his high and heavenly doctrine and in their submission to his faithful rebukes. Sin, even scandalous sin, had been found amongst the professors of the pure faith in Corinth. He had not spared the offenders, though at the peril of being called their enemy, because he "told them the truth."

A minister, obtaining grace to be faithful, preaches a doctrine as humbling to the pride of man, as it is exalting to the glory of God's free and sovereign grace,—a doctrine which leaves man nothing to hope for out of Christ or in self, and which yet declares to him, that "without holiness," personal holiness, "no man shall see the Lord." Has your pastor, my dear brethren, led your souls to the pure streams of the word of life, and not to the dark and muddy pools of human tradition? Has he strove to cast down among you all imaginations, and every high thought of your own moral goodness, fitness, or strength: to lay you low at the foot of the cross—the cleft Rock of ages, in deep and painful consciousness that you were guilty before God, and without hope from self or any earthly quarter? Has he plainly told you, that from a state of guilt and pollution you must be raised to one of righteousness and purity, or remain dead in trespasses and sins, and so condemned for ever? Has he roused you from your dreams of self-righteousness by the startling declaration of unsparing truth, that "cursed is every one that continueth not in all things that are written in the book of the law to do them?" Has he exalted Christ before you as "the end of the law for righteousness to every one that believeth," and as the full atonement in his blood for all "your mighty sins?" Has he invited you to come to God in Christ for mercy rich and free and sure? Has he even endeavoured to "compel" you to come in? Has he besought you "in Christ's stead to be reconciled to God," and to resign your needy souls to the justifying efficacy of a righteousness which is the pure righteousness of God, and to the cleansing efficacy of a truth and a grace which, being divine—the emanations of God the Holy Ghost—can and must regenerate, renew, and sanctify the pardoned and justified soul? Has he exhibited with equal vividness of teaching the justifying and the sanctifying grace of redemption? Has he warned the wilfully wicked man, "Thou shalt surely die?" Has he encouraged the awakened and alarmed and penitent soul by, "Son, be of good cheer: thy sins be forgiven thee?" Amidst the abounding novelties, or revived antiquities of traditional error, can he and his brethren say, "We are not as many which corrupt the word of God; but as of sincerity, but as of God, in the sight of God speak we in Christ?" We can tell him and them, that they are permitted to rejoice that they have been "found faithful."

And have you, beloved, "acknowledged" the faithful ministry of my friend, owning it to be in accordance with what you read, and what prophets and apostles wrote? Have the prayers which he and I unitedly offered up for each other and for our future flocks, when thirty years ago we bent our youthful knees together within the walls of then less guilty Oxford—have those prayers been answered, in the saving acceptance of my friend's ministry by some who sleep within the surrounding graves, and by others among your living selves? Do you love the ministry even more than the man, and the divine Master more than the human servant; while yet you have gladly accepted his service, as being of saving power to your own souls? Here then let our beloved friend, amidst the dark sorrows of this day, stand and rejoicing say, "Now we live, if ye stand fast in the Lord;" and if, as we "trust, ye shall acknowledge to the end," that the gospel we have preached unto you was the power of God unto your salvation. Yes, brethren, I thank God on your behalf and my friend's, that he has not to shake off the dust of his feet against you as a parish, for wilfully rejecting his errand of love; nor are you to be tempted to rejoice at the termination of an unfruitful and unprofitable, because unfaithful ministry. He has the joyful assurance, "through the grace of God," of the fidelity and acceptableness of his ministry amongst you.

III. But the faithful servant of the Lord Jesus Christ has another and still higher, though connected ground of rejoicing—HIS ANTICIPATION OF MUTUAL JOY WITH HIS PEOPLE IN THE DAY OF THE LORD JESUS.

That day is hastening on, and the eventful dates of our lives following each other in rapid succession, are bringing it nearer and nearer to every one of us. The *night* is far spent—that day of man and of man's judgment, which is *as night*, is far spent,—*the* day—"the day of Jesus Christ" is at hand. Now a few rays of light struggle through the thick gloom of sin and ignorance and care and woe that precedes it. That day will be all light to Jesus and his people, ushered in by a morning without clouds, and by the rising of a sun which shall never set. Now each day is sadly darkened, even to God's children, by anxieties and perplexities, and fears and doubts, and griefs and losses. But a day awaits them which will be Christ's exclusively, when they will see what now they only believe, that Christ is all and in all. THE DAY OF CHRIST! The prospect to us now is dark with excessive brightness: but then the eye will be strengthened to bear it; when "the whole earth shall be filled with His glory:" when the gates of hell shall be closed, and the gates of heaven shall be opened, and, as it were, connected with the plains of earth. As surely as the dial-plate in that tower has, from the time of its erection, been numbering on THIS day, so surely is the great dial of the heavens numbering on "the day of Christ."

The day of Christ *shall come*, when the deepest sorrows of time shall be remembered with a smile,

> As the storm, when escaped, will endear
> The retreat that the haven supplies.

My dear brethren, a day is on its approach when you and your former ministers, and your present pastor, and all who may succeed him, will and must meet. Oh! that it may be with joy and not with grief to either you or them. May none of them, after having then preached to you, themselves be cast away into outer darkness, receiving the doom of the unprofitable servant. May none of you, or your children, or your children's children be then found to have received the grace of God in the preaching of the gospel in vain. Need I solemnly, but affectionately remind you, that congregations are even now, to the eye of God, and will then be evidently to *every* eye, divided into only two classes—of them that are saved, and of them that perish. To the one of these "we are the savour of death unto death," and to the other, "the savour of life unto life." Under which of these *are* you, *will* you be classed? Oh! let it not remain a matter of dark uncertainty. As now there is no middle state or neutral ground, and your pastor leaves you either "at peace with God through our Lord Jesus Christ," or at enmity with him; and thus even now having "the wrath of God abiding on you:" so, hereafter, there will be no medium lot between theirs who are saved and theirs who perish.

But are your ministers now by you "acknowledged" as the friends and teachers and guides of your souls? Have you through them heard the voice of the Good Shepherd, and are you following Him to the green pastures of eternal life? Then, in the day of Christ, they will be your rejoicing, and you will be theirs. Till then he will feed you with food convenient for you, for all means are his to give, while his grace is not limited to any individual ministrations.

In that, his own day, Jesus will indeed himself be his people's "exceeding joy." But in the gracious generosity of his nature he will permit those who yet owe their all to Him, to share a mutual, unselfish, and exulting joy with and in each other. In the clear, undeceiving light of that day, when there will be no more danger of honouring the servant to the disparagement or neglect of the master, each saved soul will be permitted and enabled to see the varied amounts of spiritual good derived to him through one or more of the true servants of God, who have shewn the way of salvation. Did Paul plant the seed or scion of divine truth in the soul? So far *he* will be that soul's rejoicing, and that soul his. Did Apollos water and raise to maturity what Paul planted? So far *he* also will be that soul's rejoicing, and that soul his. But it will then be fully seen how entirely God himself gave the increase; and in Him therefore the saved soul, and its saving ministers, exult and triumph. But oh! my brethren, what a mighty joy will take possession of your souls in that day, if through the grace of God, you shall meet your beloved pastor amidst the one gathered flock at Christ's right hand! Your tears for ever wiped away: your sorrows for ever gone, as the clouds and storms of a dark winter's night: your last fear relieved: your last want supplied: your highest hopes more than realized: your souls—your perfected nature for ever safe and pure—the children of glory there as the children of grace here! And shall your pastor in the day of Christ stand *joyless* as to any of you? Shall he, as he beholds some of you placed on the left hand of the Great Shepherd, look on your unhappy souls and feel—"Ah! they are no 'rejoicing' to me now. For they never were in the days of my ministry. Then they grieved me by their cool indifference: their inordinate love of earthly things: their wilful ignorance and their aversion to spiritual pursuits. *They* now look back on *me* and *I* follow *them* with sorrow, not with joy, as we are being separated for ever." Oh! brethren—you that, judging by your present course of life, give too much ground for these forebodings, your minister has done his *last*—his *all* for you. It is time that you were startled up from the dreams of spiritual sleep and death, if you will not meet him in the day of Christ with terror and despair, instead of rejoicing and hope. But I will not dwell upon that fearful prospect. May it never prove a certainty! I do trust that the Lord Jesus will then reap a harvest of glory, and my friend a harvest of rejoicing, from the fields of Astley. If he can *now* ask and answer the blissful question, "What is our hope, or joy, or crown of rejoicing? are not even ye, in the presence of our Lord Jesus Christ at his coming: for ye are our glory and joy?" what will be the weight and the brightness of that crown, which he will then both *receive* from his Master's hands and *lay* at that Master's feet! Jesus, "for the joy that was set before him, endured the cross, despising the shame." A portion of that joy he will share with his faithful servants, and the more in proportion to their endurance of the cross and its attendant shame, in their efforts to bring the souls of men to grace and holiness here, and to glory hereafter.

Finally, my brethren, let this be a day of humiliation and prayer in your families and your closets. Be humbled before God for your neglect or defective improvement of your spiritual privileges: and let your separation from an earthly pastor be a means of uniting you closely and inseparably to the Great Shepherd and Bishop of souls, who says, "Lo, I am with you always, even unto the end of the world."

Follow him who leaves you and his family with your prayers. You will not soon be forgotten in their supplications. They need your sympathy, and I am sure that they have and will retain it. Receive my friend's successor too with earnest prayer, that God would pour out on him "the healthful spirit of his grace—the continual dew of his blessing, illuminating him with true knowledge and understanding of his word; that both by his preaching and living he may set it forth and shew it accordingly." Then "in the day of Christ" he who departs and he who succeeds, will rejoice together with you.

My brethren, we bid you farewell! May God, reconciled in Christ, bless you with his favour and love, which is better than wealth or life. May He be *your* father and your children's too, and you and they will have a goodly heritage. May the Lord Jesus be the grand—the supreme object of your faith and love, and you shall be his in the day when he shall make up his jewels. May "the Holy Ghost, who sanctifieth all the elect people of God," "sanctify you wholly," comfort you in your sorrows, and never suffer you to stray into error of doctrine or into unholiness of life. Let Christ be your life, its source, its strength, its end; and to you to die shall be gain, and to wake up in the day of Christ, shall be eternal glory!

HOLY PRAISE OFFERED BY MEANS OF HOLY MUSIC:
AND
THE UNION OF SACRIFICE AND SONG.

TWO SERMONS,

PREACHED IN

THE CHURCH OF THE HOLY TRINITY,

STRATFORD-ON-AVON,

IN AID OF THE FUNDS OF THE CHURCH CHOIR,

ON

SUNDAY, 11*th JUNE,* 1843,

BY

THE REV. W. H. HAVERGAL, M.A.

Late Rector of Astley, in the County of Worcester,

THE PROFITS WILL BE APPROPRIATED TO THE FUND FOR WHICH THE SERMONS WERE PREACHED.

STRATFORD-ON-AVON,

PRINTED AND PUBLISHED BY

R. LAPWORTH,

1843.

TO

THE REV. JOHN CLAYTON, M.A.

The Vicar;

TO

THE REV. S. H. PARKER, B.A.

The Curate,

OF STRATFORD-ON-AVON;

AND TO

THE CONGREGATION AND CHOIR

OF

THE PARISH CHURCH IN THAT TOWN;

These Sermons,

PUBLISHED AT THEIR EARNEST AND UNANIMOUS REQUEST,

ARE FAITHFULLY

AND

AFFECTIONATELY INSCRIBED,

BY

THE AUTHOR.

Henwick House, near Worcester,
July 1843.

MORNING SERMON.

2 Chronicles 5:13.

"It came even to pass, as the trumpeters and singers were as one, to make one sound to be heard in praising and thanking the LORD; and when they lifted up their voice with the trumpets and cymbals and instruments of music, and praised the LORD saying, For he is good; for his mercy endureth for ever: that then the house was filled with a cloud, even the house of the LORD."

THE church of the Living God has its musical history. The principal events in that history are the Passage of the Red Sea, the Dedication of the Temple, and the Nativity at Bethlehem. Each of these events is eminently interesting; but each has a character peculiar to itself. To the second of them your attention is now invited. May He guide and bless that attention, who gave to the Temple of Solomon all its glory, and who marked the music of its Dedication with such tokens of approval as have never since been seen.

The text, as to its narrative, is clear and comprehensive. Solomon at the Dedication of his Temple exhibited at once an essential and most interesting part of its future services. He appointed a large and goodly company of singers, and players on instruments, to thank and praise the GOD of all goodness and mercy. When voices and instruments uniting had attained their zenith of energy and sweetness, then the LORD of heaven came down, and filled the house with the glory of his presence. So overpowering was the splendour of this manifestation, that the ministering priests were necessitated to retire from their station, and desist from their service. "The priests could not stand to minister by reason of the cloud: for the glory of the LORD had filled the house of God." (ver. 14.)

Hence we may remark,

I. *That holy praise is an important part of divine worship.*

To *pray* to Almighty God is a duty which, so to speak, we owe to ourselves. To *praise* Him is a duty which we owe to his ineffable majesty. In prayer we seek for the relief of our own necessities. In praise we acknowledge and adore the divine perfections. By prayer we set forth our poverty and dependence. By praise we magnify the riches of the Saviour's love, and extol the independence of his almighty power. Assuredly, therefore, if prayer be a self-interested duty; praise should be our thankful delight.

A moment's glance at our position as favoured sinners will suffice to show the propriety of holy praise forming a prominent part of divine worship. All the incentives to praise which existed, when Solomon was King of Israel, exist, at this present, in a far higher degree, seeing that Jesus is exalted at the right hand of God to be a Prince and a Saviour to his church. Solomon, as the greatest of natural philosophers, (1 Kings 4:33) had, doubtless, a vast and comprehensive perception of the goodness of GOD in creation. As a man of surpassing knowledge, he must have been minutely acquainted with the history of his people, their redemption from Egypt, their rescue from subsequent oppressions, and their unparalleled privileges. And, as to the mercies which had been shewn to his father's house, and to himself especially, his impressions must have been vividly fresh and tenderly deep. Well, therefore, did it become him to station a choir in his magnificent Temple to praise and thank the LORD, and to say "For He is good; for his mercy endureth for ever!" And, surely, if GOD would not have his Jewish Church come before Him in a sorrowful and dejected attitude, how much more may his Christian Temple ring with the notes of praise, and the accents of thanksgiving! The goodness of GOD in creation is not less conspicuous than it was in the days of Solomon. The heavens are not less gorgeously arched, nor the earth less beautifully garnished now than then: neither are summer and winter, seedtime and harvest less sure than heretofore. While these things remain as they were, how far more wonderfully are other things developed! Things which prophets and righteous man in vain desired to see and hear, are unveiled and declared to us, with a plainness and force which make insensibility as guilty as it is inexcusable. Shadows are become realities, and types have issued in facts. Promises and predictions have received a glorious accomplishment; and life and immortality are brought to light by the advent of the Beloved Son of God.

Mindful of these things, the martyred compilers of our incomparable Liturgy have blended praise with prayer, in a manner as beautiful as it is consistent. As soon as the burthened heart has confessed its sin, and listened to the joyous announcement of absolution through faith in the merits of the One Great Mediator, the voice of the ministering priest gathers strength and says, "O Lord, open Thou our lips;" while congregated saints hasten to respond, "And our mouth shall shew forth *thy praise*." Then follow Psalm and Song with a plenitude and fitness which the calmest judgments must admire, and the warmest affections will readily welcome. And who is there, among the members of our church, who comes to the house of prayer, and forgets that it also is a house of praise? No one, surely, but that individual who forgets to pray. Only let the sinner feel his sin, and penitently confess it, and whose lip will then be more ready to praise Him who died to pardon it? They who find that they have much to supplicate, will soon discover that they have much, also for which to offer praise. Like Solomon, so also the humblest christian (who as a christian is greater than Solomon), will call to mind the wonderful works of his Creator. He will say "When I consider the heavens, the work of thy fingers, the moon and the stars, which thou hast ordained; what is man, that thou art mindful of him? and the son of man that thou visitest him?" (Psalm 8:3, 4.) And, then, as the unworthiest, in his own estimation of all God's *creatures*, he will praise Him for his *goodness*. But speedily, and as the ground of all his thoughts, he will think of his Father's "inestimable love in the redemption of the world, by our Lord Jesus Christ:" and then, as a ransomed *sinner*, he will arouse both heart and lip to praise Him for his *mercy*. Mercy, indeed, is the great object of the penitent sinner's adoration. He vividly sees that infinite as is the divine goodness, and boundless as its treasures are, he has no reason to expect that one particle thereof will ever descend on him, but through the mercy of God in Christ Jesus. Full well does he know that, unless Mercy and Truth had met together in Calvary, no message of reconciliation could have blessed a rebel world. While, therefore, he prays, "Shew us thy mercy; and grant us thy salvation," he "magnifies the Lord, and rejoices in God his Saviour, because He hath remembered his mercy and truth towards" Jew and Gentile. So also, as the christian worshipper walks up to the house of his God, and thinks of the mercies which have followed him all his days, or met him within the last few hours of the week, he joyfully says, "My *praise* shall be of Thee in the great congregation." It, consequently, is a delight to him to find that it is not yet become obsolete for "singers and players on instruments" "to make one sound to be heard in praising and thanking the Lord; and to say, For He is good, for his mercy endureth for ever." Hence the lively christian cordially assents to our proposition, That holy praise is an important part of divine worship.

Advancing from this proposition we present another: viz.

II. *That, in offering holy praise, instrumental music may very fitly accompany singing voices.*

The instruments of music mentioned in the text, were, it is probable, some of the many which had been provided by David as the Royal Psalmist and Sweet Singer of Israel. To those instruments frequent allusion is made in sacred history, after the first mention of them in 1 Chronicles 16:42. They are there denominated "musical instruments of God," but more literally "instruments of the song of God." Hence in the Vulgate, or Latin translation, they are called "instruments of music for singing unto God;" (omnia musicorum organa *ad canendum Deo*) meaning without much question, that they were instruments for accompanying the voices of those who sang praises unto God. Now, though these instruments are called "the instruments of David," and are repeatedly said to have been furnished by him, we are not to conjecture that he appointed the use of them in the Sanctuary without any divine warrant, at the mere dictum of his kingly pleasure, or for the gratification of a refined taste. Were we left in doubt upon this point, the opponents of instrumental music might be a little more brave than they sometimes venture to be. But the wisdom of the Great Head of the Church has taken good care to certify us that these very instruments were ordained of God. David, indeed, prepared them; but it was Jehovah who both directed them to be prepared, and then sanctioned their use in his service. The proof of these statements is found in 2 Chronicles 29:25, 26. It is there said that Hezekiah "set the Levites in the house of the Lord with cymbals, with psalteries, and with harps, according to the commandment of David, and of Gad the king's seer, and Nathan the prophet: for so was *the commandment of the Lord* by his prophets."

The use, then, of musical instrumentation in the services of the church is an ordinance of God. But, says the rather sullen objector, "It was an ordinance of the Jewish church, and, therefore, was abrogated with that church. There is no mention of its use, nor warrant for its adoption in the New Testament, nor was it practised in the primitive church." All this is very plausible; but it is not strictly consistent either with truth, or with itself. Let us briefly examine the complex objection. Instrumental music was not an ordinance of the Jewish church in the same sense in which other things were ordinances. It is not of the same class of ordinances as sacrificial rites, and typical ceremonies; but ranks with such institutions as reading and expounding the word of God, and singing his praises; all of which are more or less prior to the Jewish church, and respecting which no one presumes to say that they were abrogated with that church. Instrumental music was a devotional adjunct, and not a typical appointment. Besides, there is no injunction respecting it in the Law of Moses. Consequently, if we have the same affections as the spiritually minded Hebrews, we may reasonably enough make use of the same devotional helps: and if Moses did not injoin instrumental music, it cannot be said that Christ Jesus annulled it. If it be granted that in the New Testament no recognition of instrumental music occurs, nor any command for its adoption is recorded, it certainly may be pleaded that not a single word is written against it, neither is the slightest intimation given that it is inconsistent with christianity or displeasing to Christ. On the contrary, the beloved one of the disciples, and the last of the apostles, was commissioned to give us some anticipation of the nature of heavenly worship, by allusions to instrumental music. "I heard (says St. John the Divine) the voice of harpers harping with their harps." (Revelation 14:2.) If then, the services of the true sanctuary admit of "harpers harping with their harps," it is very hard to suppose that the use of musical instruments is ineligible or unbecoming in the church below.

To object to instrumental music on the ground of our not reading of it in the New Testament, is scarcely more reasonable than to object to the building of a church, a chapel, or a schoolroom, because the Apostles made no mention of such good works. To argue, too, that primitive congregations did not call in the aid of musical instruments, is in effect to argue that they failed to do what they had no facility for doing. They were a new and an oppressed community. They, consequently, were intent upon the plain essentials, and not upon the embellished adjuncts of divine worship. They were poor, too, and persecuted. Musical instruments were cumbersome as well as costly. Such instruments could not easily be taken to a crowded upper chamber, or to a darksome cavern, or to the lone locality of a martyr's tomb; especially when the sound of them would be a signal for an assault, or a clue to a discovery.

But apart from objections;[1]—be it the concern of British christians to make a legitimate use of that noble instrument, which, happily, is more common in our churches than heretofore. The organ, as a concentration of many instruments is well adapted to accompany and sustain the voices of either a choir or a congregation, or of both united. To the legitimate[2]

[1] Years ago, it was a favourite and frequent objection against the use of instrumental music in the house of God, that such music originated in the infidel family of Cain. Jubal, the descendant of Cain, "was the father of all such as handle the harp and organ." (Genesis 4:21.) But this objection employed as an argument proves rather more than is convenient: for, by parity of reasoning, dwellers in tents, and keepers of cattle, and workers in brass and iron would fall under puritanical prohibition; inasmuch as the father of all such dwellers, keepers and artificers, were the brethren of Jubal, and alike the descendants of Cain. Besides, Jubal's being called "the *father* of all such as handle the harp and organ," no more proves that instrumental music *originated* with him, than Jubal's being denominated "the father of such as have cattle" proves that he was the *first* person who tended a flock. "Abel was a keeper of sheep" centuries before Jubal lived.

[2] A church organ is *legitimately* used when the style of performance on it accords with the genius of the instrument itself and with the character of the edifice in which it is heard. A church organ ought not to be debased into Piano Forte, or forced to such an imitation of *stringed* instruments as ill accords with its very construction. What is called fingering and execution may well be exchanged for that steady, stately, seraphic style of performance, which alone befits the architecture of our churches, and the servant of Almighty God. Such style the older masters carefully studied, and excellently practised. They would have been shocked at hearing the crashing discords, the flighty chromaticisms, and the wanton or sickly prophesies of many a modern organist. The music of the theatre, the concert-room, or the parade is an abomination when brought to the organ of the house of God.

use of an organ may be attributed the continuance of our national style of church music. While the Roman church, by admitting modern orchestral accompaniments, has deviated into Operatic levities, our own church, by adhering to the grave and solemn tones of the organ, has pretty generally maintained, in her larger choirs at least, the original dignity, and high devotion of her holy music. The character of that music is eminently vocal. A simple organ accompaniment, while it requires no mean skill, allows that character to remain. But where elaborate instrumentation takes the place of more simple accompaniment, attention is divided, and devotion lowered. Experience, at least, proves such to be the fact. Mere pleasure may follow from splendid or elegant instrumentation; but, is the spirit of piety thereby quickened, or does it swell the current of that feeling which is essential to genuine worship? Possibly not. And here let me caution my hearers against confounding things which materially differ, but which difference, unhappily, is not always discerned, and, certainly, not always maintained. Sacred music, as it is called, is not necessarily *ecclesiastical* music. Much, indeed, that passes for *sacred* music is utterly unfit for the church.[1] What may be suitable for an Oratorio may be out of character in divine service; and what may be allowable for the chamber may be very inappropriate for the church. In the one we may legitimately indulge a refined though hallowed taste; but in the other we are bound to cultivate the best affections of the heart. The topic, however, is, in its bearings, too extensive for an occasion like the present: yet it is clear, that our church community stands very much in need of a little wholesome admonition respecting it.

Recurring more directly to our present proposition, suffice it to add, that when a congregation has the advantage of a superior organ, that congregation is not to regard the organ as a substitute for their singing, but as an auxiliary to it. He who is silent because the organ sounds, is an indolent and, therefore, an irreverent worshipper. I can well understand how the rich tones of an organ, as they float full and deep through the aisles of a venerable fabric, may thrill the very soul of the devout worshipper, and for a moment choke his aiding voice, but, then, the momentary pause will be followed by a more ardent effort to join the praises of the Saviour whom he loves. If, dear brethren, you have a better organ than you had, see that your vocal efforts bear a corresponding improvement. Grudge not to take a little pains, not merely when at church, but in your families at home. It is worth a churchman's best while to do all he can to make the public worship of God an admiration to others and a comfort to himself. At the Dedication of the Temple, the people were not wholly silent; but, at a proper season, joined the stated singers in their sublime chorus of praise. "And when all the children of Israel (it is said) saw how the fire came down, and the glory of the LORD upon the house, they bowed themselves with their faces to the ground, upon the pavement, and worshipped and praised the Lord, saying, For he is good; for his mercy endureth for ever." (2 Chronicles 7:3.)

In primitive times such was the ardour of congregational praise, that St. Augustine said "The voices flowed in at my ears, truth was distilled in my heart, and the affection of piety overflowed in sweet tears of joy." And such, at one period, was the full-toned and magnificent character of the Psalmody of our own church, that organs have, as it were, been drowned and pavements shaken, by the voices of assembled worshippers.[2] God grant that the increased union of instrumental with vocal music, in this congregation, may largely increase his praise and your comfort.

Consecutively our next remark is

III. *That in offering holy praise, the union of vocal and instrumental music, if accompanied with the gracious affections of the heart, is peculiarly pleasing to God.*

We arrive at this conclusion from the fact which, with great precision, is stated in the text. For the Dedication of the Temple there had been a goodly series of preparatory services. There had been the stately procession, the multitudinous sacrifice, and the joyful elevation of the ark to its resting place. Still, no token of the divine presence was vouchsafed. As soon, however, as the white-linened choir struck up their chorus of praise, and instruments and voices were as one, then "*even*" then, it is emphatically said, "the glory of the LORD filled the house." Such honour did God put upon the religious union of instruments and voices.

In a musical point of view the text, though interesting, is not explanatory, as to the long pending question about ancient harmony. Whether the Hebrew minstrels knew and practised that combination of sounds which we call harmony or

[1] Many of HANDEL's (sacred) Oratorio Songs are of this description. Either the music of them is too secular, or the words not sufficiently hallowed. Neutrality in either language or music does not befit the worship of God. Hence the unseemliness of such selections as "Angels ever bright and fair," "From mighty kings," and "O lovely peace," for some extra singers on charitable occasions, on a Lord's Day. Across the Channel they descend to even such *things* as "Angels of Life," and "The Last Man," and that in a metropolitan cathedral. The church should have a style of music all her own. That style is developed in the compositions of the Elizabethan worthies, and their successors prior to the day of Oliver Cromwell.

[2] Master Thomas MACE, in his quaint and good tempered book entitled "Music's Monument," describes the singing of Psalms at York Minster, in the year 1644, as "the most remarkable and excellent of any known or remembered, and infinitely beyond all verbal expression or conceiving." "The organ, I say, when the Psalm was set before the sermon, being let out in all its fulness of stops, together with the quire, begun the Psalm. But when that vast concording unity of the whole congregational chorus came, as I may say, thundering in, even so it made the very ground shake under us. Oh the unutterable ravishing soul's delight!"

counterpoint, the text, dispassionately construed, can hardly be said to decide. We are, indeed, told that "the trumpeters and singers were *as one*, to make *one sound* to be heard in praising and thanking the Lord;" but, whether by that "*one* sound" we are to understand sweet and perfect accordance in unisons and octaves, or rich and faultless harmony, with component chords, I will not venture to decide.

Jehovah, in testifying his approbation of the union of instruments and voices, may have designed us to learn a great moral lesson. *Everything is to be devoted to his praise.* He is Lord of all,—of all things as well as of all beings. He is the God of creation,—inanimate as well as animate. All creation, then, is to praise Him. Now that self-same Spirit which said, "Let everything *that hath breath* praise the LORD;" said also, "Let the *fields* rejoice, and all that is therein. Then shall *the trees of the wood* sing out." Consequently when we bring to the house of God, or set up in it, musical instruments made of the produce of the field and the wood, we honour Him as *the Lord of creation*: and when we sing to Him, with our own voices, we honour Him as *the Lord of redemption.* Thus the union of instrumental with vocal music perfects our praise, so far, at least, as the external act is concerned: for God, as the God of *all* harmony, beholds his animate creatures forming *musical* harmony by means of his inanimate creatures, at once for his own honour and glory.

That the eternal God, who has thronged the place of his presence with beings who have never been unlovely or impure, should delight in the praises of sinners afar off from his throne, is not only a mystery which we must always adore, but an act of condescension which we never can adequately admire. Marvellous, indeed, is it that He should permit Himself to be addressed as the God "who inhabiteth the praises of Israel;" (Psalm 22:3.) as One who taketh such delight in the songs of his people that their praise, rather than the temple in which it is offered, should be considered as his pavilion. But, let it never be forgotten that, pleasing as external acts may be when reverently performed for the honour and praise of Almighty God, they, nevertheless, carry with them no inherent excellency. The most splendid celebration of divine song is odious discord if unaccompanied with the breathings of a renewed heart. The gentlest sigh of a contrite spirit will penetrate the ear of our Divine Mediator, while the loudest chorus without faith and godliness will fail to reach it. When we sing elsewhere for our intellectual pleasure, or rational refreshment, we do not indeed assume the attitude of worshippers, though we should never forget that we are christians:[1] but, when we come to the house of God, we stand in a very different position. Every performer and every singer, and every auditor, too, is in the presence of God. While the one plays or sings for God, the other is to hear for God. If the professional man comes as a mere professional man to take his part, he is little better than a heathen. And if an auditor comes as a mere auditor *to be amused*, in what does he differ from a sacrilegious intruder? Brethren, if we would praise God acceptably, whether in the congregation or the choir, we must praise Him from the heart.

Should there be any among you who, through natural infirmity or defective habit, are unable to take part in congregational singing, or who enter but little into the hallowed pleasure of having in their church a superior organ and an efficient choir, let me kindly admonish them not to undervalue what others can enjoy. We are not all moulded alike as to capacity, taste, or sentiment; but we all have a common interest in common praise as well as in common prayer. Let, then, such individuals as are now alluded to, turn their infirmities or deficiencies to a good account, by making them stimulants for the exercise of good will, and, if they have ability, of generous contribution, for the comfort and edification of their fellow worshippers.

And should there, also, be any who feel real interest in the hallowed proceedings of this high and holy day, and yet are oppressed with sorrow, sickness, or any other adversity, and, therefore, cannot elicit their interest; let them be cheered by the thought that the offering of acceptable praise is not restricted to the medium of vocal or instrumental music, or any other single mode. That God who said, "Whoso offereth me praise glorifieth me;" and who "out of the mouth of babes and sucklings, hath perfected praise," will not assuredly disregard the less vocal or even the totally silent offerings of his aged or afflicted servants. The melody of a sanctified heart can ascend to heaven, even through the barrier of a sorrow-closed lip.

And now, christian friends, need I marshal arguments for storming your purse? Need I even *ask* you to contribute towards the cost which has been incurred for the better accommodation of your very commendable choir, in aiding the congregation to thank and praise the Lord? *Need* I ask you? Not, indeed, if you reckon holy praise an important branch of divine worship. Not, indeed, if you deem instrumental music a becoming adjunct to singing voices. Not, indeed, if you are intent on making that adjunct a means of grace which brought into Solomon's Temple not only the hope but a sight of the divine glory. Not, indeed if you venerate all that the Bible sanctions and the church loves. Not, indeed, if looking beyond the vanities of life, and this vale of tears, you are living and even

[1] Meetings for the practice of church music, in preparation for church service, require judicious management, especially where the singers are not confined to one sex. Secularity and levity are too apt to intrude. They who practise for holy service should be careful to observe a devout and reverent demeanour. The attendance of the clerical precentor, or parochial minister, cannot be otherwise than salutary, as well as encouraging. Cases are extant where a prayer, short and fervent, precedes the singers' practice.

dying daily, as the servants of the Triune God, and are exercising a "good hope through grace," that you shall one day enter a Temple which is greater than Solomon's, and join a song which shall know no end.

EVENING SERMON.

2 Chronicles 29:27.

"And when the burnt offering began, the song of the LORD began also."

KING Hezekiah, as a man of God, was zealous for the house of God. In the very first month of the first year of his reign, he did to the Temple at Jerusalem, what has recently been done to this church. He cleansed, repaired, and beautified it. On a set day, he assembled his princes and people; and "went up into the house of the LORD." And there, while some Priests and Levites offered burnt offerings and sin offerings, other Priests and Levites sounded musical instruments; and "the singers sang."

Those instruments had originally been prepared by King David "at the commandment of the LORD." Their use had become obsolete; at least in the Temple-service. If they had at all been used, it was in the abominable idolatries of Baal. But now the good Hezekiah restored their use in the worship of his God. On the great day of assembling in the renovated Temple, he either so arranged, or so restored, the parts of the service, that, as soon as the burnt offering began to blaze, the beautiful "song of the LORD" struck up.

In dependence, then, on the grace of the Eternal Spirit, let us turn our thoughts to that *union of sacrifice and song*, which the text describes, which union was and is, and, in one respect, ever will be, the grand peculiarity of that worship which alone is acceptable to the Trinity in Unity.

It is purposed, through God's assistance, to consider,

I. *The union of sacrifice and song, under the Jewish Dispensation.*

Song is older than sacrifice; inasmuch as holiness preceded sin. At the immaculate creation of the world, "the morning stars sang together, and the sons of God shouted for joy." It is likely that Adam, supreme in the paradise of Eden, would sing of the *goodness* of his Creator, while as yet the *mercy* of a Redeemer was needless and unknown. The interval between the commission of the first sin, and the revelation of the only Saviour, must have been as songless as it was dreadful. But, as soon as "the seed of the woman" was announced, it was time for "the song of the LORD" to begin. As to when it really did begin, curiosity must be content to wait, till we know even as we are known: for, from the creation of the world to the time of Jubal, no allusion is made to music. It is, however, intimated that as early as even his day, instrumental music, which usually follows vocal music, was perfectly common. For ages onward, all allusion to both the one and the other is dropped; 'till Laban complained of not having been allowed to send Jacob away, "with mirth, and with tabret and harp." But it is not 'till the passage of the Red Sea, that we read of any musical performance of a distinctly sacred character. As to *that* performance, it is more than probable that it was only one of many which preceded it. The Hebrews must have been accustomed to choral music, to be able to sing and play such a Song as the Song of Moses, at short notice, and *antiphonally*[1] too; for Moses and the men formed one choir, and Miriam and the women formed another. Subsequent incidents, such as their singing before the

[1] Simplicity, no doubt, united with energy and expression, was the characteristic of this performance. Whether or not it was the *first* instance of *antiphonal* performance, it unquestionably shews that antiphony, or singing responsively in turns, by two separate companies, is older than the establishment of the Jewish polity. That it was continued all through the existence of that polity is clear, from the arrangements of David, (1 Chronicles 25:8.) and the renewal of them by Nehemiah. (Nehemiah 12:24.) A very earnest advocate for antiphonal singing may refer not only to the vision of Isaiah, (Isaiah 6:3.) for a celestial recognition of the practice; but to the very first song of all, coeval with creation itself, "when the morning stars sang together, (as one choir) and the sons of God shouted for joy," as another choir. Certain it is that it became, at a very early period, the practice of the christian church. Antioch, where church choirs were first regularly formed, as well as where believers were first called christians, is generally reputed as the birth place of christian antiphony. Hence the error of regarding the antiphonal singing of our cathedrals as "a relique of popery."

See Hooker's Eccles. Pol. Book v, ch. 39, (2.)

golden calf, shew that they were habituated to mingle song with sacrifice. Upon the establishment of the Tabernacle-service, arrangements for musical worship, and the blowing of trumpets, were systematically made. But it was reserved for David, as the sweet singer of Israel, to enlarge and prepare for perfection, the Psalmody of his national church. Then, indeed, "the song of the LORD" abounded; and the courts of the Sanctuary rang with gracious mirth.

We need only allude to the number and excellency of the instruments made by Solomon, for they were made on the eve of degenerate days. (2 Chronicles 9:11.) "There were none such seen before in the land of Judah." After short lived revivals, sacrifice gradually ceased, and holy song ceased with it. Hezekiah at length arose, a further-reformer in Judah. He restored the offering of burnt sacrifice, and the performance of divine song. When he kindled the altar, he awoke the choir. As before intimated, he, most likely, followed the arrangement which David, as God's inspired servant, had defined. "When the burnt offering began, the song of the LORD began also, with the trumpets and with the instruments ordained by David, King of Israel."[1] And, verily, in this scene, there must have been much to affect and elevate the heart of the pious Hebrew. When he saw the sacrificial victim, he was reminded at once of the pardon of his sin, and of the joyous peace which passeth all understanding. When, also, the sound of the song ascended with the smoke of the sacrifice, it intimated to him not only that without shedding of blood there is no remission, but that without acceptable sacrifice there can be no acceptable thanksgiving. It obscurely told him a truth which, in later days, has clearly been told to us, that the atonement of the One Great Mediator is both the only basis of spiritual praise, and the grand subject of that praise. It taught him, too, the momentous difference between the most imposing ceremonies, and the renewed affections of the heart. Hence said David, "I will praise the name of God with a song, and will magnify him with thanksgiving. This, also, shall please the Lord better than an ox or bullock that hath horns and hoofs." (Psalm 69:30, 31.)

The perfection of Hebrew worship was the union of sacrifice and song with corresponding devoutness of soul. Doubtless this union will, at the last great day, be found to have existed among many a "seven thousand in Israel." God will shew that He had a people formed for his praise, amidst the scantiness of revelation, and the imperfections of ritual worship.

After the harp of Judah had hung, for many a long year, on the willows of Babylon, the burnt offering and "the song of the LORD" were renewed, under Ezra and Nehemiah. The provision which was made for the choir, in the second Temple, is rather minutely recorded. The singers were privileged persons; as much so as the ministers of the sanctuary. "It shall not be lawful (said the King of Persia) to impose toll, tribute, or custom, upon them." (Ezra 7:24.) "It was the King's commandment concerning them, that a certain portion should be for the singers, due for every day." (Nehemiah 11:23.) Their services were continued, amidst sundry interruptions, 'till that age in which Simeon and Anna waited daily in the Temple, for the coming of the Redemption of Israel. And when the lowly Redeemer did come, He himself attended the Temple-service, and gazed on the type of his own sacrifice, and listened to the song, which, though little suspected by those who were singing it, was indeed composed for his own praise. Messiah was the true burden of that song, inasmuch as He was the antitype of every sacrifice. But, when He with incarnate eyes beheld the burnt offering, the time was come for its flame to expire; but *not* for "the song of the LORD" to cease. That song is continued to this day; and eternity is not destined to witness its end. It will be everlasting, and yet ever new.

And here, before we proceed to the second part of our subject, two remarks may, from the character of the times and our present opportunity, be appropriately introduced. 1st. It has become the fashion, in what is called the musical world, to decry the ancient Hebrew music. Even persons of education have ventured to say that "The music of the Temple must have been insufferably coarse; and had Mozart heard it, he would have been horrified and shocked."

They who assert such things forget or conceal certain facts, before which their "great swelling words" shrink into native insignificance. They forget that they cannot define what Hebrew music really was. They overlook the fact that the Hebrew music school was on a scale both as to numbers, training, and stipend, which no church in christendom ever had the heart to attempt. They do not bear in mind that Hebrew trumpets were of silver, and that Jewish harps and other instruments were of the choicest manufacture. They, also, quite overlook one omnipotent consideration,—*The days of Hebrew music were days of divine inspiration.* He who inspired mechanics to construct the Sanctuary was, at least very likely to inspire musicians to sing and play in it.[2] That such inspiration was extant is more

[1] "And even in thy daily sacrifices each morning and evening, I find a heavenly mirth; music, if not so loud, yet no less sweet and delicate: no fewer than twelve Levites might be standing on the stage, every day, singing a divine ditty over thy sacrifice; psalteries, not fewer than two, nor more than six; pipes, not fewer than two, nor more than twelve; trumpets, two at the least, and but one cymbal: (Maimonides) so proportioned by the masters of thy choir; as those that meant to take the heart by the ear."

Bishop Hall's Soliloquies, lxxvi.

[2] "Kircher supposes that the Hebrew musicians were inspired with the knowledge of vocal and instrumental music, and that their performance was equal to their skill. He doubts not but that there were many, especially in the time of King Solomon, who were skilled in divine music; for that the most

than probable. What instrument in modern days can produce such effects as the harp of even the youthful David? Or what military band ever awed an opponent army, and gave a decisive turn to the battle, like that company of sacred musicians whom Jehoshophat led into the field? (2 Chronicles 20:21, 22.) Verily, in spite of semi-infidel surmises, there must have been something wonderfully touching, or strikingly beautiful, or overwhelmingly grand, in the music of the Hebrew church. How the holy and all-wise God testified his approbation of it, we heard in this morning's discourse.

Europe is now gazing on Palestine; and the Jews are in the eye of the world. But it is remarkable that God has constantly set his ancient people not only before the eye, but in the *ear* of the world. The voices of the seed of Abraham have always attracted attention.[3] For sundry generations of late, a Jew or Jewess has stood in the very first rank of European singers.[4] And, if Jewish voices be so splendid in the days of their degradation, what may they not have been in the time of their glory? and what may they not yet be on their coming restoration? (Romans 11:12, 15.) Jerusalem may yet hold the empire of song; and exhibit a model of christian music to Christ's holy catholic church.

2nd. The other remark proposed for introduction is this: We are too apt to regard the service of the Hebrew church as a dark, dull, and irksome service. We think of the dying victim, the fuming altar, and the sprinkled blood; and picture to ourselves a scene of humiliation, tedium, and cold formality. But far different was the real state of things. The service of the Temple though a mingled service was singularly cheerful. Enough has been said of its singing and instrumentation to show that it was far more spirited and lively than anything we are accustomed to witness. "The song of the LORD," under various modifications of historic recital, prophetic declaration, and devotional breathing, was kept up, day and night, in the Sanctuary, even when no sacrificial offerings were going on. (Psalm 134:1.) Thus by far the greater part of the Temple service was of a very exalted and joyous character;—a fit emblem of the worship of that "Tabernacle which God hath pitched and not man." For, as in heaven so on earth, while God will have his redeemed ones mindful of their sins, He designs them to be thankful for his mercies. This will of God was largely in the mind of our Reformers, when they modeled our invaluable Liturgy. Hence *we* have a cheerful service, and yet such an one as becomes a company of "miserable sinners."

Our next relative topic is,

II. *The union of sacrifice and song under the Christian Dispensation.*

That dispensation began with a song, but in anticipation of a sacrifice. "Glory to God in the highest," sang the angelic choir, because "a Saviour" from *sin* was announced. That beloved Saviour habitually kept his sacrifice in view: and though his disciples could but little understand it, yet did He soothe and cheer them with considerations drawn from the mysterious consequences of it. On the night of his betrayal, He virtually abolished that grand sacramental type of his own sacrifice,—the Passover. He ate of it for the last time; and then instituted and ordained another sacramental service significative of his death. This service he closed by singing a hymn. Whether that hymn was the great Hillel, *i.e.* the Passover selection of Psalms from the hundred-and-thirteenth to the hundred-and-eighteenth inclusive, or another hymn properly so called, may admit of question; seeing the Passover was abolished when it was sung, and the Lord's Supper established in its stead. Be the fact as it may, our church has followed this very first model of eucharistic service, and put in the lips of her communicants a noble and glorious song,[5] just before they rise up to go away.

Subsequently to our Lord's crucifixion and ascension, when the Spirit had been poured out from on high, somewhat of the worthiness of his sacrifice began to be seen and felt. Hearts exulted with the love of Christ, and tongues were eloquent in rehearsing the wonders and virtues of his death. That death was, in fact, the all comprehensive event which was to be told to a ruined and a wretched world; and from which that world was to take up a new song, and gather new hopes and joys.

excellent music was fittest for the wisest of mortals, and that of the Hebrews must have been more efficacious in exciting the affections, than that of the Greeks, or of later times."

Sir J. Hawkins's Hist. Mus. Vol. 1, p. 258.

[3] The Babylonians were compelled to admire the singing of their Jewish captives. (Psalm 137:3.) The Romans, who besieged Jerusalem, are described as little less than enchanted with "the music which they heard played, many a night, upon the high walls of the city, with hautboy, clarion, and dulcimer. I never," says one of them, "heard any music like the music of the Jews. Why, when they came to join the battle, their trumpets sounded so gloriously that we wondered how it was possible for them to be driven back. And, then, when their gates were closed, and they sent out to beg their dead, they would play such solemn awful notes of lamentation, that our plunderers stood still to listen, and their warriors were delivered to them, with their mail on, just as they had fallen."

Lockhart's Valerius in loco.

[4] There was so much ambiguity respecting the parentage of the wonderful Madam Mara, that, among other surmises, she was suspected of being by birth a Jewess. Mrs. Bland captivated all ears by the sweetness of her singing. Some fifty years ago, all London was going to the Jewish Synagogue to hear Leoni chant. In earlier life, Braham surpassed his competitors of every nation, with as much ease to himself as, perhaps, envy to them. And now, on all great occasions, and for all the most important bass songs, whether delicate, difficult, or scientific, who does not look to Henry Phillips?

[5] The Gloria in Excelsis of our Communion Service is better sung than said. It can easily be so versicled as to be used with a chant. Tallis is the only composer in Boyce's Cathedral Music, who has set it for singing.

Because Jesus was bound, the prisoner was to be loosed. Because He was smitten, the ailing were to be healed. Because He wept, the sorrowful were to rejoice. Because He cried with a loud and grievous cry, the tongue of the dumb was to speak the language of praise. In a word, because Jesus died, the church is to live. Consequently, be the lot or state of individuals what it may, they are to bring the burthen of their griefs and woes to the Lamb of God. On Him they are, with the hand of faith, to cast the weary load; and, then, with the song of praise to laud and magnify his holy name. The first christians could say, "Believing we rejoice with joy unspeakable and full of glory." Through their faith in the crucifixion, the dungeon was turned into a choir, the rack into a psaltery, and the stake into a music staff. And, verily, from the time that believers began to say each one for himself, "God forbid that I should glory, save in the cross of our Lord Jesus Christ," there never have been wanting a succession of faithful souls to sing the song of their crucified Lord. "Thou art the King of glory, O Christ! When thou hadst overcome the sharpness of death, Thou didst open the kingdom of heaven to all believers!" This joyous confession has yielded corresponding consolation to christians in all climes, and under all circumstances. It has animated them in perplexing life, and cheered them in the dark valley of death. And what, indeed, but the atoning death of the Lord can give energy to "the song of the LORD"? That man must be very angelic or very antichristian who thinks he can offer welcome praise, without holy faith in the sacrifice of Christ. Angels may sing of the Lord's *goodness*, but if man come to sing of his *mercy*, it must be on ground upon which angels may gaze, but on which they cannot stand. The shade of the cross is the area for human rejoicing. There the contrite sinner may kneel; and while repentance fills his eye with a tear, faith may charge his lip with a song. Sorrow may be as the softening dew which falls upon that area, but joy is the bright atmosphere which surrounds it.

Right happy should we deem ourselves at being the members of a church, in the services of which, the sacrifice of Christ is most unequivocally made the basis of all prayer and praise. Whether we ask any petition, or offer any thanksgiving, we are taught to look for acceptance only through the merits and mediation of our Lord and Saviour Jesus Christ. So true is it that, when our Reformers cast away the crucifix, they the more joyfully embraced the *doctrine* of the cross. It is remarkable, too, that in the very arrangement of "The Daily Service" of our church, it may almost be said that,—when the burnt offering begins, the song of the Lord begins also: for scarcely is our sin acknowledged, and the sacrifice of prayer kindled into a flame, when the Minister says, "Praise ye the Lord"; and presently a Psalm succeeds. And, Oh, blessed be the God of our fathers, for restoring to us "the song of the LORD" in its scriptural purity, and in our own mother tongue! Our Liturgy is clean swept of the idolatrous or deceitfully dangerous compositions with which it was once defiled. We retain "the Song *of* the blessed Virgin Mary, in English," because she uttered that song under the inspiration of the Holy Ghost; and because in it she *magnified* her Saviour and our Saviour, her God and our God. But we have no hymn *to* the Virgin, no "Audi, Mater," no chanted invocation to the queen of heaven, no musical worshipping of angels, no lauding of wafers;—nothing that is offensive to a holy and jealous God, who cannot give his glory to another.

Assuredly it cannot be out of place or season to say, Let Protestant musicians be on their guard against the wiliness of the Romish church, in linking beautiful music to idolatrous or equivocal words. The thin gauze of the Latin tongue is not of sufficient texture to shield their consciences from guilt, or their conduct from the charge of inconsistency. Let the most beautiful music go for naught, if it cannot be separated from language and sentiments which endanger souls, and insult the God of heaven.[1]

On an occasion, too, such as the present, it may be far from inappropriate to offer a remark or two upon topics inseparable from the use of an organ in the house of God. The petulant controversy about such use, though, as you know, here and there kept up, is happily on the decline. Truth has prevailed, pretty generally, at least, in England. But religious good sense will be requisite to maintain the conquest. If our church-organs are used for mere display, or for something like congregational amusement, they will merit the sharp rebuke

[1] Cathedralists and Members of large choirs will do well to be a little more circumspect than hitherto has been common. Mischief is being done by admitting the compositions of *modern* Romanists, under the specious garb of adaptations as anthems and other choral forms. Those compositions are utterly opposed to the genius and style of our own church music. They are essentially Operatic: for with the almost compulsory exception of here a phrase and there a modulation, they very little differ from the Operas of the very same authors. Truly it is appalling, and to our older worthies it would have been little short of maddening, to hear our choirs singing the harlot strains of a Roman Opera-Mass; while the noble organ is debased to "a chest of viols," and made to imitate all the levities and puerilities of a fantastical accompaniment. As an illustration of these remarks, it is sufficient to name generically one very *popular* anthem, "*Plead thou my cause.*" It is an adaptation from a Kyrie Eleeson of MOZART, and worthy of him as an Opera writer, but not as an *ecclesiastical* composer. "*Pretty*" it certainly is; but its prettiness is its fault, being as much out of place, in the house of God, as a Corinthian screen in a gothic cathedral, or the taudry dress of a Madonna in front of marble sculpturings. The evils of admitting such music into our cathedrals are great and various. Good taste is gradually vitiated; perception of proprieties is dulled; familiarity with incongruous style is increased; and the line of demarcation between the church and the world is in the way to be obliterated. Besides, such musical adaptations prepare the public ear for the decoy performances at Papal chapels. Romanists themselves fail not to boast of our borrowings, but take good care not to borrow in return. A LUTHERAN tune cannot be tolerated in a Popish service.

which, in the second part of the Homily "Of the place and time of Prayer," is passed upon the instrumental music of our churches just before the Reformation.[1] The use of an organ is to aid devotional singing, not to overpower or seduce it. Hence an organist should be a devout person, ever vigilant to adapt the powers of the instrument, and the style of playing it, to the varying circumstances of divine worship. Skill is not more requisite than discretion in using a tune, adapting a symphony or playing a voluntary.[2] As to what, generally speaking, should be the style of parish-church music, there is no difficulty in determining. The difficulty lies in bringing persons of musical feeling, but not of musical knowledge, to consent to that determination. They have been accustomed to tunes in a most faulty style, and, consequently, cannot soon be induced to like such as are legitimate and good.[3] Common, indeed, is it, to hear psalms and hymns sung in our churches, to tunes of really illiterate origin, and vulgar construction. Some of those tunes are song-like, march-like, ballad-like, while others are of such a nondescript character as to be like nothing but their own unecclesiastical selves. And yet, if an intelligent and right minded organist selects such a tune as Luther and our forefathers liked, it is called dull, prosy, and intolerable. The main cause of this evil has been the want of competent oversight, especially during the past and present generation. Our parish-church music has been suffered, like our parish-church architecture of a somewhat earlier period, to become debased. We blame the churchwarden for the one, and the parish-clerk for the other; but, in candour, we must come a little nearer to the reading-desk and pulpit, to find the blame of both. The remedy is one, as well in architecture as in music, viz. to go back to older models. But in using the older tunes we must bear in mind this fact;—they are in their very structure adapted for large congregations, for masses of voice. Hence, if all who can sing *will* sing, the fine old melodies and rich harmonies of the sixteenth and seventeenth centuries will no longer appear dull and over grave. Only let them be sung not drawlingly but with becoming vivacity,[4] and we shall presently determine on their incomparable superiority for devotional purposes. In a word, we must be content to let the world have its *pretty* tunes, while the church holds fast the *good*: for it is fitting and highly proper that there should be a marked difference between the music of the church, and of the world. "Religious harmony" (said one who well understood its nature) "must be moving, but noble withal; grave, solemn, seraphic; fit for a martyr to play, and an angel to hear." (Jeremy Collier.)

There remains a consideration of a somewhat more practical cast. It is desirable to have in our churches, not only good music, but grateful hearts and ready voices. An organ and a choir of singers are not to be regarded as substitutes for the voices of the congregation. It will, however, readily be conceded that occasionally, and as extra service may demand, the organ and the choir alone may praise the Lord "*skilfully*," for such was a common practice in the Jewish church, under the inspiration of the Holy Ghost. (Psalm 33:3.) Nor is it an ill thing for us to be reminded that, although the Majesty of heaven will mercifully listen to the poorest praises of the simplest heart, yet the best that human skill can offer is far too mean for the worthiness of his great and glorious name. Still in our customary worship, while the organ and the choir make suitable harmony, and both lead and sustain it, the mingled voices of the congregation should follow, and give that noble fulness which nothing else can give. To transfer the work of praise wholly to the lips of other persons, can never be consistent, unless we transfer

[1] An objection against the reformed church-service is represented as being uttered by one woman, in conversation with another. "Alas, gossip, what shall we now do at church, since all the goodly sights, we were wont to have, are gone; since we cannot hear the like piping, singing, chanting, and playing upon the organs, that we could before?" Upon which the preacher interposes, and says, "But, dearly beloved, we ought greatly to rejoice, and give God thanks that our churches are delivered out of all those things which displeased God so sore, and filthily defiled his holy house, and his place of prayer."

[2] It is not discreet to choose for a psalm or hymn of many verses, a tune in triple time with sundry divisions of the accented part of each bar; nor a tune in any time, in which lines or half lines are repeated. Too many Organists violate all propriety and unity by the style of their interludes, or symphonics, between each verse. To such Organists, the last note of the tune is but a starting post for running into all the fripperies or whinings of some light and chromatic Opera music. Hence, between the style of the tune and the style of the symphony, there is the widest possible diversity.

Few things shew the *good* Organist more than *good keeping* in all he plays. His symphonics will never divert the thoughts, nor his voluntaries, after a solemn service, dispel all serious feelings.

[3] Till the beginning of the last century, the excellent tunes of the Elizabethan age as published by Ravenscroft and afterwards by Playford, were universally used. Even new tunes were composed after their model. It is curious and painful to see how, about a century ago, tunes of lighter but less simple character began to be introduced. Many a locality had its wiseacre in concocting and publishing new, wretchedly *new*, "Psalm and Hymn tunes." Volume after volume sprung up; and though they speedily withered, yet each left some evil roots or cast some noxious seeds. Still, many of the good old tunes survived; as may be seen in such publications as are kept for curiosities. But, of late years, these remnants of better psalmody have nearly all disappeared. "The Old Hundredth Psalm Tune" is, perhaps, the *only* Elizabethan tune which is now commonly known. "*Bedford*," "*Hackney* or *St. Mary's*," "*St. Ann's*," and all the tunes in triple time of more solid structure, though generally considered as old tunes, are of a date long subsequent to the age of Elizabeth. The tunes of her age were uniformly simple and easy, yet sober and chaste. They were, also, *syllabic*, having a note for a syllable and a syllable for a note; without repetitions, and mostly in common time. Probably some of these tunes, if not all, with their original harmonies, will, ere long, be published.

[4] It is a great mistake to suppose that because a tune is old it should be sung or played very slowly. The old tunes were always sung, in older days, rather briskly. Hence ten or twelve verses were not thought too long. The Old Hundredth, now esteemed so solemn, was formerly the specimen of a lively and most cheerful tune, as all the older Prayer Books testify.

See "*Directions about the Tunes*," etc.

our benefits also. Devout and thankful individuals who from long, and, perhaps, faulty disusage, think that they cannot themselves sing, will yet discover such an interest in the singing of others, as will virtually make it their own. But, when persons, who can sing blithely enough in their homes, are habitually silent in the house of God, there must be something wrong in either their frame of mind, or their estimate of the duties and privileges of a christian worshipper. Besides, to be able to sing, and yet to refrain from singing, in even "an humble and lowly voice," is as unwelcome a sign of mere half-churchmanship, as not joining in the responses. In all the old editions of our metrical psalms, it is stated that they were set forth "to be sung of *all* the people *together*." So well had this hint been taken even before it was so given, that christians of the Reformation were noted for singing in crowds, even six thousand together at Paul's Cross,[1] the version newly made by STERNHOLD of some of the Psalms of David. No singing can be dull, when the voice of a congregation is "as the sound of mighty waters." Nor can it be more the duty than the interest of a congregation, to help forward the blessed "song of the LORD."

> "For this our *truest interest* is
> Glad hymn of praise to sing."
> (Psalm 135:3. *New Ver.*)

The Hebrews were of old exhorted to join their choir; and christians are bidden to abound "in psalms and hymns and spiritual songs;" singing, at the same time, with grace in their hearts, and understanding what they sing. As, therefore, advancement in holy comfort is one great end of such singing, they who use it best and most, as a means of grace, will proportionably find it an auxiliary to the hope of glory.

It remains for us to contemplate,

III. *The union of song with sacrifice, retrospectively considered in the world to come.*

"The souls of the faithful," as our Burial Service testifies, "after they are delivered from the burden of the flesh are with Christ in joy and felicity." Their bodies, meanwhile, though sentenced to dust, are sleeping in peace. In the morning of the last day, they shall awake in the glorified likeness of their Redeemer; and "they shall awake *in tune*." They shall awake with mighty and instant capacity to begin the song which will be already prepared for them: for thus saith the prophet, "Thy dead men shall live, together with my dead body shall they arise. *Awake* and *sing*, ye that dwell in dust." (Isaiah 26:19.) But though ready to begin their immortal song, they will hear a voice which, while it singles them from the countless crowd, will remind them of the sacrifice by which they were saved. "Our God," says the Psalmist, "shall come. He shall call to the heavens from above, and to the earth, that He may judge his people. Gather my saints together unto me, those that have made a covenant with me *by sacrifice*." (Psalm 50:3–5.) And then, when the Judge shall bid his good and faithful servants enter into *the joy* of their Lord, a song shall commence at which the very heavens shall be astonished, and the angelic hosts delighted. But that song will still be "the song of the LORD," "great, wonderful and holy:" and it will still be a song of sacrifice; for it will be "the song of the Lamb." "Thou wast slain," will say the sanctified choir, "and hast redeemed us to God *by thy blood*, out of every kindred, and tongue, and people."

Startling as it may seem to us, when wrapt in comfortable meditation, it nevertheless is plainly true, that *in heaven there will be a constant remembrance of former sin*. But it will not be such a remembrance as there is, or ought to be, on earth. It will be a remembrance not of sin to be repented of, but of sin abundantly pardoned. The saints of God will never forget their sins. David will remember his adultery, and Peter his denial. Else, how will they adore the Lamb as slain for them, and as having *washed* them from their *sins* in his own blood? But, by an arrangement, as admirable as it is mysterious, "all tears will be wiped from all faces," and every fresh recollection of sin will be followed by a flood of joy, and a burst of song. "Unto Him that loved us, and washed us *from our sins* in his own blood; and hath made us kings and priests unto God and his Father; to Him be glory and dominion, for ever and ever." (Revelation 1:5, 6.)

Such will be the song of those, who placed *all* their hope of salvation in the sacrifice of Christ. May we hear it; may we join it! But, bear in mind the solemn fact;—they alone will hear it, they alone will join it, who begin it now. In the exercise of godly sorrow, we must seek the Saviour's mercy, and sing of it too. Our song, however, must not be confined to the lip; it must spring from the heart, and be echoed in every part of the life. Unutterably sad will it be, should the case be found otherwise with us. If "the song of the LORD" shall have dwelt

[1] In a letter from Bishop JEWEL to PETER MARTYR, dated London, March 5th, 1560, that admirable prelate says, "Religion is now somewhat more established than it was. The people are everywhere inclined to the better part. The practice of joining in church music has very much conduced to this. For as soon as they had once commenced singing in public, in only one little church (*a*) in London, immediately not only the churches in the neighbourhood, but even the towns far distant, began to vie with each other in the same practice. You may now sometimes see at Paul's Cross, after the service, six thousand persons, old and young, of both sexes, all singing together and praising God. This sadly annoys the Mass-priests and the devil: for they perceive that by these means the sacred discourses sink more deeply into the minds of men, and that their kingdom is weakened and shaken at almost every note."

Zurich Letters, p. 71.

(*a*.) St. Antholin's, where, in September, 1559, the new morning prayer began, the bell ringing at *five* o'clock (!!!) when a psalm was sung by all the congregation together.

on our lip, and not have found its way to our heart, we never shall find our way to heaven. In vain will it prove, at the great assize, to say "Lord, Lord, have we not prophesied in thy name?" have we not *sung* in thy name? You know what the answer will be. God in infinite mercy grant that it may not be addressed to us!

But, there will be another peculiarity in "the song of the LORD" in heaven. On earth we are accustomed to sing, "Hallelujah, Amen!" In heaven they say "Amen, Hallelujah!" Of this fact we are certified throughout the Apocalypse. (Revelation 19:4.) But, as to the reason of this inversion, nothing is told us. If, however, we may indulge an humble surmise, the reason, possibly, is this:—The angelic choir are in some way, mysterious to us, affected by the Incarnation of Christ. They perpetually celebrate its wonders. Let us suppose that, at every fresh inspiration, they pause. With their mighty intellect, they grasp, at a glance, the whole history of Redemption. They behold the deep and affecting mystery of the cross. They survey the infinite love of Him who hung upon it. They see the amazing wisdom of God's dealings with man. They trace the intricacies of his providence, and understand the chastisements of his church. And then, approving, admiring and adoring, the entire scheme of grandeur and of grace, they say of it, "Amen!" and quickly their everlasting "Hallelujah" ascends before the throne of the Lamb.

Brethren, think of these things: and if your hearts and lives are in good tune, you will love the melody of a good work. You will, for Christ's sake, generously remember the fund for the liquidation of certain costs, connected with the accommodation of those, who stand in this "holy and beautiful house," to bless and praise the LORD. You will see in your voluntary choir, not merely a goodly company of those who freely offer their services to the Lord, but a lively representation of that better choir which fills heaven with rapture. In your organ, also, you will see a type of what the church below should be, and of what it is above; viz. a wonderful combination of little and great, feeble and strong to make up one harmonious hymn to Christ. You will, also, learn what is better than the best earthly music, for your death-pillow,—the love of that Name which angels and archangels, cherubim and seraphim incessantly admire and adore. And if in the interim you meet with "trouble, sorrow, need, sickness or any other adversity," "you shall have a song, as in the night, when a holy solemnity is kept; and gladness of heart, as when one goeth with a pipe to come into the mountain of the Lord, to the Mighty One of Israel." (Isaiah 30:29.)

Shareshill Parsonage and Church. This was W.H.H.'s last church that he pastored, being invited here after he needed to resign from St. Nicholas Church in Worcester because of his health. This was drawn by his eldest child, Miriam Crane.

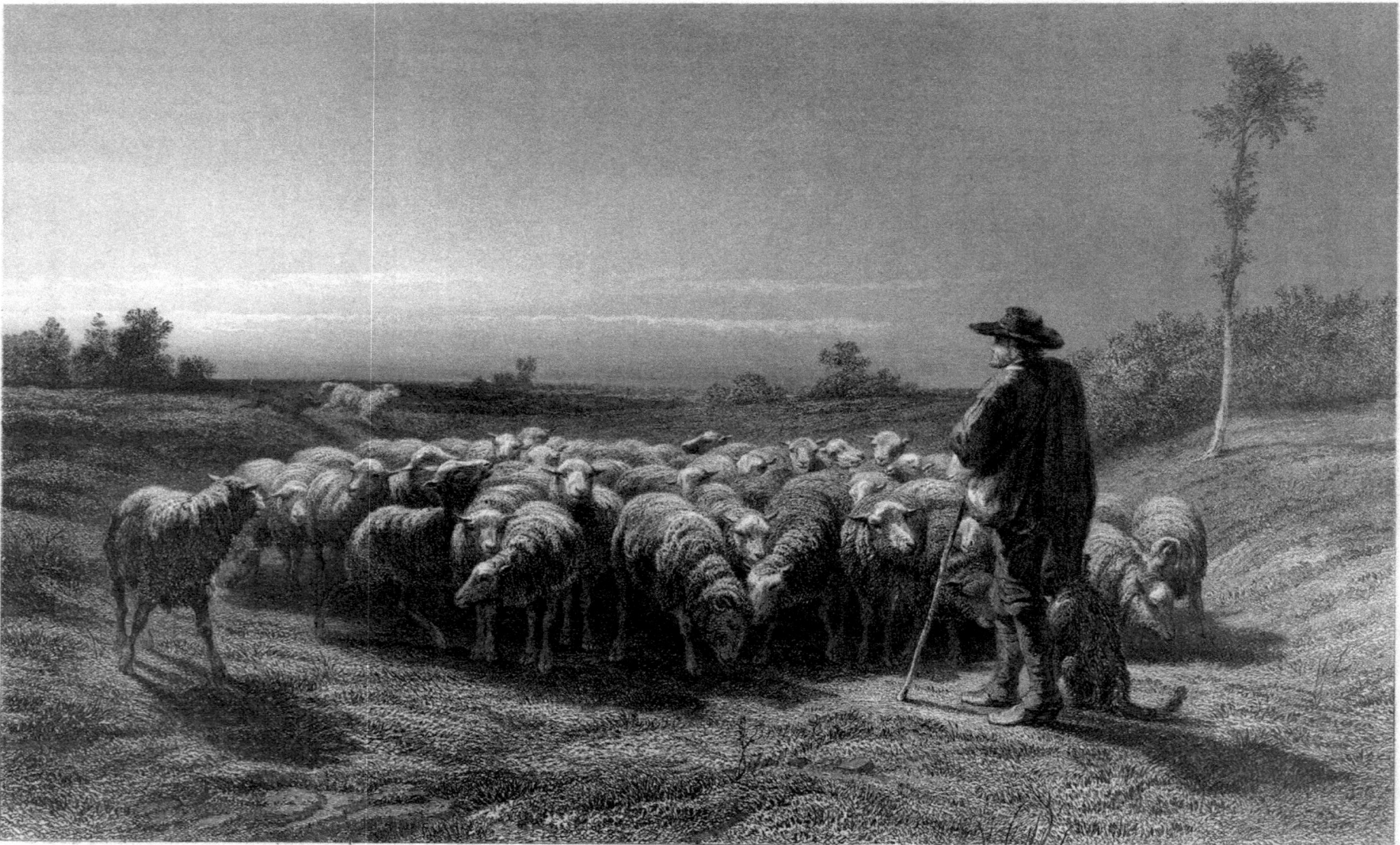

ROSA BONHEUR. PINXᵗ C. COUSEN. SCULPᵗ

"The Shepherd" by Rosa Bonheur.

"THE SHEPHERD OF THE SHEEP."

A SERMON,

PREACHED IN THE

CATHEDRAL CHURCH OF WORCESTER,

AT THE GENERAL ORDINATION HELD BY

THE LORD BISHOP OF WORCESTER,

ON TRINITY SUNDAY, 1845,

BY THE

THE REV. W. H. HAVERGAL, M.A.,

RECTOR OF ST. NICHOLAS, WORCESTER.

"As to the subject of the sermon, it is required that it relate to this occasion: for nothing is more comely or more profitable than '*a word spoken in season.*' It is very fit, at this time, to instruct the candidates in the several parts of their duty, and the nature of their office, that they may weigh and consider well the great charge they are about to undertake."

—Dean Comber on the Ordination Service.

WORCESTER:

CHILD; EATON AND SON; AND STRATFORD.

1845.

Published in compliance with the earnest wishes of many of the candidates.

A SERMON.

John 10:3.

"He calleth his own sheep by name, and leadeth them out."

THESE words are a part of our Lord's description of a shepherd who is not a hireling. The entire discourse is one of the gospels, which our church has discreetly appointed to be read at the ordering of her priests. The occasion of the discourse was this:—The Jewish authorities had questioned the right of the lowly Jesus to teach and to preach, because he had not sought for licence from them. Instead of engaging in any profitless parley, the despised preacher seized the axe, and laid it at the root of the tree. By a parable of singular beauty, he boldly left his cavillers to infer that, in spite of their authority, they were but "hirelings," "thieves, and robbers," and not true shepherds of the Hebrew sheep. Himself, he startlingly said, was "the door of the sheep." Unless, therefore, men entered the sheepfold by that door (*i.e.*, by virtue of a holy faith in him, and of a spiritual union to him) they were not genuine shepherds, but "grievous wolves."

Thus our divine Teacher would have us understand, that, for the *perfection* of the Christian ministry, spiritual qualification is as essential as official appointment. This doctrine our blessedly reformed church holds firmly, and teaches plainly.

In pourtraying the character of a spiritual pastor, our Lord refers to sundry customs, which, though not common among us, are still familiar to shepherds in eastern climes. Two of those customs are named in our text. They can hardly be misunderstood by those students of the New Testament to whom the present discourse will be especially addressed.

Beloved, your position, at this present, is as solemn, as interesting, as affecting as the worth of souls and the verities of eternity can make it. You are waiting for authority, either to advance to the inner sheepfold, or to minister at its portal. Labour and responsibility are before you: endless honour, or endless shame will inevitably follow you. In this your expectancy, many eyes are upon you; and many hearts, I trust, are lifted up for you. I pray you, therefore, to give earnest heed to such admonitory remarks as the text will justify, and a little practical experience can recommend.

The faithful and good shepherd, then, whom our Lord describes, "calleth his own sheep by name, and leadeth them out."

I. "*He calleth his sheep by name.*"

This custom of the oriental shepherd implies knowledge and tenderness; because sheep, to be called by distinctive names, must be well known; and the use of such names is always associated with somewhat of the fond, the gentle, the kind.

1. One of the first duties of the spiritual pastor is, to become acquainted with his flock. "I know my sheep, and am known of mine," is what we, after the pattern of the great Shepherd, should be able to say. In large and busy districts, such knowledge is very difficult; but if, under any circumstances, we make our pulpit our only watchtower, and the pews of our church our only field of observation; we can never be well-informed as to the real state of our flocks. Apart from all the forms of more polished society, there should be, after the manner of St. Paul, in Asia, the domestic visit, the teaching "from house to house." (Acts 20:20.)

Suffer me, my dear younger brethren, to apprize you that advantage must be taken of time and season for knowing your flocks. When sickness, bereavement, "or any other adversity" has befallen them, you will generally find an easier access to minds which, "in health and wealth," had closed the avenues of intercourse. Wait not to be sent for, when afflictions, which are always lying in ambush, have overtaken any of your people. Your ready proffer of pastoral sympathy, counsel, or prayer, will be the more acceptable, and the more deeply impressive.

And here let me advise you not to spurn opportunities of knowing even those in your parish who do not conform to our communion. Discretion will define your measure of intercourse with such individuals: but, never let a cold or impolitic demeanour provoke their antipathy, or rivet their dissent. Possibly they will have much claim on your pity; for their separation may have been occasioned by some of those causes which every sound churchman deplores. At all events, therefore, stand not aloof from any "over whom the Holy Ghost hath made you overseers." Their refusal of your oversight should only urge you to greater affection, greater patience, and a greater vigilance to minister to them in private, that you may the sooner win them back to your fold.

Especially let me advise you to know *the lambs* of your flock. O call *all* of *them* by name! They will soon love you, and listen to you; and, in after-life, remember you as the guide of their happiest days. Such remembrance has, I well know, not only been productive of the most beneficial effects, but has led to some of the most refreshing incidents in the life of the spiritual pastor.

2. Coupled with a knowledge of your flock, let there be a kind and gentle manner towards them. Such manner is peculiarly becoming in younger pastors. It is sure to be appreciated by even the most rugged tempers, and will generally be responded to by cheerful attention and ready obedience. Expect to meet with little roughnesses; but let your preparation for them be "the meekness and gentleness of Christ." His endurance of "contradiction" will, if remembered aright, be a pole-star to guide us through any altercation which the malice of Satan or the infirmity of men raise around us.

Whether, therefore, you wish to reprove or advise, dissuade or exhort, be assured of finding much valuable truth in the maxim of one who, in India and Persia, laboured much for God, viz., "*The power of gentleness is irresistible.*" [1]

Armed with that power, the discreet pastor can paralyze banded opponents, and disperse the dissolute and the excited, when opposite means entirely fail. It was the power of St. Paul among the besotted Thessalonians. "We were *gentle* among you" (he reminded them), "even as a nurse cherisheth her children." (1 Thessalonians 2:7.) In a word, let the proverbial tenderness of the shepherd be the rule of your demeanour. It will adorn your faith and facilitate your work. It will encourage the trembling penitent, and awe the cavilling sinner. Altogether, it will enable you to resemble him, whose heart was meekness, and whose lips were grace.

Allied to tenderness towards your flock, let there be "*fervent charity*" towards each brother shepherd. You are entering the church at an excited and boding period. Every where around us are "great thoughts of heart." It is impossible to look with apathy at those things which are coming upon us. Hence, we shall do well to stand in an even phalanx, and with an united spirit. Give, therefore, the hand of fellowship wherever you can. Be friends with all good and earnest men. Think not of little varieties, but look at sterling excellences. The day may come, sooner than we suspect, when, as ministers of our church, we shall need the truest affection for one another, and that resolute union which alone, by God's grace, can prove a tower of strength.

The other custom of the oriental shepherd, by allusion to which our Lord, in the words of the text, pourtrays the spiritual pastor, is this:

II. "*He leadeth out his sheep.*"

The sheep, after being safely folded for the night, were *led* out (not *driven* out) by the shepherd; who walked before them, and conducted them to "green pastures," or "still waters." Applied to the spiritual shepherd, this custom intimates that he is duly to feed his flock, practically to set them an example, and vigilantly to guard them from danger.

"And who is sufficient for these things?" No mere man is, or ever was. What, then, shall *we* do? There is but one alternative. Let us be meekly sensible of our unworthiness and inability: let us be diligent in prayer and study, and make the eternal Spirit our strength, and then our insufficiency will be crowned by the sufficiency of God. (2 Corinthians 3:5.)

1. *We are duly to feed our flocks.* And how shall we best do this? There are two ways marked out for us by the word of God, and charged upon us by the church; viz., holy worship, and faithful preaching.

(1). The ordinances of our Saviour Christ, as existing in his holy catholic church, are the pasture-fields of his spiritual sheep. His worship and his sacraments are gracious institutions. To them, it is your part earnestly to call your people, and carefully to lead them through the same. It is our privilege to minister with formularies which, even our dissentients themselves, being judges, have as little imperfection as any known compositions of their kind. The majestic simplicity, the chastened fervour, and, above all, the heavenly piety of those formularies, demand your deepest, your devoutest attention. In every ministration, therefore, aim at true earnestness and genuine devotion. The very aim will profit yourselves and animate your people.

Beware of descending to that low, earthly, romanistic notion which regards, or *seems* to regard, exercise of body more than fervency of spirit, and little ceremonies more than lively worship. Take, rather, the high and invigorating position of our protestant church, viz., *the doing all things "decently and in order,"* but esteeming the communion of the soul with its God infinitely more important than the nicest ritual observance.

Shun, too, the arrogant conceit of ministerial mediatorship in the liturgy of the church. That liturgy is not a manual of mediation, but a book of common prayer—of prayer common to all parties, the minister as well as the people. So carefully is this fact wrought up in the very frame-work of that most beautiful book, that the wonder is how any honest mind can mistake it. No where is there the slightest trace of an appeal from the people to the priest as mediator. They say not to him, "Sir, pray for a blessing!" [2] but he repeatedly says to them, "Let us pray!"

(2). In leading out our sheep to the stated pasture-field of holy worship, we are required also to feed them by the faithful preaching of Christ's holy gospel. "Go," said the angel to the apostles—"go, stand and speak in the temple to the people, all the words of *this life.*" (Acts 5:20.)

[1] Henry Martyn.

[2] Roman Breviary.

Without preaching, or an oral exposition of God's lively truth, there never was any great revival of piety in either the Jewish or the Christian church. And no marvel, seeing that always, and especially since the day of Pentecost, the gospel of Christ has been "the power of God to salvation, to every one that believeth." (Romans 1:15, 16.) To the end of time it will be an irresistible and an encouraging fact, that "it pleaseth God by the foolishness (*i.e.*, the *humanly accounted* foolishness) of preaching to save them that believe." (1 Corinthians 1:21.)

And *what* shall we preach? Exactly that which the apostles, priests, and deacons of the first days of the church constantly preached, and which their successors, the martyred or persecuted fathers of our own church, desired us to preach. With one voice, though taking St. Paul as chief speaker, they all exclaim, "We preach CHRIST CRUCIFIED!" (1 Corinthians 1:23.) Then let *us* habitually preach Christ as "the end of the law for righteousness" to every contrite believer, Christ as the source of sanctification through the Spirit, Christ as the all-in-all of the sinner, the helpless, the miserable, the broken-hearted sinner.

The sheep of Christ, dear brethren, must be fed with that soul-nurturing food, the body and blood of their Shepherd. Any thing substituted for that, their proper nutriment, will only distemper or deaden them. "The good Shepherd giveth his life for the sheep." (John 10:11.) The *doctrine* of this wondrous and affecting fact, as well as the sacramental symbols of it, must form the staple good of the flock.

But, beloved, in preaching Christ crucified, be not content with a mere exhibition of the doctrine, however lucid or truthful. You must study to convey it to "the bosom and the business of every man." You will have to apply it in a great variety of ways, for it is medicine as well as food. Consequently, you will have so to mould this one comprehensive truth as to prepare it for every man's conscience, whether for exhortation, counsel, or comfort.

And here suffer me, in this excited and unsteady day, to urge you to drop all comparisons between prayers and preaching. Neither make, nor countenance, any remarks to the disparagement of either. Set forth both exercises in their true and proper light. Encourage neither the formalist nor the flippant. Should the one speak of prayers as all-sufficient, declare the necessity of preaching; and should the other allude to preaching as the chief object of interest, assert the bounden duty of common prayer.

In the selection of subjects for your discourses, you will, I am sure, do well, as often as practicable, to derive them from such portions of holy writ as are read in time of service. The practice will encourage your flocks to listen with lively interest to the reading of psalms, lessons, and other scriptures, as well as prove to those flocks that their pastors are thoughtful churchmen.

The leading out of sheep next implies that—

2. *We are to set our people a holy example.* As the shepherd of the east calmly walks before his sheep, so the spiritual pastor is to walk holily and unblameably before his flock. That flock is to follow him as he follows Christ; for Christ hath left both ministers and people "an example that they should follow his steps." (1 Peter 2:21.)

How *reasonable* it is for the minister to be a pattern to his people, is easy to be comprehended. How *important* such a pattern must always be, we can never too vividly recollect. The minister of a parish is emphatically the parson, *i.e.*, *the chief person* of that parish. All eyes are upon him: his conduct will be noticed. The complexion, so to speak, of that conduct will necessarily give a shade to the conduct of his people. The words of the Holy Ghost will, in a sense, be verified: "As with the priest, so with the people." (Isaiah 24:2; Hosea 4:9.)

The young pastor, therefore, must look well to all his ways. His people will be observant of them. Should they see in him a worldly conversation, or an open, or even a covert, adhesion to earthly things, the bad among their number will be encouraged, and the good deeply grieved. No merely official correctness can be substitute for personal consistency. A clergyman who stakes his claim to respect mainly upon the fact of his ordination, is not worthy of the name he bears. Christ may not leave the verbal and sacramental ministrations of such a man void of efficacy to his faithful ones; but upon the man himself there hangs a curse of unprofitableness, a doom of endless desolation.[1]

Let, therefore, every young man who enters the church be careful *not to linger on the verge of worldly conformity.* (Romans 12:2.) His severance from it should be decided and complete. At his ordination he becomes *at once* a minister of Christ. He should, therefore, cease *at once* from the world, and from whatever good men, in all ages, have accounted worldly. Hence, midnight amusements, or boisterous diversions, or scenic displayings, will present no attractions to that pastor who fears to offend the weakest of his flock, and who is mindful of that solemn account which will be exacted of him in the last great day. In a word, the young minister of Christ Jesus can hardly be too sensitive on the score of personal conduct. The world will tolerate his preaching as an angel, if he will but live as a hireling. The calm eloquence of a holy life is that appeal to the conscience which worldly minds can least endure. By such eloquence the youngest and most diffident pastor may speak loudly for his Saviour. Holiness will give him a dignity beyond his years. "Let no man" (said one who well knew this fact), "let no man despise thy *youth*; but be thou an *example* of the believers, in word, in conversation, in charity, in spirit, in faith, in purity." (1 Timothy 4:12.)

[1] Art. XXVI. [26th Article of the 39 Articles of the Church of England]

In addition, the leading out of sheep implies that—

3. *We are to protect our people from spiritual dangers.* The eastern shepherd carried with him both rod and staff, that no evil beast might worry his flock. While they were following or feeding, he was looking around and watching. Thus we, brethren, are "set for the defence of the gospel" and the protection of souls. If we espy pernicious opinions or dangerous practices prowling about our field or fold, we are to warn our sheep against them. If, after our faithful warning, those sheep shall court destruction, their blood will not be on our heads. (Ezekiel 33:5.) How distressingly such opinions and such practices have, of late, beset our church, the heart of every sound Christian has felt. Whether those evils have fled outright, or retired only to muster force for renewed assaults, our duty is plain. We are to avoid all tampering with them, and to be increasingly earnest in promoting peace on the basis of truth. But, inasmuch as no reasonable man doubts the near approach of either very critical times, or the end itself of present times, our attitude should be that of prayer and watchfulness. That "perilous times" are come, and that many are giving heed to "seducing spirits," and that the very spirit of the great apostacy is flapping its dark wings in hope of triumph, cannot, without infatuation, be denied. "If thou put the brethren in remembrance of these things" (said Paul the aged to Timothy the young), "thou shalt be a good minister of Jesus Christ." (1 Timothy 4:6.)

But, in banishing "erroneous and strange doctrines," whether papal or pelagian, it is well for young preachers to be as little controversial as possible. The elucidation and enforcement of truth should constitute their chief study. Would the shepherd have his sheep withdraw from poisonous pastures or injurious associates? his object will be best achieved by setting before them ample store of wholesome provender, and exhibiting to them a safe and quiet fold.

In all cases, however, study, my dear younger brethren, to *lead* your people, and not to *drive* them. That shepherd who, through fond conceit, or private interpretation, or feverish conscience, divides and disperses his flock, must eventually suffer the keenest self-reproach, even should he escape that woe which God, by Jeremiah, has denounced against the pastors who do such things. (Jeremiah 23:1, 2.)

In fine, if we would lead out our sheep aright, and successfully labour for them, we must daily seek the supply of the Spirit of the great Shepherd. That supply is the sole spring of all strength, and the real secret of all usefulness. It must be sought by fervent and untiring supplication—by such supplication as entwines itself with our very thoughts, and becomes habitual whenever we are about to enter any company, engage in any study, or fulfil any duty.

Finally, brethren, let us turn our tide of thought from the immediate future, to the present, and the *great* future. You are on the threshold of a service which, more than any thing in adult existence, will introduce you to the realities of eternity. You are about to stake your own souls, in taking charge of the souls of others. (Hebrews 13:17.) If, through your negligence, the souls committed to your pastoral care shall die, "a horrible punishment," as you will presently hear, awaits you. If, through your willing ministry, they live, a crown of life, the fairest in all heaven, will be awarded you. (1 Peter 5:4.) Then pause, and once again, even at this latest minute, glance at your motives for standing where you are. Your testimonials have been approved, and your examination has been successful; but, remember, *that is not all!* No ordaining officer can discern your spirit, nor any examiner search your heart. Your real character and your inward motives are known to the great Judge: they will be discussed at another tribunal.

Still, however, even at this present, you have yet to be asked a series of momentous questions. They are most carefully prepared by the church, as fences against hireling intruders. Be thankful for such stringent interrogations; because they are based on the most anxious charity for your own immortal interests: they are intended to spare you from insulting the eternal Spirit. O say not, in even its most mitigated sense, that "you *trust* you are inwardly moved by the Holy Ghost," unless you have pondered those words deeply, and prayed over them fervently. Better will it be to retire from this hallowed fane,[1] than to stay in it and "treasure up wrath against the day of wrath." Better be an honest Nethinim, than a heartless Levite, or an unsanctified priest.

These things are said to you in consciousness of much affection, and in full belief of their propriety; because your bishop, after every documentary and relative testimony, has still, even at this extremest point, to appeal to one, and all in this congregation, respecting your fitness or unfitness for holy orders.[2]

But, let no young man of humble faith and tender-heartedness be cast down. Only let him, from his inmost soul, look up, and, with trembling Peter, say, "Lord, thou knowest all

[1] fane: temple

[2] The anxiety of the church to prevent intrusion into holy orders is very remarkable. That anxiety, when the act of ordination approaches, becomes intense. After the utmost preliminary caution, the end is made as searching as though that caution itself needed revisal. Notwithstanding all that has been effected by documentary testimonials, and strict examinations, and personal questionings, and admonitory addresses, and even after the candidates, upon satisfactory investigation, have virtually received a promise of ordination, the church requires the entire process to be synthetically repeated in the house of God and in presence of the people. The reason for this repetition is not very occult. The whole preceding investigation has been, comparatively, in private; but, as the best appearances may be fallacious, a final appeal, *after a preparatory sermon*, is made to the heart and conscience of each candidate, in the very house of God, before the outspread table of the Lord, and the

things: thou knowest that I love thee!" (John 21:17.) then may he, with a good courage, undertake to feed the sheep of the Lord's pasture, and the lambs of his bosom.

great congregation. Thus, if any thing has been omitted, it may now be supplied; or, if the heart and conscience of any candidate have not hitherto been faithful, opportunity is once more given for their honest exercise. Should no omission appear, or no candidate quietly withdraw, each individual is then left to God and his own soul. No excellency of human counsel can surpass this method of the church. It may have escaped modern observation, but it is one of our "good old paths." It is, in fact, the rule of the church; for similar method is followed in the celebration of the Lord's Supper, and in the solemnization of holy matrimony.

And now, "good Christian people," let me admonish you to join heartily in our holy service. Lift up your prayer, with great earnestness, for those who are about to take upon them the most solemn of all offices. For this purpose you are supposed to be assembled, and not for curious gazing. In your respective localities obey the pastors who are set over you; pray for them, and "esteem them very highly in love, for their work's sake." Take heed of being as sheep gone astray, lest the roaring lion come upon you unawares, and tear you in pieces, when there is none to deliver. Return to the Shepherd and Bishop of souls. Abide in him: so, when he shall appear, you shall be gathered into his heavenly fold.

A GOOD AND SATISFIED OLD AGE.

SOME ACCOUNT OF

GEORGE VAUGHAN,

Who Died February 13th, 1847, Aged 98 Years:

BEING THE SUBSTANCE OF

A SERMON,

PREACHED IN THE PARISH CHURCH OF SAINT NICHOLAS,

WORCESTER,

BY THE REV. W. H. HAVERGAL, M.A.,

RECTOR OF THAT PARISH, AND HONORARY CANON OF THE CATHEDRAL IN THAT CITY.

LONDON: LONGMAN & CO.

WORCESTER: T. STRATFORD.

1847.

INTRODUCTORY REMARKS.

EXTREME old age always commands attention. When coupled with true piety, it claims the greatest veneration. The individual, to whom these pages especially refer, was both a very aged and a very good man. Though among the poorest of the poor, he was one of the richest of the " rich in faith."

In the Worcester newspapers, the following account was reported of him. " February 13, 1847, died George Vaughan, of the Butts, in the parish of St. Nicholas, in this city. He was 98 years of age; and had worked as a tallow-chandler, in one warehouse, fifty years. Notwithstanding his great age, his hair was not grey; neither was his sight or his hearing impaired. To the last, his mental faculties were clear. He had never been taught to read; but, by diligently attending Church, after an alarming illness in middle life, and subsequently, for many years when confined to his chamber, by requesting visitants to read to him, he knew Holy Scripture with abundant 'patience and comfort.' Rarely have things so lovely and of such good report,—such simplicity, purity, and thankfulness, been seen, as were daily visible in this '*nice old man.*' He died as he had lived, full of tranquillizing hope in the one only Saviour."

As soon after his burial as convenient, the following Discourse, comprising some account of him, was delivered to a crowded and an attentive congregation, in his Parish Church. It is now printed, only in compliance with earnest extensive request.

SERMON.

Genesis 25:8.

He " died in a good old age, an old man, and full—".

OLD age is either a great honour, or a great curse. If " the hoary head " be " found in the way of righteousness," it " is a crown of glory: " but if it be dwelling in " the house of the wicked," it is a grievous shame. Though " the sinner be a hundred years old," and repent not; his great age will not exempt him from punishment, but will rather expose him to greater judgment. His respite having been longer and his opportunities more numerous, make his ingratitude more flagrant, and his guilt more fearful. But if the righteous man be spared to " a good old age," and his faculties spared too, he is highly honoured in being a calm witness for the grace of his God, and a living monument of his mercy and truth.

Such a man was Abraham, " the father of the faithful," of whom our text speaks: and such a man, though, of course, in a far humbler degree, was George Vaughan,—one of the recently departed of his spiritual sons, and of whom it will be my endeavour to give you some edifying account.

But, first, of Abraham, as mentioned in the text. He " died," it is said, " in *a good old age.*" That he should so die, he had been certified, full eighty years before. " Thou shalt go to thy fathers in peace; thou shalt be buried in a good old age." (Genesis 15:15.) Thus, for an extended period, he had lived in that confidence and security as to life, which God has granted to very few, and which He never grants in our day. But, when God granted it to Abraham, He granted it where He knew it would not be abused. Alas, did men generally know that they certainly should not die, till they have attained extreme old age, what a set of daring adventurers would there spring up in the world! How reckless would sinners be of dangers, crimes, and vices! Even real christians could hardly expect to be the better or the happier for any such certainty. Their ignorance, as to whether their lives will be short or long, has a sanctifying tendency. It keeps them careful, humble, and watchful. They know not when their Lord will come. Such uncertainty we may be sure is best for us.

It is not said, Abraham died in a *great* old age, but in "a *good* old age." The difference is immense. A *good* old age certainly means a *great* old age, but it means something vastly more. It means that the great age is marked with goodness,—with all the goodness which the grace of God can confer. It may, indeed, imply a great amount of personal comfort and temporal enjoyment; but, above all, it signifies an enviable degree of spiritual welfare, and that peace and prosperity of soul which is above all price. What corroborates this opinion is the fact that the expression, "*a good old age*," is, in Scripture a rather rare expression, and never applied to a graceless person. Abraham, Gideon, and David are, I believe, the only individuals of whom it is used. As the last of the three was not a very aged man, being only 70, it must be that by "a *good* old age," is meant old age piously and peacefully "*good*."

"An *old* man" Abraham, indeed, was; for he was 175 years old when he died. It seems, too, that he was blest with a sort of renovated vigour, after his arrival at an age, which was usually accounted old. For, at the birth of Isaac, he had seen a hundred years; and was as St. Paul says, "as good as dead." And yet, to have lived 75 years, a sort of second old age, after this; and to have become the sire of a numerous progeny, was surely a very unusual mark of the divine favour towards him. This is proof to us that God at any time can elongate our lives, and add unusual vigour to great age. The love of life is, by God's appointment, inherent in our nature. Seldom is it that we grow tired of life, so long as He spares health, and grants prosperity. Still, earthly life, in its best estate, is but vanity; and happiest are they who, in the faith of Jesus, quit it the soonest.

But another form of expression is used to describe the blessedness of the aged patriarch. He was, says the text, "an old man and full." "Full *of years*," say our translators: but, by reference to your Bibles, you will see that those words, "*of years*," are printed in italics, to intimate that, not being in the original, they are supplied to express the sense, according to the translators' opinion. It may be interesting to you to hear how earlier translators understood the passage. In Archbishop Cranmer's Bible, of 1561, before the verses were formed, the sentence reads thus: "And these are the dayes of the yeares of Abrahames lyfe whych he lyved an hundredh and thre score and fyftene yeare and than fel sycke and dyed in a lusty age (when he had lyved ynough)." In the Bishops' Bible, as it is called, some years later, the verse stands in this form: "And then Abraham warying away, dyed in a quiet age, beyng an olde man, when he had lyved yenough."

Thus, both these old translations (and Coverdale's is the same) give the meaning of the word "*full*" as "having lived long enough," *i.e.* as long as he wished, and to his entire satisfaction. Hence we may well say, as there is ample authority for saying, he "died—an old man and satisfied"—satisfied, to the full, of life, and all its comforts and pleasures, so as to be glad to quit it.[1] But, as a man of God, Abraham must have been satisfied not only with life itself, but with the things and dealings of God, which had blessed or befallen him in it. Doubtless, he was satisfied with all the way in which God had led him; with all his trials of him; and with all the goodness and the truth which he had experienced from Him. Now, it is this interpretation of the verse which induced me to select it, for the present occasion, in preference to many which I might have chosen. It accurately expresses what formed a remarkable feature in the character of that good old man, George Vaughan. He truly was "an old man and full"—full of life, and quite *satisfied* with everything which had met him in it. "I am very satisfied." "I am well content;" were simple sayings which his placid lips constantly breathed. Indeed, his patience, calmness, and thankfulness, through a long and wearisome decay, struck everybody who knew him, as, truly, they might; for they very remarkably distinguished him, as an aged man, who was as well satisfied even to *suffer* God's will, as he was to *enjoy* it. It was a common saying of his, when anything was carried to him; "I take it all from the Lord. It is He who sends it to me. The Lord bless you for it. He will pay you again." And, then, he used to add, "I am very happy. The Lord makes me so. He sends his Spirit to comfort me. He is nigh to me; thanks be to his holy name;" or, with a meek and reverent bow, "thank the Lord Jesus for it." It was this spirit of satisfaction, this genuine contentment, which made the great age of the aged one so morally beautiful. But, it was not always thus with him. Like Abraham he had spent the earlier years of his life, without any concern about eternal things. It was not, till he had reached the midst of his days, that any serious thoughts settled in his mind. Nor was it till some few years since, that those thoughts were accompanied with that light and sanctification which made him what he was. Born in this parish about 98 years ago, he spent between 40 and 50 of those years before he was at all aroused to bethink himself. Up to that time, he was, as he told me, a thoughtless and careless man; not what people call a bad wicked man, but a spiritually careless man; fond of a holiday in rambling about; and, alas, of spending his Sundays a-fishing in the Severn. About the period alluded to, when, as he used to express it, rambling one day in the fields, he was seized with giddiness, in the act of getting over a style. This giddiness was the precursor of a fit. In that fit he continued some time; but, the recollection of what passed before his mind, during the fit, made a deep and salutary impression on him. He fancied that the day of judgment was fearfully come; and that the fiery pit was yawning before him. The scene and its terrors, had, at

[1] Poole's Synopsis *in loco.*

least, this good effect upon him,—he forsook his godless habits on the Lord's Day, and regularly went to Church. He attended to what he heard; and the recollection was afterwards of great service to him. At length, when the Lord opened his heart, as was said of Lydia, and as he used to say of himself; then, like a shock of corn, which is under rain and cloud, the greater part of the day, he seemed to be ripened by an evening sun. Thenceforward, he also seemed to live in an atmosphere of holiness; and to love nothing and care for nothing, so much as the good things of the gospel of Christ. There was no mistaking the character of his religion. It was marked with such purity, such simplicity, such unaffected gentleness, and, yet, with such earnestness, as made you feel,—"This *is* a good man, an honest man, an illiterate but *real* Christian." No one ever said Old George was a hypocrite: for, though strangers, calling suddenly upon him, could never see him to advantage, because he then seemed abashed or slightly flurried, yet, all who really knew him could not but feel that there is a power in true godliness, which awes even the wicked, and commands their respect. In him it was strikingly the case; because, though his sayings were of the simplest sort, and often mixed with quaint or grotesque words, yet the very tone and manner of the old man testified the real dignity of christian sincerity.

That his old age was "a good old age," the following facts will prove.

1. *He hated bad things, and was grieved for them*, and that, not in other persons only, but in himself. He never spoke of his earlier life, but with sorrow. It was pain and grief to him to think of his many misspent Sundays and other days. Alas, to how many persons does the recollection of early sins give no pain at all! They either try to forget those sins, as though God would, therefore, forget them; or they take a wicked delight in recounting them to younger sinners. What more melancholy and detestable sight can there be, than when some grey headed reprobate, excited by his pipe and his liquor, details to younger profligates the debaucheries and wanton acts of his youthful days! For a man to exult in telling those things, for which God will bring him into judgment, is awful and shocking indeed! How common this odious offence is, some of you very well know.

Poor old George was accustomed to say, with mingled plaintiveness and gratitude, "I thank the Lord for looking on me in my rambling ways, and bringing me to Him. He must have thought of me, when I did not think of Him. Thanks be to his holy name for it!" And, then, when sitting at his window, if he heard any brawls, or saw any vice, he used to be *very* sorry for it. "I don't meddle with them, Sir," he would say; "but I am very sorry for them; and I pray the Lord to forgive them, as well as I know how." This was a christian's part. But how unlike that which some of you take! You stand by at a quarrel, and encouragingly look on; or it may be, you *laugh*, and make bad worse. And, then, who thinks of *praying* for bad neighbours, and silently doing for them the best which can be done? Oh that you may learn to do, in such cases, as our aged friend did!

2. He not only thus hated what was evil, *but dearly loved what was good.* Nothing gave him so much pleasure as for any one to read God's Holy Word to him; or to tell him of a Sermon; or to converse about spiritual things. It was a frequent remark of his, when a chapter, or part of one, was read to him, "Ah that's very good. I love it dearly. The Lord puts good thoughts about it into my mind, after you are gone. I bless his Holy Spirit, because *He* teaches me." Not unfrequently has he said somewhat thus; "I long for you to read to me. I shall be very *proud* for you to tell me a good word or two. I would rather have one of your *handsome* prayers, than all else you give me." Love for the Saviour shone out in all that the good old man usually said. His name was constantly on his lips; and that with a reverence which proved that he *felt* what he said. Hence, his faith in Him was beautifully strong. He never seemed to have a doubt of the Saviour's love to him. "I am very weak," he would say, "but I am with Jesus, and I am sure He is with me. I am so happy, for He draws me to him. I have yielded up myself to the Lord; and He *won't* leave me; He *will* take me. He is my hiding place in all my troubles; and his time will be best." Was not this a *good* old age? Indeed it was.

3. He not only loved what is good, *but enjoyed what is good.* Indeed? you will say; what had he to enjoy, so old and ailing and poor as he was? True, of some things which you call good, he had not much. He had nothing but what was given to him: but, then, he *did* enjoy it; both because it was *given* to him, and because he was *thankful* for it. Many, you well know, have much of the good things of this life, but *never* enjoy them. They fret over what they have, and want something more or something else. But, this good old man always *enjoyed* what was given to him; because he felt that it came from God; and was always satisfied when it came. I have told you what he used to say, when anything was carried to him. God was the first object in his thoughts and on his lips. "I thank *the Lord* for it, and *you* for giving it, or bringing it." And, here, let me tell my poorer friends a truth, and a secret,—a truth which few believe, a secret which many will not understand. "They that fear the Lord shall want no good thing." That is the truth. The secret is, "Seek the kingdom of God and his righteousness *first*," and, except under some extraordinary judgment, you shall never be otherwise than happy. Now, consider what I can declare to you; I have never known any *godly* persons but what had friends found for them, in time of need. Their God *will* send them such friends. Poor old George often had but little, and sometimes, for a few hours, nothing at all. But, as he used to

say, "I *thought* the Lord would send me *something*, because I had *nothing*. I am sure *He* won't fail me." Nor did *He* ever fail him; but rather, towards the last, caused abundance to be provided for him. Hence, my poorer friends, be assured that, as I often tell you, it is *sin* which makes you really poor. Sin makes you feel your poverty. You never get over it, because you will not learn how to begin. You begin at the wrong end. You begin with complaining, or frequently trying to do something or to get something, as though all depended on yourselves. You should begin with God. Remember that *beautiful* verse of the 34th Psalm, New Version, which many of you have heard me repeat,

> "Fear Him, ye saints, and ye will then,
> Have nothing else to fear;
> Make ye his service your delight,
> He'll make your wants his care."

But, further, our aged friend did enjoy many good things on his death-bed. Long was he on that bed; but God spared his faculties to the very last; and did not allow him to be brought into any bodily discomfort. Altogether, the closing months of his life were marked by that gentleness of decay, which had been going on for many years. Rarely were Dryden's descriptive lines more applicable than in his case:

> "Of no distemper, of no blast he died,
> But fell, like autumn fruit that's mellow'd long,
> E'en wondered at he fell no sooner.
> Providence seemed to wind him up for fourscore years;
> But he ran on nine winters (twice nine winters) more,
> Till, like a clock, worn out with eating time,
> The wheels of weary life—at last—*stood still!*"

But, ere his clock stood still, it chimed many a pleasant hour. There he lay, "an old man and full" *of grace*, telling of the goodness of the Lord to him, and waiting till his change should come. When asked at sundry times, about his inward state, and the prospect of his departure, he said, "I am full willing to go, when the good Lord shall call me; but I wait for *Him* to call me. There's not one in a hundred old men *so near the sky* as I am. I think, too, I am ready and fit to go, but" (recollecting himself, as though that was more than he ought to say, he emphatically added) "I pray the Lord to pardon me for *saying that*." In the early part of his last day, the Curate saw him, and told him, that, on the evening of the following day, *i.e.* Sunday, he meant to preach from our Lord's words to the penitent thief, "This day shalt thou be with me in paradise." The dying man raised his head from his pillow, and with a joyful countenance exclaimed, "I am not afraid to die. I hope He'll come and take *me*." And then, the Curate while going down stairs, heard him repeating the words, "*This day*, in paradise—*this day!*" And he *did* reach paradise *that day*, for he breathed his last quiet breath, just five minutes before midnight. Two hours previously to that period, I saw him for the last time. He was distressed with phlegm, while I was reading from *his own* Bible to him. I proposed for his head to be a little higher. He gladly assented; but there was nothing available for the purpose. At length, for his attendant was ill and occupied, I found a piece of old cloth; and still having his Bible in my hand, I said, "Well, George, you *have done* with your Bible now: there is nothing else at hand; suppose I wrap it up in this cloth, and lay it under your pillow: you have *felt* it in your heart, and now you may *die* with it under your *head!* Oh what a glance of heavenly delight did he give me! The Bible thus used as a pillow, was placed under his head; the increased elevation gave him ease; and he died upon the Blessed Book.

But, before I left, I said, "Well, George, of all your happy Sundays, I think to-morrow will be your happiest; for I see that you are now fast going to the Saviour whom you love." Though before he could hardly articulate more than yes, or no; yet, on my saying this, he made a convulsive effort, and with a full voice, cried out, "I *am* going now!" These were his last words; and kings and queens may well envy them. As I walked home, I could not help thinking, "There lies a man whose state is more to be desired than if he had the crown of England on his head, and the Bank of England at his feet! He has done with this vain world. He will soon leave it; and he *knows* whither he is going. Before morning he will begin an eternal Sabbath, and enter upon all the splendours and joys of heaven. He is, also, humbly *sure* that such an entrance will be granted him." Was not this then "a *good* old age?" Who would not die this death of the righteous? What would you not give to *know* what he knew,—to *know* that you *are* going to the bosom of the Eternal God? Many a worldly or wicked man would give *much* for this, if he had anything earthly which he could give: but he will not give his heart to God. That gift will gain him that knowledge: but, without the heart so given, there is neither hope nor heaven. Then, a word in conclusion.

1. *Be admonished*,—especially ye neighbours of George Vaughan. He prayed for you: O pray for yourselves! He lived among you: then, take care lest, in the last great day, he should be summoned as a witness against you.

You have come hither *this* evening, to hear what you will call his "Funeral Sermon." Why are you not here, *every* Sunday evening, or morning, or both? If you have come from curiosity, you can come from a sense of duty; and, then, you will be likely to come from a love of privilege. Make no excuse about not having *seats*. You have not *hearts*. That is the real, and the worse complaint. If you so loved the house of God as to be determined to come to it, God would find you a seat. He, having all hearts in his hand, would *constrain* the rich to enlarge your Church and make you seats.

In further admonition, let me ask you to recollect two things: (1.) *Want of learning is no excuse for want of religion.* Old George Vaughan was never able to read. "When I was a boy" (I have heard him say) "there were no such schools as there are now. Nobody seemed to care for poor boys *then.* I never heard of a Sunday school till I began to be an oldish man. I do not recollect ever being asked if I could read; and certain sure I am, no body ever offered to teach me." But though our aged friend never learned to read, he did learn the way of salvation. He knew that well; for he knew himself to be a "great sinner, and the Lord Jesus a great Saviour." Now you may learn the same, if like him you leave off your evil ways, come to God's Church, pray for God's grace, and ponder God's Holy Word. But, you will, perhaps, ask a question because I told you a fact. I told you he had a Bible of his own, and that he died with it under his head. "What need, you will say, had *he* of a Bible, if he could not read it?" I will tell you this also. Because it was well known, that nothing gave him so much pleasure as to listen to the reading of Holy Scripture, some kind lady gave him a good-sized Bible, that he might always have a copy ready for use, when any person called to see him.

Remember this, also, (2.) *Death is as certain as your life is real.* This may seem to you a very simple remark: but, it is as important as it is simple. You know its truth, but you do not act upon it. When you hear of a very aged person, you think you may live as long as that person, and perhaps, longer. Thus you put your dying day afar off; and, by so doing, neglect your soul and its great salvation. But, great age did not spare George Vaughan from death; nor has it ever spared any man. Of Methuselah it said, "*And he died;*" though he saw nearly a thousand years. As assuredly, then, as your aged neighbour is gone, so assuredly must you go. But, your death will not be like his, unless you live as he lived.

2. Be *encouraged* ye inquiring or aged poor. What God did for George Vaughan He *can* do for you: and He *will* do the like, if you do as George Vaughan did. Here is a full salvation provided for you in Christ Jesus. Come at once to it. It is made ready for you, and offered to you "without money and without price." Talk not of bettering yourselves, or of waiting till you are less encumbered with worldly things. Pardon and peace are to be accepted, not merited. They are to be accepted, too, without delay; because life is false. Till you accept them, you will never be better, holier, or happier. The Good Lord give you grace to repent, believe and pray! You need be earnest and instant; because it is not a very common thing for elderly persons to become eminent christians. The Lord generally favours them most, who seek Him in their earliest and best years.

3. *Be gladdened and grateful,* christian friends, at any tidings of God's grace working among us. Such instances, as this of George Vaughan, are sent for our truest cheer. They are intended to encourage the pious neighbour as well as the faithful minister. They may well excite us to increasing thankfulness, for the continuance of our Blessed Church, as "a witness and keeper of Holy Writ." In that Church, every poor person may hear abundance of Holy Scripture;—yea the very portions which enlightened and comforted our departed veteran.

Let us, also, learn to prize true piety among even the poorest of our neighbours. The piety of the poor is always of the utmost value to the community: and their "short and simple annals" not unfrequently comprise more real worth, than many an elaborate history. And let us all "die daily." Then, whether our years be many or few, we shall die in the Lord, and be with Him "in joy and felicity."

"Death came, but Death could not surprise
Him who had watched, each day with prayer,
Waiting with longing eyes,
To show his Lord a faithful servant's care.
When called, the bridegroom and his friends to meet,
No oil to buy—no labour to begin:
With burning lamp—girt loins and peace-shod feet,
Thus, hand in hand with Death, he entered in,
And found a bridal garment and a seat!"

"Poorest of all, O aged saint, wert thou!
Yet not *for* poverty we deem thee now
Safe in God's keeping, till the latter day:—
But that thy lot with meekness thou didst bear,
And sought for heaven, in heaven's appointed way."

From Snow's Epitaphs.

DEATH FOR MURDER,

THE DOCTRINE OF ALL HOLY SCRIPTURE.

A DISCOURSE,

DELIVERED IN THE

PARISH CHURCH OF SAINT NICHOLAS,

IN THE CITY OF WORCESTER,

On the Evening of Thursday, March 22nd, 1849,

BY

THE REV. W. H. HAVERGAL, M.A.,

RECTOR OF THAT PARISH, HONORARY CANON OF THE CATHEDRAL,
AND CHAPLAIN TO THE SHERIFF OF THE COUNTY.

PUBLISHED AT GENERAL REQUEST.

WORCESTER:
T. STRATFORD, THE CROSS.
AND
LONGMAN & CO., LONDON.
1849.

ROMANS 13:4.

"He beareth not the sword in vain."

IT can never be inopportune for the ministers of God's Word to defend principles, which the good and the wise, in all ages, have derived from his word. When honest interpretations of it have become patent and popular, it is venturous to tamper with them, and more than venturous openly to dispute them. Though the motives of persons who do thus may be pure and generous, yet will they hardly escape suspicion, in the minds of those who have followed the bright and broad lights of that word which is infallible. At the same time, the unsettling of the popular mind which, on any subject, has been well settled on that word, can hardly take place without some advantage being thrown into the scale of infidelity. It is, therefore, with regret that I have witnessed a local disposition to deny the lawfulness of capital punishment for murder: and, truly, it is with anything but welcome feelings, that I undertake, this evening, to substantiate the truth of what is so denied.

To facilitate the object in view, it will be my endeavour to reduce the question to as narrow limits as possible. Capital punishment for murder only, and not for any other crime, will be the simple point. Nothing need be said, especially at this present and in this place, about the secularities of the topic. Allusions to juries,[1] executions, and criminal statistics may well be omitted. All such portions of the subject will be waived in favour of the main and simple question,—*Is it, or is it not, the bounden duty of the christian magistrate to inflict death for the crime of murder?* That such *is* his bounden duty, it will be the object of the present lecture to prove. If that be proved, all incidental circumstances must yield to its force: for, if we only arrive at a clear knowledge of the will of God, as revealed in the Old and New Testament, we may, in obeying it, safely leave all issues with Himself.

My plan of procedure will be, first, to state and examine the arguments of those who deny what we affirm; and then to substantiate our affirmation, by such considerations as our opponents either under-weigh, or altogether overlook. May the God of life and death, the God of holiness and love, send us his abundant grace, that our present exercise may be for his greater glory among us all!

I. *The arguments of those who deny the duty of the magistrate to punish murder with death* are commonly these:—That, during the world before the flood, murder was not punished with death;—that God's language to Noah, when properly interpreted, does not require such punishment;—that murder was not so punished by the patriarchs;—that all the commands for capital punishment, under the Jewish Dispensation, were part only of a *typical* code, and so were abrogated by the death of Christ;—that our Lord, in his sermon on the mount, abolished the "lex talionis," or law of retaliation, prevalent among the Jews, and so abolished, also, whatever had been practised by the Jews as to the infliction of death for murder;—and, lastly and summarily, that, as there is no command for such infliction, nor anything to sanction it, in the New Testament, the practice is altogether opposed to the genius and spirit of the gospel.

I may here be allowed to state, that, as far as the shortness of time has admitted, I have been at some pains to collect all that is locally at hand, in the shape of book, pamphlet or tract, on the negative side of the subject; and that I am most anxious to give to every plea the fullest force which can be desired for it. By far the cleverest and most recent work with which I have met, on the negative side, is a Letter intitled, "Capital Punishments unsanctioned by the Gospel, and unnecessary in a Christian State." The author is "The Rev. Henry Christmas, M.A., F.R.S., F.S.A., late of St. John's College, Cambridge." But, elaborate and clever as the production is, it does not satisfy the reader that the author is himself satisfied with it. Independently of certain admitted misgivings, the author discards, as of no consequence, things of the first importance; leaves untouched the Apostolic Epistles; and frankly allows that, after all his struggles with the question, it is one of great difficulty. But, to argument.

1. Murderers, it is said, before the Deluge, were not punished with death: for in the case of Cain on the murder of Abel, "not a single word was spoken concerning death as a legal punishment:" and in the case of Lamech, though "the arguments cannot be so strong as from that of Cain," yet "it seems generally understood that whether a murderer or not, Lamech had shed the blood of man, and did not, so far as we hear, suffer any judicial punishment for it." (Christmas, p. 14.) Nothing is gained by this argument; for, in the case of Lamech, who might have shed blood in self-defence, its weakness is confessed; and, as to that of Cain, a few words may suffice.

Though Cain was exempted from death, as a *legal* punishment, yet was he conscious of deserving it as a *moral* retribution. "Every one that findeth me (said the murderer) shall *slay* me." Which intimates the existence of some understood right for the slaying of murderers. Whether God, however, had, from the first, denounced murder, and specified its penalty, or whether He did so at all, before the flood, is wholly unknown to us. Only, the words of Cain are favourable to the supposition that God had said *something*. Plain it certainly is that God, as the Sovereign Arbiter, inflicted on Cain *a living death*,—a sort of punishment which the guilty one felt to be more intolerable than instant death. "My punishment (he said) is *greater* than I can bear." Thus murder was punished, we are not told

[1] How juries, who, in palpable cases of child-murder, give a verdict of "*Not guilty*," can maintain "a conscience void of offence towards God and towards man," is a fearful question. As to *public* executions, the author has long been of opinion that, in the present state of society in its lower grades, they are far more injurious than beneficial. Where one less hardened heart is appalled or affected by the spectacle, thousands are brutally excited, and rendered more callous than ever. It is a well ascertained fact, that almost all executed criminals have themselves witnessed an execution. Were executions to be confined to the interior precincts of a prison, and, besides the proper officers, the prisoners alone to be allowed to witness the melancholy scene, some good might be effected, and certainly much ill avoided. The profligacy in our city and its vicinities, on the evening after the execution of the murderer Pulley, at our county gaol, was shocking in itself, and humiliating to all who toil for the instruction and improvement of the poorer classes.

how, but by a mode of God's devising, as unique, perhaps, as it was terrible. *Why* He spared Cain it may be presumptuous to inquire: but, if we regard Abel as a type of Christ, and Cain as a type of the Jews who slew their Brother, we see at least a resemblance, and possibly a reason for the mark on the criminal and his temporary exemption from vengeance. At all events, a case so unique is no guide for our conduct.

2. God's language to Noah, it is asserted, when properly interpreted, does not require the magistrate to shed the blood of a murderer. Jehovah's words, as they stand in our translation, are these, "Whoso sheddeth man's blood, by man shall his blood be shed; for in the image of God made he man." (Genesis 9:6.) This version has been constantly accounted accurate in itself, and positive in its sense, as declaring the duty of magistrates to shed blood for blood.

But, this declarative sense is disputed, and a mere prophetic intention assigned to the words. Thus it is asserted, that "It is not, let him be put to death," or anything of the sort; but simply "his blood *shall* be shed;" as though God had said, "I *will* not allow crime to be unpunished;—whoso committeth violence, I *will* cause him to fall by violence." (Christmas, p. 10.) It is next proposed to substitute another translation of the words. Among several suggestions, that of Ostervald, a Swiss Divine who wrote about a century and a half ago, is preferred. (It was, however, suggested before Ostervald was born.) It is this, "Whoso sheddeth the blood of man that is in man, his blood shall be shed." It is then concluded that, as "the difficulty lies" in the proper rendering of the second occurrence of the word "*man*," whether it should be "*in* man," or "*by* man," "this most formidable text is too doubtful in its meaning, and susceptible of too many interpretations, (*which is not exactly the case!*) to be taken as the chief support of capital punishment." (Christmas, p. 13.) Now, it is an old device to conjure a mist or raise a dust, when it is not convenient for the clear and stern face of truth to be seen. How easily all these supposed perplexities may be unravelled, and how thoroughly they were anticipated and unravelled 200 years ago, can best be shewn to you, by quoting a lucid passage, not from any authority on my own ecclesiastical side, but from an opposite quarter. In the Assembly's Annotations (A.D. 1657) upon the verse in question, it is thus said,

> Murder or killing is to be punished with death, like for like.—Some read the words thus, "*whosoever sheddeth the blood of man* IN *man*," and the original text will allow it; and so the sense may be, "*Whoso* letteth the blood out of man, which is and should remain in man, his blood shall be shed." But the first letter *Beth* in the latter word, signifieth variously, according to the sense of the place, either *in*, or *with*, or *for*, or *by*; and that instrumentally, as in this place both the construction of the words and the Hebrew accent do import; so that we may read the word as our last translation doth, *By* man, that is ordinarily by the magistrate to whom is committed the sword of Justice for that purpose especially. (Romans 13:4)—The Anabaptists (who deny the legal and military use of the sword, yet sometimes use it against those who favour not their fancies) will have the text for punishing offenders to be taken not preceptively but prophetically, because the words are phrased in the future tense, so as to imply not a command, but a bare commination: whereas, if so, being general they would contain an untruth, for many bloody malefactors often do escape the sword they deserve: besides, it is usual in the Hebrew to put the future tense for the imperative mood. (as the very sixth commandment itself, "Thou shall not kill," for "Kill not.") This and such like texts, do not only justify the use of the magistrate's sword as *lawful*, but require it as a *duty*; and in such a case mercy to a bloody man may become cruelty to many innocent persons; as, where pardons for murders are easily granted, there murders are exceedingly multiplied; as in France, in ten years space, no fewer than six thousand gentlemen have been slaughtered,—as appeareth by the Court Roll of the King's pardons: against which merciful cruelty, the Chaplains of Kings should often remember them.[1]

To these pithy remarks may be added the following consideration:—When God, in the early age of his Church, announced any standard promise or precept, it was his custom, as time advanced, to unfold and explain it by further revelations of his will. It was thus with the first promise made to Adam; and it was equally thus with the first precept to Noah relating to man. Succeeding revelations brightened up the promise of "the seed of the woman;" and succeeding injunctions manifested the full force of the law respecting murder. If one prohibition, and one penalty for violating it, was more clearly urged than another, it was the law against murder, and the absolute death of the murderer. The Mosaic code may be said to be charged with the subject at every turn of its Roll. So repeated, indeed, so explicit, and so peremptory were the regulations respecting it, and so numerous were the historical[2] recognitions of it after Moses, that any ingenuous mind would impulsively suspect that, as in the case of the Passover, something more than mere temporary type *must* be intended. "Ye shall take *no* satisfaction for the life of a murderer," was strong language—strong enough to last for ever. If a murder occurred in Israel, and the perpetrator of it could not be discovered, the Elders and Judges of the land were aroused. They ascertained the nearest city to which the corpse was found lying, and then left the Elders and the Priests of it to go forth to some fitting spot, and perform a solemn ceremony in token of their innocency of the crime, and of their prayer that God would absolve them from its charge. (See Deuteronomy 21:1–9.) All which institutions

[1] There is much fallacy in the boasted diminution of *convictions* for murder. It would be a truer thing to boast that there are more *acquitals!* Is there a shadow of proof that there really are *fewer murders?*

[2] See Judges 20:8, etc. [likely meaning verse 8 and the following verses]

were so many after illustrations of the sense, in which God intended his original command always to be taken. And thus, as we have not ceased to be interested in the first promise to man, for its fulfilment is still progressing, so have we not ceased to be bound by the first precept concerning the life of man. That precept is no more Jewish than the law against murder itself, or the law for the observance of the Sabbath, is Jewish. It is a primæval and fundamental law, and so not repealable.

3. "There is no proof," it is said, that during the patriarchal age, "the punishment of death was ever inflicted by the hands of the law, and it is more than probable that such penalty was neither commanded nor contemplated." (Christmas, p. 15.) Wherein the probability consists is not shown. As to the need of a command to the patriarchs, there was none, because the command had been given. Hence, to assert that there probably was no contemplation of such a command, is not only a mere assertion, but an assertion in the face of evidence to the contrary. The instance selected for illustration of the asserted fact, about the patriarchal age, is that of Jacob's sons, Simeon and Levi, who, in their bitter anger for a bitter provocation, slew the Shechemites. This is called "a treacherous and brutal murder;" and it is added, "It is true that the family of Jacob had been insulted, but the insult had been the doing of *one* man, and *all* the men of the city were slain for it." It is easy to construct arguments, if we fail to consider facts. To say that the insult, in the rape of Dinah "was the insult of *one* man," is not saying the *whole* truth. The insult, no doubt, was primarily and principally that of Shechem; but, it is clear that his father, and the mass of the male population treated it lightly, sided with the perpetrator, and so made themselves participators in his crime. The conduct of Simeon and Levi, though most unjustifiable, was an excess of justice rather than an ordinary murder. And, as such, God treated it. Because the Shechemites were the offenders, and also licentious idolaters; and because Jacob and his family were, as a whole, the heirs of the land, and the stock of the Church, Jehovah did not punish his sons for murder, but for wrath and treachery. This He did by reserving a curse for them, on the lips of their dying father. See Genesis 49:5, 7. At the time of the event, too, God allayed the fears of Jacob, as to the safety of his family, by removing him from the vicinity of the crime to his favourite Bethel. Thus this instance cannot fairly be taken for a proof of the fact alleged.[1] And, yet, the actual existence of patriarchal power to inflict death for crimes even less than murder, is overlooked by the writer whose opinions we are questioning. Not only does he forget that Job, one of the earliest patriarchs, mentions "*the murderer* rising with the light:" (Job 24:14.) but that Judah claimed that power, when, suspecting his daughter-in-law of harlotry, he said, "Bring her forth, and *let her be burnt!*" (Genesis 38:24.) It is, also, overlooked that Reuben *pledged the life* of his two sons, for the safe return of Benjamin. (Genesis 42:37.) And well, also, might it have been recollected that, at this early date, the power of life and death was magisterially exercised in Egypt; for Pharaoh's baker was hanged; and Moses afterwards fled through fear of death, when he had zealously killed an Egyptian. These historic facts are, at least, presumptive of the right interpretation of the original command to Noah, in its traditional spread among his varied descendants.

4. It is further argued that the punishment of death for murder, under the Mosaic economy, was, like all other ritual deaths, for all propitiation: and "that thus the punishment of death inflicted upon the offender assumes as direct an aspect of expiatory sacrifice as the offering of a bull or of a goat for sin." (Christmas, p. 8.) It is, then, confidently concluded that death for murder, being *typical* in character, was repealed by the incarnation of Christ as the true antitype. (p. 18.) The writer, whose words and sentiments are thus quoted, contrives to make confusion with expiation and type, as though the terms or the things were synonymous: and, therefore, assuming that they are synonymous he leaps to a conclusion at once most lame and impotent. In a word, his notion of the *expiatory* and *typical* character of a murderer's death, is a mere presumption; and, so far as the argument is concerned, is a grand and fatal mistake. It originates, as intimated, in confounding things which differ. Every act of expiation was not a type, any more than every type was an expiation. Besides, the infliction of death upon a murderer, apart from retribution on himself, was a *lustration* for the land, and not, as in other cases, an expiation or propitiation for the crime itself. The blood of the murderer was to be shed not by the priest but by the magistrate. It was, therefore, a political rather than an ecclesiastical procedure. Nay more, a murderer might be slain without judge or jury, and without a moment's delay. Even in the case of the most innocent homicide, the next of kin to the deceased was at liberty to kill the unfortunate culprit, provided he found him outside a city of refuge. This was vengeance rather than expiation; but such vengeance, as apart from human passion, was dictated by conventional reverence for God's image in man. Nothing but the stern force of the original mandate, and of the reason appended to it, could have justified the expedient.

Thus the notion of a type, in the death of a murderer, is abhorrent to everything which we know of holy type or figure under the Old Dispensation. The blood of a murderer was polluted blood, guilty and detestable blood; and, so far, utterly unfit to be a type of that blood which is so holy and estimable as

[1] God as a Sovereign may do as He will with his own laws; but no such power is delegated to us. We are not to ask, Why did He not punish David with death for adultery, or any one else for any other crime for which He had appointed death as the penalty? We are to be silent when He acts, but obedient when He commands.

to suffice for the cleansing of a world. It was only clean and pure blood which could typify the blood of Christ. Hence, when by his own death He abrogated every type, no abrogation was on that account made respecting the law of death for murder. That law was no type, and therefore, received no repeal. The law of death for mere man-slaughter was repealed, because that and the city of refuge for it *were* types of other things. But the case of murder remained as it was.

5. Proceeding somewhat chronologically, we next come to the assertion, true enough in itself, that Christ, in his Sermon on the Mount, "*abolished the law of retaliation which had pervaded the Jewish mind.*" (p. 19.)

This notion of *revengeful* retaliation, "an eye for an eye and a tooth for tooth," had, indeed, pervaded *the Jewish mind*; but it did not pervade *the Jewish Law.* That law was God's own law,[1] and therefore high above all such selfish debasement; and yet the arguer's argument covertly assumes that it was not. True, he does not *avow* it, indeed he rather contends, and that very properly, for the spirituality of the divine law; but his entire argument proceeds on its tacit assumption. For how, in fact, is it *possible* to *abolish* a law which is found only *in mind?* It must exist in some legible, tangible, or ascertainable form. What our Lord did was this: He repudiated the unhallowed notions and feelings with which the Jews carried out the law; but He left the holy law itself untouched. What are the facts of the case? They are these;—The Jewish Doctors looked no farther than the mere letter of the law. Our Lord unfolded to their view its deep and searching spirituality. They took into their account mere outward acts alone. He added to it inward thoughts. Hence, when he said, "Ye have heard that it was said by them of old time, thou shalt not kill; and whosoever shall kill shall be in danger of the judgment: but I say unto you, that whosoever is angry with his brother without a cause shall be in danger of the judgment: and whosoever shall say to his brother, Raca, shall be in danger of the council: but whosoever shall say, thou fool, shall be in danger of hell fire." (Matthew 5:21, 22.) He no more abrogated the infliction of death for murder, than He abrogated the law against murder itself. In fact, He made no allusion to the abrogation of either. Granting, therefore, in another case, for the sake of argument, that, because He refused to condemn the woman who was taken in adultery, He thereby annulled the punishment of death for adultery, we by no means grant, as it is by insinuation claimed, that He *therefore* annulled the like punishment in the case of murder. The cases are totally distinct, and stand on totally different grounds. The plea set up, by the author of the publication alluded to, is that because Christ decided against the non-infliction of death in the instance of adultery, "we may fairly assume that the genius of christianity is opposed to *capital punishment.*" (p. 22.) It is in this *general* way that the plea against death for murder is supported. The pleader is afraid to say, "*therefore* the genius of christianity is against capital punishment *for murder,*" because he is too good a mathematician not to know that this would be like attempting to prove that the less includes the greater, or some of the parts comprise the whole. And, yet, this, after all is really what we are wanted to believe.

6. This contrariety to the genius of christianity is said to be manifested by the fact that *there is no command for the infliction of death on murderers, nor anything like a sanction for it, in the New Testament.* That there is no *command* must be, as it well may be, readily allowed; because, forsooth, there was no need for it. Such a command would have been out of character as well as superfluous. The rule was extant, of long standing and common knowledge, still acted upon, and, as we shall presently shew, satisfactorily recognized by our Lord's apostles. The fact of that recognition is in every counter-publication which has met my own eye, positively passed over as though it were a non-entity—a something of which no theologian had ever dreamed. Singular to say, though the author, whose sentiments have been canvassed, speaks much of "the genius of christianity," he shews no disposition to consult it. He mentions the *Gospels* of the Evangelists, but does not so much as glance at *the gospel*, as more fully expounded by the Apostles. He does not even allude to our Lord's remark to Peter, "they that take the sword shall perish by the sword:" *i.e.* they who unjustifiably kill by the sword, shall die by the sword of war or justice.[2]

But, ere we pass, from "the genius of christianity," to other considerations, suffer me to admonish you against a mode of exhibiting it, and of contending for it, in the argument before us, which every devout and reverent heart must abhor. In a widely and warmly circulated Tract, intitled "Cold Blooded Homicide," sent abroad as "Sparks from an Anvil," an imaginary case of a murderer on the day of execution is described, in terms which cannot be otherwise than revolting to all who love the decency of truth, and the exalted sanctity of the word of God. To recite to you more than a brief portion of what the Tract contains, would be a waste of time, and a desecration of place. The talented but misguided writer says,

> We have heard of cold-blooded murders, perpetrated with slow premeditation, but none like those of the scaffold.[3] Let us consoli-

[1] "The *equity* of which law is still continued in force, as suitable to the law of nature; and ought to be more observed than it is."—Dr. Owen, Epistle to Hebrews 10:28, 29.

[2] See Matthew Henry's Commentary, *in loco.*

[3] Could the writer be aware of the high insult which this language commits against our Queen, and all her judicial representatives in the kingdom? If he means what his words imply, then are all, who take part in the sentence

date a christian community into one christian man. He has got his man (the criminal) into his power. He is solicitous for the salvation of his soul, and labours for his eternal happiness. The murderer is melted into the deepest contrition. He becomes a new creature in Christ Jesus. The light and loving kindness of a pardoning God shine into his heart, and give him songs of joy in the night. His executioner joins in these songs. The day draws near, and the hour, when the twain must be separated; when this christian communing must be broken off on earth, by one of the communicants deliberately breaking the neck of his brother with the halter, and all in love *prepense.* The sad hour of separation has come; and the christian executioner comes,—with a rope in one hand, and the emblems of a Saviour's broken body and shed blood, in the other.

But, I refrain from quoting more of this unhallowed burlesque. Only, I must add that the writer of it asks this question, "Is there a human conscience—which could contemplate such a case of private deliberate homicide without a thrill of horror?" Now, I stay not to remark upon the sad disingenuousness of representing a judicial execution as an act of personal hypocrisy and "*private*" revenge; but I hasten to answer this pitiful question; and I tell the man who asks it, that, there *is* essentially *just such a case,* as he imagines to be so horrible, written by the pen of inspiration for our consciences and our learning. Just such a case, in all essential points, is the case of Achan; in which the God of truth and love was the prime mover, and his faithful Joshua the chief agent. Achan had committed a crime, and was detected. Joshua said to him, "*My son* give *glory* to the God of Israel, and *make confession* unto him!" He did make confession, most frank and most penitent confession; and thus gave glory to the God of Israel, by exhibiting all the tokens of such a gracious change as the American writer describes. But what did Joshua do? *Exactly that* which this writer abominates as "a monstrous inconsistency in that christian executioner to put to death—one whom he believed—God had pardoned and accepted." Joshua and all Israel brought Achan and all his family to the valley of Achor, and there, after stoning them to death, burnt them and all that belonged to them with fire. Yet will God be clear when He is judged by puny man. His servants, too, will be justified by Him. Doubtless I shall be told, "Oh, all this is *only* Old Testament doctrine, not that of the New!" Let me reply, The God of the Old Testament is the God of the New. He changes not. What his *nature* was in the days of Joshua, it still is in this day of Jesus. It was holiness and love then, and it is holiness and love now. The different manifestations of it make no difference in itself. His procedure may alter, but his perfections do not change. It is only our dullness and selfishness which refuse to see how He can be adorably amiable, and yet unbendingly righteous. And, let me further tell those who, in questions of this sort, are accustomed to say, "It is *only* the *Old* Testament which says so and so;" that the spirit of such a remark hovers nearer to Infidelity, than they, most likely, either imagine or fear. The Old Testament is as much the word of the Spirit as is the New. The slightest reflection cast upon its *instructive* intention, is a libel upon the inspiration of the New. If we are unwilling to derive our principles from the one, we shall not be very likely to shape our practice according to the other.

In pursuance of the subject it remains for me to notice,

II. *The arguments for the lawfulness and duty of punishing murder with death,* which are either not duly weighed, or not even touched, by those who deny that lawfulness and that duty.

1. It is a fact, and therefore the basis of an argument, that, upon the affirmative side of our question, there is a singular unanimity of opinion among all the old divines of all orthodox denominations. All our great translators and commentators, whether episcopalians or noncomformists, either agree in using our authorized version of God's words to Noah, or in adopting that sense of them which determines the duty of the magistrate to punish murder with death.[4] An army of high and worthy names, to say nothing of our 37th Article, could easily be mustered. But, time will only allow me to pledge my veracity for the fact. The inference from it is this;—If such singular unanimity of tenet among the holy and the wise of all times, ages, and persuasions, is to be superseded by some new fancy of present time, what guarantee have we that the next novelty will not be a little more latitudinarian than the most liberal christian can tolerate? Let us learn, then, to hold fast what has been well proved, and long tried. How nearly allied the denial of the justice of death for murder is to the denial of the atonement of Christ for sin, I have only to refer you to Dr. Owen's Dissertation on the Divine Justice, and to the fact that Unitarians, as they call themselves, and Freethinkers of every grade, almost to a man, take the negative side of our question. I venture on this remark, only to warn hearers of what they may not suspect; and not to cast any reflection upon honest minds which mistake humanity for truth, or which have been led into that mistake by contact with erroneous opinions.

2. It is not duly considered that *the reason* of a *moral* law is, virtually, *the law itself.*

Now the reason, why murder should be punished with death, is both because murder is the same *crying*[5] sin as ever;

and execution of a murderer, cold-blooded homicides! No reprobation of the entire Tract can be too severe. Such a publication is utterly inexcusable.

[4] Hence, the author of this Discourse contends for no new or "*private*" opinion.

[5] "The voice of thy brother's blood *crieth* unto me from the ground." Genesis 4:10.

and because God and man are *unchanged.* The Scripture, on which this remark is based, meets with no attention from the Reverend author to whose arguments so much allusion has been made. He was obliged to notice it; but, he dismisses it with rapid and summary indifference. The reason which God Himself assigns for the death of him who murders man, is this plain fact, "*For* in the image of God made He man." All that our author says of this most important fact is, that "It sheds no light at all on the previous words." Strange assertion truly! On the contrary, it sheds a blaze of light on the previous words, and leads us at once to the only safe conclusion to which we can come. Man must not kill man, because he is God's image and type. Spite of his fall, he retains enough of his original impress for God himself to acknowledge the likeness. His creation presented him to the world as an all perfect gold-coin. The King's image upon it was exact and beautiful. Man's fall changed the gold into brass, but left the image and superscription as they were. Divine grace restores the gold; and all will eventually be rendered more perfect than ever. Hence, he who kills man dishonours his Creator. He is like a traitorous felon, who contemptuously mars the king's likeness on the king's coin. For this crime on man, says the King of kings, "Let him die the death!" This was the law in Noah's day. It is not changed, because *there is no change in the reason of it.* God is the same, and man is the same. He, therefore, who wilfully and maliciously kills man, as the image of God, is to be put to death.

3. As the opponents of the tenet, for which I contend, deny the existence of any evangelical recognition of it, *I beg to adduce what they strangely overlook.*

That the old duty of the magistrate is repealed by some new command, they, certainly, are bound to shew. But, it never has been shewn, except by the assertion of a nonentity,—for, such is the notion that the slaying of a murderer was a typical act, and that as such it was abrogated by the death of Christ. Aware that the ground on which I am now stepping is the Mars' hill of the subject, the very Broad Stone of the whole field of debate, I beg your renewed attention to what is about to be advanced. There is, then, as I am to shew, as much recognition of the old obligation to punish murder with death, as can reasonably be expected, *when that obligation was not a question.* There is as much recognition of it as there is of the christian sabbath; and far more than there is of either the practice of infant baptism, or of the admission of females to the Lord's Supper.

In Acts 25:11, we hear St. Paul saying, before a Roman tribunal, "If I be an offender, or have committed anything *worthy of death, I refuse not to die.*" Now the Roman tribunal, before which St. Paul made this avowal, was accustomed to punish other crimes besides murder with death. But, St. Paul well knew that an accusation of murder was not even imagined against him. He, therefore, must have supposed the *possibility* of some other inferior crime, for which, had he committed it, he would not refuse to submit to the arm of the executioner. What, then, was this but a recognition, and a very palpable recognition, of the right of the magistrate to punish grievous crimes with death?—and, if crimes below murder, how much more murder itself? Let me next read to you Romans 1:28–32. But, because it is not clearly determined whether the Apostle, by the phrase "*worthy of death,*" means penal death or eternal judgment, I raise no argument upon it. Only, it is not without importance in the settling of the question.

In Romans 5:7, the same Apostle says, "For scarcely for a righteous man will one die; yet peradventure, for a good man some would even dare to die." Would a modern disputer of the old doctrine be likely to talk in this strain? Would he not say,—It is against the genius of christianity for one man deliberately to sacrifice his own life for the sparing of another, especially if the magistrate be a tyrant who presumes on holding the power of life and death? And yet, the very chief of the Apostles speaks counter to all such sickly notions about the genius of christianity. He knew what tyrants were in his day, and the histories of those fraternal friends who had been willing to die for others.

And now we arrive at our text and what stands on record with it. "For rulers are not a terror to good works, but to the evil. Wilt thou then not be afraid of the power? do that which is good, and thou shalt have praise of the same: for he is the minister of God to thee for good. But if thou do that which is evil, be afraid; for he beareth not the sword in vain: for he is the minister of God, a revenger to *execute* wrath upon him that doeth evil." (Romans 13:3, 4.) "He beareth not the sword in vain," *i.e.* as the worthies of christendom, episcopal, presbyterian or independent, have hitherto been accustomed to say,—the magistrate, under God, holds the lawful power of inflicting death for grievous crimes. He holdeth the sword not "*in vain,*" as a mere bauble in a pageant or procession, but as a real executive power in a court of justice. Hear only what one sober and universally esteemed Nonconformist says of the expression before us, "This strongly intimates the lawfulness of inflicting capital punishment, which to deny is subverting *the chief use of magistracy.*" A host of similar expositions could quickly be brought into the field; but, if this one, from the pen of the amiable and kind hearted Doddridge, will not suffice, ten thousand would not be enough.

But, mark the remainder of the sentence, "He (the magistrate) is *the minister* of God, *a revenger* to execute wrath upon him that doeth evil." "The *minister* of *God*:" this is why superior magistrates "are called *gods.*" "There be gods many, and lords many." Such magistrates are God's vicegerents and delegates among men. His power is intrusted to them for the due and just administration of his laws. So say all who have shone as lights in the world.

Concerning the magistrate, the Apostle further describes him as "*a revenger to execute wrath.*" Our God claims the sole right of vengeance. "Vengeance is mine; I will repay, saith the Lord." But, God makes the magistrate his instrument for executing it upon guilty individuals. So that it is God's vengeance, and not *private* revenge, which the magistrate inflicts. The instrument of execution is "*the sword,*" which no sane person can deny to be the symbol of power to take away life; for culprits are not flogged by the sword, nor merely maimed nor wounded by it, but cut off from present existence.

Saint Paul said what he said, to Roman citizens, in whose commonwealth capital punishment was horribly common; and in which he himself eventually, but of course unjustly, suffered death. His language therefore, to such citizens would not accord with candour and honesty, if he meant by it something very foreign to what they would be sure to attach to it. We may, therefore, be *sure* that he meant to recognize the duty of the magistrate to inflict death, when deserved.

Here I might close the argument, were I not apprized that it may be pertinaciously said,—What Saint Paul deemed allowable in a pagan commonwealth, he might not have allowed in a christian state. Such an objection is hardly worth answering: and those who will rashly allege it, would not be very likely to waive it, though St. Paul were to rise from the dead to deny it. Suffice it to say, It is morally impossible that the Apostle could have been conscious of any such distinction. No where does he lay down one rule of conduct, or one code of law, for the pagan and another for the christian. The Great Lawgiver addressed his law to Noah, as the father of the new world in all its diversities of population and character. And all the world fostered a right impression, because it was the original impression, respecting the duty of dealing death to every real murderer. Such dealing has been universal custom. But, if the doings of the good and the just in this world are not enough, then let me point to the very pavement of heaven, and bid you behold "the noble army of martyrs" prostrate before the throne of the Lamb, and saying, "How long, O Lord, Holy and True, dost Thou not judge and avenge our blood, on them that dwell on the earth?" (Revelation 6:10.) Those martyrs were *murdered* believers; and, when made perfect in heaven, and placed beyond the reach of human passion, they recognized *the justice of blood being shed for blood,*[1] no matter by whom or what, whether by the soldier, or the magistrate, or the pestilence. What more can be required? Whither shall we further go? I know not, unless we descend to the gloom-covered Calvary, and there witness the murderous death of the Beloved Son of God. Ere He expired He prayed for his murderers, though He infallibly foresaw that his Apostles would charge them with his murder, and that vengeance would fall upon them for it. Let us not forget, from His loving example, to pray for all murderers, especially for him[2] who has stained our county with innocent blood; that God will shew him abundant pity, and perfect all the good hopes which are encouragingly entertained concerning his soul's health.

And now, to recapitulate and to conclude:

1. The present defence of the law of our land, in the article of capital punishment, pertains *only* to real murder. Every humane heart will rejoice at the abolition of such punishment for all crimes, which do not amount to it. But to abolish it for the crime of murder will be itself a crime. Were there no divine law, how gladly would we say, Let there be no death! If it be, however, the mind of God that death for murder should be the law, as long as human life continues, then must it be high insult to His sovereignty to tamper with His law, either by discarding it, or substituting ought else for it.[3] That He intended such law, and intended it to be perpetual, is not only clear from the concurrent opinion of all christendom, according to what has been argued from His words to Noah,[4] but, also, from this collateral consideration,—that, when He spake to Noah about shedding blood for blood, He was speaking of other things, also, but of *only* such other things as were to last as long as the world lasts. Man's multiplication of his race, his dominion over the animal world, his abstinence from cruelty, (not

[1] "It contains an humble expostulation about the long delay of avenging *justice.* Even *the spirits of just men made perfect* retain a proper resentment of the wrong they have sustained by their cruel enemies; and though they die in charity, praying as Christ did, that God would forgive them, yet they are desirous that, for the honour of God and Christ, and the gospel, and for the terror and conviction of others, God will take a just revenge upon the sin of persecution, even while he pardons and saves the persecutors."—Matthew Henry's Commentary, *in loco.*

[2] Robert Pulley, who has since been executed for the murder of Mary Ann Staight. His confession was full, and his end hopeful. In Bishop Hall's Works is a Letter to "W. J., Condemned for Murder. Effectually preparing him (and under his name whatsoever malefactor) for his death." Epistle 54. The letter is interesting and admirable; well worthy, also, of the attention of those who deny the propriety of death for murder.

[3] No considerations of *expediency*, deduced from the altered state of society, abuses, evils, circumstantial evidence, or statistics of any sort, can be warrant for our departure from a positive law of universal obligation. Our part is not to abolish the law, but *to amend our mode of fulfilling it.*

[4] It is remarkable that The Religious Tract Society, to which many of the opponents of the subject of this Discourse belong, continues to print a Bible "Commentary," in which are contained the strongest expressions of Scott and Henry on the duty of punishing murder with death. In that Commentary there is no mincing or mystification of God's words to Noah. It is therein regarded as a command of lasting obligation. Has this suggestion ever been well weighed? viz., That, if our Lord *intended* to abrogate the punishment of death, it would have been a fitting opportunity for Him to convey some intimation to that effect, when the crucified thief acknowledged the *justice* of his own mortal sufferings. "We indeed *justly!*"

being allowed to eat *live*-flesh,—flesh with the *life* blood reeking in it,[1]) the continuance of the seasons, and the exemption of the earth from second deluge, were all to continue to the end of time. Marvellous and surpassingly strange, then, would it be, if, amidst such a cluster of continuances, the shedding of blood for blood were designed to be only temporary, and that without a syllable to indicate such an exception! The whole argument might well be left on this single consideration.[2]

Guided, further, by the divine records, we trace either the principle or the practice of the original law, all through the patriarchal and the Levitical ages. The supposition of type, in the shedding of a murderer's blood, is a mere fantasy: and the attempt to prove the abolition of the shedding of such blood, by anything which our Lord said or did, is equally groundless. While, "the genius of the gospel" cannot, in the nature of things, be contrary to the genius of God Himself, who was *always* "the God of love." The true genius of the gospel is to be shewn not in preferring humane expedients to solemn obligations, not in tampering with the positive institutions of Jehovah, but in carrying them out in a right spirit, a christian spirit and not a Jewish spirit, and with a holy and a tender hand.[3] That genius gives every encouragement to generous sympathy, but none to morbid sentimentality. Those individuals, therefore, who inordinately quake and quail at the thought of a righteous execution, will do well to see if they are so properly affected at far more sudden deaths, by accident or disease, than any execution presents, as to be deeply concerned for the souls of the living, and above all for their own souls, which, may be called into eternity ere a second pulse can beat. They must take care, also, lest they aspire to be more amiable than the very God of love, and lest they unintentionally arraign His wisdom in *ever* having sanctioned death for crimes, as well as in continuing to permit *any* sudden deaths; and, further, lest they dictate to or limit His grace in any instance. God has many ways of humbling and renewing sinners. Ignominy and judicial death, as external monitors, are unquestionably a part of those ways. Then, let us "be still."

As to the testimony of Saint Paul, respecting the duty of the magistrate to execute wrath by the sword, and his own willingness to submit to it, there has, I think, been much culpable inattention. What has now been urged in elucidation of it, is presented with no fond suppositions of peculiar weight, or uncommon originality. It will stand on its own footing, and claim such consideration as an honest mind may ask, and a candid mind will give.

2. Finally, never let us forget that, spiritually, we all are murderers, and that there is one who constantly seeks to murder us. We know who "was a murderer from the beginning." That same subtle spirit traverses the earth for the murder of souls. "But for God's grace," too, as Bradford the martyr partly said, we might be guilty of any crime, and doomed to any punishment. Then, be thankful for past upholdings, and pray for future deliverances.

Every impenitent sinner is chargeable with the blood of Christ, and the blood of his own soul. Sentence of death is passed upon him;—it is passed upon each one of *you* who are living in sin! O "repent and believe the gospel!" You will then find the guilt forgiven, and the sentence withdrawn. The cross will annihilate the sword: and "the city of refuge" will receive you instead of the prison and the pit.

[1] See Matthew Henry's clear exposition of this matter in his Commentary on Genesis 9:4. The author's reasons for referring to Nonconformist writers, will be obvious to his readers.

[2] The mixing up of capital punishment for lighter crimes, with that for murder;—the arguing from by-gone instances of mistake, when capital punishment was frequent for lighter crimes;—the classing of Jewish punishment for adultery and Sabbath-breaking with God's *primæval* decision about murder alone: and the appealing to the feelings and passions of popular audiences; may be very ingenious modes of proceeding, but—are they *honest*? The whole country is ringing with the cry of murder, in its most revolting forms; and nothing but desperate partizanship, or infatuation, can drown either it, or the voice of God for the punishment of it.

[3] To talk of leaning to the side of mercy, as though it were a want of feeling to contend for *divine* justice, is a most culpable, because a most unscriptural, procedure. The pleas against death for murder, which are set up on the ground of duty to love *all* men,—to do to others as we would have them do to us,—to forgive as we hope to be forgiven, and not to take away what we cannot restore, are pitiful mistakes with some persons, but odious and dangerous sophistries on the lips and pens of others. Such pleas can only be maintained by the sacrifice of holy truth at the shrine of spurious charity. Such charity always pities "the *poor* murderer" more than the innocent victim; though the one is dashed into eternity, and the other is allowed time to prepare for it. The transition from such sophistries and sentimentalities to the denial of God's punitive justice in any case, especially in the eternity to come, is easier and nearer than many imagine. Infidelity has its insidious approaches, as well as its bolder assaults. To assert that death for murder might be right, under the Jewish Theocracy, but that it is wrong or unsafe, under a christian government, is little else than an *indictment* of God's superintending Providence, in the conscientious administration of His laws by His appointed rulers. Those rulers *may* mistake or be deceived; but, if they act in the fear of God, He *will* overrule the worst for ultimate good, though beyond our present discernment.

ELISHA AND THE MINSTREL:

A SERMON,

PREACHED ON THE MORNING OF THURSDAY,
NOVEMBER 29, 1849

AT THE

OPENING OF A NEW ORGAN,

IN THE

PARISH CHURCH OF ST. MICHAEL, BATH,

BY THE

REV. W. H. HAVERGAL, M.A.,

RECTOR OF ST. NICHOLAS', WORCESTER,
AND HONORARY CANON OF THE CATHEDRAL IN THAT CITY.

PUBLISHED BY REQUEST.

LONDON:
HATCHARD & SON, PICCADILLY.
MDCCCXLIX.

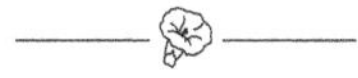

WITH THE ACCUMULATED FRIENDSHIP OF MORE THAN THIRTY YEARS,

THIS SERMON

IS AFFECTIONATELY INSCRIBED TO

THE REV. JOHN EAST, M.A.,

THE RECTOR OF THE PARISH IN WHICH IT WAS PREACHED,

BY

THE AUTHOR.

THE PROFITS ARISING FROM THE SALE OF THIS DISCOURSE ARE TO BE GIVEN TO THE FUND FOR ERECTING THE NEW ORGAN IN ST. MICHAEL'S CHURCH, BATH.

Elisha and the Minstrel:

A SERMON.

2 Kings 3:15.

"But now bring me a minstrel. And it came to pass, when the minstrel played, that the hand of the Lord came upon him."

THESE words are part of a very remarkable narrative. The king of Israel and the king of Judah, in company with the king of Edom, marched, in hostile array, against the king of Moab. The three confederate kings, in order to come upon their adversary unawares, took a circuitous course, through a wilderness. After a march of seven days, the combined armies halted, in consequence of the want of water. In their fearful extremity, the sovereigns held a council. Jehoshaphat, the king of Judah, very properly inquired whether any prophet of the Lord were present. On learning that Elisha had, unknown to them, accompanied the army, they reverently went to him. The good prophet rather warmly reproached Jehoram, king of Israel, with the idolatries of his family: indeed, he boldly told him, that unless a better man than himself, meaning Jehoshaphat, had been with him, he would not so much as look at him. But, though more than a little ruffled, the holy prophet forgat neither his humanity nor his religion. Recollecting himself, he called for the soothing influence of music, that he might thereby be the sooner fitted for receiving from God such communications as would benefit the fainting troops. In the language of the text, he said, "But now bring me a minstrel." Instantly it is added, "And it came to pass, when the minstrel played, that the hand of the Lord came upon him." The result was, that Elisha foretold the preservation of the perishing host by a supernatural supply of water.

Now, apart from other considerations, and with an eye to the special object of this morning's service, what is the plain truth which the text sets before us? Is it not that a man of God, at that time the most eminent saint on earth, sought, by means of holy music, a revival of holy feelings and spiritual affections? Such is the fact. If, then, God was found of the prophet, and the prophet was found of God, through the use of devout music, can we be wrong in concluding that such music, in a Christian church, is favourable to all the devotional exercises of that church? Answering that question in the affirmative, it will be the object of the present discourse to illustrate the affirmation in such manner as, by God's sanctifying grace, may edify and profit all who hear it. The introduction of a few historic and correlative remarks will, it is thought, be justifiable and expedient on an occasion like the present. Above all things, however, may that "hand" which came upon Elisha come on us, and so touch and tune our hearts that all our minstrelsy in the church on earth may fit us for the songs of "the church of the firstborn in heaven"!

I. With the fact before us of Elisha's calling for a minstrel to soothe his mind, and to prepare his soul for the inspiration of the Holy Spirit, it is meet that we should be correctly informed respecting the minstrel and the nature of his performance.

The Jewish minstrel, as our best students think, was not merely "a player on instruments" (Psalm 87:7), but a singer also,—one who accompanied his voice with the tones of a lyre, or of some instrument of that sort. Hence it has been suggested, that the minstrel, whom Elisha wished to be called, was not a rhapsodist or strolling bard, but a Levite skilled in the music of the temple, both vocal and instrumental, as arranged by David, according to the commandment of his God.

Such a minstrel (and such alone would the good Jehoshaphat seek), well knowing the character of Elisha and the purpose for which he desired his performance, would not fail to adapt his selection of both words and strains to the occasion for which he was employed. To suppose the contrary would be the imagining of things hardly credible. Assuming, then, the performance of the minstrel to be both hallowed and *suitable*, we may, thus early, suggest to every church minstrel the propriety of studying to adapt his performance, whether vocal or instrumental, to the varying circumstances before him. The times and seasons of our church, and the diverse character of the words selected for singing, should induce him to study *suitableness*,[1] and that sort of adaptation which the intelligent discern and the devout approve.

II. When Elisha said, "Bring me a minstrel," he said nothing which excited surprise. The minstrel was soon brought, for the case was well understood. The reason was, the Jews were,

[1] Too many organists still play most *unsuitable* interludes between the verses of a psalm or hymn. Such interludes prove the bane of *good* singing. They elongate the service, divert attention, and engender ill taste. Happily, it is becoming common to omit them altogether.

in a remarkable degree, a musical people. Indeed they seem always to have been such; while the spirit of song, which once beautified their temple, has certainly lingered among them in all their judicial dispersions. By their exquisite quality of voice, Jehovah, for the last half-century, has been setting them in the ear,[1] and so before the eye, of a vain world, which is too willing to forget His purposes respecting them. In the days of their tenure of Palestine, it was a prevailing belief among them that music had a mysterious power over the soul, and that it prepared the mind for prophetic inspiration. Hence, as Bishop Lowth[2] and Dr. Gray[3] assert, it is a well-authenticated fact, that the Jewish prophets were familiar with musical instrumentation as well as vocal strains. In the ordinary modes of prophesying, they were accustomed to compose their odes, hymns, and other poetical effusions, to the sound of some sweet instrument, either touched by themselves or more commonly played upon by an attendant symphonist.[4] Elisha, therefore, acted in accordance with ordinary usage. He desired the spirit of power and of prophecy. He consequently called for a minstrel. The minstrel came, and the Divine Spirit condescendingly followed.

III. Much might, from this circumstance, be said of *the natural fitness of music* to bring the minds of men into certain moods. It is, however, sufficient for us to recollect that the God of our souls and of our salvation prescribed the use of music, instrumental as well as vocal, for his church, and that not a whisper of the revocation of that prescription was ever heard. Before the establishment of the Jewish ritual, music was a religious exercise;[5] and, long after the establishment of that ritual, the Spirit of God devised means for the larger introduction of both vocal and instrumental music into the services of the sanctuary. It is expressly asserted that David, "at the command of God," prepared an abundance of musical instruments and a numerous company of singers. The selfsame Spirit, too, inspired him to compose divine songs, and, according to the title of some Psalms and the "Selah" of others, even to direct the manner in which they should be sung and the instruments with which the singing should be accompanied. As we are sure also that such music as Elisha invited was agreeable to "the mind of the Spirit," for, otherwise, the Spirit would not have followed it; and as we further know that the Eternal Spirit is unchangeable, and that human hearts are precisely what they were; is there any reason why the same blessing should not attend the same means? The question gathers strength from the fact of holy music being not a typical but a moral ordinance. It formed no item in the Jewish ritual, as delivered by Moses: not a word is said in that ritual about music or singing as a part of divine worship, for the blowing of trumpets by the priests was a signal for worship, rather than an act of worship. Holy music, therefore, does not rank with sacrificial observances, which ceased to be requisite when the One Great Sacrifice was offered, but with such spiritual institutions as the offering of prayer and the reading of Holy Scripture.

IV. Objections to the use of instrumental music, in public worship, have often been made, but never substantiated. The New Testament is, in vain, appealed to for the support of objections; and early ecclesiastical history is summoned for the same purpose, but not really with any better success.

The main argument of the Church of Scotland, against the use of instrumental music in public worship, is this,—That, as instrumental music was employed, not in any synagogue, but only in the tabernacle and the temple, and there *only* at the time of offering sacrifice, such music was plainly ceremonial; and, being such, was abolished, when Christ, "the true temple," came down from heaven.[6] Now, this argument, if such it may be called, has two capital defects;—it assumes that to be a fact, which is not a fact, and then proves a little too much.

Instrumental music was no more ceremonial, because it accompanied a sacrifice, than was vocal music, which, also, began when a sacrifice began. There is no intimation to be found of such music, either separate or united, being typical only; while, as we have already heard, no music at all, as a part of Divine worship, was recognised in that exposition of the

[1] Older readers will recollect the names of Billington and Leoni Lee; while those of Braham, Henry Phillips, and Mdlle. Rachel, are still familiar. The present idol of our oratorial orchestras—Felix Mendelssohn—was, by family, *a Jew*. Bishop Lavington, when a canon of Worcester, preaching there, September 8, 1725, at the anniversary of the three choirs, said thus: "The Jews have a tradition of extraordinary music at their future conversion, when, on the restoration of Jerusalem, '*all her streets shall say, Hallelujah!*'" But "*we* have a more sure word of prophecy" in the Revelation of St. John, where *music and singing* are the constant attendants on the increase of Christ's kingdom. At the *fall*, also, of *Anti-Christianism*, contemporary with the Jews' conversion, those, who had gotten the victory over "*the Beast*," are represented with the "*harps of God*," and singing "*the song of Moses, and the song of the Lamb*." The *Lamb*, the legislator of the New Testament, has *his song*, as well as Moses.

[2] Prælectiones Poet. P. 18.

[3] Key. P. 357.

[4] Ezekiel's remark in chap. 33, ver. 32 is thought to be an allusion to it.

[5] The singing of Israel at the Red Sea is proof that the people, under even the depressing power of captivity, had attained a high degree of skill in the practice of choral antiphonal music.

[6] See "A Treatise on the Use of Organs, etc.: by the Rev. J. Begg, Glasgow, 1808;" in which the strength and *weakness* of the Scotch Church is plainly shown. The *right* of that church to decline the use of instrumental music is not likely to be denied; but to argue against its *lawfulness* in any church is somewhat of an infringement upon a neighbour's *liberty*. Singular enough, since the prevalent introduction of the piano-forte, many pious Scotch families sing their morning or evening psalm to that instrument; though *not* on the Lord's-day! This is one among other symptoms of an abatement in the severity of early prejudice.

typical services of the Jews which was made by Moses. Besides, if the argument proves anything, it proves what its advocates do not approve,—the abolition of music altogether, *vocal* as well as instrumental, in the house of God. It must do this, because, at the offering of a sacrifice, while the instrumentalists played, *the singers sang.* Whether or not the Jewish worshippers abstained from playing and singing, in a synagogue, or used both only on sacrificial occasions, is of little consequence, as they are not topics of divine authenticity. Whereas, we are divinely certified that the Hebrew believers did use holy music for holy purposes, in other places than the temple.[1] Our text is proof of that.

It is remarkable that, while the New Testament in no way discountenances the use of instrumental music, in congregational worship, it does indirectly sanction it. Not only do the apocalyptic harpings, whether past historical, millennial, or celestial, favour the views of those who contend for the use of such music; but, the very text which, on the other side, is adduced as the strongest plea against it, will, upon examination, be found the weakest. The expression, "singing and *making melody in* your *heart* to the Lord," instead of disfavouring instrumental music, actually makes, in the original Greek, such allusion to it as is altogether favourable to its use. The Greek word which is translated, "making melody," means *playing on an instrument*, or *singing with an instrument*; and, as every scholar knows, "*in* your heart" may just as properly be rendered "*with* your heart."[2] Thus, the entire phrase may literally stand in this way, "*instrumentizing*, or *psalming*, *with* your heart (or heartily) unto the Lord." Such a choice of words would hardly have been made, if the Holy Ghost had intended christian believers to forget and forego the use of instrumental music in their hallowed assemblies.

Nothing but *the abuse* of such music can furnish any plea against it. Wherever that abuse occurs, or is likely to occur, let vigilance and vigorous discipline be applied. This is what the early fathers did; and our own reformers followed their example. Surrounded by a heathen population, madly bent on the music of the theatre, some christian fathers interdicted the use of instruments in church-singing: while others, more remote from danger, encouraged it.[3] Because, too, of grievous perversions in the time of Edward the Sixth, honest Latimer boldly put down, for a season, both singing and playing in the cathedral of my own diocese. By one vote alone, among our reformers, and that given by proxy, were church-organs allowed to remain. Godly minds were reasonably offended at the lengthened interludes, and the wanton or over-curious performances of organists or choirs.[4] Allusions to these grievances will be found in the second part of the "Homily of the place and time of Prayer;" and in that part of the Preface to our Book of Common Prayer, which is intitled "Concerning the Service of the Church."

Happily, by God's blessing on the wisdom, piety, and moderation of our holy reformers, things took a better turn. A foundation was laid, though not without godly jealousy, for that grave, decent, and devotional style of church music which has long marked the English choir. But the jealousy of other days must not be suffered to sleep in the present day. The performance of good music is not, alas, always associated with the practice of true piety. Our clergy, therefore, will do well always to exercise that power over the musical part of the service, which the Church most unequivocally lodges with them. At the same time, we must be prepared to bear with the infirmities of tender minds. It can be no marvel that such minds are sensitive at any change or addition in the musical part of the congregational worship, however good in itself, seeing that attention to church music has sometimes been a stepping-stone to church apostacy.[5] While, however, we bear with such likely sensitiveness, we must not permit it to become unreasonable. We must shew that we know how to discriminate between the

[1] There was *instrumental* music *outside* the tabernacle, when David carried up the Ark to it (Psalm 24, etc.); and a *psalm* was sung on closing the doors in the evening, and on opening them in the morning (see Bishop Patrick on Psalm 134 and 135.) Other occasions, on which instrumental music was used, apart from all *typical* reference, are too obvious to require mention.

A fellow of Balliol college, in the 17th century, turned the table of *this* notion of *type* against the opponents of instrumental music in his day. He contended that David, as a musical king, was a type of a musical Messiah; and that the many instruments made by the one were intimations of the abundance which should be used during the reign of the other.

[2] "Be filled *with* the Spirit" is the same form of expression. That the Apostle could *not* mean any *silent* melody *within* the heart, as opposed to audible sounds by the lips, is evident from his wishing christians to speak to and admonish one another by *the act of singing.*

[3] St. Basil, Hom. in Psalm 1; Clemens Alexadrinus, Pœdag., Lib. ii. c. 4; St. Augustine in various works; St. Cypr. Epist. ad Donatum, "Prolectat aures religiosa *mulcedo*."

[4] Profane liberties, such as descanting all sorts of lewd ballads on the plain song, became so gross and enormous, that the Pope and the Council of Trent were obliged to interfere. Romanist writers rather freely admit the horrible fact. Some of our own choristers and singing-men are not altogether innocent on such score.

[5] The gradation has been somewhat thus: the antique (without distinguishing between the true and the false) is venerable. The Gregorian music is very antique, and therefore very venerable. But the Church of Rome alone retains and practises it; and so that Church is worthy of every musical man's veneration. Another step or two completes the fatal plunge.

The *talk* of younger aspirants about Gregory and Tallis is sometimes painfully amusing; while the attempts, in certain quarters, to foster Gregorianism, are based neither upon truth nor common sense. The practice, also, of organists and editors calling certain modified versions "Gregorian chants," is as delusive in itself as it is contemptible in the estimation of Romanists. Who would exhibit a jeweller's trinket as a specimen of *native* Californian gold?—or describe a fleece of wool by shewing a piece of broadcloth?

safe and the unsafe,—between what is good as well as lawful, and what *is*, certainly in these unsettling days, *not* expedient. In a word, we may hold fast to the fact, which, in spite of efforts to wrest it from us, is still a fact, that our ecclesiastical authorities never contemplated what is called "*full cathedral service*" being the order for *parish* churches.[1]

V. As a mechanical combination of instruments, an organ is admirably adapted to supply the place of Hebrew minstrels. At an early period organs, such as they were, found admission into the Christian church. The precise date, however, of their admission is so conflictingly stated by historians that no certain conclusion can be formed. With the exception of a vague quotation by the Venerable Bede, we meet with nothing on the subject before the year 650. Other writers carry it on to the year 820.[2] But, it is tolerably certain that, although St. Dunstan, as he is called, was the great patron of organs in the tenth century, their use in the cathedrals and larger churches of England was not common till just before the blessed Reformation. Indeed, it is not two centuries ago since lutenists, or minstrels, were as much in office as organists now are.

The advance of skill, and the increase of facilities, have brought organs into almost all our parochial churches. And now that an organ of larger contents and better quality than before is erected within your own elegant and beautiful church, the friend of your beloved pastor may well congratulate you. He, I am sure, has not, in its erection, sought to provide his flock with either attraction or amusement; but rather to put the choral part of divine service under such auxiliary guidance as will help you, with increased freshness and exhilaration, to laud and praise that holy Saviour to whom alone all song is due.

VI. Henceforth, then, because of your greater facilities for singing the praises of the Lamb, you will be under greater responsibilities to promote such singing, either by studying to join in it, or, if that be impracticable, by listening, *with all your heart*, to the singing of others.

If, in the same hallowed temper, as Elisha said, "Bring me a minstrel," you have said, "Build us an organ," you may reasonably expect that the God of Elisha will visit you, not indeed with the spirit of prophecy, but with the spirit of grace and edification. You may expect your God to bless the use of that organ, for your greater composure of mind, sanctity of spirit, and fervency of affection, as often as you come up to worship Him within these inviting walls. Remember, also, that what Elisha sought, in the use of a minstrel, was nothing less than the inspiration of the Holy Spirit. For that selfsame Spirit we are to seek, not only in every act of our lives, but in the worship of God especially. We are admonished to "walk in the Spirit," and to abound in "the fruits of the Spirit," as daily parts of our christian calling: but, when we apply ourselves to the direct worship of the Triune God, then is it that we most need the hand of the Lord to come upon us. "God is a Spirit; and they that worship him (whether with prayer or praise) must worship him in spirit and in truth." Consonant with these words of our Lord, the words of his apostle may now, in a modified sense, be understood and applied, "I will sing with the Spirit," and "I will pray with the Spirit:" not that we by them mean to express any expectation of being so inspired, or wrought into such a rapture, as was common in the pentecostal age, when members of the church were enabled to stand forth and pray or sing extemporaneously, in a marvellously lofty, edifying, and hallowing manner. No. This is not our expectation: but we are bound to seek the grace and power of the Spirit, to kindle in us warm and steady affections; that the melody of the heart may find its tuneful outlet by the lips, and that what we sing with our lips may, by a becoming reaction, edify our hearts,

Taught by our Scriptural Church to learn true doctrine from Holy Scripture alone, and to pray for the cleansing of our hearts by the inspiration of the Holy Spirit, we, surely, after the example of Elisha, may seek for the grace of that Spirit by the same means as he sought it. "It came to pass, when the minstrel *played*, the hand of the Lord came upon him." This, undoubtedly, certifies us that there is in holy music a power which the Spirit of God can use for the loftiest purposes. Christians are too prone to give way to the policy of Satan in underrating the true value, and in lowering the real dignity, of genuine music. They regard it chiefly as sensuous, and therefore capable of acting only on the animal feelings. With this low view of a divinely elevating medium, we cannot wonder that they meet, with timidity and suspicion, any excitation of which they may be sensible, from the power of musical sounds, in a church or a cathedral. But, all such reluctance to avail themselves of a scripturally legitimate means of calming, elevating, or hallowing their minds, is like giving up a large space of vantage ground to the wily god of this world. So long as he, by music, can exhilarate the votaries of folly, and keep the children of God in fear of being cheered by it, so long will he be gaining a certain advantage over them. If, however, he, by "*pretty* tunes,"

[1] See a Sermon by Dr. Thomas Bisse, Chancellor of Hereford, in the cathedral of that city, at the anniversary of the three choirs, Sept. 7, 1720. That learned divine and sound churchman was of opinion, that "*saying*" is *fitter* than "*singing*" for our liturgical service in parish churches. Chanting of the prayers, as it is called, is based, he argues, on *necessity*, in large and resonant buildings, and not on any supposed inherent fitness.

[2] See the History of Music, by Dr. Burney, and that by Sir J. Hawkins, in loco. An ancient organ, at Munich, was a sort of monster bagpipe, being formed of an elephant's hide and twelve bored box trees!

can call up all sorts of passions in his dupes and devotees, do let us, in the use of good and hallowed tunes,[1] be willing for the hand of the Lord to come upon us!

The reasonable expectation of this blessed result from holy music was, most likely, the ground of that ancient custom which Queen Elisabeth recognised, when she sanctioned the singing of a hymn, or such like song, at *the beginning*, as well as at the end, of common prayer. Universal custom, also, (and it is still sedulously observed in our universities) has recognised the same ground, in the singing of a psalm or hymn, always *before* the homily or sermon. In our cathedrals, soft and sweet playing has, of late years, been substituted for singing then; because, it would seem, much has been previously sung. In either case, the principle is, and the expectation ought to be, the same. Our Reformers, however, went much beyond many among us, in approaching the mark which the text sets before us. They encouraged singing, not only before sermon, but after it. We are wont to think that singing is apt to diminish the impression of a sermon, but they thought it would deepen it. This difference arises from our giving way to that lax and low view (unintentional, I can believe) to which allusion has been made. How one of our Reformers, yea, that one to whom we are as much indebted as to any, expressed himself on this topic, you shall hear, by an extract of a letter of Bishop Jewel to Peter Martyr, dated London, March 5, 1560.

> Religion is now somewhat more established than it was. The people are everywhere exceedingly inclined to the better part. The practice of joining in church music has very much conduced to this. For, as soon as they had once commenced singing in public, in only one little church[2] in London, immediately not only the churches in the neighbourhood, but even the towns far distant, began to vie with each other in the same practice. You may now sometimes see at Paul's Cross, *after the service*, six thousand persons, old and young, both sexes, singing together and praising God. This sadly annoys the mass-priests and the Devil. For they perceive that by these means the sacred discourses sink more deeply into the minds of men, and that their kingdom is weakened and shaken at almost every note. (Zurich Letters, Parker Soc., p. 71.)

Now discourses cannot sink deeply into the minds of men, unless the hand of the Lord come upon them. Bishop Jewel was of opinion that that hand did come upon hearers, in his day, by means "of joining in church music." Here, therefore, as churchmen, you have authority, and, as christians, encouragement.[3] May it, then, be that henceforward your increased attention to the pleasant duty of vocal and instrumental praise shall witness the coming of the hand of the Lord upon you, at once for your more perfect perception of divine truth, and for your greater consolation in it.

VII. But, when we speak thus of singing, and of the Holy Spirit, let our thoughts firmly apprehend him who is "worthy" of every song, and by whom alone we receive the Spirit—the Holy Lamb, the Lord Jesus, "who taketh away the sin of the world." He is the grand object of all adoration and all praise. To Him Elisha, as one in "the goodly fellowship of the prophets," "gave witness." Never should it be out of mind with us, that our sins cost his sorrows, and that by those sorrows we have songs. But for his crying, with a loud and lamentable voice, "It is finished," no sound of minstrel-song would ever have been heard in our world. Unless the Eternal Father had heard that voice, "lamentation, and mourning, and woe," would have been the doleful melodies of unredeemed mankind. Because, also, after his atoning death and glorious resurrection, he ascended up on high and received gifts for men, we may hope for the grace of the Holy Ghost to come upon us, in the exercise of that minstrelsy with which we are invited to come into his presence.

VIII. Nor should we ever cease to recollect that, as there is "the *prayer* of faith," so also must there be the *song* of faith. No petition can ascend to heaven "without faith" in the One Great Mediator; and no praise can glorify God but such as is offered in the name of his beloved Son. Elisha, we may be assured, did not look for the coming of the hand of the Lord upon him *merely* by the agency of minstrel-music: doubtless the fingers and lips of the minstrel were not more intently employed than was the heart of the prophet,—while the one was performing, the other was seeking, desiring, believing. Thus, in all our offerings of holy song, there must be the conformable affections of the heart,—that spirit-sung melody, which, wafted on the breath of faith, mounts to the ear of God. While that song is progressing, the soul is to be communing with its Saviour, or glancing with ethereal rapidity at eternal realities, or grasping some precious truth, vividly seen and intensely felt. It is not, perhaps, too much to assert, that some of the most thrilling emotions of which the sanctified heart is capable are experienced during the singing of a psalm or hymn in the great congregation. Apart from some merely tender or touching associations, what more elevating or affecting consideration

[1] The progress of the restoration of *good* tunes to our parish churches is slow, but, seemingly, sure. Wherever the *old* tunes of the Church, or new ones *like* them, are introduced, congregational singing flourishes. A revised and an enlarged edition of "Old Church Psalmody," by the Author, is in the press, printed and published by J. Hart, 109, Hatton Garden, London.

[2] St. Antholin's; where the people used to assemble, at five o'clock, every morning.

[3] The beautiful hymns in our Ordination Service are hymns to the Spirit and *for* the Spirit.

can be presented to those who join in singing than this?—"I am now engaged," each helper of the song may say, "in that work which occupies my departed fellows, my holy kindred, above;—in that which shall be the delight of the whole earth, in its millennial age;[1]—in that which shall be the business and the bliss of the elect of God to all eternity!" Oh! may the hand of the Lord come upon us more frequently than ever for the production of these blessed effects! Such desire is necessary; because singing without spiritual-mindedness, or any musical service without vital religion, will but insult the Saviour and cheat the soul.

IX. Let me not wind up this discourse without reminding you that the sight and sound of your new organ should freshen your attention to a great moral truth. *Our God is a God of order, harmony, and love.* He has made *everything* in his church subservient to *something*; while the well-arranged and well-ordered whole is subservient to himself. From this order follows harmony. He loves his saints, and they are to love one another.

Now, an organ is a fair type of such arrangement. It is composed of various materials, of sundry parts, of many kinds of pipes, some large and some small, some loud and some soft; and yet, though everything in it is dependent on something, the whole is fitly joined together, and capable, at the touch of a master-hand, of yielding goodly harmony. Let it not, then, be deemed inopportune to say, that your parish, your church congregation, your individual souls, should henceforth be more and more like your new organ. "Seek peace, and ensue it." Let every man, in that station of life in which it hath pleased God to call him, strive for moral harmony and spiritual brotherhood. Let him who is placed in an humble station, like some tiny, and obscure pipe, be *content*; and him who stands on a greater scale, in the front of society, be *useful*: and let all "love as brethren." So, also in what is the core and vitality, the very essentiality of the moral organ,—*the church congregation*,—let the same principle be carried out. Assembling under one roof, where "one Lord, one faith, one baptism" is acknowledged, there let every worshipper, like Elisha, when calling for a minstrel, desire to forget all rufflings and perturbations, seeking only the spirit of love, "peace, unity, and concord." Such spiritual harmony is always grateful to the ear of Him who heareth not as man heareth. Nowhere, too, is it more grateful than when practised around his own table, where, "with angels and archangels and all the company of heaven, we laud and magnify his glorious Name."

And, what shall we say to the man of the world who loves music, but who does not love religion;—who, perchance, likes both sacred and ecclesiastical music, but does not like to be told that he may, almost with rapture, hear or perform such music, and yet "lose his own soul"? We pity that person, whether male or female, who is in this case, because there is something winning, something sympathetic, in even the love of music. But it is grievous, even to anguish, to think that such individuals are loving that which will not only not last them long, but which must be exchanged for something appallingly opposite. They dream of being musical for ever, and frivolously fancy that they shall hear the songs of heaven: but it is a fearful dream, and a terrific fancy. Unless the hand of the Lord come upon them *now*, and create in them a new heart and a new spirit, they will never become jubilant minstrels in the choirs above, but wailing fiends in the dungeons below. No tuneful sound will ever be heard by them there; but their own voice, and every other voice around them, will be, more truly than was fantastically said in another instance, *the horrid "concentration of a thousand screams."* "There shall be weeping, and wailing, and gnashing of teeth." God grant to all, who hear this note of warning, "repentance unto life."

X. And, now, "beloved in the Lord," is there need of exhortation to elicit your generous contributions? I trust not. Christian generosity should never require "the enticing words of man's wisdom" to call it forth. It should be as free to give, as your new organ is to speak. A touch on that is enough: a word with you should be sufficient. And it will be sufficient with all, who see in the minutest parts of the enlightened worship of the Saviour a dignity and an importance, which surpass all earthly splendours. When that sight strikes the mental eye, it will be even joy to the heart to forward whatever sets forth the honour or the praise of the only Redeemer. Your help is this day asked, not only for the bringing of minstrel-power into your church, but for furnishing seats for little scholars, who, it is presumed, will soon learn to follow its sounds, and swell your congregational songs. The singing of children in a church is always interesting. Something of the sort once pleased the ear of him whom, though not seen, you love. Their little voices will be heard in the Lord's house long after ours are silent in the dust. Themselves also will remember the opening, on this day, of your organ, when our memories have left us, or we have left the world. These thoughts should touch us. Especially should we be touched by the music of that Name, which "is as ointment poured forth." It will cheer us by day, and give us "songs in the night." It will prepare us, too, for a song which is prepared for us, when all earthly scenes are ended, and when the hand of the Lord shall so come upon us that we shall sing and not be weary, and shout everlastingly to the Lamb, and yet not be faint. Amen and Amen.

[1] "Perhaps the singing and music at the sanctuary were mentioned, as external expressions of that joy and praise, *which would most abound in the church*, after the coming of the Messiah." Scott, on Psalm 87:7.

THE DIVINE INHABITATION OF THE PRAISES OF ISRAEL:

A SERMON,

PREACHED IN THE

ABBEY CHURCH, TEWKESBURY,

ON THE MORNING OF

FRIDAY, the 28th of JUNE, 1850,

BY THE

REV. W. H. HAVERGAL, M.A.,

RECTOR OF ST. NICHOLAS, AND HONORARY CANON, WORCESTER.

The Proceeds towards the cost of enlarging the Organ in the Abbey Church.

J. BENNETT, TEWKESBURY;

AND

DEIGHTON, EATON, AND CHILD, WORCESTER.

1850.

TO THE REV. C. G. DAVIES, M.A.

TO HIS CURATES,

AND TO HIS OTHER KIND FRIENDS,

WHO JOINED IN URGING ITS PUBLICATION,

THIS SERMON

IS RESPECTFULLY INSCRIBED, BY

THE AUTHOR.

SERMON.

Psalm 22:3.

"O thou that inhabitest the praises of Israel."

THE title of this Psalm is as singular as it is poetical. "*Aijeleth Shahar*" is, in the margin, interpreted to mean "The Hind of the Morning." This is variously explained. Some expositors regard it as a musical phrase, denoting either *the style* in which the Psalm should be sung, or the *chant* itself which should be used for it. Others believe, that "The hind of the morning" means a Psalm intended to be sung with freshened alacrity in the morning. But, not a few (and among them Bishop Horne and Bishop Horsley) are of opinion, that the title describes the prophetic subject of the Psalm—even the Messiah, who, like some gentle hind, was, from the very morning of his life, and especially in the morning of his last day, as said in the 16th verse, "compassed by dogs, and inclosed by the wicked."

Of one thing we are certain,—parts of the Psalm are in the New Testament, quoted of Christ, and others can properly be referred only to Him.

Hence, in allusion to the time, when He "visited us in great humility," the entire Psalm alternates with sorrow and comfort. And, thus, after the model of her only Master, the Church has her plaintive notes as well as her jubilant strains. But, whether plaintive or jubilant, if only sounded by the voice, or struck by the finger, of faith, they are heard, yea *inhabited*, by the Eternal God.

O thou that inhabitest the praises of Israel.

Apart from any notice of the many critical renderings of our text, and well satisfied with that rendering which our judicious translators have adopted, let us seek for edification, in such an appliance of it as is suited to the occasion of the present service. And may the Spirit of truth and holiness supply to us that edification for our lasting profit!

The text admits of a very simple division of its parts;—"the praises of Israel," and the inhabitation of them by the God of Israel.

I. "*The praises of Israel,*" as offered to the True and Triune God, were, in the days of David, the praises of the Church in Israel. Confined as that Church then was, to a scanty territory, it is now, by the advent of its Lord, expanded to the utmost limits of the globe. Hence, what was spiritually true of the literal Israel, is now equally true of the spiritual Israel,—the genuine Church of Christ,—the company of the faithful scattered up and down the earth. The Almighty God inhabits their praises, and so inhabits ours.

1. What the praises of the Church were, before the time of David, we can be hardly said to know. Beyond a few incidental notices, very little is revealed. Whether the two or three Psalms attributed to Moses were statedly sung in the Tabernacle, or whether there was any singing at all in its services, we have no authentic means of ascertaining. Certainly we read not in the Mosaic Ritual of any instruments of music for accompanying voices; though mention is made of a few such instruments, prior to the revelation of that Ritual.

On certain occasions, the sons of Aaron were to "blow with trumpets *over* the sacrifices;" but we hear not of any *singing* at those sacrifices, as in after days, especially, according to what is said, on the restoration of the Temple-services by Hezekiah, "when the sacrifice began, *the song of the Lord began also.*"

Of course, the song of Moses and the response of Miriam, on the passage of the Red Sea, are not forgotten. Neither is the singing of the people around the golden calf, and at the springing of the well, overlooked. But, these instances only shew the aptness of the Hebrews for choral singing, without *proving* anything with regard to the Tabernacle-service.

2. In the days of David, and 'till the times of the Messiah, "the praises of Israel" consisted of Psalms and other inspired songs. These divine compositions celebrate the perfections of God, as displayed in the works of Creation, in the mercies of ordinary life, in the manifold deliverances of the nation, and the signal destruction of its enemies. At the same time, they convey much of the mind of the Spirit upon doctrinal and practical topics; while they especially abound with prophetical delineations of the character of the Messiah, and with vivid descriptions of the varied emotions of his people.

After the day of Pentecost, the praises of the Church were no longer confined to Old Testament compositions. Those compositions were, indeed, still continued; but, the Holy Ghost supplied additional forms. "Hymns and spiritual songs" became frequent in the assemblies of Christians. But, what those "hymns and spiritual songs" really were, no writer has clearly defined. It is, indeed, commonly said, that by "*Psalms,*" we are to understand the Psalms and other lyrical poems of the Old Testament;—by "*Hymns,*" such newly inspired compositions as the Benedictus and Magnificat; and by "*Spiritual Songs*," or Odes, sundry human compositions of a highly devotional cast.

These distinctions may be very convenient, but, when brought to the test of Apostolic record, they fail of being proved correct. By "a Psalm," St. Paul meant, not always a Psalm of David, or *any* in the Book of Psalms, but a new Psalm or Christian Song, the product of that spiritual gift which was then extant in the Church. By no means, also, are the terms, "Psalm, Hymn and Spiritual Song" used, in the Apostolic Epistles, with that nicety of distinction which some desire to find. The precise meaning of each is nowhere set down. In fact, it is highly probable that the praises of the Apostolic age were not only diversified in their structure, but that they were of a character peculiar to that age. The Spirit of inspiration hovered over the Church; and church members, endued with its power, both prayed and sung in a lofty and rapturous strain.

As time advanced and that Spirit receded, the Church set about the task of compilation. Gathering up the fragments of the feast of song, holy men seem to have moulded them into a set and permanent form. But, what, in the hymns of the early Church, are indeed fragments of inspired composition, and what are not, no Seer remains to tell. Two of the finest specimens are retained by our own Church,—the Te Deum and Veni Creator, or the Ordination Hymn. Others of great beauty have been translated, and inserted in some of the more choice of those many Selections of Psalms and Hymns, with which modern times have burthened our Church. Unquestionably all reasonable latitude is given, under the rubrical term "Anthem," for singing almost anything which sound discretion may approve, and to which the Bishop of the Diocese may not object. The strong word "*unquestionably*" is used, on the ground of a fact which, in the controversy about authorized psalms and hymns, escaped observation. It is now, from closer search and clearer recollection, a well ascertained fact, that, less than two hundred years ago, our Cathedrals and Chapels Royal understood, by the term "Anthem," [1] not only a selection of scripture words, but a string of non-inspired metrical verses, such indeed as we should now hardly dignify with the name of hymns, but rather of *carols*.[2]

3. "The praises of Israel" were offered to Jehovah generally by an union of instruments and voices. Vocal music is, of course, the standard vehicle of praise; but instrumental music is, on the authority of God himself, an auxiliary to it.

The introduction of instrumental music into the Jewish Church was a gradual work. In the days of Moses there were only two silver trumpets in use. In the time of Joshua, they were multiplied to seven. On the settlement of Israel in Canaan, the tabret, psaltery and harp were constantly heard in the celebration of divine service. But, it was reserved for David to model the Jewish music upon a broader and grander scale. Exercising his own refined taste, under the inspiration of the Holy Ghost, he constructed musical instruments of many sorts, and in great numbers. But, lest it should be supposed that he did thus of merely his own will, the Church of Israel was again and again certified that all he did was by the express command of his God. (2 Chronicles 29:25.)

Hence instrumental music, in "the praises of Israel," is an ordinance of God: and because it is an adjunct of pure devotion, and not a part of a ritual code, it is as eligible under the New Testament as it was under the Old. It was not, however, 'till the reign of Solomon, that the music of Israel attained its highest point. At the dedication of the Temple, there was a choir, such as, for numbers at least, Christendom has never seen, or heard.

That the praises of the Christian Church were not, at first, accompanied by instrumental music, cannot be construed into a wonder or an objection. The first Christians were called to face the fury of persecution, and not to sit beneath the shade of their fig tree. They had to carry in their hand, not their psaltery or harp, but their very lives. Consequently they had no leisure for the joyous embellishments of divine worship. It was hard task enough for them to enjoy its quietest simplicities. Their only leisure was to plant the doctrine of the Cross, and then to water it with their blood. Hence, if the adoption of instrumental music in a Christian assembly be objected to, on the plea of its not being recognized in the Acts of the Apostles, the same objection must apply to the building of a church, a chapel, or a school-room.

Because of the abuses of instrumental music, in the theat-

[1] The authority for these remarks is Clifford's "Divine Services and Anthems, usually sung in His Majesties Chappell, and in all Cathedrals and Collegiate Choires, in England and Ireland." (2nd edition, 1664.) The "Imprimatur" and the Dedication, the former by "Joh. Hall, R. P. D. Episc. Lon. à sac. Domest." and the latter to "the Rev. Walter Jones, D.D. Sub Dean of his Majesties Chappell Royal," place the authenticity of the volume on the broadest ground,—especially as Dr. Walter Jones was the most distinguished church musician of his day. Some of the most doggrel of the metrical verses alluded to, are set to music by our greatest and gravest masters. Anthem CXXIV. for Twelfth Eve, *In Bethlehem Town, O happy Town*, is set by ADRIAN BATTEN; and Anthem CXXXIV. *O Jesu meek, O Jesu sweet*, by THOMAS MORLEY.

[2] The usual derivation of the word CAROL, is from the Italian *Carola*. But Blount, in his Glossographia, 1674, derives it from the Saxon *Kyrriole*, a Christmas Song. "It comes (he says) from a verb *to sing*, and *rola*, an interjection, expressing joy; for, heretofore, in the burden of delightful songs, and when men were jocund, they were wont to sing *Rola! Rola!*"—The Rev. Arthur Bedford, however, cir. 1720, who is no mean authority in such matters, says that "Christmas *Carols* were so called, because such were much in use, in King *Charles* the First's reign, *Carolus* Rex."

rical exhibitions of a pagan population, primitive Bishops were slow in admitting it into churches. What Ambrose and Gregory did for its furtherance, between the fourth century and the seventh, has often of late been repeated. And, though, as to the period when *organs* were first used, chroniclers tell such conflicting tales, that truth can hardly speak for herself, yet we know, for certain, that early organs were most uncouth and cumbersome contrivances, for eliciting about an octave and a half of drawling sounds, to supply the wind for which required the lusty efforts of half as many men.

Had the character of the so-called St. Dunstan been worthy of a saint, or had his temper been as tuneful as his taste, posterity would, doubtless, have thought more, than it has, of *his* patronage of organs.

How grievous were the abuses of organs and other musical instruments, in the churches of our land, prior to the blessed Reformation, may be read in "The second part of the Homily of the Place and Time of Prayer," in which the ungodly "piping and playing upon organs" is severely and even ironically censured.

Happily the wisdom and energy of our Reformers prevailed for the correction of abuses, and the furtherance of all that is excellent in the practice of church music. When the original portions of your own venerable organ were constructed, things must have been on a superior footing, as to that music; especially in the chapel of a college for the choral service of which munificent provision had been made. And though an interval of desolation ensued, and later times have witnessed a sad declension in all that constitutes not only good choral service, but good psalmody, yet is there reason to hope that improvement is begun, and, in many places has made great advance.

4. It must not be forgotten that, although, in "the praises of Israel," instrumental music was largely blended with vocal, the voices of those who sang formed the chief basis and central beauty of the whole. The entire band of Levites, with their sons and daughters, studied music in private, and performed it publicly in the courts of the Lord's House. What the style of their singing really was, we cannot tell. But, with the sweet flexibility of the Jewish voice, and with the inspiration of the Spirit attending it, the effect must have been both beautiful and elevating.

The skilful singing, however, of the choir, did not constitute the whole of "the praises of Israel." They comprised, also, the voices of "the great congregation." At fit times, and in suitable parts of the service, the people joined in chorus, or took up the national Hallelujah. So, in the early Christian Church, the voices of the multitude pealed the praises of the Incarnate Saviour. They were even told that their voices were the real psalteries, tabrets, and harps, of the new dispensation. During the reign of Popery in our land, the people were *naved* off in silence, and the *chancelled* choir alone permitted to sing. But, on the restoration of primitive truth and practice, our forefathers burst the spell of centuries, and sang merrily unto God. Psalmody began in London, and soon spread through the land. It has been slumbering for the last hundred years; but it is waking up afresh; and the modest choir and the tuneful congregation are beginning to understand their mutual relations and interests. May the revival of good congregational singing help forward the gospel of Christ, as Bishop Jewell said it did in his day.

5. From having heard *what* "the praises of Israel" were, and *how* and by *whom* they were offered, let us glance at their seasons and localities.

The joy of harvest was always great in Israel. Their nuptials were celebrated with singing. The 45th Psalm is a grand epithalamium[1]. On marching out to battle, the Hebrews set an example, which Christendom overlooks. Instead of inspiriting their soldiery with heathen-like pæans and ballad strains, they turned the whole host into a choir, and honoured "the God of battles," by singing "Hallelujah." In travelling, also, from remoter districts, to keep high festival at Jerusalem, their friendly bands sang as they went, while a musical instrument cheered their steps. (Isaiah 30:25.[2])

But, the grand locality of "the praises of Israel" was the Sanctuary of Jehovah. There, by night and by day, in one ceaseless round, the high praises of their God were celebrated. Monasticism has attempted feeble and short-lived imitations of this "perpetual praise." "Psalmody Island" was so called, in the diocese of Nismes, because the monks, who were stationed in it, sang psalms by day and night without intermission.[3]

On commemorative occasions, however, the courses which relieved one another, in "the praises of Israel," united in one; and, joined by the multitudinous assembly, sent up their volume of song to the Mighty God of Jacob.

Upon like principles, though not in like manner, the House of God is still the chief locality of holy praise. Be our homes as tuneful as they may, with the songs of the Lord, it will hardly be questioned that his temples are the fittest and meetest places for "psalms and hymns and spiritual songs." Where the Saviour has recorded his Name, there ought He to hear his people sing his praise. "*Let us come before his presence with a song*," should be the watch-word of all Christian worshippers.

After thus imperfectly contemplating "the praises of Israel," let us turn our thoughts to Him who inhabits them.

II. *The divine inhabitation of the praises of the Church* is as cheering as it is wonderful.

[1] epithalamium: nuptial song or poem honoring the bride and bridegroom

[2] After earnest searching, the correct reference W. H. H. meant here has not yet been found. D.C.

[3] See Dr. Burney's History of Music, vol. II, p. 9.

1. Viewing the text as it stands in our present version, we perceive that our poor praises form, as it were, a pavilion for the God of our salvation. It is as though the space, which their sound occupies, constitutes an aerial palace for his special dwelling. Yea, so delighted is He with it, that He condescends to make it his permanent abode. Certainly there is great sublimity in this inspired representation of an encouraging fact. But, oh! the condescension of that God who presents it to us! For, is it not condescension of the most wonderful and adorable order, that the High and Lofty One, who inhabiteth the mansions of eternity, should stoop to dwell in the evanescent canopy of our unworthy song? Is it not marvellous that the ear, into which angels pour their sweetest lays, and seraphim their burning strains, should take pleasure in listening to the lisping notes of "babes in grace," and the sorry chantings of "miserable sinners"? It is marvellous, and we should adore the marvel. Nevertheless, we should take courage from it, to persevere in offering praise.

2. What encouragement there is for such perseverance, we may learn from what God once did, and what he has often said.

At the dedication of the Temple, He gave an overwhelmingly visible proof of his inhabiting "the praises of Israel." "The elders of Israel, the heads of the tribes, and the chief of the fathers," with king Solomon in the midst, were all in attendance. "The priests brought in the ark," and the Levites assisted in "sacrificing sheep and oxen, which could not be told or numbered for multitude." Still, no token of the divine presence was manifested. But, as soon as "the trumpeters and singers were as one to make one sound to be heard, in thanking and praising the Lord," *then*, even then, and *not 'till* then, "the house was filled with a cloud: so that the priests could not stand to minister by reason of the cloud; for the glory of the Lord had filled the house of God."

With such a testimony of the divine approbation, who will be silent in the temples of our Israel? Who will not stand to the high aim of forming a palace of praise for the inhabitation of Him who is above all blessing and all praise? Especially, too, when we are certified that "praise is comely;" and that "It is *a good thing* to give thanks unto the Lord, and to sing praises unto the Name of the Most High." Besides, that Most High has said, for the cheer of his lowliest worshippers, "*whoso* offereth praise, glorifieth Me."

3. Let, then, any memento of the enlargement and improvement of your interesting organ, (interesting from its historical associations) be a memento for the freshening of your praise within these spirit-stirring walls.

It is a Christian's duty to praise his Saviour with the best member that he has: while the earnestness of a churchman may well be summoned to make the services of his church as inviting and as edifying as he can.

Here, indeed, apart from the din of ecclesiastical controversy, we may take a quiet stand, and rejoice at feeling that we all are agreed. The pleasant duty of praise commends itself to every upright heart. It is that duty which, unlike prayer, devolves on *all* that part of the universe where Mercy prevails. Creatures that cannot pray, and beings who have no need to pray, are yet called upon to *praise* the God who made them, or the Lamb who redeemed them. The Holy Spirit calls on inanimate creation, as well as on all creatures which have breath, to "*praise* the Lord," but never to *pray* to Him. The praises of the ransomed hosts of God's elect will roll on with eternity, while their prayers will cease with the end of time.[1] Let those praises be with us as earnest as they ought to be: and, knowing that God in Christ still inhabits the praises of his people, let us study to render them a fit habitation for so awful and yet so gracious a guest. For this purpose, let all be ready to do their best,—to join in church-singing when they can, and to countenance and encourage others, when they cannot. Speaking as to a parochial and not to a collegiate congregation, allow me to recommend vigilant attention in the selection of chants and tunes of a becoming style. Let not the praises of our Israel be sung to the strains of the world: but let them be offered through the medium of such sounds as comport with the dignity, sobriety, and chastened fervour, of Christian worship. At the same time, let the tendency of the age to extremes be avoided. In shunning what is secular, there is no need to take refuge in what is uncouth. There is a true *via media* in church music, as there is in other church matters. The style, both for chant and psalm tune, which forms that *via media*, will, as nearly as practicable, be found in the music of the earlier half of the seventeenth century. Airy, trashy, ballad-like, chants and psalm tunes, found no admirers then; and, yet, the singing in our churches was both more choral and more congregational, than, for many a long year, it has since been.

4. But, in every effort to augment the praises of our Israel, let us never forget that, *without a lively and a holy faith in the One Great Mediator, our songs cannot please God.*

There is much practical oblivion on this point. Professional skill, and individual taste, are alike in danger of that oblivion. It is too easy for the members of a choir to sing or play,

[1] There is some pathos, and much true piety, in the following version of Psalm 146:2.

> "I'll praise Him, while he *lends* me breath;
> And, when my *voice* is *lost* in death,
> Praise shall employ my *nobler* powers:
> My days of praise shall *ne'er* be past,
> While life, and thought and being last,
> Or immortality endures!"

without a due recollection of the really solemn responsibilities which rest upon them. They professedly engage in the services of God's House. To that God they must give account of the state of heart in which they render their services. They may advance the edification of others; but unless they sing or play, in the spirit of true piety, they will never advance their own. To some ears it may seem a startling novelty to be told that, "as well the singers as the players on instruments," must sing and play in *faith*, if they would have their performance accepted by Almighty God. But, such is the fact; and there is no controverting it.

It is a singular and striking remark, in the Book of Proverbs, that "Burning lips and a wicked heart are like a potsherd covered with silver dross;" (Proverbs 26:23.) meaning, that when a glowing voice proceeds either musically or eloquently, from an unsanctified breast, the strain is as unseemly as a fragment of coarse earthenware covered with frosted silver. Brethren, let there be no such potsherds in our Sanctuaries! Let the vessels of our praise be sound and clean; that, ever mindful of our grievous sins, and of the Saviour's atoning sufferings, we may praise our God "with a pure heart and fervently." Such a state of heart will be followed by all those proprieties which elevate our singers and our organists, and which render our congregations "comely," because of the acceptable praise they offer.

To plead with you in any *urgent* manner, preparatory to the collection which is about to be made, can, I trust, be hardly necessary. The mere history of your organ is enough, one would think, to elicit the contents of any purse for the liquidation of the debt, which hangs upon it. One of the reliques of our Church before its grand disruption, in the days of fanaticism, rebellion and usurpation,—spared from destruction by the last man in the world, who could be thought to "have music in his soul,"—curiously conveyed to an outraged palace for his stealthy gratification,—upon his death, restored to its original home in Oxford,—and, now, standing, renovated and enlarged, in one of the most beautiful "bulwarks of our land,"—surely that organ speaks, with a speechless voice, to the *heart* of every English Churchman, more stirringly than the most consummate skill could make it speak to the ear![1] If more be wanting,—then let Poetry come to the aid of History, and tell you that her bard of bards, the glory of godly verse, must, in all probability, have listened to its tones. There can be little doubt that, if not at Magdalen College, yet at Hampton Court, your organ was often heard by MILTON. If, too, on this auspicious day, the anniversary of the coronation of the best of Queens, the debt on your organ should be more than cancelled, the act will be graceful in itself, and may fittingly be regarded as an expression of our gratitude for the safety of her crown, and the preservation of her life. May no Cromwell ever tear down your organ, or insult[2] our Queen.

But, let me end, by bringing back your thoughts, from all sublunary considerations, to that with which this Sermon commenced, viz. the "*Aijeleth Shahar*," or true "Hind of the Morning,"—the Suffering Son of God. It is He who, in his eternal majesty and infinite love, is at once the object and the medium of all praise. It is He in whom Jehovah, as "God in Christ," did inhabit, and ever will inhabit, the praises of his people. It is He whom angels and archangels, cherubim and seraphim, with all the justified and sanctified, will incessantly admire and adore. "Let Him be your praise" now; let everything be done in his Name; and you shall see Him, and praise Him for ever!

[1] "Oliver Cromwell was fond of music; and, what may seem surprising, was particularly fond of the music of an organ: as appears from the following remarkable anecdote. In the grand Rebellion, when the organ at Magdalen College in Oxford, among others, was taken down, Cromwell ordered it to be carefully conveyed to Hampton Court, where it was placed in the great gallery; and one of Cromwell's favourite amusements was to be entertained with this instrument, at leisure hours. It continued there 'till the Restoration, when it was returned to its original owners, and was the same that remained in the choir of that college 'till within these last twenty years."—*Note in Rev. T. Warton's* "Observations on the Fairy Queen of Spenser," vol. 2, p. 278.—The organ was purchased of Magdalen College for the use of the congregation in the Abbey Church of Tewkesbury, in the year 1737, and was renovated and enlarged in 1848, by Mr. Henry Willis, of London.

[2] The unhappy man, Pate, had lifted his hand against Her Majesty, a few days before.

THE FAITHFUL SERVANT.

A SERMON,

PREACHED IN THE

PARISH CHURCH OF ST. MICHAEL, BATH,

ON SUNDAY, FEBRUARY 24, 1856,

ON THE

DEATH OF THE REV. JOHN EAST, M.A.,

RECTOR OF THE PARISH.

BY

WILLIAM HENRY HAVERGAL, M.A.,

HON. CANON, AND RECTOR OF ST. NICHOLAS, WORCESTER.

BATH:

R. E. PEACH, 8, BRIDGE STREET.

SERMON.

JOSHUA 1:2.

"Moses my servant is dead."

THESE are plain and emphatic words; and truly we require to be told with plainness and emphasis what we believe with difficulty and receive with reluctance. Notwithstanding all that we certainly know, we feel it hard to *realize* the fact that he who, only a Sunday or two ago, occupied this pulpit as your faithful pastor is now no more. Our beloved East "*is dead*!" The comparative suddenness of the event, and the strange intensity of our feelings on the occurrence of it, spread over our minds such a mist as nothing but a thunder-clap can disperse. The disciples of our blessed Redeemer once stood in need of the same plainness of speech as that which we hear in the text. They heard him speak of his friend Lazarus as having fallen asleep after sickness. They fondly hoped that it was anything but death. At length "Jesus said unto them *plainly*, Lazarus is dead."

He who spake thus of his friend Lazarus was the same holy and gracious Being as spake, in the words of our text, of his servant Moses; for it is not to be doubted that the Angel Jehovah, who "spake to the fathers in the wilderness," was afterward the incarnate Jesus. "No man hath seen God *at any time*: the only begotten Son, who is in the bosom of the Father, He hath *declared* Him." Now we know that he, who spake so plainly of the death of Lazarus, wept also most tenderly at the grave of Lazarus: and who, among all the thousands of Israel, when mourning for thirty days, sorrowed more deeply and wept more feelingly than Joshua, who heard from the lips of Jehovah what our text declared? It was likely that Joshua would thus sorrow and thus weep, because for full forty years he had been intimately associated with Moses, and had gone in and out with him in all the great transactions of Israel.

May not I therefore fitly mingle my mourning with yours, or even ask you to mourn with me, when I tell some and remind others, that for exactly three and forty years I called him my brother, whom you now lament as your departed pastor? When but youths in our teens we were introduced to each other at college. We then read together, we walked together, we prayed together, and we shook hands together with the best of the Russian czars, the former Alexander. From that time to his latest hour we were constantly as one—one in heart, in feeling and theological opinion, and one in sentiment with regard to all the great questions of the day, whether affecting the church or the world. Years ago he was ready to mourn over me when taken up for dead. But he is now taken away before me; and I am left to say over him, "I am distressed for thee, my brother Jonathan: very pleasant hast thou been to me: thy love was wonderful."

To preach then to you over his grave, in a church full of bleeding hearts, and surrounded by "a widowed city," is indeed a task and a strain, at which, not without warning, I inwardly tremble, especially as from diminished sight I am still unable to read any manuscript. Help me therefore with your prayers; lest even a strong under-current of feeling should not suffice to carry me through the billows of sorrow with which I find myself encompassed.

With hallowed instinct you have already, no doubt, made a correct application of our text; but for more direct instruction and edification let me invite you to contemplate from it.

I. *The honourable title by which Moses was designated.* Jehovah calls him His servant. "Moses *my servant* is dead."

1. To be a servant of God is the *highest honour* to which a human being can aspire. Men may be "as gods;" but, if they are not servants of the one true God, they have neither happiness nor honour. To be the Lord's servant is the noblest style of our nature; for, if we are called to be his servants, we are previously made his sons, and so become partakers of his nature. No man can be an approved servant of God without being born of God, and further chosen and sanctified for his service. To be employed as God's servants is an object sufficiently ample for the loftiest aspirations of angelic hosts. When the apostle John bowed a little too reverently before the revealing angel, that angel said to him, "See, thou do it not; for I am *thy fellow-servant!*"

2. *All true believers* are servants of God; but all God's servants are not called to the *same* service, neither are they elevated to the same dignity. For, like as "we have many members in one body, but all members have not the same office," so does God employ many servants, but not in the same service; and, like also as "one star differeth from another star in glory," so the servants of God surpass one another in honour. Still *all* may serve him in that state of life in which he has placed them; and *all* are truly honourable, in even the humblest state, provided only they do him faithful service. It has been well said, somewhat after this manner, that, if two angels were to come from heaven for the service of God on earth, they would not care to choose which should sweep the streets, or which should frame a code of laws.

3. Moses was a servant of God in *a special sense*, and after a *prëeminent manner*. He was what the bishop of Rome is not, and what no other man was ever appointed to be, namely, the vice-gerent of Jehovah, and the very vicar of Messiah on earth. All scripture recognises the fact. His name is placed on even the verge of Deity itself, and associated with the eternal Name as no other name ever was. On the shores of the Red Sea it was known that "the people feared the Lord, and believed the Lord *and* his *servant* Moses;" and in the apocalyptic vision it is said, "They sing the song of Moses the servant of the Lord, *and* the song of the Lamb."

4. Of the *devotedness* and *fidelity of* Moses who ever entertained a doubt? All Israel knew and *felt*, at the time, what the Holy Ghost, in after years, testified by the pen of St. Paul, namely, that "Moses was *faithful* in all his house." If at any season men of unsound and selfish hearts disputed the truthfulness and integrity of Moses they were either shamed by divine rebuke or silenced by deathly judgment.

And who, *in their hearts*, ever doubted that our departed friend and brother was a devoted and faithful servant of the triune God? I say, "*in their hearts*," because the conscience of many a scoffer and defamer belies the words which he shoots from his lips against the honest servants of the holy God. Our beloved East was so manifestly the servant of God, as to require no demonstration of the fact. The livery of his divine Master was always and everywhere visibly upon him: whether in the desk or the pulpit, the committee-room or the platform, the cottage or the mansion, the school-room or the sick chamber, the street or the railway, he was always the recognised but unostentatious servant of the Saviour whom he loved. He was not ashamed of his Master, or of his name, or to speak a word for him, or to do an act for him, whenever a favourable or fitting opportunity presented itself. Was he not "*your* servant for Christ's sake?" Did he not as such teach you, advise you, admonish you, sympathize with you, and to the utmost of his means aid those of you who stood in need of aid? He did; and many a heart responds, at this moment, to what is thus asked. And was he not seen and known and read, as it were, of all, as the honest and single-minded man—as a man who thought but little of his own personal interests and bodily infirmities,[1] in comparison with the welfare of his people and the honour of his ministry? And did not the purity, simplicity, integrity, and sanctity of his whole life impress on the minds of even gainsayers the irresistible conviction, that he was indeed the servant of God—a genuine servant of the Lord Jesus Christ?

5. As God moulds his servants and deals with them according to a general rule, heart answering to heart, and character to character, as faces in a glass, we may justifiably, and I trust profitably, compare the ancient history of one servant of God with the more recent history of another. Suffer me therefore to call your attention to an humble comparison between some *phases* in the life of Moses, and certain phases in the life of one who was not the least of his successors in the service of God.

(*a.*) Moses, though called of God to serve him, made *a deliberate choice* of his service. Under the influence of a holy and valiant faith, he "refused to be called the son of Pharaoh's daughter," and by that refusal severed himself, as is thought, from the regal rights, or at least from the princely honours of Egypt. He did this from a heavenly motive, "*choosing rather* to suffer affliction with the people of God, than to enjoy the pleasures of sin for a season."

Your departed pastor took his first step in the path to your fold, by relinquishing worldly interests, and resolutely *choosing* the service of Christ. He had a fine opportunity of doing well in the world. But he willingly renounced the world; and, in spite of impediments and kindly-urged remonstrances, resolved to devote himself to the work of the ministry.

[1] Though always a weakly subject, he was a most *indefatigable* labourer. During his yearly holiday, commonly in August and September, he cannot be said to have rested; it was but a *change* of labour, for he generally was engaged to preach where he sojourned, and almost always prepared fresh sermons for the occasion. When at home, for his own pulpit, he was responsible for three sermons every week: but, surprising as it may seem, it is a veritable fact that he seldom or never preached an old sermon. He fed his flock with the food on which he daily fed himself.

The chief auxiliary to this resolution was the blessed converse of one whose almost angelic piety he ardently admired, before he himself well knew what true piety really is. That fervently pious one was too wise not to discern his intrinsic excellencies, and too holy not to urge the dedication of himself to the service of the only Saviour. The dedication once made was never for a moment regretted. How it was accepted, and how it prospered, yourselves know.

(*b.*) Moses was *trained* of God for the office which he filled. Solid learning and patient endurance contributed to make him, by his Master's grace, "a workman who needed not to be ashamed." "He was *learned* (as Stephen tells us) in all the wisdom of the Egyptians."

It is but justice to the memory of our beloved East to state that he was the pattern, perhaps the paragon, of a Christian student. His industry and perseverance were most exemplary. With sound talents and prayerful diligence, he attained no mean elevation in the scale of literature. At the close of his final examination in the schools at Oxford, I was one of those who heard the principal examiner address him thus, "Mr. East, we have great pleasure in saying that what you have done is done unusually well." This compliment, as contemporaries know, was not very common.

Our friend's theological views, which never changed their first colour, were matured under the ministry of the venerated Biddulph of Bristol. From that distinguished servant of Christ he learned, as I had also learned, what sort of doctrine and what sort of churchmanship can alone stand in the day of fiery trial—I mean the doctrine and churchmanship of our martyred reformers.

(*c.*) Moses, in serving God, encountered much opposition, but was acknowledged of God wherever he went, and toward the close of his service enjoyed a peaceful season. The story of Korah and his company, and of Dathan and Abiram, is read to us by our church. Other instances of "the contradiction of sinners" which Moses endured will occur to your recollection. Out of all such trials however the Lord delivered his faithful servant. Every place in which he sojourned bore testimony to his righteous and beneficent character, till at length the storms of former years subsided, and the desired tranquility ensued.

In of course a mitigated degree a similar lot marked the ministerial career of our friend and brother. From the first and for long afterward he was called to sustain no small amount of spiritual warfare. He was made the *soldier* as well as the servant of Christ. A continued series of ministerial trials befell him. What his entrance was amongst you, some of you can recollect, when, twenty-three years ago, last Sunday, he preached his first sermon and administered his first baptism in the old Saint Michael's Church. He came at that time as an humble curate, in much fear, in much trembling, and much weakness. He came, as you know, in the midst of many who were too ready to cast the cold word of scorn, and too slow to give the warm hand of fellowship. With all this however he bore. He put up with the mistakes, the prejudices, or the wrong tempers of those with whom he had to deal. But he lived to see many an opponent turned into a friend, or put aside in silence. On all fitting occasions, but never with unseemly forwardness, did he manfully battle with the vices and frivolities of his locality; while he never was backward to unmask either popery, infidelity, or formalism.

In one of his early curacies, about the year 1818, he sustained no small share of obloquy and opposition, simply because he preached the truth of Christ, as he was wont to preach it among you, and warned the people to flee from the wrath to come. A company of profligates, in a retired and darksome town, banded together for the purpose of deterring him from his "work of faith and labour of love." They went so far as to form an effigy of him, which they hung and burnt in an open street, through which the bishop of the diocese was expected to pass on his way to a confirmation. But these pitiable opponents, by affixing a largely inscribed label round the neck of the effigy, unwittingly condemned themselves and honoured him. The inscription was, "*See what* PREACHING *has brought me to.*" That apostolic man, bishop Ryder, beheld the spectacle, and in an hour or two after greeted the young preacher with these words, "Be of good cheer, dear brother, count this all joy. It can do you no harm, but may do your Master much honour." The words of the good bishop were singularly verified. An abundant measure of blessedness followed this act of opposition,[1] as could easily be testified, did time and place permit.

Wherever else our beloved brother subsequently went, whether at Stogursey, Bristol, or Croscombe, he did the work of an evangelist, and obtained full and honourable witness of being a devoted servant of Christ.

As time passed on, after his firm settlement in this city, the Lord smoothed his path, till opposition gradually died away. Still, as we all know, he was never the man to flinch from a duty, or to shrink from an enemy when that enemy set himself right before him. He stood forth, with simplicity, as the champion of the cross, ready to defend his Master's truth, and to put his foes to the blush.

[1] By it the fame of the young preacher spread to neighbouring places, and elicited many a devout heart. Among other individuals, it brought to light the late Mr. James Wylie, and his sister Miss Wylie, of Broadway, who afterward spent their lives and property in doing spiritual good. One of their first acts, after the hanging and burning, was to travel by a stage-coach to London, on purpose to deposit with the Rev. Josiah Pratt the sum of five hundred pounds, for the benefit of the Church Missionary Society.

Toward the closing years of his too short life, you know the comparative tranquility which reigned around him. He who once stood almost alone was, in the providence of God, ultimately surrounded by a large company of fellow-labourers, who called him either father or brother.

This procedure of his divine Master with him is frequently the lot of the servants of God, but is as frequently reversed. Trials first or trials last come as God pleaseth; for not only does he put the younger minister to great troubles and afflictions, and place him, when older, in a quiet path, but frequently reverses the method, by leading many a servant, first along a smooth and tranquil path, and then, when years begin to tell upon him, in a rough and thorny road. In all such diversities, however, God has some benign purpose to answer. And if, with regard to our departed friend, he did not a few months ago obtain that honourable preferment which appeared to be destined for him, it only was, as we now discern, because God, his Father and his Master, had reserved some better thing for him. For all the honours of the church below are as nought in comparison with being taken to the world of everlasting honour above.

(*d.*) Moses is historically associated with *the tabernacle which he built in the wilderness.* And who was the *real* builder of this most beautiful tabernacle, in which we now are assembled, none of us are ignorant. Yonder brass plate points to him as the last and the least in the erection of this masterly fabric; but, in truth and reality, he was the first and the greatest. Without him this noble edifice, humanly speaking, would never have been built. While therefore it is the ornament of your parish and city, it is his own truest *monument.* With far deeper and more solemn truthfulness than any which can be coupled with the celebrated inscription in St. Paul's cathedral, may it be said to any of you, if you seek for a monument of the builder of this fabric, "*Circumspice!*" LOOK AROUND!

Well do I remember, when this church was in progress, the deep and daily increasing interest which he took in it as its walls were rising to completion. Easy would it be, were my sight better than it is, to quote the beautiful description which he gave me of the touching scene of that day, when the top-stone of the spire was raised to its final position. But he, dear brethren, had loftier thoughts than the erection of an earthly temple, however superlative in character. He was thinking of you as the spiritual stones of a better and more enduring temple, in the fitly framing together of which he hoped to be an humble but successful workman. Long too will it be remembered that he, who was the main and the motive instrument in the building of this church, was also the principal means of making Bath what, in the providence of God, it now spiritually is. "Look around," and see what has been done by him and through him, in many a district besides his own!

(*e.*) Moses, though charging himself with not being "eloquent," was in reality *a great historian, preacher, and poet.* You are familiar with the proofs of this assertion. The Pentateuch is the true foundation of all the literature in the world.

In even these respects, as attributed to Moses, your late minister was no ordinary man. How many a little history has his pen most beautifully sketched. In a style peculiarly his own he could commend even a simple narrative to the warm interest of a reader. This he did not unfrequently; because, in the language of quaint Master Fuller, he was a careful observer of incidents and providences, and so never was in want of incidents and providences to observe. Even Royalty itself, as I am well assured, admired and graciously commended the pen of our friend, when exercised in a matter of domestic biography. Yes, a widowed Queen read, with deep and fervent interest, what he had written as a widower.

As a preacher, how many effective sermons did he first preach and then print! How many told on you! For did he not from this pulpit vividly set forth Christ crucified before you, and upon many another topic touch you to the very quick? How many an individual has left this church, whispering to himself, that preacher is in my secret; he knows me well; he has told me all that I feared of my own heart! And what a master of domestic exposition was our friend! Who could take the family Bible, as our beloved East, and turn to the very chapter which was most fitting and most appropriate for the occasion? And who, like him, could unfold the hidden scenes of the word of God, and bring out their latent truth in terms so sweet, so beautiful, and so telling on the heart, that all who heard cannot easily forget?

And, then, as to poesy, who like our friend could cull its flowers so readily and choicely, either to weave them into a garland by themselves, or to twine them around plants of plainer growth in the garden of truth? All who observed him could not fail to perceive that there was much habitual eloquence, neatness, precision, and even poetic feeling in what he ordinarily said, or preached, or wrote. Indeed there was not only the pious but the pleasant remark always hanging on his lips, and ready to fall with much that was often very touching and beautiful.

(*f.*) Moses was distinguished not only for fidelity but for *prayerfulness.* He was a servant who prayed much to his Master. His habitual *realization* of the divine presence was truly remarkable. Such realization is inseparable from the spirit of supplication. The exercise of that spirit secured for Moses both wisdom and success. The lifting up of his hands brought down victory to Israel, when Amalek marched into the battle field against him.

And was not your beloved pastor a man of pliant knee and ready hand, before the throne of grace? Have not many thought him the very pattern of an offerer of prayer?[1] Who that has heard him pray can forget the sweet flow, the solemn diction, and the calm fervour of his prayer? Let those who had the privilege of kneeling with him in prayer remember him as a bright example for them to follow, and be thankful for the much precious dew which distilled from his suppliant lips.

6. In all that has thus far been said, do not mistake my meaning. No *flattery* of our deceased brother is intended. He would say, "Pay no compliment to me, transfer all the honour to my Master and my Saviour." But let us admire the Master in what we see to admire in the servant, for it was his God who made him what he was.

To describe our friends as faultless is itself a fault. No man is faultless, for "there is not a just man upon earth who doeth good and sinneth not." Moses had his failings. They were marked and even reproved by the God who loved him. But they are not remembered against him; neither, as will be the case with every true penitent, shall they ever be mentioned to him again. The great Master, who is infinite in mercy, passes by all the transgressions of his faithful servants—casting them, not into the shallows of the sea from whence they may be floated back again, but into the very depth of the ocean from which there is no return.

That our beloved and exemplary East was without failings would be impious in even his dearest friend to say. He was but a man, though a man of God. Consequently, like all other men of God, he was not so angelic as to cease to be human.

And here I may remark to you, that many persons, not knowing him well enough to know his *real* self, were disposed to think that there was a dash of the austere—a little shade, a little tinge, or a little film of severity in his manner. If such appeared to be the case, it was only an appearance; for a man of a more tender and affectionate spirit, or with a warmer and more generous heart (and you know the liberal hand which he always carried), there never was than John East. This supposed austerity was but the indication of a manly mind conversant with solemn topics and fixed principles. If it were a film, it was but the film-like bloom of the plum or the grape, which no good judge of the fruit would rudely remove, because he knows that it will vanish at a touch, when the ripened sweetness which it conceals is about to be tasted.

But it is time to address our thoughts to

II. The *manner in which the death of Moses was announced.* It was, as you heard me say, a very plain and emphatic

[1] On his return from the north last autumn, he commenced a series of week-day discourses on this subject, "The men of God as *men of prayer.*" He dwelt particularly on the case of Moses, and enlarged upon even the words of our text.

manner: "*Moses my servant is dead.*" How few are these words, but how full of meaning! Their very simplicity best accords with the majesty of him, who does not burthen the genuineness of his servants with pompous titles or swelling epithets.

In the words then of our text God announces to Joshua the death of Moses,

1. *As a very natural event, and one which is not at all surprising.*

God's servants are but "dust;" and he tenderly "*remembers*" that they verily are such, and that at the destined hour they will return to their native element. He therefore *hires* them for only a season. That season is never very long while to themselves it is always very uncertain.

When the labour of their day is done, the Master calls his servants to their home and to their rest. This is his settled method, and their acknowledged expectation. Hence the death of Moses was a *routine* occurrence. It was a matter of course, and contained no element of surprise.

And such is the death of *every* servant of God. They all are removed at the proper season. Such was the removal of our beloved brother. He knew that he was not to stay for ever, and we had no power to detain him at our pleasure. His friends know that he was a man who habitually and even longingly anticipated death; and that, though he was willing to live for his Master's work, he longed to depart to his Father's home.

As the *time* of his departure unsuspectedly drew nigh, it now seems, by circumstances which occurred, that he had, as many a servant of God has had, a sort of inward presentiment of the near approach of his end. That presentiment was not so clear and vivid as to be openly expressed to others; but things which he said and did are now seen to be indicative of converse on the subject inwardly with himself.[1]

[1] On the day on which his illness set in he visited an invalid, through the window of whose apartment the spire of his church could be seen. The invalid remarked that it was a pleasure to gaze on that beautiful spire, because of the associations connected with it. His ready reply was, while pointing to the church, "Yes, it will soon be my home and your home."—In the very sermon which he wrote on the Saturday, on the evening of which he was taken ill, and which he intended to preach on the following morning, occurs this remarkable passage: "Now if the disciples had been asked, if they had questioned each other, if they had enquired within their own breasts, 'How is it that we feel in this journey to Jerusalem as we never felt before?' they probably would not have been at all able to account for it. The humblest and most spiritual would perhaps have said, 'These deep thoughts—this solemnity of soul, must come from God. He sees what will be the consequences of this passover visit to Jerusalem, and by his Spirit he is stirring our minds with new and peculiar emotions.' How often may we ourselves have been so affected when taking any new step in life, and especially when, though at the time unknown to ourselves, we were doing some accustomed thing for the last time! The Lord seems to send down upon our hearts a peculiar influence, which is afterwards explained by the event."

But the death of Moses is announced,

2. *As an event with which God was perfectly acquainted.*

Yes, Jehovah knew it well, because he had *arranged* it all. He had foreordained all its details, and then superintended even its minutest incidents. He had said to Moses, "Get thee up into this mountain Abarim; and *die* in the mount whither thou goest up." To this it is added, "So Moses, the servant of the Lord, *died there* in the land of Moab, *according to the word of the Lord.*"

Very like this was the case of our beloved brother, on the evening of Saturday, the ninth instant. Up to that period, he had been occupied as usual in his master's work, and his Master knew it. The day before had, it appears, been with him a day of more exertion than he ought to have encountered; and it no doubt added to that exhaustion of the poor bodily frame, which subsequently ensued.

But, when the evening of the *Saturday* was come (a fitting day, you will say, for the close of work), he found himself unable to continue his preparation for the ensuing Lord's day. He was about to retire to his bedroom, when the arrival of his devoted curate delayed him. Faintness overpowered him, and he sank down in that chair, on which might appropriately be inscribed, "In weariness oft." With great difficulty he reached his bedroom, the ascent to which was then like a mountain-steep to him. He went up to die; for he never left that room till he was carried from it to his grave. During the few days which succeeded this first seizure, weakness and exhaustion came on so rapidly as to allow very little to transpire which could edify you to hear. All that we need say is, that his heart was with God, and his entire demeanour was characteristic of a servant of God. As far as could be ascertained, his thoughts dwelt upon the one great business of his life—the glory of his Redeemer in the comfort and salvation of his soul.

But in even these his last days he was not wholly without trial. He suffered much from distracting dreams and distracting thoughts, but not, as he thankfully said, from "sinful thoughts." With firmness he was enabled to add, "*In the multitude of my thoughts within me* Thy *comforts refresh my soul.*"

As the closing scene rapidly and unexpectedly drew nigh, for fatal erysipelas advanced by strides, he was heard to say, what was the last audible sound from his lips, "*Home, Home.*" This perhaps was but the wandering of the poor weakened mind; but his medical attendant gave a happy turn to the words by saying, "Yes, my dear sir, you are indeed going home—to the home of the righteous—to the home where Jesus is." He seemed to hear and understand what was said, for a slight movement of the right hand, in *an upward* direction, impressed all present with the belief that he meant to say, "I know that *I am going home!*"

This *last* word "home" falls on my ear with a thrilling force which I can hardly convey to you; for, singular to say, it is the *first* remembered word which passed between him and me. The word "home" was, so to speak, the altar around which our friendship and fidelity were sworn to each other. "*East, do you love home?*" was the first sentence which he recollected ever to have been uttered by myself. He always bore it in mind, and frequently referred to it, fondly and affectionately in after days. There is no marvel in this; for our East was a thorough man of home. He loved it with hallowed intensity, and only feared, as I have heard him say, that he loved it too much. Never could it be said of him, that he was not at home what he was in society. His brightest excellencies shone out at home. Fitly therefore did a glance of his eternal home waken up his sinking thoughts.

And now the end drew nigh. But what an end was East's—so gentle, so calm, so peaceful, so child-like! Without the slightest struggle, without even a sigh, and with hardly any perceptible indication of the solemn but blessed change, did he enter into that home which, from the first, had been prepared for him, and for which he was unequivocally prepared.

Further the death of Moses was announced.

3. *As an event which, in its results, must necessarily be very blessed.*

Will Jehovah take away a faithful servant, and not take him to himself? Will he end that servant's work, and not comfort him with rest and crown him with reward? Shall he say, "Moses is *dead*," and not add, "Behold, he *liveth*"? Impossible—our God never acts unworthily or unrighteously. Hence, when as a servant Moses died, the Lord as his Master took charge of him, as well with regard to his body as his soul.

(*a.*) The Lord *took careful charge of the body of Moses.* "He buried him in a valley in the land of Moab." He provided for him both a grave and an escort of angels to convey him to it. The place of his grave was kept a profound secret, possibly from even Satan himself, in order that the Hebrews might not be tempted idolatrously to reverence it, and that no encouragement might be given to the veneration of reliques in after ages. The angelic escort was necessary, because the body had to be conveyed from the summit of a mountain, to the recesses of a valley. "Michael, the archangel," headed that escort. Altogether it was such a burial as no man, either, before or since, ever had. It was too as honourable as it was unique.

And what a burial was that which your eyes beheld on the morning of Thursday last! The whole city was moved on the occasion of it. Bath has seldom beheld such a spectacle. It was an especial honour which God, in his providence, caused to be paid to the memory of his faithful and devoted servant. We do not deal in dreams and fond imaginings about angels hovering here or hovering there; but you and I know that the angels of many churches did accompany his corpse to its last resting place.[1] Some sixty clergymen, headed by a bishop and an archdeacon, were in attendance. What a contrast was this end of the servant with the beginning of his service! Few regarded him at that beginning, but all revered him at the end. When the children of Israel went down into Egypt, they were an abomination to the Egyptians; but, when they departed from it, not a dog moved his tongue.

(*b.*) He who took care of the body of Moses, took charge also of his soul. He lodged it in his own bosom and recompensed it with his own presence. For it was as infallibly true then as it is now, that "*blessed are the dead which die in the Lord;*" seeing we are not to conclude that, because it is said of that sentence, "Write, *from henceforth,*" the holy dead were not previously blessed. They were always blessed—equally blessed. Only St. John, in the apocalyptic vision, was directed to intimate that, at or after a certain period in the history of the church, the doctrine of the blessedness of the holy dead should no longer be concealed by the darkness of popery, but should "from henceforth" be clearly preached and known for the comfort of Christ's true servants.

The transfiguration on mount Tabor revealed the fact, that he who died on mount Abarim was with the Lord in joy and felicity. Moses was seen, with the glorified Elijah, conversing with the incarnate "Lord of glory."

Where Moses then is, we joyfully believe that our departed friend is also. No one feels the slightest doubt of his having joined "the spirits of the just, the innumerable company of angels, and Jesus the Mediator of the new covenant." He beheld "the fair beauty of the Lord" as often as he worshipped in this beautiful temple; but now he is seeing the King his Master in all his unclouded beauty. Let not the thought of this flit by you, without your detaining it sufficiently long to join with it a prayerful resolve to love and serve that King and Master, as he loved and served him.

Still further the death of Moses was announced,

4. *As a loss in which Jehovah sympathized, but at which he was not disconcerted.*

Our God loves his servants, and holds their death right dear and precious. He knows the effect which their departure has on those who are left behind. He knows their sorrows; and

[1] The following account of his funeral was given in the "Bath Chronicle," February 28th, 1856:—

"The occasion was one of the most solemn of the kind that ever fell under our notice. It engrossed the attention of the whole city, not only in the immediate neighbourhood of the mournful ceremonial, but everywhere within the walls of Bath the subject held a chief place in the thoughts of our fellow-citizens. It was in strict reality a public grief which affected the people of Bath; that grief was of the strongest and most absorbing character; and, while it honoured the departed, reflected honour on those by whom it was so sincerely manifested."

not only sees their tears, but puts them in his memorial bottle. He saw all Israel mourning, for thirty days, at the foot of the mountain on which Moses died, and both sanctioned that mourning and sympathized with it. Dear brethren, he sees your grief, and is himself "*acquainted*" with it. But the loss at which we grieve disturbs only ourselves. It cannot disconcert him. He can not only supply any lack of service, but can do without any servants at all. None are necessary to him, after the manner of human necessity.

To be persuaded of this is, first, a duty, and then a comfort. God will have us confess that, although we may be workers together with him, he alone can work in us both to will and to do, and that every work is subject to his sovereign pleasure. Practically convinced of this, we are sure of all comfort. The work of the Lord shall be accomplished, notwithstanding that his righteous servants seem to perish. The death of Moses was no hindrance to the crossing of Israel into Canaan. A successor was in readiness, not another Moses, but another servant of the Lord's choosing.

In like manner the work of God in this parish church will not really be hindered by the withdrawal of its late most able minister. The Lord of this church knows his own mind as to who shall be his next servant in it. Happily the character of the trusteeship of this living secures you from painful anxiety as to the *character* of him who will next hold it. Another East you can hardly expect; but for another man of his grace and his spirit you may reasonably hope. Still, though God *can* raise up servants out of stones, yet is not this his ordinary procedure. He looks for your prayers, and waits to be inquired of, that he may send you such a pastor as your hearts desire.

Further yet the death of Moses was announced,

5. *As an event from which Joshua was to take up fresh energy and zeal.*

When God told him of the death of Moses, it was not so much to inform him of a fact, as to convey to him a call; for, when he said, "*Moses my servant is dead,*" he instantly added, "Now therefore *arise, go over this Jordan.*" This was as though he had said, "Now arise to new and increasing efforts for the completion of that journey, and the ending of that work, which Moses had begun."

Thus ought it to be with you and me and all. The providence which has taken away our East from his post calls on us to "*arise,*" and to brace up our energies for the furtherance of those works of enlightened piety and evangelical charity in which he so heartily engaged.

Once again the death of the great legislator and greatest of servants was announced.

6. *As a fact which certifies us that all God's servants must die.*

His best servants still have a sinful nature. They all are born in sin; and, though their sin may be cleansed and pardoned, they still inhabit a body of sin and death. Ere they can be fitted for a better service in a world where death never enters, they must themselves die, not to pay the debt of nature, but the appointed penalty of sin.

Why Enoch and Elijah were *translated*, and Abraham and Moses *died*, we presume not to inquire. God had justifiable reasons for conferring the honour on the former two and not on the latter; but he has not revealed them to us. If however such a "friend" as Abraham, and such a "servant" as Moses, were not exempted from the common lot, how dare we dream of escaping it ourselves? Then let it be settled in our hearts, that it will inevitably be said of each of us, He or she "*is dead.*" Yes, "*dead;*" for it is a great mistake, which some religionists are fond of perpetuating, to *evade* the word "*death,*" and substitute the word "*sleep.*" The evasion is made under colour of following the diction of the New Testament in preference to that of the Old. A little, very little examination of the text of both Testaments will show that death and sleep are as convertible terms in the one as in the other. If therefore we console ourselves with the figurative word *sleep*, we must prepare ourselves for the solemn reality. There is no sleeping in Jesus without dying the death.

And what shall now be said to you in practical conclusion? Time requires me to be brief; but my position here this morning requires me to be faithful.

1. You knew and heard him who, Sunday after Sunday, stood where I now stand. Then "remember him who hath spoken unto you the word of God." Remember him, not merely as the man, but as the minister. Remember what he preached to you, and how he prayed for you. Remember what he may have said to you in private. Remember that he had your salvation at heart, and was always in earnest about your immortal souls. Remember him therefore, not only with respect and affection, but with fervent gratitude for the mercies which you have received, and for the privileges which you have long enjoyed through him.

But be assured that no remembrance of him will benefit you unless you remember his Master and remember yourselves. His Master must be your Master; and you must yourselves seek all that the departed servant told and intreated you to seek.

2. You are further left *as witnesses* of what his faith and what his service was. Know then, that "*by it he being dead yet speaketh.*" This consideration ought to arouse and fix your attention. Your minister is gone, but his ministry will remain as long as you remain to recollect it. Personally he will preach to you no more; but relatively, as to what he did preach, he will preach to you as often as you call to mind his preaching. Even more than this, whether you call to mind his service or not, you cannot do away with it. It *will* speak to you. It cannot be

silenced; for he who accepts the servant immortalizes the service; so that "by it" the servant, "being dead, *yet* speaketh."

To many who are present in this crowded assembly it may too truly be said, You came not *regularly* to hear him speak from this pulpit when you ought to have come: let me, then, ask, why come you now? is it curiosity or conscience which prompts you to come now? Depart not then from this sanctuary, without reflecting that for all you saw in him and heard from him, as your example or monitor, *you must give account!*

3. You owe *a large debt of sympathy* to them to whom he was something more than your servant for Christ's sake. If your loss be great, what is that loss to his nearest and dearest ones? It could only depreciate it were I to attempt to describe it. Many of you do, at this moment, vividly perceive the magnitude of that loss. You know somewhat of those riches of prayer, counsel, tenderness, and comfort, which are departed with him, and which nothing can restore to his home.

Let then your choicest sympathies abound. Pray the more for them for whom he can no longer pray himself. For such sympathy, and for many another sort of sympathy, your earnest affection will find ample scope. And fail not to send that better sort, by God's telegraph, across the widest seas, where the tidings of a father's death will be bitter indeed.

4. Finally, with great propriety you may *comfort one another* over the grave of him whom you this day lament as "dead." For, though he "is dead," he sleeps in Jesus. Him therefore shall God bring with Jesus in the morning of his return to gather in his elect. In that morning all the faithful ones of this flock shall meet their beloved pastor, not indeed for a renewal of his ministrations, but for the participation of his joys. Then shall you realize to the full the blessed results of the precious blood, the everlasting righteousness, and the true holiness, which he habitually declared to you. Then also shall you see him, who turned many to righteousness, shining in the glorious beauty of his Saviour and your Saviour. Moreover you shall hear that Saviour say to him, "*Well done, thou good and faithful servant, enter thou into the joy of thy Lord.*" Yes,

"*Servant* of God, well done!
Now lay thy burthen down:
Thy day is o'er; thy race is run;
Receive thy joy and crown!"

THE CHARGE OF THE DYING PASTOR,

AND

THE PRESENCE OF THE GOD OF PEACE.

A SERMON,

ON THE

DEATH OF THE REV. JOHN DAVIES, M.A.

RECTOR OF ST. CLEMENT'S, WORCESTER;

PREACHED IN THE CHURCH OF THAT PARISH,

ON THE MORNING OF SUNDAY, JULY 25TH, 1858,

BY

W. H. HAVERGAL, M.A.

RECTOR OF ST. NICHOLAS, AND HONORARY CANON.

PREFATORY NOTE.

The following Sermon was preached, of necessity, without any manuscript aid. The author has since found it easier to recollect what, from previous study, he intended to say, than what, at the time of preaching the Sermon, he actually said. He, nevertheless, believes it to be a faithful transcript of its oral delivery.

Philippians 4:9.

"Those things which ye have both learned, and received, and heard, and seen in me, do: and the God of peace shall be with you."

THOUGH it has been arranged for me to preach, this morning, on behalf of your Parochial Schools, yet, how *can* I direct either your attention or my own, *principally*, to them?

Considering who founded those schools, and where he now is, and where, only a few weeks ago, he intended to be at this very hour, I should certainly put an intolerable chain on my own feelings, and most likely on yours, were I to be silent, or even spare, respecting him whose loss we all are lamenting.

According to the present Sunday—the Eighth Sunday after Trinity, it is exactly thirty-five years ago to-day, since I first stood in this pulpit. I was then, as a young man, merely the friendly substitute of your late beloved pastor. Let me now be his fervent but faithful witness. A similar opportunity, for such a purpose, can never return. It would, therefore, be almost criminal to let the present occasion pass, without an effort to turn it to the best account.

Suffer me, then, to combine a reference to our departed friend, and your consequent position, with an appeal on behalf of your Sunday and Week-day Schools.

It will, I trust, be allowed me to premise, that the text announced to you is not the text from which I originally intended to address you. I had selected what is said of the Apostle Barnabas, in Acts 11:24, "*He was a good man, and full of the Holy Ghost, and of faith.*" The selection was made, because there is much in the character of Barnabas which was reflected by our departed brother. Like him he was, indeed, "*a son of consolation,*"[1] a man of self-denying generosity, (Acts 4:36, 37,) and of great "brotherly kindness," (Acts 9:27,) remarkable also for the practice and power of "*exhortation,*" (Acts 11:23,) and for all those spiritual and social qualities which make the "*good man,*" and elevate him above the ordinarily "*righteous man.*" (Romans 5:7.)

This said text, though selected and studied, was relinquished, on incidentally hearing that a brother clergyman had preached from it on Sunday evening last; while, as was afterwards learned, another brother had preceded him with the same text, in the morning. These minute incidents are not without their value; inasmuch as they form "a threefold cord" of testimony, from one text, to the honour of departed excellence.

Turning, then, from what was said of Barnabas, to what was said by Paul, his companion in travel and fellow-labourer in the Gospel, I am desirous of applying the words of the latter Apostle to you; and, in so doing, of being the echo of his voice, who, but a little while ago, might most justly have urged them upon you, with his own earnest utterance. Let it, therefore, be as though, at this moment, you were listening to his parting charge and heard him say, "*Those things which ye have both learned and received, and heard, and seen in me, do: and the God of peace shall be with you.*"

May that very "God of peace be with us" *now*, and enable us, by his Holy Spirit, rightly and profitably to consider—

I. *The reference, which the Apostle makes, to his past "preaching and living.*" "Those things which ye have both *learned*, and *received*, and *heard*, and *seen* in me."

[1] This is the Syriac sense of the name Barnabas; but Barnabas also means, according to Hebrew derivation, "*a son of a prophet.*" The late Rector of St. Clement's was the son of a pious clergyman. The clerical circumstances of the family are somewhat peculiar. The four sons of the good father were born in the same county, educated at the same college, ordained as curates, and settled as incumbents within a short distance of each other, and still in the same county.

St. Paul, like every honest man, knew his own integrity. He neither ostentatiously paraded it, nor fastidiously concealed it. When need required, he becomingly referred to it. Thus to the Corinthians he said, "*Our rejoicing is this, the testimony of our conscience, that in simplicity and godly sincerity, not with fleshly wisdom, but by the grace of God, we have had our conversation in the world, and more abundantly to you-ward.*" (2 Corinthians 1:12.) To the Thessalonians he appealed thus, "*Ye are witnesses, and God also, how holily and justly and unblameably we behaved ourselves among you that believe.*" Elsewhere he speaks to the same effect. So, also, in the same spirit, and for a similar purpose, may *every* minister of Christ speak, when occasion requires.

May I not, then, most fitly, speak thus for one, who, as we all believe, might most worthily speak thus for himself? And, yet, it is morally certain, that, if he knew anything was about to be said of himself, his injunction would be that of a venerable friend,[1] many years ago, "Say as little of *me* as you can, but as much of my MASTER as you like!"

As, however, we are to glorify God in his servants, (Galatians 1:24,) I may opportunely remind you of some, at least, of "*those things which you have learned and received, and heard, and seen in him.*"

You have "*learned*" from him the truth of the Triune God. He preached that truth to you in its simplicity and entirety. He was not the man to hold parley with error, to handle the word of God deceitfully, or to keep back anything that was profitable for you. The Gospel which he declared was not "another gospel," but that one, pure, lucid Gospel, which those noble successors of the apostles, the martyred Reformers of our Church, have handed down to us. He preached the love of God in Christ to sinners, *and loved to preach it.* To tell such how they may be justified freely, and sanctified wholly, and saved eternally, was his study and delight.

He was not, what is usually called, a controversial preacher; but he did not fail to guard you against tenets and practices which stealthily, though too surely, have led many back again to the darkness and thraldom of popery.

What he preached and taught you have "*received.*" Would that this were true of all in its real and permanent sense. Some, it is certain, have so done; because, blessed be God! his ministry was not fruitless, but confessedly successful. The dew of the Spirit fell copiously on his tillage, especially during the middle years of his willing labour.

Many of you, now present, have indeed "*received,*" or, as that word properly means, *appropriated and applied to yourselves,* the doctrine which he taught you. Here the result has been your instruction, or your edification, or your comfort. They, who are practically conversant with these benefits, will know how to be grateful for them.

Among wayfarers and the working classes, usefulness was unquestionably great. But, we must wait for the developments of The Great Day to know the full details of that usefulness. A man who, for two-and-forty years, laboured, as he did, "in season and out of season," and was always on the watch to win souls, is very likely to have been an instrument of saving good to far more individuals than we can venture to surmise.

There are things, too, which you have "*heard*" from him and of him. Apart from his public ministrations, you have, more or less, "*heard*" his private discourse, and, especially his private prayer. His converse, as a friend and counsellor, must have conduced to your pleasure or profit: while his supplications in your sick chamber, or in an hour of trouble, could not be otherwise than refreshing and invaluable. Never forget his hallowed wisdom in habitually saying, at the mention of any anxious or important matter, "*Well, we must look up.*"

How much has always been kindly and truly "*heard*" *of* him, yourselves well know. The very things which, at the beginning of this chapter, the apostle commends to universal thought and attention, were constantly "*heard*" of him. Things "*pure, honest, lovely, and of good report,*" have long been associated with his very name.

Not long ago, however, he was, as you too well recollect, subjected to rather sudden reproach and insult. It was but a passing storm. Still it affected him deeply; because with innocent David he could say, "What have I now done?" But that which was intended, perhaps, for his hurt, was turned to his greater honour. God took care of the character of his righteous servant, who prayed earnestly for those who tried to injure it, and caused a testimony to it to be "*graven with an iron pen.*"

Such things "*are common to the brethren.*" They occur in the history of most good men. For, when Satan is jealous at the position or prosperity of a Christian minister, and is angry at the inroads made upon his kingdom, he will aim to stir up strife against him. He will assail him by open opponents, insidious agents, or selfish partizans, who, if they cannot find facts to distort, will invent fables to delude. Just as good Master Thomas Fuller quaintly says, so it is; "When the enemy meeteth not with a hole in the sleeve of a good man's coat, he presently setteth about *to pick one.*"

But, trials such as these are necessary for the man of God. They form a salutary check to him against "*thinking of himself more highly than he ought to think;*" and, in any case, save him from that woe, of which our Lord warned his disciples when He said, "Woe unto you when all men shall speak well of you." (Luke 6:26.)

Now, however, that our beloved brother is taken from us, who does not hear of him things which seldom grace the his-

[1] The Rev. S. Knight, of Halifax.

tory of those, whom the world calls great? The best word on the public lip is lavished on him, and his genuine worth is proclaimed in every gate. Assuredly, his memory will not want a monument, so long as we live, or this Church and your Parochial School Rooms shall last.

What has been recently written and spoken of his having built them, I need not repeat. Neither am I disposed to trench upon what was becomingly said, from this pulpit, on the morning and evening of Sunday last, but rather to call your attention to such incidents as have not been mentioned, or are but very partially known.

When your departed pastor was presented to this living, in the year 1816, it was regarded by many as a singularly providential event. They saw in it a remarkable answer to fervent prayer. At that date it was vividly remembered that strange things had, many years before, occurred in the parish. A devout and faithful clergyman, the father of that late eminent servant of Christ, the Rev. Thomas Tregenna Biddulph, of Bristol, was curate of your parish. His fervent piety and forcible preaching raised a storm of opposition, not only against himself, but against all his devoted hearers. Deeds of violence were perpetrated, and many persons were "*shamefully entreated*."[1] As the opposition was not confined to "lewd fellows of the baser sort," Mr. Biddulph was compelled to retire from the curacy of St. Clement's. Before, however, he quitted Worcester, he one day walked to the hills which lie to the eastward[2] of our city, and which command a view of it. He there, in some quiet nook, knelt down, and solemnly and fervently prayed that God would, in mercy, remember Worcester, and that, sooner or later, the Gospel might be preached in St. Clement's Church, as he had humbly endeavoured to preach it himself. Years passed away; but not without tokens that this prayer was deposited in God's vial.

At length, a grandson of this Mr. Biddulph married into the Stillingfleet family, the venerable Prebendary of which name presented to the rectory of St. Clement's that "good man," who, as your hearts know and your tears testify, has, for the last forty-two years, faithfully preached the Gospel of salvation in this church.

When he first entered on the duties of your parish, he was, as a young minister, *greatly* helped forward by the bright example and sage counsel of that heavenly man, the Rev. John Greig, who though possessing an ample fortune, was, for several years, curate of St. Nicholas. Mr. Greig, by the singular beauty of his reading, and the calm but apostolic fervour of his preaching, attracted general attention, and, by God's blessing, aroused many souls from the lethargy which too generally prevailed. Witnesses to the power which attended his ministry are, if I mistake not, to be found among yourselves. The quiet firmness and gentle dignity of this superior servant of God,[3] much encouraged his younger friend in the ministry, and cheered him under the remains of former opposition to evangelic doctrine. This opposition had not quite died out in Worcester, when Mr. Greig left it for "a city which hath foundations." His funeral sermon was preached by the relative of your late rector, the Rev. John Cawood, of Bewdley, in the parish church of St. Nicholas, on Trinity Sunday, A.D. 1819. Though that sermon was full of "*truth and soberness*," and was, in character, the same as has long been preached to you every Lord's Day, yet, because of it, the preacher was politely inhibited from preaching again in St. Nicholas. He, however, outlived the inhibition, and, on one occasion, in his declining years, testified the truth of God in that church.

It was, therefore, as some of you long have known, a standing comfort to your venerable pastor, to feel that the latter half of his ministry was entirely exempt from that antagonism which occasionally beset his earlier labours. Let it not be that you cease to be thankful for the peaceful privileges which you still enjoy.

[1] When Mr. Davies first came to the parish, a good old man, one of the fruits of Mr. Biddulph's ministry, was still living in it. The poor man kept as a memento his front teeth, which had been knocked out, when encountering a mob who attempted to throw him into the river, as he was going to St. Clement's old church.

The state of things in Worcester, at this period and for some years after, may seem incredible to the present generation. It is, however, a fact, of which witnesses are still living, that the estimable father of an alderman of Worcester was hunted like a wild beast, with all sorts of missiles, along the High-street, because he had befriended a preacher in Lady Huntingdon's Connexion.

[2] It is said to have been *Dean Hill.*

A similar but far more memorable circumstance is recorded of John Bradford the Martyr. In the "Biographical Notice," prefixed to his "Writings," and published by the Parker Society, the following statement is made:—

"Local tradition even yet points to the spot in Blackley, where the country people say that Bradford, during his last visit to Manchester, at the close of 1552, knelt down and made solemn supplication to Almighty God. His request at the throne of grace was that the everlasting Gospel might be preached in Blackley, (his native village) to the end of time, by ministers divinely taught to feed the flock with wisdom and knowledge. The martyr's prayer, it is alleged, has been answered, in the continuance, with scarcely an exception, of faithful men in that place."

[3] The benefits which this excellent man conferred in the parish of St. Nicholas, can hardly be appreciated by its present inhabitants. Much of the daring profligacy which then marked it, was either checked, or shamed into retirement. He raised the congregation, at church, from a handful to a crowd, and the sacramental collections from *pence* to pounds. With almost incredible pains, he adjusted the charity accounts of the poor, laboriously examining musty deeds and faded documents, and transcribing, with his own clear pen, a full statement of all particulars, for the future guidance of the minister and churchwardens. He also selected and bequeathed about a hundred volumes, mostly of our standard divinity, for the sole use of the rector or curate of the parish. The whole are deposited in a neat case in the vestry, with a labelled key, and neatly written catalogue, containing suitable remarks. His avowed intention was, that no successor of his, in the cure of the parish, should be without means of referring to such theological works as would be likely most to benefit himself and his people.

It may, with all fairness, be said, that your lamented minister was the local father of all the great religious societies which were extant *among you*, prior to the year 1820.[1] He was, in succession, secretary to most, if not to all, of them. His interest in them was, to the last, unabated; nor were his exertions on their behalf diminished, except in proportion to the diminution of his physical powers.

About fifteen years ago, he did, through his concern for you, a noble act of self-denial. It is, probably, not known to you, for he was not a seeker of his people's applause. It might not have been known to myself, but from circumstances which constrained him to inquire of me. At the date mentioned, when he began to feel the desirableness of a more quiescent post, he was offered an eligible living in Somersetshire. As I knew the locality, I confirmed the favourable report which he had heard of it. Shortly after, he came and said these words, or fully to this effect, "I cannot accept the nice little living, because I have reason to fear that, if I resign St. Clement's, it will fall into other hands than I could wish: whereas the living in Somerset, will, if I decline it, be given to some better man than I am." Not a few of you, I am sure, properly appreciate this fact.

Though he seems to have glided away from us, as the danger of his short illness was not much suspected, and though circumstances drew a curtain round his dying couch, yet can a few sweet testimonies of his faith and sanctification be narrated to you. But oh for the spirit of delicacy, and of strong self-possession, in making the narration! Above all, may the Eternal Spirit sanctify it to us!

One, whom he loved with strong affection, says thus of him:—

My dear brother's life was such, that, had he been assured any day would be his last, he would have done just as he was doing. He would have been more *impressed*, but he would have gone on with the duty he had in hand.

What a lovely commentary is this upon those words of the Saviour, "*Blessed is that servant whom his Lord, when He cometh, shall find so doing.*" (Matthew 24:46.)

My dear brother lived for eternity. His faith was always a realizing power. His heart was most affectionate, and full of holy love, through the power of the Holy Ghost.

When I first saw him, in his last illness, nine days before his death, he was well enough to be up. Before I left him, he knelt down by his bed-side, and, though very weak, prayed most fervently for us all by name, then for his congregation, and then for the boatmen.

On arriving at his bed-side, the Saturday before his death, which took place early on the following Monday, he first placed one hand and then both hands on my head, solemnly but tenderly, saying, "*The Lord bless thee, my dearest brother!*"[2] He then rested on his pillow, often pointing with his feeble hand to heaven, and saying, "*He doeth all things well. Nothing too hard for the Lord.*"

When I reminded him of our beloved mother's simple but habitual prayer, "*Wash me and I shall be whiter than snow:*" "*cleanse me in the blood of the Lamb,*" he took up, *most devoutly*, portions of the 51st Psalm, and made them his prayer, ending with the words, "*The sacrifices of God are a broken spirit, a broken and a contrite heart, O God, thou wilt not despise.*"

On my saying to him, in a low voice, "The Lord is your supporter," he raised his hands devoutly, and looking up steadfastly, replied, "*My supporter! Yes, he is my Supporter, my Helper, my Stronghold!*"

Shortly after I observed to him, "*Jesus Christ is the same yesterday, to-day, and for ever!*" he earnestly responded, "Yes, indeed, for ever!"

Presently after, holding my hand, he feelingly said, "*David, say that again.*" I said it; and he seemed to feel *delighted* with it.

What a touching testimony is this for you, dear brethren, of the truth of those words of a well-known hymn,

"How *sweet* the *name of Jesus* sounds,
In a believer's ear!"

The same devoted brother proceeds to say,

Upon my adding, "You have a Shepherd full of loving-kindness," he firmly exclaimed, "*I have; indeed I have!*"

Afterwards, he seemed, when not dozing, to be always praying, though we could not always ascertain what he said. Frequently looking upwards, and, though extremely weak, lifting his hand in the same direction, he appeared to have a joyful and realizing view of the heavenly world.

Other portions of the closing scene of your beloved minister's life, I need not detail to you; as you heard them, from this pulpit, on Sunday last.

What you have now heard is but "as the gleaning of grapes when the vintage is done:" and, yet, what a rich produce of satisfaction do these smaller clusters present to us! May He who counts the death of his saints precious, make these statements very profitable to you!

There are things, also, which you have "*seen*" in your departed pastor.

These are in consistent keeping with what you have "*heard.*" You habitually saw in him great kindness of heart, and unusual singleness of eye. These, with his acknowledged

[1] Shortly after this date, when an Association was commenced in aid of the Incorporated Society for the Propagation of the Gospel in Foreign Parts, Mr. Davies was the *first* local subscriber.

[2] He gave a similar blessing to his other beloved brother, on the evening before his death. It occupied only a brief period of consciousness, but seemed to afford him much satisfaction.

honesty and candour, were the cardinal points of his elevated character. It was impossible, for even a casual observer, not to be struck with his simplicity, openness, and thorough unselfishness. All who knew him more intimately, *felt* him to be "a good man," a transparent man, a type of English honesty and Christian benevolence. As you well know and have often proved, he was a man of those solid parts, and of that good understanding, which qualified him to be a judicious and very safe adviser. He eminently possessed, what a poet, with felicitous diction, calls,

"*Good sense*, the fairest gift of heaven."

Altogether, he was a man of true wisdom, because he was a man of true godliness—"*a scribe well instructed in the kingdom of heaven.*"

With the life and death of such an one before us, you cannot but exclaim with me, How great is the moral force of true piety—the majesty of sterling religion! The world may laugh at religion as a theory; but when it is compelled to witness such a practical embodiment of it as was, every day, to be seen in "John Davies," that world cannot find audacity to laugh. Was not our whole city moved, on the day of his burial, by the secret influence of his acknowledged integrity? What was the impulse which then swayed the vast concourse of all classes, but the actings of public conscience? Was not that concourse the spontaneous homage of society to pure and holy character? It was; and long may it be ere the recollection of it fade away!

This feeble effort to bear witness to the moral worth of our departed brother, is made in the hope of gathering up some of the pearls of character which he left behind him, and of setting them deeply and firmly in your grateful memory.

Possibly, however, some captious spirit may say, Was he *faultless* then? I answer, How could he be? seeing that "*there is not a just man upon earth, who doeth good and sinneth not.*" But, whatever his faults may have been, they were not the faults which dull the simple lustre of true piety, or give to surviving friends a moment's pain. At most they were the faults of a good-natured man, and of one whose temperament was strongly tinged with that "*charity*" which "*thinketh no evil, hopeth all things, believeth all things.*"

Who will cast a stone at such faults as these, or wish them banished from the world? Let me point out a more excellent way, by inviting you to consider,—

II. *The exhortation, which the Apostle grounds upon the reference which he made to himself.*

"*Those things*," the things, especially, which had been heard and seen in him, he exhorts others *to do*. "Those things," he says, "DO!" What emphasis is here! Our short Saxon word of two letters sets a volume of admonition before us. The original Greek, though it could not be more pithily translated, injoins us *practise* what things the Apostle names, and to carry them out in a consistent and continuous performance.

Yes, "dearly beloved brethren," you may safely adapt yourselves to the model of your lamented pastor. He, as a good shepherd, was one who could with meekness and confidence say, as St. Paul says in chapter 3:17, of this Epistle, "*Brethren, be followers together of me!*" Yes, he could face his flock, and, without fear of rejoinder, speak thus to them—"Not only do as I *say*, but do as I *do!*" There was no discrepancy, as our Apostolical Church prays there may never be, between his "life and doctrine," "preaching and living." He was, indeed, an ensample to his flock.

Let, then, the light of his path, which shone more and more unto the perfect day, be reflected in your own future course. Though he is gone down to the grave, yet the oblivion of it should long be warded off, by the lustrous memento of "*your good conversation in Christ Jesus.*" Vain, indeed, will it be for you to have taken part in the demonstration of last Friday week, unless you follow it up by habitually shewing that him whom you then honoured, you continue to imitate.

"*Suffer*," then, in your respective classes, "*the word of exhortation.*" 1. Let the *superiors* of this parish and congregation take the lead, in *doing* the things which are binding on them to do.

He who so untiringly laboured among you, had your best interests at heart. Whatever he did for others had a reference to your comfort; for we cannot improve the habits of the poor, without conferring some benefit on their wealthier neighbours. You have owed many a good servant to him, and frequent exemption from many annoyances. For, certainly, in his efforts to stem the tide of immorality, to dislodge immoral persons, or put a hindrance on resort to immoral places, he aimed not only to promote the cause of morality itself, but, by so doing, to advance your own domestic quietude and comfort. Do, then, what he did. Support what he supported. Walk as he walked: and, in all things, follow him as he followed Christ.

2. Let the *Teachers* and the *Children* of his schools "*do*" as he did. He, I well know, *felt* the kindness of the one, and was always deeply interested in the welfare of the other. No clergyman knew, better than he, the value of a good Sunday-school Teacher. He was thankful for having many such in his schools. May there never be wanting such, to continue the good work which he began; for the Sunday Schools of this parish were either the first, or among the first, which were established in Worcester. Let, then, dear Teachers, his everlasting cessation from labour, be a fresh impulse to you in carrying on your work of love.

And you, dear Children—you indeed, are bound to be good and to "*do*" good. You have had no common blessing in being placed as God, in his providence, has placed you. You have been the lambs of a good shepherd's flock. He has cared for you, and prayed for you. You must, henceforth, remember him, and the lessons which he taught you. It may be an honour to you, half a hundred years hence, to say that you were brought up in his school. Let your conduct always be worthy of that honour; especially as you saw his funeral, and have heard his funeral sermon, and will have to tell of them, when all we, who took part in them, are no longer in this world.

That you may have a little fact, on which to fix your tender thoughts, let me tell you an incident in the early life of his distinguished relative, the late excellent Bishop Daniel Wilson, of Calcutta. That eminent prelate thought it worth while to record the following circumstance: "I shall never forget," the Bishop says, when writing of the Rev. Basil Wood, "the impression which his evident cheerfulness and happiness of mind made on me, in early life. I have often, when a boy, wished myself to be *as good a man as he*; and this, long before any serious impressions occupied my own mind." The wish of the good Bishop was very largely fulfilled. Hence, my dear children, think of your departed pastor, and prayerfully wish that you each may become "*as good as he*."

3. Let *Servants and the Poor* "*do*" as he would have them do. You, indeed, have lost a friend. No man could surpass him in kindness to the servant or poor parishioner. Often have you "heard and seen" him: but how ready was he always to hear and see you! How ready was he to hear your tale of difficulty or distress, and to advise or aid you as best he could! And how glad was he to receive your little contributions, for any pious object, and present them in your stead, with such kindly words as were likely to prompt others to "do likewise."

In a word, let all his hearers and parishioners strive after that power of spiritual life, by which alone they can effectually "*do*," as St. Paul exhorted, and as your pastor did.

May they also, who knew him only by the eye, be witnesses to the truth of a Latin proverb[1]—"The sight of a good man does good." His very appearance in our streets was a local benefit. It was a living sermon to many a heart. The good have been cheered by it, and the bad have been checked in some meditated sin.

It remains for me to remind you of—

III. *The promise which, by Divine authority, the Apostle appends to his exhortation. "And the God of peace shall be with you."*

The blessedness of this promise is as great as it is important. It is so great as to comprise all that is valuable in time and for eternity. It is so important that nothing can be substituted for it, and no one can dispense with it.

1. The "*peace*" here promised is emphatically "*the* peace,"—the one true peace which the Lord Jesus purchased for his people, and which He lives to bestow on them who seek it.

It is that peace which was previously mentioned, in the seventh verse of this chapter, as "*the peace of God which passeth all understanding*." This peace, though surpassing all finite understanding, as to its affecting purchase, and wondrous powers, is not beyond our practical knowledge or personal realization. It can keep or *garrison* our hearts and minds from the assaults of Satan, when he aims to subvert us by temptations, cares, or afflictions. Without it we can neither be happy in life nor safe in death.

2. But, it is not the mere possession of this peace which is held out to us. Something greater is intended. We are promised the presence itself of the very "*God of peace*." Not only will peace be our guest, but the Author of peace will be with us: as though God in Christ would be both the bearer and preserver of his own inestimable gift. There is a strong necessity for this procedure; because our hearts can receive no divine gift unless God, by his Spirit, shall first come to open them, and then stay in them to keep what He has bestowed upon them. We should soon lose every spiritual treasure, were He not to dwell with us, and guard it for us.

This "God of peace" is the God of gracious power, and of watchful providence. By the knowledge of Him, in these capacities, we chiefly realize his "blessing of peace." For, when we realize his grace within us, and his watchfulness over us, must not our souls dwell at ease, and be secure from fear?

3. The promise, however, which has been thus expounded to you, is made only to those who "*do*" as the Apostle has exhorted.

Receive, then, I pray you, what, on this point, has been urged upon your attention. If, as faithful adherents of the truth of God in Christ, you "*do*" as your profession requires, you will find that, although you have not, for a short interval, the presence of a settled minister among you, "the God of peace" will not fail you. He can give you such peace, both personally and parochially, as will prove that many a dying prayer has been offered up for you. Your God can send such quietude and prosperity throughout your parish, as will call for your wonder and gratitude. And, then, as to the future position of affairs among you, leave them all in the hands of the Great Head of the Church. Be calm, quiet, and prayerful.

And, now, grant me the ear of your heart, for a conclusion which must necessarily be brief.

1. With the expression of my own sympathy, I make no doubt that *I may offer you the sympathy of multitudes.*

[1] "Rari quippe boni: *illos, tamen, videre profuit.*"
[Few, certainly, are the good: *those, nevertheless, will be profitable to see.*]

Your loss is a public loss. That loss has respect not only to instances which have been enumerated, but to one instance especially. We have lost a PUBLIC INTERCESSOR! If prayer for a locality, under the varied aspects of its population, depends, for its success, on the faith and fervour of the heart which offers it, then have we indeed sustained a loss; for he, whom we lament, was pre-eminently a man of prayer for the people. The good Lord deliver us from the coming of a time, when we may be forced to say, We have no longer that good man to pray for us!

2. Let it be your care to remember that, as your privilege has been great, *your responsibility is great also.* The beacon-light of salvation has been held up before you, with a steady hand, and for an unusually long period. You must give account to Him who sent it among you. Many of you have rejoiced in that light: but others, alas, are none the better for it, and have no hearty concern about it. God, in mercy, send upon their souls some strong light of grace, this day; or shoot into their dull hearts some arrow of conviction from the quiver of his love! Great pains did your departed minister take to impress awakening truth upon you. It was his habit frequently to repeat the same texts of Scripture to you, in the hope that, if his own word did not arrest you, some word of God might abide with you.

3. It may be salutary to recollect, as often as you enter this Church, that he, whom you saw so statedly in it, is now sleeping beneath it. He cannot pray for you now; but you can worship the God whom he worshipped and is still worshipping; for, in truth, as his last hours testified, "*Jesus Christ is the same yesterday, to-day, and for ever.*" While, therefore, you think with solemnity of the resting of his body beneath your feet, let your hearts follow him to his brighter rest above. He is gone from this church, which bears the name of "CLEMENT," to the church where "CLEMENT" is, and others, also, whose names, as is said in the third verse of this chapter, "*are written in the Book of Life.*" Oh the joy of that morning when we shall join him in "the church of the first-born!" There will the Lord Jesus bring together every faithful shepherd and every sanctified sheep. They shall for ever occupy one fold; and the Great Shepherd shall crown them with glory and honour. No friend shall be taken from them, and no enemy shall come among them. Their beloved Saviour will be with them, and as He is so shall they eternally be.

Need I, then, *plead* for the Schools of your Parish? They were *his*, who is now in heaven! With that plea, I make sure of your generous contributions. In return for them, let me desire for you what he has fully realized—

"A hand Almighty to defend,
An ear for every call;
An honoured life, a peaceful end;
And heaven to crown it all."

FINIS.

A single-verse poem to W.H.H. by F.R.H. this fair copy autograph was found in F.R.H.'s Manuscript Book Nº III. January 18th, 1859 was W.H.H.'s 66th birthday. *See the next page, 288.*

'Tis fully known to One, by us yet dimly seen,
The blessing thou hast been;
Yet speaks the silent love of many a mourning heart,
The blessing that thou art;
While traced on coming years in faith & hope we see,
A blessing thou shalt be;
Then here in holy labour, there in holier rest,
Blessing, thou shalt be blest.

For Papa's birthday.
Jan 18. /59.

This is a photograph of William Henry Havergal, obviously cut out from the complete photograph, placed in a Photograph Album which Maria Vernon Graham Havergal gave to the Church Missionary Society in 1886. Maria wrote "1869" next to the photograph, with flowers and leaves placed on the page around the photograph of W.H.H., and to the right of him was placed the quotation from Isaiah 52:7, "How beautiful upon the mountains are the feet of him that bringeth good tidings, that publisheth peace." See also page 291 for another part of this same page in Maria's Photograph Album.

This is the single-verse poem in the manuscript on the previous page:

Tis fully known to One, by us yet dimly seen,
  The blessing thou hast been,
Yet speaks the silent love of many a mourning
  The blessing that thou art; [heart,
While traced on coming years in faith & hope we
  A blessing thou shalt be; [see,
Then here in holy labour, there in holier rest,
  Blessing, thou shalt be blest.
For Papa's birthday
Jan 18. /59

FURTHER COMMENTS AND DETAILS CONCERNING WILLIAM HENRY HAVERGAL

This ends the final volume of published sermons by William Henry Havergal. He very likely was ready to publish many more if an opportunity were given, but among his extant works these are exceptional in the fulness of presentation. He almost certainly preached well more than 2,000 sermons over more than five decades: a true labor of love, a heart work, sermons taught to him by God, diligently prepared, preached to parish congregations and other audiences.

Writing about William Henry Havergal's practice of preparation to preach his sermons, his daughter Maria V. G. Havergal wrote these comments at the bottom of an announcement sheet of Two Sermons on behalf of the Church Missionary Society on Sunday, October 21, 1860 in the Parish Church of Shareshill:

> One Sermon always written by Wednesday p.m. – the 2nd by Saturday before breakfast. ! (No "hours of darkness" work! N.B. It was my father's rule to carefully look over all the Scripture, for each Sunday's service, & select his text from these. (Exceptions – also). He generally did so after each Sunday's work over. So getting a clean week to meditate on his texts ! !

Remember that he was a true Anglican, and thus would have been mindful of the Scripture lessons to be read in church each Sunday morning and evening through the calendar year.

In the biography *Records of the Life of the Rev. William Henry Havergal, M.A.* by his daughter Jane Miriam Havergal Crane (London: Home Words Publishing Office, 1882, original book page 29, page 370 of this book), this quotation is given from a letter dated October 23, 1821, early in his ministry:

> My parish has called me out a good deal, while my indoor hours have been fully occupied in attending to my pupil and in preparing sermons. In this latter employment my thoughts have little rest. I am an *anxious* sermon writer. Few things are more painful to me than to be obliged to preach a sermon I have used before, and it is so for two reasons: first, every old sermon skeleton rather pains me by its defects; and secondly, I love to preach that which I have felt and desire, and desire to feel that which I preach, and these things are only effected when the heart and the head and the hand have been engaged in the work of preparation.

In the same biography (*Records*, original book page 330, page 439 of this book), Miriam wrote this of him near the end of his ministry:

> My father was again alarmingly ill early in January, 1869, and expressed himself as distressed at not being able to preach at Christ Church for Dr. Bickmore, as arranged for the very day after his illness began. He frequently preached for his friends in Leamington when at all able to do so, especially at Milverton and Holy Trinity, in which district he resided. He used in his study a folio Bible on a lecturn, and having looked out his text would ruminate on it for a day or two, and then write down the heads of the subject; but in the pulpit delivering the sermon without notes, and enlarging upon it extemporaneously.

One very important part of William Henry Havergal's work was his strong effort over decades to present to many the work and the need of the Church Missionary Society and to raise awareness and support—money and prayer—for the missionaries bringing the good news of Christ to foreign lands. His daughter Maria, in 1886 before she died in 1887, gave to the Church Missionary Society an invaluable collection of manuscripts and other items by F.R.H. and W.H.H. (now kept in the C.M.S. Archives at the University of Birmingham in England). Among these items was a travelling case with this label handwritten by Maria: "Rev[d] W. H. Havergal's travelling case for C.M.S. in 1824–1828. Many C.M.S. papers & outlines of his speeches were kept in this till his rest from labours. April 19, 1870 Bequeathed to the C.M.S. M.V.G.H. 1886." This case contains handwritten notes, letters, and other manuscripts and items. There was also a bound volume (of pages originally blank, like a bound diary) of W.H.H.'s handwritten notes for sermons, and Maria wrote this on a label on the front cover: “One of my beloved father’s (Rev[d] W. H. Havergal’s) Sermon cases, about 1817. Outlines of his C.M.S. sermons herein, bequeathed to that Society. My father extemporized his carefully prepared thoughts. Bequeathed to the C.M.S. 1886. M.V.G.H.” Maria also bequeathed to the C.M.S. another bound volume with this label handwritten by her on the front cover: “Rev. W. H. Havergal’s life prints. ‘A faithful minister in the Lord.’ — The Record of texts & sermons – from March 31.1816. to Janry 3.1869. Sermons from June 5. to Sept 12.1869. not entered’. The last text “The Lord Jesus Christ be with thy spirit.” Preached at Pyrmont – Waldeck Sep 1.1869 Bequeathed to the C.M.S. 1886. (M.V.G.H.” This is a golden volume of W.H.H.’s handwritten record of sermons he preached: the first sermon recorded was dated March 31, 1816, preached at Durston on Acts 4:12, and the last sermon recorded was dated January 3, 1869, preached at Milverton in Leamington on Deuteronomy 33:16. This volume in his handwriting is a record of 160 pages of sermons he preached, recording the place, date, and Scripture text for each sermon. At the end, one of his children wrote this entry:

> My father’s last Sermon was preached at Pyrmont Waldeck [in Germany] (C.C.C.S.) Sept 12 1869. text “The Lord Jesus Christ be with thy spirit.” 2 Timothy IV.22.

All these items were copied in the research on the Havergal edition, but now after years of effort, the lack of time, means, and energy preclude for now the transcription and publication of the true gold in these manuscripts of W.H.H.

The bound volume of his handwritten record of his sermons (bequeathed by Maria V. G. Havergal to the Church Missionary Society) had another part: the record of the sermons did not take nearly all of the pages of the volume, and W.H.H. turned over the volume and wrote from the back side forward (inversely from the front, effectively making two books of the single bound volume) 19 pages of handwritten notes on a book entitled *The Art of Logic. on Simple Terms.* This was apparently his notes and reacting comments to John Milton’s Latin treatise *Artis Logicae* published in 1672. W.H.H. was a breathtakingly brilliant man, and a true scholar with wide interests. This and indeed all of these comments are only a glimpse of him, his life and work.

Among the Havergal manuscripts and papers was found a copy of *The Work of Jesus Christ, as an Advocate, Clearly Explain’d, and Largely Improv’d, for the Benefit of All Believers. From I John ii.1.* by John Bunyan, this copy printed in London for John Marshall, 1725. In the front of the book this is signed: W. H. Havergal. S[t] Nicholas, Worcester 1847. Below his signature, his widow Caroline Ann Havergal wrote “Last book finished by my blessed husband 1870.” See page 476 of this book.

Please see also the Preface on W.H.H. on pages vi–ix of this book.

William Henry Havergal was a finely gifted poet, and many of his poems are very edifying, truly glorifying God and enriching His people.

Like his daughter Frances Ridley Havergal, W.H.H. was a musician to the core, a rarely and finely gifted one. He was offered a professorship in music at Oxford University, a very high honor in that day, but he declined that and a career in music to be a pastor. Few could so well compose music, yet he preferred to write a sermon than to compose a score. Though music was so very important to him, and he used music to enrich his ministry and benefit his hearers, yet music was a secondary pursuit to him, an enjoyment and relaxation, unless his physical health precluded pastoral work. He was the foremost church musician of his day in England, and was very highly regarded by knowledgeable people for his compositions and his knowledge of music. He led the reform of church music, and few today realize the value of his efforts and publications to improve the practice of music in church worship. A generous sample of his published scores has been published in Volume V of the Havergal edition (*Songs of Truth and Love: Music by Frances Ridley Havergal and William Henry Havergal*). He was a remarkably, finely gifted singer, organist and pianist, a valuable composer, and a true scholar of music.

There is an abundance of rich treasure of W.H.H. in the Havergal edition: the definitive, valuable biography *Records of the Life of the Rev. William Henry Havergal, M.A.* by his eldest child Jane Miriam Crane, other accounts of his life and work by ones who knew him, and the Sermons—true gold—are given in Volume IV; a very generous number of his poems are given in Volume I; his account *A Wise and Holy Child* is given in Volume III; and several of his published music scores (as well as his edition of Thomas Ravenscroft’s Psalter and W.H.H.’s musicological treatise *A History of the Old Hundredth Psalm Tune*) are given in Volume V.

This edition has not been an exhaustive pursuit to find everything extant by W.H.H. (There has been a strong desire and earnest, diligent effort to find everything extant by F.R.H.) Other music scores by W.H.H. remain extant today that have not been copied in this research nor printed in this edition, and several handwritten manuscripts (of Sermons, etc.) of W.H.H.

that have been found and copied in this research have not been transcribed and published in this edition. The reason for this is not a lack of desire, but a lack of time, means, and energy: after years of earnest, diligent effort, I am severely depleted, and the complete or perfect should not be the enemy of the good and the needful.

Much more can be said of W.H.H., a genuine disciple of the Lord Jesus Christ.

He was a man truly blessed by God and used by Him to bless many others. Similarly to Robert Murray M'Cheyne, J. C. Ryle, Horatius Bonar, Alexander Bonar, and other godly ministers of his time more widely known today, W.H.H. is a vast, rich gold-mine full of true treasure from the Lord. Thanks be to God. David Chalkley

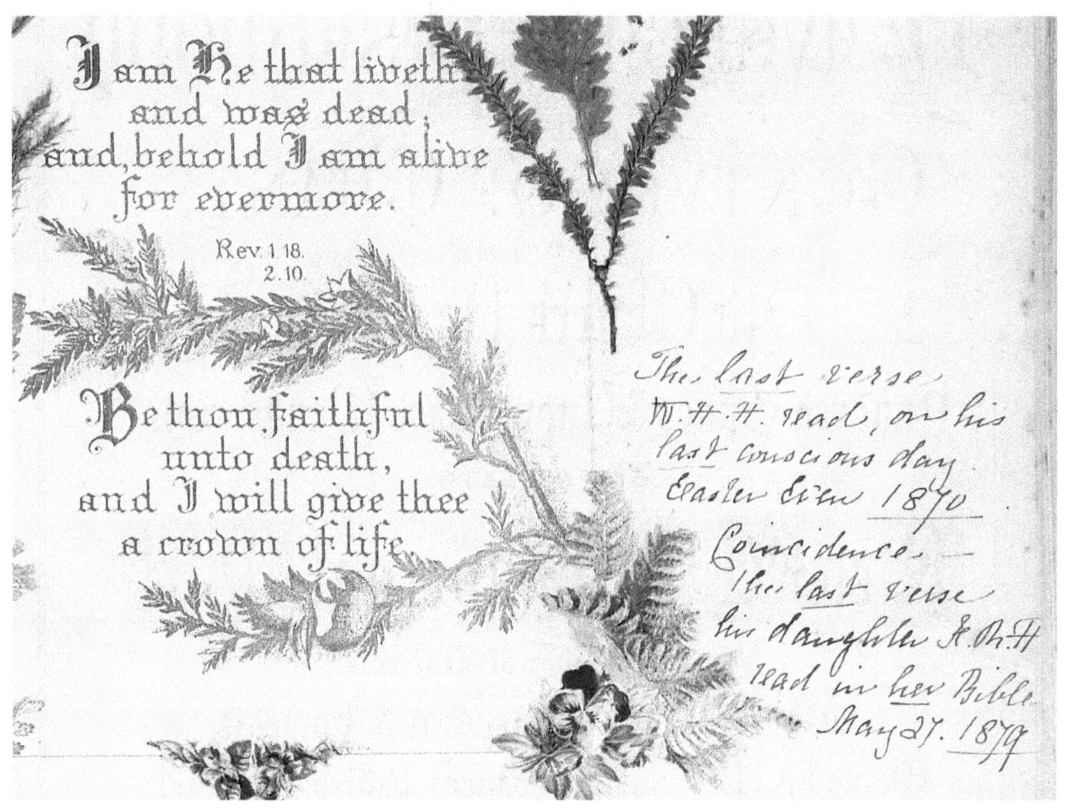

In 1886 Maria Vernon Graham Havergal donated to the Church Missionary Society very important items of William Henry Havergal and Frances Ridley Havergal. One of these was a "Photographs" album, of which one page had portraits of William Henry Havergal with glued-on flowers and hand-written details done with obvious love. This photograph of W.H.H. was taken in 1869, and is copied on page 288. Beside a printed card of Revelation 1:18 and 2:10, Maria wrote this note:

The last verse
W.H.H. read, on his
last conscious day.
Easter Even 1870.
Coincidence —
the last verse
his daughter F.R.H
read in her Bible
May 27. 1879

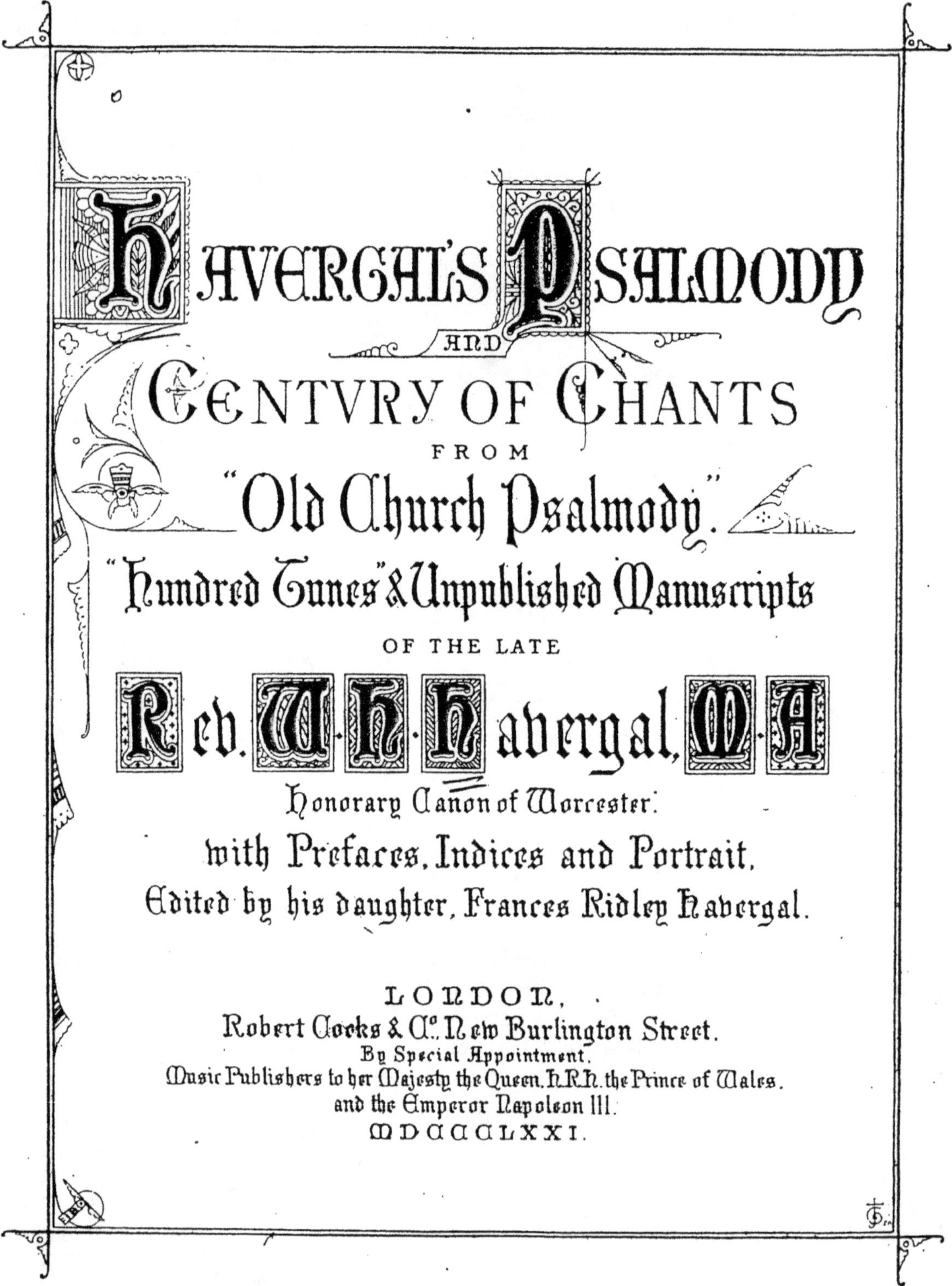

HAVERGAL'S PSALMODY
AND
CENTURY OF CHANTS
FROM
"Old Church Psalmody."
"Hundred Tunes" & Unpublished Manuscripts
OF THE LATE
Rev. W. H. Havergal, M.A.
Honorary Canon of Worcester.
with Prefaces, Indices and Portrait.
Edited by his daughter, Frances Ridley Havergal.

LONDON,
Robert Cocks & Co. New Burlington Street.
By Special Appointment.
Music Publishers to her Majesty the Queen, H.R.H. the Prince of Wales.
and the Emperor Napoleon III.
MDCCCLXXI.

William Henry Havergal was the foremost church musician and composer of sacred music in England in his generation. (Dr. William Crotch was the generation before W.H.H., and William Sterndale Bennett was not primarily a church musician.) Called to be a pastor, he declined a career in music and used music as a benefit to his church ministry, and for rest and pleasure. He would rather write a sermon than compose a score, though few had his ability and love to write and perform music at that level. He was a true scholar both in the Bible, theology, and music, and his ministry to others was a true example of Matthew 22:37–40. When his physical health removed him from pastoral work, he concentrated more on composition of music. See Volume V of the Havergal edition, Songs of Truth and Love: Music by Frances Ridley Havergal and William Henry Havergal, *which has all of* Havergal's Psalmody and Century of Chants *and several other scores by W.H.H..*

A WISE AND HOLY CHILD.

AN ACCOUNT OF

ELIZABETH EDWARDS,

BEING AN ENLARGEMENT OF

AN ADDRESS

TO THE CHILDREN AND TEACHERS OF THE SAINT NICHOLAS SUNDAY SCHOOL, WORCESTER,

ON THE AFTERNOON OF SUNDAY, 11TH MARCH, 1849;

BY THE REV. W. H. HAVERGAL, M. A.,

RECTOR OF THAT PARISH AND HONORARY CANON OF THE CATHEDRAL, IN THAT CITY.

LONDON:
J. GROOM, BAZAAR, SOHO SQUARE;
AND 185, BROAD STREET, BIRMINGHAM.

A WISE AND HOLY CHILD.

My Dear Children,

The great object of your Sunday School is, not merely for us to bring you together, and to teach you to read, and to take you to Church, but to impart to you such a knowledge of divine things as will, by God's grace, lead you to everlasting salvation. That object has, I fully believe, been answered among you in, at least, one instance: and, God grant that it may be answered in many more! Most of you know that a little girl of our School departed this life, on Thursday last; and that, because it is necessary to bury her speedily, she will be carried to her grave this afternoon. Other children of our School have died, and been carried to their graves; but never did I know such a child as Elizabeth Edwards. Though so young, for she was only eleven years old, yet was she so thoughtful, so prayerful, so holy, and so heavenly, that I cannot wonder at her being taken to the bosom of her Saviour. Hence, dear children, though, Sunday after Sunday, I address you, yet, on no Sunday have I had to say to you such things as I am about to say.

Little Elizabeth was admitted to our School, on Sunday, January 18, 1846. She was then about eight years old. It is recollected, as well as noted down, that she was a remarkably attentive and orderly child: but no signs of better things discovered themselves, till some months after; when, blessed be God, in this very room, her little heart was touched by his grace, and she became conscious of a stirring change. You shall hear, in her own words, the account of what took place. "One Sunday (she has often said) when Mr. H. could not come to close the School, Mrs. H. read to us the hymn which begins with these lines,

'Why should I say, 'tis yet too soon
To seek for heaven, or think of death?'

She spoke to us about death, and about delaying to think of it. And then, at the close of School, we sung the hymn, and she prayed with us too. It all struck me so, that somehow I could not forget it. It seemed to lodge in me: and I began to think much of death, and heaven, and of Jesus as the only way to it."

Now, many of you, my dear children, sang this hymn with her, and heard all that passed about it. But, did you, like her, *attend* to it, and did holy and anxious thoughts arise in your minds from it? Remember, you must give account of *all* you hear; and that the same Holy Spirit who blessed her hearing, can bless yours, and *will* bless it, if you pray earnestly for his blessing.

Though, as I told you, Elizabeth was always a good sort of child, yet, after that Sunday, she became a still better child; because, whatever grace had been given to her before, it was then for the first time, consciously at least to herself, stirred up within her. The change showed itself in many ways; but, as her sorrowing mother says, especially in these ways:—She began to speak openly of good things; and to set her face against all ill things. She became very exact and careful in preparing her lessons for her daily School, and to take real delight in learning all that was required of her at her Sunday School. No solicitations to play, or any thing else, could induce her to *put off* attention to these things. Though fond of reading her Bible and good little books, and always glad for her morning and evening prayer-time to come, yet Sunday was her great joy. She was eager, on its morning, to set out for School, and earnest in encouraging others to be in time. On her return, in the afternoon, she would regularly sit down by her mother's chair, and tell her all that she had been taught at School, what was read, and what was said, and what was sung, and what she *enjoyed.*

And here, dear children, let me remind you how much good you may gain for yourselves, and give to others, by doing as Elizabeth did. If, when you return from School, instead of sauntering about, or playing with thoughtless children, you were to tell your parents or relatives at home, such things as she used to tell, how much better and pleasanter would it be! Or, you might go into some neighbour's house, and tell the like to an aged or ailing acquaintance, and thus contribute to their good, by calling to their recollection what they had once learned, or by repeating something which they ought to know, and which may benefit them for ever. Years ago, I knew a little girl in Somersetshire, who used to do thus every Sunday, to the great profit of an aged and bed-ridden grandfather.

Two other things of Elizabeth, which her affectionate mother has told me, as the effects of the memorable Sunday, I must also tell you. At Church, she used, by permission, to sit with her mother; which is always desirable when practicable. During the prayers, the dear child behaved as a praying child is sure to behave: but, during the sermon, she used to place her hand in her mother's hand; and, at every sentence which struck her or pleased her, she would squeeze it affectionately, and sometimes look at her "angelically," for she was a sweet-eyed child, and the grace of Jesus always makes beauty more beautiful.

Do, dear children, mind your own behaviour at Church. Go to it as indeed the House of God; and, then, you will find it, as your school-fellow did, "the very gate of heaven."

The other thing which I must tell you of her is this:—Before she came to our School, a near relative had been accustomed, as a kindly sort of treat, to take her, with another or two, to some part of the races in Pitchcroft. But, the next time of their occurrence, after the Sunday mentioned, when the same treat was proposed to her, she resolutely declined it; and begged that it might be exchanged for a pleasant country-walk. So earnest was she, that she obtained her wish, enjoyed her walk, and came home delighted to tell her mother, that she had been where nothing vain or wicked was to be met with. Oh that you, dear children, would do likewise; and have the resolution, as I have often entreated and charged you, to stay away from those scenes of folly and sin, which prove the injury or ruin of thousands! Recollect, it is no *excuse* for you, though older persons, may offer to take you with them to such places. You are told better, and will be judged of God by what you are faithfully told.

All the things which, as you hear, manifested themselves in your little schoolfellow, were God's preparation of her, for what she has now triumphantly passed through.

Last July she was taken ill with typhus fever, together with a brother and a sister considerably older than herself, and one sister who was younger. I can hardly describe to you what a scene of affliction her home presented, when all four were laid low at once, and all so ill as to be in the greatest danger. But, do not forget that such a scene, and even worse, may come to the home of any one of you, at any time. If it should, what do you think you should do? Are you prepared for Death to stand at your bed-side, and to threaten every hour to carry you into eternity? If not, you are neither safe nor happy.

In the midst of this strange and deep affliction, Elizabeth, though a great sufferer, was a solace and pattern to all around her. She used to comfort her wearied mother; and call out to her little sister to think of Jesus, and to pray earnestly to Him. Her own prayers were often over-heard, and they were always those of a gracious child, fervent in spirit, and loving the Lord. Frequently have I gone to the room where, with her younger sister, she was lying, helpless and distressed: but I was sure to find her calm, peaceful, and thankful; more like a little patient, unbleating lamb, than any thing else to which I could compare her. She always greeted me with a bright look and a cheerful smile. Though at times she was not able to say much to me, yet what she did say was always that which I was glad to hear her say. I will tell you the sum of it in few words: "Yes, (she used to say,) I *am* a sinner. I *know* it. But Jesus is good to me. He enables me to trust Him for every thing. I do hope my sins are forgiven. Oh yes, I cannot doubt it, only *sometimes* when I seem as if I couldn't help it. I have no desire to live, no, not at all: nor can I say that I fear to die, I *long* to be with Jesus in heaven."

One day, your kind Curate said to her, Would you rather die, Elizabeth, or live? "*Die!*" she replied instantly and firmly. Well, said he, and leave father and mother, sister and brother, and all your dear ones? "Jesus, (she answered) is more and better than all." And, why do you think you *shall* go to Him? "Because I love Him!" was her ready and scriptural reason.

So ill was she that no one thought she *could* live. Indeed, more than once, I took leave of her, under the full impression that I should never see her again alive. It pleased God, however, to hold her back from the grave, and to take her brother James. He was a good lad, and, like her, had been seeking the Lord before illness came. He, too, loved his Church, and never willingly missed it. What he heard at it was blessed to him; and he used to talk much about it, with all at home who would join him. He died full of humble confidence in the one only Saviour. I was with him just before his departure, and can testify that he "witnessed a good confession."

This event was very affecting to poor Elizabeth; but she knew how to rejoice in the sure hope of her brother's blessedness. She wept but, as she said to me, "It is only, Sir, because I *cannot* help it. I am not really grieved, but rather rejoice to think that dear James is now with the Lord Jesus." At first, however, she did not shed a single tear; because, as she was heard to say, she hoped, before another week, to be with him in heaven.

Here, dear children, I will introduce and commend to your attention some notes of conversations with her, by a teacher who was accustomed to visit her. But, do not suppose that she was a *talkative* child. Far otherwise. She was very retiring; and would talk freely only to those whom she knew intimately.

September 5. "Tell me, Elizabeth, how you are." Eliz. "I am very weak, Miss, but very happy." Teacher. "And what makes you happy, dear child." E. "Jesus Christ makes me happy. My sins are forgiven by Him. Jesus came into the world to save sinners. He can save any body; and He *has* saved *me.*" T. "Then, Elizabeth, you are not afraid to die?" E. "Oh no. I have no fear. I think He will take me up to heaven very soon." T. "But, if you should get well, Lizzie, what then?" E. "Then I must live to the glory of God. I must not forget the peace He gives me now; or, perhaps, He will send me some more affliction by and by."

Sept. 7. T. "Are you strong enough to read, dear Lizzie?" E. "No, Miss; but mother reads a Psalm very often, and that's so beautiful. While I could read, my Bible was all my comfort. I have read some little books, too, about children who went to heaven. There's Jane, the Little Cottager,—such a pretty book! But the Bible is the *best* book. When I can't read, then I pray and am so happy." T. "Tell me, Lizzie, some of your happy thoughts when you have been praying." E. "I feel Jesus the Lord is *within* me. He's *fixed* to me; and I think I shall go to Him. Mother must not grieve for me. I hope she will have strength to bear all her troubles. She must look to the Lord to support her under them. Ah! I know what trouble and sorrow she has with ——. He has been naughty and wicked, but we must pray for the wicked. He does not know how I pray for him; but the Lord does, and perhaps He will answer my prayers for him when I am gone."

Sept. 9. In answer to a remark, the dear child, in a very sweet manner, said, "Ah! there is *such* comfort in Jesus. We may *all* find peace in Him."

Sept. 15. Again the dear child greeted me, with these words, "Ah! dear Miss, I am still very ill, but still *very* happy." T. "Tell me, dear child, what you have been thinking about to make you happy." E. "Why, Miss, though my poor head has been, as mother says, a little wandering, yet it seemed as though many angels were all around my bed, and Jesus standing at the bottom. There's a crown of glory waiting for me. We should *always* be thinking of heaven. It is so beautiful to know that we shall go there." T. "And, what do you think you will do in heaven?" E. "I shall sing praises to God, and learn the new song which no one on earth knows. If I get well, I must not put Jesus from me. If I forsake Him, He will send me more affliction; and perhaps He won't send me the comfort He does now."

Sept. 17. Again the dear little girl greeted me, in her usual animated way. After my speaking to her of the love of the Lord Jesus, she said, "Oh yes, it is so nice to love *Him.* I *do* love Him, and He loves me. I have done nothing to deserve His love. He helped me to call upon Him, and it is He who has put all my love for Him into my heart."

She then spoke of her brother James, "Ah, my dear brother is now in heaven. He is happy,—singing praises." T. "Yes, Elizabeth, and *my* dear mamma is there too. Do you remember her?" E. "Oh yes, Miss: I shall never forget her closing the School, on *that* Sunday, when Mr. H. was out. It is some time ago; but it's all as fresh as yesterday." We then talked of her much-loved Sunday School; and she said, "I am afraid there are some naughty girls in the School, and in my class too. They don't care about their souls. They waste their time in the streets. They will be going to the fair next week, when it is so noisy, and there's so much cursing and swearing, and foolish talking. I would rather be lying here in affliction, than going to any pleasure or merry-making. It's only for a season. I wish my school-fellows would mind what they are taught, and pray to believe in Jesus: then, when they come to a bed of sickness like mine, their hymns and texts will comfort them more than any thing."

One day before, I had repeated to her the hymn,

"How sweet the name of Jesus sounds
In a believer's ear!"

when I finished the last two lines,—

"And may the music of thy name
Refresh my soul in death!"

she repeated them several times.

Looking upwards she said, "Yes, *Jesus* is *sweeter* than *music.* I love music; but music soon leaves off, and goes away; but Jesus never goes away from us. He will never leave *me.* Music soon tires one; but we can't get tired of *Him.* Oh, no, I never shall be tired of Jesus my Saviour. It is so beautiful to think of Him, and to know that I am going to Him."

Sept. 23. At first, the dear child seemed too weak to talk; but, the mention of *heaven* aroused her to speak of it. "'Tis so beautiful (she said) to *think* of heaven, and to know that I shall go to it. Jesus loves me and I love Him. I am sure He loves me; so I *can't* be afraid to die. But oh, I am *so* unworthy of Him! Tomorrow is Sunday. I cannot go to Church, but Jesus will be near. In heaven, they are always singing praises to God. Sundays have *no end there.*"

Another kind teacher, in whose class she had last been, reports of her thus: "The dear child always received me with a sweet smile, generally saying, 'I am so happy in Jesus.' One day on asking her why she loved the Lord Jesus, she replied, 'Because He first loved me.' 'But is that the only reason?' 'Oh no, Jesus suffered and died, that I might live for ever with Him.' Her afflicted mother told me much concerning her child's love for Christ, and how she talked of the Sunday School, her teacher, and fellow scholars, and how she used to pray that they may become good and holy children. 'It is not enough,' she would say, 'for scholars to read and repeat Holy Scripture, they should *hide* it in their hearts, and that will serve them when they cannot read it with their eyes.'"

Another devoted teacher, who, as opportunity offered, went to see her, asked her, "What is it that makes you so happy?" "Nothing but Jesus," she replied. "I suffer a great deal of pain; but He helps me to bear it. He suffered much more for me."

At another time, on asking her how she was, she replied, "Very weak, thank you: but,

'When I am weak, then am I strong;
Grace is my shield, and Christ my song!'"

On Monday, the 25th September, a messenger came to let us know that there was a great change for the worse, as *we* say, in little Elizabeth. Hastening to her bedside, I found her apparently dying. Without my asking any question, the dear child said, "I am going very soon now. I am going to see Jesus face to face. I shall soon be there. There's a crown of glory prepared for me. I want, oh I want to go! Jesus died for me. He died for all who come to Him. Mother mus'n't cry: she will come to me there, and my brother will be there too."

Then, adding, "I *am* happy! happy! *happy!*" she sunk into a gentle doze. Soon waking up, she exclaimed, with a joyful voice, "The Lord Jesus is coming for me very quickly!" Her elder sister said, "Lizzie, why do you think you are going to die *now?*" She replied, "Somehow, Jesus tells me so. Ah, I long to see Him!"

But, whatever were the manifestations of Christ to the spirit of this singularly wise and holy child, when she thought her end was approaching, her Lord did not come for her just then. It was his will to stay the wheels of his chariot; and to appoint for her a further course, very different to what we had expected.

Contrary to even medical opinion, the little sufferer revived; and, like an apparently withered flower which shoots up afresh, she so far rallied as to give hope of her ultimate recovery. But the hopeful appearances soon vanished; and the termporary smile of the sweet flower only proved the near approach of fatal decay.

Other maladies succeeded the cessation of the original disease; and Elizabeth again became a sufferer, but of a far more agonizing character than before. Absence from home, and then indisposition, prevented my seeing her during the interval of her improvement, as I otherwise should; but, I constantly heard of her, to the same effect as what you now have been hearing. Soon after Christmas, all her symptoms were fearfully aggravated. Frequent sickness, incessant cough, and expectorations of blood, quickly brought her to the nearest edge of the grave. At times, and for hours together, her pangs were dreadful, and her writhings under them were distressing to witness. Still there was not a murmur on her lip; nor the trace of any thing contrary to "the meekness and gentleness of Christ." She could seldom say much; but, the little which she did say showed that the work of grace was deepened and ripened in her soul.

The last week of her life was one of bitter anguish. But, on Wednesday evening last, the evening before her death, she was easier for awhile, and seemed delighted with an opportunity for breathing out her whole heart's love for the Lord Jesus, and the things of heaven. She repeated, with singular energy and correctness, several passages of Holy Scripture, hymns, and other sacred poetry. Among them, she recited the whole of the twenty-third Psalm, repeating and dwelling on the last words, *"for ever! for ever!"* She also went through, as accurately as if she were reading it, a long and deeply experimental piece of poetry, called "The Sinner's Refuge." You shall hear two stanzas of it:

"When up he lifts his downcast eyes,
O'erwhelmed with shame and grief;
And seeks, with bitter tears and sighs,
For pardon and relief;
Whither shall he for comfort flee,
Redeemer, Jesus, but to Thee?

"To ease his pains and soothe his woe,
To smooth the rugged way;
To raise him from the scenes below,
To realms of endless day;
To whom shall he for succour flee,
Redeemer, Jesus, but to Thee?"

On this stanza she lingered with much feeling. "Ease his *pains,*" and "*endless day,*" passed her lips as though they would not leave them. She began, however, another favourite piece; "The Dying Child's Farewell," the burthen of which is,

"Weep not for me, mother,
I go to the home of the blest:"

but, her temporary strength was gone, and the sands of her glass began rapidly to run down. The night was one of unmitigated bodily torture; and the spirit was too heavily fettered to expand its wings.

In the morning, that is of Thursday last, her sleepless mother, hardly knowing what to do for her, brought her, babylike, downstairs, and laid her in her lap by the fire. In this position I found her about eleven o'clock. The kind teacher, of whom I told you first, was standing by, and had heard her say, "Peace, peace!" A glance was sufficient to tell me that the little lamb was actually dying. So we knelt *at once;* and, in the beautiful words of our Church, as far as my memory served, I offered up our last prayer for her. On rising, I despatched the teacher to bid a friendly neighbour lend the tried mother the requisite help. Meanwhile, the mother began to express to me her fears, lest, at the time of departure, her beloved one should be called through struggle and agony. While these fears were finding themselves words, I saw the little saint suddenly and gently breathe her last breath. A slight gurgling of the throat showed me that her spirit had then mounted to the bosom of her God. I gazed, for a quiet second or two, on the enviable sight,—*a sainted child going to heaven from her mother's lap!* While her mother was still speaking, I staid her with my hand, and said, "Indulge not another fear. There will be *no* struggle. Do not be alarmed. Your Lizzie *is* in heaven!" The mother looked, and it was so. But I cannot tell you the rest, only, *all was well.*

And now, my dear children, let these things sink into your inmost souls. Follow your departed school-fellow in her "faith and patience," in her spirit of prayer, in her deep humility, and, above all, in her love for Christ. You *know* what a good and holy child she was. Yourselves observed her. She always set you an example; and you could not but acknowledge it. Her mother says of her that she was always *so good* a child, such a wise, and sweet, and holy *companion*, that she has no recollection of *ever* having had occasion to reprove her. What an honour! And yet how differently did the little humble one think of herself! "I *am* a sinner. Yes, I *know* it!" Yes, yes, dear children, the best people are always the first to feel their sinfulness. Then, follow your little friend, as she followed Jesus, "the Friend of sinners." Do not let your tears end in nothing. Death in your School, recollect, is a solemn visitation. There *will* be *some one's* turn *next!* And, *whose* will it be? Let each, *each* heart put the question to itself. Then, also, ponder the hymn which you have just been singing; and let it be Elizabeth's voice to you. It was made a blessing to her, and will be made a blessing to you, if you begin, from this hour,

"To seek for heaven, and think of death."

Finally, let our dear kind teachers join me in thanking God, and taking courage. *Some* good *has* been done in our School! One soul has been saved within these walls! Words, as simple as any which you ever speak have gone to the heart of a child; and that child now "in joy and felicity" with her Saviour and our Saviour, with her God and our God. Then, look up, and be of good cheer. Such narratives as these may be counted "foolishness," and pronounced "extravagance," by a cold and perverse generation; but, with all their defects, they are "right precious" in the estimation of those who are "not of this world." Let me, therefore, bid you go forward. Continue in patience with the children of your charge, and in prayer for them too; "abounding in the same with thanksgiving." Yes, "continue in *prayer!*" Consider me as laying especial stress on this duty. You will be sure to succeed, if you do but make sure to *pray.* Tell your children that you indeed pray for them; and encourage them to pray for themselves. In doing this, never forget that there is but *one* true religion for you and for the children. It is the same in kind for you both. It differs only in degree. Hence, it must have struck you, that the sayings of our little departed one are, in substance, the spiritual experience of an older believer. Let this thought be with you, in giving instruction. The manna, which you gather and eat yourselves, may be freely given to them. The seed, which grows in your own field, is to be sown in theirs. Be confident, also, that you *shall* reap in *due* time if you faint not. Persevere in well-doing, and the Lord will do well unto you. In watering others, Himself will water you: and, when He "shall appear the second time without sin unto salvation," you will find that He has not forgotten your reward. Amen and Amen!

Hymn.

"He shall gather the lambs with his arm, and carry them in his bosom."—Isaiah 40:11.

To praise our Shepherd's care,
His wisdom, love, and might;
Your loudest, loftiest, songs prepare,
And bid the world unite!

Supremely good and great,
He tends his blood-bought fold:
He stoops, though throned in highest state,
The feeblest to uphold.

He hears their softest plaint;
He sees them when they roam:
And, if his meanest lamb should faint,
His bosom bears it home.

Kind Shepherd of the sheep!
A weakly flock are we;
And snares and foes are nigh; but keep
The lambs who look to Thee.

And if, through death's dark vale,
Our feet should early tread;
Oh may we reach thy fold, and hail
The love which us has led!

In her biography *Records of the Life of the Rev. William Henry Havergal, M.A.*, Jane Miriam Crane quoted this hymn that he wrote for the wedding of his daughter Ellen Prestage Havergal to Giles Shaw:[1]

> My father composed a hymn to be sung when the guests were in their places at the wedding breakfast, and as such a musical grace was a novelty, a copy is given.

NUPTIAL GRACE.

For G.S. and E.P.H.

February 5, 1856.

"*Holy Matrimony — instituted of God in the time of man's innocency, signifying unto us the mystical union that is betwixt Christ and his Church; which holy estate Christ adorned and beautified with his presence, and first miracle that He wrought, in Cana of Galilee.*"

O Thou, whose presence beautified
Poor Cana 's nuptial board,
By Thee let ours be sanctified,
And Thou shalt be adored.

Thyself to us, ourselves to Thee
In mystic union join;
And grant us greater things to see
Than water turned to wine.

Thy glory show, our faith make strong,
Like rivers be our peace:
And seat us where Thy Marriage Song
Shall never, *never* cease!

To Him who wove the marriage tie,
In Eden's thornless bower,
To Him, the Christ of God Most High,
Be glory, praise, and power!

This grace was sung to a tune then called St. Nicholas, but named Eden in Havergal's Psalmody, No. 38. [This was also the music score for Hymn No. 68 in *Songs of Grace and Glory*.]

[1] *Records of the Life of the Rev. William Henry Havergal, M.A.* by his daughter Jane Miriam Crane (London: Home Words Publishing Office, 1882), original book pages 211–213, pages 635–636 of Volume IV of the Havergal edition. The quotation before the hymn is taken from the Book of Common Prayer. The hymntune " Eden " in *Havergal's Psalmody and Century of Chants* is found on page 188 of Volume V, and also in Hymn No. 68 in *Songs of Grace and Glory* on page 584 of Volume V.

Poems and Hymns by William Henry Havergal

This section of poems William Henry Havergal does not include the 27 that are given in his daughter Miriam's essay "Hymns by the Rev. W. H. Havergal, M.A." on pages 392–402 of this volume, a set of such valuable hymns, heartily recommended to the reader. These poems in this section were found in these sources: *Red Letter Days* by Frances Ridley Havergal (London: Marcus Ward & Co., 1879); *Life Echoes* by F.R.H. (London: James Nisbet & Co., 1883); a few from the biography *Records of the Life of the Rev. William Henry Havergal, M.A.* by Jane Miriam (Havergal) Crane (London: Home Words Publishing Office, 1882). *Life Echoes*, a posthumous volume of poems by F.R.H., also had several poems by W.H.H., clearly indicated with his initials printed at the end of the poems by him. At the end of this set, there are 13 hymns found in printed announcement sheets of sermons concerning foreign missions, apparently never published before the Havergal edition; the next-to-last poem was found on a printed leaflet; and the last poem given in this section was found on a handwritten manuscript.

Easter Hymn.

All hail, Thou Resurrection!
All hail, Thou Life and Light!
All hail, Thou Self-Perfection,
Sole source of grace and might!
Thy Church, O Christ, now greets Thee,
Uprising from the grave,
And every eye that meets Thee
Beholds Thee strong to save.

All hail, belovèd Jesus!
For Thou indeed art He
Whose death from sin now frees us,
Whose life brings liberty.
Hence let our faith embrace Thee
With warmest hand and eye,
And then delight to trace Thee
Ascending up on high.

O Saviour, come in glory
To raise Thy holy dead,
And end redemption's story,
With crowns upon Thy head.
Then robed in white before Thee,
Without one stain or tear,
Shall all Thy saints adore Thee,
'Midst wonder, love, and fear.

Missionary Hymn.

Remember, Lord, Thy word of old,
The promised flood of grace;
When earth Thy blessing shall behold,
As streams in every place.

The barren wild and thirsty soil
Thy Spirit, Lord, await;
Oh, pour it forth, and crown our toil
In every heathen gate!

Where thorns and briers choke the ground,
And withering idols reign,
There let Thy Spirit's dew abound,
And Eden bloom again.

O Holy Ghost! on every heart,
In every land descend!
Thy fertilizing gifts impart,
And bring a glorious end.

Thee, with the Father and the Son,
Thy sainted hosts shall praise;
Those hosts by Thee in Christ made one,
For everlasting days.

Summer-tide.

Summer-tide is coming,
With all its pleasant things;
Every bee is humming,
And every songster sings.

Mornings now are brightsome,
Inviting student thought;
Evenings too are lightsome,
With balmy quiet fraught.

Hearths no longer lure us,
The fields instead we roam;
Hearts albeit insure us
A happy, happy home.

Summer-tide, I hail thee,
The empress of the year!
But thou soon would'st fail me,
Were not thy Maker near.

He thy course disposes,
Thy light, thy scent, thy glow;
He tints all thy roses,
And paints thy brilliant bow.

Laud Him, all creation,
The sinner's mighty Friend;
Near Him be our station,
Where summer ne'er shall end.

Gentle Dew.

"I will be as the dew unto Israel."—Hosea 14:5.

Softly the dew in the evening descends,
Cooling the sun-heated ground and the gale:
Flow'rets all fainting it soothingly tends,
Ere the consumings of mid-day prevail.
Sweet, gentle dewdrops, how mystic your fall;
Wisdom and mercy float down in you all.

Softer and sweeter by far is that Dew,
Which from the Fountain of comfort distils;
When the worn heart is created anew,
And hallowed pleasure its emptiness fills.
Lord, let Thy Spirit bedew my dry fleece;
Faith then shall triumph, and trouble shall cease.

And when at last we fall on sleep,
Nor heart shall throb, nor eye shall weep;
Then, blessèd Saviour, let it be,
That Thou shalt write, "They rest in Me!"

For ever and for ever, Lord.

"He shall reign for ever and ever."—Revelation 11:15.

For ever and for ever, Lord,
Thy kingdom shall endure;
Thy holy, lofty, sovereign word
Its glory doth secure.

Bring on, bring on the promised day,
Oh, speed its eagle wing,
When earth, like heaven, shall Thee obey,
And all the nations sing!

Grant us in firmest faith to stand,
Full certain of the end,
And with Thy valiant little band
Thine ancient truth defend.

O Jesu, be Thy cross our all,
Thy crown our highest meed,[1]
Nor saint nor angel will we call
To help in time of need.

Thy Spirit give, and we will then
Return Thee fervent praise;
And when Thou shalt come back again,
A nobler song we'll raise!

1866.

Invocation.

Holy and blessèd Redeemer, we pray Thee,
Succour and help us in all time of need:
Trusting in Thee and Thy promise, O may we
Always find solace and always succeed.
Speak what Thou wilt, we will ever obey Thee,
Honour and fear Thee in thought, word, and deed.

Thou art Almighty, All-wise, and All-gracious,
Make us all humble, devoted, and true;
Clad in Thine armour, no foe will dare face us,
Danger and trouble will cease to pursue.
Once let the soft arms of Mercy embrace us,
Peace shall pervade us like sweet falling dew.

Blessèd and holy Redeemer, we laud Thee,
Source of all succour, help, comfort, and joy:
While in yon heaven bright angels applaud Thee,
We with their echoes our tongues will employ.
None of Thy glory shall ever defraud Thee,
All, in its fulness, Thy saints shall enjoy.

This is another version by W.H.H. of "God Save the Queen."

God save our noble Queen!
Long live Old England's Queen;
God save the Queen!
Great and victorious,
Happy and glorious,
May she reign over us;
God save the Queen!

On her anointed head,
Blessings on blessings shed,
    Constant and rare:
Robe her with truth and might,
Health, peace, and holy light;
Save her from faction's blight,
    And withering care.

" Give peace in our time; "
Spare us from blood and crime;
    Up for us stand!
Nursed by our " Gracious Queen,"
May our Church e'er be seen
Waving like evergreen,
    Over the land.

God save our youthful Queen!
Long live Old England's Queen;
    God save the Queen!
Upward with joyous spring,
Let every heart take wing;
And the whole nation sing,
    God save the Queen!

A New National Hymn

Especially for March 10, 1863.

God save the Prince of Wales;
Bless Thou the bride he hales,
    Make them Thy care!
Where England's name prevails,
Where sweet homes scent her gales;
Where Ocean bears her sails;
    There be this prayer.

God of the bridal band,
Fast be each heart and hand
    Bound in Thine Own:
Cheer them in sorrow's hour,
Spare them if troubles lower,
Gird them with truth and power
    Sent from Thy throne!

Then, when long years have fled;
Still be Thy favours shed
    On them and theirs:
Where dwells not sin nor sigh,
Where weeps not widow's eye,
There with our Christ on high,
    Be they " joint heirs."

In *Records of the Life of the Rev. William Henry Havergal, M.A.*, this account is given (April 30, 1857): After seeing this verse pencilled on a train station wall,

> " Love not, love not—what you love will die;
> Love God—He will not die."

W.H.H. instantly said this:

> " Love not too well—the dearest one will die;
> Love Him who loves, and lives on high;
> And then you'll love eternally."

The following acrostic by W. H. H. was copied by Mrs. Clement in 1858 when she was 86 (copied by Mrs. Clement for W.H.H.'s second wife, Mrs. Caroline A. Havergal), written decades earlier by W.H.H. for Mrs. Clement's son when he was a little boy. This is found in *Records of the Life of the Rev. William Henry Havergal* by Jane Miriam (Havergal) Crane (London: Home Words Publishing Office, 1882), Chapter 10. See pages 642 and 644 of Volume IV of the Havergal edition.

D ear Jesus, teach a little child,
A nd kindly hear me when I pray;
V ouchsafe to me Thy mercy mild,
I nstruct me early in Thy way.
D raw, dearest Lord, my heart to Thee.

C leanse it from every youthful sin,
L et not the least impurity
E ntwine itself for ill within.
Make me as David was when young,
E nriched by grace, beloved by Heaven;
N or let my heart, or hand, or tongue,
T ransgress the precepts Thou hast given.

Double Acrostic.

" A wise son maketh a glad father, but a foolish son is the heaviness of his mother."—Proverbs 10:1

J ointly, age and youth,
H ear this standard truth!
S ons who fathers gladden
H onours shall receive;
A ll who mothers sadden
W ill be sure to grieve.

W isdom loves to favour
A ll who favour her;
H e who is the Saviour,
S hall grace for grace confer.
H im, the joy of all your days,
J oin to magnify and praise.

The Shortest Day.

Poem on the Birthday of Caroline Anne Havergal.

The shortest day in a foreign land
Would be one of lengthened sadness,
Were it not my spirit has at hand
A lamp of sunny gladness.
O Thou who, forty years ago,
Didst give that lamp its natal spark,

Calm the Scene—Carol.

Calm the scene—the winds scarce breathing,
Shepherds watch their flocks by night;
Angels glad their heaven at leaving,
Burst on earth in floods of light.
Bethlehem's plains now bright with glory,
See! the angel folds his wing;
Soon he tells the wond'rous story,
Christ is born, a Saviour—King!

Loudly sweet they hymn their chorus,
"Glory be to God on high,
Peace on earth, good will towards us"—
See! they soar beyond the sky.
Did these angels praise the Saviour,
Who a Saviour do not need?
Let us not be silent ever;
He for us was born indeed!

God Incarnate! Mighty Jesus!
Lord of all above—below!
Thee we bless, who cam'st to free us
From the chains of sin and woe.
Once a babe,—now King of Glory!
Thee no seraph's thought can scan;
But, dear Saviour, we adore Thee,
Son of God, and Son of Man.

Let Thy wond'rous Incarnation
Soon throughout the world be sung;
Let the praise of Thy salvation
Dwell on every heathen tongue.
Oh! remember Abraham's offspring,
Joyless scattered o'er the earth!
Saviour—God, we know rejoicing
They shall celebrate Thy birth!

"Christians, awake to joy and praise!"

Christians, awake to joy and praise!
Happy, happy, happy be our Christmas days.
God is the God of truth and love,
He has sent His only Son down from above.

Hark how the holy angels sing!
Blessing, blessing, blessing on the Infant King!
Let us repeat their noble song,
Cherubim and Seraphim the strain prolong.

Glory to God, our God on high!
Peace to them on earth who are condemned to die;
Good-will to all the tribes of men;
Glory, glory, glory, sing all Heaven! Amen.

O for that Vision!—Carol.

O for that vision! so fair yet so fearful,
O for that chorus! so sweet and so loud;
Shepherds, rejoice! no longer be tearful,
Sing like the angels in yonder bright cloud.
O for that sight! so startling, so cheerful,
O for the sound of that glorious crowd!

Then when we went as the angel had told us,
Lo! we beheld the Babe of the skies,
Shepherd of shepherds, He comes now to fold us,
Lord of all souls, Delight of all eyes.
All that He is can never be told us,
Wonderful, Counsellor, God only wise.

Blessing and honour and high adoration
Be to the Babe of pure virginal birth;
He is our hope and our only salvation,
Henceforth the theme and the crown of our mirth.
Joy to all people, each tongue and each nation,
Glory in heaven, and good-will on earth!

No Arm has Power to Raise.

"So soon as I shall see how it will go with me."—
Philippians 2:23.

No arm has power to raise
The curtain of to-morrow;

No eye can ken what future days
May bring of joy or sorrow.

Vain man, though wise, is veiled,
He walks as one benighted;
But oft he sees how hopes have failed,
And all his flowerets blighted.

Then what is man? a worm,
But does his God forget him?
Oh no! throughout his longest term
His God has often met him.

That worm, O Lord, am I,
Thick darkness is my vision;
But in the sunshine of Thine eye
I walk with all precision.

Though sightless as to what
To-morrow's dawn may call me,
I will rejoice in any lot
Which may from Thee befall me.

How it will go with me,
Shall form no anxious musing;
Full rather will I follow Thee,
In ways of Thine own choosing.

If Thou shouldst choose me pain,
Or silence or decaying,
Thou wilt my faith and love sustain
In holy praise and praying.

And when at last I see
How all has been Thy favour,
It will indeed go well with me,
Before Thy throne, my Saviour.

Coblentz, 1865.

A New National Bridal Hymn.

(Especially) for March 10, 1863.

God save our gracious Queen;
Long live our noble Queen;
God save the Queen!
Grant her victorious,
Happy and glorious,
Long to reign over us;
God save the Queen!

God save the Prince of Wales;
Bless Thou the bride he hails;
Make them Thy care!
Where England's name prevails,
Where sweet homes scent her gales,
Where ocean bears her sails,
There be this prayer.

God of the bridal band,
Fast be each heart and hand
Bound in Thine own!
Cheer them in sorrow's hour,
Spare them if troubles lower,
Gird them with truth and power
Sent from Thy throne.

Then, when long years have fled,
Still be Thy favours shed
On them and theirs!
Where dwells not sin nor sigh,
Where weeps not widow's eye,
There with our Christ on high
Be they "joint heirs."

Nuptial Grace.

For G. S. and E. P. H.[1]

"Holy Matrimony—instituted of God, in the time of man's innocency, signifying unto us the mystical union that is betwixt Christ and His Church; which holy estate Christ adorned and beautified with His presence, and first miracle that He wrought in Cana of Galilee."

O Thou, Whose presence beautified
Poor Cana's nuptial board,[2]
By Thee let ours be sanctified,
And Thou shalt be adored.

Thyself to us, ourselves to Thee,
In mystic union join;
And grant us greater things to see
Than water turned to wine.

Thy glory show, our faith make strong,
Like rivers be our peace;
And seat us where THY Marriage Song
Shall never, *never* cease!

To Him who wove the marriage tie,
When man was innocent,
To God, our Triune God, Most High,
Be all our praises sent!

[1] For Giles Shaw and Ellen Prestage Havergal. William Henry Havergal wrote this poem and set it to music for his daughter Ellen's wedding, February 5, 1856. See page 299.

[2] meal, a board or table on which food is provided (as in "room and board")

A Bridegroom's Song.

Song of Solomon 2:10.

"Rise up, my love, and come away!"
It is, it *is*, thy bridal day:
God's watchers bright
Await the sight,
And joy to chant their sweetest lay.

Come, come, my fair one, come away!
Fled is the dark and cloudy day:
Wintry night
And withering blight
Too long have held thee 'neath their sway.

Rise up, my love, from thy loneliness!
Thy harass and thy deep distress:
Sorrow and care
No more shall scare
Thy spirit's native loveliness.

'Tis God Who hath prepared thy way
To reach this blest and blessing day;
'Twas He Who trained
When most He pained,
For He meant to chase thy tears away!

Then rise, my fair one, come away
To a home of love, by night and day;
Peace and prayer
Await thee there,
And praise shall tune her song alway!

A home! yes, in it welcome stands
To bless thy feet, and kiss thy hands;
And children's love
Shall greet their dove,
And listen to her soft commands.

Yes, my own love, my home is thine,
In it shall all thy virtues shine;
But, O be wise,
Turn to the skies,
And let our nuptials be a heavenly sign!

A sign of that transcendent day
When thou shalt hear *The* Bridegroom say,—
And I the while
Stand by and smile,—
"Rise up, my love, my fair one, come away!"

To Miss M. Vernon.

I thank you, dear Mary,
For playing the fairy,
And knitting the mittens you send me;
They fit to a trice,
And are thoroughly nice,
So be sure they will warmly befriend me.

Though scarlet and white,
They are clerical quite,
For remember the surplice and hood;
And the colours, you know,
Are emblems also
Of blessings eternally good.

You may see what I mean
In that fine verse eighteen,
Chapter I. of Isaiah the great;
May what you there read
Be *your* blessing indeed,
During life, whether early or late!

1862.

Good Night.

Good night, good night!
Care take his flight,
And Peace, all bright,
Possess thee quite,
Through Christ our Light!
Good night, good night!

Good Morning.

Good morn, good morn, good morning!
Be many a smile to-day!
May we, the truth adorning,
Pass safely on our way.
When sin's fell thorn made us forlorn,
Christ came one morn, and joy was born.
Blest morn, blest morn, blest morning!
Good morn, good morn, good morning!

Grace before and after Meat.[1]

I.

No earthly gifts can yield us good,
Without, O Lord, Thy heavenly grace;
Then sanctify our present food,
And lift on us a Father's face.

II.

All praise to Him Who died to give
The Bread by which the dying live;
Our praise for all things pure shall be,
When face to face Himself we see.

I.

Jesus, Lord of earth and sky,
What Thou givest sanctify;
Always let our souls be fed
With Thyself, the living Bread.

II.

Jesus, seated on Thy throne,
Thee we bless and Thee alone;
Thee we bless for food and friends,
Every gift Thy mercy sends.

Coleridge, 1867.

Grace before Meat.

Thou, gracious Father, dost provide
All blessings in the Crucified;
What now Thou givest, sanctify,
And make us meet to feast on high.

Grace after Meat.

All praise to Him Who food supplies,
Through Christ's atoning sacrifice!
For gifts received our hymn we raise,
And hope to join in endless praise.

Penzance, October, 1868.

To Ellen, on her Third Birthday.[1]

19th February 1826.

Come, my pretty little love,
Sweet and harmless as the dove;

[1] Ellen Prestage (Havergal) Shaw, his third daughter.

You, my February Queen,
Paper-crowned, with pink and green,
Happy, happy may you be
Often as this day you see!
Onward as through life you go,
May the Bible you well know!
And when days and years are fled,
And you sleep among the dead,
May your spirit happy be
With the Great and Holy Three,
Clad in robes of holiness,
Crowned with everlasting bliss!

The Red-Streaked Apple.

Two colours on the apple glow,
Why, little friends, why is it so?
If I may guess, I'll tell you, dears,
The cause may well excite your tears.

When Eve, who vainly wise would be,
Plucked from the one forbidden tree;
The apple blushed! the tinge remains,
And still our guilt and woe proclaims.

But, little friends, come list again,
Now hear the pleasure 'midst the pain;
The red-streaked apple may be proved
To indicate our guilt removed.

When Jesus bowed His sacred head,
And died on Calvary in our stead,
His spotless side was stained with blood,
The source of our eternal good.

Hence in the apple white you see
The Saviour's stainless purity;
The reddened streak describes His blood,
Through which we're justified by God.

For Evelyn, Constance, and John Crane.[1]

Children, while you gather flowers,
Think how fleeting are your hours;
Think again in heavenly bowers,
You may cull unfading flowers.

Jesus is the sweetest flower:
Give to Him each passing hour,

[1] Three grandchildren, by his eldest daughter, Jane Miriam (Havergal) Crane. June, 1858.

He will then in Eden's bower
Make you each a fadeless flower.

Morning.

I LOVE, I love the morning!
With purple tints adorning
The mountain brow, the woodland scene,
The deep and lone ravine;
Oh, then in hallowed gladness,
My bosom drops its sadness,
And heaves in prayerful ecstasy
To the Triune Deity.
The thoughts may be grave, but the heart cannot grieve,
When day brings to nature a joyous reprieve.

The lingering mist of whiteness,
The orient streaks of brightness,
The fleecy cloud, the sparkling dew,
And boughs of every hue;
The torrent loudly rushing,
The fountain gently gushing,
The dulcet hum of early bee,
The lark's pure minstrelsy,
Are charms which the morn brings the eye and the ear,
While faith thrills the heart with the thought, "God is here!"

Thoughts in Song.

I LOVE, I love thy solemn roar,
Thou deep eternal sea,
While sounding on from shore to shore,
The boundless and the free.
I love the torrent flood's hoarse song,
The thunder's lordly mirth,
The midnight wind that walks along
The hushed and trembling earth.

I love the mountain lone and high,
The dark and silent wood,
The desert stretched from sky to sky
In awful solitude.
The whirlwind's ruthless rushing wing,
The stern volcano's voice,
To me an awful rapture bring:
I tremble and rejoice.

A mystic presence and a power
In scenes like these I see;
The stillness of the midnight hour
Has eloquence for me:
For, bursting then from earth's control,
My thoughts are all at flood;
I feel the stirring in my soul
Of high, immortal mood!

Poland.

PITY, grief, and indignation
Stir Old England's manly heart,
When a brave and free-born nation,
Crushed by despot domination,
Writhes beneath the cruel smart.

England, think! no fitful passion
Opes the gate whence mercy flows;
Thoughtful prayer brings down compassion,
Strong to rescue or re-fashion,
Righting wrongs and healing woes.

Poland, rise from superstition!
Who shall then thy peace destroy?
Give to God thy true submission,
He will give thee bright employ;
Lofty be thy future mission,
Loud and long thy peals of joy!

Pen-y-Bryn.

(*i.e.* "THE TOP OF THE ROCK.")

"From the top of the rocks I see him."—Numbers 23:9.

WHEN Israel lay in Moab's plain,
Outstretched in quiet splendour,
The eastern prophet saw with pain
That God was his Defender.

From lofty rocks (some Pen-y-Bryn)
He saw the nation's glory,
And vainly strove, through love of sin,
To blot the nation's story.

Small love had he for Israel's cause,
And none for Israel's Keeper,
He trampled on His gracious laws,
And sank in crime the deeper.

To me, good Lord, Thy Spirit give,
The Spirit of my Saviour,
That with Thy people I may live,
Encompassed with Thy favour.

May all who visit Pen-y-Bryn
Behold Thy saving vision,
Rejoice Thine Israel's lot to win,
And face the world's derision.

May they and I at length attain
The Pen-y-Bryn of glory,
And chant in everlasting strain
Redemption's wondrous story!

Pen-y-Bryn, near Colwyn, 1858.

Ode.

On the arrival of H.R.H. the Prince Regent, with the Allied Sovereigns the Emperor of Russia and the King of Prussia, at Oxford, June 14, 1814.

They come! they come! the illustrious Sovereigns come!
Loud let the song of triumph roll around;
Let grand and rapturous notes shake every dome,
And the wide world the sacred song resound.
They live! they come! with Peace and Victory crowned!
Tell it, Oxonia, even to worlds afar;
Blood-royal Chiefs now tread thy hallowed ground,
And with the well-earned laurels of the war
Thy classic honours claim, to deck the imperial car!

Begin, ye bards! the harmonious rites begin!
To loftiest song the swelling soul high raise;
Tune all your powers, exulting strike each string,
With earth and heaven sing Liberty! Peace! Praise!
Chant Victory's glorious song, from far arouse
The sluggish nations by the arch-tramp of Fame,
To view the meed of triumph crown the brows
Of Sovereigns peerless in their deeds, who claim
More than this nether world can give, or think, or name!

Fair Albion raises her once drooping head,
And stateliest look of smiling power puts on;
And while she sheds a tear for Heroes dead,
Exults to see her heaven-raised Regent-son.
Our sea-girt Isle hymns Alexander's praise,
And Frederick's virtues charm with power supreme;
To sing their honours due in equal lays
Demands the voice and fire of seraphim,
Or quill from angel's wing to pen the illustrious theme.

Far fiercer, far, than all the powers of song,
The birds of war, on iron wings amain,
Bore the big-battling thunder wide along,
Through carnaged Europe, and o'er hills of slain.
But they who braved the war, unchained a world,
Closed tyranny on Elba's atom-isle,
Shall hear in deathless odes their praises told,
While wondering nations on their virtues smile,
And Victory and Peace crown all their princely toil.

Yes! heaven-born Peace resumes her halcyon sway,
And downward hastes with blessings from the skies,
Opes on the earth the dawn of blissful day,
And cheers with prospects bright our war-sick eyes.
Here may she dwell, and unmolested reign,
Bid jarring kingdoms to her sceptre bend;
Ne'er may she wing her way to heaven again,
But o'er our globe her healing wings extend,
And make it her abode through ages without end!

But know, the King of Kings our praise demands,
His arm outstretched fought with our bannered hosts;
He calmed the rage of war, at His commands
Victorious Peace encircled Europe's coasts!
"These are His glorious works," not ours alone;
His be the greatness, His the majesty!
Let kings and subjects bow before His throne,
And willing, worship Heaven's dread sovereignty,
Which gave us good-willed Peace and lasting Liberty!

The Newfoundlander's Petition.

Hear, Britain! hear thou the plaint of thy children,
Lodged in the land which thy mariners found;
Far from thy bosom, on coasts all bewildering,
Toil we with nets o'er the bank or the sound.

Dark-waving pines fling their shade o'er our fountains,
Error's black wing from our souls hides the light;
Bleakly the snow-storm envelopes our mountains;
Oh! be our sunbeam all kindly and bright!

Kind hast thou been! for maternal affection
Oft for our solace her warm breast has riven,
But freely give us, of gifts the perfection,
Knowledge to teach us the pathway to heaven.

Send us the fragments that fall from the table
Round which thy home-born are bounteously fed;

Send us the manna of Him who is able
To nourish and save us "as life from the dead!"

Speak but the word! and a throng will be zealous
Quickly to launch on the wreck-covered deep;
Heralds of mercy! "come over" and tell us
Tidings of joy, in the land where we weep.

Thus, though the pine-tree fringe darkly our fountains,
Light, saving light, shall e'er beam from above;
Coldly the snow-storm may shroud all our mountains,
Warm shall our hearts be with heavenly love.

Then, Britain, hear thou the cry of thy children,
Lodged in the land which thy mariners found;
Gladdened by thee shall our coasts, though bewildering,
Loudly with song to the Saviour resound!

1827.

To Miss Caroline Kingscote.

I.

K ind are thy gifts! and welcome as showers
I N opening spring to the delicate flowers,
G rowing most sweet by thy home lovely bowers;
S o think my darlings and I.
C ould you but see their hearts in their faces,
O r witness their glee and their artless grimaces,
T would gladden thy spirit when it retraces
E ven days that smiled once and went by.

II.

E ver, then, be thy lot simplicity's pleasure,
T O wisdom more dear than miserly treasure;
C ould but the world see its own empty measure,
S urely shame would soon tinge its proud cheek.
G o, go, worthless world! and curb thy vain spirit
N ot the lofty in heart, but the lowly inherit
I ehovah's best gift, the robe of Christ's merit,
K ept for the childlike and meek.

1828.

For Miss Sarah Stenning.

I.

A s the blithe and busy bee
L oves to sip the honied flower,
B e each pen as choice as she,
U nlocking with simplicity
M any a fair and balmy flower

II.

M ark, then, friends, sweet Sharon's rose,
U ndecaying as it grows;
B e your flowers of poesy
L ike its stainless purity,
A nd its heavenly fragrancy!

1830.

To John Hall Shaw.

I.

S ons who fathers gladden,
H onours shall receive;
A ll who mothers sadden,
W ill be sure to grieve.

II.

W isdom loves to favour
A ll who favour her;
H e who is the Saviour
S hall grace for grace confer.

Langen Schwallbach, 1865.

Enigma.

The Birth and Adventures of a Traveller.

I WAS a first-born son,
Born on a New Year's day,
I was my Father's readiest son
His mandate to obey.

While yet in infancy
All tender and untaught,
He sent me forth a scene to see
With dismal horror fraught.

I soon became a man;
And wonder even now,
That ere I learned to walk, I ran,
Though no one showed me how.

My Father destined me
To be a traveller,
But I became immediately
A great philosopher.

He gave, forsooth, another son
My name and quality,
And other offspring one by one
Were soon called after me.

Still at each earliest morn
I sped me on my way,
Wherever sinful man was born,
Wherever there was day.

I travelled fast and far,
Without impediment;
I went up to the morning star,
And ranged the firmament.

But though a traveller bright,
More than most travellers are,
I seemed to some a marvel quite
Surpassing them by far.

No ear e'er heard me speak,
No eye saw me by night,
Yet I puzzled men by many a freak,
As though I were a sprite.

I skated on the moon,
I danced upon the sun,
I strode the rainbow for a boon
To get the work well done.

Some called me strange and cold,
Some called me warm and weak,
While some declare I'm made of gold,
Or still of silver speak.

But be I what I may,
The good and wise love me,
And tens of thousands every day
Long much my face to see.

All sinners bear me hate,
They take me for their foe;
Though Lucifer was once my mate,
He dreads me now, I trow.

Who then am I? come say!
I love each godly friend,
And hope with you to spend a day
Which is to know no end!

Enigma No. 22.

I AM a word so self-contained,
That out of me none else is framed;
And yet I wear a double face,
For I the good and bad embrace;
Indeed, both good and bad I'm called,
Though sometimes breathed and sometimes howled;
But good folk do at times refuse
My very name at all to use;
My very being they dispute,
And bid all tongues for me to be mute;
They say I'm not a Bible word,
Though oft at church I'm seen and heard.
So, if the pious me refuse,
The parsons can't themselves excuse;
I wish, then, you may prove my power,
In my best phase some happy hour.

Enigma No. 23.

A MUSICAL " MULTUM EX PARVO," OR GAMBOLS[1] WITH THE GAMUT.

I. A List[2] of Old Songs.

1. *Canons for Young Ladies.*

"Blooming Virgins" *Athalia.*

"Wise men flattering" *Judas Maccabæus.*

2. *The Schoolmaster's* alias *the Music Master's Lament.*[3]

But oh, what art can teach ?—*Dryden's Ode.*

3. *Cotton's*[4] *subject,*[5] *and Father Matthew's answer.*[6]

What's sweeter than the *Joseph.*

Water parted[7] from the *Dr. Arne.*

II. A Ground[8] for Gratitude in Rhyme.

You may be or
Or very in
You may be or
With aching or [9]
Still you are
Nor with the
In earth's deep [10] yet

Editor's Scholia.

[1] The Viol di Gamba was formerly much used in the chapels of German princes.

[2] "List! alias Listen," verb. A List subst., that which is listened to, Etymol. Nov.

[3] A plaintive ditty.

[4] A celebrated bee-fancier of Ch. Ch. Oxon.

[5] The theme or text of any movement.

[6] The subordinate or corresponding phrase which follows.

[7] Specimen of the "wisdom of the ancients" of the eighteenth century. Spring water, alias rivers, flow from the sea!

[8] A composition of bass notes repeated to a continually varying melody.

[9] The Germans call B-natural *h*. Hence the celebrated Bach wrote a learned fugue on the letters of his name

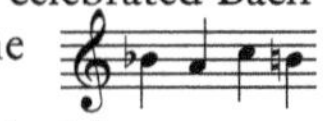

[10] Whether the Author intends this for the Jewish measure of three pints, and thence a grave in which we are measured, or the modern vehicle in which we take a nap while cabbed to our destination, perhaps the next century will be able to define.

Enigma No. 24.

I am in the Bible, but not in old Johnson,
You may know not my father, you knew not his son.
I am a true Christian, though I never was christened,
But I heard a high story, which for long I had listened.
I am not unacquainted with wedlock's high station,
And once I was used for divine revelation.
My name is most simple but strange, you will find,
Whether spelled from the front or spelled from behind,
It is of two syllables, with only two letters,
But sounds better by far than some of my betters.
I give you two articles, yet I am but one,
And I sound you three names, all meaning but one.
Yea, twist me and turn me all ways as you please,
I'll come back to myself with positive ease.
If you like, call me saint,
For it will not be quaint,
But quick tell my name,
To save your own fame.

Enigma No. 25.

A man I am, a woman too,
A husband and a wife;
As much a Gentile as a Jew,
Possessed of double life.

As man or monarch, wife or queen,
None can with me compare;
I lord it over all that's seen,
In sea, in earth, and air.

And yet I died for love of wife,
Although she died before me,
But strange to say I gave her life,
While down to death she bore me.

But stranger still, though dead and gone,
I yet on earth am living;
I pass my night without a dawn,
While bitterest trouble giving.

Though old, I goodness never learn,
But love whate'er is evil;
To Christ and His with hate I burn,
And always aid the devil.

In all good folk a foe I lie,
Though some count me a fiction;
Still well I know I'm doomed to die,
And that by crucifixion.

I need not more now signify:
My name awaits your diction.

Enigma No. 26.

My *first* is a word essential to man,
My *second* is first in a list he must scan.
When my remainder is properly put on,
Your thinkings will turn to something of mutton.
Altogether I am a multiform creature,
And yet I sustain one distinguishing feature:
Sometimes I'm — — —
A check upon evil, a hindrance of good.
I'm at home in the prison, the castle, the tavern,
The convent, the grave, the dungeon and cavern,
And yet I am honoured in Westminster Hall,
And hundreds are waiting to welcome my call.
The musician observes me, and bows to my sway,
And cannot without me well sing or well play;
I fasten your shutters, and break them to shivers,
I block up your highways, your harbours, your rivers.
I have my relations, a pretty large clan,
Not at all are they bounded by woman or man,
For I've wedded a bird, a maiden, and seaport,
And persons and places do constantly *me court;*

They always, to honour me, place me before them,
And I in return do never ignore them.
In Scripture, apostles present you my name,
A very old man and some others the same;
Yea, even to Jesus I'm nearly related,
'Tis solemn to say it, but so it is stated;
Here then I cease, without further barring,
So tell out the riddle without *further sparring.*

Enigma No. 27.

I GO with ships at sea, I haunt the forest glade,
The squatter dwells with me, Jove me a king once made.
Cut off my first, another king you'll make;
Cut off my last, and lo, your ear will shake.
If then you turn this king right round, I trow
That when you turn away I also go.
Next lop my first and last, yet leave my middle:
Oh, spare poor little Nil, but solve this riddle!

Winterdyne, March 20, 1867.

Isaiah 2:4.

"He shall rebuke many people."—Isaiah 2:4.

ART Thou, Lord, rebuking nations?
Hast Thou bared Thy glittering sword?
War, commotions, tribulations,
Are they marching at Thy word?
Shield us, Saviour,
With Thy favour,
When Thy vials are outpoured!

If Thy judgments now are waking,
Let not Thy compassion sleep;
But, while earthly powers are shaking,
Firm and free Thy kingdom keep.
Jesu, hear us,
Be Thou near us,
When the storm shall round us sweep!

Courage, saints, your fears assuaging,
Chant a bold and blissful strain!
Holy seers, of peace presaging,
Bid us hail Messiah's reign.
Strife, sedition,
Supersitition,
Then no votaries shall gain.

Warrior hosts, no longer mustering,
Cease the gleaming lance to wield:
Now they watch the fruitage clustering,
Now they crop the sunny field.
Thus shall sadness
Change to gladness
When Messiah is revealed.

Prince of Peace, let every nation
Soon Thy Spirit's empire own;
Bow the world in supplication,
Bring the heathen to Thy throne!
Earth possessing,
Boundless blessing
Then shall honour Thee alone!

1831.

Matthew 15:23.

"But He answered her not a word."—Matthew 15:23.

AND could'st Thou, blessèd One, be mute,
And turn Thy face away,
Where anguish prayed to Thee her suit,
Though never taught to pray?

How could'st Thou hear the mother cry,
"Have mercy on me, Lord!"
And then restrain Thy sympathy,
And "answer not a word?"

Belovèd Saviour, Thou art just
And wise in all Thy ways;
'Tis not for worms of murky dust
To scan Thy heavenly rays.

The mother's heart was in Thine eye,
Her faith was also there;
It was Thy will its power to try,
And then to answer prayer.

For Thou did'st bless the Canaanite,
Though cursèd was her race;
Her vexèd daughter felt Thy might,
And both adored Thy grace.

Lord, let our faith be always strong,
Though prayer may seem unheard;
Our sorrow then shall end in song,
And we will wait Thy word.

1866.

Luke 10:2.

"The harvest truly is great."—Luke 10:2.

How vast the field of souls!
Of souls that cannot die:
Where earth expands or ocean rolls,
That field invites our eye.

The harvest of that field,
How ready for our hand!
But they who well the sickle wield
Are still a little band.

Then let us earnest be
In faith for souls to care:
The Master of the field is He
Who bids us join in prayer.

Thy Spirit, Lord, forth send,
More labourers to provide;
Throughout the field be Thou their Friend,
Their Keeper and their Guide.

Then, when their toils are past,
And all Thy garner stored,
Be Thou the First, and Thou the Last,
Unceasingly adored!

Praise.

PRAISE ye the Lord! in Him rejoice,
Pour forth praises like a flood:
He in His love made us His choice,
And redeemed us by His blood.
Let all unite to laud His love,
Men below and saints above.

Praise ye the Lord! whose Shepherd-hand
Feeds and guards and guides His flock;
By Him alone can we withstand
Sorrow's storm or trouble's shock.
Let all unite to praise His love,
Men below and saints above.

Praise ye the Lord! our Brother-Friend,
Seated on His priestly throne,
There interceding without end,
He will contrite suppliants own.
Let all unite to laud His love,
Men below and saints above.

For the Shareshill Almanac, 1870.

OUR life is but a living death,
For we are born to die;
A word from God soon stops our breath,
And down to earth we lie.

Then help us, Lord, to live as they
Who live alone for Thee,
That we may reach, through Christ the Way,
A bright eternity.

O let our pleasures, sins, nor gains,
Delude us with their dross;
Lest present sweets prove future pains,
And our eternal loss.

Teach us to feel that worldly lives
No happy deaths can bring,
For sin at last the soul deprives
Of Christ the living King.

Arouse, O God, each drowsy soul,
And say with power, "Awake!"
When neighbours die, and church bells toll,
May we the warning take.

Thy Holy Spirit, Lord, impart
To cleanse and sanctify,
That we, believing with the heart,
May never dread to die.

Psalm 55:6.

"Oh that I had wings like a dove! for then would I fly away, and be at rest."
—Psalm 55:6.

O SAVIOUR, when with raptured eye
Thy glories and Thy grace I view,
My troubled spirit fain would fly,
And far from hence her course pursue.

Here darkness reigns, here grief and woe,
And foes within and fears without
Now rack my breast, and now round me throw
The chains of fear, the toils of doubt.

But, Saviour, raise Thy mighty hand,
And o'er me cast Thy favouring shield!
O crush each foe! O burst each band!
And, conquering, lead me from the field.

Then, Saviour, while on earth I stay,
To suffer or to do Thy will,
Each night, each morn, my grateful lay
Shall echo to Thy holy hill.

Invocation.

Holy and blessèd Redeemer, we pray Thee,
Succour and help us in all time of need:
Trusting in Thee and Thy promise, O may we
Always find solace and always succeed.
Speak what Thou wilt, we will ever obey Thee,
Honour and fear Thee in thought, word, and deed.

Thou art Almighty, All-wise, and All-gracious,
Make us all humble, devoted, and true; Clad in
Thine armour, no foe will dare face us,
Danger and trouble will cease to pursue.
Once let the soft arms of Mercy embrace us,
Peace shall pervade us like sweet falling dew.

Blessèd and holy Redeemer, we laud Thee,
Source of all succour, help, comfort, and joy,
While in yon heaven bright angels applaud Thee,
We with their echoes our tongues will employ.
None of Thy glory shall ever defraud Thee,
All, in its fulness, Thy saints shall enjoy.

Lord, when our Wayward Feet.

Lord, when our wayward feet
Dangers and perils meet,
Shield us from harm;
When in this world of woes,
Legions of ghostly foes
Fiercely our faith oppose,
Make bare Thine arm!

When pleasure tempts to stray,
Health chants her syren lay,
Keep us from guile;
When in affliction's hour
Waves rise and tempests lower,
Robed in Thy garb of power,
Come, Lord, and smile!

When on the verge of death,
Faintly, with faltering breath,
Comfort we crave;
Then from the gloomy flood,
O Jesus, Lamb of God,
Through Thine atoning blood,
Rescue and save!

Hymn.

"And He said unto them, that the Son of Man is Lord also of the Sabbath."—Luke 6:5.

Hallelujah! Lord, our voices
Rise in choral strains to Thee:
Son of Man, Thy Church rejoices
In her weekly jubilee!

Hallelujah! mercy beaming
Lights the path that leads to God:
Herald-lips divinely teeming
Publish blessings bought with blood.

Hallelujah! praise ascending,
Shall our faith-winged breathings stay?
Lord, before Thine altar bending,
Let the heathen hail Thy day!

Hallelujah! Saviour, hear us!
Downward send Thy quickening Dove:
May His silver pinions bear us
To the realms of rest and love!

Hymn for Good Friday.

And didst Thou, Holy Saviour, die
Upon the accursèd tree?
And was there heard Thy bitter cry
In death's last agony?

Yes, Thou didst die, most Holy One,
But not for sin of Thine;
Thy "precious death" our pardon won,
And made our face to shine.

Yes, Thou didst die, sweet Lamb of God,
To bear our sin away,
And quench in blood that fiery rod,
Which kept the heavenly way.

O Saviour, let us die with Thee,
At any cost or pain;
And through Thy glorious majesty
Eternal life attain.

Then will we chant the Father's love
And Holy Spirit's grace,
And hail Thee Lord of all above,
Sole Saviour of our race.

1867.

To a Mother.

THY lamb is safe! Thy Shepherd's love
Now bids thee follow it above.

W. H. H.

No sigh but from the harps above,
Soft echoing tones shall win;
No heart-wound but the Lord of love
Shall pour His comfort in.
Thy claim to rest on Jesu's breast
All weariness shall be,
And pain thy portal to His heart
Of boundless sympathy.

F. R. H.[1]

On Hearing of the Death of Mrs. Gross of Ayr, 1861.

REST, aged saint! Thy pilgrim staff lay down,
Now take the palm-branch and the blood-bought crown.
Rest where thy loved ones rest, and join the throng
Of those who see the Lamb, and sing His endless song.

On the Rev. S. Trist of Veryan.

T HE husband, father, pastor, friend,
R emoved from earthly sight,
I s wafted to the realms of light,
S aved by his heavenly Master's might,
T o praise Him without end.

T hy end was like the giant sun
R eclining in the west,
I t was so calm, so pure, so blest,
S ure 'twas a pledge, the brightest, best,
T hat thou with Christ are one!

RESURGEMUS.

THE MOTTO ON THE FAMILY VAULT.

T he saints who slumber in this tomb,
R aised from their granite bed,
I n fadeless glory soon shall bloom;
S oon shall their hands their harps resume
T o extol their loving Head!

NEC TRISTI NEC TREPIDE.

THE FAMILY MOTTO OF MY FRIENDS AT VERYAN.

V erily, verily cometh the hour!
E arth and the sea shall unbosom their dead;
R oused by the Saviour, renewed by His power,
Y es! we shall rise again, yes! for 'tis said,
A wake ye and sing, ye that dwell in the dust,
N ec tristi nec trepide slumber the just.

Or,

Nor sorrow nor fear haunts the tomb of the just.

Written on Hearing of the Happy Departure of Mrs. Tull of Bengeworth, July 1830.

"Mortalitati, non vitæ, valedixit." [1]

HAPPY spirit, bright and blessèd!
Thou the vale of death hast trod,
Now, with robes of light invested,
Thou behold'st the Lamb of God.

Now for ever hast thou bidden
To mortality farewell:
Perfect life, no longer hidden,
Wreathes the brow we loved so well.

Still amidst our ceaseless sorrow,
We rejoice to think of thee;

[1] "Death, not life, I have blessed."

Memory oft from thee shall borrow
Lessons of humility.

Happy spirit, ever blessèd!
Round our path thy virtues shine,
And by Jesus' love refreshèd,
May it be as bright as thine!

Henry Martyn's Last Words.

I sat 'neath the orchard's refreshing retreat,
And thought with sweet comfort and peace,
"Though no hand may cherish, tho' no voice may greet,
"His arm is my pillow, His Word is my feast."

And musing I said, "When shall time cease to be,
And the bliss of eternity gladden my breast?"
For I thought of my sin and the world's misery,
And I longed to depart where the weary find rest.

"And when (still I said) shall the new earth and heaven
Where righteousness dwelleth in glory appear?
For there no defilement, nor sin's hated leaven,
Nor sorrow, nor sighing, shall ever come near.

"No wickedness there shall debase or destroy;
And innate corruption for ever shall cease:
Oh rapturous vision! O fulness of joy!
The cross-bearing pilgrim shall reign there in peace."

Astley
Rectory,
1827.

Saviour, when from Realms Above.

William Henry Havergal wrote this poem and set it to music at the end of Frances' Autograph Album in the 1860s at the end of Frances' Autograph Album in the 1860's. See page 363 of this book.

Saviour, when from realms above,
Thou shalt come with glory 'round,
May the names of all we love,
In Thy Book of Life be found! Amen.

In that Great Day,
Lord, grant that I may
With rapture say, } "Behold I, and *the children* which God hath given me." Hebrews 2:13.

Bonn, January 18, 1866. W. H. Havergal.

Much love from
Maria V. G. Havergal

Frances Ridley Havergal

On the left, Maria Vernon Graham Havergal (1821–1887) was W.H.H.'s third child; on the right, Frances Ridley Havergal (1836–1879) was his sixth, youngest child.

These further hymns, the next 13 poems by William Henry Havergal, were found very late in the work on the Havergal edition, and are added here at the end of the section of his poems. These were found on printed announcement sheets of meetings on behalf of, for support of, the Church Missionary Society: the earliest announcement sheet found was printed for the meeting of Sunday, September 24, 1826, and the latest sheet was printed for the meeting of Sunday, October 21, 1860. These missionary hymns by W.H.H. were printed in full, to be sung in the meeting, with a Sermon, to raise awareness and support for C.M.S. missionaries in distant lands. W.H.H. for decades was a true advocate for foreign missions, travelling to many churches to preach, raising funds and presenting the need for support of the Church Missionary Society's missionaries to bring the truth of Christ to foreign lands.

"Soon the Trumpet of Salvation."

Soon the trumpet of salvation
Loudly, sweetly shall be blown;
And each kindred tongue and nation,
Shall the thrilling mandate own.

Myriads, verging on perdition,
Roused by its persuasive sound,
Shall with ardour and contrition,
Come from earth's remotest bound.

Then the wounded and the fainting,
Then the tortured idol-slave,
Then the captive exile panting,
And the borderers of the grave:

All shall haste and come believing
To the refuge of the cross;
And, the Saviour's grace receiving,
Joyous count all else but loss.

Great Immanuel! send thy spirit!
Let the gospel trump be blown;
May the Heathen know thy merit,
May they bow before thy throne!

"Heralds of the Lord of Glory."

"Say (Tell it out) among the Heathen that the Lord reigneth."—Psalm 96:10.

Heralds of the Lord of glory!
Lift your voices, lift them high;
Tell the Gospel's wondrous story,
Tell it fully, faithfully:
Tell the Heathen, 'midst their woe,
Jesus reigns, above, below!

Where the Tempter rules with terror,
Where obscene his idols stand;
Where the deathful night of error
Broods malignant o'er the land:
Heralds! there your message tell,
Jesus reigns o'er Death and Hell!

Haste the day, the bright, the glorious!
When the sad, and sin-bound slave
High shall laud, in pealing chorus
Him who reigns, and reigns to save.
Tempter, tremble! Idols, fall!
Jesus reigns, the Lord of all!

Christians! send to joyless regions
Heralds of the glad'ning word;
Let them, voiced like trumpet-legions,
Preach the kingdom of the Lord:
Tell the Heathen—Jesus died!
Reigns He now, though crucified!

Saviour! let thy quick'ning Spirit
Touch each herald-lip with fire:
Nations then shall own thy merit,
Hearts shall glow with thy desire,
Earth in jubilee shall sing—
"*Jesus reigns*"—th' eternal King!

"Widely 'midst the slumbering nations."[1]

"A light to lighten the Gentiles."—Luke 2:32.

Widely 'midst the slumbering nations,
Darkness holds his despot-sway;
Cruel in his habitations,
Ruthless o'er his prostrate prey.
Star of Bethlehem,
Rise, and beam in conquering day!

Bound and sightless, scourged and dying,
Millions throng the gaping tomb;
While the Oppressor mocks their sighing,
Reckless of the fiery doom.
Light of Israel,
Burst the bands of Gentile gloom!

[1]This text by W.H.H. differs from his text of this poem on page 393 of this book.

Where, oh where, is that effulgence
Beaming erst from Juda's fane[2]?
Idols fell;—and Rome's indulgence
Trembled, when it shone again.
Source of wisdom,
Spread Thy rays o'er every main!

Light of Light, our sole defender!
Rise with healing on Thy wing;
Rise, in all Thy soothing splendour;
Rise, and earth with joy shall ring!
Israel's Glory,
Gentiles call Thee Lord and King!

Christians, haste! The morn is breaking;
Darkness wheels his downward flight;
But, your polished armour taking,
Stand !—nor quit the waning fight.
Great Redeemer,
Guard us with Thy shield of light!

Onward, Christians, onward pressing,
Triumph in the Crucified!
Endless honor, rest, and blessing,
Wait you at His radiant side.
Cease not, cease not,
Till you see Him glorified!

"Inhabitants of Earth, Hail, Hail the Day of Rest!"

"The sabbath was made for man."—Mark 2:27.

Inhabitants of earth,
Hail, hail the day of rest!
Ye saints, who boast a higher birth,
Hail it with raptured breast!

The Sun of Righteousness
Uplifts His healing face;
And Joy and Peace unite to bless
The suppliants of His grace.

The voice of saving truth
Strikes on these hallowed walls:
Here Wisdom cries to age and youth,
And patient Mercy calls.

But lo ! 'midst deathly gloom,
The untaught heathen lies;
And trusts, though sinking to the tomb,
In refuges of lies.

No sabbath cheers his eye,
No gospel thrills his ear;
No hope of life beyond the sky
Dispels his horrid fear.

Then ye, who love the Lord,
In prayer lift up your voice:
Bestow on heathen tribes His word,
And bid the world rejoice!

"Why, Emmanuel, Wast Thou Lifted?"

"And I, if I be lifted up from the earth, will draw all men unto me."—John 12:32.

Why, Emmanuel, wast Thou lifted
On the tree of infamy?
Was it that we might be gifted
With thy life-bought liberty?
This, O Saviour,
Draws the sinner's heart to Thee.

Now enthroned above all blessing,
Bid the gods of earth retreat:
Bid mankind, Thy name confessing,
Come to Thee with holy feet.
Let the heathen
Soon Thy might and mercy greet.

Sure, no arm, but Thine, can sever
Chains which bind their souls in night;
Send Thy Spirit, Lord, or never
Will they hail Thy glorious light.
Rise, Redeemer,
Rise, and claim them as Thy right!

Draw *us* to Thee:—draw each nation,
With Thy love's mysterious cord;
So the world, in adoration,
Shall obey Thy sovereign word.
Wondrous Sufferer,
We will own no other Lord!

"Brighter than Meridian Splendour." [1]

"And let the whole earth be filled with his glory. Amen, and Amen."—
Psalm 72:19.

BRIGHTER than meridian splendor,
Beams Messiah's spotless fame:
Him we hail, our firm defender;
Him let every tongue proclaim.
He is precious;
He is gracious;
He for ever is the same.

Crowned with honor, might and glory,
See Him high in majesty!
These He won (Oh thrilling story)
By His manhood's agony.
Now adore Him;
Bow before Him;
Own His just supremacy.

Where, 'neath papal witchcraft sleeping,
Victim-souls heed not His blood;
Where, in distant darkness weeping,
Captives dread the oppressor's rod;
Where the Pagan
Clasps his Dagon;
There shall reign the incarnate God.

Lord of glory! Source of favour!
Bid Thy heralds take their stand:
Let Thy name's reviving savour
Wake each dark and drowsy land.
Saviour, hear us;
Speak and cheer us,
When we lift the suppliant hand.

Thou art all ! and all adore Thee,
Where they hymn one ceaseless song:
Soon shall earth, subdued before Thee,
Peal Thy name her tribes among.
Sons of glory,
Chant the story;
And your deep Amen prolong!

[1] This text by W.H.H. differs from is text of this poem on page 394 of this book.

[Note: At the end of these previous three hymns, in the bottom right corner of the leaflet sheet, Maria V. G. Havergal wrote this note: "F.R.H. called these 'splendid'!" See page 466.]

"In Vain the Gods of Earth and Air."

"Be still, and know that I am God: I will be exalted among the heathen, I will be exalted in the earth."—
Psalm 46:10.

IN vain the gods of earth and air
Arouse for deadly fight:
In vain their night-sprung hosts prepare
To crush the Sons of light.

In vain their weapons fast and far
Are hurled, with furious arm:
The God of gods will rule the war.
And shield His church from harm.

Then, warrior saints, "Be still ! Be still !"
Why dread the vaunted fray?
Your Captain's love and might and skill,
Shall nobly win the day.

In heathen climes, ten thousand tongues
Shall chant the Conqueror's fame;
And emulate angelic songs,
In honor of His name.

The monster-gods, who hold the earth
In darkness and dismay,
Shall hear your shout of sacred mirth,
And, vanquished, quit their prey.

Stand, Christians, stand, with crest and cross,
Your Master's Godhead own:
Your spirits then shall feel no loss,
Though worlds be overthrown.

"Arm of the Lord, awake!"

"Awake, awake, put on strength, O arm of the Lord; awake, as in the ancient days, in the generations of old. Art thou not it that hath cut Rahab, and wounded the dragon?"—Isaiah 51:9.

ARM of the Lord, awake!
Seize thy bright sword and take
Strength for the fight:
Smite, smite the dragon's[1] head,
Rome's mystic harlot-bed[2]
False gods and Mahommed,
—Offspring of night.[3]

[1] Revelation 12:9. [2] Rev. 17:5. [3] Rev. 9:1–12.

O Saviour, Son of Man!
Art Thou not He who can
Conquer and bless?
Soon let thy truth o'erthrow
Idols and every foe;
Soon let the whole earth know
Thy righteousness.

Thou art the mighty God,
And thine avenging rod
Reddens with ire:
But, Jesu, stay thine hand,
Spare, spare, thy little band,
Blood-bought, in every land,
Baptized with fire!

Then when the fight is won,
And every toil is done,
Rest on thy throne!
All thy victorious throng,
Marching the heavens along,
Shall, in one ceaseless song,
Praise Thee alone!

"Our Isle in Darkness Lay."

"The people that walked in darkness have seen a great light: they that dwell in the land of the shadow of death, upon them hath the light shined."—Isaiah 9:2.

Our Isle in darkness lay,
Remote from Judah's light;
No beam of truth, no holy ray,
Dispelled the Druid-night:

Till o'er the barrier-sea,
Came messengers of good:
They brought the lamp of life, that we
Might hope through Jesu's blood.

But, still the heathen lie
In deep and loathsome gloom;
Fast bound in deadliest misery,
And sightless of their doom.

Then up, ye favoured race,
Lift high the beacon-flame,—
The cross of Christ, His boundless grace,
His healing cheering name!

Send, send to lands of death,
That torch of living light;
And fan its blaze with prayerful breath,
The Spirit's inward might.

Rejoice we in that light,
The glory of our land;
And be our works and armour bright,
Till Christ on earth shall stand.

"In Vain the Heathen Bows."

"Neither is there salvation in any other; for there is none other name under heaven given among men, whereby we must be saved."—Acts 4:12.

In vain the heathen bows,
To gods of wood and stone;
No cruel rites or vows
Can e'er for sin atone.
No name but one,
Jehovah gave,
With power to save,
Beneath the sun.

That name! our hope below;
That name! the theme above:
Nor men nor angels know
Aught greater, than its love.
Thy power to save,
Blest Nazarene!
Is sung and seen
Beyond the grave.

All hail Immanuel!
O'er earth uplift thy face;
Let Satan's captives tell
The triumphs of thy grace.
Where idols reign,
Let prayer abound,
And faith be found,
Through thy great name!

No name but Thine shall be
Earth's solace and her song;
When heavenly minstrelsy
Shall dwell her tribes among:
When saved by Thee,
No more to weep,
Thy church shall keep
Her Jubilee.

"The God of Love, with Bounteous Hand."

"Then he said unto them, go your way, eat the fat and drink the sweet, and send portions unto them for whom nothing is provided."—Nehemiah 8:10.

The God of love, with bounteous hand,
Has scattered mercy o'er our land;
To us unsparingly are given
The means of grace, the hope of heaven.

For us an ample board is spread
Of wine and milk and living bread;
And pastors watch our souls to guide
In knowledge of the Crucified.

But millions die for lack of food,
For lack of knowing Jesu's blood:
Then, while we feast, let generous hands
Send portions meet to distant lands.

The fainting heathen perish fast;
And present time speeds on to past:
O haste we then to holiest deed,
And from our store supply their need!

O God of Love! thy Spirit grant
To turn to plenty heathen want:
May Jew and Pagan, Bond and Free,
Soon share our feast and joy in Thee!

"The King Proclaims a Feast."

"Go ye therefore, into the highways, and as many as ye shall find bid to the marriage." Matthew 22:9.*

The King proclaims a feast,
His Son's festivity:
And all, the greatest and the least,
His marriage-guests may be.

This Royal Son will give
His Bridegroom-blessing there;
And they who on that blessing live,
His highest love shall share.

Then tell the nations round,
What God the Lord has done;
How pardon, joy, and peace are found,
In his Anointed Son.

Yea tell it far and wide,
Till highway-heathen hear;
And, turning from their sullen pride,
Bow down in holy fear.

Lord, let thy bidding voice
With every heart prevail;
Let heathen-lands in Thee rejoice,
And thy salvation hail!

* In the gospel for the day.

"Wherewith, O Thou Thrice Holy God."

"Wherewith shall I come before the Lord, and bow myself before the High God! Shall I come before Him with burnt offerings, with calves of a year old! Will the Lord be pleased with thousands of rams, or with ten thousands of rivers of oil? Shall I give my first born for my transgression, the fruit of my body for the sin of my soul?"—Micah 6:7.*

Wherewith, O Thou thrice Holy God,
Shall I before Thee come?
How shall my soul escape thy rod,
For sins which strike me dumb?

The erring Jew and heathen sage,
This question asked of old:
Thy word, O Lord, in every page,
The answer can unfold.

No blood of beast, no stream of oil,
No son or daughter slain,
Can from the soul remove one soil,
Or ease one guilty pain.

But Thou, O Christ, and Thou alone
Hast brought us nigh to God;
Thou didst, by blood, for us atone,
And quench the fiery rod.

Then Christians, let the heathen know
The grace of Him who died:
Where'er a herald foot can go,
There preach The Crucified!

* In the first Lesson, Evening Service.

This next printed hymn, and the acrostic on Vowler, both by William Henry Havergal, were found very late in the work on this edition, and are added here at the end of his poems in this book.

The Protestant's Hymn.

THOU, whose uplifted arm
Fills hell with fierce alarm,
  Bend to our prayer!
Shield us from Satan's[1] guile,
ROME's threat, and harlot[2]-smile;
And, when she spreads her wile,
  Break Thou the snare.

[1] Revelation 12:9.
[2] Revelation 17:1–6.

Hear, sole Defender, hear!
Haste with Thy glittering[3] spear,
  Giant-like[4] rouse!
Let not the papal foe[5]
Vex Thy meek Church below,
Nor strike, with ruffian blow,
  Thy virgin[6]-spouse.

[3] Deuteronomy 32:41.
[4] Psalm 78:65.
[5] II Thessalonians 2:3,4; I John 2:18.
[6] II Corinthians 11:2; Revelation 21:9.

O Jesu, Lamb of God!
Look on Thy Martyrs'[7] blood
  Shed by THE[8] BEAST:
Bid all thy saints unite
'Gainst him, in holy[9] fight;
And crown their deeds of might,
  With glory's[10] feast.

[7] Revelation 6:9,10.
[8] Revelation 13:7 and 17:6.
[9] II Corinthians 10:4.
[10] Revelation 19:17.

But, ere Thy wrath[11] shall wake,
And down the burning lake
  BABYLON shall[12] fall;
Spare, spare, from torment-cries,
Souls drunk[13] with sorceries;
Help them to wake and rise,
  At Mercy's call.

[11] Revelation 6:17; II Thessalonians 2:8.
[12] Revelation 18:2,9,10.
[13] Revelation 17:2 and 18:23.

Lord![14] spread Thy sheltering wing
O'er our *anointed*[15] King;
  Cherish his days:
Bid Earth be holy[16] ground,
And, from her furthest[17] bound,
Teach her, with love, to sound
  Thy blessed[18] praise!

[14] I Timothy 2:1.
[15] II Samuel 19:21; Psalm 20:6.
[16] Isaiah 11:9.
[17] Malachi 1:11.
[18] Psalm 72:17–19.

At the bottom of this printed hymn, his daughter Maria wrote this note:

My dear father's Protestant Protest—at the passing of the Catholic emancipation bill 1829.

"The appalling treachery of our Protestant leaders, grieves me.

"The Lord help us, our King, our Country, our Church!

"The end will be glorious! Never despair with such an assurance"

"The Protestant's Hymn" (a published leaflet), and Maria's handwritten comments on this, were found on a page in a Photograph Album donated to the Church Missionary Society by Maria Vernon Graham Havergal in 1886. The next poem, an acrostic on "Vowler," was found in the same Photograph Album, hand-copied as shown in the facsimile copy. In the encircled word "copied" Maria apparently was indicating that her original copy available to her then had the first three letters of Vowler underlined, the word "vows" in line 4 double-underlined, and the two connected with the diagonal line.

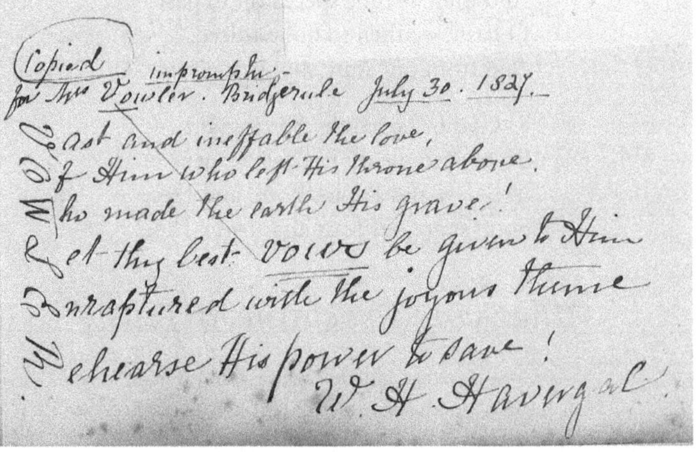
Copied impromptu
for Mrs Vowler. Bridgerule July 30. 1827.
Vast and ineffable the love,
Of Him who left His throne above.
Who made the earth His grave!
Let thy best vows be given to Him
Enraptured with the joyous theme
Rehearse His power to save!
W. H. Havergal.

Impromptu for Mrs. Vowler.

Bridgerule July 30, 1827.

V ast and ineffable the love,
O f Him who left His throne above.
W ho made the earth His grave!
L et thy best vows be given to Him.
E nraptured with the joyous theme
R ehearse His power to save!
W. H. Havergal.

In the handwritten copy copied by his daughter Maria, a line was drawn from the "Vow" in Vowler to the "vows" in line 4.

Written impromptu 13th Dec: 1869 at 9 P.M. for the little tune "Pussy cat"

Softly the Dew in the Evening descends
Cooling the sun heated ground & the gale
Flowerets all fainting it feeds and defends
Ere the consumings of midday prevail.
Sweet gentle Dew drops, how mystic your fall!
Wisdom & mercy float down in you all.

Softer & sweeter by far is that Dew,
Which from the Fountain of Comfort is shed;
When the worn heart feels itself made anew;
And its old pleasures are proved to be dead.
Lord, let Thy Spirit bedew my dry fleece;
I will then follow Thee, strong in Thy peace!

This manuscript of William Henry Havergal's poem was written on the back of a sheet (apparently advertisment or promotion) on the importance of a good piano. This poem was selected by F.R.H. to be the poem for July in her 366-day book *Red Letter Days*. See pages 941 and 1008 of Volume I of this Havergal edition. This was published, set to his music, and is given on pages 1521–1526 of Volume V of the Havergal edition. A note at the end of Chapter IV of *Starlight Through the Shadows* indicates that this was his last hymn (see page 520 of Volume II of the Havergal edition).

Written impromptu 13th Decr 1869 at 9 P.M. for the little tune "Pussy cat" [written for his granddaughter, on pages 1847–1849 of Volume V]

Softly the dew in the evening descends,
Cooling the sun-heated ground and the gale:
Flowerets all fainting it soothingly tends,
Ere the consumings of mid-day prevail.
Sweet, gentle dewdrops, how mystic your fall;
Wisdom and mercy float down in you all.

Softer and sweeter by far is that Dew,
Which from the Fountain of Comfort distils;
When the worn heart is created anew,
And hallowèd pleasure its emptiness fills.
Lord, let Thy Spirit bedew my dry fleece;
Faith then shall triumph, and trouble shall cease.

[Note: The music for this is given at the bottom of page 340 of this book.]

This list is not nearly a complete list of William Henry Havergal's music scores and works on music. This list gives only the generous number of his compositions and essays on music published in Volume V of the Havergal edition (*Songs of Truth and Love: Music by Frances Ridley Havergal and William Henry Havergal*).

Music by William Henry Havergal in Volume V of the Havergal Edition

"Just as I am,

WITHOUT ONE PLEA,"

(A MUCH APPROVED HYMN.)

Set to Music

IN FOUR PARTS, & ALSO FOR A SINGLE VOICE,

WITH

Organ or Pianoforte Accompaniment,

and, with kind permission, Inscribed to The Right Honorable

LADY HATHERTON,

BY

The Revd. W. H. Havergal, M.A.

Honorary Canon of Worcester & Incumbent of Shareshill, Staffordshire.

Ent. Sta. Hall. —— OP. 48. —— *Price 1/6*

PROFITS TOWARDS IMPROVING THE CHURCHYARD OF THE COMPOSER'S PARISH.

London,

JOHN SHEPHERD, 98, NEWGATE STREET.

This is the title page of the orignal published score of this hymn, the music composed by F.R.H.'s father, Rev. William Henry Havergal.

F.R.H. wrote an essay on Charlotte Elliott's hymns, in which she quoted this hymn. The designation of Op. 48 is apparently a mistake here (possibly a typesetter's mistake by the music printer), because W.H.H.'s Op. 48 was *A Hundred Psalm and Hymn Tunes* published by him in 1859. See *Records of the Life of the Rev. William Henry Havergal, M.A.* by his daughter Jane Miriam Crane (London: Home Words Publishing Office, 1882), page 194. See pages 618 and 680 of Volume IV of the Havergal edition.

Just As I Am, Without One Plea

Words by Charlotte Elliott
Music by William Henry Havergal

17
A
And that Thou bid'st me come to Thee; O Lamb of
T
Pno.
23
God, I come!
mf
29

2. Just as I am—and waiting not
To rid my soul of one dark blot,
To Thee, whose blood can cleanse each spot,
O Lamb of God, I come!

3. Just as I am—though tossed about
With many a conflict – many a doubt,
Fightings within, and fears without,
O Lamb of God, I come!

4. Just as I am—poor, wretched, blind,
Sight, riches, healing of the mind,
Yea, all I need in Thee to find,
O Lamb of God, I come!

5. Just as I am—Thou wilt receive,
Wilt pardon, welcome, cleanse, relieve,
Because Thy promise I believe,
O Lamb of God, I come!

6. Just as I am—Thy love unknown
Has broken every barrier down,
Now, to be Thine, yea Thine alone,
O Lamb of God, I come!

7. Just as I am—of that free love
The breadth, length, depth, and height to prove,
Here for a season, then above,
O Lamb of God, I come!

Christmas Carol.

FOR ONE VOICE OR FOUR VOICES.
W. H. HAVERGAL, M. A.
Honorary Canon of Worcester: and Incumbent of Shareshill.
Christians a - wake to joy and praise! Happy, Happy, Happy be our Christmas days: God is the God of truth and love: He hath sent his On_ly Son down from a - bove.

2

Hark how the holy Angels sing!
Blessing, blessing, blessing on the Infant King!
Let us repeat their noble song:
Cherubim and Seraphim the strain prolong:

3

Glory to God, our God on high!
Peace to them on earth, who are condemned to die:
Good-will to all the tribes of men:
Glory, glory, glory sing all heaven! Amen.

PROFITS TO LANCASHIRE DISTRESS.

"MEMENTOTE VINCTORUM."

A Musical Inverse **Palindrome**, *Composed for three Voices;*

BY THE REV.D W.H.HAVERGAL, A.M.

The Profits will be given to the West-Bromwich Anti-Slavery Association.

O Jesu! Salvator! Succurre capti-vis; so-la-re oppressos: Audi nos. Audi nos.

O Jesu! Salvator! Succurre capti-vis: so-la-re oppressos: Audi nos. Audi nos.

Published, (for the Composer,) by **JOHN SHEPHERD**, *98, Newgate Street.* *Price 1/.*

Its effect, however, may be varied by singing it, first, with the Minor third, and then, with the Major.

The peculiarity of this Composition consists in its IDENTITY. *In whatever manner it be taken, whether backwards or forwards, inverted or direct, it is the* SAME.

"MEMENTOTE VINCTORUM."

O Jesu ! Salvator ! Succure captivis; solare oppressos: Audi nos. Audi nos.
O Jesus ! Saviour ! Help the captives; comfort the crushed (or pressed): Hear us. Hear us.

O Jesu ! Salvator ! Succure captivis; solare oppressos: Audi nos. Audi nos.
O Jesus ! Saviour ! Help the captives; comfort the crushed (or pressed): Hear us. Hear us.

A Gloucester Cry!
Hot cross buns!
W: H: H
14 July 1841
Double Antiph: Chant from the subject above

A Gloucester Cry!
Hot cross__ buns!
Double Antiph. [Antiphonal] Chant from the subject above
Langs tune book
W.H.H.
14 July 1841

This is a manuscript of W.H.H.'s Double Canon on "A Gloucester Cry!" On the back side of the sheet he apparently gave an address to return this to him: "Please address to the St. Edwards [? illegible] Hall W. Glasgow."

This is reminiscent of a detail in Haydn's last Symphony, though we do not know whether W.H.H. was aware of this. (W.H.H. likely was completely original in his use of this theme, with no awareness of Haydn's adaptation of this.) It is believed that Haydn quoted or adapted a London street song "Hot Cross Buns" in the Finale of his Symphony No. 104, "The London."

We have extant two palindrome scores by William Henry Havergal, on pages 333 and 346–348 of Volume V of the Havergal edition. Palindrome scores are uncommon, very difficult to write well. Johannes Ockeghem in the 15th century wrote a number of them. There are a number of palindromes in Bach's *Musical Offering*. In the 20th century Alban Berg, Béla Bartók, and Igor Stravinsky wrote musical palindromes. Haydn's Symphony No. 47, "The Palindrome," has as its third movement a Menuetto e Trio, a "Minuetto al Roverso," in which the second part of the minuet is the same as the first part, only reversed backwards, and the Trio section is also a palindrome score.

Child's Morning Hymn

Rev[d] W.H.H.
5. Aug. 1843
Astley

My Fa-ther I thank Thee for sleep. For qui - et & peace - a - ble rest. I

7
thank Thee for stoop ing to keep An in - fant from be - ing dis - trest. Oh how can a

14
poor lit - tle crea-ture re - pay Thy fa - ther - ly kind-ness by night & by day.

2 Verse

My voice would be lisping Thy praise
My heart would repay Thee with love.
O teach me to walk in Thy ways
And fit me to see Thee above.
For Jesus said "Let little children come nigh ["]
And He will not despise such an infant as I.

3rd Verse

As long as Thou seest it right
That here upon earth I should stay
I pray Thee to guard me by night
And help me to serve Thee by day [.]
That when all the days of my life ~~have~~ shall ~~been~~ be past
I may worship Thee better in heaven at last.

William Henry Havergal wrote this hymntune at the end of F.R.H.'s autograph album in the 1860's.

Saviour, when from realms above

Each part in each strain
Per Recte et Retro
On a Ground Bass.
W.H.H.
Saviour, when from realms a-bove, Thou shalt come with glo-ry 'round. May the names of

6
all we love, In Thy Book of Life be found! A - - - - men.

In that Great Day,
Lord, grant, I may
With rapture say,

"Behold I, and <u>the children</u> which God hath given me.
Hebrews 2:13.

Bonn, January 18, 1866. W. H. Havergal

[Note: The manuscript of this is given on page 363 of this book.]

This printed score by W.H.H. was published in the fine volume *Ben Brightboots and Other True Stories, Hymns, and Music* (London: James Nisbet & Co., 1882), original book page 51, page 344 of Volume III of the Havergal edition.

Pussy cat, pussy cat, come to my lap
W. H. H.

Rev[d] W.H.H. tunes for grand children

Proper key F#.
Thank you pret - ty cow that made pleа - sant milk to soak my bread
Ev - ery day & ev - ery night Warm & fresh and sweet & white.

Frank's tune written for him when a baby W.H.H.

Oakhampton Tune written for E.C.C. C.S.C. & J.H.C. W.H.H.

Tune Frances. Written for her at Shareshill 1861 by W.H.H.

Pus-sey cat, pus sey cat come to my house. You shall have milk e nough. You shall have mouse

I will not hurt you nor tease you in play, Nor shall the naugh ty dog drive you a - way.

Pussey cat, pussey cat, come to my lap
Purr away, purr away take a sweet nap.

"Patmos." F. R. H. always sang this tune by her father to these words. Sankey's arrangement "a mournful ditty" grieved her

Words by FRANCES RIDLEY HAVERGAL.

Consecration Hymn.

Music by Rev. W. H. HAVERGAL. M.A.

Take my life, and let it be Con - se - crated, Lord, to thee.

Take my moments and my days, Let them flow in ceaseless praise.

Take my hands, and let them move
At the impulse of thy love.
Take my feet, and let them be
Swift and beautiful for thee.

Take my voice, and let me sing,
Always, only, for my King.
Take my lips, and let them be
Filled with messages from thee.

Take my silver and my gold;
Not a mite would I withhold.
Take my intellect, and use
Every power as thou dost choose.

Take my will and make it thine;
It shall be no longer mine.
Take my heart, it is thine own;
It shall be thy royal throne.

Take my love; my Lord, I pour
At thy feet its treasure-store.
Take myself, and I will be,
Ever, only, all, for thee

1/6 per 100.]

J. & R. Parlane, Paisley

A printed leaflet of the Consecration Hymn. Maria V. G. Havergal wrote this note at the top: "Patmos." F.R.H. always sang this tune by her father to these words. Sankey's arrangement "a mournful ditty," grieved her. *Maria also added "Rev." and "M.A." around her father's name.*

These next two manuscript music scores were written by William Henry Havergal on the front and back of a long piece of paper, very likely or almost certainly both the words and music by W.H.H. Both were written for his granddaughter, Frances Anna Shaw (1856–1948, the first child of Ellen Prestage Havergal Shaw, and the niece and goddaughter of Frances Ridley Havergal). Almost surely written for Francie when she was very young, she would have sung the second song to her brothers, William Henry Shaw (1858–1932) and Alfred Havergal Shaw (1859–1939).

Hark my mothers voice I hear Sweet that voice is to my ear
Ever soft it seems to tell Francie dear I love thee well—(begin again Hark my mothers voice

2 Didst not thou in hours of pain
Lull this head to ease again
With the music of thy voice
Bid my little heart rejoice
Hark my mothers voice I hear etc.

3 Ever gentle ever meek [mild?]
Didst thou nurse thy little child
Taught your [?] Francie's feet the road
Leading on to heaven & God
Hark my mothers voice etc.
For Francie to sing.

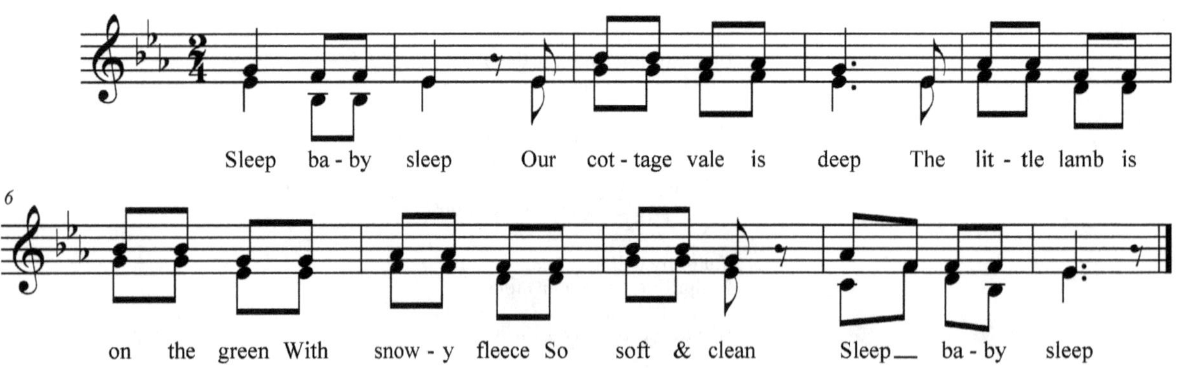

2 Sleep baby sleep
I would not, would not weep
The little lamb he never cries
And bright & happy are his eyes
Sleep baby sleep

3 Sleep baby sleep
Near where the woodbines creep
Be always like the lamb so mild
A sweet & kind & gentle child
Sleep etc.

4 Sleep baby sleep
Thy rest shall angels keep
While on the grass the lamb shall feed
And never suffer want or need
Sleep baby sleep
For Francie to sing to brothers.

Note: In an extra space below the first score (below "Hark my mother's voice I hear"), W.H.H. had started the words of his "The Worcestershire Christmas Carol," the words later crossed out and never finished: "How grand and how bright That wonderful night When angels to Bethlehem came." The words and music for Christmas hymn are found on page 1832 of Volume V of the Havergal edition.

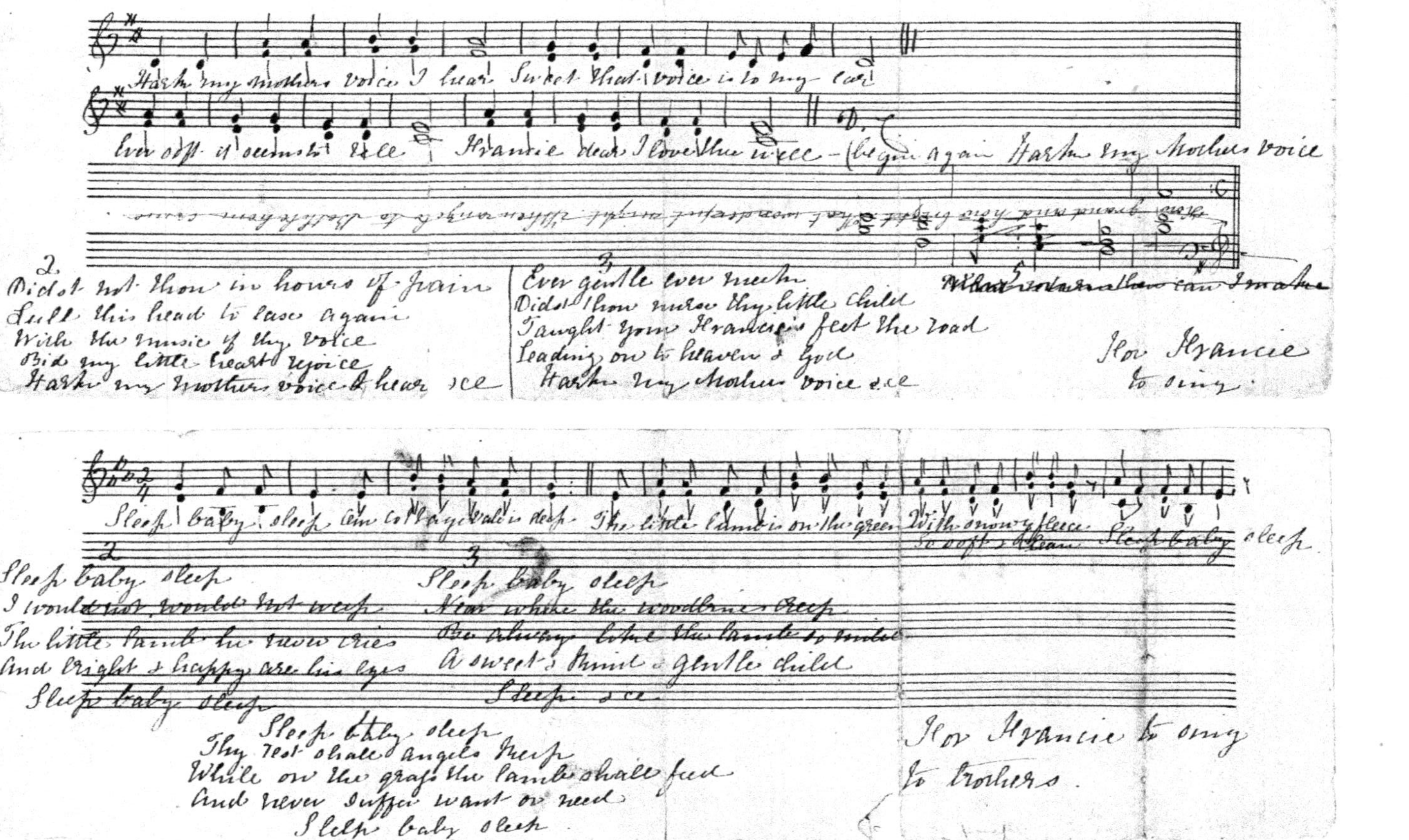

These two music scores are the front and back sides of a manuscript composed and written by William Henry Havergal for his granddaughter, Frances Anna Shaw (the oldest child of Ellen Prestage Havergal Shaw and the goddaughter of Frances Ridley Havergal). W.H.H. very likely or almost surely wrote the words as well as the music here.

"For Francie to sing."

1 Hark my mother's voice I hear Sweet that voice is to my ear
Ever soft it seems to tell Francie dear I love thee well
(begin again Hark my mother's voice [etc. repeat the first 2 lines]

2. Didst not thou in hours of pain Lull this head to ease again
With the music of thy voice Bid my little heart rejoice
Hark my mother's voice I hear [etc. repeat the chorus]

3. Ever gentle ever mild Didst thou nurse thy little child
Taught your Francie's feet the road Leading on to heaven and God.
Hark my mother's voice I hear [etc. repeat the chorus]

"For Francie to sing to brothers"

1. Sleep baby, sleep [illegible?] cottage vale is deep
The little lamb is on the green With snowy fleece so soft and clean Sleep baby sleep

2. Sleep baby sleep I would not, would not weep
The little lamb he never cries And bright and happy are his eyes Sleep baby sleep

3. Sleep baby sleep Near where the woodbines creep
Be always like the lamb so mild A sweet and kind and gentle child Sleep etc.

4. Sleep baby sleep Thy rest shall angels keep
While on the grass the lamb shall feed And never suffer want or need Sleep baby sleep.

This is Number 163 in *Havergal's Psalmody and Century of Chants*, and the tune for hymn number 4 in *Songs of Grace and Glory*.

In her article/essay entitled "Seven Clerical Hymn-Writers" (Chapter IX in the posthumously published *Specimen Glasses for the King's Minstrels*), F.R.H. presented this hymn, and at the end wrote this paragraph:[1]

> The name of the tune to this hymn—Havergal—No. 777 in "Songs of Grace and Glory," [later placed as No. 4 in *Songs of Grace and Glory*] may excite remark; but it will not be wondered that this name was chosen, when we tell that it was the last ever written by that sainted hand which now bears one of the "harps of God"—written just before the Master's voice said "Come up higher." The tune with its serene melody and rich harmony is itself an epitome of his musical work.

His oldest child Miriam (who was 19 when Frances was born, tutored her when she was two and a half, and lived 19 years after Frances died) wrote this in her biography of W.H.H.:[2]

> This Saturday [April 16, 1870] was indeed to prove my dear father's last conscious day. In a letter to a friend, written on the Monday morning, his daughter F.R.H. speaks of that day as "a very climax of peace and brightness in all respects." He twice walked out a little in front of his house, hoping to catch a young gentleman, a neighbour, to whom he thought a word in season might be useful. He also wrote his last lines, "Messiah, Redeemer!" and set them to a palindrome, and the same day he composed the beautiful tune "Havergal" to Dr. Monsell's fine Trinitarian hymn, "Mighty Father! Blessed Son!"

F.R.H. prepared this score for publication in *Songs of Grace and Glory.*

HAVERGAL.
[H. P. 163.]
4 Col. ii. 2. "The mystery of God, and of the Father, and of Christ."
Tune HAVERGAL. 777.
1 MIGHTY Father! Blessèd Son!
Holy Spirit! Three in One!
Evermore Thy will be done!
2 Threefold is Thy glorious might,
Threefold is Thy name of light,
Holy! Awful! Infinite!
3 Threefold let our praises be,
Great mysterious One, to Thee!
Undivided Trinity!
4 Mystery of mysteries!
Before whom with veilèd eyes
Songs of saints and angels rise.
5 Rainbow-like the emerald zone
That encompasseth Thy throne,
O Thou most mysterious One!
6 Thunderings and lightnings, rolled
From beneath, Thy saints enfold,
Clothed in white, and crowned with gold.
7 Holy, Holy, Holy Lord!
God Almighty! Father! Word!
Spirit! Three in One adored!
8 Threefold is Thy love to me,
Threefold let my graces be,
Faith, and Hope, and Charity.
9 Mighty Father! Blessèd Son!
Holy Spirit! Three in One!
Evermore Thy will be done.
J. S. B. Monsell, LL.D., 1863.
Note the Symbolic Form—Three lines harmonizing in each verse;—three verses in each division;—three divisions making one hymn.

[1] *Specimen Glasses for the King's Minstrels* by Frances Ridley Havergal (London: Home Words Publishing Office, 1881), original book pages 109–110, page 765 of Volume II of the Havergal edition.

[2] *Records of the Life of the Rev. William Henry Havergal, M.A.* by his daughter Jane Miriam Crane (London: Home Words Publishing Office, 1882), original book pages 354–355, page 667 of Volume IV of the Havergal edition. Miriam also wrote this near the end of Chapter VII of the same volume (original book pages 164–165, page 625 of Volume IV):

> The last lines he composed, and which he set to a Palindrome on Easter Even, 1870, are these:—
>
> [She then quoted the five-line stanza, "Messiah, Redeemer."]
>
> Earlier in the day he had composed the beautiful tune "Havergal," No. 163 in "Havergal's Psalmody." On Easter-Day he was seized with apoplexy, and remained unconscious forty-eight hours, when he quietly passed through death into life eternal the 19th of April, 1870.

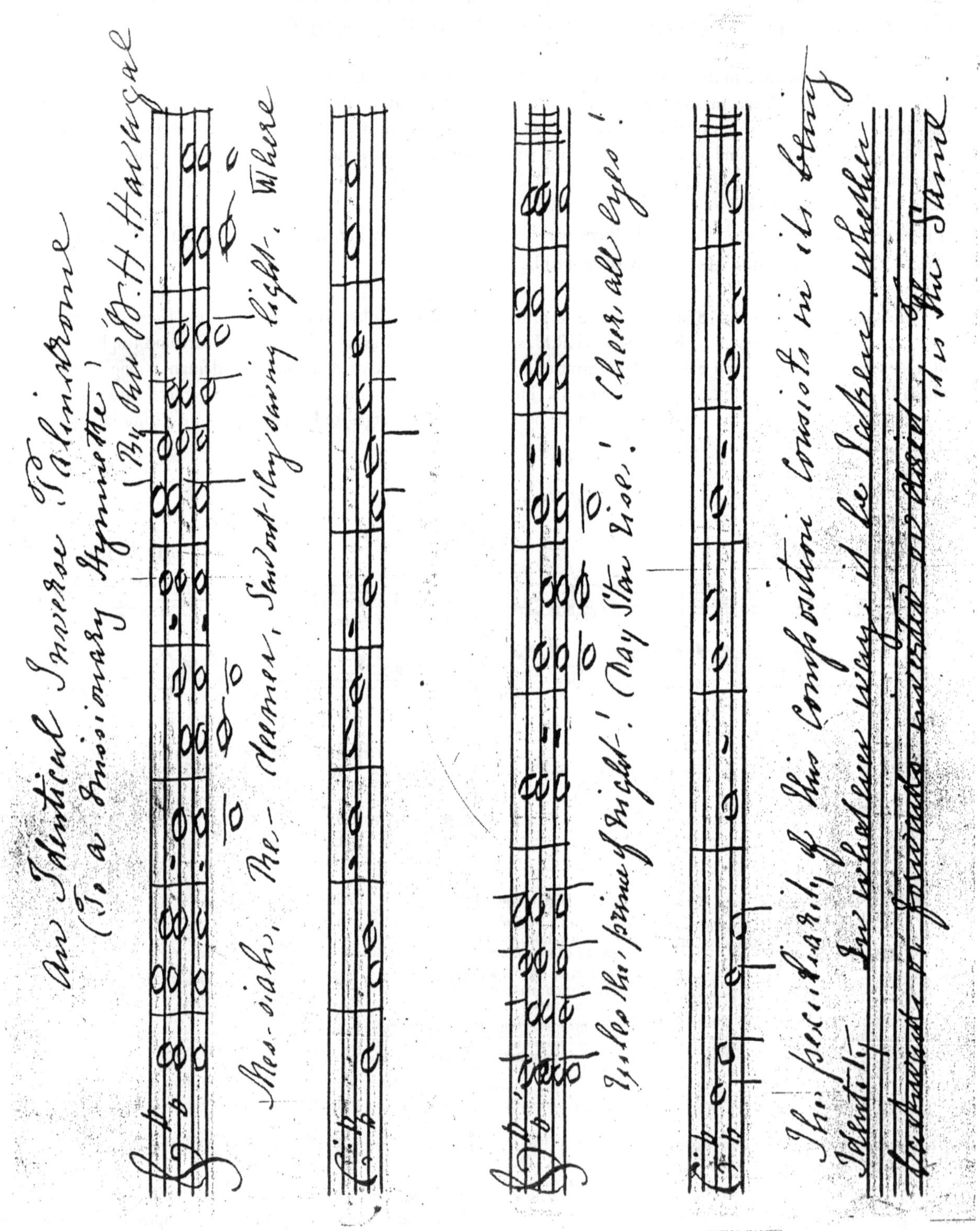

This brief stanza ("Messiah, Redeemer") was the last verse of poetry that William Henry Havergal wrote, and this palindrome score was the last music that he composed. This is newly typeset precisely as W.H.H. notated this, his last score. In the first page, the score is notated in full score; in the second page of the score, he notated the music in the four separate parts. In

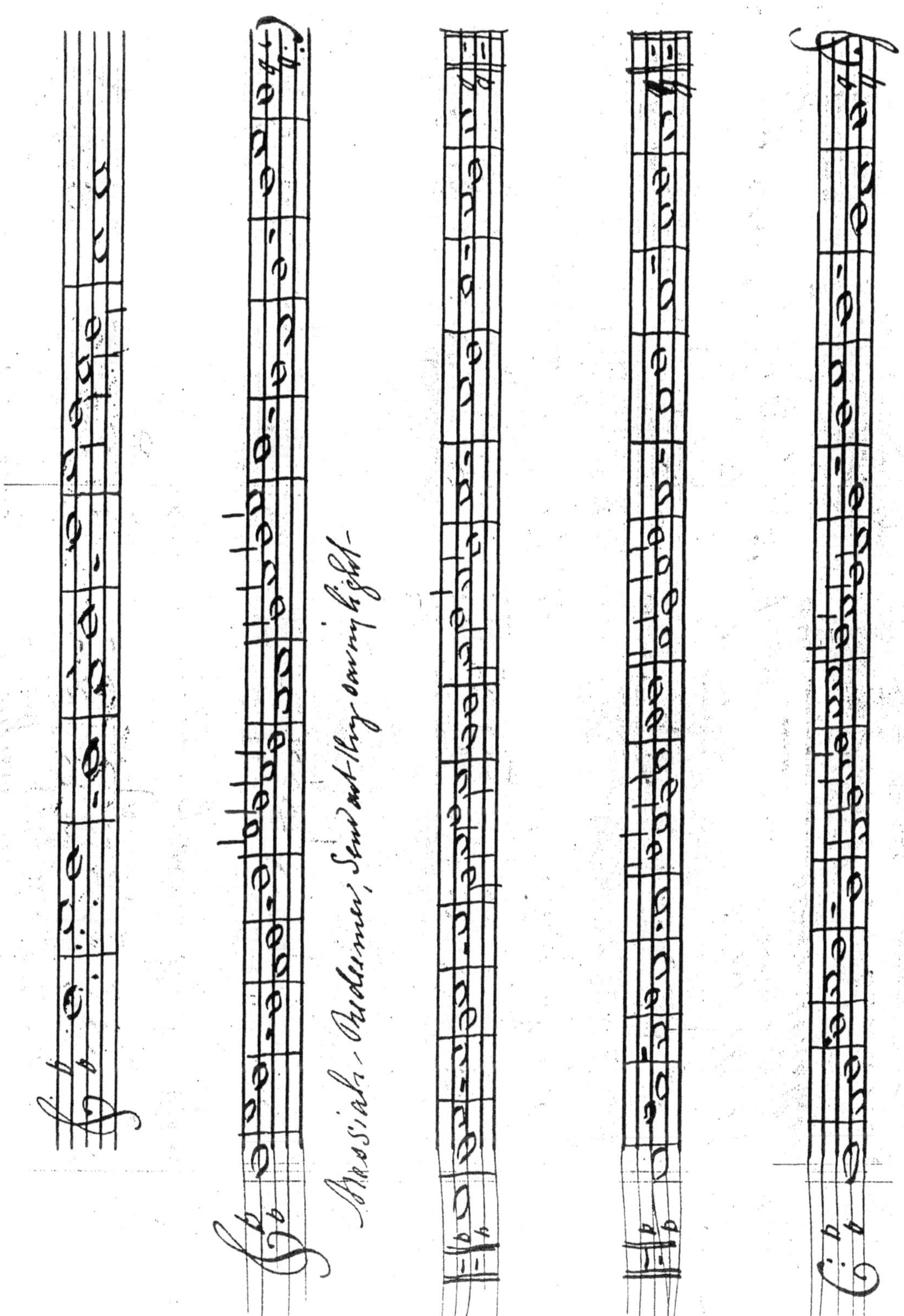

the second page, in the top treble clef, he only began but did not complete the top voice line of the four-part score (which is written in three-plus-one piano style): possibly he became distracted and later returned and re-started the top line, which is both started and completed in the second treble clef of the second page. The first page is a different score from the second

Identical Inverse Palindrome

(To a Missionary Hymnette)

By Rev W. H. Havergal

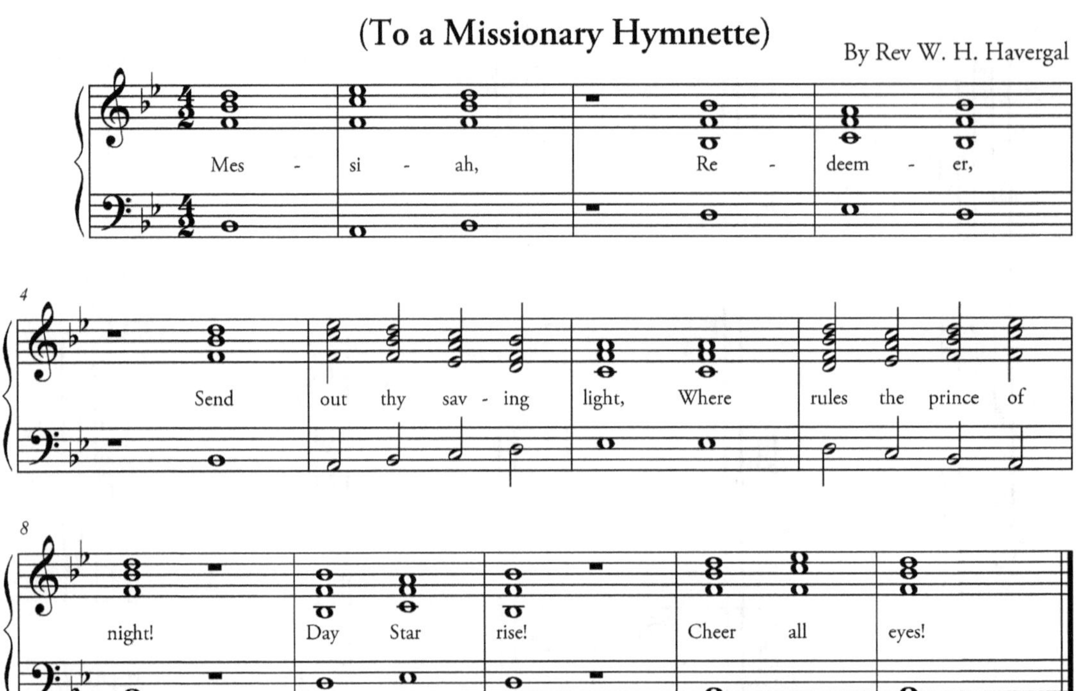
Mes - si - ah,
Re - deem - er,
Send out thy sav - ing light, Where rules the prince of
night! Day Star rise! Cheer all eyes!

The peculiarity of this composition consists in its ~~being~~ identity [.] In whatever way it be taken, whether backwards or forwards [,] inverted or direct [,] it is the same.

page: the top and bottom voice lines are identically the same on both pages, but the music for the two inner voices of the second page was completely re-written and is different—a different score—from the two inner voices of the first page. This was written on Saturday, April 16, 1870 (the day before Easter Sunday), his last full day of consciousness in this world. His daughter Frances Ridley Havergal described that day as "a very climax of peace and brightness in all respects." He had been very ill, and was weak and not well, so that a lapse or inattention is easily understood. He rose early the next morning, became unconscious (possibly a stroke, we don't know), and never regained consciousness before he died shortly before noon on Tuesday, April 19, 1870.

From the left, Henry East Havergal (1819–1875), Ellen Prestage (Havergal) Shaw (1823–1886), and Francis Tebbs Havergal (1829–1890), the second, fourth, and fifth of William Henry and Jane Head Havergal's six children. Miriam's portrait is found on page 360, and Maria's and Frances' portraits are found on page 316. The photographs of Henry and Francis (called "Frank" by the family), with such poor resolution, were the best available.

WILLIAM HENRY HAVERGAL AND LOWELL MASON.

Before the first score by William Henry Havergal (his setting of "Just as I am" by Charlotte Elliott), this is a set of quotations of correspondence between Lowell Mason and W.H.H., and other quotations and details concerning them.

Dr. Lowell Mason (1792–1872), the American composer and publisher of hymns and very prominent, important, influential leader and reformer of church music in the United States, wrote this in a letter dated "London , Jan. 9th, 1852 : "

> On Sunday morning, at 11 o'clock, we attended divine service in the parish church of St. Nicholas [Worcester], Rev. Mr. Havergal, rector. The exercises commenced by a few measures as a voluntary, or rather prelude, and the "giving out" the tune on the organ, after which all the congregation united in a single stanza sung to the old tune called "Tallis's Evening Hymn." The hymn was not read nor named, but it appeared to be a common thing for the worship to commence in the use of a stanza well known, always the same, and to the same tune. It was a hearty commencement, for every one seemed to join with full voice. The service was read by the curate. The chanting was done by the whole congregation, and the responding was between the occupants of the lower floor and those of the gallery—but the song was universal—men, women and children uniting harmonious voices. The Venite and the Te Deum were chanted responsively; the psalms were not chanted but, read in the usual manner. Two metrical hymns were sung during the service. The tunes were both of the old ecclesiastical class, and were in the same rhythmic form as St. Ann's, York , &c. appear in the *Cantica Laudis*. The first and last words of each line being long, and all the rest short. They were sung by all the people, and in very quick time; as fast as propriety would allow the enunciation of the words. They were somewhat quicker than the writer has taught this class of tunes in musical conventions and singing classes in America. Let the tune Uxbridge, for example, be sung in quick time, somewhat quicker than usual, and the crotchets will give the time of the minims in the above-named class of tunes. There were one or two organ interludes introduced in a psalm of five stanzas; but these were very short, not more than about two measures, or the length of the last line of a common metre tune. "These tunes would be popular in America," said the lady who was with me, who, though not a singer, has been accustomed for many years to give close attention to the Psalmody, and to hear criticisms and remarks concerning it. And indeed, they are as far from being dull and heavy as need be; I doubt not that many good people, with us, would think it almost irreverent to sing a hymn through with such rapidity. Yet all the people, old and young, joined—all seemed to know the tunes perfectly, and all kept well together.
>
> Mr. Havergal is himself, as is well known, much of a musical man and an excellent composer. He has once or twice obtained the Gresham prize medal for the best composition of a church service or anthem; and he is well-known by numerous sacred songs, published with pianoforte accompaniment. But it is metrical psalmody and the chant in which he is most interested, and in which he has produced some very fine specimens. He only devotes odds and ends of time to music, and never writes music when he is able to write sermons; but it has been, when weary with the labors of the day, or when travelling, that he has composed most of his popular and excellent tunes. He has many curious and valuable old books of psalmody, and is now himself writing, as he can find time, some historical notice of the "Old Hundredth Psalm Tune." [1]

He later wrote:

> . . . . The St. Nicholas Church, in Worcester, England , has the true Congregational style, and when that, which we have heretofore described, shall universally prevail, Congregational singing will be excellent and effective. [2]

This next quotation refers to Lowell Mason's second trip to England in 1850, when he visited St. Nicholas' Church, Worcester, in which William Henry Havergal both was the pastor and led the music. In the periodical *Music*, Volume IV, May, 1893 to November, 1893, in an essay entitled "Lowell Mason, American Congregational Musician" (pages 527–530), this was written:

[1] *Musical Letters from Abroad* ("Including Detailed Accounts of the Birmingham, Norwich, and Dusseldorf Musical Festivals of 1852") by Lowell Mason (New York: Mason Brothers, 1854), pages 13–14.

[2] *Musical Letters from Abroad* by Mason, pages 163–164.

> Mason went to Europe twice, in 1837, the year of the accession of Queen Victoria, and in 1850. In England he interested himself in church music and congregational singing. He found the musical service, in Rev. W. H. Havergal's church, Worcester, England, "excellent in all particulars and far in advance of anything that he heard." [3]

In the July 16, 1870 issue of *The Musical World*, in a memorial notice of "The Late Rev. W. H. Havergal" (which apparently was a quotation from another periodical, the *Tonic Sol-fa Reporter*), this was written:

> When Dr. Lowell Mason visited this country, one of his first and most sacred pilgrimages was to Mr. Havergal's house in Worcester, and we well remember the heartiness and earnestness with which Dr. Mason acknowledged the obligations of American psalmodists to this good man. [4]

Next are quotations from a number of letters between Mason and W.H.H.

Frances Ridley Havergal wrote this in her "Supplementary Remarks" in *Havergal's Psalmody and Century of Chants*: "The selections from 'Havergal's Psalmody' will be found, as experience has proved them to be, easily learnt, greatly liked, and practically adapted for congregational singing. Of one of these, Dr. Lowell Mason, the great American promoter of choral singing, wrote as follows:—"

> I have lately introduced into my choir, and sung with admirable effect, your tune "St. Nicholas" [now called "Eden," No. 38 in this volume]. The effect of it was truly magnificent. My choir consists of about sixty singers; the different parts are well sustained, and about equally balanced. I have never heard anything come nearer to my *beau ideal* of Church Music than did the singing of this tune, on a fine Sabbath morning, in a church filled with people. It made a deep impression; and the next day one and another was asking, "What tune did you sing yesterday morning?" "Where did you get that tune?" etc. The performance of "St. Nicholas" ["Eden"] makes one feel as did Jacob at Luz, and involuntarily exclaim, "This is none other but the house of God, and this is the gate of heaven." Wonderful would be the effect of Psalmody were all the people to unite in such lofty and majestic strains.—April 30, 1847. [5]

Miss Grierson wrote that Mason described "Eden" (the hymntune that had earlier been named "St. Nicholas") as "sublime." [6]

The next three quotations from letters by Lowell Mason were given in Miriam Crane's biography *Records of the Life of the Rev. William Henry Havergal, M.A.*:

(*Letters from Dr. Lowell Mason*)

> I have lately introduced into my choir and sung with admirable effect your tunes of St. Nicholas and Glasshampton. The effect of St. Nicholas was truly magnificent; I have never heard anything come nearer to my *beau ideal* of Church music than did the singing of this tune on a fine Sabbath morning, in a church filled with people. It made a

[3] *Music* ("A Monthly Magazine Devoted to the Art, Science, Technic and Literature"), Volume IV, May, 1893 to November, 1893, W. S. B. Mathews, Editor and Publisher (Chicago: Published at 240 Wabash Avenue, 1893), page 529. This ending sentence was found in two other places: In *Education* ("A Monthly Magazine, Devoted to the Science, Art, Philosophy, and Literature of Education"), Frank H. Kasson and Frank H. Palmer, Editors, Volume XIV, September, 1893—June, 1894 (Boston: Kasson and Palmer, 50 Bromfield Street, 1894), in an essay on Lowell Mason entitled "Lowell Mason, American Musician" by Rev. James H. Ross, Somerville, Massachusetts (pages 411–416), Ross wrote this same quotation (on page 415): "He found the musical service, in Rev. W. H. Havergal's church, Worcester, England, 'excellent in all particulars and far in advance of anything that he heard.'" In *The Poets of the Church* A Series of Biographical Sketches of Hymn-Writers with Notes on Their Hymns by Edwin F. Hatfield, D.D. (New York: Anson D. F. Randolph & Company, 1884), page 302, in his entry on William Henry Havergal, Dr. Hatfield wrote this same statement (only without the same quotation marks in Dr. Hatfield's text): "He [Dr. Lowell Mason] describes the musical service in Mr. Havergal's church as excellent in all particulars, and far in advance of anything that he heard in England."

[4] *The Musical World* Vol. XLVIII (London: Duncan Davison & Co., 244, Regent Street, 1870), page 483.

[5] F.R.H.'s "Supplementary Remarks" published in *Havergal's Psalmody and Century of Chants* (London: Robert Cocks & Co., 1871). She also quoted this same letter in her "Original Preface to the Musical Edition of Songs of Grace and Glory" published by Nisbet in 1876 and later re-published in the definitive "New and Enlarged Musical Edition" of *Songs of Grace and Glory* (London: James Nisbet & Co., 1880). See pages 163–164 and 528 of Volume V of the Havergal edition.

[6] *Frances Ridley Havergal Worcestershire Hymnwriter* by Janet Grierson (Bromsgrove, Worcestershire: The Havergal Society, 1979), page 63. See page 1159 of Volume IV of the Havergal edition. Miss Grierson wrote, ". . . . The tune "St. Nicholas," described as "sublime" by the American musician Dr. Lowell Mason of Boston, was appropriately re-named ' Eden ' in the posthumous publication of Havergal's Psalmody."

deep impression, and the next day one and another was asking, "What tune did you sing yesterday morning?" "Where did you get that tune?" etc.

On the Sabbath following we sung Glasshampton; this is beautiful, but St. Nicholas is sublime. The performance makes one feel as Jacob did, "none other but the gate of heaven." Wonderful would be the effect of psalmody were all the people to unite in such lofty, majestic strains.

November, 1848. My book the "National Psalmist" was completed about September last. I fear to send it you, for there is, I well know, much that you cannot approve. There is much indeed, I (who am not so orthodox as you are) do not like, but I was obliged to adapt myself to the state of things, and I introduce into my book quite as much of the real psalmody as the people are prepared for. But I have done something towards reformation. A few of your tunes which I took a little liberty with I have marked; forgive me, my dear sir, for the few instances in which I deviated a little from your copy, for the purpose of adapting them for more general use here. Much have you enriched my book. Your letters and remarks have much modified my book. For all this and much more I shall ever be truly grateful.

March, 1862. I thank you for your kind note of February 2. It has gladdened my heart, and caused me to look upon your portrait, ever before me, with renewed interest, and, if possible, with a deeper respect and affection for its original, who has been so kind to me. Ten years ago, on January 3, I saw you at Worcester; dined with you on Saturday. On Sunday I attended divine service at your church; you preached from Jeremiah 50:5. I wish you had put that sermon into your printed volumes. In the evening you preached again on Psalm 23:4. It is most pleasant to recall the remembrance of kind friends. I shall never cease to hold them dear. Now, dear sir, may the blessing of our heavenly Father ever rest upon you and yours, and at last, when you shall be called home, may an abundant entrance be ministered to you into everlasting habitations.

Yours most truly,

Lowell Mason.[7]

Miriam later quotes two letters by W.H.H. to Lowell Mason: "After an illness in the summer my father gives a short account of his autumn holiday in a letter to Dr. Lowell Mason."

Killarney, Oct. 22, 1856.

My dear Sir,

Your kind letter of the 29th ult. has overtaken me in this charming locality. An attack of poor or suppressed gout left me in an enfeebled state. As, too, I had had no holiday for fifteen months, I felt obliged as soon as practicable to take a long rest. With Mrs. Havergal and our neighbours, the Misses Nott, I have been in Ireland for more than a month, and hope to reach home again next week. The main attraction to Ireland was the new home of my dear daughter Ellen; we are thankful to say we found everything equal to our fondest wishes. We spent three weeks at Kilkee, a wild but noble spot on the western coast, where the waves and breezes of the Atlantic greatly refreshed and delighted us. I am, thank God, much benefited by the change.

While out I have been catching an hour now and then to arrange and copy a selection of my own psalm and hymn tunes, which have either never been published or are scattered in the publications of others. My children are urgent for me to do this, but it is a difficult task with my imperfect vision. I have had some very large music paper ruled on purpose for the occasion. If the accompanying MSS. will be of any service to you, all is yours ad lib. The sacred round was hit off sortie years ago. The recto et retro chant was picked by Fanny, my scribe, out of a lot of such articles. I never have time for greater things, but scraps of weary hours will lead my thoughts to some little contrivances of a short description. My dear wife joins me in very best remembrances to Mrs. Mason.

Believe me,

Most faithfully yours,

W. H. Havergal.[8]

[7] *Records of the Life of the Rev. William Henry Havergal, M.A.* by his daughter Jane Miriam Crane (London: Home Words Publishing Office, 1882), pages 188–190. See pages 630–631 of Volume IV of the Havergal edition.

[8] *Records of the Life of the Rev. William Henry Havergal, M.A.* by Miriam Crane, pages 188–190. See page 636 of Volume IV of the Havergal edition.

(*To Dr. Lowell Mason, of Boston, U.S.*)

Poppelsdorfer Allée, Bonn,
March 5, 1866.

My dear Friend,

Your letter has just been welcomed. I hasten to reply to it as well as my eyes will allow. I can hope only for less dimness of vision at the most. At this distance I dare not advise you; possibly an operation may restore you to perfect sight spite of advancing years; I have known many such instances. The good Lord favour you. I can keenly sympathize with you. I feel that I write worse than I did, and can read only large church print for a few minutes; but all these things, though trying, are but light afflictions compared with what might be. Then our great standing mercies in Christ Jesus, how precious are they! May they abound to you. Only my dear wife is now with me and one of our home servants. My parish is left in good hands. I regret to hear of the popularity of Robertson's sermons in America. There is much of splendid trifling in them, with "fair speeches" on behalf of erroneous novelties.

As to music I do but little, although I cannot keep from nibbling at chants and metrical tunes. I have fifty varied forms of the Grand Chant,* and have one hundred other chants, mostly single, ready for publication.

All that has been passing in America has engaged my anxious attention. In dear old England Church matters are perilous, though I hope for the best by reason of the Bishops having spoken out well on ultra-ritual movement.

Here, as in England, we have had no winter yet. My own parish is still mercifully preserved from cattle-plague. My old friend Dr. Hodges is gradually failing at Bristol. My dear wife is better, and joins me in best regards.

Ever faithfully yours,

W. H. Havergal.[9]

* Early in 1867 J. Shepherd published "The Grand Chant in Forty Different Forms." By the Rev. W. H. Havergal, M.A., Op. 52.

This next quotation is taken from a "Biographical Sketch" by Andrew James Symington:

Mr. Havergal's severe and classical music is often to be heard in our cathedrals; and in Scotland and America no Psalm tune is oftener sung than "Evan." The history of this tune is somewhat peculiar, and, as its authorship has been questioned, it may be well to mention the matter here, as the writer can do so authoritatively from Mr. Havergal's own words, as well as from written statements. In 1847 Mr. Havergal published an original air (a sacred song) to Burns's words, "O Thou dread Power." Dr. Lowell Mason, of New York, arranged the first half of that air as a psalm tune, altering both the time and key, and called it "Evan." Hence it is frequently given in collections with Mason's name, and at other times simply with the letter H, under which initial it first appeared, because Dr. Mason did not wish to attribute the liberty he had taken in arranging the part of a melody to the composer of the original air. This is Dr. Lowell Mason's own explanation, which we have seen. Mr. Havergal has since arranged it as it should be, and within the last month played over the tune, and gave a MS. copy of it to the writer, with its curious history noted on the sheet. It has travelled far and wide, and been claimed for many composers, and even been called an old Celtic air. We have here stated the true origin of this unprecedentedly popular tune.[10]

F.R.H. wrote this in a letter to Charles Busbridge Snepp:

Ascension Day 1871.

Do you know my father's tune "Evan"? It has been claimed as a Celtic air by some of those Celts who want to appropriate anything that can add to Celtic glory! The Andersonian Professor of Music at Glasgow has recently inserted a challenge to all Highlanders on the subject in the Scotch papers, and the result is, that it is finally and incontestably proved to be my father's own, entirely and only, and neither Celtic nor Lowell Mason's, to whom he once played and sang the melody,—which the Doctor much admired, and took it with him to America,—reducing it to a commometre tune, with only my father's initial "H." All my dear father's own tunes are wonderfully suited to large congregations.[11]

[9] *Records of the Life of the Rev. William Henry Havergal, M.A.* by his daughter Jane Miriam Crane (London: Home Words Publishing Office, 1882), pages 313–314. See page 659 of Volume IV of the Havergal edition.

[10] *The Pastor Remembered, and the Brethren Entreated A Memorial of the Rev. W. H. Havergal, M.A.* by Charles Bullock, with the "Biographical Sketch" by Andrew James Symington (London: W. Hunt & Co., S. W. Partridge & Co., and The Christian Book Society, no date, likely 1870), pages 51–52. See page 714 of Volume IV of the Havergal edition.

[11] *Letters by the Late Frances Ridley Havergal* edited by her sister, Maria V. G. Havergal (London: James Nisbet & Co., 1886), Appendix II, pages 388–390. See also page 257 of Volume IV of the Havergal edition.

His daughter Maria wrote this in her *Autobiography*:

> It was during this visit to Scotland that my father became acquainted with Dr. Laurie, of Monckton Manse, to whom he dedicated a lovely melody to "Burns's Prayer." This had a piano accompaniment, and is the original air from which the popular tune "Evan" was afterwards taken by Dr. Lowell Mason. When visiting my father, Dr. Mason was charmed with his singing it, and requested a copy. Turning to Frank, my father told him to give his copy to the Doctor, who took it to America . He wrote for permission to shorten the air to a C.M. hymn tune. My father did not think it in strict, ecclesiastical style, and would not allow his name to appear; hence it got published with his initial H. only, and, appearing in Dr. Mason's collection, soon got his name instead of my father's.
>
> Would that more had heard my father's exquisite touch and extemporized fugues and harmonies—waves of melody, now richest chords, then gentlest adagios. His voice was sweet and clear, and his long-sustained shake would hush us completely.[12]

These are only glimpses of the relation and communication between Mason and W.H.H., most of the details no longer extant. Finally, these are two more glimpses.

W.H.H.'s *A History of the Old Hundredth Psalm Tune* with Specimens was published by Mason Brothers, New York, in 1854. Mason Brothers was the publishing firm of Lowell Mason's sons Daniel Gregory Mason (1820–1869) and Lowell Mason (1823–1885), who began the publishing firm in 1853.

In the first Volume of *Sermons, Chiefly on Historical Subjects from the Old and New Testaments Preached in the Parish Church of St. Nicholas, Worcester* by W. H. Havergal, Volume I, Old Testament (London: Hamilton, Adams, and Co., and Hatchard, 1853), in the published list of subscribers of the books, this entry was given: "Mason, Lowell , Esq., Boston , U.S. Two copies." See page 1317 of Volume IV of the Havergal edition (page xiv of the original book).

This is a final note in this section on Lowell Mason and William Henry Havergal: Few today realize how remarkably prominent and successful Lowell Mason was as a musician in the 19th century. He was very famous, highly regarded, and his many editions of hymnbooks were published in the millions. He became one of the wealthiest men of his generation in the United States, enormously wealthy from the sales of his hymnbooks and other publications. (This was the generation before the U.S. railroad "robber barons" and other extremely wealthy industrialists of the last half of the 19th century.) The mention of this is not at all meant to impugn nor question Dr. Mason's ethics or integrity. William Henry Havergal never sought any financial gain from his music, only a desire to glorify God and to serve others. For one example, his daughter Maria wrote in the first chapter of *Memorials of Frances Ridley Havergal* (see page 6 of Volume IV of the Havergal edition): "My father's first published musical composition was a setting of Bishop Heber's hymn, 'From Greenland's icy mountains.' The proceeds amounted to £180, and were devoted to the Church Missionary Society." Another very representative example of this is the statement "Profits to Various Charities" at the top of a list of published music scores composed by W.H.H., found on page 1558 of Volume V of the Havergal edition. Over and over he would assign any profits from published scores to a specific church or to another work of ministry, and he freely gave his music, knowledge of music, and advice to others without price. Beyond his intentionally declining any financial gain from his published scores, W.H.H. was notably not much honored formally or famously for his work that surely must have been realized and valued by many in his day (for one example, he was a fine musicologist, abundantly worthy of a doctorate in just that area alone, and that is not as important as other areas of his interest, prominently foreign missions and the work of the Church Missionary Society): though there is no proof of this, there is a temptation—after much research—to infer that he may have been offered an honorary doctorate, knighthood, or other honor, and declined them.

[12] *The Autobiography of Maria Vernon Graham Havergal* edited by her sister Jane Miriam Crane (London: James Nisbet & Co., 1887), pages 50–51. See pages 506–507 of Volume IV of the Havergal edition. "Frank" was William Henry Havergal's fifth child, Francis Tebbs Havergal (1829–1890).

ADVERTISEMENTS.

FOURTH EDITION.

IN MEMORIAM.

HAVERGAL'S PSALMODY.

Being selections from 'Old Church Psalmody,' 'Hundred Tunes,' and unpublished manuscripts of the late Rev. W. H. Havergal, M.A., Honorary Canon of Worcester. Edited by his daughter, Frances Ridley Havergal.

A.	With full Prefaces and Portrait . .	6s. 6d.
B.	Do. without Century of Chants .	5s. 0d.
D.	Without Prefaces or Portrait . .	8s. 6d., 2s. 6d.
E.	Do. without Chants . . .	3s. 0d., 2s. 3d.
C.	and F. Chants alone	1s. 6d., 1s. 0d.

ROBERT COCKS & CO., New Burlington Street, London, W.; and through all Book and Musicsellers.

HAVERGAL'S PSALMODY contains the best results of the psalmodic labours of a lifetime in discovery, restoration, harmonisation, and original composition. All well known and valuable old tunes from English, Scotch, and German sources will be found in it, together with full supply for modern hymns and metres. There are 253 Tunes and 100 Chants, also Hymn Chants. Kyries, Glorias, &c. The Prefaces and Historical Notes are a treasury of information, and an armoury of defence of the principles of Church Music.

o

HAVERGAL'S PSALMODY ABRIDGED.

Contains 100 Tunes selected from the Full Edition. Price 4d. Cloth 6d.

Paisley: J. & R. PARLANE. London: HOULSTON & SONS.

o

RE-ISSUE OF WORKS BY THE LATE

REV. W. H. HAVERGAL, M.A.

SERMONS, CHIEFLY HISTORICAL. Vol. I. Old Test. **Vol. II. New Test. Price 8s. 6d.**

SIX LECTURES ON THE ARK OF THE COVENANT. **Price 2s.**

HAMILTON, ADAMS, & CO.; and HATCHARDS & CO., LONDON.

A HISTORY OF THE OLD HUNDREDTH PSALM TUNE, **with Specimens. Price 2s.**

SAMPSON, LOW, & CO., LONDON.

PYRMONT: AN ELIGIBLE PLACE FOR ENGLISH **Patients, who require Chalybeate or Saline Waters. Price 1s.**

JAMES NISBET & CO., LONDON.

In rich cloth, bevelled, with Portrait and Illustrations, price 6s.,

RECORDS OF THE LIFE OF THE

REV. WM. H. HAVERGAL, M.A.

By his Daughter, JANE MIRIAM CRANE.

'"Yet speaketh!" In the memory of those
To whom he was indeed "a living song."'
—Frances Ridley Havergal.

'Canon Havergal was no ordinary man. He was rich in grace as well as rich in gifts. "Who could see him and not love him?" asked a brother pastor, his friend for many years. The readers of "The Memorials of Frances Ridley Havergal" will remember how intense was her veneration for her loved father, and these pages will show how justly he held the highest place in the affections of all who knew him. This Biography is admirably written, and gives charming word-pictures of home and parish life. The illustrations include a portrait from a painting by S. Cole, and another from a bust taken by Robert Pauer, of Creuznach. Engravings are also given of Astley Church, and St. Nicholas' Church, Worcester.'—*Church Standard.*

'The Life of the Rev. W. H. Havergal (written by his daughter, J. Miriam Crane) deserves to take its place with the Memoirs of M'Cheyne. It has the same gracious interest, the same powerful unction, the same fervour, force, tender love and practical sympathy. It is written by a refined, skilful, and attractive pen. The reading of such a beautiful work as this is nothing short of a means of grace. Pastors will find in it much stimulus, inspiration, and many practical hints. Young Christians will be strengthened by its perusal, and the aged will read it with zest and delight. It is a biographical gem, and deserves a place in every Christian home.'—*Oldham Chronicle.*

'HOME WORDS' OFFICE, 1 Paternoster Buildings.

The advertisements of books by W.H.H. were found on an advertisement page near the end of a copy of Under the Surface *by F.R.H. (London: James Nisbet & Co., 1874); the advertisement of Miriam Crane's biography of W.H.H. was found near the end of a copy of* Letters by the Late Frances Ridley Havergal *(London: James Nisbet & Co., 1885, a later edition with the addition of the Appendix II ("Additonal Letters" and "Hinderers and Hinderances").* Havergal's Psalmody and Century of Chants *and his* A History of the Old Hundredth Psalm Tune *are given in Volume V of the Havergal edition.*

From a Painting
by S. Cole.
Faithfully Yrs
W: H: Havergal.
Engraved by R. & E. Taylor.

This was the frontispiece of the original book, Records of the Life of the Rev. Wm. H. Havergal, M.A.

RECORDS OF THE LIFE

OF THE REV.

WM. H. HAVERGAL, M.A.

FORMERLY RECTOR OF ST. NICHOLAS, WORCESTER, AND

HONORARY CANON OF WORCESTER CATHEDRAL.

By his Daughter,

JANE MIRIAM CRANE.

"'Yet speaketh!' In the memories of those
To whom he was indeed 'a living song.'"
FRANCES RIDLEY HAVERGAL.

SECOND THOUSAND.

London:

"HOME WORDS" PUBLISHING OFFICE,

1, PATERNOSTER BUILDINGS, E.C.

CONTENTS.

Jane Miriam (Havergal) Crane (1817–1898), oil portrait by Solomon Cole in 1845. She was W.H.H.'s eldest child. His six children are named in the third paragraph of page vi of this book.

Found among Havergal manuscripts and papers, this is very likely a portrait of William Henry Havergal, likely drawn by one of his daughters (Miriam and Ellen were especially gifted artists).

PREFACE.

"'THE memory of the just' is not only blessed in itself, but is often made a blessing to others.

"The recollection of departed excellence has in numerous instances proved a tender but powerful impulse to the practice of those things which adorn the doctrine of God our Saviour. If we would be followers of those who through faith inherit the promises, we must often remember them.

"Besides, by enlarging the list of those who through the work of faith and labour of love have 'obtained a good report,' we may hope to set up a banner of invitation to others, and to proclaim a pledge that they who honour Christ shall indeed be honoured by Him."

These remarks, by my Father, in prefacing the Memorial of a Friend, are equally applicable in presenting to the public some records of his own life.

His widow intended to prepare a memoir, but after her death it was found she had left an account of three years only and a selection of letters. His eldest daughter has now taken up the work, feeling that his grandchildren, his numerous godchildren, and the many friends and parishioners still living, should possess some written memorial of one whose life was in several respects worthy of notice and imitation.

My father's chief characteristics were accuracy, activity, industry, punctuality, and generosity. His musical touch, and voice, and handwriting, were beautiful and unique. He was eminent as a church musician. He wrote some good hymns, and his sacred songs added largely to various religious and charitable treasuries. Above all, he was a truly faithful ambassador for Christ; and his ministry was greatly blessed in guiding many into the way of peace.

Now that my youngest sister has also joined "the spirits of the just made perfect," a double interest will be felt in his memory as the father whom Frances Ridley Havergal so intensely and admiringly loved.

There are few references to her in the following pages, as her "Memorials" are so widely known, and a collection of our father's letters I had hoped to include, in which she is mentioned, are now irrecoverable.

The facts of my father's early life were given to me at various times by himself. These and other incidents I have linked together with as few words of my own as possible, preferring to let the memoranda and the letters speak for themselves.

My thanks are due to the Rev. Charles Bullock, of Blackheath, for his kindness in reading my manuscript and making some suggestions.

All who appreciate simple histories of Christian life will, I think, find some pleasure or profit in tracing the course of one who could say, "I thy servant fear the Lord from my youth."

Some stanzas by my sister Frances will appropriately conclude these few preparatory observations.

The joy of loyal service to the King,
Shone through his life and lit up other lives,
With the true fire of faith that ever strives,
Like a swift-kindling beacon, far to fling
The tidings of His victory, and claim
New subjects for His realm, new honours for His Name.

And so the years flowed on, and only cast
Light and more light upon the shining way;
That more and more shone to the perfect day,
Always intenser, clearer than the past,
Because they only bore him on glad wing
Nearer the Light of Light, the Presence of the King.

From "Zenith," by F. R. H.

J. MIRIAM CRANE.

OAKHAMPTON, NEAR STOURPORT,
September, 1882.

"So shall we ever be with the Lord."

(I Thessalonians 4:17.)

Oh, thrilling thought ! that I shall be
With Him who shed His blood for me,
 Where naught from Him shall sever;
Where I, with sainted hosts above,
O'ershadowed by the Holy Dove,
Shall banquet on His boundless love,
 And know those words, "For ever."

Oh, thrilling thought! to see Him shine,
For evermore to call Him mine,
 With heaven, all heaven, before me!
To stand where angel myriads gaze,
Amid the illimitable blaze,
While He the Godhead full displays,
 To all the sons of glory!

Rev. W. H. Havergal.

This is the last page of F.R.H.'s signature Album (containing poems, verses, and other items by her friends, 1860–1868), a score written by her father.

Each part in each strain
 Per Recte et Retro
 On a ground bass
Saviour, when from realms above,
Thou shalt come with glory 'round
May the names of all we love,
In Thy Book of Life be found! Amen.
 In that Great Day,
 Lord, grant that I may
 With rapture say,
"Behold I, and the children which
 God hath given me." Heb. 2:13.
Bonn. January 18. 1866. W. H. Havergal.

RECORDS OF THE LIFE

OF THE

REV. W. H. HAVERGAL.

CHAPTER I.

BIRTH TO ORDINATION.

Ancestry — Wycombe Sunday School — Early years — Merchant Taylors' School — Love of music — Enters St. Edmund's Hall, Oxford — Like-minded friends — Letter to the Vice-principal — Ordination — Curacy with Mr. Biddulph.

THE ancestors of my father, the Rev. WILLIAM HENRY HAVERGAL, were country people possessing small properties at Great Milton in Oxfordshire, and Great Marlow and Fawley in Buckinghamshire, where many of them are buried, and some tombs still remain. The old clerk at Fawley told my grandmother that he remembered the tattered escutcheons of the Havergal family, which finally disappeared at the restoration of the church in 1748.

The orthography of the name has varied from Heavergill, which signifies the rising of the brook, to Havergill, Havergall, or Havergal.

The first name of any babe recorded in the Fawley baptismal register is that of Ann, daughter of John and Elizabeth Heavergill, in 1694. It was probably her brother Thomas, born in 1696, who practised as a doctor at Henley-on-Thames, where he owned a street. He died in March, 1734, leaving one orphan child, John, born December 8, 1733. Through the neglect and dishonesty of his guardian John Havergall's property was greatly diminished, but he married and settled comfortably in High Wycombe. He pre-deceased his wife Ann, and left three children.

1. John, the eldest, lived and died at Great Milton; his descendants are extinct, as his elder son, Edward, who had an office in the Customs, died unmarried, and the younger, William, had only one son, William Henry, educated for the law, who died in London unmarried in 1871.

2. Ann, whose miniature exists, and who was very beautiful, died at the age of twenty-one, June 7, 1784. A tablet to her memory is inserted in the churchyard wall at Wycombe.

3. William, born March 29, 1765. He was my grandfather, and was a much respected alderman in his native town. He was an amiable and upright man, and possessed some skill in music, which so largely developed itself in his descendants. He married December 29, 1790, Mary, the only surviving child of Thomas Hopkins.

My grandmother was a woman of true piety and of superior sense and judgment. Her education was completed in a French convent, but she always remained a sound Protestant, although her chief school-friend, Miss Macdonald, was a Roman Catholic, and continued to correspond with her when abbess of the convent at Winchester.

My grandmother originated the Sunday-school at Wycombe, and continued to superintend it till she was seventy. Writing to me when a child, she said: "Within the last week I have had the pleasure of hearing six poor boys and girls repeat very correctly the following seven Psalms from the Old Testament, namely, 1, 15, 25, 37, 101, 113, 145, and for which they each obtained a handsome Bible containing the Book of

Common Prayer. You would have been pleased to behold their smiling countenances when I expressed my approbation at the conclusion."

The only son of William and Mary Havergal was my father, who was born January 18, 1793, and was baptized February 15, in the parish church. The old house in which he was born was taken down long ago. In a memorandum he writes: "I was named William after my father, and Henry from Mr. Henry Trombel, a native of France, a most excellent man, and a great friend of my grandmother Hopkins, whose maiden name was Ruth Brooksbanke."

His only sister, Mary, was born November 8, 1796; she also was a fine performer on the organ and pianoforte, and wrote a beautiful hand.

William Henry seems to have been a very good little boy: his old nurse, Nanny, who fondly remembered his long golden curls and rosy cheeks, declared that the naughtiest thing he ever did was taking the cat to bed. This fondness for animals in general and cats in particular continued his characteristic through life. There are few records of his early years. When he was eight years old he was sent to a school at Princes Risborough, from whence he wrote his first letter home in excellent round hand, but with no stops.

Princes Risborough.
16 October

Honourd Parents

I write these lines unto you hopeing you are all well as it leaves me at present if you please to send me some almonds and raisons and fireworks I love my school very well we rise about Six and go to bed at eight give my best regards to Mrs. Shaw my duty to my Grandfather and Grandmother I received the two parcels safe which you sent and I thank you very much please to give my love to my sister I remain

Honoured Parents
Your dutiful Son
William H Havergal

P.S. by the Master.—Accept my kind respects. It is necessary to say the above is Master William's own in every respect, as I make it a point never to alter the first production in any particular.

He subsequently went to Merchant Taylors' school, in London, but of his life as a public schoolboy no memoranda remain. In the holidays he cultivated music, practising on the piano and the flute, and from the age of fourteen often played the organ in his parish church, and composed several hymns for its anniversary occasions.

In an old MS. music-book the following memorandum is written by my father, dated 1870. Other books of fugues and anthems exist, written in copper-plate style.

The tunes in this book are such as were popular at the beginning of the present century. I had sung them at home and at church from my early boyhood. No one was more pleased with "Willie's" clear treble voice than his beloved mother. I began to copy the tunes when fourteen or fifteen years old, when I began to be "organ mad." It used to be my Vade Mecum when invited to play in the church at Loudwater, Beaconsfield, etc. Dear, good Dr. Slater (a most eminent physician) was always inviting me to go with him in his phaeton to Loudwater (three miles from W.) that I might play the organ there.

On leaving school, being fond of medicine as well as music, which he had contemplated as a profession, his father agreed with a surgeon, a good man, to receive him; but before the indentures were signed the doctor died suddenly. The deliberations which followed this sad event had a happy result in determining him, with a humble dependence on God's help, to commence a course of preparation for serving Him in the ministry.

My father matriculated at St. Edmund's Hall, Oxford, in 1813. Its Vice-Principal was the Rev. John Hill, of whose kindness and fitness for his office he often spoke in warm terms. The visit of the allied sovereigns to Oxford on the 14th of June, after the peace of 1814, was an event of great interest to him, and he wrote an ode to welcome their arrival, and also an Ode to Peace on the occasion, with designs for illuminated allegorical figures. He had previously joined the military drill at Wycombe when the fear of French invasion prevailed.

His time at Oxford seems to have passed pleasantly and profitably in industrious study and in intimacy with like-minded friends. One of them, the Rev. Robert Francis Walker, was then a curate in Oxford. He excelled in music and drawing, and was a remarkably sweet and heavenly-minded man. He was incumbent of Purleigh for thirty years before his death in 1854, when a memoir was published, including several poems. But his chief college friend was John East, afterwards vicar of Croscombe, and finally rector of St. Michael's, Bath, the author of many pleasing and spiritual works in prose and verse. The first he published, "Original Memorials," was dedicated to my father. In it he thus refers to their frequent country walks together in the neighbourhood of Oxford—

Bounding along in all the vivacity and vigour of youth, one in sentiment, taste, and affection, pursuing the same studies, and making our way through the initiatory discipline of the university to the same high office, we were at no loss for topics of discourse. We loved to enthusiasm

"the boundless store
Of charms which nature to her votary yields,"

calling forth quotations from the sacred and the classic page. We often conversed with the child or the cottager by the way, leaving with each an appropriate tract, and sometimes rested in friendly homes, where the voice and hand of my friend Havergal delighted the inmates with the songs of Zion.

Another dear friend and life-long correspondent was Henry Virtue Tebbs, a delightful specimen of a Christian layman, who became a proctor in Doctors' Commons, and was the last survivor of the happy trio who met for praise and prayer in each other's rooms in "that honourable hall," as Bishop Daniel Wilson termed it, because it had nurtured so many devoted ambassadors for Christ. Mr. Tebbs was also skilful with his pencil. He resided much abroad in the last years of his life, but died at Hillside in Henbury in 1876.

My father passed his final examination November 15, 1815, and took his B.A. degree February 24, 1816. On leaving Oxford he wrote the following letter to the Vice-Principal—

St. Edmund's Hall,
1st March, 1816. 10.30 p.m.

My dear Sir,

At this present crisis of my life I feel a sadness, the nature of which you can imagine. The lateness of the hour forbids many words, but I cannot leave Oxford and this revered abode, which has witnessed in me such varied and memorable feelings, without simply expressing somewhat of that high estimation and cordial gratitude which I do feel for the exceeding kindness, interest, and tenderness you have at all times shown towards me. To do this *vivâ voce* is more than my feelings would suffer; but now that I can speak in silence I rejoice to utter the affection of a heart that has minutely, though perhaps not apparently, noticed your actions of love. I have deeply valued them, and though you, dear sir, may disown them, yet our God will keep them in everlasting remembrance, inasmuch as they were done in His Name and to one of His little ones. My poor prayers for your lasting peace and universal happiness are the only return and perhaps the best acknowledgment I can make. It has been my happy privilege to have for my college tutor "a friend," a man who could feel, and I must ever regard this as among the blessings of my life. And now, my dear sir, when you pray in the Ember weeks, or any other period, for those who are about to be admitted to Holy Orders, let me entreat your special request on behalf of

Your unworthy yet most obedient friend,
Wm. H. Havergal.

Writing to his mother about the same date, he says: "I have heard considerably more about the Bristol and Somersetshire curacy. So desirable is the position considered to be that Mr. Biddulph has had no less than six applications, and I am told my letter determined the choice of candidates." Accordingly he became curate to that holy and eminent man, the Rev. Thomas Tregenna Biddulph, vicar of St. James's, Bristol, and rector of Durston and Lyng, about forty miles distant. My father's duties were to assist another curate in St. James's for the summer months, and then (exchanging with Mr. Biddulph) to take the sole charge of the country parishes in the winter. The residence then was a cottage in Creech Heathfield, two miles from the nearest church. His friendly fellow curate in Bristol was the Rev. John Swete, afterwards D.D. and chaplain to the Orphan Asylum at Redland, and rector of Blagdon.

The following most touching letter was found in my father's pocket-book after his death. It was written in pencil to him by his mother in the early morning before he left home for his ordination at Wells—

I had much to say to you last night, but my heart was too full to permit it. My earnest prayers accompany you. I trust He who has promised to be His people's Guide will direct and guide you in all you are going to undertake. You have an Almighty arm to lean on, and a faithful God to look up to. Surely these will suffice. To Him I commend you whether we meet again or not.

Do not bid me good-bye; it would upset me for the day. God abundantly bless you. Be faithful to the charge about to be committed to you. Fear the face of no man, but preach Jesus Christ alone. May God enable you to do this. My feeble petitions will accompany you. Adieu! A father's love you may some day know, but a mother's love you can never feel!

He was ordained deacon on the 24th of March, 1816, in Wells cathedral, by the Bishop of Bath and Wells. On Sunday, March 26th, he preached his first sermon in Durston Church, on Acts 4:12; and at Lyng in the afternoon his text was Colossians 1:12.

These sermons still exist, simply and forcibly setting forth the fundamental truths of the Gospel to which he adhered to the end of his ministry, untouched by the religious epidemics which arose, ever pursuing the even tenor of his way, and faithful to the Reformation principles of our Protestant Prayer Book. Even those who differed from him felt and recognized the personal nobleness of his character.

Honourd Parents
Your dutiful Son
William Havergal

This is W.H.H.'s signature when he was eight years old, at the end of the letter of 16 October 1801 (see page 588). Miriam in this biography had his middle initial in his signature, but apparently this was not on the original signature.

CHAPTER II.

MARRIAGE AND LIFE IN SOMERSETSHIRE.

Marriage — First home at Creech — The "Baring" party and Antinomianism — Ministerial success — A choir difficulty — Takes his M.A. degree — Letter from Rev. T.T. Biddulph — "A Mary and a Dorcas" — Interest in missions — Removes to Coaley.

ON the wedding day of the Princess Charlotte of Wales and Prince Leopold, being the 2nd of May, 1816, my father married, in the parish church of East Grinstead, Jane, the fifth daughter of William and Mary Head of that town. She was beautiful and graceful, and by her piety, energy, and practical ability was well fitted for a clergyman's wife. Her youngest sister, Susanna, soon afterwards married the Rev. Joshua Stratton, who was for so many years the efficient and genial precentor of Canterbury cathedral.

My mother's first home after her marriage was the cottage at Creech Heathfield, Mr. Biddulph being detained in Bristol by illness in his family. My father's sister, Mary Havergal, gives the following graphic account of the place in letters to their mother—

May, 1816.

My dear Mother,

We had pouring rain all the way. We did not reach Bath (from Maidenhead through Marlborough) till past nine o'clock. Leaving early next morning, through Wells we reached Creech St. Michael Cottage in the afternoon. It is a most lovely country with extensive views. The cottage is not so good as I had hoped, but Jane and William are contented and pleased. It has the pretty thatch and white walls so common hereabouts, and the inside is very comfortable. The garden in a great measure compensates for any disappointment I felt in the house, and we have a lovely prospect from the windows. William does not dine till after the services, and carries little lunch with him. The people are all apparently so fond of him, and seem so pleasant and kind. I like all very much, and though so quiet here and thorough country, am not at all dull. We walked to Taunton yesterday—a very pretty town, nice shops and houses, and two fine churches: St. Mary's has a beautiful tower.

William says he cannot spare time to take us about; he is always in his parish. He has, however, reluctantly accepted an invitation to dine with Mr. Snow, one of the Baring party, to-day. I hear that William is appreciated by all that set; they think him so sensible, so good, and so clever. Mrs. Baring actually preaches! She sings and plays in the cottages about Taunton. She has her harp taken where she goes, and all the country-folk go with eyes and ears and mouths open to see the wonderful lady. You would greatly smile to hear the Somersetshire dialect."

(*From the same.*)

May 30th, 1816.

We walked to Lyng on Monday. The good people are most pressing to make us eat and drink. We took tea with one family, thereby conferring a great favour! They were all so eager to hear William. He says he has great pleasure in preaching, the people are so attentive. No listlessness or staring about them, but such profound silence. He feels quite at home at Lyng, even more so than at Durston, though there one can but admire the seriousness of the people.

When service is in the afternoon at Lyng the church is crammed. Last Sunday crowds went away, not even finding room in the porch. The font and the communion table were surrounded with people; then as soon as William left the reading-desk four persons were squeezed into it, and the old clerk took some in his seat. His only fault is in preaching too fast, but he is trying to break himself of this. He possesses a large share of Daniel Wilson's animation and warmth. Many say he will not stay long here; he is too good. On Monday he is to preach for a club which is to be instituted here, and he dines with them afterwards in hope of good resulting.

(*From the same.*)

Royal Fort, Bristol,
June 24, 1816.

We came here on Tuesday, the 11th. The day was fine, the country very beautiful. We had a view of the Channel sometimes; once we were only two miles distant from it. We spent two days with Mr. Biddulph's family. He is certainly a most excellent and kind man: quiet, and what would be called reserved, but it is natural to him. He is humble and very domesticated; remarkably fond of his children, and has much cool wit and good-humour about him. A college friend of William's, who is staying here, is to preach at St. James's on Sunday; it is quite a relief to William, who feels very nervous about filling Mr. Biddulph's pulpit.

The "Baring party," to which my aunt Mary Havergal alludes, is commented on in a letter from my father to his friend Mr. Tebbs, and in the following one to his mother:—

(*W. H. H. to Henry V. Tebbs, Esq.*)

Thank you, friend beloved, for your letter. You address me with all the ardour of youth and the decision of age! "If you have *one* friend, think yourself happy," is a familiar adage. A friend I have for some time enjoyed in dear East, but my love for him is no barrier to a regard to you. The human heart is morally elastic, and when renewed by grace is capable of thrilling with affection for many friends, and heaving with pity towards "enemies, persecutors, and slanderers." That "a man may have many acquaintances and not one friend" is a truth which a celebrated wit uttered a century ago, and which the experience of every day confirms. But how many disbelieve the fact: else why do so many ingeniously cheat themselves by politely reckoning mere society, that has no union of mind, no share of heart, no trace of heaven in it, as genuine friendship. Let me remind you that his friendship is most valuable who prays most earnestly and frequently for his friend. Intercede, then, for me! and O that to our mutual intercessions the great Intercessor may say Amen, and we receive an answer of peace!

Matters as to the Antinomian heresy I found waxing worse on my return to the little sphere in which the providence of God has placed me. All I can do is to pray for penitence on their part and patience on my own. Still God spares me some whose simplicity and meekness in the faith adorn the doctrine I strive to preach. Here and there I know of a violet that bows its head to Jesus and flings its perfume into the censor of His incense; while many a gourd that grows near it scorns its beauty and frowns on its humility. I speak thus because it is painfully remarkable how arrogant and supercilious the promoters of these strange doctrines speedily become. Baring, it is said, has espoused a modification of the Sabellian heresy. I have positive evidence that he asserts that the Holy Spirit is not a party concerned in the Covenant of Redemption. Surely this virtually denies the Divinity of the Eternal Spirit, and is awfully consistent with a scheme that admits of sanctification only by imputation. Among many who call themselves Christians Antinomianism glides into the hearts of some who have long been sermon-proof, because it does not molest their hidden iniquities.

(*W. H. H. to his Mother,* 1818.)

Mr. Snow, one of the Baring party, thinks it is wrong (as he wrongly thinks) for believers to unite with unbelievers in any act of worship; he preaches consequently to his congregation generally, but prays and sings only with "the church" particularly. On the Trinitarian question he is sound; while his colleagues in the secession are going to awful lengths on that topic.

The neighbourhood of Lyng is now inundated as far as the eye can reach. Many cottages are full of water, and several small farmers have not a yard of dry ground, which is very distressing for them and the poor cattle. I wish the waters would wash away the plague of Antinomianism. That leprosy spreads, I fear; it is trying, indeed, but yet I hope and persevere.

In December, 1818, my father writes to Mr. Tebbs:—

Amidst my clerical discouragements I have had equivalent supports. A young gentleman to whom the great Head of the Church had blessed my ministrations, but who subsequently fell in with the Baring party, has returned to me, and after counting the cost, has resolved in the strength of Christ to give himself up as a labourer in the Gospel vineyard. He has accordingly commenced a preparation for Oxford University under myself. *Deo gloria.*

This young friend was afterwards ordained, and made an offer to the Church Missionary Society of his services and property, which being accepted for Sierra Leone, my father writes: "That he" (the Rev. T. R. Garnsey) "will be a shining light on the mountains of benighted Africa I do not doubt. I rejoice in the prospect of his mission to that land of the perishing."

My father was ordained priest in Wells Cathedral in March, 1817, by Bishop Ryder, when Dean of Wells, acting for Bishop Beadon.

From letters to his mother in his first curacy a few extracts are given, but space will not allow the insertion of many anecdotes of the kind feeling and growth in grace of the people around him.

Creech, Feb., 1817.

There are numbers of poor little heathens on the borders of two or three of the neighbouring parishes, and I long to take them into my Sunday School, but cannot yet awhile. How I wish you were here to foster and tend it. The arranging and planning it has straitened me much for time. I wish I could live nearer the parish. The good Bishop Ryder will preach at Gloucester on Friday for the District Society for Promoting Christian Knowledge. Of course I shall (God willing) go to hear him.

Do you know that the celebrated spot, the Isle of Athelney, where Alfred concealed himself from the Danes, is in Lyng parish, half a mile from the village? I am going to Lyng as usual this evening to teach my *singers,* as they are called, some new tunes; they get on tolerably well.

Yours, dear Mother, as "ever and ever,"

W. H. H.

Creech, Heathfield, 1818.

I have not been devoid of ministerial difficulties. A farmer in Lyng had promised the singers, or rather the *performers,* a glorious treat if they would oppose me by singing in their old way, in spite of my giving out any other psalm or hymn. The majority of the singers agreed to the bait. Accordingly, they came to the church with the intention of doing as he wished; but when it came to the point their hearts failed them, and to the chagrin of the said farmer, who had brought his whole family to hear the triumphal singing, they gave way and sang in the accustomed manner. I was not apprised of this underhand spirit of discord till I was going into the church, but providentially I had selected a suitable text (Isaiah 46:12,13), and from the former verse I took care to give them a serious castigation, without being fully aware of their wickedness until afterwards. Thus He uses His own Word! The whole matter is now exploded to my comfort and the people's wishes. I have desired the bass singers never to bring their instruments again.

My Wednesday evening lecture has been cheeringly attended. Many of my hearers come from a distance of two to four miles. In the dark and stormy nights there have been never less than forty present, and when the moon is up and the weather tolerable from eighty to a hundred. You would be surprised and rejoiced to see the number of Bibles, Testaments, and Prayer Books I am constantly selling; these must do good to present or future generations. Our flowers are lovely; we could give you handfuls of anemones, double stocks, and roses.

In June, 1818, my father and mother accepted a most kindly and pressing invitation from the Rev. J. Hill and his wife to visit them at Oxford, upon which occasion my father took his M.A. degree. At this time he had some pleasant correspondence with the Rev. C. E. De Coetlogon, author of sermons, etc., and much admired in London for his eloquence. When rector of Godstone, where my mother's eldest sister, Mrs. Stenning, lived, meeting my father there he became ardently attached to him, and intended to promote his advancement in the Church; but he did not live to fulfil his kind promises. His mother spent some weeks at Creech in the spring of 1819, and he speaks of his delight that she should "see Somersetshire in all its vernal beauty, orchards in full blossom, and banks on the way to church, twenty or thirty feet high, literally covered with violets and primroses."

His rector continued to express the great satisfaction he felt in his deputy, of which this extract from a note, written from Creech to my father in Bristol, is a specimen.

My dear Friend,

I have repeatedly mentioned how much I have been gratified by the appearance of things at Lyng. The church has been filled both at morning and evening service. From seven to ten miles round on every side people have flocked to hear, and many I have observed in tears every Sunday. Last Sunday morning, though some of the constant attendants were absent from a cause which I will presently explain, yet the seats were all occupied, and several persons (among the rest poor Philips, who was there for the first time) were much affected while I called on them to behold the Lamb of God, etc.

Those whom I have visited in private have given me the greatest satisfaction, particularly by the love they have manifested towards yourself, and the thanks which I have received as the humble instrument of bringing you among them, etc.

Very faithfully yours,

T. T. Biddulph.

My parents found some inconvenience in the frequent removals to and from Bristol, and disliked spending the summers there. The country cottage was also too small for their increasing requirements. They therefore decided early in 1820 to welcome any eligible change that presented itself. My father writes: "If a door is opened I may think seriously of it, but I shall not attempt to open the door myself. I must leave this matter entirely to the directing providence of Him who, since He placed me where I am, has given me all things necessary, and many things comfortable." Soon after, writing to his mother (always his trusted counsellor), he asks her advice about two curacies offered him. He remarks:—

One vicar said, "Among other things it is requisite for the curate's wife to be a Mary and a Dorcas." I answered, "I trust my wife is like Mary and loves our Lord Jesus Christ; and, like Dorcas, would cheerfully make clothes for the poor disciples as far as her domestic engagements and means will allow." As to myself, I really have not sufficient assurance to write to him as one coming up to the model he names. He can hear enough of me at many places round Wycombe, and here also recommendations would be plentiful. I thank my dear father, and am as much indebted to him for applying for a certain living on my behalf as if he had procured me all he wished. I indeed thank him. Publish my sermon for good old King George! Fine idea, truly! I hope I have wisdom enough not to publish sermons yet awhile. Young men had better be studying while young, and publish, if at all, when riper. Besides, a sermon made for such a congregation as mine is not at all equal to what I imagine I could produce if I had a superior congregation to preach it to. But dear mothers feel differently from strangers and publishers. Mr. Biddulph preached at St. James's from 2 Kings 2:12—a text I greatly admire; it is so patriotic, and places the character of our late king in so exalted a point of view. If you want a new work to propose for your library, let it be Morier's "Second Journey through Persia, Armenia," etc. It is an admirable volume; full of illustrations of Scripture from the present customs of the East.

In March, 1820, he says, "The Bristol Missionary Anniversary is this week. Pratt, Bickersteth, D. Wilson, Cunningham, and Mortimer are expected; the latter I do not yet know. Swete kindly invites me to his house."

Early in May, 1820, he had three offers of curacies, Astley included; but at this time he preferred Coaley, a sole charge in Gloucestershire, with a lectureship in the neighbouring town of Dursley. Writing to his mother, he says, "The Bishop of Gloucester is very solicitous I should take the lectureship, as Dursley is an important sphere, and he longs to get the truth preached in it. Mr. Biddulph and other friends have again made kindly effort to retain me for Bristol, but this cannot be. I will write again; meantime remember me in prayer."

He thus writes to his friend H. V. Tebbs on the resignation of his first charge: "Before our stay of three weeks in Bristol I took leave of my much-loved people in Somerset. I preached my farewell sermons on Sunday, the 28th of May. The trial was great, and the parting scenes in both churches very affecting. The farmers, in a really kind manner, presented me with a piece of plate as a parting memorial of their good-will."

The kind Bristol people, with many of whom my father kept up a life-long intimacy, also made him handsome farewell gifts.

CHAPTER III.

LIFE IN GLOUCESTERSHIRE.

First pupil at Coaley — Birth of a son — Revival in a dark parish — Sermon-writing — Increasing usefulness — Testimonial on leaving Coaley for Astley — Letter from the Bishop of Gloucester — Parish medical aid.

(*Letter from Rev. W. H. Havergal to his Mother.*)

Coaley, June 29, 1820.

I SEIZE the earliest opportunity of letting you know we are safely lodged in our new residence. Busy enough we have been. We are delighted with our home; it is picturesquely situated, and the view in front is very charming. The village, which is straggling for four miles, is a perfect contrast to Durston and Lyng: you would be highly pleased with its romantic scenery, and with the clean appearance of the cottages. It is a dairy country, but some cloth and edge-tools are manufactured in the parish. Coaley is three miles from Dursley, an uncommonly pretty place about twelve from Gloucester, and a mile and a half from the high road. The incumbent of Coaley resides at Bath. Mr. Biddulph first told me of the curacy, and then the good bishop corresponded with me. The people of the village already show us much kindness, sending us vegetables, etc., as we have none at present in our garden.

You will be surprised to hear that through Mr. Biddulph I have consented to receive a pupil in the autumn, a youth of fifteen, the eldest son of General Graham, now in the Mediterranean, and nephew of Sir George Cooke, Governor of Portsmouth. He will need my attention both in his studies and his amusements.

This pupil was the precursor of about eighty others during the next twenty-three years. He received from two to six at a time, some remaining only for a few months before College or Ordination; and of these eighty there were only three or four whose after life was not exemplary. His success as a tutor will be referred to in a distant page. We now continue his letters.

(*To Henry V. Tebbs, Esq.*)

Coaley, August, 1820.

On the 22nd of July my lovely little boy was born, and through mercy my dear Jane is now doing well, and our dear treasure is charmingly hearty. My heart overflows with joy, and my mouth is filled with praise. . . . Coaley is one of the parishes long considered as one of the dark and neglected parts of Gloucestershire. . . . But notwithstanding these sad things, it has pleased God to reserve many in the parish who can testify that He is gracious. The people now come with eagerness to church, and there is no small stir among them in consequence of what they hear. Five Sundays ago I commenced a lecture in the evening; from the first the congregation rapidly increased, till on the two last Sunday evenings the church was completely filled, even to the porch door; so that ministerially my prospect is remarkably encouraging. Help me with your prayers, that the Word of the Lord may indeed be glorified. Coaley has about one thousand inhabitants; the neighbourhood is beautiful, and in the extreme and higher parts of the parish the views are lovely and extensive. Our vicarage is newly built, and in a convenient situation.

About a fortnight ago I received a direct communication from poor Garnsey, at Sierra Leone. On the 4th of October their babe died, after four days' sickness. About the middle of the month Mrs. Garnsey was attacked with fever and ague, and is still distressingly weak, and he himself is so much reduced by constant attacks of fever, that the medical men urge their return to England. Dear man, he is agitated with a variety of feeling, anxious to remain, but is told his life will be the price. They have, therefore, determined to leave Africa late in March, so as to reach England when the cold of spring has passed.

(*To the same.*)

October 23, 1821.

My parish has called me out a good deal, while my indoor hours have been fully occupied in attending to my pupil and in preparing sermons. In this latter employment my thoughts have little rest. I am an *anxious* sermon writer. Few things are more painful to me than to be obliged to preach a sermon I have used before, and it is so for two reasons: first, every old sermon skeleton rather pains me by its defects; and secondly, I love to preach that which I have felt and desire, and desire to feel that which I preach, and these things are only effected when the heart and the head and the hand have been engaged in the work of preparation.

Yesterday I went to the cottage of a widow who has six children. Herself and her eldest son are following our dear Redeemer with all that delight which those who are but recently converted to Him usually feel. Six months ago they were strangers to the power of godliness, and if they now really feel it I shall never have cause to regret coming to Coaley. After some warm-hearted conversation she requested me to purchase for her four Bibles, stating that God had been gracious to her, and as she of late had had plenty of work, she was resolved to make an effort, and give her four younger children, who are from home, a Bible each! Some measure of this spirit is, I have reason to hope, spreading through the parish. The little cloud is expanding. Oh may it not pass away, but swell and burst in fertilizing showers till the wilderness around me become the garden of the Lord!

In recurring to the date of your letter, what an eventful and interesting period of our national history is the intervening time! Such a crowd of rare occurrences seldom has been pressed within so short a space; and yet when does our God leave Himself without witness? When does He not appear to be omnipotent and reigning? Never! The events of our own little history, so interesting and so dear to a feeling mind, as strikingly demonstrate the energies of His Providence as when a king is permitted to assume his crown in peace, or when such spirits as those of Buonaparte and the last Queen of England are summoned into eternity.

The table of contents in the last part of my history is somewhat like this: July 1st, opened my Sunday-school; the children are semi-pagans, as wild and uncouth as aboriginals. In August was unwell. In September set on foot a Missionary Association, printed a collection of hymns, preached charity sermons at four places, assented to the wishes of my people to continue evening services through the winter. Very busy at Dursley, and just now heard from my vicar that he has applied to the Lord Chancellor for an exchange of this living. "Arise, depart hence; this is not your rest."

(To the same.)

On the 15th of last month my dear Jane became a mother for the third time. Our newly-given treasure is a sweet little girl. Mercy has constantly attended, and though not always smiling, has not turned her face from us. . . . Truly your diary presents a series of incidents which are not undeserving of notice. The best of them probably is your Amharic engagement; may the angel of God be sent forth to minister to you in that holy undertaking.

Coaley presents little variety of incident, hemmed in by the inconveniency of wet weather; the roads are horrible, some impassable. It would be an excellent penance for a clerical exquisite to take my duties for a week or two. I preach at Dursley once on Sundays, and each other Thursday. The middle and poor people hear me gladly, but the wealthy and gay, though not hostile or unkind, are stout in prejudice and worldliness. But I "plow in hope."

The diocese of Gloucester is still in an Arctic sea, notwithstanding it has had a fine sun in its bishop for several years. Blessed, however, be God, the state of the diocese is improving; the ice is broken up in many places, and zealous adventurers are entering it. Our Sunday evening congregations are truly encouraging. My little selection of hymns, intended as a supplement to the New Version of the Psalms, gives my people great pleasure. I am of opinion that the great barrier to congregational singing in country churches is the dulness of the versions of the psalms used. Give the people words that speak, and they will soon learn to sing them.

(To his Mother.)

Jan. 16, 1822.

I have been to Hilton Park, and my visit was very pleasant. Mrs. Graham is as a high-bred lady what Mrs. Anderdon is as a gentlewoman. She is a good woman, and does a great deal of good. Now for home news. Jane is better, and so is Henry, but he has no more teeth, nor can he say any word but "Adone!" and how he learnt that we cannot tell. He takes after me in point of self-will, etc. Oh, such a boy for a book; he will follow you all day, and cry, "Tah! Tah!" in order that you may show him pictures, and talk to him about birds and lambs, etc. Miriam continues to grow, and her tongue grows too; she has an answer for everybody, and something to say upon everything. She is always reading and scribbling, and learns papa's text every Sunday.

(Letter to H. V. Tebbs, Esq.)

May, 1822.

About three months ago notice was given me that my services were no longer required at Dursley. The ostensible reasons were that the incumbent's better health would allow him to take the evening duty, and that he could no longer afford to engage help. But I suspect there is a feeling you can better imagine than I describe. The parish began to arouse, and individuals to inquire. The church was filled when I preached; some Dissenters, alas! found their way into it, and sixty subscribers to the Church Missionary Society had been readily obtained by some of my friends. At this juncture the Vicar of Coaley apprised me of his intention to resign or exchange. Thus situated, came almost simultaneously three offers: one Mr. Biddulph's cure, then a perpetual curacy near Ringwood and Christchurch, with new church and parsonage, and with zealous coadjutors in the parish. I wrote to my mother, asking her counsel about this, and also desired her to name it to dear Bradley, and Mr. Pryce of Loudwater. After much anxious deliberation, we decided to accept the offer of the curacy of Astley, in Worcestershire, which I had before declined on leaving Somersetshire. It is now arranged for us to go to Astley at Midsummer next. But "if Thy presence, O Lord, go not with us, carry us not up thence!" All that I can now tell you is, that it is a lovely spot and a promising curacy.

The church at Coaley was filled with an overflowing congregation on my father's last service, when his text was Philippians 1:27. The grateful parishioners presented him with a silver teapot and an affectionate address. His Dursley hearers set on foot a subscription for a silver basket, but he earnestly begged it might be discontinued, and his wish was obeyed. His life in Gloucestershire pleasantly closes with the following letter from his kind Bishop.

(Bishop Ryder to W. H. H.)

June 27, 1822.

My dear Sir,

I enclose the testimonial countersigned, with a letter which you may read and then wafer or seal. It will, I hope, prevent any possible doubt about the want of three years' testimonials. May it please God to supply your place with a labourer of similar views and talents! May He bless you in your new situation! The Christian love of your people was very pleasing. You have acted very wisely about the Dursley plate, as you have done in all things. With every kind and Christian wish,

I remain,

Your affectionate Brother,

H. Gloucester.

(*Letter enclosed to W. H. H. from the Bishop of Gloucester to the Bishop of Worcester.*)

June 27, 1822.

My dear Lord,

I cannot help adding to the usual testimonial in favour of Mr. Havergal, the tribute of peculiar respect and regard which his character demands from me. He is indeed a very serious loss to the parish which he served, and to the Deanery in which he resided and acted as Secretary to the Diaconal Committee as the Secretary for Promoting Christian Knowledge.

Believe me, my dear Lord,

Yours very truly,

H. Gloucester.

I may here mention that in all his country parishes my father turned his early medical studies to good account. He was skilful in treating burns and broken bones, and in prescribing for all kinds of ailment, and his remedies were generally thought more efficacious than the doctor's. Some, indeed, would not take the medicine that came from a surgery till he had tasted and approved it! The doctor who attended in Coaley warmly thanked my father for saving him so much time and trouble in unremunerative cases, and begged him to send to his house for a fresh store of medicines whenever required.

Thus did my father follow His example who went about doing good to the bodies as well as to the souls of men.

CHAPTER IV.

FOOTPRINTS OF MY FATHER WHEN CURATE OF COALEY, GLOUCESTERSHIRE, 1819–1822.[1]

Footprints — "The elders that outlived Joshua" — Eliza Workman — "Mr. Havergal is all music" — George's remembrances — "The way of transgressors is hard" — The fighting on Coaley Peak — The vicarage kitchen class — A cottage in Silver Street — "The doctrine to fill churches" — How he led "the rabble of Coaley" — Thomas Cam, the "musicianer" — The text in the "Pockrifa" — Work in the workhouse — "All the Dissenters turned to Church" — "Footprints" amongst the farmers — "His life preached."

FOOTPRINTS! Some never seen, some quickly erased, some shining indelibly, cheering and guiding others, pressing to the selfsame mark.

Soon after my dear father's death, in 1870, I determined to revisit my birthplace, Coaley, and if possible trace his footprints. The vicar kindly secured me lodgings just opposite the church and vicarage. Though my father was curate for only three years, his ministry, his life, and his visits were well remembered by many in both cottage and farm.

Sunday, July 17, 1870. The bells were chiming for church when I passed through the churchyard gate. The last time that gate opened for me I was in my christening robes! The old church is pulled down and beautifully rebuilt, the old tower remaining. Many of the tombstones bore the dates when my father must have stood there. I saw some Sunday-school children laying flowers on a grave; there were rails round it, but no stone. "Whose grave is that, dear child?" "It is our last clergyman; we bring flowers every Sunday, and when the cowslips come we put so many!"

After church I followed two aged women, hoping to find they were like "*the elders that overlived Joshua,* and which had known all the works of the Lord that He had done for Israel"

[1] This chapter has been written by my sister, Maria V. G. Havergal, who prepared the Memorials of F. R. H. for publication. (London: J. Nisbet & Co.)

(Joshua 24:31). In answer to my question, "Do you remember Mr. Havergal?" one said, "To be sure, and ha'n't never forgot him. Wasn't he kind to me and every one! I'm the widow Philamore. Dear Mr. Havergal!"

It was not kind to keep her tottering there, so I promised to call at her cottage.

It was soon known in the village that "a belonging of Mr. Havergal's" was come, and sundry visitors called, whose simple words shall now be given.

My name is Eliza Workman; you must have heard your dear father speak of me. I believe I was the first he spoke to. My mother was a dressmaker, and I remember Mrs. Havergal sending to know if she could go to work at the vicarage and sew a carpet for the study. My mother told me to go, but I was timid, and said, "Perhaps Mr. Havergal will be asking me questions I can't answer." But I went, and as soon as I saw him I was no more timid. He had such a way as won everybody. Dear Mr. Havergal! when my troubles came he was just everything to me. My mother died—his visits so comforted her. Then I went to live with grandmother, and was so cast down till Mr. Havergal called.

Mr. Havergal is printed on my mind, and will be till my dying day.

The congregations were wonderful. The church that was so empty hadn't even standing room. I've seen the road lined with horses, gigs, and carts from all parts. When the people knew he was going away they thickened to hear him; and the last sermon! not a dry eye in the church. I can show you the hymn-book Mr. Havergal made for us. We used to say, "Mr. Havergal is all music." Old Thomas Cam, the clerk, was so too; and they did have such talks. The new hymn-book was so liked that my little cousin George took some eggs to the vicarage to get one. Mr. Havergal was out, but George soon had one. The school children loved him dearly. He was the one to keep a parish right, for they took all their quarrels to him and he squared them all.

Another knock, and another visitor.

"Good evening, miss. Why, you features your father uncommon!"

"Perhaps you will tell me all you remember—it is so pleasant to find my dear father is not forgotten."

George.—I was a stiffish lad of fourteen when Mr. Havergal came to Coaley, and I went with my father to work at the vicarage garden. The vicarage was new, for the old one was pulled down after the last parson had hung himself in it. The garden was covered with rubbish. I remember Mr. Havergal would work along with us sometimes, and he could put his hand to anything. He was a lithesome man—not a lithesomer in England. Such a one to be up in the morning; and he'd set the vicarage windows open, to let out the night air. And to see him walk! why he'd be at Dursley in twenty-five minutes, and its three miles. He never touched the stiles; he'd go clean over them. When I heard you were come to the village, miss, I said to my missus, "Her father did what few would do now-a-days." There was a poor fellow, Joe Ford, convicted at Gloucester for horse-stealing. He was condemned to die, and when the 'Size was over Mr. Havergal travelled every day to see him, though it's fourteen miles, and he mostly walked it. From his condemnation to his execution Mr. Havergal saw him daily. His body was buried under the church tower; there were over three hundred at the funeral, and Mr. Havergal addressed them from the grave. The text of the sermon the next Sunday was, "The way of transgressors is hard."

I remember how people said "Mr. Havergal do be in and out of the houses all the week, and that fetched them to church on Sunday; and he do be as frequent to Dissenters as to the t'others." Why, the head man at the chapel turned over to the Church!

The old clerk, Thomas Cam, was a musicianer; he made pieces that were sung at Gloucester College. Mr. Havergal and he had mighty turns at it; and what seemed so curious to me was, that they both made tunes in their heads without stopping to play them.

Coaley Peak is one of the juttings of the Cotswold range. The long narrow lanes leading up to it are almost impassable in winter; not only "oxey" and clayey, but with water-springs overflowing the path. But through mud and water ankle deep did the pastor go after his flock. An old man remembered one night when, he said, "There was awful fighting highish up, quite at the hills. They ran to the vicarage and called him, though long past midnight. Up he went; he wasn't the sort to mind a journey night or day to do good, and he had some One to watch over him. They say when he got up to the fighting they soon dropped their hands, and he reasoned them into lambs, and got 'em all to shake hands and go home."

Returning down the lane, I saw a woman running after me, saying, "Will you please to stop, miss; there's a woman wants to see you; she says she went to his class in the kitchen."

Going into the cottage, the good woman exclaimed, "I heard talk there was some one belonging to Mr. Havergal up this hill. I never see that kitchen without remembering him."

"What kitchen?"

"The kitchen down at the vicarage."

"Who taught you there?"

"Who? him himself;" and she burst into tears. Then she continued: "He had the first class of girls every Wednesday to instruct in the Scriptures and in the answering. 'Twas him himself that tried to bring us to Christ, and if he had stopped longer we should all have come to the Lord's table. Mr. Havergal had such a sweet, lovely voice. Yes, I remember it, and the hymns and chapters he taught us. I never shall forget him. And is he gone?" And she cried afresh.

The woman went on telling how he always went to the opening and closing of the Sunday school. "And your mother, dear Mrs. Havergal, always came too; the girls were under her edication. I remember her well—such a pretty look; we thought her a lovely lady."

One of the Coaley lanes is called Silver Street. In one of the lonely cottages a woman asked me what my name was?

"Havergal."

"Havergal!" She burst into tears. "Then I count it must be him I did love; aye, I did love him well, and never heard of one as didn't. It's a few years back he called to see me; my sight was very dim, so he put out his hand and said, 'Don't you know me?' I could have fallen down before him! O I loved him, and he was so friendly to us all. I warrant he knew all the Scriptures by heart. He'd have his little Bible on the pulpit cushion, and take it up now and then, but I never saw a sarmint book in his hand."

Just then her husband came in.

"Tom, thee knowed Mr. Havergal?"

"Knowed him? aye, and loved him; and is he alive?"

"No; he's gone."

"Aye, gone to his Lord's kingdom. Many's the time I've heard him preach; but I was one of the giddy multitude, and then it took no effect of me; now I see the wall pulled down betwixt my soul and Christ. The wall must be pulled down before you can pluck roses on the t'other side. But I must give account of all his texts and sermons. Was he ill long, miss?"

"No, it was a very sudden call; he never opened his eyes to bless us, nor could he pray."

"That was done afore: he'd no need to pray then; he had lived in the Lord, and he died in the Lord, not a doubt."

They asked many questions, and listened, eagerly as I told how he sang and played that last Easter Even.

They said, "Ah, he was a musicianer; he drawed out music on paper; only he and old Cam the clerk could do that much."

Then asking them if I should sing one of my dear father's tunes, I sang "Evan," the old man joining in the tenor.

He said, "That tune is sung in all the churches and chapels round. I'll assure you we have some happy moments singing that sweet tune."

The dear old woman exclaimed, "I often think what I'll do when I get's to heaven; I'll be such a poor creatur up there! But I believe to see Jesus will be my first look out; and I shan't take any sin in with me, for the hymn says,

'Those holy gates for ever bar
Pollution, sin, and shame;
For none will gain admission there
But followers of the Lamb.'"

Passing on to a wild common, I saw a man sitting on the trunk of a tree. I said, "What a beautiful view this is!"

"Yes, 'tis uncommon grand; not that many travels to see it."

"Do you go to Coaley church?"

"Sometimes; not as I did when a young 'un. The old church was crowded then. Mother told me she often stood three Sundays running. Mr. Havergal preached then; a good minister he was, beloved by all far and near. They travelled from Uley and Dursley and Kingscote to hear him. He preached the Gospel, and that's the doctrine to fill churches. Not that I'm a possessor, and I ain't going to make any profession till I has possession. Mr. Havergal and other parsons have talked at me, but the world, the flesh, and the devil are again me; and then the trials and troubles put out the amusements of religion from my heart. I had a book lent me lately, 'Four Last Things: Death, Judgment, Hell, Eternity.' Sommat in it striking, sommat in it encouraging; it's all my own disbelief that I'm not ready."

"Have you got a Bible?"

"Yes; it was my mother's, and Mr. Havergal gave it her; it's big print. My mother was an established Churchwoman. Often and often Mr. Havergal walked up to see her; and a smartish walker he was. One of his texts is plain afore me now, 'The way of transgressors is hard,' and many another comes round to me. Not that I'm religious, mind you, nor beint going to profess it, to please any one."

One more cottage stood far on the hillside. An old man was mending shoes; the wife looked very ill. Looking keenly at the stranger, he said—

> I count as thee belongs't to Mr. Havergal; he brought her and me t'gether at Coaley church. But I didn't 'spect thee to travel so far. Mr. Havergal led the rabble of Coaley as asey as a shepherd leads his she'p dog. There was plenty of rabble when he cum'st to Coaley; and when he took to us, them that wudna hearken to nons't, ud hearken to him. There was one particular bad fellow, not over eighteen. Mr. Havergal got him put in the stocks a few hours, just as long as he thought needful to soften him. Then he took him to the vicarage, and gave him a good supper and good advice. He'd hearken to no one; but in course he hearkened to Mr. Havergal, for no one could go agen him. When my father was ill, that good parson came again and again, and he'd administer medicine to sowl as well as body—aye, a sight of medicine he guv for nothing—up till ten at night folks went for his mixtures. I remember Coaley church was cram full, not a standin' empty. He was a plain-spoken man, preaching the Gospel, and that "all our righteousness was as filthy rags." He's in my eye now—a very upstanding man, not his fellow in the pulpit, I knows.

Another day I called on the daughter of Thomas Cam, "the musicianer." She was not so communicative as some, but told me of the wonderful music her father made in his head. From her garden, just under Coaley Peak, the Severn looked almost like the sea, and she seemed pleased with my admiration of the view, exclaiming, "You may go hundreds of miles and not see such a sight! The tide comes up the Severn every twelve hours—it's ruled by the moon; it comes up like to the boil, and then lessens again; isn't it wonderful?"

I saw cottages still far away, and I knew my father's footprints would be "excelsior," and so I trudged on. Some women were churning at a cottage-door, so I could not hinder them; but I asked if they remembered Mr. Havergal.

"Yes, that I do, though I was only five years old. He preached a text mother could not find in all the Bible, so she said it must be in the 'Pockrifa;' and I remember her sending me across the fields to ask missus at the farm to please to find it out in the big Book."

"Can you tell me the words?"

"Yes: 'His head bare, and he shall put a covering upon his upper lip.'"

I assured her it was in Leviticus, but only carrying my Testament I failed to convince her it was not in the "Pockrifa."

Another footprint deep and clear! It is singular how the unobliterated track shines out unexpectedly. Returning Eliza Workman's call, she told me that my beloved father was voluntary chaplain at the workhouse. "Mr. Havergal went of his own free will to comfort and instruct them. He used to take a three-legged stool and sit down among them as freely as if he was in a palace. There was one poor creature, Kate Twirling, who had been excommunicated out of the Church. 'Twas stricter rules in those days. Poor thing! she had been a beautiful girl, but so bad. Mr. Havergal could not rest till he brought her back to the Church; and he knew that was not enough; ah, it was to Jesus he tried to bring us all. I remember after Kate died it was found that great property belonged to her. Never mind, Mr. Havergal showed her the true riches. All he did was out of love to God and free good-will to man."

Another man told me that when my father first came to Coaley, as soon as ever church was over the game of fives was played against the tower walls; but for shame they could not play after hearing such sermons. An old pilgrim, John Stiff by name, remarked: "Aye, he preached the Gospel and the marrow of the Gospel. There was mighty little of that in the Establishment then. I used to walk five miles to hear Mr. Havergal preach. And all the Dissenters turned to Church. Ah, he preached Christ and he lived Christ, and now he's with Christ for ever. He was the first to tell us about the missionaries."

Nor was it only amongst the cottagers, but in many farmhouses I found pleasant footprints. One farmer said: "I shall never forget Mr. Havergal's confirmation classes. He was beloved by all; such a nice spirited man, and no bigot. Never was a better churchman, and yet he never ran down Dissent. He was anxious to do good to every one's soul, and so won many. I remember how well he stood up in the pulpit; such a fine proportioned man, his head erect, his hand waving. And his voice! no one could ever forget it, and no one's like it. We gave him a silver teapot when he went away, though there was not a rich man in the parish. Oh, how, we wished to keep him! and as a lad I used to think I'd follow him to the ends of the earth."

An elderly lady told me of his voluntary lecture in Dursley Church on Sunday afternoons, walking four miles there and back just in time for his evening service. She said his preaching attracted large congregations, and most blessed results followed from his faithful preaching of Jesus Christ: "I was quite a child, about ten years old, when your dear father left Coaley. His sermons were the means of my dear father and mother's conversion, but I did not then know the Lord myself. I remember the effort made by my crippled father to go and hear him. How well I recollect your father's beaming face! He was so full of the love of Christ, it shone in every feature. Precious man! every one loved him, every one looked up to him, for his life preached. And it was not only his own parish he cared for, but many others; and it was Mr. Havergal who first held missionary meetings in Dursley, Uley, and other places. His correspondence was much blessed to me. For two years I had not heard from him. I used to stand before his portrait and think, 'I should like to know if you are in heaven.' I did not hear of his death for six weeks. Then I went to look at his picture, and thought, 'Now you *are* in the glory, and oh, what must your music be now!' And I knew my father would be with him, and both singing, 'Glory be to Thee, O God!' Yes, he has a glorious crown, and I can't tell you how sweetly I realize his glory."

CHAPTER V.

CURATE OF ASTLEY, 1822–1829.

Scenery of Astley — Visit to Aberystwith — Mr. and Mrs. East — First and second Church Missionary Society tours — Letter from the Rev. Thomas Kelly — The Rev. Joseph Wolff — Hebrew melody — The Newfoundland School Society — Third Missionary Tour in Cornwall and Devon — Letter to H. V. Tebbs — Notes for a missionary speech — Grandeur, difficulties, and advance of the work — Offer of secretaryship — Bishop Heber's hymns and sacred songs — Letter from the Countess Valsamachi — Indian Education Society and Moravian Missions — "Hurry and Worry" — Letter from the Rev. D. J. J. Cookes — Fourth Missionary Tour in Cornwall — The Rev. J. Cawood — *The Protestant Warder* published — Death of Rev. D. J. J. Cookes — Meets with a serious accident near Hallow Park — First letters after accident — Birth of youngest son — Baptism and sponsors — Mr. and Mrs. M. Usborne.

ON the 25th of June, 1822, my father and mother, with children and servants, arrived at Astley Rectory; a plain building, but beautified with ivy, China roses, and a vine, standing close to the old church, built in Saxon and Norman times, with a fine tower of later date. The little sloping lawn, where my mother afterwards loved to work among her flowers, was only separated from the churchyard by a grassy bank below a wire fence. The scenery of Astley, under the name of Satley, has been well described in "Trevor: a Tale for the Times," by one of the pleasant family who resided there in the early years of my father's stay. The view from the upper windows of the rectory and the church bank, before the overgrowth of the present time, was perfectly enchanting—undulating or steep wooded grounds; orchards, with here and there a cottage roof; plantations, with the glimmer of a pool; far below, a brook winding through a flowery dell; above, far away in the south, the cone of Malvern, and nearer, the graceful outlines of Woodbury, and the Abberley Hills, formed a scene unique in the character of its loveliness.

The curacy of Astley was virtually another sole charge, as the rector, though generally resident, was too great an invalid to do more than preach very rarely; but he was able for a few years frequently to attend the morning service, and often expressed his gratitude for the clearer Gospel light which my father's sermons had brought to his heart.

I have no memoranda of the first two years at Astley, except that on August 19, 1822, he made his first appearance on a platform at Stourport as a speaker for the Church Missionary Society, and the following day for the Bible Society at Worcester; that he visited the kind godmother of his little Maria at Hilton Park before her departure for Geneva; and that he added a sermon to the afternoon service, changing the hour to six o'clock in the summer, when people flocked from Stourport and the neighbouring country parishes to hear him. From one of these occasional hearers my father received the following note:—

My dear Sir,

I have delayed a few days from indisposition to inform you of the removal of my dear honoured mother to her eternal rest. She died in great peace, and the day previous requested me to give her dying love to dear Mr. Havergal, and "tell him to continue on boldly declaring full salvation in Christ Jesus. I have prayed constantly for his ministry in the dark wilderness of Astley, but his labours have been owned of God, and will again be blessed." You would have been delighted to have seen the holy peace she enjoyed, and what a glorious testimony she witnessed to the power of faith. For fifty years, she said, she had been kept in the way to the kingdom, depending on the mercy of God through faith in Christ Jesus. We are left to sorrow, but not without hope, and the same grace is free for us, and the fountain is still open; may we be sharers of its fulness!

Yours very respectfully,

E. L.

In January, 1824, after a visit to his mother, he writes: "Safely home! all and everything well, and the little ones as much rejoiced as a distant colony is when a richly laden ship arrives. You would have smiled to see them as I opened my portmanteau. Miri has your letter in lavender, Henry takes his knife to bed with him, little Ria soon hugged Dolly's head off, and baby—who is better—kicked her little legs and was satisfied with a bit of sweetie."

In June, 1824, my father and mother, with their four children and two servants, had the rare pleasure of a month at Aberystwith, my father returning home for a few days for parish duties, and to see the progress of a new study he was building. He then wrote the following letter to me:—

July, 1824.

My dear Miriam,

You cannot think how papa longs to come and see you again and kiss you all, and then for you to kiss him. I hope, my dear child, you learn your lessons, and give mamma no trouble. Tell me what is the English of this, *Ego amo te, me amas?* Is it not delightful to see the great billows of the wonderful deep? Now think how few little girls there are who are taken to see the sea, and how many men and women have never seen it. Be thankful, then, that you behold so charming a sight. Read what is said about the sea in the 104th Psalm and in the 107th Psalm. But, Miri dear, do make me some pretty verses about the sea; only think how many things you can mention—the pretty pebbles, the beautiful weeds, the waves, and the fishes, and the ships, and the lovely green colour of the water. Now if you make me some nice verses I will give you a pretty book some day. Good-bye, my dear Miri; pray to God to bless you, and be sure to pray for your

Dear Papa.

He writes enthusiastically to his mother, who had lately visited us at Astley, about the scenery at the Devil's Bridge, Barmouth, and Dolgelly, and entreated his father to take her a tour in Wales instead of going to the tameness of Brighton and Hastings. In a postscript he says, "Jane bought a couple of fine chickens for sixteen pence, and two fine soles for sixpence!" While at Prospect House, Aberystwith, he invited the other inmates to family prayer every evening, and thus made acquaintance with two Miss Ditchers, who kept a ladies' school near Wellington, in Shropshire, with whom he was so pleased that he placed me under their care in 1826.

After our return my parents received a fortnight's visit from the Rev. John East with his second bride—a most heavenly-minded woman, daughter of the Rev. W. Day, of Bristol—and his children, Jane Havergal and John Fraser East. Both the latter died young, and Mr. East published a memoir of his son under the title of "The Happy Moment," and also a life of this his second wife. Their own sweet and clever mother was a special friend of my mother. One day my father actually walked to Malvern with Mr. East, returning on the following one by "short cuts," which proved almost as long as the eighteen miles by road.

The only item remaining of 1825 is the following scrap to H. V. Tebbs:—

July 4.

I am on the Bristol coach, on my way to Cornwall, whither I am going with Garnsey and Berkins for a missionary tour. I shall be absent four Sundays, and then have to preach two Sunday-school sermons at a new church near Birmingham.

The principal events of 1826 were my father's journeys to Yorkshire and Cornwall as a deputation for the Church Missionary Society. In his travelling portfolio are still preserved hundreds of resolutions moved or seconded by him in these counties in this and other years. On the back of the resolutions are outlines of his speeches and a variety of missionary facts. The ease and elegance of his manner, and the singular sweetness and clearness of his voice, his well-arranged matter and forcible appeals, always aroused enthusiastic cheers at the close of his speeches, as his hearers have often testified. With the Rev. E. Bickersteth and the Rev. W. H. Bartlett he preached twice, or assisted at meetings, every day between June 24 and July 4, in the principal towns of Yorkshire. Then travelling rapidly down to Holsworthy, in Devon, he held a meeting July 7, and formed a lasting friendship with the chairman, the Rev. R. Kingdon, and his family. He proceeded to Jacobstow and Boscastle, and other places in the north of Cornwall, till July 24, by which time he had collected nearly £75 in his southern tour. He also attended six meetings for the Church Missionary Society in Worcestershire in this year, and preached sermons for it at his friend Mr. Bradley's living of Glasbury. He was also industrious in the musical line, and published his Op. II., "A Collection of Original Airs and Harmonized Tunes," thirty in number; and very pretty they are, though not all of the style he approved in latter years. Writing to the Rev. Thomas Kelly for permission to use some of his popular hymns, he received the following answer—

37, Dominick Street, Dublin,
Jan, 16, 1826.

Dear Sir,

Two of the hymns you mention are already set to music by myself, and belong, though for a limited period only, to Mr. Power, of Dublin: but I have reserved the right to publish them with music: so it is in my power to comply with your request respecting the following hymns, "Whence those sounds symphonious?" etc. I consider your setting them to music a compliment, and I feel thankful to the Lord whenever I hear of any of my poor productions being a comfort to any of His people. I shall be thankful for a copy of the work whenever it is published. The Lord's people know one another in one sense without a personal acquaintance. The Lord the Spirit dwells in them all, and unites them together. May we know more of His grace and power, and walk more as becometh the Gospel!

Yours, I trust, in best bonds,
Thomas Kelly.

My father also published a song, "Crown with freedom Afric's brows," for the benefit of an Anti-Slavery Association, in the autumn.

(*Letter to his Mother.*)

Astley Rectory,
Nov. 4, 1826.

Our missionary collection again increased—£25, besides a £5 note. I attended the Jews' meeting at Worcester. The lion of the day was that extraordinary man and Hebrew missionary, Joseph Wolff. He spoke for two hours! Every sentence was either sensible, interesting, or overwhelmingly exciting; we had also Marsh, Stewart, etc. Wolff recited a Hebrew chant, or air, which he used to sing at Jerusalem and Bushire with some venerable Jews. He has no knowledge of music: so by request I noted it down from his voice. This was done with difficulty, as the Eastern traveller could not be kept still or to the point; he would jump up, clasp W. H. H., kiss his forehead, and then break out in another strain or anecdote. It is a beautifully simple and pleasing air, and is to be published."[1]

(*To his Mother.*)

Nov. 17.

About a week ago I was strongly urged to quit Astley, and become the clerical secretary of the Newfoundland School Society, to reside in or near London. Upon mature deliberation I declined it, though I should prefer to labour as a preacher rather than a tutor, and am perhaps better adapted for it. I have little else to tell you. In October I went to preach two Sunday-school sermons at Kinver, about fifteen miles from hence. As to H.'s shyness, the better way is to take no notice of it. We have often seen, and others have remarked, that to urge or rebuke a child for shyness is the very way to confirm it. Age and further society is sure to rub it off. M.'s birthday was on Wednesday; the hours of course counted till its arrival; when it came she was highly pleased, but said, "Why, papa, I don't feel any older, and I don't feel any taller: how is it? It is my birthday, and now I'm five, but was only four yesterday." Such is childhood; and the expectations of many in maturity are about as rational.

In 1827 my father again made a tour in Cornwall for the Church Missionary Society, and this time as sole deputation and pioneer in some hitherto unvisited places. The following letters will give some particulars—

(*Letter to his Mother, written on the back of a C. M. S. Handbill.*)

St. Teath, near Camelford,
July 23, 1827.

From this paper you will see whereabouts I am. I left home on the 2nd and began my work in Cornwall on Sunday, the 8th. I was nearly the whole week in very delightful society at Ruan Lanyhorne, Veryan, Philleigh, Gerrans, Tregony, just above Falmouth, so that I much enjoyed the sea coast. The congregations and meetings have been very interesting. This year I am the only "foreigner" in the county, as Mr. Trist is resident with his father at Veryan, so that the whole weight of speaking at meetings falls on me as the agent of the Society. I shall finish, you see, at Launceston, an important town where a meeting has never yet been held. I am very well, and desire to be thankful for it. To-morrow and Wednesday I shall be close to the sea on the northern coast, near Boscastle. The cliffs and rocks there are very fine. I write in haste rather than not write at all; my time is constantly occupied, coming almost every day into fresh society."

[1] "Lord, build Thy house speedily." Op. 5. Profits to the London Society for Promoting Christianity among the Jews, which soon reached £100.

St. Columb major,
July 18, 1827.

My dearest Miriam,

You shall see that papa does not forget you; indeed, my thoughts amidst new scenes are often flying off towards you. Last week I spent near the sea with kind and intelligent friends. I was at Ruan Lanyhorne, and Veryan; look for them about the middle of the eastern side of Cornwall. I met with three nice little girls; two of them, Charlotte and Fanny, come from Madras. I wrote ever so much poetry for them, and some music. They send you some flower seeds, and their grandpapa a book. Where I am to-day are beautiful shrubs and flowers, a paraquet, a Java sparrow, and turtle doves. I am just going to Padstow, where Mr. Biddulph was born, and where I am to preach this evening. And now, dear M., I commend you to God and to the word of His grace. May you strive to be a really good girl, and let mamma have a pleasing account to give me.

Your affectionate Papa.

(*Letter to H. V. Tebbs, Esq.*)

August 16, 1827.

I was absent about five weeks in Cornwall and Devon. The season was laborious but refreshing to my mind. I met with much to cheer a Christian mind, and saw and associated with many excellent and friendly individuals. Many little incidents occurred to interest me, and I returned pleased with my tour and thankful to reach my home. Alluding to "incidents," I was charmed with a little brother and sister in a retired spot in Devonshire; they went last year to the first meeting of the kind there, and were so interested with what they heard me tell that they resolved to do what they could. The little boy had a lamb given to him, and he came to me and said, "My little lamb has become a sheep, and the wool sold for 3*s.*: will you please to take it? If I have a young lamb next year you shall have its wool and all its mother's." Then came the little girl, who devoted a chicken to the same cause. She had raised four shillings by her chick becoming a hen and nestling. She gave that sum with a warm expression of hope that next year she would be more successful. I was right glad, and blessed God that so much strength and praise redounded from such little ones."

W. H. H.'s Notes for a Speech at a Church Missionary Society meeting at Stratton, North Cornwall, July 31st, 1827.

I recollect saying last year, "We are assembled to lay the first stone of a moral edifice." I come as an humble agent of the greater architects to inspect its progress, to report it to them, and to accelerate it among yourselves. I rejoice at seeing an increasing number of good materials. I trust many are disposed to "arise and build." It is the union of effort which we want. Indeed, the secret of success lies in inducing individuals, as members of a body, to do their part. Moravian, Esquimaux, Indians, in bringing each a stone for a chapel, illustrates this point. Bring *your materials.*

But from our local edifice turn to the great temple that is erecting throughout the world. Turn your eye to 1st, *The grandeur of the work.* It is the work of God! Far more glorious than creation. It respects the souls of men. Six hundred millions are perishing in heathen lands.

They are scattered like the blocks of spar and granite on your heaths, rugged and misshapen. We labour to make them fit for the temple of the Lord. And, blissful sight, when the top stone shall be brought out with shoutings, and our King and High Priest adorn it with the more visible marks of his presence!

But now note also 2nd, *The difficulties that impede its progress.* Alas, how great! But Elliot's remark. Idolatry and every spiritual abomination stand in our way. View the state of society in savage and barbarian lands. Cruelty. Infanticide (Ellis). Ashantees. In more civilized countries, India. Norton's account of Alleppic. Millet's Suttee. Women. Sibthorpe's mother at the Ganges.

3rd. *The means by which we labour to remove impediments and forward the work.* By sending missionaries as wise builders. They copy that great master builder, St. Paul, and preach "Jesus Christ and Him crucified." This is the simple but the powerful and constituted means of building the house of God in all lands. The fable of Amphyon and city of Thebes. Church of Rome in vain used other means in China and South America. Moravians also, for seven years in Greenland. Story of the Makikan Indian.

4th. *The details of the C. M. S. as illustrating the advance of this work.* The Society sprang up as a labourer in 1800. Other Church Societies. No rivalry but that of love. It is a Church Society, but it maintains an affectionate and charitable temper. Honest Society. It first sent episcopates (Dr. B.'s episcopacy). Preparation at Islington. Labourers. Missions. Stations. Scholars, etc. Patronage and Funds. Africa. West Indies. East Indies. Ceylon. North America. O pray!

After this tour he was offered by the Committee the office of travelling secretary to the Church Missionary Society. After some hesitation and repeated offer he finally declined it, on which the Rev. E. Bickersteth, in the name of the Society, wrote a kind letter, ending with, "I fear that we are not likely to meet with one in whom we could so entirely confide, and with whom we could so entirely unite as yourself."

(*Letter to H. V. Tebbs, Esq.*)

August, 1827.

The sensation around you produced by Canning's death has, no doubt, been considerable. In our torpid village it is by this time almost forgotten. Oh that men were wise, etc.! Newspaper accounts of such deaths do, I conceive, much towards confirming the world in its thoughtlessness. When the nation is told that he who stood at its highest post was in his dying hours *most* solicitous about its political course, the men of this world shut their eyes and their hearts still closer against convictions of the value of the soul and the awfulness of dissolution. May we do otherwise.

In this and other years my father published many sacred songs to Bishop Heber's words, the profits being devoted to various Societies, but chiefly for Mrs. Heber's Hindoo Female Schools. After the last he set to music—"Wake not, O Mother, sounds of lamentation" (Op. 32)—he received the following letter from her:—

Sept. 4.

My dear Sir,

Although I have changed my name since I last had the pleasure of writing to you, I have not in any degree changed my feelings either for the past or the future. Your kind letter and the approbation which it expressed of my last publication gave me very sincere pleasure, and I have great satisfaction in complying with the request it contains, by enclosing you some of the handwriting of one of the most perfect beings who ever lived, and one whose memory must ever be loved and honoured and revered by me. You will doubtless have heard of my marriage about two months ago with Count Demetrius Valsamachi, secretary to the Governor of the Ionian Islands, and an English knight. He is a man well known to the members of our government, and highly respected for his talent and integrity and the services he has rendered to his country. Indeed, in every respect, whether moral, religious, or educational, his character and talents stand high in the estimation of all who know him. He loves my children as if they were his own, and his affection is even more than returned. My first and anxious wish is to bring them up to be worthy of the name of Heber. The character of their excellent father will ever be their model, and his features ever before their eyes. Should your health permit of your setting any more of his hymns to music, will you allow me and my children to partake in the pleasure you will then give the world: any parcel sent to Mr. Murray, in Albemarle Street, will be forwarded to me. I am very anxious that the Indian Female Education Society should not suffer from my temporary absence from England; as yet I have not succeeded in persuading any lady to take my place, although it will be an idle office for this year. I have myself made the necessary arrangements and purchases for the schools, and in 1832 hope to resume the situation. I hope you will never cease to befriend the Society. Accept my best wishes for your better health, and believe me ever, with much respect and esteem,

Very truly yours,

Amelia Valsamachi.

(*Letter to H. V. Tebbs, Esq.*)

Nov. 28, 1827.

My beloved Friend,

Most Christians, in these days especially, have indeed need of circumspection, both in forming opinions and in broaching them. The more I review all past things and consider the present, the more I see the necessity of labouring to unite fervency of spirit with very great caution; ready rather to act upon tried and established views than those which have not been proved, and respecting which authorities as great as any in the present day have been mistaken.

As to your request about Moravian missions, I could not bring them to the notice of my people till I have obtained their support to more objects in our own church. I have a great esteem for the Moravians, and enclose £2 as a donation to their missions, and will publish a piece of music at once on their behalf.

(*To the same.*)

Feb. 11, 1828.

Hurry and Worry sometimes visit me as well as yourself. They are sad fellows, but let us turn to the Epistle to the Hebrews and take comfort, "There remaineth a rest." This is sweet.

During these years my father maintained a voluminous correspondence with his kind rector, whose health now kept him in Devonshire. From one of the folio sheets I transcribe a part.

(*Rev. D. J. J. Cookes to W. H. H.*)

Brookfield House, Teignmouth,
April 21, 1828.

My beloved Friend,

I wish much to know the effects of your run to the metropolis, and I am anxious to hear that Dr. Farrar has been enabled to eradicate the evils, and to qualify the patients to prevent their recurrence. I am sure that much after evil might be obviated were we disposed to eye with greater suspicion incipient causes. I hope soon to receive an amended report of my twain-valued friends. The Almighty appears to have much for you to do in His vineyard, but it is better and wiser to labour with three parts out of four of our strength and ability than to lay out the whole four at an early part of the day, and at the tenth hour be thrown upon the shelf.[1] Active spirits in debilitated, or rather in *debilitatable,* frames have an additional duty imposed upon them when they well know that the useful activity of the former depends so greatly on the soundness of the latter. It is not constant restlessness in polishing that the instrument requires, and economy in husbanding the resources of the Christian guardsman and soldier is a prerequisite to length and duration of usefulness. . . . God has placed you at an early hour in His vineyard, and may He, my dear Havergal, keep you "doing" till, like the ripe fruit, you fall into the lap of the husbandman. Since I last wrote my life has appeared hovering in doubt upon "the Brink." Pray that the Lord may be the strength of my heart, and my portion for ever. . . .

I look forward to having you here with unusual delight, and hope, though the hope be feeble, that I may be enabled to accompany you in some at least of your rambles.

Yours affectionately,
Denham J. J. Cookes.

This year my father made the last of his C. M. S. tours, beginning with a sermon at Allhallows, Exeter, June 29, and a meeting in Exeter July 1; then, in company with the Revs. E. Bickersteth and Fisher, he proceeded to Linkinhorne, in Cornwall, and many other places, till the 27th of July. One letter remains referring to this journey written July 12, 1828, at Parc Behan, in Veryan—

My dear Mother,

Knowing that you will be pleased to see whereabouts I am, I enclose you a handbill of my travels. I am now in a most delightful spot and in a most charming family. To-morrow I set out again for the neighbourhood of Truro and Falmouth. I finish on the 27th at Sennen, the last parish in the kingdom, near the Land's End. I am pretty well; all the better for change and sea air, and blessed work for the Master. With much love to my father,

Yours, W.

(*To his Mother.*)

Sept. 22, 1828.

Why sleeps your pen? We half fear something is the matter, and we long to hear how our boy is getting on. Encourage him to sing. The hymns enclosed are fresh from the pen that is writing to you. Written for missionary sermons here Sept. 28. Which do you like best?[2] You have heard of good Mr. Biddulph's decease. East is gone to his new living—Croscombe, near Wells; a handsome purse of money was presented to him on leaving Bristol. My pupil, S., is better; he is at Brighton for the vapour baths, but longs to come again. My friend Abernethy told him he was a goose for having studied more hours a day than he could walk! Have you seen the "Life of Legh Richmond"? It is worth reading.

[2] The hymns were, "Hallelujah! Lord our voices": "Widely midst the slumbering nations": and "Shout, O earth! from silence waking."

(*To his Mother.*)

Dec., 1828.

I was glad to have a tolerably good account of my hopeful son. I shall be pleased if he pleases you. Tell him if he is a good boy I will probably fetch him the week after Christmas. It is late, and I have yet to write something for the *Worcester Herald.* I am just returned from a long ride on Protestant business. We are all tolerably well, for which I have to be thankful: as of late I have worked hard, head and pen constantly employed. The main business is the Protestant cause. The more I study it, and the more I study my Bible, the more important does it seem and the more imperative do exertions appear. Look at Scott on 2 Thessalonians 2:4, and Revelation 17, etc. Surely the mass of the nation is asleep, while Popery, the deadly enemy of the Church of God, is stealing upon it rapidly and deceptively. I am stirred within myself to fight manfully against it. Cawood is preaching anti-popish lectures at Bewdley, and repeating them at Birmingham on Thursday evenings; they make a commotion, which is better than stillness or ignorance. I am busy with the press; the Protestant's hymn is just out: music and words are mine, but the hymn may always be sung to the old Protestant tune, "God save the King." Send them going where you please. The Scripture references are designed to set readers on the search.

The editors of *The Protestant Warder* are Cawood and myself. I send you some prospectuses. More about it when we meet. The week before last I darted into Yorkshire, preached the missionary sermons at Ossett and Wakefield, and back on Monday; the fag was a little too great. I have asked Tebbs to come to our aid with poetry or prose in the *Protestant Warder.* I hope he is a soldier on our side.

(*To H. V. Tebbs, Esq.*)

Astley Rectory,
Feb. 13, 1829.

Beloved Friend,

You know what it is to have much to say without leisure to say it. All our first No. of *Protestant Warder* is gone, and the second also is nearly out. Whether the appalling treachery of our Protestant leaders

[1] In the 20th and 21st centuries, British people widely understand the phrase "on the shelf" to mean a woman who would never be considered for marriage, a woman certain to be a spinster, never to marry. This is not at all W.H.H.'s meaning of this phrase: here he meant the idea of a tool or utensil set on the shelf when

may deter our readers from reading, and hinder the sale of our little work, I know not. There certainly is more occasion than ever for it. I am not disposed to slacken. The Lord help us, our king, our country, our Church! "The end will be glorious." Never despair with such an assurance! You will see in our original articles compression is a leading feature. In writing mine I scribble at length, and then reduce to one-half. Nothing is lost by this in neatness, perspicuity, or sense. Diffusion is the fault of most articles in periodicals. The *Christian Observer*, for instance, might reduce by half many of its articles, and yet be quite as good. But, as you know, it is more tedious and difficult to write with perspicuous brevity than with unimportant length.

My parishioners have numerously signed a petition against the Roman Catholic Emancipation Act, and its acknowledgment has arrived with Robert Peel's signature.

(*To his Mother.*)

May 29, 1829.

On Saturday last poor Mr. Cookes was released from his sufferings. His bodily state has for months been most affecting, but his mind has been tranquil and happy.

I preached two sermons for Sunday schools at Coaley last Sunday, and contrived to visit Kingscote Park and Dursley, and reach home again on Tuesday. The distress in that neighbourhood is truly grievous from stagnation of trade. Mr. P. of Dursley is quite a changed man, and is himself persecuted for the truth which he once disliked in me! We quite look to see my father. I am expecting by and by a younger pupil than usual, a son of Mr. Ridley, the rector of Hambleden, with whom I have had some pleasing correspondence.

On the 14th of June, 1829, my father met with a most serious accident. He was driving alone to fetch me from school near Worcester; when opposite the gates of Hallow Park, nearly nine miles from Astley, the usually steady horse suddenly plunged and dashed against the opposite bank, throwing him out, and causing concussion of the brain. He was soon discovered and carried into Hallow Park, where his friends, Mr. and Mrs. Horace Mann, made every possible arrangement for his relief. They sent for my poor mother and myself, and we remained some days till it was safe to remove him home. The excellent and charming hostess was a daughter of Sir Lucius O'Brien, and one of her sisters was Archdeacon Spooner's wife, and another the Honourable Mrs. Gerald Noel.

Whilst at Hallow he was attended by old Mr. Carden, father of the late eminent surgeon, Henry Carden, of Worcester, and at Astley by Mr. K. Watson, of Stourport, in whom he had much confidence.

My grandmother spent the first weeks of her son's illness at our rectory. His nerves were so shaken by the accident that he suffered more or less from its effects for many years. After about five weeks he was able to write thus to his friend, H.V. Tebbs:—

I am getting better every day, but my progress is slow. The concussion of the spine extends to my extremities. Only within the last day or two can I hold a pen. Watson tells me escape from instant death was narrow indeed. Oh! what does my heart feel at this! And yet I want it to feel abundantly more than it does. All my desire is towards the Good Physician who has smitten, only, I trust, to renew me more and more in His own image. Pray for me, and give thanks with me! Accept a few shillings' worth of music in aid of the Moravian Missions.

On the 7th of August he was able to resume his correspondence with his mother as follows:—

My dearest Mother,

All your kindness has been deeply felt. The Lord reward you for it, and hear the prayers that ascend for you. All mercifully and happily over, and God has given us a little boy, who arrived at five o'clock, a.m. I write this wide awake though up all night, and make no delay, as I expect to feel amiss by and by. I am getting well really as fast as could be expected. I follow now my usual hours, and hope to be competent for the return of my pupils, having good assistance. I have not yet officiated. All my desire is to live wholly and constantly for Him who has spared me.

August 20th he writes to Mr. Tebbs:—

I am again on the advance. May my progress toward health be marked with greater humility of heart and devotedness of life. On Sunday I re-entered my pulpit, and preached from Isaiah 38:22. Still I am not equal to much. I earnestly wish our present babe to be called Edward or Astley Tebbs. Will you, his father's friend, become his Christian sponsor? You know that such a relationship will give me unfeigned pleasure. I cannot write so fully as I could wish; understand what my heart would reply to your refreshing letter; thanks for it. My fingers are still very capricious, but "why should a living man complain?"

The "babe" was named Francis Tebbs; the former name from his other godfather, the Rev. Robert Francis Walker, incumbent of Purleigh. Mr. Tebbs came for the baptism and made a little book full of slight but masterly sketches of Astley. After this visit, my father writes to him, September 4th:—

Your kindness, dearest friend, demands some acknowledgment from my heart. I thank you for coming hither. I thank you for all your affectionate thoughts now that you are away from us. To hear you say, "Dear Astley!" and "I was profited," makes me say, "what am I or my house that one of God's children should speak thus?" Ah! dear friend, we may be thankful even for a smile in this troublous world. Our dear E. is leaving us next week, which is a source of regret to herself and to me, for as she has I really hope entered the school of our heavenly Master, it is very delightful to become her helper and teacher. Dear girl, if prayer and fervent desire will avail with the Great Intercessor, I may taste of that spring of joy which the servants of God in converting souls alone feel.

not being used, on the shelf awaiting use. The current meaning of unattractiveness and certainty to be a spinster was not at all meant here.

The "dear girl" referred to was sponsor to my baby brother with Mr. Tebbs, and one of my mother's nieces. She married Major Usborne, Esq., and lived in London. Both died long ago, but their kindness and hospitality, especially to my father in his frequent visits to town on musical and other business, are held in grateful remembrance.

CHAPTER VI.

LIFE AS RECTOR OF ASTLEY.

Perplexities — The Rectory of Astley *in commendam* — Effects of his accident — Visit to Rev. J. East — A relapse — Preaching recommenced — Bristol riots — Great Campden House — Rejoicing with trembling — Sympathy in suffering — The Mumbles and Glasbury — Tour in Somerset and Devon — A long silence — Curates and livings — Musical publications — Letter from Sir Herbert S. Oakeley — Gresham prize medals — Affecting burial — Bereaved mothers — Birth of Frances R. Havergal — The Rev. W. H. Ridley — Request for sponsorship — New Church clock — Baptism of Frances R. Havergal — Letters on the burial service — Letter to a first-class pupil — Low spirits — Astley Church restoration — Queen Victoria's coronation-day — Rural festivities — "God save the Queen" — Visit of Dr. Edward Hodges — Musical names — Tour in Ireland — St. Asaph's Cathedral — An Irish welcome — Glendalough — Vale of Avoca — Ferns Cathedral — Vinegar Hill — Whisky and popery — Kilkenny — Limerick — Kilrush and Killarney — Illness — "Fanny full of prattle" — Reopening of Astley Church — Sermon by Rev. J. East — A happy day — At the Isle of Man — Tour in North Wales — Bangor — Carnarvon — Snowdon — The Bishop of Calcutta's charge — Taylor's "Ancient Christianity" — "A refined transubstantiation" — Rev. J. Keble as an examiner — A means of grace not "the" means — Visit to Iona and Staffa — Fire in the chancels of Astley Church — "The King of Terrors" — Sermons at Dewsbury — Visiting Paris and Canterbury — Resignation of Astley — Gift of Bibles, etc., "for ever" — Farewell Sermons — Rev. J. East — Parting Presents.

THE last four months had been a time of great perplexity to my parents. My father's invalid state rendered it possible that he might be obliged to resign his curacy and give up tuition, and consequently leave the home to which he was so much attached, as indeed a medical consultation urged him to do. Then after Mr. Cookes' death the uncertainty as to the new rector, and whether he would wish to reside in the rectory itself, naturally gave rise to very anxious feelings. But now the bow was seen in the cloud, and its silver lining became visible.

Shortly before Mr. Cookes made his last will, in July, 1828, he sent for my father to Teignmouth, and informed him that he intended to leave him the living of Astley "out and out." He naturally, and at once, remonstrated against an arrangement which would not have been just to Mr. Cookes' own children, supposing one of them might hereafter enter the ministry. Mr. Cookes acquiesced; but as a proof of the affection and esteem he felt for my father, he left him the second option of becoming Rector of Astley *in commendam*. The first option was to his old friend the Rev. Harvey Marriott, who declined it, preferring to retain his own living. These circumstances are referred to in the following letter—

My dear Mother.

I am almost afraid lest you should think we forget you and our dear child now with you (Maria V. G. H.). So many things have been in agitation. I have now a budget to open to you though I scarcely know how to begin; but I must not tantalize you or myself, but at once tell you I am to be the new Rector of Astley. As Mr. Marriott declines it, the living devolves on me; for so Mr. Cookes has left it in his will, and moreover, as Mrs. Cookes tells me, to the very last he talked of me, and expressed his hearty wish that I should become his successor in the living. Certainly *it is* remarkable, and you will say so, as you know the manner in which I refused to accept it when Mr. Cookes offered it to me. Certainly "honesty is the best policy." I shall be inducted as soon as the necessary papers can be got ready. The event brings me unnumbered congratulations, and the satisfaction of the parishioners is extreme. In mentioning the news to any one, be sure state plain facts. I hold "*in commendam*" only. I wish never to forget that it is the blessing of God alone that maketh rich: without this what will it all avail? With prosperity I may in all probability have some proportionate trial.

(*To his Mother.*)

Oct. 23rd.

I am thankful to say I am wonderfully well. Still I am not what I was. I cannot endure fatigue or excitement, I feel the taking a Sunday duty. Frank thrives so nicely, altogether a charming little fellow. Ellen is quite a nurse; she sits by the hour together and watches him when asleep, as quiet and contented by herself as can be; she is a good child, but of late has not been strong. My crop of apples is most abundant. It would grieve Buckinghamshire eyes to see what beautiful and delicious fruit is knocked down and thrown in a heap for the cider-mill.

(*To his Mother.*)

Nov. 23rd.

There will be no tithe dinner for a twelvemonth, no alteration of pulpit, or else, beyond what shall be in proper consideration for God's glory. I do not intend to dismiss my pupils, as I have an able assistant. On the 13th I was inducted, *i.e.,* put in possession of temporalities, by the Rev. H. J. Hastings, of Martley. Institution is to spiritualities, and on Sunday the 16th I read myself in, as the phrase is. I send you the skeleton of the sermon then preached. It seemed to make an impression. God grant it and deepen it. I still feel effects of my accident in my breathing and my fingers, which die very frequently.

(*To his Mother.*)

Dec. 18, 1829.

Dear East is very anxious I should visit him in his new rectory this Christmas, and be sponsor to his little boy, and open the missionary cause in his new parish. I have therefore concluded, with the Divine blessing, on starting from home on the 28th by the "Aurora" coach, which leaves Worcester at 7 a.m., goes round through Cheltenham, reaches Wycombe, I guess, about half-past five p.m. I then proceed to London. Tell Maria we do not forget her; she may tell her cousin Kate that little Frank is as soft as velvet, as merry as a kitten, and as good as a babe can be.

(*To H. V. Tebbs.*)

March 31, 1830.

I am again laid low. I have a seaton in my neck as an expedient against paralysis. Every engagement is given up and every exertion is forbidden. I am to live only as a vegetable. How difficult the task! But may I glorify God; pray that I may.

(*To the same.*)

June 1st.

Thanks be to God our Healer! My general health is better, my walking power increased. But paralytic symptoms still hang about me: any exercise of the brain, even in pleasant conversation, throws me back. But how good is the Lord! I might be in circumstances a thousand times more afflictive.

(*To the same.*)

Nov. 29th.

Beloved Friend,

What can be the occasion of your long silence? Imagination has often taken wing respecting it, but no place can she find for the sole of her foot to rest. As to myself, about a fortnight ago I had a sad relapse. Leeches, however, by God's blessing, saved me from what my head threatened.

(*To his Mother.*)

April 29, 1831.

I would always regulate my voting by patriotic feeling, *i.e.,* without the influence of mere party, I would vote for that candidate who thinks as I think upon any *vital* or important question. Tell grandpapa that Frank (nineteen months old) can sing "God save the King" quite distinctly; he catches any chant in a few minutes. I have a nice set of pupils, for which I thank God.

In July, 1831, my parents took Terrace Cottage, Malvern Wells, for a month, which was a time of great enjoyment to us all. Here my grandfather Havergal joined our party and returned with us to Astley.

(*To his Mother.*)

Nov. 24, 1831.

Through God's mercy I am stronger and better. Hitherto I have only taken my desk once on the Sunday, besides the slight occasional duty. I hope to gain permission after Christmas to preach once every Sunday. The prospect is cheering, and yet I sometimes view it with trembling. I desire to be God's servant, even in waiting for Him, and to do His will by endurance as well as by action.

You have heard, of course, of the sad tidings at Bristol. I was going thither last week, on the very days of the riots, to fetch Ellen, but some obstacle arose, and besides, I felt an extraordinary and unusual reluctance to go this journey, saying, "We shall, perhaps, see by events why it is that I feel so." Now, no one will call this superstition, but I am thankful such singular feelings befell me. If it was of God's mercy I will speak good of it.

The Bristol rabble never would have proceeded to such excesses had they not been urged on by higher individuals whom the Government court or countenance. Their cowardly and foolish bending to such infamous parties as the Birmingham Political Union is quite enough to account for these disturbances. All these things are, in my eye, scourges for our national countenance of popery and infidelity. I have been to Bristol since to meet Mr. East with Ellen, and saw some of my old friends; their alarm had been excessive. I saw the devastation in Queen's Square and the bishop's palace. It was a melancholy and affecting scene. We are quiet here, thank God, and do not anticipate any stir. The cholera, of course, and the Reform Bill are the general themes.

In the summer of 1832 my father, by the advice of the Rev. John East, sent me to the large school at Great Campden House in Kensington, presided over by the well-known and excellent Mrs. and Miss Fanny Teed. In the following year I was joined by my sister Maria, who wrote an interesting account of the school, which appeared in "The Sunday at Home" for 1863. The other sisters also went there in due course. The experiences of Frances Ridley Havergal (then unborn) at Mrs. Teed's are recorded in her "Memorials."

(*To H. V. Tebbs,* 1832.)

Since recommencing preaching I have gradually become worse, and am now strongly urged to discontinue even a single sermon. The excitement, it seems, is more than I can support. Such are the Lord's dealings with me: may I bow my proud and eager spirit to them. Thankful and happy you, I doubt not, are in the circumstances you describe to me; but oh, forget not that all our rejoicing at the possession of temporal mercies must be with fear and trembling. At no time is it perhaps more necessary to remember this is not our rest than when our hearts beat high in our first days of deliverance from tribulation. A conqueror flushed with victory has often been vigorously assailed by the vanquished party, becaused it was rightly supposed that conquest induced carelessness. Let us take heed to what the Captain of our Salvation says to us and to all, "Watch."

(*To Miss M. Bulgin.*)

Nov., 1834.

I am indeed sorry that you are again a sufferer; you have my earnest sympathy. I hoped your summer excursion would be permanently beneficial to you: but as God sees fit to appoint otherwise, I pray that His grace may suffice for your patience and comfort. All such dispensations are very trying to the flesh, but they may become sources of joy to the spirit; everything that will wean us from earth is a mercy. It is a hard task to learn contentment with a painful lot, but when the lesson is submitted to, it becomes even sweet and pleasant. So the saints of olden time found it, and so may you abundantly prove it.

In the summer I went to The Mumbles, returning through the pleasant vale of Neath to Glasbury, my dear friend the Rev. Charles Bradley's living.

(*To H. V. Tebbs, Esq.*)

Sept. 4, 1835.

I have had a month's tour with my eldest girl, taking her first to Durston and Lyng, then to Exeter, Launceston, and Bude, intending to stay with the Kingdons of Pyworthy; but on account of the death of Mrs. K. we proceeded up the coast to Clovelly and Ilfracombe. There we crossed the Channel to the Mumbles, having sent to my boy Henry to join us there. We had plenty of oysters at Oystermouth. We reached home three weeks ago, and, refreshed by my trip, I have rcommenced preaching once every Sunday. Mine has been a long silence in the midst of my years, but it has been marked by many mercies. Although my path of late has been most tangled and trying, light arises upon it, and God's countenance makes it pleasant.

One of the trials alluded to had been his frequent change of curates through unavoidable circumstances, such as being able only to make temporary engagements, or their succeeding to livings, as in the case of his valued helper the Rev. John Garwood Bull, who by the sudden death of his father became Rector of Tattingstone. But now his former clever pupil, Octavus Fox (afterwards rector of Knightwick), was ordained and remained at Astley more than three years, when he was succeeded by the Rev. Thos. Ludlam, a truly faithful pastor, but who in the next year became vicar of Ellington. He was followed by the Rev. Frederick Jeffery, whose efficient help came to an end by his marriage and appointment to the incumbency of Sway, but his faithful friendship continues to the present day. The former curates are now all deceased.

In 1836 my father published one of his popular songs, "Hark to the old bells' chime!" profits to the restoration of the Abbey Church, Malvern; and "An Evening Service in E flat," *Cantate Domino* and *Deus Misereatur,* prefaced by lengthy "Remarks on Chants and Chanting," and with the addition of "A Hundred Antiphonal Chants," selected from the many hundreds he had composed.

Two of these chants are referred to by the accomplished Professor of Music in the University of Edinburgh, Sir Herbert S. Oakeley, in a letter to Maria V. G. H.

Edinburgh, Feb. 18, 1882.

Dear Miss Havergal,

Acquaintance with your talented father, Canon Havergal, and with Mr. and Mrs. Stratton, also with your brother, is my apology for writing direct to you to thank you for the permission and the chants received through Mr. Robertson. As my selection is made up I am unable to introduce any more chants, but I have taken a copy of a very good single in G minor, changeable, in case of requiring one. I have always admired the construction and harmony of your father's admirable chants and without the "immortal Recte et Retro" in D and the E Worcester chant, no collection would be complete.

Yours very faithfully,

Herbert S. Oakeley.

In this year also appeared "An Evening Service in A," *Magnificat* and *Nunc Dimittis* (Op. 37), for which the Gresham Prize Medal was adjudged. He obtained another of these prize medals in 1841, for an anthem, "Give thanks," 1 Chronicles 16:8–10.

(*Letter to the Rev. J. East.*)

Astley Rectory, April 27, 1836.

My Beloved East,

Your letter has just reached me; it is like this very April day, dark and stormy, genial and sunny. It comes too at a singularly coincident moment: it was waiting for me as I came in from a very affecting burial. A respectable couple had followed their eldest son to the grave, a dear, affectionate, pious child of twelve years of age. The poor mother had more energy, but not less sorrow, than the spirit-broken father. He had watched the dying boy incessantly for four days, and nursed him with all the assiduity of a mother. When the bier was set down in the church he paused a moment at the door of a pew, and then followed the yearnings of his heart by throwing himself upon the coffin, and then kneeling down and embracing it during the solemnities of the Psalm and the Chapter. I omit the rest of the scene.

The death and burial of your babe—what an appendage to the earnest sorrow I have just witnessed! I can hardly touch the chord which is vibrating of itself beneath my finger. Our hearts bleed with yours; may the one Almighty and most merciful Saviour look upon you! Tell your dearest wife to look with a Protestant eye at a mother on Calvary. What a sword was that which then pierced through her very soul! And yet, though the sufferer was her Son and the Saviour of all the world, there was no other grace provided for her support than precisely that grace which is provided for every bereaved mother. All these things are trying, dearest friend, but then they are transparent. You seem to know why the Lord deals thus with you. That knowledge is part of His grace to you. Thank Him for it, and welcome each cross if it adds brightness to your Redeemer's crown.

To buy up Bath ecclesiastically is indeed a mighty work. But it is, as you say, half done. I *will* afford a £5 note, for your sake and God's glory, towards its completion. The Lord of the Church speed and prosper it! My wife's love and all my children's. C. R. Hay's, too. Let us hear soon.

Ever yours,

W. H. H.

At the close of the year 1836 an event occurred which has made the name of Astley Rectory familiar to tens of thousands. Late in the evening of December 14th the little Frances Ridley Havergal arrived, whose poetic genius and heaven-taught mind produced those writings in prose and verse which have exercised so wide an influence on the present generation. She will only be mentioned incidentally in these pages, as my sister Maria has written her "Memorials." On December 24th my father thus writes to his much beloved pupil, Wm. H. Ridley, afterwards Rector of Hambleden:—

You may be sure, dear Ridley, that it was not without cause a letter from me failed to reach you at Oxford on the day of your appointment to a Christ Church Studentship. The cause was increased indisposition; for some days I was wholly laid aside, unable to bear a sound, and am still unfit for anything. Your appointment is very, very gratifying to me. I heartily rejoice at it, and earnestly pray our heavenly Father to make it a blessing to you and to others. My dear Mrs. H. and babe (whose sisters think it the sweetest little creature in the world) are going on very nicely. We are planning the baptismal arrangements. Will you be a party to them? You have resided in our family for a longer period than any person, whether pupil or friend, it will therefore be a real pleasure to us all, but to myself especially, if you will undertake to "promise and vow three things" in the name of our last born babe. I can ask you with confidence, and I trust you will assent without any regret. As to the day of baptism, we will endeavour to fix it so as to suit your convenience, etc., etc. We think of calling our little one by a name you love, Fanny. Take my Christmas love, and may the God of Christmas give you peace and joy.

Ever affectionately yours,

W. H. H.

New Year's Day, 1837, was signalized by setting in motion the new church clock (with dials on the east and west sides of the tower) which my father presented to the parish. He arranged for it to strike the hours and quarters on the chord of G. Long may it remain

A musical memento of his love,
For time, and tune, and punctuality.

(*To his Mother.*)

Jan. 31st, 1837.

It was no little disappointment to me not to be able to spend a few days with you; indeed, I went to London with a heavy heart. As long as God is pleased to spare your lives I hope to come and see you twice a year at least, and much oftener if the bounds of my habitation were so fixed that I could. Long may your lives be spared, and more blessed and happy may they be as you approach the close of them. Oh, I thought my heart would have burst as I passed my father's house without entering it; the thought pierced me that in a few years, if I am spared, I may often have to pass that door, with the grief of knowing that I have no father or mother there! May the God of mercy put that day a long way off from me! Now that my own children are growing up I seem to feel that I am myself a son more and more. But enough. Thanks to God I am pretty well. Baby grows nicely. She was baptized on the 25th inst[1] Frances Ridley—of course we shall call her Fanny. Frank is gone to school. I took Henry on his way to Bruton. Mr. Abrahall gives him an excellent character, and we find him a conscientious, good sort of boy. What a mercy! The Lord be praised for it.

(*To his Daughter Maria V. G. H., at Great Campden House, Kensington.*)

May 28, 1837.

My dearest Maria,

I have not time to write more than is necessary to answer your question respecting a passage in the Burial Service. The objection you hear made is utterly without foundation. Observe, the clergyman does *not* say, "in sure and certain hope of his or her resurrection" but "of *the* resurrection." So that, in fact, it is simply a declaration of faith in God's promise respecting the resurrection of the just. Only transpose the words, according to the original Latin, and you will see the true sense of the passage immediately; thus it will read, "*we,* therefore (in sure and certain hope of *the* resurrection, etc.), commit his (or her) body to the ground," etc. That this is the true sense is further evident from the corresponding part of the Service for the Burial of the Dead at Sea. So long ago as 1661, at the Savoy Conference, the words were altered from *a* resurrection, etc., to *the* resurrection, etc., thus *intending* to put the question beyond all dispute. As a general rule, so far as our most excellent Church is concerned, you may safely take it as certain that all her formularies and their phraseology will, *upon examination,* be found to be far more scriptural, and far more accordant with the teaching and practice of the earliest Christians, than objectors are wont to imagine. Never forget that the men who drew up these Services were *martyrs,* holy, learned, and faithful followers of the Lord Jesus. May you and I, dear girl, one day join that company of which they constitute so noble and so conspicuous a part. Amen.

Ever your affectionate father,

W. H. H.

Dec. 1, 1837.

My dear Ridley,

"Not unto us! not unto us!" You know the words and their application. I am just now in one corner of the valley of humiliation, but I can look up, and with you rejoice and give thanks. *Truly, I am glad.* Neither do I forget to pray for you, especially that you may with alacrity and fervent affection carry your class-crown, and lay it at the feet of the Saviour. Yes, yes, dear Ridley, you have still a race to run; and a nobler crown than that which you have gained, or at Oxford still can gain, awaits your efforts through life. May you be as successful and as honourable in the Church of God as you have been enabled to be in the university! My heart goes forward for you.

It is kind of you to think of me as having lent a hand towards your success. My share of commendation in the matter is, if truth be consulted, so very scanty, that while I heartily thank you, I am in no danger of being elated. There are *two* in heaven whose earlier training far outweighs any poor services of mine. They give all glory to the Lamb. Let us learn to do the same.

(*Letter to his Mother from Bath.*)

Jan. 9, 1838.

I have been here for ten days, but was unwilling to write until I could give you a somewhat encouraging account of myself.

I have been very unwell, spirits low, and my mind disposed to dwell on the darker side of things. The new year has brought up many old thoughts, but also, I hope, some new resolutions. I have lived nearly forty-five years—none of them have been spent as they ought. My hope and desire is that the remainder, as many as God may see fit to grant, may be more entirely devoted to His glory. My very mercies humble me, because I am unworthy of them; and my trials, though not few, are light in comparison with some which many of the Lord's people are appointed to suffer. One of my greatest mercies is the promise of good among my children.

The church business is going on well, and contracts will, I expect, be soon settled. I do not recollect if I told you the parishioners were most earnest and liberal in subscriptions towards their part. I was amazed at them. I long to know how you all are faring, and how my father is. It is good to be here for better things than those which concern the poor body. East is a Christian of the best stamp. God is doing great things by him in Bath. His new church is a noble and beautiful structure. All done by his own exertions! To see it as it is, thronged from end to end, is its glory and greatest beauty. It puts my poor plans and efforts quite into the shade. However, to be able to do *anything* is an honour and a privilege.

(*To H. V. Tebbs.*)

May 13, 1838.

I have in hand a great work in the enlargement, repair, restoration, convenience, and decorous fitting up of my church. It was in a sad state, altogether unworthy of such a parish and such a living; but when finished, it will, I trust, be, if not a model of a parish church, yet such an one as will indicate a little more reverence than heretofore for the house and the honour of the eternal God. The parish contribute nobly to its restoration; for my own share I am building a new north aisle, putting in a new chancel window, and other items. It will cost me something! But I have nothing of *my own.* It is all of the Lord's giving; and in the end I shall not lose. He gives me faith in His promise, and certainly I feel strong in His strength. Come and see what we are doing; not that, Jehu-like, I care for your seeing it, but I should love to *see you.*

(*To his Daughters at Great Campden House.*)

May 7, 1838.

My dearest Ones,

The Good Shepherd carry you in His bosom. I am so unwell that, with much on my hands and head, I can say little more than, "The Lord be with you, keep you, bless you." Dear mamma is very poorly, and darling sprightly Frank too, so both, with baby and Ann, are going to Aberystwith for a month. Mr. Watson insists on this. Mr. Ludlam continues to act as I approve, and to give us just such sermons as the Lord will bless. My kindest love to your dear friends.

Ever your affectionate father,

W. H. H.

[1] inst: likely an abbreviation of "instant," an older usage meaning the present or current month. (F. R. H. was baptised on January 25, 1837, recorded in the baptismal registry of the church.)

Queen Victoria's coronation-day was suitably kept in Astley by my father's arrangement. Early in the morning the parishioners assembled at the meeting of the three roads before the western churchyard wall, where also the tables were placed, with loaves and joints of beef, and a huge barrel of cider gaily decorated. My father stood before his seraphine[1] in the churchyard above, nearly on the site of his own after-grave, with family and friends on either side. (We had all adorned ourselves with a sprig of oak for Old England, and a rose-bud for the Queen). Then, after a prayer, he made a loyal address to the people, and led their cheers. Before the distribution of provision, all joined in singing one of his versions of "God save the Queen." A copy of the hand-bill is subjoined. The school children had a dinner of roast beef and plum-pudding at 12.30 in the rectory garden.

GOD SAVE THE QUEEN.

"To be sung of all the people together" in the Parish of ASTLEY, on the morning of Thursday the 28th June, 1858; (the day of the Coronation of our MOST GRACIOUS SOVEREIGN, QUEEN VICTORIA.)

"God save our noble Queen!
Long live Old England's Queen;
God save the Queen!
Great and victorious,
Happy and glorious,
May she reign over us;
God save the Queen!

"On her anointed head,
Blessings on blessings shed,
Constant and rare:
Robe her with truth and might,
Health, peace, and holy light;
Save her from faction's blight,
And withering care.

"'Give peace in our time';
Spare us from blood and crime;
Up for us stand!
Nursed by our 'Gracious Queen,'
May our Church e'er be seen
Waving like evergreen,
Over the land.

"God save our youthful Queen!
Long live Old England's Queen;
God save the Queen!

Upward with joyous spring,
Let every heart take wing;
And the whole nation sing,
God save the Queen!"[2]

(*To the Rev. J. East.*)

My dearest E.,

The King of kings save you! After the bustle of the Coronation day, I commence a short epistle to you at half-past five this morning. Henry had no chance at Merton, twenty-four crack candidates, and the contest very close. However, my dear boy came off with great credit, and a note was sent me to that effect. I have just read Dr. Fausett's sermon before the university on the revival of popery. God be praised for it! seven-eighths of it are good, good, good.

The whole scene of yesterday was affectingly simple and beautiful. The whole village assembled by nine o'clock (but Miriam will describe all this). My dear ones had trimmed a fair flag for the church tower, and arrayed and arranged the school children, who, after the proceedings, had a dinner followed by speaking, and singing, and cheering, etc. Young and old were contented and pleased, and some, I trust, prayerful and thankful. It was just the thing that would have delighted you, for I suspect such village scenes are far more simple and pleasing than any which you can enjoy in a city. The Lord pardon all sin, and accept our prayer and praise! I have worked very hard lately, and must try and trip it to the sea, perhaps to Ireland for a little relief. The Lord afflicts, but He pours oil on the wounds. I rejoice to see my children all turned, or turning to the Lord. Oh, it is enough! Talk not of trials. "Let the children of Zion be joyful in their king." When we get our crowns we shall never think we had one trial too many, or one cross too hard to bear.

Our Poet Laureate should have put forth an authorized National Anthem. We have none worthy of such an epithet. Many foolish or party ones are afloat, and therefore I had no alternative between taking one of those or scribbling what I send you. All unite in love to you and yours.

Ever as since college days,
Yours,
W. H. H.

About this time Dr. Edward Hodges came to see us at Astley, before leaving for New York. He and my father had a great regard and admiration for each other. Dr. Hodges was a Churchman and Conservative, well read in classical and sterling literature, a witty and cheerful companion, although his life was an anxious and struggling one. He was a fine organist and a wonderful pedalist, the composer of much church music, and author of treatises on chanting and psalmody, etc. He was born in 1796, became organist at St. James's, Bristol, 1819, took his Mus. Doc. 1829. In New York he was director of music in three churches, and finally organist of Trinity

[1] The Royal Seraphine, invented by J. Green, Soho Square, was a predecessor of the harmonium. My father's instrument was one of the first ever made, and certainly the first imported into Worcestershire, where it was regarded as a great curiosity.

[2] A slightly altered version was made by my father some years after. See p. 142. [See page 396 of this book.]

church. Enfeebled by paralysis, he returned to Clifton, and there he "entered into rest" in 1866. His clever daughter, Faustina, is still an organist in America. All his children were musically named, *e.g.*, Jubal, John Sebastian Bach, Asaph, and I think there was a Miriam and a Handel.

In this summer my father made a tour in Ireland, shortly described in his various letters home.

Wicklow, July 14, 1838.

I stopped at St. Asaph to see the cathedral, which the organist showed me, and the organ, which is new and good as far as it goes. Saw my two services there; the Gresham one is in use, though it is not to be compared to the other. Saw Mrs. Heman's monument; the neighbourhood is pretty and pleasant. On Friday sailed from Holyhead. In Dublin beggary and finery abound in painful contrast. Went to Bray, a pleasant village twelve miles off, near the shore, and then came on through a Welsh-like country here. Yesterday (Sunday, July 15) was a truly singular day with me. I went early to the rocks and the sea, fine and beautiful; at nine the Popish Chapel. Oh, what a degrading, soul-stirring sight! I could have cried out, "Sirs, why do ye these things? Turn from these vanities," etc.

At 12 o'clock I went to the parish church (finely situated), and there found a respectable congregation, with a pair of most gentlemanly *Christian* pastors. The young one read, and the older one preached, much to my taste and satisfaction. They *seemed* to *eye* me. In the evening at 6 o'clock I went again. But a small congregation. To my surprise the vicar sent to me, when seated in a pew, to come into the reading desk. I briefly declined. Seeing me without a hymnbook, he sent me one. After service he came towards me before I could get to him to return the book. In an instant, all in a gentle breath, he said, "I am sure by your *head* you are a brother clergyman, so you must come home with me." A few words followed, and out came a hearty Irish welcome—"I must stay two or three days and see the country, and he would drive me," etc. So home he took me, with his family and his curate, in his barouche and pair, to a lovely residence in a sweet spot near the sea, about one and a half miles out of Wicklow, just the place to please me. He is a most gentlemanly man, about fifty-three or more, his wife a lady, with twelve children, the eldest about Miriam's age, and the youngest (a boy) about fourteen months (the rest mostly girls), altogether a decidedly Christian right-minded family. This morning his curate (a *Ludlam*-like young man) is to call for me, and both of us are going to the vicar's, and he is going to drive me to the Devil's Glen. I am to dine, and I don't know what beside. I see the daughters have a pianoforte, so I mean to take them some music, and Mrs. C. a "Memoir of John East." Altogether this is a pleasant adventure.

Mathdrum, Tuesday, I o'clock.

Yesterday was in every respect a charming day. Mr. Charnley (for such is my new friend's name) drove me, with Mrs. C., two daughters and his curate, to a place called the Devil's Glen, about six miles from Wicklow. Oh it is a lovely spot! It delighted me much. Took me, too, to Glenmaur Castle, the seat of a good man, but he was not at home. We drove back to Mr. C.'s house, dined at 5 o'clock, and spent a pleasant evening. Altogether very pleased. Felt better too. This morning I took a car (good thing for travelling, sixpence a mile and no turnpikes!) and went to Glendalough, or the Seven Churches of Kevan. Delighted! delighted! with wild mountain scenery and *genuine* Saxon architecture.

Enniscorthy, July 18, 1838.

Yesterday afternoon at Rathdrum; the weather cleared up, and after being perished with cold, I had a charming ride through the vale of Avoca to Arklow. That vale is the pride of Ireland, and a lovely vale it certainly is. Mr. Fox was highly pleased with it, and so indeed was I. Arklow is nothing of a town, though as populous as Bewdley. Such lots of *squalid*, horrid-looking females and wild children everywhere to be seen. The beach is capital for bathing. I had a ramble all along it till nearly dark. For tea I had some "*white* trout," a most delicate sort of salmonet caught in the sea at Arklow. I longed to send you some to Astley. I came through Gorey to *Ferns* to see the cathedral, as it is called, and the ruins of a fine *old* castle. I reached this place about 5 o'clock. It is a rather large town, six thousand people, with some interesting things about it. This evening I have been to the top of Vinegar Hill (easy ascent, just out of the town), the scene of the celebrated battle in which General Lake beat the Irish rebels in 1798. The ruins of a windmill still remain on which scores were hung after the battle. The view from the hill is extensive and fine. All Ireland is cursed with whiskey as well as popery—shocking. I am always at Astley! Thank God I am pretty well for me, but not up to the mark. The Lord bless!

Kilkenny, Thursday evening.

Left Enniscorthy at half-past eight this morning, over a wild mountainous district to Barris (*alias* Ballyburris), then through a more level and cultivated country to this town. No rain again to-day, but brisk wind. Kilkenny is a large place, twenty-five thousand people, and said to be the best town in Ireland. If so the green isle has not much to boast of. It is, however, an interesting place, and has some fine ruins. I have been all over the cathedral, and touched its organ. Fine old building, and delighted with it, but modern additions and abuses put me in a stew, and would make Mr. Eginton mad. Organ in miserable plight. Thank God am tolerable, but feel the effects of the *wind* in my face.

Kilhill (to the north of the mouth of the Shannon, about forty miles to the west of Limerick). Yesterday I passed through Clonmel, Cahir, and Tipperary. I reached Limerick about 5 o'clock. Thomas U—— and his wife's sister were walking in a street along which I was entering Limerick. He saw me and ran after me. Consequently I went to his house at once, for Elizabeth had apprised him of my coming. I went over Limerick with Mr. Thomas. It is really a handsome and spirited place. Was pleased with the cathedral. As good shops in some streets as are to be seen in England. Mrs. U—— touched her grand upright pianoforte. She is evidently a dashing player of the London school. They have family prayer every evening, and accordingly their servants came in, evidently as usual, and I did as I should at home. This morning at 7 o'clock I left Limerick by a splendid iron steamer down the Shannon (a fine river, truly, far beyond the Thames or Severn) as far as Kilrush, and on by cars to this place, which is the Margate of the Limerick people. It is nothing of a town, and the hotel where I am is miserable. However, here is a magnificent sea, and a *fine bold* rocky coast, as much like Bude as well can be. I have been strolling to my heart's content, delighted with some caverns, etc. The noise is great, but I bear it better than at Bude. I spend to-morrow here, and on Monday go back to Limerick, and on Tuesday to Killarney. I hope to reach home about next Wednesday week.

(*To his Mother.*)

September 7, 1838.

God be praised that I can write to you! Three weeks ago, in the act of stooping to take up baby, I was seized and sunk down, and laid for two hours unable to be moved, for the slightest motion brought on intolerable spasms of the spine. Leeches thrice repeated, and other remedies, by God's blessing, have enabled me to move about again, but I lie down as much as possible. There was great danger of paralysis, but the Lord has mercifully averted this; I am in His hands and there I desire to remain.

I am glad to hear the gout has relaxed his tyranny, and I hope he still keeps away as my father directed the last *Record*; that, however, induces me to fear that you are ill, or that you are out. In either case "the Lord hear and help." Fanny is well and full of prattle, though not twenty-one months old; she inherits my head of hair; quite *your* grandchild; God give all your desire for her. My church building goes on at a broad-wheel waggon pace, and yet I know not who to blame.

Harvest is chiefly over, plentiful and good; I preached on that last Sunday.

1839. The great event of this year in Astley was the reopening of the church on the 11th of June, St. Barnabas' Day, after its restoration by the parishioners, and the building of a handsome north aisle at my father's sole expense. The weather was very fine and pleasant, the church was crowded from far and near, and more than £90 was collected for the remaining expenses. The music of the opening anthem, Psalm 132:8, 9, "Arise, O God, into Thy resting-place," etc., the old version of Psalm 84, the hymn by Bishop Heber, "O Saviour is Thy promise fled," and "Christ is our corner stone," were all sung to my father's cheerful music. The Rev. John East preached an excellent sermon from a very appropriate text: "We are the servants of the God of heaven and earth, and build the house that was builded these many years ago" (Ezra 5:11). Afterwards there was no general gathering, but every house feasted its friends. How nice our dear mother looked in her grey silk and lace shawl as she moved among her guests with gentle courtesy! So one dream of my father's life was fulfilled, and praise and prayer with dear old friends around concluded the happy day.

After this exciting time he went to the Isle of Man, from whence he writes as follows:—

At Archdeacon Moore's,
Kirk Andreas.

My dear East,

I arrived at this quiet spot on Tuesday last, and am already better. May I be thankful for it and have grace rightly to use returning health. I never was at Scarborough or Filey, but have heard much of the former, as, in fact, the Brighton of the north. Therefore I could not fancy it. The air is bracing, situation elevated, and the sands and bathing are good. I love wilder and quieter spots. The Lord go with you wherever you go. I wanted rest, but it seems I must preach a little here. Oh for burning love to feel preaching to be both rest and refreshment. But alas for our poor earthly natures and feeble hearts. If, too, I did but feel my spiritual languor as much as I do my bodily depression sometimes, how would it be!

You decry Mona; I cannot recollect when you were in it. To me it is an interesting isle. Its mountain aspect suits my eye, and its breezes are very refreshing. Access to it now is easy. Here are many good people also. The new bishop is a kind man, ready to favour what is good, but likely to take things without pains or energy.

All at home much as of late. Ever yours,

W.H.H.

On his return he was so unwell that change of scene was again ordered, so on the 22nd of July he took Maria and myself a delightful little tour in North Wales, of which my first sketch-book forms a diary. Our brother Henry drove us to Wolverhampton, where we parted with him. But first we set out two-and-two to see the fine old church. The people stared, and one woman cried out, "Eh, but that's a pretty wedding!" which amused us much, but we never could decide which of us was considered the bride or the bridegroom. Then we took the rail to Liverpool, the first time Maria and I had thus travelled, and the next day a steamer was seven hours taking us to the Menai Bridge, also a novelty in those times. We rested at the George Hotel, near Bangor, and in the evening saw all the maids dancing with bare feet on the stone floor of the hall to the strains of an old Welsh harper with a long white beard. Next day we went to Bangor cathedral and the tiny Llandisilio church, where a notice on the door informed us that "The Holy Sacrament will be administered here next Christmas Day." We then went for a fortnight to Carnarvon, where the old daughters of a late archdeacon were very friendly, and gave us carnations and Welsh diamonds, and showed us all their curiosities. The incumbent and my father coalesced delightfully also. We met our doctor, Mr. Watson, and went up Snowdon with him, and after seeing the lovely Nant Gwynant, and the magnificent Pont Aberglaslyn, we returned *via* Liverpool. We stayed one night at Prescot Vicarage to visit Maria's friend, L. Driffield, one of a large and delightful family, and we all reached home with renewed health and spirits.

(*Letter to Rev. W. H. R.*)

November 5, 1839.

You have frequently testified your kindness by sending me books and pamphlets respecting topics which can hardly be matched in point of interest. I allude to what is rife around you in theological matters. Let me beg you to accept the recently published charge of the Bishop of Calcutta, as containing towards its close what I esteem a correct and masterly view of what is called the Oxford case. Do read it, and may God give you guidance and grace in pondering it.

Perhaps it will interest you to learn that I am increasingly interested with the subject, that I am reading the "Tracts for the Times" over and over again, as many as I possess, and that I have ordered all that have not yet reached me. Hitherto I only get deeper and deeper in my former convictions, while I gather a good deal that is excellent and valuable. I am about half through Taylor's "Ancient Christianity." It is a book of books. Do get it. Do study it. It cannot fail to repay you. I am delighted with it, because it gives just such a view of the *truth* of the case as I have always been *disposed* to entertain. One party depreciates too much that antiquity which the other party unduly exalts. Mr. Taylor sees in antiquity all that Dr. Pusey sees, *and something more.* He sees the truth in *all* its bearings. Consequently, while he entertains the highest veneration, he exercises the utmost caution.

(*To the same.*)

November 14.

I have been accustomed to say, in opposition to more heated opinions, that the Oxford divines (so called) are not Romanists *themselves* (in disguise), but well-meaning, though mistaken, theologians, contending for what they deem ancient Christianity; only that their views and doings have a direct tendency towards Romanism, *just as certain views and doings of the primitive Church itself insensibly* led to the development of Popery. This is the Bishop of Calcutta's idea. Only look again at both works and you will see it. Here my belief is as firm as my life.

"Whatsoever approaches to a part of the doctrine of the Church of Rome," etc. You decidedly *mistake* what is conventionally meant by the "Doctrine of the Church of Rome." No one, I presume, intends by that phrase any portion of *genuine Catholic* truth; but merely the additions and corruptions of Romanism. Had you but borne this in mind—for that is what Bishop Wilson means—you would have seen that your own syllogism was perfectly correct.

The Bishop quotes some expressions to which he says our ears are unaccustomed—"Sacrifice," "Oblations," etc. A short and simple reply may suffice. The Oxford divines are fond of such phrases as savour and favour the notion of *a sort of corporeal* presence in the bread and wine. Is it not so? "A refined transubstantiation," says Bishop Wilson. Now every use of the same common terms and phrases in the formularies of our Church is utterly opposed to the notion of a corporeal presence in any mode or degree. (See the protestation at the end of Communion Service.)

The *real* presence is the spiritual presence, "not in the elements themselves," as Whately says, "otherwise the wicked would have Christ in them," but by the incorporation of faith in the holy recipients. This is the sure meaning of Jewel's Latin sentence which you give me. Do, dear R——, be on your guard on this very point. There is so much refining and subtilizing on this vital point, that a little error may soon be admitted; and that, like a wedge in a block, endangers the whole framework. Keble himself questioned me in the schools on this very topic. I well remember it, and have memoranda of it. He made me define the Scriptural views of the Church of England about the real and veritable presence, as opposed to the Lutheran and Romish Churches. I stand where I did, but he, I fear, is not the same man he was then. You say, "Surely the Sacraments are the means through which grace is given." Not, dear R——, THE means, but simply "means," or "a means," as in Church Catechism. The same exclusive language about the Sacraments occurs in the very preface of the Tracts. I repudiate the notion.

(*To his Daughters, from Oban.*)

July 20, 1840.

My dearest Girls,

God bless you! Oh that I could turn my shillings into sovereigns, and take you where I have been this *blessed* day! Indeed I have seen the far and justly famed Iona and Staffa! The former is ten times what I thought it to be. The ruins would delight Henry—Early Norman and choicest Decorated. Beautiful! And then Staffa! Fingal's cave—what a temple! I could not help a burst of tears on entering. I send you some heaths, etc., growing on the rugged top of it; keep them. I am tired, but well. The day has been splendid.

Ever your

W. H. H.

Of the year 1840 few records remain. One Saturday evening in November the church stove set fire to the little north chancel, but happily, being soon discovered and speedy means used, it was quickly extinguished. The roofs of both chancels were slightly burnt, but the Winford monuments by Bacon and the old Blount altar tombs were uninjured, to his great delight. In the first week of December he went into Herefordshire to preach a funeral sermon at Llangarren Church for the eldest son of a friend, to which he thus alludes in a letter to Mr. Tebbs:—

High Wycombe,
January 4, 1841.

Your letter, dearest friend, was like sunshine on one of these piercing days, and yet to hear of the paralysis of a mother and the illness of a wife was a cold blast indeed. But "it is well"; when faith can sing that short anthem our sorrows are charmed into joy. The good Lord comfort your dear ones, and that will comfort you. He has comforted us very greatly amidst our recent circumstances of grief and excitement.

First the fire. God gave me very serviceable composure and presence of mind, so that though the roof of each chancel caught fire, not a pane of glass was broken; nor are the monuments injured. I forget the loss in the recollection of the sparing mercy. The difference of an hour or two in the night saved the entire church.

Then the King of Terrors! Oh but he was made to come with all his terrors in the background, and was compelled to acknowledge that he was vanquished. Our dear E. J—— had become a vigorous Christian, and when sickness told him of eternity he laboured manfully to do all the good he could. He did much in his locality in a way that cannot soon be forgotten. His funeral, and the attendance at my sermon after it, was such as is rarely seen. My text was the two last lines of Luke 15.

And now worse than fire or death is the probability of my leaving my pleasant flock, one of the sons for whom I hold the living *in commendam* having taken his degree. But the Lord rules, and He keeps me content—what a mercy is that! I am staying with my father and mother. I preached twice yesterday—a feat for me. The Lord make this year the best you have ever seen. My godchild! I long to see Emily and bless her. The Lord do so more abundantly!

In April, 1841, he went to Dewsbury to deliver a lecture on Church music and preach school sermons for the Rev. Thomas Albutt. In August he went to Paris, and on his return visited his brother-in-law, the Rev. J. Stratton, in the Precincts, Canterbury.

In December a son of his former rector was ordained priest, and being thus "qualified" to take the living of Astley, my father expressed his intention of resigning in three months' time, the period specified in the deed of resignation. My father devoted the last quarter's income of the living to supplying the parishioners of Astley, through the Society for Promoting Christian Knowledge, with Bibles, Prayer-books, and Homilies on the Second Sunday in Advent "for ever."

The last time he officiated in Astley Church was the afternoon of the first Sunday in March, 1842, when he re-delivered the first sermon he preached there in 1822, on Colossians 1:28, his object being, as he began and continued, so to end "with setting forth and setting forward the salvation of sinners and the perfecting of believers only through Jesus Christ the Lord." He wrote a farewell sermon for the next Sunday morning, March 13, but becoming too ill to leave the house, he sent for his kind friend, the Rev. John East, to deliver it for him. The text was Acts 20:32, and the sermon concluded thus:—

Astley has been a land of brotherly love and kind-heartedness to me and mine. Never shall I forget the friendliness of past days and the willingness to oblige which all classes have shown. Of late, also, when trials of no common bitterness have come upon me, I have intensely felt the hearty sympathy of every one who has seen me or my family. The simple sayings, too, of many an humble parishioner have gone to my very heart. Brethren and friends, for myself and my family I thank you, I *thank* you! My office will soon cease, but my affection cannot cease. Many of you I have baptized, many of you I have led to confirmation, and to many also I have administered the most comfortable sacrament of the body and blood of our Saviour Jesus Christ. Not a few of your nearest kindred or dearest friends have I tended on a sick-bed, and consigned to the silent tomb. All which things are ties so fastened by years of kindly intercourse as not to be dissolved by any earthly severance.

Brethren, farewell! Pray for me and for mine. Live for Christ, and you shall die in Christ. Live also in peace and love among yourselves, and the God of love and peace shall be with you, Amen, and amen.

In the afternoon Mr. East preached himself on the occasion from 2 Corinthians 1:12–14. These sermons were afterwards published.

The parishioners of Astley were most generous in their parting presents to my parents—massive silver candlesticks, handsome inkstand, cake-basket.[1] Handsomely bound large books, including the Hexapla, also were presented, and a pocket Bible in which two hundred and twenty names of the kind donors of these gifts were written by the late John Wright, Esq.

At the end of this list my father has written the text Matthew 25:40, "Inasmuch," etc., and

"May all whose names are written here
In the Lamb's Book of Life appear!"

The dear school children also gave me a silver pencil-case, with "Astley" engraved on its jasper stone.

[1] The inscription on the silver cake-basket specially given to my mother was this: "A token of grateful affection from the parishioners of Astley to Mrs. W.H. Havergal, in remembrance of her uniform kindness during her residence among them of nearly twenty years. March 8, 1842."

CHAPTER VII.

HYMNS BY THE REV. W. H. HAVERGAL, M.A.

Missionary hymns — Astley Wake Sunday — Hymns for Sunday-school sermons — Harvest hymn — The National Anthem, new version — Christmas Carols — Hymns written in illness — "Jerusalem the Golden" — "The Rock of Ages" — "My times are in Thy hand" — "Summertide is coming" — "Just as Thou wilt" — "Rest in the Lord" — Palindrome on Easter Even — "A Fireside View of Sunset."

AS the greater number of my father's hymns were written before he left Astley, the notice which is due to them is given here by the reprint and enlargement of a paper which appeared in *The Day of Days* magazine for March and April, 1882—

It was the intention of my lamented sister, Frances Ridley Havergal, to write a concluding chapter of "Specimen Glasses" on the hymns of her father. The Editor of *The Day of Days* has asked me to prepare such a paper, and in doing so I have chosen for notice some of the hymns which I think she would have been likely to select.

From his boyhood my father was fond of rhyming, chiefly with a view to amuse and brighten his own home circle; and even in his riper years many were the poetical and playful epistles to his young friends, and acrostics on their names.

His hymns seem almost invariably to have been called forth by special occasions; and many of these were printed on handbills (as was formerly the custom), to be sung at the annual sermons for the Church Missionary Society, in his beloved church of Astley, Worcestershire. He always composed a tune for each new hymn. It should be remembered that these were times when but few missionary hymns had been written, and the deep interest he took in Missionary work was very exceptional. Fifty or sixty years ago a missionary sermon would have been considered in many of our churches no slight innovation.

A specimen hymn, simple yet spirited, is given, which was sung, after a sermon by the Rev. I. Lamb, D.D., Master of Corpus Christi College, Cambridge, on the 23rd of September, 1827, when nearly £21 was collected—a goodly sum for a country congregation.

"HERALDS OF THE LORD OF GLORY."

"Say (Tell it out) among the heathen, that the Lord reigneth."
—Psalm 96:10.

Heralds of the Lord of glory!
  Lift your voices, lift them high;
Tell the Gospel's wondrous story,
  Tell it fully, faithfully;
Tell the heathen 'midst their woe,
Jesus reigns, above, below.

Haste the day, the bright, the glorious!
  When the sad and sin-bound slave
High shall laud in pealing chorus
  Him who reigns, and reigns to save.
Tempter, tremble! Idols, fall!
Jesus reigns, the Lord of all!

Christians! send to joyless regions
  Heralds of the gladdening word,
Let them, voiced like trumpet-legions,
  Preach the kingdom of the Lord:
Tell the heathen—Jesus died!
Reigns He now, though crucified.

Saviour, let Thy quickening Spirit
  Touch each herald-lip with fire,
Nations then shall own Thy merit,
  Hearts shall glow with Thy desire,
Earth in jubilee shall sing.
Jesus reigns, the eternal King.

Several of the most poetical and popular of his missionary hymns are the following. The first was a special favourite with his daughter, Frances Ridley Havergal.

"SHOUT, O EARTH! FROM SILENCE WAKING."

"And men shall be blessed in Him: all nations shall call Him blessed."
—Psalm 72:17.

Shout, O earth! from silence waking,
  Tune with joy thy varied tongue;
Shout! as when, from chaos breaking,
  Sweetly flowed thy natal song:
Shout! for thy Creator's love
Sends redemption from above.

Downward from His star-paved dwelling
Comes the incarnate Son of God;
Countless voices, thrilling, swelling,
Tell the triumphs of His blood:
Shout! He comes thy tribes to bless
With His spotless righteousness.

See His glowing hand uplifted!
Clustering bounties drop around;
Rebels e'en are richly gifted,
Pardon, peace, and joy abound!
Shout, O earth! and let thy song
Ring the vaulted heavens along.

Call Him blessèd on thy mountains,
In thy wilds and citied plains;
Call Him blessèd where thy fountains
Speak in softly murmuring strains.
Let thy captives, let thy kings
Join thy lyre of thousand strings.

Blessed Lord, and Lord of blessing!
Pour Thy quickening gifts abroad;
Raptured tongues, Thy love confessing,
Shall extol the living God.
Blessed, blessed, blessed Lord!
Heaven shall chant no other word.

THE LIGHT OF LIFE.

"In Him was life; and the life was the light of men."—John 1:4.

In doubt and dread dismay,
'Midst Superstition's gloom;
The heathen grope their way,
And joyless reach the tomb:
No holy light,
No balmy ray
Of Gospel-day
Has blessed their sight.

Then, Star of Life, arise!
And on thy healing wing,
With blood of sacrifice,
Thy great salvation bring:
Let heathen lands
Thy brightness see:
Oh set them free
From cruel bands.

With searching beam explore
The dark strongholds of sin:
And on the prisoners pour
Transforming light within.
Bright morning Star!
Unveil thy face,
And shed thy grace,
In realms afar.

O Jesu, Light of Life!
Arouse the world from sleep;
Send holy love in place of strife,
And joy to those who weep.
Great King of Kings!
Thy Spirit give!
Let Gentiles live,
Beneath thy wings.

"CHRISTIANS, HASTE! THE MORN IS BREAKING."

"Until the day dawn, and the Day-star arise."—2 Peter 1:19.

Widely 'midst the slumbering nations,
Darkness holds his despot sway;
Cruel in his habitations,
Ruthless o'er his prostrate prey.
Star of Bethlehem!
Rise and beam in conquering day!

Light of Life, our sole Defender,
Rise, with healing on Thy wing;
Rise, in all Thy soothing splendour;
Rise, and earth with joy shall sing!
Israel's Glory!
Gentiles call Thee "Lord and King!"

Christians, haste! the morn is breaking;
Darkness wheels his downward flight;
But, your polished armour taking,
Stand! nor quit the waning fight.
Great Redeemer!
Guard us with Thy shield of light.

Onward, Christians, onward pressing,
Triumph in the Crucified!
Endless honour, rest, and blessing,
Wait you at His radiant side.
Cease not, cease not,
Till you see Him glorified!

"NO DAWN OF HOLY LIGHT."

"The Dayspring from on high hath visited us, to give light to them that sit in darkness, and in the shadow of death."—Luke 1:78, 79.

"To turn men from darkness to light, and from the power of Satan unto God."—Acts 26:18.

"I am the Light of the world."—John 8:12.

No dawn of holy light,
No day of sacred rest,
E'er breaks upon the heathen's sight,
To soothe his troubled breast.

But lo! with healing ray,
The Dayspring meets our eye:
And Christians, on their Master's day,
Rejoice to feel Him nigh.

To Him let praise be given,
The noblest, sweetest, best;
For He has brought us light from heaven,
And hope of endless rest.

Lord, let Thy saving light,
Thy day of glorious rest,
Soon chase from earth the toilsome night
And soothe each wearied breast!

REDEMPTION.

"Who gave himself a ransom for all, to be testified in due time."
—1 Timothy 2:6.

Redemption! Oh the thrilling word!
It tells of joy in woe;
Of more than prophets saw or heard,
Of all that *we* can know.

Redemption! God's great charity
To man imprisoned long;
The world's reprieve; the sinner's plea;
And heaven's eternal song.

Redemption! but—its countless cost!
It cost the blood of Him
Who spread the heavens, and rules the host
Of flaming Seraphim.

Redemption! be its joy proclaimed
By men of every tongue,
Where Christ has never yet been named,
Where Satan's power is strong.

REDEEMER, Thou who diedst *for all!*
Let all Thy love adore:
Let Jew and Heathen join to call
Thee—*Lord* for evermore!

"BRIGHTER THAN MERIDIAN SPLENDOUR."

"The Sun of Righteousness."—Malachi 4:2.

Brighter than meridian splendour,
Beams Messiah's spotless fame;
Him we hail our firm Defender,
Him let every tongue proclaim.
He is precious,
He is gracious,
He for ever is the same.

Lord of glory! Source of favour!
Bid Thy heralds take their stand:
Let Thy name's reviving savour
Wake each dark and drowsy land.
Saviour, hear us;
Speak and cheer us,
When we lift the suppliant hand.

Thou art all! and all adore Thee,
Where they hymn one ceaseless song:
Soon shall earth, subdued before Thee,
Peal Thy name her tribes among.
Sons of glory,
Chant the story,
And your deep Amen prolong!

For several years the Church Missionary sermons were preached on the Astley Wake Sunday, a day my Father was anxious to redeem from the intemperance and revelling with which it was kept; and the first hymn at the morning service was always the following, which he wrote in 1834.[1] The notes accompanying the hymn are subjoined.

ASTLEY WAKE.

Many persons require to be informed, and others to be reminded, that a parish Wake is properly a Religious Festival. It was originally the Feast of the Dedication of the Parish Church; and was kept by watching, or waking, unto prayer and praise, during the whole of the preceding night, till sunrise.

"Blow up the trumpet in the new moon, in the time appointed, on our solemn feast-day."—Psalm 81:3.

Our festal morn is come,
And, Lord, we come to Thee;
Thy house shall be our joyful home,
Thy name our melody.

"These temples of Thy grace,
How beautiful they stand!
The honours of our native place,
And bulwarks of our land."

Our fathers built this fane,[2]
And watched the livelong night:
They sleep in death; but we remain
To hail a purer light.

Then blow the trumpet, blow:
The psalm, the psaltery take:
Let every heart with praise o'erflow,
And every lip awake.

[1] The second verse is quoted from Dr. Watts. [2] fane: temple

Sound, sound that sweetest strain,
The gospel-jubilee,
Till, bursting from their idol-chain,
The heathen shall be free.

Thus let us keep the feast,
Thus wake to righteousness:
And teach the world, from sin released,
The Lord our God to bless.

In the Jewish Church, notice was given of feasts, jubilees, etc., by sound of trumpet. We have now our religious feast-days. On these and all other solemn occasions, let the evangelical trumpet give a sound of victory over death, of liberty from sin, of joy and rejoicing in Christ Jesus our Saviour.—*Bishop Horne.*

My Father delighted to sing to children, and with them, his own nursery rhymes, and short hymns suited to their understanding.

He led the child-singers in Astley Church with his singularly sweet and penetrating voice, accompanying on his seraphine (a precursor of the harmoniums of to-day).

From the hymns he wrote for the annual Sunday-school sermons, three are selected. The first two are sweet and tender strains; the other a song of spiritual and inspiriting praise.

THE HOLY CHILD.

"He was subject unto them."—Luke 2:51.

Blessed Jesus, Lord and Brother,
Once thou wast a lowly child,
Subject to Thy Virgin-mother,
"Holy, harmless, undefiled";
Wisdom, favour, grace, and truth,
Graced, like morning stars, Thy youth.

Great Redeemer, Mediator!
Now Thou art enthroned in light;
But Thou wearest still our nature,
And all heaven admires the sight.
Lord, to tender years impart
Mercy's boon, the tender heart.

Jesu, by Thy childhood's favour,
By Thy manhood's agony,
Fill us with Thy Spirit's savour,
Train us for eternity;
With the glittering hosts above,
May we sing Thy boundless love!

THE GOOD SHEPHERD.

"He shall gather the lambs with His arm, and carry them in His bosom."
—Isaiah 40:11.

To praise our Shepherd's care,
His wisdom, love, and might;
Your loudest, loftiest songs prepare,
And bid the world unite!

Supremely good and great,
He tends His blood-fought fold;
He stoops, though throned in highest state,
The feeblest to uphold.

He hears their softest plaint,
He eyes them when they roam;
And if His meanest lamb should faint,
His bosom bears it home.

Kind Shepherd of the sheep!
A weakly flock are we,
And snares and foes are nigh; but keep
The lambs who look to Thee.

And if through death's dark vale
Our feet should early tread;
Oh, may we reach Thy fold, and hail
The love which safely led!

"HOSANNA!"

"Hosanna to the Son of David."—Matthew 21:15, 16.

Hosanna! raise the pealing hymn
To David's Son and Lord;
With Cherubim and Seraphim
Exalt the Incarnate Word.

Hosanna! Lord, our feeble tongue
No lofty strains can raise:
But Thou wilt not despise the young
Who meekly chant Thy praise.

Hosanna! Sovereign, Prophet, Priest,
How vast Thy gifts, how free!
Thy blood, our life: Thy word, our feast;
Thy name, our only plea.

Hosanna! Master, lo! we bring
Our offerings to Thy throne;
Not gold, not myrrh, nor mortal thing,
But hearts to be Thine own.

Hosanna! once Thy gracious ear
Approved a lisping throng;
Be gracious still, and deign to hear
Our poor but grateful song.

O Saviour! if, redeemed by Thee,
Thy temple we behold,
Hosannas through eternity
We'll sing to harps of gold!

Among hymns composed for parochial occasions, a Harvest Hymn, written in 1863, for his parish of Shareshill, Staffordshire, is truly admirable for its doctrinal and practical character—

HARVEST HYMN.

"He will gather His wheat into the garner."—Matthew 3:12.

Our faithful God hath sent us
A fruitful harvest-tide;
He summer boons hath lent us,
And winter wants supplied.

The fields, at His ordaining,
Stands thick with golden sheaves;
And man, full oft complaining,
New bounty now receives.

Though Mercy largely giveth,
Is justice pacified?
We live through Him who liveth,
The "Corn of Wheat" that died.

Then full be our thanksgiving,
And clear each note of joy;
While faith and holy living
Our earnest thoughts employ.

And at the last great reaping,
When Christ His sheaves will own,
May we, no longer weeping,
Be garnered near His throne.

Praise we the Godhead-Union,
The Eternal Three in One;
With them may our communion
For ever be begun.

My father's strong feeling of loyalty was shown by versions of our National Anthem in language more graceful and becoming than

"Confound their politics,
Frustrate their knavish tricks."

Those on the Coronation and Widowhood of the Queen, the Marriage of the Prince of Wales, and for the Festivals of the St. Nicholas Sunday-schools, at Worcester, are worthy of reprint for similar occasions.

THE NATIONAL ANTHEM.

New version for the schools assembling in Worcester Cathedral on Whit-Monday.

God save our noble Queen;
Long live Old England's Queen;
God save the Queen!
Great and victorious,
Happy and glorious,
May she reign over us:
God save the Queen!

On her anointed head,
All choicest blessings shed
Forth from Thy hand:
Let her be Thy delight;
Make her path always bright;
And in Thy Word and might,
Firm be her stand!

While nations rage and groan,
Stablish her sacred throne
In sure repose:
Where'er our banners wave
O'er land or ocean-cave,
There all our warriors save:
Forgive our foes!

Send peace in this our time;
Spare us from strife and crime;
Strengthen each band!
Nursed by our gracious Queen,
May our Church e'er be seen
Planted, like evergreen
Throughout the land.

Sovereign of earth and sky,
Hear Thou our Nation's cry,
Bless, bless our Queen!
Grant us, through her, to be,
In Thee and all for Thee,
"Great, glorious, and free":
God save the Queen!

The following verses were composed on the death of the Prince Consort. My father's arrangement of the National Anthem in the minor key is, I believe, unique.

"WEEP WITH OUR QUEEN."

Let Britain's prayer ascend,
Let mournful voices blend,
Weep with our Queen!
God of our country, see
How England bows the knee,
How suppliants cry to Thee,
God save the Queen!

In sorrow's withering hour.
When droops the smitten flower,
Be Thy might seen:
God of the bleeding heart,
Heal Thou the bitter smart,

Thy Spirit's grace impart,
Comfort our Queen!

Chase every cloud away,
Turn all her night to day,
Bright but serene:
God of the widow, hear,
Dry up her burning tear,
Strong for her help appear;
God save the Queen!

Lord, let Thy husband-arm
Be her life's heavenly charm,
Felt, though unseen:
Long as her days extend,
Her home and throne defend,
And give a glorious end;
God save the Queen!

While he was Rector of St. Nicholas, musical and poetical compositions were a great resource in his failing eyesight, for which he twice obtained leave of absence to be under the care of the great Prussian oculist, Dr. de Leuw, at Gräfrath.

Writing from Langen Schwalbach, in May, 1862, my father says:—"My version of 'God save the Queen,' in the minor key, makes its way in the goodwill of the loyal and musical, here and in Prussia, where the tune is claimed as a native and national melody; the minorizing is much liked, no one seems to have thought of thus treating it."

My father wrote some lively Christmas Carols, the first published being:—

THE WORCESTERSHIRE CHRISTMAS CAROL.

"The glory of the Lord shone round about them."—Luke 2:9.

How grand and how bright
That wonderful night,
When angels to Bethlehem came!
They burst forth like fires,
They struck their gold lyres,
And mingled their sound with the flame.

The shepherds were 'mazed,
The pretty lambs gazed
At darkness thus turned into light:
No voice was there heard
From man, beast, or bird,
So sudden and solemn the sight.

And then, when the sound
Re-echoed around,
The hills and the dales all awoke:
The moon and the stars
Stopped their fiery cars,[1]
And listened while Gabriel spoke:

"I bring you," said he,
"From the Glorious Three,
Good tidings to gladden mankind;
The Saviour is born,
But He lies all forlorn
In a manger, as soon you will find."

At mention of this,
(The source of all bliss),
The angels sang loudly and long;
They soared to the sky,
Beyond mortal eye,
But left us the words of their song:

"All glory to God,"
Who laid by His rod,
To smile on the world through His Son;
"And Peace be on earth,"
For this wonderful birth
Most wonderful conquests has won:

"And Good-will to man,"
Though his life's but a span,
And his thoughts all evil and wrong:
Then pray, Christians, pray;
But let Christmas-Day
Have your sweetest and holiest song.

Another favourite carol is "A Bethlehem Shepherd-Boy's Tale," in which, with unconscious poetic feeling, the child describes his unusually good thoughts and pleasant feelings through the previous day, with which the sights and sounds of Nature seem in unison, and he feels as if this must be the prelude to something uncommon. Then he describes the calm loveliness of the night, the "musical breeze" of distant angel-notes, the sudden blaze, the heavenly message, and the walk to Bethlehem to see the wonderful Babe.

A BETHLEHEM SHEPHERD-BOY'S TALE.

"Those things which were told by the shepherds."—Luke 2:18.

So happy all the day
Had I been without play;
And such good thoughts had come o'er my mind:
That I wondered what it meant,
Or for why it was sent;
As I ne'er had felt aught of the kind.

And the birds, all day long,
Had kept trilling their song;
And the sun had gone down, oh so red!
We had folded the sheep,
And were talking of sleep,
But, somehow, we cared not for bed.

[1] car: archaic usage, meaning chariot, carriage, or cart

The stars were all drest
In their brightest and best;
And the moon showed a streak of her gold:
'Twas a glorious night;
And we thought of the sight
Of which David our father has told.

A sound struck our ear,
Sweet, joyous, and clear,
It seemed like a musical breeze:
But, ere we could gaze,
We were all in a blaze,
And found ourselves down on our knees.

A bright one then said,
('Twas like life from the dead),
"Good tidings, good tidings I bring!
Messiah's come down;
In your own little town
You will find Him a Babe and a King!"

And then the whole choir,
Rising higher and higher,
Sang of "glory, sweet peace, and good-will,"
The sheep seemed to dance,
And the mountains to prance,
And the stars could no longer stand still.

Then onward we sped,
To find out the bed,
Where the Saviour in lowliness lay:
Near Bethlehem's inn,
(Oh shame on their sin!)
We found Him midst cattle and hay.

But we saw the blest sight;
'Twas our Judah's delight;
And Mary and Joseph were there:
And soon we made known
To all in the town
What we heard the good angel declare.

And now, every day,
I sing and I pray
To the Babe who is Saviour and all:
May His wonderful birth
Be known through the earth,
And cheer both the great and the small!

The last Carol he composed is also original in idea. A shepherd who had seen "the glory of the Lord," and heard the melody of the "heavenly host," calls upon his companions to celebrate with prayer and song the first anniversary of the Saviour's birth.

THE FIRST ANNIVERSARY OF CHRISTMAS.[1]

Come, shepherds, come, 'tis just a year
Since sweetest music woke our ear,
And angels blessed our sight.
Come, lift your heart, and tune your voice,
And bid the hills and vales rejoice,
As on that glorious night.

'Tis just a year ago, we say,
When night shone out as clear as day,
And Heaven came down to earth.
How we did fear, how we did gaze,
Surrounded by the sudden blaze,
And thrilled with sounds of mirth!

Ah! see you not that angel-choir?
And hear you not that mighty lyre
Which hushed our bleating sheep?
And, oh, that voice of sweetest awe,
Which told us all we after saw;
Who now would silence keep?

Come, shepherds, come, with prayer and song,
This night to be remembered long,
Rejoice to celebrate.
With reedy pipe chant forth who can
To God all glory, love to man,
And peace in every gate!

'Tis just a year ago to-night,
From heaven came down the Prince of Light,
Our guilty world to bless,
Let Gentiles now with Israel sing
Our Saviour, Brother, Friend, and King,
Our promised righteousness!

From a manuscript volume entitled, "Forty Hymns from Subjects in the book of Genesis," written at Langen Schwalbach during a season of illness, in August and September, 1865, I transcribe the two following:—

"IS ANYTHING TOO HARD FOR HIM?"

"Is anything too hard for the Lord?"—Genesis 18:14.

Is anything too hard for Him,
Whom Cherubim and Seraphim
Incessantly adore?
No! He, the everlasting Son,
Made countless worlds their course to run,
And reigneth evermore.

[1] For the words and music of these Carols, see the Musical Editions of "Songs of Grace and Glory" (J. Nisbet & Co., 21, Berners Street). [See Volume V of the Havergal editon, *Songs of Truth and Love: Music by Frances Ridley Havergal and William Henry Havergal.*]

He stooped from highest heaven and died,
That every want might be supplied
Of all who own His power.
His gracious eye, His mighty hand,
Are always waiting faith's command,
In trial's darkest hour.

He can the hardest heart subdue,
The most corrupted soul renew,
The driest bones make live;
He can the bruised reed bind up,
The bitter take from every cup,
And strength to weakness give.

Then blessed be Thy glorious might,
Thou God-man! Saviour! Infinite!
Whom Abram longed to see,
When by Thy arm we rise from death
Our chant shall be, with ceaseless breath,
Nought was too hard for Thee!

BETHEL.

"And he called the name of that place Bethel."—Genesis 28:19.

Lonely wilds and woodland mazes,
Spots remote from human din,
God can make His holy places,
And reveal himself therein:
Dread Jehovah,
Contrite hearts Thou dwellest in.

Jacob weary, sad, and fearful,
Chose a spot for sleep by night:
All was soon divinely cheerful,
Heavenly visions blessed his sight;
Henceforth Bethel
Was his watchword and delight.

Everywhere, good Lord, be near us,
Let us many a Bethel see;
By Thy one great vision cheer us,
Christ the Ladder-Path to Thee,
Gate of heaven
Now to all believers free.

God of Jacob, God of Jesus,
Standing at the ladder's height,
Soon from pilgrim toils release us,
Rest us in Thy home of light:
Blessed Saviour,
Thine the glory, ours the sight!

The next hymn is one rich in comfort to the tried believer.

"O CAST ON CHRIST YOUR MIGHTY CARE."

"Casting all your care upon Him for He careth for you."—1 Peter 5:7.

O cast on Christ your mighty care,
However great it be;
He knows it well, and can prepare
Some sure relief for thee.

Thy surging thoughts and spectral fears
Thy boding dreams of ill,
Thy sighings, and Thy silent tears,
Are all within His will.

Lay these upon His holy arm,
For He can all sustain:
He'll end thy cares, as with a charm,
And lift thee up again.

Sustaining grace waits His command,
And He awaits thy call;
Then pray, and down within thine hand
Shall strength and comfort fall.

I, Lord, would cast on Thee my care,
And nothing anxious be;
Content if Thou, who hearest prayer,
Wilt care, O Lord, for me.

The following beautifully worded hymn will, I think, bear comparison with the well-known versions of the ancient hymn by Bernard de Morlaix on the heavenly Jerusalem.[1]

REVELATION XXI.

Jerusalem the Golden
The home of saints shall be;
What eyes have not beholden,
They shall for ever see!
Those gem-built walls of wonder,
Those pearly gates of praise,
Those harps of sweetest thunder,
Those streets of sunless blaze.

By them shall Christ in glory
Be always seen and heard,
And His Redemption-story
Shall be their household word.
Apostles, prophets, martyrs,
Shall their companions be,
And loved ones shall be partners
Of their felicity.

[1] The comparison is, we think, considerably in favour of Canon Havergal's hymn. Much that is "fanciful" in this case gives place to the substantial and the real, and there is no falling off in poetic power.—The Editor of *The Day of Days*.

Each golden street and dwelling
 Shall teem with happy throngs,
In holiness excelling,
 And chanting lofty songs:
The Lamb! the Lamb, once dying,
 They worship on His throne,
And fall before Him crying,
 Thou, Thou art Lord alone!

Great Bridegroom of the City,
 The Maker, Lord, and Light,
Grant us, in tender pity,
 To walk with Thee in white!
So while on earth we linger,
 All joyous in thy love,
Our hearts shall watch Thy finger
 To beckon us above.

Toplady's immortal hymn, "The Rock of Ages," *seemed* to my father to confound the rock which Moses smote for water (Exodus 17:6) with the rock in which he was hidden for shelter (Exodus 33:22). Each separate case, he thought, suggested a separate train of ideas. This led him to write the next hymn.

"THE ROCK OF AGES."

Part I.

"Rock of Ages, cleft for me,
Let me hide myself in Thee,"
While the glory passeth by,
Keep me as the tenderest eye:
Keep me, for I dare not gaze
On that glory's awful blaze:
All unholy and impure,
I its light cannot endure.

When my sins, a mighty sum,
Threaten me with wrath to come:
When, to crush me, draweth near
Tyrant Doubt, or giant Fear;
When my hopes, now few and faint,
Seem to mark the almost saint:
Rock of Ages, unto Thee
I for instant shelter flee.

Rock of Ages, in Thy side
Let me joyfully abide:
Then my daily boast shall be,
Thine, Incarnate Deity:
Then no wily tempter's skill
Shall entangle me with ill:
Then nor earth nor hell shall harm,
Thou wilt shield from all alarm.

Rock of Ages, cleft for me,
Cleft from all eternity;
Hidden here, I fully share
All the Father's love and care:
Hidden here, the Spirit's might
Shall my darkness turn to light;
Rock of Ages, one with Thee,
All Thy glory I shall see.

Part II.

Rock of Ages, cleft for all,
Who for saving shelter call,
Who, forsaking selfish pride,
Stoop to enter and abide.
Cleft for all! Oh joyous sound!
Chant it long and loud around:
All may thither now repair:
Mercy meets the sinner there.

Rock of Ages, Rock of God,
Smitten not by human rod:
Opened from eternity,
Heaven's profoundest mystery!
Hidden in its wondrous cleft,
Though of all things else bereft,
Sinners find a mine of wealth,
Riches, honour, endless health.

Rock of Ages, Christ my Lord,
Hidden here, by faith's accord,
Guilty souls at once possess
Pardon, peace, and righteousness,
Though thy glory passeth by,
They may gaze and yet not die:
Yea, thy glory they shall see
In its full intensity.

Rock of Ages, Rock of Life,
Hide me in the last dread strife:
And when suns shall cease to roll,
Let thy life light up my soul!
Then, as all things pass away,
Let my raptured spirit say,
"Rock of Ages, cleft for me,"
Ever shall I dwell with Thee.

The next two hymns have been much appreciated, and well illustrate the devotional and cheerful spirit of the writer.

"MY TIMES ARE IN THY HAND."

"My times are in Thy hand,"
 Their best and fittest place;
I would not have them at command
 Without Thy guiding grace.

"My times," and yet not mine;
I cannot them ordain;
Not one e'er waits from me a sign,
Nor can I one detain.

"My times," O Lord, are Thine,
And Thine their oversight:
Thy wisdom, love, and power combine
To make them dark or bright.

I know not what shall be,
When passing times are fled;
But all events I leave with Thee,
And calmly bow my head.

Hence, Lord, in Thee I rest,
And wait Thy holy will:
I lean upon my Saviour's breast,
Or gladly go on still.

And when my "times" shall cease,
And life shall fade away,
Then bid me, Lord, depart in peace
To realms of endless day.

"SUMMERTIDE IS COMING."

Summer-tide is coming,
With all its pleasant things:
Every bee is humming,
And every songster sings.
Mornings now are brightsome,
Inviting student thought;
Evenings too are lightsome,
With balmy quiet fraught.
Hearths no longer lure us,
The fields instead we roam;
Hearts albeit insure us
A happy, happy home.

Summer-tide, I hail thee,
The empress of the year!
But thou soon wouldst fail me,
Were not thy Maker near.
He thy course disposes,
Thy light, thy scent, thy glow;
He tints all thy roses,
And paints thy brilliant bow.
Laud Him, all creation,
The sinner's mighty Friend:
Near him be our station,
Where summer ne'er shall end.

Among the pieces my father wrote of a more experimental kind, I quote one which was dictated in severe illness in 1860. It was apparently an impromptu; and the occasion—a sigh. Being asked if it arose from any fresh pain, he replied: "Oh, no! I feel it a little relief; but do not think I repine: I should be ashamed. Repine? No, nor change aught, though suns and stars were mine. How busy are my heart and brain!" He then repeated in whispers the following "specimen" of complete resignation.

"JUST AS THOU WILT!"

Just as Thou wilt, O Lord, do Thou!
I to Thy sovereign purpose bow;
On brightest day or darkest night
Whate'er is Thine is right.

Just as Thou wilt! O Lord, perform
Thy counsels 'midst the raging storm;
Not for the earth would I complain
Of sorrow, cross, or pain.

Just as Thou wilt! Be all to me,
E'en when Thy hand smites heavily;
Not for the stars would I repine,
If only Thou art mine.

Just as Thou wilt! Should anguish fierce
With scorpion stings my body pierce,
I'll praise Thee, if on me Thou'lt shine
And whisper, I AM thine!

Just as Thou wilt! In death's dark hour,
Should Satan's cloud around me lower,
If Thou, O Christ, wilt be my Guide,
No ill can me betide.

Just as Thou wilt! When Thou shalt come
And take of souls the mighty sum,
Then, blessed Saviour, let mine be
Among Thy family!

Another hymn, written at the same time, is entitled

"REST IN THE LORD."

"Rest in the Lord."—Psalm 37:7.

"Rest in the Lord!" Sweet word of truth,
A word for age, a word for youth,
A word for all the weary world,
A banner-word by love unfurled.

Then cease, ye wearied ones of earth,
To slave for pleasure, gain, or mirth;
Cast down your load of vanities,
And welcome God's realities.

"Rest in the Lord!" Sweet word of grace,
To all the Saviour's new-born race;
'Tis music, light, and balm to them,
An hourly guiding apothegm.

Then, Lord of rest, we rest in Thee,
For all our daily destiny;
Our mighty guilt, our grief, our care,
We cast (strange act!) on Thee to bear.

For Thou, dear Lamb of God, wast slain,
To bear each load, and ease each pain;
And now Thy blood and righteousness
Are rocks of rest in all distress.

And when at last we fall on sleep,
Nor heart shall throb, nor eye shall weep;
Then, blessed Saviour, let it be,
That Thou shalt write, "They rest in Me!"

Some years after this illness he felt obliged to give up parochial work, and obtained leave of absence from Shareshill. In the autumn of 1867 he bought a house at Leamington, and called it Pyrmont Villa, after his favourite resort in Germany. This was his last home; but he was able to return to Pyrmont, and take Sunday services for the English visitors in the summer of 1869.

The last lines he composed, and which he set to a Palindrome on Easter Even, 1870, are these:—

Messiah, Redeemer!
Send out Thy saving light;
Where rules the prince of night,
Day-star rise!
Cheer all eyes!

Earlier in the day he had composed the beautiful tune "Havergal," No. 163 in "Havergal's Psalmody." On Easter-Day he was seized with apoplexy, and remained unconscious forty-eight hours, when he quietly passed through death into life eternal the 19th of April, 1870.

One of his lovely little pieces in "Fireside Music" will fitly close this list of "Specimens."

A FIRESIDE VIEW OF SUNSET.

How calmly sinks the sun
Beneath the western deep,
When day his giant course has run,
And storm is hushed to sleep.

So, like the sun, would I
In tranquil eve descend,
And watch with softly waning eye
The footsteps of the end.

But though in darkness set,
The sun seems lost awhile;
He will his shroud shake off, and yet
Arise with joyous smile.

Thus, like the sun, may I
Descend to rise again,
And meet my Saviour in the sky,
With all His glorious train.

CHAPTER VIII.

LIFE AT HENWICK.

Henwick House — At Cologne — A Marriage in Hallow Church — Remarks on the Compilation of Church Music — Architecture and Music — Ravenscroft's "Whole Booke of Psalmes" — "New Church Music, but no New Style" — Charity Sermons and Musical Lectures — Letter to Rev. J. East — Visits the Isle of Arran — Ordination Sermon at Worcester — Appointed Rector of St. Nicholas', Worcester — Names of Pupils — System of Training adopted — A Pastoral Visit.

IN the last week of March, 1842, my parents removed with children, pupils, and servants to Henwick House, in a suburb of Worcester, but belonging to the parish of Hallow, of which the Rev. W. J. Phillpotts, now Archdeacon of Cornwall, was vicar. It was a cheerful and commodious residence, with a large garden and terrace-walk, half in sun and half in shade, much longer when the merry little Fanny R. H. raced up and down than it is now. There was also an arbour at the north end, looking over the Severn and its meadows towards Worcester, where she loved to sit and read. It has disappeared like the grave of her little dog Flora; but the snowy Mespilus above it still adorns the lawn. In May my father wrote to a friend:—

"Thank the God of all gods we are thus far on our pilgrimage. Passing through Astley was very pleasant, but leaving it was trying indeed. Our new residence suits us well. May we be thankful for our many comforts. I am not a settled tutor, but an expectant, waiting for any permanent post in the Church which I am equal to take. A living has already been offered me, but I shrink from its weight, and others do so for me."

The only record of his summer holiday this year is the following letter to my mother:—

COLOGNE, 18 July, 1842.

MY DEAR JANE,

We spent our Sunday at Aix, and heard an excellent sermon from a Rev. Mr. Clifton (not one of the Worcester clan). The Sunday was more marked than at Paris by massing and profanation: the churches crammed, and yet the streets full of buyers, sellers, and idlers. Close to the cathedral lots of shopping of all sorts are in full exercise. The world and the Church have no barrier between them.

This place of delicious *eau de Cologne* is fully equal to its reputation for dirt and evil odours. It contains many fine churches. It has been so hot that I could not get about except along the bridge of boats this evening. We are to embark for Bonn to-morrow. We have given up Geneva, as I cannot enjoy bustling about, having been very poorly. We mean to make Mayence the bourne of our trip, and beat about Frankfort, Wiesbaden, etc. We intend to begin to descend the Rhine in ten days, see Amsterdam and The Hague, and be at home about August 6. Direct to Rotterdam if necessary. I am oftener at home than anywhere else. The God of Jacob be there constantly. I can only send earnest love, love, love, to each and all.

Ever your

W. H. H.

In the October of this year the first home-bird left the nest. I was married in Hallow Church by my uncle Stratton, vicar of Graveney and rector of Goodnestone, to Henry Crane of Oakhampton, in Astley, who had been my father's churchwarden for many years.

At the close of this year my father had some correspondence with the Rev. J. Faucett (who consulted him about his compilation of Church music) from which extracts are given.

HENWICK HOUSE, WORCESTER,
Dec. 8, 1842.

DEAR SIR,

As I told you, there is trouble enough in your undertaking. And you have not done yet. You want a competent hand to edit every piece that is sent you. I have done it only cursorily and generally. The fact is that most of the articles sent you are got up hastily, as their authors sometimes acknowledge, and as other cases plainly show. Some also are sent you at random without care or concern, *ex. gr.*, dear ——. Hence one half of the pieces, though more or less decent, are hardly fit for publication. Lots of little things want seeing to, altering, amending, correcting: otherwise, when the volume is out and has slept a little, it will be found full of oversights and imperfections. Bear, too, in mind that many of your contributors are not *Church* musicians, as —— and ——, etc. Consequently they make a mess when they attempt a style they really do not understand. There is as much difference between styles in music as in architecture. Many a man who can manage a Grecian or an Italian structure well, is at sea in Gothic buildings. And this is a fact which I want to ding-dong in everybody's ears till they see and *feel* it.

Again, too, many of our cathedral, collegiate, and large parish-church organists are but poorly educated men, in music as well as in letters. They can play and, as they think, compose; but really they do not know what they are about. They have had no theoretical education, and in after life are too busy with teaching or performing to allow them to study, read, write, and *think*. Consequently many of them, ——, and even —— and —— pen trash, nonsense, and that in a thoroughly secular style. In truth they do not understand *style*; they do not discriminate.

Hence while many of your contributors show latent *power*, very few evince practical *skill*. They could compose Church music if they knew how. The consequence is they send you a lot of stuff, all very pretty and taking with the musical commonalty, but utterly unfit for Church service. Instead of music of a stately, dignified, majestically plaintive or devotionally warm character, they write things in the style of the tavern or concert-room—things which would have horrified the worthies of Queen Elizabeth's days.

All this applies to all the sorts of music you intend to comprise in your volume. Therefore, dear sir, keep a sharp look-out. Chants, for instance, are among the most meretricious doings of the present day. "Everybody thinks he can write a chant," and yet to write a good chant is *now* one of the most difficult things in the musical world.

One other general remark, and then to particulars. Most of your greater contributors are accustomed to send their contributions for a little pecuniary consideration. When they send gratis they send careless things. See Dr. C.'s shrewd hint at the end of his chants.

* * * * *

Further, I send for your inspection an introit anthem, "Arise, O Lord." It wants a little furbishing, which I will see to *if* you wish to have it. And now I beg to send you my Evening Service in E flat and one hundred chants; *Te Deum* to match, with sixteen chants; and Gresham Prize No. 6—I won't say as a present, but in exchange for a copy of your forthcoming volume. Read my preface on chants, etc. Any of those chants are at your service; if you wish it I will tell you which I deem the best. Now I would willingly dock the hundred by fifty or more. We grow wiser by time. So you see I cut up myself as well as others. But a truce, for I am tired. God's blessing.

Ever yours,

W. H. H.

P.S.—I do not exactly like *our* collects set to music, so I am not solicitous for your having any.

(*To the same.*)

Dec. 23rd.

——'s Chants are not worth your notice. Mr. —— is a clever and a capable man, and a superior organ-player; but from what I hear of him I am very wary how I put myself in his way. I did venture to point out to —— the crudities and incongruities of certain pieces of his, in consequence of which he threw them out of the second edition and sacrificed the costs. How different is the style of all our great English composers—Handel, Greene, Arne, Boyce, Crotch, etc. With them all is natural, simple, beautiful.

Some persons seem always to be wanting brisk and lively tunes—just as though they can drink nothing but champagne.

Some composers, A. and G. to wit, cannot harmonize a tune without seeking for discords at every step. They keep the ear in torment, teasing it at every turn; like persons who, in laying out grounds, place stiles and gates at every step for mere whim.

I should like to see anything of Gibbons and Palestrina's. They most likely would do for you. I send you a Decalogue Response, which will give you my idea of what *such* a Response ought to be, simple, plaintive, masculine, devout, without prettiness or repetition.

(*Letter to another Musical Editor.*)

The accompanying hymn tune is essentially good, but its arrangement is careless and irregular. Will you induce the author, whoever he may be, to reconsider his effusion? It has the faults of the great majority which are submitted to me. Men compose now, as architects built in the last century, without due attention to *style*. Hence we have so many ugly churches and so many bad tunes. Style is an appointment of God in both nature and art. He follows it Himself. Men discover it in art and follow it too, if they are wise. Hence I do mean to contend for the common-sense propriety of musicians discriminating certain styles, and shaping their productions in accordance with them. What may be allowable in one style of architecture, painting, or even language, may be quite out of place in another. *So is it in music.* If a composer sits down to write, let him be in keeping with his aim. Now in church music the worthies who formed our church style always shunned the doings which I have marked in the MS. The chord of 6.4.3 was used by no good master till after Handel's day. To begin a strain as the last one in the tune begins, with a 6.4, is the veriest modernism of the day. The great Beethoven, I believe, in one of his half-mad and self-willed freaks, was the first to start it.

The foregoing are the only remnants of my father's musical correspondence while at Henwick House. His chief musical publication at that time was a reprint of Ravenscroft's "Whole Booke of Psalmes," 1621, which he brought out in 1844. He prefaced it by short notices of "the authors which composed the tunes of the Psalmes into four parts," and by an account of Thos. Ravenscroft himself, who was born 1594 and took his degree of Bachelor of Music at Cambridge when only fourteen years old, and was yet in his teens when he published "Melismata; or, Musical Phansies fitting the Court, Citie, and Countrey Humors." The preface continues with remarks on the tunes and on the decay of the grand style of Elizabethan Psalmody and the peculiarities of its harmony. He makes practical observations and admonitions to observe Dr. Crotch's rule, "new church music, but *no new style*," and concludes with Ravenscroft's own excellent words:—"Thus I end, humbly wishing to all true Christian hearts that sweet consolation in singing praises unto God here upon earth, as may bring us hereafter to bear a part with the choir of angels in the heavens."

Although in his three years' residence at Henwick my father had no regular Sunday duty, he frequently preached for his brother clergy in its parish and neighbourhood, and was much in request for charity sermons and musical lectures. In June, 1843, he preached two sermons in aid of the funds of the choir of Holy Trinity Church, Stratford-on-Avon. They were published, by request, with notes, and contain interesting accounts of Jewish and Christian sacred song. These sermons were referred to in a letter from the Rev. J. East, which obtained the following reply from my father in December, 1843—

Prosperity to your kind-hearted people; they are "noble" Bathites. Of all my gift-books I value most Bagster's English Hexapla. And now for the sermons and your specks in them. But first hearty thanks for my brother's "smiting." I love the motive and honour it. With a lens out of my poor telescope perhaps the specks will no longer seem deformities.

1st. As to a side blow at the divines of the Puritan age, I had not the remotest idea; I merely showed the fallacy of a favourite argument, rife even so late as the last edition of the Eastcheap lectures in 1810. These good men were, as I and thousands think, decidedly wrong about instrumental music; I therefore aimed a blow at their error in *that* respect. Besides, it still is the error of the Scottish Church. Did they not dogmatize on the subject we might leave them alone.

The "glimpse of the martyr's tomb." Again you startle me. I only alluded to a well-known fact that the persecuted Christians were wont to worship where they could, or where their tearful affection would naturally lead them. The upper chamber, the darksome cavern, the martyr's grave were their resorts. Certainly I should not say that St. Paul favoured pilgrimages, mendicantism, or hermitages, or naked and dirty devoteeism, because he alluded to *facts* when he spoke of wanderings and caves, and sheep and goat-skin coverings, etc. As to the cloud of glory which filled the house being a token of Divine complacency, surely no Puritan ever disputed that. But should a Puritan say, "The cloud came to stop the music," then I reply, "If it came to stop the music, it came also to stop the sacrifice—for 'the priests could not minister.'" Besides, the musicians did not stand *in* the house! So hush, dear friend, especially as the music either continued or began again

(2 Chronicles 7:3). God to stop the praises of Israel when He "inhabits them"? Impossible! "The trees of the wood," etc. I think the idea analogous to the words of the Psalmist, who exhorts not merely all creatures to praise God, but ourselves to praise Him by His creatures. I once mentioned the idea to Mr. Faber, who is very musical, and he was much taken with it. But now as to oratorios I am wrong, not in what I said, but only in not saying more. I should have said as I have elsewhere, and on which I have always acted, viz, that oratorios in themselves are perfectly legitimate, but conducted as they generally are they receive no help from me. I have never doubted that we can do more good by battling against abuses, and not weakening our force by mixing the legitimate with the inexpedient.

(*To the same.*)

Brodick, Isle of Arran,
July 6, 1844.

My dearest E.,

Hitherto! After preaching twice at Bradford, in Yorkshire, and visiting my father, Maria and her young friend Augusta Walker arrived with me here on Thursday last. We sailed from Liverpool; the voyage was splendid, and mercies were abundant. We are in cottage lodgings, homely, but as good as this remoter district affords. A lovely bay, with Glasgow shipping constantly passing, lies before us. Behind is the Black Glen, and on one side the beautiful Goatfell rising 3000 feet above us. Altogether it is a lovely spot; sea, wild hills, and deep glens all about us. God who made them all grant us His presence! At home all were well, but discomposed at not hearing from your Annie after her return to Bath. We think of crossing to Ardrossan on the 25th, and I hope by rail to give my young travellers two days' peep at Edinburgh; then take ship at Glasgow and wend homewards by August. Say how it fares with James's eyes. You and yours are all, I hope, singing of mercy and strong in health. We are three days' post from you at Tenby, I think. Maria is all I can wish; she sends love to each. The blessing of our long-tried Father be with you all.

Ever affectionately yours,
W. H. Havergal.

In this year a living in Derbyshire was offered to him through Archdeacon Moore, but the population being too large for his strength, it was, after consultation with his friends, declined.

On Trinity Sunday, May 18, 1845, he preached in Worcester cathedral the ordination sermon,[1] from John 10:3, which was published by request of the candidates, and about that time the bishop preferred him to an honorary canonry in that cathedral, being the third he had appointed since their commencement. Still further to mark his appreciation of my father's merits, Bishop Pepys presented him to the living of St. Nicholas, in Worcester, vacant by the resignation of his chaplain, the Rev. J. H. Stephenson, on his promotion to the living of Hallow. It was when walking into Worcester when the bells of St. Nicholas were welcoming him that the beautiful hymn tune called at first by that name came into his mind. It is now called Eden, No. 38 of Havergal's Psalmody.

On leaving Henwick House in June, he gave up taking pupils, but retained one for a short time to read with my youngest brother. Many pupils had come and gone in these long years, and there are some still living who would gladly testify their sense of his ability as a tutor, and who feel they owe him more than advancement in mere earthly knowledge.

Several took high honours at Oxford, some few died young—the polished H. R. Slade, the amiable Fitzhardinge Kingscote, the promising Henry Emva, drowned in his first term at Oxford, the gentle C. R. Drury, etc. The names of others, who, I believe, continued laymen, are J. and T. Bagnall, R. Blackburn, E. Burton, brother of the traveller, Lord Crofton, S. Charrington, Right Hon. Hugh C. E. Childers, A. J. S. French, W. L. Grant, F. Grote, H. C. Vernon Graham, W. K. Heseltine, L. L. Haslope, W. W. Hozier, R. A. F. Kingscote, Walter Long, Lord Louth, J. and T. Fuller Maitland, A. Macalister, A. Tod, S. W. Maul, R. B. Mansfield, J. Scott, Gerard Spooner, D. H. Rucker, W. W. Carus-Wilson. Of the remainder, forty-one became clergymen; among them are (or were, for some have entered into rest) T. Albutt, R. W. Barnes, J. S. Broad, P. H. Boissier, Ed. Bradley, Hon. H. O'Brien, J. Cawood, Octavus Fox, V. G. Faithful, Geo. Greig, C. Rae Hay, W. Hulme, Jas. Jones (of Naseby), John Antes Latrobe, F. Simcox Lea, Archdeacon J. C. Moore, J. W. Neat, Edward Pollard, J. E. ("Dictionary") Riddle, W. H., and N. J. and O. M. Ridley, G. Ed. Walker. Of many of the above my father would say, "I have no greater joy than to hear that my children walk in truth."

He was peculiarly fitted to guide young men, by his quick insight into character (although bodily short-sighted), by his kindness of heart, sense of justice, order, method, accuracy, and punctuality. His conversational powers also were of much use with them; he never seemed at a loss for a topic on which to descant gravely or gaily, forcibly or pathetically. After I left school I felt it a great advantage to listen to the meal-time conversations between my father and successive clever assistants and the young men preparing for college, or ordination at Astley Rectory. The political and religious topics of the day were invariably discussed, and university affairs also, with keen interest; new books from the Stourport Reading Society were

[1] "The solemn character of the ordination service was much heightened by the presence of so many clergy on the platform, and the striking suitableness of the noble cathedral with all its furniture and ornaments. The rural deans assisted the bishop in the imposition of hands. All the candidates were presented by the archdeacon. The only novelty of variety in the service which we noticed on this occasion was the use of the second and longer hymn, *Veni, Creator Spiritus,* the bishop singing the two first lines in each verse, and the clergy and others answering as directed in the rubric. The tune used is that composed for this hymn by our great cathedralist, T. Tallis; of which one of the best of modern composers (the Rev. W. H. Havergal) has remarked—"A child may sing the tune, while manly genius may admire it."—*Extract from the Worcester Journal.*

commented on. But the breakfast conversations, the greater part of each week, were always on Scriptural subjects. Every Sunday morning my father wrote on a half-sheet of paper in his clear and distinct hand six or eight questions on some Scripture character, or incident, or doctrine. The pupils were expected to spend their leisure hours on Sunday in searching Bibles and commentaries to enable them to answer those, and any questions arising out of them, on the week-day mornings. In this way much critical and historical knowledge and a store of spiritual ideas were early and pleasantly acquired. Many at the close of their university career informed my father of the advantage they had found from their recollection of his skilful and exhaustive handling of the Sunday questions. One first-class man declared he thought his divinity examination turned the scale from a second to a first class, for which he thanked my father as having so well prepared him when at Astley.

The chapter at morning prayers was always followed by the pupils with their Greek Testaments, and in the short interval before breakfast they were expected to show up a short sentence neatly written on a slip of paper from any Greek or Latin author; and at breakfast, before the Scripture question for the day was propounded, each had to quote a text, with chapter and verse. So that a large amount of knowledge was gently imbibed by nine o'clock every morning.

Great attention was paid to English composition; the wherefore of each correction in a theme was always thoroughly explained.

Such of the pupils as were fitted for it, especially those preparing for the ministry, were encouraged to take classes in the Sunday school, in which their help proved most valuable, and also to visit old or invalid people selected by himself.

It was a great comfort to him to think of these young messengers of mercy turning their daily walks to good account, when he was unable, from the state of his head, to visit the poor himself. How welcome and cheering his calls were when made many a one could tell.

When quite a child I remember accompanying him on a pastoral visit to a young woman at Astley Burf. It was evening: there was no conversation; a kindly greeting, a reverent recital of appropriate passages of Scripture, a prayerful blessing, and we silently left; but the soothing sound of his voice in the deepening twilight, the flickering firelight on the cottage wall, the calm face of the dying girl, made a pictured impression on my mind never to be effaced.

CHAPTER IX.

LIFE IN WORCESTER.

St. Nicholas' Rectory — Letters to the Rev. J. East — Elizabeth Edwards and George Vaughan — Letters from Dr. Lowell Mason — Marriage of the Rev. H. E. Havergal — Illness and Death of Mrs. Havergal — "Old Church Psalmody" — "A Century of Chants" — "Havergal's Psalmody" and "Songs of Grace and Glory" — Special Sermons — Death of his Mother — Letter to the Rev. J. East — Second Marriage — Lansdowne Crescent, Worcester — Failing Eyesight — Consults Prussian Oculist — "Sermons on Historical Subjects from the Old and New Testament" — Letters from the Rev. G. S. Faber and the Rev. Charles Bradley — "A History of the Old Hundredth Psalm Tune" — Dr. Wainwright's Preface — Marriage of his Daughter Ellen — "Nuptial Grace" — Death of the Rev. John East — The last word "Home" — Visit to Killarney — Letter from the Rev. S. B. James — Death of the Rev. John Davies — Resignation of St. Nicholas' — Generous gifts — The Parish Schools — Letter to the Churchwardens — Parting Address.

AT Midsummer, 1845, my parents, with their younger daughters and son, took up their residence in St. Nicholas' Rectory, Worcester. It was a very dreary abode compared with their former homes, overshadowed on one side by the tall Doric church, and on the other by the houses from which it retreated, behind a strip of ground which extended to the street. A Banking Company now occupy the new building erected on its site a few years later. Notwithstanding this unpleasant change as to residence, our dear mother was quite content, and congratulated herself on having a smaller household to care for than the former she had managed with so much tact and ability, and looked forward to finding more time to work among the poor and visit her friends generally. She little knew how soon she would have to prove her faith by patient suffering instead of by active service.

In a letter to a friend my father described his new sphere as "arduous, but promising." Not much more can be gathered from the few letters that remain of this time.

(*To the Rev. J. East.*)

Oct. 16, 1845.

My heart rose into joy as I glanced at your improved handwriting. It seems all yourself again, and comes to me itself a bulletin. But I startle at hearing you say that the sensation in your leg returned as you stood in your pulpit. Now that sensation is a text and a sermon to you! Read it well, and preach to yourself about it continually. You should go out again for full nine months, to make up the year. I am most serious, because, with that sensation, you are not sound.

Thanks for your invitation to preach; I cannot and dare not accept it. You must not tempt me to violate the rule you lay down for me, "Be not righteous over much." If I fail in that point, it shall be in my own parish. The fact is, to make exceptions is a difficult task. Hence I have said, Nay, I must not go anywhere. In addition, I find much interest in my own pulpit; other things render it highly expedient for me to stay in Worcester my first year. It was only yesterday that I refused to preach for George Bull, of Birmingham. A wisdom tooth has prevented my eating these ten days, but is recovering its folly.

"The times," indeed! One of the worst features of them is the supineness of our bishops. Poor Jordan is hauled up and racked for indiscretion only, while Pusey is left in open heresy to enjoy his dignities. We shall be interested with the letters of your naval son. I should like a talk with you, and a long one.

(*To the same.*)

April 20, 1846.

The Lord uphold and comfort you, dearest East, under your sore trial. No doubt these dark ways are all right, and are only parts of a bright plan. But one cannot help thinking of poor Bagot and the diocese. Somehow I dread to hear of the death of good men. One has a boding idea that their departure is a loss to the Church not to be supplied. Well, the more reason why we should strive to the utmost while we can. But oh! to sleep in Jesus away from sin, turmoil, and anxiety. And yet it is foolish to be anxious. I know it, but too often fall into it . . . Your letter has only just reached me, as I interdict delivery on the Lord's Day.

(*To the same.*)

Isle of Man,
Jan. 19, 1847.

I am staying with the Archdeacon of this island, and have only a few minutes to reply to your announcement. Truly I can sympathize with you. I know the sort of pain and the sort of pleasure which you now experience. May our God turn the one into the other, and crown all with His abundant blessing. My love to your dear girl, and tell her to believe that I do wish her all joy in the prospect before her. But these things, dear brother, tell *us* that life is but a dream, except so far as we keep our eye on eternity. We pass from stage to stage, and the last scene soon comes. In our real home we shall meet where distance and separation will not be known.

May we rejoice, no wanderer lost,
A family in heaven!

My father met with much encouragement in his work among the poor of St. Nicholas', and published a little account of Elizabeth Edwards, a Christian child, and also of George Vaughan, "an old disciple," who died February 13, 1847, aged 98 years. Many other instances of holy lives and happy deaths among the poor in his parish who were rich in faith, may be found in his daughter Maria's record of her "walks and talks" among them in her "Pleasant Fruits." [1]

His musical correspondence of course continued. I insert an extract of a letter from the American musician, Dr. Lowell Mason, of Boston, April, 1847, and from others of later date.

(*Letters from Dr. Lowell Mason.*)

I have lately introduced into my choir and sung with admirable effect your tunes of St. Nicholas and Glasshampton. The effect of St. Nicholas was truly magnificent; I have never heard anything come nearer to my *beau ideal* of Church music than did the singing of this tune on a fine Sabbath morning, in a church filled with people. It made a deep impression, and the next day one and another was asking, "What tune did you sing yesterday morning?" "Where did you get that tune?" etc.

On the Sabbath following we sung Glasshampton; this is beautiful, but St. Nicholas is sublime. The performance makes one feel as Jacob did, "none other but the gate of heaven." Wonderful would be the effect of psalmody were all the people to unite in such lofty, majestic strains.

November, 1848. My book the "National Psalmist" was completed about September last. I fear to send it you, for there is, I well

[1] London: J. Nisbet & Co.

know, much that you cannot approve. There is much indeed, I (who am not so orthodox as you are) do not like, but I was obliged to adapt myself to the state of things, and I introduce into my book quite as much of the real psalmody as the people are prepared for. But I have done something towards reformation. A few of your tunes which I took a little liberty with I have marked; forgive me, my dear sir, for the few instances in which I deviated a little from your copy, for the purpose of adapting them for more general use here. Much have you enriched my book. Your letters and remarks have much modified my book. For all this and much more I shall ever be truly grateful.

March, 1862. I thank you for your kind note of February 2. It has gladdened my heart, and caused me to look upon your portrait, ever before me, with renewed interest, and, if possible, with a deeper respect and affection for its original, who has been so kind to me. Ten years ago, on January 3, I saw you at Worcester; dined with you on Saturday. On Sunday I attended divine service at your church; you preached from Jeremiah 50:5. I wish you had put that sermon into your printed volumes. In the evening you preached again on Psalm 23:4. It is most pleasant to recall the remembrance of kind friends. I shall never cease to hold them dear. Now, dear sir, may the blessing of our heavenly Father ever rest upon you and yours, and at last, when you shall be called home, may an abundant entrance be ministered to you into everlasting habitations.

Yours most truly,

Lowell Mason.

The chief event of domestic interest in 1847 was the marriage of my eldest brother, the Rev. Henry East Havergal. He had been chaplain of New College and Christ Church, Oxford, successively, and had published a few musical works, and two editions of Geo. Wither's "Hymns of the Church." He was now vicar of Cople, near Bedford. On the 16th of September he married, at Norton-juxta-Kempsey, Frances Mary, the eldest daughter of Geo. J.A. Walker, Esq., J.P. and D.L., who was heartily welcomed among us.

Our dear mother was then, to our inexpressible grief, languishing in her last illness; but in bridal attire they came to her bedside for a blessing, which she gave in the words of Numbers 6:24–27, and saying, "You, my dear children, are beginning life, I am ending it. It is such a relief to me to see you united; I so feared being the means of preventing your happiness"; adding some sweet counsel which was not recorded.

Many sweet expressions of resignation and holy joy were throughout her illness written down by another sister. I will unveil one page only of her diary.

The earliest dawn always found my father at my dear mother's side, even before the night-nurse left, with words refreshing as the dew. Once kneeling by her, with her hand upon his head, she repeated many times, "My dear, dear husband." "Yes," he said, "but One is with you dearer still; He does more for you than I can." *My Mother*: "It has so troubled me to-night that Satan has power to keep me from dying, and so hinder me from my rest." "Oh, no! that cannot be; life and death are in the Lord's hands alone. 'My times are in Thy hand,' and there is a glorious comfort that Christ alone has the key of death—'He openeth and no man shutteth.'" At another time she said to him, "How wonderfully God has blessed us through life and in our dear children. Goodness and mercy have indeed followed us." Pointing to some camellias from Oakhampton, she said, "How beautiful! but not *perfectly* white; soon I shall be in garments whiter than snow." *My Father*: "Yes, and see your Saviour, who is altogether lovely. What a change awaits you! Into what joy will you soon enter! You have joy now, knowing Jesus is with you, and that He will remain with you."

Our beloved mother lingered in great suffering, too dreadful to dwell on, till July 5, 1848, when her spirit was released to be "for ever with the Lord." She was buried in the crypt beneath the church of St. Nicholas, and a tablet to her memory was placed on the chancel wall with the inscription:—

Jane, the beloved wife of the

Rev. W. H. Havergal,

Rector of this Parish, and Hon. Canon of

Worcester Cathedral;

Died in holy peace, July 5, 1848.

Aged 54 years.

"I give unto them eternal life."

Her daughter Frances thus alludes to her burial-place in "Travelling Thoughts."[1]

"There in a busy city,
  A crypt all dark and lone,
A name engraven on our hearts
  Is traced upon a stone.

Not *there* the sainted spirit!
  She dwells in holy light,
Within the pearl-raised portals,
  With those who walk in white.

May all her children follow
  The path she meekly trod,
And reach the home she rests in now,
  And dwell like her with God."

After this heavy bereavement we all went together to Aber, in North Wales, for some weeks, lodging in a farm-house named Tyn-y-coed.

[1] "The Ministry of Song," p. 147. [See page 102 of Volume I of the Havergal edition.]

In November, 1847, my father published "Old Church Psalmody," a collection of old English tunes and others of foreign origin which he esteemed a *desideratum,* as he believed there was no existing volume which contained only such tunes and such harmonies as strictly accord with the style of those times when psalmody was best understood, and of which the date of T. Ravenscroft's Psalter, 1621, he considered the zenith. No composition of a later date which did not accord with that style was admitted, nor any tune by a living author.

"Old Church Psalmody" contained remarks on harmony, style, rhythmical form, the time and pitch in which the tunes were sung, followed by notes of information respecting many of them.[1]

He received numberless testimonies from America and Scotland, as well as England, of the high estimation in which this now standard work was held. It passed through five editions, and has since been incorporated with the next mentioned volumes. He published, in 1859, "A Hundred Psalm and Hymn Tunes," Op. 48. These tunes were selected from very many of his own composition, and are all constructed on the principles set forth in his "Old Church Psalmody." They are named from the natural geography of the Bible, as Amana, Bethany, Carmel, etc., a system which had not before been adopted, and is a distinctive mark of his later tunes. My sister Frances in like manner named her published tunes from the names of St. Paul's friends, as Claudia, Euodias, Hermas, etc. The preface to the "Hundred Psalm and Hymn Tunes" contains remarks on the secularities too prevalent in psalmody, etc., insisting that in music, as in architecture, the church should have a style of her own. In January, 1870, he published "A Century of Chants," with a preface, and a "Supplemental Note" on the career of Dr. Crotch.

When an Oxonian my father had the advantage of hearing Dr. Crotch on the organ in his best days, and of imbibing his musical ideas, for which he always retained the utmost veneration. In later years Dr. Crotch often expressed his high opinion of my father's compositions, and his respect for his judgment and learning.

In 1871, the year following his death, the above works were incorporated in one volume, entitled "Havergal's Psalmody," and published by his widow; but it was entirely prepared and arranged by his daughter Frances R. Havergal, with the addition of many of his other tunes, some kyries, and glorias, and also some of her own tunes, to which she afterwards added an appendix. Finally the Rev. C. B. Snepp published in 1875, by permission, another edition as a musical companion to his "Songs of Grace and Glory." This also my sister Frances arranged, adding new tunes by herself and other composers.

The only record of 1849 is that my father preached, on the 22nd of March, a sermon which was published by request, entitled "Death for Murder," a subject which was then much agitated in Worcester and elsewhere. His text was, "He beareth not the sword in vain" (Romans 13:4), on which he founded an able defence of our present law. He was then chaplain to the High Sheriff of the county. On the 29th of November he preached at the Rev. J. East's church, St. Michael's, Bath, on the opening of a new organ, an appropriate sermon, also published, entitled "Elisha and the Minstrel," from 2 Kings 3:15.

The year 1850 brought one of the great trials of my father's life. In February he was summoned to the death-bed of his mother, who had been seized with apoplexy. He thus writes to his daughters:—

My dear Ones,

You will be anxious to hear. Dr. H. and Mr. J. again saw my mother this morning. They say, as I feared, that life diminishes—in fact, that recovery is hopeless. It becomes increasingly difficult for her to swallow, so that all is against her as to the body, but all, rather, is forwarding the soul to its blessed home. I would not detain her, although I see the loss to myself. Her living prayers have been my sheet-anchor. Aunt Mary arrived last evening from Norwich. The nurse is efficient and a good woman, my father's tenant the last twenty-five years. P.M.—Symptoms no better. The Lord see and hear! Though my dear dying mother can say nothing, yet sometimes her meaning can be caught. It is quite clear that she anticipated a seizure, from what she said to Kate and the directions she gave her. It is clear also that she is enjoying full peace and assurance. Her strong Protestant feelings are singularly fresh to the last. On my saying to her, "Dear mother, would you like me to administer the Lord's Supper?" she emphatically muttered "No! no!" She added another word, which at last we found to be "Rome." Her meaning was, as I found, that she had always been a communicant; and did not wish by any deathbed act even to appear to countenance the notion of the sacrament of the Lord's Supper being *necessary* to a dying person. No passport—no! no!

She died on the 24th of February, aged nearly seventy-eight years. Afterwards my father writes:

Frank has arrived, also Edward. Yesterday was a most sad day with my poor father. Alternations between gushes of sorrow and mental wanderings. His last leave of the blessed dead was very affecting; I had to sustain him and myself too. The Lord helped! The last earthly scene was off our eyes (never to be off my heart) about midday. Mr. Paddon read the service—oh what a service!—very nicely. Many neighbours followed. I hear the whole town feels the event. All seem to know she *was* a good woman. I think much of you. The Lord think of us all!

[1] In 1859, as in some other years, my father had much correspondence with the Rev. C. H. Davis, then of Nailsworth, who kindly gave him much assistance in preparing for the press one of the editions of "Old Church Psalmody," etc.

My grandfather survived his wife more than four years, dying of old age (having worn out the gout), September 2, 1854, aged eighty-nine years and a half. Their only daughter Mary, Mrs. Prestage, died March 21, 1874, leaving three children—Catherine, Edward, and George. She had long been a widow, as Mr. Prestage died at Tunbridge Wells in 1848.

(*Letter from W. H. H. to Rev. J. East.*)

Worcester, March 22, 1850.

My dearest East,

Heart thanks for your earnest solicitudes and sympathies. I am, thank the God of my mercies, as well as I can reasonably expect. The loss of my mother—such a mother as she was—will ever be a loss which cannot be repaired. I feel that I have lost my *praying* mother! I have been so accustomed to send to her to "undertake for me," that it is with me now as when a ship parts with its sheet-anchor. Lord, help me to look more to Thyself!

The bracing weather is the instrument of my better health, spite of incessant fag to the full. My Lent lectures are nobly attended. Let the Saviour be praised! Maria and Fanny are pretty well, though the former is like a sparrow on the housetop without her Ellen, who, as Theophilus told you is gone on a guardian visit to my poor father. Splendid indeed is your mission list. Poor Archdeacon Thomas of bygone days! Thank the Lord our archdeacon will (D.V.) preach for the society in my church next month, and take the chair at the meeting. Is *our* great battle at hand? It looks like it. "The sword of the Lord" and the articles! All love to all.

Ever yours,

W. H. H.

On the 28th of June in this year my father preached in the Abbey Church at Tewkesbury, for the enlargement of its organ, from Psalm 22:3. I have no memoranda of any family event till the next summer.

In July, 1851, my father married Caroline Ann, daughter of John Cooke, Esq., of Gloucester (then deceased), and sister of John Russell Cooke, Esq., of Newent, who made him an affectionate and devoted wife. The first weeks after their marriage they spent at Slindon, near Arundel, where in August my sisters joined them, excepting Fanny, who had gone to school at Powick Court, near Worcester, which is described in her "Memorials," also her visit with her father and step-mother to Colwyn in North Wales the following summer.

In 1852 my father delivered Lent lectures on "The Ark of the Covenant," which were published some time afterwards.

The site of St. Nicholas' Rectory being required for business purposes, and the plan of building a new rectory being deferred, my father, after his second marriage, took up his abode at Lansdowne Crescent, Rainbow Hill, within easy distance of his parish, but on higher ground. It was an advantage to him to live in purer air, and the new home commanded a lovely and extensive view, looking over the city and the Severn to the beautiful range of the Malvern Hills. His eyesight had for some time been failing, and now became so seriously affected that, having obtained leave of absence from the bishop, he left England in November with Mrs. Havergal and my sister Fanny, to consult the renowned Prussian oculist, Dr. de Leuw.

The Hofrath, as he was locally called, pronounced the case to be one of incipient cataract, which he hoped to absorb and disperse by his remedies if my father could remain within reach. Accordingly, after staying a few weeks at Gräfrath, they wintered at Düsseldorf, placing Fanny at the Louisenschule there. Mrs. Havergal's birthday was on the shortest day of the year, and my father always commemorated it by a poetic offering. That for this year is given as a specimen.

The shortest day in a foreign land
   Would be one of lengthened sadness,
Were it not my spirit has at hand
   A lamp of sunny gladness.
O Thou who, forty years ago,
Didst give that lamp its natal spark,
Keep bright its own ethereal glow,
No day shall then with me be dark!

W. H. H.

Düsseldorf, Dec. 21, 1852.

[Note: December 21 was the winter solstice, the shortest day of 1852.]

My father in this winter wrote a little book (published by Hatchard) on the Hofrath and his surroundings, entitled, "The Prussian Oculist." In the spring he made excursions to Munster and other places, and returned to England in December, 1853, with improved sight and a distant prospect of complete cure. Of this first long sojourn abroad his MS. "Facts and Scraps" will form a chapter by themselves.

Ever industrious, even under difficulties, my father had, while abroad, published in London two volumes of "Sermons chiefly on Historical Subjects from the Old and New Testament, preached in the Parish Church of St. Nicholas, Worcester."[1] He was assisted in their selection by his friend the Rev. S. R. Waller, then incumbent of Mitton, Stourport.

Many favourable notices in papers and magazines followed their publication, but it will be sufficient to quote from the letters of two friends, who were excellent writers and preachers themselves.

(*From the Rev. G. S. Faber, Canon of Durham.*)

Sherburn House, Durham,
July 17, 1853.

My dear Sir,

My two copies of your sermons I have received. I read one every

[1] London: Hamilton, Adams, & Co.; and Hatchards.

morning in the course of my ordinary devotions, and without compliment I think them both very original, and, what is much better, calculated to be eminently useful. In my perfectly sober judgment, 1 think them some of the best I have ever read—sound in doctrine, eminently practical in application. In a mechanical point of view they are most comfortable reading. You adopt the plan I always follow, that of numbering the divisions and subdivisions of the subject by figures, instead of writing in unmarked continuity, which greatly increases a reader's difficulty of comprehension. . . .

Yours most truly,

G. S. Faber.

(*From the Rev. Charles Bradley.*)

My dear Havergal,

I have received your sermon, and thank you for it. It is pleasant, nice reading. But the Sermons! Their chief value in my eyes is their suggestiveness. They contain "seeds of thought." Of course to ordinary lay readers this excellence in them might not be perceived; but there are other excellences which the commonest mind might discover. Your mind is eminently practical; may I say, though logical it is not metaphysical? On historical subjects you are unrivalled; no author that I know, save Bishop Hall, comes near you. Your style is racy, and has quaintnesses which some would think might be removed; but I like the raciness, and moreover we preachers like a new word now and then as well as a new idea. I am sure we shall find your sermons very helping.

The time with me is very short; I feel as though I had never preached my Master's Gospel fully yet, and long to preach it before I die. Pray for me.

Yours gratefully and affectionately,

Charles Bradley.

In this year also my father wrote "A History of the Old Hundredth Psalm Tune with Specimens," for which the Right Rev. J. M. Wainwright, D.D., Bishop of New York, wrote a preface, and it was published there in April, 1854. In the last month of his life my father began to write a preface for a new edition.

Dr. Wainwright's prefatory note so well portrays the merits of this work, and the estimation in which my father's character and talents were held, that an extract may here be given:—

There is probably no musical composition, with the exception of the ancient Ambrosian and Gregorian tones, that has been so universally sung by worshipping assemblies as the Old Hundredth Psalm tune, and certainly none so familiar to the ear of Protestant communities. It has proved equally acceptable to the instructed and uninstructed musical taste. When in any congregation, through ignorance or bad taste, it has been for a time laid aside to make way for more modern yet more feeble tunes, it has been taken up again, after the intermission, with increased interest; and as its strains have been given out by the organ, and its first tones raised by the choir or clerk, devout affections have been roused, and voices which have been long silent have swelled the loud chorus of praise. It has been known in this country from its first settlement. It was in all probability used by the earliest Church of England missionaries in Virginia, and it was certainly one of the songs of the Puritan fathers of New England, since we find it in Ainsworth's Psalms, the book of Psalmody which they brought from Holland. It was, therefore, one of the tunes to which the wild forests in this new world were first made vocal with the praise of God. Nor was its use confined to the early European settlers; its lofty strains were taught by them to the inhabitants of the forest they found here; it was sung by the new-made converts of the missionary, John Elliot; and in the various missionary settlements amongst the Indians it may yet be heard.

The history of such a composition must be a matter of interest not only to the musician but to all who have the slightest taste for musical art, and especially to those who take delight in the service of song in the house of the Lord. Mr. Havergal has performed a most acceptable work in his curious researches. He has carefully hunted up, probably, everything that can be discovered relating to its origin, and has established its authorship as satisfactorily as can now be done. We think it will be generally conceded that William Franc must hereafter be entitled to the credit of *composing* this most remarkable of all metrical tunes. But the result of Mr. Havergal's researches is perhaps of more practical importance considered with reference to the form of the tune. This, it seems, has been greatly changed, and hence the heaviness and almost tediousness which sometimes attends its performance. Could its old rhythm be restored, the tune would more fully accord with the joyful character of the psalm by which it is called, and would not fail to be even more popular and useful than heretofore.

The most estimable author of this work, a clergyman of the Church of England, is well known in the United States as well as in England for his devotion to the cause of sacred music; and no one in our day has contributed more than he has done to the revival of a taste for pure ecclesiastical melodies and harmonies.

The introductory part of the volume is devoted to an inquiry into the versions of our early psalters and Psalms, in which the tune is inserted, and in which is shown how deep have been his researches into this interesting subject. He then enters into an examination of the works of the several foreign composers—Luther among the number—to whom has been attributed " the composition of the tune, establishing clearly that to William Franc the merit of the composition belongs; not so much that he was the original composer as the fragmental compiler, my father clearly tracing each phrase of the tune to sundry Gregorian hymns.

It having, however, been the subject of controversy, whether an Englishman—Thomas Ravenscroft or John Douland—was not the composer of the tune, he enters into the discussion of this point with his usual acumen, and thus satisfactorily disposes of the surmise in relation to both:—

In consequence of Ravenscroft having prefixed the name of John Douland to the tune, as the harmonizer of it, Douland has been considered its author. The erroneous notion seems to have taken its rise from some vague remarks of Dr. Pepusch, about the beginning of the last century. The surmise that Douland was the composer of the tune spread among the editors of many local collections of tunes of the ensuing generation. At length the Rev. W. Bowles, Canon of Salisbury, in his interesting "History of Bremhill" (p. 206, etc.), advocated the surmise, and detailed many arguments in support of it. The process which the estimable poet, historian, and divine thought fit to follow is this. Considering that there is no authority for attributing the tune to Luther, he endeavoured to prove that it is "originally English." The tune, he argues, so exactly suits the accentuation of the first verse of our hundredth psalm, old version, that it must have been composed to those words. In an old book of his own, the title of which is not given, the worthy Canon found the name of John Douland at the head of the tune. Ravenscroft also, as he thought he had discovered, assigned it to that eminent musician. But "after," as Mr. Bowles supposes, "Ravenscroft published the air as Douland's he saw it in a French book of psalms, and, without sufficient examination, retracted in the index what he advanced in the body of his work" (p. 208). This is the sum of a rather long argument. A breath would suffice to demolish it, and the deserved repute of the pleader of it requires a little more formality in its annihilation.

It is singular that a man like Canon Bowles should have so slurred over facts which he was perfectly competent to investigate. He furnishes, however, another proof of what has been so often proved, that a superior mind, without a special turn, is not always equal to every task. Had the poet been more of a musician he could hardly have failed, as he has, in handling a point of musical history. A very easy glance at any of the old psalters, which must have been within his reach, would have sufficed to convince him that his argument about the accentuation of the words was but a mere cobweb, and that it was far more likely that the words were written to the tune than that the tune was composed for the words; especially as there are many tunes to the same metre in the foreign psalters, but only this one set of words in our own *old* psalter.

But apart from all arguments and surmises, it is plain fact Douland was not the author of the tune, for he was born in 1562, and the tune was printed in an English psalter at Geneva in 1561.

In relation to the time in which the tune should be sung, he makes the following appropriate remarks:—

The time in which the tune is now sung furnishes an instance of alteration as remarkable as any in its entire history. Originally, and till a comparatively late period, the tune was regarded as the liveliest and most cheerful in the whole Psalter.

On the publication of Tate and Brady's New Version, the Old Hundredth Psalm tune was singled out as a model tune "for psalms of praise and cheerfulness." As such it is still recognized in the "Directions concerning tunes" printed at the end of some recent editions of that Version. But time, which changes so many things, has witnessed a strange alteration in the mode of singing this tune. Instead of being regarded as a joyous and animating melody, it is reckoned a solemn and even a funeral strain. It consequently is no longer sung in a spirited and sprightly style, but doled forth with the utmost length of syllabic utterance. So inveterate, too, has this singular change become, that not even the extremely jubilant character of the Hundredth Psalm itself is sufficient to awaken attention to the anomaly. Though choirs and other singers are familiar with the old title of the Psalm, "*Jubilate* Deo," and repeat its translation, "O be *joyful* in the Lord," in the Morning Service of our Church, they, nevertheless, fail to see the inconsistency of singing the tune to its metrical version in a drawling and sleepy manner. Not even when using the old or new version, and repeating lines which call on all the dwellers upon earth to rejoice in praising, lauding, and blessing Jehovah, do they perceive the incongruity; but continue to sing those lines with the same sleepy slowness as they would sing a dirge in a graveyard. The reason of this perversion may perhaps be found, nowadays at least, in the very antiquity of the tune itself. It has become a popular notion that all old tunes must be sung in proportionably slow time. How groundless and inaccurate this notion is, there would be no great difficulty in proving at large. It is sufficient to state that, in the year 1621, Thomas Ravenscroft, the great oracle for this species of church music, directed "That Psalms of Rejoicing be sung with a loud voice, and *a swift and jocund measure*." This, no doubt, was in accordance with what had been the custom of the Elizabethan age; for unless such custom had existed, how were our forefathers to get through twelve or sixteen verses, the usual partition of the longer psalms? Even Dr. Isaac Watts, who composed many of his "Imitations of the Psalms of David" to suit the measure of our fine old church tunes, remarked, about the middle of the last century, that "If the method of singing were but reformed to *a greater speed* of pronunciation, we might often enjoy the pleasure of a longer psalm, with less expense of time and breath; and our psalmody would be *more agreeable to that of the ancient churches*, more intelligible to others, and delightful to ourselves."

Before giving twenty-eight specimens of this celebrated tune, of different ages and harmonies, my father thus concludes his observations:—

Considered as Gregorian in its texture, the Old Hundredth Psalm tune is indeed very old, much older than is commonly imagined. Its sacred strains had been sung by Christian voices not only a thousand years before Luther was born, but for centuries before the Papal system was developed.

Viewed in this light, the old tune assumes a new interest, and its antique notes vibrate with freshened impulse. May the fervour with which it used to be sung at St. Paul's Cross, soon after its first importation into England, be speedily revived in all our parish churches.

1856 was signalized by a very happy domestic event. My sister Ellen was married by the Rev. Charles Bradley in St. Nicholas' Church to Giles Shaw, Esq., of Celbridge Lodge, County Kildare, where they resided till December, 1866, when they came to Winterdyne, near Bewdley—a home of Christian word and work.

My father composed a hymn to be sung when the guests were in their places at the wedding breakfast, and as such a musical grace was a novelty, a copy is given.

NUPTIAL GRACE.

FOR G. S. AND E. P. H.

February 5, 1856.

"Holy Matrimony—instituted of God in the time of man's innocency, signifying unto us the mystical union that is betwixt Christ and his Church; which holy estate Christ adorned and beautified with his presence, and first miracle that He wrought, in Cana of Galilee."

O THOU, whose presence beautified
 Poor Cana's nuptial board,
By Thee let ours be sanctified,
 And Thou shalt be adored.

Thyself to us, ourselves to Thee
 In mystic union join;
And grant us greater things to see
 Than water turned to wine.

Thy glory show, our faith make strong,
 Like rivers be our peace:
And seat us where Thy Marriage Song
 Shall never, *never* cease!

To Him who wove the marriage tie,
 In Eden's thornless bower,
To Him, the Christ of God Most High,
 Be glory, praise, and power!

This grace was sung to a tune then called St. Nicholas, but named Eden in Havergal's Psalmody, No. 38.

A few days after this "model of a Christian wedding," as I heard it called,

"So swift treads sorrow on the heels of joy!"

my father received the news of the dangerous illness of the Rev. John East, who for forty-three years had been his most affectionate and devoted friend, whose funeral sermon he preached in St. Michael's, Bath, February 24th, from "Moses my servant is dead" (Joshua 1:2).

The last word Mr. East uttered, pointing upward, was "Home!" On this my father remarked,

This last word "home" falls on my ear with thrilling force, for it is the first remembered word which passed between him and me. "Home" was the altar round which our friendship and fidelity were sworn to each other. "East, do you love home?" was the first sentence which he recollected ever to have been uttered by myself. He frequently referred to it affectionately in after days. Our East was a thorough man of home; he loved it with hallowed intensity, and only feared that he loved it too much. Never could it be said of him that he was not at home what he was in society. Fitly, therefore, did a glance of his eternal home waken up his sinking thoughts.

After an illness in the summer my father gives a short account of his autumn holiday in a letter to Dr. Lowell Mason.

KILLARNEY, Oct. 22, 1856.

MY DEAR SIR,

Your kind letter of the 29th ult. has overtaken me in this charming locality. An attack of poor or suppressed gout left me in an enfeebled state. As, too, I had had no holiday for fifteen months, I felt obliged as soon as practicable to take a long rest. With Mrs. Havergal and our neighbours, the Misses Nott, I have been in Ireland for more than a month, and hope to reach home again next week. The main attraction to Ireland was the new home of my dear daughter Ellen; we are thankful to say we found everything equal to our fondest wishes. We spent three weeks at Kilkee, a wild but noble spot on the western coast, where the waves and breezes of the Atlantic greatly refreshed and delighted us. I am, thank God, much benefited by the change.

While out I have been catching an hour now and then to arrange and copy a selection of my own psalm and hymn tunes, which have either never been published or are scattered in the publications of others. My children are urgent for me to do this, but it is a difficult task with my imperfect vision. I have had some very large music paper ruled on purpose for the occasion. If the accompanying MSS. will be of any service to you, all is yours *ad lib.* The sacred round was hit off some years ago. The *recto et retro* chant was picked by Fanny, my scribe, out of a lot of such articles. I never have time for greater things, but scraps of weary hours *will* lead my thoughts to some little contrivances of a short description. My dear wife joins me in very best remembrances to Mrs. Mason.

Believe me,
Most faithfully yours,
W. H. HAVERGAL.

It is somewhat remarkable that two of my father's curates at Worcester were ordained on the same day at York, little thinking they would be called to what they both considered the high privilege of serving at different times under the same rector. One of them, the Rev. Charles Bullock, his successor at St. Nicholas', and now the editor of *Home Words* and other magazines, will be alluded to later on; the other, the Rev. S. B. James, is now vicar of Northmarston. He is the author of sermons and lectures, etc., and a well-known contributor to periodical literature. He was my father's esteemed coadjutor from September, 1856, to February, 1858. He thus writes to me concerning him:—

So unselfish, single-hearted, generous, and transparently upright a friend and rector I think it would be difficult to find. It seemed to me, when he was taken home, I should never be able to fill the blank in my correspondence, my thoughts, and my heart. He so entirely mourned with me when I mourned, and, what is far rarer, rejoiced with me when I rejoiced, that I viewed him with almost filial affection.

I have his pocket Communion Service, as my child has his accomplished daughter's writing-desk. I have books with his well-known autograph; I had very many precious letters of his, but, by a sad mischance, they are lost to me. I have his portrait and other valued mementoes, and as long as I live shall cling to his memory and all its associations.

I remember his disappointment at my remaining unbeneficed, and ending a letter with, "Ah, there's nothing left but the Great Patron." And when somebody attacked one of my sermons, he remarked, "Have you never noted, friend James, that whenever the great serpent is angry the little snakes are sure to hiss!"

His generosity was ever in advance of a curate's expectations. On one occasion he wrote thus: "Your last letter is before me; I value it and thank you. The good Lord return for me all its kindness to you. Herewith I enclose a cheque, and henceforth you must let me name £—' (an advance of £20) "as the stipend, because I fear I am likely to task you a little more than heretofore. Even that little increase will exhaust the proceeds of my gradually exhausting living." And he would take no refusal.

He was keenly appreciative of the regard and honour which I strove to indicate by outward acts. "With you," said he, "it is always 'My rector and I;' it is not so with all curates." I think my reply was an allusion to Wolsey's "*Ego et rex meus.*"

He was, as friend, as rector, as man of business with me—and, as I verily believe, in all relationships to others—a man of a thousand and of ten thousand.

One little note of 1857 has been preserved, written to his daughter, Mrs. Shaw, on the first anniversary of her wedding-day.

My dearest Ellen,

As many happy returns to you of this your happy day as the God of Abraham and Sarah may see fit to grant you! My best love to your dear husband. We enjoyed the thought of your unexpectedly seeing dear Frank; we long to hear all about his visit. Kiss the babe for me. Our God fix his smile on her!

Ever yours,

W. H. H.

I have no other records of this year, but my father's widow has left a little diary of his home sayings and pastoral doings from January, 1857, to March, 1860, extracts from which will form a separate chapter. She died at Pyrmont Villa, Leamington, May 26, 1878.

Not only did my father support in his own and other dioceses Home and Foreign religious and charitable societies, but he collected large sums for any unusual distress wherever it occurred. Lists and receipts remain with grateful letters from Scotland, Ireland, Lancashire and other English counties. Worcestershire seems to have been very liberal to the Highlanders in 1847, when he collected £276 for their destitution.

In 1858 the Rev. John Davies (one of four estimable brothers in holy orders), Rector of St. Clement's, Worcester, died. My father preached his friend's funeral sermon from Philippians 4:9, on July 12th, and afterwards published a small volume entitled, "Memorial Notices of the Rev. J. Davies, M.A.," including his own and other sermons preached in Worcester on the death of this kindly and holy man. The profits were given towards the erection of a church for the watermen on the Severn, for whose spiritual welfare Mr. Davies had so warmly interested himself.

In this year, and at other times, my father had some musical correspondence with Mr. S. G. Hatherly, Mus. Bac. Oxon., an acute and scientific musician, who had published several compositions, dedicating one to "A kind Friend and learned Musician, the Rev. W. H. Havergal." Mr. Hatherly is now a priest in the Greek Church, the only Englishman, I believe, who has become one.

(*To his Danghter, Mrs. Shaw.*)

Jan. 11, 1858.

My dearest Ellen,

The God of life be praised! May He make this new token of His love and care a blessing to each of you! All I trust will be well with you, as day succeeds day, in your upward progress.

Babies are solemn joys; you know it. Be the knowledge sanctified to you in training another immortal for the house of Jesus! Dear Grannie cannot pen a line to-day, as she is in all haste to be at the school; it is a new commencement under a new mistress. But she joins me in earnest love to Mr. S. and yourself. Kisses to the new one.

Ever affectionately yours,

W. H. H.

To my father's second sojourn abroad to be under the care of the Prussian oculist, and to shorter holidays in Derbyshire and Somersetshire, reference will be found in Mrs. Havergal's diary. In 1859 he began to long for a country parish of small extent suited to his failing powers; and having good ground for hoping that his kind bishop would offer St. Nicholas' to his dear and valued curate, the Rev. Charles Bullock, he prepared to resign that living and accept the incumbency of Shareshill, in Staffordshire. This was in Lord Hatherton's gift; but Hilton Park, the residence of his friend, Henry C. Vernon, Esq., being in the parish, he kindly accepted that gentleman's nomination of my father, who thus writes to Mr. Vernon's sister on the occasion:—

Lansdowne Crescent, Worcester,
Dec. 28, 1859.

My dear Miss Vernon,

And so I am to settle at Shareshill! Well I have written to Lord Hatherton, and have his courteous reply. I trust the step will prove a wise one, at least a blessed one for the people of the pasture. Some who desired better things for me, as the world's balance weighs them, would have had me wait. But higher motives, something better than the best of earthly boons, have decided me. Not a little do I think of *her,* who, with an irresistible look of heavenly sweetness, would have said, "Do, dearest Mr. H; oh, *do* come." I am sure there is a large phial yet to be poured out of the prayers of herself and her sainted sister. And you, too, will be a little host to me, will you not? Amen! and may the great Advocate add His omnipotence to it.

Should it be fine to-morrow we hope to be at Shareshill as before. Our best love.

Ever faithfully yours,

W. H. Havergal.

At different times the generous parishioners of St. Nicholas' made handsome presents to my father, either in the shape of money for the poor or in articles for his own use. In 1850 the Sunday-school teachers gave him a writing-case, "as an affectionate and grateful acknowledgment of his ministerial faithfulness, uniform kindness, and untiring zeal in the promotion of the spiritual and temporal happiness of both teachers and children."

In 1854 some "friends and parishioners," on account of his failing eyesight, and as an expression of their heartfelt sympathy in the "strange trial which has happened unto him," sent him "Macklin's Illustrated Bible," in 6 vols. folio, bound in Russia leather and gilt.

Before one of his journeys to Gräfrath a purse of £130 was presented, to be used in the recovery of his eyesight.

Both W. Laslett, Esq., M.P., and J. W. Dent, Esq., made very liberal offers for certain parochial plans, which, however, were not carried out, at least in my father's incumbency. One proposal, however, from a worthy and wealthy parishioner took happy effect.

One morning an early rap at his study door announced Mr. John Wheeley Lea; he had come to inform my father that it was a jubilee-day with him. For fifty years God had prospered him commercially, and now he was come to propose a thanksgiving offering; and to show his appreciation of my father's ministry, he wished him to choose in what way it should be applied. "Schools! schools!" was the reply. A borrowed room on Sunday, and a wide scattering of the children on weekdays, had long been a grief to the kind pastor, and doubtless this sudden answer to prayer called forth an "Alleluia! Amen." The jubilee schools were nobly and picturesquely built and arranged according to my father's ideas. Some years afterwards most comfortable almshouses were also built by Mr. Lea.

Now that his term of ministry in Worcester was drawing to a close, farewell gifts flowed in. The more wealthy of his people presented him with a purse of 160 guineas on a handsome silver salver, with a very gratifying address on the termination of his pastoral care during fifteen years. He replied to the churchwardens, T. B. Burrow, Esq., and Geo. Grainger, Esq., in writing.

My dear Sirs,

In the midst of much weakness I can find no words strong enough for the adequate expression of those grateful feelings which wellnigh overwhelm me. The gold and the silk and the silver, and the beautiful words brought me from my most kind and generous parishioners and a few other friends, are all too much and too good for one so unworthy as myself. I acknowledge them all to Him "whose I am and whom I serve." May He write in His own book all the names which you have given in writing to me!

Unworthy as I am, yet my dear ones, and especially *the one,* cannot be unworthy of the reference which your address makes to them; they have indeed laboured in the parish.

I will not attempt to say more at present, as I hope when somewhat stronger more fully to express both my gratitude and thoughts to my beloved people. I am, my dear sirs,

Faithfully and gratefully yours,

W. H. Havergal.

Lansdowne Crescent,
March 21, 1860.

My sisters, Maria V. G. Havergal, and Frances R. Havergal, also received gold watches with inscriptions.

Of the poorer parishioners one hundred and fifty contributed for a handsome library table; Mrs. Packman and Mrs. Walton of the Trinity almshouses being deputed to wait on him with an address, which he suitably acknowledged.

The teachers and children of the parochial schools presented my father and Mrs. Havergal with framed views of the church and schools, and my sisters with handsomely bound books.

And so ended my father's term of nearly thirty-eight years in Worcestershire. Its close was gladdened by the knowledge that from the effects of his ministry many would hereafter arise and call him blessed.

The following parting address expresses the feelings with which he left St. Nicholas'.

PARTING ADDRESS

On Resigning the Rectory of St. Nicholas, Worcester.

My dear Parishioners and other kind Friends,

It has pleased God to mingle for me the cup of disappointment as regards my taking leave of you. He has seen fit, by illness which has not yet passed away, to prevent my doing any of the things which I intended to do. It was my intention to preach to you and to call upon you; to meet our Sunday-school teachers and district visitors; to assemble our poor and their children in our beautiful and generously given schoolrooms; and to hold such intercourse as would be opportune in itself, and by God's blessing profitable to all. But these things I am compelled to forego.

One thing, however, I was permitted to do which I had little thought of doing. Late in the clear evening of a stormy day, characteristic, perhaps, of my time of life, I was driven very slowly through all the accessible parts of the parish. As I passed each well-known locality, and as far as practicable rapidly thought of you all, prayers and supplications and thanksgivings in your behalf were with many tears poured forth before Him, who alone knew the intention of that secret drive. The only other thing which I can do is now to address to you a few remarks, which I doubt not will be received in the same loving spirit with which they are written.

I. *I am deeply grateful for your exceeding kindness to me.* I have not to complain of any lack of esteem for my work's sake. Many generous acts in acknowledgment of it have often humbled and wellnigh overpowered me. I can never forget the liberality which met me on my first return as an eye-patient from Germany. In the autumn of 1857, at a time of common loss in our city, my need was supplied by Bank of England notes sent with untraceable privacy. Similar instances of kind feeling have at other seasons reached me. I venture on this acknowledgment of them, as no other opportunity may ever again occur.

But what shall I say of that *rain* of kindness, which in the shape of letters and presents has been coming down on mine and me for the last few weeks? May it return on yours and you with the richest luxuriance of blessedness.

And then, as to the offerings of the rich followed by those of the poor in the week preceding the last, what words can suffice to tell you the half of what I feel? The pounds of the one and the pence of the other, with the touching addresses of each, have much the same effect on me as the waggons and gifts of Joseph had upon the patriarch Jacob. At first I seem ready to faint. Then I revive with a full heart to exclaim, "It is enough!"—yea, more than enough, my beloved people. Good Lord, accept it all as done in Thy Name and given to Thyself, through the medium of the most unworthy of all Thy servants! That which puts a glow upon the whole of this moral picture is the fact of which I have been certified—that all has been done, not only without solicitation, but as with a spontaneous burst of the most hearty feeling.

In some way, which I do not understand (for I am pleasantly told not to ask any questions), it seems that a few "grateful ones in secret" have been doing a noble thing. My heart says, "O Thou who seest in secret, reward them openly and abundantly!"

My best thanks are earnestly given to our Sunday-school teachers, who have devised and effected such liberal and tasteful gifts for their fellow-helpers in my family, as well as for myself. Each article will be often viewed with the most affectionate esteem. To those teachers and our district visitors I owe much for their indefatigable exertions.

And now, last of all, but by no means the least, I thank those aged and holy women who have habitually assembled together to make prayer and supplication for me, whenever they have heard that illness or trial has come upon me. The God of all grace help them, as they have helped me.

II. *Kind as your thoughts of me may have been, my own thoughts often trouble me on your account.*

I have done nothing for you as I ought to have done. Whatever I have preached, or said, or done, is so full of stain and imperfection, that it is all as nought without the cleansing of that blood which alone "cleanseth from all sin." At the best I am but an unprofitable servant. Often have your commendations driven me to inward shame and self-abasement; for though we serve not an austere Master, yet must we give account to an infinitely holy God.

Notwithstanding, however, my countless shortcomings, I can with humble but fearless integrity say, as St. Paul said, "Our rejoicing is this, the testimony of our conscience, that in simplicity and godly sincerity, not with fleshly wisdom, but by the grace of God, we have had our conversation in the world, and more abundantly to you-ward" (2 Corinthians 1:12). Never also have I omitted, at the table of the Lord or at other suitable opportunities, to say with Zacchæus, "If I have done any wrong to any man, I restore fourfold" (Luke 19:8). In other words, if I have done any person the slightest wrong, I shall be but too glad to make the utmost amends, provided the wrong *can* be pointed out.

That *all* my parishioners are of one mind towards me cannot be expected. Were it so, I should be in a perilous position; for our Divine Lord has said, "Woe unto you when all men shall speak well of you" (Luke 6:26). Consequently, if there be in the parish any who cherish wilful mistake or thoughtless prejudice, or, alas, a secret desire to make a stumbling-block for an excuse, may He "who willeth not the death of a sinner" grant them "repentance unto life."

But ere I pass on from noticing your kind thoughts of myself, who am unworthy of them, let me assure you that there is one on whom your kindest thoughts may deservedly rest. It is but common justice for me to avow that all the hidden work of the parish—the management of the schools, of the Christmas charities, of the accounts connected with clubs and associations, have devolved on her who has always laboured to the utmost of her strength, and too often beyond it. Kind friends and all others will therefore please to understand, that her utter inability to call on any of them for the purpose of taking leave has arisen from her devotedness to me in sickness, from her sole supervision of our removal, and from the desire to leave all accounts intended for my successor in the best possible order.

III. *Let me assure you that my resignation of the living of St. Nicholas is not a matter of choice, but of necessity.*

After having been in the county and diocese for thirty-eight years, fifteen of which have been spent among you, it was likely I should wish to continue in one at least, or both. Failure of sight and constantly diminishing health have compelled me to feel that the advice of medical friends to seek comparative repose ought to be taken. While pondering that advice, the little living which I have accepted was, with others, most unexpectedly offered me. The offer came with every mark of providential intervention. One thing I especially beg you to observe—that I do not leave you for *any sort of gain.* I well know that many, among my poorer friends especially, imagine that I might still retain St. Nicholas', and leave my present most excellent and willing curate to do all, or nearly all the work. The friends to whom I allude must implicitly believe me when I say *this cannot be.* I have no space for explanation of this point, nor of others which might be named.

To leave you, even as I now leave you, with every conviction of propriety in so doing, occasions me no ordinary sorrow. Upon this I cannot dwell further than to remark that with me it is not only a sorrowful but a very solemn event. It is the closing of a spiritual account which has to be examined in the last great day. When, in that day, "the books shall be opened," the paragraph of my fifteen years' service among you will be found minutely recorded. May you and I hear it, not with anguish and sorrow, but with pleasure and joy. God grant in the present acceptable time speedy repentance to all who, during my humble ministry, have been careless or negligent. Let me affectionately warn them of the bitter consequences of personal irreligion and Sabbath desecration. Conscience will some day turn like a serpent upon them, and the recollection of the much study and the daily pains so long devoted for them may bring unavailing distress in the next hour of sickness: or plant a thorn in the inevitable death-pillow. May these few sentences be the means of inducing timely self-examination, and an honest effort to enter on a better course. To those of my people with whom, as "followers of the Lamb," I have been accustomed to "take sweet counsel," I would briefly but emphatically say, "Abide in Him!" and "Continue in prayer" for me and all mine.

IV. *It remains for me to offer a brief but kind hint or two, and to add a few parting words.*

Whoever my successor may be, I beseech you to receive him "with all readiness of mind," with the utmost candour, and with fervent and constant prayer.

Remember that he cannot carry on your parochial schools successfully unless you support them liberally. Never let him lose much precious time in repeatedly calling for your subscriptions. As the rent of the rectory-house cannot again be received, your enlarged contributions to his personal means will be the more necessary. I can thus speak for him what I could not say for myself.

Let me also affectionately counsel you to continue your support to those religious associations which for the last few years have steadily advanced among you.

And now, "dearly beloved in the Lord," having written thus far to you, in much weakness, let me assure you that whatever concerns your best interests will always be very near my heart. It will be the great joy of my remaining days to know that all your days are given to Him whose days were shortened on the cross for you. May His Spirit be largely poured out upon you, so that there may be a great awakening among you, to the diminution of all worldliness, and the increase of vital godliness. And then, in "that day," when all pastors and people must stand before the righteous Judge, may we be among the number of those who hear Him say, "Come, ye blessed children of my Father, receive the kingdom prepared for you from the beginning of the world."

Meanwhile I pray you to remember how I have endeavoured to preach and to teach the things which alone belong to your everlasting peace. My unworthy lips have declared to you not "another Gospel," but the one, pure, simple Gospel of our Lord and Saviour Jesus Christ. His atoning blood, His all-perfect righteousness, and His sanctifying grace, have been constantly and honestly set before you. On those great truths we must build for time and eternity.

"And now, brethren, I commend you to God, and to the word of His grace, which is able to build you up, and to give you an inheritance among all them which are sanctified" (Acts 20:32).

"Only let your conversation be as it becometh the Gospel of Christ: that whether I come and see you, or else be absent, I may hear of your affairs, that ye stand fast in one spirit, with one mind, striving together for the faith of the Gospel" (Philippians 1:27).

In a few days I shall cease to be your rector; but never shall I cease to be

Your grateful and faithful friend,

W. H. Havergal.

Worcester,
April 5, 1860.

CHAPTER X.

EXTRACTS FROM THE DIARY OF MRS. CAROLINE A. HAVERGAL, 1857–59.

Birthday — The "shepherd of the flock" — The school and parish — Preaching and God's Word — The Preparation Day — At Matlock — Journey to London — At Spa and Gräfrath — Serious illness — "I die daily" — Day of Humiliation — Return home — At Clevedon — Visits Durston and Lyng — Illness at Worcester — Thanksgiving Day — On Oratorios — Repeated illness.

JANUARY 18, 1857.—The birthday of my precious husband. It was the Sabbath, but, as usual, little mementoes of love, respect, and affection, given to me for him, were arranged ready for his receiving on his first rising. On seeing the various little packets he said, "Alas! how is the unworthy one remembered! God remember each. May the great Giver abundantly bless each giver!" On coming to his breakfast, on his plate was another small parcel. Guessing it to be from his little granddaughter Cecilia, then staying with us, he took it up before her and kissed it, saying, "The Lord bless the giver, whoever it is." This little fact the dear child loves to remember. He took the morning school; could not read as he hoped and intended, but preached in the evening; text, "God shall bruise Satan," etc. It was a sermon of his own dear style, a text few could handle as he.

Few know his deep inward breathings, how he lives on his God and draws all from Him. He said to-night, in answer to a question from myself, "Happy? oh yes, truly happy! But then, dear love, as you say, there will come little storms and trials—the dark opposition to truth and such like. But we have much to enjoy; yes, and we will enjoy it. Only let us try to enjoy all more in Him, and be more watchful and earnest than ever."

January 25th.—One of his beautiful sermons, all given to me *vivâ voce* before going to preach it, on St. Paul's conversion. At the afternoon school he addressed the children on the same subject. During the week an incident showed his benevolent spirit. A respectable widow with five children, who worked hard at dressmaking, was behind in her rent. The landlord would not wait, and threatened to have her things sold. On the case being brought to the "shepherd of the flock," he instantly set about to rescue his sheep from the thorny hedge, and in the course of two days collected a great part of the sum, and adding the rest set the poor widow free.

The small tenements belonging to the rectory having been sold, he now ceases to be landlord. To each tenant, on ceasing to be his, he has presented either a Bible or his own two volumes of sermons, with an appropriate address. It is sweet to hear the poor blessing him.

February 1st.—Self taken ill: so I can only note the exquisite tenderness of my devoted husband, who waits on me and administers my medicines with his own hands. I cannot put down all his holy sweetnesses, and much regret they should be lost. "Ah, dear love, I cannot say, Take up thy bed and walk. But One can; you are in better hands than mine, and He who afflicts loves you with better love than mine."

Sunday, February 22nd.—A most earnest and faithful sermon from Luke 5: the leper. He followed it up closely in the afternoon address at the school, bidding the children tell him of Gehazi's lie and consequent leprosy, and bringing home to the conscience of a boy he knew had been very guilty during the week, the consequence of a lie. This was unknown to any one in the school save the boy himself.

February 28th.—Greatly troubled in consequence of a gin-palace being opened in his parish. O Lord, forgive! Earnest in prayer for them. Saw a parishioner coming from an hotel tipsy; went next day and told him of his sin, and also to the inn.

March 6th.—Evening prayers: "Call us, O Lord, by Thy Spirit, by Thy Word, by Thy doing; call us, and awake our hearts to Thy call: and awake us to-day!"

His wont is to devote his Saturday morning uninterrupted to his sacred work on the coming Sabbath. After four o'clock he does what needful visiting there may be. Every Saturday in our evening prayers he refers to it. To-day he prayed for a blessing, "that all who had been or were diligently labouring for their work might be enlarged in heart, and greatly revived in themselves, and made a blessing to others; and that all who were about to be ordained on the morrow might be faithful," etc. On his return from the parish in the evening spoke of nurse W. "She is in a precarious state, may not recover, but she is safe." This poor woman always calls him "The Father," meaning the father of the parish.

Sunday, March 8th.—In the evening spoke to me of his constant feeling—and said he thought it must be that of every preacher—that the more he preached and dug into the ever deepening mine of God's Word, how poor all his preaching seemed, how empty it was in comparison with the fulness of God's Word. "I seem to wish all unsaid that I might say it better." Hearing his curate (Mr. James) commended as having kept nicely to his text, he said, "Yes, only as we keep to God's Word and give the Spirit's meaning in those words can we expect a blessing. The less of our own thoughts or reasoning, the more of God's. It must be Christ we preach, and not ourselves; not the nice phrase or essay, but Christ and His Gospel."

March 9th.—At evening prayer he began thus: "O Lord, we bow before Thy throne of grace now; grant that we may be of those who shall bow before Thy throne of glory."

He is in his study as soon as it is light, and visits in his parish for two or three hours in the morning, and nearly the same in the evening. He often visits twenty a day, praying with the sick, and leading all to seek Him who is the alone Saviour. On Saturdays he never enters the town till afternoon, and then only to visit urgent cases, feeling the day before the Sabbath should be a "preparation" day. In our usual Saturday evening meeting for prayer, having finished the prophet Amos, he was asked what we should next take. "Go on, you cannot err; all in *that* Book is *good*." Prayed, "Even by infirmity may we glorify Thee."

Visiting a poor woman, rather an invalid; a bitterly cold day. She had just returned from her daughter, who was ill in the infirmary. She was suffering from her walk in the cold, but said she had again to go out to take work home which must go, and to be paid for it. "Oh no," said the kind pastor; "put the work in my pockets, and I will take it." The poor woman hesitated, but he was firm, and asking how much she had to receive for it he quietly paid it, and not it alone. The poor woman told me all this herself, speaking of him as her "heavenly minister;" and, with many a tear, saying he was "like his Divine Master, that he was."

April 25th.—The fourth Lent lecture, 2 Samuel 23:5. A lady calling, expressing her thanks to him for his sweet and comforting sermon, he meekly answered, "The Lord make it profitable, and then take all the praise." Another thanking him said it was a precious sermon. "Nothing in itself," he said, "all nothing; but the Lord can make it precious, and may He do so."

April 30th.—Dearest husband left Matlock this morning for London. He purposes to be at home May 2nd. He prayed that we might be mercifully preserved in our going out and coming in, that His presence might be with those who stay and those who go, bringing us together again to recount the loving-kindness of our God. On leaving Matlock, at the station some one had pencilled this verse on the wall—

> "Love not, love not—what you love will die;
> Love God—He will not die."

He instantly changing it said—

> "Love not too well—the dearest one will die;
> Love Him who loves, and lives on high;
> And then you'll love eternally."

Writing his little granddaughter Cecilia's name in a book he gave her, he added this: "May she love the Word of grace here, and hereafter live in the world of glory."

June 23, 1857.—Fanny leaving for some long-promised visits in Germany, to return, as we anticipate, with ourselves, who are (D.V.) expecting to visit the oculist in August. I accompanied her to the station for London, where she joins her travelling companions. He came to the point of the road, watching us out of sight, with hand pointing upward to signify his heart was ascending for the traveller. Who can ever tell what mercies others have received from his ever-ascending supplications! Eternity only will reveal.

July 2nd.—He was not quite well, and on lying down complained he could not get on with his sermons. He then referred to Mr. C. and himself as agreeing on general points, "but not always as to sermons." "Dear Bradley and myself have always been of one mind. Often, in comparing our feelings, the one has felt that the other just entered into all; and as to sermons, we seem ever to take the same view of a text—treat it the same, divide it the same, and both look back with increasing dissatisfaction on every sermon, always aiming at something better, and yet no sooner preached than we feel ashamed of it. How vast the treasury, and how little do we get at a time, of the Word of God."

We left home for Spa and Gräfrath, August 26, 1857. Before leaving his usual prayer ascended, that for the Saviour's sake God would be very gracious, and as He had often taken us out and brought us back, so He would graciously again; commending his dear people, curate, children, and servants to his Heavenly Father's care and blessing, and ascribing all praise to Him who is the only wise Disposer and Preserver of men.

Meeting with Lord Shaftesbury on board the vessel from Dover to Calais, and sitting by his side, he soon commenced conversation. Afterwards he said to me: "It is something to be permitted to travel with such a man; may God bless him!" We fell in with his lordship's courier and Lady S.'s maid. He spoke to them, and told them to prize such a master, and that England did not possess a better or nobler man. He then gave them each a "George Vaughan."

He was not well all the journey. At Ghent we rested all night and part of the next day. At Spa, as soon as he was in his room, he thanked God for preserving, travelling mercies.

Sunday, August 29th.—Went to the English service, where his sweet voice rose as usual in praise to his God. He was grieved with seeming irreverence of the preacher, and emptiness of his sermon. Evening, still more grieved with the haste and lightness of the preacher's manner. He said, "How important that such a place as this should have a good, consistent, holy pastor." Hoped that Lord Shaftesbury, as a member of the Continental Society, would be able to effect some good.

August 30th.—He started for Gräfrath; his care for me not allowing me to go with him, as the place was crowded, and we were expecting Fanny. He was absent four days, poorly all the time, and he arrived again at Spa September 4th, so ill as greatly to alarm me. Dr. de Leuw had prescribed. He was fearfully ill, but, thank God, measures were blessed, and he improved till Tuesday the 11th, when bad symptoms came on. The doctor came constantly; for days he had medicine every hour. My hope seemed all gone, and so I saw was his. He said, "Not my will; I ask not life. I know in very faithfulness Thou has afflicted me." His tenderness and anxiety for me were more than I could bear.

We had almost telegraphed for Mr. Carden from Worcester, but the *bureau* was closed. Fanny came from her visit in Düsseldorf, but could not be allowed to see him.

September 19th.—A better night; hope increased. He dozed a little and then said, "Oh, my Carrie, how little can you know the depth of unworthiness I feel; deep, oh how deep! In time of affliction how little avail is all, save the simple first principles: as a little child you must fall back on those. Oh, when they say to me, 'How you have comforted and nourished others,' how sad it makes me. To look back I see nothing but to make me ashamed. My emptiness, my emptiness!"

In the evening he was not so well again, but after a while was better, and said, "'In all their affliction he was afflicted, and the Angel of His Presence saved them.' Do you know those lines of Ambrose Searle's?—they suit me so—

'Not equal grace by Paul obtained,
Nor Peter's pardon I desire,
But what upon the cross was gained
For the poor thief, is my desire.'"

Sunday, 20th.—After breakfast he said, "The dear school! The Lord be there!" When others were preparing for church he said to me, "I so wished last Sunday that I could send a winged message to my assembling dear people." "What should it be?" I said. He replied, "Your unworthy absent pastor earnestly asks the prayers of his dear people during his time of dangerous illness." I whispered, "Your wife has sent a message, and perhaps at this time their supplications are ascending." He looked on me and said, "One in spirit; thank you, sweet love. May their prayers be returned by a thousand-fold blessing in their own hearts."

At intervals I read a sermon preached by the Rev. C. Forster in Canterbury Cathedral, one of a series entitled "Perilous Times, or Rationalism in the Church," on "The faith once delivered to the saints." He said, "It is an able sermon; I thank God for it."

Wednesday, 23rd.—He was fully dressed for the first time. A kind message from his curate (the Rev. S. B. James) elicited, "I thank him from the depths of my heart, and pray the Lord to sustain and comfort him." Poor Fanny had had an alarming attack of erysipelas,[1] brought on by imprudence, but as she was recovering he said, "God is better than our fears." I have omitted one little thing: as Fanny one evening bent over him to bid him good-night, saying to him, "What a gem you are!" he said, "Hush, hush, my child, your father is unworthy, unworthy—a worm and no man."

Thursday, 24th.—Sent to his daughter Fanny this message: "Her father's love, crowned by the blessing of Him who is able to do exceeding abundantly above all that we can ask or think."

Sunday, 27th.—He was wrapped in his plaid for one minute to breathe under the canopy of heaven. Tears suffused his eyes and a prayer of thanksgiving arose, exclaiming, "Oh, the beautiful hills! the beautiful sun!" In the evening he said, "We must realize this, 'I die daily.' I used to think I did; but oh, it is quite different to feel on the verge than when in health. Here I am a monument of His mercy, as I trust I am of His grace. May we live more as monuments."

Tuesday, 29th.—First time he breathed the air in the garden. Came in and fell on his knees to thank God.

October 1st.—A sweet letter from the Rev. C. Bradley to myself. He said, "Dear, dear Bradley! he is a good friend, the Lord comfort him; but it is of little consequence what he calls me, or what any one does, so that I am called by God as His."

October 7th.—The day appointed for fast and humiliation. He did not sleep the night previously, but seemed like a watchman in Israel; and when he thought I slept, I could hear his heavenly musings: "May all my people and all mine be humbled before Thee. May the hearts of all be bowed down as one man. May it be no lip service. I need to be humble. Lord, hear; O Lord, forgive. Let Thy Name be known, Thy righteousness acknowledged, Thy praise be extended over the whole earth!"

October 16th.—Left Spa for Gräfrath. Attended morning service there on the 18th, where he met clerical friends, and enjoyed converse with them. Left on the 19th, full of gratitude for the mercy to eyesight there. Stayed at Aix, and spent Sunday 26th at Liege. Arrived at Folkestone October 30th, where we stayed a fortnight, and returned to Worcester November 13th, greatly benefited and his heart deeply thankful.

January, 1858.—While all his people rejoiced at his return, none so welcomed him as the sick. One poor man, J. Packman, had prayed to be spared to see his dear minister again on earth, as he "could then die happy." He was spared, and thanked him for all he had taught him, and for bringing him to Christ. He died before a second visit could be paid him.

Dear Mrs. Usborne died suddenly February 4th. On the 10th she was interred, and my darling kept the hour with ourselves assembled in his study. He read Psalms 90 and 89, and prayed most solemnly, often utterance choked by feeling. She was a favourite niece. Morning and evening he continued to pray for the bereaved family.

April 16th.—At evening prayer he prayed that all, especially his people, should sanctify the Sabbath-day. "May they fly as doves to the windows, crowd Thy holy house, and be filled with Thy holy Gospel."

September 22nd.—Came to Clevedon.

Sunday, October 10th. Afternoon, the preacher's text, "The joy of the Lord is your strength." Afterwards my dear husband said, "The first thing here is the joy of the Lord: in what does it consist? then what is it opposed to? how comes it ours? and what have we if we possess it?" etc.; but good Mr. —— only spoke of its possession and its opposite. It is the principal thing to expound 'the *joy* of the *Lord*.' Here so many young preachers fail, laying hold of a part, and not expounding the whole of a text. We should strive to know the mind of the Spirit in every text, and be very fearful of giving any interpretation of our own."

[1] erysipelas: an acute disease of the skin, streptococcal infection causing red inflammation of the skin and mucous membranes

October 12, 1858.—Darling took me to visit the parishes of Durston and Lyng, to which he was ordained in 1816. As we entered the parish from the station, standing still and looking up to heaven he said, "The Lord look upon us and bless us; go before and follow us with His blessing."

Several old people we visited recognized him with untold joy. One good Mrs. Clement cried for joy and blessed him. He was her spiritual father, and she could hardly find words to express her feelings. She is now eighty-six, but wrote out for me the following acrostic, which my husband had composed for her son when a little boy.

D ear Jesus teach a little child,
A nd kindly hear me when I pray;
V ouchsafe to me Thy mercy mild,
I nstruct me early in Thy way.
D raw, dearest Lord, my heart to Thee,

C leanse it from every youthful sin,
L et not the least impurity
E ntwine itself for ill within.
M ake me as David was when young,
E nriched by grace, beloved by Heaven;
N or let my heart, or hand, or tongue,
T ransgress the precepts Thou hast given.

We went to see Mrs. Anderdon, of Henlade House, who used to come four miles every Sunday to hear him preach. She is now eighty-four, a true Christian. Her joy at having him once more under her roof was very great. She urged him to continue bold as ever in the faith, reminding him of what he had done.

On the 23rd we went to the house of kind Mr. Wood; and from thence he went to preach at Lyng in the morning, from Acts 15:36. Then we stayed at good Mr. and Mrs. Wills, who dated their conversion to his ministry. To Durston for afternoon; crowded churches; young and old with eager gaze, and such attention; text, Acts 14:7. Crowds after to speak and claim him as their pastor, and praying blessings on him, some walking miles to hear him. His humble gratitude is so beautiful.

A retired tradesman, who formerly never frequented church, spoke of him thus: "Ah, nobody preaches like Mr. Havergal; he teaches me what I want. I tell you what he does: he takes a text, picks it all to pieces, and shows us what is inside it, and then makes us feel it."

From morning family prayer, January I, 1859.—"And though Thy promises are new every morning, yet are they old as the everlasting hills; help us therefore ever to trust them."

February 2nd.—My precious husband was taken alarmingly ill on his return from his parish walks in the evening, and I sent for Mr. Carden. He was better before night, and took family prayer as usual, praying "the Great Physician to take soul and body under His Divine care, to do with both as He saw best, and prepare all for any event, enabling each to lie in His hands in full and perfect hope."

February 3rd.—He was very ill again. Mr. Carden ordered perfect quiet and great care.

Friday, 4th.—On my telling him of the kindness of our good curate, Rev. Charles Bullock, and his wife, he said, "Ah, they are very pleasant, but God will have us learn the danger of all pleasant things on earth; and so sends a crook in the lot, and on the right person too. Oh yes, He knows who needs it."

February 5th.—A nice little dish made and brought for him by Mrs. Bullock. He said, "The Lord make *all* good things theirs, and reward them sevenfold."

Sunday, 6th.—The bell ceasing for service, he said, "Now hush!" closed his eyes and clasped his hands: "Now, Lord, be *there,* help Thy servant, bless Thy Word, sow the seed, water it, and make it bring forth abundantly."

February 9th.—He sat up for first time. Presently he said, "Ah, my sweet, I want—ah, I want *a trinity.* I want to be all thankfulness, all holiness, all devotedness."

February 22nd.—He was able to be moved to Clevedon. Many kind presents and inquiries followed us. During our three weeks' holiday I read to him Mrs. Schimmelpennick's Autobiography. He was deeply interested, but thought there was too much false liberality in the early part of it; he knew her. Also read "Godfrey Massy, the Faithful Shepherd." He was so pleased with it he wrote to the author, and a pleasing correspondence began.

May 1, 1859.—Thanksgiving Day. A wondrously powerful sermon; it cost him much study and prayer; 2 Samuel 22:48–50. So bold and truthful, warning against frivolity, etc., a ball having taken place in the week, and some of his congregation present. In the evening he said, "How little do the mass of our people look on these momentous times otherwise than with political eyes. How different the Christian. The former can have no rest or comfort; all must be vague. Not so the Christian. With his Bible in his hand he watches all, guided by this unerring Word. He sees how all must be fulfilled, and how all is being fulfilled; he feels all will go on till the all is accomplished, but he remains in peace, unmoved in spirit, while around there is turmoil."

December 3rd.—Speaking of a poor woman, one of Christ's rich ones, whom he had been praying with, he remarked, "Ah! she is a blessed one—one wing in heaven, though a foot yet on earth."

December 4th.—He had preached on the Bereans, being the second Sunday in Advent, and remarking on some good poor people he said, "They are God's gentry. As I said in preaching, many of God's kings and queens live in cottages."

Speaking of an intended visit to the Bishop on particular business, he said, "I shall want great grace and wisdom for my interview. I cannot do without."

On Oratorios.—Not as singing in worship—different. Allowable to use Scripture so, known to have converted men. One instance related by Dr. Hodges: in the chorus "He shall reign," a Socinian was so converted; in tears he went home, studied his Bible, and was converted. An artist represents Scripture scenes; some look on with a right eye, others only artistically. So with oratorios: one goes as a sacred pleasure to hear holy words given in their sweetest and most winning manner; others only listen to the music artistically;—because all see not aright, that is no argument why it is wrong.

January 31, 1860.—On my adult class of lads presenting me with a touching testimonial, he bid me thank God and take courage; and remarked how sweet it was to him for me to have this gift.

February 18th.—He said, "What can I do—how preach a farewell sermon? Lord, help me!" Miss Passey sent a beautiful *déjeûner* tray to us unitedly. On my placing it before him, he said, "The Lord reward her abundantly, and give her to drink constantly of the cup of His love and consolations."

March 3rd.—He was very poorly this morning, but set out to see an old parishioner, now living in another parish, who is ill, and sent for him. Knowing she was in danger, and so feeling no time must be lost, he made the effort when not equal to it. The consequence was, he became so much worse he was obliged to take a cab in Worcester and return home. Medical help sent for, and our anxieties are somewhat appeased. He is feverish and restless, yet often in silent prayer. On his saying, "O Lord," I asked what was the petition; he quietly answered, "He knows the thoughts and desires that crowd around His holy Name." Often in a little gentle tone, as dear Maria says, like an Æolian harp, he breathes them forth.

CHAPTER XI.

"CONTINENTAL FACTS AND SCRAPS."

Protestantism in Rhenish Prussia — "Common Prayer" — Cemetery at Düsseldorf — Burial of the dead — Church bells — Romish intolerance — A Continental Sunday — The true Decalogue kept out of sight — Romish "Confirmation" — Architecture and Romanism — Gregorian music — Bell-ringing — Romish priests — "Tawdry modernisms" — The Jews and the Sabbath — Baptisms — Wedding at Heidelberg — Marriages — Sunday schools — Holy Communion — Rome out-Romed — Condition of the Jews — A Jewish Service — Notes: Civic, Rural and Miscellaneous. — Minima.

THE following notes were written by my father at different places when visiting the continent. He entitled them "Continental Facts and Scraps, chiefly relating to Rhenish Prussia, Baden, and Nassau."

I. Protestantism in Rhenish Prussia has a mean existence hardly worthy of its name. Pastors and people seem alike listless in its peculiarities, as opposed to Popery. Many good ministers preach evangelical truth with even clearness and energy, but generally in such a way as to leave the dark errors around them to propagate and prevail as though they were of little consequence, or else of too much strength to be opposed. Something may be said to excuse or account for this. 1. The political influence of Popery is so great that any vigorous exposure of its errors or devices is sure to be followed by legal troubles or penalties. Practically, pastors must hold their tongues. 2. The majority of the population almost everywhere being popish, and the entanglements of marriage, trade, etc., being great,

Protestant fervour is sadly cooled, and men cease to oppose that which in so many ways becomes familiar to them.

II. Roman Catholics on the continent seem to be either profoundly devout or capable of singular abstraction. The tinkling of bells at the altar, the coming in and going out of other worshippers, and sometimes the loud vocal service of the season, seem to have no effect in diverting their attention from the pages of their breviary. Nowhere, however, may the English churchman so vividly perceive the force of the expression "Common prayer" as by contrast in a Roman Catholic church. There is no common prayer, *i.e.,* prayer engaged in by all the worshippers at once, engaged in as a common custom by all at one and the same time. Occasionally and at some set service there is something of the sort, but the general custom is otherwise. Constantly is one priest seen massing at one altar and another mumming at another, the people variously engaged; some are kneeling before neither altar, but at one of the many image shrines; some are using one set of prayers and others silently praying; while going out and coming in, with no concern about noisy doors, is constantly proceeding. At Munster we observed that while high mass was being celebrated by the bishop and a capital orchestra in the choir, a priest was celebrating "dry" or silent mass in the nave, which was filled with a crowd of persons on their knees, beginning and ending their prayers according as they came in, with no reference to the other proceedings. Oh the beauty of the holiness of our common prayer in a congregation of earnest worshippers!

III. In some of the litanies of the Roman Catholic Church the manner in which the people respond is truly admirable; they speak out and keep good time, and that without any clerk to lead them. The like may be said of their metrical singing. Many of their tunes are the same as those used in the Lutheran and Evangelical Churches; and, as also in those churches, they sing only in unison, rather slowly, but it is earnest and universal, though generally loud and coarse.

IV. The cemetery at Düsseldorf is worth inspection, if only to see how pretty and interesting a graveyard can be made. It is less than a mile from the town, in a dry and pleasant situation a little above the right bank of the Rhine; it is about four hundred yards long and forty wide. In the middle is a lofty crucifix; the monuments are cruciform, excepting some belonging to Protestant families; many of them are elegant and costly. A considerable number of graves or vaults are fenced in with ornamental rails, having a little gate (with a lock) to admit of friends entering to train flowers or shrubs, or suspend fresh wreaths on the birthday or deathday of the deceased. On the evening of All Saints' Day the cemetery is said to present a striking and an affecting appearance. Wax candles are lighted all round each tomb. The lights being on the ground give a singular aspect to the scene as sorrowing friends and relatives pace the walks or kneel at the graves. The mixture of excited grief and promenading fashion forms a strange scene. The Church reaps a harvest from it, by the stirring of affection among surviving relatives, and the consequent payment of fees for fresh masses for the souls of the deceased.

V. Judging from what is habitually to be seen at Düsseldorf, the R. C. undertakers are marvellously clever in making the burial of the dead a very picturesque affair, having many devices to disguise death and divert attention from ideas usually associated with a corpse. The hearse is an elegant and rather fantastic-shaped vehicle, black indeed, but not sad looking; the driver wears a cocked hat. The sides of the hearse are covered with festoons of evergreen; occasionally these are joined to leafy chains, which are held by gaily dressed young girls walking by the sides. Then follow boys in white or coloured attire, carrying tall wax candles entwined with artificial wreaths of various colours; other lads and men carrying censers, holy water bucket, banners and crosses. The priests, often six or more in number, of course are the principal figures. Then comes a long train of friends and neighbours, generally bareheaded and joining aloud in a chanted litany or hymn; their train is also interspersed with banners and gold or silver crucifixes. The coffin itself is ornamentally fashioned with ribs and flutings, with a ridge-like lid, painted green, with gold or silver striping on it so as to form a cross. All these things make up a picturesque scene, and harmonize with anything but English notions of a *solemn* funeral.

VI. There are church bells throughout Rhenish Prussia of rich and beautiful tone, but there is no such thing as "bell-ringing;" occasionally three or four may be rung in gamut succession, but the ordinary practice is to ring either the whole peal or part of it pell-mell, without any order or regard to relative succession. All is confusion. Sometimes two or three men will ring eight or ten bells at once; they tie the ropes to the clapper and pull several at a time as fast as they can. It is a childish jingle, unworthy of the noble metal.

VII. It is curious to observe the policy of the Church of Rome in the exercise of her native intolerance. Where the population is considerably Protestant she is quiet; but if she is mistress of the majority, all is noise, pomp, holiday and arrogance. At Düsseldorf the two Protestant churches are built in narrow yards aside from the main streets, and not visible to passers-by. Some say they were so built because the Roman Catholics of former days would not allow them to occupy any conspicuous parts. Others say the Protestants chose these spots as being sheltered from Popish mobs, and affording less scope for missiles against the windows. Both accounts may be true—the one originally, the other by consequence. So also for safety's sake the Protestant schools are obliged to give a holiday on certain Popish festivals, or else their windows would be broken in the course of the day.

VIII. The desecration of the Lord's day is frightfully common on the continent, excepting in Holland. In Rhenish Germany and Prussia among Protestants and Papists alike this sin prevails. The Sabbath is made a sort of merry day, sobered a little in the fore-part by religious service. With very few exceptions the shops are dressed as if for a fair; it is, in fact, the chief shopping-day of the week. Country people come in to the towns to make their principal purchases, and the shopkeepers are dressed in their gayest clothes to welcome them. Hotels, beer-gardens, railroads and steam-boats, and carriages all prepare for extra occupation. Hence, in proportion to those who spend the day in pleasure is the number of those who are forced to engage in extra labour—so true is the remark, "Sunday pleasure-taking is Sunday labour-making." As a matter of course, in all the larger places, Sunday evenings are given up to all that the god of this world can desire. Theatres, concerts, balls, gamblings, and every sort of revelry and laxity have throngs of eager devotees.

Even those Protestants who profess spiritual religion are far behind English Christians in the observance of the Sabbath. Indeed, both among pastors and people there is a low tone both of feeling and conduct, and the customary violations of the day pass without any protest against them. The fairs are always held on Sunday, often close to the church, and bales of goods are lodged close to the doors, and yet the pastor walks home through the fair as though no transgression were being perpetrated under his very eyes.

IX. What reasons may be assigned for this almost universal desecration of the Lord's day? The following facts may partly account for it. The true Decalogue is kept out of sight, and rarely comes within hearing. In neither Protestant nor Roman Catholic Churches is any transcript of the Ten Commandments to be seen. Occasionally a copper-plate ornamental copy is hung on the wall in a Roman Catholic house, but then the version of the Commandments is false and treacherous, the second commandment being altogether omitted and the fourth abbreviated to "Remember the festivals!"

Thus is Jehovah insulted by the omission of all allusion to His own day, and thus are the people brought to regard the festivals of the Church in the same light as the Sabbath. The people even call a Church holiday Sunday—*e.g.*, the market people may be heard to say, "There will be no market on Tuesday (or some other ordinary day), because it is Sontag," *i.e.* Sunday. Thus by bringing down the Lord's day to a mere holiday, and elevating the mere holiday into a Sunday, the people are induced to spend all alike; *i.e.,* they do no regular work, put on their best clothes, go to mass in the morning, and spend the rest of the day in some sort of pleasure. This laxity has a benumbing and lowering effect on the mind.

Protestant pastors, say the French, when occupying the provinces, did much harm by bringing the people to a worse state than before. This may be, but the people too evidently love the evil, and the pastors do not set a good example in this respect. At Bonn, on one Sunday morning in this August, 1853, a Protestant pastor preached himself in, as the phrase is, and afterwards joined a hundred persons, clerical and lay, at a grand dinner in Key's Hotel to celebrate the event. Altogether the Sabbath question is one of melancholy import on the continent.

X. Confirmation is a somewhat different thing in the Roman Catholic Church to our own. The candidates are generally not more than ten or twelve years old. Whatever else they learn, they are taught to carry and behave themselves with effect. The crossed hands, the bended head, the undiverted look are admirably performed. While we lament for them we may well learn from them. Our candidates should behave better than they sometimes do. The female candidates at a Roman Catholic confirmation are attired in white with a long hood-like scarf or veil. In this conspicuous dress they walk about the rest of the day, and generally seem to fancy that is very fine and themselves very attractive. It is also common for the younger sisters of the candidate to be decked in the same style on the confirmation day. Hence children soon learn to connect personal finery with church solemnity.

XI. Confirmation in the Reformed Church also differs in some respects from our own. It comprises a more laborious preparation than is common in England; it is the work of a whole year. Confirmations are generally held in the summer. When one is over, candidates for the next are requested to come forward. "The pastor meets them once a week in the church for catechetical instruction. Each candidate purchases a large and usually well-bound and lettered book, in which are carefully written down answers to theological questions and notes on Scripture topics. These books are from time to time inspected by the pastor, and the amount of labour is considerable. On the final day of public examination the girls appear in black dresses. The examination too often elicits the clever girl and leaves the good one in the shade. On the following Sunday morning all the females appear at church in white dresses, which, like the black examination dresses, are scrupulously new, and in the making and the wearing receive too much attention. The confirmation service is said to be solemn and decorous. The candidates as soon as confirmed receive the Lord's Supper. After this the pastor gives to each an ornamentally engraved certificate of the fact of confirmation and communion; he also writes on it a text of Scripture, which is regarded as the motto text of the candidate for life. This certificate is generally framed and hung up in the house; great importance is attached to it, and without it parties incur difficulty in case of wishing to marry.

XII. There is a sad sort of feeling abroad among young people respecting confirmation. The year of examination is looked forward to as the dark and wintry year of their youth. To get the confirmation well over is like the passing of a barrier or fence which separates the young traveller from some longed-for country. When it is passed and done with, the young person dreams of being at liberty to follow any pleasures or gaieties which suit the taste. The certificate too is secured, and marriage is made easier. Thus, as in many another instance, well-intended regulations are perverted or rendered worse than useless.

XIII. Many a little parish along the Rhine has an interesting old church, generally Byzantine in style and of an early date, perhaps not later than the 11th century. The arches and pillars resemble our Norman ones of about the same date; the towers are strong and square, with blunt diagonally-formed spires. Architecturally the interiors are unimportant, but they form an historical protest against some of the now most essential marks of popery. There is no room for canopies, banners, or processions, and certainly none for the side altars the priests are so fond of setting up. Consequently the present garniture of these old churches ill befits the original structure. So much for the antiquity of the papal forms of worship. Old churches were not built for them.

XIV. What there is to admire in the strictly Gregorian part of the Romish service, one musical ear at least cannot discern. It is generally a gruff, noisy affair, difficult to do correctly, and when done correctly not worth the doing. When performed with the aid of the organ, it is sometimes pleasant enough; but then it is no longer strictly Gregorian, it is no more like its original self than a piece of dyed broadcloth is like a fleece of wool. The talkers about unearthly Gregorian beauties concoct an article of their own out of some original stuff, and twist and shape it into some Anglican mould or other. They then admire what Gregory never compiled, and what his successors never heard.

XV. At Obercassel we were much amused with the style of bell-ringing on the vigil of any particular day. One man would be the performer. The method was to tie the ropes of three bells to their respective clappers. These three bells formed a common chord, as the treble notes F, A, C, so that however they might be jingled the effect could not be inharmonious. But the fun of the thing was, that with two hands and a foot one man used to edify the faithful for the space of an hour by jingling petty changes on these three bells, and then tang them all together after the manner of a small Kentish fire. But this ludicrous jingling was an ecclesiastical form, a notification of a special service in the morning.

XVI. There are clever-looking and even gentlemanly-looking men among the Roman Catholic priests, but a great number are ill-looking, sly, and low-looking men of the coarsest manners, with no aspect of purity or religion about them. Some few are even interesting, from their pensive and abstemious demeanour. We have seen some curiosities of priesthood, for instance, on the deck of a steamer, when three or four priests have been walking together and talking, smoking and conning the breviary at the same time. This last exercise is a frequent practice in travelling. Whether it is done to make up for lost time, or to fulfil a certain *quantum* of duty, is best known to themselves. Oh that they all may come to the Light!

XVII. All sorts of ill-taste and desecrations are to be met with in and around the noble cathedrals and churches of the Rhineland. To say nothing of tawdry modernisms in the interiors, the walls are completely encased with paltry secularities. At Aix-la-Chapelle petty shops of all kinds are built close to the Dom or Minster church; at the east end is a dirty liquor-shop, close at the back of the wall behind the altar. At Mayence the fine massive cathedral is completely hemmed in by mean houses built into its walls. At Heidelberg a line of tinkers' shops occupies the spaces between the buttresses of the large church of the Holy Ghost.

XVIII. The Jews set a striking example to the Christians with regard to the Sabbath-day. They close their banks or shops entirely on Saturday, in rare instances only keeping a Gentile agent to do what is barely requisite. At Godesberg the principal butcher was a Jew. With his handsome wife he went regularly to synagogue on Saturday, and not a pound of meat would he sell till the evening, when the Jewish Sabbath ends. They were perfectly surprised when I told them English butchers did not sell on the Christian Sabbath. "Ah so, dat is goot!" said they. They seemed to have no idea that Christians anywhere kept Sunday with any strictness. How sadly chargeable are Protestants as well as Roman Catholics on the continent with the guilt of obstructing the conversion of the Jews! No marvel that a Jew thinks a Christian can have no religion because he keeps no Sabbath.

XIX. What the form of baptism is among Roman Catholics I had no opportunity of observing. Among Protestants it is too frequently administered in private, especially among the superior classes. At Obercassel I saw the child of a small farmer baptized by Pastor Schulzeberge. After the sermon the pastor descended to the communion table in an open space before the pulpit. The table was covered with a white linen cloth; into a basin on it the pastor poured water from a bottle. The young mother, carrying her babe, went up to the table with two young men who were the sponsors. The pastor read a form of words from a book, asked a few questions of the sponsors, and then proceeded with the service, the sponsors retiring to their seats.

In all the large Evangelical churches there are stone fonts, some of them very handsome.

XX. Marriage near the Rhine is differently conducted to what it is in England, and the betrothal is more formal. When two persons agree to wed, their agreement is made public and is considered binding. Tidings of it are sent to relatives and friends in all quarters, and the pastor names it from the pulpit and asks the prayers of the congregation for the parties. They then appear together in public, are greeted as happy ones, and allowed to associate as they please. For the actual marriage a civil contract is made at the Rath House; the bride and bridegroom then proceed to church for a religious ceremony in much the same style as with us. I saw a wedding at Heidelberg in the church of the Holy Ghost. The bridal party walked from the house of a respectable tradesman to the church. There were first four young women, including the bride, all neatly and similarly dressed in white, with wreaths of oak-leaves on their hair; then five young men, including the bridegroom, all dressed exactly alike in black, excepting white waistcoats and ties. On entering the church they went to the vestry, where they continued some time. At length they came into the body of the church, and ranged themselves before the communion table, in front of which stood the pastor, all in black, with large white bands and a new black service book. The ladies stood together on the pastor's right hand, and the gentlemen on the left. The bride and bridegroom then stepped forward alone, and went close to the railing, the others standing a little on each side. At this instant a burst of men's voices proceeded from an opposite gallery. They sang in madrigal style a soft, pleasing composition, with occasional loudness. When this was ended the pastor read a rather long address. He asked the bridegroom a question, to which he replied "Ja!" (yes); the like was done with the bride. The pastor joined their hands, made another address, gave a blessing and then retired. The sacristan then came forward with a plate and collected money from each of the bridal party. The chorus of men again burst out in louder and more chromatic composition. They sang well for a few minutes, and then all left the church. There was a considerable crowd of lookers on.

XXI. It is everywhere observable that R. C. priests encourage marriage between members of their church and Protestants, especially when the woman is one of their body. In this case she is always instructed to stipulate that, in the event of issue, the daughters at least will be brought up in her faith. When the husband is a R. C. too often the bargain is that all the children shall be educated in his religion. So vigilant and so wily is Popery in the old game of aggression. And so provident of certain injury was the wisdom of God in prohibiting mixed marriages among the Jews. God knew that the danger would always be on the side of the Jew or Jewess. It now always is on the side of the Protestant. None know this better than the priests; they calculate on gaining something for their church sooner or later.

XXII. The non-existence of Sunday schools in Germany is a sad blot on its ecclesiastical annals. They can hardly be expected to originate in the R. C. Church, for that seems only to adopt the Sunday-school system when impelled by jealousy of other religious bodies, or as a means of self-defence. But the Protestants of the Rhine nowhere, alas, provoke them to any sort of emulation, for they have no Sunday schools. They give religious instruction on other days, and seem to think that is enough.

XXIII. The position of the communion table in the Reformed Churches in Germany seems to correspond in some degree with the intention of our own Reformers, as to its position "in the body of the church." It frequently so stands in the continental churches, and generally in front of the pulpit, either close to its base, or so as to admit of walking round it.

At Langen Schwalbach the Holy Communion was solemnly administered on the first Sunday in October, 1853, which was kept as a sort of harvest festival. After an address was read to the communicants, and other parts of the service ended, the men advanced in a line to what we should designate as the north corner of the table. The minister stood at that corner with the bread, and administered a portion to two at once, repeating certain words. These two walked onwards round the east corner of the table, moving on as other two communicated, till the three sides were filled. The minister then took a cup in each hand and pronounced a short form of words, gave one cup to each of the two individuals, who retired as soon as they had drunk of the cup, and were succeeded by two others, the whole line gradually moving onwards, all the communicants standing. Then the women came up in like manner, headed by the pastor's wife. The same order was followed as before. The women took off their bonnets and left them in their seats when they went forward to the table. There were no candles on the table or elsewhere; the organist played a soft movement, and a few singers sang a hymn while the communicants were at the table. The entire scene was reverential and devout.

XXIV. There is more scrupulousness in England, at least among certain parties, than among Roman Catholics in Germany with regard to the position of chancel and pulpit. The chancel is not always towards the east, nor is the pulpit always on the north side of the nave. Instances are so common as hardly to require mention; still it may be noted that the church of the Jesuits at Düsseldorf has the chancel about due west, and the large church by the post-office has it due south. And as to the pulpit, it is as common on the south as on the north side. A practical lesson may be learned from these facts: we must not out-Rome Rome in trifles!

XXV. It is a rare thing to hear a good boy's voice in Germany—they are all thin and wiry; the voices of the men are loud and rough. The effect of the combination sometimes may be described as if a herd of bulls of Bashan were vociferating in company with a tribe of wild cats! In the orchestra, at some high mass, the effect is often very different, the sopranos being always females.

XXVI. The condition of the Jews is in many respects different from what it is in England. Here, except in London, they hold a very inferior position in the mercantile community. In Germany they hold the first commercial positions; they are among the first-rate shopkeepers of all kinds, and often the chief bankers in every place. In agriculture and artizanship they seldom engage. To find a Jewish family in an English village is very unusual; in Germany there is scarcely a village without them, and in tolerable-sized villages they are sure to have a synagogue. In such localities they are generally shopkeepers, butchers, or cattle-dealers. There is something singular in this, as in Germany no man seems spiritually to care for the Jews, whereas in England great efforts are made for the dissemination of Christianity among them. The Romanists merely pronounce an annual curse on the Jews, and the Reformed Churches take little interest in them; they either spiritualize the magnificent prophecies concerning them, applying them to the Christian Israel, or regard them in some way as fulfilled.

England alone cares for the souls of the Jewish people, and she will have her reward. They are generally in a thriving state, poverty is rare among them, and fine features and beautiful faces are to be seen among them everywhere. Like other things pertaining to the Jew, may not their singular beauty be an indication of innate national greatness which future days are to develop. In Sabbath observance, as before stated, they set an example to Christians.

XXVII. At Frankfort on the Maine there is a regular old Jewry, chiefly consisting of a long, narrow, and dirty street. The houses are lofty and black with age, built of wood which once was painted; here the Jews are huddled together. The synagogue is a plain building; adjoining it is the original one, said to be four hundred years old. It is a low, stone, arched chamber, with a gallery for the women. Only the shorter P.M. services are held in it.

On the afternoon of their Sabbath, October 15, 1853, we were politely shown in by one of the rabbis. There were about fifteen persons present, besides two women in the gallery. It was the most irreverent, heartless, and despicable mode of religious worship that is probably anywhere to be seen. The rabbis seemed low sort of men; not a knee was bent, nor a hat taken off: the service seemed to have no distinct beginning or end, but all begun and ended in saunter and talk. A rabbi in plain clothes and grey cap was the chief reader, or sing-songster, for it could not be called chanting; then our polite friend in a white wide-awake hat recited a few sentences and stooped down to kiss the large folio; a slight humming response was made. Whoever went up to read first put round his neck a sort of grey speckled shawl, and threw it off as soon as he came down. The parchment copy of the Law was then brought out of the sanctuary cupboard to the platform on which the reader stood, and after some mysterious handling of it, was carried back on the rabbi's shoulder; two or three young persons touched it in passing, and then kissed the fingers with which they touched it. Altogether the scene was childish and contemptible. The Jew is blind indeed. On one side of the synagogue is the very Gadara of Frankfort, for it is the pig-market held on Saturday, said to have been fixed on as an annoyance in old time to the Jews. Here were scores and scores of little pigs, chiefly sucklings in hampers, some asleep amid the din of the others. Unless the Jews have no sensibilities, or secretly love pork, the Sabbath market must be an odious insult.

XXVIII. It is singular that in the Roman Catholic Church in Germany there is no uniform practice as to the posture of worshippers when singing. They sit, stand, or kneel on most occasions, though in some one posture or other is most commonly observed. In cathedrals the principal ecclesiastics *sit* in their stalls, while chanting the psalms, with their caps on, but pull them off when they come to a *Gloria Patri*. Oh, the holy beauty of the arrangements which our Reformers made for England's Church!

II.—CIVIC, RURAL, AND MISCELLANEOUS.

I. An Englishman cannot enter a Rhenish city or town without being struck by the backward state of things as compared with even the ordinary towns of his own country. Inconveniences and nuisances which have long ceased in England meet him at every turn. The absence of a foot pavement in the streets is as common as it is annoying. Open gutters by the sides and across even the principal streets, the rush of spouts and dropping of eaves in rainy weather, with all sorts of odious scents, are some of the common inferiorities of these towns and cities to our own.

II. There are strange inconsistencies in the buildings of our continental neigbours. They build strong, airy, handsome houses, but care nothing for their situation. It is common to see such houses in the course of erection, or under substantial repair, in the narrowest lanes or just opposite to a focus of nuisances. They finish the ceilings of their rooms superbly or prettily, but yet have no carpet on the floor. They may have a good well and pump, but close to a cesspool. They have lots of *eau de Cologne* and flowers, and beautifully-worked articles looking so nice, and yet their passages and corridors are filled with pestilential vapours.

Then, again, they are almost rudely strict about the removal of a corpse within three days for burial and yet have no drainage, but allow heaps of pestiferous filth to accumulate close to their dwellings. At Königswinter, the house of the principal medical man was surrounded with these abominations.

III. The streets of most towns are generally clean, being always swept by women in the early morning; but as in other things, so in this the German cleanliness is superficial. There is abundance of filth where the scavenger's broom never comes.

IV. Everywhere, both in town and country, there are many taverns and places for drinking, and there seems to be quite as much drinking going on as in England. But there is not the same amount of *open* drunkenness, nor does there appear to be so much consequent disease. This I cannot account for, especially as ardent spirits are varied and cheap.

V. German shops have neither the neatness nor the exhibition of the English. It is a rare thing to see a handsome shop; usually they are mere rooms, with only the ordinary windows of a dwelling-house. There is a sad propensity to vary prices, and to impose on the English. It seems to be a popular axiom, "To cheat English customers is no crime." Those who speak French are more likely to meet with fair dealing, as they will not be taken for "English fools."

VI. The Prussians are said to be "thieves," and, as the phrase goes, "from the king downwards." Some things occurred to ourselves which did not tend to remove this odious impression. We sustained some annoying losses under circumstances which occasioned much suspicion of even respectable parties. We have also heard of instances which more than matched our own.

VII. The Germans generally have an ugly fashion of putting their right fore-finger to their nose when speaking to any one. Even a lady does this when talking in the street or at table. As soon as she begins talking at all seriously or knowingly, pop goes her fore-finger to one side or along the ridge of her nose. It looks very peculiar.

VIII. The Rhine is remarkable as being different from most rivers, in being widest and looking noblest about the middle of its length. From Mentz to Mannheim, four hundred miles or more from its outlet at Rotterdam, it is often so broad and contains so many large islets that it seems more like a lake than a river. But to talk of the "blue Rhine" is German dreaming, at least till it flows near Switzerland. For ten months of the year it is of a whity-brown colour, and so thick and impure as to have no transparency. In a calm autumn there are azure gleams in places at times.

IX. *Table d'hôte* is the soul of every German hotel. Everything gives place to it, and everything must be squared by it. And yet there is hardly anything on the continent more disagreeable to a person who values time and health. It is a tedious, messy affair, to say nothing of grease, raw ham, and raw herrings. The German order of things is first soup, then vegetables, then pudding, then meat—which often proves annoying to the Englishman who has partaken heartily of pudding.

X. The varieties of money current in Germany are occasions of inconvenience and annoyance to foreigners. Almost every petty state has some coinage or "notage" of its own. On the frontiers, natives are sometimes puzzled themselves in reckoning from one standard to another, so that people generally carry a pencil to apply on every little reckoning. These varieties of money are also an occasion for cheating strangers, especially at post-offices and railway-stations. The writer could tell of infamous frauds in this way.

XI. When cholera invades Germany, the wonder is not that so many fall, but that so many escape. Nowhere is there anything like freedom from all those habits and filthy accumulations which invite cholera. The marvel is that it does not always exist. True, many of the German streets and rooms in houses are beautifully clean; but all is superficial; the streets have no sewers, and the rooms are close to horrid receptacles of filth. Nothing but the fine climate can instrumentally preserve it from raging pestilence.

XII. The Germans are by no means an equestrian people. Saddle-horses are not common among any class. As for ladies on horseback, it would be a perfect phenomenon in many districts; only where the English resort is a side-saddle seen now and then. There is a plentiful supply of carriages in most places. Generally speaking they are roomy and convenient vehicles, commonly drawn by two horses. Their hire is cheap; four of us went from Remagen to Altenahr—about eighteen English miles—in an excellent carriage with a capital pair of horses, and returned next day; for this we paid 13s. 6d. of our money. The driver was well content with 1s. 6d. We have nothing like this in England.

XIII. It is hardly possible to have what we call "a sweet walk" in the agricultural districts of Germany during the spring months, as the people save up their liquid manure for applying it to their haricot (?) beans, of which they plant a great many. The detestable odour is so great that even windows are obliged to be closed to keep out the scent. They have also the irrational custom, now exploded in England, of leaving manure on the fields to be washed in by the rain.

XIV. "The rule of the road" all over Germany is just the contrary of our own. Thus a carriage meeting another drives to the right, and goes to the left in passing one. This difference as to the road is matched by the rule of the wife's ring: she wears it on the fourth finger of the right hand.

XV. Oxen and kine are used both in German town and country for draft. Though slow, they are very docile and efficient. Instead of pulling by a heavy wooden yoke on their shoulders, they are taught to pull with their heads. A spar of wood, padded to fit the forehead, is tied below the horns, and the trace-ropes are fastened to it. The oxen generally draw in pairs, attached to a high and roughly-built four-wheeled waggon. Both oxen and horses are kept in good condition, but they are smaller than in England. The cow is everything to a cottar or peasant farmer; with but one cow he ploughs and hauls, feeds his family, and rears calves, and at last supplies the butcher.

XVI. All pastures in Germany are mown or hand cut. No animals are consequently to be seen grazing in meadows as with us, they are all stall-fed; even sheep are kept in a pen or a hovel, excepting in some parts of Saxony, where another system is followed. The unnatural one is very convenient as preventing the necessity of partitions and gates, but must be very unhealthy for the poor animals. Their food, too, is of the coarsest description, everywhere women are seen cutting for them the rank and dusty grass and weeds on the roadside.

XVII. The absence of cattle from the fields is a great drawback to the rural scenery. The rarity, too, of a bird or any wild animal is strikingly singular. Nightingales and other singing-birds may be heard in particular spots; but during the whole spring and summer of 1853, though taking daily walks in various parts of the country, we seldom saw a bird, and only once a rabbit. No rooks nor even saucy sparrows met our gaze, and the only partridges we saw were in a butcher's shop at Heidelberg.

XVIII. Certain viands in Germany are always excellent. Capital ox-beef may be had almost everywhere, but not so large or fat as in England. Pork also is excellent; but mutton is too often lean or woolly, no doubt from the sheep having little air and no exercise. Bread is good of its sort, but the sort is seldom good; the white bread is too spongy, and the black bread, chiefly made of rye, is close and sour. Excellent coffee everywhere, and always freshly roasted. Every little shopkeeper roasts coffee each other day. The Germans do not boil their coffee, but scald it.

XIX. Some of the commodities of life are dearer than in England, as bread, sugar, salt, and candles; but meat, oil, coffee, and spices are cheaper. Oranges and lemons are very dear—a *good* orange costs fourpence. Common vegetables, fruit, eggs, and poultry are as cheap again as with us. Lodgings are also lower, and when a person can speak the language and has mastered the manners and customs of the people, so as not to be imposed upon, he may live much more cheaply than in England.

XX. In Prussia, particularly, the compulsory education of the poor is a blessing to the poor themselves and a benefit to all classes. A little consideration will enable any one to discern wherefore. German servants are on a totally different footing to English ones; they are less dissociated from their original selves, their mode of living and their style of dress. They are never spoiled by superior food and fine clothes; they are not allowed butter, white bread, nor generally meat, but live as at their own homes. The Germans do not cook large joints which servants finish, but only small portions, just enough for one meal. Maid-servants wear neither caps or bonnets, and £4 per annum is considered good wages. They easily fall back to their home style of living, because they have never deviated much from it, and yet there is more familiarity with the family than is usual in England.

III.—MINIMA.

1. The Prussians turn their apples and pears to good account. They grow them in great abundance, and instead of making cider and perry they make a delicious *kraut,* by squeezing out the juice as for cider and boiling it down to a thick treacle-like substance. They also make jam or apple jelly of a superior quality by paring the fruit, boiling and straining it.

2. The Germans have vast numbers of walnut trees; they extract an inferior salad oil but superior lamp oil from the fruit, and use the wood for articles of furniture. Why do we not grow more walnut trees?

3. The German maidens have a very pretty way of dressing their long hair: they braid it into two long plaits behind, and bring them in wreath-like style to the top of the brow, with various fastenings, either combs or silk, etc. Light flaxen hair is the prevailing sort; curls would be unsuitable, as the middle and lower class of women go about in all weathers without cap or bonnet.

4. The universal custom in Prussia is to take off the hat on entering a shop and to keep it off till you depart, even if a little girl only or a servant-of-all-work is behind the counter. Is this real politeness or unmeaning habit?

5. From Obercassel a market-boat goes every week-day to Bonn. As soon as they come opposite to the old church (Roman Catholic) of Obercassel the boatmen sing out, "In the name of God!" and instantly all the Roman Catholic heads are bowed and a short prayer muttered.

6. Smoking is carried on to an odious extent throughout all Germany. Tobacco is grown in great quantities in Baden, etc., and six cigars may be bought for a penny. Boys not in cloth, of even eight years old and under, may be seen puffing a cigar—sad to see; and wives like their husbands to smoke because, forsooth, it keeps them quiet!

7. The life of German women and girls of the lower class is incomparably more laborious than anywhere in England. They do all sorts of field-work, even the heaviest. It is piteous to see girls of fifteen or sixteen with knitted brows and furrowed foreheads, as the effect of pressure from the enormous burdens of wood and of the grass they carry for the cows. The palm for

good looks must be given to our own poor countrywomen. The German women soon get haggard, squalid, and swarthy.

8. The Germans do not understand our clerical prefix "Reverend." They call a clergyman "Pastor," and his wife, "Pastorinn." Roman Catholic priests are plebeianly called "Holies!"

9. As a people the Germans are dirty. Few wash themselves on dressing in the morning; they leave it till mid-day.

10. Germany is the land of soup. Everybody swallows it daily, and it disagrees with nobody. The secret can be told.

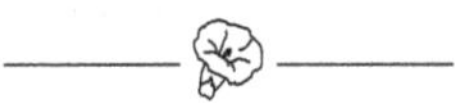

CHAPTER XII.

LIFE IN STAFFORDSHIRE.

Shareshill — Marriage of son — Birthday Letters — Rev. W. Marsh, D.D. — Parish Almanack and Address — "Firstfruits" — Letters to grandchildren — The Archaeological Institute — Ritualistic services — Lord Hatherton — Death of the Rev. James Knight — Letter to Mrs. Knight — Home letters — Letter to Dr. Lowell Mason — Return to Shareshill — Services at Pyrmont — Letters on Music — Memoranda by Mrs. (C. A.) Havergal — Restoration of St. Nicholas' Church — Retirement from Shareshill.

IN the last week of March, 1860, my father and Mrs. Havergal removed to Shareshill Parsonage, my sisters Maria and Fanny remaining with me at Oakhampton for some weeks. It was a comfortable modern dwelling in a rather picturesque country, about six miles from Wolverhampton. There was a garden and a pleasant lawn looking over green fields to the tall trees of Hilton Park; a door in an ivied wall close to the house opened into the churchyard. The body of the church having been rebuilt in the "no-century style" was not such as to gratify my father's architectural taste, but the plain old tower remained and some curious, antique monuments. It had lately been discovered that the circular end of the chancel, in the line of the wainscot, forms a whispering gallery.

The next event of interest was the fourth entrance into the state of matrimony among his children. On the 6th of September, in Hereford Cathedral, assisted by his brother-in-law, the Rev. J. Stratton, of The Precincts, Canterbury, he had the pleasure of uniting in marriage his youngest son, the Rev. Francis Tebbs Havergal, with Isabel Susan, only surviving child of Mrs. and Colonel William Martin, late of the 57th Regiment Bengal Native Infantry. Sir Frederick G. Ouseley, Bart., of musical fame, was my brother's best man. The bride was half a "Scotch lassie," and her relatives of the Mar and Kellie and Lawrence families were present. Frank, as we always call him, was then Vicar Choral of Hereford Cathedral, and shortly after became Vicar of Pipe and Lyde, and is now Vicar of Upton Bishop and Prebendary of Colwall in Hereford Cathedral. He is author of "Fasti Herefordenses," and other antiquarian works; and, like his eldest brother, himself built his own church organ.

For the next two years my father seems to have led a retired life, visiting his children only, and his kind old friends at Hilton Park, and making acquaintance with his other parishioners, who soon began to appreciate his ministry. A few letters must supply the want of other information.

(*Birthday Letters from her Father to F. R. H.*)

December 14, 1858.

I have not forgotten you. There is One who knows how you have been in my thoughts. May you be much in His, and He in yours! Another year of mercies past, and another of obligations on you. Every blessing!

December 13, 1860.

To-morrow! You know what it will be. I do not forget it. May He who gave it you at the first renew it for many a long year.

But you must be wise, without *always* having to learn the *same* sort of wisdom. You should consider your promise to *take care* as a solemn vow, and look to God to enable you to keep it.

December 13, 1861.

Every year will be sure to introduce some new trial or other to test your faith or practice. New forms of worldly*ism* are ever meeting us, and we always need new grace to "resist" them. God grant you, by His Holy Spirit, abundant peace, strength, and steadfastness.

(*To W. H. H. from Rev. Dr. Marsh.*)

Beckenham, Kent,
July 26, 1860.

Dear Mr. Havergal,

How kind of you to think of me! Since the operation for cataract, I have been able by spectacles to read the smallest print with ease. I often think what cause we have to thank God for the ingenuity given to man to help his fellowman. Many thanks to you likewise for your affecting Farewell Address, and for the beautiful missionary hymns.

You may yet live as a witness for your Redeemer's love and power. May His blessing be on you and yours! Lift up your heart for me, that I may finish my course with deep humility and fervent gratitude.

I am heartily glad to hear that our friend Mr. Bullock was your successor. You will pray for the Bishop of Worcester. I hope his health is returning.

Yours faithfully,
Wm. Marsh.

At the close of the year 1860 my father wrote the following address to his parishioners for the Shareshill Parish Almanac, which he presented to them:—

My dear Friends and Parishioners,

A few months only have passed since I came to "watch for your souls," as one "that must give account."

Life is advanced with me, and time may be very short with you. Let us, therefore, "pray without ceasing," that "the word of Christ may have free course" in our parish, "and be glorified." To forward that course, I beg to present you with an Almanac, which may help you for time and eternity.

Suffer me to commend to your consideration a few important subjects.

1. Let the salvation of your souls be the great business of your lives. Pray for the Holy Spirit to keep you from a "*dead* faith," and to make you Christians "*in deed* and *in truth*."

2. Let the Bible be the Book of your hand and heart. Let it also be the lamp and guide of your house, if you wish your children to be obedient, and your servants honest.

3. Make every effort to keep the Lord's-day holy. Avoid all *unnecessary* occupation, visiting, and travelling. Come to church regularly, and as often as possible. Manage for every servant to come at least once every Sunday. Pay weekly wages early—on a Friday, if practicable. Labourers, shopkeepers, and others should count it a shame to buy or sell on Sundays.

4. Love your Prayer-book. It was made by Reformers, who died or suffered for it. Observe its directions about kneeling and responding. Do your best to join in singing. Engage not in worldly conversation on leaving church. Always pray for a blessing on the whole service.

5. In these days of change and beguilement, hold fast to the Protestant principles of our forefathers. As your station may allow, observe "the signs of the times." "Watch and pray." "Distress of nations" may be coming. Death and judgment will come.

"Finally, brethren, be of one mind; live in peace; and the God of love and peace shall be with you."

Always your faithful friend and servant,
W. H. Havergal.

The only item of family affection which remains on record for 1861 is the present of a handsome silk cassock, in which is sewn a piece of parchment, bearing the following inscription in my father's own handwriting:—

THE LOVING GIFT

OF MY

LOVING DAUGHTER

FANNY,

THE FIRSTFRUITS OF HER PEN,

1861.

(*To his Grandchildren at Oakhampton.*)

Langen Schwalbach,
June 10, 1862.

My dear little Loves,

God Almighty bless you much through His dear Son! We often think and speak of you. Aunt Fanny will tell you where we now are, and about the waters we drink. They are sparkling and very pleasant, especially when the weather is hot. We go to the well by seven o'clock a.m. Grandmamma is very much better, and I also as to bodily health; but I always want to be better in heart and soul and as to the things of heaven.

An excellent band of stringed and wind instruments plays near us two or three times a day. The music is often first-rate. They begin by six o'clock every morning with some fine old chorale which I very much enjoy. The gardens are thronged with people of all nations, ages, and ranks. Some of their dresses are very funny and fine. I often pass a group of little Russian boys, sons of great personages; they dress most curiously. Just fancy Johnnie dressed up in a red and blue cap, white knickerbockers, with long black boots and red tops, black velvet frock coat and red sash, or in hot weather with handsome short sleeves, bare arms, a velvet vest, and strange looking appendages. At the baths are a lot of shop-recesses for all sorts of articles, stationery, boots, Tyrolese gloves, and Swiss articles carved most beautifully in ivory and wood, and lots of the most funny toys you can imagine. I must end. I hope to hear you are all of you very good, and give no one any trouble. Give my love to dear papa and mamma. God again bless you!

Ever affectionately yours,
W. H. H.

(*To his Grandson, J. H. Crane, aged six years and six weeks.*)

My dear John,

I thank you for your questions. But neither I nor any one else can *quite* answer them. Though we know when Adam died, yet it is not known *exactly* how many years have passed from that time till the 18th of the present month; learned men are not agreed on that point. It is impossible to say how many men were killed in David's reign, as every death is not recorded. No one also can say *how* wise the wise men were who came from the East to see the infant Jesus. But we know that they were "wise unto salvation." This is what I pray my dear little Johnny may be. Yes, I shall rejoice to see him become a wise and holy child, growing in grace and wisdom as he grows in stature, and in favour with God and man.

Give my love to Miriam, and Evelyn, and Constance. Tell Nanna I thank her for her kind hop pillow. I have used it and so has dear grandmamma. Come and see us in the spring.

Ever your affectionate G. P.,
W. H. Havergal.

(*To the same when just seven years old.*)

My dear John,

I thank you for your nicely written and prettily embellished letter. When I was a little boy I used to write well. I had, too, one of the best of mothers, who used to take pains with me and teach me all that was good. I bless her memory.

Like you, I was an only son, and had only one sister; you have three; my love to them all. My grandfather's name was John, and so also was my only uncle. I thank you for your Latin, only you should have written, Dulcis est libertas, not Dulce. Now let me give you a little bit. Libertas est dulcis, sed Pater et Mater et sorores dulciores sunt, Christus antem est Dulcissimus. God bless you, my dearest John, always, and may His Holy Spirit teach and strengthen. A really happy new year to you all.

Ever affectionately yours,
W. H. H.

(*From the Precentor of Lincoln to W. H. H.*)

June 16, 1863.

My dear Mr. Havergal,

I am hoping to visit Worcester next Friday to survey the ground for our proposed Archæological Meeting next July. I wish I could have had the pleasure of meeting you there, and of renewing my acquaintance with one of the earliest and truest friends of my dear wife and my excellent father-in-law, whose name has always been associated in my mind with all that is friendly and kind. But if this gratification is denied me now, I heartily hope I may enjoy it "when I next visit your city (*for yours* I must still call it), in July.

And now let me convey the request of the Committee of the Archæological Institute, that you will not only favour us with your presence and patronage at our approaching meeting, but also gratify us by giving an illustrated lecture on the subject with which you are probably better acquainted than any man in England—our early Protestant Psalmody.

Last year at Peterborough we had a very interesting lecture on the music of the Sarum Breviary, and other early Roman Catholic ecclesiastical compositions, which, though very much could not be said for the melodies themselves, greatly pleased our friends. We now wish for a pendant to that lecture; and meeting at the city of whose cathedral you are a Canon, we feel we have a claim upon you for such an illustration of our more glorious Protestant Church music, as may show the superiority of Protestants in this as in every other essential respect.

It would gratify us very much if I could receive a few lines from you announcing your kind willingness to take this matter into your consideration. A more formal request shall then be forwarded to you by our secretary, Mr. Albert Way, who has begged me to indicate to you thus unofficially the wishes of our Institute. With Caroline and Emily's sincerest regards,

I remain, dear Mr. Havergal,
Yours very truly,
Edmund Venables.

(*Description by W. H. H. of the services he attended at All Saints' Church, Margaret Street, in February,* 1863.)

Saturday, Feb. 21, 5 p.m.

Three excellent bells tolled briskly for ten minutes before service. When they ceased I heard from towards the clergy-house a mutter followed by an amen of boys' voices intoning. This I took to be a sort of priests' introit near the entrance. As soon as the four officiating clergy entered the congregation rose, when they kneeled the congregation knelt. This is neither an English or a Romish custom. Some but not all bend the knee and bow towards the (so-called) altar. This is Popish, and was done just as is common on the continent. A bearded priest began intoning; his voice was a rough tenor without feeling. On coming to the Lord's Prayer he pronounced the words "Our Father" alone, the response commencing "Which art in heaven." The same process was observable in the Creed, "I believe," by the priest alone, etc. This is neither English nor Romish, but in my judgment incorrect. The chant to the Psalms was (so-called) Gregorian, the organ playing steadily, but with very equivocal harmonies now and then. At the *Gloria Patri* the Priest Precentor turned right round to the east, as did some of the congregation, and all bowed their heads, and held them so till the Amen. This is neither home nor foreign. The *Magnificat* and *Nunc Dimittis* were chanted to another Gregorian; the effect to me was sing-songy, and the slurring of some two or three notes together was distasteful. This sort of Gregorianism is mongrel and hybrid. It is not in use on the continent, and certainly it cannot be like what it was in the 6th or 7th centuries.

After "Lighten our darkness," a hymn was sung in unison by choir and congregation very neatly and in good time. The service altogether did not impress me as *devotional.*

Sunday morning, Feb. 22. Full church. All much the same as the preceding evening till after the Creed. Only the Psalms were more gabbled and the *Benedicite* sung to a Gregorian, which offended me much. The mixture of triplets in the *Benedictus* was most odious; I felt the want of that noble distinctness and masculine pleasantness which marks our best Anglican chants. The harmonized responses in the Suffrages, "O Lord, let thy mercy," etc., were new to me, and dramatized by softening and swelling. In the preceding "Lord, have mercy upon us," a liberty of repetition was taken, which I had not before even heard of, and the words were toned down in a sort of *Miserere* style. For the anthem we had a hymn, "Forty days and forty nights." It was well sung by all, and the tune was worthy of "Old Church Psalmody." After it came the prayer of St. Chrysostom, and "The grace of," etc., a sort of shortening quite new to me.

The choir sang twice without the organ; it seemed to want bass.

Then came the sermon. The text was Matthew 18:19. The sermon was chiefly on the duty of prayer during the Ember week. Many good things and some ill ones were said in a free and easy style, *e.g.*, "Prayer and patience are the weapons of our victories." I thought of faith which overcometh the world. He also said, "The effectual, fervent prayer of a righteous man, viz., one who is wistful of being righteous," etc.! Not a syllable about Who is to help us to pray. Much said about truth, but no definition given nor any holding up of Christ. Altogether the overwrought place and its modes sadden me.

W. H. H.

Among my father's pleasant ministrations during his residence at Shareshill were his visits to Lord Hatherton, the patron of his living. In his long illness he requested an interview at least once a week, and with thoughtful kindness provided a carriage for the long drive to Teddesley Park. He much valued the conversations and prayers on these occasions, and on the last visit emphatically thanked him, saying, "Mr. Havergal, you have taught me two things, that I am a great sinner, and that Jesus Christ is my great Saviour."

On one or more occasions, by Lord Hatherton's wish, my sister Frances accompanied her father, that, in an adjoining room, he might hear her voice and touch on his piano. Thus was her skilful "Ministry of Song" appreciated by the solitary invalid, as it was in following years by assembled hundreds.

After Lord Hatherton's death both his son and heir and his widow wrote in most grateful terms to my father. Lady Cavan wrote:—

Having perused with the deepest interest the little sketch you have so kindly drawn out of your interviews with my dearest father, in which an uplifted Saviour brought peace and joy to his soul, I cannot refrain from sending you a word of thanks most earnestly felt; for though Mr. Fell was most faithful and affectionate and my father highly prized his visits, "In the mouth of two witnesses shall every word be established," and "The Lord is with them that uphold my soul"; and the ever "new song" needs often repetition to be learnt here below.

Among all classes in Shareshill, and especially among the "poor and needy," my father was most assiduous in pastoral visits. I regret that no written anecdotes or observations on these remain, but doubtless many hearts still rejoice in their remembrance, and many lives are benefited and enlivened by their effects.

In August of this year died the Rev. Jas. Knight, to whose widow he thus writes:—

Shareshill, September 1, 1863.

My dear Mrs. Knight,

Lucy was right in saying that you knew I should sympathize with you. How could it be otherwise? I have known and loved him for forty-eight years.

From 1815, as you know, I have felt that in him I had a true-hearted brother. But our great elder brother of all had a gracious right to call him to Himself sooner than we expected. *It is well.* That is enough for a sorrowing heart, if said in full faith and in unfeigned submission.

Yes, I know, without fear of presumption, that it *is well* with him. We have no power even to imagine the real blessedness of the change to him. Only let us press on to know it ourselves, through the Saviour's love to our own souls. May it be well, *well* with you, dear friend, now that a widow's lot is assigned you. It *must be* well, for you have also the widow's God. He is nowhere called the God of the *widower,* but only of the widow. There must therefore be a special blessedness in that new relation to our God on which you now have entered.

And may it be well with all your dear children. May they follow Christ as their father followed Him. Thus will they be comforted under all trials: he had many. They will be loved by the wise and good, and at length come to an honourable end and a crown of glory after it. My love and sympathy to them all. Tell them that, for their dear father's sake, I shall always be glad to see them or hear of them. My dear wife weeps with you, for she loved and admired her husband's friend. God's best and lasting blessing.

Ever faithfully yours,

W. H. H.

Mr. Knight was for thirty-six years the Incumbent of St. Paul's, Sheffield, which living he resigned four years before his death. He and my father ran an amicable race in buying up rare editions of the Bible, and wrote to one another when a fresh Biblical treasure was added to their collections.

In 1864, owing to the ill-health of his wife and himself and the difficulty of finding a suitable curate, my father seems to have thought of resigning his living, and saw the Bishop of Lichfield on the subject, for whom he had a great regard, and often said he felt towards him as a real "Father in God."

In the absence of other memoranda some letters must now carry on the history.

(*From Dr. Kempe.*)

Hereford,
July 8, 1864.

Rev. and dear Sir,

Accept my grateful acknowledgments for your valuable present of sermon and music. I shall treasure them up as relics representing the labours of one whose name and compositions are identified with my first sympathies for contrapuntal studies.

As a pioneer in resuscitating our ecclesiastical music from the degrading and meaningless flippancy of the last and beginning of the present century, it must be gratifying to you to witness the vast and increasing hold which the church music of a former century is obtaining on the public mind. May you long live to see its influence extending, and

Believe me to remain, dear sir,
Yours most respectfully,
Geo. Kempe.

Shareshill,
July 9, 1864.

My eldest and not least beloved Granddaughter,

Monday next will be the day of your natal majority. It will be an important day to you. May the good Lord make it a blessing to you. He has kept and prospered you hitherto, in all the youthful and domestic scenes through which you have passed, and He alone can make all your future days honourable and happy. Then, dearest Miriam, spend this day *with Him*. Amidst all the congratulations that will be sure to meet you, let Him be your first and last Friend. Seek His Holy Spirit. Ask for much softness of heart and earnestness of mind, that you may see present life in its true colours, and aim at securing the future life just as His Gospel tells you how to seek it. You will in future days be a *happy* woman just in proportion as you are a true Christian. It seems but a few weeks since I became twenty-one. "So soon passeth it away and we are gone." Never forget this fact, and *time* will then always be right with you.

But, dearest Miriam, all is haste to-day, as mamma will tell you. My precious one cannot write to you, nor can we send you our little birthday tokens, but in a while.

Ever most affectionately yours,
W. H. H.

Langen Schwalbach,
September 9, 1864.

My dear and much loved Children,

Your father has you all in his heart—you, I know, have him also in your hearts. May the Spirit of our only Saviour be constantly on all. As I am to write as little as possible, I will be brief as possible, and leave my devoted one to tell you all general things. Thanks to God, she is wondrously well. I too am now much better, but my eyes are not greatly improved. Dr. Meuser says they are not essentially worse, but that they are very weak and extremely sensitive. I must be more careful to avoid light, and hence I am to wear blue glasses whenever I go out in fine weather. This is an exception to a general rule; I already find great comfort from them. All this you will, I know, like to hear.

(*To his Children.*)

Langen schwalbach,
September 14, 1864.

At length my eyes seem on the mend. The utmost I must expect is not to lose ground and to secure strength for the eyelids, which are the most troublesome part. Let Him who "made the eye" do as He will. A remark of Dr. Müller of this place led me to ask him, "Well, and how old do you think I am?" He replied, "Oh, between fifty and sixty." When I told him the reality he looked incredulous astonishment. "Well, there's not such a man in all Germany!" How great, my dear ones, ought my gratitude to be! But oh! what an unprofitable servant have I been! Lord, make my coming days, if any, better than hitherto they have been! These things are ever uppermost in my thoughts; I know my years cannot be many. My spirit is painfully stirred within me on the subject of clerical representatives of our Church on the continent. Such inefficient chaplains! Would that I were more at liberty than at S—— as to absence!

I am concerned at Frank's rheumatism. It is what I dread for him in his ever residing on the clay at his living of P. and L. May the God and Father of our Lord Jesus Christ give to all of you just that grace which you severally need. This poor life must soon pass away. Let us strive more and more for the blessed assurance of an *abundant* entrance into the everlasting home.

Ever most affectionately yours,
W. H. H.

(*To his Daughter, F. R. H.*)

Shareshill,
May 3, 1865.

Darling Fan,

Give all your pretty musical plans to Æolus to make harmonic sport with, for I am not at all competent to meet them. If we come to Oakhampton it will be on Tuesday next, and home on Saturday. You will, I guess, see some alteration in me. I do not regard myself as ill or broken, but a little shaken and warned. It is all right and well, even if I do not fully rally again as Dr. M—— thinks I shall. For some time past I have been in an unfixed state, and that has done me ill. What to do for the future as wisest, discreetest, best, I see not yet: you shall hear when we come (D.V.) Dear Maria is not well. The Notts go to Bayton tomorrow. We were pleased with Arthur: God spare and bless him. All love to all. Papa always thinks of, loves, and prays for his dear little Fan more than she supposes.

Ever your
W. H. H.

(*To his Son, Rev. F. T. H.*)

Elizabeth's Ruh, Ems,
July 19, 1865.

My dear Frank,

We arrived here late on Saturday. Fearfully hot travelling. Saw the Hofrath, Dr. Spengler, on Monday. I drink 6 oz. of the water at

6 a.m., another 6 oz. at 7, and take a bath of 80° at 9.30; and 6 oz. water at 5 p.m. This I am assured will do me good. Ems is a most lovely spot, a vale closely surrounded by wooded hills, with a sweet river. Hours are early. A capital mixed band near the drinking-fountain. A beautiful little Gothic church, but a Romanizing chaplain. I am indignant. Upon the whole I am rather better, but feel the heat banefully. We are here for three weeks at least. If you can take a trip we will board and lodge you. From London to Antwerp, on by rail *via* Cologne, and on return go down the Rhine. See the *Record* of Monday last for a letter of mine about Ostend. Love from all to Isabel and you. God's blessing!

Ever your

W. H. H.

(*To the same.*)

Ems, August 5, 1865.

My dearest Frank,

This is likely to reach you on your birthday. The God of life bless it to you! May He long spare you to be a blessing to many souls, and to us and all yours. Learn more and more to see all things in the light of Gospel truth, Christ the only Redeemer and the great Providential Preserver. All else is vain; I find it so. We all longed for your coming in the fine weather; now we have such cold rains. The change falls sadly on many here. I wished you to see Ems because it would give you a synopsis of the whole continent. The noble band is a charm for me; the morning chorale at 7 is fine indeed. Dear C. is, thank God, again herself, and Miss Nott is flourishing. All say I look better, but the main evil is not removed. We go to Schwalbach on Tuesday (D.V.); I long to be there. All love to you and all.

Your

W. H. H.

(*To his Children.*)

Langen Schwalbach,
September, 1865.

My beloved Children,

You have heard how the God of love has been dealing with me. He is righteous, even when He tries most severely. I, no doubt, was very ill, but again I am better; I am feeble and thin: all this of external things, the internal I can but little recount. My days of illness were days of deep humbling. I found I was a "worm and no man." I wish to lie at the lowest step of the saints' gallery. I thought intensely of each one of you—what if I should never see you again? But I was not distressed; I could leave all with confidence in the Saviour's hand. All is of the Lord. I bow, amen. Only pray for me: I need all grace. I have had the most tender, sedulous nursing by night and by day.

Your

W. H. H.

(*To his Son, F. T. H.*)

Poppelsdorfer Allée, Bonn,
Dec. 6, 1865.

My dearest Frank,

We have not heard of you since you left Edinburgh. Did you see Dr. Hodson, and what did you make of him? Before this reaches you you will have seen Miss Nott, and have heard all she can tell. Bonn suits us, myself especially. As Fanny is to start on the 18th on her way to us, please send to her any reading you may like us to see. Alas for Dr. Pusey's "Irenicon;" I hoped better things after his noble stand against neology. Nothing will ever stand but the simple truth in Christ. The *Elijah* in German was performed here a week since. I dared not go. The weather has been fine and open, no such winds and rains as have been in England.

The cathedral has some fine bells, which I much enjoy—I mean as to the harmonics, *ex. gr.*, in pitch according to Novello, Bass E flat, D, C, B flat. They are jingled and jumbled, not rung in sequence, and only half up, *i.e.*, in a swinging style. The largest bell takes four men. Dear C. hopes you have the *pro bono* letters she sent.

(*To his Grandchildren at Celbridge Lodge, County Kildare.*)

Bonn, Jan., 1866

My dear little Loves,

I cannot write to each of you separately, so I write to you all as one. The Bible, you know, is just in that way. It is God's Word to each and all at once. I thank you for your nice birthday texts. May the Holy Spirit cause all their blessings to come on you! I often think of and always pray for you. I long to hear of not one ever being naughty, but each always good. You are, my dear little ones, more highly blessed than most children. Few have such parents and such a home as you. Be thankful, and remember you must give account. Give my kind wishes to Harriet. You must be very good to her as she belongs to my parish. The God of love bless you!

Ever your affectionate

Grandpapa.

(*To his Grandchildren at Oakhampton.*)

Jan. 24, 1866.

My dear, dear Grandchildren,

I pen a few lines to you all as one. I thank you for your nicely-chosen texts on my birthday. May all the blessings they contain be fully realized by you, through the grace of the Holy Spirit by whom they were inspired. Be assured that I fail not to pray for you, that every failing may be diminished, and every indication of good abundantly increased. But you must pray for yourselves; unless you do no other prayers are likely to benefit you. You have the kindest parents; you must love, honour, and obey them.

I am your most affectionate

Grandpapa, W. H. H.

(*To his Son, F. T. H.*).

Bonn, Jan. 24, 1866.

Dearest Frank,

Fanny is to start to-morrow, sleeping at a friend's at Lille, and hoping to be in London on Friday. She has been well, and says Bonn always agrees with her. She has won more musical laurels in Germany than I care for her to wear. It has been a great disappointment that I have not been able to sing with her, or go out much with her, as I have had influenza and toothache. I am ashamed of the scurrility and childishness, not to say popery, of such papers as the *Church Times.* What babies men can be! All blessings on you and yours.

Ever your

W. H. H.

(*To Dr. Lowell Mason, of Boston, U.S.*)

Poppelsdorfer Allée, Bonn,
March 5, 1866.

My dear Friend,

Your letter has just been welcomed. I hasten to reply to it as well as my eyes will allow. I can hope only for less dimness of vision at the most. At this distance I dare not advise you; possibly an operation may restore you to perfect sight spite of advancing years; I have known many such instances. The good Lord favour you. I can keenly sympathize with you. I feel that I write worse than I did, and can read only large church print for a few minutes; but all these things, though trying, are but light afflictions compared with what might be. Then our great standing mercies in Christ Jesus, how precious are they! May they abound to you. Only my dear wife is now with me and one of our home servants. My parish is left in good hands. I regret to hear of the popularity of Robertson's sermons in America. There is much of splendid trifling in them, with "fair speeches" on behalf of erroneous novelties.

As to music I do but little, although I cannot keep from nibbling at chants and metrical tunes. I have fifty varied forms of the Grand Chant,[1] and have one hundred other chants, mostly single, ready for publication.

All that has been passing in America has engaged my anxious attention. In dear old England Church matters are perilous, though I hope for the best by reason of the Bishops having spoken out well on *ultra*-ritual movement.

Here, as in England, we have had no winter yet. My own parish is still mercifully preserved from cattle-plague. My old friend Dr. Hodges is gradually failing at Bristol. My dear wife is better, and joins me in best regards.

Ever faithfully yours,

W. H. Havergal.

(*To his Daughters, M. V. G. H. and F. R. H., at Oakhampton.*)

Shareshill, April 16, 1866.

Dearest Maria and Fan,

All mercy and goodness, blessed be the Name! I hasten to sketch you a little of yesterday. At 11 a.m. found the tidy church well filled. Began with the morning hymn on the "grinder," which is far better than I expected. Mr. Rushton in the desk. The Vernons all there. Guess my surprise to hear the *Venite* chanted in good style to "Havergal's Worcester Chant:" the same to the *Glorias.* Then Dr. Boyce's chant to the *Te Deum* and *Jubilate* in really fair mood. Then the metrical psalm, lo and behold, to St. Nicholas! and the L.M. hymn to Waldeck. Much the same in the afternoon—my tune, Astley Wake, S.M., etc.

You can hardly picture my pleasure and astonishment. I afterwards found, from a list of the barrel tunes, that with few exceptions all are from my "Old Church Psalmody," and all the chants such as we had at St. Nicholas'.

I was marvellously helped through my sermon, new, from the old text, Hebrews 13:17. Afternoon, from 2 Corinthians 4:5. All most attentive. Treble the congregations that used to be, I am afraid to tell you how cheery and promising all things seem. There must be a crook in the lot. Amen. All love to all.

W. H. H.

(*To Mr. and Mrs. Shaw.*)

Pyrmont, May 30, 1866.

My beloved Son and Daughter S.,

What mean ye to break mine heart? Yes; but not with any hammer of iron, but with the soft mallet of love. The God of my life bless you both abundantly, and especially my good son, for all that has been and is in your hearts! I am unworthy of the least goodness from the Triune God of our salvation. I thought that my dear E. clearly understood what I said before you left us last week, when she mentioned her husband's wish to pay the stipend of my curate. I distinctly but affectionately declined the proposal, and begged that it might not be entertained or mentioned.

Accept an excellent book, "End of All Things," by Mr. Grant, editor of the *Morning Advertiser*. Heart's love.

Ever yours,

W. H. H.

(*To H. V. Tebbs, Esq.*)

Geneva, Sept. 8, 1866.

Thanks for yours last evening on arriving. I am heartily glad to hear from you after so long silence. We wintered at Bonn, went to Pyrmont, and, after further benefit, have reached thus far through Switzerland on our way home; but my *locum tenens* is obliged to leave on account of his wife's illness, and spite of all efforts no curate can be found for me, though I offer £120 for assistance only. My poor eyes prevent my writing about wonders and beauties. Suffice it to say the daydream of life has been favourably realized.

(*To the same.*)

Shareshill, Oct. 8, 1866.

Our God brought us home on Tuesday last all safe and well, excepting a check from a slip downstairs at Oakhampton the preceding evening. It shook me much; blessed be the unseen Hand for holding me up from a more serious fall. As no help could be obtained I took my whole two services. My worthy clerk read the lessons, and the Lord helped me marvellously. Yours to Shareshill reached me safely. Yes, Bonn, not Rome. I would not willingly winter at the latter place; the expectation of its "millstone"-like destruction is always before me. The predicted reality cannot be far distant. "Eternal city!" vain appellation—its very vanity is a part of its doom. Loving thanks for all your kind plannings. You amuse me with your old combination of playful imagination and sound judgment. The difficulty of

[1] Early in 1867 J. Shepherd published, "The Grand Chant in Forty Different Forms." By the Rev. W. H. Havergal, M.A. Op. 52.

finding a good helper is great indeed, and I cannot give a title now. I can only be still and trust.

(*To his eldest Daughter.*)

Feb. 12, 1867.

May all your daughters, dearest Miriam, be to you as you are to me! The Lord the Spirit can do this for them and you. I thank you for all your thoughtful kindness. The good Lord return it to you. Just now I am busy in expectation of a new *locum tenens* curate. Fanny will tell you all about this and other matters; I shall be glad of quiescence as to them all. I consulted Professor Plito about my old Bohemian *Gesang Buch,* and sent it to Professor Kraft, who is enthusiastic about it, and thinks it is unique and a first-rate gem. My heart's best love to you and each of yours.

In February, 1867, my father published a little book entitled, "Pyrmont, an Eligible Place for English Patients who require Chalybeate or Saline Waters." (J. Nisbet & Co.) The profits were devoted towards preparation for English service at Pyrmont; thither he proceeded with Mrs. Havergal in June, and remained nearly three months.

(*Memoranda by W. H. H. at Pyrmont, 1867.*)

Arrived on Saturday, June, 15. No English besides ourselves, nor English-speaking visitors.

Speedily got the large inner room of the Friends' or Quakers' meeting-house put in a tidy state. It had been closed for many years, except as a storeroom for grain and garden produce. When Mrs. Elizabeth Fry "held forth" in it, there were, it is said, three hundred persons closely packed together. The use of this room was obtained chiefly by the kind intervention of Herr W. J. Seebohm.

In 1866 we had found many Americans and others who could speak English lodging in the town. But this season the Paris Exhibition was thought to forestall everybody. Still, a printed notice was prepared; but no arrivals were announced in the *Kur-Liste.*

At length, in the week preceding August 18, we heard of several. Accordingly, in the afternoon of that day, after sending word to all we could discover, Church of England service was, for the first time in the history of the building and even of the town itself, held at 4 o'clock. A goodly and grateful congregation of nineteen made the "little sanctuary" look encouragingly pleasant. My text was Matthew 18:20, "Where two or three," etc. We had previously sung "Jesus, where'er Thy people meet." Many of the few seemed to feel that the promised Presence was indeed granted.

Sunday, August 25th.—Congregation, twenty-three.

September 1st.—Only eight were present—Miss Pollard being one—as a severe storm of thunder, hail, and rain set in just before the time for service. Commenced a collection this P.M., which amounted to three thalers.

September 8th.—Congregation, twenty-one. Mr. and Mrs. Johnson from New York, Mrs. Knight and mother from Copenhagen, Mr. Collins from Harefield, etc. Great attention. May it have been watered with *the* dew! Collection, 6 th. 8 gr.

September 15th.—Rainy and dark; congregation, twenty.

September 22nd.—No service. A sharp east wind had made many invalids. Half our expected congregation were unable to go out. I was ill in bed and Mrs. Havergal also. When God deals thus decidedly with us, we may well submit and be patient.

Sunday, September 29th.—Congregation, seven. Boisterous wind and driving rain, but the "pilgrims" came. The Lord was indeed with us. Glory to Him! Amen.

(*To the Rev. J. P. Metcalfe, of Bilbrough Rectory.*)

September, 1867.

My dear younger Friend,

With reference to Dr. Monk, I can only say I am open to any aid which I can render in the cause of Church music, but my ability is sadly lessened by failure in eyesight. My inability to read, especially choice music, is a great trial. Others can read *words* to me, but I must read *music* myself to thoroughly understand it. All your kind sayings I shall cherish. I thank you for the handsome volume of "Catches," etc., and for your introduction to Mr. Macfarren. About this time last year I saw your good brother, Dr. M., at Geneva. The interview was I think mutually agreeable. Of course Canterbury was a rallying-point of conversation. Your account of the change in Mr. M. deeply interests me. May the God of all grace perfect the work thus begun. Dr. R. is no great musician, but a first-rate antiquary. I have lots of little anthems, but they are scattered in print or MS. "Mr. Havergal composes *pretty* tunes," etc. Well you shall have some of them when I am able to look them up. My royal round is one of several. Our school-children used to sing it ringingly. I fancied the little introit canon would please you. I have very funny things of that sort and carols also. In the forty Grand Chant specimens are things of the kind in abundance, so that ears that like perpetual repetitions may revel. "*Ars celare artem,*" is my motto in such doings. I like no art in music unless it is sensible and pleasing. Because so many of the Psalms are artificially composed, I like a little of the same principle brought to bear in chants to them.

I have a theory of popular, and I think primitive, chanting, of which you shall hear some day; but I dare not go on. All through life I have looked on music only as a pleasant means to a gracious end. I see many abuses and watch them. In these days we need vigilance.

Ever faithfully yours,

W. H. Havergal.

Respecting March and April, 1867, Mrs. (C. A.) Havergal has left a sheet of memoranda.

March 24th.—Reading the second lesson for evening service. "A faithful and precious chapter; the Canaanite woman's prayer is mine. Strange that I should so have preached to and for myself." In allusion to this and his last Sunday morning sermon, preaching for first time after five Sundays' seclusion from laryngeal attack.

March 27th.—Through the day often in quiet prayer. So calm and trusting. At the usual time for our reading he asked for it, fancying I was thinking him too poorly to hear.

March 28th.—Dr. Millington visited; darling prayed for a rich reward on him. No anxiety visible, but knows his precarious state.

March 30th.—Being told of poor children praying for him, he said, 'The Lord hear them for themselves.' Very anxious about a sick parishioner.

March 31.—Very drowsy, the effect of medicine. Sent messages to Mrs. Vernon on her sending him some flowers: "May He give her the leaves of the tree of Life." And on reading to him a message from her, "The Lord bless and comfort her, and make her peace as a river."

Talking of children being from their youth allowed to read the Bible in full, and how far it would be good they should have extracts. "No, abide by what God Himself says, 'Thou shalt teach them thy children,' etc.; and 'It shall come to pass when thy children ask thee what meaneth this, thou shalt,' etc.; and to Timothy, 'That from a child,' etc. Keep to God's directions. How many children die before they would have a whole Bible. To how many is it their only learning time. How many learn by rote, and when older, in sickness or trial, it is brought home to them."

April 9th.—Had he been well he was to have preached—by the special request of his former curate, the Rev. Charles Bullock—a re-opening sermon or sermons at St. Nicholas', Worcester, after the Restoration of the Church. The Bishop took the morning sermon and Mr. Fisk the evening. He said in the course of the day, "Ah, had I preached I should have taken a well-known text, 'Where two or three are gathered together in my Name, there am I in the midst of them.' Divided thus: 1. Where two or three. 2. In my Name. 3. There am I."

The necessity of frequent visits to Germany, both to consult his oculist and for Mrs. Havergal and himself to take the waters of Pyrmont, his increasing inability to fulfil his parochial duties, even with the aid of a curate, had long caused my father to feel it to be his duty either to resign the living of Shareshill, or to procure leave of absence for an indefinite time, and place a *locum tenens* in his parsonage. Having heard of one he had formerly known in whose hands he could safely leave his flock, and whose wife would be a true helpmeet in tending it, he chose the latter plan. The Bishop kindly assented to it, and the Rev. Robert Butcher became my father's curate in 1867, till his death about three years afterwards, when the patron acceded to the wish of the parishioners and presented him to the living.

The inhabitants of Shareshill, on my father's retirement from active service among them, presented him with a purse of gold, and an easy-chair with an inscription ending with the simple and touching words, "In weariness oft." Doubtless his rest in it was often sweetened by the remembrance of their thoughtful kindness.

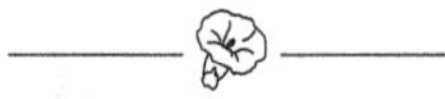

CHAPTER XIII.

LIFE IN LEAMINGTON.

Pyrmont Villa — Services at Pyrmont — Illness — Diary by Mrs. Havergal — His musical powers — Last visit to Pyrmont — Letters — Rev. A. K. Cherrill's pamphlet — Letter on oratorios — Closing days.

ON leaving Shareshill my father and Mrs. Havergal removed to apartments in Leamington, from whence they visited Shrewsbury and other places in search of a home. They finally decided to remain at Leamington, and my father bought a newly-built semi-detached house in Binswood Terrace—which he named "Pyrmont Villa," from his favourite foreign resort—now numbered 43, in which they took up their abode on Saturday, December 28, 1867. When settled he diminished his library by parting with some books and making presents of others to his family and friends. He retained such as were endeared to him by association or beauty; also his valuable collection of old Bibles and rare musical and theological books, which were a pleasure to him to exhibit and discourse on to his friends, and to form eventually memorial treasures to his children. At Leamington he had more leisure for musical correspondence, but none of 1868 has been preserved except a copy of a letter from Mr. J. Bickers, of Glasgow, to a mutual friend.

January 20, 1868.

My dear Sir,

Allow me to thank you most heartily for the criticism on St. Rowan's and the holograph score—which I value greatly—by your much beloved Mr. Havergal. I did not look for this kindness, and I feel that I owe it entirely to you. I am half amused at the care you take to let the stroke of the Nestor fall lightly on me. But I am by no means so deeply in love with myself as that this should occasion you the slightest anxiety. Blame from such a man is to me of more account and use than praise from half a hundred of the ordinary run of musical amateurs. I have well considered every one of his remarks and made note of them. That about the interval of a minor seventh being "so secular" as *never* to be found in any authenticated Church tune is quite new to me. Moderns have yet much to learn in the matter of Church music.

You will perhaps permit me to say, that I saw Jeremiah Clarke's "Nottingham" for the first time a *good while after* writing "St. Rowan's," and the opening is therefore in all fairness as entirely mine as it was, and is, the notable Jeremiah's. After the discovery I would fain have altered, but was strongly urged by certain musical friends to retain the phrase, on the ground that the character of the tune would be destroyed by any alteration. If you have any opportunity of communicating soon with Mr. Havergal, I would like him to know this, as he might think me of that kind of bird which goes about in borrowed feathers. Do me the favour at the same time of conveying to him the sense of obligation which he has called forth—not in these inelegant words, but in your own. You can't go wrong, for I really feel grateful to him.

I am yours most sincerely,
James Bickers.

(*Memoranda of Sunday Services at Pyrmont held by my Father, continued.*)

Arrived at Pyrmont June 18, 1868. On the following Sunday no service, because no congregation was ready.

Sunday, June 28th, at 6 p.m.—Misses Pollard and Soames, Miss Nicol from Glasgow, present, and several Germans—thirty-three in all. God grant that some word of His may have touched the foreign hearts. Unfavourable weather.

Sundays, July 5th and 12th.—Congregations much the same. Mr. and Mrs. Wason there.

July 19th and 26th.—More English than before. Burkes from Dublin, Mr. Cross from Valparaiso.

August 2nd.—Misses Garner, Stewart, Thompson, and Mr. A. Wilson from Walthamstow. *Master* Burke, of the Common Pleas, Ireland, read the lessons in a nice devout style. Hearers seemed interested.

August 9th.—About twenty-three of the congregation real English. Mr. and Miss Lawrence Walker. Rev. James Beatie, from Perth, read the lessons. Singing quite agreeable.

August 16th.—Collection, 3 th. 17 gr. But an anonymous hand deposited two sovereigns towards costs. Lord repay it largely!

August 23rd.—Text, "Jezebel and the portion of Jezreel." The little flock seemed interested with the novel subject in evangelical and Protestant grounds. Miss Jane Murray. Collected 5 th. 9gr. The Germans seem to have little idea of contributing.

August 30th.—The English diminish, only fourteen.

Sunday, September 6th, 4.30 p.m.—Text, Job 7:20: "O thou preserver of men." Two pounds added to the collection for *ad lib.* expenses, which I sent to the C. C. Society itself. As only one English visitor was expected to remain, this was the last service for the season of 1868. Whether the unworthy chaplain will be spared to return for another season is known only to that sovereign but beloved Saviour to whom, as his Redeemer, Job plaintively looked up and said, "O thou preserver of men!" All praise to Him for the mercies and encouragements of this season!

W. H. H.

(*From a Letter of August* 21, 1868.)

My dear Children,

Yesterday week I was very ill, but since then, with the exception of two ailing days from the epidemic malady, I have been making decided progress. These wonderful waters seem to be the very thing for me. Still I dare not boast, but I do desire to give great thanks and take good courage. No doubt it is a great help to me not to be anxious about a parish, or under necessity for immediate return. For work I am certainly not yet competent. Another month will show whether I am really better or not. I want for nothing here. My love to all, I am always thinking of you. I send a little *impromptu* for the birthday festivities, literally such, on hearing Proverbs 10:1.

DOUBLE ACROSTIC.

"A wise son maketh a glad father, but a foolish son is the heaviness of his mother."—Proverbs 10:1.

oin to magnify and praise.	J	ointly, age and youth,
im, the joy of all your days,	H	ear this standard truth!
hall grace for grace confer.	S	ons who fathers gladden
e who is the Saviour,	H	onours shall receive;
ll who favour her:	A	ll who mothers sadden
isdom loves to favour	W	ill be sure to grieve.

My father was again alarmingly ill early in January, 1869, and expressed himself as distressed at not being able to preach at Christ Church for Dr. Bickmore, as arranged for the very day after his illness began. He frequently preached for his friends in Leamington when at all able to do so, especially at Milverton and Holy Trinity, in which district he resided. He used in his study a folio Bible on a lecturn, and having looked out his text would ruminate on it for a day or two, and then write down the heads of the subject; but in the pulpit delivering the sermon entirely without notes, and enlarging upon it extemporaneously.

I will now give extracts from the short diary for four months (at intervals) of Mrs. Caroline A. Havergal.

January 9th.—Still very ill. He said, "Let us give thanks. I seem not to have a care; my parish is well supplied; no business to attend to. Here I may be in peace. It is easy to lie calmly in Jesus' arms when we have everything we want, and all is made so nice for us. How little my suffering to that of many an honoured servant of God; how much have I to be humbled for, how much to be thankful for."

January 13th.—Such a succession of dark days. Some one said, "I think the sun has ceased to shine!" His answer was—

"'My God, who makes the sun to know
His proper hour to rise.'

It shines still!" and then went on to compare it to sin and grace.

January 16th.—Such bad nights; I often hear him in whispered ejaculatory prayer, always full of humility, but sure confidence in Christ. So calm and thankful. "My thoughts always busy, wondering how this one or that is doing. I pray that many may be taught and blessed for their work on the morrow—dear Frank, dear Henry; my old curates, Jeffery, James," etc.

Sunday, January 24th.—"I hope all my dear ones will remember me to-day when they pray for all sick folk. Wearisome nights are appointed me, but how tenderly relieved. Lesson, a.m., Genesis 1. 'Day' is literal, twenty-four hours, as in Fourth Commandment; no doubt of it, cannot be strained to years; but 'In the beginning' may mean some prior time to present formation of the earth; but now all arranged as on each day. Vain men would be wise, etc., and to meet their difficulties will try and alter God's word."

February 1st.—"So much of the past comes to me. I live over again so many scenes—Wycombe especially. How I pray for light to be given and continued there, and in all my parishes. My head is full of texts and preaching, and what I would do. Music and poetry, too, all come busying me."

February 2nd.—A little sleep granted. On awaking, "Oh, praise and thank the Lord, He has given sleep. Now, Lord, again grant it."

February 6th.—First day he went out. Soon tired and rested in the porch: "I am standing at the wicket, where I would be always standing, waiting and watching."

February 9th.—On my saying "My treasure!" he said, "What a poor earthly one; but I have treasure given me now in an earthen vessel; it will be a glorious one some day. How wonderful for a worm to be made at last like unto *Him*."

February 14th.—On awaking he said, "I have just repeated Dr. Watts's hymn—

'This is the day when Christ arose.'"

This shows the value of such, for once learnt how they come back to the mind; none of the more sentimental hymns can supply their place; they are hooks on which to hang the thoughts.

Eastbourne, February 27th.—Alluding to some troublesome law business which fidgeted and distressed him, he said, "I prayed earnestly, 'Lord, I would cast this and all my cares at Thy feet, and leave them there;' and He did help me, and I was quieted; and I have thought of something on which to act, and I will, believing His Spirit has suggested it."

March 7th.—After reading Genesis 43: "How full that chapter is of the Gospel! The Lord Jesus, in the person of Joseph, makes Himself known to His brethren; they come to buy, but he gives; he yearns over them, but they know it not. How did Jesus show Himself to His disciples; yet they understood not. John, the youngest, especially loved—so Benjamin. In Egypt the Israelites learned to know their brother as their saviour; so the Jews, in their scattered state, will learn to know Jesus, and return to their own land, to tell they have found Him whom they once sold and hated."

March 12th.—"I was thinking in the night of St. Paul and the Hebrews; though writing especially to the Jews, yet what an entire absence of allusion to the music of the temple services. The silence of the Epistles on this, on the Virgin Mary, etc., shows how the Holy Spirit by silence left all Christians to infer the insignificance of form and ceremony. There is also only a single reference to the Lord's Supper in the Epistles."

April 14th.—"The eyes of the Lord be ever smiling on you," was his wish. "The doctrine of imputed righteousness is very clear and strong. Christ's active and passive obedience was necessary. Praise Him for His *perfect* obedience, His holiness, and His atoning blood. Never may I say, or do, or think anything but what an angel from heaven should witness, approve, and bless. May actions always speak for me when words are few."

On his return from Eastbourne my father resumed his usual quiet avocations, enjoying short calls only from his friends, for he was soon tired of talking or of hearing others talk. His musical correspondence was continued at intervals. Among those who succeeded Dr. Crotch and Dr. Hodges and Mr. Couchman in these later years, I find the names of Dr. W. Horsely, W. Marten Cooke, K. J. Pyne, J. D. Glennie, H. Mayo Gunn, W. Ewing, W. Locke, Miss Hackett, Dr. Rimbault, Professor Taylor, Rev. John Antes and Peter La Trobe, Sir John Goss, Otto Goldschmidt, T. A. Walmisley, H. E. Dibdin, E. G. Monk, Rev. G. Quirke, and Rev. C. H. Davis. He was still able to sit down for a short time at his piano or harmonium, and with his never-to-be-forgotten touch and voice would "discourse sweet music;" but his hand was soon fatigued, and his voice had lost its volume and some of its sweetness. But I will transcribe the eloquent account of a musical friend who heard him in some former year.

To hear Mr. Havergal improvise, seated at a good harmonium with many stops, given him by his parishioners, was a rare treat; something higher, deeper, and more than a pleasure—a thing, or rather a spiritual experience, which cannot be forgotten. Sweet-flowing melody, accompanied with strange, unexpected combinations of harmony full of mysterious chords and curious synchronous and successive felicities, each part capable of being resolved into a perfect and separate composition—fugues chasing each other, turning, meeting, and then passing through the theme in quite opposite directions, meeting again, then twining lovingly together, and, like the strands of a new cable, finding strength in unison—starry phrases of melody echoed from heavenly heights till lost in the distance; then vast galaxies of chords "swim into ken," dependent on and perfectly balanced by other galaxies, controlled even to the perturbation of a satellite, till all is light and motion; while Handelian shakes, like auroras, at intervals gleam and dart across the blue starlit dome. Yet with all this there is no hesitation, no confusion, no fear; ruled by the genius of a master, every phrase, chord, and movement progresses with stately grandeur and precision towards the evolution of the one idea which informs and pervades the whole marvellous performance. Sometimes we wander far away through wild intervals into weird discords; and then these, ere they become too painful, are resolved with consummate skill, and we mark "lines of different method" all meeting "in one full centre of delight," as we find ourselves led on and on, and ever by new and unexpected ways, home again at last to the key-note.

The firmness, precision, and delicacy of Mr. Havergal's touch were each and all remarkable, both in kind and degree. These several characteristics were strikingly brought out in his improvizations, which never by any chance contained anything approaching the commonplace. Instead of that, his every combination was original, often a surprise even to himself; many lovely transient effects thus flashed and faded that could not be repeated. Compositions of daring originality and perfect rounded beauty—now bold and strident, like the tramp of a giant army, and now ethereally delicate, like the dying cadences of an Æolian harp—streamed from the keys at the magic "touch" of that "vanished hand" we shall hear no more on earth.

Although Mr. Havergal's ecclesiastical music is of the very highest type and severe in style, he has also written many beautiful songs, rounds and catches for the young, which are full of childlike life and bird-like glee; also numberless carols, hymns, and sacred songs, composing both the words and the music.

Mr. Havergal's severe and classical music is often to be heard in our cathedrals; and in Scotland and America no psalm tune is oftener sung than "Evan." The history of this tune is somewhat peculiar; and, as its authorship has been questioned, it may be well to mention the matter here, as the writer can do so authoritatively from Mr. Havergal's own words, as well as from written statements. In 1847 Mr. Havergal published an original air (A Sacred Song) to Burns's words, "O Thou dread Power." Dr. Lowell Mason, of New York, arranged the first half of that air as a psalm tune, altering both the time and key, and called it "Evan." Hence it is frequently given in collections with Mason's name, and at other times simply with the letter H, under which initial it first appeared, because Dr. Mason did not wish to attribute the liberty he had taken in arranging the part of a melody to the composer of the original air. This is Dr. Lowell Mason's own explanation, which we have seen. Mr. Havergal has since arranged it as it should be; and within the last month played over the tune, and gave a MS. copy of it to the writer, with its curious history noted on the sheet. It has travelled far and wide, and been claimed for many composers, and even been called an old Celtic air. We have here stated the true origin of this unprecedentedly popular tune.

Of the *Hundred Tunes* it is not too much to say that they are a monument of learning and industry; and are all, or nearly all, in entire agreement with the principles which its author so long and so successfully propounded.

Handel, Corelli, and our great Cathedralists, were his masters. His aim was to preserve purity of style, and put down musical vanities. Notoriously liberal to publishers of music, he has been equally willing to aid, by scientific criticism and research, all who applied to him.

My father visited Pyrmont for the last time in the summer of 1869, and continued the diary of his Sunday services.

Sunday, July 4th at 6 p.m.—Congregation nineteen; text, Philippians 4:19. Favoured with a bright evening, and the presence of God seemed to make this new beginning pleasant and hopeful. Found myself better able to read, preach, and sing than I expected. All glory to the Saviour! Germans speaking English were the majority in the little company.

July 11th.—Congregation twenty-six; text, John 6:37. No British but ourselves and Consul Crauford, of Grimstadt, a fine Scotchman, but married and settled in Norway. Some of the Germans responded and sung well. Blessed Jesus, let all "come" to Thee!

July 18th.—Text, "But He answered her not a word." Still no more English, but some very excellent Dutch people. The power of the Lord seemed present to heal and bless. Lord, be it so!

July 25th.—Congregation twenty-five; text, 1 Kings 19:12. Three English ladies present, but only passers-by. An Old Testament subject seemed a novelty to our Dutch friends, but it proved interesting and edifying to them. Lord, let Thy "still small voice" prevail!

August 1st.—Text, Hebrews 4:14: "Seeing then that we have a great High Priest," etc. After service a somewhat singular circumstance was detailed to me respecting my text. Madame de Weirt, who takes much interest in my unworthy sermons, dreamed on Saturday night that I selected Hebrews 4:14, the very text I did take. In the morning she told the dream to her family and a devoted friend, all of whom assured me of the fact. None of them could have known my intention; they had no English calendar, and know nothing of our lessons. Who can account for the dream?

August 8th.—Text, Hebrews 11:7. At length a rainy afternoon, and the congregation only fifteen. Much feeling and attention. All glory to our faithful God!

August 15th.—Favoured with a fine evening; twenty-three present. Text, "Man did eat angels' food." The Duke of Buckingham and Chandos and some of the Grenville scions present. His Grace, at his own most kind request, read the lessons very nicely indeed. The Misses Rose and Mrs. Fretwell were there. The sermon seemed to interest all present. He who alone knows all things knows how far it was blessed to any or all.

August 22nd, 4 p.m.—Text, John 10:9. Drizzly and chilly weather; the same individuals present as on Sunday last. The Duke of Buckingham again read the lessons very reverently. May our God make the word read, as well as the word preached, profitable to all!

August 29th.—Text, John 10:11. Again favoured with splendid weather. Thanks to Him who sent it. Again the Duke read the lessons excellently well. The hymn nicely suited the text, and was sung heartily to Vienna. Much attention. Be thou exalted, O Lord!

September 5th.—Text, Acts 10:43. Congregation eighteen; collection 3 th. 3 gr. Fine weather. The Duke read the lessons as before. Oh that he and all may be blessed as was Cornelius and his company. Lord, make all to understand and receive!

September 12, 1869, 4 p.m.—Text, "The Lord Jesus Christ be with thy spirit" (2 Timothy 4:22). Congregation fourteen; collection, 9 th. 23 gr. Equinoctial wind and rain; branches blown off and trees blown down. As we passed by, a large tree had just fallen on the Roman Catholic chapel. The Duke read the lessons as before. My humble sermon seemed to tell on the last congregation in our little sanctuary. Shall I ever again resume such service? O Lord Jesus Christ, only be with my spirit, and all the praise shall be Thine!

This was the very last service my dear father held in Pyrmont. His labours were thus alluded to in the Report of the Church Continental Society in the autumn of 1870:—

PYRMONT.

The Committee are happy to state that the late Rev. W. H. Havergal, who took such a deep interest in the Chaplaincy at this place, has had, during the last summer, a successor in the Rev. A. Lockwood, who has entered into the work and carried it on in the faith and spirit of his predecessor. They would also gratefully mention the interest which Mrs. Havergal continues to take in the work which was so dear to her late husband. Mr. Lockwood writes in his report:—

"In sending the accompanying book, recording the services held at Pyrmont during the season now closing, it is well perhaps that I should inform the Committee of the result of my observations of the place as a fitting sphere for the Society's operations. I have no hesitation in saying that it is one in which much good may be done. The number of English visitors this season has been less than was anticipated, owing to the unexpected breaking out of the war. Nevertheless, the attendance during the last two months, as will be seen from the record book, has, on the whole, been fairly sustained.

"A new railway from Hanover will be opened next June, and as one or two works on Pyrmont are shortly to be published in England, it is confidently expected that English invalids, in greater numbers than hitherto, will be induced to try its waters, which are acknowledged to be of greater variety and potency than any in Germany.

"There are a few English and American residents at Pyrmont. By these, as well as by the visitors, the services have been greatly appreciated, and to some there is reason to believe they have been blessed by the Great Head of the Church.

"There is one obstacle to the successful conduct of the services to which I ought to refer—the situation of the Friends' Meeting House, which is so far from the town, and is so concealed from view that few visitors at first have been able to find it. No other room, however, is available; but it has occurred to me that a small iron church, if this could be obtained, would best meet the necessities of such a place as Pyrmont. A site might, without difficulty, be secured in a central position. I have thought of suggesting the erection of such a church to the numerous friends of the late Mr. Havergal, to whose memory it would be a graceful tribute. Would the Society be prepared to contribute a sum of money towards its purchase?

"I cannot close this report without referring to the labours of the venerable servant of God just mentioned. His influence in Pyrmont was great. From all classes of people I have heard of him—English and German alike, whom he visited in their houses, and to whom he had been wont to speak on the way, whenever he met them, never omitting an opportunity for doing good. The testimony which all bear to the example and labours of that good man is one of affectionate gratitude. Thus it was Mr. Havergal sought to do good. He secured the confidence and good-will of the people, and used the influence thus gained to bring them to the Saviour. If his example were followed by the many Chaplains who visit the Continent annually, they would not fail, on their return home at the close of each season, of leaving a mark behind them—one which would speak well for our English Christianity, and would be reflected back upon England in the form of regard and thankfulness from many a true German heart."

My father, with Mrs. Havergal, spent the month of November, 1869, at Oakhampton and Winterdyne, and these were his last visits to his married daughters. He proceeded to London Nov. 30th, and after writing the following letter he was taken ill at his hotel, but was soon able to return to Leamington.

(*To Rev. F. T. H.*)

London, Dec. 2, 1869.

My dearest Frank,

Yesterday I sent a packet for the darling boys. I principally wished them to have each a copy of good old Watts's "Divine Songs," as published nearly a century ago by the S. P. C. K. My blessed mother taught me to say and sing them. Your own mother taught you and all her children to do the same. I should like your dear little ones to thread their early steps in the same safe and excellent path.

I have been hearing much of that most remarkable man the Armenian Archbishop, who, through our Prayer-book chiefly, has become a Protestant, and is learning English more perfectly in a garret in Jerusalem under Bishop Gobat. A letter from the Archbishop was read to me. Here is a noble fellow, indeed, and I hope one of the signs of the times. Amen! ....

Ever affectionately yours,

W. H. H.

(*To Rev. W. H. H., from the Rev. Joseph Powell Metcalfe.*)

Bilbrough Rectory.
Dec. 29, 1869.

I really was very much touched by your kind little Christmas remembrance of me, so appropriate to the blissful season when "a child was born to us," in its very simplicity a fit Christmas gift from a Christian Gresham Prizeman.

I am blest with two merry little children of four and five years old. "The Bethlehem Shepherd Boy's Tale" has been appropriated, words and tune, with marvellous relish by them. The strain only gets interrupted with crying, "I *do* like it so," emphasized with a shake of the curly head against which there is no appeal. It would give us very great pleasure to hear from you or any kind deputed scribe. Miss F. R. H.'s note lies before me, a member of my musical treasury. It speaks of your failing eyesight. It almost seems as though faulty vision was decreed as the doom of unusual musical sensibility. Old Mr. Goss complains of eyes to be nursed. Geo. Macfarren has long wholly lost his sight; but this can scarcely be laid to the charge of our dear mistress Music, since a brother of his, a scene painter, is also blind. What should we do without music, especially we country parsons? I have been blessed with a wife of musical capabilities. Somehow I always connect the Psalmist's "voice of joy and gladness" with fireside strains. I do believe many a moody thought and inner grumble that might hatch into family bickerings is exorcised, like Saul's evil spirit, by home music. We always fancy there can be no kitchen mischief brewing so long as the work is done to a tune.

(To Rev. W. H. H., from Rev. Charles Rae Hay, Vicar of Ridlington, writing from Leven, Fife.)

Again I have to thank you for so kindly sending me your Lectures on the Ark of the Covenant, and for the affectionate words you have written on the first page. It greatly surprises us that you can write so well as you do!

If Miss Fanny is better, which I sincerely hope she is by this time, and if her poetical and other compositions allow the time, I should esteem it a favour if she would kindly take the trouble to copy your old chant No. 4 for us. I mean the one of which the organist of Worcester Cathedral used to say it was "the best chant ever composed." I want to introduce it into our little chapel here, and we unfortunately left the book put away somewhere at home. There was also another chant, No. 92, I believe, which we frequently had at Astley; I have known some persons prefer it to the other. It used to be a great favourite with our friends, Sir Christopher and Lady Lighton. I will give your message to V. G. Faithful when next I see him.

(To his eldest Daughter.)

Pyrmont Villa,
Jan. 24, 1870.

My dearest Miriam,

Thank you for all kind words and deeds. I much enjoyed the sight and sound of your dear boy. He *is* a dear little bud, and will, I trust and pray, be kept from the evils of a public school. I thought of him and you on Friday last at Harrow. Glad shall I be to learn that the "great Angel" was indeed sent before you and with you. Yesterday I had another physical lesson; I found myself suddenly chilly, and other symptoms. However, thank God, I am better this morning, though tired and listless. Thus I alternate, but all praise be to Him who does not lay any burden of a heavier sort.

Your affectionate
Father.

(To his Son, Rev. F. T. H.)

Feb. 22, 1870.

My dearest Frank,

I have been some time getting through Mr. Cherrill's pamphlet,[1] as our best one has been so distressingly ill. I have been marvellously upheld, and Fanny is flourishing. "The Musician" has tuned his pipe in a sharp key as regards cathedral Dons. It will, I hope, awaken them to such duties as are incumbent on them. In allusion to a remark in the Hereford article, let me remind you that the elder of the two Halls, who were organists *circa* 1700, was ordained to a Vicar-Choralship in conjunction with his office of organist.

Cherrill's pamphlet surprises me. He must have read much and well. He can also not only analyse, but condense when it suits his purpose. On all the main questions between Papists and Protestants, Ritualists and sound Churchmen, he is not only clear but forcible. Here some of his hits are really clever. But I am disappointed at finding him wavering on certain non-essential topics, but which have essentially wrong tendencies; *e.g.*, all he says about the oblation of bread and wine *presentio* (properly placed) on the table, just before the Church militant prayer, is utterly groundless. As Dean Goode and others have well shown, "oblations" are "the other devotions of the people," and not the elements. He enlarges very unnecessarily on the Jewish sacrifices and the fable of vegetable offerings in Paradise, and all covertly to defend the application of the term sacrifice to our Communion. He acknowledges that neither the Bible nor the Church so apply it, and yet suicidally pleads for it. So he takes up the Popish interpretation of Malachi 1:11, and Hebrews 13:10, forgetting that Malachi says too much for him, as he prophesies of incense as well as of meat-offering, and that the great Reformation commentator, Dr. Fulke, fully proved that the words of the epistle refer not to any ecclesiastical altar. Then he cannot let the Ritualists go without an excusing and even commendatory word at the last. He forgets that our Lord did not so with those who, in His day, were *very earnest and painstaking* in making one proselyte. But it is rather significant that Cherrill says not a word about the Popish heresy of receiving the elements only fasting, so speciously followed by the Ritualists under the title of early celebration—*i.e.*, at a fasting hour, and not merely at an early hour.

Neither does he touch on the modern absurdity of forbidding an *evening* celebration, of which S. W., now of Winchester, is, as far as I know, the only episcopal advocate. Cherrill had better, when he was on the subject, have handled the whole of it; an extra page would have sufficed. Alas! alas! that the Church of Christ should be troubled with such trifles while weightier matters are always at hand.

Ever affectionately your
W. H. H.

(To Miss Emma P. Vernon.)

March 23, 1870.

"An old disciple" of 77 may well "set" his papers "in order." Among my heaps I find the enclosed reserves. I have not the heart to destroy them, hence I commit them to you. How fast do years flit on! What a span does it seem since these foreign letters were first opened by me! Lord, make us meet for the home where time and infirmity shall be no more! Your letter this morning has been eagerly

[1] "The Sacrament of the Lord's Supper, considered with reference to recent Controversies." Oxford and London: James Parker & Co.

read. The Good Shepherd direct my godson to some choice fold; my kindest sympathy to him. All happiness to the anticipated twain. I have been indoors since Dec. 6th. I sigh to see Shareshill again.

(*To his eldest Daughter.*)

Pyrmont Villa,
April 14, 1870.

My dearest Miriam,

To-day *was* my beloved mother's birthday. I always used to associate it with your own, as standing in the calendar so near to her. Had she been alive she would have been 99, and my father would have been 105 on Monday last. The good Lord hear and answer my prayers for you! I do not make much progress; I have not been out since that one trial on the 6th. Just now I tried the garden, but hastened in as I found it damp. As to the future the *vista* is full of odd shapes and the atmosphere is strange, as though something were about to occur out of the usual course. Pyrmont beckons invitingly, but a sort of haze hangs over it. One little matter is that it will not be so easy to arrange about lodgings as before. But "the God of my life" will bless and comfort. Dearest wife improves, but is not well. You are most filially thoughtful; my heart thanks you. May my Father and your Father, my Saviour and your Saviour, always remember you and yours.

Ever your
W. H. H.

The following letter, written on the same day as the preceding, was the last he ever wrote. Like his mother, he was Protestant to the end.

(*To Hyla Holden, Esq.*)

Pyrmont Villa, Leamington,
April 14, 1870.

My dear Sir,

For my eyes' sake, which soon fail, you must kindly pardon brevities. I cannot sign the address to the Dean and Chapter of Worcester as it stands. In the love of architecture I yield to no one. But "grandeur" without purity is as naught to me. "Images defile the temple of God," is an adamantine adage. "Ye saw no similitude," "Thou shalt not make unto thee," etc. If in restoring a cathedral *such* images are set up as our Reformers pulled down, and our Homilies forbid, no pure grandeur can exist.

The "dignity" of Divine worship in a noble cathedral is very dear to me. But oratorios, *as at present conducted,* are a burlesque of such worship, and the use of such books as "Hymns Ancient and Modern" both musically and theologically debase it. Some declaim bravely about ecstatic worship in the performance of oratorios. All facts belie this. Pleasurable feeling is mistaken for reverential worship. Handel, as can be proved, did not write any oratorio, not even the "Messiah," with an eye to *worship*. The performers show no consciousness of it, and the mass of the audience never dream of it.

And yet I am humbly of opinion that more may be said for an oratorio in a cathedral than, as far as I know, has been said. I cannot now attempt to say what that *more* is. Suffice it to add, that if an oratorio could be held in a cathedral, apart from worldly adjuncts, and so performed as to elevate the best emotions of the mind in listening to a fine and forcible representation of Scripture facts and truths by means of musical expression, then our highest style of Churchmanship may be fostered and refreshed. I could wish that the original *idea* of "The Meeting of the Three Choirs" were resuscitated as a basis for new and better arrangements. At present that principle languishes. Early morning service, followed by a full oratorio, is not a very eligible mode; it cramps the service and enfeebles the oratorio in some of its parts. Years ago, before the existence of the present cathedral management, I laboured hard and long to correct grievous desecration and bring on a less objectionable state of things. Success followed. For a few years the Tuesday morning service, in grand and solemn style, with opportunity for a dignified psalm tune and an edifying sermon, gave general satisfaction, especially when the "Grand Ball" was separated from cathedral announcements.

In a word, I am sorry that I do not sign the address, but feel that fairly I cannot. With every good wish,

I am, my dear sir, faithfully yours,
W. H. Havergal.

His wife made the following memorandum on this letter: "This was written on Thursday, but kept, as he wished to make a little alteration. He attempted it on Saturday, on another sheet, but felt unequal to the effort, and laid it aside unfinished. His work was finished, and he soon heard the 'Well done, good and faithful servant.'"

This Saturday was indeed to prove my dear father's last conscious day. In a letter to a friend, written on the Monday morning, his daughter F. R. H. speaks of that day as "a very climax of peace and brightness in *all* respects." He twice walked out a little in front of his house, hoping to catch a young gentleman, a neighbour, to whom he thought a word in season might be useful. He also wrote his last lines, "Messiah, Redeemer!" and set them to a palindrome, and the same day he composed the beautiful tune "Havergal,"[1] to Dr. Monsell's fine Trinitarian hymn, "Mighty Father! Blessed Son!"

But the music of earth now ceased for him, and the singularly beautiful voice was heard no more in songs of praise. The next morning was Easter day. He rose early as usual, but soon after was seized with apoplexy. The kind and attentive Dr. A. Thursfield came immediately, but pronounced the case a dangerous one. His children arrived on Easter Monday, to behold their beloved father unconscious. His devoted wife never left his side, and his faithful friend Miss Nott was often in attendance. My brother Frank at times relieved the solemn silence by reading consolatory passages of Holy Scripture; and the Rev. J. S. Ruddach came in the evening, offering a few kind words of sympathy and a sweet and soothing prayer, giving thanks to God for the grace which had enabled His servant so to glorify Him in the life which was now closing.

[1] Tune "Havergal," No. 163 in "Havergal's Psalmody."

Our dear father continued unconscious, and a few minutes before noon on Easter Tuesday, April 19th, 1870, he almost imperceptibly passed into "the rest that remaineth for the people of God."

"When the rest of faith is ended, and the rest in hope is past,
The rest of love remainth, Sabbath of life at last:
No more fleeting hours, hurrying down the day,
But golden stillness of glory, never to pass away."

F. R. H.

CHAPTER XIV.

CONCLUSION, AND MEMORIAL NOTICES.

The resting-place at Astley — Letter of F. R. H. — Memorial tablet — Letters of condolence — *The English Churchman* — *The Hereford Times* — Sermons at Shareshill and St. Nicholas' — "The Pastor Remembered" — "Yet speaketh."

MY dear father had often said he should like to be buried in the west corner of the churchyard in Astley, where the longest portion of his ministerial life was spent, and so he was laid there in a rock-hewn grave "till *the* day break and the shadows flee away." On Saturday, April 23rd, the Rev. R. Butcher, his successor at Shareshill, read the burial service, surrounded by mourning relatives and old parishioners. His eldest daughter raised a white marble tomb over his grave, where his second wife was also laid eight years after; and in June, 1879, Frances, his youngest and most gifted daughter, was added to that little sanctuary of the blessed dead. This dear sister thus wrote of his departure:—

My beloved father's death is a dream as yet, but rather solemn than terrible; and after it—"when I awake, I am still with Thee!" I think He will let me prove that. It has been the very best for papa, and therefore I don't think any of us would have it otherwise. It was apoplexy, and he never moved or spoke again—lay as in a deep sleep till Tuesday at noon, and then the breathing ceased. That was all—no struggle, no pain, only gone to *rest*. Was it not merciful, so? Not any pang for him, not a good-bye, or the possibility of a troubled thought—not an hour's conscious illness—then sleep, then glory. We could not have chosen better for him. And for us, everything that could soften and sustain has been given. All were in time to see him. There was no human element, and so no evil, no bitterness; it was only God's hand! . . . If I loved my father less, I should grieve *more*; but his comfort was truly first, and that is everything. And now he is "with Him," and I think that includes *all*. And I can look at *that* and even be glad. I did not think God *could* make it so easy to bow and trust and say, "Thy will be done."

"Death
Has only parted us a little while,
And has not severed e'en the finest strand
In the eternal cable of our love:
The very strain has twined it closer still,
And added strength."

A memorial brass tablet, designed by his son, the Rev. F. T. Havergal, with a harp on either side of the sacred monogram "I.H.S.," a symbolical crown above, and a surrounding border of appropriate Scripture texts, was placed in one of the niches in the arcade of the S.E. transept of Worcester Cathedral, and similar ones in the churches of St. Nicholas, Worcester, and Shareshill, Staffordshire. The inscription is as follows:

To the Glory of God
and in remembrance of His Servant
William H. Havergal.
Born at High Wycombe, Jan. 18th, 1793
Died at Leamington, April 19th, 1870
in holy peace,
Resting in Astley Churchyard.

Rector of Astley, 1829–42
and of St. Nicholas, Worcester, 1845–60.
Vicar of Shareshill, 1860–70.
Honorary Canon of this Cathedral.

Erected by his Widow and Children.

This mural brass is well described in the letter of his life-long friend, H. V. Tebbs, Esq., who survived him for six years.

Hill-side, Westbury-on-Trym,
November 8, 1870.

Dear Mrs. Havergal,

Many thanks to you for your letter of this morning, and for the photograph of the memorial brasses in the Cathedral and Churches.

The design is marked by good taste; I like it much. That simple record of the name, birth, death, and position in the Church of my beloved friend, how much better than a long statement of intellectual powers, moral qualities, and professional labours. The verses from the holy Book sufficiently allude to these, and the harps of the Psalmist and of a redeemed one most gracefully recall those gifts which so distinguished him, and which he ever used to the glory of God.

The evangelistic emblems at each corner suitably proclaim that chief theme of his ministry, the Gospel of the grace of God. The angel-figure with the writer's pen; the sacrificial ox; the lion, strong but calm, bearing in his front the holy Book, not sealed, its page spread open to proclaim its peace; and then the noble eagle, with its wings outstretched to carry it through all the world. One only suggestion had I seen it in time I might have ventured to make. . . . Still, there is abundant reference to that blessed Being, the Alpha and Omega—the cross with His monogram and the crown with its glory. So let me again thank you for awakening my recollections of the beloved friend with so many pleasant thoughts. With my wife's kind regards,

Believe me ever yours sincerely,
H. V. Tebbs.

Among the letters of condolence on my lamented father's death are the following:—

(*From the Rev. J. S. Broad, now of Pentney Vicarage, Swaffham.*)

Brampton House, Newcastle-under-Lyme,
April 23, 1870.

My dear Mrs. Havergal,

It was with sorrow I saw the announcement of the departure of my dear old tutor and friend; not indeed unlooked for in the course of nature, but yet a cause of deep and sincere grief to all that loved him;—and who that knew him could help loving him? It is now upwards of forty years since I first became acquainted with him, and from the moment I saw him I honoured and loved him. Doubtless you have been prepared for the severance of the earthly tie; but when it actually takes place it is felt as a wrench of affection, as a deep and trying affliction. But "blessed are the dead who die in the Lord"; blessed are they who "sleep in Jesus," or, as the word really means, "are laid asleep by Jesus."

Of the beloved one just gone we know that he has entered into life in its best sense, and that he is, and for ever will be, with the Lord. As one indebted to him for instruction and example in early life, I can truly say that both instruction and example have been impressed upon me and valued throughout life; and I would desire to emulate his faithfulness and devotedness, his calmness of temper, his kind affability, his holy cheerfulness, so as to adorn as he did the doctrine of God our Saviour.

We must look onward to the future when the faithful shall all meet around the throne, and join in that praise, that holy song, in which he delighted in the Church on earth. I trust and pray that you and those of his who are left behind may experience the consolations of God, which are neither few nor small, and find Him to be "the Father of mercies and the God of all comfort." With sincere condolence with you in your loss, and with kindest remembrances to any old Astley friends who may be with you, believe me, dear Mrs. Havergal,

Yours faithfully in Christ,
John S. Broad.

(*From the Rev. Frederic Simcox Lea, now Rector of Tedstone Delamere, to the Rev. W. H. Havergal's eldest daughter.*)

Trinity Parsonage, Bow Road,
April 21, 1870.

My dear Mrs. Crane,

Reginald's letter this morning tells me of the close of a life so bright and saintly that to have been brought in any way within its influence is a gift to thank God for. That the end should have come by a sudden stroke is what the recollection of 1842 had prepared me to expect; though the immediate blow is more hard to realize even to me, and much more must it be so to you. His epitaph is written in Astley churchyard: you know the inscription on the tomb of his predecessor, Mr. Geers, about a hundred years ago; and those words I associated with Mr. Havergal the first time that I read them. And now the "Mortalitati, non vitæ, valedixit" is realized.

About, or soon after, the time we came to Astley my love for the "Christian Year" began to grow, and one of its pictures of Christian character has ever since belonged to him. Whether I ever heard him quote the verse I cannot now remember, but it seemed drawn from the life as his.

"There are, in this loud stunning tide
Of human care and crime,
With whom the melodies abide
Of th' everlasting chime;
Who carry music in their heart," etc.

There has been something so even and unchanging about him, the latest recollections are so exactly the same with the earliest ones, it seemed as though the passing of years left him unaltered, excepting the ageing of the outward man, like the sight of the hills or the sound of his own church bells. Reginald tells me that he will be buried in Astley churchyard; it is just what we should all have desired, and have missed, I think, if it had not been so. My wife asks me to add the assurance of her deep and affectionate sympathy. Will you remember me most kindly to Henry and Frank and your sisters, as well as to Mr. Crane and your own home circle, and believe me,

Very sincerely yours,
F. Simcox Lea.

(*To Frances Ridley Havergal, from the Rev. William Jones* [*extract*].)

I had the privilege of being your father's curate at Shareshill about ten years ago, and should be ungrateful indeed if I could ever forget either his kindness to me personally, or the pattern which he gave me of faithfulness and single-heartedness as a preacher and a pastor. He told me that one always remembered one's first curacy, and he made mine such that I have good reason to remember it with gratitude.

(*To the Editor of "The English Churchman."*)

AVENUE MARBŒUF, PARIS,
May 17, 1870.

SIR,

Will you allow me to endorse the sentiments of your correspondent the Vicar of Bourton in reference to the late Rev. W. H. Havergal, as expressed in the last number of your journal. His musical attainments, especially in regard to Church music, have never been adequately appreciated; but it is not chiefly on account of these that I wish he had been better known. I became acquainted with the late Mr. Havergal in Bath more than twenty years ago, and although since that time I have enjoyed but few opportunities of personal intercourse with him, I have never ceased to entertain for him the warmest feelings of affection and regard. About the year 1855 I passed many happy and profitable hours in his society at Bonn-on-the-Rhine. His remarks on the controverted questions of the day were peculiarly interesting and edifying, and were always characterized both by wisdom and love. But that which chiefly impressed me in him was his meek and cheerful acquiescence in the painful dispensation of Providence under which he was at that time suffering, viz., that of failing sight. Though unable to read, he was occasionally ready to preach when his health permitted him. A dear friend of my own has frequently expressed to me her deep and lasting obligations to Mr. Havergal for the spiritual benefit she derived from his conversation and letters. I have often thought that it is a strong demonstration of the anomaly in our system of Church patronage that a man of his high character and attainments should never have received greater preferment than the Vicarage of Shareshill.

I shall be thankful if you will allow me to offer, through your columns, this feeble tribute to the memory of one whom I so much admired and esteemed as the late Rev. W. H. Havergal.

I remain, sir, yours faithfully,

GEORGE G. GARDINER.

(*From a Correspondent of "The Hereford Times."*)

With sincere regret we recorded in our last the death of the Rev. W. H. Havergal, for fifteen years the earnest and pious Rector of St. Nicholas', Worcester, and subsequently of Astley, Worcestershire. The deceased was well known as amongst the foremost of the evangelical ministers of the Church of England. As a preacher he was powerful in argument and eloquent in appeals, with lofty intelligence; he was for ever ready to "contend for the faith once delivered to the saints," and he boldly encountered the infidel or any one who dared to rob the Scriptures of one text of its immortal truths. He was a trenchant controversialist, using all his artillery of learning and long experience against the modern innovations and tawdry embellishments of the Church.

With the simple but everlasting truths of the Gospel he used to scatter to the winds all the mummeries which interfered with the simplicity of Church of England worship. He was ever happy in proclaiming broad truths for which the Reformers shed their blood, and with zealous earnestness he was accustomed to charge all under his care never to swerve from those truths. It needs scarcely to be added that he strongly opposed any approach to Romanism.

The sublime simplicity of the Revelation of God to man was his theme of delight, and never was he more joyful than when speaking its words of solace or imparting its blessed consolations to those who were in trouble, sickness, or adversity. He was an eminent scholar, a poet, and a musician, and from long study was ready on most subjects to give well-considered opinions. He was often consulted on occasions of difficulty, and indeed it was his great comfort to mix with his parishioners, doing all in his power to cement their mutual esteem. Being thus usefully engaged in his parish, and always of very thoughtful and studious habits, he interfered little with the outer world. The line of the temple and its services were indeed his highest happiness and privilege. As a preacher he was poetic and eloquent in diction, as well as clear and forcible in argument, explaining the Gospel plan of salvation with a power that would arrest the attention of the most careless listener.

For many years his sight had been impaired, and it was his wont once a year to repair to Germany to get the most able advice for his eyes. When he occupied the pulpit in the evenings, the gas had to be so lowered that he and his congregation were scarcely visible to each other. In the midst of that darkness he would preach, without note or Bible, most erudite and valuable discourses. Though without reference, there was no tautology in his style, but all was so compactly built together as to form a body of divinity and eloquence. He was very vehement against any human interposition between the sinner and the Saviour, and always when the subject was opportune strongly denounced saint and man-worship. Nothing but the Bible satisfied him, and his constant aim was to bring forth its treasures in all simplicity, declaring "the whole counsel of God." He was of a very humble mind and benevolent nature, and thought little of himself in comparison with his great mission. Many of the poor in Worcester can bear testimony to his great kindness, being always ready to give a helping hand to those who were in need. Indeed, he watched over the poor with a Christian love and affection which were well known to many in the parish of St. Nicholas. The deceased published two volumes of "Historical Sermons," which are valued by all who have read them for their great and glorious truths. He was about publishing some of his lectures, when death seized him. We still hope to see many of his works yet given to the public.

Few men have done more to restore the musical portion of our service. His anthems for May services are well known in our Cathedral. He was fond of congregational singing, on which he bestowed much of his time, also frequently admonishing his congregation on the duty of praise to God. About sixteen years ago he brought out his "Old Church Psalmody," which is one of the best collections of Church Psalmody extant. The tunes are good, simple in structure, always of devotional strains, and free from too many discords (of which he had a great abhorrence). The work was a great *boon* to the

Church, for in all parts it has found a hearty welcome. Some years ago the deceased wrote a history of the Old Hundredth Psalm Tune, a subject to which he had given much research.

The writer of this imperfect sketch knew of Mr. Havergal's great respect for the late Rev. J. J. Waite, of Hereford, and how much he eulogized Mr. Waite for his laborious exertions in rescuing Psalmody from the sing-song style into which it had fallen, and raising it to a higher level. It is now about eighteen years since Mr. Havergal preached the funeral sermon of his old friend the Rev. John East, of Bath. Also, eight years later, he likewise preached a funeral discourse on that good and faithful servant the Rev. John Davies, Rector of St. Clement's, Worcester. On leaving Worcester he was presented to the living of Shareshill, near Wolverhampton, but on many occasions he assisted his many clerical brethren at Leamington, at which town he resided for a short time previous to his death. That mournful event occurred when he had reached the ripe age of seventy-seven; his death being caused by apoplexy. He leaves a widow, four daughters, and two sons, one of whom, the Rev. F. T. Havergal, is Minor Canon of our cathedral, and Vicar of Pipe and Lyde.

In Leamington, at Shareshill, and many other places, funeral sermons were preached on the death of my beloved father. His successor at St. Nicholas', Worcester, gave an admirable sermon, which he afterwards published with notes and hymns and a biographical notice, forming a volume entitled, "The Pastor Remembered." [1]

My own little labour of love in collecting and uniting the scattered records of his life cannot be more appropriately concluded than by quoting the first part of this sermon by the Rev. Charles Bullock, the intimate and valued friend both of the Rev. William Henry and Frances Ridley Havergal.

THE PASTOR REMEMBERED.

2 *Thessalonians* 3:1.

"Finally, brethren, pray for us, that the word of the Lord may have free course and be glorified."

The Pastor Remembered; the brethren entreated. To utter words of affectionate recollection and words of earnest exhortation: this is my purpose, this is my desire.

Brethren, pray for me! and pray that the Holy Spirit may so "direct and rule" all our hearts, that our recollections of the past and our resolves for the future may conduce to our spiritual edification and profit.

First, then, I am anxious to utter in this sanctuary words of affectionate remembrance.

It is not, indeed, in my power to attempt any adequate sketch or estimate of the character and ministry of the "faithful" pastor, whose memory, though years have elapsed since he laboured amongst us, will ever be deeply and lovingly cherished. My words will be few: but still I trust they will, in some measure, give expression to those feelings of veneration and appreciation in which all who knew him so fully shared.

He was truly no ordinary man. His personal endowments were distinguished. A true "poet of the sanctuary" and an enthusiastic lover of "holy music," his contributions to the Psalmody of the House of God ranked him amongst the foremost musical authorities of the age. His "Old Church Psalmody" will always be a standard book of reference, and scarcely can a collection of tunes be found which is not enriched with his original compositions. But he was rich in grace as well as rich in gifts. His heart and his life were in good tune, and he loved above all other harmony the melody of good works.

I have enjoyed the friendship of many ministers, but I have never met with one whose Christian character in the Church and in the home shone more brightly than his. "Who could see him and not love him?" asked a brother pastor, who had known him for many years. "One of the kindest rectors and one of the most unshrinking friends a curate ever had," [2] is the grateful testimony of a former fellow-labourer in the ministry: a testimony which my own privileged experience enables me to repeat if possible in yet stronger terms. His spirit was eminently tender and affectionate, and his heart warm and generous. In society, and especially the society of home, he was full of cheerful anecdote and profitable suggestion. To use words which he applied to another, "There was not only the pious but the pleasant remark always hanging on his lips, and ready to fall in with much that was often very touching and beautiful." He was in very truth the sunshine of the home circle; and his kindly influence extended to every member of the household, so that he possessed, as he richly merited, the title of "the kindest and best of masters." But whether in the home or in the parish, thoughtfulness for others, in little things as well as in great things, was the law of his daily life; no personal interest or indulgence was ever allowed to stand in the way, if by the sacrifice he could further the spiritual interests of his people.

Not, indeed, that he was without faults or failings, for "there is not a just man upon earth that doeth good and sinneth not;" but Gospel grace wrought so manifestly in him "the fruits of the Spirit," that, to a remarkable degree, he "adorned the doctrine of God his Saviour:" so that it would be difficult for those who knew him best to specify what those faults and failings were.

In all that he did he was emphatically "real." There was harmony in his character; the counterpart of that harmony of

[1] "The Pastor Remembered: a Memorial of the Rev. W. H. Havergal, M.A." By the Rev. Charles Bullock, B.D. London: *Home Words* Office, Paternoster Buildings, E.C.

[2] "Sermons and Lectures," by S. B. James, B.A., formerly Curate of St. Nicholas'. See Dedication. London: Bell and Daldy.

musical genius which gave him a world-wide reputation. None could fail to recognize his "godly sincerity." He preached and said what he felt: and *from* the heart he spoke *to* the heart, as if he really *had* a message from God to deliver. He was *always* the pastor. His was not the ministry of official routine: it was the ministry of the life. His testimony respecting his friend, the Rev. John East, of Bath, when preaching his funeral sermon, applies most truly to himself:—

> The livery of his Divine Master was always and everywhere visibly upon him. Whether in the desk or the pulpit, the committee-room or the platform, the cottage or the mansion, the schoolroom or the sick chamber, the street or the railway, he was always the recognized but unostentatious servant of the Saviour whom he loved. He was not ashamed of his Master, or of His Name, or to speak a word for Him, or to do an act for Him, whenever a favourable or fitting opportunity presented itself.

He advised, he admonished, he sympathized; and, to the utmost of his means, he aided those who stood in need of aid. And throughout his ministry he was eminently "faithful." He did not hesitate, though he well knew the cost, to battle manfully with the vices and frivolities of the day. None could hearken to his conversation and think it possible to "serve God *and* mammon."

As a preacher his words were ever impressive and weighty, because they were always Scriptural; and, for the same reason, they were always easily understood. Possessing a mind of no ordinary compass and power, his imagination rich, his literary attainments varied, there was no display of gifts, but an evident desire to preach so that all might profit. He loved especially to welcome the pious poor to the House of God; often did he regret the lack of fitting accommodation for them, and heartily and liberally did he aid us in later years in making our church, in a truer sense, the house of prayer where "the rich and poor meet together." But whatever might be the character of the congregation, his aim was simply to "preach the Word." The Bible and the Bible only was his storehouse for spiritual instruction; and that storehouse could not fail. Never shall I forget his remark on one occasion, when I had referred to his lengthened ministry and the possible difficulty of selecting new texts and topics. His answer was, "The longer I live the more I am impressed with the unsearchable, inexhaustible fulness of the Word of God."

It was no slight privilege to listen for a season—only too short—to his impressive and striking expositions of Scripture; and highly do I value the notes which I was in the habit of taking down at the time. Many parishioners, I know, possess the volumes of sermons which have been published. They are models of natural and unaffected eloquence, rich in poetic feeling; but they are chiefly remarkable for close adherence to the written Word. The text contains the sermon, instead of, as is sometimes the case, the sermon merely containing the text. The prayerful study of these sermons could not fail, under God's blessing, to conduce to the spiritual edification of the reader. They preach the Gospel to the poor; and, at the same time, they are clearly the fruit of diligent labour, and frequently embody, without show of scholarship, the results of intellectual research and critical investigation. They afford proof that he did not, as a pastor, offer to his people that which "cost him nothing" in the way of preparation and careful study. It was his regular practice, unknown to others, as long as he could see, to read or write his sermons on *bended knee*. He often used to say, "I am not going to make my sermon now: that I have been doing every day; but only to write down what I have thought and done." Nor did he relax in this diligent habit of preparation when in later years his sight failed him so far that he could not use either manuscript or notes of any kind. Indeed, many considered that the marked order and precision of thought in the arrangement of his sermons, and the clearness and fulness of his expositions, became only more striking. But the secret of his preaching power was undoubtedly the Scriptural testimony which he bore, combined with his prayerful spirit of dependence on the Divine blessing.

Humility was a distinguishing trait of his character. It marked him amongst men. Whilst honouring, as we have seen, the Word of God, he ever manifested as a preacher of that Word the deepest sense of his own inability to preach it as he felt it ought to be preached. In his last sermon at Astley he said, "Often have I taken my freshly written sermon and locked it up as soon as I have left the pulpit, because I have been ashamed of its poverty and weakness, in comparison with the richness and strength of the Gospel of our salvation." He had set himself to preach "the Word," and whoever does this will be prepared to make a similar record. And this humility, which went with him into the pulpit, pervaded his whole life and conversation. He knew how to condescend, in the Gospel sense of the word, to men of low estate. He put on "lowliness of mind," and there was no affectation in his lowliness; it sat on him like a garment which had been long and constantly worn; and his native dignity only graced his humility.

It was this trait of character which made him content to abide where God had placed him. His celebrity as a musical authority, as well as his pastoral gifts, might justly have led him to look for some fitting recognition of his work. But he was not one to seek position or promotion; and after a ministry in the diocese of more than half the allotted age of man, when compelled by failing health to seek a less burdensome post, he only found in another diocese, and that through the kindness of a personal friend, a small incumbency, the income of which barely sufficed to secure the needed help of a brother pastor. Yet I never heard him complain. He was not ambitious of honours or of fame. He knew that "promotion cometh neither from the east nor from the west;" and that it becomes the Christian to

> "Scorn the highest place on earth,
> For *yonder higher place*."

And thus, in close alliance with his genuine humility, we note his noble *disinterestedness* and *integrity*; his superiority to the place-seeking spirit; that uprightness of character which ever kept him on the "crown of the road," indifferent, so far as the claims of duty were concerned, to the smiles or the frowns of men.

I say in close alliance with his humility; for, whilst he was emphatically one who "held his integrity fast"—as every honest man must hold it fast—this integrity, this consciousness of disinterestedness, in no way derogated from his humility. It was grace—grace abounding to him as a sinner—grace in which he gloried—it was grace gave him the high standard of integrity at which he aimed, and *by grace alone* did he hope to take a single step towards that standard. But, so far as grace *did* enable him to advance, whilst his shortcomings always kept him deeply humble, he gave glory to God, and he felt that the credit of the Gospel was, as it were, at stake in his person. Like St. Paul, accounting himself "the chief of sinners," he knew nevertheless what the grace of God had done for him, and he would not have the Master dishonoured by any palpable inconsistency of life or conversation. "Our rejoicing is this, the testimony of our conscience, that in simplicity and godly sincerity, not with fleshly wisdom, but by the grace of God, we have had our conversation in the world, and more abundantly to you-ward" (2 Corinthians 1:12).

Yet his consciousness of integrity never went beyond the truth, or beyond the testimony which others, who knew him best, would bear concerning him: and it was always accompanied with the ready acknowledgment of "countless shortcomings." And so, in his farewell sermon at Astley, after noting the importance of this ministerial integrity in order to ministerial usefulness, and referring to the stirring appeal of Samuel the Prophet at the close of his life to the people of Israel, he continued—

> Confident as I am, that, could your answer be openly given to me, it would resemble the answer of the Israelites to Samuel, I nevertheless disclaim, with the deepest humiliation, all self-complacency before you, and all idea of merit before God. I have been but an unworthy steward. I have indeed *aimed* to advance your comfort, and God's glory in that comfort [mark the consciousness of integrity]: but this it was my *duty* to do. I see ten thousand imperfections in my few little doings, and feel that I have urgent need to look up and say, "O Lord, cleanse Thine unworthy servant! accept what is Thine own, and pardon all that is mine!"

Yes, he knew and groaned under the "plague of his own heart." He felt cause enough to lie low before God, whilst he was conscious of his integrity before man; and it was this combination of integrity and humility which gave such power to his testimony to the Gospel of God's grace, and made him not only a preacher in the pulpit, but a preacher in the world—a preacher of what Herbert has beautifully styled "the visible rhetoric of a holy life."

The substance of his ministerial teaching, as I have said, was ever the testimony of the written Word. He did not take the waters of life at second-hand from human or ecclesiastical cisterns, but went direct to the Fountain of living waters. As a Bible Churchman, he was a genuine successor of our best Reformers. His soul beat in true harmony with Hooper and Latimer, and Cranmer and Bradford. He was faithful to his ordination promise, "out of the Scriptures to instruct the people committed to his charge;" and never forgot that the Church of England placed the Bible in his hand and bade him be "a faithful dispenser of the Word of God."

Hence the pole-stars of his teaching were, "Repentance towards God, and Faith towards our Lord Jesus Christ." In one of his sermons, "The Shepherd of the Sheep," at an ordination in Worcester, in 1845, after dwelling upon the importance of "the faithful preaching of Christ's holy Gospel, the oral exposition of God's lively truth, without which there never was any great revival of piety in either the Jewish or the Christian Church," he thus answers his question, "And *what* shall we preach?" "Let us habitually preach Christ, as the end of the law for righteousness to every contrite believer; Christ as the source of sanctification through the Spirit; Christ as the all-in-all of the sinner—the helpless, the miserable, the broken-hearted sinner."

Such was the soul-nurturing food with which he ever sought to feed the flock; and hence, amidst all the doctrinal fantasies of the age, and the clashing of opinions in the Church, in closing a ministry of nearly twenty years at Astley, before he came to Worcester, he was able to testify, "I am not conscious of the slightest change of sentiment upon any topic of importance since the day I first came amongst you." The "*truth*" could not change, and his testimony never changed. And up to the last, his opinions remained firm and unshaken. All were founded upon the Divine Word; and the only alteration was the daily continuous growth of his own *experimental* knowledge of those doctrines of Grace which caused an apostle to exclaim, "O the depth!" and into which "the angels desire to look."

He preached a doctrine as humbling to the pride of man as it is exalting to the glory of God's free Grace: a doctrine which casts down all imaginations and every high thought of moral goodness, fitness, or strength, and lays the sinner low at the foot of the Cross, the cleft Rock of Ages, in deep and painful consciousness of guilt before God and without hope from self or any earthly helper: that Evangelical doctrine which, in the pregnant and comprehensive words of Archbishop Leighton, "lays low the sinner, exalts the Saviour, and promotes holiness." He exalted Christ as "the end of the law for righteousness to every one that believeth," and pointed to His blood as the full Atonement for all "our mighty sins." He exhibited with equal clearness the Justifying and Sanctifying grace of redemption. What he said of good John Davies, of St. Clement's, we say of him: "He preached the love of God in Christ to sinners, and he *loved to preach it*: to tell such how they might be justified freely, and sanctified wholly, and saved eternally, was his study and delight." And so he defines the ministerial work, in one of his published sermons, in these striking words:—

> Repentance and Faith constitute the high road which leads to the Saviour; and the Bible and the ministers of the Gospel are appointed by God to direct inquirers in the right way. What St. Paul said of himself applies to every minister: "Woe is unto me, if I preach not the Gospel!" If we preach any other refuge but Christ, or direct men wrongly to that refuge, their blood will be required of us. The Great Saviour Himself waits to be gracious, and condescendingly and cheeringly says, "Him that cometh unto Me I will in no wise cast out." His atoning death, and His sanctifying Spirit, leave us in want of nothing but faith to apply them, and love to be grateful for them. And faith He will give if we ask it: and love He will shed abroad if we cleave to Him, and walk with Him, and pray to Him.

Could a more perfect summary of Gospel truth be expressed in simpler or clearer language?

Of the closing days of a life thus eloquent for grace, and truth, and goodness, it is needless to speak. He "walked with God, and he was not: for God took him." The first intelligence I received of his translation was conveyed to me in the simple touching words, "He is at Home"—the home in heaven of which so truly he made his earthly home a type and earnest.

The sunset of life was calm and peaceful: and on Easter-day, "very early in the morning," the joyful thoughts of Resurrection glory fresh in his mind, the Master's message reached him—the stroke of apoplexy from which he never rallied. He lay without consciousness or suffering till noon on Tuesday, and then only ceased breathing, and was at *home*. He slept in Jesus, who is "The Resurrection and the Life." "There were no good-byes for the bereaved, only *welcomes to come* in the Father's House above."

"Before one tear was wept below,
Joy filled the courts above;
No parting pang was he to know:
God took him from a world of woe
To His own world of love."

The yearning thought of *another*, expressive of more touching sympathy and precious comfort for the bereaved than words which we could frame, was to be true of him:

"Dear ones! shall it be *mine* to watch you come
Up from the shadow and the valley mist,
To tread the jacinth and the amethyst;
To rest and sing upon the stormless height,
In the deep calm of love and everlasting light?"
(F. R. H.)

May this thought prove "the bright light" in the dark cloud which hangs so heavily over loving and sorrowing hearts, especially to *one* whose grief can only be measured by her own affectionate devotedness and the irreparable loss she has sustained. "The riches of prayer and counsel, tenderness and comfort," nothing can restore to the home on earth: but that home is bereaved to help to form the Home in Heaven; and "the day is at hand."

"Soon and for ever, the breaking of Day,
Shall chase all the night-clouds of sorrow away;
Soon and for ever, our union shall be
Made perfect, our glorious Redeemer, in Thee;

When the sins and the sorrows of time shall be o'er,
Its pangs and its partings remembered no more;
Where life cannot fail, and where death cannot sever,
Christians with Christ shall be, soon—and for ever!"

Brethren, I meant these words of affectionate remembrance to be few: but "out of the abundance of the heart the mouth speaketh," and well I know the testimony I have borne will be grateful to many ears. You who knew him loved him, and to you his memory will be blessed.

He was truly "a good man, and full of the Holy Ghost, and of faith":—"an Israelite indeed, in whom was no guile." The grace of God in him issued in the formation of a character full of beauty and goodness, and in the living of a life which was the spring of purest happiness to himself and of real and abiding usefulness to others.

The contemplation of such a path, conducting to such a conclusion—

"An honoured life, a peaceful end,
And Heaven to crown it all,"—

must constrain from every heart the wish, the prayer—"Let my experience, my life, my end, be like his"; let it equally impress upon our minds the Inspired counsel—applicable to all who walk as he walked—"Be ye followers"—imitators—"of them who through faith and patience inherit the promises."

"Yet Speaketh."

"He obtained witness that he was righteous, God testifying of his gifts: and by it he being dead yet speaketh."—Hebrews 11: 4.

"Yet speaketh!" though the voice is hushed that filled
  Cathedral nave or choir, like clearest bell,
With music of God's truth, that softly thrilled
  The silence of the mourner's heart; that fell
So sweetly, oh so sweetly, on the ear
Of those to whom that voice was dearest of the dear.

"Yet speaketh!" For the echo lingers yet
  Where fifty years ago his voice was heard,
And old men weep, who never can forget
  Their early gladness through his faithful word;
O'er all the waves and storms of life between,
That voice floats on for them, still powerful and serene.

"Yet speaketh!" Glowing hymns, like heavenly breeze,
  That stir us, and our soft Hosannas lift
To Hallelujahs; holy melodies,
  Enrobed in grand sweet harmonies, a gift
Laid wholly on the altar of his God,
Without one thought or care for this world's vain applaud.

Deep teachings from the Word he held so dear,
  Things new and old in that great treasure found,
A valiant cry, a witness strong and clear,
  A trumpet with no faint, uncertain sound:
These shall not die, but live; his rich bequest
To that beloved Church, whose servant is at rest.

"Yet speaketh!" In the memories of those
  To whom he was indeed a "a living song,"
The voice, that like fair morning light arose,
  Rings on with holy influence deep and strong;
Rings on, unmingled with another sound,
The sweetest, clearest still among all others found.

"Yet speaketh!" By that consecrated life,
  The single-hearted, noble, true, and pure,
Which, lifted far above all worldly strife,
  Could all but sin so patiently endure.
O eloquence! by this he speaketh yet;
For who that knew and loved could evermore forget?

"Yet speaketh!" E'en the shadow, poor and dim,
  Of sun-traced portrait, and the cold white stone
(All that the stranger-artist guessed of him),
  Speak to our hearts in gentle spirit-tone,
Vocal with messages of faith and love,
And burning thoughts that fall like swift stars, from above.

"Yet speaketh!" There was no last word of love
  So suddenly on us the sorrow fell;
His bright translation to the home above
  Was clouded with no shadow of farewell;
His last Lent evening closed with praise and prayer,
And then began the songs of endless Easter *there.*

"Yet speaketh!" O my father, now more dear
  Than ever, I have cried, "Oh, speak to me
Only once more, once more!" But now I hear
  The far-off whisper of thy melody;
Thou art "yet speaking" on the heavenly hill,
Each word a note of joy,—and shall we not "be still"?

FRANCES RIDLEY HAVERGAL.

Thou art yet speaking on the heavenly hill,
Each word a note of joy — and shall we
not "be still"?

✻ A blind girl who heard two or three of his last sermons, said "He was a living song to me." She is now in heaven.

Our Own Fireside Aug/72
P.B.H.W. June /72.

Easter. 1872.

This is the end of F.R.H.'s fair copy autograph of "Yet Speaketh" in her Manuscript Book Nº VI, written at Easter, 1872, two years after William Henry Havergal died. Her notations at the bottom left are two periodicals that published this poem. "P.B.H.W." was likely the Perry Barr Magazine *published by Charles Bullock's* Home Words, *that this poem was published in that magazine in June, 1872. Frances added this note:*

⋇ A blind girl, who heard two or three of his last sermons, said "He was a living song to me." She is now in heaven.

ST. NICHOLAS' CHURCH, WORCESTER.

From a Sketch taken in 1848.

On the left side, this print of St. Nicholas Church was given in the original Records of the Life of the Rev. Wm. H. Havergal, M.A. *W.H.H. was the rector of St. Nicholas at the time of this sketch. On the right is an undated 19th century photograph of St. Nicholas Church, Worcester..*

TESTIMONIAL

TO THE

REV. W. H. HAVERGAL,

HENWICK HOUSE,

BY THE PARISHIONERS OF ASTLEY,

WORCESTERSHIRE,

(Upon his Resignation of the Living of that Parish;)

PRESENTED ON WEDNESDAY, SEPTEMBER 7TH, 1842.

EXTRACTED FROM

THE WORCESTER HERALD

OF SEPTEMBER 10TH, 1842.

THE present consists of an Inkstand, a Coffee Pot, a Sugar Bason, a pair of Candlesticks, all of massive silver and elegant pattern, fully bearing out the reputation of Mr. Keeley, of Birmingham, by whom they were manufactured. Each article bears a comprehensive inscription, which is more largely expressed in an introductory leaf in the following Books attached to the present of Plate:—The English Hexapla (Bagster's edition), and reprint of Miles Coverdale's Bible, and the Oxford reprint of the original authorised edition printed by Barker, each bound in purple morocco, with a small Pocket or Pulpit Bible and Liturgy, bound in purple velvet, with silver clasps and edgings. The inscription in these being—

"Presented to the Rev. W. H. HAVERGAL, M.A., by the Parishioners of Astley, on his resignation of the Living, March 18, 1842, as a memorial of gratitude for the zeal and fidelity with which, as Curate and Rector, he laboured among them during a period of nearly twenty years."

An elegant and costly Silver Cake Basket was at the same time presented to Mrs. W. H. HAVERGAL, with the annexed inscription:—

"A token of grateful affection from the Parishioners of Astley, to Mrs. W. H. HAVERGAL, in remembrance of her uniform kindness during a residence among them of nearly twenty years. March 18, 1842."

A neat Pencil Case was also presented to Miss HAGERGAL from the Children in the Sunday School of Astley.

The two Churchwardens, accompanied by T. Simcox Lea, Esq., with other principal Inhabitants, constituted a deputation, and Mr. Lea, in an address of much neatness and feeling, alluded to three kindred feelings—of gratitude, esteem, and affection, which had prompted the present tribute of respect. "If," said he, "various little incidents which had occurred during the progress of the subscriptions, could be mentioned, he should be readily believed in declaring that no body of parishioners could be found more generally and more zealously influenced by those feelings, and with such enthusiastic desire to manifest them by some memorial: that memorial was the unanimous and freewill offering of all classes in the parish, and contained both the pounds of the rich and the not less acceptable pence of the poor." The Rev. Gentleman responded to Mr. Lea in terms both chaste and elegant, and which will not soon be forgotten by those who heard him, and in a manner well worthy of all that his parishioners testified of him.

STATEMENTS OF APPRECIATION AND ARTICLES ABOUT WILLIAM HENRY HAVERGAL.

TO THE

REV. W. H. HAVERGAL,

HENWICK HOUSE,

BY THE PARISHIONERS OF ASTLEY,

WORCESTERSHIRE,

(Upon his Resignation of the Living of that Parish;)

PRESENTED ON WEDNESDAY, SEPTEMBER 7th, 1842.[1]

EXTRACTED FROM

THE WORCESTER HERALD

Of September 10th, 1842.

The present consists of an Inkstand, a Coffee Pot, a Sugar Bason, a pair of Candlesticks, all of massive silver and elegant pattern, fully bearing out the reputation of Mr. Keeley, of Birmingham, by whom they were manufactured. Each article bears a comprehensive inscription, which is more largely expressed in an introductory leaf in the following Books attached to the present of Plate:—The English Hexapla (Bagster's edition), and reprint of Miles Coverdale's Bible, and the Oxford reprint of the original authorised edition printed by Barker, each bound in purple morocco, with a small Pocket or Pulpit Bible and Liturgy, bound in purple velvet, with silver clasps and edgings. The inscription in these being—

"Presented to the Rev. W. H. Havergal, M.A., by the Parishioners of Astley, on his resignation of the Living, March 18, 1842, as a memorial of gratitude for the zeal and fidelity with which, as Curate and Rector, he laboured among them during a period of nearly twenty years."

An elegant and costly Silver Cake Basket was at the same time presented to Mrs. W. H. Havergal, with the annexed inscription:—

"A token of grateful affection from the Parishioners of Astley, to Mrs. W. H. Havergal, in remembrance of her uniform kindness during a residence among them of nearly twenty years. March 18, 1842."

A neat Pencil Case was also presented to Miss Havergal from the Children in the Sunday School of Astley.

The two Churchwardens, accompanied by T. Simcox Lea, Esq., with other principal Inhabitants, constituted a deputation, and Mr. Lea, in an address of much neatness and feeling, alluded to three kindred feelings—of gratitude, esteem, and affection, which had prompted the present tribute of respect. "If," said he, "various little incidents which had occurred during the progress of the subscriptions, could be mentioned, he should be readily believed in declaring that no body of parishioners could be found more generally and more zealously influenced by those feelings, and with such enthusiastic desire to manifest them by some memorial: that memorial was the unanimous and freewill offering of all classes in the parish, and contained both the pounds of the rich and the not less acceptable pence of the poor." The Rev. Gentleman responded to Mr. Lea in terms both chaste and elegant, and which will not soon be forgotten by those who heard him, and in a manner well worthy of all that his parishioners testified of him.

[1] This was published on a full, large page, given in facsimile on the facing page, found among Havergal manuscripts and papers.

To the Reverend William Henry Havergal. M.A. [1]

Rector of Saint Nicholas Worcester, and
Honorary Canon of Worcester Cathedral.

Reverend and Dear Sir,

It would be needless for us to employ many words to express the deep regret felt by the Members of your Congregation in the prospect of your removal from them.

Your faithfulness, zeal and devotedness in the discharge of every Ministerial duty: your pastoral counsel and sympathy so kindly dispensed in the more private relations of social and family life; the place which we are conscious we have occupied for so many years in your prayers both public and private: These are grounds of attachment and gratitude which cannot but make us feel how great will be our loss. At the same time we trust that the change will be advantageous to yourself and that the comparative rest of a Village charge may under God be found conducive to your better health.

As a small token of our deep appreciation of the many spiritual privileges which we have through you enjoyed for the lengthened period of fifteen years, we beg your acceptance of the accompanying Salver and Purse, you will permit us also to convey to Mrs. Havergal and the other Members of your family our hearty thanks for the devoted interest they have taken in promoting, in the Parish, every "work of Faith and labour of Love."

That the Lord whom you serve, may return "the sevenfold blessing" into your own bosom, and that you may long be spared to render your invaluable services to the Congregation, whose privilege it will be to welcome you, is the sincere wish of your faithful, affectionate, and grateful flock, as also of

Reverend and Dear Sir,
Yours most sincerely,
Thomas B. Burrow,
George Grainger
Churchwardens of
Saint Nicholas.

21st March 1860.

LIST OF SUBSCRIBERS.

"Grateful ones in Secret"

Mr. John Stallard
The Misses Nott
Lea and Perrins

Mr. J. W. Lea
Mr. W. Perrins
Mr. R. T. Rea
Mr. John Jones
Mr. Carden

Mrs. Hill & Mrs. Taylor
Mr. Tho. Cook
Mrs. Malpas
Mr. E. Malpas
Dr. Maxwell
Mr. Shrimpton
Mr. Jabez Jones
Mrs. Hill, Broad Street
Miss Hill, do.
Mrs. Roach
Mr. Hartin
Mr. Preedy
Mr. Skarratt
Mr. Ranson
Mrs. Parsons
Mr. Harrison
Mr. Reece
Mrs. Bayliss
Mr. Wells
Miss Birch
Mr. W. Wilson
Mr. S. Taylor
Miss Wood
Mr. F. W. Clark
Mr. Bosley
Mr. H. Rowe

---

[1] This set of papers, testimonies of appreciation from the congregation of St. Nicholas Church upon the resignation of Rev. William Henry Havergal, March, 1860, is given here newly typeset and also in facsimile in the following pages.

———

Rev. David Davies
Mrs. Guise & Mrs. Whitcombe
Mr. Stratford
Mr. Higgs

———

Sir C. Hastings, M.D.
W. Haigh, Esq., The Mayor
Mr. Aldrich
Mr. I. Garmstone
Dr. Davis
Messrs. Hobbs
Mr. Turk
Mr. Gaunt
The Misses Hudlestone

———

Rev. Dr. Phillips
Rev. C. Evans
Rev. D. W. Evans
Rev. C. Bullock
Mr. Thomas B. Burrow
Mr. George Grainger
Mr. T. Drake
Parry and Co.
Mr. H. Perkes
Mrs. N. Perrins
Miss Harris, St. Georges Square
Miss Hobbs
Mr. Robertson
Mr. G. Finch
Mr. Wakeman

———

Mr. Laslett
Mr. Bedford
Mr. Appleyard
Mr. G. Skinner
Mrs. Plant
Mrs. Perry
Mr. Corbett
Miss Allies
Mr. John Hill
Mrs. Manning
Mr. Harriss

———

Miss Harriss
Miss Malpas
Mr. Gough
Mr. Tho. Hopkins
Mr. F. Manning
Mrs. Clark
Mr. W. Woodward
Mr. C. Hill

———

Miss Smith
Mr. Gilbert
Mr. Henry Davis
Mr. Whitgrove
Mrs. Bunn
Miss Day
The Misses Barnes
Mr. Edwards
Miss Edwards
Mrs. Newland
Mr. Hobday
Mr. Mucklow
Mr. Norman
Mr. Jackson
Mr. T. A. Wilson
Mr. Henry Williams
Mrs. Gummery
Mr. C. Taylor
Mrs. Carroll

———

Mr. Arnold

———

Miss Hill, Nicholas Street
Mrs. Cole

———

Mr. Merryman
Mr. Honess
Mrs. Coombs
Mr. John Smith
Mrs. Insolb
Mr. Haycock

Thomas B. Burrow
George Grainger
} Churchwardens of Saint Nicholas, Worcester

To the Reverend William Henry Havergal. M.A.

Rector of Saint Nicholas Worcester, and
Honorary Canon of Worcester Cathedral.

Reverend and Dear Sir,

As the poorer Parishioners of Saint Nicholas we are anxious to assure you of our deep regret at the close of your earnest ministry amongst us.

We have, indeed, had many special proofs of your faithful and affectionate interest in our highest welfare, and we know how fervently you have ever desired for us " the best gifts."

As a small acknowledgement of the great debt we owe to you for spiritual and temporal exertions on our behalf, may we ask you to accept a Library Table which we trust may prove a useful piece of Furniture in your study at Shareshill.

That you, and the beloved members of your Family, to whom we owe so much, may long be spared to be a blessing in your new Parish is our earnest desire, and asking a continued interest in your Prayers.

We remain
Reverend and Dear Sir
Your grateful and attached Parishioners.

Ellen Packman
John Harris
Emma Watts
Mary Green
Mrs. Walton
Eliza Walton
Mrs. Bouldring
Francis Dyke
Harriet Dyke
Eliza Bouldring
Mr. Grainger
A well wisher
M. Malpas
Mrs. Collard
Mrs. Quorman
Fanny Knowles
Mrs. Jenkins
Mary Jenkins
Anne Jenkins
Samuel Hughes
John Hemming
Tho. and Jane Passey
B. Holmes
M. A. Wainwright
M. Combs
L. Williams

Mr. Grainger
Mr. Langford
Mrs. Wood
Mary Fidoe
Hannah Fidoe
Mrs. Williams
Eliz Williss
Mrs. Williss
Mrs. John Wood
Mrs. Gould
Sarah Combs
Catherine Dyke
Mr. E. Dyke
Mrs. E. Dyke
Mr. Bishop
Mrs. Bishop
Mr. Barker
Mrs. Barker
Mrs. Bullock
John Bullock
E. Woodward
Mary Thomas x }
Children }
Mr. Hyam
A Friend
Mrs. Lanford

Mrs. Smith, widow
Mrs. Matthews
Mrs. Groomridge, W. I.
Mrs. Rogers
Mrs. Fosbury
Eliz Jee
Sarah Hale
Mrs. Wheeler
Ann Reynolds
Mrs. Hallier
Jane Quorman
Harriet Jee
Mary Jee
Richard Jee
Mrs. Hughes
Ann Kendrick
Edward Dovey
Mrs. E Dovey
Eliz Berrow
Betsey Berrow
Jane Doughty
Mary Johnstone
Ann Watts
Mrs. Bourne
John Packman
Mrs. Gardner

I. L. Stockhall
Cha. & H. Smith
Elizabeth Tipper
George Priest
Hannah Whittle
Mrs. Jones
Esther Morris
Mrs. Yarnold
Mrs. Finch
Edw. Tillbrook
Mary Gibbons
Eliz Franklin
Ann Phillips
Lucy Tyler
Eliza Smith
Mrs. Sexton
Mrs. Soley
Richard Herbert
Mrs. Lee
Sarah Wilkins
C. H. Smith
Mrs. Tilbrook
Eliz Fosbury
Mary Withers
Mary Bowen
Mrs. Phillips (W.)

Mrs. Handley	Mrs. Stokes	Mrs. Merriman	Eliza Teague
Jane Walton	Maria Birbeck	C. Holland	Ann Helf
Eliz Evans	Mrs. Birbeck	L. Jee	Mr. Jordan
Miss Osbaldeston	Mrs. Hite	Julia Cheverton	A Friend
Thos. Hope	Ann Pardoe	M. A. Cheverton	Mrs. Dyke
Nurse Bedford	Mary Taylor	Mrs. Pugh	Mrs. Whittle
Susanna Webley	Mr. Gillams Hourkeeper	Mary Walton	Mr. Insole
Mary Anthony	A well wisher	Mrs. Williams	Mary Yarnold
Mary Cole	Rebecca Lawrence	Mrs. Newell	Mrs. Cretchley
Mrs. Waters	John Lawrence	Mrs. Robertson	Miss Wood
Mrs. Mitchell	Ann Roach	Mary Thomas	Mr. Thomason
Mrs. Surman	Mrs. Taylor	A Friend	
Eliz Sherwood	Mrs. Rickets	Mrs. Dyke Senior	

The District Visitors have the pleasure of adding a small sum to that collected among themselves by their poor people and whilst sympathising with them in every feeling expressed above, "bear them record that to their power, yea and beyond their power they were willing of themselves praying us with much intreaty that we would receive the gift and take upon us the fellowship of the ministering to the Saints."

Worcester
March 24th, 1860

C. Allies
Harriet Prekzall
Elizabeth Hobbs
Sarah B. Hill
Elizabeth Nott

Note: In the list of names above, the donation numbers are not given here, and the column format is not precisely identical. See the copy of the original document in the immediately following facsimile pages. Next is a final article of appreciation for W.H.H.

[*From the* Worcester Herald *of March* 31, 1860.]

Another Testimonial to the Rev. W. H. Havergal.—In addition to the silver salver and purse containing 160 guineas recorded last week as having been presented to Mr. Havergal on his retirement from this city, the poorer parishioners of St. Nicholas, [crossed out, illegible] have since testified their esteem of the reverend gentleman by contributing a handsome mahogany library table. Widow Packman and Mrs. Watson, both of the Trinity, were on Saturday deputed to wait upon Mr. Havergal, at Landsdowne-terrace, with an address, of which the following is a copy:—

"To the Rev. William Henry Havergal. M.A., Rector of St. Nicholas and Hon. Canon of Worcester Cathedral.

"Rev. and dear Sir,—As the poorer parishioners of St. Nicholas, we are anxious to assure you of our deep regret at the close of your earnest ministry amongst us. We have indeed had many special proofs of your faithful and affectionate interest in our highest welfare, and we know how fervently you have ever desired for us 'the best gifts.' As a small acknowledgment of the great debt we owe to you for spiritual and temporal exertions on our behalf, may we ask you to accept a library table, which we trust may prove a useful piece of furniture in your study at Shareshill. That you, and the beloved members of your family, to whom we owe so much, may long be spared to be a blessing in your new parish, is our earnest desire, and asking a continued interest in your prayers,

"We remain,
"Rev. and dear Sir,
"Your grateful and attached Parishioners."

Mr. Havergal acknowledged in suitable terms this further proof of the high estimation in which his ministrations in St. Nicholas' parish are held; and after he had expressed a fervent hope that the names of all the subscribers might be recorded in the Lamb's Book of Life, the deputation withdrew.—On Monday, Mr. and Mrs. Havergal were presented with neatly-framed photographic views of St. Nicholas church and the parochial schools, and the two Misses Havergal were each presented with a handsomely-bound book, all of which had been subscribed for by the teachers and children of the parochial schools, in order to mark their esteem for Mr. Havergal and his family.
[Added below in handwriting:] (and gold watches)

To the Reverend William Henry Havergal. M.A.

Rector of Saint Nicholas Worcester, and

Honorary Canon of Worcester Cathedral.

Reverend and Dear Sir.

It would be needless for us to employ many words to express the deep regret felt by the Members of your Congregation in the prospect of your removal fom them.

Your faithfulness, zeal and devotedness in the discharge of every Ministerial duty: your pastoral counsel and sympathy so kindly dispensed in the more private relations of social and family life; the place which we are conscious we have occupied for so many years in your prayers both public and private: These are grounds of attachment and gratitude which cannot but make us feel how great will be our loss. At the same time we trust that the change will be advantageous to yourself, and that the comparative rest of a Village charge may under God be found conducive to your better health.

As a small token of our deep appreciation of the many spiritual privileges which we have through you enjoyed for the lengthened period of fifteen years, We beg your acceptance of the accom- [illegible]

[illegible]

As a small token of our deep appreciation of the many spiritual privileges which we have through you enjoyed for the lengthened period of fifteen years, We beg your acceptance of the accompanying Salver and Purse, You will permit us also to convey to Mrs Havergal and the other Members of your family our hearty thanks for the devoted interest they have taken in promoting in the Parish, every "Work of Faith and labour of Love."

That the Lord whom you serve, may return "The sevenfold blessing" into your own bosom, and that you may long be spared to render your invaluable services to the Congregation, whose privilege it will be to welcome you, is the sincere wish of your faithful, affectionate, and grateful flock, as also of,

Reverend and Dear Sir,
Yours most sincerely,
Thomas B. Burrow,
George Grainger
Churchwardens of
Saint Nicholas.

21st March 1860.

List of Subscribers.

"Grateful ones in Secret"

Mr John Stallard.
The Misses Nott.
Lea and Perrins.

Mr J. W. Lea.
Mr W. Perrins.
Mr R. T. Rea.
Mr John Jones.
Mr Carden.

Mrs Hill & Mrs Taylor.

Revd David Davies.
Mrs Guise & Mrs Whitcombe
Mr Stratford.
Mr Higgs.

Sir C. Hastings, M.D.
W. Haigh, Esq., The Mayor.
Mr Aldrich.
Mr J Garmston.

Mr Thos. Cook.
Mrs Malpas.
Mr E Malpas.
Dr Maxwell.
Mr Shrimpton.
Mr Jabez Jones.
Mrs Hill, Broad Street.
Miss Hill, do.
Mrs Roach.
Mr Hartin.
Mr Preedy.
Mr Skarratt.
Mr Ranson.
Mr Robertson.
Mr G. Finch.
Mrs Wakeman.

Mr Laslett.
Mrs Bedford.
Mr Appleyard.
Mr G. Skinner.
Mrs Plant.
Mrs Perry.

Mrs Parsons.
Mr Harrison.
Mr Reece.
Mrs Bayliss.
Mr Wells.
Miss Birch.
Mr W. Wilson.
Mr S Taylor.
Miss Wood.
Mr F W Clark.
Mr Bosley.
Mr H Rowe.

Mr Whitgrove.
Mrs Bunn.
Miss Day.
The Misses Barnes.
Mr Edwards.
Miss Edwards.
Mrs Newland.
Mr Hobday.
Mr Mucklow.
Mr Norman.

Dr Davis.
Miss Hobbs.
Mr Turk.
Mr Gaunt.
The Misses Hudlestone.

Revd Dr Phillips.
Revd C Evans.
Revd D W Evans.
Revd C Bullock.
Mr Thomas B Burrow.
Mr George Grainger.
Mr T Drake.
Parry and Co.
Mr H Perkes.
Mrs N Perrins.
Miss Harris, St Georges Square
Miss Hobbs.

Mr Corbett.
Miss Allies.
Mr John Hill.
Mrs Manning.
Mr Harriss.

Miss Harriss.
Miss Malpas.
Mr Gough.
Mr Thos Hopkins.
Mr F. Manning.
Mrs Clark.
Mr W. Woodward.
Mr C. Hill.

Miss Smith.
Mr Gilbert.
Mr Hy Davis.

Mr Jackson.
Mr J. A. Wilson.
Mr Hy Williams.
Mrs Gummery.
Mr C. Taylor.
Mr Carroll.

Mr Arnold.

Miss Hill, Nicholas Street,
Mrs Cole.

Mr Merryman.
Mr Horness.
Mrs Coombs.
Mr John Smith.
Mrs Insoll.
Mr Haycock.

Thomas B. Burrow
George Grainger } Churchwardens of Saint Nicholas, Worcester.

To the Reverend William Henry Havergal, M.A.

Rector of Saint Nicholas Worcester and

Honorary Canon of Worcester Cathedral.

Reverend and Dear Sir

As the poorer Parishioners of Saint Nicholas We are anxious to assure you of our deep regret at the Close of your earnest Ministry amongst us.

We have, indeed, had many special proofs of your faithful and affectionate interest in our highest welfare, and we know how fervently you have ever desired for us "the best gifts."

As a small acknowledgment of the great debt we owe to you for spiritual and temporal exertions on our behalf, may we ask you to accept a Library Table which we trust may prove a useful piece of Furniture in your Study at Shareshill.

That you, and the beloved Members of your Family, to whom we owe so much, may long be spared to be a blessing in your new Parish is our earnest desire, and asking a continued interest in your Prayers.

We remain

Reverend and Dear Sir

Your grateful and attached Parishioners.

Ellen Hickman.	1	.	Brought forw.d £1.	11.	7	Brought forw.d £2.	16.	4	Brought forw.d £3.	9.	4	Brought forw.d £4.	2.	3	Brought forw.d £4.	19.	6
John Harris.	1	.	Mrs Wood.	.	6	Mrs Rogers.	.	4	Hannah Whittle.	.	3	Nurse Bedford.	1	.	Mary Walton.	2	6
Emma Watts.	.	6	Mary Fidoe.	.	1	Mrs Fosbury.	.	1	Mrs Jones.	.	4	Susanna Webley.	.	6	Mrs Williams.	.	6
Mary Green.	1	.	Hannah Fidoe.	.	1	Eliz.th Fee.	.	6	Esther Morris.	1	.	Mary Anthony.	.	4	Mrs Newell.	2	6
Mrs Walton.	2	.	Mrs Williams.	.	6	Sarah Hale.	.	6	Mrs Yarnold.	1	.	Mary Cole.	.	6	Mrs Robertson.	.	3
Eliza Walton.	2	6	Eliz.th Williss.	1	.	Mrs Wheeler.	.	6	Mrs Finch.	.	3	Mrs Waters.	.	6	Mary Thomas.	.	6
Mrs Bouldring.	1	.	Mrs Williss.	1	.	Ann Reynolds.	.	6	Edw.d Tillbrook.	1	.	Mrs Mitchell.	.	6	A Friend.	.	6
Francis Dyke.	1	.	Mrs John Wood.	.	6	Mrs Hallier.	.	3	Mary Gibbons.	.	6	Mrs Surman.	.	6	Mrs Dyke Senr.	2	6

Name	s.	d.
Harriet Dyke	1	-
Eliza Bouldring	1	-
Mrs Grainger	1	-
A well wisher	2	6
Mr Malpas		6
Mrs Collard		6
Mrs Quorman		6
Fanny Knowles	1	-
Mrs Jenkins	2	6
Mary Jenkins	2	6
Anne Jenkins	2	6
Samuel Hughes		2
John Hemming		2
Thos & Jane Passey		6
B Holmes	2	6
M A Wainwright		3
M Combs		6
S Williams		6
Mr Grainger	1	-
Mr Langford		6
car'd forw'd £1.	11.	7

Name	s.	d.
Mrs Gould	1	-
Sarah Combs	1	-
Catherine Dyke	1	-
Mr E Dyke	2	6
Mrs E Dyke	2	6
Mr Bishop	1	-
Mrs Bishop	1	-
Mr Barker	-	6
Mrs Barker		6
Mrs Bullock		6
John Bullock		6
E Woodward		6
Mary Thomas & children	3	-
Mr Hyam	1	-
A Friend	1	-
Mrs Sanford	2	6
Mrs Smith widow		3
Mrs Matthews		6
Mrs Groomridge [illegible]	-	4
car'd forw'd £2.	16.	4

Name	s.	d.
Jane Quorman		3
Harriet Jee		6
Mary Jee	1	-
Richard Jee		6
Mrs Hughes		2
Ann Hendrick	1	-
Edward Dovey		6
Mr & E Dovey		6
Eliz Berrow		1
Betsey Berrow		1
Jane Doughty		6
Mary Johnstone		2
Ann Watts		6
Mrs Bourne		6
John Packman		6
Mrs Gardner		3
J L Hockall	1	-
Chas & M Smith		2
Elizabeth Tipper		2
George Priest	2	-
car'd forw'd £3.	9.	4

Name	s.	d.
Elizth Franklin		4
Ann Phillips		2
Lucy Tyler		1
Eliza Smith		6
Mrs Sefton		3
Mrs Soley		6
Richard Herbert		6
Mrs Lee		2
Sarah Wilkins		2
C H Smith		3
Mrs Tilbrook		6
Elizth Fosbury		2
Mary Withers		4
Mary Bowen		1
Mrs Phillips (Row)		2
Mrs Handley		3
Jane Walton	2	6
Elizth Evans		6
Miss Osbaldeston	1	-
Thos Hope		2
car'd forw'd £4.	2.	3

Name	s.	d.
Elizth Sherwood		6
Mrs Stokes		6
Maria Birbeck		6
Mrs Birbeck		6
Mrs Hite		6
Ann Pardoe		2
Mary Taylor		6
Mr Gillams Housekeeper	1	-
A Well wisher	2	-
Rebecca Lawrence		6
John Lawrence		6
Ann Roach		3
Mrs Taylor		3
Mrs Ricketts		3
Mrs Merriman	2	-
G Holland	1	-
S Jee	1	-
Julia Cheverton		6
M A Cheverton		6
Mrs Pugh		6
car'd forw'd £4.	19.	6

Name	s.	d.
Eliza Teague		7
Ann Hill		6
Mr Jordan	1	-
A Friend		3
Mrs Dyke	1	-
Mrs Whittle	1	-
Mr Insole	2	
Mary Yarnold		6
Mrs Critchley	1	-
Miss Wood	1	-
Mr Thomason	2	6
£6.	0.	1.

The District Visitors have the pleasure of Adding a small sum to that collected [2nd] among themselves [1st] by their poor People and whilst sympathising with them in every feeling expressed above, "bear them record that to their power, yea and beyond their power they were willing of themselves praying us with much intreaty that we would receive the gift and take upon us the fellowship of the ministering to the Saints."

Worcester.
March 24th 1860

C Allies
Harriet [illegible]
Elizabeth Hibbs
Sarah B Hill
Elizabeth Mott.

William Henry Havergal was a strong advocate for the Church Missionary Society, the Church of England's organization to send and support preachers of the Gospel in foreign lands. He travelled extensively, speaking in many churches on their behalf, to raise awareness and support for the missionaries and their work. He wrote at least twenty-one missionary hymns, three of them printed on this announcement sheet (see pages 2085–2102 of Volume V of the Havergal edition, and also the section of poems by W.H.H. on pages 1003–1083 of Volume I). Very much like him, foreign missions was very important and dear to F.R.H. The funds raised for the C.M.S. and his initials are W.H.H.'s handwriting. The note in the bottom right corner is almost certainly Maria Vernon Graham Havergal's handwriting: F.R.H. called these "splendid"!

See page 319.

Collected after the Sermon — 16. 6. 6
Pupils' Box — 2. 2. 0
A friend (Miss N.) — 15. 0
£19. 3. 6

ON SUNDAY MORNING, THE 26th OF SEPTEMBER, 1830,

A Sermon,

ON BEHALF OF THE CHURCH MISSIONARY SOCIETY,

WILL BE PREACHED IN

THE PARISH CHURCH AT ASTLEY;

BY

~~THE REV. W. H. HAVERGAL, A.M.~~

HYMN I.

"The sabbath was made for man." Mark II. 27.

Inhabitants of earth,
Hail, hail the day of rest!
Ye saints, who boast a higher birth,
Hail it with raptured breast!

The Sun of Righteousness
Uplifts His healing face;
And Joy and Peace unite to bless
The suppliants of His grace.

The voice of saving truth
Strikes on these hallowed walls:
Here Wisdom cries to age and youth,
And patient Mercy calls.

But lo! 'midst deathly gloom,
The untaught heathen lies;
And trusts, though sinking to the tomb,
In refuges of lies.

No sabbath cheers his eye,
No gospel thrills his ear;
No hope of life beyond the sky
Dispels his horrid fear.

Then ye, who love the Lord,
In prayer lift up your voice:
Bestow on heathen tribes His word,
And bid the world rejoice!

W. H. H.

HYMN II.

"And I, if I be lifted up from the earth, will draw all men unto me." John XII. 32.

Why, Emmanuel, wast Thou lifted
On the tree of infamy?
Was it that we might be gifted
With thy life-bought liberty?
This, O Saviour,
Draws the sinner's heart to Thee.

Now enthroned above all blessing,
Bid the gods of earth retreat:
Bid mankind, Thy name confessing,
Come to Thee with holy feet.
Let the heathen
Soon Thy might and mercy greet.

Sure, no arm, but Thine, can sever
Chains which bind their souls in night;
Send Thy Spirit, Lord, or never
Will they hail Thy glorious light.
Rise, Redeemer,
Rise, and claim them as Thy right!

Draw *us* to Thee:—draw each nation,
With Thy love's mysterious cord;
So the world, in adoration,
Shall obey Thy sovereign word.
Wondrous Sufferer,
We will own no other Lord!

W. H. H.

HYMN III.

"And let the whole earth be filled with his glory. Amen, and Amen. Psalm LXXII. 19.

Brighter than meridian splendor,
Beams Messiah's spotless fame;
Him we hail, our firm defender;
Him let every tongue proclaim.
He is precious;
He is gracious;
He for ever is the same.

Crowned with honor, might and glory,
See Him high in majesty!
These He won (Oh thrilling story)
By His manhood's agony.
Now adore Him;
Bow before Him;
Own His just supremacy.

Where, 'neath papal witchcraft sleeping,
Victim-souls heed not His blood;
Where, in distant darkness weeping,
Captives dread the oppressor's rod;
Where the Pagan
Clasps his Dagon;
There shall reign the incarnate God.

Lord of glory! Source of favor!
Bid Thy heralds take their stand:
Let Thy name's reviving savor
Wake each dark and drowsy land.
Saviour, hear us;
Speak and cheer us,
When we lift the suppliant hand.

Thou art all! and all adore Thee,
Where they hymn one ceaseless song:
Soon shall earth, subdued before Thee,
Peal Thy name her tribes among.
Sons of glory,
Chant the story;
And your deep Amen prolong!

W. H. H.

MARY NICHOLSON, PRINTER, BRIDGE STREET, STOURPORT.

F. R. H. called these "splendid"!

St. Edmund Hall, Oxon.

Matriculated — 10th July 1812.
Responded — — 12. Feby. 1814
Passed the final Examination — } 15. Novr. 1815.
Proceeded to A.B. 24 Feby. 1816.
Ordained Deacon 24 March 1816
Do. — Priest — 23. March 1817.
Proceeded to A.M. 25 June 1819

Revd. W. H. Havergal

My dear Father's autograph record. The first C.M.S. Sermon was at Astley Sept. 1823 preached by his friend Revd. John Davis of St. Clements Worcester

M. V. G. H.

Memoranda de Concionibus

1816.

March 31st M. Durston } My first Sermons { 4 Acts 12.
— — — N. Lyng. — 1. Col. 12.
June 16. N. St. James's Bristol 36. Ezek. 26.
July 21st M. Keynsham — 1. Col. 12.
— 28. M. Brislington — 36. Ezek. 26.
— — N. Do. — — 10. Acts 43.
Augt. 18. M. Clifton Church — 1 Tim. 1st. 11.
Sepr. 15. M. Bedminster — 85 Ps. [illegible] 7.

1817

Jany. 19. M. Wellington — Do. — Do.
[illegible] 1. Saml. 2. d. 30.
26. M. Do. 16. Acts 14.
*Sepr. 14. M. St. Mary Le Port Bristol
Novr. 16. [illegible] Durston 57. Is. 19.
[illegible] 19. E. Lyng 2. Saml. 14. 14.
*July 1. E. — St. James's Bristol [illegible] Lecture 22 Matt 4. [illegible]

1818

June [illegible] Wellington [illegible] A.3. Phil. 8. [illegible]
Hampton Gay — 45. Is. 22.
Oct: 27. E. Wellington — 2 Kings 19. 14.
Sepr. 13. M. Burstow — 3 Philip: 8. [illegible]

1868

Jany. 22. M. [illegible] Ch. John XIII. 34
— — 29. [illegible] John XIII. 5.
April 5. M. Trinity Ch. Matt. XXVI. 18
[illegible]
April 19. E. [illegible] I. Peter III. 18
— 26. M. [illegible] XXI. [illegible]
May [illegible] M. St. Mary's — Ps. LXII. 16.
— 17 [illegible] Zech. XIII. 5
— 24. [illegible] Luke XXIV. [illegible]
E. — Do. — I. Cor. VII. 16
[illegible] Ch. [illegible] Acts XIX. 17
[illegible] Ch. [illegible] IV. 18
Octr. 18. — Do. Do. John XII. 20
— — 25. M. [illegible] Do. Do.
— — — N. Do. Do. Eph. V. 2.

1868

Novr. 15. M. [illegible] Prov. XI. 30.
— — 22. M. [illegible] Phil. II. 3
29. M. [illegible] Isaiah I. 18.
Decr. 3. M. [illegible] Col. III. 4.
— — 6. M. St. [illegible] [illegible] III. 16
10. M. [illegible] Luke X. 6.
— 13. M. Trinity Ch. — Col. I. 27.
— 20. M. [illegible] Eph. IV
[illegible] Zech. X. 4.
27. Do. Do. — I. John I. 7.

1869

Jany. 3. [illegible] Ch. [illegible] XXXIII. 16

and this was the last he ever preached in Leamington — also [illegible] [illegible] — for he was engaged at Christ Church for the 6th but taken [illegible]

These are the first two pages of sermons recorded, and the last two pages of sermons recorded in W.H.H.'s handwriting, in his Sermon Record Book. He wrote in this book the date, place, and text of Scripture for each sermon, more than 150 pages of entries, from 1816 to 1869. See also pages 41, 133, and 476 of this book.

THE REV. W. H. HAVERGAL, M.A.
From a Bust by Robert Pauer of Creuznach in 1868.
Engraved by W. Ballingall.

*This print in the original book (*Records of the Life of the Rev. William Henry Havergal, M.A.*) shows the sculpture of William Henry Havergal, which his daughter Miriam thought a good likeness of him. The same sculpture was photographed in 2002. His daughter Maria, in her Photograph Album that she gave to the Church Missionary Society wrote that this sculpture was made in 1869.*

BIOGRAPHICAL SKETCH.[1]

OF

REV. W. HAVERGAL, A.M. Editor of "OLD CHURCH PSALMODY."

Note.—The following sketch of his friend's life, by the Editor of the present SUPPLEMENT, is reprinted from THE MUSICAL AMATEUR for June 1861. To make clear an allusion to the previous notice of GLUCK, a portion of the last sentence in the "sketch" of that master's life is here added:—"We may consider him as indeed a great musician, worthy the memorial the son of Sirach invites: 'Let us now praise famous men, such as found out musical tunes. There be of them that have left a name behind them, that their praises might be reported.'" *Ecclus.* xliv. 1, 5, 8.

HAVERGAL.

WE closed the notice of Chevalier GLUCK in our last number with a quotation from the book of *Ecclesiasticus,* which we considered peculiarly apt in reference to that gifted individual. Its aptitude we consider equally great, excepting in one particular, in regard to the subject of our present notice. In that one particular, however, we hope for a long time to be at fault, and many, we are sure, concur with us in that hope. But though we cannot say of the subject of our present notice that he is "of them that have left a name *behind* them," it is by all but universal consent that "his praises are reported" as a most learned Ecclesiastical Musician and the greatest Psalmodist of this generation.

Rev. WILLIAM HENRY HAVERGAL, A.M., Incumbent of Shareshill, and Hon. Canon of Worcester, was born in the last decade of the last century, in Buckinghamshire. His public education commenced at Merchant Tailors' School, from whence so many "famous men" have emanated. His early tastes fluctuated between Medicine and Music. Making the acquaintance of Dr. CROTCH, while on a visit to Oxford previous to entering the University, he was recommended by the Doctor, who approved the skill evinced in his early compositions, to graduate both in Arts and Music, as did subsequently the late Professor at Cambridge, Dr. T. A. Walmisley, and as has done still more recently, the present Professor of Oxford, Sir F. A. Gore Ouseley, Bart, and a few others. He did not, unfortunately, act upon the advice given, but, intending to enter the church, and being a member of St. Edmund Hall, graduated in Arts only, as Bachelor in 1815, as Master in 1819.

In 1816 he was ordained, but it was not until his second Curacy, in Gloucestershire, that his taste for musical composition (laid aside for a time to make place for other subjects of study) revived. The singular musical skill of his Parish Clerk, who had a considerable local celebrity, was the immediate provocative of this revival. After removing to the Rectory of Astley, in Worcestershire, a distressing and all but fatal accident disabled him from the severer duties in which he was engaged. During several years of clerical silence, the result of that accident, his studious and active mind found relief in Music, the taste for which had so happily returned. His first published composition was an anthem-like setting of *From Greenland's Icy Mountains,* the proceeds of which, amounting to £160, were devoted to a Missionary Society. Other compositions rapidly followed, and their proceeds were always devoted in the same liberal spirit, to some charitable object. Considerable sums have been thus raised, and many, indifferent to the charms of musical notes, have doubtless oft-times been gladdened by cashing the same. Several of these earlier pieces have become popular, and all are characterized by great sweetness of melody and skill of construction. They never sustained an unfavorable criticism.

In 1836 appeared Op. 35, *An Evening Service in E flat, and 100 Antiphonal Chants.* Of the *Evening Service* it may be said that it is one of the modern glories of cathedral music. Of the *100 Antiphonal Chants,* their writer, as time rolled on, and a more correct Ecclesiology prevailed, did not judge so favourably. In 1849, Mr. HAVERGAL published an announcement to the effect that he was willing to devote nine-tenths of them to the fire, and after that halve the remainder. For ourselves we may say that the *Antiphonals* were greatly in advance of the parochial chants prevalent twenty-five years ago, and were, in common with all the works of our author, noted for their skillful and pleasing construction. One of them, a "*Recte et Retro*" Chant in C, (now commonly printed in D, and sometimes called "Worcester Chant,") is as widely known as the language, and, short though it be, possesses all the elements of musical immortality.

In the same year as the above (1836), the Gresham prize medal was adjudged to him for *An Evening Service in A,* Op.

[1] This published article was found among Havergal manuscripts and papers.

37. In 1841 a second medal was gained by an anthem *Give Thanks,* Op. 40, decidedly one of the best compositions of the kind in existence. Upon thus gaining two prizes, the umpires ruled that henceforth no candidate should receive more than two. Other Anthems and Services proceeded at various times from the pen of our author, who, we must never forget, was, with renewed strength, constantly and untiringly engaged in the arduous duties of a minister of religion.

But it is in the restoration of Metrical Psalmody to its original purity, that Mr. Havergal has rendered himself so illustrious, and for which he will be long justly venerated. He has certainly done more and to better purpose in this way than any living Musician. Those whose labours come nearest his in greatness will be the first to confirm this. From Dr. Crotch he caught the true idea on this subject, which has greatly developed in his hands. He first of all published a reprint of Ravenscroft's scarce work, *The Whole Booke of Psalmes,* in 1844. At the close of an elaborate preface of 21 pages, he there promises,—"It is the intention of the editor, as speedily as practicable, to publish a selection of the tunes, with the cantus and tenor inverted or of necessity altered, to suit our present mode of singing. To such selection will be added other tunes, principally for other metres; but strictly in the same generic style of melody and harmony." This promise was redeemed in 1847 by the publication of *Old Church Psalmody,* Op. 43, of which most persons can speak as approvingly as ourselves. It is the best, and best principled book of Psalm tunes of which Protestantism can boast, representing as we believe, and as far as is now possible, the true ideal of the Reformation and its time. All compilers since 1847 have drawn largely upon the *Old Church Psalmody.* It is now in its fourth edition. In 1854 appeared a highly interesting volume, *A History of the Old Hundredth Psalm tune, with Specimens.* In this it is proved, and as Bishop Wainwright in the Prefatory note says, "we think it will be generally conceded, that William Franc must hereafter be entitled to the credit of *composing* this most remarkable of all metrical tunes." The thanks of the archaeological as well as musical world are due to Mr. Havergal for this excellent *History.* In 1859 was published, *A Hundred Psalm and Hymn Tunes,* Op. 48, entirely of his own composition. This was due to his reputation acquired in this walk of Church music, for excepting in scattered publications by other compilers, no Psalm tunes of his own construction had been published. The *Old Church Psalmody* eschewed all modern compositions, as its name would lead readers to suppose. Its preface says:—"No composition of any living author is introduced." Of the *Hundred Tunes,* it is not too much to say that they are a monument of learning and industry; and are all, or nearly all, in entire agreement with the principles which so long and so successfully our author has propounded.

Handel, Corelli, and our great Cathedralists, are his masters. His aim is to preserve purity of style, and put down musical vanities. Notoriously liberal to publishers of music, he has been equally notorious in aiding, by scientific criticism and research, all who have applied to him. He has written and kept back far more than he has published. He is not a mere musician, but a theologian also, as his two volumes of sermons and other works of that class prove. These, as we know, are read with pleasure by persons widely differing from their writer's views.

In 1852 he all but lost his sight, which has been only partially restored. He is unable to read a note of printed music or decipher his own handwriting. Through weakened health, he has lately resigned a city Rectory (St. Nicholas, Worcester), and retired to the quiet of a small country parish. Long may he be spared to witness the growth of the principles he has so vigorously inculcated, and to receive the respect which all within his immediate influence so justly feel for him.

Note: This "Biographical Sketch" is unsigned, but the next piece, an article by Andrew James Symington, has passages which are identical, suggesting that Symington almost surely was the author also of this piece. This piece and the next article in the London *Morning Advertiser* have long passages that are identical also to the "Biographical Sketch" by Symington in *The Pastor Remembered and the Brethren Entreated* (pages 489–492 of this book).

THE LATE REV. W. H. HAVERGAL, M.A., ETC., HON. CANON OF WORCESTER CATHEDRAL.

(From a notice in the London *Morning Advertiser*, by Andrew James Symington.)

Havergal has gone to his rest. After that long life-service to the great Master for which he was truly made meet, he was peacefully called away on Tuesday, April the 19th, at noon. The church on earth is poorer for the change, but the Church in Heaven is richer by one. His memory will be lovingly and fondly cherished by the parishioners to whom he successively ministered at Astley, Worcester, and Shareshill; by those to whom he occasionally preached in later days at Leamington; at Pyrmont, in Germany, where for some years he officiated during the summer months; and by all those who in any degree enjoyed the great privilege of his personal acquaintance; for he was pre-eminently a good pastor and a faithful friend.

As an ecclesiastical musician and psalmodist he was, without question, the first man of his generation,—indeed, the Ravenscroft of the nineteenth century. His loss is deeply felt and deplored by the musical world.

He was born in Buckinghamshire, in 1793; was educated at St. Edmund's Hall, Oxford, where he graduated B.A. in 1815, and M.A. in 1819. His early tastes fluctuated between medicine and music.

Among his university contemporaries were Archbishop Longley, Bishop Hampden, Dr. Arnold, Lord Westbury, Professor Baden Powell, Archdeacon Creyke, and the Hon. G. Pellew, late Dean of Norwich.

In 1816 he was ordained by Bishop Ryder, for Dr. Beadon, Bishop of Bath and Wells; and, having served some minor offices in the Church, he was, in 1829, presented to the rectory of Astley, near Bewdley.

Here he met with a distressing and almost fatal accident which laid him aside from his clerical duties for several years, and indeed seriously affected his vision for life. During that period his studious and active mind found relief in music, for which art he naturally had both taste and genius.

His first published composition was an anthem-like setting of Heber's "From Greenland's Icy Mountains," the proceeds of which, amounting to £180, were devoted to the Church Missionary Society. Other compositions rapidly followed, and their proceeds were always devoted in the same liberal spirit to charitable objects. Many of these early pieces have become popular, and all of them are characterised by great sweetness of melody and skillful construction.

In 1836 appeared Op. 35, "An evening Service in E flat and One Hundred Antiphonal Chants." One of these, a "Recte et Retro" Chant in C (now commonly printed in D), and sometimes called "Worcester Chant," is as widely known as the language, and possesses all the elements of musical immortality.

In the same year as the above (1836), the Gresham prize medal was adjudged to him for an Evening Service in A, Op. 37. In 1841 a second medal was gained by an anthem, "Give Thanks," Op. 40, decidedly one of the best compositions of the kind in existence. Upon thus gaining two prizes, the umpires ruled that no man should receive more than two. Other anthems and services proceeded at various times from the pen of our author, who, we must never forget, was, with renewed strength, constantly and untiringly engaged in the arduous duties of a minister of religion.

But it is in the restoration of metrical psalmody to its original purity that Mr. Havergal has rendered himself so illustrious, and for which he will be long justly venerated. He has certainly done more and to better purpose in this way than any other musician. Those whose labours come nearest his greatness will be the first to confirm this. From Dr. Crotch he caught the true idea on this subject, which has greatly developed in his hands. He first of all published a reprint of Ravenscroft's scarce work, *The Whole Booke of Psalmes,* in 1844. At the close of an elaborate preface of 21 pages, he there promised,—"It is the intention of the editor, as speedily as practicable, to publish a selection of the tunes, with the cantus and tenor inverted, or of necessity altered, to suit our present mode of singing. To such selection will be added other tunes, principally for other metres, but strictly in the same generic style of melody and harmony.

In 1845 he was presented by Bishop Pepys to the rectory of St. Nicholas, Worcester, and to an honorary canonry in the cathedral.

In 1847 he published the *Old Church Psalmody,* Op. 43. It is the best book of Psalm tunes of which Protestantism can boast, representing, as we believe, and as far as is now possible, the true ideal of the Reformation and its time. All compilers since 1847 have drawn largely upon the *Old Church Psalmody.* In 1854 appeared a highly interesting volume, *A History of the Old Hundredth Psalm tune, with specimens.* In this it is proved, and as Bishop Wainwright in the prefatory note says, "we think it will be generally conceded, that William Franc must hereafter be entitled to the credit of composing this most remarkable of all metrical tunes." The thanks of the archaeological as well as the musical world were accorded to Mr. Havergal for his excellent history. A few days before his last illness he was engaged in writing a preface for a new edition of this work. In 1859 was published *A Hundred Psalm and Hymn Tunes,* Op. 48, entirely of his own composition. This was due to his reputation acquired in this walk of Church music, for, excepting in scattered publications by other compilers, no Psalm tune of his own construction had been published. The *Old Church Psalmody* eschewed all modern compositions, as its name would lead readers to suppose. Its preface says:—"No composition of any living author is introduced." Of the *Hundred Tunes* it is not too much to say that they are a monument of learning and industry; and are all, or nearly all, in entire agreement with the principles which so long and so successfully its author propounded.

Handel, Corelli, and our great Cathedralists, were his masters. His aim was to preserve purity of style, and put down musical vanities. Notoriously liberal to publishers of music, he has been equally willing to aid, by scientific criticism and research, all who applied to him. He has written and kept back far more than he has published.

He was not a mere musician, but a theologian also, as his two volumes of sermons and other works of that class prove.

In 1852 he all but lost his sight, which was afterwards only partially restored. He for long was unable to read a note of printed music or decipher his own handwriting. Through weakened health, in 1860, he resigned his charge at Worcester, on being nominated by Lord Hatherton, to the rectory of Shareshill, a small country parish near Wolverhampton. In 1868, from increasing infirmities, he had to lay aside all regular parish work, and removed to Leamington, where, with the exception of visits to the Continent, he resided until his death.

For some years he was in the habit of frequenting Pyrmont, in Germany, during the summer months, for the sake of its mineral waters; and while there he was able to conduct the English service and preach in the Friends' meeting-house, for the benefit of his fellow-countrymen and others who were also sojourners there. No opportunity for sowing the good seed or uttering a kindly human word of help or cheer did he ever neglect; and so highly were his ministrations valued by strangers from various parts of Europe, that the fact of Mr. Havergal being there in several instances decided that parties should go to Pyrmont rather than elsewhere. This summer he had arranged to go there in May.

To hear Mr. Havergal improvise, seated at a good harmonium with many stops, given him by his parishioners, was a rare treat, something higher, deeper, and more than a pleasure—a thing, or rather a spiritual experience, which cannot be forgotten. Sweet-flowing melody, accompanied with strange, unexpected combinations of harmony, full of mysterious chords and curious synchronous and successive felicities, each part capable of being resolved into a perfect and separate composition—fugues chasing each other, turning, meeting, and then passing through the theme in quite opposite directions, meeting again, then twining lovingly together, and, like the strands of a new cable, finding strength in union—starry phrases of melody echoed from heavenly heights till lost in the distance; then vast galaxies of chords "swim into ken," dependent on and perfectly balanced by other galaxies, controlled even to the perturbation of a single satellite, till all is light and motion; while Handelian shakes, like auroras, at intervals gleam and dart across the blue starlit dome. Yet with all this there is no hesitation, no confusion, no fear; ruled by the genius of a master, every phrase, chord, and movement progresses with stately grandeur and precision towards the evolution of the one idea which informs and pervades the whole marvellous performance. Sometimes we wander far away through wild intervals into weird discords; and then these, ere they become too painful, are resolved with consummate skill, and we mark "lines of differing method" all meeting "in one full centre of delight," as we find ourselves led on and on, and ever by new and unexpected ways, home again at last to the key-note.

The firmness, precision, and delicacy of Mr. Havergal's touch were each and all remarkable, both in kind and degree. These several characteristics were strikingly brought out in his improvisations, which never by any chance contained anything approaching the commonplace. Instead of that, his every combination was original, often a surprise even to himself; many lovely transient effects thus flashed and faded that could not be repeated. Compositions of daring originality and perfect rounded beauty;—now bold and strident, like the tramp of a giant army, and now ethereally delicate, like the dying cadences of an Æolian harp—streamed from the keys at the magic "touch" of that "vanished hand" which we shall hear no more on earth!

Although Mr. Havergal's ecclesiastical music is of the very highest type, and severe in style, he has also written many beautiful songs, rounds, and catches for the young, which are full of childlike life and birdlike glee; also numberless carols, hymns, and sacred songs, composing both the words and music. Here is one of his songs for the young, written for his grandchildren. It is in keeping with that incoming season which its gifted author loved, but which he needs not now:—

SUMMERTIDE IS COMING.

I.

"Summertide is coming,
    With all its pleasant things,

Every bee is humming,
And every songster sings.
Mornings now are brightsome,
Inviting student thought;
Evenings, too, are lightsome,
With balmy quiet fraught!
Hearths no longer lure us,
The fields instead we roam;
Hearts albeit insure us
A happy, happy home.

II.

"Summertide, I hail thee,
The Empress of the year!
But thou soon would'st fail me
Were not thy Maker near.
He thy course disposes,
Thy light, thy scent, thy glow;
He tints all thy roses,
And paints thy brilliant bow.
Laud Him, all creation,
The sinner's mighty Friend;
Near Him be our station,
Where summer ne'er shall end!"

W.H.H.

The genius of poetry and music has descended and been largely developed in Mr. Havergal's youngest daughter, whose recent volume, *The Ministry of Song,* has been so extensively and favourably noticed throughout the Press, and been admired by all lovers of true poetry.

Mr. Havergal's severe and classical music is often to be heard in our cathedrals; and in Scotland and America no Psalm tune is oftener sung than "Evan." The history of this tune is somewhat peculiar, and, as its authorship has been questioned, it may be well to mention the matter here, as the writer can do so authoritatively from Mr. Havergal's own words, as well as from written statements. In 1847 Mr. Havergal published an original air (a sacred song) to Burns's words, "O Thou dread Power." Dr. Lowell Mason, of New York, arranged the first half of that air as a psalm tune, altering both the time and key, and called it "Evan." Hence it is frequently given in collections with Mason's name, and at other times simply with the letter H, under which initial it first appeared, because Dr. Mason did not wish to attribute the liberty he had taken in arranging the part of a melody to the composer of the original air. This is Dr. Lowell Mason's own explanation, which we have seen. Mr. Havergal has since arranged it as it should be, and within the last month played over the tune, and gave a MS. copy of it to the writer, with its curious history noted on the sheet. It has travelled far and wide, and been claimed for many composers, and even been called an old Celtic air. We have here stated the true origin of this unprecedentedly popular tune.

Mr. Havergal throughout his life has subordinated genius and every talent to the work of the Christian ministry, and was in every respect the model of what a faithful pastor and a gospel preacher should be, giving no uncertain sound, but delivering his message in its fulness and freeness from the heart to the heart, without fear or favour. He studied medicine that he might attend to the bodies as well as the souls of his country parishioners, instructed them in sanitary matters, inculcated habits of domestic and general economy, organised charities, and, in short, was a loving and beloved father and friend to all his people.

As genial as he was gentlemanly, refined in his tastes, high-souled and gifted, his own immediate home circle, relatives, and numerous friends were all perfectly devoted to him; and no one could possibly approach him, even in a casual way, without feeling the radiation of Christian light and warmth from his heart and beaming face; for to the core he was a true man: true to God, and true to his fellow-men.

Bible societies, district visitation, Bible reading, home and foreign missions, and all philanthropic schemes had ever his cordial support and co-operation. Loving freedom, he was from of old an earnest and urgent advocate for the abolition of slavery; and for the same reason he constantly resisted both the open and the insidious aggressions of the Roman Catholic system, as being a conspiracy subversive of all *civil* liberty, to say nothing of religion; and the very last use made of his pen was to append his signature to a petition in favour of Mr. Newdegate's motion for the inspection of convents and nunneries.

On Saturday, the 16th, three days before the end, Mr. Havergal felt even better than his wont,—was able to be twice out of doors, went to bed as usual, and slept fairly; but very early on Easter morning, after complaining of pain in the head, he was instantly and entirely unconscious. It was apoplexy, and consciousness never returned. He lay without any suffering till noon on Tuesday, when, at the age of 70, he fell asleep in Jesus. He fully realised the wish so beautifully expressed in his own characteristic lines given below for a peaceful departure. He was even spared the pain of a parting farewell to his dear ones around him.

On Saturday, the 23rd, Shakespeare's birthday, he was borne to Astley Churchyard, and there he peacefully rests amid the scenes of his early labours, awaiting the joyous and certain welcome, "Well done, good and faithful servant," which awaits him on the resurrection morn. Truly the memory of the just is blessed!

MY TIMES ARE IN THY HAND

(By the late Rev. W. H. Havergal.)

My times are in Thy hand,
Their best and fittest place;
I would not have them at command
Without Thy guiding grace.

" My times," and yet not *mine,*
I could not them ordain;
Not one e'er waits from me a sign,
Nor can I one detain.

" My times," O Lord, are Thine,
And Thine their oversight:
Thy wisdom, love, and power combine
To make them dark or bright.

I know not what shall be
When passing times are fled;
But all events I leave with Thee,
And calmly bow my head.

Hence, Lord, in Thee I rest,
And wait Thy holy will;
I lean upon my Saviour's breast,
Or gladly go on still.

And when " my times " shall cease,
And life shall fade away,
Then bid me, Lord, depart in peace
To realms of endless day!

[*From the* Worcester Herald *of Saturday, April* 23, 1870.]

THE LATE REV. W. H. HAVERGAL.

This venerated, highly-gifted, and beloved minister of our Church, for 14 years the rector of St. Nicholas' parish, in this city, has been gathered to his rest, "a shock of corn in its season."

He was no ordinary man. A true " poet of the sanctuary," his contributions to the " Psalmody " of the House of God ranked him amongst the foremost of our musical authorities. His " Old Church Psalmody " is a standard book of reference, and scarcely a collection of tunes can be found which is not enriched with his original compositions.

As a preacher and a pastor, the motto of his life might have been, " This one thing I do," so entirely did he devote himself to his ministerial labours. His sermons were models of natural and unaffected eloquence, rich in poetic feeling, and evincing the intellectual powers of a well-stored mind. But they were chiefly remarkable for close adherence to the Written Word. The pole stars of his teaching were " Repentance towards God," and " Faith towards our Lord Jesus Christ." Hence, amidst all the doctrinal fantasies of the age, and the clashing of opinions in the Church, in closing a ministry of nearly 20 years at Astley, before he came to Worcester, he was able to testify, " I am not conscious of the slightest change of sentiment upon any topic of importance since the day I first came among you." The "*truth*" could not change; and his only aim had been to preach " the truth " in all its Scriptural simplicity. Thus honouring the Word of God, he ever manifested, as a preacher of that Word, the deepest personal humility. In his last sermon at Astley he said, " Often have I taken my freshly-written sermon and locked it up as soon as I have left the pulpit, because I have been ashamed of its poverty and weakness in comparison with the richness and strength of the Gospel of our salvation." Yet those who were privileged to enjoy his ministry were especially impressed with the clearness and fulness of his expositions. During later years sight failed him so far that he could not use either manuscript or notes of any kind, but the marked order and precision of thought in the arrangement of his sermons became only more striking. Two volumes of sermons have been published, and a year or two since a smaller work containing a course of Lent lectures.

As a pastor he was " in labours more abundant," but ever ready to acknowledge " ten thousand imperfections " in his ministry, and " his urgent need to look up and say, 'O Lord cleanse Thine unworthy servant: accept what is Thine own, and pardon all that is mine."

It was the writer's privilege for a time to witness in the parish of St. Nicholas, Worcester, his single-minded and thorough-hearted devotedness to the spiritual interests of his people. Never has he met one whose Christian character shone more brightly. The integrity, disinterestedness, and purity of his motives, marked "the holy and humble man of heart." His spirit was eminently tender and affectionate, and his heart warm and generous; but "in godly sincerity," uninfluenced by fear or favour, he never shunned to declare "the whole counsel of God." He excelled in uttering "words in season." His testimony respecting the Rev. John East, of Bath, when preaching his funeral sermon, applied most truly to himself: "There was not only the pious but the pleasant remark always hanging on his lips, and ready to fall in with much that was often very touching and beautiful."

His *home* sympathies were very strong. In the funeral sermon just mentioned, a passage occurs which brings this trait into touching prominence. No words could better describe his own home-character, than the closing sentences of the paragraph. The last audible sound from the lips of his beloved friend, John East, was "Home, Home." Referring to this, the preacher said:—

This *last* word "home" falls on my ear with a thrilling force which I can hardly convey to you: for, singular to say, it is the *first* remembered word which passed between him and me. The word "home" was, so to speak, the altar around which our friendship and fidelity were sworn to each other. *"East, do you love home?"* was the first sentence, which he recollected ever to have been uttered by myself, in the early days of our school-life. He always bore it in mind, and frequently referred to it, fondly and affectionately in after days. There is no marvel in this: for our East was a thorough man of home. He loved it with hallowed intensity, and only feared, as I have heard him say, that he loved it too much. Never could it be said of him, that he was not at home what he was in society. *His brightest excellencies shone out at home.* Fitly therefore did a glance of his eternal home waken up his sinking thoughts.

One in heart and spirit, the "friends" have been one also in the similarity of the closing scene. East's end was "gentle, calm, peaceful, child-like." So with his now departed brother in the faith. For some years he had been unequal to any active ministerial charge, although, on resigning the rectory of St. Nicholas, Worcester, he accepted the small incumbency of Shareshill, near Wolverhampton. Through the last winter he had been at Leamington; and there he died. Last Saturday, three days before his death, we are told, was "his best and brightest day for months." He was out twice, and seemed peculiarly *happy*. He slept fairly, but on Easter morning, "very early," after complaining of pain in the head, he fell back, and was instantly and entirely unconscious. It was apoplexy, and consciousness never returned. He lay without any suffering till noon on Tuesday, and then only ceased breathing and was *at home*. There were no goodbyes for the bereaved—only *welcomes to come* in the Father's House above.

"*Servant of God*, well done!
Rest from thy loved employ:
Thy day is o'er, the victory won:
Enter thy Master's joy."

—*Communicated.*

"So shall we ever be with the Lord."

(I. THESS., IV. 17.)

O thrilling thought, that I shall be
With Him who shed His blood for me,
Where nought from Him shall sever;
Where I with sainted hosts above,
O'ershadowed by the Holy Dove,
Shall banquet on His boundless love,
And KNOW those words,—"for ever."

O thrilling thought, to see Him shine,
For evermore to call Him mine,
With heaven, ALL heaven, before me!
To stand where angel myriads gaze,
Amid the illimitable blaze,
While He the Godhead full displays,
To all the sons of glory!

BY THE LATE REV. W. H. HAVERGAL, M.A.

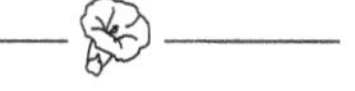

In Remembrance of
William Henry Havergal, M. A.,
Vicar of Shareshill, and Hon. Canon of Worcester Cathedral,
Who entered into Life Eternal
APRIL 19th, 1870; AGED 77 YEARS.

"FAITHFUL UNTO DEATH."

His remains were interred, April 23rd, at Astley, of which Parish he was Rector, 1829 *to* 1842.

A memorial card printed to give to family and friends after his death.

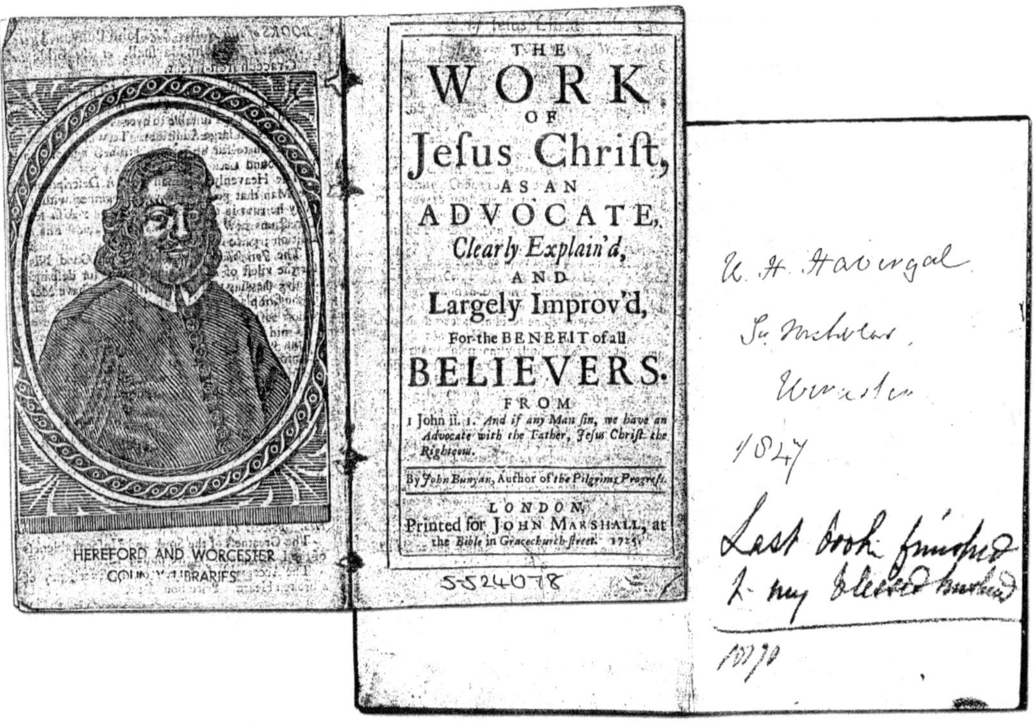

THE
WORK
OF
Jesus Christ,
AS AN
ADVOCATE,
Clearly Explain'd,
AND
Largely Improv'd,
For the BENEFIT of all
BELIEVERS.
FROM
1 John ii. 1. And if any Man sin, we have an Advocate with the Father, Jesus Christ the Righteous.

By John Bunyan, Author of the Pilgrims Progress.

LONDON,
Printed for JOHN MARSHALL, at the Bible in Gracechurch-street. 1725.

HEREFORD AND WORCESTER
COUNTY LIBRARIES
5524078

W. H. Havergal
St. Nicholas.
Worcester
1847

Last book finished
by my blessed husband
1870

On the inside of the book, near the front cover, William Henry Havergal wrote: W. H. Havergal St. Nicholas Worcester 1847. Below that, his widow Caroline Ann Havergal wrote: Last book finished by my blessed husband 1870.

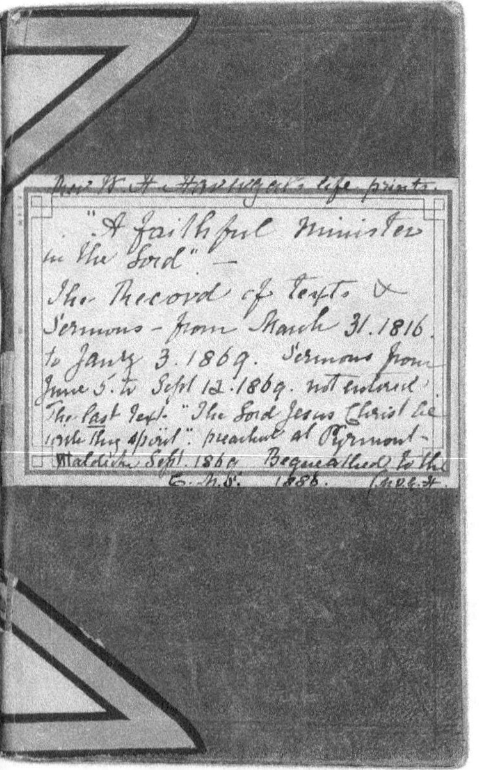

Rev W. H. Havergal's life prints.
"A faithful minister in the Lord" —
The Record of Texts & Sermons – from March 31. 1816. to Janry 3. 1869. Sermons from June 5. to Sept 12. 1869. not entered. The last Text "The Lord Jesus Christ be with thy spirit". preached at Pyrmont-Waldeck Sept. 1869. Bequeathed to the C.M.S. 1886. (M.V.G.H.)

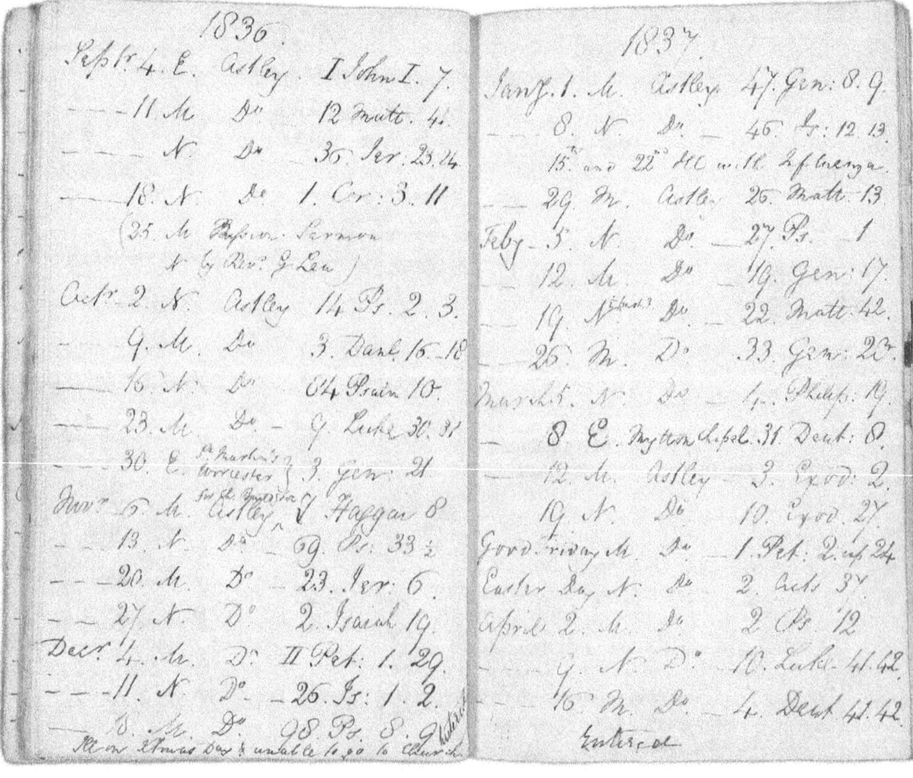

1836.

Sept. 4. E.	Astley	I John I. 7.
— 11. M.	Do	12 Matt. 4.
— N.	Do	35. Jer. 23. 24
— 18. N.	Do	1. Cor: 3. 11
(25. M. Mission Sermon N. by Revd. G. Lea)		
Octr. 2. N.	Astley	14 Ps. 2. 3.
— 9. M.	Do	3. Danl. 16–18
— 16. N.	Do	84 Psalm 10.
— 23. M.	Do	9. Luke 30. 31
— 30. E.	St. Martin's Worcester	3. Gen: 21
Novr. 6. M.	Astley	Haggai 8
— 13. N.	Do	69. Ps. 33½
— 20. M.	Do	23. Jer. 6.
— 27. N.	Do	2. Isaiah 19.
Decr. 4. M.	Do	II Pet: 1. 29.
— 11. N.	Do	26. Is: 1. 2.
— 18. M.	Do	98 Ps. 8. 9

Xmas Day & unable to go to Church

1837.

Jany. 1. M.	Astley	47. Gen: 8. 9.
— 8. N.	Do	46. Is: 12. 13.
15th and 22d ... Influenza		
— 29. M.	Astley	26. Matt. 13.
Feby. 5. N.	Do	27. Ps. 1
— 12. M.	Do	19. Gen: 17.
— 19. N.	Do	22. Matt. 42.
— 26. M.	Do	33. Gen: 20.
March 5. N.	Do	4. Philip: 19.
— 8. E.	Mytton Chapel	31. Deut: 8.
— 12. M.	Astley	3. Exod: 2.
— 19. N.	Do	10. Exod. 27.
Good Friday M.	Do	1. Pet: 2. up 24
Easter Day, N.	Do	2. Acts 38
April 2. M.	Do	2. Ps. 12
— 9. N.	Do	10. Luke 41. 42.
— 16. M.	Do	4. Deut 41. 42.

Entered

The front cover and two pages of the Sermon Record Book of William Henry Havergal. He wrote in this book the date, place, and text of Scripture for each sermon, more than 150 pages of entries, from 1816 to 1869. Maria wrote on the cover: Rev W. H. Havergal's life prints. "A faithful minister in the Lord." The Record of Texts and Sermons from March 31.1816. to Janry 3.1869. Sermons from June 5 to Sept 12.1869. not entered. The last text "The Lord Jesus Christ be with thy spirit." Preached at Pyrmont Waldeck [illegible, preached at Waldeck in Germany] Sept.1869 Bequeathed to the C.M.S. 1886. (M.V.G.H.) See also pages 41, 133, and 467 of this book.

The Pastor Remembered,

AND

The Brethren Entreated.

A MEMORIAL OF

THE

REV. W. H. HAVERGAL, M.A.,

FORMERLY RECTOR OF ST. NICHOLAS', WORCESTER;

BY THE

REV. CHARLES BULLOCK,

RECTOR OF ST. NICHOLAS', WORCESTER, AUTHOR OF "THE WAY HOME," ETC.

WITH

Biographical Sketch,

BY

ANDREW JAMES SYMINGTON,

FELLOW OF THE ROYAL SOCIETY OF NORTHERN ANTIQUARIES, COPENHAGEN.

LONDON:

W. HUNT & CO., 23, HOLLES STREET, CAVENDISH SQUARE.
S. W. PARTRIDGE & CO., 9, PATERNOSTER ROW.
THE CHRISTIAN BOOK SOCIETY, 22, KING WILLIAM STREET, STRAND.

Downtown Worcester at or near the time of William Henry Havergal. St. Nicholas Church has the tall spire, on the right. See also page 453 of this book.

"The memory of the just is blessed."

"So shall we ever be with the Lord."

(1 Thessalonians 4:17.)

Oh, thrilling thought! that I shall be
With Him who shed His blood for me,
Where naught from Him shall sever;
Where I, with sainted hosts above,
O'ershadowed by the Holy Dove,
Shall banquet on His boundless love,
And know those words, "For ever."

Oh, thrilling thought! to see Him shine,
For, evermore to call Him mine,
With Heaven, all Heaven, before me!
To stand where angel myriads gaze,
Amid the illimitable blaze,
While He the Godhead full displays,
To all the sons of glory!

By the late Rev. W. H. Havergal, M.A.

A TRIBUTE

TO

The Memory

OF A

VENERATED PASTOR AND BELOVED FRIEND,

WHOSE LIFE

IN THE HOME, THE CHURCH, AND THE WORLD,

ADORNED THE DOCTRINE

OF

GOD HIS SAVIOUR.

"Thou hast made him most blessed for ever: Thou hast made him exceeding glad with Thy countenance." Psalm 21:6.

"He was a good man, and full of the Holy Ghost and of faith." Acts 11:24.

CONTENTS.

Church
Missionary Society
27. Sept. 1835.
Collected
after a Sermon by
Rev. W. H. Havergal
£14. 6. 0.
Text
1. Tim: II. 6.

This is one of many collections after sermons by W.H.H., who travelled and preached very extensively to raise awareness and support for the Church Missionary Society. Text 1 Timothy 2:6. Foreign missions and the preaching of the gospel of Christ to lost people was very important and dear to W.H.H. *See page 480.*

"Be ye followers of them who, through faith and patience, inherit the promises."

"Lord of the church, we humbly pray."

Lord of the Church, we humbly pray
For those who guide us in Thy way,
And speak Thy Holy Word;
With love Divine their hearts inspire,
And touch their lips with hallowed fire,
And needful grace afford.

Help them to preach the truth of God,
Redemption through the Saviour's blood;
Nor let the Spirit cease.
On all the Church His gifts to shower,
To them a messenger of power,
To us of life and peace.

ANON.

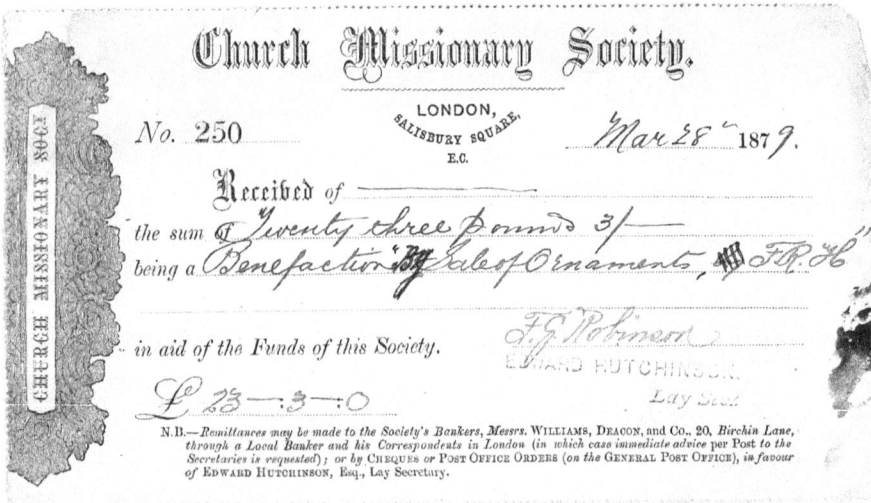

Church Missionary Society.

CHURCH MISSIONARY SOCY.

No. 250 LONDON, SALISBURY SQUARE, E.C. Mar 28th 1879.

Received of

the sum of Twenty three Pounds 3/–

being a Benefaction By Sale of Ornaments, by F.R.H.

in aid of the Funds of this Society. F.G. Robinson EDWARD HUTCHINSON, Lay Secy.

£23—3—0

N.B.—*Remittances may be made to the Society's Bankers, Messrs.* WILLIAMS, DEACON, and Co., 20, *Birchin Lane, through a Local Banker and his Correspondents in London (in which case immediate advice per Post to the Secretaries is requested); or by* CHEQUES *or* POST OFFICE ORDERS (*on the* GENERAL POST OFFICE), *in favour of* EDWARD HUTCHINSON, Esq., Lay Secretary.

Very much like W.H.H., F.R.H. also deeply loved and supported the work of foreign missions. The March 28, 1879 receipt shows the money for the C.M.S. from the sale of F.R.H.'s jewellery late in her life. She would have wanted to go to India as a missionnary, if her physical health had been equal to that.

CDyl. 11/12/78. 10/12/78

£50 from Miss Havergal which entered as "Profits on books & sale of ornaments – from Miss F. R. Havergal –"

This receipt, dated 10/12/78 and 11/12/78, was almost surely signed by Mr. Wright of the Church Missionary Society, whose work and missionaries she deeply loved. The "ornaments" almost certainly were the sale of her jewellery that she donated and sold for money to the C.M.S. .

£50 from Miss Havergal which entered as "Profits on books & sale of ornaments – from Miss F. R. Havergal –"

I.

The Pastor Remembered,

AND

The Brethren Entreated.

A SERMON PREACHED IN ST. NICHOLAS' CHURCH, ON SUNDAY, MAY 1st, 1870.

---

2 Thessalonians 3:1.

"Finally, brethren, pray for us, that the Word of the Lord may have free course, and be glorified."

THE PASTOR REMEMBERED: THE BRETHREN ENTREATED. To utter words of affectionate recollection and words of earnest exhortation and entreaty—this is my purpose, this is my desire. Brethren, pray for me! Pray that I may be guided by the wisdom which descendeth from above, and pray that the Holy Spirit may so "direct and rule" all our hearts that our recollections of the past and our resolves for the future may alike conduce to our spiritual edification and profit.

First, then, I am anxious to utter in this sanctuary, WORDS OF AFFECTIONATE REMEMBRANCE.

It is not, indeed, in my power to attempt any adequate sketch or estimate of the character and ministry of the "faithful" pastor, whose memory, though years have elapsed since he laboured amongst us, will ever be deeply and lovingly cherished. My words will be few: but still I trust they will, in some measure, give expression to those feelings of veneration and appreciation in which all who knew him so fully shared.

He was truly no ordinary man. His personal endowments were distinguished. A true "poet of the sanctuary" and an enthusiastic lover of "holy music," his contributions to the Psalmody of the House of God ranked him amongst the foremost musical authorities of the age. His "Old Church Psalmody" will always be a standard book of reference, and scarcely can a collection of tunes be found which is not enriched with his original compositions. But he was rich in grace as well as rich in gifts. His heart and his life were in good tune, and he loved above all other harmony the melody of good works.

I have enjoyed the friendship of many ministers, but I have never met with one whose Christian character in the Church and in the Home shone more brightly than his. "Who could see him and not love him?" asked a brother pastor, who had known him for many years. "One of the kindest rectors and one of the most unshrinking friends a curate ever had,"[1] is the grateful testimony of a former fellow-labourer in the ministry: a testimony which my own privileged experience enables me to repeat, if possible, in yet stronger terms.

His spirit was eminently tender and affectionate, and his heart warm and generous. In society, and especially the society of home, he was full of cheerful anecdote and profitable suggestion. To use words which he applied to another—"There was not only the pious but the pleasant remark always hanging on his lips, and ready to fall in with much that was often very touching and beautiful." He was, in very truth, the sunshine of the home circle: and his kindly influence extended to every member of the household; so that he possessed, as he richly merited, the title of "the kindest and best of masters." But, whether in the home or in the parish, thoughtfulness for others, in little things as well as in great things, was the law of his daily life; and no personal interest or indulgence was ever allowed to stand in the way if by the sacrifice he could further the spiritual interests of his people.

Not, indeed, that he was without faults and failings, for "there is not a just man upon earth who doeth good and sinneth not;" but Gospel grace wrought so manifestly in him "the fruits of the Spirit," that, to a remarkable degree, he "adorned the doctrine of God his Saviour;" so that it would be difficult

[1] Sermons and Lectures, by S. B. James, B.A., formerly Curate of St. Nicholas'. See Dedication. London: Bell and Daldy.

for those, who *knew him best* to specify what those faults and failings were.

In all he did he was emphatically "real." There was harmony in his character; the counterpart of that harmony of musical genius which gave him a world-wide reputation. None could fail to recognize his "godly sincerity." He preached and said what he felt: and *from* the heart he spoke *to* the heart, as if he really *had a* message from God to deliver. He was *always* the pastor. His was not the ministry of official routine: it was the ministry of the life. His testimony respecting his friend, the Rev. John East, of Bath, when preaching his funeral sermon, applies most truly to himself:—

> The livery of his Divine Master was always and everywhere visibly upon him. Whether in the desk or the pulpit, the committee-room or the platform, the cottage or the mansion, the school-room or the sick chamber, the street or the railway, he was always the recognized but unostentatious servant of the Saviour whom he loved. He was not ashamed of his Master, or of His Name, or to speak a word for Him, or to do an act for Him, whenever a favourable or fitting opportunity presented itself.

He advised, he admonished, he sympathized; and, to the utmost of his means, he aided those who stood in need of aid. And throughout his ministry he was eminently "faithful." He did not hesitate, though he well knew the cost, to battle manfully with the vices and frivolities of the day. None could hearken to his conversation and think it possible to "serve God *and* mammon."

As a preacher his words were ever impressive and weighty, because they were always Scriptural: and, for the same reason, they were always easily understood. Possessing a mind of no ordinary compass and power, his imagination rich, his literary attainments varied, there was no display of his gifts, but an evident desire to preach so that all might understand and profit. He loved especially to welcome the pious poor to the House of God; often did he regret the lack of fitting accommodation for them; and heartily and liberally did he aid us in later years in making our Church, in a truer sense, the House of Prayer where "the rich and the poor meet together." But, whatever might be the character of the congregation, his aim was simply to "preach THE WORD." The Bible and the Bible only was his storehouse for spiritual instruction: and that storehouse could not fail. Never shall I forget his remark on one occasion, when I had referred to his lengthened ministry, and the possible difficulty of selecting new texts and topics. His answer was:—"The longer I live the more I am impressed with the unsearchable, inexhaustible fulness of the Word of God."

It was no slight privilege to listen for a season—only too short—to his impressive and striking expositions of Scripture: and highly do I value the notes which I was in the habit of taking down at the time. Many parishioners I know possess the volumes of his sermons which have been published.[1] They are models of natural and unaffected eloquence, rich in poetic feeling; but they are chiefly remarkable for close adherence to the Written Word. The text contains the sermon, instead of, as is sometimes the case, the sermon merely containing the text. The prayerful study of these sermons could not fail, under God's blessing, to conduce to the spiritual edification of the reader. They preach the Gospel to the poor; and, at the same time, they are clearly the fruit of diligent labour, and frequently embody, without show of scholarship, the results of intellectual research and critical investigation. They afford proof that he did not, as a pastor, offer to his people that which "cost him nothing" in the way of preparation and careful study. It was his regular practice, as long as he could see, to read or write his sermons on *bended knee*. He often used to say, "I am not going to make my sermon now: that I have been doing every day; but only to write down what I have thought and done." Nor did he relax in this diligent habit of preparation when in later years his sight failed him so far that he could not use either manuscript or notes of any kind. Indeed, many considered that the marked order and precision of thought in the arrangement of his sermons, and the clearness and fulness of his expositions, became only more striking. But the secret of his preaching power was undoubtedly the Scriptural testimony which he bore, combined with his prayerful spirit of dependence on the Divine blessing.

Humility was a distinguishing trait of his character. It marked him amongst men. Whilst honouring, as we have seen, the Word of God, he ever manifested, as a preacher of that Word, the deepest sense of his own inability to preach it as he felt it *ought* to be preached. In his last sermon at Astley, he said:—"Often have I taken my freshly-written sermon, and locked it up as soon as I have left the pulpit, because I have been ashamed of its poverty and weakness *in comparison* with the richness and strength of the Gospel of our Salvation." He had set himself to preach THE WORD, and whoever does this will be prepared to make a similar record. And this humility, which went with him into the pulpit, pervaded his whole life and conversation. He knew how to condescend, in the Gospel sense of the word, to men of low estate. He "put on lowliness of mind," and there was no affectation in his lowliness; it sat on him like a garment which had been long and constantly worn: and his native dignity only graced his humility.

It was this trait of character which made him content to abide where God had placed him. His celebrity as a musical authority, as well as his pastoral gifts, might justly have led

[1] Sermons, Chiefly on Historical Subjects, from the Old and New Testaments. London: Hamilton, Adams, and Co.; and Hatchard's.

him to look for some fitting recognition of his work. But he was not one to seek position or promotion; and, after a ministry in the diocese of more than half the allotted age of man, when compelled by failing health to seek a less burdensome post, he only found, in another diocese, and that through the kindness of a personal friend, a small incumbency, the income of which barely sufficed to secure the needed help of a brother pastor. Yet I never heard him complain. He was not ambitious of honours or of fame. He knew that "promotion cometh neither from the east nor from the west;" and that it becomes the Christian to

"Scorn the highest place on earth,
For *yonder higher place*."

And thus, in close alliance with his genuine humility, we note his noble *disinterestedness* and *integrity*: his superiority to the place-seeking spirit: that uprightness of character which ever kept him on the "crown of the road," indifferent, so far as the claims of duty were concerned, to the smiles or the frowns of men.

I say in close alliance with his humility; for, whilst he was emphatically one who "held his integrity fast"—as every honest man must hold it fast—this integrity, this consciousness of disinterestedness, in no way derogated from his humility. It was grace—grace abounding to him as a sinner—grace in which he gloried—it was grace that gave him the high standard of integrity at which he aimed, and *by grace alone* did he hope to take a single step towards that standard. But, so far as grace *did* enable him to advance, whilst his shortcomings always kept him deeply humble, he gave glory to God, and he felt that the credit of the Gospel was, as it were, at stake in his person. Like St. Paul, accounting himself "the chief of sinners," he knew nevertheless what the grace of God had done for him, and he would not have the Master dishonoured by any palpable inconsistency of life or conversation. "Our rejoicing is this, the testimony of our conscience, that in simplicity and Godly sincerity, not with fleshly wisdom, but by the grace of God, we have had our conversation in the world, and more abundantly to you-ward" (2 Corinthians 1:12).

Yet his consciousness of integrity never went beyond the truth, or beyond the testimony which others, who knew him best, would bear concerning him and it was always accompanied with the ready acknowledgment of "countless shortcomings." And so, in his farewell sermon at Astley, after noting the importance of this ministerial integrity in order to ministerial usefulness, and referring to the stirring appeal of Samuel the prophet at the close of his life to the people of Israel, he continued:—

Confident as I am, that, could your answer be openly given to me, it would resemble the answer of the Israelites to Samuel, I nevertheless disclaim, with the deepest humiliation, all self-complacency before you, and all idea of merit before God. I have been but an unworthy steward. I have indeed *aimed* to advance your comfort, and God's glory in that comfort [mark the consciousness of integrity]: but this it was my *duty* to do. I see ten thousand imperfections in my few little doings, and feel that I have urgent need to look up and say, "O Lord, cleanse Thine unworthy servant! accept what is Thine own, and pardon all that is mine!"

Yes, he knew and groaned under "the plague of his own heart:" he felt cause enough to lie low before God, whilst he was conscious of his integrity before man: and it was this *combination* of humility and integrity which gave such power to his testimony to the Gospel of God's Grace, and made him not only a preacher in the pulpit but a preacher in the world—a preacher of what Herbert has beautifully styled "the visible rhetoric of a holy life."

The substance of his *ministerial teaching*, as I have said, was ever the testimony of the Written Word. He did not take the waters of life at second-hand from human or ecclesiastical cisterns, but went direct to the Fountain of living waters.[1] As a Bible Churchman, he was a genuine successor of our best Reformers. His soul beat in true harmony with Hooper and Latimer, and Cranmer and Bradford. He was faithful to his Ordination promise, "*out of the Scriptures* to instruct the people committed to his charge:" and never forgot that the Church of England placed the BIBLE in his hand and bade him be "a faithful dispenser of THE WORD OF GOD."

Hence the pole-stars of his teaching were "Repentance towards God," and "Faith towards our Lord Jesus Christ." In one of his sermons, "The Shepherd of the Sheep," at an Ordination in Worcester, in 1845, after dwelling upon the importance of "the faithful preaching of Christ's Holy Gospel, the oral exposition of God's lively Truth, without which there never was any great revival of piety in either the Jewish or the Christian Church," he thus answers the question, "And *what* shall we preach?"—"Let us habitually preach Christ, as 'the end of the law for righteousness' to every contrite believer, Christ

[1] Scarcely can it be necessary to say that the modern innovations and tawdry embellishments of Ritualism were strongly reprobated by Mr. Havergal: as they must be by all who have true sympathy with the Evangelical teaching of the Articles and Formularies of the Church of England. A writer in the *Hereford Times* remarks:—"He had a great horror of what is called High Churchism [placing the Church *above* the Bible—the ecclesiastical *above* the spiritual]: and, with the simple but everlasting truths of the Gospel, the truths for which the Reformers shed their blood, he used to scatter to the winds all the mummeries which interfered with the simplicity of Church of England worship. He was very vehement against any human interposition between the sinner and the Saviour: and always, when the subject was opportune, strongly denounced saint and man worship. Nothing but the Bible satisfied him, and his constant aim was to bring forth its treasures in all simplicity, declaring 'the whole counsel of God.'"

as the source of sanctification through the Spirit, Christ as the all-in-all of the sinner—the helpless, the miserable, the broken-hearted sinner."

Such was the soul-nurturing food with which he ever sought to feed the flock; and hence, amidst all the doctrinal fantasies of the age, and the clashing of opinions in the Church, in closing a ministry of nearly twenty years at Astley, before he came to Worcester, he was able to testify—"I am not conscious of the slightest change of sentiment upon any topic of importance since the day I first came amongst you." The "*truth*" could not change: and his testimony never changed. And, up to the last, his opinions remained firm and unshaken. All were founded upon the Divine Word: and the only alteration was the daily continuous growth of his own *experimental* knowledge of those doctrines of Grace which caused an Apostle to exclaim, "O the depth!" and into which "the angels desire to look."

He preached a doctrine as humbling to the pride of man as it is exalting to the glory of God's free Grace: a doctrine which casts down all imaginations and every high thought of moral goodness, fitness, or strength, and lays the sinner low at the foot of the Cross, the cleft Rock of Ages, in deep and painful consciousness of guilt before God and without hope from self or any earthly helper: that Evangelical doctrine, which, in the pregnant and comprehensive words of Archbishop Leighton, "lays low the sinner, exalts the Saviour, and promotes holiness." He exalted Christ as "the end of the law for righteousness to every one that believeth," and pointed to His blood as the full atonement for all "our mighty sins." He exhibited with equal clearness the justifying and sanctifying grace of redemption. What he said of good John Davies, of St. Clement's, we say of him:—"He preached the love of God in Christ to sinners, and he *loved to preach it*: to tell such how they might be justified freely, and sanctified wholly, and saved eternally, was his study and delight." And so he defines the ministerial work, in one of his published sermons, in these striking words:—

Repentance and Faith constitute the high road which leads to the Saviour: and the Bible and the ministers of the Gospel are appointed by God to direct enquirers in the right way. What St. Paul said of himself applies to every minister: "Woe is unto me, if I preach not the Gospel!" If we preach any other refuge but Christ, or direct men wrongly to that refuge, their blood will be required of us. The Great Saviour Himself waits to be gracious, and condescendingly and cheeringly says, "Him that cometh unto me I will in no wise cast out." His atoning death, and His sanctifying Spirit, leave us in want of nothing but faith to apply them, and love to be grateful for them. And faith He will give if we ask it: and love He will shed abroad if we cleave to Him, and walk with Him, and pray to Him.

Could a more perfect summary of Gospel truth be expressed in simpler or clearer language? [1]

[1] In estimating the zealous and outspoken avowal of the grand fundamental truths of the Gospel by the pastors of a former generation, it should be remembered that they had to pay the cost of faithfulness. Not only did the preaching of "Christ crucified" present almost an insuperable barrier to ecclesiastical promotion or advancement, but it subjected those who proclaimed the obnoxious doctrines to no slight measure of persecution and "shameful entreaty." Mr. Havergal, in his sermon on the death of the Rev. John Davies, Rector of St. Clement's, Worcester, records some strange things which have occurred in our city. The following extract will be read with interest:—

"When your departed pastor was presented to this living [St. Clement's] in the year 1816, it was regarded by many as a singularly providential event. They saw in it a remarkable answer to fervent prayer. At that date it was vividly remembered that strange things had, many years before, occurred in the parish. A devout and faithful clergyman, the father of that eminent servant of Christ, the Rev. Thomas Tregenna Biddulph, of Bristol, was curate of your parish. His fervent piety and forcible preaching raised a storm of opposition, not only against himself, but against all his devoted hearers. Deeds of violence were perpetrated, and many persons were shamefully entreated. When Mr. Davies came to the parish, a good old man, one of the fruits of Mr. Biddulph's ministry, was still living in it; and he kept as a memento his front teeth, which had been knocked out when encountering a mob who attempted to throw him into the river, as he was going to St. Clement's old church. The state of things in Worcester at this period, and for some years after, may seem incredible to the present generation. It is, however, a fact, of which witnesses are still living (1858), that the estimable father of an alderman of Worcester was hunted like a wild beast, with all sorts of missiles, along the High Street, because he had befriended a preacher of Lady Huntingdon's Connexion.

"As the opposition to Mr. Biddulph was not confined to 'lewd fellows of the baser sort,' he was compelled to retire from the curacy of St. Clement's. Before, however, he quitted Worcester, he one day walked to the hills which lie to the eastward of our city (it is said to have been *Dean Hill*), and which command a view of it. He there, in some quiet nook, knelt down, and solemnly and fervently prayed that God would, in mercy, remember Worcester: and that, sooner or later, the Gospel might be preached in St. Clement's Church as he had humbly endeavoured to preach it himself.

"Years passed away; but not without tokens that this prayer was deposited in God's vial. At length, a grandson of this Mr. Biddulph married into the Stillingfleet family, the venerable prebendary of which name presented to the rectory of St. Clement's that 'good man' who, as your hearts know and your tears testify, has, for the last forty-two years, faithfully preached the Gospel of Salvation in this church."

Referring to a period three years after the appointment of Mr. Davies, Mr. Havergal further records an incident connected with the parish church of St. Nicholas. "The Rev. John Greig, although possessed of an ample fortune, had been for several years the curate of St. Nicholas. The apostolic fervour of his preaching attracted general attention, and, by God's blessing, aroused many souls from the lethargy which too generally prevailed. He raised the congregation at church from a handful to a crowd, and the sacramental collections from pence to pounds. During his ministry much of the daring profligacy which then marked the parish was either checked or shamed into retirement. On his death his funeral sermon was preached by a relative of the then Rector of St. Clement's, the Rev. John Cawood, of Bewdley, on Trinity Sunday, A.D. 1819. Though that sermon was full of 'truth and soberness' [a copy remains in the library case of books in the vestry of St. Nicholas, bequeathed by Mr. Greig for the use of the rector and curate of the parish], yet, because of it, the preacher was inhibited by Bishop Cornwall from preaching again in St. Nicholas.' He, however, outlived the inhibition, and, on one occasion, in his declining years, testified the truth of God in that church."

Of the closing days of a life thus eloquent for grace and truth and goodness, it is needless to speak. He "walked with God, and he was not: for God took him." The first intelligence I received of his translation was conveyed to me in the simple, touching words, "He is at Home"—the Home in Heaven of which so truly he made his earthly home a type and earnest.[1] On his last day of consciousness on earth, although there were indications of suffering, he appeared at times brighter and better. He was out twice, and seemed peculiarly happy. Before the evening prayer, he played over a beautiful *Palindrome*, to the following words, which he had just composed:—

"Messiah, Redeemer,
Send out Thy saving light
Where rules the prince of night!
Day-Star, rise! Cheer all eyes!"

The sunset of life was calm and peaceful: and on Easter day, "very early in the morning," the joyful thoughts of Resurrection glory fresh in his mind, the Master's message reached him—the stroke of apoplexy from which he never rallied. He lay without consciousness or suffering till noon on Tuesday, and then only ceased breathing, and was at *home*. He slept in Jesus, who is "The Resurrection and the Life." "There were no good-byes for the bereaved, only *welcomes to come* in the Father's House above."

"Before one tear was wept below,
Joy filled the courts above;
No parting pang was he to know:
God took him from a world of woe
To His own world of love."

The yearning thought of *another*, expressive of more touching sympathy and precious comfort for the bereaved than words which we could frame, was to be true of *him*:—

"Dear ones! shall it be *mine* to watch you come
Up from the shadow and the valley-mist,
To tread the jacinth and the amethyst;
To rest and sing upon the stormless height,
In the deep calm of love and everlasting light?"[2]

May this thought prove "the bright light" in the dark cloud which hangs so heavily over loving and sorrowing hearts, especially to *one* whose grief can only be measured by her own affectionate devotedness and the irreparable loss she has sustained. "The riches of prayer and counsel, tenderness and comfort," nothing can restore to the home on earth: but that home is bereaved to help to form the Home in Heaven; and "the Day is at hand."

"Soon and for ever, the breaking of Day,
Shall chase all the night-clouds of sorrow away;
Soon and for ever, our union shall be
Made perfect, our glorious Redeemer, in Thee;
When the sins and the sorrows of time shall be o'er,
Its pangs and its partings remembered no more;
Where life cannot fail, and where death cannot sever,
Christians with Christ shall be, soon—and for ever!"

Brethren, I meant these words of AFFECTIONATE REMEMBRANCE to be few: but "out of the abundance of the heart the

[1] His *home* sympathies were very strong. In the funeral sermon on the death of the Rev. John East, which has been mentioned, a passage occurs which brings this trait into touching prominence. No words could better describe his own home-character than the closing sentences of the paragraph. The last audible sound from the lips of his beloved friend, John East, was "Home, home." Referring to this the preacher said:—

"This *last* word 'home' falls on my ear with a thrilling force which I can hardly convey to you: for, singular to say, it is the *first* remembered word which passed between him and me in the early days of our school life. The word 'home' was, so to speak, the altar around which our friendship and fidelity were sworn to each other. '*East, do you love home*?' was the first sentence which he recollected ever to have been uttered by myself. He always bore it in mind, and frequently referred to it fondly and affectionately in after days. There is no marvel in this, for our East was a thorough man of home. He loved it with hallowed intensity, and only feared, as I have heard him say, that he loved it too much. Never could it be said of him that he was not at home what he was in society. *His highest excellencies shone out at home*. Fitly, therefore, did a glance of his eternal home waken up his sinking thoughts."

[2] The closing verse of some exquisitely beautiful lines, by a gifted daughter, which, by a remarkable coincidence, after a lapse of some months from the time they were received, were inserted in the May number of a magazine edited by the writer. The entire poem reads thus:—

ON THE COL DE BALM.

Sunshine and silence on the Col de Balm!
I stood above the mists, above the rush
Of all the torrents, when one marvellous hush
Filled God's great mountain temple, vast and calm,
With hallelujah-light, a seen though silent psalm:

Crossed with one discord, only one. For Love
Cried out, and would be heard, "If ye were here,
O friends, so far away, and yet so near,
Then were the anthem perfect!" And the cry
Threaded the concords of that Alpine harmony.

Not vain the same fond cry if *first* I stand
Upon the mountain of our God, and long
Even in the glory, and with His new song
Upon my lips, that you should come and share
The bliss of heaven, imperfect still till all are there!

Dear ones! shall it be *mine* to watch you come
Up from the shadow and the valley-mist,
To tread the jacinth and the amethyst,
To rest and sing upon the stormless height,
In the deep calm of love and everlasting light?

FRANCES RIDLEY HAVERGAL.

mouth speaketh," and well I know the testimony I have borne will be grateful to many ears. You who knew him loved him, and to you his memory will be blessed.

He was truly "a good man, and full of the Holy Ghost, and of faith:"—"an Israelite indeed, in whom was no guile." The grace of God in him, issued in the formation of a character full of beauty and goodness, and in the living of a life which was the spring of purest happiness to himself and of real and abiding usefulness to others.

The contemplation of such a path, conducting to such a conclusion—

"An honoured life, a peaceful end,
And Heaven to crown it all,"—

must constrain from every heart the wish, the prayer—"Let my experience, my life, my end, be like his;" let it equally impress upon our minds the Inspired counsel—applicable to all who walked as he walked—"Be ye followers"—imitators—"of them who through faith and patience inherit the promises."

But, brethren, I have still to utter WORDS OF EARNEST EXHORTATION AND ENTREATY; words which I would commend to you, as a Congregation, in the earnest hope that by God's blessing they may conduce to our highest—our spiritual interests.

As you will have inferred, I have chosen my text with this end in view. I was anxious that our reminiscences of the past might leave upon our minds *a message for the present*—such a message as your once venerated pastor would have given us; and this my text seemed to furnish. I have felt that, if words *could* have been uttered by our loved friend before God bade him "Come up higher," words to reach *your* ears, his mind would have fastened at once on *the ministerial relation between pastor and people*; and no words could more fittingly have expressed his fervent desire for *our spiritual prosperity as a Congregation*, than the Apostle's entreaty in my text: "Finally, brethren, pray for us"—pray for those who minister to you the words of Gospel life which *I* once ministered—"that the Word of the Lord may have free course, and be glorified!"

I say his fervent desire for our prosperity as a Congregation: for, although after the tie between himself and his people had once been broken, his state of health and his sensitive spirit hindered those repeated visits I had fondly anticipated, his interest in all that concerned his old parish was unchanged. When he left us he did not forget us. If ever pastor identified himself with his people, he was that pastor. Long and earnestly did he seek counsel of God before he would think of a removal to a less arduous sphere of labour: although others saw the change to be most necessary, if health, and indeed life, were not to be entirely sacrificed. And when at length he felt constrained to contemplate the step, his anxiety was intense that a simple Gospel testimony might be borne in this sanctuary when he was gone. Well do I remember, at a season of doubt and uncertainty, his committing the issue in earnest prayer to God in the vestry of our Church. Personally I could not but shrink from such a charge: and if ever, certainly at that time, I prayed that the disposing of the lot might be in Higher Hands than ours. But *his* anxiety was a token of pastoral faithfulness; it conveyed a lesson which I trust I valued, and shall never forget; and it is well that *you* should be acquainted with it. It may help you to attach additional solemnity and weight to the appeal in my text—a word, as it were, from the pastor in Heaven—commending to you, *as the surest and only pledge of spiritual prosperity in the Congregation*, PRAYER FOR THE MINISTRY, "that the Word of the Lord may have free course, and be glorified."

I have no lengthened comment to make on this appeal. It is expressed so plainly that it is impossible to mistake its meaning. I would only offer two considerations suggestive of the main grounds upon which the appeal rests. May these considerations, by God's blessing, prompt in many hearts the hallowed resolve, We *will* henceforth abound more in PRAYER FOR THE MINISTRY.

I. The first consideration is this:—

Such prayer will dispose you, as Hearers of the Preached Word, to HEAR ARIGHT.

It is dangerous, brethren, to attend critically upon the ministrations of the sanctuary. I mean critically as to the mode in which Divine truth is presented, or the particular gifts of the ministry presenting it.

Hearers, indeed, cannot be too careful *what* they hear. They cannot examine too closely the Holy Scriptures in order to see whether the preacher's testimony accords with the testimony of the Oracles of God. If Repentance and Faith, man's Ruin by sin, Christ's Redeeming work, and the Spirit's enlightening, convincing, quickening, and renewing work, form not the staple of our ministry, then beware lest human teaching lead you far astray. But if there is a clear and full and experimental witness borne to these fundamental verities, then *pray* for that ministry, and criticise not the mode or the manner in which the Word of the Lord is delivered.

You want to *feed on truth*, not to sit and hear and criticise the preacher. His feeblest word, if God the Spirit bless, shall send you to your home "rejoicing with joy unspeakable and full of glory;" his most laboured effort, unblessed, however the intellect or the imagination may have been gratified, will leave you "poor, and wretched, and miserable, and blind, and naked." Buy the truth—"the truth as it is in Jesus;" seek "the hid treasure;" secure "the pearl of great price." Think not of "the earthen vessel;" the excellency of the power *must* be of God. Come not only before the preacher, but before the preacher's God. Look from the pulpit below to the throne above. Pray that "the Word of the Lord"—not the word or the opinions or the gifts of man—"may have free course and be glorified." So praying, you will not fail, as hearers of the preached Word, to *hear aright.*

II. The second consideration, I would mention, points to ministerial need:—

Such prayer for the Ministry will afford no uncertain pledge and security that the Ministry will PREACH ARIGHT.

The very entreaty, "Brethren, pray for us!" is a token of a right sense of the work of the Ministry. He can know little of the true nature of the ministerial charge, who has not often upon his heart the question—"Who is sufficient for these things?" And he who asks that question will duly value his people's prayers.

It should never be forgotten that the mission of the pastor is a *spiritual* one. We are to aim at spiritual results. If we have a lower aim, we shall depend less upon prayer and more upon ourselves.

The Apostle is the best exemplar we could have of ministerial character. He was no ordinary minister of the Gospel. He possessed special gifts which we never can possess. He was an inspired writer, a worker of miracles. But he knew his true mission was to accomplish "greater things than these." He knew that the ministry he had received was designed "to open the eyes" of the spiritually "blind," to "turn them from darkness to light, and from the power of Satan unto God." Therefore *he* asked that question, "Who is sufficient for these things?" and *he* urged the entreaty, "Finally, brethren, pray for us, that the Word of the Lord may have free course, and be glorified!" If to open literally the eyes of a blind man is beyond human power, who shall open the eyes of the spiritually blind?

The Apostle knew that whatever gifts he possessed, *God has reserved to Himself the quickening energy of spiritual life and power*; and he knew that PRAYER—the *token of human weakness and the confession of human impotence*—was the appointed, the necessary condition, in order that "the Word of the Lord might have free course, and be glorified."

And, brethren, the deeper our ministerial experience, the more conscious do we become of this need of Divine power to work *in* us and *through* us. We increasingly feel that so far as *spiritual* results are concerned we can do nothing. We cannot overcome the difficulties in our *hearers.* The proclamation of the Law, "holy, just, and good," will not change the heart. The invitations of the Gospel, "the glorious Gospel of the Blessed God," will not change the heart. The Lord Himself, the Divine Spirit, must "open the heart," must give "the new heart," or our preaching is vain. And then the difficulties in *ourselves!* Our personal infirmities, how they hinder us! How humbling are the lessons of our own weakness and sinfulness, which we are continually learning! And, though we preach the truth, how feebly we preach it! How dependent we are upon God for spiritual insight into the doctrines of the Word! How we often feel our eyes want opening to enable us to behold the "wondrous things" in God's Word! How little power we seem to have to silence the gainsayer, to encourage and direct the enquirer, to "divide rightly the Word of Truth!" How fittingly might we follow the example of humility which has been set before us by our remembered pastor, and "lock up our freshly-written sermons as soon as we have left the pulpit, because we are ashamed of their poverty and weakness, *in comparison with* the richness and strength of the Gospel of our Salvation!"

Brethren, this is the experience which makes those who possess it "able ministers of the New Testament!" They who thus learn to "put no confidence in the flesh," will learn also to put all confidence in God. And whilst seeking to work as Paul worked—bearing in mind his exhortation to Timothy, "Be instant in season, out of season; preach the Word; reprove, rebuke; watch in all things, endure afflictions, do the work of an evangelist, make full proof of thy ministry,"—they will cast themselves, as Paul cast himself, upon the power of prayer, their own prayers and the prayers of the brethren, "that the Word of the Lord may have free course, and be glorified." So preaching, they will assuredly not fail to *preach aright.*

Such are the practical issues depending upon the heed given to the Apostle's entreaty as expressive of ministerial desire. Can we doubt for one moment that a people *so hearing* and a ministry *so preaching* "the Word of the Lord," would speedily furnish a marvellous testimony to the power of the Grace of God in the Gospel of His Son to secure spiritual results in the hearts and over the lives of men?

If prayer is the Christian's "vital breath," prayer for the Ministry is the Church's "vital breath." Such prayer would bring our people into closer sympathy with the Divine purpose to bless men through the Gospel. Such prayer would increase their love to God and their love to their fellow-men. Such prayer would kindle zeal for ever-increasing efforts for the spiritual good of others—not zeal unenlightened and misdirected, but zeal conscious from past experience that activity for God must ever spring from fresh strength received at the Throne of Grace. And assuredly such prayer, in the gracious answers that would be vouchsafed, would endue the Ministry with "power from on High." Our own sense of weakness and infirmity and sinfulness would be met by the abundant supply of the grace of God. Our question, "Who is sufficient for these things?" would find its ready answer: "I can do all things through Christ which strengtheneth me." In our sense of insufficiency we should realize God's all-sufficiency: and the language of praise would oftener be on our lips—"Thanks be unto God, which always causeth us to triumph in Christ, and maketh manifest the savour of His knowledge in every place."

Then, brethren, LET SUCH PRAYER ABOUND. I believe the special and urgent need of the Church of Christ at this time, is a deep earnest soul-penetrating conviction of *the absolute necessity of the Divine influence of the Holy Spirit for the right-doing of Christian work, and of the Holy Spirit's blessing to make that work effectual.* We want to apply this conviction especially to the work of the Ministry. It is not enough that we who minister hold the truth, and are zealous for the truth, and faithfully preach the truth. All this is well: but we need *more* than this. The truth of the Gospel itself must be quickened by the Spirit, or it will not turn men's hearts to God; it will not bring out of the moral chaos of man's ruined state a creation of moral order, life, and beauty; it will not prove the power of God to the salvation of souls. The Divine Spirit is "the Lord and Giver of spiritual life;" and even the Word of the Gospel inspired by the Spirit, which we preach, must be quickened by the Spirit, or it will not convey the life of God into the soul of man.

Ministers in themselves are powerless. The faithful ministry of the venerated pastor who has been called to his rest did not profit *all.* Paul may plant, Apollos may water; but, as in the natural, so in the spiritual world, God only gives the "increase." That increase He gives in answer to PRAYER. He will be "enquired of" for the blessing which He is waiting to bestow. If we would hear "the Word of the Lord" in the sanctuary: if that Word is to have "free course and be glorified:" the petition must be in our hearts and on our lips, "Speak, Lord, for Thy servant heareth." We are not "straitened in God," nor is "the fulness of the blessing of the Gospel of Christ" in any way diminished or restrained. But "the preparation of the heart" is needed, and that preparation is "from the Lord."

If, then, as Gospel hearers, we have *not* hitherto tasted true Gospel blessedness, let us learn to wait more on the Lord before we expect anything from the Ministry. Begin with God. Ask Him—"Teach Thou me." The still small voice will soon be heard: the heart will be opened: and then "the Word of the Lord" which we preach will have "free course and be glorified."

So, also, of the Ministry of the Word as a means to "growth in grace"—the edification and instruction of believers: the same teachable spirit—the same prayerful spirit, is still needed. "*Help the preacher to preach aright—help me to hear aright—the message of Thy Word!*" If such prayer prevailed in our congregations, the promise would speedily be fulfilled—"I will open you the windows of heaven, and pour you out a blessing, that there shall not be room enough to receive it." The Gospel would come unto us, as it came to the praying converts of Thessalonica, "not in word only, but also in power, and in the Holy Ghost, and in much assurance;" and a similar record of Christian influence and missionary zeal might be given of us—"For from you sounded out the Word of the Lord not only in Macedonia and Achaia, but also in every place your faith to Godward is spread abroad; so that *we need not to speak any thing*" (1 Thessalonians 1:5–8). Mightily indeed would "the Word of the Lord" "grow and prevail," if thus the voice of the living Church of true believers sustained, and almost rendered *needless*, the testimony of the Gospel Ministry!

Ponder these considerations, brethren; ponder them, as they bear upon yourselves as individuals; ponder them, as they bear upon our spiritual prosperity as a Congregation; and, as you feel increasingly their solemnity and weight, remember and act upon the earnest exhortation and entreaty:—

"Brethren, pray for us, that the Word of the Lord may have free course and be glorified!"

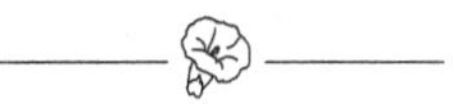

"Shout, O Earth! from silence waking."

Shout, O earth! from silence waking,
Tune with joy thy varied tongue;
Shout! as when from chaos breaking
Sweetly flowed thy natal song:
Shout! for thy Creator's love
Sends redemption from above.

Downward from His star-paved dwelling
Comes the Incarnate Son of God;
Countless voices thrilling, swelling,
Tell the triumphs of His blood:
Shout! He comes thy tribes to bless,
With His spotless righteousness.

See His glowing hand uplifted!
Clustering bounties drop around;
Rebels e'en are richly gifted;
Pardon, peace, and joy abound.
Shout, O earth! and let thy song
Ring the vaulted heavens along!

Call Him blessed! on thy mountains,
In thy wilds and citied plains;
Call Him blessed! where thy fountains
Speak in softly murmuring strains.
Let thy captives, let thy kings
Join thy lyre of thousand strings.

Blessed Lord, and Lord of blessing!
Pour Thy quickening gifts abroad;
Raptured tongues, Thy love confessing,
Shall extol the living God:
Blessed, Blessed, Blessed Lord!
Heaven shall chant no other word.

W. H. H.

II.

Biographical Sketch.

By ANDREW JAMES SYMINGTON,

AUTHOR OF "THE BEAUTIFUL IN NATURE, ART, AND LIFE."

"My Times are in Thy hand."

My times are in Thy hand,
Their best and fittest place,
I would not have them at command
Without Thy guiding grace.

"My times," and yet not *mine*,—
I could not them ordain;
Not one e'er waits from me a sign,
Nor can I one detain.

"My times," O Lord, are Thine,
And Thine their oversight:
Thy wisdom, love, and power, combine
To make them dark or bright.

I know not what shall be
When passing times are fled;
But all events I leave with Thee,
And calmly bow my head.

Hence, Lord, in Thee I rest,
And wait Thy holy will;
I lean upon my Saviour's breast
Or gladly go on still.

And when "my times" shall cease,
And life shall fade away,
Then bid me, Lord, depart in peace
To realms of endless day!

W. H. H.

HAVERGAL has gone to his rest. After that long life-service to the great Master for which he was truly made meet, he was peacefully called away, on Tuesday, April 19th, at noon. The Church on earth is poorer for the change, but the Church in Heaven is richer by one. His memory will be lovingly and fondly cherished by the parishioners to whom he successively ministered at Astley, Worcester, and Shareshill; by those to whom he occasionally preached in later days at Leamington; at Pyrmont, in Germany, where for many years he officiated during the summer months; and by all those who in any degree enjoyed the great privilege of his personal acquaintance; for he was pre-eminently a good pastor and a faithful friend.

As an ecclesiastical musician and psalmodist he was, without question, the first man of his generation,—indeed, the Ravenscroft of the nineteenth century. His loss is deeply felt and deplored by the musical world.

He was born in Buckinghamshire, in 1793; was educated at St. Edmund's Hall, Oxford, where he graduated B.A. in 1815, and M.A. in 1819. His early tastes fluctuated between medicine and music.

Among his university contemporaries were Archbishop Longley, Bishop Hampden, Dr. Arnold, Lord Westbury, Professor Baden Powell, Archdeacon Creyke, and the Hon. G. Pellow, late Dean of Norwich.

In 1816 he was ordained by Bishop Ryder, for Dr. Beadon, Bishop of Bath and Wells; and, having served some minor offices in the Church, he was, in 1829, presented to the rectory of Astley, near Bewdley.

Here he met with a distressing and almost fatal accident, which laid him aside from his clerical duties for several years. During that period his studious and active mind found relief in music, for which art he naturally had both taste and genius.

His first published composition was an anthem-like setting of Heber's "From Greenland's Icy Mountains," the proceeds of which, amounting to £180, were devoted to the Church Missionary Society. Other compositions rapidly followed, and their proceeds were always devoted in the same liberal spirit to charitable objects. Many of these early pieces have become popular, and all of them are characterized by great sweetness of melody and skilful construction.

In 1836 appeared Op. 35, "An Evening Service in E flat and One Hundred Antiphonal Chants." One of these, a "Recte et Retro" Chant in C (now commonly printed in D), and sometimes called "Worcester Chant," is almost as widely known as the language, and, short though it be, possesses all the elements of musical immortality.

In the same year as the above (1836), the Gresham prize medal was adjudged to him for an Evening Service in A, Op. 37. In 1841 a second medal was gained by an anthem, "Give Thanks," Op. 40, decidedly one of the best compositions of the kind in existence. Upon thus gaining two prizes, the umpires ruled that no one should receive more than two. Other anthems and services proceeded at various times from his pen, whilst, with renewed strength, he was constantly and untiringly engaged in the arduous duties of a minister of religion.

But it is in the restoration of metrical psalmody to its original purity that Mr. Havergal has rendered himself so illustrious, and for this he will be long justly venerated. He has certainly done more and to better purpose in this way than any other musician. Those whose labours come nearest his greatness will be the first to confirm this. From Dr. Crotch he caught the true idea on this subject, which has greatly developed in his hands. He first of all published a reprint of Ravenscroft's scarce work, *The Whole Booke of Psalmes*, in 1844. At the close of an elaborate preface of twenty-one pages, he there promised,—

> It is the intention of the editor, as speedily as practicable, to publish a selection of the tunes, with the cantus and tenor inverted, or of necessity altered, to suit our present mode of singing. To such selection will be added other tunes, principally for other metres, but strictly in the same generic style of melody and harmony.

In 1845 he was presented by Bishop Pepys to the rectory of St. Nicholas, Worcester, and to an honorary canonry in the cathedral.

In 1847 he published the *Old Church Psalmody*, Op. 48. It is the best book of psalm tunes of which Protestantism can boast, representing, as we believe, and as far as is now possible, the true ideal of the Reformation and its time. All compilers since 1847 have drawn largely upon the *Old Church Psalmody*. In 1854 appeared a highly interesting volume, *A History of the Old Hundredth Psalm Tune, with Specimens*. In this it is proved, and, as Bishop Wainwright in the prefatory note says, "we think it will be generally conceded, that William Franc must hereafter be entitled to the credit of composing this most remarkable of all metrical tunes." The thanks of the archæological as well as musical world were accorded to Mr. Havergal for this excellent history. A few days before his last illness he was engaged in writing a preface for a new edition of this work. In 1859 was published A *Hundred Psalm and Hymn Tunes*, Op. 48, entirely his own composition. This was due to his reputation acquired in this walk of Church music, for, excepting in scattered publications by other compilers, no Psalm tune of his own construction had been published. The *Old Church Psalmody* eschewed all modern composition, as its name would lead readers to suppose. Its preface says:—"No composition of any living author is introduced." Of the *Hundred Tunes* it is not too much to say that they are a monument of learning and industry; and are all, or nearly all, in entire agreement with the principles which its author so long and so successfully propounded.

Handel, Corelli, and our great Cathedralists, were his masters. His aim was to preserve purity of style, and put down musical vanities. Notoriously liberal to publishers of music, he has been equally willing to aid, by scientific criticism and research, all who applied to him. He has written and kept back far more than he has published.

He was not a mere musician, but a theologian also, as his two volumes of sermons and other works of that class prove.

In 1852 he all but lost his sight, which was afterwards only partially restored. He for long was unable to read a note of printed music or decipher his own handwriting. Through weakened health, in 1860, he resigned his charge at Worcester, on being nominated by Lord Hatherton to the vicarage of Shareshill, a small country parish near Wolverhampton. In 1868, from increasing infirmities, he had to lay aside all regular parish work and removed to Leamington, where, with the exception of visits to the Continent, he resided until his death.

For some years he was in the habit of frequenting Pyrmont, in Germany, during the summer months, for the sake of its mineral waters: and while there he was able to conduct the English service and preach in the Friends' meeting-house, for the benefit of his fellow-countrymen and others, who were also sojourners there. No opportunity for sowing the good seed or uttering a kindly human word of help or cheer did he ever neglect; and so highly were his ministrations valued by strangers from various parts of Europe, that the fact of Mr. Havergal being there in several instances decided that parties should go to Pyrmont rather than elsewhere. This summer he had arranged to go there in May.

To hear Mr. Havergal improvise, seated at a good harmonium with many stops, given him by his parishioners, was a rare treat: something higher, deeper, and more than a pleasure—a thing, or rather a spiritual experience, which cannot be forgotten. Sweet-flowing melody, accompanied with strange, unexpected combinations of harmony, full of mysterious chords and curious synchronous and successive felicities, each part capable of being resolved into a perfect and separate composition—fugues chasing each other, turning, meeting, and then passing through the theme in quite opposite directions, meeting again, then twining lovingly together, and, like the strands of a new cable, finding strength in unison—starry phrases of melody echoed from heavenly heights till lost in the distance; then vast galaxies of chords "swim into ken," dependent on and perfectly balanced by other galaxies, controlled even to the perturbation of a single satellite, till all is light and motion; while Handelian shakes, like auroras, at intervals gleam and dart across the blue starlit dome. Yet with all this there is no hesitation, no confusion, no fear; ruled by the genius of a master, every phrase, chord, and movement, progresses with stately grandeur and precision towards the evolution of the one idea which informs and pervades the whole marvellous performance. Sometimes we wander far away through wild intervals into weird discords; and then these, ere they become too painful, are resolved with consummate skill, and we mark "lines of different method" all meeting "in one full centre of delight," as we find ourselves led on and on, and ever by new and unexpected ways, home again at last to the key-note.

The firmness, precision, and delicacy of Mr. Havergal's touch were each and all remarkable, both in kind and degree. These several characteristics were strikingly brought out in his improvisations, which never by any chance contained anything approaching the commonplace. Instead of that, his every combination was original, often a surprise even to himself; many lovely transient effects thus flashed and faded that could not be repeated. Compositions of daring originality and perfect rounded beauty,—now bold and stridant, like the tramp of a giant army, and now ethereally delicate, like the dying cadences of an Æolian harp—streamed from the keys at the magic "touch" of that "vanished hand" which we shall hear no more on earth!

Although Mr. Havergal's ecclesiastical music is of the very highest type, and severe in style, he has also written many beautiful songs, rounds, and catches for the young, which are full of childlike life and birdlike glee; also numberless carols, hymns, and sacred songs, composing both the words and the music.[1] Here is one of his songs for the young, written for his grandchildren. It is in keeping with that incoming season which its gifted author loved, but which he needs not now:—

SUMMER-TIDE IS COMING.

I.

"Summer-tide is coming,
  With all its pleasant things;
Every bee is humming,
  And every songster sings.
Mornings now are brightsome,
  Inviting student thought;
Evenings, too, are lightsome,
  With balmy quiet fraught:
Hearths no longer lure us,
  The fields instead we roam;
Hearts albeit insure us
  A happy, happy Home.

II.

"Summer-tide, I hail thee,
  The Empress of the year!
But thou soon would'st fail me
  Were not thy Maker near.
He thy course disposes,
  Thy light, thy scent, thy glow,
He tints all thy roses,
  And paints thy brilliant bow.
Laud Him, all creation,
  The sinner's mighty Friend;

[1] Many of these Sacred Songs and Carols will be remembered as contributions which appeared in the earlier volumes of "Our Own Fireside." They have since been published under the title, "Fireside Music" (W. Hunt and Co.): and a Second Edition has been prepared. They include "Summer-tide is Coming." [See Volume V of the Havergal edition.]

Near Him be our station,
Where Summer ne'er shall end!"

W. H. H.

The genius of poetry and music has descended and been largely developed in Mr. Havergal's youngest daughter, whose recent volume, *The Ministry of Song*, has been so extensively and favourably noticed throughout the Press, and been admired by all lovers of true poetry.

Mr. Havergal's severe and classical music is often to be heard in our cathedrals; and in Scotland and America no Psalm tune is oftener sung than "Evan." The history of this tune is somewhat peculiar: and, as its authorship has been questioned, it may be well to mention the matter here, as the writer can do so authoritatively from Mr. Havergal's own words, as well as from written statements. In 1847 Mr. Havergal published an original air (A Sacred Song) to Burns's words, "O Thou dread Power." Dr. Lowell Mason, of New York, arranged the first half of that air as a psalm tune, altering both the time and key, and called it "Evan." Hence it is frequently given in collections with Mason's name, and at other times simply with the letter H, under which initial it first appeared, because Dr. Mason did not wish to attribute the liberty he had taken in arranging the part of a melody to the composer of the original air. This is Dr. Lowell Mason's own explanation, which we have seen. Mr. Havergal has since arranged it as it should be: and within the last month played over the tune, and gave a MS. copy of it to the writer, with its curious history noted on the sheet. It has travelled far and wide, and been claimed for many composers, and even been called an old Celtic air. We have here stated the true origin of this unprecedentedly popular tune.

Mr. Havergal throughout life subordinated genius and every talent to the work of the Christian ministry, and was in every respect the model of what a faithful pastor and a Gospel preacher should be; giving no uncertain sound, but delivering his message in its fulness and freeness from the heart to the heart, without fear or favour. He studied medicine that he might attend to the bodies as well as the souls of his country parishioners, instructed them in sanitary matters, inculcated habits of domestic and general economy, organized charities, and, in short, was a loving and beloved father and friend to all his people.

As genial as he was gentlemanly, refined in his tastes, high-souled, and gifted, his own immediate home circle, relatives, and numerous friends, were all perfectly devoted to him; and no one could possibly approach him, even in a casual way, without feeling the radiation of Christian light and warmth from his heart and beaming face; for to the core he was a true man: true to God, and true to his fellow men.

Bible societies, district visitation, Bible reading, Home and Foreign Missions, and all philanthropic schemes, had ever his cordial support and co-operation. Loving freedom, he was from of old an earnest and urgent advocate for the abolition of slavery; and for the same reason he constantly resisted both the open and the insidious aggressions of the Roman Catholic system, as being a conspiracy subversive of all *civil* liberty, to say nothing of religion; and the very last use made of his pen was to append his signature to a petition in favour of Mr. Newdegate's motion for the inspection of convents and nunneries.

On Saturday, the 16th of April, three days before the end, Mr. Havergal at times felt even better than his wont, and was able to be twice out of doors. Before prayers, on this his last Saturday night, he played over a beautiful *Palindrome* to the following words, which he had just composed:—

"Messiah, Redeemer,
Send out Thy saving light
Where rules the prince of night!
Day-star, rise! Cheer all eyes!"

W. H. H.

He went to bed as usual, and slept fairly; but very early on Easter morning, after complaining of pain in the head, he was instantly and entirely unconscious. It was apoplexy, and consciousness never returned. He lay without any suffering till noon on Tuesday, when, at the age of 77, he fell asleep in Jesus. He fully realised the wish for a peaceful departure, so beautifully expressed in his own characteristic lines:—"My Times are in Thy Hand." [See pages 623–634.] He was even spared the pain of a parting farewell to his dear ones around him.

On Saturday, the 23rd, he was borne to Astley Churchyard, and there he peacefully rests amid the scenes of his early labours, awaiting the joyous and certain welcome, "Well done, good and faithful servant," which awaits him on the resurrection morn. Truly the memory of the just is blessed!

III.

The Pastor's Testimony.

"Rest in the Lord."

Psalm 37:7.

"REST in the Lord!" Sweet word of truth,
A word for age, a word for youth,
A word for all the weary world,
A banner-word by love unfurled.

Then cease, ye wearied ones of earth,
To slave for pleasure, gain, or mirth;
Cast down your load of vanities,
And welcome God's realities.

"Rest in the Lord!" Sweet word of grace,
To all the Saviour's new-born race;
'Tis music, light, and balm to them,
An hourly guiding apothegm.

Then, Lord of rest, we rest in Thee,
For all our daily destiny,
Our mighty guilt, our grief, our care,
We cast (strange act!) on Thee to bear.

For Thou, dear Lamb of God, wast slain,
To bear each load, and ease each pain;
And now Thy blood and righteousness
Are rocks of rest in all distress.

And when at last we fall on sleep,
Nor heart shall throb, nor eye shall weep;
Then, blessed Saviour, let it be,
That Thou shalt write, "They rest in Me!"

W. H. H.

A FEW brief extracts, gathered from "Sermons Chiefly on Historical Subjects from the Old and New Testaments," are added here to those given on former pages. They will, in some measure, illustrate the remarkable Scriptural clearness and fulness of the PASTOR'S TESTIMONY. It is hoped that ere long a Memoir will be prepared, which will embody much valuable material, notes of conversation, letters, etc., which are in the hands of relatives.

THE PREACHING OF THE WORD.

"Recollect how entirely we depend on God for all we preach to you, or say among you. Our preaching is very much like drawing a bow at a venture, the arrow of which God alone must direct. Often, like the Syrian bowman, we shoot our words 'in our simplicity,' without aim at any individual, and in utter unconsciousness of the mark which they may hit. But, we know that, by such means, many a heart has been infixed by an arrow which God has made the death of sin. Often has the utterance of some Scripture text or simple speech been carried home to the inmost bosom, and made a blessing beyond what worlds can give. Oh that many such arrows may be shot from this pulpit! Pray that many may."

SELF-KNOWLEDGE AND SELF-ABASEMENT.

"No man who views himself in the glass of God's Word, will entertain a particle of admiration of himself. He will soon say as Job said, 'Behold, I am vile: I abhor myself.' He will, if honest with himself, always discover enough evil in his breast to make him ashamed, and to keep him humble. Instead of 'laying any flattering unction to his soul,' he will rather bemoan himself with Ephraim, and be lowly in his own eyes. Nor will he omit to seek the daily renewal of his heart; for he will find that it is not to be trusted, and that, on this side the grave, it is never cleansed so perfectly as he wishes. He still finds that, when he would do good, evil is present with him, and that nothing but the Saviour's grace can keep him pure, or uphold him from falling.

"He is not, therefore, one of those who substitute external acts for internal operations—'the putting away of the filth of the flesh,' for 'the answer of a good conscience towards God.'

He trusts not in the ceremony, but anxiously looks for the grace which faith finds in it. He knows that the dislodgment of evil from his heart is the work of his life; and, as he lives by faith, so does he pray that God will purify his heart by faith. He loves that prayer of our Church—'Cleanse the thoughts of our hearts by the inspiration of Thy Holy Spirit.' He prays for that cleansing because he knows that the absence of it in man is the cause of all crime, disorder, and misery."

THE NEED OF RENEWING GRACE.

"Nothing but the grace of the Spirit of God can affect the heart of man in that way which will make him a new creature. Without that Spirit we shall continue dead while we live, and fall into a living death when we die. * * * Neither sacramental dedication, nor education, nor official institution, nor even the profession of a correct creed, is any proof of, or any substitute for, a participation of saving grace. No outward station, compliance, or calling, can impart that grace. It must come from another quarter. The Spirit of Christ is the only Agent of the grace of Christ in the heart of a sinner."

THE ONE ONLY HEALER.

"To feel our spiritual misery, and to go to our great Intercessor for its removal, are the first steps in the path of restoration to that health which is destined to end in a glorious immortality. The good Lord open many a prayerful heart in this congregation! Then will no prayer fail of its earnest desire. But, till we feel the smart of our sin, and cry to the one only Healer to have mercy on us, we shall be but as the dying Israelites, who perished before help came to them, or who refused it after it had come."

THE DEATH OF THE PRINCE OF LIFE.

"The death of 'the Prince of Life' may well as a fact have its anniversary; but, if that anniversary be set up in the place of daily recollection, man's appointment will only do sad dishonour to God's intention. Never can it be said that we fulfil the Divine intention, unless the Crucifixion of the Saviour is the grand thought and leading principle of our hearts. * * * We must rest all our hopes upon it, as well as trace all our mercies to it. It is to be our stay in life, and our song in death. Well indeed may we make it such, because it will be the germ of that life, and the burthen of that song, which await us after death. 'Thou wast slain!' will be an eternally repeated declaration, amid the throngs who will be assembled around the throne of the risen Redeemer."

PERSONAL FAITH INDISPENSABLE.

"There was no looking by substitute or proxy on the brazen serpent; and, verily, there is no such thing as believing for salvation in another's stead. It is all a cruel fable to substitute priestly faith for personal belief. Faith in Christ for eternal safety must be our individual act and deed. The stipulation in the wilderness was that the anxious sufferer should look not on the pole, but on the typical serpent. So in the Gospel it is Christ, and not the Church, on whom the eye of faith is to dwell. The Church is but as the pole to the brazen serpent,—it is but a means to an end,—a means for the fitting elevation of Him who alone can save. Mark well the mighty difference."

THE SPIRITUAL AND THE VISIBLE CHURCH.

"A greater mistake can hardly be made than the confounding of the true Israel with the nominal Israel, the spiritual Church with the visible Church. Holy Scripture labours to keep men mindful of the distinction between the two: but unrenewed minds are unwilling to see the distinction, and teachers who borrow their light from earthly sources are perpetually mistaking and mis-stating the simple truth."

"LIGHT IN THE DWELLING."

"The Israel of God, as opposed to the families of the world, have light in their dwellings. Truly Christian families are conducted upon principles of light. They set up the Bible as the lamp of their household, and study to work and walk in its light: whereas, in a worldly family, where is only nominal Christianity but no religion, the light of the Scriptures sheds no sanctifying and calming ray. The Bible may indeed be in the house, but it is there to no purpose. It is a light put under a bushel. It is put away on the shelf, in the drawer, or the closet, and if wanted is hard to be found. And, as for the reading of it daily before the entire family of children and servants, that each may, as it were, kindle their lamp afresh in the midst of a dark world,—how few, alas, practise this!"

ONLY "TWO OPINIONS."

"In the present day, as in every other day, there are but 'two opinions,' two states, two sides, opposed to each other. Light and darkness, holiness and sin, Christ and Belial, still divide the world: and every man is in reality ranged on the one side or the other.

"The difference between the 'two opinions' is broad and very definite. It stands not in any niceties of ecclesiastical or theological sentiment. It does not consist in holding this view or that view—in joining this party or that party. It is altogether of *another sort* of difference. It is a *spiritual* difference, discernible indeed by its effects, but not always so clearly as to be determined by the human eye. The heart is its seat: and He alone who searches the heart can accurately discern the opinion or *thought*, as the word also means, which most sways the heart. But He *does* discern it. He knows if it inclines to Himself or to another master,—if it sides with holiness or with sin—with the love of heavenly or of earthly things. He knows, too, what we are so unwilling to admit, that all the shades and varieties of moral thought and opinion, range themselves into one or other of those two, and only two, classes. We are of opinion that 'the Lord He is God,' or that some Baal of our own making is worthy of being our God. We are either serving the creature, in some shape or other, or giving up ourselves to the One only Creator. Quibble, and plead, and refine as we may, we cannot make more 'opinions' than Divine infallibility has made. There are but 'two.'"

THE RAINBOW A TOKEN OF PEACE.

"The bow, as used among men, is an instrument and a symbol of *war*, but the *rainbow* is eminently a token of *peace*. God's bow, when suspended in the heavens, is a bow without either string or arrow. It, therefore, is not intended for war, but altogether for peace. It is God's picture of the Gospel, hung up in the heavens to cheer the heart of His contrite ones on earth. It is, in fact, a representation to the eye of what the song of the angels at Bethlehem was to the ear. The declaration of both is the same, namely 'Peace on earth, goodwill towards men.'

"It may not be inopportune to mention that even among barbaric nations a bow well strung, and a bow unstrung, were anciently the heraldic symbols of war and peace. In the Cambrian Antiquities it is stated that such bows were sent round the country, as proclamations of war or peace, according to the circumstances of the case.

"The representation of 'a rainbow *round about the throne*,' as seen by St. John, indicates that He who sits upon the throne is a reconciled God, a God at peace with penitent sinners. And because 'a rainbow was *upon the head*' of Jesus, He is thereby marked out as the Divine and glorified Reconciler of such, yea, 'the Prince of Peace,' the Mediator of 'the Covenant of Peace.'"

FALSE PEACE.

"Let no man say, 'Peace, peace, when there is no peace.' The rainbow is so strikingly beautiful, that thousands admire it without thinking of Him who looks upon it, or that they can be saved only by what it represents. Thus the Gospel has its attractions; and many see its beauties, and hear its glorious truths, and even admire and assent to them, without deriving any saving benefit from them. They see the bow, and in a certain way welcome its peace; but they never receive it in a broken and sanctified heart. The consequence is, that after all they have no true peace. The name contents them, and they delude themselves by it. Then awake; search and try your ways, and know that there is no peace without repentance and the pardon of the great Peace Maker."

THE HUMILITY OF JOHN THE BAPTIST.

"What an amount of pride is there in our wicked world! How full of it are our hearts, our streets, our drawing-rooms, and even our halls, and the many far inferior dwellings of our land! How little sense of unworthiness marks the demeanour of many persons as they enter a church, or take their seat in a pew! How little do they *seem* to think themselves *unworthy* to loose the latchet of Messiah's shoe! Let us apply these brief words to *ourselves*, and not add sin to sin by fancying how applicable they are for other persons.

"John the Baptist thought meanly of himself: but his Master said that among all who had been born of woman there had not been a greater than he. Yes, the Lord hath respect to the lowly: He will deal with them as He deals with valleys; that is, let the flowing rains fertilize them, while the towering hills lift their heads with only *barren* grandeur. And as life advances, and sanctification increases, they shall find good evidence of their acceptance with God in the ease with which their souls bend and bow to His will. A fruitless branch will shoot aloft; but that which is laden with fruit bends downwards. The increase of humility is a sign of a nearer approach to Heaven. At an early period in his ministry St. Paul said, 'I am unworthy to be called an apostle:' just before his martyrdom, 'I am the chief of sinners.'"

TRUE HUMILITY.

"We never can know what true humility is, till we know the Lord Jesus Christ as the Mighty God and the Sorrowful Man. 'Voluntary humility,' both in heathendom and Christianity, has done its feats and gained its honours; but true humility has only been obtained when the soul has been filled with that love for Christ and admiration of Him, which are followed by the laying down of every honour at His feet. We accordingly find that in the New Testament the study of Christ is enjoined as the sole method of learning humility (Philippians 2:5–12)."

"THE PRAISES OF ISRAEL."

"Marvellous, indeed, is it that the eternal God should permit Himself to be addressed as the God 'who inhabiteth the praises of Israel' (Psalm 22:3); as One who taketh such delight in the songs of His people that their praise, rather than the temple in which it is offered, should be considered as His pavilion. But, let it never be forgotten, that, pleasing as external acts may be when reverently performed for the honour and praise of Almighty God, they, nevertheless, carry with them no inherent excellency. The most splendid celebration of Divine song is odious discord if unaccompanied with the breathings of a renewed heart. The gentlest sigh of a contrite spirit will penetrate the ear of our Divine Mediator, while the loudest chorus without faith and godliness will fail to reach it."

WEEP NOT.

"'When the Lord saw her, He had compassion on her, and said, Weep not.' Amid the mournful throng the bereaved one seems at once to have caught and fixed the eye of Him who alone could help her. It may be that her grief, and her mourning veil, prevented her seeing Him till she heard His voice. But He saw her. He knew, too, all the bitterness of her soul, and that keen smart which she smothered to enable her to follow the last journey of her son. And then He showed that He *felt for her* too. He proved Himself to be one of us, having as man all our kindliest and tenderest feelings, without one of our imperfections or infirmities. It does not appear that He began any conversation, or uttered any preliminary remark, but that He at once said to her, '*Weep not!*' The early Christians cherished a tradition that our Lord was remarkable for a most sweet and tenderly thrilling voice. Can we imagine it ever to have been more so than when He uttered those two simple but soul-soothing words, '*Weep not!*' There must have been a power of sweetness in their utterance which no tongue can define. Ah! dear brethren, anything from Christ, be it but a look, a touch, or a word, carries with it a world of might, and penetrates where nothing human can."

LAST HOURS BEST HOURS.

"It is not the transient flush of hasty profession, but it is the uniform and habitual cultivation of holiness, which makes last hours best hours; and which, amid the darkness of dissolution, gilds the surrounding scene with the calm brightness of a 'good hope through grace.'"

THE CHRISTIAN'S GRAVE.

"The grave is now a sanctified repository for the bodies of the saints. Christ, by entering the grave as our Head and Representative, consecrated it for our safe reception. Instead of a prison, it is become a passage to a blessed Home. 'Fear not,' then, ye who walk softly, 'to go down into this Egypt.' Jesus has gone thither before you. He will be with you, and bring you up again from it.

"The Christian sepulchre is but a quiet chamber in which our bodies rest awhile till their redemption cometh. It may be likened to the workshop of a superior mechanist, in which our bodies, so fearfully and wonderfully made, are taken to pieces preparatory to their being fashioned by the great Artificer, 'like unto His own glorious body.'

"Are you, then, 'in bondage to the fear of death'? Take a near view of Jesus in the Sepulchre of the Garden; and believe that, if you 'only believe,' your rest in the grave will be as safe and as peaceful as His. 'Death is yours!' saith the Apostle; for Christ has made him your servant: and therefore the grave also is yours."

The Good Lord be
always with you!
W: H: Havergal

William Henry Havergal, and his second wife Caroline Anne (Cooke) Havergal, married in July, 1851. A devoted wife till his death April 19, 1870, she lived until May 26, 1878, aged 65. After W.H.H. died in 1870, his youngest child, Frances Ridley Havergal, and Caroline Anne continued to live in the home at Leamington Spa. She was F.R.H.'s step-mother, whom Frances always addressed and <u>truly</u> honored as "Mother". Both photographs are undated.

THE HAVERGAL FAMILY.

SOME LINGERING MEMORIES.[1]

BY THE REV. S. B. JAMES, D.D., VICAR OF NORTHMARSTON, BUCKS; FORMERLY CURATE TO THE REV. CANON HAVERGAL, AT ST. NICHOLAS', WORCESTER.

I.

OLD letters of long ago stir the heart, if it is a sensitive and sympathetic heart, more deeply than many an almost emotional interview. Here are these letters, preserved with unaccountable caprice, while many others of more tender interest and even more characteristic impressiveness, from members of the same richly gifted family, have gone the way of a rather large amount of the writer's correspondence. He has of late, to prevent unmanageable accumulations, almost indiscriminately and quite recklessly, burned letters as they come and are read, in some cases are once or twice re-read—burned them with a self-accusing pang sometimes, but burned them on ruthless principle, which may be utterly indefensible, and which certainly he does not care to defend.

Why have these forty or fifty letters been kept, while a hundred others have been destroyed? Ah, well, here they are; and as the writer was taking a last look at them on a winter day before a brightly burning fire, and intending to commit them to its flames; he hesitated with a sort of loving hesitation. The faces of the writers came up before him very vividly indeed; he heard most clearly the rich, deep tones of his old rector's voice, and he felt as if he could not destroy at once those memorials of an undying friendship. It seemed to him as if, by the shadow of the screen, there stood the well-remembered figure, the grave dignity of the at times almost solemn face irradiated by the half-humorous gleam that often passed across its expressive features. "Yes, burn them, my brother; burn them all, but do not forget their writers," the fancied Eidolon seemed to say, with a wave of the hand and a well-remembered straightening up of the shoulder.

Thank God for memories of those who have "emigrated," distinct recollections of how they looked and imaginations of how they "would have looked," the tones of their voice, their ways of doing things, the shade of disapproval and the radiance of pleasure on their countenances that came and went, their downsitting and uprising in and from the familiar chair, the swing of the arm, the action of the hand, all the innumerable "characteristics" that make the difference between one human brother or sister and all other human brothers and sisters!

And these letters, some on thin Continental paper and others on ordinary tissue, brought back to me their writer's personality. It is so almost impossible to realize "dead and gone" with the letter in your hand speaking to you still, not telephonically—that is too weird and uncanny, that bottling up a man's living words to be uttered again by his very voice after he has died,—but naturally and with the light of other days in his face and the sound of old affection in his voice. One of the chief reasons, or perhaps "excuses" would be the more modest word, for giving a few extracts from Canon Havergal's letters to a public which may take comparatively little interest in their subject matter, is that they show a strong attachment—perhaps unusually strong would not be too presumptuous an expression—between rector and curate.

They mostly commence with "My dear Br. James" (always the abbreviated "Br."), varied by "My dear, dear friend," and in one of the last of all, as if with tender prescience of the end, "My beloved Br. James." And their endings are sometimes the expressively truthful "Yours faithfully," but far more often "Yours affectionately," or "ever affectionately," or "most affectionately," with here and there a playful ending linked on to the sense of what goes before. And they are full of good cheer, never a gloomy line: always, even in describing trying circumstances, a noble strain of hope and trust.

But the introductory point I am making is that it is often so easy, and never quite impossible, for rector and curate to "love as brethren," if they are pitiful, if they are courteous. Many a case of friction between a "chief" and his curate or staff of curates is owing to the unhappy inability of the one, even after preaching very forcibly about "doing as you *would* be done by, and not as you *are* done by," to put himself in the place of the other. I do not mean by "the one" a rector, nor by "the other" his curate; but either expression is applied to either of the high (or low) "contracting parties." May, then, this little

[1] Rev. S. B. James was a curate (assistant pastor) under William Henry Havergal at St. Nicholas Church, Worcester, 1856–58. This essay was published in the weekly periodical *The Fireside*, published in two separate sections. The dates are not known.

memorial paper be applied by any rectorial or curatorial reader, at variance, or simply not on cordial terms, with his curate or his rector, to self, and thought over, perhaps even (if the writer might be so bold as to say it) prayed over, by such a reader.

Another preliminary "excuse" lies in the fact that whatever relates to the family bearing the honoured name of HAVERGAL is interesting simply as relating to that family. The letters are from various members of Canon Havergal's house and home, and whatever comes therefrom is of value as well as interest—of lasting value and of unfading interest.

And yet another influence upon the writer's mind is that full justice was never done to the distinguished merits, the musical genius and the ministerial eloquence and excellence, as well as the considerable mental power in all directions, of Canon Havergal while he lived, and composed, and wrote, and ministered. This inadequacy of recognition was owing partly, perhaps chiefly, to his own grand humility—some would call it noble pride—in shrinking from, and sometimes refusing public recognitions and acknowledgements of his work. He appeared always to prefer the designation "Mr. Havergal" to "Canon Havergal," because (though he richly merited a residential canonry) his canonry was only honorary. And the world, the ecclesiastical world, resembling in this as in many other particulars the world from which the Church is supposed to be separate, allowed so good and great a man to live and die without any suitable recognition of his true position. He was happy enough without such recognition, but one at least of his curates has never ceased to feel an indignant regret at such ungrateful and unappreciative treatment. Pushing and much inferior men not only make their way in the world—that is natural enough—but, which is unnatural and inconsistent, in the Church of England.

The letters are all written *currente calamo*, marvellous in their calligraphy, remembering that his sight was all but gone. And there is, varying their frequently deep solemnity and invariable absence of flippancy, oftentimes a quaint and very taking pleasantry and humour about them.

From Shareshill, 1861: "I am on the shelf.[1] For the last five or six days I have been there with a touch (hardly an attack) of poor internal gout. This is mercy to me; be it glory to God. Amen. Well, let me book you for one pulpit and one desk on Sunday, August 25. All will be most glad to see you. Only fix your day and hour for being at Wolverhampton. Fanny is at home, and sends love; Maria still in Ireland. Bring mother, babe, and eldest born, if you can. Best love."

From London: "Arrived here last evening. Frightful sea weather; we were in peril and misery. Thank God, all has ended well. Can you run up and look at us, and report progress about the Lectures? I am wonderful, but need care. My eyes have been examined by the greatest German oculist. Alas! no hope: some portions are *dead*. I have worked when I ought to have rested. Now, must *do* nothing. All love."

From Shareshill, 1862: "I have been half deluged with gift sermons on passing events. It is only at a slow pace that I can get rowed through them all. Well, I like yours, on the whole, better than any. It is yourself, and I am not surprised that you published it. But one thing. You seem to regard Solomon as the chief of all human mourners. Poor I, in my old-fashioned style, have always looked on David as at the head of those who severally say, 'Every night wash I my bed and water my couch with my tears.' Things with us parochially much as usual; many mercies and few trials."

From Shareshill, 1863, in reply to a letter asking advice about accepting a small benefice: "My humble advice is, By no means accept. Take these reasons: 1. You are better off already; 2. You would be instantly shelved; 3. The incumbency is most likely in the North. That will not suit Mrs. James; 4. You are worth being presented with more. Even I may have an opportunity of saying so some day. Besides, a tolerable curacy is always less expensive than a small living. Only wait patiently, and go on as you are going, and the Great Patron will be found to have reserved some better thing for you."

From Shareshill, 1863: "It is a fact that, in elderly people especially, an excess of intention produces a failure of execution. It is often so with me. When I thought of writing to you yesterday, the leading idea in my mind was to sympathize with yours and you under your painful visitation. The very strength of intention pushed itself out of my sensorium. I knew as I was fastening the letter that I had something special to say, but could not think of it. Pardon all. Again, God bless you, and Good-bye."

From Shareshill, 1864, in reply to a letter respecting an unkind review of a volume of my sermons: "Good Ambrose Serle said, 'When the young snakes hiss, it is a sure sign that the Old Serpent is displeased.' Stick to your divinity."

From Pyrmont, in 1867: "No English here; only a few Americanized Germans. I resolved to resign my benefice, and at the patron's request sent in the names and addresses of three friends as eligible. I put yours first, with everything I could say. He quietly ignored all three, and offered it to one utterly antipodal to, etc. Happily I was able to withdraw my intention, and the upshot is etc., but I should have been really glad to be quite free."

(*To be continued.*)

[1] In the 20th and 21st centuries, British people widely understand the phrase "on the shelf" to mean a woman who would never be considered for marriage, a woman certain to be a spinster, never to marry. This is not at all Frances' meaning of this phrase: here she meant the idea of a tool or utensil set on the shelf when not being used, on the shelf awaiting use, in F.R.H.'s case caused by illness. The current meaning of unattractiveness and certainty to be a spinster was not at all true of F.R.H.

II.

IN editing Canon Havergal's "Ark of the Covenant," I had ventured to remonstrate respecting a strong denounciation of the Church of Rome, and this was the reply: "I return your suggested version of a stringent but truthful passage, in testimony of my respect for yourself. I used to hear the late G. S. Faber speak and even write far more strongly. I believe things are as I say, and the Apocalypse *warrants* all. The times demand plain speaking, but send the amended paragraph at once, else charge will be made after proof." With regard to the same editorship: "Christian or christian; the former when it refers, as a noun, to persons; when an adjective, it is seldom used with a capital." The same: "'Gentlemanly honour:' Fudge, as applied to Romanists *within* the Church, charitably allowable to those who honestly leave it. If I have said anything of the sort you seem to imply, alter it. You do not intimate that you *approve* the sentiments and teaching of the Lectures." The reason was that I thought any expression of my approbation would be presumptuous.

Starting again for Pyrmont from Leamington (he had resigned his benefice): "In the midst of many things to be done, and rather poorly, I pen a hurried line to waken you up ere we go. I have been sustained and permitted to preach for some one or other most Sundays. Thus I am spared from rusting out. Amen. Our hearts' love to you both. All blessings from above."

From Pyrmont: "The Bishop of—— *preaches* more or less evangelically, but has just appointed for his examining chaplain a decided opponent of evangelical truth. In this halting, half-and-half way, too many bishops proceed. But," etc. In 1869, from Eastbourne: "I love you, but I do not love your present state of mind. You are not the Rev. S. B. J., curate of St. Nicholas'. You and I differ. I stand just where I was; you diverge from me. You repudiate the Church Association; I heartily receive it. After this plain speaking, which *you* will approve, let me request you to read the enclosed letter from my dear old friend Bradley. I offer no advice, but commend you to the Great Counsellor and the word of His grace."

It was a letter from Canon Havergal's most intimate friend, the Rev. Charles Bradley, "prince of sermon-writers," and father of the present Dean of Westminster, respecting a benefice.

From Leamington, 1869: "As to the gleam of hope from the Dean and Chapter of Windsor, I cease not to hope for you in God's own way. Whenever you can, let us hear as to which way God's wind is blowing for you. Fanny wonders if you received a copy of her vol., which was sent to you from London in July. She is much lauded for it by reviews. May she be kept at the footstool." This alludes to a book of poems by his daughter, Frances Ridley Havergal.

From Leamington, March 2, 1870: "Thanks for your ghost of a letter. You promised to send a full, true, and particular account of your new home. None has arrived. Thanks for the copy of *Churchman's Shilling Magazine*. The article has been read to me, and approved by me. I want to know if the Duke of Buckingham has any property in your parish, because I shall be writing to his Grace in a week or so, and will mention you," etc. That was always his thought, "How can I help?"

Canon Havergal's last letter is dated 1870. Not very long after it was received the writer was at Oxford, and the announcement met him first thing in the reading room of the Union that his best of friends was taken to his rest, leaving many disconsolate friends to mourn his loss far more truly than is mourned the loss of many a more eminent man. There was an innate grandeur of magnanimity about him, a loving tenderness of heart, a most touching and delicate sympathy in joy and sorrow, which the writer saw almost in a moment, and which grew upon his perception through all the years. He has never yet found, to his mind, the equal of William Henry Havergal, rector of St. Nicholas', Worcester; and he fears that now he never will. Kindest of readers, do not smile, or if you do, let it be an unsarcastic smile, at this renewed placing of the wreath of exuberant affection upon his cherished memory.

Frances Ridley Havergal was also a frequent correspondent, but seldom dated her letters with more than the day of the month, leaving the year to be taken for granted; sometimes not even putting the day of week or month. She was sponsor to my daughter, and sent her writing-desk to her godchild, with many other tokens of interest and affection. Every letter she wrote was worth preservation, though so few have been preserved. I had reviewed her sister's "Pleasant Fruits" and her own "Bruey" in the *Church of England Magazine*, then under my editorship, and she says:

I must write at once, not only to thank you for so kindly noticing the little books, but to tell you with what great interest and pleasure I have read your leader on Penny Readings, and the account of your mission services. I so entirely and exactly agree with the former, and think it such a sorely needed dose, and am so exceedingly interested in the Mission Service movement, that nothing that has come by post for a long time has given me such pleasure. I do think these mission weeks are just the counteractive needed for all the worldly tendencies of the day. So few are really living as if there were eternal things *certainly* before them. "The things which are seen," "temporal" though they are, fill up the whole foreground, and hide the tremendous background of eternity. And as for "amusing" folks in order to get good influence, it is worse than going to London round by Land's End. Sweet words about Jesus, clear and direct and fervent, will make more glad hearts than all the "entertainments" in the world. I have met Mr. Neville Sherbrooke, and my sisters know him intimately. I wish there were more of that sort. I have had *such* a pleasure. Nisbet tells me that "Bruey" is the most successful book on his list this season. I never expected that, or anything like it. I am sorry your successor may not do as much good as you might if you continued it. I hope my godchild is flourishing. I have *very* seldom forgotten her in the Litany whenever read.

As regards the sponsorship, the writer had reminded F.R.H. that, though distant in body, she might be near in spirit and in prayer, and she writes: "I think it so kind of you to care to have me as sponsor. I think I may almost promise that I shall *never* forget my little godchild when the 'young children' are remembered. I have a fancy that I should like her to have a 'Ministry of Song,' and a 'Sacred Songs for Little Singers,' as both will probably be out of print long before she is able to read either. So if you will let me have a line to say *where* I am to address them to, I will send them. I will enclose a wee book for yourself by a dear friend of ours, of which, at least, the dedication will interest you. Your notice" (an *In Memoriam* of her father) "was a singular solace and delight to me. I like it best of *any*. It is so characteristic, both as to writer and subject so thoroughly natural, so *real*. Dear papa! how few have such natural gifts of mind and character, and how few that have consecrated them so *wholly* as he did! It *was* beautiful, was it not? Anything so perfect, so entirely saintly, as his patience and sweetness all last winter I never imagined, let alone saw."

One more "scrap" about the baptism. Would that all Christian people were so ready to undertake friendly sponsorship, instead of so often making difficulties; and would that all sponsors were so mindful of their solemn promises: "I accept the office with real pleasure. Your letter reached me early this morning; so the special topic of my own morning prayer was that dear little Susan Katharine might be 'Christ's faithful *soldier* and *servant* unto her life's end,' with emphasis on both; for there is need of both. I was wishing to write and thank you for your beautiful notice in the *C.S.M.* I am working at high pressure just now. I will write again when I get breathing time. Yours always most truly."

In the Lent season of the year 1890, the writer preached for the present Dean (Stubbs) of Ely, then rector of Wavertree, one of a series of sermons on "Seven Good Women,"—the one selected by me being Frances Ridley Havergal—the other six being Catherine Tait, Agnes Jones, Elizabeth Barrett Browning, "Sister Dora," Mary Carpenter, and Florence Nightingale. The following extract from that subsequently printed sermon may be not out of place here:

I have quoted none of F.R.H.'s beautiful and devout poetry to you this afternoon, although looking into various volumes (personal gifts with valued autographs and manuscript corrections). I prefer to dwell on the sweet and holy poem of her life. She was a poet and a singer, a preacher and a prophet, and so she is interesting, and we are glad to hear and think about her. But it was because she was more than that that she and the constellation which has shone upon your Lenten season this year was selected for your notice. We cannot all be poets and singers, preachers and prophets. And so I am commissioned to put her bright example before you as one of God's saints, a burning and shining light of righteousness. Dear brethren, let us aim at holy living, let us seek to promote God's glory, let us become less self-seeking and worldly from this time forward; let us realize, as sinners for whose redemption Christ died, that we have received or that we need the pardon of our manifold transgressions. I will to believe that I have merely taken my little journey hither from my humble Buckinghamshire parish to renew an old friendship with your rector, nor to proclaim the merits and describe the genius of one whom I so affectionately esteemed, and who honoured me with so much of her affectionate regard, and who is lost a while from earthly sight; but I will hope and pray, and so will you, that we all—you, my hearers, and I your preacher—may be stimulated by our contemplation of a saintly and beautiful life to become ourselves more weaned from earthly and grovelling thoughts and ways, more studious of the glory of God, more thoughtful of the true ends of this passing life, more convinced that we are not our own to live for our own ignoble ends, but that we are Christ's own, bought with the price of His precious blood—heirs of God and joint-heirs with Christ, suffering with Him, if it be His will, that we may be also at last glorified together with Him and reign with Him, world without end. Amen.

Respecting the last days of this sweetest of sweet singers, her sister, Maria V. G. H. Havergal, wrote most touchingly and pathetically from the Mumbles, Swansea:

Dear Mr. James,—Hundreds of letters, floods of sympathy. I pass heaps by; it would *kill* me. But a few, and *yours*, I single out. I know you feel, and Mrs. James; and her godchild has lost *her* prayers, but many have gone to the Throne for her. I don't wish her back, and *won't*. I told her so, and she said, "You darling for saying that!" She was overworked, overwritten too, and specially the correcting of a new edition of "Songs of Grace and Glory," a great daily burden which hindered her exercise and rest for months. We were *so* happy in her chosen seaside nest; all but the post-bag! She worked in every cottage: sailors, donkey-boys, her new temperance regiment of 150, all adored her; and she led many straight to Jesus. Her loving words pierced old stony hearts, and men and women wept as she spoke of the atoning blood that had washed her, that would wash them. On the day before Ascension she stood on the village bank (by promise), with sailor-men and boys all round her. It was an east wind, in which she stood for an hour and a half, and came home chilled and exhausted. Ascension Day, out again, to see a sailor going to sea. Friday, chills and doctor. Saturday, high fever, then inflammation, then peritonitis—the whole fragile frame burning in the fever furnace, constant sickness, etc., up to the last hymn she sang in almost death. Her peace and joy shone clear and clearer. It was not doctrines, it was Christ, her King, meeting her almost visibly. She said, "Spite of the breakers, God's love and mercy are all true. Not one thing hath failed me." To her doctor, when he said "Good bye, I shall not see you again," "Then you think I am going?" "Yes." "Today?" "Possibly." "Beautiful; too good to be true." On Whit-Monday, to her brother, "Let it be a sacramental service," and it was. After she had received, he was going on with the words individually, when she solemnly stopped him: "Say the words *once* for all of us." Then, "It is *not* the rite—no safety in that; I wished it in obedience to *His* command."

After that, she asked us to go in her study, and on her harp piano play papa's tune, "St. Chrysostom," and "Jerusalem, my happy home"; "but we must sing from the copy, 'Jesus my Saviour dwells'; it is Jesus so good, so dear to me." The Vicar of Swansea came up, by her wish. By him she sent this message to Mr. W. H. Aitken—"Give my love to Mr. Aitken, and tell him to preach Jesus Christ; tell him to urge *all* the younger clergy to be ambassadors for Christ, to win souls for Christ; and you too, Mr. Morgan, oh, tell Mr. Aitken to speak bright words about Jesus; do, do." She told us only a deal coffin; it was covered with white cashmere, and on it a crown and stars; no *crosses*; she never chose them. We took her to Astley Church. Papa's tomb was opened, and there, under *his* grand old fir-tree, in sight of her birth-window, we laid her to rest. 1 John 1:7 she chose for her tomb. She died at daybreak, her eyes shining gloriously. He took her, and she rests, and sings, and waits for *you*, and me, and dear Mrs. James, and godchild. Yours ever.

Some letters from the late Mrs. Havergal, widow of Canon Havergal, are too strictly personal and private for reproduction. The foregoing extracts are culled and garnered with care, and, it is hoped, with discrimination. They are very precious, and some of them solemn and sacred "remains" of a family of very dear friends, a family not only of celebrity and genius, but of seldom equalled worth and piety. They served God diligently before they fell on sleep. The writer has felt very keenly, sometimes almost bitterly, his loss and so far loneliness, in recording the memories he loves so well, and reading over once more the words that used to cheer his heart and lighten some heavy hours. Those spirits of the just with whom he held much converse for many years are now made perfect, their toils and troubles—they had them, for they were God's own children—are over for evermore. Pardon is asked of all readers, and of every reader, to whom it may seem that this record of some of the "loved and lost" was obtrusive or out of place; and indulgence is asked for all its errors, egotisms, and faults of every kind.

Preach the Gospel to every creature" "Lo I am with you alway, even unto the end of the world.

Elizabeth Clay

Punjab Village Mission

Winterdyne Sept 26th. 1884.

This is an entry by Elizabeth Clay in the Visitors' Album of Giles and Ellen Shaw. This Album has the entries of several missionaries to distant lands, often with entries in other languages as well as English. Ellen Shaw was W.H.H.'s third daughter. His youngest daughter, Frances Ridley Havergal, was a very close friend of Elizabeth Clay from 1851 to 1879 (when Frances died). Elizabeth Clay was a missionary with the Zenana Missionary Society, laboring among women in a rural part of India. F.R.H. was ready to join Elizabeth there, but her health prevented her. Taking the truth of Christ to those in foreign lands was a work very dear to W.H.H., and to his daughters, and this is only a glimpse of that.

www.ingramcontent.com/pod-product-compliance
Lightning Source LLC
Chambersburg PA
CBHW062031090426
42740CB00016B/2881
* 9 7 8 1 9 3 7 2 3 6 2 7 4 *